Frommer's®

Europe by Rail

4th Edition

WILEY

Wiley Publishing, Inc.

Published by:

WILEY PUBLISHING, INC.

111 River St.

Hoboken, NJ 07030-5774

ISBN 978-0-470-64994-7 (paper); ISBN 978-1-118-03348-7 (ebk); ISBN 978-1-118-03349-4 (ebk); ISBN 978-1-118-03350-0 (ebk)

Editor: Naomi P. Kraus
with Susan Barnes, Andrea Kahn, and Davis MacMillan
Production Editor: Heather Wilcox
Cartographer: Liz Puhl
Photo Editor: Richard Fox
Production by Wiley Indianapolis Composition Services
Front Cover Photo: ICE high-speed train going through the Bavarian Alps, Loisach Valley, Germany.
©H. P. Huber / fototeca9x12
Back Cover Photo: The Brienzer Rothorn steam-powered cog railroad in the Bernese Oberland.
©Christof Schuerpf / Swiss Image

For information on our other products and services or to obtain technical support, please contact our Customer Care Department within the U.S. at 877/762-2974, outside the U.S. at 317/572-3993 or fax 317/572-4002.

Wiley also publishes its books in a variety of electronic formats. Some content that appears in print may not be available in electronic formats.

Manufactured in the United States of America

5   4   3   2   1

CONTENTS

List of Maps viii

1 TOURING EUROPE BY RAIL 1

1-Week Itineraries 1

ITINERARY 1: EUROPE'S BEST CASTLES & PALACES 2

ITINERARY 2: SMALL CITIES OF THE BENELUX 4

ITINERARY 3: RIDING THE SCENIC ROUTE 6

ITINERARY 4: EASTERN EUROPE 9

ITINERARY 5: EXPLORING THE SCANDINAVIAN TRIANGLE 11

2-Week Itineraries 13

ITINERARY 6: EUROPE FOR HISTORY & CULTURE BUFFS 13

ITINERARY 7: EUROPE'S BEST ART & ARCHITECTURE 16

ITINERARY 8: EUROPE FOR FOOD LOVERS 19

ITINERARY 9: GREAT CITIES OF EUROPE 23

ITINERARY 10: THE GRAND TOUR 26

2 PLANNING YOUR EUROPEAN RAIL TRIP 29

Visitor Information 29

When to Go 32

WHAT TIME IS IT, ANYWAY? 33

Finding Your Rail Route 35

Choosing the Train That's Right for You 36

CLEANING UP 46

The Price of Rail Travel 46

NO PASSES PLEASE, WE'RE BASQUE 49

The Train Passes 51

VALIDATING YOUR PASS 60

The Rail Experience 61

When a Train Just Won't Do 63

THE RULES OF THE ROAD: DRIVING IN EUROPE 65

Getting to Europe 70

Money Matters 72

Tips on Accommodations 75

3 AUSTRIA 79

Essentials 81

FESTIVALS & SPECIAL EVENTS 82

RIDING HISTORIC RAILS 84

FAST FACTS: AUSTRIA 85

Vienna 87

CITY TRANSPORTATION ON THE CHEAP 94

BOATING ON THE "BLUE" DANUBE 101

COFFEEHOUSES INSIDE THE RING 104

THE HEURIGE OF GRINZING 107

Salzburg 108

A PANORAMIC STROLL 114

CAFE SOCIETY 117

Innsbruck 119

THE MOST BEAUTIFUL SPOT IN TYROL 123

4 BELGIUM 126

Essentials 127
FESTIVALS & SPECIAL EVENTS 128
FAST FACTS: BELGIUM 130
Brussels 132

SPECIAL BRUSSELS EXPERIENCES 139
HEADING OUT TO WATERLOO 145
Bruges 149
Liège 156

5 THE CZECH REPUBLIC 164

Essentials 165
FESTIVALS & SPECIAL EVENTS 166
USEFUL CZECH TRAIN & TRAVEL TERMS 167
TRAIN DESIGNATIONS IN THE CZECH REPUBLIC 168
FAST FACTS: CZECH REPUBLIC 169
Prague 171

KAVÁRNA SOCIETY 185
AN EXCURSION TO KARLŠTEJN CASTLE 188
Western & Southern Bohemia 188
SPA CURES & TREATMENTS 190
SEEING THE ČESKÝ KRUMLOV CHÂTEAU 194
FOR BEER LOVERS: TOURING A BEER SHRINE 197

6 DENMARK 198

FESTIVALS & SPECIAL EVENTS 200
Essentials 200
FAST FACTS: DENMARK 202
Copenhagen 204

THE OLD SAILORS' PORT AT NYHAVN 213
THE TOWN'S HOTTEST DATE: HALF WOMAN, HALF FISH 215
Highlights of Jutland 222
FERRIES TO SWEDEN & NORWAY 225

7 FINLAND 226

FESTIVALS & SPECIAL EVENTS 228
Essentials 228
FAST FACTS: FINLAND 231
Helsinki 232

PAYING HOMAGE TO FINLANDIA & SIBELIUS 238
OLYMPIC MEMORIES & A FLYING FINN 240
EXPLORING THE FORTRESS OF FINLAND 241
TRAVELING ON TO ST. PETERSBURG 243

8 FRANCE 245

Essentials 247
FESTIVALS & SPECIAL EVENTS 248
FAST FACTS: FRANCE 251
Paris 253
SAVING ON TRAVEL 259

THE FAMOUS CAFES OF PARIS 275
The Loire Valley 281
NATURE & ART IN CHAUMONT-SUR-LOIRE 294
Provence & the Riviera 295

9 GERMANY 320

FESTIVALS & SPECIAL EVENTS 322
Essentials 322
FAST FACTS: GERMANY 326

Berlin 327
A NEW WALL 342
Munich 351

More Highlights of Germany 371

A CRUISE ON THE ELBE 379

TRAVELING THE ROMANTIC ROAD BY BUS 382

10 GREAT BRITAIN & IRELAND 389

FESTIVALS & SPECIAL EVENTS 390

Essentials 392

FAST FACTS: GREAT BRITAIN 394

London 397

DISCOUNT TRANSPORTATION PASSES 402

Edinburgh 419

THE EDINBURGH FESTIVAL: ART & TATTOOS 432

Irish Rail Essentials 433

FESTIVALS & SPECIAL EVENTS 433

FAST FACTS: IRELAND 437

Dublin 438

WHICH DUBLIN STATION? 442

11 HUNGARY 455

Essentials 455

FESTIVALS & SPECIAL EVENTS 456

USEFUL HUNGARIAN TRAIN TERMS 458

FAST FACTS: HUNGARY 459

Budapest 460

COFFEEHOUSE CULTURE 475

MUSIC FOR A SUMMER EVENING 477

12 ITALY 482

FESTIVALS & SPECIAL EVENTS 484

Essentials 484

FAST FACTS: ITALY 487

Rome 490

I LEFT MY HEART ON THE PIAZZA NAVONA 500

ANCONA & BARI: GATEWAYS TO GREECE 506

Naples 510

SICILY: LAND OF MYTH & LEGEND 514

Florence & Tuscany 517

Venice & the Northeast 535

A RIDE IN A GONDOLA 544

Milan & the Northwest 552

13 THE NETHERLANDS 564

Essentials 565

FESTIVALS & SPECIAL EVENTS 565

FAST FACTS: THE NETHERLANDS 568

Amsterdam 569

SPECIAL AMSTERDAM EXPERIENCES 580

SMOKING COFFEE SHOPS 586

The Hague 587

Maastricht 592

14 NORWAY 595

FESTIVALS & SPECIAL EVENTS 596

Essentials 597

THE ESSENCE OF NORWAY 598

FAST FACTS: NORWAY 600

Oslo 601

SCANDINAVIA'S GREATEST PAINTER 607

RINGING THE DOORBELL AT IBSEN'S APARTMENT 609

Bergen 614

STROLLING MEDIEVAL BERGEN 618

NORWAY'S MOST DRAMATIC TRAIN RIDE 620

15 PORTUGAL 624

FESTIVALS & SPECIAL EVENTS 625
Essentials 626
FAST FACTS: PORTUGAL 630
Lisbon 632
STROLLING THE ALFAMA 639

TO MARKET, TO MARKET . . . 641
IF IT SWIMS, IT'S HERE 642
THE SONGS OF SORROW 646
NORTHWARD HO! 648
The Algarve 652

16 SPAIN 657

FESTIVALS & SPECIAL EVENTS 660
Essentials 660
FAST FACTS: SPAIN 663
Madrid 665
DEATH IN THE AFTERNOON 675
TASCA-HOPPING IN MADRID 680

THE EXOTIC SOUND OF FLAMENCO 683
Seville 686
Granada 694
Barcelona 700
RAMBLING LA RAMBLA 710
A TASTE OF CATALÁN BUBBLY 712

17 SWEDEN 718

Essentials 719
FESTIVALS & SPECIAL EVENTS 720
SWEDEN'S MOST FAMOUS RAIL
    JOURNEY 722
FAST FACTS: SWEDEN 722

Stockholm 723
A WALK BACK IN TIME 732
Gothenburg 740
SCENES FROM GOTHENBURG LIFE 745
A PICNIC IN THE PARK 747

18 SWITZERLAND 750

Essentials 752
FESTIVALS & SPECIAL EVENTS 753
FAST FACTS: SWITZERLAND 755
Zurich 757
A SUMMER WALK ALONG THE QUAYS
    OF ZURICH 762
DISCOVERIES ALONG MEDIEVAL
    STREETS 764
SAILING LAKE ZURICH 765

Bern 768
BERN: A CENTER FOR RAIL TRIPS 770
ON THE HOOF THROUGH BERN 774
Lausanne 776
A WALK THROUGH THE MIDDLE AGES 780
Geneva 782
SAILING THE WATERS OF LAC LÉMAN 791
Switzerland's Famous Scenic Rail
    Lines 794

19 EASTERN EUROPE, GREECE & THE BALKANS 799

Bulgaria 799
Croatia 803
Greece 806
Macedonia 809
Poland 811

Romania 813
Serbia & Montenegro 816
Slovakia 818
Slovenia 820

20 USEFUL TERMS & PHRASES 824

Glossary of French-Language
Terms 824

Glossary of Italian-Language
Terms 829

Index 833

LIST OF MAPS

Itinerary 1: Europe's Best Castles & Palaces   3

Itinerary 2: Small Cities of the Benelux   5

Itinerary 3: Riding the Scenic Route   8

Itinerary 4: Eastern Europe   10

Itinerary 5: Exploring the Scandinavian Triangle   12

Itinerary 6: Europe for History & Culture Buffs   15

Itinerary 7: Europe's Best Art & Architecture   17

Itinerary 8: Europe for Food Lovers   21

Itinerary 9: Great Cities of Europe   25

Itinerary 10: The Grand Tour   27

Austria   81

Vienna   88

Vienna Public Transport   93

Salzburg   109

Innsbruck   121

Belgium   127

Brussels   134

Bruges   151

Liège   157

Luxembourg City   160

The Czech Republic   165

Prague   172

Scandinavia   199

Copenhagen   206

Finland   227

Helsinki   234

France   247

Paris   254

The Loire Valley   283

Orléans   285

Tours   287

Avignon   297

Aix-en-Provence   303

Cannes   305

Nice   309

Monaco   317

Germany   321

Western Berlin   328

Berlin Mitte   331

Berlin U-Bahn & S-Bahn   334

Munich   352

Munich U-Bahn & S-Bahn   356

Dresden   377

Great Britain & Ireland   391

London   398

Edinburgh   420

Ireland   435

Dublin   440

Hungary   457

Budapest   462

Italy   483

Rome   492

Florence   518

Venice   536

Milan   554

The Netherlands   567

Amsterdam   570

The Hague & Scheveningen   589

Oslo   602

Bergen 615

Portugal 627

Lisbon 633

The Algarve 653

Spain 659

Madrid 666

Madrid Metro 668

Seville 687

Granada & the Alhambra 695

Barcelona 702

Barcelona Metro 705

Stockholm 724

Gothenburg 741

Switzerland 751

Zurich 758

Bern 769

Geneva 784

Eastern European Rail Routes 801

ABOUT THE AUTHORS

Amy Eckert's love affair with travel began on a train in Europe and hasn't stopped yet. As a college student, Amy lived and worked in Southern Germany; as a travel writer, she has returned many times since, traveling by train through a dozen countries, including Germany, France, the Benelux nations, Italy, and Scandinavia.

Dardis McNamee is editor-in-chief of the *Vienna Review* and an assistant professor of Media Communications at Webster University Vienna. In her long career in journalism, she has been a correspondent for the *New York Times, Condé Nast Traveler, Wall Street Journal Europe,* and *Die Zeit,* as well as a speech writer to two U.S. ambassadors to Austria. She has lived in Vienna for 15 years.

After graduating with a degree in French, **Christopher Anderson** left North Carolina, traveled across Siberia, and taught English in France and Austria. In addition to travels in over 40 countries (and counting), he has worked as managing editor of the *Vienna Review* and as a reporter at the 2010 World Cup in South Africa. He unpacks his bags in Vienna, Austria.

George McDonald has lived and worked in both Amsterdam and Brussels as deputy editor of the KLM in-flight magazine and as editor-in-chief of the Sabena in-flight magazine. Now a freelance journalist and travel writer based in Germany, he is the author of *Frommer's Amsterdam* and *Frommer's Belgium, Holland & Luxembourg.*

Mark Baker is a long-time American expat who lives in Prague. He's one of the original editors of *The Prague Post* and was for years a foreign correspondent and editor for Radio Free Europe/Radio Liberty, based in Prague. He is now a freelance writer and reporter. He is the author of *Frommer's Prague* and *Prague Day by Day* and coauthor of *Frommer's Eastern Europe* and *Frommer's Poland.*

Ryan James earned a doctorate in International and Multicultural Education from the University of San Francisco. He has been living in Budapest, Hungary, since 2001, and has been a full-time instructor in the American Studies Department at Eötvös Loránd University since 2002. He has traveled to 45 countries so far.

Darwin Porter, a native of North Carolina, was assigned to write the very first edition of a Frommer's guide devoted solely to one European country. Since then, he has written many bestselling Frommer's guides to all the major European destinations. In 1982, he was joined in his research efforts by **Danforth Prince,** formerly of the Paris bureau of the *New York Times,* who has traveled and written extensively about Europe.

Native New Yorker **Naomi Kraus** is a senior editor at Frommer's, a former travel agent, and a graduate of the Columbia Graduate School of Journalism. She has logged lots of miles on European trains over the years and rides the rails whenever she can.

ACKNOWLEDGMENTS

Many people worked behind the scenes and lent us a helping hand to keep this book on track. I'd like to give special thanks to **Beth Demarte, Samina Sabir, Meredith Marks,** and **Paul Kaufmann** for their invaluable assistance. You can't ask for a better cartographer than **Liz Puhl,** the woman behind all the maps in this book. Major kudos to **Andrea Kahn** at Frommer's for her enthusiastic assistance with both maps and text, to **Cate Latting** for her help on the maps, and to **Susan Barnes** and **Davis Macmillan** for pitching in where needed. And thanks to my family for making sure I stayed sane while juggling rail maps, timetables, and train itineraries for 6 months.

—Naomi Kraus

HOW TO CONTACT US

In researching this book, we discovered many wonderful places—hotels, restaurants, shops, and more. We're sure you'll find others. Please tell us about them, so we can share the information with your fellow travelers in upcoming editions. If you were disappointed with a recommendation, we'd love to know that, too. Please write to:

Frommer's Europe by Rail, 4th Edition
Wiley Publishing, Inc. • 111 River St. • Hoboken, NJ 07030-5774
frommersfeedback@wiley.com

AN ADDITIONAL NOTE

Please be advised that travel information is subject to change at any time—and this is especially true of prices. We therefore suggest that you write or call ahead for confirmation when making your travel plans. The authors, editors, and publisher cannot be held responsible for the experiences of readers while traveling. Your safety is important to us, however, so we encourage you to stay alert and be aware of your surroundings. Keep a close eye on cameras, purses, and wallets, all favorite targets of thieves and pickpockets.

FROMMER'S STAR RATINGS, ICONS & ABBREVIATIONS

Every hotel, restaurant, and attraction listing in this guide has been ranked for quality, value, service, amenities, and special features using a **star-rating system.** In country, state, and regional guides, we also rate towns and regions to help you narrow down your choices and budget your time accordingly. Hotels and restaurants are rated on a scale of zero (recommended) to three stars (exceptional). Attractions, shopping, nightlife, towns, and regions are rated according to the following scale: zero stars (recommended), one star (highly recommended), two stars (very highly recommended), and three stars (must-see).

In addition to the star-rating system, we also use **five feature icons** that point you to the great deals, in-the-know advice, and unique experiences that separate travelers from tourists. Throughout the book, look for:

🎁 **special finds**—those places only insiders know about

📷 **special moments**—those experiences that memories are made of

✎ **insider tips**—great ways to save time and money

🏷 **great values**—where to get the best deals

⚠ **warning**—traveler's advisories are usually in effect

The following abbreviations are used for credit cards:

AE	American Express	DISC	Discover	V	Visa
DC	Diners Club	MC	MasterCard		

TRAVEL RESOURCES AT FROMMERS.COM

Frommer's travel resources don't end with this guide. Frommer's website, **www.frommers. com**, has travel information on more than 4,000 destinations. We update features regularly, giving you access to the most current trip-planning information and the best airfare, lodging, and car-rental bargains. You can also listen to podcasts, connect with other Frommers. com members through our active-reader forums, share your travel photos, read blogs from guidebook editors and fellow travelers, and much more.

TOURING EUROPE BY RAIL

R ich, ancient, and incredibly diverse, the nations of Europe offer a vast array of sights, climates, cultures, and cuisines. The 10 trips outlined below show the full reach of the European rail system; feel free to mix and match parts of them to create your ideal vacation.

Where possible, we use overnight trains on these trips, as they save you the cost of a hotel night, maximize your sightseeing time, and are experiences in and of themselves. Remember that overnight trains, many high-speed lines, the Eurostar trains, French TGV trains, and Eurostar Italia require extra reservation fees over the price of your railpass. (See p. 40 for more on overnight trains.) Also note that advance reservations on high-speed rail lines and night trains are becoming more essential every day. If your itinerary depends on making specific connections or catching trains that run on specific schedules, reserve your seat or sleeping car as soon as possible (see "The Price of Rail Travel," in chapter 2, for more information on making train reservations).

We recommend railpasses for those itineraries below that would make good use of them; where point-to-point tickets are cheaper, we note that as well. (For an overview of when to buy a pass and when to go point to point, see p. 32.)

Exact train times and prices are subject to change—the details in these pages were accurate as of December 2010, but you should double-check all train schedules when plotting out your journey. For more on navigating rail schedules, see p. 35.

1-WEEK ITINERARIES

The average North American vacation is a mere 7 days long (we know, too short!). To help you make the best of your time in Europe, we've put together six 1-week rail itineraries that will give you a taste of some of the best Europe has to offer. Whether you're a royalty fanatic who can't get enough of the Continent's magnificent palaces or a nature buff who'd rather tackle the magnificent scenery of Scandinavia, you'll find an itinerary below that will suit your needs. And if you happen to have more than a week to spend (lucky you!), you can mix and match these itineraries or check out the 2-week itineraries we offer in the next section.

ITINERARY 1: **EUROPE'S BEST CASTLES & PALACES**

DURATION:	**8 days, 7 nights**
BEST TIME OF YEAR:	**Spring or fall**
RECOMMENDED PASSES:	**Second-class Eurail France–Germany 4-day railpass, plus Eurostar ticket**
ARRIVE IN:	**London**
DEPART FROM:	**Munich**

Europe is practically overflowing with medieval castles and ornate palaces. And many of these world-famous residences (and former residences) are open to exploration by those of us whose blood isn't royal blue. Touring all these bastions of nobility could take years, but we've put together an itinerary that will introduce you to a few of the most noteworthy castles and palaces on the Continent and in London.

Day 1

Arrive in London (you'll need to take the red-eye, so catch some z's on the flight). After checking into your hotel, head for a tour of **Buckingham Palace** in the morning, if it's open (only in summer); otherwise, take in the adjacent **Royal Mews** and the magnificent **Queen's Gallery,** both of which are open year-round and feature lots of fabulous royal treasures. Spend the afternoon exploring the **Tower of London,** an imposing castle complex built by William the Conqueror and home to Britain's fabulous crown jewels. If you have time, indulge in a traditional afternoon tea, or try a night out at the theater. See "London" in chapter 10 for more sightseeing options in this historic city.

Day 2

Fortify yourself with a good English breakfast before taking the Eurostar train on a jaunt (trip time: 2 hr., 15 min.) to Paris. If you've got time once you've settled into your hotel, visit the **Louvre,** which would be the largest palace in the world, if it were still a palace and not one of the world's greatest art museums. Pay homage to the *Mona Lisa,* the *Venus de Milo,* and 300,000 or so of their fellow artworks. It's a royal treat, palace or not. See "Paris" in chapter 8 for other things to do in the city.

Day 3

Get an early morning start and take the RER C-line commuter train (show your railpass at the ticket booth and get your Métro ticket—the pass itself isn't enough) out to **Versailles Rive Gauche** (p. 280) and spend a half-day touring Louis XIV's masterpiece, a structure so magnificent that building it practically bankrupted the state treasury. Return to Paris in the afternoon for a stroll or some other sightseeing before taking an evening TGV high-speed train for the ride (1 hr., 15 min.) to **Tours,** in the Loire valley. Check into your hotel (see "Tours" in chapter 8 for accommodations options) and rest up.

Day 4

If ever there were a spot for castle lovers, it's the **Loire Valley.** Unfortunately, it's not the most train-friendly locale in France, so the best way to see the region's famous castles is to get up early and take a full-day bus tour of the Loire châteaux. Tours leave at 9am daily from the city's tourist office, but, alas, Tours sightseeing tours aren't covered by railpasses. Should you wish to explore on your own, a few châteaux are reachable from Tours by rail. Try the Gothic and Renaissance **Château Royal d'Amboise** or the historic **Château Royal de Blois.** Stay in Tours a second night. See "Tours" in chapter 8 for more châteaux excursions out of Tours.

Day 5

More châteaux! Take a 25-minute train ride to **Chenonceaux** (p. 293), noted for its startling river-spanning castle. Return to Tours and take the 4:11pm train to St-Pierre-Des-Corps, then hop immediately on the TGV to Gare Montparnasse in Paris, arriving at 5:20pm. Grab a quick bite, then connect to the

8:20pm overnight train from Paris Est station to **Munich,** which arrives at 7:16am. (***Note:*** You'll have to get from Montparnasse to Paris Est station by Métro or taxi, but you've got plenty of time to make the connection.)

Day 6

Check into your hotel upon arriving in Munich, then head off to the **Nymphenburg Palace** (p. 362), Germany's largest baroque palace. If the weather's good, be sure to stroll the surrounding Nymphenburg Park. At night, you can raise a stein or two inside of the city's famous beer halls. For other nightlife options, check out "Munich" in chapter 9.

Day 7

You've got a busy day. From the Munich Hauptbahnhof, take an early morning train to **Füssen** (trip time: 2 hr.). Take one of the hourly buses to **Neuschwanstein** (p. 369), Mad King Ludwig's fairy-tale folly. (This was the model for Walt Disney's Cinderella Castle, and the real thing is a heck of a lot better!) Next up is nearby **Hohenschwangau** (p. 369) and its famous murals. Tour that castle (waiting in line to get in should eat up the rest of your day), and then return to Munich for the evening.

Day 8

If you have an afternoon flight, you can tour the downtown **Residenz Palace** before heading off to the airport. Otherwise, your castle-hopping will come to an end as you fly home from Munich.

ITINERARY 2: **SMALL CITIES OF THE BENELUX**

DURATION:	**8 days, 7 nights**
BEST TIME OF YEAR:	**Summer**
IDEAL PASSES:	**Point-to-point tickets or Eurail Benelux Pass (more convenient, though more expensive)**
ARRIVE IN:	**Amsterdam Schiphol**
DEPART FROM:	**See below**

Relaxing, romantic small cities can be an antidote to the typical European big-city bustle. Tack part of this itinerary onto a Paris or Amsterdam trip for a change of pace, or do the whole thing for a truly intimate week. All the Dutch and Belgian destinations in this itinerary are within a few hours of Amsterdam or Brussels, and you won't have to worry about catching a train at a specific time because all trains run on at least an hourly basis.

Day 1

Arrive at Amsterdam Schiphol airport, and take a train from the station beneath the airport terminal directly to The Hague, about 35 minutes away. Check into your hotel for a 3-night stay. Once you're settled in, head for **Madurodam,** a fascinating scale-model replica of dozens of Dutch landmarks and attractions. After you've had your fill of miniatures, and if you still have time, take tram 1 all the way up to the beach resort of **Scheveningen** to see how the Dutch spend sunny days. See p. 587 more information on The Hague.

Day 2

Take local tram 1—not the train—from The Hague to **Delft** and spend the day in that charming city, strolling its atmospheric canals, touring its two churches, and visiting its renowned **Stedelijk Museum Het Prinsenhof** (p. 592). Head back in the evening to The Hague and relax.

Day 3

In the morning, grab a train to **Haarlem,** a compact town just 35 minutes away that's ideal for strolling. Start first at its impressive **Grote Markt (market square)** and catch a recital on the 98-foot-tall (29m) organ inside the **Church of St. Bavo.** Finally, take in the city's finest attraction, the **Frans Hals Museum,** which sports both great art and a charming 17th-century setting. For more information on Haarlem, see p. 586. In the afternoon, head back to The Hague and tour the **Mauritshuis,** whose must-see art collection includes the quintessential Benelux city landscape—Vermeer's *View of Delft*—as well as Vermeer's famous *Girl with a Pearl Earring.*

Day 4

It's time to leave The Hague behind. Take a morning InterCity train from Den Haag HS to Antwerp's Centraal Station (trip time: 1 hr., 25 min.), store your luggage there, and then lose yourself on the streets of Antwerp, a hidden gem that's the capital of Europe's diamond trade. Don't miss the largest church in the Benelux, the **Cathedral of Our Lady,** situated right off the city's medieval and picturesque **Grote Markt.** For a touch of culture, visit the impressive **Rubens House,** where artist Peter Paul Rubens once lived and worked. For more on Antwerp, see p. 147. In the evening, head back to the rail station and catch a train (trip time: 1 hr., 43 min.) to the city of Liège in the heart of Belgium's Wallonia province; you'll need to change trains in Bruxelles Nord unless you opt for a slower direct train. Check into your hotel and give yourself a well-earned rest.

Day 5

Spend your day exploring the "Passionate City" of Liège. Don't miss the **Museum of Walloon Life** (p. 158), especially its fabulous puppet collection. The Romanesque **Church of St. Bartholomew** has a 12th-century baptismal font that's regarded as one of the greatest treasures in Belgium. For more options in Liège, see p. 156.

Day 6

Eat an early breakfast before catching a train to your final base in the Benelux—the World Heritage city of **Bruges.** The trip will take about 2 hours. Once you've settled into your hotel, wind your way through the medieval streets of Bruges, making sure to visit the city's famous **Belfry and Market Halls,** the **Begijnhof,** and the **Church of Our Lady,** with its sculpture by Michelangelo. See p. 149 for more on the city.

Day 7

If you can draw yourself away from Bruges for the day, get on a train for the 23-minute ride to **Ghent,** another breathtaking medieval city. Make sure to see its **St. Bavo's Cathedral,** the **Belfry,** and the grim **Castle of the Counts,** and then stroll along Graslei. Return to Bruges before dinner and spend the rest of the evening soaking up the city's medieval atmosphere. For more on Ghent, see p. 145.

Day 8

Bruges is close to several international airports: Brussels is about 1½ hours away, Amsterdam Schiphol is just under 3½ hours, and Charles de Gaulle in Paris is about 3 hours (an advance reservation is required for this train). Fly home from whichever airport works best for you.

ITINERARY 3: **RIDING THE SCENIC ROUTE**

DURATION:	**8 days, 7 nights**
BEST TIME OF YEAR:	**Spring; arrive on a Sunday or Monday so you can ride the Semmering Pass weekend train**
IDEAL PASSES:	**Second-class point-to-point tickets (cheapest) or first-class 6-day, three-country Eurail Select Pass (most comfortable and flexible, and only a little more expensive)**

ARRIVE IN:	**Milan**
DEPART FROM:	**Vienna**

There's some intense rail riding on this weeklong trip, but you'll be rewarded with a number of the world's most thrilling and dramatic rail journeys as you travel across the Alps. Two noteworthy trains you'll be riding are the magnificent Centovalli Railway traversing Italy and Switzerland, and one of the few railways deemed worthy of UNESCO's World Heritage Site designation, the Semmering Pass Railway in Austria.

Before leaving home: Call to make reservations to see Leonardo's *Last Supper* in Milan.

Day 1

Arrive in Milan in the morning. After checking into your hotel, see the **Duomo,** and then head for the *Last Supper* if you nabbed a reservation. Spend the afternoon in the **Brera Picture Gallery** and checking out the shops and antiques stores on the side streets off of **Via Brera,** which are open until 7:30pm on most evenings. See p. 552 for more information on the city.

Day 2

Today you head off on of the best railroad journeys in Europe: a ride on the **Centovalli Railway.** Grab the 9:10am EuroCity train to Bellinzona, arriving at 10:34am. Connect there to an 11am train to Locarno, arriving at 11:27am, and then get on the Centovalli Railway to Domodossola, one of the lesser-known scenic treasures of the Alps. The hourly frequency of the Centovalli line means you can get off at any of the charming villages it serves (we recommend Verdasio or Intragna, for their cable cars) and get back on again. No matter how many stops you choose to make, make sure to get back on the train to arrive in Domodossola no later than 7pm so you can catch the 7:48pm Cisalpino (reservations required) to **Bern,** where you'll arrive around 9:30pm and can check into your hotel for a well-earned rest.

This itinerary may sound very complicated, but the views offered by the Centovalli trains are exceptional, and there are common and frequent connections. The conductors on any of the trains we mention above will tell you where to go if you ask. And if you miss a train, there will usually be another one along in an hour or so.

Day 3

Bern is lovely, but the best railway scenery is in nearby Interlaken. In the morning, make the 53-minute journey to the Interlaken Ost train station, and you'll get a view of the mountains in the distance, the 13,000-foot (3,900m) peaks of the **Jungfrau** (p. 797). An intricate network of railways climbs these mountains, and you can ride one or two of them today out of the Interlaken station; a railpass doesn't cover these trains, but passholders do get a 25% discount. Rail Europe also sells Jungfrau tickets. Once you've had your fill of the magnificent scenery, head back to Bern and have dinner in one of the city's wine taverns. See p. 775 for more Bern nightlife options.

Day 4

Say goodbye to Bern, grab your luggage, and head back to Interlaken Ost. The famous **Golden Pass Line** (p. 795) heads through the mountains outside of Interlaken along an incredibly scenic route to Luzern (Lucerne). Take the 10:04am **Golden Pass Panoramic** train (reservations needed) from Interlaken Ost to Luzern (you'll arrive at 12:04pm), connecting there to Zurich.

From Zurich, make the 3¾-hour trip to Innsbruck, Austria (you will probably end up on the 4:40pm out of Zurich and won't arrive in Austria until after 8pm, so consider eating on the train, or wait to eat a late dinner after you check into your hotel). If you have some energy left (or you managed to snag an earlier train out of Zurich), take a tram to the **Hungerburg cable railway** (p. 123), which takes you up a mountain overlooking the city and offers especially beautiful nighttime views of Innsbruck. For more on the city, see p. 119.

Day 5

Spend the morning strolling the beautifully preserved **Altstadt** (Old Town) in **Innsbruck.** After an early lunch, catch the 1:54pm train to **Salzburg,** a 2-hour ride through spectacular Alpine scenery. Check into your hotel and then stroll through this picturesque city and see the **Residenz State Rooms,** where Mozart once played for royal guests. For more options in Salzburg, see p. 108.

Day 6

Take the 9:02am train from Salzburg to Vienna. After you arrive at 11:40am, check into your hotel and eat lunch. Spend the afternoon visiting the **Schönbrunn palace,** summer seat of the Habsburg dynasty. For more on this city, see p. 87. Have a piece of the city's famous dessert, the *Sacher torte*—you've earned it.

Day 7

Trying to experience the 150-year-old **Semmering Pass Railway**—the rail line on UNESCO's list of World Heritage sites—on a speedy modern train is a lost cause. The best way to see it is to take a round-trip excursion on an old-fashioned Experience Train out of Vienna, though these depart only on Saturday and Sunday mornings. For more on this historic railway, see p. 84. Have dinner in a Viennese wine tavern and, if you can, attend a concert or theater performance. If you're an opera fan, the **Staatsoper (Vienna State Opera)** is one of the best in the world.

Day 8

If there's time in the morning, try to see **St. Stephen's Cathedral,** in the heart of Vienna. Climb its south tower for a panoramic view of the city, and then stroll down Kärntnerstrasse, the main shopping street, before flying home out of Vienna.

ITINERARY 4: **EASTERN EUROPE**

DURATION:	**8 days, 7 nights**
BEST TIME OF YEAR:	**Summer**
IDEAL PASSES:	**Point-to-point tickets**
ARRIVE IN:	**Prague**
DEPART FROM:	**Budapest**

Liberated and bustling, but also ancient, Eastern Europe is blooming as a rail destination. And, compared to Western Europe, it's cheap, too. This weeklong jaunt takes you to three very different but easily accessible capitals on both sides of the former Iron Curtain: hip Prague, historic Budapest, and cultured Vienna.

Day 1

Arrive in **Prague** in the morning. After checking into your hotel, walk the city's famous Royal Route, touring **Prague Castle** before walking across the Charles Bridge into **Old Town.** From there, head for **Wenceslas Square,** site of the demonstrations that led to the Velvet Revolution in 1989. See p. 171 for more on the city.

Day 2

Prague's greatest strengths are its architecture and atmosphere; both are best experienced by strolling and wandering the city's streets. So spend your day exploring Prague's **Old Town** and **Jewish Quarter** in more depth. In the Jewish Quarter (Josefov), be sure to visit the **Old Jewish Cemetery.**

Day 3

Take an early morning train to beautiful, medieval **Český Krumlov,** changing trains in České Budějovice. Grab the 8:16am from Prague (not Sun or mid-/late Dec), which will get you into Krumlov around 12:07pm. Spend the day exploring this World Heritage Site (be sure to see the city's famous castle) and stay overnight. For more information on this picturesque town, see p. 192.

Day 4

It's another very early start. Hop the 8:35am train from Krumlov back to **České Budějovice** (Mon–Fri only; not July/Aug). You'll have about 2½ hours to explore this former fortress town and original home of Budweiser beer. See p. 196 for sightseeing options in the town. Make sure you're back in the station in time to catch the 12:02pm train to Linz. You'll connect there to a train to Vienna and should arrive in the Austrian capital around 4:25pm. Check into your hotel, have dinner (don't skip dessert in this city renowned for its pastries!), and perhaps take in a concert. For more on Vienna, see p. 87.

Day 5

See Day 7 of the "Riding the Scenic Route" itinerary on p. 9.

Day 6

Take the 8:04am train out of Vienna West to Budapest. After arriving at 10:49am, check into your hotel and eat lunch. Spend your afternoon exploring the **Inner City** and **Central Pest.** Walk down **Vaci útca,** the city's trendiest shopping street. Then stroll along the Danube to the neo-Gothic **Parliament** building. Have a hearty Hungarian dinner and, if you're an opera fan, join the rest of Budapest at the **Hungarian State Opera.** See p. 460 for more information on the city.

Day 7

Today focus on Budapest's Castle District. Be sure to see the 13th-century **Matthias Church** and the **Budapest History Museum.** On your way back into Pest, stop for coffee and a slice of *dobos torta* (layer cake) at **Auguszt,** one of the city's classic coffeehouses. Then drop in at **St. Stephen's Church,** the country's largest, before heading over to the striking Moorish and Byzantine **Dohány Synagogue,** the largest in Europe. After dinner, take in one the city's many musical concerts.

Day 8

Fly home from Budapest.

ITINERARY 5: EXPLORING THE SCANDINAVIAN TRIANGLE

DURATION:	**8 days, 7 nights**
BEST TIME OF YEAR:	**Summer**
IDEAL PASSES:	**Point-to-point tickets or 5-day Eurail Scandinavia Pass**
ARRIVE IN:	**Copenhagen**
DEPART FROM:	**Stockholm**

Summer in Scandinavia brings days that stretch forever. Take advantage of all those sunny hours to explore three of the region's key cities: Copenhagen, Stockholm, and Oslo.

Day 1

Arrive in Copenhagen in the morning and check into your hotel. Take a couple of hours to stroll the old city's cobblestone streets and its many canals. Spend the late afternoon at **Christiansborg Palace.** Early in the evening, sample the rides and entertainment at the city's famous **Tivoli.** See p. 210 for more sightseeing options.

Day 2

In the morning, visit **Amalienborg Palace,** see the changing of the guard there, and then walk to the statue of the **Little Mermaid.** In the afternoon, see the treasures of the **Nationalmuseet,** and in the evening, drop in on one of the city's many jazz clubs.

Itinerary 5: Exploring the Scandinavian Triangle

Day 3

Spend your morning perusing works by the Old Masters at **the Statens Museum for Kunst,** then leave Copenhagen on the 12:17pm IC train to Gothenburg, and switch there to the 5:42pm train to Oslo (Sat 4:10pm). You'll arrive in Oslo at 9:45pm. Check into your hotel and get some rest.

Day 4

After breakfast, stroll past the **Akershus Castle and Fortress** before catching the bus to the Bygdøy peninsula for the city's renowned ship museums. In the afternoon, if you have time, take in the **Edvard Munch Museum** or head to the **Tryvannstårnet** tower for a panoramic view of Oslo. See p. 607 for more information.

Day 5

Get up early and spend your morning viewing the masterpieces hanging in the **Nasjonalgalleriet.** Then hop the 3:49pm IC train to Stockholm, which will put you in the Swedish capital at 10pm. See p. 723 for information on Sweden's capital.

Day 6

Get an early start and take a ferry to Djurgården to visit the **Royal Warship Vasa** and the **Skansen** folk museum. In the afternoon, head to the **Royal Palace & Museums** and check out the Swedish crown jewels, among other royal treasures. Have dinner in Old Town and, if you can, take in a performance in the exceptional **Drottningholm Court Theater.**

Day 7

Take a morning train to **Uppsala**—trains leave around every half-hour and take 57 minutes—and spend some of the morning walking around the university and visiting its famous Gothic cathedral. After lunch, take the local bus to historic **Gamla Uppsala** and explore the archaeological remains there. For more sightseeing options, see p. 738. Return to Stockholm by train before dinnertime. For dinner, try the smorgasbord-style buffet at the **Grand Verandan.**

Day 8

If your flight doesn't leave until the afternoon, spend the morning in the **National Museum of Art.** Catch the 20-minute Arlanda Express train to the airport and fly home.

2-WEEK ITINERARIES

Though you can do a 1-week rail vacation in Europe if you limit your travels to a small region, if you want to cut a wider swath, you'll need at least 2 weeks to see things without feeling rushed. In this section, we offer a couple of specialized itineraries for architecture buffs, history fans, and food lovers, as well as a few "grand tour" suggestions for travelers who want to sample Europe's various regions and cities at a reasonable pace.

ITINERARY 6: **EUROPE FOR HISTORY & CULTURE BUFFS**

DURATION:	**14 days, 13 nights**
BEST TIME OF YEAR:	**Spring or fall**
IDEAL PASSES:	**First-class 6-day, five-country Eurail Select Pass, plus Eurostar tickets**
ARRIVE IN:	**London**
DEPART FROM:	**Vienna**

There's no shortage of history to be found in the cradle of Western civilization. This ancient and beautiful continent is home to numerous cultural and historical diversions, many of which hold great meaning even today. This 2-week trip takes you to historic battlefields, sacred sites, and monuments to mankind's cultural and scientific achievements.

Day 1

Arrive in London (you'll need to take the red-eye, so catch some z's on the flight). After checking into your hotel, head for **Westminster Abbey**, where all but two of England's monarchs have been crowned, and many a scientist and poet has been laid to rest. Spend the afternoon exploring the bounty of the British Empire at the **British Museum.** Then it's time for a night of cultural indulgence at one of the city's famous theaters. See "London" in chapter 10 for more sightseeing options in this historic city.

Day 2

Fortify yourself with a good English breakfast in the morning and then tackle the **Tower of London,** whose history is loaded with intrigue, suspense, and more than a few famous beheadings. Have some lunch and then catch the Eurostar train (trip time: 2 hr.) to Brussels. Check into your hotel, then head to off to the city's historic **Grand Place,** where you can revel in the World Heritage site's medieval atmosphere (especially at the **Hôtel de Ville**) and explore the city's history at the well-curated **Musée de la Ville de Bruxelles.** Have dinner in one of the city's many cafes and call it a day. See p. 132 for more on Brussels.

Day 3

Spend the morning taking in the surprisingly intact (and moving) battlefield at **Waterloo,** the European version of America's Gettysburg. Return to Brussels and take the 2:37pm train from Brussels Midi to Paris Nord. You'll arrive at 4pm. Check into your hotel for 3 nights, and then spend the early evening strolling through one of the city's historic neighborhoods (**The Marais** and the **Latin Quarter** are good options) before dinner. Cap your night off with a drink at one of the city's wine bars or a night at the opera or ballet. See "Paris" in chapter 8 for nightlife options in the city.

Day 4

Depart Paris on the 9:16am TGV train to **Avignon,** in Provence (arriving at 11:56am). Not only do you get history in the form of the magnificent **Palais des Papes (Palace of the Popes),** but you get some culture as well at **La Fondation Angladon-Dubrujeaud.** Oh, and did we mention some excellent dining as well? Have an early dinner, because you'll need to hop the TGV back to Paris at 9:03pm to arrive at 11:40pm. Fall into bed and get a well-deserved night's sleep. See p. 298 for dining options in the city.

Day 5

For a lesson in the historical extravagance that spurred on the French Revolution, get an early morning start and take the RER C-line commuter train (show your railpass at the ticket booth and get your Métro ticket—the pass itself isn't enough) out to **Versailles** (p. 280) and spend a half-day touring Louis XIV's masterpiece. Then head back to Paris and tour the atmospheric **Conciergerie,** where the indulgent nobility awaited their date with Madame La Guillotine during the Reign of Terror. For some culture, visit the stunning **Ste-Chapelle** (attend a concert here in season) and then dine in one of the city's many sidewalk cafes.

Day 6

Few buildings sum up the history of a nation the way **Notre-Dame** does of France. Hit the cathedral in the morning, do a little shopping (that counts as culture in Paris), and then spend your afternoon with the artifacts and art of the

Louvre. Get in an early dinner before catching the 6:54pm Artesia Night Train out of Paris Bercy to Rome. You'll arrive there about 10am in the morning.

Day 7

Check into a hotel for 2 nights. See Day 9 of "Europe's Best Art & Architecture."

Day 8

Catch the 9am Eurostar train to Naples out of Stazione Termini (except Sun); upon arrival, board the **Circumvesuviana Railway** to Herculaneum (easier to cover in shorter time than nearby Pompeii). Spend a few hours exploring the ruins, then head back to Naples for lunch (pizza!). Finish up your day of history with a visit to the **Museo Archeologico Nazionale (National Archaeological Museum),** then hop a Eurostar train back to Rome. For more on sightseeing and dining options in Naples, see p. 511.

Day 9

See Day 2 of "Great Cities in Europe." Be sure to be at Stazione Termini by 7:05pm to catch the City Nightline train to Munich.

Day 10

You'll arrive in Munich's Hauptbahnhof at 6:30am. Check into your hotel. Wander the city's historic **Altstadt (Old Town),** and then explore the world's largest and oldest technical museum, the **Deutsches Museum von Meisterwerken der Naturwissenschaft und Technik.** End your day sampling Munich's famous nightlife and beer halls. For more on the city, see "Munich" in chapter 9.

Day 11

Rise early and head off to **Nymphenburg Palace,** a testament to 4 centuries of Wittelsbach reign over Bavaria. Have a quick lunch, then end your time in Germany on a somber note by visiting one of history's most infamous sites: **Dachau.** Eat dinner, then hop the late-night train to Vienna.

Day 12

You've done the British and Roman empires; now it's time to tackle the Austro-Hungarian one. Arrive at 6am and check into your hotel. Spend the morning wandering the **Alstadt** and visiting Empress Maria Therese's extravagant **Schönbrunn** (you'll be in good company—Mozart was a guest here way back when). Coffeehouse culture is an integral part of Viennese society; for a truly historic culinary experience, indulge in a slice of *Sacher torte* in **Café Sacher,** the very place where the famous dessert was invented. Follow that up with a visit to the **Kunsthistorisches Museum (Museum of Fine Arts),** a repository of the Habsburgs' finest art and artifacts. For more sightseeing options in the city, see p. 96.

Day 13

Spend your morning scouting the historic and cultural treasures of the **Hofburg Palace Complex.** Have a late lunch and then opt for a unique cultural experience by visiting either the **Spanische Reitschule** (Spanish Riding School) or (if they are performing while you're in town) the **Wiener Sängerknaben (Vienna Boys' Choir).** Vienna has a vibrant nightlife, so end your time in Europe by attending one of its many cultural offerings—the fabulous **Wiener Staatsoper** being a noteworthy choice—and cap off your evening with a drink in one of the city's famed wine cellars (the **Augustiner Keller** combines excellent wines with quite a bit of history).

Day 14

Fly home from Vienna.

ITINERARY 7: **EUROPE'S BEST ART & ARCHITECTURE**

DURATION:	**15 days, 14 nights**
BEST TIME OF YEAR:	**Spring**
IDEAL PASSES:	**First-class 6- or 8-day, four-country Eurail Select Pass (most comfortable, and only a little more expensive than second class)**
ARRIVE IN:	**Brussels**
DEPART FROM:	**Venice**

This trip lets you bury yourself among the masterpieces of European art—it's a museum buff's dream. You'll hit four of the world's greatest museums—the Louvre, the Prado, the Vatican, and the Uffizi—as well as three open-air museums filled with great architecture in Bruges, Barcelona, and Venice.

Day 1

Arrive at Brussels National Airport, then take the train into Brussels Midi station and immediately connect to a train to **Bruges;** the entire train trip should take about 1½ hours. In Bruges, tour the medieval streets and enjoy the city's unique architecture. If you opt for the 6-day pass, then just buy a point-to-point ticket for this trip. See p. 149 for more on Bruges.

Day 2

Take one of the hourly trains that leave Bruges for Brussels, and then catch a Thalys trains to Paris. If you time it right, the entire trip should take about 2½ hours. Once you're settled in **Paris,** start off at the **Arc de Triomphe,** then stroll down the Champs-Elysées to the **Egyptian obelisk** at the Place de la

Concorde. Next up is the **Eiffel Tower.** Around sunset, head for **Notre-Dame Cathedral** to top off your Paris monuments tour. See p. 253 for more on the City of Light.

Day 3

If you're a fan of great art, then we don't have to tell you that the **Louvre** warrants an entire day. But if you need a change of pace in the afternoon, the **Centre Pompidou** will yank you into the 21st century.

Day 4

So many riches: The **Musée National Auguste Rodin?** The **Musée Picasso?** How about the **Musée d'Orsay?** Choose two, and enjoy one in the morning and one in the afternoon. After an early dinner, head to Paris's Austerlitz station for the 7:47pm overnight train to Madrid's Charmartín station, arriving at 9:10am. This train, the *Francisco de Goya,* is an Elipsos Trenhotel (p. 43) and one of Europe's most luxurious rides (operates daily only in high season).

Day 5

Check into your hotel, then start your day in Madrid at the **Royal Palace** and work your way east to the **Monasterio de las Descalzas Reales.** Spend the night as locals do by Tasca-hopping. See p. 680 for more on information.

Day 6

How does the **Museo del Prado** compare to the Louvre? Today's your day to find out. If there's time, head over to the **Museo Nacional Centro de Arte Reina Sofia,** home of Picasso's famous *Guernica.* If you aren't too exhausted, take in a flamenco show after dinner.

Day 7

Take the 10:30am high-speed train from Charmartín station to **Barcelona Sants,** arriving at 1:22pm. Spend the afternoon and evening strolling the **Barri Gòtic,** the city's Gothic quarter, or the famous promenade of **La Rambla.** For more sightseeing options in Barcelona, see p. 707.

Day 8

Start your morning with a tour of **La Sagrada Família;** then either head to **Parc Güell** for more Modernist masterpieces or take in the **Fundació Joan Miró** or **Museu Picasso** museums. (This is a good time to take a break from museums and lounge on a bench in Parc Güell staring at the sky.)

Take the 7:38pm Euro Night train out of Estacio de França to Torino Porta de Susa in Italy, where you'll transfer to the 8:35am Eurostar Italia train bound for Rome, arriving at 12:35pm on Day 9. The timing on this route is very exact and the Euro Night train only departs Barcelona on Tuesday, Thursday and Sunday, so be sure you have your seats and sleeping arrangements reserved well in advance.

Day 9

Check into your hotel in **Rome** and spend the afternoon and evening touring the ruins of Ancient Rome, starting at the **Capitoline Hill** and walking along the **Via dei Fori Imperiali** to the ruins of the **Colosseum.** See p. 496 for more sightseeing options in the city.

Day 10

Spend the entire day perusing the contents of the **Vatican Museums.** Seeing the **Sistine Chapel** is a given, but don't miss the **Pinacoteca** (picture gallery), which is loaded with masterpieces.

Day 11

Say goodbye to Rome and take a morning train—trains run twice an hour and reservations are necessary—for the 95-minute journey to **Florence.** Florence is fortunately compact, so once you've checked into your hotel, you can spend your day strolling the axis from the **Basilica di Santa Maria Novella** to **Il Duomo,** the **Palazzo Vecchio,** and **Giotto's Bell Tower.** See p. 517 for further details on the city.

Day 12

Check out of your hotel, stash your bags at the train station, and spend your entire day, if possible, submerged in the art of the **Galleria degli Uffizi.** Tear yourself away from the museum's masterpieces in order to grab your bags and board the 7:30pm train to Venice, arriving at 9:33pm. (Either have an early dinner in Florence or eat in the Eurostar Italia train's dining car.) See p. 535 for more details on Venice.

Day 13

Venice *is* art. Explore the **Piazza San Marco** in the morning—be sure to stop in at the **Ducale Palace & Bridge of Sighs** and **St. Mark's Basilica**—and then wander the city's many canals and bridges in the afternoon.

Day 14

Museum buffs should hit the **Galleria dell'Accademia** for older art, the **Collezione Peggy Guggenheim** for newer works, and **Ca' d'Oro,** where a multitude of masterpieces are hung in a grand setting in a former palace. If you prefer architecture to museums, take a *vaporetto* (water taxi) ride along the Grand Canal and visit several of Venice's beautiful churches and guild houses.

Day 15

Bid farewell to Europe and fly home out of Venice.

ITINERARY 8: **EUROPE FOR FOOD LOVERS**

DURATION:	**15 days, 14 nights**
BEST TIME OF YEAR:	**Spring or fall; note that the Hotel Elipsos train from Milan to Barcelona runs only on Monday, Wednesday, and Friday, so you'll need to time your trip from Milan to Barcelona on the night of Day 12 to coincide with the train schedule**
IDEAL PASSES:	**First-class three-country Eurail Select Pass (5 or 6 days, depending on the side trips you take), plus Eurostar ticket**
ARRIVE IN:	**London**
DEPART FROM:	**Barcelona**

This 2-week trip features a walk through some of the best and most recognized regional cuisine and dining experiences in Europe. We start you off in London, where you can take afternoon tea or dine on classic pub grub, then head off to indulge in the renowned food mecca of Paris plus the celebrated cuisines of Tuscany and Spain, with a side trip to Provence as a bonus. Loosen your belt as you eat your way through Europe.

Before you leave: If you don't want to be left out in the cold, it is crucial to make dinner reservations by phone in advance before you leave home.

Day 1

Arrive in the morning in **London.** The city is actually a center of global cuisine where you can eat a different country's food every day for weeks—it's an often-underrated foodie capital that's about a lot more than fish and chips (though you should have those too!). Spend the day visiting the sites of Westminster: **Westminster Abbey, 10 Downing Street, Big Ben,** and the **Houses of Parliament.** For dinner, dine at the ultra-British but thoroughly modern cuisine at **Rules Restaurant.** Top off the evening with a pint at a pub near your hotel. See p. 405 for more on dining and sightseeing in the city.

Day 2

Today's a royal day in London. Spend a long morning at the **Tower of London,** have lunch, and then head off to **Kensington Palace.** Grab a pretheater dinner at the festive **Mela,** then head off to the West End and see a show.

Day 3

In the morning, visit the **British Museum.** Shop a bit in Covent Garden and stop in at one of Soho's many patisseries (**Maison Bertaux**'s our favorite) for a traditional afternoon tea. Then head off to South Kensington and pop in at the **Victoria & Albert Museum.** On your final night in London, indulge your palate with a splurge meal at **Gordon Ramsay** (be sure to make reservations well in advance!).

Day 4

After a good English breakfast, take a morning Eurostar train (trip time: 2 hr., 15 min.) ride to Paris. Your Eurail Select Pass gives you a discount on this speedy but expensive train. (See p. 392 for more on the Eurostar.) Spend the afternoon at the **Louvre** and have dinner in a traditional French brasserie. See p. 272 for dining options in Paris.

Day 5

Get acquainted with monumental Paris. Begin at the **Arc de Triomphe** and stroll down the Champs-Elysées to the **Egyptian obelisk;** then either stand in line for the Eiffel Tower or explore the **Ile St-Louis** and the **Quartier Latin.** Take a break at a Left Bank cafe for coffee and pastries, and around sunset, head for **Notre-Dame Cathedral** to top off your Paris monuments tour. Have dinner in a Left Bank bistro.

Day 6

Explore a Parisian food market this morning to see where chefs get their inspiration. Then visit **Fauchon,** the ultimate gourmet food store, for the ingredients of a picnic lunch. Spend the rest of the day exploring the sights of the **Ile de la Cité** and **Le Marais** before seeing what all that three-star Michelin stuff is about at **L'Ambroisie** (just be prepared to empty your wallet). Get some rest—you'll have an early start and a very long day tomorrow.

Day 7

Depart Paris on the 10:20am TGV train to **Avignon** (doesn't run on Sun), in Provence (arriving at 1:47pm). This former capital of Christendom offers excellent dining and the magnificent **Palais des Papes (Palace of the Popes)** for touring. Have an early dinner, because you'll need to hop the TGV back to Paris at 9:03pm to arrive at 11:40pm. Fall into bed and get a well-deserved night's sleep. See p. 298 for dining options in the city.

Day 8

Sleep in a little, have a leisurely breakfast, and then spend the day at the **Musée d'Orsay** and **Centre Pompidou.** Have lunch in one of the city's celebrated cafes (the avant-garde **Café Beaubourg** is just across from the Pompidou). You can bring along Parisian takeout or have dinner on the 6:54pm overnight train (out of Gare de Bercy) to Florence, your base for Tuscany. You'll arrive at 7:13am on Day 9.

Day 9

Work up your appetite today by strolling **Florence** from the **Basilica di Santa Maria Novella** to the Duomo, the **Palazzo Vecchio,** and finally Santa Croce. Have lunch at a simple Italian restaurant such as **Buca dell'Orafo.** For dinner, eat at the legendary Tuscan restaurant **Paoli.** See p. 527 for more on dining in the city.

Day 10

It's excursion time: Catch the 9:27am train to the Tuscan city of Pisa. You'll arrive at 10:29am and should immediately set out for the famous **Leaning Tower.** For lunch, sample excellent Pisan cuisine at **Antica Trattoria Da Bruno,** near the tower. Then tour the **Duomo** and the **Baptistery** before returning to Florence on the 5:32pm train (arriving 6:33pm). Sample some more delectable Tuscan cuisine at dinner, then have dessert and coffee at one of the city's many sidewalk cafes and people-watch.

Day 11

Spend the morning at the **Boboli Gardens** and the **Palazzo Pitti.** Take a long lunch at **Cantinetta Antinori,** sampling the wines. After a siesta, do some shopping and have a final Tuscan dinner at **Trattoria Garga.**

Day 12

Get up early and spend the day in the **Galleria degli Uffizi,** one of the world's greatest art museums. Take the 5pm express train from Florence to Milan, where you'll have a 55-minute layover before connecting to the 7:40pm Hotel Elipsos train to Barcelona. Have dinner on the train or grab something in Milan's station before you depart. You'll arrive in Barcelona at 9:40am.

Day 13

Barcelona has an embarrassment of riches, both culinary and architectural. Check into your hotel and then start your day off at **La Sagrada Familia** cathedral, the city's famous cathedral, and wander the city's Gothic Quarter. Take lunch at **La Gardunya,** located in the back of Catalonia's best food market, before visiting the **Museu Picasso.** Retire to your hotel room for a siesta, then eat a late dinner and spend the night downing bubbly at Barcelona's numerous *cava* (champagne) bars. See p. 711 for more on dining in the city.

Day 14

Start your day off by visiting the **Parc Güell** and the **Fundació Joan Miró.** Spend a relaxing afternoon sipping cava and munching tapas at **El Xampanyet,** and eat a late dinner at one of Barcelona's excellent Catalonian restaurants— **Can Ravell** is a foodie favorite.

Day 15

Say *adios* to Europe and fly home from Barcelona.

DURATION:	**15 days, 14 nights**
BEST TIME OF YEAR:	**Spring or fall**
IDEAL PASSES:	**First-class 5-day, four-country Eurail Select Pass, plus Eurostar tickets**
ARRIVE IN:	**Rome**
DEPART FROM:	**Berlin**

Europe has been the center of many a globe-girdling empire. This 2-week trip gets you to the heart of the Continent's great cities—and gives you as much time as possible to explore their sights and sounds—and to meet their people.

Day 1

Land at Rome's Fiumicino airport, starting your European rail journey with the train shuttle to the Roma Termini Station (don't waste a day on your railpass for this ride, though—the ticket is very cheap). Check into your hotel before starting your exploration of ancient Rome, beginning at the **Capitoline Hill** and walking along the Via dei Fori Imperiali to the ruins of the **Colosseum.** Nearby you'll find the ruins of the **Roman Forum** and the **Palatine Hill.** Have dinner near the **Pantheon** and visit the **Trevi Fountain.** See p. 490 for more on the city.

Day 2

Spend today exploring the treasures of the Vatican. Take in St. Peter's Basilica in the morning and the Vatican Museums in the afternoon. Have dinner in Trastevere.

Day 3

During the morning, shop and stroll around the **Spanish Steps.** In the afternoon, take in another museum, such as the **Galleria Borghese,** or enjoy people-watching on the Piazza della Rotonda near the Pantheon. Around 5pm, head to Stazione Termini for your first major rail trip: the **Artesia France-Italy Night train,** departing at 6:20pm from Rome, arriving at 9:16am the next morning in Paris.

Day 4

Get acquainted with Paris. Begin at the **Arc de Triomphe** and stroll down the Champs-Elysées to the **Egyptian obelisk;** then either stand in line for the **Eiffel Tower** or explore the **Ile St-Louis** and the **Latin Quarter.** Around sunset, head for **Notre-Dame Cathedral** to top off your day. Eat dinner in a Left Bank cafe. See p. 253 for more information on Paris.

Day 5

Start your day off exploring the **St-Germain-des-Prés** area. Move on to the Ile de la Cité before heading to the **Place de la Bastille.** Finish your day off by touring fashionable Le Marais. Then eat dinner at a brasserie and spend the night people-watching at a sidewalk cafe.

Day 6

Spend the day at the **Louvre;** if you want a change of scenery, tack on a visit to the magnificent **Musée d'Orsay.** Be sure to indulge in some Parisian pastries before the day is through.

Day 7

Grab a croissant on the way to the Gare de Nord and take a morning Eurostar train to London. The just-over-2-hour journey rockets across France at up to 180 mph (290kmph). It may appear costly, but the passholder fare is no more expensive (and far more comfortable) than the combined fare for a high-speed ferry from Calais to Dover and a local train from Dover to London. (See p. 392 for more on Eurostar.)

You'll arrive in **London** around lunchtime. Leave your bags at your hotel and grab lunch at a nearby pub. Spend the afternoon touring the sights of Westminster: **Westminster Abbey, 10 Downing Street, Big Ben,** and the **Houses of Parliament.** Have dinner in Covent Garden. See p. 397 for more on the British capital.

Day 8

If you couldn't get into Westminster Abbey on Day 7, try again. Otherwise, spend the morning at the **British Museum,** and after lunch head over to the **Tower of London.** If you have time, take a ride on the **British Airways London Eye,** just across the river. After a quick dinner, head over to the West End and catch a show.

Day 9

If one of your days in London is a weekend, spend some time at one or two of the major markets, such as Portobello Road. If you're here midweek, wave hello to the lions in **Trafalgar Square** and tour the **National Gallery,** one of Europe's finest art museums (and it's free!). Grab some lunch, shop a bit at Covent Garden, and end your day at the **Victoria & Albert Museum**—home of the world's greatest collection of decorative arts (don't miss the British Galleries).

Day 10

Fortify yourself with a good English breakfast this morning before heading to St. Pancras station for the 8:27am Eurostar to **Brussels,** the capital of the European Union. The trip takes 2 hours, but you'll arrive just before noon, thanks to a 1-hour time difference. See p. 132 for more on Brussels.

Once you arrive, stash your luggage at Gare du Midi, then hop a train to Gare Central and head to the medieval **Grand-Place,** a World Heritage Site, for some of the city's famous seafood and mussels. After dinner, head back to Gare du Midi and get on the 7:18pm InterCity train for the 2¾-hour trip to Amsterdam. You'll get in late, so take a cab to your hotel. We suggest staying near Centraal Station, at a hotel such as the **Hotel Amsterdam-De Roode Leeuw** or the **Amstel Botel.** See p. 574 for more hotel options.

Day 11

You've got only 2 days in Amsterdam, so focus on the city center. Explore the core of the city either by foot or on a canal boat, stopping at the **Dam Square,** the picturesque **Flower Market** at **Muntplein,** the immense market at **Waterlooplein,** and the lively **Leidseplein.** After a late lunch, stop at the renowned **Rijksmuseum** to see its current "greatest hits" exhibition of Dutch art. For dinner, sample one of the city's **Indonesian rijsttafel buffets.** After dinner, if you dare, take an evening walk through the Red Light District on the way back to your hotel—it only gets livelier as it gets later.

Day 12

Check out of your hotel early, store your luggage, and head to the western part of the city this morning, past the Dutch Renaissance–style **Westerkerk,** to the haunting **Anne Frank House.** Have lunch at **De Prins,** right across the canal. Unwind with a coffee and "brown-cafe" style food while people-watching along the canal.

Make sure to be at Schiphol Station in time to catch the 2:49pm InterCity train to Berlin (alas, there are no decent overnight trains from Amsterdam to the German capital). Have dinner on the train and arrive in Berlin at 9:20pm. Check into your hotel and get a good night's sleep.

Day 13

In the morning, visit the **Brandenburg Gate,** symbol of Berlin, then walk down Unter den Linden and enjoy breakfast at one of the cafes that line the street. Head to the store-lined **Ku'damm** to witness German capitalism in action. In the afternoon, visit the Greek and Roman antiquities in the **Pergamon Museum,** then head south to explore the charming 16th-century **Nikolai Quarter.** If they are playing when you are in town, the **Berlin Philharmonic Orchestra** is one of the best in the world. For more on Berlin, see p. 327.

Day 14

Visit the masterpieces at the **Gemäldegalerie,** then tour **Charlottenburg Palace** and its museums. Spend any leftover time strolling through Berlin, perhaps stopping at the Cold War's **Checkpoint Charlie.** Or take a day trip to beautiful **Potsdam,** just 20 minutes away by train (trains depart throughout the day), and explore the **Sans Souci Palace** and its surrounding parkland. After dinner, do as Berliners do and have a drink at a Kneipe, the local version of a British pub.

Day 15

Fly back to your home from Berlin.

ITINERARY 10: **THE GRAND TOUR**

DURATION:	**15 days, 14 nights**
BEST TIME OF YEAR:	**Any time**
IDEAL PASSES:	**First-class 15-day Eurail Global Pass or point-to-point tickets (cheapest)**
ARRIVE IN:	**Lisbon**
DEPART FROM:	**Berlin**

The European Union may have a single currency (well, minus a few pesky holdouts here and there), but it's got more than a dozen unique cultures. A dozen in 15 days is a bit too much of a challenge for us, but this long-distance journey lets you experience six distinctly different flavors of Europe without having to change your money once—the most diversity and least hassle you can get in 2 weeks. Note that the five rail legs used in this itinerary are night trains, so you'll save on hotel rooms but will have to budget for sleeper supplements.

Day 1

Time your flight to arrive in Lisbon as early as possible. Start your day with a stroll through the **Alfama,** the most atmospheric quarter of Lisbon. Visit the city's 12th-century cathedral and take in a view of the city and the river Tagus from the **Miradouro de Santa Luzia.** Climb up to the **Castelo de São Jorge** and take in another breathtaking view from the castle's observation platform. Consider a nap before spending a late night at a **fado club** in the Alfama. See p. 632 for more information on the Portuguese capital.

Day 2

Head to the suburb of Belém to see the **Mosteiro dos Jerónimos,** the **Torre de Belém,** and the **Museu Nacional dos Coches.** After lunch, see the artworks at the **Museu de Fundação Calouste Gulbenkian,** or shop at the open-air **Feira da Ladra.** Take the overnight *Lusitania* hotel train to Madrid (p. 629).

Day 3

Drop your luggage at your hotel, then start your day in Madrid at the **Royal Palace** and work your way east to the **Monasterio las Descalzas Reales.** After checking into your hotel, snack your way around the many tapas bars in the Plaza Mayor area. See p. 665 for more on Madrid.

Day 4

Check out the masterpieces at the **Museo Lázaro Galdiano** in the morning and shop the El Rastro flea market in the afternoon. Or take a day trip to explore the Moorish architectural riches of **Córdoba**—frequent AVE express trains leave from Madrid's Atocha station for the just-under-2-hour journey. See p. 692 for more on this Moorish city.

Day 5

Spend your last day in Madrid at the **Museo del Prado,** and take the overnight *Francisco de Goya* train to Paris. This train, one of the Elipsos series, is one of Europe's most luxurious regular trips; even the most basic accommodation is a four-berth sleeper, not a six-berth couchette room like those on many other trains (p. 257). **Note:** The train only runs daily in high season.

Day 6

See Day 4 of the "Great Cities of Europe" itinerary (p. 23).

Day 7

See Day 5 of the "Great Cities of Europe" itinerary (p. 23).

Day 8

Spend the day immersed in art at the **Louvre** and the **Musée d'Orsay.** Grab some gourmet French takeout at **Fauchon** for dinner and take the overnight train to Florence, departing Paris Bercy at 6:52pm and arriving at 7:13am.

Day 9

Florence is all about art. Spend your day strolling the city from the **Basilica di Santa Maria Novella** to the **Duomo,** the **Palazzo Vecchio,** and finally **Santa Croce.** Florence is all about food, too, so load up on Tuscan cuisine at dinner. See p. 527 for dining options in Florence.

Day 10

Allot the entire day for the **Galleria degli Uffizi,** one of the world's greatest art museums. If you need a change of scenery, stroll the **Boboli Gardens** and take in the art at the **Palazzo Pitti.** Take the 9:52pm overnight train to Vienna, arriving at 8:34am.

Day 11

See Day 7 of the "Riding the Scenic Route" itinerary (p. 9).

Day 12

Explore other major Vienna attractions, such as the **Kaiserliche Hofburg (Imperial Court Palace)** and the **Kunsthistorisches Museum.** Get to the train station in time to take the 10:08pm overnight train to Berlin (arriving at 9:09am).

Day 13

You'll get to **Berlin** by breakfast time, so head for **Unter den Linden** and enjoy breakfast at one of the cafes that line the street. Head to the store-lined **Ku'damm** to shop until you feel like eating lunch. In the afternoon, visit the Greek and Roman antiquities in the **Pergamon Museum,** then head south to explore the charming 16th-century **Nikolai Quarter.** If they are playing, when you are in town, the **Berlin Philharmonic Orchestra** is one of the best in the world. For more on the city, see p. 327.

Day 14

Visit the masterpieces at the **Gemäldegalerie,** then tour **Charlottenburg Palace** and its museums. Spend any leftover time strolling through Berlin, perhaps stopping at the Cold War's **Checkpoint Charlie.** Top off your trip with a drink at one of Berlin's vaunted wine cellars.

Day 15

Fly home from Berlin.

PLANNING YOUR EUROPEAN RAIL TRIP

Rails are the veins of Europe. When you travel on the Continent's speedy, affordable, and surprisingly complete rail system, you'll cross terrain where no cars go; make friends you would never otherwise have met; travel without the worries of traffic, parking, and airport security—and perhaps enjoy a good night's sleep, too.

Speedy trains zip across Northern Europe at speeds up to 186 mph (300kmph); slower trains stop in the depths of Swiss mountain valleys and meander past quaint Dutch villages. And somehow, trains make people open up in ways they never would if they were traveling by air, bus, or car. In a car on a French night train, we once met a college student from Nashville, an artist from Florence, and five members of an Ethiopian soccer team. Riding a high-speed train along the backbone of Italy, we were charmed by a young man, heading to his exams for the *carabinieri,* who led us patiently through the chaos of Rome's Termini Station.

Thousands of students first see Europe from the inexpensive perch of a six-berth couchette, but more mature travelers who seek luxury are sure to find it in Europe's top-class trains, where cabins include private showers and waiters bring restaurant-quality meals straight to your room as the Pyrenees or the Mediterranean coast slide by your window.

Those who haven't traveled on European trains in a while will be startled by the range of ticket classes and the bewildering number of trains. But traveling by train doesn't have to be confusing: Take a deep breath, leave yourself some time at the station, and enjoy traveling the way Europeans do.

Modern trains are romantic, comfortable, and an easy way to get around, and they even get you to where you're going on time. What more can you ask?

VISITOR INFORMATION

Your first step in planning your Europe trip should be to decide which countries or regions you'd like to visit. Browse chapters 3 through 19 of this book to get an idea of the highlights of each major European country. The 39-nation **European Travel Commission** produces a customized electronic travel planner on its website that is also useful. (c/o Spring, O'Brien and Co., 50 W. 23rd St., 11th Floor, New York, NY 10010; ✆ 212/620-7100; www.visiteurope.com). Should you want more detailed information to help you make your selections, contact the **European tourist offices** in your own country; for a complete list, see below:

Austrian National Tourist Office

www.austria.info

IN THE U.S. & CANADA P.O. Box 1142, New York, NY 10108 (✆ 212/944-6880; fax 212/730-4568; travel@austria.info). No visitors.

Belgian Tourist Office

www.visitbelgium.com

IN THE U.S. & CANADA 220 E. 42nd St., Ste. 3402, New York, NY 10017 (✆ 212/758-8130; fax 212/355-7675; info@visitbelgium.com). Open Monday to Friday 9:30am to 4:30pm.

Visit Britain

www.visitbritain.com

IN THE U.S. & CANADA 551 Fifth Ave., Ste. 701, New York, NY 10176 (✆US: 800/462-2748; CANADA: 888/VISIT-UK [847-4885]; travelinfo@visitbritain.org). Open Monday to Friday 9am to 5pm.

Bulgarian State Agency for Tourism

www.bulgariatravel.org

IN BULGARIA 1, Sveta Nedelia Sq., 1040 Sofia, Bulgaria (✆ 359/2-933-5845; fax 359/2-989-6939; info@bulgariatravel.org).

Croatian National Tourist Board

http://us.croatia.hr

IN THE U.S. & CANADA 350 Fifth Ave., Ste. 4003, New York, NY 10118

(✆ 212/279-8672; fax 212/279-8683; cntony@earthlink.net).

Czech Tourist Authority

www.czechtourism.com

IN THE U.S. 1109 Madison Ave., New York, NY 10028 (✆ 212/288-0830; fax 212/288-0971; info-usa@czechtourism.com). Open Tuesday, Wednesday, and Friday 10am to 5pm; Thursday 10am to 7pm.

IN CANADA 2 Bloor St. West, Ste. 1500, Toronto, ON M4W 3E2 (✆ 416/363-9928; fax 416/972-6991; info-ca@czechtourism.com). Open Monday to Friday 8:30am to 4:30pm.

French Government Tourist Office

www.franceguide.com

IN THE U.S. 825 Third Ave., New York, NY 10022 (✆ 514/288-1904; fax 212/838-7855; info.us@franceguide.com).

IN CANADA 1800 av. McGill College, Ste. 1010, Montréal, QC H3A 3J6 (✆ 866/313-7262 or 514/876-9881; canada@franceguide.com). Open Monday to Friday noon to 3pm.

German National Tourist Office

www.cometogermany.com

IN THE U.S. & CANADA 122 E. 42nd St., Ste. 2000, New York, NY 10168 (✆ 212/661-7200; fax 212/661-7174; office-usa@germany.travel).

Greek National Tourism Organization

www.greektourism.com

IN THE U.S. Olympic Tower, 645 Fifth Ave., Ste. 903, New York, NY 10022 (☎ **212/421-5777;** fax 212/826-6940; info@greektourism.com).

IN CANADA 1500 Don Mills Rd., Toronto, ON M3B 3K4 (☎ **416/968-2220;** fax 416/968-6533; grnto.tor@on.aibn.com).

Hungarian National Tourist Office

www.gotohungary.com

IN THE U.S. & CANADA 350 Fifth Ave., Ste. 7107, New York, NY 10118 (☎ **212/695-1221;** fax 212/695-0809; info@gotohungary.com).

Tourism Ireland

www.discoverireland.com

IN THE U.S. & CANADA 345 Park Ave., New York, NY 10154 (☎ **800/223-6470** or 212/418-0800; fax 212/371-9052).

Italian Government Tourist Board

www.italiantourism.com

IN THE U.S. 630 Fifth Ave., Ste. 1565, New York, NY 10111 (☎ **212/245-5618;** fax 212/586-9249). Open Monday to Friday 9am to 5pm.

IN CANADA 110 Yonge St., Ste. 503, Toronto, ON M5C 1T4 (☎ **416/925-4882;** fax 416/925-4799). Open 9am to 5pm.

Luxembourg National Tourist Office

www.visitluxembourg.com

IN THE U.S. & CANADA 17 Beekman Place, New York, NY 10022 (☎ **212/935-8888;** info@visitluxembourg.com).

Macedonian National Tourism Office

www.exploringmacedonia.com

IN MACEDONIA Partizanski odredi 62, 1000 Skopje, Macedonia (☎ **389/2-311-8498;** fax 389/2-3075-333; contact@exploringmacedonia.com).

National Tourist Organization of Montenegro

www.visit-montenegro.com

IN MONTENEGRO Postanski fah, 28, 85310 Budva, Montenegro (☎ **382/3340-2030;** fax 382/3340-2031; info@visit-montenegro.com).

Netherlands Board of Tourism

www.holland.com

IN THE U.S. & CANADA 215 Park Ave. S., Ste. 2005, New York, NY 10003 (☎ **212/370-7360;** fax 212/370-9507; information@holland.com).

Polish National Tourist Office

www.poland.travel

IN THE U.S. & CANADA 5 Marine View Plaza, Hoboken, NJ 07030 (☎ **201/420-9910;** fax 201/584-9153; info.na@poland.travel).

Portuguese Trade & Tourism Office

www.visitportugal.com

IN THE U.S. 590 Fifth Ave., 4th Floor, New York, NY 10036 (☎ **646/723-0200;** tourism@portugal.org).

IN CANADA 60 Bloor St. West, Ste. 1005, Toronto, ON M4W 3B8 (☎ **416/921-9870;** tourism@portugal.org).

Romanian National Tourist Office

www.romaniatourism.com

IN THE U.S. & CANADA 355 Lexington Ave., 8th Floor, New York, NY 10017 (✆ **212/545-8484;** info@romaniatourism.com).

Scandinavian Tourist Boards (Denmark, Finland, Norway & Sweden)

www.goscandinavia.com, www.visitdenmark.com, www.visitfinland.org, www.visitnorway.com, or www.visitsweden.com

IN THE U.S. & CANADA 655 Third Ave., Ste. 1810, New York, NY 10017 (✆ **212/885-9700;** info@goscandinavia.com).

National Tourism Organization of Serbia

www.serbia.travel

IN SERBIA Čika-Ljubina 8, 11000 Belgrade, Serbia (✆ **381/11 6557 127;** fax 381/11 2097 828; info@serbia.travel).

Slovak Tourist Board

www.slovakia.travel

IN THE SLOVAK REPUBLIC Námestie Ĺ. Štúra 1, P.O. Box 35, 974 05 Banská Bystrica, Slovak Republic (✆ **421/48-413-61-46;** fax 421/48-413-61-49; sacr@sacr.sk).

Slovenian Tourist Board

www.slovenia.info

IN SLOVENIA Dimičeva 13, SI-1000 Ljubljana, Slovenia (✆ **386/1 5898 550;** fax 386/1-5898-560; info@slovenia.info).

Tourist Office of Spain

www.spain.info

IN THE U.S. 666 Fifth Ave., 35th Floor, New York, NY 10103 (✆ **212/265-8822;** fax 212/265-8864; nuevayork@tourspain.es).

IN CANADA 2 Bloor St. West, 34th Floor, Toronto, ON M4W 3E2 (✆ **416/961-3131;** fax 416/961-1992; toronto@tourspain.es).

Switzerland Tourism

www.myswitzerland.com

IN THE U.S. 608 Fifth Ave., New York, NY 10020 (✆ **877/794-8037;** fax 212/262-6116; info.usa@myswitzerland.com).

IN CANADA 926 The East Mall, Toronto, ON M9B 6K1 (✆ **800/794-7795;** fax 416/695-2774; info.caen@myswitzerland.com).

Turkish Government Tourist Offices

www.tourismturkey.org

IN THE U.S. & CANADA 2525 Massachusetts Ave., Washington, DC 20008 (✆ **202/612-6800;** fax 202/319-7446; info.dc@tourismturkey.org).

WHEN TO GO

Europe is a continent for all seasons, offering everything from a bikini beach party on the Riviera to the world's finest skiing in the Alps.

Europe has a continental climate with distinct seasons, but you can expect great temperature variations from one region to another. Northern Norway measures its snow in meters, while southern Italy remains far warmer in the winter. Still, the Gulf Stream keeps weather more temperate across the continent than you might imagine. Scandinavia is seldom colder than the northern U.S., and it's not unheard

WHAT time IS IT, ANYWAY?

Based on U.S. **Eastern Standard Time (EST),** Britain, Ireland, and Portugal are 5 hours ahead of New York City; the rest of the countries in this book are 6 hours ahead of New York. For instance, when it's noon in New York, it's 5pm in London and Lisbon; and 6pm in Paris, Amsterdam, and Berlin. The European countries observe daylight saving time, but the time change doesn't occur on the same day as in North America, so the time difference can vary by up to 2 hours during those weeks between time changes.

If you plan to visit Ireland or continental Europe from Britain, keep in mind that the time will be the same in Ireland and Portugal and 1 hour later in the other countries in this guide.

Note: Departure and arrival times on train schedules are always given in 24-hour military time. So a train leaving at 1:23pm would be listed as leaving at 13:23.

of for snow to fall even on the Greek Islands in winter. Generally speaking, expect European temperatures to be somewhat warmer than those in similar North American latitudes.

The **high season** lasts from mid-May to mid-September, with most tourists hitting the Continent from mid-June to August. In general, this is the most expensive time to travel except in Austria and Switzerland, where prices are actually higher during the ski season. And because Scandinavian hotels depend on business clients instead of tourists, lower prices can often be found in the fleeting summer, when business travelers are scarce and a smaller number of tourists take over.

You'll find smaller crowds, fair weather, and moderate prices at hotels in the **shoulder seasons,** from Easter to mid-May and mid-September to mid-October. **Off season** (except at ski resorts) is from November to Easter, with the exception of December 25 to January 6. Much of Europe, especially Italy, traditionally takes August off from work, and August 15 to August 30 is vacation time for many locals. Some cities may well be devoid of natives, many of whom are flocking to the beaches instead, though this trend is slowly changing as Europeans step up efforts to attract a global tourism market.

As with any international travel, it's also a good idea to keep an eye on currency and economic fluctuations. When the euro is weak or the economy is down, it's often easier to find a European bargain, whatever the season.

Weather

BRITAIN & IRELAND   Everyone knows it rains a lot in Britain and Ireland. Winters are rainier than summers; August and from September to mid-October are the sunniest months. Summer daytime temperatures average from the low-60s Fahrenheit (teens Celsius) to mid-60s (20s Celsius), dropping to the 40s (single digits Celsius) on winter nights. Ireland, whose shores are bathed by the Gulf Stream, has a milder climate and the most changeable weather—a dark, rainy morning can quickly turn into a sunny afternoon, and vice versa. The Scottish Lowlands have a climate similar to England's, but the Highlands are much colder, with storms and snow in winter.

CENTRAL EUROPE   In Vienna and along the Danube Valley, the climate is moderate. Summer daytime temperatures average in the low 70s Fahrenheit (20s Celsius), falling at night to the low 50s (teens Celsius). Winter temperatures are in the 30s Fahrenheit (below 0 Celsius) and 40s (teens Celsius) during the day. In Budapest, temperatures can reach 80°F (25°C) in August and dip to 30°F (0°C) in January. Winter is damp and chilly, spring is mild, and May and June are usually wet. The best weather is in the late summer through October. In Prague and Bohemia, summer months have an average temperature of 65°F (18°C) but are the rainiest, while January and February are usually sunny and clear, with temperatures around freezing.

FRANCE & GERMANY   The weather in Paris is approximately the same as in the U.S. mid-Atlantic states, but like most of Europe, there's less extreme variation. In summer, the temperature rarely goes above the mid-70s Fahrenheit (mid-20s Celsius), though heat waves (such as the one that struck all of Europe in 2006) can occur. Summers are fair and can be hot along the Riviera. Winters tend to be mild, in the 40s Fahrenheit (teens Celsius), though it's warmer along the Riviera. Germany's climate ranges from the moderate summers and chilly, damp winters in the north to the mild summers and very cold, sunny winters of the Alpine south.

NORTHERN EUROPE   In the Netherlands, the weather is never extreme at any time of year. Summer temperatures average around 67°F (20°C) and the winter average is about 40°F (5°C). The climate is rainy and windy, the skies gray, with the driest months from February to May. From mid-April to mid-May, the tulip fields burst into color. The climate of northern Germany is very similar. Belgium's climate is moderate, varying from 73°F (23°C) in July and August to 40°F (5°C) in December and January. It does rain a lot, but the weather is at its finest in July and August.

SCANDINAVIA   Summer temperatures above the Arctic Circle average around the mid-50s Fahrenheit (mid-teens Celsius), dropping to about 14°F (–10°C) during the dark winters. In the south, summer temperatures hover around 70°F (22°C) and drop to the 20s Fahrenheit (below 0 Celsius) in winter. Fjord and ocean swimming is often possible in summer, but rain is frequent. The sun shines 24 hours in midsummer above the Arctic Circle, where winter brings semi-permanent twilight. Denmark's climate is relatively mild by comparison. It has moderate summer temperatures and winters that can be damp and foggy, with temperatures just above the mid-30s Fahrenheit (0 Celsius).

SOUTHERN EUROPE   Summers are hot in Italy and Spain, with temperatures around the high 80s Fahrenheit (30s Celsius) or higher in some parts of Spain. Along the Italian Riviera, summer and winter temperatures are mild, and except in the Alpine regions, Italian winter temperatures rarely drop below freezing (although Mediterranean winds can be cold). The area around Madrid is dry and arid, and summers in Spain are coolest along the Atlantic coast, with mild temperatures year-round on the Costa del Sol. Seaside Portugal is very rainy but has temperatures of 50° to 75°F (10°–25°C) year-round.

SWITZERLAND & THE ALPS   The Alpine climate is shared by Bavaria in southern Germany, the Austrian Tyrol, and the Italian Dolomites. Winters are cold and bright, and spring comes late, with snow flurries well into April. Summers are mild and sunny, though the Alpine regions can experience dramatic changes in weather any time of year.

FINDING YOUR RAIL ROUTE

Thousands of trains run across Europe every day, and on many routes you can just show up at the station and be assured a train will leave pretty soon. But there are many reasons to plan your trip in advance. Some trains require advance reservations, some run only a few times a day, and most lines have both fast and slow trains. You will want to be especially mindful of reservations if you want a sleeping car, plan to travel along particularly popular routes (such as Frankfurt to Berlin), or plan to travel via high-speed trains like Thalys and Eurostar.

The **Rail Europe** website (**www.raileurope.com**) produces train schedules for routes between major European destinations. But many smaller towns and cities are missing from their site, and if you want to check intermediate stops on a given train, you'll have to look elsewhere. The site also offers prices for point-to-point tickets (a major plus when budgeting for a trip), seat reservations, passes when purchased in North America (some passes can be purchased only on this side of the Atlantic), and a list of accommodations on night trains.

A better site for detailed timetables—and our personal favorite—is produced by the German railway **Die Bahn (DB)** at **www.bahn.de** (select the English option at the top of the Web page). The DB site covers all major rail lines in most Eurail countries. It also features many bus and ferry services, will tell you which trains require reservations, and within Germany provides train prices and tells you at which tracks your train is expected to depart and arrive. If you click the little "Mobility Check" box near the bottom of the screen, you can even compare travel times and the environmental impacts of making your preferred trip via car, train, or airplane.

But even the DB site is missing some small stations and lines, and it can be hard to find the correct station for smaller cities when the station name doesn't match the location name (we had a heck of a time getting the correct routing for some towns in Hungary). Note also that, although the DB site does a pretty good job of translating, like most European sites, it relies on local spellings rather than North American ones. In other words, you'll be looking for Firenze and Wien, not Florence and Vienna.

If the DB site doesn't meet your needs, try the national rail site for your travel destination. Choose your desired country from the "National Railway Websites & Phone Numbers" chart on the next page, or from a more comprehensive list at **www.railfaneurope.net/links.html**. Many of the national rail sites display prices for domestic itineraries only; if you are traveling through several countries, you'll need to call the national rail company or check Rail Europe's website, keeping in mind that some European rail sites don't have English language pages.

Off-line, the ultimate bible for European rail schedules since its first printing in 1873 is the **Thomas Cook European Timetable.** At over 500 pages, it's clunky, but it covers every major railway line on the Continent, as well as many bus and ferry services. It's updated twice a year, with the summer edition including railpass information as well as embassy and tourist info contacts. Order the timetable online from Thomas Cook Publishing (allowing 2 weeks for delivery, **www.thomascook publishing.com**) for £15 plus shipping to the U.S. (approx. $30 total). To order by phone (it'll cost you about 10% more), call ℂ **44/1733-416-477.**

National Railway Websites & Phone Numbers

Country	Website	Phone Number (International)
All countries	www.raileurope.com	800/622-8600 (E)*
Austria	www.oebb.at	43/1-930-000
Belgium	www.b-rail.be	32/2-528-2828
Bulgaria	www.bdz.bg	359/2-932-41-90
Croatia	www.hznet.hr	385/60-333-444
Czech Republic	www.cd.cz	420/840-112-113
Denmark	www.dsb.dk	45/70-13-14-15 (E)
Finland	www.vr.fi	358/9-2319-2902 (E)
France	www.sncf.com	33/892-35-35-35 (E)
Germany	www.bahn.de	44/8718-80-80-66 (E)
Great Britain	www.nationalrail.co.uk	4/20-7278-5240 (E)
Greece	www.trainose.com	30/210-529-8829
Hungary	www.mav.hu	36/1-444-44-99
Ireland	www.irishrail.ie	353/1-836-6222 (E)
Italy	www.trenitalia.com	39/06-684-75-475
Luxembourg	www.cfl.lu	352/2489-2489
Netherlands	www.ns.nl	31/900-202-11-63
Norway	www.nsb.no	47/815-00-888, ext. 9 (E)
Poland	www.pkp.pl	48/22-511-6003, ext. 1 (E)
Portugal	www.cp.pt	351/21-854-5212
Romania	www.cfr.ro	40/256-793-806
Serbia & Montenegro	www.zeleznicesrbije.com	381/360-28-99
Slovak Republic	www.slovakrail.sk	421/181-88
Slovenia	www.slo-zeleznice.si	386/1-29-13-332
Spain	www.renfe.es	34/902-15-75-07
Sweden	www.sj.se	46/771-75-75-75 (E)
Switzerland	www.sbb.ch	41/512-20-11-11
Turkey	www.tcdd.gov.tr	90/212-527-7085

Note: All phone numbers above are shown as you would dial them from North America (dial the international access code 011, then the number as listed above).

* Phone numbers marked with an "E" respond immediately in English. For other countries, you'll have to wait through a taped message in the local language. Hang on—the operators usually speak, or can find someone who speaks, English.

CHOOSING THE TRAIN THAT'S RIGHT FOR YOU

If your time in Europe is limited, then speed will be an issue when selecting a train. There are many high-speed options that will zip you around the Continent, but it's admittedly hard to enjoy the scenery when you're flying by at 186 mph (300kmph), so consider a slower train now and then. (Those who suffer from motion sickness may find high-speed trains harder to take than the local lines.)

If your budget allows, you may enjoy the amenities and extra space in first class; those who prefer to spend their money on other things will find that second-class cars are a perfectly clean, comfortable option. And those who prefer to travel while they sleep will find a plethora of sleeping options on Europe's vast array of night trains. In this section, we outline all of the major train and accommodations options you'll encounter when traveling through Europe by rail. Read through the descriptions and then choose the train that best suits your needs.

High-Speed Trains

Note: See the tear-out map at the back of this book for a look at all of the major high-speed routes in Europe.

Europe's high-speed trains are true marvels, traversing the countryside at speeds of 186 mph (300kmph) and faster. Some of them, such as the Pendolino and X2000 trains, tilt so they can glide through curves without having to slow down (trust us, you'll hardly feel a thing). In many cases, traveling on high-speed trains is faster than flying!

Italy, Germany, France, and Spain offer the most developed high-speed networks, but most European countries have some form of high-speed service. These trains are worth seeking out: TGV and Eurostar trains, especially, can turn a full day's journey into a 3-hour trip. In fact, in some cases, it is difficult to travel between two major European cities any other way but via high-speed train.

You'll pay extra for the privilege of riding on one of these rail rockets, but shelling out the extra cash is often worth it. An express ticket from Munich to Berlin, for instance, is 79€ ($101) if bought online, with the ride taking about 5½ hours. You can pay as little as 33€ ($42) for a regular ticket, but you'll be forced to spend more than 11 hours of your vacation on a train! However, it pays to check schedules closely. In some cases—particularly in the Benelux nations—high-speed trains don't travel any faster than their regional counterparts.

High-speed trains tend to be more comfortable and posh than regional and local trains. First-class accommodations might include a newspaper, free drinks and meals, outlets for powering up cellphones and laptops, Wi-Fi access, or onboard music channels. So if you're purchasing a railpass and you want legroom and luxury, go for first class.

For passholders, most high-speed trains require reservations and, therefore, a reservation fee (and some include extra fees on top of that). You'll still get a large discount over what nonpassholders pay, but the ride won't be free. (For the passholder fares listed below, we assume you've got a pass that covers all the countries the train travels through. For more on reservation fees, see p. 47.) In the "High-Speed Trains in Europe" chart that follows, we detail the high-speed trains in all of the Eurail-covered countries and the starting point for seat reservations. We list second-class, one-way adult fares on the chart because those are what most leisure travelers with point-to-point tickets buy; first-class fares tend to be around 50% more. Most trains also have discounted children's, youth, and senior fares.

High-Speed vs. Regular Trains

Route	Fastest Regular Train	High-speed Train	Time Saved
Paris–Avignon	8 hr., 57 min.	2 hr., 38 min.	6 hr., 19 min.
Rome–Florence	2 hr., 30 min.	6 hr., 3 min.	3 hr., 33 min.
Munich–Berlin	5 hr., 46 min.	11 hr., 6 min.	5 hr., 20 min.
London–Paris	9 hr., 20 min.	2 hr., 22 min.	7 hr., 12 min.

High-Speed Trains in Europe

Country & Train Name	Route	Time	One-Way Fare (2nd Class)	Minimum Pass Res. Fee (2nd Class/1st Class)	Reservations
Belgium Thalys	Brussels–Paris Brussels–Cologne Brussels–Amsterdam*	1 hr., 22 min. 1 hr., 50 min. 1 hr., 50 min.	$73 $26–$75 $74–$88	$36/$56 $12/$12 $44/$70	Yes Yes Varies with departure time
Denmark X2000	Copenhagen–Stockholm	5 hr., 3 min.	$210	$28/$13	Yes
England Eurostar	London–Paris London–Brussels	2 hr., 20 min. 2 hr., 6 min.	$74–$205 $74–$130	$78/$137 $78/$137	Yes Yes
Finland Pendolino	All major cities	Varies	Varies	$20/$20	Yes
France Artesia TGV	Paris–Milan Paris to many major cities	7 hr., 5 min. Varies	$82–$130 Varies	$25/$28 $21/$25	Yes Yes
Germany ICE	All major cities	Varies	Varies	$12/$12	Varies
Italy Eurostar Italia (ES)	Milan–Basel Venice–Geneva All major cities	4 hr., 7 min. 6 hr., 43 min. Varies	$103 $123 Varies	$14/$14 $21/$21 $14/$14	Yes Yes Yes
Portugal Alfa	Lisbon–Porto	2 hr., 35 min.	$33	Open seating	No
Spain AVE	All major cities	Varies	Varies	$14/$33	Yes
Sweden X2000	All major cities	Varies	Varies	$13/$13	Yes
Switzerland	Served by Trenitalia International trains from Italy, TGV and Artesia trains from France, ICE trains from Germany, and RailJets from Austria.				

* We recommend against spending extra to ride the high-speed train on this route, as the trip takes just as long as it would on a normal express train.

Express, Regional & Local Trains

Typically, there are four levels of trains below the posh, high-speed services, though some countries may have fewer or more (Germany has seven). As all of these trains typically cost the same—and all are included in a railpass—you should just take whichever is the fastest train that stops at your destination.

EuroCity (EC) trains are express trains, typically crossing borders. EC trains sometimes require reservations and additional supplements, so make sure to ask when booking your ticket.

InterCity (IC) trains are express trains, stopping at major cities. Some require reservations, so make sure to check.

Regional or **Local** trains have different names in every country. In Belgium they're "L" trains, in the Netherlands they're "stoptreins," and in Germany they're "Regional Bahn." Whatever they're called, these are the slow trains that stop at every tiny station, and you should avoid them whenever possible. (In Germany, there is another class of middling express trains called Regional Express. These essentially split the difference btw. express and regional trains.)

Suburban trains connect major cities and nearby destinations, and may leave from a different train station than long-distance trains. Some of these may **not** be covered by a railpass, such as the Paris RER system (except for Paris RER line C) and Stockholm's S-togs. Also not covered are **local city transport systems** such as buses, trams, and subways.

Getting the Quickest Trip

Before you assume that the very next train for Amsterdam is the one you want, take a close look at the train's arrival time. You may discover that the next fast train—perhaps one with a departure time 30 minutes later—actually delivers you to your desired destination *before* its slower counterpart.

First vs. Second Class

Most European trains have two classes of seats: first and second class.

On **local, regional,** and most **express trains,** there's not as much difference between the classes as there is on the high-speed and premier trains. First-class cars usually have either three seats per row (a seat on one side of the aisle, two seats on the other) or six seats per compartment; second-class cars have four seats per row

Fabulous in First

Country	Train	First-Class Bonus
Belgium/France/Netherlands	Thalys	Free meals, wine, and Wi-Fi; credit card phones; and taxi-booking service
England/Belgium/France	Eurostar	Free meals, wine, and newspapers; power ports; Wi-Fi lounges; dedicated check-in desk; and business cars
Germany	ICE	Free newspapers, laptop ports, in-seat music, and dedicated quiet zones
Italy	Eurostar Italia	Free drink, snacks, and Italian newspaper
Italy/Switzerland	Cisalpino	In-seat music system, power ports, drinks, and snacks
Italy/France	Artesia	Free welcome drink, newspaper, and wake-up service on night trains
Norway	Signatur	Meals, phones, in-seat music, and power ports
Spain	AVE	Free meals, drinks, newspapers, and audio/video services; and free 24- or 48-hour parking
	Talgo	In-seat audio/video system
Sweden	X2000	Free meal, coffee/tea, in-seat music, and Swedish newspaper

First-class compartment, Euromed train. *(photo: Courtesy of Rail Europe)*

First Class

The photo features the standard first-class configuration on most modern European trains; older trains (such as the Corail trains in France) have compartment seating, but these are gradually being phased out.

(two on each side of the aisle) or eight per compartment. First class has more legroom, and the upholstery may be plusher or better kept.

Note that second class tends to fill up a lot faster than first class, so if you're traveling second class on a major route where reservations are not required, you'll want to show up early at the train station to guarantee yourself a seat.

The major difference between first and second class on most trains is the clientele; the folks in the first-class compartment will be older and include more business travelers. Most families and young travelers will be in second class. Both classes, of course, get to their destinations at the same time.

On **high-speed trains,** first class often includes airline-style amenities (see "Fabulous in First," on preceeding page, for some examples) and very spacious seating. In the individual country chapters in this book, we point out where the difference between second class and first class isn't enough to justify paying the higher fee. And we also point out instances where going first-class (on older trains in Greece, for example) is almost a must if you want to have anything approaching a comfortable ride.

If you feel like switching classes, first-class pass and ticket holders can sit in second class any time they like. Second-class ticket holders can upgrade on board the train by paying the price difference if a seat is available.

Night Trains

Most major European cities that are at least 7 hours apart by rail are connected by night trains. Not only do night trains save you the price of a hotel, but they also give you more time to sightsee. And some night trains even have hotel-style amenities, such as private bathrooms with showers. We recommend taking night trains whenever possible.

Second-class compartment, panoramic car on Switzerland's Glacier Express. *(photo: Courtesy of Rail Europe)*

Second Class

The photo features the second-class configuration on most modern panoramic European trains. Second-class seats on high-speed trains are usually far more comfortable than those on local and regional trains.

The average European night train will have sleeper cars, which sleep between one and four people; couchettes, which are affordable compartments for four to six people with less comfortable but serviceable bunk beds; and airline-style reclining coach seats. True cheapskates can sleep in coach seats on trains that offer this option, but because a berth in a six-bunk couchette costs passholders as little as $35, there's no need to give yourself a neck cramp. Keep in mind that some trains require that you have a first-class pass to sleep in certain types of cabins. Except in France and Italy, however, there are no first-class couchettes—you can go second class only. Note that we've had enough reports about substandard conditions in second-class couchettes in several countries (and theft issues in certain countries) that we recommend you stick to either first-class couchettes or sleeper cars. **Note:** Couchettes, except in a few countries (see p. 44), are not gender specific.

Sleepers offer a somewhat more posh travel experience than other train sleeping arrangements: You have a steward to deliver snacks, drinks, and (possibly) a complimentary breakfast to your room. All sleeper cabins also have sinks (and some have bathrooms with showers), while couchette cabins don't.

Whether you're traveling in a couchette or sleeper, the compartment you sleep in will start out with benches or sofas during the evening (unless your departure is after 10pm). At some point after dark, an attendant will come by to snap down the bunks and make them up as beds (or give you the necessary equipment to make your own), with sheets included. The attendant will also take your passport if you're traveling across a border with passport control so there's no need to wake you for it later (this doesn't apply at Eastern European borders).

Trenhotel restaurant car. *(photo: Courtesy of Rail Europe)*

Restaurant Cars

Though most long-distance trains feature some type of dining option, premier trains, such as Spain's luxurious Elipsos Trenhotel, feature top-quality restaurant cars.

After the bunks are down, everyone's expected to be quiet. In couchettes, nobody undresses; just stash away your shoes, curl up under the covers, and let the rocking of the train lull you to sleep. (Be sure to cuddle up with your valuables or you may wake up without them!)

The attendant will wake you up in time for your stop, but if you want to have control over your morning, you can bring your own alarm clock. Forget sleeping in: When morning comes around, the attendant will return to the car to turn the bunks back into seats.

If you're a woman creeped out by the idea of sleeping near strangers of the opposite sex, French and Austrian couchettes offer the option of women-only cars. (Sorry,

 Tasty Train Rides

Unless you're traveling in some Eastern European countries, if you don't have time to eat before you get on the train, don't worry: Long-distance trains in Europe have dining cars or will send an attendant past your seat with a rolling cart serving up drinks and snacks, which, while not always healthy, are at least edible. Expect prices to be very high for what you get.

Premium-class tickets on many high-speed and night trains (for instance, on AVE, Eurostar, and Thalys) include a welcome drink and meals, and if you're in a first-class sleeper on one of the premier night trains, they'll even serve you breakfast in your cabin. Ask about food arrangements when making your reservation.

Snack bar on Eurostar train. *(photo: Courtesy of Rail Europe)*

Snack Bars

Most new or upgraded high-speed and international trains have a fast-food snack bar where passengers can get a quick bite.

guys, you don't get any couchette cars to yourselves.) Otherwise, your only option is to get a bed in a sleeper: Sleepers are segregated by sex unless you're booking the whole sleeper at once.

All sleeping compartments are supposed to have locks, but with the number of strangers coming in and out of a couchette, you shouldn't count on the lock to protect your valuables. Lock your bags and chain them to seats or bunks if possible.

Parents concerned about their children's safety in bunk beds can request "safety nets" on French sleepers at no charge; this webbing prevents the kids from rolling out of bed. Still, if you want complete control over your environment, get a sleeper rather than couchettes or reserve the entire compartment. (**Note:** You will need a ticket for each berth in that case.)

Luxury Sleepers

A few luxury sleeper services don't have couchettes, which means you have to either settle for a reclining seat or shell out for a bunk in a four-berth room. Here's a selection of some of the best luxury options in Europe:

o **Elipsos Trenhotel.** The bane of the budget traveler, but absolutely perfect for someone looking for a high-end rail travel experience, this super-classy overnight service is available between Paris and Madrid, and Barcelona and Zurich/Milan/Paris. The train has a full restaurant on board and individually air-conditioned sleepers. Opt for the top "Gran Class" and you'll get all meals and a private bathroom with shower. The minimum passholder fare on those routes during the tourist high season is $67 for a second-class (Tourist Class) reclining seat; to stay in a second-class (Tourist Class) four-bed sleeper, the price runs $100 and climbs to

$289 for a single Gran Class cabin. Find out more at **www.elipsos.com** or **www. raileurope.com**.

○ **Artesia Night Train.** This train runs between major French and Italian cities, including Paris, Chambery, Dijon, Rome, Milan, Florence, and Venice. Six-person couchettes begin at $35 for passholders. Double sleepers in first class begin at $124 for passholders.

○ **CityNightLine.** These trains run various routes through Germany, Switzerland, France, Italy, Denmark, the Netherlands, and Austria. The trains offer deluxe single and double sleeper cabins with private bathrooms and showers, as well as economy six-bed cabins with shared bathrooms and reclining seats. All cabins have electronic locks, and are air-conditioned and nonsmoking. Passholders can get a reclining seat reservation starting at $14. A bed in a four-berth sleeper starts at $64 for passholders; double sleepers start at $82 a person. To find out more, check out **www.raileurope.com**.

Other luxury night trains include Swedish night trains (Stockholm–Malmo/Oslo; the latter in peak season only), Spanish night trains (Madrid–Santiago de Campostela, and Barcelona–Granada), the Lusitania Trenhotel (Lisbon–Madrid), and Paris–Germany night trains (Paris to Munich, Hamburg, Berlin, or Hannover). For more information, check out **www.raileurope.com**.

TYPES OF ACCOMMODATIONS

If the last time you rode on a European night train was as a college student, crammed into a six-berth couchette compartment, you'll be pleasantly surprised by the range of accommodations on modern night trains. At their best, they bring back the classic age of train travel, with a uniformed attendant serving you an aperitif as you board, air-conditioning, private showers, and attendant-call phones in every room. Of course, a top-class bed will cost you; a full-fare ticket for a single, private, top-class compartment from Paris to Madrid costs nearly $700.

Not every train has every one of these accommodations, but the range of accommodations on night trains usually includes the ones listed below.

Seats are the cheapest way to travel overnight. These are airline-style seats, with toilets and sinks at one end of the car. Reservations will usually cost you around $20. (Elipsos' reclining seats cost $67 on overnight trains.) We recommend you add another $15 to upgrade to a couchette. But, as always, compare prices, as they may vary by destination and time of year.

Couchettes (aka **T6**) are the sleeping cars of the masses, and they're where you'll find most budget travelers. Second-class couchette accommodations cost $35 for passholders on most European trains. The compartment has two long, benchlike seats during the day, with three people sitting on each side and two top bunks up near the ceiling; at night, the back of each bench snaps up to become a middle bunk. Couchette cars have toilets and sinks at one end, but no showers.

First-class couchettes are offered on some French trains. They seat and sleep four (two on each side) and usually cater to an older, more business-oriented clientele than second-class couchettes.

Four-berth sleepers (aka **T4**) have two beds on each side. These are most often seen on high-class night trains such as the Elipsos hotel trains, which don't offer couchettes. On those trains, these are the cheapest beds.

Triple sleepers (aka **T3**) have three beds that fold down from one side of the compartment, with a table and a sink on the other side. These are gender specific unless occupied entirely by one group.

Train Sleeping Accommodations

Regular sleeper, Spanish night train

REGULAR SLEEPERS

- One to four beds per cabin
- Secure compartments with reserved bathrooms
- Available in either first- or second-class (On some trains)
- Air-conditioning in most cabins
- Sink, mirror, and luggage storage space
- Mineral water
- Breakfast often included in the rate

Deluxe sleeper, Trenhotel Elipsos

DELUXE SLEEPERS

- One to three beds per cabin
- Secure compartments with private attendant
- Private bathroom with shower and toiletries
- Sitting area (only on some trains)
- Electronic door locks, luggage storage areas, panoramic windows, individual climate controls
- Mineral water
- Breakfast always included in rate

cleaning UP

If you can't stand the idea of an overnight ride without a shower, these trains provide showers:

PRIVATE SHOWERS
○ Spanish hotel trains between Barcelona and Granada
○ Paris–Germany night trains between Paris and Munich, Frankfurt, Bremen, Hamburg, Hannover, and Berlin
○ Elipsos trains from Madrid to Paris, Barcelona to Paris, Barcelona to Zurich, and Barcelona to Milan in "Gran" class

○ Lusitania Trenhotel from Madrid to Lisbon in "Gran" class
○ CityNightLine trains throughout Germany, Switzerland, Austria, and the Netherlands in "Deluxe" two-bed cabins
○ Sweden's Northern Arrow from Gothenburg or Stockholm to Östersund in "Exclusive" class

Some other night train accommodations offer corridor showers. In certain cars, you'll find washbasins as well as one shower at both ends of each coach. And if all else fails, many large European train stations provide showers for a nominal fee.

Double sleepers (aka **T2** or **Double**) offer two bunk beds, a table, and a sink. These are always gender specific unless occupied entirely by one group.

Single sleepers (aka **Special** or **Sgl**) give you the most personal space you'll have on a train: a compartment all to yourself, complete with sink and locking door.

Top-class or **deluxe sleepers** are available on hotel trains such as the Elipsos and CityNightLine series. Many of these have private showers, and you're sure to get very attentive service.

THE PRICE OF RAIL TRAVEL
Reservations & Supplements

A railpass means you've paid up front and can just hop on a train, right?

Alas, no. Most high-speed trains (including some EuroCity and InterCity), scenic trains, and all sleepers require reservations—and reservation fees will cost you over and above the price of your railpass. Some fast trains have "Passholder Fares," which are essentially reservation fees.

Some exceptions: Reservations aren't necessary on German high-speed trains (although they're helpful, especially on popular routes, as they guarantee you a seat). They're also unnecessary on certain Spanish, Portuguese, and British trains (except on some routes to Scotland) and Swiss trains (except certain scenic trains).

We say, don't nickel and dime yourself to avoid reservation fees. The difference in speed—and comfort, as with overnight trains—between regular and high-speed trains is so striking that your extra $20 will seem money well spent.

You can often reserve within just a few hours of departure at European train stations, and you probably won't have to worry about most trains selling out (a major exception: TGV and other French-run trains during peak periods, when only a very limited number of seats are allocated to Eurailpass holders). You'll also likely save money by making reservations in Europe: While the reservation fee on most trains begins at $12 if booked from the U.S., it can be as little as 4€ ($5.20) if you're booking in Europe.

Reservation Fees*		
Country	**Train**	**Res. Fee/Pass Fare in US$**
England–France/Belgium	Eurostar	From $78
France	TGV	From $13
France–Belgium/Netherlands	Thalys	From $43
France–Italy	Artesia (day)	From $18
Italy	Eurostar Italia	From $16
Italy–Switzerland	Cisalpino	From $17
Most countries	Night trains	From $36 (couchette)
Most countries	High-speed trains	From $12
Spain	AVE	From $14
Spain	Altaria	From $14
Spain–France/Italy	Elipsos night trains	From $67
Spain–Portugal	Lusitania	From $48 (T4)
Switzerland	Glacier Express	From $40
Switzerland	William Tell Express	From $44
Switzerland	Bernina Express	From $19
Switzerland	Golden Pass Line	From $17

* Unless otherwise noted, all reservation fees were calculated for second-class seats and accommodations.

There are cases when you will want to reserve before you leave home. If you're traveling on popular routes (especially night trains) in the summer or during a holiday period, we advise you to reserve in advance through **Rail Europe** (© **888/438-7245** in the United States, © 800/361-7245 in Canada; www.raileurope.com). We let you know in the individual country chapters when a reservation should be made before you leave home. You can make reservations up to 120 days in advance for Eurostar and CNL; up to 90 days in advance for most countries/high-speed routes; only up to 60 days in advance for trains in Spain, Poland, and the Czech Republic. Reservations in Bulgaria, Greece, Portugal, and Ireland can't be made from North America. Serbia, Hungary, and Romania only allow international train reservations, not domestic service.

Note: If you did reserve a seat, there is one quirk you might want to watch out for. Some countries (Greece, for example) don't mark seats as reserved and confusion occasionally reigns when people occupy seats they didn't know were reserved. If you show up at your reserved seat and someone's sitting in it, politely but firmly inform him or her that you have a reservation and ask him or her to vacate. Don't let anyone talk you out of your own seat (and some people will try to do just that). Ask a porter if you need assistance.

Passes vs. Point-to-Point Tickets

Ah, the great debate: to buy a pass or to buy point-to-point tickets?

That depends on what kind of traveler you are. If you're on a tight budget, are staying in only a few cities, or plan out your trip in advance and travel second class,

Protecting Your Pass

Railpasses are expensive and may be lost or stolen. Get peace of mind through Rail Europe's Rail Protection Plan, which reimburses you for your pass's remaining value if the pass disappears. We strongly recommend buying the Rail Protection Plan for Eurail Global Passes and Eurail Select Passes ($20), and for single-country and regional passes ($16). Rail Europe also sells a Rail Protection Plan for individual tickets, for $9 per ticket. While that's a great idea for a $269 round-trip IC ticket, you can probably do without it for a $15 hop from Amsterdam to Delft. *Note:* The Rail Protection Plan doesn't cover sleepers or reservations, so keep a very close eye on that $677 Gran Class sleeper ticket from Madrid to Paris.

you may find that point-to-point tickets are cheaper. But if you plan to cover a lot of territory, love the freedom of traveling on a whim, crave convenience, or want to know with some certainty how much your European adventure is going to cost you, you'll find railpasses will likely save you money and time. Rail Europe's website (**www.raileurope.com**) has an interactive railpass finder that will help you compare point-to-point tickets up against a pass.

PASS PLUSES

o **Passes allow for spontaneity.** Many itineraries are cheaper if you buy point-to-point tickets rather than a pass. But what a pass gives you is the flexibility to dodge ticket lines and vending machines, and often to ignore schedules—you simply show up at the station to hop onto the next train to anywhere.

  If you're a peripatetic traveler who wants to see every new day in a different city, or a spontaneous traveler who wants to follow your whims, railpasses are for you. You'll still have to make reservations for high-speed or overnight trains, but if you choose to avoid the reservation counter entirely, you may find your trip made more spontaneous on a slower train that stops in fascinating small towns along the way.

  Consider also that a single full-fare TGV round-trip between Paris and Avignon will cost at least $220. That's only $70 less than a full-fare 3-day France Railpass, and only $28 less than a second-class France Railpass, either of which will allow you 3 days of unlimited travel throughout the country within a 30-day period. Clearly, the pass is the way to go if you're traveling long distances.

o **Speedy trains mean big savings for passholders.** Generally, if you're traveling several long-distance legs on high-speed trains, especially within large countries such as France or Germany, a single-country pass will pay off. The triangular route of Berlin–Munich–Frankfurt–Berlin will cost $360—and a whopping $476 in high season—for second-class, point-to-point tickets. But a 4-day second-class German Rail Pass will run only $245—a big cost savings, and you'll have an extra rail day left on the pass.

o **If you're staying in one or two countries and taking long trips, passes are winners.** The France–Italy Pass is a good deal because it reduces the huge fare on overnight trains between those two countries to a cool $35 (if you're sleeping in a couchette). Even if you're just going from Paris to Rome and Venice and back, you end up spending just $20 more by getting a France–Italy Pass over buying point-to-point tickets—and you enjoy the added flexibility that a railpass offers.

- **Railpasses are usually discounted if you buy in volume.** BritRail has a Guest Pass for adult passengers, offering a 50% pass discount for two traveling together. Many Eurail passes offer "saver" varieties for two or more people traveling together; these discount the per-person rate.
- **Railpasses lock in your transportation costs.** If you're waffling between buying point-to-point tickets or railpasses, consider this: You can purchase a railpass up to 6 months in advance of your trip, while most European trains won't sell tickets sooner than 30 to 60 days prior to travel. Buying in advance means you can firm up your budget early and head off currency fluctuations.

POINT-TO-POINT ADVANTAGES

- **If you're not traveling far, don't bother with a pass.** It's almost impossible to make the Benelux Pass pay off because trips in Belgium and the Netherlands are so short and cheap. Even if you cram Antwerp, Bruges, Ghent, Brussels, Luxembourg, Amsterdam, Haarlem, Leiden, Delft, and the Hague into your trip, you'll spend only around $122 on point-to-point tickets if you buy in Europe—far less than the $220 you'd pay for a Benelux Pass.

  In Italy, a 3-day Italy Pass starts at $186 (plus reservation fees if you're taking Eurostar Italia trains). But if you plan to travel between only two or three cities (say, Rome to Florence to Venice—an itinerary that costs only $128 in point-to-point tickets), you're not covering enough ground to warrant the purchase of a pass.
- **A quick trip across a border is best done point-to-point.** If you're just slipping from the Benelux into Germany, a Eurail Benelux–Germany Pass is overkill. Get a single-country pass for the country you're spending more time in, and supplement it with a point-to-point ticket or two. Look into getting two one-country passes (or two-country combo passes such as the France–Italy or France–Spain passes) only if you're spending considerable time in two countries. Some international high-speed trains offer pass rates that are valid when only one of the countries you're traveling through is covered by a railpass.
- **Eastern Europe is really cheap.** Point-to-point tickets in Eastern Europe are so inexpensive that railpasses become difficult to justify unless you're continually hopping on and off trains or traveling very long distances.

NO PASSES PLEASE, WE'RE Basque

Some trains in Europe won't take *any* railpass. You'll have to buy point-to-point tickets on these trains whether or not you have a pass:

- Regional trains in Spain not run by RENFE (trains along the northern coast, in the Basque country, and around Valencia, and FGC-run trains around Barcelona) don't take passes. You'll have to pay cash for these tickets, and you can't buy the tickets from Rail Europe.
- The private InterConnex train in Germany isn't covered by

railpasses and Rail Europe will not book tickets on this train. The good news: Regular EC and IC trains also ply the InterConnex routes, and they *are* covered.
- Scenic private railways in Switzerland and Austria don't take passes. A number of scenic railways (the famous Jungfrau trains in Switzerland, for example) aren't covered by your railpass, though it will get you a discount. Rail Europe will help book these rail tickets.

HOME OR AWAY?

If you're buying point-to-point tickets, you've got to decide whether to get them while you're in North America or when you arrive in Europe. We'd advise buying all tickets on high-speed or overnight trains from Rail Europe. For other tickets, it's up to how adventurous you feel.

It's always a good idea to buy long-distance tickets as far in advance as you can, whether through Rail Europe's website or a local European rail company's website. For a full list of European rail websites, see p. 36.

Rail Europe's prices are generally competitive with European prices for high-speed trains such as the French TGV and German ICE. For other trains, you may want to compare Rail Europe's website prices to the prices on a local European rail site. Most European rail companies, including the railways in France, Spain, Italy, Great Britain, and Germany, let you buy tickets through their websites with a credit card and print them out on your home printer, pick them up at the train station, or simply send the tickets to your smartphone. If you buy tickets in advance and can tolerate a few restrictions, you can get some amazing discounts.

For instance, a ticket from Paris to Milan for the next day bought at a train station can run you up to $147 if the train isn't entirely sold out (which happens during the summer). On Rail Europe's website, a Paris–Milan ticket bought a month in advance costs $125. Buy that advance-purchase ticket through **www.voyages-sncf.com** (the French rail website) and it can be as little as $77.

Dealing with local European railway sites, however, isn't for the timid. If you buy your tickets through Rail Europe, you deal with friendly, English-speaking agents who know the needs of North American travelers and will make sure you get all your tickets and necessary reservations before you leave home. Accommodations arrangements on night trains, especially, can be complicated. And inexperienced visitors to Europe may relish a patient walk-through from an experienced agent.

> ### Don't Wait Until the Last Minute!
>
> If you wait until the last minute to order your railpass from Rail Europe, you'll incur a $36 overnight shipping fee. It pays to plan ahead.

If you're taking short trips—practically any train in Belgium or the Netherlands, from Denmark to Sweden, or on local trains in Spain and Italy will qualify—it makes sense to buy the tickets on the spur of the moment from a vending machine at a local train station. So much sense, in fact, that Rail Europe doesn't sell certain short-distance tickets online, such as rides between Barcelona and Girona in Spain, or between Delft and Haarlem in the Netherlands. In Europe, you can generally buy unreserved tickets at vending machines, avoiding long lines at ticket counters. (Make sure to have enough change, though, as some vending machines don't take bills.) Even the short-haul tickets that Rail Europe does sell are usually much cheaper in Europe than they are in North America.

Fare Discounts

There's one other advantage to buying tickets in Europe: You can get discounts that aren't offered when you're buying your tickets in North America. Often these discounts require buying tickets in advance, but you can usually buy them over the phone, with a credit card, by calling the relevant national rail system's phone number,

Pricing the Difference: Fast vs. Slow Trains

Route	Rail Europe Price	Sample European Price (Next-Day Travel)
Fast or Long-Distance Trains		
Munich–Berlin	$171	$149
Paris–Avignon	$88	$133
Madrid–Seville	$108	$104
Rome–Venice	$100	$94
Paris–Milan	$125	$147
London–Paris	$177	$189
Slow or Short-Distance Trains		
Amsterdam–Haarlem	$7	$3
Bruges–Ghent	$12	$7.50
London–Cambridge	$38	$34
Nice–Monaco	$11	$4.50
Cologne–Aachen	$29	$19

through the rail system's website (see the "National Railway Websites & Phone Numbers" chart on p. 36), or even via mobile phone.

A few other notable discounts apply whether you buy your tickets in person, over the phone, or over the Internet. **German** trains offer two big discounts. The "Sparpreis 25" fare gives you 25% off a round-trip ticket bought at least 3 days in advance. The "Sparpreis 50" fare bumps the discount up to 50% if you stay over a Saturday night. Both special fares require that you make reservations, and both are of limited availability and nonrefundable. Tickets connecting Germany to certain international destinations also enjoy these price reductions. **British** trains have a complex system of advance-purchase fares (now available from Rail Europe); rest assured that the further you buy in advance, the lower the fare will probably be.

European nations differ in the ages eligible for **children's fares,** but most offer considerable discounts, charging approximately 50% the adult fare for kids between ages 4 and 11. Kids under 4 usually ride free. In Belgium, the "Large Families" discount card (which costs 6€, or $7.75) is available to parents with three children under age 25: Adults and children age 12 and over get 50% discounts on first- and second-class tickets, while children under 12 get a 50% discount in first class and travel free in second class, even if they are traveling alone. In the Netherlands, the Railrunner ticket is just for kids ages 4 to 11 and costs only 2.50€ ($3.20) when accompanied by an adult. In Sweden, all children under 16 ride for 5 SEK (70¢) when accompanied by an adult and booking online; when booking tickets at the station, you'll pay just 25 SEK ($3.50) per child. Wherever your journeys take you, if your travel includes children, ask about available discounts.

THE TRAIN PASSES

So you've decided you're going with a pass. Rail Europe offers dozens of passes, and the choices can be overwhelming. Decide on the appropriate railpass by answering four questions:

1. **How much ground do you want to cover?**

If you want to stay in one country, look for a single-country pass (or point-to-point tickets; see p. 47). For up to five countries, look for a multiple-country pass, such as the Eurail Select Pass. For six or more countries, look at the Eurail Global Pass.

2. **Will you be continually on the move, or do you want to linger in some places for a few days?**

If you're continually on the move, **a consecutive-day** pass allows unlimited travel during a specified period. If you'll be staying in cities for several days at a time, a **nonconsecutive** pass gives you a certain number of travel days and lets you stay put for the rest.

Once you've determined your best kind of railpass, answering two more questions will help you get the best price:

3. **How old are you?**

If you are under 26, **youth passes** are available. Children travel at reduced rates, usually half-price or free. If you are at least 60, discounted **senior passes** (where available) are the way to go.

4. **How many people are you traveling with?**

If at least two people are traveling together, look for **two-person and group discounts.**

In this section, we divide all the passes into five categories so you can find the one that's best for you, and then we describe youth, senior, and group savings options.

One-Country, Consecutive-Day Passes

Consecutive passes are available for whirlwind journeys within the U.K. or Switzerland. As with all one-country passes, they're not always cheaper than point-to-point tickets, especially for brief trips, but they offer ultimate flexibility.

BritRail Consecutive Pass: Covers 3, 4, 8, 15, or 22 days, or 1 month of unlimited travel in England, Scotland, and Wales. **First-class prices:** Start at $289 for 3 days. **Second-class prices:** Start at $199 for 3 days. You may use the tickets for rail service between Heathrow, Gatwick, and Stansted airports to London. Special passholder fare available on Eurostar to Paris and Brussels.

BritRail England Consecutive Pass: Covers 3, 4, 8, 15, or 22 days, or 1 month of unlimited travel in England. **First-class prices:** Start at $229 for 3 days. **Second-class prices:** Start at $159 for 3 days. Special passholder fare available on Eurostar to Paris or Brussels.

Swiss Pass: Covers 4, 8, 15, or 22 days, or 1 month of unlimited travel in Switzerland. **First-class prices:** Start at $361 for 4 days. **Second-class prices:** Start at $241 for 4 days. **Discounts & Bonuses:** Includes discounts on most mountain railways and private scenic trains. Free entrance to 400 museums. Discounts on city tours, hotels, and events available through RailAway, a travel and events company run by the Swiss Federal Railways.

One-Country, Nonconsecutive Passes

If you're planning to explore one country for a week or two, this is the kind of pass to get. Watch out when buying these passes: In many cases, especially with short pass durations or in very small countries (such as the Netherlands), point-to-point tickets will be cheaper.

Is the U.K. Okay?

The one glaring omission from the Eurail system is that its passes don't touch England, Scotland, or Wales. But there are still several railpass options for travelers going to Britain. **BritRail** passes cover the mainland U.K.; the **BritRail England Pass, BritRail London Plus Pass,** and **Scottish Freedom Pass** focus on specific parts of the kingdom. The **BritRail Pass + Ireland** lets you roam freely in all of the U.K. and Ireland, and includes a round-trip by ferry.

If you're traveling with children in the U.K., be sure to request the **BritRail Family Pass,** which allows one child age 5 to 15 to travel for free with each fully paying adult or senior. Additional children age 5 to 15 pay approximately half-price, and all children under 5 ride for free.

One-country passes can also be used as add-ons to regional passes or stacked on top of each other for a two-country trip. If you're going to France and Germany, for instance, the combined price of two one-country passes can often be cheaper than point-to-point tickets.

All passes covering Britain or France give you access to the special passholder fare on Eurostar.

Austrian Railpass: Covers 3 to 8 days of travel within a 1-month period. **First-class prices:** $202 for 3 days. **Second-class prices:** Begin at $141. **Discounts:** Discounts on certain ferries (p. 64) and Danube River trips.

BritRail Flexipass: Covers 3, 4, 8, or 15 days of travel within a 2-month period in England, Scotland, and Wales. **First-class prices:** Start at $359 for 3 days. **Second-class prices:** Start at $255 for 3 days.

BritRail England Flexipass: Covers 3, 4, 8, or 15 days travel within a 2-month period in England. **First-class prices:** Start at $289. **Second-class prices:** Start at $205.

BritRail London Plus Pass: Covers 2 or 4 days of travel within an 8-day period or 7 days of travel within a 15-day period in Southeast England. **First-class prices:** Start at $199. **Second-class prices:** Start at $139.

Britrail Scottish Freedom Pass: Covers 4 days of travel within an 8-day period or 8 days of travel within a 15-day period throughout Scotland. Includes discounts on certain island ferry routes. **Second-class prices only:** Start at $235.

Bulgaria Pass: Covers 3, 4, 6, or 8 days of travel within a 1-month period. **First-class prices:** Start at $98. **Second-class prices:** Start at $74.

Croatia Pass: Covers 3, 4, 6, or 8 days of travel within a 1-month period. **First-class prices:** Start at $136. **Second-class prices:** Start at $109.

Czech Flexipass: Covers 3, 4, 6, or 8 days of travel within 1 month. **First-class prices:** Start at $136. **Second-class prices:** Start at $101.

Denmark Pass: Covers 3 or 7 days within a 1-month travel period. **First-class prices:** Start at $172. **Second-class prices:** Begin at $112. **Discounts:** Up to 50% in discounts on private railroads and ferries to Sweden and Norway.

Finland Pass: Covers 3, 5, or 10 days of travel within a 1-month period in Finland. **First-class prices:** Start at $243. **Second-class prices:** Start at $164. **Discounts:** Receive up to 50% off ferry crossings to Stockholm or Rostock, Germany.

France Railpass: Covers 3 to 9 days of travel within a 1-month period. **First-class prices:** Start at $291. **Second-class prices:** Start at $248. **Discounts:** A wide variety of discounts apply, ranging from scenic ferries (p. 64) and Seine River cruises to museums, shopping, scenic trains, skiing, theme parks, hotels, wine tastings, and cooking workshops, as well as free passage on certain Paris RER underground trains.

German Railpass: Covers 3 to 10 days of travel within a 1-month period. **First-class prices:** Start at $299. **Second-class prices:** Start at $228. **Discounts & Bonuses:** Free travel on KD Rhine and Mosel River cruises. Discounts on Zugspitze train tickets, Lake Constance cruises, sightseeing ferries (p. 64), Romantic Road Europabus routes, and Expressbus service between Nuremberg and Prague.

Greece Pass: Covers 3 to 10 days of travel within a 1-month period. **First-class prices only:** Start at $128. **Discounts & Bonuses:** Price reductions on certain high-speed ferries to Greek isles and Italy, cruises, sightseeing excursions, and hotels.

Hungary Pass: Covers 5 within 15 days of travel or 10 days travel within a 1-month period. **First-class prices only:** Start at $96. **Discounts & Bonuses:** 50% reduction on admission to the Hungarian Heritage Railway Park.

Ireland Pass: Covers 5 days of travel within a 1-month period. **First-class prices:** Cost $350. **Second-class prices:** Cost $280. **Discounts & Bonuses:** 30% reduction on select ferry crossings to France and the U.K.

Italy Pass: Covers 3 to 10 days of travel within a 2-month period. **First-class prices:** Start at $229. **Second-class prices:** Start at $186. **Discounts & Bonuses:** Free passage on the Leonardo Express train between Fiumicino Airport and Roma Termini rail station for first-class pass holders. Free or discounted passage to all passholders on select ferries to Sicily, Greece, Spain, and Tunisia (p. 66).

Norway Pass: Covers 3, 4, 5, 6, or 8 days travel within a 1-month period. **Second-class prices only:** Start at $242. **Discounts:** Reduced fares on select private railways, bus travel, and ferries to Denmark. (p. 66).

Poland Pass: Covers 5, 8, 10, or 15 days of travel within a 1-month period. **First-class prices:** Start at $148. **Second-class prices:** Begin at $115.

Portugal Pass: Covers 3, 4, or 6 days of travel within a 1-month period. **First-class prices only:** Start at $129.

Romania Pass: Covers 5 or 10 days of travel within a 2-month period. **First-class prices only:** Start at $174.

Slovenia pass: Covers 3, 4, 6, or 8 days within a 1-month period. **First-class prices:** Begin at $82. **Second-class prices:** Start at $62.

Spain Pass: Covers 3 to 10 days of travel within a 2-month period. **First-class prices:** Start at $248. **Second-class prices:** Start at $198. **Discounts:** 50%

And Norway Connects to Denmark . . .

The Eurail Select Pass applies to "adjoining" countries. Most of these are obvious—countries that share a border, such as France and Germany, are adjoining. But there are a few tricks. Ireland and France are considered adjoining, as are Greece and Italy; Norway and Denmark; and Germany, Sweden, and Finland—all of those countries are connected by ferry lines. Norway and Finland share a border, but they're *not* considered adjoining, as no rail or ferry line crosses that border.

reduction on Catalonian rail lines, hotel discounts, and reductions in fares for certain ferries to Italy and the Balearic islands (p. 66).

Sweden Pass: Covers 3, 4, 5, 6, or 8 days of travel within a 1-month period. **First-class prices:** Begin at $315. **Second-class prices:** Start at $242. **Discounts & Bonuses:** Free and discounted travel on certain trains to Denmark and Norway and on certain private railways. Up to 50% discounts on passage on select ferries throughout Sweden and Scandinavia.

Swiss Flexipass: Covers 3 to 6 days of travel within a 1-month period. **First-class prices:** Start at $347. **Second-class prices:** Start at $231. **Discounts & Bonuses:** Includes discounts on most mountain railways and private scenic trains. Free entrance to 400 museums. Discounts on city tours, hotels, and events available through RailAway, a travel and events company run by the Swiss Federal Railways.

Regional, Nonconsecutive Passes

Most travelers on 1-week or 2-week trips are going to go for this kind of pass, which lets you take a few defined trips covering a specific chunk of Europe.

The king of the regional passes is the do-it-yourself **Eurail Select Pass.** The Select Pass allows you to cover 3 to 5 adjoining countries for 5, 6, 8, 10, or 15 days of travel within a 2-month period. The following count as one country: the Benelux (Belgium/the Netherlands/Luxembourg), Croatia–Slovenia, and Serbia/Montenegro. The ultimate do-it-yourself pass, the Select Pass will satisfy most desires for trips up to a month long.

There are many other predefined regional passes that are cheaper than the Select Pass, as listed below. Unless otherwise indicated, discounts and bonuses for individual country passes transfer to these regional passes. For example, bonuses for the Austria–Germany Pass include those discounts included in the separate "Austrian Railpass" and "German Rail Pass" listed above.

Austria–Croatia–Slovenia Pass: Covers 4 to 10 days of travel within a 2-month period in Austria, Croatia, and Slovenia. **First-class prices only:** Start at $240.

Austria–Czech Republic Pass: Covers 4 to 10 days of travel within a 2-month period in Austria and the Czech Republic. **First-class prices only:** Start at $227.

Austria–Germany Pass: Covers 5, 6, 8, or 10 days of travel within a 2-month period. **First-class prices:** Start at $364. **Second-class prices:** Start at $310.

Select a Price

Pricing on the Eurail Select Pass depends both on how many days of travel you want and on how many countries you will be traveling in. Further complicating things, there are discounts for couples, groups, and people under 26. At press time, the prices for one adult over age 26 traveling first class with a 5-day pass were as follows: three countries from $408, four countries from $456, and five countries from $503. Passes are also available for 6, 8, 10, and 15 days of travel within a 2-month period. For more information, check out **www.raileurope.com**.

Austria–Hungary Pass: Covers 4 to 10 travel days within a 2-month period. **First-class prices only:** Start at $227.

Austria–Switzerland Pass: Covers 4 to 10 travel days within a 2-month period. **First-class prices only:** Start at $343.

Balkan Flexipass: Covers 5, 10, or 15 days of travel within a 1-month period in Bulgaria, Greece, Macedonia, Montenegro, Romania, Serbia, and Turkey. **First-class prices only:** Start at $249. **Discounts & Bonuses:** Includes discounted hotel stays in Bulgaria, Macedonia, and Serbia, as well as discounts on certain ferries (p. 66) and sightseeing excursions in Greece.

Benelux Pass: Although they're considered a single country for purposes of a regional railpass, the Benelux Pass covers 5 days of travel within a 1-month period throughout the countries of Belgium, the Netherlands, and Luxembourg. **First-class prices:** Cost $322. **Second-class prices:** Cost $220. **Discounts:** Discounts on certain Dutch ferries (p. 66) and reductions on Eurostar fares between Brussels and Paris or London.

Benelux–France Pass: Covers 4, 5, 6, 8, or 10 days travel within a 2-month period in Belgium, the Netherlands, Luxembourg, and France. **First-class prices:** Start at $335. **Second-class prices:** Start at $281.

Benelux–Germany Pass: Covers 5, 6, 8, or 10 days of travel within a 2-month period in Belgium, the Netherlands, Luxembourg, and Germany. **First-class prices:** Start at $379. **Second-class prices:** Start at $286.

BritRail Pass + Ireland: Covers 5 or 10 days of travel within a 1-month period in the U.K. and Ireland. **First-class prices:** Start at $665. **Second-class prices:** Start at $469.

Croatia–Slovenia–Hungary Pass: Covers 5, 6, 8, or 10 days of travel within 2 months. **First-class prices only:** Start at $220. **Discounts & Bonuses:** For bonuses see "Hungary Pass," p. 54.

Czech Republic-Germany Pass: Covers 5, 6, 8, or 10 days within a 2-month travel period. **First-class prices:** Begin at $353. **Second-class prices:** Start at $290.

Denmark–Germany Pass: Covers 4, 5, 6, 8, or 10 days of travel within 2 months. **First-class prices:** Start at $309. **Second-class prices:** Start at $253.

Denmark–Sweden Pass: Covers 4, 5, 6, 8, or 10 days of travel within 2 months. **First-class prices:** Begin at $343. **Second-class prices:** Start at $264.

European East Pass: Covers 5 days of travel within a 1-month period in Austria, the Czech Republic, Hungary, Poland, and Slovakia. **First-class prices:** Start at $294. **Second-class prices:** Start at $205. **Additional days:** $32 in first class, $28 in second class. **Discounts:** Bonuses include discounted fares on select Danube River cruises in Austria and discounts on the Berlin–Warsaw Express train.

Finland–Sweden Pass: Covers 4, 5, 6, 8, or 10 days of travel within 2 months. **First-class prices:** Begin at $347. **Second-class prices:** Start at $268.

France–Germany Pass: Covers 4, 5, 6, 8, or 10 days of travel within a 2-month period. **First-class prices:** Start at $366. **Second-class prices:** Start at $328.

France–Italy Pass: Covers 4 to 10 days of travel within 2 months. **First-class prices:** Start at $335. **Second-class prices:** Start at $286.

France–Spain Pass: Covers 4 to 10 days of travel within a 2-month period. **First-class prices:** Start at $335. **Second-class prices:** Start at $286.

France–Switzerland Pass: Covers 4 to 10 days of travel within a 2-month period. **First-class prices only:** Start at $360.

Germany–Poland Pass: Covers 5, 6, 8, or 10 days of travel within a 2-month period. **First-class prices:** Start at $373. **Second-class travel:** Begin at $321.

Germany–Switzerland Pass: Covers 5, 6, 8, or 10 days of travel within a 2-month period. **First-class prices only:** Start at $385.

Greece–Italy Pass: Covers 4 to 10 days of travel within a 2-month period. **First-class prices:** Start at $319. **Second-class prices:** Start at $255.

Hungary–Romania Pass: Covers 5, 6, 8, or 10 days travel within 2 months. **First-class prices only:** Start at $239.

Train Pass Tip

If you are not a European resident and have already arrived in Europe and want to buy a pass, in the U.K., contact Rail Europe at ℂ 08708/306-050; in Germany, contact Euraid at ℂ 089/593-889.

Italy–Spain Pass: Covers 4 to 10 days of travel within a 2-month period. **First-class prices:** Start at $335. **Second-class prices:** Begin at $287.

Norway–Sweden Pass: Covers 4, 5, 6, 8, or 10 days of travel within a 2-month period. **Second-class prices only:** Start at $281.

Portugal–Spain Pass: Covers 3 to 10 days of travel within a 2-month period. **First-class prices only:** Start at $284.

Scandinavia Pass: Covers 4, 5, 6, 8, or 10 days of travel within a 2-month period in Denmark, Finland, Norway, and Sweden. **Second-class prices only:** Start at $296.

All-Europe, Consecutive-Day Passes

The classic Eurail Global Pass is best if you want the ultimate in flexibility or you're covering very long distances. With the 15-day pass, you've got to take some very long trips or be on the train constantly for the price to make sense, but as the pass durations get longer, the Eurail Global Pass compares better and better to point-to-point tickets.

Eurail Global Pass: Covers 15 or 21 days, or 1, 2, or 3 months of consecutive travel. **First-class prices only:** Start at $648. For a complete list of bonuses and discounts, refer to Rail Europe's website at **www.raileurope.com**.

All-Europe, Nonconsecutive Passes

Plot your trip out before comparing the prices for the Eurail Global Pass and the Eurail Global Pass Flexi. For many trips, you'll find the original Global Pass is a better deal. The Flexi is good, for instance, if you're visiting eight cities over the course of 2 months without taking many side trips.

Eurail Global Pass Flexi: Covers 10 or 15 days of travel within a 2-month period. **First-class prices only:** Start at $764. For a complete list of bonuses and discounts, refer to Rail Europe's website at **www.raileurope.com**.

An Add-On Pass: The Swiss Card

The **Swiss Card** adds a trip from the Swiss border station or airport to one Swiss destination and back within 1 month's time. The card also nets you 50% discounts on all Swiss railways, lake steamers, postal buses, and excursions to most mountaintops for the length of the pass. The price is $236 for first class, $169 for second class. Compare the price of this pass with that of a single round-trip ticket into the country, then factor in the savings you'll receive from additional discounted travel to see whether it makes sense for you.

Rail-Drive Passes

Not all of Europe is accessible by train—many charming small towns and rural areas are best visited by car, and you've got to take a boat or a plane to get to the Greek Islands. So Rail Europe offers a range of passes combining car rentals or plane tickets with railpasses. Remember to factor in gas, though, which can exceed US$6 per gallon. *Note:* Unlike a regular car rental, car days on a rail 'n drive pass need not be used consecutively.

The price of rail 'n drive passes is based on the class of car you drive, and the available cars vary from country to country, so check out **www.raileurope.com** for the full details. Generally, you'll pay a big premium for an automatic transmission.

Car rentals in Europe are generally much more expensive than in North America, and although these passes are discounted, U.S. and Canadian travelers may get hit by sticker shock. For instance, an add-on car day for a tiny economy car with the Eurail Global Pass 'n Drive is $57; for a car with automatic transmission, you'll pay $117 a day. Single-country passes vary widely in affordability and the availability of automatic transmission. In Germany, an economy car is $56 per day and a full-size is $154; in Spain, an economy car will cost you only $46, but a full-size car costs $140 per day. France charges just slightly more for an economy car ($47), but you can get

---

Point-to-Point-to-Point

Unreserved point-to-point tickets in Europe let you get off and back on again at any number of stops, as long as you start and end your trip on the same day. So you don't need to book two tickets or use a pass if you want to visit Orléans on the way from Paris to Tours. If you're using high-speed trains, though, you'll need separate reservations for each segment of the journey.

a premier automatic for only $116 per day. Still, rental car prices are no bargain in Europe. Before you rent a car, make sure you can't get where you need to go by train or bus.

These passes are all for nonconsecutive days. **Rail 'n drive** passes include:

EurailDrive Pass 'n Drive: Covers 4 to 10 days of train travel and at least 2 days' car rental within a 2-month period in Austria, Benelux, Bulgaria, Croatia/Slovenia, Czech Republic, Denmark, Finland, France, Germany, Greece, Hungary, Ireland, Italy, Norway, Portugal, Romania, Serbia/Montenegro, Spain, Sweden, and Switzerland. Manual and automatic-transmission cars are available through Hertz, although automatics are not available in every city. **Price:** From $552 and up. **Discounts:** Includes all the bonuses listed under the single-country passes detailed above.

Eurail Select Pass 'n Drive: Covers 2 to 15 days of train travel and at least 2 days' car rental within a 2-month period in 3, 4, or 5 adjoining nations from the list above (see "EurailDrive Pass"). Beware that, while you can drive in Bulgaria, Romania, Serbia, and Montenegro, cars may not be rented there. **Price:** From $363. **Discounts:** Bonuses available, depending on the countries selected.

BritRail Pass 'n Drive: Covers 4 to 8 days of train travel and at least 2 days of car rental within a 2-month period in England, Scotland, and Wales. **Price:** From $557. **Discounts:** Special passholder fare on Eurostar.

France Rail 'n Drive: Covers 2 days of train travel and at least 2 days' car rental within a 1-month period. **Price:** From $319. **Discounts:** For bonuses, see "France Railpass," earlier.

German Rail 'n Drive: Covers 2 to 4 days of train travel and at least 2 days' car rental within a 1-month period. **Price:** From $284.

Italy Rail 'n Drive: Covers 3 to 10 days of train travel and at least 2 days of car rental within a 2-month period. **Price:** From $399. **Discounts & Bonuses:** For discounts, see "Italy Pass" above.

Discounts
YOUTH & SENIOR DISCOUNTS
Many railpasses offer discounted versions for travelers under 26 and over 60.

All **youth passes** except the Balkan, BritRail, French, Greek, Romanian, and Swiss versions are for second-class travel only, but they offer big savings. There are youth versions of all of the multiple-country passes we discuss, with the exception of the BritRail Pass + Ireland, the European East Pass, all Benelux Passes, and all Portugal Passes. In the U.K., you can take advantage of the BritRail Consecutive Youth Pass, BritRail Flexipass Youth, BritRail England Consecutive Youth Pass, and BritRail England Youth Flexipass. There are also youth versions of most single-country passes, excluding those from Belgium, BritRail London, Finland, Luxembourg, the Netherlands, Portugal, and Spain. Eurail Global and Eurail Select Youth Passes are also available.

Senior passes, for travelers over 60, are just like the standard versions—but cheaper. Senior passes include the France Pass, Ireland Pass, and Romania Pass, as well as the BritRail Consecutive Senior Pass, BritRail Senior Flexipass, BritRail England Consecutive Senior Pass, and BritRail England Senior Flexipass. Only the Eurail Ireland Pass is available in either first or second class; all other passes offer only first-class senior pricing.

validating YOUR PASS

You must validate your railpass before you step on your first train. Head to a ticket office at any European train station and ask the ticket agent to validate your pass. The agent will write in the first and last days you can use your pass, and you're on your way.

Single-country passes and multicountry have to be validated in the country they're being used for (except when using the passholder rate on the Eurostar). For instance, if you've got a France Railpass and you're heading to the Riviera from Barcelona, buy a ticket from Barcelona to the border; then the French conductor will validate the pass and you can use it for the rest of your journey.

If you're using a Saverpass or another kind of pass that affects more than one person, all the relevant people must be present when the pass is validated—but not necessarily every time it's used (except in France).

If you're using a nonconsecutive day pass such as a Eurail Select Pass, there's one more thing you have to do after validation. Each day you plan to use the pass, write the day and month in ink in one of the boxes below "Last Day." If you're taking an overnight train that leaves after 7pm, write in the next day's date. (You get the evening part of the train free!) This is called the **7pm Rule,** but it may not apply to all passes; inquire at time of booking. All trips must be completed in the days marked on your pass. Be sure to write in the date before you get on the train or you might get fined when the conductor comes around.

Note: Dates should be entered European style—date first, then month. So May 10 would be written 10-5 and not 5/10.

Children get discounted rates on most passes, usually 40% to 50% off the adult rate. Qualifying ages vary by country. Adults with a Swiss Pass, Swiss Flexipass, or Swiss Card can also get the free Swiss Family Card, which will let them tote along any number of their own children under 16 at no additional charge. Adults holding any type of BritRail Pass can request the free BritRail Family Pass, which allows one child, age 5 to15, to travel free with each full-paying adult.

If you're supplementing your railpass with an occasional point-to-point ticket, be sure to ask about local discounts on rail tickets for youths, seniors or families.

COUPLE, GROUP & FAMILY DISCOUNTS

If more than one person is traveling, more discounts are available. Saver and Party passes offer discounts to small groups (including couples). Generally, if you're under 26, the youth discount is better than the saver discount, so go with a youth pass instead. If there's no youth pass available in the country you want to visit, check out the group passes.

Saver passes or group discounts include the following multicountry and regional passes: All rail 'n drive passes, Eurail Global Pass, Eurail Select Pass, all Austria passes, all Benelux passes, all Croatia passes, all Denmark passes, all France passes, all Germany passes, all Hungary passes, all Italy passes, all Norway passes, the Portugal–Spain Saverpass, all Sweden passes, and the Scandinavia Saverpass, as well as BritRail passes (which offer the fun-sounding Party Passes). Notable exceptions are the Balkan Flexipass, BritRail + Ireland, and the European East passes.

Single-country passes that do not allow for group discounts include Bulgaria, the Czech Republic, Finland, Greece, Ireland, Poland, Portugal, Romania, Slovenia, and Spain.

Note: If you are traveling with a group of 10 or more people, Rail Europe's Group Department can assist you through **groups@raileurope.com**. British passes require three or more people to constitute a group; other passes require only two.

THE RAIL EXPERIENCE
At the Train Station

If you're traveling Europe by rail, you'll spend a lot of time in train stations. That's not a bad thing. Many European train stations are masterpieces of architecture—glorious palaces of stone, glass, and light that will inspire your wanderlust. In practical terms, European stations are generally clean, safe, and well kept, though you should keep an eye on your bags in any public place.

Many European cities have more than one train station: Paris has six, London has nine, and Brussels has four. Make sure you know which station your train leaves from, as they can be miles apart and stations aren't necessarily connected to each other by efficient means. If you have to transfer between stations in a major city, check the appropriate country chapter in this book to see how long it takes to switch stations.

In some cases, the station most trains come into isn't the most convenient one for downtown tourist attractions. See if you can hop a short-distance train to get to the more central station. In Madrid, for instance, you can take the local *cercanias* trains (valid with a pass) between the Chamartin and Atocha stations.

If you're in town for just a few hours, most large train stations offer lockers for around $5 per day. Some lockers take credit cards, but most require coins, so make sure you've got change on you. Train station lockers can fit even sizeable suitcases. Some stations have luggage checkrooms rather than lockers where you can leave your bags. If a station has porters, they'll be uniformed. Never hand your bag over to a guy on the platform who isn't wearing a clearly identifiable uniform.

Feeling hungry? Most train stations have fast-food restaurants (or at least a vending machine or two). Larger stations have sit-down restaurants and pubs. Some stations have mini-groceries—ideal for buying picnic essentials. If you need cash, stations generally have ATMs and (in major cities) currency-exchange windows. ATMs offer the best exchange rate and they work just like at home; if you need to use an exchange window, local banks generally have a better rate than train stations.

When you need to use the restroom, check your pockets. While European train stations have bathrooms, they almost all cost money to use. (Usually, the price is around 50¢.) Paid toilets mean clean, safe, and well-attended toilets; the pay turnstile will often be handled by a live attendant, who makes sure things are kept neat and tidy. Larger stations offer showers, also for pay.

As you go to buy your ticket, remember that many stations have separate domestic and international reservations counters. Even though some European countries are tiny, "International" still means just that—a ticket from the Netherlands to Belgium must be booked at the international counter.

To help you find the right train, stations offer printed schedules and departure boards. Printed schedules are usually posted up on gigantic boards, both by the tracks and in the main hall of the station. Departure schedules are usually on a yellow background; arrival schedules are on a white background. On the schedules, train

---

Special Needs

Many, but not all, trains and stations in Europe have accessible toilets, ramps, and elevators for mobility-impaired passengers. If you think you'll need help or want to scope out the situation in advance, ask Rail Europe or your	travel agent when you make your train reservation. Station staff is willing to help travelers with mobility issues to the best of their abilities, but help must be reserved in advance.

---

times are shown according to a 24-hour clock, with fast trains in red and slower trains in black. Departure and arrival tracks are also listed. Larger stations have computerized departure boards.

You'll find local transport, like trams, buses, and taxis, outside the stations; subway lines typically share the same station as the train you came in on. Taxi touts working inside stations may be scam artists. Walk past them to the official taxi stand instead.

Getting on Board

Be on the platform a few minutes before your train is due to arrive. European trains are seldom early—don't worry if you see no sign of your train even 2 minutes before its departure. On the other hand, trains wait for no one, and stops can be as short as a minute.

When your train shows up, don't just jump into the first door you see (unless you're in a real hurry). While you're safe with most short-distance trains, some long-distance trains tend to split and rejoin, with different cars going to different destinations. Ask a conductor on the platform which cars are going your way. If you're in a hurry, get on board and ask the conductor once the train leaves which car you need to be in—you'll be able to move between cars using the connecting doors (except on some high-speed trains).

You'll also need to pay attention to whether you're in a first-class or second-class car: Classes are marked by a big "1" or "2" on the side of the carriage. There may also be a yellow stripe on the car for first class and a green stripe for second class. And if you are sensitive to smoke, be sure you get yourself into a nonsmoking car or section. In most European nations, trains are entirely smoke-free, but that isn't true everywhere on the continent and NO SMOKING signs tend to be ignored more in Europe than they are in North America.

If you have a reservation, you can locate your car by checking the train diagram (*composition de train*) on the platform so you'll know just where to stand when the train pulls into the station. Once on board, you'll need to match up your car number and seat number. Car numbers are listed right by the outside car doors. Seat numbers are usually over the seats, inside the train. If you're in a hurry, jump onto the train and sort things out after the train gets moving.

Most train cars have a space for luggage near the entrance and baggage racks above the seats. If you have more baggage than you can handle, check it; we don't recommend letting your bags out of your sight. Theft is common enough that you'll need to be vigilant. If you're traveling by rail in Europe, also remember that you'll be walking along a lot of long platforms and up and down a lot of stairs—escalators, ramps, and elevators aren't nearly as common in Europe as in North America. Try not to travel with any luggage that you can't handle yourself.

WHEN A TRAIN JUST WON'T DO

Trains are the best way to see Europe, but there are times when you find alternative forms of transportation will get you someplace faster; in some of the more remote locations, a train may simply not be an option. Sometimes a quick trip by air, a short bus leg, a ferry ride, or a rental car can save you a long, roundabout trip by train—and it may save you a little money, too.

When to Fly

Trains are usually the cheapest and most efficient way to get from Point A to Point B in Europe. But scheduling a flight can help you cover a great distance very quickly (for instance, from London to Italy, or from Dublin to pretty much anywhere else) if you're short on time. So if you want to travel to a number of countries that aren't all that close together and have a limited amount of time in Europe, a quick flight used in conjunction with your railpass may make sense.

The lowest one-way fares in Europe are available from **low-fare airlines** that offer no meal service, no intercontinental connections, no first class, and often fly from satellite airports well outside their target cities. It's not uncommon to get a flight halfway across Europe for as little as $40 to $70, including taxes and fees.

The two biggest low-fare players in Europe are **Ryanair** (℃ **353/1-248-0856,** with toll-free numbers in many European countries; www.ryanair.com) and **easyJet** (www.easyjet.com). Both are profitable, solid carriers. Ryanair has major bases in Dublin, London, Frankfurt, Milan, Rome, Stockholm, and northern Spain. easyJet offers the most flights out of London and Berlin, but both airlines cover dozens of European destinations.

A wide array of smaller budget carriers blankets Europe as well, with nearly every country having its own budget-flight solution. To find out where these carriers fly and get links to their websites, go to **www.flybudget.com**, an independent and regularly updated guide to low-fare airlines. **SkyScanner** (www.skyscanner.com) is another good site, offering a map of low-fare airlines' routes and tools to help you figure out the best days to fly for the best fares.

Warning: When pricing and timing planes against trains, factor in the price of getting to the airport, any baggage or meal fees, and the time you'll need to spend in the airport before getting anywhere. For example, even though it isn't fully covered by the Eurail Global Pass, the Eurostar is actually a far more economical choice than flying from London to Paris once you've factored in the time and cost of getting to the airport.

When to Take a Bus

Local buses pick up where the rail network leaves off, and they can be lifesavers. Taking a train from Portugal's Algarve to Spain's Costa Del Sol is a 19-hour agony; by bus, the ride is a mere 1½ hours. Many small towns in Ireland, archaeological sites in Greece, and small villages in Eastern Europe are also reachable only by bus.

The most useful bus services for rail travelers are small, local outfits that will be discussed in each of the following country chapters. Likewise, the best way to get information about their routes, schedules, and prices is to contact them locally. The

major international bus company **Eurolines** (*©* 44/870-514-3219; www.euro
lines.com) will hook you up with routes in Ireland and some Eastern European countries, but not anything in Greece.

When to Take a Ferry

Many ferries are covered by the Eurail Global Pass, including international routes
from Italy to Greece, from Germany to Sweden, from Denmark to Norway, and from
Germany and Sweden to Finland. The Global Pass also offers discounted fares on
several other routes, including ferries from Ireland to France. On many routes—especially the Scandinavian, Mediterranean, and Adriatic ones—the modern, comfortable
ferryboats are great ways to cross borders while you sleep. Note that in order to take
advantage of discounted tickets, your pass must be valid in either the country of
departure or the country of arrival. For free tickets, your pass must be valid in **both**
the country of departure and the country of arrival. For either free or reduced travel
within a single country, your pass must be valid in that country. Free tickets require
the use of 1 travel day on your pass (the day of either departure or arrival).

European ferries are generally even more plush than European trains. They may
have onboard swimming pools, movie theaters, sit-down restaurants, or even casinos.
On the Adriatic ferries, accommodations range from chaises on the deck to luxurious
private cabins equipped with showers, refrigerators, TVs, and spectacular views. In
colder waters, nobody's forced to sleep on the deck—accommodations start with
reclining, airline-style seats or four-berth cabins and work their way up to two-berth
cabins with a view.

Note, however, that your railpass usually covers only the lowest possible fare.
Depending on the route, that may give you an unreserved seat, a bed in a four-berth
cabin, or a little space on the deck overnight. If you want better accommodations,
you'll have to pay more. You'll also likely have to pay port fees (6€–20€) and/or high-
season supplements, even if you have a railpass. These fees are usually payable at the
port when you're about to board the ferry, so have some cash on you.

Keep an eye on schedules, too. Ferry schedules vary from season to season,
and some ferries don't run every day. You can get schedules from the individual ferry
firms' websites (see "Major European Ferry Lines," later, for the major ferry company
websites).

If possible, reserve your ferry in advance. Ferries do sell out, just like overnight
trains. Many ferry companies allow you to book seats and cabins online; though you
usually can't book online if you're holding a railpass, you can make a reservation by
calling the ferry company direct.

Complicating the issue, a growing number of ferry companies now offer airline-
style pricing. Irish Ferries, for instance, has seven price levels, varying by individual
sailing. If you're intending to take a ferry, you can save lots of money by planning
ahead and getting on one of the cheap sailings—dropping the fare from Ireland to
France from 110€ to 60€.

Two of these ferry routes are so well trodden by low-fare airlines and other options
that they're not worth taking unless you're unwilling to plan ahead. The ferries
between Ireland and France are 19-hour trips, and they don't even leave daily. But if
you plan ahead and book a flight on low-fare Ryanair well in advance, you can shrink
that trip to 2½ hours for as little as 25€.

Aside from the major international ferry routes, your railpass also gives you discounts on a wide range of sightseeing boats. None of these smaller boats are the most efficient way to get from Point A to Point B, but many are scenic. Discounts on these scenic options include:

Austria: Twenty percent off DDSG Blue Danube Schiffahrt GmbH (📞 **43/ 1-588-80;** www.ddsg-blue-danube.at) boats between Melk and Krems, boats between Vienna and Dürnstein (Sun), and sightseeing trips by boat in Vienna. Special price on Wurm and Köck steamers (📞 **43/732-783-607;** www. donauschiffahrt.de) between Linz and Passau (Germany). Fifty percent off BSB, SBS, and ÖBB boats on Lake Constance from May to October.

Germany: Free passage on KD German Rhine Line (📞 **49/2-21-20-88 318;** www.k-d.com) between Köln and Mainz on the Rhine and between Koblenz and Cochem on the Mosel. Fifty percent off BSB, SBS, and ÖBB boats on Lake Constance from May to October. Special price on Wurm and Köck steamers (📞 **49/ 851-929-292;** www.donauschiffahrt.de) between Linz (Austria) and Passau.

Greece: Twenty percent off 1-day cruises from Athens to Aegina, Poros, and Hydra with Ionian Travel (📞 **30/210-452-6900;** www.greeka.com).

When to Drive

Train and bus services honeycomb much of Europe, but there are still rural areas where you might want to drive—especially in such countries as Ireland, Portugal, and Greece, where the rail networks aren't as comprehensive as in the rest of Europe. We recommend using a car only to explore small towns and wilderness areas—traffic and parking in major European cities can be nightmarish and expensive!

Though we mostly stick to the rails in this book, there are a few spots in Europe that we point out are better explored by car (the Ring of Kerry in Ireland, for example). This is when the rail 'n drive passes we detail on p. 58 may come in handy.

THE RULES OF THE ROAD: driving IN EUROPE

- First off, know that European drivers tend to be more aggressive than their American counterparts.
- Drive on the right except in England, Scotland, Wales, and Ireland, where you drive on the left. And *do not drive* in the left lane on a four-lane highway; it is truly only for passing.
- If someone comes up from behind and flashes his lights at you, it's a signal for you to slow down and drive more on the shoulder so he can pass you more easily (two-lane roads here routinely become three cars wide).
- Except for the German autobahn, most highways do indeed have

speed limits of around 60 to 80 mph (100–135kmph).

- Remember that everything's measured in **kilometers** here (mileage and speed limits). For a rough conversion, 1 kilometer = .6 mile.
- Be aware that although gas may look reasonably priced, the price is per liter, and 3.8 liters = 1 gallon—so multiply by four to estimate the equivalent per-gallon price. (Gas prices in North America don't look so bad now, do they?)
- Never leave anything of value in the car overnight, and don't leave anything visible any time you leave the car (this goes double in Italy, triple in Naples).

Major European Ferry Lines

Countries	Routes	Ferry Line	Contact
Denmark–Norway	Hirtshals–Larvik	Color Line	www.colorline.com; ✆ 47/22 94 44 00
	Hirtshals–Kristiansand	Color Line	www.colorline.com; ✆ 47/22 94 44 00
	Copenhagen–Oslo	DFDS Seaways	www.dfdsseaways.com; ✆ 45/3342-3010
Denmark–Sweden	Frederikshavn–Gothenburg	Stena Line	www.stenaline.nl; ✆ 31/174 315 811
	Grenå–Varberg	Stena Line	www.stenaline.nl; ✆ 31/174 315 811
Finland–Germany	Helsinki–Rostock	Talink Silja Oy	www.tallinksilja.com; ✆ 358/600 15 700
Finland–Sweden	Helsinki–Stockholm	Vikings Line	www.vikingline.fi; ✆ 358/600 41 577
	Turku–Stockholm	Vikings Line	www.vikingline.fi; ✆ 358/600 41 577
	Helsinki–Stockholm	Talink Silja Oy	www.tallinksilja.com; ✆ 358/600 15 700
	Turku–Stockholm	Talink Silja Oy	www.tallinksilja.com; ✆ 358/600 15 700
France	Cannes–Île Ste. Marguerite	Trans Côte d'Azur	www.trans-cote-azur.com; ✆ 04/92 98 71 30, ✆ 04/93 99 37 67
Germany	Rhine River, 32 stops between Mainz and Cologne	KD Rhine Line	www.k-d.com; ✆ 49/2 21 20 88 3 18
	Mosel River, 7 stops between Koblenz and Cochem Cologne	KD Rhine Line	www.k-d.com; ✆ 02/21 20 88 3 18
	Nearly 50 stops on Lake Constance	Bodensee-Schiffsbetriebe	www.bsb-online.com; ✆ 49/7531 3640 389
Greece	Numerous Greek ports	Blue Star Ferries	www.bluestarferries.com; ✆ 30/210 891 9800
	Patras–Corfu	Minoan Lines	www2.minoan.gr; ✆ 30/281 039 9800
	Piraeus–Heraklion	Minoan Lines	www2.minoan.gr; ✆ 30/281 039 9800
Greece–Italy	Patras–Brindisi	HML	www.greekislands.gr; ✆ 30/2810 346 185, ✆ 30/2810 330 598
	Patras–Ban/Ancona	Superfast/Blue Star Lines	www.bluestarferries.com; ✆ 30/210 891 9800
Ireland–France	Rosslare–Cherbourg	Irish Ferries	www.irishferries.com; ✆ 353/818 300 400
	Rosslare–Roscoff	Irish Ferries	www.irishferries.com; ✆ 353/818 300 400

* Sailings may be reduced or cancelled on holidays or in off season. Check schedules before departing.

Length of Trip	Frequency	Passholder Discount/Regular One-Way Fare
3 hr., 45 min. (day and overnight)	1–2 daily*	50% off day crossings only/9€–31€
3 hr., 15 min.	2–3 per day*	
16½ hr. (overnight)	1 per day*	25% discount on all cabins except Commodore Class/from 63€
3 hr., 30 min. (day and overnight)	Multiple sailings per day*	20% discount on full fares/20€–39€
4 hr., 25 min.–5 hr., 30 min. (day and overnight)	1–2 per day*	20% discount on full fares/13€–29€
26–29 hr.	4 per week*	30% discount/73€–159€ plus cabin
16 hr. (overnight)	2 per day*	50% discount/40€–70€
10 hr. (morning and overnight)	4 per day*	50% discount/10€–50€
16½ hr. (overnight)	1 per day*	50% discount/122€–408€ plus cabin
10 hr. (morning and overnight)	2 per day*	50% discount/11€–71€ mornings, 75€–119€ overnight
4½–5½ hr.	8 per day*	Buy one, get one free/12€
Varies by destination	2–8 per day*	Free transportation on Rhine and Mosel River boats/2.70€–53€ one-way
		Free transportation on Rhine and Mosel River boats/2.70€–53€
Varies by destination	4–12 per day*	50% reduction on all boats/5€–40€
Varies by destination	Varies by destination	30% discount on all domestic routes/10€–226€
7 hr. (overnight)	4 per week*	20% discount/31€–127€
7 hr. (daily and overnight)	Daily to 1 per week*	20% discount/19€–117€
14 hr. (overnight)	Daily*	30% reduction on standard fares and cabins, mid-June to mid-Sept/58€–200€
17–21 hr. (overnight)	Daily	100% reduction/from 53€
19½ hr. (overnight)	Up to 4 per week*	30% discount/from 64€
19½ hr. (overnight)		

Continues

Major European Ferry Lines

Countries	Routes	Ferry Line	Contact
Ireland-England	Dublin–Holyhead	Irish Ferries	www.irishferries.com; 353/818 300 400
	Rosslare–Pembroke	Irish Ferries	www.irishferries.com; 353/818 300 400
	Dun Laoghaire–Holyhead	Stena Line	www.stenaline.nl; 31/174 315 811
	Rosslare–Fishguard	Stena Line	www.stenaline.nl; 31/174 315 811
Italy–Sicily	Villa S. Giovanni–Messina	Trenitalia	www.trenitalia.com; 39/06 6847 5475
Italy–Spain	Civitavecchia–Barcelona	Grimaldi Ferries	www.grimaldi-ferries.com; 39/06 42 01 01 69
Italy–Tunisia	Civitavecchia–Tunis	Grimaldi Ferries	www.grimaldi-ferries.com; 39/06 42 01 01 69
	Palermo–Tunis	Grimaldi Ferries	www.grimaldi-ferries.com; 39/06 42 01 01 69
Netherlands–England	Hoek van Holland–Harwich	Stena Line	www.stenaline.nl; 31/174 315 811
	Amsterdam–Newcastle	DFDS Seaways	www.dfdsseaways.com; 45/3342 3010
Spain	Barcelona or Valencia–Balearic Islands	Baleària	www.balearia.com; 34/902 160 180
Sweden	Nynäshamn–Visby	Destination Gotland	www.destinationgotland.se; 46/771 22 33 00
	Oskarshamn–Visby	Destination Gotland	www.destinationgotland.se; 46/771 22 33 00
Sweden–Estonia	Stockholm–Tallinn	Talink Silja Oy	www.tallinksilja.com; 358/600 15 700
Sweden–Latvia	Stockholm–Riga	Talink Silja Oy	www.tallinksilja.com; 358/600 15 700

Warning: Those rail 'n drive passes don't include any of the following: gas, the collision damage waiver (CDW—included on the Italy 'n Drive pass only), personal accident insurance (PAI), other insurance options, fees for an additional and/or young driver, airport surcharges, registration tax, or car group upgrades made locally. Note that the minimum age for rentals on a rail 'n drive pass ranges from 23 to 25 depending on the country you're visiting. Also note that, in some countries, or for a few car groups, a service charge is due on one-way rentals. And keep in mind that, unlike North America, most rental cars in Europe have manual transmission; automatic will cost you more.

When reserving your car, be sure to ask what these extras cost, because they can make a big difference in your bottom line. Gasoline is very expensive in Europe. The CDW and other insurance might be covered by your credit card if you use the card to pay for the rental; check with your card issuer to be sure.

Length of Trip	Frequency	Passholder Discount/Regular One-Way Fare
1 hr., 49 min.	Up to 4 per week*	30% discount/from 30€
3 hr., 45 min	2 per day*	30% discount/from £26
2 hr.	2 per day*	30% discount/28€
2–3½ hr.	2–3 per day*	30% discount/28€
40 min.	25 per day	Free
20 hr. (overnight)	1 per day*	20% off/15€–50€
24 hr.	1 per week*	20% off/70€–120€
10 hr. (overnight)	1–2 per week*	20% off/29€–50€
5½ hr. (midday and overnight)	2 per day*	30% off/15€
15½ hr. (overnight)	1 per day*	25% discount on all cabins except Commodore Class/from 34€
Varies by destination	Varies by destination	20% discount/varies by destination
3-4 hr.	1–6 per day*	Various discounted rates/SEK152–SEK505
3 hr.	1–3 per day*	Various discounted rates/SEK152–SEK505
16 hr. (overnight)	1 per day*	50% discount/144€–194€ plus cabin
18 hr. (overnight)	1 per day*	50% discount/103€–163€ plus cabin

If your credit card doesn't cover the CDW (and it probably won't in Ireland), **AIG Travel Guard,** P.O. Box 47, Stevens Point, WI 54481 (✆ **800/826-4919;** www.travelguard.com), offers it for as little as $7 per day. Avis and Hertz, among other companies, require that you purchase a theft-protection policy in Italy.

Should you wish to rent a car on your own for a day trip, the U.S. contact information for main car-rental companies are **Avis** (✆ **800/230-4898;** www.avis.com), **Budget** (✆ **800/527-0700;** www.budget.com), **SIXT** (✆ **888/749-8227;** www.sixt.com), **Hertz** (✆ **800/654-3131;** www.hertz.com), **Dollar** (✆ **800/232-3301;** www.dollar.com), and **National** (✆ **877/222-9058;** www.nationalcar.com).

U.S.-based companies specializing in European rentals are **Auto Europe** (✆ **888/223-5555;** www.autoeurope.com) and **Kemwel** (✆ **877/820-0668;** www.kemwel.com). Kemwel and **Renault Eurodrive** (✆ **888/532-1221;** www.renaultusa.com) also offer a low-cost alternative to renting for longer than 17 days: **short-term leases** in which you technically buy a fresh-from-the-factory car and then sell it back when you return it. All insurance and taxes are included, from liability and theft to personal injury and CDW, with no deductible. And unlike many rental agencies, who won't rent to anyone under 25, the minimum age for a lease is 18.

The **AAA** (**www.aaa.com**) supplies good maps to its members. **Michelin** maps (www.viamichelin.com) are made for European visitors. The maps rate cities as "uninteresting" (as a tourist destination), "interesting," "worth a detour," or "worth an entire journey." They also highlight particularly scenic stretches of road in green and have symbols pointing out scenic overlooks, ruins, and other sights along the way.

But for easy mapping on the go, nothing beats traveling with a portable GPS. The biggest names in North American mobile devices are also present in Europe, and they're nearly always equipped with English-language capability. Ask about the price and availability of adding a GPS to your rental car, or consider bringing your own system with you overseas—after making sure that it is equipped with current European mapping software.

GETTING TO EUROPE
Flying from North America

There's no train from North America to Europe (that pesky ocean gets in the way), so you'll have to fly. Most major airlines fly to Europe, but fares can vary wildly depending on the time of year and who's having a sale at any given moment.

Railpass travelers have unusual flexibility in choosing their destination; if you're going to be covering five or six countries, you can choose the cheapest one to fly into. Generally, flying into a capital city (such as Paris) is cheaper than flying to a provincial city (such as Marseille), but there are exceptions: For Germany, you'll often find better fares into **Frankfurt** than into Berlin, and fares to Milan and Rome are often the same.

London is usually the cheapest European destination to fly to from North America, followed by **Brussels, Frankfurt,** and **Munich. Amsterdam** and **Paris** are also competitive hubs. If you're heading for Eastern Europe, **Prague** may be cheaper than Vienna or Budapest.

The time of week and time of year you fly is critical. Midweek flights are almost always cheaper than weekend flights. **Low season** stretches from November to March, except December 14 to January 1, and fares of around $600 from the East Coast of the U.S. to various European destinations are the norm. **Shoulder season** is from April to May, mid-September to October, and December 14 to January 1. In **high season,** from June to early September, expect to pay at least $1,000 for a round-trip ticket to Europe.

As with all air travel, however, prices vary widely, sometimes from one day to the next (and even from one seat to the next!). Follow airfares into a couple of acceptable European cities over the course of several weeks so you know what airfare norms are. Then you'll recognize a deal when you see one.

Note: The cheapest way to fly to Europe is usually to fly into and out of the same city—flying into one city and out of another can sometimes add several hundred dollars to your airfare. The best way to travel by rail, however, is usually to start off in one city and end your journey in another, and unless you're covering a small region, backtracking to your starting point could cost you valuable travel time. We suggest you add up the costs and time of doing your rail trip as both a one-way or round-trip journey and then decide which option works best for your schedule and budget.

Check the "Essentials" section in chapters 3 through 19 for a list of the major airlines that service each European country's major cities out of North America.

Finding the Lowest Fares Online

Shopping online provides an easy way of finding low fares. The "big three" online travel agencies, **Expedia.com, Travelocity.com,** and **Orbitz.com,** sell most of the air tickets bought on the Internet. (Canadian travelers should try expedia.ca and travelocity.ca.) Each has different business deals with the airlines and may offer different fares on the same flights, so it's wise to shop around. Expedia and Travelocity will also send you **e-mail notification** when a cheap fare becomes available to your favorite destination. **Kayak** (www.kayak.com) is another popular "aggregator," pulling together other websites' fare results and allowing you to specify not only when and where you want to travel, but how long the layover between flight segments.

Also remember to check **airline websites.** Don't neglect checking prices on low-fare carriers such as easyJet or Ryanair, whose fares are often misreported or simply missing from travel agency websites. And even the major airlines reserve their best deals for their own websites. Check the consolidator sites to compare prices, but before you purchase, visit the carriers' own websites to see if you can shave even more money off the price. Finally, be aware that the best available prices are available almost only through **booking online.** Most airlines now offer online-only fares that even their phone agents know nothing about.

If you're willing to give up some control over your flight details, use an **opaque fare service** such as **Priceline** (www.priceline.com; www.priceline.co.uk for Europeans) or **Hotwire** (www.hotwire.com). Both offer rock-bottom prices in exchange for travel on a "mystery airline" at a mysterious time of day, often with a mysterious change of planes en route. The mystery airlines are all major, well-known carriers—and the possibility of being sent from Philadelphia to Paris via Chicago is remote; the airlines' routing computers have gotten a lot better than they used to be. But your chances of getting a 6am or 11pm flight are pretty high. Hotwire tells you flight prices before you buy, while Priceline makes you play its "name your price" game for the best deals; Priceline will, however, also let you buy non-opaque fares at smaller discounts.

Package Tours & Travel Agents

Packages aren't guided tours—rather, they're a way to save by buying your airfare, railpass, and accommodations from the same agent. Especially during high season, you can often get a better deal this way than if you book all the pieces independently.

 Alternative Airlines

A few airlines fly between the U.S. and Europe from destinations you'd never think of, and often at lower fares than U.S. or European carriers. The most reliable include:

Singapore Air (800/742-3333; www.singaporeair.com), which flies from Newark and New York's JFK Airport to Frankfurt.

Air India (800/223-7776; www.airindia.com), which flies from Newark and Chicago to Frankfurt and from Toronto to London.

Air New Zealand (800/262-1234; www.airnz.com), which flies between London and numerous North American cities.

Air Tahiti Nui (877/824-4846; www.airtahitinui-usa.com), which flies from Los Angeles to Paris.

You lose some freedom, though, and the hotels chosen by packagers are usually personality-free international-style boxes. Getting a travel agent to construct a custom package may cost a bit more, but it can take a lot of stress out of the planning process and you'll get exactly the trip you want.

The **Society of International Railway Travelers** (© **800/478-4881**; www. irtsociety.com) knows so much about rail that they publish an online newsletter entirely about great train journeys. They offer organized rail tours and are also willing to function as a travel agent to design your ideal air/hotel/rail combination.

MONEY MATTERS

The U.S. dollar has traveled a rocky road against every European currency for several years now. During the 2005–06 period, the dollar dropped by about 5% against the euro and the British pound, while in 2010 Europe's economic doldrums have worked to push the dollar back up. Eastern Europe, once seen as an inexpensive, undiscovered jewel for adventurous North American travelers, isn't nearly such a hidden secret anymore. As a result, prices in the more remote European countries just aren't the bargains they once were. It's simply difficult to predict how far your money will take you on your European journey.

Even if the **euro,** Western Europe's joint currency, batters your wallet, it is convenient. As long as you stay in Austria, Belgium, Finland, France, Germany, Greece, Ireland, Italy, Luxembourg, the Netherlands, Portugal, Slovakia, Slovenia, and Spain, you won't need to change your money (or pay all of those change fees) more than once. Montenegro also uses the euro because that country refuses to use the Serbian dinar.

One euro is broken into 100 cents. There are coins of 1, 2, 5, 10, 20, and 50 cents, and 1 and 2 euros; bills are 5, 10, 20, 50, 100, 200, and 500 euros. (Five-hundred-euro bills, a common counterfeiters' target, aren't accepted at many shops.) Bills look the same in every euro country, but each country is allowed to design one side of its euro coins. They're like the "50 states" U.S. quarters—interchangeable, but collectable—and if you're traveling with kids, it's a great game for them to try to find all 96 varieties.

At press time, 1€ equaled 77 cents. The exchange rate directly affects the planning of your rail journey—when the euro is low, it becomes much cheaper to buy some point-to-point tickets in Europe than to buy them at home. Check the latest currency rates in your local newspaper's business pages or by going to **www.oanda.com** before traveling.

Other Foreign Currency

Fourteen other countries in this book don't use the euro. Great Britain, Denmark, and Sweden are members of the European Union (E.U.) that have "opted out" of the euro. Bulgaria, the Czech Republic, Hungary, and Poland are new members of the E.U. who are still aligning their economies to ready themselves for the euro. Croatia, Macedonia, Norway, Serbia and Montenegro, Switzerland, and Turkey are not members of the E.U. (Some non-E.U. businesses post prices in euros or dollars and will accept both the posted currency and their own local cash—but don't expect a great exchange rate.) Here's how the "outsider" currencies break down and their rates against the U.S. dollar at press time:

Getting Cash

The proliferation of ATMs means that international travelers don't necessarily have to exchange money before leaving home (your arrival airport will definitely have an ATM), though if you want to, you can do so at your local American Express or bank. If you're far away from a bank with currency-exchange services, **American Express** (✆ **800/528-4800**; www.americanexpress.com) offers traveler's checks and foreign currency, though you'll pay ordering and shipping fees.

But fewer European businesses accept traveler's checks nowadays. Instead, the easiest and best way to get cash away from home is from an ATM. They are as ubiquitous in Europe as they are in North America. The **Cirrus** (✆ **800/424-7787** or 636/722-7111 collect from anywhere in the world; www.mastercard.com) and **PLUS** (✆ **800/847-2911**; www.visa.com) networks span the globe. Look at the back of your bank card to see which network you're on, then call or check online for ATM locations at your destination. Be sure you know your personal identification number (PIN) before you leave home and verify your daily withdrawal limit before you depart.

Also keep in mind that most banks impose a fee every time a card is used at a nonmember bank's ATM. Those fees are usually higher for international transactions (up to $5 or more) than for domestic ones and, on top of this, the bank from which you withdraw cash may charge its own international conversion fees. While these costs are impossible to avoid entirely, you can keep them at a minimum if you estimate in advance how much cash you are likely to need while traveling and make one withdrawal every week, for example, rather than each day.

You can also get cash advances on your credit card at an ATM. Keep in mind that credit card companies protect themselves from theft by limiting the funds someone can withdraw outside their home country. Call your credit card company before you leave home to learn their policy regarding overseas card use.

NON-EURO COUNTRIES

Bulgaria	Leva (BGN)	100 stotinki	$1 = 1.51 BGN
Croatia	Kuna (HRK)	100 lipa	$1 = 5.59 HRK
Czech Republic	Koruna (Kč)	100 haléru	$1 = 19Kč
Denmark	Krone (DKK)	100 øre	$1 = 5.77 DKK
Hungary	Forint (Ft)	No smaller unit	$1 = 222 Ft
Macedonia	Denar (MKD)	100 deni	$1 = 47 MKD
Norway	Kroner (NOK)	100 øre	$1 = 6.17 NOK
Poland	Zloty (Zl)	100 groszy	$1 = 3.11 Zl
Romania	New Lei (RON)	100 bani	$1 = 3.31 RON
Serbia	Dinar	100 para	$1 = 81 Dinar
Sweden	Krona (SEK)	100 oüre	$1 = 7.30 SEK
Switzerland	Franc (CHF)	100 centimes	$1 = 1.05 CHF
Turkey	New Lira (TRY)	100 kurus	$1 = 1.52 TRY
United Kingdom	Pound (£)	100 pence	$1 = 0.65£

Credit Cards

Credit cards are a safe way to carry money, they provide a convenient record of all your expenses, and they generally offer good exchange rates. You can also withdraw cash advances from your credit cards at banks or ATMs, provided you know your PIN. If you've forgotten yours, or didn't even know you had one, call the number on the back of your credit card and ask the bank to send it to you. It usually takes 5 to 7 business days, though some banks will provide the number over the phone. However, you should beware that you'll be charged interest from the day you withdraw your cash, not from the day your credit card bill is due, as is the case with credit card purchases. If you charge foreign purchases to your card, your bankcard company will likely charge a commission (1% or 2%) on every foreign purchase you make. Try not to sweat this small stuff, though. For most purchases, you'll still get the best deal with ATM withdrawals and credit card purchases when you compare them to the high price of traveler's checks.

Within Europe, Visa and MasterCard are almost universally accepted (though some smaller establishments or places in rural areas still insist on cash). American Express is useful, although less widely accepted than the Big Two. Leave your Discover Card at home.

Note: Some European credit card companies, most notably those in France and the U.K., have introduced "Smartcard" or "Chip and PIN" micro technology to their credit cards. These cards include chips that can be programmed with user information and a PIN, making it more difficult for thieves to use the cards. At this writing, most merchants in Europe still readily accept the older magnetic strip cards commonly issued in the U.S. But the new technology, while reducing headaches for some credit card users, can introduce new ones to overseas travelers.

Value-Added Tax (VAT)

All European countries charge a **value-added tax (VAT)** of 15% to 34% on goods and services—it's like a sales tax that's already included in the price. Rates vary from country to country (as does the name—it's called the IVA in Italy and Spain, the TVA in France, MOMS in Sweden, and so on), though the goal in E.U. countries is to arrive

---

 Dear Visa: I'm off to Paris!

It used to be commonplace for overseas travelers to notify their credit card companies prior to an impending trip. This preventive measure made sure that their unusual spending behavior didn't look suspicious to bank personnel and result in blacked accounts. These days most bank companies insist this is no longer necessary, that high-tech tracking software is supposed to make these calls unnecessary. But if you've ever been stranded in Stockholm without cash or embarrassed in England because of a credit card company's rejection, you'll never forget it. Play it safe and notify your bank company before you leave home. And remember that if things go wrong, you can always call the toll-free emergency number printed on the back of the card. Be doubly safe and carry more than one card with you on your trip. After all, a card might not work for any number of reasons and you'll be glad to have the backup.

at a uniform rate of about 15%. Citizens of non-E.U. countries can, as they leave the country, usually get back most of the tax on purchases (not services) if they spend above a designated amount (usually $80–$200) in a single store (and, in some cases, if they don't use the items while in the country in which they were purchased).

Regulations vary from country to country, so inquire at the tourist office when you arrive to find out the procedure. Ask what percentage of the tax is refunded and whether the refund is given to you at the airport or mailed to you later. Look for a TAX FREE SHOPPING FOR TOURISTS sign posted in participating stores. Ask the storekeeper for the necessary forms and, if possible, keep the purchases in their original packages. Save all your receipts and VAT forms from each E.U. country to process at the **"Tax Refund"** desk in the airport of the last country you visit before flying home (allow at least an extra 30 min. at the airport to process forms).

To avoid VAT refund hassles, ask for a **Global Refund form** at a store where you make a purchase. When leaving a European country, have it stamped by Customs, after which you take it to the Global Refund counter at more than 700 airports and border crossings in Europe. Your money is refunded on the spot. For information, contact **Global Refund** (© **866/706-6090;** www.globalrefund.com).

TIPS ON ACCOMMODATIONS

Traditional European hotels tend to be simpler than American ones and emphasize cleanliness and friendliness over amenities. For example, even in the cheapest American chain motel, free cable is as standard as indoor plumbing. In Europe, however, few hotels below the moderate level have cable TV.

Unless otherwise noted, all hotel rooms in this book have **private bathrooms.** However, the standard European hotel bathroom might not look like what you're used to. For example, some very basic European hotels create a shower out of little more than a nozzle in the bathroom wall and a drain in the floor. Shower curtains are optional, and in some cramped private bathrooms, you'll have to relocate the toilet paper and towels before turning on the shower to keep them dry. Another interesting fixture is the "half tub," in which there's only room to sit rather than lie down. The half tub usually sports a shower nozzle that has nowhere to hang—so your knees get very clean and the floor gets very wet. Hand-held shower heads are quite common in Europe; little bottles of hair conditioner and body lotion are not. And in the most basic of hotels, hot water may be available only once a day and not on demand, as heating water is so costly.

A few other differences to note:

○ **Think small.** European hotel rooms are generally smaller than hotel rooms in North America. Many have been squeezed into historic and older buildings. As a result, these hotels offer an atmosphere that more modern hotels lack, but they also occasionally end up with some odd room configurations.

○ **Double up.** Or not. When we use the term "double" in referring to hotel rates inside this book, we mean a room for two people. However, if you ask for a double room in Europe, what you'll likely get is a room with one double bed. A twin room, on the other hand, has two beds. King beds are exceptionally rare.

○ **Cooling off.** Air-conditioning is far from common in most European hotels, and the hotels that do have it tend to fall into the top price categories. If you must have air-conditioning, be prepared to pay for it.

- **A sense of adventure goes a long way.** Remember that the chief reason you've gone to Europe is because it is so different from what you would experience on a vacation anywhere in North America. Learning to appreciate the differences and laugh at unexpected surprises will go a long way toward keeping your European adventure fun.

The **rack rate** is the maximum rate that a hotel charges for a room. Hardly anybody pays this price, however. To lower the cost of your room:

- **Ask about special rates or other discounts.** Always ask whether a less expensive room than the first one quoted is available, or whether any special rates apply to you. You may qualify for corporate, student, senior, or other discounts. Find out the hotel policy on children—do kids stay free in the room (this is uncommon in Europe) or is there a special rate? Do you get a discount if you book a minimum number of days?
- **Dial direct.** When booking a room in a chain hotel, you'll often get a better deal by calling the individual hotel's reservation desk than the chain's main number.
- **Book online.** Many hotels offer Internet-only discounts to Priceline, Hotels.com, Lodging.com, Kayak.com, or Expedia at rates much lower than the ones you can get through the hotel itself.
- **Shop around!** A little-known gem, **Travelaxe** (**www.travelaxe.com**) offers a free, Web-based price-comparison program that will make your hotel search easier. The program searches a host of discount travel websites for the best hotel prices (including major European cities) on your travel dates. Click on the price you like, and the program will send you straight to the website offering it. And, unlike most websites, Travelaxe prices almost always include hotel tax, so you actually see the total price of the room.
- **Remember the law of supply and demand.** Many hotels have high-season and low-season prices, and booking the day after "high season" ends can mean big discounts. For example, Paris hotel rates usually drop in August as natives leave town en masse for their summer vacations, and if you hit the Netherlands right after the major tulip bloom season, you'll still see plenty of colorful flora but will pay a whole lot less for your hotel room.
- **Avoid excess charges and hidden costs.** When you book a room, ask whether the hotel charges for air-conditioning (some do in the Mediterranean countries). Use your own cellphone (keeping in mind that you'll need to buy an international plan once you leave North America), pay phones, or prepaid phone cards instead of dialing direct from hotel phones at exorbitant rates. If you must call for dinner or theater reservations, ask the front desk to make the call for you—they'll be happy to help and it will cost you nothing. Leave your room's minibar locked. Most hotels charge through the nose for water, soda, and snacks. Finally, ask about local taxes and service charges, which can increase the cost of a room by 15% or more.

Hotel Booking Services

When you arrive in town, don't be snookered by hotel hawkers who peg you as a traveler as soon as you hop off the train—they're probably scam artists. A desk in the train station or at the tourist office (marked by an *i* sign for *information*) acts as a central reservation service for the city. Tell them your price range, which neighborhood you'd like to stay in, and even the style of hotel, and they'll use a computer database to find a room that meets your demands.

A Traveler's Tip

If you call a hotel from home to reserve a room, *follow up with a confirmation fax or e-mail* as printed proof that you've booked a room. Keep the language simple—state your name, number of people, what kind of room (such as "double with bathroom and one bed" or "twin with bathroom and two beds"), how many nights you'd like to stay, and the starting date for the first night. Remember, Europeans abbreviate dates day/month/year, not month/day/year.

The advantages of booking services are that they do all the room-finding work for you—for a nominal fee—and always speak English, while individual hoteliers may not. When every hotel in town seems to be booked up (during a convention or festival or just in high season), they can often find space at inns not listed in guidebooks or other main sources. On the downside, hotels in many countries often charge higher rates to people booking through such services. Our recommendation: Unless you're the happy-go-lucky type, plan an itinerary and make your hotel reservations in advance, even if it's only a few days in advance. And remember that even inexpensive hostels accept online reservations.

Railpass Hotel Bonuses

If you've got a European railpass, you can get discounted rates at many European hotels. Be aware, though, that the discount almost always applies to the hotel's sky-high rack rates and the final price may still be higher than what you'd get through an online reservation service such as hotels.com or Priceline.

Eurail Global Pass, Eurail Global Pass Flexi, and Eurail Select Pass: Discounts of up to 50% of room rates in many major European cities. See the country-specific discounts listed below, including passes in Austria, Benelux, Germany, Greece, Romania, and Spain.

Austria and Germany Railpasses: Discounts of 10% on rooms at Meininger Hotels (✆ **49/30-666-36-100;** www.meininger-hotels.com).

Balkan Flexipass: Discounted prices at the Hotel Beograd (11070 10 Vladimira Popovica) in Belgrade, Serbia; the Hotel Zeleznicar in Vrnjacka Banja; and the Klimetica in Ohrid, Macedonia. Discount of 15% off hotels in Athens booked via Ionian Travel (✆ **30/26610-99403;** www.ioniantravel.gr).

Benelux and Spain Passes: Ten percent discount at HUSA-Hotels (✆ **34/902-100-710;** www.husa.es; login: Rail Pass; password: eurailinterrail).

France Passes: Discounts on Accor Group Hotels (✆ **33/1-46-62-44 40;** www.accorhotels.com; reservation code: France Rail Pass) and at Citadines Apart'hotels (✆ **65/6272-7272;** www.citadines.com).

Greece Passes: Up to 15% off select Athens hotels booked via **Ionian Travel** (✆ **30/26610-99403;** www.ioniantravel.gr).

Romania Passes: Fifty percent off rooms at the Crowne Plaza Bucharest (✆ **40/212-240-034)** and 30% off rooms at the Hotel Europa and Asian Health

Spa in Eforie Nord. All are members of the Ana Hotels Group (☎ **40/241-741 710;** www.anahotels.ro). The Hotel Alexandros in Busteni also offers 30% off room rates to passholders (☎ **40/244-320-138;** www.hotel-alexandros.ro).

Swiss Passes: Ten percent discount on Swiss Budget Hotels (☎ **41/848-805-508;** www.rooms.ch), Minotel hotels (☎ **800/365-3346;** www.minotel.com), Best Western Swiss Hotels (☎ **800/528-1234;** www.bestwestern.ch), Sunstar Hotels (☎ **800/222-1140;** www.sunstar.ch), Unikat Hotels (☎ **41/566-645-684;** www.unikathotels.ch), and several other Swiss hotel chains. Details are available at Rail Europe's website, **www.raileurope.com**.

Mobile Phones

The three letters that define much of the world's wireless capabilities are **GSM** (Global System for Mobile Communications), a big, seamless network that makes for easy cross-border cellphone use throughout Europe and dozens of other countries worldwide. In the U.S., T-Mobile and AT&T Wireless use this quasi-universal system; in Canada, Microcell and some Rogers customers are GSM, and all Europeans and most Australians use GSM. GSM phones function with a removable plastic SIM card, encoded with your phone number and account information. If your cellphone is on a GSM system, and you have a world-capable multiband phone, such as many Sony Ericsson, Motorola, or Samsung models, you can make and receive calls across civilized areas around much of the globe. Just call your wireless operator and ask for "international roaming" to be activated on your account. Unfortunately, per-minute charges can be high—usually $1 to $2 in Western Europe.

For some, **renting** a phone can be a good idea. Although you can rent a phone from any number of overseas sites, including kiosks at airports and car-rental agencies, we suggest renting the phone before you leave home. North Americans can rent one before leaving home from **InTouch USA** (☎ **800/872-7626;** www.intouch global.com) or **RoadPost** (☎ **888/290-1606** or 905/272-5665; www.roadpost. com). InTouch will also, for free, advise you on whether your existing phone will work overseas; simply call ☎ **703/222-7161** between 9am and 4pm EST, or go to **http:// intouchglobal.com/travel.htm**.

Buying a phone can be economically attractive, as many nations have cheap prepaid phone systems. Once you arrive at your destination, stop by a local cellphone shop and get the cheapest package. Local calls are usually cheap, and in many countries incoming calls are free.

AUSTRIA

Rivaled only by Switzerland for its soaring Alpine peaks and scenic grandeur, Austria is one of the world's greatest destinations for rail travelers. Much of the country's spectacular scenery can be seen outside your window as you ride the rails in this once-great empire that was a major world power during the 18th and 19th centuries. You'll pass unspoiled mountain villages, baroque doorways fronting golden-yellow facades, onion-domed churches, and miles and miles of rugged scenery in a country that is 75% mountainous.

Though Austria is just smaller than the state of Maine, its geography is among the most varied in Europe. Castles and dense forests disappear as ancient glacial lakes come into view, nestling gracious old spas bordered by hillside vineyards. Still, nothing can compete with the Alps, with some of the most panoramic and dramatic mountain peaks in the world—most of which you'll be able to see and reach easily through the country's extensive rail system of some 3,400 miles (5,474km) of track.

Austria lies today, as it has since ancient times, at the crossroads of Europe—an embarrassment of riches for the rail traveler in a reunited continent. Bordered by Germany and the Czech Republic to the north, Slovakia and Hungary to the east, Slovenia and Italy to the south, and Switzerland and Liechtenstein to the west, Austria is at the heart of most of Europe's rail networks, easily connected to almost anywhere, including by tunnel and ferry to Britain and Scandinavia. One of the oldest rail systems in Europe dates in places back to 1837; by 1884, a 5,103km rail network reached south to Trieste, west to Bregenz, and east to Budapest and beyond.

Today Austria's rail system is among the most intricate, efficient, and sophisticated anywhere; even in the mountains, travel is easy and fast because of remarkable engineering advances in rail technology, including aerial cableways.

Another plus: Language is rarely a barrier, as most Austrians begin learning English in grade school. A final allure: Austria is an all-season country, attracting hikers and cyclists in summer, skiers in winter, and cultural tourists all year. Legendary ski resorts Kitzbühel, St. Anton, and others—rivaling anything in neighboring Switzerland—are all easy to reach by rail.

Highlights of Austria

Austria's top destinations of Vienna, Salzburg, and Innsbruck are all on major rail lines, which rarely suffer snow delays or closures during the popular winter ski season. These are just the beginning, however, and the dramatic routes south through the Semmering Pass to Italy or through Graz to the Balkan capitals of Ljubljana (Slovenia) or Zagreb (Croatia) are all memorable, now reachable through comfortable, modern service several times a day. Vienna also lies on the route of legendary **Orient Express** from Paris to Istanbul, a romantic 3-day adventure possible again with a little intelligent planning; see "Austria by Rail," below, for more on this route.

The capital city of **Vienna** lies in one of modern Austria's easternmost provinces, on the north-south rail line from Prague to Budapest and the Balkans, rather than the more highly traveled routes from Frankfurt to Verona and Rome. This seeming oddity is a legacy of its central place in an empire that stretched south to the Adriatic and east to the Black Sea, and the travel patterns of a Europe divided by the Iron Curtain. If you're flying into Austria or arriving by rail from Eastern Europe, this will assuredly be your first stop in the country and is, therefore, where we start you off in this chapter. And if your rail trip will include an overview of Europe (western, central, and eastern) as a whole, then designate Vienna your crossroads: A dividing point between the Continent's western and eastern frontiers, it makes an ideal stopover of at least 3 days, especially if you're traveling by rail farther east to such cities as Budapest or Prague.

Vienna is one of Europe's great capitals, majestic and yet engaging, a lively modern city where tradition, culture, and contemporary life are in nearly perfect balance. Here imperial grandeur is softened by lovingly tended gardens, as bicycles roll past along tree-lined alleys; ancient cobbled lanes lead you to hidden courtyards hung with flowers, and everywhere cafes and restaurants spill out onto the sidewalk. In their 7 centuries of royal and imperial rule, the Habsburgs left an astonishing legacy of palaces, parks, squares, and monuments, along with some of Europe's greatest orchestras, opera houses, theaters, and museums, an intellectual and artistic heritage among the richest of any in the West. Along with New York and Geneva, Vienna is the third headquarters city of the United Nations, which for 30 years has drawn a growing international community and helped make the city again a place of cosmopolitan energy and ideas.

The second most popular destination for travelers to Austria, **Salzburg,** is easily reached by rail from Vienna, Innsbruck, Munich, Zurich, or Milan. As a rail destination, it's particularly convenient for travelers to Bavaria and parts of Italy on the same journey. Allow at least 2 days for a quick visit to this city of Mozart and the von Trapps, made famous in the 1965 film musical *The Sound of Music.* Rich with the ornate charm of the baroque era, Salzburg is one of Europe's most loved architectural jewels, undamaged in World War II and world famous for one of the Continent's most prestigious music festivals.

Most rail passengers entering Austria from the west also make a stopover in **Innsbruck,** the capital of the federal state of Tyrol. It's a two-season city, being both a summer destination for its architectural and natural beauty, and a winter ski center full of Alpine flavor. Its Old Town has a distinct medieval flair, with mountain peaks soaring above the rooflines virtually everywhere you look. Innsbruck is perhaps the most central of the major Austrian cities, a stopover on the east-west rail link between Zurich and Vienna, and the north-south line between Munich and Verona, making it an ideal introduction to the Alpine grandeur of this small nation. Most rail visitors usually settle for a 2-night visit to Innsbruck before heading off to other countries, with the promise of a return on another occasion.

ESSENTIALS

Getting There

From the United States and Canada, you can fly directly to Vienna on **Austrian Airlines** (✆ **800/843-0002** in the U.S. and Canada; www.aua.com), the national carrier of Austria. There's nonstop service from New York; Washington, D.C.; and Toronto to Vienna. **British Airways** (✆ **800/AIRWAYS** [247-9297] in the U.S. and Canada; www.ba.com) provides excellent service to Vienna through London. Flights on **Lufthansa** (✆ **800/645-3880** in the U.S. and Canada; www.lufthansa.com), the German national carrier, depart from North America frequently for Frankfurt and Munich, with connections to Vienna.

Austria by Rail

Rail travel is superb in Austria, with fast, clean trains taking you through scenic regions. Trains will carry you nearly every place in the country, except for some remote hamlets tucked away in almost-inaccessible mountain districts. Many other services tie in with railroad travel, among them car or bicycle rentals at many stations, bus transportation links, and package tours, including boat trips and cable-car rides.

FESTIVALS & special events

In Austria, music is the national sport, the way, say, cricket or soccer is in England and bullfighting in Spain. Since the 1920s, the **Salzburg Festival,** held the end of July to the end of August, has been one of the premier cultural events of Europe, sparkling with opera, chamber music, plays, concerts, appearances by world-class artists, and many other cultural presentations. Always count on stagings of Mozart operas. Performances are staged at various venues throughout the city. For tickets, contact the **Salzburg Festival,** Postfach 140, A-5010 Salzburg (✆ **0662/8045-500;** www.salzburgfestival.at), several months in advance.

Other big annual events include the **Wiener Festwochen (Vienna Festival;** www.festwochen.at), in May and June, featuring primarily new and avant-garde theater productions, as well as jazz and classical concerts and art exhibits; and the **Donauinselfest (Danube Island Festival;** www.donauinselfest.at), a gigantic open-air party held in Vienna the last weekend in June on the banks of the Danube, complete with rock, pop, and folk music and an evening fireworks display. And then there's **JazzFest** in early July, **ImpulsTanz** in July and August, the **Wienerlied Festival** in September, the **Klezmer Festival** in October, and much more. For more information on Vienna's many events, contact **Vienna Tourist Information** (✆ **01/24 555;** www.vienna.info).

Inaugurated in 2009, the **Railjet** is Austria's high-speed answer to Germany's ICE and France's TGV, connecting Zurich, Innsbruck, Munich, Vienna, and Budapest at speeds of up to 125 mph (201kmph). High-tech **InterCity Express (ICE)** trains, complete with electrical outlets at every seat and video displays in first class, connect Vienna with all major cities in the country, including Salzburg and Innsbruck, with express IC trains on other lines. **EuroCity (EC)** trains also connect cities within Austria, as well as with several international trains. A few **EuroNight (EN)** and **CityNightLine (CNL)** trains travel through the night to connect Vienna with Venice, Florence, Rome, Zurich, Berlin, and other international destinations. Avoid the slower RegionalExpress and RegionalBahn trains unless you have no other alternative, as the other rail options in the country are faster and have more amenities.

One memorable outing is an evening or day journey on the Vienna-based *Magestic Imperator,* the most elegant train in Europe, re-creating the spirit and style of the Royal Court Train of the Kaiser Franz Josef. Reassembled and restored by owner Gottfried Rieck, the Majestic Imperator is a train of six period cars—including a Salon car dating from 1905—collected from rail yards all over Europe and restored in the same Ringhofer-Smirchow works in the Czech Republic. One prime journey takes you along the Danube through the lush wine country of Wachau, considered one of the most beautiful landscapes in Austria, stopping at Krems, Durnstein, Weissenkirchen, and Spitz. Trips can be booked up to 2 days in advance at the cost of 89€ per person, including wine and hors d'oeuvres. Special outings include guided tours of historic Duernstein, where Richard the Lionhearted was held prisoner by the Duke of Babenburger on his way back from the Crusades; a gala five-course dinner at Schloss Durnstein for 59€ a person, or a vintner's buffet and wine tasting at the Baroque Keller Schloessel for 39€. At Weissenkirchen and Spitz, travelers can wander through the streets of these picture-perfect villages and have dinner at any of the many local Heuriger wine taverns. Or try something on your own: Passengers are free to leave and reenter the train at any station and plan their own programs. For complete information on this and other routes and offers, see **www.imperialtrain.com**.

Another noteworthy route is the 8-hour **Zurich–Vienna alpine run,** which passes through sweeping, panoramic valleys and magnificent Alpine vistas, especially around the Arlberg Pass. This trip runs past some of the most beautiful and unspoiled villages in Europe before stopping at Innsbruck and Salzburg as the train heads east toward Vienna. At either Innsbruck or Salzburg, you can change trains and head north to Munich or south to Venice, Verona, or Rome.

For more information, to order tickets, and to obtain schedule information, go to the **Austrian Federal Railroad (ÖBB)** website at www.oebb.at. In Austria, information on trains and schedules can be obtained by calling ℂ **05/1717** from anywhere in the country.

TICKETS & PASSES

For information on the **Eurail Global Pass, Eurail Select Pass, Eurail Global Pass Flexi,** and other multicountry options, see chapter 2. In addition to these popular passes, the **Austria Railpass** grants 3 to 8 days of nonconsecutive unlimited train travel in a 15-day period, with a choice of first- or second-class seats. Bonuses built into this pass include various discounts, including Danube river trips between Melk and Krems and between Vienna and Dürnstein. The 3-day pass starts at $205 in first class or $139 in second class. There is also an **Austria–Switzerland Pass,** valid for 4 to 10 days of nonconsecutive unlimited train travel within 2 months, with the 4-day pass costing $349 for first class.

All of the passes mentioned should be purchased in North America prior to your departure. To buy a pass, contact **Rail Europe** (ℂ **888/438-7245** in the United States, ℂ 800/361-7245 in Canada; www.raileurope.com) or your travel agent.

Note: Children under 6 travel free in Austria; kids ages 6 to 12 are offered a discount. Other discount fares and tickets available in Austria at most rail stations include:

ÖBB VORTEILSCARD   The VORTEILScard Classic provides a 50% reduction on domestic train fares and 25% reduction on international travel through most European countries. Price of the card is 100€ and is valid for 1 year; a photo is required. Seniors (women 60 years of age and over and men age 65 and over) can have the same benefits with the VORTEILScard Senior, which costs 27€ and requires proof of age along with a passport photo. All VORTEILScard are available at all railroad stations.

FOREIGN TRAIN TERMS

English speakers should have no trouble getting around and riding the rails of Austria. The people in the urban centers of Austria, including those who run the rails, are typically highly proficient in English and willing to lend a hand.

It's helpful to know that the Austria Federal Railroad is called **Österreichische Bundesbahn (ÖBB)** and that yellow poster-size signs announce departure times, called *Abfahrt,* and that white signs announce arrivals, known as *Ankunft.* For more train terms in German, see chapter 9.

PRACTICAL TRAIN INFORMATION

TICKETS   Any train depot in Austria will sell you an individual ticket. At major stations, these are also sold at automated machines with English-language options.

You can often hop aboard a train, seek out the conductor, and purchase a ticket, although you're assessed a small surcharge (usually 3€) for this service. Nearly all major stations accept credit cards such as American Express, Visa, and MasterCard.

For more on Austria's railways, check out the ÖBB's website at **www.oebb.at**.

RESERVATIONS Although not always required, it is still advisable to make a reservation for travel on an Austrian rail line. A seat reservation is not guaranteed even with a railpass, and it's worth the 3.50€ extra investment for the greater security in travel. During holiday seasons or busy times—such as the peak winter ski season in Innsbruck—reservations are imperative. Your railpass will cover most high-speed trains, such as EuroCity or InterCity, and though no supplement is charged within Austria, you may be charged a supplement for the portion of your travels outside the Austrian border.

Austria is a relatively small country, and you can usually get where you're going without any long overnight hauls, so sleeping arrangements are rarely a factor. If, however, you're heading for an international destination, you might consider getting a *couchette* (a fold-down bunk bed; see chapter 2 for more details). These are usually clean and comfortable on Austrian trains. Reservations can be made through travel agents or in person at any rail station in Austria. Most seat reservations require only a few hours' notice. However, for a couchette reservation, a few days' notice is advised, especially during high season. ***Note:*** Because the price of couchette and seat reservations is the same in the U.S. as it is in Austria, if you have a firm travel itinerary, we recommend getting your train reservations from Rail Europe (see above) before you leave North America. Another option, if you wish to travel in style, is to

 ## RIDING historic RAILS

One of the most breathtaking and dramatic train rides in Alpine Europe is the **Semmering Pass Railway ★★★**, one of the world's greatest feats of railway engineering. This UNESCO-protected site (the only rail line on UNESCO's Heritage list) dates from 1842 and still pays tribute to the engineers of imperial Austria.

Through limestone cliffs with craggy rocks and across wide valleys, the rail lines take you across 16 viaducts, through 15 tunnels, and across 129 bridges, a distance of 25 miles (40km). The railway, for the most part, is wholly preserved in its original state. The Semmering Pass itself is 56 miles (90km) southeast of Vienna and marks the boundary between the provinces of Styria and Lower Austria. At the peak of the pass, constructed on terraces between 3,231 and 3,973 feet

(969–1,192m), is a winter sports center and mountain spa.

The Semmering rail links Vienna's Südbahnhof with the city of Leoben, 106 miles (171km) southwest of Vienna. Although modern trains make this run, the best way to experience this breathtaking ride is aboard the slower **Erlebniszug** (Experience Train), a regular engine with old-fashioned coaches. Most seasons it departs Vienna's Südbahnhof every Saturday and Sunday morning and travels through Semmering to Mürzzuschlag before heading back to Vienna, with more than a dozen stops along the way. Passengers can get off the train wherever they like and reboard it later in the day on its return trip to Vienna (passholders can ride for free). For more information and other Erlebniszug offerings, call ℂ **05/1717** or go to **www.erlebnis-bahn-schiff.at**.

Trains & Travel Times in Austria

From	To	Type of Train	# of Trains	Frequency	Travel Time
Vienna	Salzburg	Railjet, ICE, IC, EC, EN	37	Daily	2 hr., 39 min. to 3 hr., 9 min.
Vienna	Innsbruck	Railjet, ICE, IC, EC, EN	14	Daily	4½ hr.
Salzburg	Innsbruck	Railjet, ICE, EC, EN	16	Daily	2 hr.

splurge on your own private sleeper compartment, complete with bathroom, on the EuroNight or City Nightline trains that cross the country or pass through it.

SERVICE & AMENITIES All InterCity and EuroCity trains have dining cars. And all, except for local commuter trains going to the suburbs of Vienna, feature minibars—which on European trains is a trolley-style snack bar (also serving liquor) that's rolled on wheels through the train carriages.

The bad news is that drinking and dining on Austrian railways is prohibitively expensive for travelers on strict budgets, who are better advised to bring along some food and drink and have an on-train picnic while taking in all that panoramic Austrian scenery. Most stations have well-stocked kiosks that are only slightly more expensive than regular supermarkets. In Vienna, food or drink is no problem, as the two big stations have delicatessens and small shops that keep long hours, even on Sundays.

[FastFACTS] AUSTRIA

Area Codes The country code for Austria is **43.** The area code for Vienna is **01;** for Salzburg, **0662;** and for Innsbruck, **0512.**

Business Hours Banking hours vary according to the region. In Vienna, they're open Monday to Friday 8am to 3pm (to 5:30pm Thurs). The exchange counters at airports and railroad stations are open longer (from the first to the last plane at airports), including weekends. Shop hours are generally Monday to Friday 9 or 9:30am to 6:30 or 7pm, and Saturday from 9am to 5 or 6pm. Shops in small towns or outside city centers may close for lunch from noon to 1 or 2pm.

Most businesses and shops are closed on Sunday, but convenience stores at train stations are open and sell basic necessities.

Climate In Austria, the temperature varies greatly depending on your location. The national average ranges from a low of 9°F (–13°C) in January to a high of 68°F (20°C) in July. However, in Vienna, the January average is 32°F (0°C), for July 68°F (20°C). Snow falls in the mountainous sectors by mid-November, but it rarely affects the major rail routes. The winter air is usually crisp and clear, with many sunny days. The winter snow cover can last from late December through March in the valleys, from

November through May at about 6,000 feet (1,800m), and all year at above 8,500 feet (2,550m). The ideal times for visiting Vienna are spring and fall, when you'll find mild, sunny days. "Summer" generally means from Easter until about mid-October. By the end of July, Alpine wildflowers are in full bloom.

Documents Required Americans, Canadians, and Australians need only a valid passport for travel to Austria. European Union (E.U.) citizens traveling to Austria face lesser requirements. In general, a national identity card with photo ID will be sufficient. But check with a travel agent or the Austrian embassy in your home country to be absolutely certain.

Electricity Austria operates on 220 volts AC (50 cycles). That means that U.S.-made appliances that don't come with a 110/220 switch will need a transformer (sometimes called a converter) and an adaptor plug. Many Austrian hotels stock adapter plugs but not power transformers.

Embassies & Consulates The main building of the Embassy of the **United States** is at Boltzmanngasse 16, A-1090 Vienna (𝄐 **01/31339-0**). However, the consulate is at Parking 12a, A-1010 Vienna (𝄐 **01/31339-7573;** U-Bahn: Stadtpark); it handles lost passports, tourist emergencies, and other matters, and is open for emergency services Monday to Friday 8:30am to 5pm.

The Embassy of **Canada,** Laurenzerberg 2, third floor (𝄐 **01/531 38-3000;** U-Bahn: Schwedenplatz), is open Monday to Friday 8:30am to 12:30pm and 1:30 to 3:30pm.

Health & Safety You'll encounter few health issues while traveling in Austria. The tap water is generally safe to drink, the milk is pasteurized, and health services are good. Occasionally, the change in diet and water may cause some minor gastric disturbances, so you may want to talk to your doctor. As for safety, no particular caution is needed, other than what a discreet person would

maintain anywhere. Compared to the rest of the world, Austria is a very safe country in which to travel.

Holidays Bank holidays in Austria are as follows: January 1, January 6 (Epiphany), Easter Monday, May 1, Ascension Day, Whitmonday, Corpus Christi Day, August 15, October 26 (Austria National Day), November 1, December 8, and December 25 and 26.

Legal Aid If arrested or charged with a crime, you can obtain a list of private lawyers from the U.S. Embassy to represent you.

Mail **Post offices** (*Das Postamt*) in Austria are usually located in the heart of the town, village, or urban district they service. If you're unsure of your address in any particular town, correspondence can be addressed c/o the local post office by labeling it either POST RESTANTE or POSTLAGERND. If you do this, it's important to clearly designate the addressee, the name of the town, and its postal code. To claim any correspondence, the addressee must present his or her passport.

The postal system in Austria is, for the most part, efficient and speedy. You can buy stamps at a post office or from the hundreds of news and tobacco kiosks, designated locally as Tabak-Trafik. Mailboxes are painted yellow. Both postcards and airmail letters weighing less than 20 grams cost 1.40€ for delivery to North America.

Police & Emergencies Dial 𝄐 **133** anywhere in Austria to summon the police. Emergency phone numbers throughout the country (no area code needed) are as follows: 𝄐 **133** for the police, **144** for an ambulance, and **122** to report a fire.

Telephone If you're on a tight budget, do not dial abroad directly from your hotel room unless it's an emergency. Austrian hotels routinely add 40% surcharges, and some will add as much as 200% to your call. If you do place a call from your room, for help dialing, contact your hotel's operator. Alternatively, dial 𝄐 **09** for placement of long-distance calls within Austria or for information about using a telephone company credit card, dial 𝄐 **1611** for directory assistance, and dial 𝄐 **08** for help in dialing international long distance.

Telephone booths can be found all over Austria. Despite the increasing automation of many aspects of local life, many public phones (some with video displays) are still operated by coins instead of by credit card. It costs .10€ to make a 1-minute local phone call, but you must insert a minimum of .20€ to place the call. Insert several coins to prevent being cut off. The phone will return whatever unused coins remain at the end of your call (in theory, at least).

Avoid carrying lots of coins by buying a **telephone card,** called **Eco+,** available at post offices for 10€ or 15€. It offers savings on domestic and international calls, with those to U.S. and Canada costing .07€ per minute. There are also cheaper telephone cards for 3.60€ and 6.90€, but these do not provide discounts.

Tipping A service charge of 10% to 15% is included on hotel and restaurant bills, but it's a good policy to leave something extra—about 10% of the bill—for waiters and 2€ per day for your hotel maid.

Your hairdresser should be tipped 10% of the bill,

and the shampoo person will be thankful for a 2€ gratuity. Toilet attendants are usually given .50€, and coat-check attendants expect .50€ to 1.50€, depending on the establishment.

VIENNA ★★★

From the time the Romans selected the site of a Celtic settlement for the location of one of its most important Central European forts, *Vindobona,* the city that grew up in the Vienna Basin of the Danube has played a vital role in European history. Austria developed around the city into a mighty empire, but the Viennese character that formed during the long history of the country is a rich amalgam of the blending of cultures that have made Vienna what it still is today: a cosmopolitan city whose people devote themselves to enjoyment of the good life. It is also one of Europe's most visually striking capitals.

The Habsburgs, Austria's rulers for 6 centuries, left a rich architectural legacy of magnificent baroque and rococo buildings and palaces, beautifully landscaped gardens, and fabulous art collections from the far corners of their empire. Music, art, literature, theater, architecture, education, food, and drink (perhaps wine from the same slopes where the Romans had vineyards in the 1st c. A.D.)—all contribute to the warm congenial atmosphere, the *Gemütlichkeit,* of Vienna.

For the rail traveler exploring Austria, Vienna should, and likely will, be your introduction to the country. Most flights into Austria from North America land here, and the city is the center hub for the Austrian rail system. In addition, it's a springboard for travel to or from Budapest, Prague, and other Eastern European destinations.

Station Information
GETTING FROM THE AIRPORT TO THE TRAIN STATION
Vienna International Airport (✆ 01/7007-22233; www.viennaairport.com) is 12 miles (19km) southeast of the city center. For a list of air carriers flying into Vienna, see "Getting There," earlier in this chapter.

A branch office of the **Vienna Tourist Information Office,** located in the arrivals hall, is open daily 6am to 11pm. A shuttle bus, the **Vienna Airport Line** (✆ **01/7007 32300**), departs every 30 minutes for Schwedenplatz, in the heart of the city. The trip takes about 20 minutes, and Schwedenplatz is easily connected to the rest of the city via tram, bus, and U-Bahn (subway). Shuttle buses also depart the airport every 20 minutes for Wien Meidling (a 30-min. trip) and the Westbahnhof (a 45-min. trip), currently Vienna's two train stations. In any case, the cost of the shuttle to Schwedenplatz or the train stations is 6€ one-way or 5€ if you have the Vienna Card (see "City Transportation on the Cheap," p. 94).

A cheaper alternative is to take **Schnellbahn (Rapid Transit) 7** from the airport to Wien Mitte, a train/subway station located just east of the Old City. The trip costs 3.60€ one-way and takes about 25 minutes, with departures every half-hour. But if

Vienna

ACCOMMODATIONS ■
Altstadt Vienna **3**
Aviano **14**
Graben Hotel **15**
Hotel Am Schubertring **33**
Hotel Mailberger Hof **31**
Hotel-Pension Arenberg **24**
Hotel Wandl **19**

König von Ungarn **28**
Pension Nossek **18**
Pertschy Hotel **17**

DINING ◆
Griechenbeisl **23**
Gulaschmuseum **27**
Kantine **4**

Palmenhaus **11**
Pizza Bizi **21**
Settimo Cielo **30**
Trzesniewski **16**
Wiener Rathauskeller **2**
Wrenkh **20**
Zwölf Apostelkeller **22**

ATTRACTIONS ●

Albertina **12**
Burgkapelle **9**
Haus der Musik **32**
Hofburg **8**
Kaiserappartements **6**
Kunst Haus Wien **26**
Kunsthistorisches Museum **5**

Leopold Museum **4**
MUMOK **4**
Prater/Riesenrad **25**
Schatzkammer **7**
Schönbrunn **1**
Silberkammer **6**
Sisi Museum **6**
Spanische Reitschule **10**

Stephansdom **29**
Staatsoper **13**

Navigating Vienna's Evolving Rail Network

Many of Vienna's rail hubs are undergoing reconstruction, replacing the temporary post–World War II eyesores with modern, efficient stations. The most ambitious of them all is at the site of the former Südbahnhof (South Station), where the future Hauptbahnhof (Main Station) is rising from the rubble and slated to begin operation in 2012. With much of the rail traffic shifted to Westbahnhof and the temporary station at Meidling, both locals and travelers must navigate through construction zones and readjust to the new layout. Yellow signs indicate the provisional entrance and exits at Westbahnhof, and blue signs with the letter i indicate where the English-speaking staff of ÖBB can be located.

you're in a hurry, you can take the same trip aboard the **City Airport Train** (CAT; www.cityairporttrain.com), which delivers you to Wien Mitte in 16 minutes for 9€, 7.50€ for Vienna Card holders, with departures every 30 minutes.

Taxis charge about 32€ to 35€ for the same trip the shuttle buses make.

INSIDE THE STATIONS

Vienna has two main rail stations that offer frequent connections to all Austrian cities and towns and from all major European cities. For train and station information, call ✆ **05/1717** from anywhere in Austria.

The **Westbahnhof (West Station),** Mariahilferstrasse 132, serves trains arriving from western Austria, France, Germany, Switzerland, and some Eastern European countries (Hungary, for one). It has frequent links to major Austrian cities such as Salzburg, Innsbruck, and Linz, with longer connections to such cities as Hamburg, Amsterdam, Munich, Zurich, and Budapest. Trains arrive on the second level of the two-level station. For reservations, rail information, and pass validation, head for the ÖBB office on the upper level. It's open daily 5:20am to 10:45pm. The Westbahnhof also has a money exchange office and Western Union located to the left of the escalators on the main level, which is open daily from 8am to 9pm. There are lockers for luggage. Westbahnhof connects with local trains, the U3 and U6 underground lines (also known as the *U-Bahn*), and several tram and bus routes.

Vienna's **Meidling** station has become a temporary hub for destinations in southern and eastern Europe, while the former Südbahnhof (South Station) makes way for the future Hauptbahnhof (Main Station). Offering regular service to Italy, Zagreb, Budapest, Prague, and Warsaw, the eight-platform station is located at the Philadelphiabrücke stop on the U6, just four U-Bahn stops away from the Westbahnhof. Its ticket office (*Reisezentrum*) is open 5:30am to 10:30pm and located below the street and platform level. Next door is the exchange office, open Monday to Thursday 9am to 1pm, 1:30 to 5:30pm, and Friday 9am to 1pm and 1:30 to 4pm.

At the site of the future Hauptbahnhof is the **Ostbahn,** a small station useful for shorter trips in southern and eastern Austria, as well as Bratislava. Although lacking an exchange office and the amenities of the other stations, its **Reisezentrum** (✆ **05/1717**) is open Monday to Friday 6:15am to 6pm and weekends 7:15am to 5:10pm.

3

Vienna

AUSTRIA

Information Elsewhere in the City

For a free map, brochures, and details on Vienna (including the current showings and times for the opera, theater, Spanish Riding School, and Vienna Boys' Choir), drop by the main office of **Vienna Tourist Information,** on the corner of Albertinaplatz and Maysedergasse (✆ **01/24 555;** www.vienna.info; U-Bahn: Stephansplatz), off Kärntner Strasse behind the Staatsoper. It will book hotel rooms for 2.90€. Be sure to pick up the free monthly *Wien-Programm*—it tells what's going on in Vienna's concert halls, theaters, and opera houses. If you're looking for detailed historic information on Vienna's many beautiful buildings, be sure to buy the 3.60€ English-language booklet *Vienna from A to Z.* Its listings are keyed to the unique numbered plaques affixed to the front of every building of historic interest. You'll spot these plaques everywhere: They're heralded by little red-and-white flags in summer. The tourist office is open daily 9am to 7pm.

Further information and event listings can be found in the monthly *Vienna Review,* the city's only English-language newspaper, available at tobacconists.

City Layout

Vienna's **Altstadt (Old City)** is delightfully compact, filled with tiny cobblestone streets leading to majestic squares. In the center is **Stephansplatz,** with Vienna's most familiar landmark, Stephansdom (St. Stephen's Cathedral). From here, it's a short walk to the Hofburg (official residence of the Habsburgs) and its many attractions, the Kunsthistorisches Museum (Art History Museum), and MuseumsQuartier Wien, one of the largest museum complexes in the world and home to the prestigious Leopold Museum. **Kärntner Strasse,** much of it pedestrian, is the main shopping street, leading from Stephansplatz past the Staatsoper to Karlsplatz.

Circling the Altstadt is "the Ring," as Vienna's **Ringstrasse** is commonly called. This impressive circular boulevard, 2½ miles (4km) long and 187 feet (56m) wide, was built in the mid-1800s along what used to be the city's fortifications (hence its shape as a circle around the Altstadt). Trams run along the tree-shaded Ring. Everything inside the Ring is known as the first *Bezirk* (District), denoted by the 1010 postal code in addresses and the 1 preceding street names on signs. The rest of Vienna is also divided into various districts, designated on the free map the Vienna Tourist Information distributes.

Schönbrunn, Vienna's top sight, is a few miles southwest of the city center, easily reached by U-Bahn from Karlsplatz.

Getting Around

Vienna's transit network consists of five U-Bahn (subway) lines, trams, buses, and several rapid transit and commuter trains. The free map given out by the tourist office shows tram and bus lines, as well as subway stops, although you'll need a magnifying glass to read it. Luckily, most of Vienna's attractions are within walking distance of one another.

For details on Vienna's public transport system, visit the **Informationsdienst der Wiener Verkehrsbetriebe,** in the underground Opernpassage at Karlsplatz, in the U-Bahn station at Stephansplatz, at the Meidling railway station, or at the Westbahnhof U-Bahn station. All four are open Monday to Friday 6:30am to 6:30pm, and all except the Meidling office on Saturday, Sunday, and holidays 8:30am to 4pm.

The staff can answer questions, such as which bus to take to reach your destination. You can also call ℂ **01/79 09-100** or check the website at **www.wienerlinien.at**.

A **single ticket** (good for the tram, day and night buses, S-Bahn, or U-Bahn) costs 1.80€ if bought in advance and permits as many transfers as you need to reach your destination, as long as you keep moving in the same direction. You can buy advance tickets from automated ticket machines in U-Bahn stations and ticket booths or tobacconists. Tickets bought on board from bus or tram conductors, on the other hand, cost 2.20€. For all tickets, you must validate them yourself by inserting them into little boxes at the entry of S-Bahn and U-Bahn platforms or on buses and trams. Children up to 6 can travel free, while those 7 to 14 travel for half-fare, except on Sunday, holidays, and Vienna school holidays, when they travel free.

U-BAHN (SUBWAY) Most of the top attractions in the Inner City can be seen by foot, tram, or bus, but the U-Bahn is your best bet to get across town quickly or to reach the suburbs. It consists of five lines labeled as U1, U2, U3, U4, and U6 (there is no U5). The most useful U-Bahn line for visitors is the U4, which stops at Schwedenplatz and Karlsplatz before continuing to Kettenbrückengasse (site of Vienna's outdoor market and weekend flea market) and Schönbrunn. The U2 travels around part of the Ring, to the Prater with its Ferris wheel (Riesenrad), past the stadium, and over the Danube, while the U1 and U3 have stations at Stephansplatz (U3 connects the Westbahnhof with Stephansplatz). U4, U2, and U1 all converge at Karlsplatz. The subway runs daily 6am to midnight and every 15 minutes all through the night on Friday and Saturday nights, as well as nights before public holidays.

TRAM (STREETCAR) Although the U-Bahn and buses have taken over most of the tram (*Strassenbahn*) routes, the city's red-and-white trams are not only a practical way to get around, but they're also a great way to see the city. They're heavily used for traveling around portions of the Ring (trams 1 and 2) and for transportation between the Südbahnhof and the Ring (tram D).

A specially designated yellow **Vienna Ring Tram** (ℂ **01/7909 121**) plies the entirety of the Ring for sightseeing purposes, allowing riders to enjoy the Ring without having to change trams. Departures occur every half-hour from Schwedenplatz between 10am and 6pm. The 24-minute ride costs 6€, 4€ children. A 24-hour Kombi ticket that includes the yellow tram and the rest of the normal public transport is also available for 14€.

BY BUS Buses (*Autobus*) traverse Vienna in all directions and operate daily from 5 or 6am to around midnight, depending on the route. However, only 1A, 2A, and 3A (mostly minibus size) travel inside the Ring Monday to Saturday. Numerous buses operate throughout the night from Schwedenplatz, Oper, or Schottentor to the suburbs (including Grinzing), with departures every half-hour.

BY TAXI Taxis are easy to find within the city center, but be warned that fares can add up quickly. The base fare is 2.50€, plus 1.20€ per kilometer. For night rides after 11pm, and for trips on Sundays and holidays, the base fare is 2.60€, plus 1€ for each additional kilometer. There is an additional charge of 2€ if ordered by phone. The fare for trips outside the Vienna area (for instance, to the airport) should be agreed upon with the driver in advance, and a 10% tip is the norm. Taxi stands are marked by signs, or you can call ℂ **01/31 300,** 60 160, or 40 100.

BY BIKE Public bicycles, named **Citybike** (ℂ **0810/500 500;** citybikewien.at), are available at any one of 12 stands in the first district and over 50 in the remainder of Vienna. Bikes can be removed from the terminal with the swipe of a Citybike

Vienna Public Transport

Tourist Card available at Royal Tours, Herrengasse 1–3, open 9 to 11:30am and 1 to 6pm, as well as at selected hotels. Base charge is 2€ per day; free for first hour, 1€ for the second hour, 2€ for the third hour, and 4€ for each subsequent hour.

Where to Stay

Note: Vienna hotels use seasonal pricing reflecting the opera, concert, and theater calendar and, to a lesser extent, the temperate weather in spring and fall. Thus, high season is usually September to mid-November and April through June, as well as the week between Christmas and New Year's. Low and middle seasons are in summer, before Christmas, and in midwinter. Check each hotel's website for details.

CITY TRANSPORTATION ON THE cheap

The **Vienna Card** is useful when traveling a lot by public transportation within the city limits. It's extremely flexible and functional for visitors because it allows unlimited travel on Vienna's subways, buses, and trams for 72 hours, along with nominal discounts at city museums, attractions, restaurants, and shops. You can purchase a Vienna Card valid for 72 hours for 19€ at tourist information offices, public transport centers, and some hotels.

Another option if you plan to ride a lot on the city's transport system is to buy transportation-only tickets. A ticket valid for unlimited rides during any 24-hour period costs 5.70€; an equivalent ticket valid for any 72-hour period

goes for 14€. There's also a green ticket, priced at 29€, that contains eight individual partitions, each good for 1 day of unlimited travel (an individual can opt to use all eight of the partitions for his or her own use, thereby gaining 8 days of cost-effective travel on the city's transport system; or the partitions can be subdivided among a group of several riders, allowing—for example—two persons 4 days each of unlimited rides or three persons 2 days each of unlimited rides).

These tickets are available at Tabak-Trafiks, as well as vending machines in underground stations, at the two main train stations, and the airport.

Graben Hotel   Established in 1918 at the collapse of the Austrian empire, this well-run hotel on a quiet side street off the Graben was once a favorite hangout of some of Vienna *Kaffeehausliteraten,* writers such as Peter Altenberg, Franz Kafka, and Max Brod, and is just across from the pleasingly threadbare and justly famous Café Hawelka. The mostly Art Nouveau, minimalist hotel bedrooms are a bit small and spartan, but individually designed and with high ceilings that make them feel bigger. It's a longtime favorite of those who like the atmosphere of the old city, surrounded by good restaurants (including the fine Trattoria San Stefano in the building), galleries and antique shops, and insider destinations such as Tresniewski's sandwich shop, the Dorotheum Auction House, the Jewish Museum, or Doblinger Musikhaus.

Dorotheergasse 3, A-1010 Vienna. ⓒ **01/512 70 41-0.** Fax 01/512 15 31-20. www.kremslehnerhotels.at. 41 units. 150€–180€ double. Rates include buffet breakfast. AE, DC, MC, V. U-Bahn: Karlsplatz. **Amenities:** Restaurant; smoke-free rooms. *In room:* No A/C.

Hotel Am Schubertring ★   This handsome hotel on the Ring near the opera and the lovely Stadtpark has stayed truer to Austrian style and old-world tradition than many of its nearby competitors, its mostly midsize rooms decorated in the 1840s Biedermeier or turn-of-the-century Jugendstil (the Austrian version of Art Nouveau), and its staff attentive and personal. Popular with U.N. regulars, the hotel's accommodations are all located on the top floor (some with kitchenettes) and offer views over the rooftops or skylights that on clear days flood the well-appointed rooms with sunshine.

Schubertring 11, A-1010 Vienna. ⓒ **01/717 02-0.** Fax 01/713 99 66. www.schubertring.at. 39 units. 128€–218€ double. Rates include buffet breakfast. AE, DC, MC, V. U-Bahn: Karlsplatz or Stadtpark. **Amenities:** Bar.

Hotel Altstadt Wien ★★   The Altstadt Wien is a true original, a sophisticated urban hostelry that treats its guests like friends of the family. Converted from a century-old private residence by art connoisseur Otto Wiesenthal, each room is original, combining the traditional architecture with dramatic uses of color and design. The whole is innovative and stylish, with many charming personal touches— as if you were staying in a private home of someone with extremely good taste. The breakfast buffet is renowned, with fresh bread and rolls, local cheeses and jams, and much more. There's occasional live piano music in the very comfortable and well-used lounge.

Kirchengasse 41, A-1070 Vienna. ✆ **01/522 66 66.** Fax 01/ 523 49 01. www.altstadt.at. 63 units. 139€– 179€ double. Rates include buffet breakfast. AE, DC, MC, V. U-Bahn: Stephansplatz. **Amenities:** Bar; smoke-free rooms. *In room:* No A/C (in some rooms).

Hotel Mailberger Hof ★★ 🏨 This property dates from the 14th century and once served as a residence for the Knights of Malta. It was converted into a small baroque palace in the 17th century before being recast in 1976 as a stately hotel and listed on the registry of historic buildings. On a charming side street off Vienna's elegant Kärntnerstrasse in the pedestrian zone, it is an easy walk or subway ride to almost anything. Many old-fashioned touches remain, with paneled doors and wall sconces, vaulted ceilings, and a cobblestone courtyard. The public rooms are stunning, the atmosphere is intimate and cozy, and the midsize bedrooms have been comfortably modernized with a bit of style.

Annagasse 7, A-1010 Vienna. ✆ **01/512 06 41.** Fax 01/512 06 41 10. www.mailbergerhof.at. 40 units. 98€–220€ double. Rates include buffet breakfast. AC, DC, MC, V. U-Bahn: Karlsplatz. **Amenities:** Restaurant; bar; smoke-free rooms. *In room:* No A/C (in some rooms).

Hotel-Pension Arenberg ★★★ This small, quaint hotel, under the Best Western banner, occupies the second and third stories of a six-floor apartment house dating from the late 1890s. A few minutes from the Danube canal, the well-run family hostelry has many handsome rooms, some with balconies and all with soundproof windows and well-appointed bathrooms. There's a certain old-fashioned charm here, though the attempt to integrate both modern and antique furnishings doesn't always work.

Stubenring 2, A-1010 Vienna. ✆ **800/633-6548** in the U.S., or 01/512-52 91. Fax 01/513 93 56. www.arenberg.at. 22 units. 98€–258€ double . Rates include breakfast. AE, DC, MC, V. U-Bahn: Schwedenplatz or Stubentor. **Amenities:** Restaurant; smoke-free rooms. *In room:* No A/C (in some rooms).

Hotel Wandl ★★ Halfway between the cathedral (some rooms have a view of St. Stephen's) and the Hofburg, this comfortable inn has been run by the same family for generations. The rooms are simple yet attractively furnished, and the hotel is of the best values for the money in central Vienna, with top savings going to those who don't mind sharing a bathroom. It's right around the corner from the famed **Café Korb,** a popular hangout for journalists, writers, and other deviants.

Petersplatz 9, A-1010 Vienna. ✆ **01/534 550.** www.hotel-wandl.com. 138 units. 170€–220€ double; 240€ suite. Children up to 6 years old stay free in parent's room. Rates include buffet breakfast. AE, DC, MC, V. U-Bahn: Stephansplatz. *In room:* No A/C.

König von Ungarn ★★★ A top choice in boutique hotels within the Ring, this property dates from 1746 and hosted Hungarian royalty during the days of the Austro-Hungarian empire. The overall atmosphere is of a dignified, up-scale country inn. Its lounge fills a handsome courtyard atrium topped by a glass cupola, while guest rooms—no two alike—are attractively decorated with chandeliers, rich fabrics, walk-in closets, and large bathrooms with two basins. Its location, near Stephansplatz, is superb, and the staff is attentive and professional.

Schulerstrasse 10, A-1010 Vienna. ⓒ **01/515 84-0.** Fax 01/515 848. www.kvu.at. 33 units. 219€ double. Rates include breakfast. AE, DC, MC, V. U-Bahn: Stephansplatz. **Amenities:** Restaurant; bar.

Pension Aviano ★ 🍴 This popular, centrally located pension, between Stephansplatz and the opera just off Kärntner Strasse, offers comfortably elegant rooms, tasteful traditional furnishings with baroque accent pieces, and all the modern conveniences. Some rooms have kitchen nooks and offer double-pane windows overlooking Kärntner Strasse on one side or the Neuer Markt on the other.

Marco-d'Aviano-Gasse 1 (off Kärntner Strasse), A-1010 Wien. ⓒ **01/512 83 30.** Fax 01/512 83 30-6. www.secrethomes.at. 17 units. 148€–169€ double high season; 124€ to 140€ double middle and low seasons. Rates include buffet breakfast. AE, DC, MC, V. U-Bahn: Stephansplatz or Oper. *In room:* No A/C.

Pension Nossek On the Graben overlooking the extraordinary Plague Monument, this authentic, family-run pension has large rooms with high, ornamental ceilings, and it's filled with pleasing old things; it's genuine rather than posh, with friendly and attentive service. It has an unbeatable central location, a generous breakfast, and (sometimes unreliable) Wi-Fi in the rooms.

Graben 17, A-1010 Vienna. ⓒ **01/587 55 18.** Fax 01/535 3646. www.pension-nossek.at. 30 units. 115€–1,200€ double; 280€ suite. Rates include buffet breakfast. No credit cards. U-Bahn: Stephansplatz. *In-room:* No A/C.

Pension Pertschy ★★ 🍴 Inside the Ring between the Hofburg and St. Stephan's, the Pertschy occupies several floors of a 1723 palace built for a count that is now a historic landmark. Rooms are outfitted in updated Biedermeier style of the 1840s, with high, vaulted stucco ceilings; chandeliers; and modern bathrooms. Some rooms have kitchenettes. To get from room to room, you walk along an enclosed catwalk on a balcony tracing around a courtyard, giving the pension a certain old-world charm.

Habsburgergasse 5 (a few steps off Graben, near Stephansplatz), A-1010 Wien. ⓒ **01/534 49-0.** Fax 01/534 49 49. www.pertschy.com. 55 units. 100€–177€ double. Rates include buffet breakfast. AE, DC, MC, V. U-Bahn: Stephansplatz. **Amenities:** Smoke-free rooms. *In room:* No A/C.

Top Attractions & Special Moments

After deliverance from the dreaded plague and the equally dreaded Turks, the empire entered into a period of great power and prosperity that reached its zenith under the long reign of Empress Maria Theresa from 1740 to 1780. Many of the sights we describe below can be traced directly to that great empress of the Age of Enlightenment, who welcomed Mozart to her court at Schönbrunn when he was only 6 years old—a child prodigy, indeed.

SCHÖNBRUNN PALACE

Schönbrunn ★★★ 😊 🎒 A baroque summer palace with an astounding 1,441 rooms, the lovely Schönbrunn was built between 1696 and 1730 and is an absolute must-see for the Vienna visitor. Empress Maria Theresa left the greatest imprint on the palace. In the course of having 16 children (one of whom was the ill-fated Marie Antoinette) in 20 years, running the country, and fighting a war for her right to sit on the Austrian throne, she found time to decorate and redesign the palace (1744–49), and it remains virtually as she left it. Franz Josef I, who was born in the palace and reigned for 68 years, was the last emperor to live here. His wife, Elisabeth, popularly known as Sisi, was famed for her beauty (her hair reached to the ground), intelligence, and independent spirit.

You can tour the inside of the predominantly white-and-gilt palace on your own, choosing either the 50-minute **Grand Tour** through 40 state rooms or the 35-minute **Imperial Tour** through 22. Both include use of an English-language audio guide and allow you to see the **private apartments** of Franz Josef and Elisabeth; **Maria Theresa's nursery,** with portraits of her children; the **Hall of Mirrors,** where the 6-year-old Mozart played for Maria Theresa; the exotic **Chinese Cabinets,** with inlaid lacquerware; the **Hall of Ceremonies,** with a portrait of Maria Theresa; the impressive **Large Gallery,** fashioned after a room in Versailles and used in a 1961 meeting between Kennedy and Khrushchev; and more. The Grand Tour then continues on through, among others, the **Chinese Lacquered Room** and the **Millions Room,** decorated with 260 precious parchment miniatures brought from Constantinople and set under glass in the paneling.

If you have children in tow, they can have their own tour of Schönbrunn, called the **Schloss Schönbrunn Experience,** which is both educational and fun. After dressing in period clothing, children are led by English-speaking guides (make reservations online or by phone) through original rooms outfitted with hands-on displays that give an insider's view of court life, from why people wore wigs to how folding fans were used to communicate intentions. Tours are given daily during school vacations and only on weekends and holidays the rest of the year. Contact the palace for times.

Be sure to explore the 500 acres (200 hectares) of **palace grounds,** one of the most important baroque gardens in the French style. At the top of the hill opposite the palace is the **Gloriette,** a monument to soldiers and the site of a cafe with glorious views of Schönbrunn and the spread of Vienna beyond. Among the many other things to see, standouts include the **Wagenburg,** a museum with 36 imperial carriages, and the beautifully designed **Tiergarten Schönbrunn,** founded in 1752 and considered the world's oldest zoo.

Schönbrunner Schlossstrasse. (C) **01/811 13-239.** www.schoenbrunn.at. Imperial Tour 9.50€ adults, 8.50€ students, 6.50€ children 6–18 (free for children 5 and under). Grand Tour 13€ adults, 11€ students, 8.90€ children. Schönbrunn Palace Experience 6.50€ adults, 4.50€ children. July–Aug daily 8:30am–6pm; Apr–June and Sept–Oct daily 8:30am–5pm; Nov–Mar daily 8:30am–4:30pm. U-Bahn: Schönbrunn.

THE HOFBURG PALACE COMPLEX

The Hofburg was the Imperial Palace of the Habsburgs for more than 6 centuries, during which time changes and additions were made in several architectural styles—Gothic, Renaissance, baroque, rococo, and classical. The entire Hofburg occupies 47 acres in the heart of Vienna; it's a virtual city within a city, with more than 2,600 rooms.

Hofburg Kaiserappartements (Imperial Apartments), Hofburg Silberkammer (Imperial Silver Collection), and Sisi Museum ★★★

The Imperial Apartments, Silver Collection, and Sisi Museum share the same entrance and are included in the same ticket price. The **Imperial Apartments,** which served as the winter residence of the Habsburgs, might seem a bit plain if you've already seen the splendor of Schönbrunn, but the Hofburg is so conveniently located, it's a shame to pass it up. You can wander at leisure through 19 official and private rooms once belonging to Franz Josef and his wife, Elisabeth. Known as Sisi, she was talented, artistic, and slightly vain—she wouldn't sit for portraits after she turned 30. She was an excellent rider, and in the Hofburg is her own small gymnasium, where she kept in shape (much to the disgust of the court, which thought it improper for a lady). The **Sisi Museum** describes her somewhat tragic life and includes many personal mementos.

She came from the Wittelsbach family of Munich in 1854 to marry Franz Josef at 16. Her son, Crown Prince Rudolf and the only male heir to the throne, committed suicide in a hunting lodge at Mayerling with his young mistress. Elisabeth was assassinated in 1898 by an anarchist in Geneva.

Dating from the 15th century onward, the **Imperial Silver Collection** of silverware, dinnerware, and tableware provides insight into the imperial household, royal banquets, and court etiquette. It displays items of daily use, as well as valuable pieces, everything from cooking molds and pots and pans to table linens, elaborate centerpieces, crystal, silver serving sets, gilded candelabras, silverware, and porcelain table settings.

Michaelerplatz 1. ℂ **01/533 75 70.** www.hofburg-wien.at. Admission 9.90€ adults, 8.90€ students and Vienna Card holders, 5.90€ children. Daily 9am–5:30pm (to 6pm July–Aug; you must enter 1 hr. before closing). U-Bahn: Stephansplatz or Herrengasse. Tram: 1, 2, or D to Burgring.

Schatzkammer (Treasury) ★★ The Schatzkammer displays a stunning collection of the secular and ecclesiastical treasures of the Habsburgs. Its priceless imperial regalia and relics of the Holy Roman Empire include royal crowns inlaid with diamonds, rubies, pearls, sapphires, and other gems (the two most impressive are the Crown of the Holy Roman Empire from ca. 962 and the Austrian Emperor's Crown from 1602), as well as swords, imperial crosses, jewelry, altars, christening robes, coronation robes, and other richly embroidered garments. However, because descriptions are only in German, it's worth forking over the extra 3€ for an audio guide.

Two prized heirlooms are believed to have mystical and religious significance: the **Agate Bowl (Achat Schale),** carved in Constantinople in the 4th century from a single piece of agate and once thought to be the Holy Grail; and the **Ainkhörn,** a huge narwhal tusk, considered a symbol of the unicorn and associated with the Virgin Mary and Christ. Other objects on display include the Holy Lance, which was once thought to be the lance used to pierce Christ's side during the crucifixion; and a reliquary containing what's regarded as a piece of the cross.

Among other great Schatzkammer prizes is the **Burgundian Treasure,** seized in the 15th century and rich in vestments, oil paintings, gems, and robes. The artifacts connected with the Order of the Golden Fleece, that romantic medieval order of chivalry, are the highlight of this collection.

Schweizerhof 1, Hofburg. ℂ **01/533 79 31.** www.khm.at/en/treasury. Admission 12€ adults, 11€ Vienna Card holders, 9€ seniors/students, free for children 18 and under. Wed–Mon 10am–6pm. U-Bahn: Stephansplatz or Herrengasse. Tram: 1, 2, or D to Burgring.

Spanische Reitschule (Spanish Riding School) ★★★ This prestigious school has roots dating back more than 400 years, when Spanish horses were brought to Austria for breeding. The famous graceful Lipizzaner horses are a cross of Berber and Arabian stock with Spanish and Italian horses. They're born with dark coats that turn white only between the ages of 4 and 10. In addition to being beautiful, they are the world's most classically styled equine performers. Many North Americans have seen them in the States, but to watch the Lipizzaners perform their "airs above the ground" dressage to the music of Johann Strauss or a Chopin polonaise in their baroque, chandeliered 18th-century hall is a pleasure you should not miss.

There are several ways to see the Lipizzaners at work. Most impressive are the 80-minute regular performances. However, tickets for these often sell out, so it's best to order them in advance online. The least expensive and easiest way to see the horses is at their regular Morning Exercise Sessions with music. When the horses are out on tour, the Horses' Workout features youngsters who come to the school when they're

4 years old and spend the next 6 years training. Tickets for the Morning Exercise and Horses' Workout are sold on a first-come, first-served basis at the visitor center, Michaelerplatz 1, Tuesday to Saturday from 9am to 4pm, and in the inner courtyard of the Imperial Palace at Josefsplatz, gate 2, on days of morning exercise. Finally, you can also join a 1-hour guided tour for a look behind the scenes of the Spanish Riding School (reservations suggested).

Josephsplatz, Hofburg. ✆ **01/533 90 31.** www.srs.at. Regular performances, seats 47€–173€, standing room 23€–31€; Morning Exercise Sessions 12€ adults, 9€ seniors, 6€ students/children; Horses' Workout 6€ guided tours 16€ adults, 13€ seniors, 8€ students/children. Children 2 and under not permitted. Regular performances Feb–June and Sept–Oct, most Sun at 11am, and occasionally Fri or Sat at 11am or Fri at 7pm; Morning Exercise Sessions Feb–June and Sept–Oct and Dec, Tues–Sat 10am–noon; Horses' Workout Nov to mid-Dec Tues–Sat 10am–noon; guided tours year-round Tues–Sun (no tours given on days of performances) usually at 2, 3, and 4pm. U-Bahn: Stephansplatz or Herrengasse.

Wiener Sängerknaben (Vienna Boys' Choir) ★★★   The Vienna Boys' Choir was founded in 1498 to sing at church services for the Royal Chapel of the Imperial Palace. Joseph Haydn and Franz Schubert sang in the choir, which now consists of four choirs, two of which are usually on world tours. January to June and mid-September to Christmas, you can hear the choir, accompanied by Vienna State Opera orchestra members, every Sunday and some religious holidays at 9:15am Mass in the Burgkapelle of the Hofburg. Order seats at least 10 weeks in advance by contacting the Hofmusikkapelle, Hofburg, A-1010 Wien (fax 01/533 99 27-75; whmk@chello. at). Don't enclose money or a check, but rather pay and pick up your ticket at the Burgkapelle on the Friday preceding the performance 11am to 1pm or 3 to 5pm, as well as Sunday 8:15 to 8:45am. Unsold tickets go on sale at the Burgkapelle on Friday 11am to 1pm and 3 to 5pm for the following Sunday. (It's wise to get there at least 30 min. before tickets go on sale.) Otherwise, standing room is free, but there's room for only 20 people on a first-come, first-served basis.

Burgkapelle, Hofburg (entrance in Schweizerhof). ✆ **01/533 99 27.** Fax 01/533 99 27-75. www.wsk.at, www.hofburgkapelle.at for tickets. Mass: Seats 5€–29€, standing room free. Mass performed Sun and some religious holidays at 9:15am mid-Sept to June. U-Bahn: Stephansplatz or Herrengasse.

THE TOP MUSEUMS

Albertina Museum ★   Occupying the southern tip of the Hofburg, this museum features a fine collection of works spanning 130 years, from French Impressionism and Fauvism, to Expressionism and the Russian avant-garde. Artists include Monet, Renoir, Matisse, Picasso, Klee, Kandinsky, and Chagall. The museum's renowned graphic arts collection of hand-drawn sketches, drawings, posters, and lithographs by Raphael, Rubens, Rembrandt, Michelangelo, da Vinci, and Dürer is no longer on display, but selected reproductions hang in their place for admiration. Exhibitions change every 3 months, drawing on the museum's own collection and international contributions. Several elegant State Rooms are also open for viewing.

Albertinaplatz 1. ✆ **01/534 83-540.** www.albertina.at. Admission 9.50€ adults, 8€ seniors, 7€ students, free for children 18 and under. Daily 10am–6pm (to 9pm Wed). U-Bahn: Karlsplatz, Stephansplatz. Tram: 1, 2, or D to Oper.

Haus der Musik   For a one-stop lesson in the origins of sound, the history of the Vienna Philharmonic Orchestra, and the lives of Austria's most famous composers, take in this unique hands-on museum. Exploring the world of sound through audiovisual displays, visitors can play futuristic instruments, conduct an orchestra, listen to the gnashing of teeth (and other bodily functions), create a CD (for an extra fee), and listen to an audio guide as they wander through rooms devoted to Haydn, Mozart, Beethoven, Schubert, and other famous composers.

Seilerstätte 30. ℂ **01/516 48-50.** www.hdm.at. Admission 10€ adults, 8.50€ students/seniors, 5.50€ children. Daily 10am–10pm. U-Bahn: Stephansdom or Karlsplatz.

KunstHausWien ★★ 👕 This one-of-a-kind museum showcases the lifelong works of painter/designer Friedensreich Hundertwasser, famous for his whimsical, fantastical, and dramatically colorful paintings, prints, and architecture. Created from a former Thonet chair factory, the museum houses about 300 of his works, including paintings, prints, tapestries, and architectural models. Temporary shows feature the works of international artists. Typical of Hundertwasser (who died in 2000), the building itself is one of the exhibits, a colorful protest against the mundane gray of modern cities. Be sure to see the **Hundertwasser Haus,** an apartment complex Hundertwasser designed on the corner of Kegelgasse and Löwengasse in the mid-1980s (about a 5-min. walk away). On Kegelgasse is also **Kalke Village,** another Hundertwasser architectural conversion, this time a former stable and gas station turned into a small shopping complex.

Untere Weissgerberstrasse 13. ℂ **01/712 04 91.** www.kunsthauswien.com. Admission 9€ adults, 7€ seniors/students, 4.50€ children 10–18, free for children 9 and under; temporary exhibits extra, 50% discount Mon (except holidays). Daily 10am–7pm. Tram: 1 or O to Radetzkyplatz.

Kunsthistorisches Museum (Museum of Fine Arts) ★★★ This great museum owes its existence largely to the Habsburgs, who for centuries were patrons and collectors of art. There are several collections, of which the **Egyptian-Oriental Collection**—with sarcophagi, reliefs, statues, and portraits of kings—and the **Picture Gallery** are the most outstanding. Other displays feature coins and medals, as well as sculpture and applied arts from the medieval, Renaissance, and baroque periods. The Picture Gallery, on the first floor, contains paintings by **Rubens, Rembrandt, Dürer, Titian, Giorgione, Tintoretto, Caravaggio,** and **Velázquez.** The high point of the museum is the world's largest collection of **Bruegels,** including the *Turmbau zu Babel* (*Tower of Babel*), *Die Jäger im Schnee* (*The Hunters in the Snow*— you can hardly believe it's not real), the *Kinderspiel* (in which children have taken over an entire town), and *Die Bauernhochzeit* (*The Peasant Wedding*—notice how the bride is isolated in front of the green cloth, barred by custom from eating or talking).

Maria-Theresien-Platz. ℂ **01/525 24-4025.** www.khm.at. Admission 10€ adults, 7.50€ seniors/students/children, 20€ families, free for children 6 and under. Tues–Wed and Fri–Sun 10am–6pm; Thurs 10am–9pm. U-Bahn: Volkstheater or MuseumsQuartier. Tram: 1, 2, or D to Burgring.

Leopold Museum ★★★ The centerpiece of the MuseumsQuartier, Vienna's impressive museum district, is this outstanding collection of Austrian modernist masterpieces covering movements from the late Romantic period to the mid-1900s, including art produced during the Jugendstil, Secessionist, and Expressionist periods. Major works by Gustav Klimt, Oskar Kokoschka, Richard Gerstl, Herbert Boeckl, Alfred Kubin, Ferdinand Georg Waldmüller, and Anton Romako are on display, but the absolute highlight of the museum is the world's largest collection of paintings by **Egon Schiele,** who produced 330 oil canvases and more than 2,500 drawings and watercolors before dying at 28; the museum owns some 200 of his works. Also on display are major objects of Austrian arts and crafts, such as furniture and glassware from the late 19th and 20th centuries, with works by Otto Wagner, Adolf Loos, Josef Hoffmann, Kolo Moser, and Franz Hagenauer. A must-see.

BOATING ON THE "blue" Danube

Contrary to legend, the Danube is not generally blue, except in the bright, clear days of January, when reflection off the crisp azure winter sky shimmers off the powerful current. But none of that matters when it comes to enjoying this broad, majestic river that has been the principal artery of Central Europe since the Middle Ages, and many visitors to Austria view a day cruise along the Danube as a highlight of their trip. Until the advent of railroads and highways, the Danube played a vital role in Austria's history, helping to build the complex mercantile society that eventually became the Habsburg Empire.

Some of the best cruises are operated by the **DDSG Blue Danube Steamship Co.** (✆ **01/588 80-0;** www. ddsg-blue-danube.at). Boats cruise the Danube during the warmer months, departing from a pier next to the Schwedenbrücke (U-Bahn:

Schwedenplatz) or from the Reichsbrücke (U-Bahn: Vorgartenstrasse). Various tours are available, from standard sightseeing trips costing 17€ to themed cruises such as the Sound of W.A. Mozart tour, featuring musical entertainment and a three-course meal for 38€. DDSG also offers cruises to Budapest.

Those interested in traveling to Bratislava, Slovakia (p. 819), can enjoy a cruise on the **Twin City Liner** (✆ **01/ 588 80;** www.twincityliner.com). Departing from a new passenger terminal at Schwedenplatz, catamaran-style boats ply the waters and pass through the only lock in the 37-mile (60km) trip, in just over an hour. From March to October, there are 4 trips daily, and only one the rest of the year. A single journey costs 30€ on weekends and holidays, 28€ during the week, and 17€ on the final boat from Vienna and the first from Bratislava from March to October.

Museumsplatz 1. ✆ **01/525 70-0.** www.leopoldmuseum.org. Admission 11€ adults, 8€ seniors, 7€ students/children. Wed–Mon 10am–6pm (to 9pm Thurs). U-Bahn: Volkstheater or MuseumsQuartier.

MUMOK (Museum of Modern Art Ludwig Trust Vienna) ★★   This museum in the MuseumsQuartier showcases international 20th-century art, with an emphasis on "classical modern" art, from Expressionism and Cubism to abstraction, pop art, photo realism, and contemporary media art. The museum's biggest contribution to the art world is its preservation of Viennese Actionism, which emerged in the 1960s at the same time as performance art was gaining attention in the United States and shocked audiences with its aggressive attacks on social taboos. Works by Picasso, Kokoschka, Kandinsky, Warhol, Rauschenberg, Roy Lichtenstein, Nam June Paik, Joseph Beuys, Günther Brus, and many others are presented in both permanent and temporary exhibits.

Museumsplatz 1. ✆ **01/525 00.** www.mumok.at. Admission 9€ adults, 7.20€ seniors, free for students and children. Daily 10am–6pm (to 9pm Thurs). U-Bahn: Volkstheater or MuseumsQuartier.

OTHER LEADING ATTRACTIONS

Prater ☺   Prater is Vienna's amusement park, opened to the general public in 1766 on the former grounds of Emperor Maximilian II's game preserve. Most notable is its **Riesenrad,** a giant Ferris wheel constructed in the 1890s (then rebuilt after its destruction in World War II). If you saw the film classic *The Third Man,* you may recall the park's Ferris wheel in the scene where it appeared that Orson Welles was going to murder Joseph Cotton. Measuring 200 feet (60m) in diameter, it offers 20-minute rides and great views of Vienna, especially at night. An adjoining museum presents miniature model cityscapes of how Vienna would have looked at various periods of its long history. In the Prater park itself, there are also some 200 booths and both old and new attractions, including the usual shooting ranges, amusement rides ranging from bumper cars and miniature train rides to roller coasters and a bungee ejection seat, game arcades, restaurants, beer halls, and beer gardens (only a limited number of attractions, including the Riesenrad, operate in winter). Compared to today's slick amusement parks, Prater seems endearingly old-fashioned; kids, of course, love it.

Prater Hauptallee. ℘ **01/728 05 16.** www.prater.wien.info. Park free; amusement rides vary (the Ferris wheel and its museum cost 8.50€ adults, 7.50€ students, 3.50€ children). May–Sept daily 9am–11:45pm; Mar–Apr and Oct daily 10am–9:45pm; Nov–Feb daily 10am–7:45pm. U-Bahn: Praterstern.

Stephansdom (St. Stephen's Cathedral) ★★   In the heart of old Vienna, Stephansdom is the city's best-known landmark. Built in the 12th century and then enlarged and rebuilt over the next 800 years, it's Vienna's most important Gothic structure and boasts staggering dimensions—352 feet long (106m), with a nave 128 feet high (38m). The highest part is its 450-ft.-high (135m) **south tower,** completed in 1433, with 343 spiral steps. From its high vantage point, watchkeepers of earlier days kept vigil over the city. This tower is open to the public (entrance outside the church on its south side) and affords one of the best city views. If you don't like to climb stairs, you can take an elevator (entrance inside the church) to the top of the **north tower,** which was never completed and is only about half as high as the south tower, but contains the **Pummerin,** the third-largest bell in Western Europe, weighing in at nearly 20 tons.

Stephansdom is inextricably linked with Viennese and Austrian history. It was here that mourners attended Mozart's "pauper's funeral" in 1791, and it was on the cathedral door that Napoléon posted his farewell edict in 1805. The chief treasure of the cathedral is the carved wooden **Wiener Neustadt altarpiece** dating from 1447, richly painted and gilded, found in the Virgin's Choir. The **catacombs** contain copper urns bearing the intestines of the Habsburg family. May to November, organ concerts are given every Wednesday at 8pm; there are also choirs and other concerts throughout the year (pick up a brochure at the cathedral).

Stephansplatz. ℘ **01/515 52-3689.** www.stephanskirche.at. Left aisle of cathedral interior, including Wiener Neustadt altarpiece, free; remainder of cathedral interior and treasury with audioguide 7.50€ adults, free for children 13 and under; south tower 3.50€ adults, 1€ children; north tower elevator 4.50€ adults, 1.50€ children 6–12; catacombs 4€ adults, 1.50€ children. Cathedral Mon–Sat 6am–10pm, Sun 7am–10pm; south tower daily 9am–5:30pm; north tower daily in summer 8:15am–6pm, daily in winter 8:15am–4:30pm; catacombs Mon–Sat 10–11:30am and 1:30–4:30pm, Sun and holidays 1:30–4:30pm. U-Bahn: Stephansplatz.

Where to Dine

Bizi ⬧ ITALIAN   This popular self-service restaurant is a top choice for many Viennese in search of a quick, tasty meal inside the Ring. It offers a variety of pizzas and pastas, such as ravioli, gnocchi, tagliatelle, and tortellini, all with a choice of sauces. There's also a salad bar, daily specials, and a selection of wines and beer. The decor is upbeat and pleasant, with modern art on the walls, and there's even a non-smoking section (now required at many restaurants).

Rotenturmstrasse 4 (at the corner of Wollzeile, north of Stephansplatz). ℘ **01/513 37 05.** Main courses 5.50€–7€. No credit cards. Daily 10:30am–10:30pm. U-Bahn: Stephansplatz or Schwedenplatz.

GriechenBeisl ★ AUSTRIAN   All Viennese know the GriechenBeisl, and many of their ancestors probably did, too—it dates from the 15th century, built on Roman foundations inside the Ring. Prominent diners have included Beethoven, Schubert, Wagner, Strauss, Brahms, and Mark Twain, who lived in and near Vienna for 2 years, from 1897 to 1899. Housed in an ancient-looking vine-covered building, Vienna's oldest restaurant offers typical Viennese food from its English menu, including *Tafelspitz* (boiled beef with vegetables), Wiener schnitzel, Gulasch, and ragout of venison with burgundy sauce. There's live music from 7:30pm each evening and, in summer, outdoor seating.

Fleischmarkt 11. ℂ **01/533 19 77.** Main courses 15€–20€. AE, DC, MC, V. Daily 11:30am–11:30pm (last order). U-Bahn: Stephansplatz or Schwedenplatz.

Gulaschmuseum AUSTRIAN   Despite its name, this is not a museum dedicated to that favorite Austrian dish imported from Hungary, but it does offer walls covered with fine art for customers to gaze upon as they dine on more than a dozen variations of Gulasch (goulash). Probably the world's only restaurant dedicated to Gulasch, it serves traditional Hungarian Gulasch (a spicy beef and paprika ragout), as well as innovative renditions like fish or mushroom Gulasch. A large selection of desserts rounds out the English menu.

Schulerstrasse 20. ℂ **01/512 10 17.** Reservations recommended for dinner. Main dishes 8.30€–14€. MC, V. Daily 10am–midnight. U-Bahn: Stephansplatz.

Kantine AUSTRIAN/CONTINENTAL   Of the handful of restaurants in the MuseumsQuartier, this casual bistro is one of the most inviting, with seating at tables or on sofas and a long bar under a high vaulted ceiling. Its very "lived-in" atmosphere is that of a coffee shop, diner, and bar rolled into one (maybe that's why it says *"essen, trinken und mehr"* ["eat, drink and more"] on its menu). You can order breakfast until noon (to 6pm on weekends) or opt for one of the pita sandwiches, soups, salads, or meat or vegetarian selections. You'll find it next to the Prachner bookshop, on the east end of MuseumsQuartier.

Museumsplatz 1. ℂ **01/523 82 39.** Main courses 5€–10€. AE, DC, MC, V. Mon–Sat 9am–2am; Sun 9am–midnight. U-Bahn: MuseumsQuartier.

Palmenhaus ★ MODERN AUSTRIAN   This stylish, airy restaurant is a good place for a meal on an overcast day—of which Vienna has many in the long winter months. It occupies the middle section of the Schmetterlinghaus (Butterfly House) at the Hofburg, an early 1900s Jugendstil greenhouse, set in the midst of the formal Burggarten. On fine summer days, you can dine on the outdoor terrace overlooking tree-shaded lawns and lovingly tended gardens. It offers a variety of fresh grilled fish and daily specials, as well as what could be described as nouveau Austrian cuisine. On Fridays, there's a DJ from 9pm on.

In the Schmetterlinghaus, Burggarten, Opernring. ℂ **01/533 10 33.** Main courses 10€–19€. DC, MC, V. Daily 10am–11:30pm (last order). Closed Mon–Tues Jan–Feb. U-Bahn: Karlsplatz, Stephansplatz, or MuseumsQuartier. Tram: 1, 2, or D to Opernring or Burgring.

Settimo Cielo ★ 🍽 ITALIAN   Walk through the lobby of the Hotel Royal on Singerstrasse to elevators that will whisk you to "seventh heaven"—a glass-enclosed restaurant serving up fine northern Italian cuisine, with great views over Vienna's rooftops. The menu focuses on fresh fish, lobster, and seafood, but such traditional dishes as chicken with sage are also definitely worth trying.

Hotel Royal, Singerstrasse 3. ℂ **01/512 38 75.** Reservations recommended. Main courses 18€–26€. AE, DC, MC, V. Mon–Sat noon–2:30pm and 6–11:30pm. U-Bahn: Stephansplatz.

Trzesniewski ★ SANDWICHES   This cafeteria is a Viennese institution—and rightly so. It's so small that the mealtime line often snakes through the entire store; try coming at off-peak times, as seating is limited. Trzesniewski is a buffet of small open-face finger sandwiches covered with spreads like salami, egg salad, tuna fish, hot peppers, tomatoes, and two dozen other selections. This is a most satisfying choice unless you are ravenously hungry or want a leisurely meal.

Dorotheergasse 1 (just off Graben). ℭ **01/512 32 91.** Sandwiches 1€. No credit cards. Mon–Fri 8:30am–7:30pm; Sat 9am–5pm. U-Bahn: Stephansplatz.

Wiener Rathauskeller ★★ AUSTRIAN   The Rittersaal (Knights' Hall), in the cellar of Vienna's City Hall, offers elegant a la carte dining in a historical setting. The attractive decor features medieval-style murals on the vaulted ceilings, stained-glass windows, beautiful lamps, and flowers and candles on the tables. The English menu lists traditional Viennese dishes, as well as such in-house specialties as grilled loin of veal. In the evenings, there's live classical music. Farther down the hall, in the Grinzinger Keller, the **Austrian Dinner Show** (ℭ **01/274 90 46**) features a fixed-price meal with traditional Viennese entertainment, offered mid-April to mid-October Tuesday to Saturday from 8 to 10:30pm.

Rathausplatz. ℭ **01/405 12 10.** www.wiener-rathauskeller.at. Reservations recommended for fixed-price meal with traditional entertainment. Main courses 8.30€–18€; Austrian Dinner Show 39€. AE, DC, MC, V. Mon–Sat 11:30am–3pm and 6–10pm (last order). U-Bahn: Rathaus. Tram: 1, 2, or D to Burgtheater/Rathausplatz.

Wrenkh ★ VEGETARIAN/INTERNATIONAL   If you're a vegetarian or simply tired of Austria's meat obsession, head to this hip restaurant and treat yourself to innovative dishes influenced by Mediterranean and Asian cuisine. You might start with one of the tofu dishes (like the appetizer plate of smoked tofu with five spices),

coffeehouses INSIDE THE RING

As Paris has its sidewalk cafes, Vienna has its coffeehouses. All offer newspapers for leisurely perusal, and many also offer live classical music a few times a week. Introduced 300 years ago by the Turks during their unsuccessful attempt to conquer Vienna, coffee as served in Viennese coffeehouses has become an art form. Among the many kinds are the *kleiner Schwarzer,* a small cup without milk; *kleiner Brauner,* a small cup with cream; *Melange,* a large cup with frothy milk; *Melange mit Schlag,* coffee topped with whipped cream; *Mokka,* strong black Viennese coffee; and *Türkischer,* Turkish coffee boiled in a small copper pot and served in a tiny cup. Coffee is always served with a glass of water.

Founded in 1785 by a pastry chef who later served as the pastry supplier to the royal family, **Demel,** Kohlmarkt 14 (ℭ **01/535 17 17-0;** www.demel.at; U-Bahn: Stephansplatz), is Vienna's most expensive and most famous coffeehouse. Its elegant interior looks like the private parlor of a count, and in summer there's sidewalk seating. It's open daily 9am to 7pm.

Equally famous is the 19th-century **Café Sacher,** in the Hotel Sacher Vienna behind the Staatsoper, Philharmonikerstrasse 4 (ℭ **01/514 56-0;** www.sacher.com; U-Bahn: Karlsplatz), where you can taste the famous *Sacher torte,* created in 1832 by 16-year-old Franz Sacher, whose son later founded this hotel. The cafe is open daily 8am to midnight.

followed by glass noodles in a tomato-coconut sauce. There are also seafood dishes, such as the tuna on spinach and red beets in caramel, with a honey-mustard sauce. The chef of this restaurant has become so well known, he even has his own cooking school next door.

Bauernmarkt 10 (west of Stephansplatz). (𝄐 **01/533 15 26.** Main courses 13€–16€. AE, DC, MC, V. Mon-Fri noon–4pm and 6–11pm; Sat 6–11pm. U-Bahn: Stephansplatz.

Zwölf Apostelkeller ★ 🍴 TRADITIONAL AUSTRIAN   This Stadtheuriger, or city wine tavern, is the most romantic of these traditional eateries in central Vienna that serve *heurigen* (meaning "this year's") wines, usually from their own vineyards. The Twelve Apostles is in an ancient cellar of a former Jesuit monastery dating from 1339, where lanterns glow under the heavy stone arches, for a varied and artfully prepared traditional buffet of hot and cold meats, cheeses, spreads, fresh bread, and salads. Group events are by arrangement and served at table on vast platters. There's an excellent wine list from half a dozen local vintners, including the award-winning Krems Sangrube vintages, and live "Schrammelmusik" daily from 7pm on.

Sonnenfelsgasse 3. (𝄐 **01/512 67 77.** Meals 12€–20€, with wine. AE, DC, MC, V. Daily 11am–midnight. U-Bahn: Schwedenplatz.

Shopping

Vienna's most famous **shopping streets** are inside the Ring in the city center, including the pedestrian-only Kärntner Strasse, Graben, Kohlmarkt, and Rotenturmstrasse. **Ö.W. (Österreichische Werkstatten),** Kärntnerstrasse 6 (𝄐 **01/512 24 18;** U-Bahn: Stephansplatz), a three-floor, well-run store, sells hundreds of handmade art objects from Austria. Leading artists and craftspeople throughout the country organized this cooperative to showcase their wares, and it's only half a minute's walk from St. Stephen's. There's an especially good selection of pewter, along with modern jewelry, reproduction Art Nouveau jewelry, glassware, brass, baskets, ceramics, candles, and more.

If during your exploration of Vienna you should happen to admire a crystal chandelier, there's a good chance that it was made by **J. & L. Lobmeyr,** Kärntnerstrasse 26 (𝄐 **01/512 05 08;** www.lobmeyr.at; U-Bahn: Stephansplatz). Established in 1823, Lobmeyr was named as a purveyor to the imperial court of Austria in the early 19th century, and it has maintained an elevated position ever since. In addition to chandeliers of all shapes and sizes, the store sells hand-painted Hungarian porcelain, along with complete breakfast and dinner services.

If you prefer to wear your crystal, stop by the elegant **Swarovski Store Wien,** Kärntnerstrasse 8–9 (𝄐 **01/512 90 32**), Vienna's outlet for the famous Tyrolean crystal manufacturer. The well-stocked **Steffl Kaufhaus,** Kärntnerstrasse 19 (𝄐 **01/514 31-0;** U-Bahn: Stephansplatz), rising five floors above the pedestrian traffic of inner Vienna's central shopping street, is the first district's most prominent department store of leading international brands.

The state-owned **Dorotheum,** Dorotheergasse 17 (𝄐 **01/515 60-0;** www. dorotheum.com; U-Bahn: Stephansplatz), is Europe's oldest auction house, founded by Emperor Joseph I in 1707 as place where impoverished aristocrats could fairly (and anonymously) get good value for their heirlooms. The objects for sale cover a wide spectrum, including exquisite furniture and carpets, delicate objets d'art, valuable paintings, and decorative jewelry.

If flea markets are more your style, then visit the city's best known, held just past the Naschmarkt outdoor market on **Linke Wienzeile,** near the Kettenbrückengasse

U-Bahn station. This is the most colorful (and crowded) place to look for curios, antiques, jewelry, ethnic clothing, and junk. Be sure to haggle. It's open Saturday about 8am to dusk (about 6pm in summer). It's also worth a trip to the adjoining **Naschmarkt,** Vienna's outdoor food-and-produce market, open Monday to Friday 6am to 6:30pm and Saturday 6am to 5pm.

Nightlife

Vienna is a city of theaters, with some 140 active stages for music, drama, dance, and cabaret, not counting a seemingly endless number of small performance venues tucked away in the cellars and side rooms of taverns and coffeehouses all over town. It is home to three great opera houses (the Wiener Staatsoper, the Volksoper Wien, and Theater an der Wien) and five leading orchestras (the Wiener Philharmoniker, the Wiener Symphoniker, the Radio Symphonieorchester [RSO], the Tonkünstler, and the Klangforum), along with numerous smaller ensembles.

One of the world's leading opera houses, and under the musical direction of Franz Welser-Möst since 2010, the **Wiener Staatsoper,** Opernring 2 (✆ **01/514 44-2250;** www.wiener-staatsoper.at; U-Bahn: Karlsplatz), stages over 50 operas and ballets a season, including 10 premieres, from September through June, accompanied by musicians from the Viennese Philharmonic. It's a lavish undertaking, with a staff of about 1,200—including the stage crew, singers, and production workers—and a 5,300-square-foot (488-sq.-m) stage area, making it one of Europe's grandest, even larger than the parquet seating area of the opera house. The smaller **Wiener Volksoper** (Währinger Strasse 78 (✆ **01/514 44-30;** www.volksoper.at, U-Bahn: Wahringerstrasse), under the direction of Robert Meyer, has greatly enriched its program, adding opera, dance, and musicals to the traditional Viennese operetta unequalled anywhere, with Johann Strauss's beloved *Die Fledermaus* beginning each season and ringing in the new year. Regular seasons for all houses run from September through June. The Vienna State Opera and the Theater an der Wien each now also mount a summer production, as does the charming Schlosstheater at the Schönbrunn Palace. Other summer musical offerings include the **Rathaus Film Festival** (www.wien vienna.com/rathaus-film-festival-2010), the renowned **ImpulsTanz Festival** (www.impulstanz.com), and the Aron Quartet's chamber music series, **Kammermusikfestival Schloss Laudon** (www.schlosslaudon.at).

For advance ticket sales, head to the **Bundestheaterkassen,** cater-cornered from the opera at Operngasse 2 (✆ **01/5144-7880;** U-Bahn: Karlsplatz). It's open Monday to Friday 8am to 6pm, and Saturday, Sunday, and holidays 9am to noon. Tickets for most productions are 10€ to 240€. There are also hundreds of standing-room tickets available only on the night of the performance that cost 3€ to 4€.

Almost equally dear to the Viennese heart are the city's many historic wine cellars. With a history stretching back to the 19th century, the **Augustiner Keller,** located below the Albertina Museum at Augustinerstrasse 1 (✆ **01/533 10 26;** U-Bahn: Karlsplatz or Stephansplatz), boasts wooden floors, a vaulted brick ceiling, and a long, narrow room that once served as a monastery cellar. A *Heuriger* (wine tavern) serving wine from its own vineyards, it offers free traditional *Heurigenmusik* daily starting at 6:30pm and a menu of traditional Austrian specialties. It's open daily 11am to midnight. The **Zwölf Apostelkeller,** Sonnenfelsgasse 3 (✆ **01/512 67 77;** U-Bahn: Stephansplatz), detailed earlier under "Where to Dine," is a huge wine cellar two levels deep. Its Apostel wine is the specialty of the house. It's open daily 11am to midnight, with *Heurigenmusik* filling the vaults beginning at 7pm.

Heurige are Viennese wine taverns featuring this year's ("heurigen") local Viennese wines. The tradition dates back to 1784, when Emperor Joseph II gave Austrian wine growers the right to sell their own wine and provisions on the premises without the prohibitive cost of a restaurant license. Today there are about 400 families still cultivating some 770 hectares (1,900 acres) of vineyards within the city limits, spread over several wine-growing districts on the outskirts of town.

Of these, **Grinzing,** at the edge of the Vienna Woods, is probably the best known, with about 20 heurige clustered together along a charming main street lined with fairy-tale-like houses, their thick walls built around inner courtyards where grape arbors shelter Viennese wine drinkers on summer nights. Almost all heurige also offer evening *Heurigenmusik* and a buffet with cold cuts, cheeses, salads, and meats such as grilled chicken, smoked pork, and Schweinsbraten. Or you can just buy a quarter-liter mug of wine and linger as long as you want. Most heurige are open 4pm to midnight, and although some are closed November to March, you'll always find heurige that are open. Look for the sprig of pine, usually hung above the entrance, and a small plaque with EIGENBAU written on it, which means the grower serves his or her own wine.

Although it's probably easiest to wander about and choose a heuriger that suits your mood, you might try the **Altes Presshaus,** Cobenzlgasse 15 (✆ **01/320 02 03**), uphill from the tram stop. Built in 1527, it's the oldest heuriger in Grinzing, with an interior of dark wood paneling and pleasantly worn furniture, and a charming garden terrace that blossoms throughout summer. **Mayer am Pfarrplatz,** Pfarrplatz 2 (✆ **01/370 33 61**), has been owned by the Mayer family since 1683. The house remains unchanged since Beethoven lived here in the summer of 1817, when he is said to have worked on his Ninth Symphony here.

Grinzing is only 5 miles (8km) from the city center. From Schottentor, take tram 38 to the last stop, a 20-minute ride.

Loos American Bar, Kärntnerdurchgang 10 (✆ **01/512-3283;** U-Bahn: Stephansplatz), is one of the most unusual and interesting bars in the center of Vienna. Once a private men's club designed by famed architect Adolf Loos in 1908, this closet-size establishment now welcomes a crowd that tends to be multilingual and very hip, often from Vienna's arts and media scene. It's open daily noon to 4am. On the opposite end of the spectrum is **Esterházykeller,** Haarhof 1 (✆ **01/533 34 82;** U-Bahn: Stephansplatz), a brick-vaulted cellar with scarred wooden tables and permeated with the aroma of endless pints of spilled beer and smoke (there is, however, a no-smoking section). Famous since 1683, it attracts a mostly older crowd and offers a self-service food counter selling meat dishes and snacks. If you decide this place is for you, choose the left entrance (*not* the right entrance), grip the railing firmly, and begin your descent down very steep stairs. It's open Monday to Friday 11am to 11pm.

Somewhere in between is the plebian **Bermuda Bräu,** Rabensteig 6 (✆ **01/532 28 65;** U-Bahn: Schwedenplatz), which caters to a mixed professional crowd with a varied international menu and beer on tap, while the next-door **Krah Krah,** Rabensteig 8 (✆ **01/533 81 93**), is famous for its large selection of beer. Both are located in **Rabensteig,** about a 3-minute walk north of Stephansplatz, in the center of the Ring's most popular nightspot, popularly referred to as the Bermuda Triangle. Both bars are open daily 11am to 2am.

Jazzland, Franz-Josefs-Kai 29 (✆ **01/533-2575;** www.jazzland.at; U-Bahn: Schwedenplatz), is the oldest and most famous jazz pub in Austria, noted for the quality of its U.S. and Central European–based performers. Open for more than 35 years, it's in a deep 200-year-old cellar and is open Monday to Saturday 7pm to 1am, with music beginning at 9pm. Cover charge is 11€ to 18€. You can get good tavern meals. Seating is first come, first served; no reservations.

SALZBURG ★★★

Salzburg, surrounded by magnificent Alpine scenery, boasts one of the world's most striking cityscapes—a medieval fortress perched above a perfectly preserved baroque inner city filled with architectural wonders. With only 150,000 inhabitants, Salzburg is also one of Europe's leading cultural centers, especially for classical music. Mozart was born here, and Salzburg boasts one of the best-known classical music festivals in the world.

For passengers doing a rail tour of the Continent, Salzburg stands at the crossroads of Europe. It makes a grand stopover on the lines running between Munich and Italy, and also lies on the main rail route linking Switzerland in the west with Vienna (and, ultimately, Budapest) in the east. Because Vienna is somewhat remotely located in the east end of Austria rather than its center, Salzburg is actually a more convenient gateway into the country if you're arriving by rail.

On the most rushed of itineraries, Salzburg (at least, its highlights) can be viewed in a day, though it's better to devote at least 2 days to explore its architectural treasures and soak up its refined atmosphere. The best months to visit—unless you're planning a winter ski trip in the region of Salzburg, one of Europe's greatest winter playgrounds—is from May to September, though the sight of Salzburg covered in a delicate layer of snow is equally breathtaking. On the downside, all this *Sound of Music* atmosphere and great beauty carries a high price tag, as Salzburg is one of the most expensive cities in Central Europe.

Getting There

For some visitors, Salzburg—not Vienna—is their aerial gateway to Austria. Once in Salzburg, it's possible to begin a rail journey not only to the urban centers of Vienna and Innsbruck, but to all the remote corners of this little Alpine nation.

Salzburg Airport–W.A. Mozart, Innsbrucker Bundesstrasse 95 (✆ **0662/8580;** www.salzburg-airport.com), 2 miles (3.2km) southwest of the city center, has regularly scheduled air service to Vienna and Graz, as well as London, Frankfurt, Berlin, and other major European destinations. Major airlines serving the Salzburg airport are **Austrian Airlines** (✆ **0662/85 45 33**), **Lufthansa** (✆ **0810/1025 8080**), and **British Airways** (✆ **01/79 567 567**).

Station Information

GETTING FROM THE AIRPORT TO THE TRAIN STATION

There is no direct rail service from the airport into the city center. Bus no. 2 runs between the airport and Salzburg's main rail station, while no. 8 goes to Hanuschplatz and the *Altstadt* **(Old Town).** Departures are frequent, and the 20-minute trip costs 2€ one-way. By taxi, it's only about 15 minutes, but you'll pay at least 13€ to 15€.

Salzburg

3

AUSTRIA | Salzburg

(i) Information
☒ Post office

0 — 150 yds
0 — 150 m

ACCOMMODATIONS ■
Altstadthotel
  Goldene Ente **12**
Altstadthotel
  Kasererbräu **13**
Amadeus **3**
Bergland Hotel **2**
Der Salzburger Hof **1**
Trumer Stube **4**

DINING ◆
Café Bazar **5**
Café Tomaselli **11**
Carpe Diem Finest
  Fingerfood **8**
Restaurant Herzl **7**
Sternbräu **10**
Stiftskeller
  St. Peter **14**

ATTRACTIONS ●
Hellbrunn Palace **21**
Hohensalzburg Fortress **20**
Mönchsberg **19**
Mozarts Geburtshaus **9**
Mozart-Wohnhaus **6**

Museum der Moderne
  Salzburg **22**
Panorama Museum **18**
Residenz **16**
Salzburg Cathedral **15**
Stiftskirche St. Peter **17**

INSIDE THE STATION

Salzburg's main rail station, **Salzburg Hauptbahnhof,** Südtirolerplatz, is connected to all the major rail lines of Europe, with frequent arrivals not only from all the main cities of Austria, but also from a host of European cities, especially Munich (see "Munich," in chapter 9). Trains from Vienna arrive approximately every hour or so (trip time: 3 hr. or less) and from Innsbruck every hour or so (trip time: 2 hr.). From Munich, trains arrive every hour or less (trip time: 2 hr. or less).

Like the stations in Vienna, the Salzburg rail station is undergoing reconstruction that is slated to last until 2014. Many of the amenities have been transferred to temporary locations on the Südtirolerplatz in front of the construction site. Follow temporary yellow signs to navigate through the site to the square. There's a **Reisezentrum** with train information, open Monday to Saturday 5:30am to 9:10pm, as well as luggage-storage lockers. There's a small tourist information office in the InfoBox on the square, along with an exhibition about the reconstruction, where you can obtain a free map, buy a more detailed city map for .70€, or make hotel reservations by paying a 2.20€ fee and a 12% deposit. The office is open daily 8:15am to 7:30pm.

From the train station, buses depart to various parts of the city, including the Altstadt and Hellbrunn Palace. Or you can walk from the rail station to the Altstadt in about 20 minutes.

Information Elsewhere in the City

A larger **Salzburg Tourist Office (Tourismus Salzburg)** is in the heart of the Altstadt, at Mozartplatz 5. May to September, it's open daily 9am to 7pm; October to April, hours are Monday to Saturday 9am to 6pm. The office also books hotel rooms; sells city maps; stocks brochures; and sells sightseeing, concert, and theater tickets. Be sure to pick up a free copy of *Veranstaltungen,* a monthly brochure listing the concerts in Salzburg's many music halls. For more information, call ⓒ **0662/889 87-0** or check the website **www.salzburg.info**.

Getting Around

Walking around Salzburg, especially in the Altstadt, with its many pedestrian zones, is a pleasure. In fact, because Salzburg is rather compact, you can walk to most of its major attractions. Otherwise, buses provide quick, comfortable service between the Hauptbahnhof and Altstadt and to Salzburg's outskirts. When purchased from a machine *(Automat),* a ticket for a single journey, including transfers to reach your final destination, costs 1.90€ for adults and 1.10€ for children (children under 6 travel free). From the driver, expect to pay .20€ more. If you think you'll be traveling a lot by bus, consider buying a 4.20€ **24 Stundenkarte,** valid for 24 hours of unlimited travel. If you purchase tickets in advance (not from the bus driver, but from tobacco shops or vending machines at the train station), prices are slightly cheaper: 6.50€ for a booklet of five single journey tickets and 3.20€ for the 24-hour ticket. For more info about the **public transportation system,** call ⓒ **0662/44 801 500.**

You'll find taxi stands scattered at key points all over the city center and in the suburbs. In and around the Altstadt, convenient taxi stands are at Hanuschplatz, Residenzplatz, Max-Reinhart-Platz, and the Mönchsberg Lift; on the opposite side of the river, taxi stands are at the train station, Makartplatz, and Auerspergstrasse. Fares start at 3€; 10pm to 6am and all day Sundays and holidays, fares start at 3.70€. To phone for a **taxi,** call ⓒ **8111.**

Top Attractions & Special Moments

Most of Salzburg's attractions are on the left bank of the **Salzach River,** in the **Altstadt (Old City).** Much of the Altstadt is a pedestrian zone, including picturesque Getreidegasse, with its many shops; Domplatz; and Mozartplatz. This is where you'll find such attractions as Mozart's Geburtshaus (Mozart's Birthplace), the Festival House complex, the cathedral, the Catacombs of St. Peter, and Salzburg's landmark, the **Hohensalzburg.** In fact, it's this fortress, towering above the Altstadt on a sheer cliff, that makes Salzburg so beautiful, even from afar. It's lit up at night, making a walk along the Salzach river one of the most romantic in Austria.

Just a short walk across the Salzach from the Altstadt is the **Neustadt (New City),** though even it boasts medieval buildings and Mozart's Wohnhaus (Mozart's Residence), as well as the pretty Mirabellgarten.

Festung Hohensalzburg (Hohensalzburg Fortress) ★★★, Mönchsberg 34 (✆ **0662/84 24 30 11;** www.salzburg-burgen.at), is Salzburg's overwhelming landmark. Dominating the city from a sheer cliff, this impressive medieval fortress was built between the 11th and 17th centuries as a residence for the prince-archbishops who ruled Salzburg for more than 500 years. It has the honor of being both Central Europe's largest completely preserved fortress and Europe's largest fortress from the 11th century. It contains the **State Rooms** of the former archbishops and two related museums, which you can visit on a guided tour in which each participant receives an audio guide that describes the most important rooms. There's even an audio guide geared toward kids, with less history and more anecdotes. The tour takes you through dark corridors and unfurnished chambers, including a dismal torture chamber filled with hideous instruments of pain. You'll also see the archbishops' living quarters, with carvings of gold leaf and a late Gothic porcelain stove from 1501—the most valuable item in the fortress—as well as a huge open-air barrel organ (dating from 1502) once used to signal the daily opening and closing of the city's gates.

Included in the tour is a visit of the **Rainermuseum,** a military museum displaying armor, swords, uniforms, and other related items. You'll also tour the **Burgmuseum (Fortress Museum),** which provides a historic overview of the fortress with displays of weapons used in peasant revolts, furniture from the 14th and 15th centuries, and a macabre collection of medieval torture devices. And, finally, you'll see the **Sound and Vision Show,** a multimedia presentation of the fortress's history, and

Welt der Marionetten, a museum displaying marionettes from Salzburg and around the world.

The easiest way to reach the fortress is by **funicular,** but if you want a workout, you can hike to the fortress. A path leading from the Altstadt and winding up the hill, offering changing vistas on the way, makes for a pleasant and slightly strenuous walk. As an alternative, you might want to go up by funicular and descend on foot.

A combination ticket for the funicular, fortress tour, and museums costs 11€ adults, 6€ children ages 6 to 14, and 24€ families. It's open daily October to April 9:30am to 5pm, and May to September 9am to 7pm (you must enter at least half an hour before closing).

Below the fortress, in the heart of the Altstadt, is the 180-room **Residenz,** Residenzplatz 1. It dates from the mid–12th century but was rebuilt extensively in the 16th, 17th, and 18th centuries, offering a tour through 200 years of classical architecture. It served as the official residence of the archbishops when it was deemed safe for them to move down from the fortress into the city. (After you've toured both places, you won't blame them for preferring the more elegant Residenz.) You can tour 15 **Residenz Prunkräume** (**State Rooms;** ✆ **0662/80 42 26 90;** www.salzburg-burgen.at) with the aid of an audio guide; you'll see the throne room (the most beautiful, and one of several in which Mozart performed), the bedroom of the archbishop, the library, the audience chamber (the most lavishly decorated, with original furnishings), and other chambers, most with inlaid wooden floors, marble portals, ceiling frescoes relating the heroics of Alexander the Great, tapestries, and precious furniture.

Also in the Residenz is the **Residenzgalerie** (✆ **0662/84 04 51 0;** www.residenzgalerie.at), a 15-room gallery of European art from the 16th to the 19th centuries, with works by Dutch, French, Italian, and Austrian baroque artists, including **Rembrandt, Bruegel, Friedrich Loos, Ferdinand Georg Waldmüller,** and **Hans Makart.** Of special interest are paintings depicting Salzburg through the centuries.

A combination ticket for both the State Rooms and Residenzgalerie is 8.50€ adults, 6.50€ seniors/students, and 2.70€ children. The State Rooms are open Tuesday to Sunday 10am to 5pm (open Mon during holidays and the Festspiele). The Residenzgalerie is open Tuesday to Sunday 10am to 5pm.

At the south side of Residenzplatz, where it flows into **Domplatz** (here you'll see a 1771 statue of the Virgin Mary), stands the **Dom (Salzburg Cathedral)** ★ (✆ **0662/80 47 18 60**), world renowned for its 4,000-pipe organ. When a previous edifice was destroyed by fire in 1598, Prince-Archbishop Wolf Dietrich followed up the start of work on the Residenz by commissioning construction of a new cathedral, but his overthrow prevented the finishing of the project. His successor, Archbishop Markus Sittikus Count Hohenems, commissioned the Italian architect Santino Solari to build the present cathedral, which was consecrated in 1628 by Archbishop Paris Count Lodron. Hailed as the "most perfect" Renaissance building in the Germanic countries, the cathedral has a marble facade and twin symmetrical towers. This is where Mozart was baptized and engaged as a court organist. The interior is in rich baroque style with elaborate frescoes, the most important of which, along with the altarpieces, were designed by Mascagni of Florence. The Dom, free to the public, is open daily 8am to 7pm (to 5pm in winter).

Although the Dom is Salzburg's most commanding cathedral, the **Stiftskirche St. Peter (St. Peter's Church)** ★★, St.-Peter-Bezirk (✆ **0662/84 45 78 0**), boasts the most picturesque setting, nestled at the foot of Mönchsberg and surrounded by

The Hills Are Alive . . .

Bob's Special Tours (✆ 0662/84 95 11; www.bobstours.com), which has specialized in personable English-language tours for more than 45 years, offers personalized tours in buses seating 8 to 20. The 4-hour *"Sound of Music* Tour" includes a short city tour and takes in most of the major film locations, such as the Schloss Leopoldskron (which served in part as the von Trapp film home), the lake district where the opening scene was filmed, and the gazebo at Hellbrunn Palace. It costs 40€ for adults and 35€ for children, and sometimes adds a toboggan ride for 4.50€.

one of the prettiest cemeteries you're likely to see anywhere. Many of the aristocratic families of Salzburg are buried here, as well as many other noted persons, including Nannerl Mozart, sister of the composer. Four years older than her better-known brother, Nannerl was also an exceptionally gifted musician. It's also possible to take a tour through the early Christian catacombs in the cliff above the church cemetery, where you'll see rooms and chapels carved into the cliff, the first dating from A.D. 250 and built by Roman Christians for secret religious ceremonies (be forewarned, there are lots of stairs to climb). Admission to the cemetery is free; the catacombs cost 1€ adults, .60€ children. The cemetery is open daily 6:30am to 7pm. The catacombs are open May to September Tuesday to Sunday 10:30am to 5pm, October to April, Wednesday and Thursday 10:30am to 3:30pm and Friday to Sunday 10:30am to 4pm.

Of course, the reason many music fans are drawn to Salzburg is the city's most famous citizen: Wolfgang Amadeus Mozart. The most heavily visited attraction in Salzburg is the **Mozart Geburtshaus (Mozart's Birthplace)** ★, Getreidegasse 9 (✆ **0662/84 43 13;** www.mozarteum.at), located in the heart of the Altstadt on its most picturesque street. Mozart was born in this simple third-floor apartment in 1756 and lived in these four rooms with his family until 1773. The museum contains his clavichord, a copy of his pianoforte (he started composing when he was 4), and the violin he played as a boy. Of the several paintings of Amadeus; his sister, Nannerl; and his family, only one is known to be a true likeness of the Wunderkind—the unfinished one by the pianoforte, done by his brother-in-law. Another is thought to be of the musician when he was 9. In addition to the rooms where the family lived, there are a few adjoining rooms decorated in the style of a typical burgher's house in Mozart's time. You'll also find changing exhibits related to Mozart's works.

More worthwhile, however, if you have time for only one Mozart attraction, is the **Mozart-Wohnhaus (Mozart's Residence)** ★★★, Makartplatz 8 (✆ **0662/87 42 27-40;** www.mozarteum.at), on the other side of the Salzach River in the Neustadt. It strives to chronicle the musician's life and the influence his family—particularly his father—had on his career, making it more informative than his birthplace for those who know little about the genius's life. A teenaged Mozart and his family moved from their small Getreidegasse home to this more spacious, elegant residence in 1773; it dates from 1617 and was once used for dancing classes for the aristocracy. Mozart lived here until 1780, composing symphonies, serenades, piano and violin concertos, and sacred music. His father died here in 1787. Today the home, heavily damaged during World War II and completely rebuilt, contains a museum dedicated to Mozart and his family, period furniture, Mozart's pianoforte, and original music

A panoramic STROLL

For the best view of Hohensalzburg Fortress towering above Salzburg and the Salzach River, hike along the heavily forested ridge that stretches from the fortress to **Mönchsberg.** The hike takes about 30 minutes and features changing vistas along the way. On Mönchsberg is the **Museum der Moderne Salzburg Mönchsberg** (© 0662/84 22 20-401; www.museumdermoderne.at), which features changing exhibitions of art and photography from the 20th and 21st centuries. It's open Tuesday to Sunday 10am to 6pm (to 9pm Wed) and charges 8€ adults and 6€ seniors, students, and children.

From here, you can take the **Mönchsberg Lift** (© 0662/44 80-9772; www.moenchsbergaufzug.at) back down to the Altstadt. It operates daily 8am to 7pm (to 9pm Wed), except in July and August, when it's open daily 8am to 9pm. It costs 1.80€ one-way for adults and .90€ for children.

Or, for more scenic hiking, continue walking west another 20 minutes to the **Augustiner Bräustübl,** Salzburg's famous brewery and beer garden (see "Nightlife," below).

scores. Best, however, are the audio guides that are automatically activated by the various displays, complete with music, and the movie depicting the child prodigy's life in Salzburg and his tours of Europe. You can spend the better part of an hour here, more if you're a Mozart fan.

Both the Geburtshaus and Wohnhaus are open September to June daily 9am to 6pm and July and August daily 9am to 8pm (you must enter 30 min. before closing). A combination ticket to both costs 12€ adults, 10€ seniors and students, 4.50€ children 15 to 18, 3.50€ children 6 to 14 (free for children under 6), and 26€ families. Otherwise, a ticket to either costs 7€, 6€, 3€, 2.50€, and 17€, respectively.

If you're in Salzburg between April and October, it's worth a trip 3 miles (5km) south of the city to see the unique **Hellbrunn Palace and its trick gardens ★★,** Fürstenweg 37 (© 0662/82 03 72-0; www.hellbrunn.at). Built as a hunting lodge/summer residence for Salzburg's prince-bishops in the early 17th century, this Italian Renaissance–style country villa is an impressive example of the luxury enjoyed by absolute rulers during the Renaissance. The most intriguing features are its water gardens—dozens of trick fountains and water sprays hidden in the large Renaissance gardens, with mysterious grottoes and mythical statues. (You almost invariably get doused, to the delight of children.) Guided tours of the garden last 30 to 40 minutes and depart every half-hour daily: April and October 9am to 4:30pm (last tour); May, June, and September 9am to 5:30pm; and July and August 9am to 9pm. During July and August, evening guided tours that take in only the illuminated trick fountains are also given at 7, 8, 9, and 10pm.

The cost of the tour is 9.50€ adults, 6.50€ students, 4.50€ children, and 24€ families. Included in the price (except during the evening tours), is a visit to the palace, which you tour on your own with an audio guide. To reach the palace, take bus no. 25 to Hellbrunn.

Finally, history buffs may want to see the **Panorama Museum,** located next to the post office at Residenzplatz 9 (© 0662/620 808-730). It displays Salzburg's first advertising campaign, a huge 360-degree panorama of Salzburg painted in 1829 by J. M. Sattler, who then traveled to Munich, Vienna, Prague, Dresden, Berlin, Amsterdam, and beyond to promote his masterpiece. An interactive display allows visitors to compare the Salzburg of 1829 with today, but most fun are the 24 *cosmoramas* (panoramas) of cities from around the world as they looked in the 19th century, identified only by number so you can guess which cities they represent. It's open daily 9am to 5pm (to 8pm Thurs) and charges 2€ adults, 1.70€ seniors and students, and 1€ children.

Where to Stay & Dine

Located in the heart of the Altstadt in a 650-year-old house, **Altstadthotel Goldene Ente,** Goldgasse 10 (*©* **0662/84 56 22;** www.ente.at; bus: 3, 5, 6, 7, 8, or 25), looks as ancient as it is, with thick walls, worn stone stairways attesting to centuries of use, tiny bathrooms, and wood furnishings. The entire house is nonsmoking, and there's a ground-floor restaurant serving traditional Austrian cuisine. Doubles are 125€ to 160€, including buffet breakfast (there's a computer with free Internet use). There's a 10% discount for paying in cash.

A few blocks from the Dom (cathedral), **Altstadthotel Kasererbräu,** Kaigasse 33 (*©* **0662/84 24 45;** www.kasererbraeu.at; bus: 3, 5, 6, 7, 8, or 25), is a 670-year-old house constructed on Roman walls in the center of the city. Each of its 45 rooms is different; those decorated with baroque and Biedermeier furnishings have more character than those with modern furniture. Guests have free access to a steam room and sauna, and on the ground floor there's a pizzeria and a cinema—one of the oldest in the country. Some units are large enough to be classified as apartments and are suitable for two to four persons. Double rates are 89€ to 224€ and include buffet breakfast. Apartments cost 169€ to 264€. Free wireless in all the rooms.

Occupying a 15th-century building and owned by the same family for three generations, **Amadeus** ★★, Linzer Gasse 43–45 (*©* **0662/87 14 01;** www.hotel amadeus.at; bus: 1, 3, 5, 6, or 25), has a great location in the city center, across the river from the Altstadt. You have your choice of rooms facing either a pedestrian shopping street or a peaceful cemetery (where Mozart's wife is buried). Rooms are pleasant, with both traditional furniture and modern touches. There's a computer in the lobby with free Internet use as well as Wi-Fi, and the hotel's second-floor terrace overlooking the cemetery is a good place to relax in the sun or spend an evening with drinks. Double rates are 180€ to 200€, and 125€ to 150€ in the off season. Rates include a substantial buffet breakfast.

Der Salzburger Hof, Kaiserschützenstrasse 1 (*©* **0662/46 97-0;** www.der salzburgerhof.at), is a worthy and convenient choice for rail travelers, as it lies only 2 blocks from the Hauptbahnhof. It's a small, older hotel, with a friendly staff and 32 theme-decorated rooms, ranging from Mozart to the *Sound of Music.* Its restaurant offers Austrian, Indian, and Italian cuisine. Room rates are 92€ to 187€ double and include buffet breakfast.

Trumer Stube ★★, Bergstrasse 6 (*©* **0662/87 47 76;** www.trumer-stube.at; bus: 1, 3, 5, 6, or 25), is a 22-room, personable hotel-pension on the right bank of the Salzach River in the Altstadt and within a 5-minute walk of both Mozart's Birthplace and Residence. Ideal for couples and families, it's managed by friendly Marianne Hirschbichler, who speaks English well and is happy to give sightseeing tips, make restaurant and guided tour reservations, and do whatever else guests desire. The pension offers cheerful, cozy, and spotless rooms (all nonsmoking) with flowers in the windows, as well as free Wi-Fi and a lobby computer guests can use. Doubles are 96€ to 135€.

Although not as conveniently located as those above, another good choice is the **Bergland Hotel,** Rupertgasse 15 (© **0662/87 23 18-0;** www.berglandhotel.at; bus: 2, 4), a nonsmoking hotel owned by the Kuhn family since 1912. A 15-minute walk from the train station and a 10-minute walk from the Altstadt (rental bikes are available), it is managed by the friendly English-speaking Peter Kuhn, who has decorated the pension with his own artwork, oversees breakfast, and is on hand most evenings to converse with guests in the cozy bar/lounge. There's an outdoor terrace available for relaxing and free Wi-Fi. Doubles here are 83€ to 125€, including buffet breakfast.

A dining favorite, **Restaurant Herzl ★★**, Getreidegasse 35 or Karajanplatz 7 (© **0662/8084 889;** bus: 1, 4, 8, or 24), stands next door to the city's most glamorous hotel, Goldener Hirsch, and is entered from either Karajanplatz or Getreidegasse in the center of the city. It's especially popular during the Salzburg Festival, drawing some of the leading performers with its relaxed country-inn atmosphere and its finely tuned take on Austrian and Viennese specialties. Come here for old-fashioned favorites such as Wiener schnitzel and Nürnberger sausages with sauerkraut. Main courses run 7.50€ to 24€. It's open daily 11:30am to 10pm.

The Austro-Hungarian army used to eat at **Sternbräu,** Griesgasse 23 (© **0662/84 21 40;** bus: 1, 4, 8, or 24), opened more than 500 years ago as a brewery. Located in the Altstadt, it's a huge place, with various dining halls and two courtyard gardens, including a beer garden shaded by chestnut trees. The Austrian food is more hearty and filling than refined, but that—and the brew served here—is why the place is so popular. Main courses with side dishes cost 8€ to 16€. It's open daily 10am to 11pm.

Stiftskeller St. Peter ★★, near St. Peter's Monastery at the foot of the Mönchsberg, St. Peter-Bezirk (© **0662/84 12 68-0;** bus: 3, 5, 6, 7, 8, 25, or 26), is probably Salzburg's most popular first-class restaurant. It's under the management of St. Peter's Monastery and was first mentioned in documents dating from 803, making it Europe's oldest restaurant. There are various dining rooms, each unique but all with a medieval ambience. The changing English menu lists international dishes as well as local specialties, such as fresh mountain trout, boiled beef with chives, veal schnitzel, and numerous daily specials. For wine, you might select the Prälatenwein (prelate's wine), the grapes of which are grown in the convent's own vineyards in Wachau. The traditional desserts are great—try the *Salzburger Nockerl,* a dessert soufflé made of eggs, flour, butter, and sugar. For a real splurge, there's the Mozart Dinner Concert, held in the restaurant's elegant Baroque Hall and featuring Mozart music played by period-costumed musicians and a three-course meal based on traditional 17- and 18th-century recipes, costing 51€. Otherwise, main courses here are 12€ to 25€. It's open daily 11:30am to 2:30pm and 6 to 10:30pm.

Although it looks out of place in the Altstadt, the trendiest restaurant for casual dining is **Carpe Diem Finest Fingerfood,** Getreidegasse 50 (© **0662/84 88 00;** bus: 1, 4, 8, or 24), where you can try famous chef Jörg Wörther's innovative finger food, served mostly in crispy cones and ranging from cream of avocado with carrots tempura and gazpacho with prawns, to beef tartar with potato purée and rocket salad in a potato cone. Most cones cost 4.90€ to 8.90€, and the restaurant is open daily 11:30am to 11pm.

Shopping

Austrian artisanship is of high quality, with correspondingly high prices for Austrian traditional **sweaters, dirndls, leather goods, jewelry, petit point,** and other local

cafe SOCIETY

Salzburg, like Vienna, is famous for its coffeehouses and pastry shops, where you can linger over pastry and coffee or a glass of wine, read the newspapers (including the *International Herald Tribune*), and watch the passersby. In summer, most cafes have outdoor seating. **Café Bazar,** Schwarzstrasse 3, on the Neustadt side of the Salzach near the Staatsbrücke (© **0662/87 42 78**), is a stunning Jugendstil Kaffeehaus, with lustrous wood paneling and brass fittings, large windows, and a great terrace with stunning views of the river and fortress, and is popular with locals. It serves breakfast all day, as well as snacks and daily specials, and is open

Monday to Saturday 7:30am to 11pm and Sunday and holidays 9am to 6pm.

Opened in 1705, and one of Austria's oldest coffeehouses in Salzburg, **Café Tomaselli,** in the heart of the Altstadt at Alter Markt 9 (© **0662/84 44 88**), is still going strong—so popular you might have to wait to get a seat. In summer, seating spills out onto the cobblestone square, an upstairs balcony, and a shady area around a nearby kiosk. Have a *Melange* (a large coffee with frothy milk) and dessert, or choose from the pastry tray or display case. It's open Monday to Saturday 7am to 9pm (midnight during the Salzburg Festival).

goods, including **chocolates.** Most shops are concentrated in the Altstadt along **Getreidegasse** and **Alter Markt,** as well as across the river along **Linzergasse.** Most stores in Salzburg are open Monday to Saturday 9am to 6pm. Some shops may close an hour or two at noon or Saturday afternoon.

Established in 1408 and owned by the same family for four generations, **Jahn-Markl,** Residenzplatz 3 (© **0662/84 26 10**), is a small and elegant store with a forest-green facade trimmed with brass and wrought-iron detailing. Located in the center of the Altstadt, it carries Lederhosen for all sizes and sexes, leather skirts, and a full line of traditional Austrian coats and blazers.

Salzburger Heimatwerk, Residenzplatz 9 (© **0662/84 41 10**), is one of the best places in town to buy regional handcrafts. It's a dignified stone building next to the post office and the Panorama Museum. Items for sale include Austrian silver and garnet jewelry, painted boxes, candles, glassware, woodcarvings, copper and brass ceramics, tablecloths, and patterns for cross-stitched samplers in Alpine designs. A new wing offers Austrian culinary specialties.

Wiener Porzellanmanufaktur Augarten Gesellschaft, Alter Markt 11 (© **0662/84 07 14**), is the premier shop in Salzburg for Austrian porcelain made at the factory at the Augarten Palace in Vienna. Its most famous design is a black-and-white coffee set created by architect/designer Josef Hoffmann.

Nightlife

As the birthplace of Mozart and site of the Salzburg Festival, the city boasts a musical event almost every night of the year. To find out what's going on where, stop by the **City Tourist Office,** Mozartplatz 5 (© **0662/889 87-0**), to pick up a free copy of the monthly *Veranstaltungen.*

The cheapest way to secure theater tickets is by buying them directly at the theater box office. Otherwise, the **Salzburg Ticket Service,** which charges a 20% commission, is at the City Tourist Office on Mozartplatz (© **0662/84 03 10**). Selling tickets for all concerts, it's open Monday to Friday 9am to 6pm and Saturday 9am to noon (mid-July to Aug Mon–Sat 9am–7pm and Sun 10am–6pm).

All the premier opera, ballet, and concerts are staged at the **Festspielhaus,** Hofstallgasse 1 (℃ **0662/80 45-0;** bus: 1, 3, 5, 6, 7, 15, 25, or 26), as are major events of the Salzburg Festival. Performances are in the 1,324-seat Haus für Mozart or the 2,170-seat Grosses Haus (Large House), and it's best to buy tickets in advance—for the Salzburg Festival, months in advance for major performances. The box office for the Salzburg Festival is at Herbert-von-Karajan-Platz (℃ **0662/80 45-500**). It's open Monday to Friday 9:30am to 3pm, except from July 1 to the start of the festival, when it's open Monday to Saturday 9:30am to 5pm, and during the festival, when it's open daily 9:30am to 6:30pm. For orchestra concerts, given September to June, you'll find the box office at Kulturvereinigung, Waagplatz 1A (℃ **0662/84 53 46**), near the tourist office. It's open Monday to Friday 8am to 6pm; performances are usually at 7:30pm. Tickets for orchestra concerts start at 8€, while opera tickets begin at 22€.

Orchestra concerts and chamber music are presented in the **Mozarteum,** Schwarzstrasse 26 (℃ **0662/87 31 54;** bus: 1, 3, 5, 6, or 25). The Mozarteum is on the river's right bank, near Mirabellgarten. Its box office is open Monday to Thursday 9am to 2pm and Friday 9am to 4pm. Performances are at 11am and/or 7:30pm, with most tickets at 9€ to 38€.

The **Salzburger Schlosskonzerte (Salzburg Palace Concerts)** take place year-round in the Marble Hall of Mirabell Palace, Mirabellplatz (℃ **0662/84 85 86;** www.salzburger-schlosskonzerte.at; bus: 1, 3, 5, 6, 51, or 25). The chamber-music series presents mostly Mozart's music, as well as music by other renowned composers such as Haydn, Beethoven, Schubert, and Vivaldi. Concerts, generally at 8 or 8:30pm 3 to 7 nights a week, are held in intimate baroque surroundings, much as they were in Mozart's time. The box office, at Theatergasse 2, is open Monday to Friday 9am to 5:30pm. Tickets are 29€ to 35€ adults, 16€ students, 10€ children under 10.

Salzburg's landmark, the **Hohensalzburg Fortress,** Mönchsberg 34 (℃ **0662/82 58 58;** www.mozartfestival.at; take the funicular from Festungsgasse), features concerts called the **Salzburger Festungskonzerte** in the medieval Prince's Chamber, performed by the Salzburger Mozart-Ensemble, as well as guest musicians. The box office, at A.-Adlgasser-Weg 22, is open daily 9am to 9pm; performances are given almost daily at 7:30, 8, or 8:30pm. Tickets are 31€ or 38€, 20€ or 28€ for children and students. Both the Salzburg Palace and Fortress concerts can be combined with preconcert dinners.

The **Salzburger Marionettentheater,** Schwarzstrasse 24 (℃ **0662/87 24 06;** www.marionetten.at; bus: 1, 3, 5, 6, or 25), was founded in 1913 and tours the world as one of Europe's largest and most famous marionette theaters. Using recordings made by top orchestras and singers, it presents operas and operettas Easter through September, during Christmas, and some dates in January, including *The Magic Flute, Die Fledermaus, The Barber of Seville, The Marriage of Figaro,* and *Don Giovanni.* The box office is open Monday to Saturday 9am to 1pm and 2 hours before the start of each performance; performances are usually Monday to Saturday at 7:30pm, with occasional matinees and short performances at 2pm in July and August. Tickets run 18€ to 35€.

Outside the cultural venues, the most entertaining evenings in Salzburg are at the **Augustiner Bräustübl,** Augustinergasse 4 (℃ **0662/43 12 46;** bus: 27). Founded in 1621 by Augustine monks, this brewery, about a 10-minute walk from the Altstadt, is a Salzburg institution and a great place for a meal in the huge outdoor beer garden or upstairs in one of the huge beer halls. Counters sell sausages and cold cuts, cheese, pretzels, hamburgers, grilled chicken, soup, salads, boiled pork with horse-radish, beef with creamed spinach and potatoes, and more. It's a crowded, noisy place, as a brewery should be. It's open Monday to Friday 3 to 11pm, and Saturday and Sunday 2:30 to 11pm.

INNSBRUCK ★★

Rivaling Vienna and Salzburg for the title of Austria's most beautiful city, Innsbruck is the capital of the federal state of Tyrol, one of the world's greatest Alpine playgrounds. Its name—translated as "bridge over the Inn," the Inn being the river that flows through the city—is testimony to its importance as a major crossroad through the centuries, and today it serves as a major rail transportation hub for western Austria. But it is also a destination in itself, boasting a picture-perfect medieval Old Town (Altstadt) of narrow cobbled streets and Gothic, Renaissance, and baroque buildings in kaleidoscopic colors, with majestic mountain peaks rising above the rooftops virtually everywhere you look. Little wonder the Winter Olympics were held here in 1964 and 1976—it's a skier's paradise almost year-round, due to the nearby Stubai Glacier, and is the rail gateway to such winter ski resorts as Seefeld, Zell am Ziller, and Kitzbühel. In summer, the surrounding countryside offers hiking and other fair-weather pursuits.

In short, Innsbruck is a perfect place to unwind and escape the big city (pop. 120,000), and is also a convenient stopover for those doing a grand rail tour of Europe. By train, the German border is only 45 minutes to the north, while the Italian frontier is just 30 minutes to the south. While its major attractions can be seen in a day, 2 days are needed to do the city justice. And though it's not cheap, it's less expensive than Salzburg.

Station Information

GETTING FROM THE AIRPORT TO THE TRAIN STATION

Although its airport is much smaller than Munich's and Salzburg's, Innsbruck's airport, **Flughafen Innsbruck-Kranebitten,** Fürstenweg 180 (℗ **0512/22525;** www.innsbruck-airport.com), serves as a gateway for air passengers who prefer to begin their rail journey of Austria in the Tyrolean Alps. Though there is no direct service from North America, there is regularly scheduled air service from Frankfurt, London, Vienna, and a few other cities on flights operated by **Austrian Airlines** and **Air Alps** (℗ **0039/06 222;** www.airalps.net). From the airport, 2 miles (3.2km) west of the city, there is no direct rail service into town, but bus F travels to the main train station in the exact center of town in 18 minutes. Tickets cost 1.80€. A taxi ride takes about 10 minutes and costs 10€ and up, depending on traffic.

MORE STATION INFORMATION

Innsbruck is connected to all the major cities of Europe by international railway links. At least eight direct trains arrive daily from Munich (trip time: 1 hr., 50 min.) and 16 direct daily trains from Salzburg (2 hr.). Train travel from Vienna ranges from 4½ hours to about 5 hours, depending on the train you take. Trains arrive at the recently remodeled main railway station, the **Hauptbahnhof,** Südtiroler Platz, about a 10-minute walk from the Altstadt and connected to the rest of the city by tram and bus. Call ℗ **05/1717** for rail information or visit the **Reisezentrum,** open daily 6:30am to 8:45pm.

There's an **Innsbruck Information Office** in the press stand in the main hall, where you pick up city maps for 1€ and reserve accommodations for free. It's open daily 9am to 6pm. A bank (open weekdays only), post office, and lockers are also in the train station.

Information Elsewhere in the City

Innsbruck-Information, Burggraben 3 (*�C* **0512/59850**), in the Altstadt just off Maria-Theresien-Strasse, is open daily 9am to 6pm. Here you can stock up on printed information about Innsbruck (and other parts of Tyrol) and ask questions about virtually any feature of the town. You can also buy bus tickets, exchange money (even on weekends), purchase tickets to concerts and cultural events, and book hotel rooms for free. You can visit Innsbruck's home page at **www.innsbruck.info**.

Getting Around

Most of Innsbruck's major sights are clustered in or around the Altstadt, within easy walking distance from one another. Otherwise, trams and buses provide public transportation around Innsbruck and its environs. A **single ticket,** which permits transfers, costs 1.80€ and can be bought from the driver. Other options, available from the tourist information office, tobacco shops, and automated vending machines, include a **24-hour transportation pass** for 4.10€ or a **group of four tickets** for 5.90€. Best for tourists, however, is the **Sightseer,** a red bus that travels to the Alpenzoo, the Altstadt, and other tourist attractions, with runs every 40 minutes in summer and every hour in winter. A single ticket costs 3€, but best is the **Day Ticket** for 6€ that includes travel on public transportation. For information about various routes, call the **Innsbrucker Verkehrsbetriebe** (*℃* **0512/5307-500;** www.ivb.at).

Otherwise, the best deal that combines transportation and sightseeing is the **Innsbruck Card,** available for 24, 48, or 72 hours for 29€, 34€, and 39€, respectively (children pay half-fare). It provides unlimited transportation (including the Sightseer and shuttle bus to Swarovski Kristallwelten), along with free entry to all Innsbruck's attractions.

Taxi stands are scattered at strategic points throughout the city, or you can call a radio car (*℃* **0512/5311**).

Top Attractions & Special Moments

First mentioned in 12th-century documents, Innsbruck gained international stature under Maximilian I, who became German emperor in 1507, made the town the seat of the Holy Roman Empire, and constructed the most important buildings. Today these buildings stand at the center of the compact medieval **Altstadt,** which contains most of the city's main attractions.

Most striking is Innsbruck's famous landmark, the **Goldenes Dachl (Golden Roof),** Herzog-Friedrich-Strasse 15, easily recognized by its gleaming balcony made of 2,657 gilded copper tiles. Built in the early 15th century by Emperor Maximilian to celebrate his marriage to his second wife, Bianca Maria Sforza, it was used as a royal box for watching civic events in the square below, including tournaments between armored knights, dances, and theatrics. If you look closely at the building's reliefs, you can see images of Maximilian and his two wives. (His first wife, Mary of Burgundy, died in a riding accident and was much grieved; his second wife brought him great wealth and went largely ignored.) Today the building's facade is the most photographed sight in Innsbruck. In August, Tyrolean Folk Art Evenings are staged in the square on Thursday at 8:30pm.

Just a stone's throw away is the **Stadtturm (City Tower),** Herzog-Friedrich-Strasse 21 (*℃* **0512/56 15 00**), built in 1450 and, at 185 feet tall (56m), still one

ACCOMMODATIONS ■
Weisses Kreuz **9**
Weisses Rössl **4**

DINING ◆
Cammerlander **11**
Ottoburg **3**
Weisses Rössl **4**

ATTRACTIONS ●
Alpenzoo **1**
Bergisel **12**
Goldenes Dachl **2**
Herzog-Friedrich-
Strasse **5**
Hofburg **6**

Hofkirche **7**
Stadtturm **10**
Tiroler Volkskunst-
museum **8**

ⓘ Information
✉ Post Office

Salzburg
Vienna✷
AUSTRIA
●Innsbruck

of the Altstadt's highest structures. Its viewing platform, reached via 148 stairs, offers magnificent panoramic views of the city and Alps. It's open daily 10am to 5pm (to 8pm in summer), and admission is 3€ adults, 2.50€ seniors/students, 1.50€ children, and 6€ families.

Innsbruck's most imposing building remains the **Kaiserliche Hofburg (Imperial Court Palace)** ★★, Rennweg 1 (© **0512/58 71 86;** www.hofburg-innsbruck.at). It's to Innsbruck what Versailles is to Paris—but on a much smaller scale. Built in 1460 and enlarged by Emperor Maximilian in the 1500s as a residence for his second wife, it was reconstructed in the baroque style by Empress Maria Theresa in the mid–18th century. On view are the **Kaiserappartements** used by Maria Theresa and her family whenever they visited, including the royal chapel, dining rooms, and bedrooms, all with original furnishings, tapestries, paintings, and portraits. The most fascinating of the 20-some open rooms is the **Giant's Hall**, lavishly decorated in rococo style with elaborate stucco designs and a painted ceiling. What's most striking about the room, however, are the portraits of Maria Theresa and her 16 children, including her youngest daughter, Antonia, who went on to become that ill-fated queen of France, Marie Antoinette. Admission is 8€ adults, 6€ seniors and students, and free for children under 19. It's open daily 9am to 5pm (you must enter by 4:30pm).

A minute's walk east of the Kaiserliche Hofburg is the **Hofkirche (Court Church)**, Universitätsstrasse 2 (© **0512/58 43 02**; www.hofkirche.at), conceived by Maximilian as his memorial and place of burial. Inside is his elaborate tomb, decorated with reliefs depicting scenes from the emperor's life and surrounded by 28 larger-than-life bronze statues representing his ancestors, relatives, and peers, including his father, two wives, son, and daughter; two of the statues are from designs by German artist Albrecht Dürer. The tomb, however, is empty—Maximilian died before the church was built and was buried in Wiener Neustadt. Several other important figures are interred here, however, including Tyrolean freedom fighter Andreas Hofer and Archduke Ferdinand II. You'll find Ferdinand's final resting place up the stairs in the **Silberne Kapelle (Silver Chapel)**; just outside the chapel's iron gate is the tomb of Ferdinand's wife, Philippine Welser, who, as a mere commoner, wasn't allowed to be buried beside her husband. It's open Monday to Saturday 9am to 6pm, and Sunday and holidays 12:30 to 6pm, with admission at 4€ adults and 2€ children.

For adults, the best deal is to buy a combination ticket for 8€ that also includes a visit to the **Tiroler Volkskunstmuseum (Tyrolean Folk Art Museum)** ★★★ (© **0512/594 89-510**; www.tiroler-volkskunstmuseum.at), housed in a former monastery adjoining the Court Church (and sharing the same entry). Our favorite museum in Innsbruck, it's one of Austria's best folk art museums, with a collection of items used by common folk in the Tyrol from the Middle Ages to the 20th century. Included are sleighs; a beautiful collection of painted furniture (*Bauernmöbel*); ornamental bells for sheep, goats, and cows (you should see the size of some); farming tools and cooking utensils; religious artifacts; traditional clothing; glassware; displays on cottage industries ranging from weaving to woodcarving; and a fascinating collection of nativity scenes (*Krippe*). It also contains more than a dozen reconstructed Tyrolean rooms taken from inns, farmhouses, and patrician homes and furnished in Gothic, Renaissance, and baroque styles. It's open daily 10am to 6pm. A *Kombiticket* that includes the Folk Art Museum, Court Church, the Ferdinandeum and Zeughaus costs 8€ for adults and 4€ for children and students.

Although it's not in the Altstadt, very much worth a visit—especially if you have children in tow—is Europe's highest-elevation zoo, the **Alpenzoo (Alpine Zoo)** ★, Weiherburggasse 37 (© **0512/29 23 23**; www.alpenzoo.at), boasting great views from its location above the city on the slopes of the Hungerburg. This is the place to see all those animals native to the Alps and Alpine region, such as European bison, wolves, lynx, marmots, otters, beavers, vultures, owls, eagles, buzzards, elk, Alpine ibex, rabbits, brown bears, and local fish. There's also a section devoted to domesticated Alpine animals, including cows, goats, and sheep. Admission to the zoo, open daily 9am to 6pm (to 5pm Nov–Mar), is 8€ adults, 6€ seniors/students, and 4€ children. Combo ticket with the Nordkettenbahn (see below) is also available for

THE MOST BEAUTIFUL SPOT IN Tyrol

The **Hungerburg** ★★ mountain plateau, at 2,860 feet (858m), must be one of the most beautiful spots in Tyrol, affording the best view of Innsbruck, especially on summer nights, when much of the city, including fountains and historic buildings, is brightly lit. Beyond it is the Hafelekar, a paradise for snowboarders and skiers alike.

To reach the Hungerburg plateau, take the new funicular from Congress Innsbruck, located in downtown Innsbruck just north of the Altstadt, 25 minutes to the mountain. Once you reach the plateau, you progress even farther into the Alpine wilds via the **Nordkette cable railway (Nordkettenbahn).** It will take you up to the Seegrube and the Hafelekar 7,401 feet (2,220m) for a sweeping view of Alpine peaks and glaciers. This is the starting point of high mountain walks, climbing expeditions, and skiing. A round-trip ticket for the railway from Congress to Hungerburg; the cable car up to Hafelekar costs 26€ for adults, 21€ for students/seniors, and 13€ children ages 6 to 15. The funicular runs Monday to Friday 7am to 7:30pm (8am–7:30pm Sun and holidays), while cable cars run daily 8:30am to 5:30pm, with the final return departure from Hafelekar at 5pm. For schedules and information, call ✆ **0512/29 33 44** or go to **www.nordpark.at**.

Note: None of the railways above are covered by railpasses.

10€, 8.50€, and 5€, respectively. To reach the zoo, take bus W or the Sightseer to the Alpenzoo bus stop.

If you're staying overnight in Innsbruck, we highly recommend an excursion to nearby **Wattens** to visit the fantastic **Swarovski Kristallwelten (Crystal Worlds)** ★★★, Kristallweltenstrasse 1 (✆ **05224/51080;** http://kristallwelten. swarovski.com), which you can reach in about 15 minutes by bus from the Innsbruck Busbahnhof (next to the Hauptbahnhof). Buses depart for Wattens every 30 minutes (every 60 min. on Sun and holidays); get off at the Kristallwelten stop. There is also a Swarovski shuttle bus four times a day from Innsbruck's Hauptbahnhof, at a round-trip fare of 8.50€.

Even if you know what Swarovski is—the world's leading producer of full-cut crystal—you won't be prepared for this experiment in fantasy, with theatrical three-dimensional displays that give this attraction a Disneyesque quality and have catapulted it into the region's top tourist draw. Kristallwelten itself is subterranean, hidden from view by a man-made hill but attracting attention with a giant head spouting water. Designed by Viennese multimedia artist Andre Heller, the interior consists of more than a dozen magical cavernlike chambers, with displays relating to crystal. You'll see the world's largest cut crystal (137 lb.); a glass-enclosed wall containing 12 tons of crystal; works by artists ranging from Salvador Dalí to Keith Haring; and costumes, art, and other displays about crystal, including a crystal dome that gives one a pretty good idea of what it would be like to be encapsulated inside a crystal. New Age music adds a dreamlike quality. Admission is 9.50€, free for children under 12. Open daily 9am to 6:30pm (you must enter by 5:30pm).

Where to Stay & Dine

If you can afford it, stay in the Altstadt, just a 10-minute walk from the train station (or tram 3 to the second stop, Maria-Theresien-Strasse). A top pick is the **Weisses**

Kreuz ★★, Herzog-Friedrich-Strasse 31, 6020 Innsbruck (© **0512/59 4 79**; www.weisseskreuz.at), with an enviable location down the street from the Goldenes Dachl and boasting a 500-year history. Mozart stayed here when he was 13, during a 1769 journey with his father to Italy. Although the inn has been updated with modern conveniences, including an elevator, it remains true to its historic atmosphere, offering 40 white-walled rooms furnished with modern or traditional pine furniture and free Wi-Fi. Doubles here are 70€ to 132€, including buffet breakfast.

Also in the Altstadt is the **Weisses Rössl** ★★, Kiebachgasse 8, 6020 Innsbruck (© **0512/58 30 57**; www.roessl.at). This delightful inn, built in 1410 and recently renovated to enhance its rustic splendor, offers 12 rooms that have been updated in a contemporary style yet retain their medieval simplicity. A restaurant features local favorites. Rates are 110€ to 130€ double, including a breakfast buffet.

For hearty, reasonably priced Austrian cuisine, head to the restaurant of the **Weisses Rössl,** described above. Up on the first floor, this old-fashioned restaurant with a covered outdoor terrace offers an English menu with photographs of Schnitzel, *Gröstl* (a local stew made of potatoes, beef, and onions), and other meals costing 9€ to 18€. Be sure to top off your meal with homemade Apfelstrudel. It's open Monday to Saturday 11:30am to 2:30pm and 6 to 10pm; it's closed for 2 weeks in April and November.

For a splurge, there's no better place for a taste of Tyrolean history and cuisine than the atmospheric medieval-era **Ottoburg** ★, Herzog-Friedrich-Strasse 1 (© **0512/58 43 38**), in the Altstadt between the Goldenes Dachl and the Inn River. First mentioned in 12th-century documents, when it was listed as an apartment house (Maximilian lived here for a year), it was converted to a restaurant 150 years ago. The building is topped by a 1494 Gothic tower and contains four intimate dining rooms with carved wooden ceilings and neo-Gothic decor. In summer, there's outdoor seating on the Altstadt's most famous pedestrian lane. Local and house specialties on the English menu include Gulasch, Wiener schnitzel, and Ottoburg pork filet and steak with an herb sauce and Austrian-style gnocchi, with meals costing 13€ to 27€. It's open Tuesday to Sunday from 11:30am to 2pm and 6 to 10pm, closed 2 weeks in January.

If you're tired of the hearty and somewhat heavy Austrian cuisine, try the **Cammerlander,** Innrain 2 (© **0512/58 63 98**), conveniently located beside the Inn River and offering an outdoor terrace in summer with a view of the mountains. It serves a variety of international dishes, including pizza, pasta, salads (including a salad bar), Schnitzel, fish, Japanese-style noodles, steaks, and more, with most dishes priced 7.90€ to 19€. It's open daily 11:30am to midnight.

A Leap of Faith

Less than a mile from the center of Innsbruck, easily reached by the Sightseer bus and then funicular (8.50€ adults, 4€ children), looms the sleek, futuristic-looking **Bergisel** (© **0512/589 259**; www.bergisel.info). Its raison d'être is its famous ski jump, first built in 1925, but the new tower also beckons with an observatory and the Café im Turm, offering continental food, snacks, and desserts. Enclosed by glass on three sides, the cafe boasts panoramic views of Innsbruck, lofty mountain peaks, the ski jump, and, at the bottom of the hill, Innsbruck's largest cemetery. Bergisl is open daily 9am to 5pm (9:30am–6pm in summer).

Shopping

On their home turf, you can purchase such Tyrolean specialties as lederhosen, dirndls, leather clothing, woodcarvings, loden cloth, and all sorts of skiing and mountain-climbing equipment. Stroll around such shopping streets as the **Maria-Theresien-Strasse,** the **Herzog-Friedrich-Strasse,** and the **Museumsstrasse,** ducking in and making discoveries of your own.

Here are two recommendations if you're seeking something special:

Tiroler Heimatwerk, Meraner Strasse 2 (✆ **0512/58 23 20**), is one of the best stores in Innsbruck for such handcrafted Tyrolean items as sculpture, pewter, textiles, woolen goods, hand-knitted sweaters, lace, and bolts of silk for do-it-yourselfers. You can purchase regionally inspired fabrics and dress patterns, which you can whip into a dirndl (or whatever) as soon as you get home. Also for sale are carved chests, mirror frames, and furniture.

Zillertaler Trachtenwelt, Brixner Strasse 4 (✆ **0512/58 09 11**), is the closest thing you'll find to a department store in Innsbruck devoted to regional Tyrolean dress. Most of the goods are made in Austria, including a full array of lederhosen, coats, dresses, dirndls, and accessories for men, women, and children. Be sure to check out the basement as well.

Nightlife

The **Tiroler Landestheater,** Rennweg 2 (✆ **0512/52 07 44;** www.landestheater. at), is Innsbruck's most important venue for performances of opera, operetta, and theater. Tickets for opera run 9.50€ to 55€, with standing room tickets from 3€ to 5€. The box office is open Monday to Saturday 8:30am to 7pm and, on night of performances, Sunday and holidays 5:30 to 7pm.

For an evening of Tyrolean entertainment, including traditional music, yodeling, and folk dancing, see the **Tiroler Abend** (✆ **0512/263 263;** www.tirolerabend. info), held in the Gasthaus Sandwirt am Inn, Reichenauerstrasse 151. Held daily at 8:30pm May through October, it costs 27€, including a free drink, or 43€ with a three-course dinner and drink.

South of the Altstadt is a very popular microbrewery, **Theresien-Bräu,** Maria-Theresien-Strasse 51 (✆ **0512/58 75 80**). It offers an Austrian menu and is open Monday to Wednesday 10am to 1am, Thursday to Saturday 10am to 2am, and Sunday 10am to midnight. Nearby, at Maria-Theresien-Strasse 9, is **Limerick Bill's Irish Pub** (✆ **0512/58 20 11**), a popular tri-level gathering place for English speakers; it's open daily 4pm to 6am.

In summer, there's no finer place to be—judging by the crowds—than the **Hofgarten Cafe** (✆ **0512/58 88 71**), located in the Hofgarten just north of the Altstadt and offering indoor and outdoor seating and live music. Many natives make it a tradition to stop off for a beer after work—and then perhaps another, and another. In summer, it's open daily 11am to 2am; in winter, hours are Tuesday to Saturday 6pm to 2am.

BELGIUM

The home of continental Europe's first railway, built way back in 1835, Belgium has one of Europe's most extensive rail networks—nearly 2,200 miles (3,500km) of track. About the size of Maryland and with 10 million inhabitants, Belgium is a small country, but not so small that if you blink you'll have missed it—it does take almost 4 hours to cross by train, after all. But it's compact enough that a couple of hours of riding the rails will get you from the capital, Brussels, to just about any corner of the realm you care to mention. Yet the variety of culture, language, history, and cuisine crammed into this small space would do credit to a country many times its size, making this the ideal destination for the rail traveler on a tight time budget.

4

Belgium's diversity is a product of its location at Europe's cultural cross-roads. The boundary between the Continent's Germanic north and Latin south cuts clear across the country's middle, leaving Belgium divided into two major ethnic regions, Dutch-speaking Flanders in the north and French-speaking Wallonia in the south. (No matter where you end up on your journey, however, you'll likely find someone who speaks English.)

The country stands at the crossroads of some of Europe's major rail networks and serves as a major hub for international train travel. If you're planning a grand jaunt across the Continent, Belgium makes an easy and convenient transfer point—don't miss it.

Highlights of Belgium

Because **Brussels** has Belgium's only real international airport and is the country's rail net hub, it's likely you'll visit this centrally located city first. That's not a bad proposition. Brussels may not be the Continent's most exciting city, but the "capital of Europe" has its fair share of history and world-class attractions, and much to savor when it comes to dining and drinking. If you can set aside a few days for Belgium on your rail trip, devoting one to Brussels will be time well spent, though ideally you need 2 or 3 days to do the place any kind of justice.

If, instead, you want to head straight to a historic Flemish city of art and culture, you can do no better than **Bruges.** Art, history, and Gothic architecture are what this marvel of a city is all about. It's less than an hour from Brussels by train and is small enough to be doable in a day, if all you want is to soak up the atmosphere and visit a few of its highlights.

Ghent and **Antwerp** are even closer to Brussels than Bruges. Though these two handsome Flemish cities can't boast as much sheer old-fash-ioned charm as Bruges, each one is brimming with art and history yet has far less of a tourist-swamped, museum-exhibit setting.

To compete with the Flemish art cities and the Flanders region's North Sea coast, the Wallonia region offers fresh air and scenic landscapes in the Ardennes and the Meuse River valley. Sadly, the sparsely populated Ardennes has few rail lines, and travel by bus is slow. You really need your own transportation there and the time to take advantage of it. For a taste of francophone Belgium, a day trip to a Meuse River city like **Liège** is an acceptable substitute easily done by train from Brussels.

As a final option, a fairly easy side trip is **Luxembourg.** The Grand Duchy may be a pocket-size nation, but size isn't everything. Its capital, Luxembourg City, is one of Europe's small, hidden gems—off the beaten track, but worth a visit in its own right.

ESSENTIALS

Getting There

Carriers with flights to Brussels from North America include **Air Canada** (© 888/247-2262; www.aircanada.ca), **American Airlines** (© 800/433-7300; www.aa.com), **Continental Airlines** (© 800/231-0856; www.continental.com), **Delta** (© 800/241-4141; www.delta.com), **United** (© 800/538-2929; www.united.com), and **US Airways** (© 800/428-4322; www.usairways.com).

A major event in Brussels is the **Omme-gang,** a historic pageant that takes place on the Grand-Place on the first Tuesday and Thursday in July. It represents the "joyous entry" into Brussels of Emperor Charles V and his entourage in 1549. For more information, contact **Brussels International Tourism & Congress** (© **02/513-89-40**).

A striking spectacle that should not be missed if you're in town when it's on is the **Carpet of Flowers,** on the Grand-Place, Brussels. During this event—held in mid-August in even-numbered years—the historic square is carpeted with two-thirds of a million begonias arranged in a kind of tapestry. Contact **Brussels International Tourism & Congress** (© **02/513-89-40**).

Finally, if you're in Bruges on Ascension Day (5th Thurs after Easter), don't miss the **Procession of the Holy Blood.** A relic of the blood of Christ is carried through the streets, while costumed characters act out biblical scenes. Contact **Toerisme Brugge** (© **050/44-46-46**).

Brussels Airport (© **0900/70-000** in Belgium, or 02/753-77-53 from abroad; www.brusselsairport.be), at Zaventem, 7 miles (11km) northeast of the city center, is Belgium's principal airport and handles virtually all the country's international flights. From here there is direct train service to Brussels, where you can travel onward to Bruges, Ghent, Antwerp, and all other points in Belgium, as well as to Paris, Amsterdam, and Cologne. There's a desk of **Brussels International Tourism & Congress** (© **02/513-89-40;** www.brusselsinternational.be) in the Arrivals Hall.

Belgium by Rail

Four different kinds of high-speed trains zip into Belgium from neighboring countries: The **Eurostar** linking Great Britain to the Continent runs from London to Brussels in 2 hours; **Thalys** links Brussels, Antwerp, Liège, and other Belgian cities with Paris, Amsterdam, and Cologne (trip times to Brussels from these three cities are, respectively, 1 hr., 20 min.; 1 hr., 45 min.; and 1 hr., 47 min.); **ICE** trains speed into Brussels from Cologne (1 hr., 45 min); and **TGV** trains arrive in Brussels from around France. In addition, Belgium is linked to most European capitals by slower **EuroCity (EC)** and other international trains.

Although one or more high-speed services stop at several Belgian cities, distances inside the country are so short and local trains fast enough that using the fast-movers is rarely worth the additional expense and ticket regulations. Besides, all important tourist destinations in Belgium can be reached easily in a day trip by train from Brussels on the excellent rail network of the **Société Nationale des Chemins de Fer Belges/SNCB,** also known as NMBS in Dutch (Belgian Railways; © **02/528-28-28;** www.b-rail.be). There are the fast and comfortable **InterCity (IC)** trains, the somewhat slower and less comfortable **Inter-Regional (IR)** trains, and the **Local (L)** trains that stop at every station on the way and can get uncomfortable over long distances (or what passes for long distances in Belgium).

Note that many train stations around the country have bicycles for rent.

PASSES

For details on purchasing multicountry options, such as the **Eurail Pass,** see chapter 2. The **Benelux Pass** allows 5 days of unlimited travel in 1 month in Belgium, the Netherlands, and Luxembourg for $221 in second class and $325 in first class.

4

Essentials

BELGIUM

Two to five adults traveling together should purchase instead the **Benelux Saverpass,** to benefit from a discount of around 18%. For passengers ages 12 to 25, the **Benelux Youth Pass** (available in second class only) costs $148. Children ages 4 to 11 pay around half the adult fare, and children ages 3 and under 4 ride free, so long as they share a seat or berth with an adult. These passes must be purchased in North America and can be obtained from **Rail Europe** (*C* **888/438-7245** in the United States, *C* **800/361-7245** in Canada; www.raileurope.com) or through your travel agent.

Valid only in Belgium, and available from train stations in Belgium, the **Rail Pass** is valid for 10 single journeys anywhere on the Belgian Railways network (except for stations at international borders), for 74€ in second class and 113€ in first class. The same pass for passengers ages 4 to 25 (traveling in second class only) is called a **Go Pass** and costs 50€.

In addition to Belgian Railways's regular one-way (*billet simple/enkele reis*) and round-trip (*aller et retour/retour*) tickets, look for discounted **B-Excursion** and **Weekend Ticket** options. These various tickets are valid only in Belgium and can be purchased only at train stations and other sales points in Belgium.

Note: Tickets should be purchased onboard Belgian trains only if the station where you board has no sales point; if you were merely in too much of a hurry, you need to inform the train conductor before boarding or immediately after, in which case your ticket will cost an additional 3€. The fine for riding a train without a valid ticket is 13€ when paid on the spot, and 60€ for adults and 30€ for minors, when paid within 14 days, plus the fare.

FOREIGN TRAIN TERMS

A train is *un train* in French and a *trein* in Dutch. Class is *classe* in French and *klas* in Dutch. Second class is *deuxième classe/tweede klas,* and first class is *premier classe/ eerste klas.* A station is a *gare/station.* In big cities like Brussels and Antwerp, which have more than one station, the main station is called *Gare Centrale/Centraal Station* (Central Station). Platform is *quai/spoor* (in Dutch, it rhymes with "boar").

In French, departure and arrival are pretty easy: *départ* and *arrivée.* In Dutch, you'll need to get by with *vertrek* and *aankomst* (announcements are also made in English in the most important stations). Information is *Renseignements* in French and *Informatie* in Dutch.

PRACTICAL TRAIN INFORMATION

Belgian trains are often crowded, and because reservations for individual passengers are not available, it makes sense not to travel during peak hours, when you may need to stand (reservations are available on international trains). On the other hand, distances between stations are short, and a bunch of people are sure to get out at whatever the next one is, so you could just wait and grab a seat when it becomes vacant.

All trains, even the smallest, have a first-class section or cars. Smoking is forbidden both on trains and in stations.

Due to the country's small size, no Belgian trains have restaurant cars (international trains generally do), but on long-distance InterCity trains, an attendant pushes around a small cart, from which coffee, tea, mineral water, sandwiches, potato chips, and other snacky items are dispensed. These cost more than the same things bought from a supermarket, so if you are on a tight budget, buy them before traveling. Similarly, a lack of long-distance lines means there are no sleeper cars on trains within Belgium.

Some trains, employed most often during rush hours in urban areas, are doubledeckers; these often get very crowded, but an upstairs window seat affords a great view of whatever there is to be seen.

Train Frequency & Travel Times in Belgium*

	Ghent	Antwerp	Bruges	Liège
Time	35 min.	34 min.	1 hr., 2 min.	58 min.
Train frequency**	4	4	2	3

* Travel times are calculated using Brussels Gare Centrale as the departure point and assume you'll be traveling by the fastest InterCity train.

** Frequency is average number of trains out of Brussels Gare Centrale per hour during daytime (for Ghent, Antwerp, and Liège, these may include slower InterRegional [IR] and Local [L] trains).

Note that Belgium has two main national languages, French and Dutch (there's also a small community of German speakers who provide a third national language). Depending on where you are in the country, a station might be listed or announced using a name you are not familiar with. Station name boards are written in the local language, except in Brussels, where they are in both French and Dutch. The following are some common examples:

English	French	Dutch
Brussels	Bruxelles	Brussel
Bruges	Bruges	Brugge
Ghent	Gand	Gent
Antwerp	Anvers	Antwerpen
Liège	Liège	Luik
Ostend	Ostende	Oostende
Namur	Namur	Namen
Ypres	Ypres	Ieper

[FastFACTS] BELGIUM

Area Codes When making phone calls within Belgium (and this includes calling another number within the same area code), you always need to dial the area codes shown in this chapter. The area code for Brussels is **02.** Other area codes are: Bruges **050,** Ghent **09,** Antwerp **03,** Liège **04.** Luxembourg has no area codes; when calling a local number from anywhere within the Grand Duchy, you need only dial the local number.

Business Hours Banks are generally open Monday to Friday from 9am to 1pm and 2 to 4:30 or 5pm, and some branches are also open on Saturday morning. Stores generally are open Monday to Saturday from 10am to 6pm, though some also are open on Sunday. Most department stores stay open on Friday to 8 or 9pm.

Climate Belgium's climate is moderate, with few extremes in temperature in either summer or winter. It rains a lot. You're well advised to pack a fold-up umbrella at any time of year. Likewise, carry a raincoat (with a wool liner for winter). Temperatures are lowest in December and January, when they average 42°F (6°C), and highest in July and August, when they average 73°F (23°C). Pack a sweater or two (even in July) and be prepared to layer your clothing at any time of year. Don't worry: May through October, you're allowed to leave some space for T-shirts, skimpy tops, and sneakers.

Documents Required For stays of up to 3 months, U.S. and Canadian citizens need only have a valid passport. For stays longer than 3 months, a visa is required.

Electricity Belgium runs on 230 (220–240) volts electricity (North America uses 110 volts). So for any small appliance, you need to take a small voltage transformer (available in drug and appliance stores and by mail order) that plugs into the round-holed European electrical outlet and converts the Belgian voltage from 230 volts down to 110 volts.

Embassies These are both in Brussels. **U.S.:** bd. du Régent 27 (✆ **02/811-40-00;** www.usembassy.be; Métro: Arts-Loi). **Canada:** av. de Tervueren 2 (✆ **02/741-06-11;** www.canada international.gc.ca/belgium-belgique/index.aspx; Métro: Merode).

Health & Safety For day or night emergency medical service in Brussels, call **Médi Garde** (✆ **02/479-18-18**) or **SOS Médecins** (✆ **02/513-02-02**); for emergency dental service, call ✆ **02/426-10-26.** For both prescription and non-prescription medicines, go to a pharmacy (*pharmacie* in French; *apotheek* in Dutch). Regular pharmacy hours are Monday to Saturday from 9am to 6pm (some close earlier on Sat). Each pharmacy has a list of late-night and weekend pharmacies posted on its door; schedules are also available by calling ✆ **0900/10-500** or heading online to www. pharmacie.be.

Holidays January 1 (New Year's Day), Easter Sunday and Monday, May 1 (Labor Day), Ascension Day, Pentecost Sunday and Monday, July 21 (Independence Day), August 15 (Assumption Day), November 1 (All Saints' Day), November 11 (World War I Armistice Day), and December 25 (Christmas). In Flanders

only, July 11 is Flemish Community Day. In Wallonia only, September 27 is French Community Day.

Mail Postage for a priority-mail *(Prior)* postcard or standard letter to the U.S. and Canada is 1.15€, and for nonpriority mail 1.05€.

Police & Emergencies For emergency police assistance, call ✆ **101;** for an ambulance or the fire department, ✆ **100.**

Taxes On top of a 16% service charge, there's a value-added tax (TVA) of 6% on hotel bills and 21% on restaurant bills. The higher rate is charged on purchased goods, too. If you spend over 125€ in some stores and you are not a resident in a European Union country, you can recover it from some stores by having the official receipt stamped by Belgian Customs on departure and returning the stamped receipt to the store. Your refund should arrive by check or be credited to your credit card within a few weeks. Not all stores participate in this scheme, so it pays to ask first, particularly for major purchases.

Telephone **To call Belgium:** If you're calling from the United States, dial the international access code (011), followed by the country code for Belgium (32), then the area code (2 for Brussels) and the number. So the whole number you'd dial would be **011-32-2-000-0000.**

To make international calls: To make international calls from Belgium, first dial

00 and then the country code (U.S. and Canada 1). Next you dial the area code and number.

For information in English, both in Belgium and international, dial ✆ **1405.**

You can use pay phones with a Belgacom *télécarte* (phone card), which costs 5€, 10€, and 25€ from post offices, train ticket counters, tourist information offices, some tobacconists, and newsstands. Some pay phones take credit cards. A few pay phones take coins, of .10€, .20€, .50€, 1€, and 2€.

To charge a call to your calling card, dial **AT&T** (✆ **0800/100-10**), **MCI** (✆ **0800/100-12**), **Sprint** (✆ **0800/100-14**), or **Canada Direct** (✆ **0800/100-19**).

Tipping The prices on most restaurant menus already include a service charge of 16%, so it's unnecessary to tip. If service is good, however, it's usual to show appreciation with a tip. It's enough to round up the bill to the nearest convenient amount, if you wish, rather than leave a full-fledged tip. Otherwise, 10% is adequate (and more than most Belgians would leave). Service is included in your hotel bill as well. Taxis include the tip in the meter reading. You can round up the fare, if you like, but need not add a tip unless you have received an extra service like help with luggage. For other services: Leave 20% for hairdressers (with the cashier when you pay up) and 1€ to 2€ per piece of luggage for porters.

BRUSSELS

A city with a notable history, Brussels is carving out a bright future for itself and is unquestionably the place to start your train journey through Belgium. The "capital of Europe" has begun to act like Europe's Washington, D.C., a focus of economic and political power, where decisions are made that affect the lives of people around the world. Headquarters of the European Union (E.U.), Brussels both symbolizes the Continent's vision of unity and is a bastion of officialdom, a breeding ground for the regulations that govern and often exasperate the rest of Europe.

Bruxellois have ambivalent feelings about their city's transformation into a power center. At first, the waves of Eurocrats brought a new cosmopolitan air to a somewhat provincial city, but old neighborhoods have been leveled to make way for office towers, leaving people wondering whether Brussels is losing its soul. After all, this city doesn't only mean politics and business—it helped inspire surrealism and Art Nouveau, worships comic strips, prides itself on handmade lace and chocolate, and serves each one of its craft beers in its own unique glass.

Fortunately, not all of Brussels's individuality has been lost in this transition, and though the urban landscape has suffered from wanton "development," the city's spirit survives in traditional cafes, bars, bistros, and restaurants. Whether elegantly Art Nouveau or eccentrically festooned with posters, curios, and knickknacks, such centuries-old establishments provide a warm, convivial ambience that is peculiarly Belgian.

Station Information

GETTING FROM THE AIRPORT TO THE TRAIN STATION

Brussels Airport Express trains depart from Brussels Airport (see "Getting There," earlier in this chapter) to the capital's Gare du Nord, Gare Centrale, and Gare du Midi stations every 15 minutes or so between 5:30am and 11:30pm, for a one-way fare of 6.70€ in first class and 5.10€ in second class. The ride is free if you hold a validated train pass. Most airport trains have wide corridors and extra space for baggage and are the best and easiest way into town. The ride to Gare Centrale takes 16 minutes with the fastest trains.

You'll find **taxi** stands in front of the airplane terminal building, if you prefer to head into town that way. All taxis from the airport are metered. Expect to pay around 35€ to get to the center city.

INSIDE THE STATIONS

Brussels has three major train stations. High-speed Eurostar trains from London; Thalys from Paris, Amsterdam, and Cologne; TGV from France; and ICE from Germany arrive at the city's main station, **Bruxelles-Midi/Brussel-Zuid,** rue de France, south of the city center. A few blocks from the Grand-Place, **Bruxelles-Central/Brussel-Centraal,** Carrefour de l'Europe, is the station closest to many attractions in the city center. **Bruxelles Nord/Brussel-Noord,** rue du Progrès, is north of the center of town. Trains arriving from around Belgium generally stop at all three stations.

Boards and screens provide constantly updated train departure and arrival information. Note that Bruxelles-Central does not have a train information desk, and you cannot make train reservations or validate a railpass here. Bruxelles-Central and Bruxelles-Midi have room reservations desks that do not accept phone bookings. Tourist information is available in the main hall at Bruxelles-Midi station.

All three stations offer currency exchange, luggage storage, waiting rooms, fast-food restaurants, bars, cafes, snack kiosks, and stores, with Bruxelles-Midi being the best-outfitted in all these services.

Note: Watch out for pickpockets and for your bags, in particular at Bruxelles-Midi, but at the other two stations as well. The environs of Bruxelles-Midi have been popular with muggers preying on international travelers, and though this is less of a problem than it once was, it might still be better to access and depart the station by public transportation or taxi than on foot. The north exit from Bruxelles-Nord leads into Brussels's scuzzy red-light district and is best avoided; the south exit has some slightly classier red-light haunts mixed in with upmarket hotels and modern office towers and is generally okay.

Both Bruxelles-Midi and Bruxelles-Nord have stops for tram (streetcar) lines and a bus station; Bruxelles-Central has an adjacent Métro (subway) station and multiple bus stops outside. All three stations have taxi stands outside.

Information Elsewhere in the City

The most central city office of **Brussels International Tourism & Congress** is at the Hôtel de Ville (Town Hall), on the Grand-Place (✆ **02/513-89-40;** www.brussels international.be; Métro: Gare Centrale; Apr–Oct daily 9am–6pm; Nov–Dec Mon–Sat 9am–6pm, Sun 10am–2pm; Jan–Mar Mon–Sat 9am–6pm). Other offices are at rue Royale 2 (tram: 92 or 94; daily 10am–6pm), and at rue Wiertz 43, in the European District (bus: 22 or 54; Mon 1–5pm, Tues–Thurs 9am–5pm, Fri 9am–noon).

Getting Around

Once in town, your feet are almost always the best way to get around, and the center of town is small enough to allow you to use your own leg power. Be sure to wear good walking shoes, as those charming cobblestones on the sidewalks and streets will get under your soles and onto your nerves after a while. When crossing the street, watch out for trams and bikes.

Maps of the integrated public transit network—Métro, tram, and bus—are available free from the tourist office; from offices of the public transportation company, **STIB,** Galérie de la Toison d'Or 15 (✆ **070/23-20-00;** www.stib.be); and from the Porte de Namur, Rogier, and Gare du Midi Métro stations. In addition, all stations and most tram and bus stops have transit maps. The full system operates from 6am to midnight, after which a limited night-bus service takes over.

The **Métro** (subway) net covers the center city and reaches out to the suburbs and to the Bruparck recreation zone in the north of town. Stations are identified by signs with a white letter m on a blue background. An extensive network of **tram** (streetcar) lines provides the ideal way to get around the city. Trams are generally faster and more comfortable than **buses.**

A one-ride ticket costs 2€ when purchased from tram and bus drivers, and 1.70€ when purchased before boarding. It costs 7.30€ for a five-ride ticket, 12€ for a 10-ride ticket, 4.50€ for a 1-day ticket, and 9.50€ for a 3-day ticket. The 5-ride, 10-ride, and 1-day tickets cannot be purchased onboard trams or buses of the STIB city transit authority, but only from sales points and ticket machines; they can, however, be purchased onboard buses of the regional transit companies De Lijn and TEC that have stops inside the city limits. The 3-day ticket can be used only with STIB and must be purchased before boarding. Finally, whatever ticket you want, if you plan to use it on Métro trains, you must purchase it before boarding.

Brussels

ACCOMMODATIONS ■
Albert **10**
Brussels Welcome Hotel **7**
Floris Arlequin
 Grand-Place **15**
Hotel George V **2**
Hotel Métropole **8**
Hotel Mozart **20**
Hotel Sabina **11**
Le Dixseptième **23**

DINING ◆
Au Vieux Bruxelles **27**
In 't Spinnekopke **3**
La Manufacture
 Restaurant **1**
L'Auberge des
 Chapeliers **22**
Restaurant de l'Ogenblik **14**
Restaurant François **6**
Restaurant 't Kelderke **19**
Scheltema Brasserie
 Restaurant **13**

ATTRACTIONS ●
Atomium **5**
Cathédrale des Sts-Michel-
 et-Gudule **12**
Centre Belge de la
 Bande-Dessinée **9**
Grand-Place **16**
Hôtel de Ville **18**
Manneken-Pis **21**
Mini-Europe **4**
Musée de la Ville
 de Bruxelles **17**
Musées Royaux des Beaux-
 Arts de Belgique **25**
Palais Royal **26**
Parc de Bruxelles **24**

4

BELGIUM | Brussels

Bruxelles-Nord

quai de Willebroek

av. de l'Héliport

Yser
place de l'Yser

bd. d'Ypres

chaussée d'Anvers

Jacqmain

rue du Marché

rue du Progrès

bd. Baudouin

bd. St-Lazare

place Rogier

Rogier

bd. du Jardin Botanique

quai au Foin

rue de Laeken

rue du Pélican

bd. Émile

bd. Adolphe Max

rue Neuve

rue du Marais

bd. Pacheco

Botanique

place de la Reine

rue Verte

rue de la Poste

rue Royale

chaussée de Haecht

rue Van Dyck

rue du Moulin

rue Tiberghien

rue du Méridien

rue de la Limite

rue Potagère

Fish Market Square (Marché-aux-Poissons)

quai au Bois à Brûler

quai aux Briques

rue de Flandre

Sainte-Catherine

7

6

place Ste-Catherine

place de Brouckère

De Brouckère

8

place de la Monnaie

place des Martyrs

10

9

bd. Royale

place de la Liberté

11

Madou

chaussée de Louvain

bd. Bischoffsheim

Théâtre Royal de la Monnaie

Galeries Royales St-Hubert

rue de l'Écuyer

rue des Bouchers

bd. de Berlaimont

rue de la Croix de Fer

rue de Louvain

av. des Arts

rue Marie-Thérèse

place de la Bourse

Bourse

rue du Midi

i

15

17 16

i

Grand-Place

18

19

20

21

rue du Lombard

22

place St-Jean

23

place de l'Albertine

BOZAR

13

14

12

Palais de la Nation

Parc

rue de la Loi

Gare Centrale

Bruxelles-Central

PARC DE BRUXELLES

24

Arts-Loi

rue de la Loi

rue Joseph II

rue du Commerce

EUROPEAN UNION DISTRICT

rue Belliard

bd. Anspach

rue du Chêne

rue des Alexiens

bd. de l'Empereur

25

UPPER TOWN

place du Grand-Sablon

place de la Chapelle

rue du Miroir

rue des Capucins

rue Haute

rue de Minimes

rue Allard

rue de la Régence

place du Petit-Sablon

place Poelaert

Palais de Justice

rue aux Laines

bd. de Waterloo

Louise

rue Jourdan

av. de la Toison d'Or

av. Louise

place Royale

Palais Royal

place des Palais

bd. du Régent

av. des Arts

Trône

rue de l'Industrie

rue de Luxembourg

rue de Namur

Porte de Namur

IXELLES

bd. de Waterloo

rue des Strassart

rue des Chevaliers

chaussée

rue du Prince Royal

rue Concorde d'Ixelles

rue de la Science

rue Montoyer

d'Arlon

place du Luxembourg

rue du Trône

rue Sans-So

rue Goffart

135

You validate your ticket by inserting it into the orange electronic machines that stand inside buses and trams and at the access to Métro platforms. Though the ticket must be revalidated each time you enter a new vehicle, you are allowed multiple transfers within a 1-hour period of the initial validation, so you can hop on and off Métro trains, trams, and buses during that time, and only one journey will be deducted from your card by the electronic scanner. If more than one person is traveling on one ticket, the ticket must be validated each time for each traveler. Children under 12 ride free on the STIB transit network.

STIB has introduced an electronic stored-value card, the **MOBIB,** available from KIOSK and BOOTIK sales points at some rail and Métro stations. It is more complicated to purchase and use this card compared with the ordinary tickets detailed above and, for short-stay visitors, may currently not be worth the extra hassle. Still, there's a saving of around 10% over the price of ordinary tickets, for those ticket classes that have a MOBIB option.

Taxi fares start at 2.40€ from 6am to 10pm, and at 4.40€ between 10pm and 6am, increasing by 1.35€ a kilometer inside the city (tariff 1) and 2.70€ a kilometer outside (tariff 2)—make sure the meter is set to the correct tariff. Taxis cannot be hailed on the street, but there are stands at prominent locations around town. Call **Taxis Bleus** (🕿 **02/268-00-00**), **Taxi Orange** (🕿 **02/349-49-49**), or **Taxis Verts** (🕿 **02/349-49-49**). You can round up the fare if you like, but you need not add an extra tip unless there has been extra service, such as helping with heavy luggage.

Where to Stay

Albert ★ 🍴   A modern hotel next to the bronze-domed 19th-century Eglise Royale Ste-Marie and close to an enclave of the most authentic Turkish restaurants in town (which should more than compensate for its lack of an in-house restaurant), Albert has clean, bright rooms with a touch of design flair and tiled bathrooms. Although the hotel is on the outer edge of the city center, trams from a nearby stop take you straight to the Royal Palace, the Royal Museums of Fine Arts, and the Sablon antiques district.

Rue Royale-Ste-Marie 27–29 (off place de la Reine), 1030 Bruxelles. 🕿 **02/217-93-91.** Fax 02/219-20-17. www.hotelalbert.be. 19 units. 70€–75€ double; 75€–90€ studio apartment. Rates include continental breakfast. MC, V. Tram: 25 to Lefrancq; 92 to Robiano; or 94 to Sainte-Marie. **Amenities:** Bar. *In room:* No A/C.

Brussels Welcome Hotel ★★   The smallest hotel in the center city, this little gem of a place lives up to its name in full. You can think of it as a country *auberge* (inn) in the heart of town, on the old Fish Market square. Rooms are styled on individual themes—Savannah, Provence, Japan, Thailand, India, Tibet, Bali, and Laura Ashley—and furnished and decorated from both local designer and antiques stores with what can best be described as tender loving care.

Quai au Bois à Brûler 23, 1000 Bruxelles. 🕿 **02/219-95-46.** Fax 02/217-18-87. www.hotelwelcome.com. 15 units. 95€–115€ double. Rates include buffet breakfast. AE, DC, MC, V. Métro: Ste-Catherine. **Amenities:** Lounge.

Floris Arlequin Grand-Place   You can't get closer to the heart of the city than this, with the restaurant-lined rue des Bouchers right outside the hotel's back entrance, and fine views from some rooms of the Town Hall spire on the neighboring Grand-Place, and of the Old City's rooftops and narrow medieval streets from the top-floor breakfast room. The guest rooms themselves are not quite so spectacular, but all are tastefully contemporary and most get plenty of natural light.

Rue de la Fourche 17–19, 1000 Bruxelles. 🕿 **02/514-16-15.** Fax 02/514-22-02. www.arlequin.be. 92 units. 100€–230€ double. Rates include buffet breakfast. AE, DC, MC, V. Métro: Bourse. **Amenities:** Bar; lounge.

One of the city's best discounts is the **Brussels Card,** available from the Brussels International tourist offices and from hotels, museums, and STIB city transit authority offices. Valid for 1, 2, or 3 days, the card costs 24€, 34€, and 40€, respectively. It affords free use of public transportation; free and discounted admission to 30 city museums and attractions; and discounts at restaurants and other venues, and on some guided tours.

Hôtel George V This agreeable little hotel is located on the edge of the city center, in an area that is being reborn as a trendy shopping-and-eating district. Situated in a renovated town house from 1859 within easy walking distance of the Grand-Place, the George has rooms that are plain but clean and have new furnishings.

Rue 't Kint 23 (off place du Jardin aux Fleurs), 1000 Bruxelles. ℃ **02/513-50-93.** Fax 02/513-44-93. www.hotelgeorge5.be. 17 units. 80€–100€ double. Rates include buffet breakfast. AE, MC, V. Métro: Bourse. **Amenities:** Bar.

Hôtel Métropole ★★★ An ornate marble-and-gilt interior distinguishes this late-19th-century landmark from 1895 (Brussels's sole surviving 19th-c. hotel), just a few blocks away from the Grand-Place. Soaring ceilings, potted palms, and lavishly decorated public spaces on the ground floor add to the Belle Epoque allure. The spacious rooms, some in Art Deco style, have a mix of classic and elegant modern furnishings. Both the French restaurant **L'Alban Chambon** and the **Café Métropole** are worth a visit in their own right.

Place de Brouckère 31, 1000 Bruxelles. ℃ **02/217-23-00.** Fax 02/218-02-20. www.metropolehotel.be. 298 units. 275€–450€ double. Rates include buffet or continental breakfast. AE, DC, MC, V. Métro: De Brouckère. **Amenities:** Restaurant; lounge; cafe.

Hotel Mozart Grand-Place ★ Can you guess which famous composer's music wafts through the lobby here? The Mozart is located a flight of stairs up from the busy, cheap eats at street level, a block away from the Grand-Place. Salmon-colored walls, plants, and old paintings create a warm, intimate ambience that's carried into the rooms. Furnishings are in Louis XV style, and exposed beams lend each unit a rustic originality. Several are duplexes with a sitting room underneath the loft bedroom. Top rooms afford great views.

Rue du Marché aux Fromages 23, 1000 Bruxelles. ℃ **02/502 66-61.** Fax 02/502-77-58. www.hotel-mozart.be. 50 units. 100€–150€ double. AE, DC, MC, V. Métro: Gare Centrale. **Amenities:** Lounge.

Hotel Sabina This small hostelry off place des Barricades is like a private residence, presided over by hospitable owners. A grandfather clock in the reception area and polished wood along the restaurant walls give it a warm, homey atmosphere. Rooms vary in size, but all are comfortable and simply yet tastefully done in modern style with twin beds. Three rooms have kitchenettes.

Rue du Nord 78, 1000 Bruxelles. ℃ **02/218-26-37.** Fax 02/219-32-39. www.hotelsabina.eu. 24 units. 60€–90€ double. Rates include buffet breakfast. AE, DC, MC, V. Métro: Madou.

Le Dixseptième ★★ This graceful, 17th-century house was once the Spanish ambassador's official residence and stands close to the Grand-Place in a neighborhood of restored dwellings. Rooms have wood paneling and marble chimneys and are as big as suites in many hotels; some have balconies. All are in 18th-century style and are named after Belgian painters from Bruegel to Magritte. Two elegant lounges are decorated with carved wooden medallions and 18th-century paintings.

Rue de la Madeleine 25, 1000 Bruxelles. (©) **02/517-17-17.** Fax 02/502-64-24. www.ledixseptieme.be. 24 units. 100€–200€ double. Rates include buffet breakfast. AE, DC, MC, V. Métro: Gare Centrale. **Amenities:** Lounge.

Top Attractions & Special Moments

THE GRAND-PLACE ★★★

Ornamental gables, medieval banners, gilded facades, sunlight flashing off gold-fili-greed rooftop sculptures, a general impression of harmony and timelessness—there's a lot to take in all at once when you first enter the **Grand-Place** (Métro: Gare Centrale or Bourse), a World Heritage Site. Its present composition dates mostly from the late 1690s, but the Town Hall dates from the early 1400s. Don't miss the cafes lodged within the opulent wooden interiors of old guild houses; their upper-floor windows overlooking the Grand-Place afford some of the best views in Europe.

And be sure to take in the *son-et-lumière* (see "Special Brussels Experiences, below) on summer evenings on the Grand-Place. Or stop by at noon, when the Maison du Roi's tower bells play golden carillon chimes reminiscent of an earlier European era.

THE PRINCIPAL MUSEUMS

Musée de la Ville de Bruxelles (Museum of the City of Brussels) ★★   In
the neo-Gothic Maison du Roi, this museum documents the history of Brussels. Among the most fascinating displays are old paintings and modern scale reconstructions of the historic center, including some that depict activity along the now-vanished Senne River. There also are exhibits on traditional arts and crafts, such as tapestry and lace. The museum's pride, however, is its collection of 780 costumes—including an Elvis outfit—donated to clothe Brussels's famous *Manneken-Pis* statue (see "Key Monuments & Public Buildings," below), each equipped with a strategically positioned orifice so that the little sculpture's normal function is not impaired.

Grand-Place 1. (©) **02/279-43-50.** www.brucity.be. Admission 3€ adults, 2.50€ seniors and students, 1.50€ travelers with limited mobility and children 6–15, children 5 and under free. Tues–Sun 10am–5pm. Métro: Bourse.

Musées Royaux des Beaux-Arts de Belgique (Royal Museums of Fine Arts of Belgium) ★★★   In a vast museum of several buildings at place Royale,
this complex combines the **Musée d'Art Ancien** and the **Musée d'Art Moderne** under one roof (connected by a passage). The collection shows off works, most of them Belgian, from the 14th to the 20th centuries, including Hans Memling's portraits from the late 15th century, which are marked by sharp lifelike details; works by Hieronymus Bosch; and Lucas Cranach's *Adam and Eve*. Be sure to seek out the rooms featuring Pieter Bruegel, including his *Adoration of the Magi* and *Fall of Icarus*. Don't miss his unusual *Fall of the Rebel Angels*, with grotesque faces and beasts. But don't fear—many of Bruegel's paintings, such as those depicting Flemish village life, are of a less fiery nature. Later artists represented include Rubens, Van Dyck, Frans Hals, and Rembrandt.

Next door, in a circular building connected to the main entrance, the modern art section has an emphasis on underground works—if only because the museum's eight

SPECIAL Brussels EXPERIENCES

o **Watching the Son-et-Lumière on Summer Evenings in the Grand-Place.** This sound-and-light show in which a series of colored lamps on the Hôtel de Ville (Town Hall) are switched on and off in sequence to a piece of appropriately grand music is admittedly kind of kitsch. But who cares? It's also magical.

o **Snapping Up a Bargain at the Flea Market.** Each day, from 7am to 2pm, the Marché aux Puces on place du Jeu de Balle in the Marolles district offers everything from the weird to the wonderful at rock-bottom prices.

o **Pigging Out on Belgian Chocolates.** Those devilish little creations—handmade Belgian pralines—are so addictive they should be sold with a government health warning attached. Try the Wittamer chocolatier on place du Grand Sablon, and eat your fill.

floors are all below ground level. The overwhelming collection includes works by van Gogh, Matisse, Dalí, Tanguy, Ernst, Chagall, Miró, and local boys Magritte, Delvaux, de Braekeleer, and Permeke.

Rue de la Régence 3. (C) **02/508-32-11.** www.fine-arts-museum.be. Admission 8€ adults, 5€ seniors, 2€ students, free for children 12 and under; free for all visitors 1st Wed afternoon of the month (except special exhibits). Tues–Sun 10am–5pm. Métro: Parc.

KEY MONUMENTS & PUBLIC BUILDINGS

Two blocks from the Grand-Place, the famous *Manneken-Pis* **statue** ★, on the corner of rue du Chêne and rue de l'Etuve, is Brussels's favorite little boy, gleefully doing what a little boy's gotta do. It's known that the boy's effigy has graced the city since at least the time of Philip the Good, who became count of Flanders in 1419. Among the speculations about his origins are that he was the son of a Brussels nobleman who got lost and was found while answering nature's call, and also that he was a patriotic Belgian kid who sprinkled a hated Spanish sentry passing beneath his window. Perhaps the best theory is that he saved the Town Hall from a sputtering bomb by extinguishing it with the first thing handy.

Atomium ★ ☺ There's nothing quite like this cluster of giant spheres representing the atomic structure of an iron crystal enlarged 165 billion times. The model was constructed for the 1958 World's Fair. It rises 335 feet (102m) like a giant plaything of the gods that's fallen to earth. The view from the viewing deck is marvelous, and you can even wander around inside the spheres.

Bd. du Centenaire, Heysel. (C) **02/475-47-77.** www.atomium.be. Admission 11€ adults; 8€ students, seniors, children 12–18; free for children 11 and under. Daily 10am–6pm. Métro: Heysel.

Cathédrale des Sts-Michel-et-Gudule ★ Begun in 1226, this magnificent Gothic church, off boulevard de l'Impératrice 2 blocks west of Gare Centrale, was officially consecrated as a cathedral only in 1961. The 16th-century Emperor Charles V donated its superb stained-glass windows. Aside from these, the spare interior decoration focuses attention on its soaring columns and arches, and the bright exterior stonework makes a fine sight.

Parvis Ste-Gudule. ℂ **02/217-83-45.** www.cathedralestmichel.be. Admission: Cathedral free; crypt 1€, treasury 1€, archaeological zone 2.50€; in all cases, free for children age 13 and under. Mon–Fri 7am–7pm (Oct–Mar 6pm), Sat–Sun 8:30am–7pm (Oct–Mar 6pm); tourist visits not permitted during services Sat from 3:30pm, Sun until 2pm. Métro: Gare Centrale.

Hôtel de Ville (Town Hall) ★★ The facade of the dazzling Town Hall, dating back to 1402, shows off Gothic intricacy at its best, complete with dozens of arched windows and sculptures—some of them, such as the drunken monks, a sleeping Moor and his harem, and St. Michael slaying a female devil, display a perfectly medieval sense of humor. A 215-foot (65m) tower sprouts from the middle, yet it's not placed exactly in the center. A colorful but untrue legend has it that when the architect realized his "error," he jumped off the summit of the tower. The building is still the seat of civic government of the Brussels *commune,* and its wedding room is a popular place to tie the knot. Its spectacular Gothic Hall, open for visits when the aldermen are not in session, is replete with baroque decoration. In other chambers are 16th- to 18th-century tapestries; one depicts the Spanish duke of Alba, whose cruel features reflect the brutal oppression he imposed on the Low Countries; others show scenes from the life of Clovis, the king of the Franks.

Grand-Place. ℂ **02/279-43-65.** Admission (for guided tours in English) 3€ adults, 2.50€ seniors and students, 1.50€ children 6–15, children 5 and under free. Apr–Sept Tues–Wed 3:15pm, Sun 10:45am, 12:15pm; Oct–Mar Tues–Wed 3:15pm. Métro: Gare Centrale.

Palais Royal (Royal Palace) The palace, which overlooks the Parc de Bruxelles, was begun in 1820 and had a grandiose Louis XVI–style face-lift in 1904. The older wings date from the 18th century and are flanked by two pavilions. Today the palace is used for state receptions. It also contains the offices of King Albert II, though he and Queen Paola do not reside here.

Place des Palais. ℂ **02/551-20-20.** www.monarchie.be. Free admission. 3rd week July to late Sept (exact dates announced yearly) Tues–Sun 10:30am–4:30pm. Métro: Parc.

POPULAR CITY ATTRACTIONS

Centre Belge de la Bande-Dessinée (Belgian Center for Comic-Strip Art) ★★ ☺ Dubbed the CéBéBéDé, the center, off boulevard de Berlaimont, is dedicated to comic strips and takes a lofty view of its "Ninth Art." As icing on the cake, it's housed in a restored Art Nouveau department store from 1903, the Magasins Waucquez, designed by Victor Horta. A model of the red-and-white checkered rocket in which Tintin and Snowy flew to the Moon, long before Armstrong and Aldrin did it in mere fact, takes pride of place at the top of the elegant staircase.

 A Neat Little Park

Once a hunting preserve belonging to the dukes of Brabant, the **Parc de Bruxelles (Brussels Park),** rue Royale (Métro: Parc), between Parliament and the Royal Palace, was laid out in the 18th century as a landscaped garden. In 1830, Belgian patriots fought Dutch troops here during the War of Independence. Later it was a fashionable place to stroll and to meet friends. Although not very big, the park manages to contain everything from carefully trimmed borders to rough patches of trees and bushes, and has fine views along its main paths, which, together with the fountain, form the outline of Masonic symbols.

The working-class Marolles district is a special place where the old Brussels dialect *Brusseleir* can still be heard. It's a generally poor community, threatened by encroachment and gentrification from neighboring, wealthier areas. Most visitors to Brussels get their Marolles initiation by visiting the daily flea market on place du Jeu de Balle, which opens at 7am and closes at 2pm (take the Métro to Porte de Hal and then walk several blocks up rue Blaes). Here the weird and wonderful is commonplace. It makes a refreshing change to wander around for an hour or two in this other Brussels, a simple neighborhood of homes, welcoming cafes, and great, inexpensive restaurants.

Beyond is a comic strip wonderland. All the big names appear in a library of 30,000 books and in permanent and special exhibits, including Tintin, Asterix, Thorgal, Lucky Luke, the Smurfs, Peanuts, Andy Capp, Suske and Wiske—yes, even Superman, Batman, and the Green Lantern—along with many lesser heroes.

Rue des Sables 20. *©* **02/219-19-80.** www.cbbd.be. Admission 7.50€ adults, 6€ students and seniors, 3€ children 5-12, free for children 4 and under. Tues-Sun 10am-6pm. Métro: Gare Centrale.

Mini-Europe ★ Stroll among highlights from European Union member states, all meticulously detailed at a scale of 1:25. There's London's Big Ben, Berlin's Brandenburg Gate, the Leaning Tower of Pisa, the Bull Ring in Seville (complete with simulated sounds of fans yelling ¡Olé!), and Montmartre in Paris, as well as more modern emblems of continental achievement such as the Channel Tunnel and the Ariane rocket. Mt. Vesuvius erupts, gondolas float around the canals of Venice, and a Finnish girl dives into the icy waters of a northern lake.

Bruparck, Heysel. *©* **02/478-05-50.** www.minieurope.com. Admission 13€ adults, 9.80€ children under 13, children under 4 ft. (1.2m) accompanied by parents free. Late Mar to June and Sept daily 9:30am-6pm; July-Aug daily 9:30am-8pm (except Aug Sat-Sun 9:30am-midnight); Oct-Dec and 1st week Jan 10am-6pm. Closed rest of Jan to late Mar. Métro: Heysel.

Where to Dine

Au Vieux Bruxelles ★ BELGIAN/SEAFOOD Opened in 1882, this convivial, brasserie-style restaurant specializes in mussels, which it serves in 15 different of ways. In Belgium, the personality of the humble but tasty mussel is a staple of conversation, and people assess the quality of each year's crop with the same critical eye that other countries reserve for fine wines. Should you not wish to sample the mussels, you can get great steaks like *steak au poivre flambé* (flamed pepper steak), *escargots* (snails), and crepes.

Rue St-Boniface 35 (close to Porte Namur). *©* **02/503-31-11.** www.auvieuxbruxelles.com. Reservations not accepted. Main courses 15€-21€. AE, MC, V. Mon-Thurs 6:30-11:30pm; Fri-Sat 6:30pm-midnight; Sun noon-3pm and 6:30-11:30pm. Métro: Porte de Namur.

In 't Spinnekopke ★★ 🍴 TRADITIONAL BELGIAN Occupying a 1762 stagecoach inn off rue Van Artevelde, "In the Spider's Web" is just far enough off the beaten track downtown to be frequented mainly by those in the know. You dine in a tilting, tiled-floor building, at plain tables. This is one of Brussels's most traditional cafe/restaurants—so much so, in fact, that the menu lists its hardy standbys of regional Belgian cuisine in the old Bruxellois dialect.

4

BELGIUM | **Brussels**

Place du Jardin aux Fleurs 1. ⓒ 02/511-86-95. www.spinnekopke.be. Main courses 13€–30€; *plat du jour* 12€. AE, DC, MC, V. Mon–Fri noon–3pm and 6–11pm; Sat 6pm–midnight (bar Mon–Fri 11am–midnight; Sat 6pm–midnight). Métro: Bourse.

La Manufacture Restaurant ★ FRENCH/INTERNATIONAL   Even in its former incarnation, this place was a purveyor of style—it used to be the factory of chic Belgian leather goods maker Delvaux. Fully refurbished, with hardwood floors, leather banquettes, polished wood, and stone tables set amid iron pillars and exposed air ducts, it produces trendy world cuisine on a French foundation. On sunny days in summer, you can dine outdoors on a terrace shaded by giant bamboo plants. It's something of a hike from the Bourse Métro station, past place du Jardin aux Fleurs, but well worth the walk.

Rue Notre-Dame du Sommeil 12–20. ⓒ **02/502-25-25.** www.manufacture.be. Main courses 12€–31€; *menu du jour* (lunch only) 15€; fixed-price menus 35€–55€. AE, DC, MC, V. Mon–Fri noon–2pm and 7–11pm; Sat 7pm–midnight. Métro: Bourse.

L'Auberge des Chapeliers ★ 🍴 TRADITIONAL BELGIAN   In a 17th-century building off the Grand-Place that was once the hatmakers' guild house, the Auberge preserves its historic charm. Behind a venerable brick facade, the first two floors are graced with timber beams and paneling and connected by a narrow wooden staircase. The food is typical hearty Belgian fare, with an accent on mussels in season and dishes cooked in beer.

Rue des Chapeliers 1–3. ⓒ **02/513-73-38.** Reservations recommended on weekends. Main courses 10€–18€; set-price menus 15€–22€. AE, DC, MC, V. Mon–Thurs noon–2pm and 6–11pm; Fri noon–2pm and 6pm–midnight; Sat noon–3pm and 6pm–midnight; Sun noon–3pm and 6–11pm. Métro: Gare Centrale.

Restaurant de l'Ogenblik ★ FRENCH/BELGIAN   Set in the elegant Galeries Royales St-Hubert, this restaurant supplies good taste in a Parisian bistro-style setting. It often gets busy, but the ambience in the split-level, wood-and-brass-outfitted dining room, with a sand-strewn floor, is convivial, though a little too tightly packed when it's full. Look for garlicky meat and seafood menu dishes, and expect to pay a smidgeon more for atmosphere than might be strictly justified by results on the plate.

Galerie des Princes 1. ⓒ **02/511-61-51.** www.ogenblik.be. Main courses 23€–32€; *plat du jour* (lunch only) 11€. AE, DC, MC, V. Mon–Thurs noon–2:30pm and 7pm–midnight; Fri–Sat noon–2:30pm and 7pm–12:30am. Métro: Gare Centrale.

Restaurant François ★★ SEAFOOD   A bright and cheerful ambience complements fine cuisine at this restaurant on the ground floor of a 19th-century *maison de maître* (town house). The building has housed fishmongers since 1922, and that tradition is taken seriously. The presentation is professional yet relaxed. In fine weather, you can dine on a great sidewalk terrace across the street out on the old Fish Market square. If you're dining indoors, try to get a window table overlooking the square.

Quai aux Briques 2. ⓒ **02/511-60-89.** www.restaurantfrancois.be. Main courses 23€–58€; fixed-price menu 25€–55€. AE, DC, MC, V. Tues–Sat noon–2:30pm and 7–11:30pm. Métro: Ste-Catherine.

Restaurant 't Kelderke ★★ TRADITIONAL BELGIAN   Despite being on the Grand-Place—the square that is the focus of tourism in Brussels—this is far from being a tourist trap. As many Bruxellois as tourists throng the long wooden tables in a 17th-century, brick-arched cellar, and all are welcomed with time-honored respect. Memorable traditional Belgian fare, with little in the way of frills, is served up from an open kitchen. This is a great place to try local specialties.

Grand-Place 15. ⓒ **02/513-73-44.** www.restaurant-het-kelderke.be. Main courses 9€–27€; *plat du jour* 9€. AE, DC, MC, V. Daily noon–2am. Métro: Gare Centrale.

Scheltema Brasserie Restaurant ★ BELGIAN   This is one of those solid restaurants in the Ilot Sacré district off rue des Bouchers that keep going day in, day out, year after year, serving up much the same fare but never forgetting that quality counts. Good service and fine atmosphere complement the seafood specialties at this brasserie-style restaurant, which in some ways is similar to others in the district but always goes the extra mile in terms of class and taste.

Rue des Dominicains 7. (✆ **02/512-20-84.** www.scheltema.be. Main courses 19€–41€; seafood platter 52€. AE, DC, MC, V. Mon–Thurs noon–3pm and 6–11:30pm; Fri–Sat noon–3pm and 6pm–12:30am. Métro: Gare Centrale.

Shopping

One of Europe's oldest malls, the **Galeries Royales St-Hubert** (Métro: Gare Centrale) is a light and airy triple-galleried arcade hosting boutiques, cafe terraces, and street musicians playing classical music. Built in Italian neo-Renaissance style and opened in 1847, architect Pierre Cluysenaer's gallery offers shopping with a touch of class and is well worth strolling through even if you have no intention of shopping. The gallery is near the Grand-Place, between rue du Marché aux Herbes and rue de l'Ecuyer, and split by rue des Bouchers.

Among the finest—and most addictive—of Belgian specialties are the country's handmade pralines. Two good places to buy these are **Neuhaus,** Galerie de la Reine 25–27 (✆ **02/512-63-59;** Métro: Gare Centrale), and **Wittamer,** place du Grand Sablon 12 (✆ **02/512-37-42;** tram: 92 or 93). And while you're in sweet-tooth mode, for spicy *speculoos* cookies (made with cinnamon, ginger, and almond) and *pain à la grecque* (a thin, spicy biscuit), check out **Dandoy,** rue au Beurre 31 (✆ **02/511-03-26;** Métro: Bourse).

Lace isn't far behind as a Brussels shopping highlight. Two fine, centrally located stores that retail top-quality handmade Belgian lace are **Maison Antoine,** Grand-Place 26 (✆ **02/512-48-59;** Métro: Gare Centrale), and **Manufacture Belge de Dentelles,** Galerie de la Reine 6–8 (✆ **02/511-44-77;** Métro: Gare Centrale).

For kids, pick up some Tintin mementos from **Boutique de Tintin,** rue de la Colline 13 (✆ **02/514-51-52;** Métro: Gare Centrale).

At the **Flea Market** on place du Jeu de Balle (Métro: Louise), a large square in the Marolles district, you can find some exceptional decorative items, many recycled from the homes of the "recently deceased," as well as unusual postcards, clothing, and household goods. The market is held daily from 7am to 2pm.

Every weekend, place du Grand Sablon hosts a fine **Antiques Market** (tram: 92, 93, or 94). The salesmanship is low-key, the interest pure, the prices not unreasonable (but don't expect bargains), and the quality of the merchandise—which includes silverware, pottery, paintings, and jewelry—high. The market is open Saturday from 9am to 6pm and Sunday from 9am to 2pm.

Near the Grand-Place, at the top end of rue du Marché aux Herbes, in a square loosely called the Agora, there's a weekend **Crafts Market** (Métro: Gare Centrale), with handmade jewelry and other items, mostly inexpensive.

Nightlife

The superb and historic **Théâtre Royal de la Monnaie** ★★, place de la Monnaie (✆ **070/23-39-39;** www.lamonnaie.be; Métro: De Brouckère), founded in the 17th century, is home to the Opéra National and l'Orchestre Symphonique de la Monnaie. Ballet performances are also presented here. The present resident dance company is local choreographer Anne Theresa de Keersmaeker's Group Rosas. **BOZAR** (or, to purists, the Palais des Beaux-Arts), rue Royale 10 (℡ **02/507-82-00;** www.bozar.be; Métro: Gare Centrale), is home to Belgium's National Orchestra.

Théâtre Royal de Toone, in a room in the Toone cafe, is the latest in the Toone line of puppet theaters, which dates from the early 1800s—the title being passed from one puppet master to the next. At Toone, Puppet Master Nicolas Géal presents his adaptation of such classic tales as *The Three Musketeers, Faust,* and *Hamlet* in the Brussels dialect, but also in English, French, Dutch, and German. Impasse Schuddeveld 6, Petite rue des Bouchers 21 (℡ **02/511-71-37;** www.toone.be; Métro: Gare Centrale). Ticket prices and performance times vary.

Jazz is a popular scene. **L'Archiduc,** rue Antoine Dansaert 6 (℡ **02/512-06-52**), puts on jazz concerts on Saturday and Sunday. **Le Sounds,** rue de la Tulipe 28 (℡ **02/512-92-50**), has daily jazz concerts and a workshop on Mondays at 7:30pm. For those who like their licks a tad restrained, there's a jazz brunch at the **Airport Sheraton Hotel,** facing the terminal building (℡ **02/725-10-00**), every Sunday from noon to 3pm.

BARS & CAFES   A Brussels favorite, **A la Mort Subite,** rue Montagne aux Herbes Potagères 7 (℡ **02/513-13-18**), is a bistro of rather special character whose name translates to "Sudden Death," which is also the name of a beer you can buy here. The decor consists of stained-glass motifs, old photographs, paintings, and prints on the walls, and plain wooden chairs and tables on the floor.

Hidden away at the end of a narrow alleyway, **Au Bon Vieux Temps,** impasse St-Michel, rue du Marché aux Herbes 12 (℡ **02/217-26-26**), is a gloomily atmospheric old tavern that seems to hearken back to a bygone era. You should try the appropriately named *Duvel* (Devil) beer here. **A l'Imaige de Nostre-Dame,** impasse des Cadeaux, rue du Marché aux Herbes 8 (℡ **02/219-42-49**), is a decent, quiet place to drink and read or reflect if you're alone, or to converse with a companion without having to compete with a blaring jukebox.

A legendary 1904 Art Nouveau tavern, enlivened with a dash of Art Deco and rococo, **Le Falstaff,** rue Henri Maus 19 (℡ **02/511-87-89**), has stunning decor, stained-glass scenes in the style of Pieter Bruegel the Elder depicting Shakespeare's Falstaff tales, and reasonably priced brasserie food. **Rick's,** av. Louise 344

 Puppet Shows

A special sort of theater—that of the wooden marionettes, like those of the Théâtre Royal de Toone VII—has entertained Belgians for centuries. In times past, puppet theaters numbered in the hundreds nationwide (Brussels alone had 15), and the plays were much like our modern-day soap operas. The story lines went on and on, sometimes for generations, and audiences returned night after night. Performances were based on folklore, legends, or political satire.

Specific marionette characters came to personify their home cities: A cheeky ragamuffin named Woltje (Little Walloon) was from Brussels; Antwerp had the cross-eyed, earthy ne'er-do-well Schele; Pierke, from Ghent, was modeled on the traditional Italian clown; and Liège's Tchantchès stood only 16 inches high and always appeared with patched trousers, a tasseled floppy hat, and his constant companion, the sharp-tongued Nanesse (Agnes).

HEADING OUT TO Waterloo

The Battle of Waterloo was Europe's Gettysburg, and the battlefield remains much as it was on June 18, 1815. To visit it, you don't go to the town of Waterloo, 6 miles (10km) south of Brussels. A stretch of rolling farmland dotted with stoutly built manor-farmhouses several miles to the south is where the battle was actually fought. By bus from Brussels, take TEC line W from Bruxelles-Midi train station to the **Centre Visiteur (Visitor Center) ★**, route du Lion 252–254 (*☎* **02/385-19-12;** www.waterloo 1815.be), where an audiovisual presentation on the tactical background plus an extract from a fictional film version of the conflict will give you an idea of the battle's immense scale.

The view from atop the **Butte du Lion (Lion Mound),** next to the Visitor Center, is worth the 226-step climb, though it takes an active imagination to fill the peaceful farmland below you with slashing cavalry charges, thundering artillery, and 200,000 colorfully uniformed, struggling soldiers. Across the road from the Visitor Center is the **Musée des Cires (Waxworks Museum),** where Napoleon, Wellington, Blücher, and other leading participants appear as wax figures. Also

next to the Center is the **Panorama de la Bataille (Battlefield Panorama),** featuring a painted diorama of the massive French cavalry charge led by Marshal Ney. It was a sensation in the pre-cinema era.

These four sites are open daily April to October from 9:30am to 6:30pm; and November to March from 10am to 5pm. Admission to the Visitor Center is free. Admission to its audiovisual presentation and the four on-site attractions is 12€ for adults, 9€ for seniors and students, 7.50€ for children ages 6 to 17, and free for children 5 and under.

In Waterloo itself is the well-ordered **Musée Wellington (Wellington Museum),** chaussée de Bruxelles 147 (*☎* **02/354-78-06;** www.museewellington.be), in an old Brabant coaching inn that was the Duke's headquarters. It was from here that Wellington sent his historic victory dispatch. The museum is open daily April to September from 9:30am to 6:30pm; and November to March from 10am to 5pm. Admission is 5€ for adults, 4€ for students and seniors, 2€ for children ages 6 to 12, and free for children 5 and under.

(*☎* 02/647-75-30), brings a touch of Humphrey Bogart and Ernest Hemingway, accompanied by American and Mexican food, to the stylish avenue Louise.

An Excursion to Ghent ★★

When it comes to tourism, Ghent (Gent) is often considered a poor relation of Bruges (p. 149). Its historical monuments and townscapes are not quite as pretty as those in its sister city and are to be viewed only if there is time after visiting Bruges. There is some truth in this—but not too much. An important port and industrial center, Ghent compensates for its less precious appearance with a vigorous social and cultural scene.

ESSENTIALS

GETTING THERE Ghent is just a half-hour train ride from Brussels (trains depart from all three of Brussels's main stations), and there are around four trains an hour from the capital. The city's main train station, **Gent-Sint-Pieters** (or Gand-Saint-Pierre, as you also may see it written in French on timetables), on Koningin

Maria-Hendrikaplein, 1½ miles (2.4km) south of the center city, dates from 1912 and has a more-than-decent station restaurant. For schedule and fare information, call ☎ **02/528-28-28.**

To get quickly and easily to the heart of town, take tram 1 from the nearest tram platform under the bridge to your left as you exit the station, and get out at Korenmarkt—it may be just a bit too far to walk there, and the way is none too interesting.

VISITOR INFORMATION   The **Toerisme Gent Infokantoor (Ghent Tourist Information Office)** is in the cellar of the Belfry and Cloth Hall, Botermarkt 17A (☎ **09/266-56-60;** www.visitgent.be). It's open April to October daily from 9:30am to 6:30pm, and November to March daily from 9:30am to 4:30pm.

TOP ATTRACTIONS & SPECIAL MOMENTS

Even if you see nothing else in Ghent, you shouldn't miss **Sint-Baafskathedraal (St. Bavo's Cathedral) ★★★**, Sint-Baafsplein (☎ **09/269-20-45;** www.sint baafskathedraal-gent.be), a mix of Romanesque, Gothic, and baroque styles. The interior has priceless paintings, sculptures, screens, memorials, and carved tombs. About midway along the vaulted nave is a remarkable pulpit in white marble entwined with oak, reminiscent of Bernini. St. Bavo's showpiece is Jan van Eyck's 24-panel altarpiece *The Adoration of the Mystic Lamb,* completed in 1432. The cathedral is open April to October Monday to Saturday from 8:30am to 6pm, and Sunday from 1 to 6pm; November to March Monday to Saturday from 8:30am to 5pm, and Sunday from 1 to 5pm. Admission to the cathedral is free; to the *Mystic Lamb* chapel, 3€ for adults, 1.50€ for children ages 6 to 12, and free for children 5 and under.

Across the square from the cathedral, the richly ornate Gothic **Belfort en Lakenhalle (Belfry and Cloth Hall) ★**, Emile Braunplein (☎ **09/269-37-30**), together form a glorious medieval ensemble. The Cloth Hall from 1425 to 1445 is where cloth was stored and traded and was the gathering place of wool and cloth merchants. A UNESCO World Heritage Site, the Belfry, dating from 1313 to 1380, is 298 feet high (89m) and has a gilded copper dragon at its summit. It holds the great bells that have rung out Ghent's civic pride down through the centuries. Take the elevator up to the Belfry's upper gallery, at a height of 215 feet (65m), to see the bells and fantastic panoramic city views. The attraction is open mid-March to mid-November daily from 10am to 12:30pm and 2 to 6pm (and mid-Nov to mid-Mar for pre-booked guided tours for groups) only. Admission is 3€ for adults, 2.50€ for seniors and students, and free for children 12 and under. Free guided tours are available May to October at 2:10, 3:10, and 4:10pm.

Grim is the word that springs to mind when you first see the **Gravensteen (Castle of the Counts) ★**, Sint-Veerleplein (☎ **09/225-93-06**). The fortress, built by Philip of Alsace in 1180, crouches like a gray stone lion over the city. If the castle's 6-foot-thick (1.8m) walls, battlements, and turrets failed to intimidate attackers, the count could always turn to a well-equipped torture chamber inside. Climb to the ramparts of the high building in the center, the donjon, where your reward is a great view of Ghent's rooftops and towers. The castle is open April to September daily from 9am to 6pm, and October to March daily from 9am to 5pm. Admission is 8€ for adults, 6€ for seniors and visitors ages 19 to 26, and free for visitors 18 and under.

WHERE TO DINE

In a town where the Middle Ages are *big,* **Brasserie Pakhuis ★★**, Schuurkenstraat 4 (☎ **09/223-55-55;** www.pakhuis.be), located down a narrow lane off Veldstraat,

> **Graslei** and **Korenlei** ★★, two elegant canal-side rows that face each other across a waterway that once formed the city's harbor, are home to towering, gabled guild houses built between the 1200s and 1700s. To appreciate their majesty, walk across the connecting bridge over the Leie to view each one from the opposite bank, then return to stroll past each.

is almost modern. In a vast, beautifully restored 19th-century warehouse, it's replete with painted cast-iron pillars, soaring wrought-iron balconies, and oak and marble tables with specially designed table settings, and has a granite mosaic floor. Although maybe too conscious of its own sense of style, Pakhuis is all stocked up in matters of taste and serves excellent Flemish cuisine. Main courses range from 11€ to 21€.

Convivial and trendy, **Keizershof Brasserie** ★, Vrijdagmarkt 47 (℗ **09/223-44-46;** www.keizershof.net), on the historical market square, has an attractively informal ambience and a good menu of continental fare. Behind its narrow facade are plain wood tables on multiple floors around a central stairwell. The decor beneath the timber ceiling beams is spare, tastefully tattered, and speckled with paintings by local artists. Service for office workers doing lunch is fast; in the evenings you're expected to linger. In summertime, you can dine alfresco in a courtyard at the back. An entree will set you back 15€ to 21€.

An Excursion to Antwerp ★

Antwerp, the acknowledged "Diamond Center of the World," is one of Western Europe's most hidden gems. Many people think of it only as a port and center of the diamond trade, yet it is also easygoing, stylish, and filled with the monuments of a wealthy medieval and Renaissance period. Only 40 minutes by train from Brussels and compact enough for walking, it's an ideal day trip out of the capital city.

ESSENTIALS

GETTING THERE You can count on around four trains an hour from Brussels. Antwerp's main station is **Antwerpen Centraal Station** (or Anvers-Central, as you may see it written in French on timetables), 1 mile (1.5km) east of the Grote Markt, on the edge of the city center. Centraal Station is a domed, cathedral-like edifice constructed between 1895 and 1905, and recently refurbished. A 2009 article in *Newsweek* magazine named the station the world's fourth most beautiful (behind London's St. Pancras, New York's Grand Central, and Mumbai's Chhatrapati Shivaji). Antwerp is on the **Thalys** high-speed train network that connects Paris, Brussels, and Amsterdam. Reservations are required for Thalys. For schedule and fare information, call ℗ **02/528-28-28.**

To get quickly from Centraal Station to the heart of the Old Town, take tram 2, 3, 5, or 15 and get out at Groenplaats. It's a short walk from there to the Grote Markt.

VISITOR INFORMATION There is an **Info Desk** of the Antwerp Tourist Office inside Antwerpen Centraal Station that is open the same hours as the main office. The main **Antwerp Tourist Office (Toerisme Antwerpen),** Grote Markt 13, 2000 Antwerpen (℗ **03/232-01-03;** www.antwerpen.be), is open Monday to Saturday from 9am to 5:45pm and Sunday from 9am to 4:45pm.

4

BELGIUM | Brussels

TOP ATTRACTIONS & SPECIAL MOMENTS

Housed in an impressive neoclassical building, the **Koninklijk Museum voor Schone Kunsten Antwerpen (Antwerp Royal Museum of Fine Arts)** ★★★, Leopold de Waelplaats 2 (✆ **03/238-78-09;** www.kmska.be), has a collection of paintings by Flemish masters that is second to none in the world. Among them are more Rubens masterpieces in one place than anywhere else. To view them, pass through the ground-floor exhibits of canvases by modern artists (including works by Ensor, Magritte, Permeke, and Delvaux). Ascend to the second floor, where you'll find works by Rubens, Jan van Eyck, Rogier van der Weyden, Dirck Bouts, Hans Memling, the Bruegel family, and Dutch artists Rembrandt and Frans Hals. The museum is open Tuesday to Saturday from 10am to 5pm and Sunday from 10am to 6pm. Admission is 6€ for adults, 4€ for seniors and students, 1€ for persons ages 19 to 25, and free for children 18 and under; admission on the last Wednesday in the month is free.

A masterpiece of Brabant Gothic architecture, the towering **Onze-Lieve-Vrouwekathedraal (Cathedral of Our Lady)** ★★, Handschoenmarkt (✆ **03/213-99-51;** www.dekathedraal.be), off the Grote Markt, is the largest church in the Low Countries. Begun in 1352 and completed by around 1520, it has seven aisles and 125 pillars, but of the original design's five towers, only one was ever completed. This one is the tallest church spire in the Low Countries, 403 feet (121m) high. A mix of baroque and neoclassical, the cathedral houses four Rubens altarpieces. Our Lady is open Monday to Friday from 10am to 5pm, Saturday from 10am to 3pm, and Sunday and religious holidays from 1 to 4pm. Admission is 5€ for adults, 3€ for seniors and students, and free for children 11 and under.

To touch Antwerp's cultural heart, a visit to the **Rubenshuis (Rubens House)** ★★, Wapper 9–11 (✆ **03/201-15-55;** www.rubenshuis.be), a short walk east of the center, is essential. Antwerp's most illustrious son, the artist Peter Paul Rubens (1577–1640), lived and worked here. Rubens amassed a tidy fortune from his paintings that allowed him to build this impressive mansion in 1610, along what was then a canal, when he was 33. Today you can stroll past the baroque portico into its reconstructed period rooms and through a Renaissance garden, and come away with a good idea of the lifestyle of a patrician Flemish gentleman of that era. Examples of Rubens's works, and others by master painters who were his contemporaries, are scattered throughout. The house is open Tuesday to Sunday from 10am to 5pm. Admission is 6€ for adults, 1€ for persons ages 19 to 26, and free for seniors and children 18 and under; admission on the last Wednesday in the month is free.

The Diamond Quarter

Some 80% of the world's rough diamonds, 50% of cut diamonds, and 40% of industrial diamonds are traded here annually. The diamond cutters of Antwerp are

---

 Cruising the Harbor

Do take a cruise around Antwerp's awesome harbor, which handles 16,000 ships and 100 million tons of cargo a year. Most departures are from the Steen waterfront on the Scheldt. Flandria Line (✆ 03/231-31-00;

www.flandria.nu) runs a varied program of harbor cruises. Their signature 2½-hour cruise is 13€ for adults, 11€ for seniors, 8.50 for children ages 3 to 18, and free for children 2 and under.

world-renowned for their skill, which you can admire in the Diamond Quarter, a surprisingly down-at-the-heels-looking area, only steps away from Centraal Station. More than 12,000 cutters and polishers work here in hundreds of workshops, serving thousands of firms, brokers, and merchants. Browsing the various store windows in the quarter is a highly enjoyable activity and won't cost you a thing.

WHERE TO DINE

The magnificent brasserie **De Foyer** ★, Komedieplaats 18 (✆ **03/233-55-17;** www.defoyer.be), is in the foyer of the 19th-century Bourla Theater. With its ornately painted dome, potted palms, red velvet drapes, and marble columns, you would expect prices to be a lot higher than they are. The bargain daily lunch buffet includes an array of fish and vegetable salads, soup, several hot dishes, cheese, and pastries. Reservations are recommended on weekends. Light meals are 9€ to 14€; the lunch buffet is 16€.

Rooden Hoed Restaurant ★, Oude Koornmarkt 25 (✆ **03/233-28-44;** www. roodenhoed.be), a pleasant, old-fashioned restaurant is the oldest in Antwerp, having been in business for more than 250 years. It serves good, hearty food—a mix of old-style regional cuisine and trendy new forms—at moderate prices. Mussels, a delicious *choucroute d'Alsace* (sausages with sauerkraut and mashed potatoes), chicken *waterzooï*, and fish specialties are all featured on the menu. Try an aperitif, or a snack, in the medieval cellar under the restaurant. Main courses run 21€ to 27€.

A location amid the delightful 16th-century Vlaeykensgang courtyard's jumble of cafes, restaurants, and antique apartments all but guarantees a pleasant atmosphere at **Restaurant Sir Anthony Van Dijck** ★★, Oude Koornmarkt 16 (✆ **03/231-61-70;** www.siranthonyvandijck.be). Owner/chef Marc Paesbrugghe operates this relaxed French brasserie-restaurant in a sparely elegant setting that's flooded with light that streams in from the old-world Vlaeykensgang courtyard through big, arched windows. Another plus is its commitment to good food. Main courses run 34€ to 35€.

BRUGES ★★★

The graceful, small city of Bruges (Brugge) has drifted down the stream of time with all the self-possession of the swans that cruise its canals. To step into the old town is to be transported back to the Middle Ages, when Bruges was among the wealthiest cities of Europe. UNESCO has recognized the cultural importance of the historic center by awarding it World Heritage status. The city is the pride and joy of all Flanders.

Medieval Gothic architecture is the big deal here. Sure, there's a layer of Romanesque; a touch of Renaissance, baroque, and rococo; a dab of neoclassical and neo-Gothic; and a smidgen of Art Nouveau and Art Deco. But Gothic is what Bruges provides, in quantities that come near to numbing the senses—and likely would if it weren't for the city's contemporary animation.

Getting There

Trains arrive every half-hour or so from Brussels, Antwerp, and Ghent, and from the North Sea resort and ferry port of Ostend (Oostende) and the ferry port of Zeebrugge. Journey time is about 1 hour by train from Brussels and Antwerp, 30 minutes from Ghent, and 15 minutes from Ostend and Zeebrugge.

From Paris, you can take the Thalys high-speed trains through Brussels to Bruges, or just travel to Brussels and then change there for a domestic train to Bruges. A train to/from Lille in northern France connects at Bruges or Ghent with the Eurostar trains through the Channel Tunnel to and from London. From Amsterdam, you can go via Antwerp or Brussels, either on the Thalys or on the hourly InterCity trains.

Station Information

Although the city is called Bruges in English and French, in Dutch it's "Brugge," and that's what the train station destination boards say. The station is on Stationsplein, about 1 mile (1.6km) south of the center of town. You can even get started on sight-seeing here—inside the station is a large wall mural depicting scenes from Bruges's history and everyday life. And when leaving, the elegant **Brasserie Perron** is a good place for a pretrain snack or drink. For schedule and fare information, call ✆ **02/528-28-28.** There's a small booth for tourist information and hotel bookings inside the train station.

It's a 20-minute walk to the town center or a short bus or taxi ride—choose any bus labeled CENTRUM from the bus stops outside the station and get out at the Markt.

Information Elsewhere in the City

Bruges's main tourist information office, **In & Uit Brugge,** Concertgebouw, 't Zand 34, 8000 Brugge (✆ **050/44-46-46;** www.brugge.be), is inside the city's ultramodern Concert Hall, about midway between the train station and the heart of town. The office is open daily from 10am to 6pm (Thurs until 8pm).

Getting Around

Narrow streets fan out from two central squares, the **Markt** and the **Burg.** A network of canals threads its way to every section of the small city, and the center is almost encircled by a canal that opens at its southern end to become a swan-filled lake, the **Minnewater**—this translates as Lake of Love, though the name actually comes from the Dutch *Binnen Water,* meaning Inner Harbor—bordered by the Begijnhof and a fine park.

Walking is by far the best way to see Bruges, since the center of town is traffic-free (but wear good walking shoes, as those charming cobblestones can be hard going). A bicycle is a terrific way to get around. You can rent a bike from the train station for 10€ a day, plus a deposit. Some hotels and stores rent bikes, for 8€ to 12€ a day.

De Lijn city buses (✆ **070/22-02-00;** www.delijn.be) depart from the bus station outside the train station and from the big square called 't Zand, west of the Markt. Several bus routes pass through the Markt. There's a taxi stand outside the train station (✆ **050/38-46-60**) and another at the Markt (✆ **050/33-44-44**).

Top Attractions & Special Moments

In the **Markt (Market Square),** heraldic banners float from venerable facades. This square, along with the Burg (see below), is the heart of Bruges and the focal point of your sightseeing. Most major points of interest in the city are no more than a 5- or 10-minute walk away.

A part of the **Belfort en Hallen (Belfry and Market Halls)** ★★, Markt (✆ **050/44-87-11**), the bell tower was, and is, the symbol of Bruges's civic pride. The tower itself stands 272 feet (82m) high. Its lower section dates from around 1240, with the corner turrets added in the 14th century and the upper, octagonal section in the 15th century. If you have the stamina, climb the 366 steps to the Belfry's summit for a panoramic view over Bruges and the surrounding countryside. Its

Bruges

ACCOMMODATIONS ■
Egmond **23**
Fevery **2**
Lucca **4**
Rosenburg **15**
Ter Duinen **1**

DINING ◆
Bhavani **16**
Brasserie Erasmus **12**

Breydel-de-Coninck **11**
De Stove **9**
Lotus **8**

ATTRACTIONS ●
Basiliek van het Heilig Bloed **14**
Begijnhof **22**
Belfort en Hallen **10**
Brouwerij De Halve Maan **21**
Bruggemuseum-Brugse Vrije **7**

Burg **6**
Groeninge Museum **17**
Gruuthuse Museum **18**
Kantcentrum **3**
Markt **5**
Memling in Sint-Jan **20**
Onze-Lieve-
  Vrouwekerk **19**
Stadhuis **13**

magnificent 47-bell carillon peals out every quarter-hour. From the 13th to the 16th centuries, much of the city's commerce was conducted in the Hallen. These halls have recently been brought back into use for exhibits by a consortium of local art dealers. The complex is open daily from 9:30am to 5pm. Admission is 5€ for adults, 4€ for seniors and persons ages 13 to 25, and free for children 12 and under.

The **Burg,** a public square just steps away from the Markt, holds an array of stellar buildings. On this site, Baldwin Iron Arm, Count of Flanders, built a fortified castle (or "burg"), around which a village grew up that developed into Bruges.

A Romanesque basilica with a Gothic upper floor, the **Basiliek van het Heilig Bloed (Basilica of the Holy Blood)** ★, Burg 10 (🕿 050/33-67-92; www.holy blood.com), houses a venerated relic of Christ. Since 1149, it has been the repository of a fragment of cloth embedded in a rock-crystal vial and stained with what is said to be the coagulated blood of Christ, wiped from his body by Joseph of Arimathea after the crucifixion. Every year, in the colorful Procession of the Holy Blood on Ascension Day, the bishop of Bruges carries the relic through the streets, accompanied by costumed residents acting out biblical scenes. The basilica is open April to September daily from 9:30 to 11:50am and 2 to 5:50pm; October to March Thursday to Tuesday from 10 to 11:50am and 2 to 3:50pm, and Wednesday from 10 to 11:50am. Admission to the basilica is free; to the museum, 1.50€ for adults, 1€ for students, and free for children 12 and under.

Bruges's unmatched Gothic **Stadhuis (Town Hall)** ★, Burg 12 (🕿 **050/44-87-11**), the oldest town hall in Belgium, dates from the late 1300s. Don't miss the upstairs **Gotische Zaal (Gothic Room)** ★★ and its ornate decor, wall murals depicting highlights of the town's history, and the illuminated vaulted oak ceiling from 1385 to 1402, which features scenes from the New Testament. The Town Hall is open daily from 9:30am to 5pm. Admission is 2€ for adults, 1€ for seniors, and free for persons 25 and under.

Next door, the **Bruggemuseum–Brugse Vrije (Bruges Museum–Liberty of Bruges),** Burg 11 (🕿 **050/44-87-11**), dates mostly from 1722 to 1727, when it replaced a 16th-century building as the seat of the Liberty of Bruges—the Liberty being the medieval name for the district around Bruges. The palace later became a courthouse and now houses the city council's administration. Inside, at no. 11A, is the **Renaissancezaal (Renaissance Hall)** ★★, the Liberty's council chamber, which has been restored to its original 16th-century condition. The hall has a superb black-marble fireplace decorated with an alabaster frieze and topped by an oak chimney piece carved with statues of Emperor Charles V, who visited Bruges in 1515, and his grandparents: Emperor Maximilian of Austria, Duchess Mary of Burgundy, King Ferdinand II of Aragon, and Queen Isabella I of Castile. The palace is open daily from 9:30am–12:30pm and 1:30 to 5pm. Admission is 2€ for adults, 1€ for seniors, and free for persons 25 and under.

The **Groeninge Museum** ★★★, Dijver 12 (🕿 **050/44-87-11**), ranks among Belgium's leading traditional museums of fine arts, with a collection that covers painting in the Low Countries from the 15th to the 20th centuries. The Gallery of Flemish Primitives holds some 30 works by painters such as Jan van Eyck, Rogier van der Weyden, Hieronymus Bosch, and Hans Memling. Works by Magritte and Delvaux also are exhibited. The museum is open Tuesday to Sunday from 9:30am to 5pm. Admission is 8€ for adults, 6€ for seniors, and free for persons 25 and under.

Lodewijk van Gruuthuse, a Flemish nobleman and herb merchant who was a counselor to the Dukes of Burgundy in the 1400s, lived in this ornate Gothic mansion, now the **Gruuthuse Museum** ★, Dijver 17 (𝄞 **050/44-87-11**). Among the 2,500 antiques in the house are paintings, sculptures, tapestries, lace, weapons, glassware, and richly carved furniture. The museum is open Tuesday to Sunday from 9:30am to 5pm. Admission is 6€ for adults, 5€ for seniors, free for persons 25 and under.

In the former Sint-Janshospitaal (Hospital of St. John), where the earliest wards date from the 13th century, is housed the **Memling in Sint-Jan** ★, Mariastraat (𝄞 **050/44-87-11**). Visitors come primarily for the magnificent paintings by the German-born artist Hans Memling (ca. 1440–94), who took up residence in Bruges in 1465 and became a prominent city artist. Among his masterpieces here is the three-paneled altarpiece of St. John the Baptist and St. John the Evangelist. The museum is open Tuesday to Sunday from 9:30am to 5pm. Admission is 8€ for adults, 6€ for seniors, and free for persons 25 and under.

It took 2 centuries (13th–15th c.) to build the **Onze-Lieve-Vrouwekerk (Church of Our Lady)** ★★, in Mariastraat (𝄞 **050/34-53-14**), whose soaring 396-foot (119m) spire can be seen from miles around. Among the many art treasures within is an outstanding Carrara marble *Madonna and Child* ★★★, by Michelangelo. This sculpture, created in 1504, was the only one of Michelangelo's works to leave Italy during his lifetime. It was bought by a Bruges merchant, Jan van Mouskroen, and donated to the church in 1506. In addition, there's a painting, the *Crucifixion,* by Anthony Van Dyck, and the impressive side-by-side bronze **tomb sculptures** of the Duke of Burgundy, Charles the Bold, who died in 1477, and his daughter, Mary of Burgundy, who died at age 25 in 1482. The church is open Tuesday to Saturday from 9am to 5pm (Sat 4:45pm) and Sunday from 1:30 to 5pm. Admission to the church and *Madonna and Child* altar is free; to the chapel of Charles and Mary and the museum, it costs 2€ for adults, 1€ for seniors, and free for persons 25 and under.

A combination workshop, museum, and sale room, the **Kantcentrum (Lace Center)** ★, Peperstraat 3A (𝄞 **050/33-00-72;** www.kantcentrum.com), is where the ancient art of making lace by hand gets passed on to the next generation. The center is open Monday to Saturday from 10am to noon and 2 to 6pm (Sat 5pm). Admission is 2.50€ for adults, 1.50€ for seniors and children ages 7 to 12, and free for children 6 and under.

Through the centuries, since it was founded in 1245 by the Countess Margaret of Constantinople, the **Prinselijk Begijnhof ten Wijngaarde (Princely Beguinage of the Vineyard)** ★★, Wijngaardstraat (𝄞 **050/33-00-11**), at the Lake of Love, has long been one of Bruges's most tranquil spots. *Begijns* were religious women, similar to nuns, who accepted vows of chastity and obedience but drew the line at poverty, preferring to earn a living by looking after the sick and making lace. The begijns are no more, but the Begijnhof is occupied by the Benedictine nuns of the

4

BELGIUM | Bruges

 Strolling the Back Streets

You don't need to visit the top 10 highlights to enjoy Bruges. Shut your guidebook, put away the street map, and just wander, taking time out to make your own discoveries. Bruges's inhabitants live their everyday lives in absurdly beautiful surroundings and aren't always engaged in putting on a show for the tourists.

Be sure to take a **boat trip ★★★** on the canals, onboard one of the open-top tour boats that cruise year-round from five departure points around the center, all marked with an anchor icon on maps available from the tourist office. The boats operate March to November daily from 10am to 6pm. A half-hour cruise is 6.90€ for adults, 3.20€ for children ages 4 to 11 accompanied by an adult, and free for children 3 and under.

Monasterium De Wijngaard, who try to keep their traditions alive. This handsome little cluster of 17th-century whitewashed houses surrounding a lawn with poplar trees and flowers makes a marvelous escape from the hustle and bustle outside. The Begijnhof courtyard is always open and admission is free.

A fine example of the *godshuizen* (houses of God, or almshouses), built by the rich in Bruges from the 13th century onward as refuges for widows and the poor, is the **Godshuis de Vos (De Vos Almshouse),** from 1713, at the corner of Noordstraat and Wijngaardstraat, near the Begijnhof. The moneybags weren't being entirely altruistic, since the residents had to pray for their benefactors' souls twice a day in the chapel that was an integral part of an almshouse's facilities. The pretty courtyard garden here is surrounded by a chapel and eight original houses, since converted to six, which are owned by the city and occupied by seniors. Admission is not permitted, but you can view the complex from over a low wall out front.

The **Brouwerij De Halve Maan (Half-Moon Brewery) ★**, Walplein 26 (📞 050/33-26-97; www.halvemaan.be), has been turning out ale since at least 1546. Today it produces Bruges's famous Straffe Hendrik beer, a strapping blond brew that can be sampled in the brewery's own brasserie, after a perusal of the facility. Admission is 5.50€. Hourly guided visits are conducted April to October Monday to Friday from 11am to 4pm, Saturday and Sunday from 11am to 5pm; and November to March Monday to Friday from 11am to 3pm, and Saturday and Sunday from 11am to 4pm.

Where to Stay

Hotel Egmond ★   There are just eight rooms in this rambling mansion next to the Minnewater Park, but the lucky few who stay here will find ample space, plenty of family ambience, abundant local color, and lots of peace and tranquillity. All rooms are furnished in an individual style, and all have views on the garden and the Minnewater Park. Every afternoon, free coffee and tea are served on the garden terrace or in the lounge.

Minnewater 15, 8000 Brugge. 📞 **050/34-14-45.** Fax 050/34-29-40. www.egmond.be. 8 units. 89€–140€ double. Rates include buffet breakfast. MC, V. **Amenities:** Smoke-free rooms (all rooms).

Hotel Fevery   A family-owned hotel, the Fevery is on a quiet side street off Langerei in a quiet part of town. Its modern and comfortably furnished guest rooms are cheery and immaculate, with new bathrooms and monogrammed pressed sheets. The proprietor, Mr. Asselman, is a wealth of local information and clearly takes great pride in his establishment.

Collaert Mansionstraat 3, 8000 Brugge. 📞 **050/33-12-69.** Fax 050/33-17-91. www.hotelfevery.be. 10 units. 50€–90€ double. Rates include buffet breakfast. AE, MC, V. **Amenities:** Lounge; smoke-free rooms (all rooms).

Hotel Lucca ⚜ This mansion right in the heart of romantic Bruges was built in the 14th century by a wealthy merchant from Lucca, Italy. The high ceilings and wide halls convey a sense of luxury—not that this is entirely backed up by reality, though the guest rooms are in reasonable condition and sport pine furnishings. Breakfast is served in a cozy medieval cellar decorated with antiques.

Naaldenstraat 30 (off Sint-Jakobsstraat), 8000 Brugge. ℂ **050/34-20-67.** Fax 050/33-34-64. www. hotellucca.be. 19 units, 14 with bathroom. 53€ double without bathroom; 68€–88€ double with bathroom. Rates include buffet breakfast. AE, DC, MC, V. *In room:* No TV (some units).

Hotel Rosenburg ★★ This ultramodern brick hotel is set alongside a lovely canal, a short walk west from the center of Bruges. The hotel is an artful combination of old Bruges style and contemporary amenities and fittings. Its spacious guest rooms are restfully decorated in warm colors like peach and furnished with bamboo and rattan beds. Most have views of the canal at Coupure.

Coupure 30, 8000 Brugge. ℂ **050/34-01-94.** Fax 050/34-35-39. www.rosenburg.be. 27 units. 100€– 170€ double. AE, DC, MC, V. **Amenities:** Smoke-free rooms.

Hotel Ter Duinen ★★ This charming hotel is an ideal marriage of classical style and modern conveniences. Guest rooms are ample in size, brightly decorated, and have modern furnishings. Some rooms have wooden ceiling beams, and some have a great view overlooking the tranquil Langerei canal, just north of the town center and an easy walk away. Proprietors Marc and Lieve Bossu-Van Den Heuvel take justified pride in their hotel and extend a friendly welcome to guests.

Langerei 52, 8000 Brugge. ℂ **050/33-04-37.** Fax 050/34-42-16. www.terduinenhotel.be. 20 units. 139€–159€ double. Rates include full breakfast. AE, DC, MC, V. **Amenities:** Lounge.

Where to Dine

Bhavani INDIAN For a change from traditional Belgian food, try this traditional Indian restaurant. It's a consistently fine performer across a wide range of Subcontinental cuisine—thali, tandoori, curry, vegetarian, and seafood—without being exactly outstanding in any category. A mix of coziness, colonial atmosphere, Indian music, and exotic charm marks a setting that gives traditional Indian motifs a modern slant.

Simon Stevinplein 5 (off Oude Burg). ℂ **050/33-90-25.** www.bhavani.be. Main courses 16€–25€; fixed-price menus 19€–27€. AE, DC, MC, V. Daily 4:30pm–12:30am. Bus: 6, 12, or 14.

Brasserie Erasmus FLEMISH Small but popular, this is a great stop after viewing the cathedral and nearby museums. It serves a large variety of Flemish dishes, all prepared with beer. Try the typically Flemish souplike stew dish *waterzooï,* which is very good here and is served with fish, as it's supposed to be, although they also make it with chicken, a style that has become the norm elsewhere.

Wollestraat 35. ℂ **050/33-57-81.** www.hotelerasmus.com. Main courses 15€–25€. MC, V. Daily noon–3:30pm and 6–10pm.

Breydel-de-Coninck SEAFOOD The wood-beam ceilings and plaid upholstery here are cheerful, but the real attraction is the seafood. The specialties are mussels, eels, and lobsters prepared with white wine, cream, or garlic sauces that enhance the seafood without overwhelming it. Try a pail full of plain mussels, or go for something with a little more zest, such as the *moules Provençal* (mussels in a light red sauce with mushrooms, peppers, and onions).

Breidelstraat 24. ℂ **050/33-97-46.** Main courses 11€–23€. AE, MC, V. Thurs–Tues noon–3pm and 6–9:30pm.

Lotus ★ VEGETARIAN Even nonvegetarians will likely enjoy the inventive food here. There are just two menu options—but at least you can choose from a small, medium, or large serving—each with a hearty assortment of imaginatively prepared ingredients, served in a tranquil but cheery Scandinavian-style dining room.

Wapenmakersstraat 5. ℂ **050/33-10-78.** Fixed-price lunch menus 9€–12€. No credit cards. Mon–Sat 11:45am–2pm.

Restaurant De Stove ★★ FLEMISH/SEAFOOD This small (there's space for just 20 diners), family-owned restaurant combines a rustic atmosphere with a more contemporary style than is usual in Bruges. The seafood specialties are well worth a try, particularly the Flemish fish stew, and the menu of the month is always well considered.

Kleine Sint-Amandsstraat 4 (close to the Markt). ℂ **050/33-78-35.** www.restaurantdestove.be. Reservations recommended on weekends. Main courses 17€–32€. AE, MC, V. Fri–Tues noon–1:45pm and 6:30–9:30pm.

LIÈGE

Fervent, lively Liège—its nickname is *Cité Ardente* (Passionate City)—exudes the aura of an aging industrial gloom, but that seems to fade next to its gracefully down-at-the-heels 19th-century monuments and remnants from the time of its powerful prince-bishops.

Getting There

There are between two and four trains an hour to Liège from Brussels and Antwerp, one an hour from Maastricht (Holland) and Cologne (Germany), and one every 2 hours from Luxembourg. The Thalys high-speed train arrives via Brussels, from Paris, and direct from Cologne; ICE high-speed trains arrive from Cologne and Brussels.

Station Information

The main train station is **Liège-Guillemins,** rue des Guillemins, just south of the center of town. In 2009, the old Guillemins station, a crumbling concrete relic from 1958, which had superseded a Belle Epoque gem from 1905, was replaced by a spectacular new, domed structure designed by Spanish architect Santiago Calatrava Valls. A smaller, more centrally located Liège station, **Liège-Palais,** on rue de Bruxelles, is used by some local and connecting trains. Both stations are served by multiple bus lines. For schedule and fare information, call ℂ **02/528-28-28.** There is no tourist information office at either station.

Information Elsewhere in the City

The city tourist office, the **Office du Tourisme,** Féronstrée 92, 4000 Liège (ℂ **04/221-92-21;** www.liege.be), is open Monday to Friday from 9am to 5pm, Saturday from 10am to 4:30pm, and Sunday from 10am to 2:30pm.

Getting Around

The **Old City,** which has most of Liège's sightseeing attractions and nighttime entertainment in the student-filled **Carré** district, is on the west bank of the Meuse, bounded by rue de l'Université, boulevard de la Sauvenière, and rue Pont-d'Avroy. On the east bank, the **Outremeuse** (Across the Meuse) district has a big choice of lively bars, dance clubs, and cabarets. Along the river are tree-lined walkways.

Liège

Legend:
- Church
- *(i)* Information
- ✉ Post office

ACCOMMODATIONS ■
Best Western Univers **8**
Le Campanile **1**

DINING ◆
Bruit Qui Court **2**
Tchantchès & Nanesse **7**

ATTRACTIONS ●
Eglise St. Barthélemy **6**
Musée de l'Art Wallon **5**
Musée de la Vie Wallonne **4**
Palais des Princes-Evêques **3**
Val Saint Lambert **9**

Sightseeing highlights in the Old City are close together, so downtown Liège makes for easy walking, though traffic can be frenetic. **Buses,** useful for getting to sights outside the Old City, cost 1.40€ for a ride. You can buy discounted eight-ride tickets from booths at major route stops and at train stations. The excellent bus system is not hard to figure out, since many stops have network maps posted. Place St-Lambert, an important interchange point and meeting place downtown, is reached from Liège-Guillemins train station by lines 1, 2, 3, and 4. City bus information is available from **TEC** (✆ **04/361-94-44;** www.infotec.be). For a taxi, call **Liège-Tax** (✆ **0800-32-200** or 04/367-50-40).

Top Attractions & Special Moments

A small but impressive collection of works by Walloon (French-speaking Belgian) artists from the 16th century to the present graces the **Musée de l'Art Wallon (Museum of Walloon Art)** ★, Ilot St-Georges, Féronstrée 86 (✆ **04/221-92-31**), by the river in the center of town. Among these artists are Paul Delvaux, Constant Meunier, Antoine Wiertz, Félicien Rops, René Magritte, Roger Somville, and Pierre Alechinsky. The museum is open Tuesday to Saturday from 1 to 6pm and Sunday from 11am to 4:30pm. Admission is 5€ for adults; 3€ for seniors, students, and children ages 12 to 18; and free for children 11 and under.

An incredible array of exhibits bring to life the days of 19th-century Walloons and their traditions and customs, at the refurbished **Musée de la Vie Wallonne (Museum of Walloon Life)** ★★, Cour des Mineurs (✆ **04/237-90-40**), north of place St-Lambert in the center of town. Housed in a 17th-century former Franciscan convent, the collection features examples of popular art, crafts, recreation, and even the workings of a coal mine. Here, too, is a marvelous puppet collection, which includes the city's beloved Tchantchès. The museum is open Tuesday to Sunday from 9:30am to 6pm. Admission is 5€ for adults, 4€ for seniors and students, 3€ for children ages 6 to 18, and free for children 5 and under.

The twin-towered Romanesque **Eglise St-Barthélemy (Church of St. Bartholomew),** place St-Barthélemy (✆ **04/221-89-44**), dates from 1108. Its **Fonts-Baptismaux (Baptismal Font)** ★ is counted among "Belgium's Magnificent Seven" most important historical treasures. The copper-and-brass font, a masterpiece of Mosan Art cast in the early 1100s by master metalsmith Renier de Huy, rests on the backs of 10 sculpted oxen and is surrounded by five biblical scenes. The church is open to visitors Tuesday to Saturday from 10am to noon and 2 to 5pm, and Sunday from 2 to 5pm. Admission is 2€ for adults, 1.25€ for seniors, .75€ for students, .50€ for children ages 6 to 18, and free for children 5 and under.

The prince-bishops, who ruled the city and the surrounding territory from 980 to 1794, constructed for themselves the largest secular Gothic structure in the world. Of primary interest at the **Palais des Prince-Evêques (Palace of the Prince-Bishops)** on place St-Lambert are the two inner courtyards, one lined with 60 carved columns depicting the follies of human nature, and the other housing an ornamental garden. Today this historic building houses the courtrooms and offices of Liège's Palace of Justice. The palace is open Monday to Friday from 10am to 5pm. Admission to the courtyards is free; contact the tourist office for guided tours.

A side trip to the suburb of Seraing, next to the Meuse River, just southwest of Liège, allows you to visit the factory of **Val Saint Lambert,** rue du Val 245, (✆ **04/330-38-00;** www.val-saint-lambert.com), makers of the renowned, hand-blown Val Saint Lambert crystal. The workshop is sited within a complex that contains the remains of a 13th-century Cistercian abbey, a 16th-century Mosan

Renaissance château, and examples of industrial archaeology from the 18th and 19th centuries. Housed in the château, the **Cristal Discovery** (✆ **04/330-36-20;** www.cristalpark.com) exhibit features some of Val Saint Lambert's craftsmen at work and displays particularly fine antique pieces. It's open daily from 9am to 5pm. Admission is 12€ for adults, 10€ for seniors, 6€ for children ages 6 to 18, and free for children 5 and under. You can buy finished crystal—including slightly flawed pieces at a considerable discount—from the factory store.

Where to Stay

The 51-room **Best Western Univers** ★, rue des Guillemins 116 (✆ **04/254-55-55;** www.bestwestern.com), close to Gare des Guillemins, is a reasonably good value. The guest rooms are modest in decor but quite comfortable. Though there's no restaurant on the premises, several are within walking distance. Rates here are 80€ to 140€ double.

Guest rooms at **Hotel Campanile Liege,** rue Jean-Baptiste Juppin 17 (✆ **04/224-02-72;** www.campanile-liege.be), are spacious and comfortable, if not much inflected with character at this modern hotel, which has a reputation for its value. The suburban setting won't appeal to anyone who wants to be in the heart of town, but it's just 5 to 10 minutes by bus to the city center. Rates run 75€ to 125€ double and don't include breakfast.

Where to Dine

An imposing 19th-century building, formerly a bank, houses **Bruit Qui Court,** bd. de la Sauvenière 142 (✆ **04/232-18-18;** www.bruitquicourt.be), and confers upon it a certain amount of class, which is matched by a refined cuisine. Light menu dishes, such as salads and quiches, predominate and mix flavors in a manner that often is unexpected. You can even dine in the ground-floor strong room, behind the original heavily armored door. A main course runs 11€ to 21€.

Named after two local folklore characters, **Taverne Tchantchès & Nanesse,** rue Grande-Bêche 35 (✆ **04/343-39-31;** www.taverne-tchantches.be), is a Liège institution and one of the best addresses in town for Walloon specialties, such as grilled *boudin* sausage with potatoes, the warm *salad liégeoise,* the world-famous (in Liège) meatballs with french fries in syrup, pigs' kidneys flamed in *peket* (gin), chicken in beer, and hot blood sausage (black pudding) with sour cherries. Main courses are 8€ to 16€.

Shopping

On Sunday mornings, a **street market** is strung out for about a mile along the quai de la Batte on the bank of the Meuse. You'll find brass, clothes, flowers, foodstuffs, jewelry, birds, animals, books, radios, and more; the list is simply endless. Shoppers from as far away as Holland and Germany join what seems to be at least half the population of Liège.

An Excursion to Luxembourg City ★★

Luxembourg City, the Grand Duchy's diminutive capital, is a marvelously contrasting mix of the old and the new. The old part of town runs along a deep valley beneath brooding casemates, while the more modern part of town crowns steep cliffs overlooking the old. The city is the headquarters of the European Court of Justice and of the European Investment Bank, and is one of the three seats of the European Parliament

Luxembourg City

ACCOMMODATIONS ■
Hôtel Français 1
Hôtel Le Châtelet 9

DINING ◆
Chiggeri 6
Mousel's Cantine 8

ATTRACTIONS ●
Bock Casemates 7
Cathédral de
Notre-Dame 3
Musée National
d'Histoire et d'Art 5
Palais Grand-Ducal 4
Pétrusse Casemates 2

NORTH
SEA

NETHERLANDS
Amsterdam

BELGIUM
Brussels

LUXEMBOURG

Luxembourg ✴

✝ Church
ⓘ Information
⊠ Post office

1/4 mi
0.25 km

(along with Brussels and Strasbourg). Despite the many banks and the Euro-office towers, Luxembourg City has retained plenty of small-scale, provincial ambience.

GETTING THERE Luxembourg City has good rail connections from Belgium, Germany, and France (a high-speed TGV service from Paris). From Brussels, the fastest time by **InterCity** train (departing from Bruxelles-Midi station) is just under 3 hours.

STATION INFORMATION The **Gare de Luxembourg** (✆ **49-90-49-90**), the main train station, in the southern part of town, has a currency-exchange office and luggage-storage facilities inside. The Luxembourg National Tourist Office operates a **Bureau d'Acceuil (Welcome Desk)** at the station (✆ **42-82-82-20**; www. visitluxembourg.lu). This information desk is open June to September Monday to Saturday from 9am to 7pm, and Sunday from 9am to 12:30pm and 1:45 to 6pm; October to May daily from 9:15am to 12:30pm and 1:45 to 6pm. Buses run frequently from outside the station to the center of town. For train information (and bus service outside Luxembourg City), contact **Chemins de Fer Luxembourgeois** (✆ **24-89-24-89**; www.cfl.lu).

VISITOR INFORMATION In addition to a national tourist office desk inside Luxembourg Gare (see above), **Luxembourg City Tourist Office,** place Guillaume II 30, 1648 Luxembourg-Ville (✆ **22-28-09**; www.lcto.lu), is open April to September Monday to Saturday from 9am to 7pm, and Sunday from 10am to 6pm; and October to March Monday to Saturday from 9am to 6pm, and Sunday from 10am to 6pm.

GETTING AROUND Because of the city's small size, you may have little need to use the **bus** network. Service is extensive and efficient but infrequent on some lines. The fare (valid for 1 hr.) is 1.50€; a 10-ticket pack costs 12€. A money-saving **day ticket** for 4€ and a 5-day pack for 16€, available from train stations and the airport, can be used on buses and trains throughout the Grand Duchy. Luxembourg City bus information is available from **AVL** (✆ **47-96-29-75**; www.vdl.lu). **Taxi** service is available from **Benelux Taxis** (✆ **800/2-51-51**; www.beneluxtaxi.lu).

TOP ATTRACTIONS & SPECIAL MOMENTS

Luxembourg City grew up around Count Sigefroi's 10th-century castle at Montée de Clausen on the Bock promontory. In time, there came to be three rings of battlements around the city, 15 forts, and an exterior wall interspersed with 9 more forts, 3 of them cut right into the rock. Even more impressive than these aboveground fortifications were the 16 miles (25km) of underground tunnels that sheltered troops by the thousands, as well as their equipment, horses, workshops, artillery, arms, kitchens, bakeries, and even slaughterhouses. Legend says that within the fortress's tremendous rocky walls sits a beautiful maiden named Mélusine, whose knitting needles control the fate of Luxembourg. In 1867, the Treaty of London ordered the dismantling of all these battlements, and what you see today represents only about 10% of the original works. The **Casemates** (✆ **22-28-09**) are open March to October daily from 10am to 5pm. Admission is 3€ for adults, and 2.50€ for children ages 6 to 18, and free for children 5 and under.

The oldest part of the **Palais Grand-Ducal (Palace of the Grand Dukes)** ★★, rue du Marché aux Herbes (✆ **47-96-27-09**), dates from 1572. Its "new" right wing was built in 1741. Next door is the Chamber of Deputies (Luxembourg's Parliament). Guided tours are conducted mid-July to mid-September Monday to Friday from 2:30 to 5pm (in English at 4:30pm only), and Saturday from 10 to 11am (not in English).

Admission is 6€ for adults and 3€ for children; tickets are available from the Luxembourg City Tourist Office on place Guillaume II.

The **Musée National d'Histoire et d'Art (National Museum of Art and History)** ★, Marché aux Poissons (✆ 47-93-30-1; www.mnha.lu), is set in the 120-plus rooms of a strikingly modern building of white stone and glass. This museum in the oldest part of town holds archaeological, geological, and historical exhibits, and decorative and popular art. Highlights of the collections are the exhibit on the Fortress of Luxembourg, two watercolors by J.M.W. Turner depicting the Old Town in the 19th century, and works of art by later artists including Cézanne, Picasso, Magritte, and Luxembourg's own Joseph Kutter. The museum is open Tuesday to Sunday from 10am to 5pm. Admission is 5€ for adults, 3€ for seniors and students, and free for children 17 and under.

A magnificent Gothic structure built between 1613 and 1621, the **Cathédrale de Notre-Dame (Notre-Dame Cathedral)** ★, boulevard F.D. Roosevelt (entrance also on rue Notre-Dame), contains the royal family's vault and a remarkable Treasury (it can be viewed only on request). This is the offsetting for the **Octave of Our Lady of Luxembourg,** an annual ceremony on the fifth Sunday following Easter, when thousands of pilgrims arrive to pray to the miraculous statue of the Holy Virgin for protection. They then form a procession to carry the statue from the cathedral through the streets to an alter covered with flowers in avenue de la Porte Neuve, north of place d'Armes. The cathedral is open daily from 10am to noon and 2 to 5:30pm. Admission is free.

WHERE TO STAY

Small and central, the **Hôtel Français** ★, place d'Armes 14 (✆ **47-45-34;** www.hotelfrancais.lu), is a nice, moderately priced hotel. The 21 guest rooms are decorated in a bright, modern style, though some are on the small side. The hotel is in a pedestrian-only zone, but cars and taxis are allowed to drop off and pick up people and baggage. Rates run 125€ to 140€ double and include continental breakfast.

The **Hôtel Le Châtelet** ★★, bd. de la Pétrusse 2 (✆ **40-21-01;** www.chatelet.lu), close to the Pétrusse Valley, is a longtime favorite of visiting academics and businesspeople. Its 40 rooms are divided between two lovely old Luxembourg homes; all have modern, comfortable, and attractive furnishings. Rates are 105€ to 175€ double and include a buffet breakfast.

WHERE TO DINE

The remarkable **Chiggeri** ★, rue du Nord 15 (✆ **22-99-36;** www.chiggeri.lu), off Grand-Rue, is in a rambling mansion on a quiet side street. The main dining room employs African-influenced decorative motifs and has a friendly but professional style. The menu changes seasonally, and the Mediterranean dishes with Asian influences are always inventive. When the weather's good, you may want to dine on the cafe section's outdoor terrace. Main courses in the cafe cost 11€ to 14€, and in the restaurant 17€ to 23€.

Next door to the Mousel Brewery, down beside the Alzette River, the excellent **Mousel's Cantine,** Montée de Clausen 46 (✆ **47-01-98;** www.mouselscantine.lu), is a great place to sample regional treats. The decor is rustic, with plain wooden tables and oil paintings in the back room, and the front room overlooks the quaint street outside. The menu majors on hearty portions of Luxembourg favorites such as sauerkraut with sausage, potatoes, and ham. To wash this down, try a stein of the unfiltered local Mousel brew. A main course will set you back 13€ to 25€.

THE CZECH REPUBLIC

The Czech Republic, comprising the ancient kingdoms of Bohemia, Moravia, and Silesia, is the westernmost of the former Soviet satellite countries and probably the easiest way to explore what used to be the other side of the Iron Curtain. The republic is actually a lot more modernized than most of its former East Bloc neighbors. The European Union put the Czech Republic at the head of its new intake of states in May 2004.

Three years into E.U. membership, the Czech Republic has been included in the Schengen border-free zone. In January 2008, the country's borders with all neighboring countries were opened, making passport checks obsolete. Although the euro won't be adopted here before 2015, this country already has the attitude of a mature Western European state, and the tourists and investments keep flowing in.

For rail travelers, however, the republic still has some work to do in the modernizing department. New SuperCity Pendolino trains now serve riders on several top routes within the country and to neighboring Vienna. But with the exception of a handful of international trains crisscrossing the country, most local routes in the country are served by ubiquitous, prompt, and cheap-but-oh-so-grungy trains. On the positive side, the Republic is now covered by the Eurail Global Pass, few countries in Europe can match its rich mix of history, and it's renowned as a value destination, so rail travelers' dollars will go a lot further here than in many other countries.

Highlights of the Czech Republic

The capital, **Prague,** is widely regarded as one of the most beautiful cities in Europe. This quirky and compact heart of Bohemia is a jumble of architecture. Gothic bestrides baroque, Renaissance adjoins Cubist, with a splash of Socialist Realism and postmodern kitsch thrown in for good measure. It's also unquestionably the first stop on any rail traveler's itinerary. Most international trains arrive here, and it's the only Czech city that welcomes direct flights from North America.

But Prague isn't the Czech Republic's only draw. For castle-hoppers, the majestic **Karlštejn Castle** (p. 188) is an easy day trip by train from Prague and one of the country's most popular destinations. And visitors are venturing more and more into West Bohemia, where one of the world's best-known spas **(Karlovy Vary)** has been restored to its Victorian-era splendor, and where castles abound in the surrounding countryside. These are old-world spas—not New Age health farms—villages where you

The Czech Republic

get your system replenished by drinking the waters, strolling the promenades, and soaking up the ambience. And though some of the Czech Republic isn't efficiently accessed by rail—hence the absence of Moravia from this chapter—the cities in this region generally make for easy rail trips out of Prague. In addition to the spa towns, if you have the time in your schedule, don't pass up the opportunity to visit Southern Bohemia's jewel of cities, **Český Krumlov,** named a World Heritage Site by UNESCO for its magnificent old-world architecture and atmosphere. You can reach this town on your way through **České Budějovice,** the hometown of the original Budweiser brand and a convenient rail base for exploring southern Bohemia.

ESSENTIALS

Getting There

BY PLANE   CSA Czech Airlines (**www.csa.cz/en**), the national airline, offers flights to Prague from a number of U.S. cities, including New York, Atlanta, Chicago, Los Angeles, and Washington, D.C. From Canada, you can fly to Prague out of Toronto and Montréal.

5

THE CZECH REPUBLIC

Essentials

FESTIVALS & special events

The world-famous **Prague Spring International Music Festival** is a 3-week series of classical music performances and concerts that usually takes place the last 3 weeks of May. Details on the festival can be found online at **www.festival.cz**. There is also an autumn version of the festival in September (**www.pragueautumn.cz**), with a similarly impressive mix of internationally recognized orchestras, conductors, and soloists.

After being banned during communism, **The Festival of the Five-Petaled Rose** in Český Krumlov has made a triumphant comeback and is now in its 22nd year. It's held each year on the summer solstice. Residents of Český Krumlov dress up in Renaissance costume and parade through the streets. Afterward, the streets become a stage, with plays, chess games with people dressed as pieces, music, and even duels "to the death." Information is available online at **www.ckrumlov.cz**.

To make a reservation in North America, call toll-free ℂ **800/223-2365.** For more information, call the nonstop call center in Prague, ℂ **011-420/239-007-007.**

The only major U.S. airline that flies to Prague (though always with a stopover somewhere in Europe) is **Delta Airlines** (ℂ **800/241-4141;** www.delta.com). Other airlines that service Prague out of Europe and that offer connecting services to several major U.S. airlines include **Lufthansa** (ℂ **800/645-3880;** www.lufthansa.com) and **British Airways** (ℂ **800/AIRWAYS** [247-9297]; www.ba.com).

All flights arrive in modern **Ruzyně Airport** (ℂ **00-420/220-111-111;** www.csl.cz), which is 12 miles (19km) west of the city center. At the airport, you'll find currency exchange offices Travelex, Acron, and AVE (open daily 6am–11pm); telephones; and several car-rental offices.

The Czech Republic by Rail

PASSES

Note: The Czech Republic is now covered by the **Eurail Global Pass,** as well as the **European East Pass,** the **Austria–Czech Republic Pass, Central Europe Triangle Pass, Eurail Select Pass,** and the **Czech Republic–Germany Pass** (see chapter 2 for more on these pass options).

The **Eurail Czech Republic Pass** entitles you to 3 to 8 consecutive or nonconsecutive days of unlimited train travel in a 1-month period. It starts at $145 for first class and $105 for second class. The Prague Welcome Card provides free entry to over 30 historic sights, museums, and galleries, as well as a 72-hour pass for transportation in Prague starting at $50. For other discounts included with the Welcome Card, check online. Both passes should be purchased in North America before you leave on your trip. You can buy one on the phone or online from **Rail Europe** (ℂ **888/438-7245** in the United States, ℂ **800/361-7245** in Canada; www.raileurope.com) or your travel agent.

FOREIGN TRAIN TERMS

In Prague, many of the international ticket window agents at the main train station will speak English. It may not be the most pleasant experience—Czech sales assistants in any trade tend to be surly—but you should get along fairly well.

As you get farther afield from Prague, you may not find such convenience, but with a little patience and a bit of preparation before you join the line, you should be able to be understood enough in English to get to where you want to go, and at the appropriate fare. Many destinations are often hard to pronounce, so be sure to write them down clearly on a piece of paper to show to the agent, or circle your end station in this guide book or on a train timetable.

Note that you will see signs bearing the following terms in train terminals and major attractions: **Vchod (entrance); Východ (exit); Informace (information); Odjezd/Odlet (departures);** and the all-important **Toalety (restrooms).**

PRACTICAL TRAIN INFORMATION

The train network in the Czech Republic is run by **Czech Railways (České Dráhy),** which uses a number of trains of different quality. For a list of the trains, their abbreviations on timetables, and an explanation of their features, see "Train Designations in the Czech Republic," below. Ordinary passenger trains (marked Os for *osobní* on timetables) don't require reservations or supplements and offer first- and second-class seating. They are also slow as molasses and usually very uncomfortable—avoid them, if you can. If you get stuck, splurge on first-class to make the trip as painless as possible. The Eurail Czech Republic Pass covers all national railway services, with limited exceptions.

The train network itself is pretty extensive and connects to a number of major cities in both Eastern and Western Europe. Major cities with InterCity or EuroCity connections to Prague include Vienna, Munich, Berlin, Budapest, and Warsaw. Locally, the routings are a little odd, and getting to some of the country's smaller towns and out of the way spots is, as a result, often faster by bus. Stick to the major cities and towns we discuss in this chapter, and you'll be fine. To find out about timetables of all connections within the Czech Republic and from/to abroad, go to **www.jizdnirady.cz**.

USEFUL CZECH train & travel TERMS

English	Czech	Pronunciation
Where is the . . . ?	Kde je . . . ?	gde yeh . . .
train station	nádraží	nah-drah-zhee
How much is the fare?	Kolik je jízdné?	koh-leek yeh yeesd-neh
I am going to . . .	Pojedu do . . .	poh-yeh-doo doh . . .
I would like a . . .	Chci . . .	khtsee . . .
one-way ticket	Jízdenka	yeez-den-kah
round-trip ticket	Zpáteční	zpah-tech-nee
	jízdenka	jeez-den-kah
I'm looking for . . .	Hledám . . .	hleh-dahm . . .
the city center	centrum	tsent-room
the tourist office	cestovní	tses-tohv-nee
	kancelář	kahn-tseh-larsh
Where is the nearest	Kde je nejbližší	gde yeh nay-bleesh-ee
telephone?	telefon?	tel-oh-fohn
I would like to buy . . .	Chci koupit . . .	khtsee koh-peet . . .
a map	mapu	mahp-oo

train designations IN THE CZECH REPUBLIC

NAME	ABBREVIATION	EXPLANATION
SuperCity	SC	Czech trains with a high standard of quality and consisting of modernized first-class coaches only and a restaurant car. A reservation is necessary, and special prices apply (see "Reservations" in this section for more on pricing).
EuroCity	EC	European trains that are guaranteed to meet an international standard. These have first- and second-class coaches and a restaurant car. A supplement is required, and reservations are possible but not mandatory.
InterCity	IC	These trains offer a certain level of guaranteed quality, and have first- and second-class coaches and a restaurant car. A supplement is required, and reservations are possible but not mandatory.
Express	Ex (*EN*)	Express trains offer fast connections between selected Czech cities and have first- and second-class coaches. It is a regional train. Night trains are indicated by the letters EN in a timetable. Reservations are possible. There is no supplement.

RESERVATIONS   Reservations on Czech trains are mandatory only if an R surrounded by a box is listed on the timetable next to your departure, or if you are traveling on an SC train. That said, trains can get very crowded, and if you plan on traveling in high season or on weekends, make a reservation way in advance so you can assure yourself of a seat and avoid standing in lines in the station. You can no longer print e-tickets from the online ticket site (**https://eshop.cd.cz**). Reservations on express trains must be made at least 2 hours before departure and can be made inside almost all of the Republic's train stations. A reservation costs 200Kč. Note that reservations on local trains in the Czech Republic cannot be made in North America, though you can buy open tickets through Rail Europe.

Reservations for sleeper accommodations on night trains in the Czech Republic and on international night trains to and from Prague are required. Reserve these as soon as you can (most international trains allow you to reserve up to 3 months in advance). You can reserve most international sleepers and couchettes through Rail Europe before you depart North America. Sleeper supplement prices are variable, based on availability and cost of service; a single couchette costs about 700Kč.

Note: Even if you have a railpass of any type, you'll still have to pay a travel supplement of about 150Kč one-way, when traveling on IC and EC trains, but prices again vary based on availability and cost of service.

You pay a fixed price for any route taken on an SC train, regardless of distance or time. The fee is 200Kč.

Trains & Travel Times in Czech Republic

From	To	# of Trains	Frequency	Travel Time
Prague	Karlovy Vary	9	Daily	3 hr., 26 min.
Český Krumlov	České Budějovice	9	Daily	55 min.
Prague	České Budějovice	12	Daily	2 hr., 50 min.

SERVICES & AMENITIES Generally, Czech trains do not have a very good reputation in terms of comfort and cleanness. They are old, lack most creature comforts, and run on old-style single tracks. That said, they still run pretty reliably and for reasonable prices. First-class travel (the only way to go) in the republic is far less expensive than in Western European countries. The Republic, however, has introduced more high-speed trains, and additional updates (likely more expensive ones) are on the drawing board.

Sleeping accommodations—ranging from simple couchettes to private single rooms—are available on long-haul trains within the Czech Republic and on international trains running through or terminating in Prague. Sleepers tend to be expensive (though often less than a hotel room), and the quality of the accommodations varies widely, as do prices. *Warning:* Theft is common from couchette compartments, so if you opt for a couchette, keep a close eye on your belongings.

Restaurant cars are available on SC, EC, and IC trains. They are available only on some Express trains, however, so bring lots of food—and lots of bottled water, just in case. (Do not drink tap water on trains, or anywhere else, for that matter.)

In Prague's main station, České Budějovice's station, and other selected cities' train stations, the Czech railways have a **"ČD center,"** providing complete services—reservations and ticket sales, timetable info, international train connections info, hotel booking, currency exchange, and so on. You also can call (**✆ 840-112-113**) or check their website at **www.cd.cz**, where you will find timetable information and an online reservation service.

[FastFACTS] CZECH REPUBLIC

Area Codes The **country code** for the Czech Republic is **420**. The **city codes** are connected to the local number in front, so the entire 9-digit number must be dialed locally. Numbers that begin with a 6 or 7 indicate a mobile phone.

Business Hours Most **banks** are open Monday to Friday 9am to 5pm. Pubs are usually open daily 11am to midnight. Most restaurants are open for lunch 9am to 3pm and for dinner 6 to 11pm; only a few stay open later. In smaller towns, cafes and restaurants open at 11am.

Climate Prague's average summer temperature is about 63°F (18°C), but some days can be quite chilly and others uncomfortably sultry (July and Aug can get very hot). In winter, the temperature remains close to freezing. During an average January, it's sunny and clear for only 50 hours the entire month. Pollution, heaviest in the winter, tends to limit the snowfall in Prague, though the city's been blanketed for quite a long period of winter the last couple of years.

Currency The basic unit of currency is the koruna (plural *koruny*), or crown, abbreviated Kč. Each koruna is divided into 100 haléřů, or hellers. It is usually noted as "CZK" in banks.

Documents Required

North American citizens need only passports and no visa for stays less than 90 days; passports must be valid for a period of at least 90 days beyond the expected length of stay in the Czech Republic. The Czech Reublic now has open borders. For more information, go to **www.czech.cz**.

Electricity

Czech appliances operate on 230 volts and plug into two-pronged outlets that differ from those in America and the United Kingdom. Appliances designed for the U.S. or U.K. markets must use an adapter and a transformer.

Embassies

The **U.S. Embassy** is at Tržiště 15, Praha 1 (✆ **257-022-000;** http://prague.usembassy. gov). The **Canadian Embassy** is at Muchova 6, Praha 6 (✆ **272-101-800;** www.canada.cz).

Health & Safety

You will likely feel safer in Prague than in most Western cities, but always take common-sense precautions. Don't walk alone at night around Wenceslas Square—one of the main areas for prostitution. All visitors should be watchful of pickpockets in heavily touristed areas, especially on Charles Bridge, in Old Town Square, and in front of the main station. Be wary in crowded buses, trams, and trains.

If you need any common medicine, you can purchase it from a pharmacist. Czech pharmacies are called *lékárna* and are recognized by a green cross on a white background. The most centrally located one is at Václavské nám. 8, Praha 1 (✆ **224-227-532**), open Monday to Friday from 8am to 6pm. If you need nonurgent medical attention, practitioners in many fields can be found at the **Canadian Medical Care** center at Veleslavínská 1, Prague 6, Dejvice (✆ **235-360-133;** www.cmcpraha.cz). For dental service, call **American Dental Associates,** at V Celnici 4, Prague 1, Nové Město (✆ **221-181-121;** www.americandental.cz), open 8am to 8pm Monday to Friday. For emergency medical aid, call the Foreigners' Medical Clinic, **Hospital Na Homolce,** Roentgenova 2, Praha 5 (✆ **257-271-111;** www. homolka.cz; Metro: Anděl, then bus 167).

Holidays

Official holidays are observed on January 1 (New Year's Day), Easter Monday, May 1 (Labor Day), May 8 (Liberation Day from Fascism), July 5 (Introduction of Christianity), July 6 (Death of Jan Hus), September 28 (St. Wenceslas Day), October 28 (Foundation of the Republic), November 17 (Day of Student Movement in 1939 and 1989), December 24 and 25 (Christmas), and December 26 (St. Stephen's Day). On these holidays, most business and shops (including food shops) are closed, and buses and trams run on Sunday schedules.

Mail

Post offices are plentiful and are normally open Monday to Friday from 8am to 7pm. The main post office (Hlavní pošta), at Jindřišská 14, Prague 1 (✆ **221-131-111**), is open 24 hours a day. Mailboxes are orange and are usually attached to the side of buildings. If you're sending mail overseas, make sure it's marked "Par Avion" so it doesn't go by surface. If you mail your letters at a post office, the clerk will add this stamp for you. Mail can take up to 10 days to reach its destination. For a regular letter to a European country, you need about a 18Kč stamp, and you need a 19Kč stamp to send a regular letter to North America.

Police & Emergencies

Dial the European emergency number ✆ **112** from any phone in case of emergency. You can reach Prague's police and fire services by calling ✆ **158** or **150.** For an ambulance, call ✆ **155.**

Telephone

The **country code** for the Czech Republic is **420.** The **city codes** are connected to the local number in front, so the entire number is dialed locally and has nine digits. To make a direct international call from the Czech Republic, dial 00 plus the country code of the country you are calling and then the area code and number. For directory assistance in English and for information on services and rates for calling abroad, dial ✆ **1181.**

The majority of pay phones operate with a

phone card, available from post offices and news dealers in denominations ranging from 200Kč to 500Kč. There are few coin-operated pay phones left. The more efficient phone-card telephones deduct the price of your call from the card. Charging a call to your phone credit card from a public telephone is often the most economical way to call home.

You can also dial abroad from the main post office (see "Mail," above).

Tipping At most restaurants and pubs, locals just round the bill up to the nearest multiple of 10 koruny. When you're given good service at tablecloth places, a 10% tip is proper. Washroom and cloakroom attendants usually demand a couple of koruny, and porters in airports and rail stations usually receive 20Kč per bag. Taxi drivers should get 5% to 10%, unless they've already ripped you off.

PRAGUE

More than 80 years after native son Franz Kafka's death, Prague's mix of the melancholy and the magnificent, set against some of Europe's most spectacular architecture, still confounds all who live or visit here. Its tightly wound brick paths have felt the hooves of kings' horses, the jackboots of Hitler's armies, the heaving tracks of Soviet tanks, and the shuffle of students in passive revolt. Fate tested the city once again in August 2002, when record floodwaters from the River Vltava engulfed much of Lesser Town and part of Old Town, putting many restaurants and attractions near the riverfront out of business. But the city has recovered very quickly. The 6-centuries-old Charles Bridge is today jammed with visitors and venture capitalists looking for memories or profits from a once-captive city now enjoying yet another renaissance.

For the rail traveler, Prague is *the* city to visit in the Czech Republic—if you can visit only one place in the country, this is the one you want to see. It's also the one you most likely *will* see. The central hub for most of the country's trains, the city is also a convenient stop on rail routes heading from the west into Eastern Europe. It's about 5 hours by train from Berlin and Vienna, and 7 hours from Frankfurt and Budapest.

If the Czech Republic is the first stop on your rail trip, Prague is home to the only airport that serves direct flights from the U.S. And on the convenience front, though it's cheaper than many other European capitals, it's the most modern of the Eastern European cities, so you'll have access to most of the creature comforts of home, even while surrounded by centuries of medieval architecture. If your schedule allows it, plan on spending at least 2 days here, though you could spend more than a week and not discover all of the city's treasures.

Station Information
GETTING FROM THE AIRPORT TO THE TRAIN STATION
Plenty of taxis line up in front of Ruzyně Airport (p. 166), but know that most drivers will try to take advantage of you, and getting an honestly metered ride out of the airport is next to impossible. Two cab companies are licensed to operate at the airport. The more reliable of the two is **AAA Radiotaxi** (✆ **222-333-222;** www.aaa-taxi.cz); look for the yellow cabs lined up outside both main terminals, North 1 and North 2. Fares with AAA average about 600Kč to the center. The trip normally takes about 25 minutes, but the drive can run as long as an hour during rush hour.

CEDAZ (✆ **221-111-111;** www.cedaz.cz) operates an airport minibus to náměstí Republiky in central Prague, and from that point you can take the Metro to

Prague

ACCOMMODATIONS■
Andante **34**
Hotel Cloister Inn **27**
Hotel Esplanade **33**
Hotel Meran **32**
Hotel Paříž **18**
Hotel Ungelt **19**
Palace Hotel **30**
U Krále Karla **7**

DINING◆
Bakeshop **16**
Bohemia Bagel **17**
Bonante Restaurant **37**
Café-Restaurant
  Louvre **29**
Hergetova Cihelna **9**
Kogo **24, 25**
Pivovarský dům **35**
Pizzeria Rugantino **15**
Radost FX **36**
U medvídků **28**

ATTRACTIONS●
Astronomical Clock
  at Old Town Hall **22**
Cathedral of
  St. Nicholas **8**
Charles Bridge **23**
Jewish Museum **13**
Maisel Synagogue **14**
National Gallery **20**
Old Jewish Cemetery **13**
Old-New Synagogue **12**
Old Town Square **21**
Prague Castle **4**
Royal Garden **5**
Royal Palace **3**
St. Agnes Convent **11**
St. George's Convent **6**
St. Vitus Cathedral **2**
Šternberk Palace **1**
Veletržní Palace **10**
Wenceslas Square **31**

INFORMATION●
Castle Information
  Office **2**
Prague Information
  Office **26**

5

Prague

THE CZECH REPUBLIC

all of Prague's train stations. Minibuses run regularly between the airport and the center for a flat fee of 480Kč for groups of one to four persons. CEDAZ also takes individual passengers from the airport to V Celnici street in central Prague (near Náměstí Republiky) for 120Kč per person. You can also take **city bus 119** from the airport to the Dejvická Metro station (Line A; trip time: 30 min.). Travel requires a 26Kč ticket purchased from yellow ticketing machines at the bus stop (note that the machines accept only exact change), or 30Kč if bought from the driver (exact change appreciated). Buy two tickets if you're carrying large luggage. A special **Airport Express** (designated AE on buses) runs to and from Prague's main train station and costs 50Kč per person each way. This is convenient if you are connecting directly to an international train.

INSIDE THE STATIONS

Prague has two central rail stations: Hlavní nádraží and Nádraží Holešovice.

Of the two, **Hlavní nádraží (Main Train Station),** Wilsonova třída 80, Praha 1 ℂ 224-614-071; www.cd.cz; Metro: Hlavní nádraží, line C) is grander and more popular; however, it's also seedier because it has been neglected for years. At this writing, a massive reconstruction of the station's building complex is underway. It will be a lengthy process that should bring significant changes to the station's main hall interior as well as revitalization of the surrounding areas.

Tickets for domestic and international trains are available at the windows located in the main hall on the ground level. From the train platform, you'll walk down a flight of stairs and through a tunnel before arriving in the ground-level main hall. There are also several visitor and accommodation information windows situated in the main hall. Useful is the **ČD center** (ℂ 840-112-113; www.cd.cz), run by Czech Railways. It provides domestic and international **train information,** as well as currency exchange, airline tickets, and accommodation services. It is open daily from 7am to 11am, 11:30am to 2pm, and 2:30pm to 5:45pm. Visa and MasterCard are accepted. An information window is open 3:15am to 12:40am (the train station is closed 1–3am). The **Prague Information Service (PIS)** office helps with accommodations, tickets for events, and city tours and excursions. It is generally open daily from 7am to 6pm, though, due to the construction, hours are not firmly set and are subject to change.

The station's basement has luggage lockers for 60Kč per day. They aren't secure, though, and should be avoided.

Nádraží Holešovice (North Train Station), Partyzánská at Vrbenského, Praha 7 (ℂ 224-615-865; www.cd.cz), is usually the terminus for trains from points north, especially international trains arriving from Germany, Vienna, and Budapest. It's not as centrally located as the Main Train Station, but its more manageable size and convenient location at the end of Metro line C make it a popular choice. Train information is available at ℂ 840-112-113 or on the Web at **http://jizdnirady. idnes.cz**.

Prague also has two smaller rail stations. **Masarykovo Station,** Hybernská, Praha 1 (ℂ 221-111-122; Metro: nám. Republiky), is primarily for travelers arriving on trains from other Bohemian and Moravian cities. It's about 10 minutes by foot from the main station. **Smíchov Station,** Nádražní ulice, Praha 5 (ℂ 224-617-686; Metro: Smíchovské Nádraží Line B), is used mainly for commuter trains from western and southern Bohemia, though it's a convenient station for getting to popular day-trip destinations like Karlštejn and Plzeň. The station has a 24-hour baggage check.

Reading Maps

When reading maps or searching for addresses, keep in mind that *ulice* (abbreviated *ul.*) means "street," *třída* means "avenue," *náměstí* (abbreviated *nám.*) is a "square" or "plaza," a *most* is a "bridge," and *nábřeží* is a "quay." In Czech, none of these terms are capitalized. In addresses, street numbers usually follow the street name (like Václavské nám. 25). Each address is followed by a district number, such as Praha 1 (*Praha* is "Prague" in Czech).

The site **www.idos.cz** provides an online timetable for trains and buses, including international destinations. Just type in the city (using the Czech spellings, such as "Praha" for Prague, but note that diacritical marks are not required), and you'll get a complete listing of train and bus connections.

Information Elsewhere in the City

The **Prague Information Service (PIS)**, Rytířská 31, Praha 1 (© **12444**; www.pis.cz; Metro: Můstek), makes lodging reservations, gives touring tips, and sells tickets for cultural events and tours. Its website offers regularly updated tourism information in English. It's open Monday to Saturday from 9am to 7pm. It is closed on Sundays. There are also PIS offices inside Old Town Hall.

The city's **Cultural and Information Center,** on the ground floor of the Municipal House (Obecní dům), nám. Republiky 5, Praha 1 (© **222-002-101**; www.obecnidum.cz; Metro: nám. Republiky), offers advice, tickets, souvenirs, refreshments, and restrooms. It's open daily 10am to 7pm.

On the Web, the well-designed **www.czechsite.com** offers tips on getting around, attractions, museums, galleries, and restaurants. You can book your lodging on the site.

Getting Around

In order to easily get around town, you'll first need a quick explanation of the city's layout. The River Vltava bisects Prague. **Staré Město (Old Town)** and **Nové Město (New Town)** are on the east (right) side of the river, while the **Hradčany (Castle District)** and **Malá Strana (Lesser Town)** are on the west (left) bank.

Bridges and squares are the most prominent landmarks. **Charles Bridge,** the oldest and most famous of those spanning the Vltava, is at the epicenter and connects Old Town with Lesser Town and the Castle District. Several important streets radiate from Old Town Square, including fashionable **Pařížská** to the northwest, historic **Celetná** to the east, and **Melantrichova,** connecting to Wenceslas Square (Václavské nám.) to the southeast. On the west side of Charles Bridge is **Mostecká,** a 3-block-long connection to **Malostranské náměstí,** Malá Strana's main square. **Hradčany,** the Castle District, is just northwest of the square, while a second hill, **Petřín,** is just southwest.

BY PUBLIC TRANSPORTATION   Prague's public transport network is a highly efficient, vast system of subways, trams, and buses. Adults can ride through a maximum of five stations on the Metro (not including the station of validation) or 20 minutes on a tram or bus, without transfers (on the Metro, you can change from lines A, B, and C within 30 min.), for 18Kč; children 6 to 15 years old ride for 9Kč, those 5 and under ride free. You usually won't need more than the maximum five stations

5

THE CZECH REPUBLIC

Prague

for trips in the historic districts. Rides of more than five stops on the Metro, or longer tram or bus rides, with unlimited transfers for up to 75 minutes (90 min. Sat–Sun, public holidays, and after 8pm on workdays) after your ticket is validated, cost 26Kč. You can buy tickets from coin-operated orange machines in Metro stations or at most newsstands marked TABÁK or TRAFIKA. Machines have instructions in English; push ticket type (discounted or full) and then insert money. Hold on to your ticket (which you must validate at the orange or yellow stamp clocks in each tram or bus when you get on board or at the entrance to the Metro) during your ride—you'll need it to prove you've paid if a ticket collector asks. If you're caught without a valid ticket, you have to pay a 700Kč fine to a ticket controller on the spot or 950Kč if paid later.

Warning: Oversize luggage (larger than carry-on size) requires a transfer ticket for 13Kč for each piece. You may be fined 100Kč on the spot for not having tickets for your luggage, or 200Kč if paid later. Also beware the pickpockets common on the trams and Metro.

Metro trains operate daily from 5am to midnight and run every 2 to 10 minutes, depending on the time of day. The three lines are identified by both letter and color: A (green), B (yellow), and C (red). The most convenient stations are Muzeum, on both the A and C lines at the top of Václavské náměstí (Wenceslas Sq.); Můstek, at the foot of Václavské náměstí on both A and B lines; Staroměstská, on the A line, for Old Town Square and Charles Bridge; and Malostranská, on the A line, serving Malá Strana and the Castle District.

The electric **tramlines** run practically everywhere. You never have to hail trams; they make every stop. The most popular, **no. 22** (aka the "tourist tram" or the "pickpocket express"), run past top sights such as the National Theater and Prague Castle. Regular bus and tram service stops at midnight, after which selected routes run reduced schedules, usually only once per hour. If you miss a night connection, expect a long wait for the next bus.

Passes You can purchase discounted transport passes for the public transport system. A 1-day pass good for unlimited rides is 100Kč, a 3-day pass 330Kč, a 5-day pass 500Kč, and a 30-day monthly pass 550Kč. You can buy the day passes at the DP windows at any Metro station.

BY FUNICULAR A cog railway makes the scenic run up and down Petřín Hill every 10 minutes or so from 9am to 11:30pm, with an intermediate stop at the Nebozízek Restaurant in the middle of the hill overlooking the city. It requires the same 26Kč ticket as other public transportation, and discounted transport passes are accepted. The funicular departs from a small house in the park just above the middle of Újezd (tram: 12, 20, or 22) in Malá Strana.

BY TAXI *Avoid taxis!* If you must, hail one in the streets or in front of train stations, large hotels, and popular attractions (a better idea is to call a taxi by phone or have your hotel or restaurant call one for you). Be forewarned that many drivers simply gouge tourists, though the situation has gotten slightly better over the last few years. The best fare you can hope for is 28Kč per kilometer, but twice or three times that isn't rare. The meter starts at 40Kč, 30Kč if you've ordered by phone. The rates are usually posted on the dashboard, making it too late to haggle once you're in and on your way. Negotiate a price and have it written down before getting in. Fares around the center typically run from 100Kč to 200Kč, depending on the journey. Never get into an unmarked cab, and make sure the driver puts on the meter. Better yet, go on foot or by public transport. Somewhat reputable companies with English-speaking

dispatchers are **AAA Radiotaxi** (📞 **14014** or 222-333-222; www.aaa-
Taxi (📞 **844-700-800;** www.profitaxi.cz), and **SEDOP** (📞 **841-6(**
sedop.cz). AAA operates a few dedicated taxi stands around town,
conveniently located on Václavské náměstí and Malostranské náměstí,
find honest drivers.

Where to Stay

Not so long ago, Prague used to have a shortage of hotel rooms, and if you arrived in town without reservations, there was a good chance you would be without a place to stay. That's no longer the case (though it always pays to reserve in advance if you find a good place at a good price). Hotel construction became a boom industry during the past decade, and if anything, the city now has too many beds, not too few. That's great news for travelers. It means that prices might someday start to come down from their lofty peaks. Inexplicably, hotel prices in Prague the past decade or so have been higher on average than in Paris or Amsterdam, for facilities that were usually inferior.

The combination of new hotels plus the worldwide economic recession in 2009–2010 succeeded in driving down prices somewhat, meaning that, depending on the night, it was possible to snag a good place in the center for under $100 for the first time in many years. It's not clear what the future will bring, but it always pays to shop around. Bargains are out there.

All kinds of private housing are offered by several local agencies. The leader now is Prague-based **E-TRAVEL.CZ,** which offers all types of accommodations at their main website, or you can tap their large pictured database of apartments at **www. apartments.cz.** The office is near the National Theater at Divadelní 24, Praha 1 (📞 **224-990-990;** www.travel.cz; Metro: Národní třída). Another agency, especially for those arriving late by train or air, is **AVE Travel Ltd.** (📞 **251-551-011;** www. avetravel.cz). It has an outlet at the airport (open 7am–10pm) and at the Nádraží Holešovice, open daily from 7am to 9pm.

Andante Hotel 🎗 One of the best value choices near Wenceslas Square, the understated Andante is tucked away on a darker side street, about 2 blocks off the top of the square. Despite its less-than-appealing neighborhood (it's in the local red-light district), this is the most comfortable property in the moderate price range. The clean and comfortable guest rooms have been modernized and have well-kept bathrooms.

Ve Smečkách 4, Praha 1. 📞 **222-210-021.** Fax 222-210-591. www.andante.cz. 32 units. 2,700Kč double; 3,600Kč suite. Rates include breakfast. AE, MC, V. Metro: Muzeum. **Amenities:** Restaurant; bar. *In room:* No A/C.

Hotel Cloister Inn ★ 🎗 Between Old Town Square and the National Theater (a 3-min. walk from the Charles Bridge), the Cloister Inn occupies a building that the secret police once used to hold prisoners. It sounds ominous, but the rooms are inviting. A new proprietor has taken over management from the secret police and has refurbished and expanded the hotel with smart colors and comfortable Nordic furniture. The rooms offer enough space, beds with firm mattresses, and reasonably sized shower-only bathrooms.

Konviktská 4, Praha 1. 📞 **224-211-020.** Fax 224-210-800. www.cloister-inn.cz. 73 units. 2,100Kč double. Rates include breakfast. AE, DC, MC, V. Metro: Národní třída. **Amenities:** Breakfast room.

.el Esplanade   Located on a side street at the top of Wenceslas Square and .cross from the Main Train Station, this very family-friendly hotel began life as a bank and the offices of an Italian insurance company. Rooms are bright and airy, some with standard beds, others with French provincial headboards, and others with extravagant canopies.

Washingtonova 19, Praha 1. ℂ **224-501-111.** Fax 224-229-306. www.esplanade.cz. 74 units. From 2,300Kč double; from 4,800Kč suite. Rates include breakfast. AE, MC, V. Metro: Muzeum. **Amenities:** Restaurant; bar; cafe.

Hotel Meran 🖋   This used to be part of Hotel Evropa, the bigger Art Deco landmark that draws so much attention to its gilded facade. The family-run and cozier Meran has had a face-lift to make it a fair midrange choice on Wenceslas Square, within walking distance of the Main Train Station. The lobby interior has retained some original Art Nouveau accents, although the furnishings in the spotless rooms have few.

Václavské nám. 27, Praha 1. ℂ **224-238-440.** Fax 224-230-411. www.hotelmeran.cz. 20 units. 2,400Kč double. Rates include breakfast. AE, DC, MC, V. Metro: Muzeum or Můstek.

Hotel Paříž ★★   At the edge of náměstí Republiky (very close to the Metro) and across from the Municipal House, the Paříž provides a rare glimpse back into the gilded First Republic. Each light fixture, etching, and curve at this Art Nouveau landmark recalls the days when Prague was one of the world's richest cities. For a glimpse of the hotel's atmosphere, rent the film *Mission Impossible;* you can see Tom Cruise plotting his revenge from within one of the fine suites. The high-ceilinged guest rooms are comfortable, with modern Art Deco accents.

U Obecního domu 1, Praha 1. ℂ **222-195-195.** Fax 222-195-907. www.hotel-pariz.cz. 94 units. 4,200Kč double; from 8,000Kč suite. Rates include breakfast. AE, DC, MC, V. Metro: nám. Republiky. **Amenities:** Restaurant; cafe; lounge.

Hotel Ungelt   It's not very opulent, but this family-friendly hotel offers airy, spacious suites at a great value. Each contains a living room, a full kitchen, and a bathroom. Rooms have standard-issue beds; some have hand-painted ceilings. The Old Town Square is just around the corner, and the train station is less than half a mile away.

Štupartská 7, Praha 1. ℂ **222-745-900.** Fax 222-745-901. www.ungelt.cz. 6 units. From 2,700Kč 1-bedroom suite; 3,600Kč 2-bedroom suite. Rates include breakfast. AE, MC, V. Metro: Staroměstská or on B Line nám. Republiky. **Amenities:** Bar.

Palace Hotel ★   The Palace is a top upscale property, a block from Wenceslas Square and within walking distance of the Main Train Station, although I think the nearby Paříž (see above) has far more character. The 1903 Art Deco property is nevertheless a favorite with visiting celebrities (from Caruso to Steven Spielberg) and offers excellent service. Guest rooms are some of the largest and most modern luxury accommodations in Prague, each with an Italian marble bathroom.

Panská 12, Praha 1. ℂ **224-093-111.** Fax 224-221-240. www.palacehotel.cz. 124 units. From 6,500Kč double; from 7,500Kč suite. Rates include breakfast. AE, DC, MC, V. Metro: Můstek. **Amenities:** 2 restaurants; 2 lounges; 2 rooms for those w/limited mobility.

U Krále Karla ★   This Castle Hill property does so much to drive home its Renaissance roots, King Charles's heirs should be getting royalties. Replete with period-print, open-beamed ceilings and stained-glass windows, the atmosphere is almost Disneyesque in its pretense, but somehow appropriate for this location at the foot of

Prague Castle. This is a fun, comfortable choice, with heavy period furniture and colorful angelic accents everywhere, though it is pretty far from a train station.

Nerudova-Úvoz 4, Praha 1. ✆ **257-533-594.** Fax 257-533-591. www.romantichotels.cz. 19 units. 65€–70€ double; 70€–85€ suite. Rates include breakfast. AE, MC, V. Tram: 22 or 23 to Malostranské nám. **Amenities:** Restaurant; bar; cafe.

Top Attractions & Special Moments

Most of Prague's special features are best viewed while slowly wandering through the city's heart. Except for the busy main streets, where you may have to dodge traffic, Prague is ideal for walking. Actually, walking is really the only way to explore Prague. Most of the town's oldest areas are pedestrian zones, with motor traffic restricted. If you have the time and energy, absorb the grand architecture of Prague Castle and the Old Town skyline (best from Charles Bridge) at sunrise and then at sunset. You'll see two completely different cities.

Prague Castle (Pražský Hrad) ★★★ 📷 The huge hilltop complex known collectively as Pražský Hrad encompasses dozens of towers, churches, courtyards, and monuments. A visit could easily take an entire day or more. Still, you can see the top sights in the space of a morning or an afternoon. Make sure not to miss **St. Vitus Cathedral (Chrám sv. Víta)** ★, constructed in A.D. 926 as the court church of the Premyslid princes. It was named for a wealthy 4th-century Sicilian martyr and has long been the center of Prague's religious and political life. The cathedral's architecture is a mix of Gothic, baroque, and neo-Gothic elements.

The **Royal Palace (Královský palác)** ★, in the third courtyard of the castle grounds, served as the residence of kings between the 10th and 17th centuries. Vaulted Vladislav Hall, the interior's centerpiece, was used for coronations and is still used for the inauguration of the Czech presidents and special occasions. You'll find a good selection of guidebooks, maps, and other related information at the entrance. Other must-sees include **St. George's Basilica (Kostel sv. Jiří),** which houses a museum of historic Czech art; **Golden Lane (Zlatá ulička),** a picturesque, fairy-tale street of tiny 16th-century servants' houses; and the **Powder Tower (Prašná věž,** aka Mihulka), a laboratory for the 17th-century alchemists serving the court of Emperor Rudolf II.

Tickets are sold at the **Prague Castle Information Center** (✆ **224-373-368**), in the third courtyard after passing through the main gate from Hradčanské náměstí. The center also arranges tours in various languages and sells tickets for individual concerts and exhibits.

Hradčanské nám., Hradčany, Praha 1. ✆ **224-373-368.** Fax 224-310-896. www.hrad.cz. Grounds free. Combination ticket for permanent exhibition, St. George's Basilica, Powder Tower, Golden Lane, Dali-borka Tower, the Prague Castle Picture Gallery, without guide, 350Kč adults, 175Kč students; short tour

Prague in a Day

If you are doing a quick stopover in Prague and have only 1 day to see the city, do what visiting kings and poten-tates do on a short visit: Walk the **Royal Route** from the top of the Hradčany hill (tram 22 or 23 or a taxi is suggested for the ride up unless you're very fit). Tour **Prague Castle,** and then stroll across Charles Bridge on the way to the winding alleys of **Old Town (Staré Město).**

(Royal Palace, St. George's Basilica, Golden Lane, and Daliborka Tower) 250Kč adults, 125Kč students. Tickets valid 2 days. Daily 9am-6pm (to 4pm Nov-Mar). Metro: Malostranská, then tram no. 22 or 23, up the hill 2 stops.

THE JEWISH MUSEUM

The Jewish Museum manages (☎ **221-711-511;** www.jewishmuseum.cz) all the Jewish landmarks in Josefov, the Jewish Quarter, which is the northwest quarter of Old Town. The museum offers guided package tours with an English-speaking guide as part of a comprehensive admission price. The package includes the Ceremonial Hall, Old Jewish Cemetery, Pinkas Synagogue, Klaus Synagogue, Maisel Synagogue, and Spanish Synagogue.

Maisel Synagogue   Maisel Synagogue is used as the exhibition space for the Jewish Museum. Most of Prague's ancient Judaica was destroyed by the Nazis during World War II. Ironically, those same Germans constructed an "exotic museum of an extinct race," thus salvaging thousands of objects, such as the valued Torah covers, books, and silver now displayed here.

Maiselova 10 (btw. Široká and Jáchymova 3), Praha 1. ☎ **222-317-191.** Fax 222-317-181. www.jewish museum.cz. Admission to museum sites listed above is 300Kč adults, 200Kč students. Apr-Oct tours for groups of 10 or more on the hour starting 9am (last tour 5pm). Nov-Apr tours leave whenever enough people gather in the same language, open 9am-4:30pm Sun-Fri. Metro: Line A to Staroměstská.

Old Jewish Cemetery (Starý židovský hřbitov) ★   Dating from the mid–15th century and a block away from the Old-New Synagogue, this is one of Europe's oldest Jewish burial grounds. It's also one of the most crowded because the city restricted Jewish burials—a 1-block zone is filled with more than 20,000 graves. The most renowned occupant: Rabbi Yehuda Loew (d. 1609), also known as the Maharal, who created the legendary Golem (clay creature) to protect the Jews of Prague.

U Starého hřbitova; the entrance is from Široká 3. ☎ **221-711-511.** Fax 222-317-181. www.jewishmuseum. cz. Admission to all Jewish Museum sites 300Kč adults, 200Kč students. Apr-Oct Sun-Fri 9am-6pm; Nov-Mar Sun-Fri 9am-4:30pm. Closed Sat and Jewish Holidays. Metro: Line A to Staroměstská.

Old-New Synagogue (Staronová synagoga) ★   First called the New Synagogue to distinguish it from an even older one that no longer exists, the Gothic-style Old-New Synagogue, built around 1270, is Europe's oldest Jewish house of worship. Note that this is the one site in Josefov not included in the Jewish Museum tour package.

Červená 2. ☎ **224-800-812.** www.synagogue.cz. Admission 200Kč adults, 140Kč students (if part of the package for Jewish Museum, 490Kč adults, 330Kč students), free for children 5 and under. Jan-Mar Sun-Thurs 9:30am-4:30pm, Fri 9am-2pm; Apr-Oct Sun-Fri 9:30am-6pm; Nov-Dec Sun-Thurs 9:30am-5pm, Fri 9am-2pm. Closed Sat and Jewish holidays. Metro: Line A to Staroměstská.

 Charles Bridge

Dating from the 14th century, the Charles Bridge (Karlův most) ★★★, Prague's most celebrated structure, links Prague Castle to Staré Město. For most of its 600 years, the 1,700-foot (510m) span has been a pedestrian promenade, although for centuries walkers had to share the concourse with horse-drawn vehicles and trolleys. Today the bridge is filled with hordes walking among folksy artists and street musicians. Strolling the bridge is a quintessential Prague experience and should not be missed.

THE NATIONAL GALLERY

The national collection of fine art is grouped for display in the series of venues known collectively as the **National Gallery (Národní Galerie; www.ngprague.cz).** *Tip:* Admission to all of the National Gallery's exhibits is free from 3pm to 8pm on the first Wednesday of every month.

St. Agnes Convent (Klášter sv. Anežky české) This complex of early Gothic buildings and churches dates from the 13th century. The convent, tucked in a corner of Staré Město, is appropriately home to a collection of medieval and Renaissance art.

U milosrdných 17, Praha 1.© **224-810-628.** www.ngprague.cz. Admission 150Kč adults, 80Kč children; 80Kč adults, 40Kč children after 4pm. Tues–Sun 10am–6pm. Metro: Line A to Staroměstská.

St. George's Convent at Prague Castle (Klášter sv. Jiří na Pražském hradě) Dedicated to displaying traditional Czech art, the castle convent is especially packed with Gothic and baroque Bohemian iconography, as well as portraits of patron saints. The most famous among the unique collection of Czech Gothic panel paintings are those by the master of the Hohenfurth Altarpiece and the master Theodoricus. There's also a noteworthy collection of Czech Mannerist and baroque paintings from the 17th and 18th centuries.

Jiřské nám. 33.© **257-531-644.** www.ngprague.cz. Admission 150Kč adults, 80Kč students; Reduced rates after 4pm. Daily 10am–6pm. Metro: Line A to Malostranská or Hradčanská. Tram: 22.

Šternberk Palace (Šternberský palác) ★ The jewel in the National Gallery crown, the gallery at Šternberk Palace, adjacent to the main gate of Prague Castle, was overhauled in 2002–03. It now has an exhibition of ancient Greek and Roman art, though the primary collection still features European artworks from the 14th through the 18th centuries. You'll find small sculptures mixed along with Renaissance oils from Dutch masters. Pieces by Rembrandt, El Greco, Goya, Dürer, and Van Dyck are mixed among numerous pieces from Austrian imperial-court painters.

Hradčanské nám. 15, Praha 1.© **233-090-570.** www.ngprague.cz. Admission 150Kč adults, 80Kč students and children; reduced rates after 4pm. Tues–Sun 10am–6pm. Metro: Line A to Malostranská or Hradčanská. Tram: 22.

Veletržní Palace This 1925 constructivist palace, built for trade fairs, holds the bulk of the National Gallery's collection of 20th- and 21st-century works by Czech and other European artists. Three atrium-lit concourses provide a comfortable setting for some catchy and kitschy Czech sculpture and multimedia works. Alas, the best Cubist works from Braque and Picasso, Rodin bronzes, and many other primarily French pieces have been relegated to the second floor; the museum's 19th-century collection is here as well.

Veletržní at Dukelských hrdinů 47, Praha 7.© **224-301-111.** www.ngprague.cz. Admission 200Kč adults, 100Kč students; reduced admission after 4pm. Tues–Sun 10am–6pm. Metro: Line C to Vltavská. Tram 12, 14, or 17 to Strossmayerovo nám.

FAMOUS SQUARES

The most celebrated square, **Old Town Square (Staroměstské nám.),** is surrounded by baroque buildings and packed with colorful craftspeople, cafes, and entertainers. In ancient days, the site was a major crossroad on central European merchant routes. In its center stands a memorial to Jan Hus, the 15th-century martyr who crusaded against Prague's German-dominated religious and political establishment. Unveiled in 1915, on the 500th anniversary of Hus's execution, the monument's most compelling features are the asymmetry of the composition and the

5

THE CZECH REPUBLIC

Prague

fluidity of the figures. It has been in reconstruction since 2007. Take Metro line A to Staroměstská.

The **Astronomical Clock (orloj)** at **Old Town Hall (Staroměstská radnice)** performs a glockenspiel spectacle daily on the hour from 8am to 8pm. Originally constructed in 1410, the clock has long been an important symbol of Prague. **Wenceslas Square (Václavské nám.)**, a former horse market, has been the focal point of riots, revolutions, and national celebrations. Take Metro line A or B to Můstek.

MORE ATTRACTIONS

Cathedral of St. Nicholas (Chrám sv. Mikuláše) ★ 📷 This church is critically regarded as one of the best examples of the high baroque north of the Alps. K. I. Dienzenhofer's 1711 design was augmented by his son Kryštof's 260-foot (78m) dome, which has dominated the Malá Strana skyline since its completion in 1752. Prague's smog has played havoc with the building's exterior, but its gilded interior is stunning. Gold-capped marble-veneered columns frame altars packed with statuary and frescoes.

Malostranské nám., Praha 1. ✆ **257-534-215.** Admission 70Kč. Daily 9am–5pm, concerts are usually held at 6pm. Admission around 490Kč. Metro: Malostranská, then tram 12 one stop to Malostranské nám, or take tram 20 or 32.

PARKS & GARDENS

From **Vyšehrad,** Soběslavova 1 (✆ **224-920-735;** Metro line C to Vyšehrad or tram no. 3 or 16 to Výtoň; park is open 24 hr.), legend has it that Princess Libuše looked out over the Vltava valley toward the present-day Prague Castle and predicted the founding of a great state and capital city. Vyšehrad was the seat of the first Czech kings of the Premyslid dynasty before the dawn of this millennium. Today, within the confines of the citadel, lush lawns and gardens are crisscrossed by dozens of paths, leading to historic buildings and cemeteries. From here you'll see one of the city's most panoramic views.

The **Royal Garden (Královská zahrada)** at Prague Castle, once the site of the sovereigns' vineyards, was founded in 1534. Dotted with lemon trees and surrounded by 16th-, 17th-, and 18th-century buildings, the park is laid out with abundant shrubbery and fountains. Enter from U Prašného mostu street north of the castle complex; it's open daily from 10am to 6pm in the summer season.

In Hradčany, the **Garden on the Ramparts (Zahrada na Valech)** is a park below the castle with a gorgeous city panorama. Beyond beautifully groomed lawns and sparse shrubbery is a tranquil low-angle view of the castle above and the city below. Enter the garden from the south side of the castle complex, below Hradčanské náměstí. The garden is open daily from 10am to 6pm in the summer season.

Where to Dine

The true Czech dining experience can be summed up in three native words: *vepřo-knedlo-zelo*—pork, dumplings, and cabbage. If that's what you want, try most any *hostinec* (Czech pub). Most offer a hearty *guláš* or pork dish with dumplings and cabbage for about 80Kč to 150Kč After you wash it down with Czech beer, you won't care about the taste—or your arteries. Today, thanks to a massive influx of tourist dollars, as well as rising incomes of ordinary Czechs, Prague now supports many very good restaurants, with traditional Czech places supplemented by French, Italian, Japanese, Chinese, and Indian restaurants.

Menu prices include VAT. Tipping has become more commonplace in restaurants where the staff is obviously trying harder; rounding up the bill to about 10% or more is usually adequate. Many restaurants are now accepting credit cards, but it is better to leave tips in cash to ensure that the waitstaff actually receives it.

Warning: Some restaurants gouge customers by charging exorbitant amounts for nuts or other seemingly free premeal snacks left on your table. Ask before you eat.

Bakeshop ★★ AMERICAN/DELI   Prague's lucky enough to have an American-style bakery and sandwich shop that would be the envy of many an American town or city. Bakeshop is simply the best bakery for miles. Come here for soups; salads; ready-made sandwiches; yogurt cups; and, naturally, bread, cakes, brownies, and cookies. It's one-stop shopping for a picnic lunch. You can eat in at the counter or get it to go.

Kozí 1, Prague 1. ✆ **222-316-823.** www.bakeshop.cz. Sandwiches 90Kč–145Kč. AE, MC, V. Daily 7am–7pm. Metro: Staroměstská.

Bohemia Bagel 🍴 BAGELS/SANDWICHES   The roster of golden-brown, hand-rolled, stone-baked bagels at these restaurants (the original one is at the base of Petřín Hill, located just off Old Town Square at Masná 2 [Staré Město; ✆ **224-812-560;** daily 8am–11pm; metro: Staroměstská]), near the Jewish Quarter, and one near Charles Bridge at Lázeňská 19), is stellar. Plain, cinnamon raisin, garlic, or onion provides a sturdy but tender frame for Scandinavian lox and cream cheese or jalapeño-cheddar cheese (on which you can lop Tex-Mex chili for the Sloppy Bagel). The lunch menu is filled with soups and fresh sandwiches, served on a bagel or French bread.

Lázeňská 19, Prague 1 (Malá Strana). ✆ **257-218-192.** www.bohemiabagel.cz. Bagels and sandwiches 60Kč–175Kč. No credit cards. Daily 7:30am–7pm. Metro: Malostranská plus tram no. 12, 20, or 22 to Malostranské náměstí.

Bonante Restaurant ★ INTERNATIONAL   Our favorite choice above Wences-las Square in Vinohrady, it is one of the best values in Prague and especially great for shunning the cold of an autumn or winter evening near the roaring fire in the brick cellar dining room. Bonante is a bridge between Italian cuisine and other continental foods. There are also vegetarian and low-calorie, chicken-based selections. Jazz combos play on some nights from a small stage in the corner.

Anglická 15, Praha 2. ✆ **224-221-665.** www.bonante.cz. Reservations recommended. Main courses 160Kč–410Kč. MC, V. Daily 11am–11pm. Metro: I. P. Pavlova or nám. Míru.

Café-Restaurant Louvre CZECH/INTERNATIONAL   This big, breezy upstairs dining hall in New Town is great for a coffee, an inexpensive pretheater meal, or an upscale game of pool. A fabulous Art Nouveau interior with huge original chandeliers buzzes with shoppers, businessmen, and students. Main dishes range from Czech beef goulash to grilled salmon steak. Avoid the always-overcooked pastas and stick to the basic meats and fish. In the snazzy billiards parlor in back, you can have drinks or a light meal.

Národní třída 22, Praha 1. ✆ **224-930-949.** www.cafelouvre.cz (for reservations). Main courses 130Kč–350Kč; breakfast menu 30Kč–120Kč. DC, MC, V. Mon–Fri 8am–11:30pm; Sat–Sun 9am–11:30pm. Metro: Národní třída.

Hergetova Cihelna ★★ INTERNATIONAL/PIZZA   Set inside a much-reno-vated 18th-century former brick factory *(cihelna)*, this dining complex consists of a restaurant, cocktail bar, cafe, and music lounge. One of Prague's top dining experi-ences, it's worth a splurge. The food is good; we enjoyed their homemade pizza quat-tro stagioni and Czech goulash served with herbed gnocchi. From the large summer terrace, you'll get an exciting and unforgettable view of the river and Charles Bridge.

Cihelná 2b, Praha 1. ✆ **296-826-103.** www.cihelna.com. Reservations recommended. Main courses 215Kč–695Kč. AE, MC, V. Daily 11:30am–1am. Metro: Malostranská.

Kogo ★★ 🍴 ITALIAN   This ristorante-pizzeria in the middle of Old Town is very trendy and popular. Fresh and well-prepared salads, pizza, pasta, and Italian specialties are served by an above-average waitstaff in a pleasant atmosphere. Beyond the standard and tasty pasta roster, the roasted veal is a good choice, or try the rare (for Prague) tasty mussels in white wine and garlic.

Kogo has a second, even more popular, location in the atrium of the Slovanský Dům shopping center, at Na Příkopě 22 (✆ **221-451-259**). The prices are higher here, but the location makes it a logical choice for a meal before or after taking in a movie at the multiplex cinema.

Havelská 27, Praha 1. ✆ **224-214-543.** www.kogo.cz. Reservations recommended. Main courses 210Kč–480Kč. AE, MC, V. Daily 9am–midnight. Metro: Můstek.

Pivovarský dům ★★ CZECH   Good Czech beer is not made only by the big brewers. This very popular microbrewery produces its own excellent lager, as well as harder-to-find varieties like dark beer and wheat beer. The "Brewery House" also dabbles in borderline-blasphemous (but still pretty good) concoctions such as coffee-, cherry-, and banana-flavored beer. Sharing the spotlight with the beer is excellent traditional Czech food including pork, dumplings, rabbit, goulash, and schnitzel, served in an upscale publike setting. The dining areas are all smoke-free. You'll need reservations to walk in the door—it's that popular.

Lípová 15 (corner of Ječná), Prague 2. ✆ **296-216-666.** www.gastroinfo.cz/pivodum. Reservations recommended. Main courses 135Kč–275Kč. AE, MC, V. Daily 11am–11:30pm. Metro: I. P. Pavlova plus tram no. 4, 6, 10, or 22, 1 stop to Štěpánská.

Pizzeria Rugantino ★ PIZZA   This restaurant's wood-fired stoves and handmade dough result in a crisp, delicate crust, a perfect platform for a multitude of cheeses, vegetables, and meats. The Diabolo, with fresh garlic bits and very hot chiles, goes nicely with a cool iceberg salad and a pull of Czech Bernard beer. The constant buzz, nonsmoking area, and heavy childproof wooden tables make this place near the Jewish quarter a family favorite. More spacious Rugantino II was opened at Klimentská 40, Praha 1 (✆ **224-815-192;** Metro: Florenc or Nám. Republiky), with a children's corner and plasma TV.

Dušní 4, Praha 1. ✆ **222-318-172.** www.rugantino.cz. Individual pizzas 120Kč–220Kč. AE, MC, V. Mon-Sat 11am–11pm; Sun noon–11pm. Metro: Staroměstská.

Radost FX ★★ 🍴 VEGETARIAN   In vogue and vegetarian, Radost is a club-house for hip New Bohemians that's a short walk from the Main Train Station. The veggie burger is well seasoned and substantial, on a grain bun, and the soups, such as lentil and onion, are light and full of flavor. The dining area is a dark rec room of upholstered armchairs, chaise lounges, couches from the 1960s, and coffee tables on which you eat. It serves as an art gallery and cafe as well.

Bělehradská 120, Praha 2. ✆ **603/181-500.** www.radostfx.cz. Main courses 80Kč–285Kč. AE, MC, V. Daily 11:30am–5am. Metro: I. P. Pavlova.

U medvídků ★★ CZECH   Bright and noisy, the House at the Little Bears serves a better-than-average *vepřo-knedlo-zelo*. The pub, on the right after entering, is much cheaper and livelier than the bar to the left. It's a hangout for locals, German tour groups, and foreign journalists in search of the original Czech Budweiser beer, Budvar.

Kavárna SOCIETY

Cafe life is back in a big way in Prague. From dissident blues to high society, these are the places where nonpub Praguers spend their afternoons and evenings, sipping coffee and smoking cigarettes while reading, writing, or talking with friends.

The **Kavárna (Cafe) Slavia ★**, Národní at Smetanovo nábřeží 2, Praha 1 (① **224-218-493;** Metro: Národní třída), reopened in 1997, after a half-decade sleep. The restored crisp Art Deco room recalls the Slavia's 100 years as the meeting place for the city's cultural and intellectual crowd. You'll still find a relatively affordable menu of light fare served with the riverfront views of Prague Castle and the National Theater. Reservations are possible on **www. cafeslavia.cz**. It's open daily 8am to 12am.

The biggest draw of the **Grand Café,** Staroměstské nám. 22, Praha 1 (① **221-632-520;** www.grandcafe.cz; Metro: Staroměstská), is a great view of the Orloj, the astronomical clock with the hourly parade of saints on the side of Old Town Square's city hall. It's open

daily 7am to midnight and now offers free Wi-Fi.

Of all the beautifully restored spaces in the Municipal House, the **Kavárna Obecní dům ★**, nám. Republiky 5, Praha 1 (① **222-002-763;** Metro: nám. Republiky), might be its most spectacular room. Lofty ceilings, marble accents and tables, an altarlike mantel, huge windows, and period chandeliers provide the awesome setting for coffees, teas, and other drinks, along with pastries and light sandwiches. It's open daily 7:30am to 11pm.

A New Age alternative to the clatter of the kavárnas is **Dahab ★★**, Dlouhá 33, Praha 1 (① **224-827-375;** Metro: nám. Republiky). This tearoom was founded by Prague's king of tea, Luboš Rychvalský, who introduced Prague to Eastern and Arabic tea cultures soon after the 1989 revolution. Here you can choose from about 20 varieties of tea and more than 10 kinds of coffee. Arabic soups, hummus, tahini, couscous, pita, and tempting sweets are also on the menu. It's open daily from 11am to 1am.

In high season, an oompah band plays in the beer wagon. It is a part of the Hotel U Medvídků and also includes a brewery.

Na Perštýně 7, Praha 1. ① **224-211-916.** www.umedvidku.cz. Main courses 88Kč–290Kč. AE, MC, V. Mon–Fri 11am–11pm; Sat 11:30am–1pm; Sun 11:30am–10pm. Metro: Národní třída.

Shopping

Czech porcelain, glass, and cheap but well-constructed clothing draw hordes of day-trippers from Germany. Private retailers have been allowed to operate here only since late 1989, but many top international retailers have already arrived. Shops lining the main route from Old Town Square to Charles Bridge are also great for browsing. For clothing, porcelain, jewelry, garnets, and glass, stroll around Wenceslas Square and Na Příkopě, connecting Wenceslas Square with náměstí Republiky.

For glass and crystal, try **Moser,** at Na Příkopě 12, Praha 1 (① **224-211-293;** www.moser-glass.com; Metro: Náměstí Republiky).The Moser family began selling Bohemia's finest crystal in central Prague in 1857, drawing customers from around the world. It's open daily from 10am to 8pm.

Celetná Crystal, Celetná 15, Praha 1 (𝄐 **222-324-022;** Metro: nám. Republiky), has a wide selection of world-renowned Czech crystal, china, arts and crafts, and jewelry displayed in a spacious three-floor showroom right in the heart of Prague. At **Cristallino,** Celetná 12, Praha 1 (𝄐 **224-225-173;** www.cristallino.cz; Metro: nám. Republiky), you'll find a good selection of stemware and vases in traditional designs. The shop's central location belies its excellent prices.

Havelský trh (Havel's Market), Havelská ulice, Praha 1 (Metro: Line A or B to Můstek), is on a short street running perpendicular to Melantrichova, the main route connecting Staroměstské náměstí with Václavské náměstí. This open-air market (named well before Havel became president in 1989) features dozens of private vendors selling seasonal homegrown fruits and vegetables. Other goods, including flowers and cheese, are also for sale. Since this place is designed primarily for locals, the prices are exceedingly low by Western European standards. The market is open Monday to Friday 8am to 6pm.

Nightlife

Prague's nightlife has changed completely since the Velvet Revolution—for the better if you plan to go clubbing, for the worse if you hope to sample the city's classical offerings. Still, seeing *Don Giovanni* in the Estates' Theater, where Mozart first premiered it, is worth the admission cost. Ticket prices, while low by Western standards, have become prohibitively high for the average Czech. You'll find, however, the exact reverse in the rock and jazz scene. Dozens of clubs have opened, and world-class bands are finally adding Prague to their European tours.

Turn to the *Prague Post* (**www.praguepost.cz**) for listings of cultural events and nightlife around the city; it's available at most newsstands in Old Town and Malá Strana. Once in Prague, you can buy tickets at theater box offices or from any one of dozens of agencies throughout the city center. **Ticketpro** has several offices around town, including at the **Prague Information Services** (𝄐 **221-714-444;** www.pis.cz) offices at the Old Town Hall and at Rytířská 31. Ticketpro also sells tickets at Václavské nám. 38, Prague 1 (𝄐 **296-329-999**). Other large, centrally located agencies (take the Metro to Můstek for all) are the **Prague Tourist Center,** Rytířská 12, Praha 1 (𝄐 **296-333-333**), open daily 9am to 8pm; **Bohemia Ticket International,** Na Příkopě 16, Praha 1 (𝄐 **224-215-031;** www.bohemiaticket.cz); and **Čedok,** Na Příkopě 18, Praha 1 (𝄐 **224-197-640**).

THE PERFORMING ARTS Although there's plenty of music year-round, the symphonies and orchestras all come to life during the **Prague Spring Festival,** an annual 3-week series of classical music events that runs from mid-May to early June (see "Festivals & Special Events," on p. 166). Tickets for festival concerts run from 250Kč to 2,000Kč and are available in advance from Hellichova 18, Prague 1 (𝄐 **257-312-547;** www.festival.cz).

The **Czech Philharmonic** Orchestra usually performs at the **Rudolfinum,** Alšovo nábřeží 12, Prague 1 (𝄐 **227-059-352;** www.ceskafilharmonie.cz; Metro: Staroměstská).The Czech Philharmonic is the traditional voice of the country's national pride, often playing works by native sons Dvořák and Smetana. Tickets are 120Kč to 140Kč. The **Prague Symphony** performs at the Art Nouveau **Smetana Hall ★★**, náměstí Republiky 5, Prague 1 (𝄐 **222-002-336;** Metro: Naměstí Republiky), as well as the Rudolfinum and Municipal House. It focuses more on 20th-century music, with occasional forays into Bach. Tickets are 200Kč to 600Kč on average but depend strongly on the venue they are playing at. Ticket orders and purchases can be made in advance (and you are advised to book well in advance) through the agencies listed above. Any remaining tickets are sold at the venues of the performances, which have various opening hours, but few seats usually remain within a month of the festival.

In a city full of spectacularly beautiful theaters, the massive pale-green **Estates' Theater** (Stavovské divadlo), Ovocný trh 1, Praha 1 (*©* 224-901-111; Metro: Můstek), is one of the most awesome. Built in 1783 and the site of the premiere of Mozart's *Don Giovanni* (conducted by the composer), the theater now hosts many of the classic productions of European opera and drama. Simultaneous English translation, transmitted via headphone, is available for most performances. Tickets cost 100Kč to 1,000Kč. Lavishly constructed in the late-Renaissance style of northern Italy, the gold-crowned **Národní divadlo (National Theater),** Národní třída 2, Praha 1 (*©* 224-901-448; www.narodni-divadlo.cz; Metro: Národní třída), overlooking the Vltava River, is one of Prague's most recognizable landmarks. Completed in 1881, the theater was built to nurture the Czech National Revival—a grassroots movement to replace the dominant German culture with that of native Czechs. Today classic productions are staged here in a larger setting than at the Estates' Theater, but for about the same ticket prices.

The **National Theater Ballet** performs at the National Theater. The troupe has seen most of its top talent go west since 1989, but it still puts on a good show. After critics complained that Prague's top company had grown complacent, choreographer Libor Vaculík responded with humorous and quirky stagings of off-the-wall ballets such as *Some Like It Hot* and *Psycho.* Tickets cost 100Kč to 1,000Kč. **Laterna Magika,** Národní třída 4, Praha 1 (*©* 224-931-482; Metro: Národní třída), is a performance-art show in the new wing of the National Theater. The multimedia show, which combines live theater with film and dance, was once considered radical and is not for those easily offended by nudity. Tickets for a matinee are from 250Kč to 350Kč, and for an evening performance, from 350Kč to 680Kč.

JAZZ CLUBS Upscale by Czech standards, **AghaRTA Jazz Centrum,** Železná 16, Praha 1 (*©* 222-211-275; www.agharta.cz; Metro: Můstek), regularly features some of the best music in town, from standard acoustic trios to Dixieland, funk, and fusion. Bands usually begin at 9pm, but try to come much earlier to snag one of the few places to sit. The club is open daily 7pm to midnight. **Reduta Jazz Club,** Národní třída 20, Praha 1 (*©* 224-933-487; www.redutajazzclub.cz; Metro: Národní třída), is a smoky subterranean room that looks exactly like a jazz cellar should. An adventurous booking policy, which even included a saxophone gig with a U.S. president in 1994, means that different bands play almost every night. It still has a kind of welcoming retro feel, as if Charlie Parker or Miles himself might walk in at some point during the night. It's open from 9pm (the music usually starts around 9:30) to midnight.

PUBS & BARS You'll experience true Czech entertainment in only one kind of place—a smoky local pub serving some of the world's best beer, which is uncommonly cheap, at usually less than 35Kč a pint. Remember to put a cardboard coaster in front of you to show you want a mug, and never wave for service, as the typically surly waiter will just ignore you.

Originally a brewery dating from 1459, **U Fleků,** Křemencova 11, Praha 1 (*©* 224-934-019; http://en.ufleku.cz; Metro: Národní třída), is Prague's most famous beer hall and one of the only pubs that still brews its own beer. This huge place has myriad timber-lined rooms and a large, loud courtyard where an oompah band performs. Tourists come here by the busload, so U Fleků is avoided by disparaging

By far the most popular day trip from Prague is to **Karlštejn Castle,** 18 miles (30km) southwest of Prague, which was built by Charles IV in the 14th century to safeguard the crown jewels of the Holy Roman Empire and has been restored to its original state.

As you approach the castle by train from the Prague, little will prepare you for your first view: a spectacular castle perched high on a hill, surrounded by lush forests and vineyards. The Holy Rood Chapel is famous for the more than 2,000 precious and semiprecious inlaid gems that adorn its walls, and the Chapel of St. Catherine was King Karel IV's private oratory. Both the Audience Hall and the Imperial Bedroom are impressive, despite being stripped of their original furnishings. To see the Holy Rood Chapel, you need to make a reservation (© **311-681-617;** www. hradkarlstejn.cz).

Admission for a shorter tour in English is 250Kč adults and 150Kč students, and the longer one (Tour II) with the Holy Rood Chapel is 300Kč adults, 200Kč students. It's open Tuesday through Sunday May, June, and September 9am to noon and 12:30 to 5pm; July

and August 9am to noon and 12:30 to 6pm; April and October 9am to noon and 1 to 4pm; November, December, January and March 9am to noon and 1 to 3pm; closed February. Check the website for exceptions and holiday hours.

Most trains leave from Prague's Hlavní nádraží to the castle on an hourly basis throughout the day (trip time: 43 min.) and from Smíchov Station (Metro: Line B to Smíchovské nádraží), from which the trip time is only 34 minutes. One-way second-class fare is 49Kč from the main train station or 44Kč from Smíchov station. For train schedules, go to **www.jizdnirady.cz**. The castle is a 1¼-mile (2km) walk from the train station, though the stroll uphill to the castle— and the views that come with it—is one of the main highlights of the experience.

There is no official tourist center in Karlštejn, but the ticket and castle information booth can help you. On the main street heading up to the castle itself, you will find a number of stores and restaurants. Take a break in **Restaurace Blanky z Valois** (© **608-021-250**), where pizzas range from 85Kč to 190Kč. It is open daily from 11am to 10pm.

locals who don't like its German atmosphere anyway. The pub's special dark beer is excellent, however, and not available anywhere else. It's open daily 10am to 11pm.

One of the most famous Czech pubs, **U Zlatého tygra (At the Golden Tiger),** Husova 17, Praha 1 (© **222-221-111;** www.uzlatehotygra.cz; Metro: Staroměstská or Můstek), was a favorite watering hole of ex-President Havel and the late writer Bohumil Hrabal. Particularly smoky, and not especially tourist-friendly, it is nevertheless a one-stop education in Czech culture. Then-presidents Havel and Clinton joined Hrabal for a traditional Czech pub evening here during Clinton's 1994 visit to Prague. It's open daily from 3pm to 11pm; try to arrive before 3pm to secure a table.

WESTERN & SOUTHERN BOHEMIA

The Czech Republic is composed of two geographic regions: Bohemia and Moravia. The larger of the two, Bohemia, occupying the central and western areas of the country, has for centuries been caught between a rock (Germany) and a hard place (Austria). Bohemia was almost always in the center of regional conflicts, both secular and religious. But the area also flourished, as witnessed by the wealth of castles that dot the countryside and the spa towns that were once the playgrounds of the rich and famous. The good news for the rail traveler is that the region is small enough that you can visit these towns as separate day trips from Prague, or once in the region, you can hop from one place to the other.

Karlovy Vary (Carlsbad)

The discovery of Karlovy Vary (Carlsbad), 75 miles (121km) west of Prague, by Charles IV reads something like a 14th-century episode of *The Beverly Hillbillies*. According to local lore, the king was out huntin' for some food when up from the ground came a-bubblin' water (though discovered by his dogs, not an errant gunshot). Knowing a good thing when he saw it, Charles immediately set to work building a small castle, naming the town that evolved around it Karlovy Vary (Charles's Boiling Place). The first spa buildings were built in 1522, and before long, notables such as Russian czar Peter the Great and, later, Bach, Beethoven, Freud, Goethe, and Marx all came to take the waters.

After World War II, East Bloc travelers (following in the footsteps of Marx, no doubt) discovered the town, and Karlovy Vary became a destination for the proletariat. On doctors' orders, most workers enjoyed regular stays of 2 or 3 weeks, letting the mineral waters ranging from 110.3° to 161.6°F (43.5°–72°C) from the town's 12 spas heal their tired and broken bodies. Even now, most spa guests are there by doctor's prescription.

GETTING THERE   There is no fast rail connection from Prague to Karlovy Vary, and train travel takes much longer than a trip by bus, so although it's the most popular of the towns to visit (and, thus, the one we mention first), it's actually easier to get here by bus or by train from one of the other Bohemian towns.

The train from Prague goes through the northern region of Bohemia and reaches the spa town in about 4 hours. There are two trains leaving from Prague's main station and nádraží Holešovice in the morning and two from Masarykovo station in the late afternoon. The fare is 294Kč.

Karlovy Vary's **Horní (upper) train station** is connected to the town center by city bus no. 12 or 13. If you are coming via Mariánské Lázně, there are about seven trains daily. The 1½ hour-trip costs 112Kč, and you will end up at Karlovy Vary's **Dolní (lower) nádraží.** Just a 5-minute walk from this station is the main stop for all city buses (**Městská tržnice**) and the city center.

By Bus   Taking a bus to Karlovy Vary is much more convenient if you're leaving from Prague. Frequent express buses leave from Prague's Florenc bus station and arrive in Karlovy Vary in 2¼ hours. The trip costs 140Kč. Take a 10-minute walk or local bus no. 4 into Karlovy Vary's spa center. Note that you must have a ticket to board local transport. You can buy tickets for 16Kč at the bus station stop, or, if you have no change, the kiosk across the street sells tickets during regular business hours. Alternatively, you can purchase the ticket for 20Kč from the bus driver. For timetable information, go to **www.jizdnirady.cz.**

VISITOR INFORMATION   Infocentrum města **Karlovy Vary** is located near the main Mlýnská Kolonáda, at Mlýnské nábřeží 5 (© **355-321-176**). It's open Monday to Friday from 9am to 7pm and Saturday and Sunday from 10am to 6pm. The office also has a window at the terminal of the **Dolní (lower) nádraží** bus and

Most visitors to Karlovy Vary come specifically to get a spa treatment, a therapy that usually lasts 1 to 3 weeks. After consulting with a spa physician, guests are given a regimen of activities that may include mineral baths, massages, waxings, mudpacks, electrotherapy, and pure oxygen inhalation. After spending the morning at a spa, guests are then usually directed to walk the paths of the town's surrounding forest.

The common denominator of all the cures is an ample daily dose of hot mineral water, which bubbles up from 12 springs. This water definitely has a distinct odor and taste. You'll see people chugging it down, but it doesn't necessarily taste very good. Some thermal springs actually taste and smell like rotten eggs. You might want to take a small sip at first.

You'll also notice that almost everyone in town seems to be carrying "the cup," basically a mug with a built-in straw that runs through the handle. Young and old alike parade through town with their mugs, filling and refilling them at each new thermal water tap.

You can buy these mugs everywhere for as little as 60Kč or as much as 230Kč; they make a quirky souvenir. **Warning:** None of the mugs can make the hot springs taste any better!

Most rail travelers won't have the 1-week minimum most major spas demand, but many of the local hotels also offer spa and health treatments, so ask when you book your room. Most will happily arrange a treatment if they don't provide it directly. Visitors to Karlovy Vary for just a day or two can experience the waters on an "outpatient" basis. The **Sanatorium Baths III,** Mlýnské nábřeží 7 (☎ **353-225-641**), welcomes day-trippers with mineral baths, massages, saunas, and a cold pool. It's open Monday to Friday 7am to 2pm for spa treatments, and the swimming pool and sauna are open Monday to Friday 3 to 6pm, Saturday 1 to 5pm.

For more information and reservations for spa packages, contact **Čedok,** Na Příkopě 18, Praha 1 (☎ **224-197-632/111;** www.cedok.cz), in Prague.

5

Western & Southern Bohemia | THE CZECH REPUBLIC

train station, Západní ulice (☎ **353-232-838**). These are the official town's information centers, which will answer your questions, help you make hotel reservations, sell you tickets for entertainment in the city, and so on.

Be sure to pick up the *Promenáda* magazine, a comprehensive collection of events with a small map of the town center.

For Web information on festivals and events in the city, go to **www.karlovyvary.cz**.

TOP ATTRACTIONS & SPECIAL MOMENTS

The town's slow pace and pedestrian promenades, lined with Art Nouveau buildings, turn strolling into an art form. Nighttime walks take on an even more mystical feel, as the sewers, river, and many major cracks in the roads emit steam from the hot springs underneath. A good place to start is the **Hotel Thermal,** I. P. Pavlova 11 (☎ **359-001-111**), at the north end of the old town's center, an easy walk from the bus station. The 1970s glass, steel, and concrete structure, between the town's eastern hills and the Ohře River, sticks out like a sore communist thumb amid the 19th-century architecture. Nonetheless, you'll find three important places here: its outdoor pool, the only centrally located outdoor public pool; its upper terrace, boasting a spectacular view of the city; and its cinema, Karlovy Vary's largest, which holds many of the local film festival's premier events.

As you enter the heart of the town on the river's west side, you'll see the renovated, ornate white wrought-iron **Sadová kolonáda** adorning the beautifully manicured park **Dvořákovy sady.** Continue following the river, and about 330 feet (99m) later, you'll encounter the **Mlýnská kolonáda,** a long, covered walkway housing several Karlovy Vary springs, which you can sample 24 hours a day. Each spring has a plaque beside it telling which mineral elements are present and the temperature of the water. Bring your own cup or buy one just about anywhere to sip the waters; most are too hot to drink from your hands.

When you hit the river bend, the majestic **Church of St. Mary Magdalene** sits perched atop a hill, overlooking the **Vřídlo,** the hottest spring in town. Built in 1736, the church is the work of Kilian Ignac Dientzenhofer, who also created two of Prague's more notable churches—both named St. Nicholas. Housing Vřídlo, which blasts water some 50 feet (15m) into the air, is the glass building called the **Vřídelní kolonáda.** It was built in 1974 and houses several hot springs you can sample for free daily from 6am to 7pm. There are also public restrooms, open daily 6am to 6pm and costing 10Kč. The building also holds several kiosks selling postcards, stone roses, and drinking cups. Heading away from the Vřídelní kolonáda are Stará and Nová Louka streets, which line either side of the river. Along **Stará (Old) Louka,** you'll find several fine cafes and glass and crystal shops. Crystal and porcelain are Karlovy Vary's other claims to fame. Dozens of places throughout town sell everything from plates to chandeliers. **Nová (New) Louka** is lined with hotels and the historic **Town's Theater.**

Both streets lead to the **Grandhotel Pupp.** After a massive reconstruction that erased nearly 50 years of communism (it was temporarily called the Grand Hotel Moskva), the Pupp is once again the crown jewel of the town. Regardless of capitalism or communism, the Pupp remains what it always was: the grande dame of hotels in the area. Once catering to nobility from all over Central Europe, the Pupp still houses one of the town's finest restaurants, the Grand, and its grounds are a favorite with the hiking crowd.

If you still have the energy, atop the hill behind the Pupp stands the **Diana Lookout Tower** (© **353-222-872**). Footpaths leading through the forests eventually spit you out at the base of the tower, as if to say, "Ha, the trip is only half over." If you are not up to the five-story climb, you can use the lift and enjoy the view of the town from above. Alternatively, a cable car runs to the tower from the base located right next to the Grandhotel Pupp. A one-way ticket on the cable car is 40Kč; round-trip, it's 70Kč. The cable car runs every 15 minutes June to September daily from 9:15am to 6:45pm; February, March, November, and December 9:15am to 4:45pm; April, May, and October 9:15am to 5:45pm (closed Jan).

WHERE TO STAY & DINE

Some of the town's major spa hotels accommodate only those who are paying for complete treatment, unless their occupancy rates are particularly low. The hotels listed below accept guests for stays of any length. Expect to pay about 1,500Kč for a double.

One of Karlovy Vary's best hotels, the 111-room **Grandhotel Pupp ★★★**, Mírové nám. 2 (© **353-109-111**; www.pupp.cz), was built in 1701 and is also one of Europe's oldest. The hotel's public areas ooze with splendor and charm, as do the renovated guest rooms. The best tend to be on the upper floors facing the town center; only some rooms have air-conditioning. The **Grand Restaurant** serves up as grand a dining room as you'll find, with the food to match. *Casino Royale,* the James Bond movie released in 2006, was filmed at this hotel. The hotel's rates are quoted in euros to combat the volatility of the crown and run 267€ double, from 377€ for a suite; rates include breakfast.

Parkhotel Pupp ★, Mírové nám. 2 (☎ **353-109-111;** www.pupp.cz), is housed within the same complex as its five-star cousin and was recently refurbished. The rooms are large, and all the same facilities are available. Rates are from 138€ to 161€ double, 192€ to 224€ suite. Rates include breakfast.

Less stylish but still in a great location is **Hotel Dvořák,** Nová Louka 11 (☎ **353-102-111;** www.hotel-dvorak.cz). Part of the Vienna International hotel/resort chain, the Dvořák has improved immensely, especially in terms of service. If the Pupp has the history and elegance, the Dvořák has the facilities. However, the rooms, for all their creature comforts, lack the old-world charm found at the Pupp. Rates run 3,375Kč for a double.

Family-run hotel **Embassy** ★★, Nová Louka 21 (☎ **353-221-161;** www.embassy.cz), manages to evoke the turn of the 20th century with elegantly decorated rooms. Although smaller than those at the Pupp, they're impeccably furnished and overlook the river. The restaurant downstairs is where a lot of movers and shakers at the Karlovy Vary film festival get away from the glitz and get down to business. You can stay here for about 3,130Kč for a double; 3,990Kč suite. Rates include breakfast. On the ground floor of the hotel is the **Embassy** restaurant (☎ **353-221-161**), which has a pub on one side and an intimate dining room on the other. On a cold day, the pub works wonders with a hearty goulash soup. But the dining room is the Embassy's hidden treasure. What the meals lack in flair, they make up for with sophistication. Soups cost 70Kč; main courses cost 220Kč to 600Kč

Look for the restaurant **Promenáda** ★, Tržiště 31 (☎ **353-225-648**), if you'd like to dine in an intimate atmosphere. Across from the Vřídelní kolonáda, the Promenáda serves the best food around, offering a wide selection of generous portions. The daily menu usually includes well-prepared wild game, but the mixed grill for two and the chateaubriand, both flambéed at the table, are the chef's best dishes. Soups cost around 70Kč; main courses run 290Kč to 750Kč.

Český Krumlov

If you have time for only one day trip, consider making it Český Krumlov, 96 miles (155km) south of Prague. One of Bohemia's prettiest towns, Krumlov is a living gallery of elegant Renaissance-era buildings housing charming cafes, pubs, restaurants, shops, and galleries. In 1992, UNESCO named Český Krumlov a World Heritage Site for its historic importance and physical beauty.

Bustling since medieval times, the town, after centuries of embellishment, is exquisitely beautiful. In 1302, the Rožmberk family inherited the castle and used it as their main residence for nearly 300 years. Looking out from the Lazebnický bridge, with the waters of the Vltava below snaking past the castle's gray stone, you'll feel that time has stopped. At night, with the castle lit up, the view becomes even more dramatic.

GETTING THERE   The only way to reach Český Krumlov by train from Prague is via České Budějovice (see below), a slow ride that deposits you at a station relatively far from the town center (trip time ranges from 3 hr., 46 min. to 4 hr., 41 min). Nine trains leave daily from Prague's Hlavní nádraží, and the fare is 250Kč.

Avoiding the Crowds

Consider yourself warned: Word has spread about Český Krumlov. The summer high season can be unbearable, as thousands of visitors blanket its medieval streets. If possible, try to visit in the off season—we suggest autumn, to take advantage of the colorful surrounding hills. When the crowds recede, the prices decrease, and the town's charm can really shine. Who knows? You might even hear some Czech! For more details about the town, go to **www.ckrumlov.cz**.

If you are already in České Budějovice and you want to make a trip to Krumlov, numerous trains connecting these two cities run throughout the day. It takes about 60 minutes and costs 50Kč. For timetables, go to **www.jizdnirady.cz**.

The Český Krumlov train station is situated in a northern suburb of the city. You can take a city taxi (parked in front of the station building) to get to the town center. The 10- to 15-minute ride costs about 120Kč.

VISITOR INFORMATION   On the main square, in a renovated Renaissance building, the **Infocentrum,** náměstí Svornosti 2, 381 01 Český Krumlov (*©* **380-704-622;** fax 380-704-619), offers a complete array of services, from booking accommodations to ticket reservations for events, as well as a phone, fax, and Internet service. It's open daily June through September from 9am to 7pm; in April, May, and October from 9am to 6pm; and from November to March from 9am to 5pm. For more information about Český Krumlov, visit its well-organized website, **www.ckrumlov.cz**, which features a very cool interactive map of the city.

TOP ATTRACTIONS & SPECIAL MOMENTS

Bring a good pair of walking shoes, and be prepared to wear them out. Český Krumlov not only lends itself to hours of strolling, but its hills and alleyways demand it. No cars, thank goodness, are allowed in the historic town, and the cobblestones keep most other vehicles at bay. The town is split into two parts—the Inner Town and Latrán, which houses the city's famous castle. They're best tackled separately, so you won't have to crisscross the bridges several times.

Begin at the **Regionální Muzeum** (**Regional Museum;** *©* 380-711-674), at the top of Horní ulice and to the right of the Main Square. Once a Jesuit seminary, the three-story museum now contains artifacts and displays relating to Český Krumlov's 1,000-year history. The highlight of this mass of folk art, clothing, furniture, and statues is a giant model of the town that offers a bird's-eye view of the buildings. Admission is 60Kč, and it's open daily 10am to 5pm (May, June, and Sept) daily 10am to 6pm (July–Aug), Tuesday to Friday from 9am to 4pm and Saturday and Sunday 1 to 4pm (March, Apr, and Oct–Dec).

Across the street is the **Hotel Růže (Rose;** (*©* 380-772-100; www.hotelruze. cz), which was once a Jesuit student house. Built in the late 16th century, the hotel and the prelature next to it show the development of architecture in the city—Gothic, Renaissance, and rococo influences are all present. Continue down the street to see the impressive late-Gothic **St. Vitus Cathedral;** admission is free.

As you continue down the street, you'll come to **náměstí Svornosti.** For such an impressive town, the main square is a little disappointing, with few buildings of any character. The **Radnice (Town Hall),** at nám. Svornosti 1, is one of the few

Reputedly the second-largest castle in Bohemia (after Prague Castle), the **Český Krumlov Château** was constructed in the 13th century as part of a private estate. Throughout the ages, it has passed to a variety of private owners, including the Rožmberk family, Bohemia's largest landholders, and the Schwarzenbergs, the Bohemian equivalent of the Hilton family. Perched high atop a rocky hill, the château is open from April to October only, exclusively by guided tours.

Follow the path at the entrance for the long climb up to the castle, and first to greet you is a round 12th-century tower—painstakingly renovated—with a Renaissance balcony. You'll pass over the moat, now occupied by two brown bears. Beyond it is the **Dolní Hrad (Lower Castle)** and then the **Horní Hrad (Upper Castle).** There are three guided tours. The first tour begins in the rococo **Chapel of St. George** and continues through the portrait-packed **Renaissance Rooms** and the **Schwarzenberg Barogue Suite,** outfitted with ornate furnishings that include Flemish wall tapestries and European paintings. You'll also see the extravagant 17th-century

Golden Carriage. Tour 2 includes the **Schwarzenberg portrait gallery,** as well as its 19th-century suite. Tour 3 presents the Castle's fascinating **Baroque Theater,** though with the more expensive tickets. Sadly, this is priced more for real theater aficionados than the general public. Tours last 1 hour and depart frequently. Most are in Czech or German, however. If you want an English-language tour, arrange it ahead of time (**✆ 380-704-711;** www.castle.ckrumlov. cz). The guided tours in English cost 240Kč adults, 1400Kč students (Tour 1); 180Kč adults and 100Kč students (Tour 2); and 380Kč adults, 220Kč students (Tour 3). The tickets are sold separately. The castle hours are from Tuesday to Sunday: June to August 9am to 6pm; April, May, September, and October 9am to 5pm. The last entrance is 1 hour before closing.

Tip: Once past the main castle building, you can see one of the more stunning views of Český Krumlov from **Most Na Plášti,** a walkway that doubles as a belvedere over the Inner Town. Even farther up the hill lies the castle's riding school and gardens.

exceptions. Its Gothic arcades and Renaissance vault inside are exceptionally beautiful in this otherwise run-down area. From the square, streets fan out in all directions. Take some time just to wander through them.

One of Český Krumlov's most famous residents was Austrian-born 20th-century artist Egon Schiele. He was a bit of an eccentric who, on more than one occasion, raised the ire of the town's residents (many were distraught with his use of their young women as his nude models); his stay was cut short when residents' patience ran out. But the town readopted the artist in 1993, setting up the **Egon Schiele Foundation** and the **Egon Schiele Centrum** in Inner Town, Široká 70–72, 381 01, Český Krumlov (**✆ 380-704-011;** www.schieleartcentrum.cz). The center documents his life and work, housing a permanent selection of his paintings, as well as exhibitions of other 20th-century artists. Admission 120Kč. It's open daily from 10am to 6pm.

For a different perspective on what the town looks like, take the stairs from the **Městské divadlo (Town Theater),** on Horní ulice, down to the riverfront and rent a boat from **Maleček boat rentals,** at Rooseveltova 28 (**✆ 380-712-508;**

www.malecek.cz), at 400Kč per hour. Always willing to lend his advice, the affable Pepa Maleček will tell you what to watch out for and where the best fishing is (no matter how many times you say that you don't want to fish!).

WHERE TO STAY & DINE

Hotels are sprouting up or are getting a "new" old look; PENSION and ZIMMER FREI signs line Horní and Rooseveltova streets and offer some of the best values in town. For a comprehensive list of area hotels and help with bookings, call or write the Info-centrum listed above.

We recommend **Hotel Konvice,** Horní ul. 144 (© **380-711-611;** www.boehmerwaldhotels.de), as a good value choice. If you can get a room with a view out the back, take it immediately. Rooms themselves are small but clean and comfortable, with nice parquet floors and well-appointed bathrooms. As you overlook the river and the castle on the opposite bank, you'll wonder why people would stay anywhere else. Rates are from 1,500Kč double, from 3,500Kč suite. Rates include breakfast.

Along "pension alley," **Pension Anna ★**, Rooseveltova 41 (©/fax **380-711-692;** www.pensionanna.euweb.cz), is a comfortable and rustic choice. The friendly management and the homey feeling you get as you walk up to your room make it a favorite. Forget hotels—this is the kind of place where you can relax. The owners even let you buy drinks and snacks at the bar downstairs and take them to your room. Rates include breakfast and run from 1,250Kč for a double, 1,550Kč for a suite.

For a typical Czech dining experience, visit **Hospoda Na louži,** Kájovská 66 (© **380-711-280;** www.nalouzi.cz), which offers diners good value for their money. The large wooden tables encourage you to get to know your neighbors in this Inner Town pub, located in a 15th-century house near the main square. The atmosphere is fun, and the food above average. If no table is available, stand and have a drink; the seating turnover is pretty fast, and the staff is accommodating. Main courses cost about 100Kč; credit cards are not accepted.

Located in the former cooling room of the local Eggenberg Brewery near the castle, **Restaurant Eggenberg,** Latrán 27 (© **380-711-917;** www.eggenberg.cz), is one of the few big beer halls in town, with some of the freshest drafts anywhere. Traditional meat-and-dumplings-style Czech food is augmented by vegetarian dishes. Main courses cost 98Kč to 280Kč.

 Dining at the Castle

Most visitors don't realize that, beyond the tourist sections of **Český Krumlov Château,** they can have one of the Czech Republic's finest dining experiences at **Krčma Markéta ★**, Zámek 62 (© **775-155-504;** www.auviex.cz), a Renaissance pub. To get there, walk all the way up the hill through the castle, past the Upper Castle, and past the Castle Theater. Walk through the raised walkway and into the Zámecká zahrada (Castle Garden), where you'll eventually find the pub. Going inside is like leaving this century, and the atmosphere hasn't changed much over the centuries. There's a wide variety of roasted meat on the menu. The waiter/cook will bring bread and a slab of spiced pork fat (considered a good base for drinking), but don't worry—refusing to eat it won't raise anyone's ire. Instead, wait until the entree comes. Krčma Markéta is open Tuesday to Sunday from 11am to 9pm or by appointment, and main courses cost 130Kč to 390Kč.

České Budějovice

This fortress town was born in 1265, when Otakar II decided that the intersection point of the Vltava and Malše rivers would be the perfect site to protect the approaches to southern Bohemia. Although Otakar was killed at the battle of the Moravian Field in 1278, and the town was subsequently ravaged by the rival Vítkovic family, the construction of the city continued, eventually taking the shape originally envisaged.

Today České Budějovice, hometown of the original Budweiser brand beer, is more a bastion for the beer drinker than a protector of Bohemia. But its slow pace, relaxed atmosphere, and interesting architecture make it a worthy stop for the rail traveler, especially as a base for exploring southern Bohemia or as a quick stopover for those heading on to Austria.

GETTING THERE By Train Twelve express trains from Prague's Hlavní nádraží make the trip to České Budějovice in about 2½ hours. The fare is 320Kč for first class and 213Kč for second class. From the train station, take city bus no. 2 to the city center; the ride costs 12Kč. For timetable information, go to **www. jizdnirady.cz**. You can also easily walk from the train station (it takes about 10–15 min).

VISITOR INFORMATION The **ČD center** (© 972-544-361) at the train station is open nonstop (except the lunch break 12:30–1pm and midnight–3:30am) and provides train information, makes hotel bookings, and sells event tickets.

The **Tourist Information Centre,** nám. Přemysla Otakara II 2 (©/fax **386-801-413**; www.c-budejovice.cz), in the main square, sells maps and guidebooks, and finds lodging.

TOP ATTRACTIONS & SPECIAL MOMENTS

You can comfortably see České Budějovice in a day. At its center is one of central Europe's largest squares, the cobblestone **náměstí Přemysla Otakara II.** The square contains the ornate **Fountain of Sampson,** an 18th-century water well that was once the town's principal water supply, plus a mishmash of baroque and Renaissance buildings. On the southwest corner is the **town hall,** an elegant baroque structure built by Martinelli between 1727 and 1730. On top of the town hall, the larger-than-life statues by Dietrich represent the civic virtues: justice, bravery, wisdom, and diligence.

One block northwest of the square is the **Černá věž (Black Tower),** visible from almost every point in the city. Its 360 steps are worth the climb to get a bird's-eye view in all directions. The most famous symbol of České Budějovice, the 232-foot (70m), 16th-century tower was built as a belfry for the adjacent **St. Nicholas Church.** This 13th-century church, one of the town's most important sights, was a bastion of Roman Catholicism during the 15th-century Hussite rebellion. You shouldn't miss the flamboyant white-and-cream 17th-century baroque interior. The tower is open Tuesday to Sunday (open daily in July and Aug) from 10am to 6pm. Admission is 20Kč. The church is open daily from 9am to 6pm.

WHERE TO STAY & DINE

Several agencies can locate reasonably priced private rooms. Expect to pay about 700Kč per person, in cash. The Tourist Information Centre (see "Visitor Information," above) can point you toward a wide selection of conveniently located rooms and pensions.

FOR BEER LOVERS: TOURING A
beer shrine

On the town's northern edge sits a shrine for those who pray to the gods of the amber nectar. This is where it all began, where **Budějovický Budvar** (☎ **387-705-111**), the original brewer of Budweiser brand beer, has its one and only factory. Established in 1895, Budvar draws on more than 700 years of Bohemian brewing tradition to produce one of the world's best beers. For information, contact Budvar n.p., Karolíny Světlé 4, České Budějovice (☎ **387-705-341;** http://budweiser-budvar.cz). Tours cost 100Kč.

Tours can be arranged by phoning ahead, but only for groups. If you're traveling alone or with only one or two other people, ask a hotel concierge at one of the bigger hotels (we suggest the Zvon; see below) if he or she can put you in with an already scheduled group. Failing that, you might want to take a chance and head up to the brewery, where, if a group has arrived, another person or two won't be noticed.

Trolley bus no. 2 and bus no. 4 stop by the brewery; this is how it ensures that its workers and visitors reach the plant safely each day. The trolley costs 20Kč to the brewery. You can also hop a cab from the town square for about 150Kč.

Location is everything for the city's most elegant hotel, **Grandhotel Zvon,** nám. Přemysla Otakara II 28 (☎ 381-601-601; www.hotel-zvon.cz), which occupies several historic buildings on the main square. Upper-floor rooms have been renovated and tend to be more expensive, especially those with a view of the square, which are not only brighter, but larger and nicer, too. Others are relatively plain and functional. There's no elevator, but if you don't mind the climb, stay on the fourth floor. One of the biggest improvements here in recent years has been the staff, which seems to be learning that guests like respect and quality treatment. Rooms cost 2,800Kč to 5,000Kč double.

Around the corner from the Zvon, you can find **Hotel Malý Pivovar (Small Brewery)** ★★, Ulice Karla IV. 8–10 (☎ 386-360-471; www.malypivovar.cz). A renovated 16th-century microbrewery combines the charms of a B&B with the amenities of a modern hotel. Rooms are bright and cheery, with antique-style wooden furniture. It's definitely worth consideration if being only 100 feet (30m) from the sometimes-noisy main square isn't a problem. Rates are 2,760Kč double, 3,200Kč suite. Rates include breakfast.

The town is also home to a typical Czech-style restaurant serving up hearty food at reasonable prices. **U královské pečeti (At the Royal Seal),** Karla IV 8–10 (☎ 386-360-471), which is located in the **Hotel Malý Pivovar,** has a wide main menu selection, ranging from goulash with dumplings to rib-eye steak. Main courses range from 80Kč to 290Kč.

DENMARK

With one of Europe's best rail networks, the maritime nation of Denmark is easily viewed from the window of a train. It may not offer the dramatic and often hair-raising train trips of nearby Norway, but you'll pass by sweet fishing villages, rustic hamlets with half-timbered houses, Renaissance castles, Viking ruins, and gorgeous dune-backed beaches along the North Sea.

Touring Denmark by rail has been made easier since the 1990s, thanks to the tunnel and bridge crossing The Great Belt. The "Belt" is a body of water separating the island of Zealand (on which Copenhagen sits) from the island of Funen. Funen is the island between Zealand and the peninsula of Jutland, which is connected geographically to Germany and the rest of continental Europe. These rail links mean the three landmasses can be reached without having to take the formerly unavoidable ferry. Nowadays, high-speed diesel trains link the major cities of Denmark, such as Copenhagen and Århus, at faster speeds than ever before.

The county's international rail links were also dramatically improved in the summer of 2002 when a 10-mile (16km) rail and motorway tunnel and bridge complex linked the northeast of Denmark (including Copenhagen) with southern Sweden (through Malmö).

Though Denmark is a very expensive destination for the rail traveler, its small size and extensive and efficient rail system mean you'll need only 3 to 4 days to take in its scenic highlights.

Highlights of Denmark

All visitors to Denmark seem to arrive in **Copenhagen,** the capital. It's not only the gateway to the country—by both rail and air—but also the country's major attraction. Historically known as the "fun" capital of Europe, contemporary Copenhagen focuses on all things hip, with designer hotels, bars, and restaurants springing up alongside the more functional old-fashioned equivalents. Yes, it's expensive: According to an ECA International study, Copenhagen was the eighth most expensive city in the world in 2010 (though not the most expensive city in Scandinavia: Norway's Oslo and Stavenger cost more). But it is also clean and safe (although crime is increasing) and packed with things to see and do: museums, theaters, castles, old churches, and interesting shops. Plus, there's a noticeable lack of car fumes, as half of the city's 1.7 million residents apparently prefer to pedal around their hill-free city on bikes.

If time allows, day-trip to **Helsingør,** 25 miles (40km) to the north of Copenhagen, easily reached by train. Here you'll find Hamlet's Castle, known as **Kronborg Slot.** Yes, it's true, Shakespeare never actually visited the city, but it's still one of Denmark's proudest heritage sites.

The **Roskilde Festival** in Roskilde (a half-hour from Copenhagen) is one of Europe's biggest outdoor festivals, going strong since 1971. Taking place in late June/early July, it's 4 days of big names from pop, rock, and hip-hop playing on four stages. Bring a tent. For more information or to buy tickets (about 1,675DKK), go to the official website, **www.roskilde-festival.dk**. If jazz appeals more to your musical tastes, international jazz musicians play in the streets, squares, and theaters during the **Copenhagen Jazz Festival** in early July. Pick up a copy of *Copenhagen This Week* (**www.ctw.dk**) to find the venues. For information, call ℭ **33-93-20-13** or check out **www.jazzfestival.dk**. Early July.

At **Århus Festival Week** in late August/early September, a wide range of cultural activities—including opera, jazz, classical, and folk music, as well as ballet and theater—is presented. It's the largest multicultural festival in Scandinavia. Sporting activities and street parties abound as well. For more information, call ℭ **45-87-30-83 00** or go to the festival website at **www.aarhus festuge.dk**.

Another free day? Take the train to Odense (97 miles/156km west of Copenhagen), on the neighboring island of Funen. This ancient town was the birthplace of Hans Christian Andersen, and fans can explore his humble boyhood home and a museum devoted to the master storyteller.

For most visitors, Odense will mark the end of a rail tour of Denmark. Those with more time can continue by rail into Jutland, a peninsula of heather-covered moors, fjords, farmland, lakes, and sand dunes.

Here, the most interesting city is **Århus,** 109 miles (175km) west of Copenhagen and easily reached by train. Århus is the capital of Jutland and Denmark's second-largest city, university town, and cultural center with a lively port life.

For most visitors, it's then back to Copenhagen or on to the port of **Frederik-shavn,** 238 miles (383km) northwest of Copenhagen, for overnight ferry connections to Oslo in Norway.

ESSENTIALS
Getting There

From North America, nonstop flights to Copenhagen from the greater New York area take about 7½ hours; from Chicago, 8½ hours; and from Seattle, 9½ hours.

SAS (ℭ **800/221-2350;** www.flysas.com has more nonstop flights to Scandinavia from North American than any other airline, and more flights to and from Denmark and within Scandinavia than any other airline. North American carriers flying to Copenhagen include **Air Canada** (ℭ **888/247-2262;** www.aircanada.ca), **American Airlines** (ℭ **800/433-7300;** www.aa.com), **Delta Airlines** (ℭ **800/221-1212;** www.delta.com), and **United Airlines** (ℭ **800/864-8331;** www.united.com).

In the United Kingdom, **British Airways** (ℭ **800/AIRWAYS** [247-9297] in the U.S., or 0844 4930 787 in the U.K.; www.ba.com) offers convenient connections through Heathrow to Copenhagen. Other European airlines with connections through their home countries to Copenhagen include **Icelandair** (ℭ **800/223-5500;**

www.icelandair.com), **Northwest/KLM** (✆ 800/241-4141; www.klm.com), and **Lufthansa** (✆ 800/645-3880; www.lufthansa-usa.com). Note that it's best to make your flight arrangements in North America before you go, or you might find some of these flights prohibitively expensive. If you can get a cheap flight into London, **easyJet** (✆ 0871 244 2366 in the U.K. at a rate of 10p per minute plus network charges, or 01144870/600-0000 in the U.S.; www.easyjet.com) offers no-frills, daily flights from London Stansted to Copenhagen.

Denmark by Rail
PASSES
For information on the **Eurail Global Pass, Eurail Global Pass Flexi, Eurail Denmark–Germany Pass, Eurail Denmark Pass,** and **Eurail Scandinavia Pass,** see chapter 2. Note that if you will be confining your travel to Denmark and the other Scandinavian countries, the Eurail Scandinavia Pass is your best option.

All Denmark train passes are best purchased in North America and are available from **Rail Europe** (✆ 888/438-7245 in the United States, ✆ 800/361-7245 in Canada; www.raileurope.com) or **ScanAm World Tours,** 108 N. Main St., Cranbury, NJ 08512 (✆ 800/545-2204; www.scandinaviantravel.com), which sells Eurail Scandinavia Passes if booked together with other land arrangements such as hotels.

FOREIGN TRAIN TERMS
Almost everyone in Denmark, where schoolchildren start learning English in grade school, speaks English, so there's no need to worry about a language barrier.

PRACTICAL TRAIN INFORMATION
Flat, low-lying Denmark, with its hundreds of bridges and absence of mountains, has a large network of railway lines connecting virtually every hamlet with the largest city, Copenhagen. For **information, schedules,** and **fares** anywhere in Denmark, call ✆ 70-13-14-15. Waiting times for a person at this number can be lengthy. An alternative way to gather schedules and prices, and even reserve a seat on specific trains, involves surfing over to the website maintained by the **Danish State Railways (www.dsb.dk/Rejseplan/bin/query.exe/en?L=vs_dsb&).**

A word you're likely to see and hear frequently is *Lyntog* (Express Trains), which are the fastest trains presently operational in Denmark. Be warned in advance that the most crowded times on Danish trains are Fridays, Sundays, and national holidays, so plan your reservations accordingly.

The Danish government offers dozens of discounts on the country's rail networks—depending on the age of a traveler, days or hours traveled, and destination. On any train within Denmark, children between the ages of 12 and 15 are charged half-price if they're accompanied by an adult, and up to two children under 12 can travel for free with any adult on any train in Denmark. Seniors (age 65 or older) receive a discount of 25% for travel on Fridays, Sundays, and holidays, and 50% every other day of the week. No identification is needed when you buy your ticket, but the conductor who checks your ticket may ask for proof of age.

RESERVATIONS The **Danish State Railways (DSB)** runs all train services except for a few private lines, and the outfit is one of the best and most reliable in Europe. Reservations are strongly recommended on the new, sleek **InterCity (IC)** trains unless you board after 8pm or are traveling on the line from Aalborg to Frederikshavn, where overnight ferries leave for Norway. Expect to pay a small booking fee when making the reservation.

Trains & Travel Times in Denmark

From	To	Type of Train	# of Trains	Frequency	Approx. Travel Time
Copenhagen	Odense	InterCity	Every 30 min.	Daily	1 hr., 30 min.
Copenhagen	Odense	Lyntog	Every hour	Daily	1 hr., 15 min.
Copenhagen	Århus	InterCity	Every hour	Daily	3 hr.,11 min.
Copenhagen	Århus	Lyntog	Every hour	Daily	2 hr., 51 min.
Copenhagen	Helsingør	Regional	Every 20 min.	Daily	45–50 min.
Århus	Aalborg	InterCity	Every hour	Daily	1 hr., 35 min.
Århus	Aalborg	Lyntog	Every hour	Daily	1 hr., 23 min.
Århus	Aalborg	Regional	Every 30 min.	Mon–Sat	1 hr., 42 min.
Aalborg	Frederikshavn	Regional	12 (9 on Sun)	Daily	1 hr., 20 min.
Aalborg	Frederikshavn	Lyntog	10 (6 on Sun)	Daily	1 hr., 11 min.

You can reserve both first-class or second-class cars on all IC trains. In Denmark, second-class travel is generally quite comfortable, so you may not want to pay the extra money for a first-class seat.

The other major type of train, the **Regional (R),** is upgrading its cars and aims to replace all the older ones by the time you read this. The trains are a bit slower and there is no first-class section. Seat reservations are optional on these trains, which don't tend to be crowded except at major holidays or during peak travel periods, especially July—the single biggest travel month in Denmark. In most cases, you'll be able to find a seat without a reservation, but you may not want to take that chance. Note that reservation fees aren't covered by railpasses, so you'll have to pay extra for them.

SERVICES & AMENITIES Because Denmark is so small, long overnight hauls aren't a factor. There are also no dining cars on trains, though most trains do have carts selling snacks and drinks. "Snacks" usually consist of expensive *smørrebrød* (open-faced sandwiches), though drinks are more reasonably priced.

[Fast FACTS] DENMARK

Area Code The country code for Denmark is **45.** It precedes any call made to Denmark from another country. There are no city area codes. Every telephone number has eight digits.

Business Hours Most **banks** are open Monday to Friday from 9:30am to 4pm (Thurs until 6pm), but outside Copenhagen, banking hours vary. **Stores** are generally open Monday to Thursday from 9:30/10am

to 5:30pm, Friday 9:30/10am to 7 or 8pm, and Saturday noon to 2pm (although they are allowed to stay open until 5pm on the first Sat of every month); most are closed Sunday (although they can open on the first Sun of the month and Sun in Dec).

Climate Denmark's climate is mild for Scandinavia—New England farmers experience harsher winters. Summer temperatures

average 61° to 77°F (16°–25°C). Winter temperatures seldom go below 30°F (–1°C), thanks to the warming waters of the Gulf Stream, though cold snaps and snow are common, and wintry winds can cut sharply. From a weather perspective, mid-April to November is a good time to visit.

Currency The basic unit of currency is the krone (crown), or DKK, made up of 100 øre. At this writing,

$1 = approximately 5.9DKK and £1 = 8.9DKK. Some major stores may also show prices in euros and accept euros as payment, but they are not obliged to and may give back change in kroner.

Documents Required Americans and Canadians can stay up to 3 months in Denmark with just a passport, but it must be valid for 3 months beyond their planned departure day.

Electricity Voltage is generally 220 volts AC, 50 to 60 cycles, and appliances use round two-pin plugs. In many camping sites, 110-volt power plugs are also available. Adapters and transformers may be purchased in Denmark. It's always best to check at your hotel desk before using an electrical outlet.

Embassies All embassies are in Copenhagen. The embassy of the **United States** is at Dag Hammärskjölds Allé 24, DK-2100 København (✆ **33-41-71-00;** www.usembassy.dk). **Canada**'s embassy is at Kristen Bernikowsgade 1, DK-1105 København K (✆ **33-48-32-00;** www.canada.dk).

Health & Safety You will have few health issues to worry about in Denmark. You don't need to get shots, most foodstuffs are safe, and the water in cities and towns is potable. If you're concerned, order bottled water. Prescriptions can be filled in towns and cities at any *apotek* (make sure your doctor fills out prescriptions using generic and not brand names), and nearly all areas

have English-speaking doctors in hospitals with well-trained medical staffs. Doctors will also make house calls to your hotel.

Denmark is one of the safest European countries for travelers. Copenhagen, the major population center, naturally experiences the most crime, much of it alcohol-related hooliganism, although muggings are known to occur. There are also tensions between the police and the citizens of the free state of Christiania that can erupt into rioting, as happened in 2008. If you are concerned, stay away from the area, or check the current situation with hotel staff. Crimes of violence are exceedingly rare. Exercise the usual precautions you would when traveling anywhere.

Holidays Some of the dates below may vary slightly each year, so check with a local tourist office or online at **www.visitdenmark.com**. Danish public holidays are New Year's Day (Jan 1), Maundy Thursday, Good Friday, Easter Sunday, Easter Monday, Labor Day (May 1), Common Prayers Day (4th Fri after Easter), Ascension Day (mid-May), Whitsunday (late May), Whitmonday, Constitution Day (June 5), Christmas Day (Dec 25), and Boxing Day (Dec 26).

Legal Aid While traveling in Denmark, you are, of course, subject to that country's laws. If arrested or charged, you can obtain a list of private lawyers from the U.S. Embassy to represent you.

Mail Post office opening hours vary widely. Most post offices are open Monday to Friday from 9 or 10am to 5 or 6pm. Some close on Saturdays. Others open from 9am to noon. All post offices close on Sundays and bank holidays. A standard letter weighing up to 50 grams (1.7 oz.) to North America costs 9.50DKK. Mailboxes are painted red and display the embossed crown and trumpet of the Danish Postal Society. To find post offices in Denmark, check out **www.postdanmark.dk**.

Police & Emergencies Dial ✆ **112** for the fire department, the police, or an ambulance, or to report a disaster of any kind. Emergency calls from public telephone kiosks are free (no coins needed).

Telephone At public telephone booths, use two 50-øre coins or a 1-krone or 5-krone coin only; insert the coins only when your party answers. You can make more than one call on the same payment if your time hasn't run out. Emergency calls to ✆ 112 are free.

Tipping Tips are seldom expected. Porters charge fixed prices, and tipping hairdressers or barbers is not customary. Service is built into the system, and hotels, restaurants, and even taxis include a 15% service charge in their rates. Rounding up when paying a restaurant bill or for your taxi is the norm, but you generally need tip only for special services.

6 COPENHAGEN ★★★

The capital of Denmark, home to almost a quarter of the country's population, is booming, bustling, and cosmopolitan. In summer—the time to visit—the entire city seems to flock outdoors to enjoy some precious sunshine after the gloomy, cold months of winter. Cafe culture flourishes, and locals flood the Strøget (the pedestrian-only mall in the heart of town) or go boating on the city's lakes. But mainly they bike: Danes cycle an average of 375 miles (604km) per year. At night, the Tivoli Gardens explode into a burst of light with entertainment for the masses. All this makes Copenhagen a veritable summer festival before it settles down once more in September for a long winter's nap.

For the rail passenger, Copenhagen is the gateway to all of Scandinavia, including Norway and Sweden. Trains will carry you from Copenhagen to Stockholm in just 5½ hours and to Oslo in 8½ to 9½ hours. And Copenhagen's train connections to Germany are great, especially to Hamburg and Berlin, two of Europe's best rail hubs.

Copenhagen is also the rail hub of Denmark, even though it's in the far eastern section of the country. The city offers easy rail links to all major attractions on the island of Zealand (on which Copenhagen lies) and to the eastern island of Funen, which is most often visited by those wishing to explore Odense, the birthplace of Hans Christian Andersen. You'll also find convenient connections to the major cities and towns on the peninsula of Jutland, including Århus.

Station Information

GETTING FROM THE AIRPORT TO THE TRAIN STATION

Flights into Copenhagen land at **Copenhagen Airport** (✆ **32-31-32-31;** www.cph.dk) in Kastrup, 5 miles (8km) from the center of Copenhagen. Trains link the airport with Copenhagen's Central Railway Station, in the center of the hotel zone. The trip takes a mere 13 minutes and costs 29DKK. Located right under the airport's arrivals and departures halls, the Air Rail Terminal is a short escalator ride from the gates. It has ticketing offices (where you can validate a railpass), information desks, restaurants, and fast-food chains. You can also take an SAS bus to the city terminal; the fare is 26DKK. A taxi to the city center costs between 190DKK and 250DKK, depending on the route and time of day.

INSIDE THE STATION

Trains arrive at the **København Hovedbanegård (Central Rail Station),** Copenhagen's main train hub, in the center of Copenhagen near the Tivoli Gardens and Rådhuspladsen (Town Hall Square). The station is frequently abbreviated "København H" on train schedules. Call ✆ **70-13-14-15** for local rail information.

Visitor information and hotel reservations are not available inside the rail station, but you'll find both at the Tourist Information Center, which is nearby and well marked (follow the signs from the station). Several ATMs can be found on the streets outside the station. Inside the station is a currency exchange kiosk open daily 7am to 9pm. It doesn't charge commission and will exchange any remaining kroner you have at the end of your trip if you keep your receipt. There is also an on-site luggage storage kiosk, charging 40DKK to 50DKK per bag for 24 hours; service is Monday to Saturday 5:30am to 1am, Sunday 6am to 1am. Several restaurants and a few shops are also located in the station. For more details, see **www.hovedbanen.dk**. From the Central Station, you can easily connect with the local subway system, the **S-tog.** Trains depart from platforms within the terminal.

Information Elsewhere in the City

The **Copenhagen Tourist Information Center**, Vesterbrogade, 4A (© **70-22-24-42;** www.visitcopenhagen.dk), is across from the main entrance to the Tivoli and around the corner from the rail station. The center is open 9am to 4pm Monday through Friday, and 9am to 2pm Saturday for September through April; open 9am to 6pm Monday through Saturday in May and June; and Monday to Saturday 9am to 8pm, and Sunday 10am to 6pm in July and August. It's closed Easter Monday; December 25, 26, and 31; and New Year's Day.

The staff here will make hotel reservations in person for 100DKK, or you can book a room online or over the phone for free. While here, pick up a copy of *Copenhagen This Week* (**www.ctw.dk**); its events calendar has good listings for sightseeing and entertainment.

Getting Around

Touring Copenhagen is best done on foot, but you'll need public transport to reach some of the sights. A joint fare system covers the Metro, buses, and trains, meaning you can travel on Copenhagen Transport buses, the State Railway, and S-tog trains in Copenhagen and North Zealand, plus some private railway routes within a 25-mile (40km) radius of the capital on one ticket.

BASIC FARES   The Greater Copenhagen area consists of seven different transportation zones, and fares vary depending on the zones you travel through. All bus stops and transit stations display a color-coded zone map to help you calculate your fare. A *grundbillet* (basic ticket) for both buses and trains costs 21DKK, allowing you to travel on as many different forms of public transport as you like, in two zones, for up to an hour. Up to two children ages 11 and under ride for half-fare when accompanied by an adult. For 120DKK, you can purchase a ticket allowing 24-hour bus and train travel through nearly half of Zealand; it's half-price for children 7 to 11 and free for children 6 and under.

Eurail passes and **Nordturist Pass** tickets (which can be purchased at any train station in Scandinavia) can be used on local trains in Copenhagen.

DISCOUNT PASS   The **Copenhagen Card** entitles you to free and unlimited travel by bus and rail throughout the metropolitan area (including North Zealand), 25% to 50% discounts on crossings to and from Sweden, and free admission to many sights and museums. The card is available for 1 or 3 days and costs 225DKK and 450DKK, respectively. Up to two children under the age of 10 are allowed to go free with each adult card. If you have three or more children, a 50% discount is granted. Buy the card at tourist offices, the airport, train stations, and most hotels. For more information, contact the Copenhagen Tourist Information Center (see above).

BY BUS   Copenhagen's well-maintained buses mostly leave from Rådhuspladsen, in the heart of the city. Buses run along the major routes every 10 to 15 minutes. Fares are integrated into the existing zonal systems (see "Basic Fares," above). For information, call © **36-13-14-15.**

BY METRO   In 2002, Copenhagen launched its first Metro line, taking passengers from east to west across the city or vice versa. Operating 24 hours, the Metro runs as far west as Vanlose or as far south as Vestmager. Nørreport is the transfer station to the **S-tog** system, the commuter rail link to the suburbs. Metro trains run every 2 minutes during rush hours and every 15 minutes at night. Check online at

ACCOMMODATIONS ■
Absalon Hotel **10**
Ascot Hotel **4**
Copenhagen Strand **20**
Danhostel Copenhagen
City **14**
Hotel Ansgar **12**
Hotel Fox **3**
Hotel Kong Arthur **2**
Hotel Skt. Petri **23**
Hotel Twentyseven **18**
Saga Hotel **11**

DINING ◆
Bøf & Ost **22**
Caféen I Nikolaj **21**
Divan **7**
Færgekroen **6**
Pierre André **24**
Restaurant Els **25**
Søren K **15**

ATTRACTIONS ●
Amalienborg Museum
& Palace **27**
Christiansborg Palace **19**
Christiania **16**
Frilandsmuseet **1**
The Little Mermaid **30**
Nationalmuseet **17**
Ny Carlsberg
Glyptotek **13**
Nyhavn **26**
Rådhus (Town Hall)
and World Clock **5**
Rosenborg Castle **28**
Statens Museum
for Kunst **29**
Tivoli Gardens **8**

INFORMATION ●
Tourist Information
Center **9**

http://intl.m.dk/ for a map and schedule, or call ☎ **33-11-17-00** for more info. Fares are integrated into the existing zonal systems (see "Basic Fares," earlier).

BY S-TOG   The S-tog connects the heart of Copenhagen, most notably the Central Station, with the city's suburbs. Use of the tickets is the same as on the buses and Metro (see "Basic Fares," earlier). You can transfer from a bus line to an S-tog train on the same ticket. Rail passholders generally ride free. For more information, call ☎ **70-13-14-15.**

BY TAXI   Watch for the FRI (free) sign or green light to hail a taxi, and be sure the taxis are metered. **Hovedstadens Taxi** (☎ **38-77-77-77**) operates one of the most central taxi companies. Tips are included in the meter price (although rounding up and leaving a little change is common): 24DKK at the drop of the flag and 12DKK per kilometer thereafter Monday to Friday 7am to 4pm. From 6pm to 6am, and all day Saturday and Sunday, the cost goes up to between 13DKK and 16DKK per kilometer. Many drivers speak English. ***Note:*** You will be charged more for ordering a taxi by phone—it's cheaper to hail one or find a taxi stand.

BY BICYCLE   Copenhagen is one of the most bike-friendly cities in Europe, resulting in a noticeable lack of pollution. Beware of cyclists as you walk around— they have right of way on bike paths, and if you hear a bell, move over. If you want to join the locals, there is a great rental scheme allowing you to pick up one of 2,000 bikes from one of 110 racks for a refundable deposit of 20DKK. You then return it to any bike rack across the city and get your deposit back. The scheme runs from May to November annually. See **www.bycyklen.dk** or call **45-36-16-42-33** for more info. You can also rent a bike at **Copenhagens Cyklebors,** Gothersgade 157 (☎ **33-14-07-17**). Depending on the bike, daily rates range from 60DKK to 150DKK, with deposits from 200DKK to 500DKK. Hours are Monday to Friday 8:30am to 5:30pm and Saturday 10am to 1:30pm.

Where to Stay

Note: Air-conditioning is not a standard amenity in Scandinavia, where it rarely gets very hot in summer. So, unless noted below, your hotel won't have any. And for those on tight budgets, look for hotels offering weekend packages to counteract the city's high rack rates.

Absalon Hotel ★ ✦   Long the most popular and most affordable budget hotel near the Central Station, this well-managed, family-run lodging has been putting up rail travelers since 1938. It is actually two hotels in one: the government-rated three-star Absalon Hotel and the one-star Absalon Annex. The rooms in the main building are more comfortable and spacious (best of all being the 19 luxury rooms and suites on the top floor); the Annex is more of a hostel, without private bathrooms.

Helgølandsgade 15, DK-1653 København. ☎ **33-24-22-11.** Fax 33-24-34-11. www.absalon-hotel.dk. 262 units. 835DKK–1,290DKK double with private bathroom; 750DKK annex double without private bathroom. MC, V. Closed Dec 14–Jan 2. Bus: Most lines run from nearby central station, NR 10 stops right outside. **Amenities:** Breakfast room; lounge; smoke-free rooms.

Ascot Hotel ★ ✦   One of Copenhagen's better midsize hotels, in the very heart of town, near the Central Station and a 2-minute walk from Rådhuspladsen. Dating from 1902 (with a 19th-c. ex-bathhouse annexed in 1994), it's seen many changes and alterations over the years but could now do with a little sprucing up. Bedrooms are simply furnished. The finest open onto the street, but the units in the rear get better air circulation and more light. There's also a fitness center.

Studiestraede 61, DK-1554 København. ℂ **33-12-60-00.** Fax 33-14-60-40. www.ascothotel.dk. 120 units. 1,490DKK–1,590DKK double; 2950DKK suite. AE, DC, MC, V. Bus: 2, 6, 8, 11, 14, 28, 29, 30, 34, 67, 68, 69, 150S, or 250S. **Amenities:** Restaurant; bar; smoke-free rooms.

Copenhagen Strand ★   This old brick-and-timber warehouse has been skillfully converted into a charming modern hotel. The waterfront Strand sports a vaguely maritime decor heavy on the *hygge*, a Danish word loosely translating as "cozy" or "warm," but meaning so much more. The higher-priced rooms open onto views of the harbor. Standard rooms are well furnished and on the small end of midsize; each has a well-kept bathroom with a tub (some have showers). The Strand offers guests free Internet access.

Havnegade 37, DK-1058 København. ℂ **33-48-99-00.** Fax 33-48-99-01. www.copenhagenstrand.com. 174 units. 770DKK–1,220DKK double; 1,170DKK–1,420DKK suite. Tram: 1 or 6. **Amenities:** Breakfast room; bar; babysitting; rooms for those w/limited mobility; smoke-free rooms.

Danhostel Copenhagen City ★   Staying in a hostel can be risky, but we recommend this one because it's more stylish than most. The furniture has been supplied by GUBI, the same design company chosen to furnish New York's Museum of Modern Art, *and* the whole place is clean, central (less than 1km from the rail station) and cheap compared to most Copenhagen accommodations. Private rooms sleep between four and six, but if you pay for the whole room, you can keep it all to yourself.

H.C. Andersens Blvd. 50, DK-1553 København. ℂ **33-11-85-85.** Fax 33-11-85-88. www.danhostel.dk. 192 en-suite units. 520DKK–780DKK 4-bed private room. AE, DC, MC, V. Bus: 5A. **Amenities:** Breakfast room; entire hostel is nonsmoking; rooms for those w/limited mobility. *In room:* No phone.

Hotel Ansgar   Only a 3-minute walk from the Central Station, this hotel lies in the heart of Copenhagen but on a fairly tranquil one-way street. The five-story building dates from 1885 and has recently been upgraded and extensively modernized (meaning the prices went up, but it's still good value). It's a family favorite because of its two dozen spacious rooms with extra beds. Rooms are comfortable, cozy, and modern, with Danish designs and a marble, shower-only bathroom.

Colbjørnsensgade 29, DK-1652 København. ℂ **33-21-21-96.** Fax 33-21-61-91. www.ansgar-hotel.dk. 81 units. 850DKK–1,250DKK double. Rates include buffet breakfast. AE, DC, MC, V. **Amenities:** Breakfast room; lounge; smoke-free rooms.

Hotel Fox ★★   In 2005, Volkswagen launched its new Fox car and wanted somewhere "super cool" to put up the visiting journalists and execs. They couldn't find anywhere, so they decided to equip an old hotel to suit their needs. The result was this highly recommended hotel, where all the rooms have been decorated by 21 hip local designers. Choices now range from kitsch Heidi-inspired boudoirs to boxing dens. To top it off, there's an eco-loving Nordic eatery and free Internet access throughout.

Jarmers Plads 3, DK-1551 Copenhagen. ℂ **33-13-30-00.** Fax 33-14-30-33. www.hotelfox.dk. 61 units. 1,325DKK–1,925DKK double. Rates include breakfast. AE, DC, MC, V. Bus/Metro: Noerreport. **Amenities:** Restaurant; bar; all rooms smoke-free.

Hotel Kong Arthur ★ 🦊   This 1882 hotel and former orphanage enjoys a tranquil residential setting opening out onto a string of city lakes. Completely renovated and modernized over the years, it's a very welcoming and intimate choice with a small atrium garden where breakfast is served in summer. The comfortable guest rooms have spacious tiled bathrooms. The helpful staff will do anything from cleaning shoes to getting theater tickets. It was once owned by Frommer's founder Arthur Frommer, hence the name.

Nørre Søgade 11, DK-1370 København. ✆ **33-11-12-12.** Fax 33-32-61-30. www.kongarthur.dk. 117 units. 1,840DKK double; from 3,020DKK suite. Rates include buffet breakfast. AE, DC, MC, V. Bus: 5, 7, or 16. **Amenities:** 3 restaurants; bar; spa; smoke-free rooms.

Hotel Skt. Petri   This luxe hotel is a celebrity magnet offering trendy elegance in a charming neighborhood nicknamed the "Latin Quarter." Originally a graceless modern department store, this well-renovated property offers fine views of St. Peter's Church, the old library, and the Rundetårn (Round Tower), just 2 blocks away. The rooms have all of the amenities you could wish for and marvelously comfy beds with feather pillows and cotton sheets. Prices are very high and the standard rooms are small, so definitely ask about their deals.

Krystalgade 22, DK-1172 København. ✆ **33-45-91-00.** Fax 33-45-91-10. www.hotelsktpetri.com. 268 units. 1,395DKK–2,195DKK double; from 3,395DKK suite. Breakfast buffet is an additional 165DKK AE, DC, MC, V. S-tog: Nørreport. **Amenities:** Restaurant; cafe; bar; rooms for those w/limited mobility; smoke-free rooms. *In room:* A/C.

Hotel Twentyseven ★★   Within easy walking distance of Copenhagen's central station, Hotel Twentyseven is the city's latest design hotel and a place where we like to stay. Rooms are light and bright, featuring current Scandinavian styling and unique touches such as black slate bathrooms. There's no restaurant, as such, but The Wine Room does allow for some global grazing, while the attached ice bar is an interesting experience that requires the donning of a thermal hooded cape. Free Wi-Fi is available throughout the hotel.

Løngangstræde 27, DK-1468 København. ✆ **70-27-56-27.** Fax 70-27-96-27. www.hotel27.dk. 200 units. 1,725DKK double. Rates include breakfast, coffee/tea, and light evening buffet. AE, DC, MC, V. Bus: 6a. **Amenities:** 3 bars; hotel is completely smoke-free.

Saga Hotel   Close to the rail station, this longtime budget favorite of foreign visitors and students was created in 1947 by combining two late-19th-century apartment buildings. Only 31 of the comfortably but simply furnished bedrooms have private bathrooms. The shared hallway bathrooms are adequate. Many of the bedrooms are spacious, with three to four beds—great for friends traveling together. **Warning:** The five-story building has no elevator, and the cheaper rooms are often at the top.

Colbjørnsensgade 18-20, DK-1652 København. ✆ **33-24-49-44.** Fax 33-24-60-33. www.sagahotel.dk. 79 units. 480DKK–750DKK double without bathroom; 600DKK–950DKK double with bathroom. Rates include breakfast. AE, DC, MC, V. Bus: 6, 10, 16, 28, or 41. **Amenities:** Breakfast room; lounge; smoke-free rooms.

Top Attractions & Special Moments

Like many rail travelers, you may have only 1 day to spend in Copenhagen. That's far too little time, but start the day off by strolling the old city's cobblestone streets and along its canals. Spend the afternoon at **Christiansborg Palace,** on Slotsholmen ("Palace Island"), where the queen receives guests. Early in the evening, head to the **Tivoli.** If it's winter, explore **Kongens Nytorv (King's New Square)** and the charming old sailor's quarter called Nyhavn, bristling with boats, bars, and cozy restaurants. At some point in the day, climb the Rundetårn (Round Tower) for a glorious panorama of Copenhagen.

If you have a second day, visit **Amalienborg Palace,** the queen's residence. Try to time your visit to see the changing of the guard. It doesn't have the precision or pomp of the changing of the guard at Buckingham Palace (p. 407), but it nonetheless remains a Kodak moment. Continue beyond the palace to the city's most famous statue, *The Little Mermaid,* perched upon a rock in the harbor. In the afternoon, see the art treasures of **Ny Carlsberg Glyptotek.**

Not for everybody, but worth a look, is a trip to the **Free City of Christiania**, on the island of Christianshavn (take bus no. 8 from Rådhuspladsen). Since 1971, some 1,000 squatters have taken over 130 former army barracks (spread across 85 acres/34 hectares) and declared themselves a free city, whose hippie-style liberation included communal living, ecological stewardship, hashish cafes, and general tolerance of alternative lifestyles. You can shop, dine, and talk to the natives about the experimental community, which has its own doctors, clubs, and stores. It even flies its own flag. On January 1, 2006, the settlement was sold to private developers by the Danish government, who would like to see it become "like any other neighborhood," and who hope to quash the fabled anarchic spirit of the place. This led to a riot in May 2007 and increased tension between police and residents. Caution also needs to be exercised in the area, as it's a favorite of pickpockets, and "Pusher Street" attracts just the kind of crowd its name suggests.

Amalienborg Museum and Palace ★★ Amalienborg museum is inside Amalienborg Palace, the 18th-century French-style rococo home of the Danish royal family since 1794. Amalienborg opens onto Copenhagen's most beautiful square and is the setting for the changing of the guard ceremony at noon. The ceremony takes place only when the queen is in residence, which is signaled by the raising of a swallowtail flag. In 1994, the overflow of royal treasures at Rosenborg Castle was accommodated in a museum on the ground floor, and since then, other rooms of Amalienborg have been opened to the public, revealing lavish private and state rooms. Two of the most interesting rooms are the **study of Christian IX** (1863–1906) and the **drawing rooms of Queen Louise** (1817–98). These rooms are furnished with gifts from their far-flung children in honor of their unofficial status as "parents-in-law to Europe."

Amalienborg Museum. ☎ **33-12-21-86.** www.ses.dk. Admission 60DKK adults, 35DKK students, 40DKK seniors, children 17 and under free. Oct–May Tues–Sun 11am–4pm; June–Aug daily 7am–4pm; Sept daily 11am–4pm. Closed Mon. Bus: 1, 6, 9, or 10.

Christiansborg Palace ★★★ Since 1167, five royal palaces have stood on this site on Slotsholmen, a small island separated from the heart of the city by a moatlike canal, pierced by several bridges. The present granite-and-copper palace dates from 1928. For 8 centuries, this has been the center of political power in Denmark, and the Christiansborg complex today is home to the houses of parliament, the prime minister's offices, and the Danish Supreme Court. Of more interest to visitors is a tour of the lushly decorated Royal Reception Salons, taking in such attractions as the Throne Room, the Banqueting Hall, and the Queen's Library.

In the courtyard, an equestrian statue of Christian IX (1863–1906) guards the grounds, and on the north end, you'll find the **Kongeliege Stalde & Kareter (Royal Stables & Coaches).** Especially interesting here are the regal coaches and the grand carriages used in days of yore. There's a separate admission charge to the stables of 10DKK adults, free for children under 12. The site can be visited May to October Saturday to Sunday 2 to 4pm.

Christiansborg Slotsplads. ☎ **33-92-64-92.** www.ses.dk Guided tour of Royal Reception Rooms 70DKK adults, 35DKK children 4–17, 60DKK students/seniors. Admission to castle ruins 40DKK adults, 20DKK children 4–17, 30DKK students/seniors, 185DKK family ticket (2 adults, 2 kids). Free admission to parliament. Guided tours of Reception Rooms May–Sept daily at 11am, 1, and 3pm; Oct–Apr Tues–Sun at 3pm. Ruins May–Sept daily 11am, 1, and 3pm; Oct–Apr Tues–Sun 3pm. Call to make appointment for English-language tour. Bus: 1, 2, 5, 8, or 9.

Frilandsmuseet (Open-Air Museum) ★★   Covering 86 acres (35 hectares) in Lyngby, on the fringe of the city, this museum re-creates rural Denmark in the 19th century and does so exceedingly well. It's a 2-mile (3.2km) walk around the entire compound, where you'll come across cottages once inhabited by fishermen, a farmstead from the 1700s on a remote Danish island, a primitive longhouse from the remote Faeroe Islands, and even tower windmills and a potter's workshop from the 1800s. Buildings were shipped from all over Denmark and reassembled here. Organized activities often take place here on summer afternoons. Sometimes dancers perform Danish folkloric shows, or you might see demonstrations of lace-making and loom-weaving. The park is a 9-mile (14km) ride from the Central Station, and there is a restaurant serving lunch on the grounds.

Kongevejen 100.℗ **33-13-44-11.** www.nationalmuseet.dk. Free admission. Easter–Oct Tues–Sun 10am–5pm; closed Mon. Closed rest of the year, except for select special openings; call ahead. S-tog: Copenhagen Central Station to Sorgenfri (trains leave every 20 min.). Bus: 184 or 194.

Nationalmuseet (National Museum) ★★★   One of the great museums of Scandinavia, this is the treasure-trove of Denmark, a gigantic repository of artifacts that allows visitors to stroll through 10,000 years of history in beautiful rooms that have been recently modernized without losing their charm. The vast complex takes in the Prinsens Palae, or Prince's Palace, constructed in 1744. There are six different departments in all, beginning with Danish prehistory, spanning the period from 13,000 B.C. to A.D. 1000. Among the stunning exhibits is the "Sun Chariot" found in a bog and dating from 1200 B.C. Finds from the Viking epoch include runic stones from Jutland in the 10th century. Religious objects and other exhibits, such as a 12th-century golden altar from Århus, fill a lot of the rooms devoted to the Middle Ages and the Renaissance. Lesser rooms feature the Danish collections of 1660 to 1830 (mainly antiques), Near-Eastern and Classical Antiquities, the Ethnographical Collections (among the finest in the world), and the Royal Collection of Coins and Medals. If it all seems like too much, free English audio guides can whisk you around the museum's highlights in an hour.

Ny Vestergade 10. ℗ **33-13-44-11.** www.nationalmuseet.dk. Free admission. Tues–Sun 10am–5pm. Closed Dec 24, 25, and 31. Bus: 1, 2, 5, 6, 8, or 10.

Ny Carlsberg Glyptotek ★★★   Carl Jacobsen, Mr. Carlsberg Beer himself, originally opened this major art museum behind the Tivoli more than a century ago. It's now one of the greatest art collections in Europe. Jacobsen was a feverish collector of classical art, and the museum still reflects his 19th-century taste, though the beer baron's original collection has been beefed up considerably over the years and now includes a treasure-trove of works by French Impressionists. It was started with a gift of some three dozen Paul Gaugin pieces, but today you'll also see paintings by Monet, Manet, Degas, and Renoir, as well as French sculpture, such as Rodin's *Burgers of Calais*. Cézanne's much-reproduced *Portrait of the Artist* also hangs here.

The antiquities collection is filled with sculpture and art from ancient Greece and Egypt, as well as Italy in the Etruscan and Roman eras. The most notable prize in the Egyptian collection is a prehistoric rendering of a hippopotamus. Impressive Greek originals, such as a headless Apollo and Niobe's tragic children, are on view with Roman copies of original Greek bronzes, including a 4th-century Hercules. The

Etruscan art display is especially notable, with its sarcophagi, winged lions, bronzes, and pottery. The entire museum reopened in June 2006 after a 3-year renovation that cost 100 million DKK, part of which was spent on the construction of a wing called "The Ancient Mediterranean World."

Dantes Plads 7. ⓒ **33-41-81-41.** www.glyptoteket.dk. Admission 60DKK adults, free for children 17 and under; free for everyone on Sun. Tues–Sun 11am–5pm. Closed Jan 1, June 5, and Dec 24–25. Bus: 1, 2, 5, 6, 8 or 10.

Rådhus (Town Hall) and World Clock We have never been able to work up much enthusiasm for this towering monument, the City Hall of Copenhagen. It was said to have been inspired by the main tower at the Piazza del Campo in Siena. The original is magnificent, the one in Copenhagen a bit dull. The architect, Martin Nyrop, wanted to create a building to "give gaiety to everyday life and spontaneous pleasure to all." We're not so sure he succeeded, but check it out anyway. Statues of Hans Christian Andersen and Niels Bohr (the Nobel Prize–winning physicist) are worth a look. Jens Olsen's **World Clock** is open for viewing Monday to Friday 10am to 4pm and Saturday at 1pm. Frederik IX set the clock on December 15, 1955. The clockwork is so exact that it's accurate to within half a second every 300 years. Climb the tower for an impressive view, though it's not for the faint of heart—300 steps with no elevator.

To the east of the Rådhus is one of Copenhagen's most famous landmarks, the **Lurblæserne** (Lur Blower Column), topped by two Vikings blowing an ancient trumpet called a *lur*. There's a bit of artistic license taken here. The *lur* actually dates from the Bronze Age (ca. 1500 B.C.), while the Vikings lived some 1,000 years ago. But it's a fascinating sight anyway.

Rådhuspladsen. ⓒ **33-66-25-82.** Admission to Rådhus 25DKK; 5DKK children 5–15. Guided tour of Rådhus 30DKK Mon–Fri 3pm; Sat 10 and 11am. Guided tour of tower Mon–Sat noon. Bus: 1, 6, or 8.

Rosenborg Castle ★★ Inspired by Dutch Renaissance architecture, this *slot* (castle) was constructed of red brick and decorated with sandstone, and it's rather the same as it was in 1633, except for the absence of the original moat. First laid out in

---

 THE OLD SAILORS' PORT AT Nyhavn

Nothing quite captures the spirit of maritime Copenhagen the way **Nyhavn ★★★** does. This colorful canal was dug in the late 1600s to permit seafaring vessels to go right up to Kongens Nytorv, the city's largest square, with an equestrian statue of Christian IV in the center. Here mariners would unload their cargo from the remote corners of the globe at the old warehouses once located here. Because so many sailors were in the area at night, a series of rowdy bars, cafes, and bordellos were opened to serve them.

In time, the area became gentrified and many of the most famous Copenhageners preferred to live here, including Hans Christian Andersen, who resided at various addresses: 20, 67, and 18 Nyhavn, in that chronological order. Today charming little restaurants, cafes, and a scattering of bars line the canal, and this is one of the most favored places for absorbing Copenhagen's unique flavor. The northern side of Nyhavn is a pedestrian area crowded with locals and visitors alike. High-speed craft come and go from here all day, linking Copenhagen with Malmö, Sweden.

1606, *Kongens Have* (King's Garden) remains a delightful oasis of tranquillity within the bustling city. Danish royals used Rosenborg as their summerhouse until 1710, when King Frederik IV pronounced it "too small for a king." The castle is filled with royal treasures ranging from Narwhal tusk and ivory coronation chairs to Frederik VII's baby shoes. The **crown jewels and regalia**—the single most impressive treasure—is on exhibit in the Treasury. In the Knights Hall, you can see the coronation seat and other royal relics from the 18th century. The most lavish royal bedroom, Room 3, is decorated with Asian lacquer art with a stucco ceiling. Christian IV died in this room surrounded by mourners.

Øster Voldgade 4A. ✆ **33-15-32-86.** www.rosenborgslot.dk. Admission 75DKK adults, 45DKK students, 50DKK seniors, free for children 16 and under. 20DKK to take pictures. Palace and treasury (royal jewels) Jan-Apr Tues-Sun 11am-4pm; May and Sept-Oct daily 10am-4pm; June-Aug daily 10am-5pm; Nov to mid-Dec Tues-Sun 11am-4pm. Closed Dec 17-26, Dec 31, and Jan 1. S-tog: Nørreport. Bus: 5, 10, 14, 16, 31, 42, 43, 184, or 185. Metro: Nørreport.

Statens Museum for Kunst (Royal Museum of Fine Arts) ★★★ We could spend an entire day here and always find some new artistic discovery. If you can't afford so much time, give it at least 2 hours, even more if you can spare it. The largest museum in Denmark houses painting and sculpture from the 13th century to the present. Its collection of Flemish and Dutch paintings from the 15th to the 18th centuries is especially impressive: an era of golden age landscapes and marine paintings by Rubens and his school, and remarkable portraits by every artist, from Rembrandt (in 2006, after much international research, the museum discovered two of its paintings were genuine Rembrandts) to Frans Hals. The European art section is rich in works from the Italian school from the 14th to the 18th centuries, and the French school from the 17th and 18th centuries. The Statens is also one of the grandest showcases for the development of Danish painting in the 19th century. Notable paintings, each a world masterpiece, displayed here include *Workers Coming Home,* by Edvard Munch; *Interior with a Violin,* by Matisse; *Alice,* by Modigliani; *The Guitar Player,* by Juan Gris; and *The Judgment of Paris,* by Harald Giersing. The museum also houses an impressive collection of Viking artifacts and has a sculpture garden filled with both classical and contemporary works. In 1998, a concert hall, the Children's Art Museum, and a glass wing were added, the latter devoted to temporary exhibitions.

Sølvgade 48-50. ✆ **33-74-84-94.** www.smk.dk. Admission 80DKK adults, 60DKK seniors, 25DKK students/children 24 and under. Tues and Thurs-Sun 10am-5pm; Wed 10am-8pm. Bus: 6A, 14, 40, 42, 43, 150S, 184, or 185.

Tivoli Gardens ★★★ 📷 Created in 1843, the Tivoli gardens gave Walt Disney an idea, and look what he did with it. The original is still here, standing in a 20-acre (8-hectare) garden in the center of Copenhagen. Its greatest admirers call it a pleasure park or flower garden; its critics say it's one giant beer garden.

Let's face it: The Tivoli is filled with schmaltz, but somehow, with its glitz, glamour, and gaiety, it manages to win over hardened cynics. Children prefer it during the day, but adults tend to like it better at night, when more than 100,000 specially made soft-glow light bulbs and at least a million regular bulbs are turned on—what an electric bill!

It features thousands of flowers, a merry-go-round, pinball arcades, slot machines, a Ferris wheel of hot-air balloons, an Arabian-style fantasy palace, and two dozen expensive restaurants. The latest attraction at Tivoli, "The Star Flyer," is the world's tallest carousel, at 264 feet (80m) high, giving the brave amazing views of the city below. There's also a playground for children.

THE TOWN'S hottest date:
HALF WOMAN, HALF FISH

The Little Mermaid ★ is the most famous statue in Scandinavia, and every visitor wants to see her. Described by some cynics as "Copenhagen's greatest disappointment," this life-size bronze of *Den Lille Havfrue* was inspired by Hans Christian Andersen's *The Little Mermaid,* one of the world's most famous fairy tales. Edvard Eriksen's sculpture, unveiled in 1913, rests on rocks right off the shore. In spite of its small size, the statue is as important a symbol to Copenhageners as the Statue of Liberty is to New Yorkers. The mermaid has fallen prey to vandals over the years. In the early 1900s, her arm was cut off and later recovered. She was decapitated on April 25, 1964, and the head was never returned. (The original mold exists, so missing body parts can be recast.) In January 1998, she lost her head again,

and most of the city responded with sadness. "She is part of our heritage, like the Tivoli, the queen, and stuff like that," said local sculptor Christian Moerk.

Although not taking blame for the attack, the Radical Feminist Faction sent flyers to newspapers to protest "the woman-hating, sexually fixated male dreams" allegedly conjured by the statue's nudity. The head mysteriously turned up at a TV station, delivered by a masked figure. Welders restored it, making the seam invisible.

But the japes and protests continue; since 2006, *The Little Mermaid* has sported a bra, a burka, a dildo, and various shades of paint. Copenhagen officials have responded by suggesting moving their city's symbol farther out to sea.

A parade of the red-uniformed Tivoli Boys Guard takes place on weekends at 4 and 6pm, and their regimental band gives concerts on Saturday at 2pm on the open-air stage. The oldest building at Tivoli, the Chinese-style Pantomime Theater with its peacock curtain, offers pantomimes in the evening.

For more on the nighttime happenings in Tivoli—fireworks, bands, orchestras, discos, variety acts—see "Nightlife," below.

Vesterbrogade 3. ✆ **33-15-10-01.** www.tivoligardens.com. Admission 95DKK adults, 50DKK children 3–11, free for kids 2 and under. For all rides 205DKK adults, 170DKK children 3–11. Ride ticket 25DKK. Closed mid-Sept to mid-Apr. Bus: 1, 16.

Where to Dine

Bøf & Ost FRENCH/DANISH   Popular with university students, this relatively affordable restaurant—Beef & Cheese in English—is housed in an 18th-century building with an outdoor terrace overlooking Greyfriars Square, one of the landmark plazas in Copenhagen's Old Town. Its cellars were created out of the ruins of a medieval monastery. You don't get a lot of surprises here, but you do get good, solid, home-style cooking (try the chargrilled streak) and one of the best cheese boards in Copenhagen.

Gråbrødretorv 13. ✆ **33-11-99-11.** www.boef-ost.dk. Reservations required. Main courses 190DKK–250DKK; lunch 100DKK–150DKK. DC, MC, V. Mon–Sat 11:30am–1am, kitchen closes at 10:30pm Sun–Wed, 11pm Thurs–Sat. Closed Jan 1. Bus: 5.

Caféen I Nikolaj DANISH   Set in an old church, this reasonably priced lunch and teatime venue is one of the most attractive eateries in the medieval Latin Quarter. Tables and chairs are set up outside in the summer months, while the building's large leaded-glass windows add atmosphere inside. Produce is brought in straight from the market, so the menu changes seasonally but should always include innovative dishes such as mature cheddar cheese on rye with aspic jelly, drippings, and Jamaican rum.

Nikolaj Plads, 12. ℂ **33-11-63-13.** www.nikolajkirken.dk. Reservations not accepted. Main courses 70DKK–178DKK. AE, DC, MC, V. Mon-Sat 11:30am–4pm; July-Aug and 2 weeks before Christmas Mon-Sat 11:30am–11pm.

Divan II ★★ DANISH/FRENCH   Established in 1843, this Tivoli landmark mixes audacious Danish cuisine with a setting that includes lush gardens, gorgeous fountains, and a greenhouse-inspired decor. Both the food and the service are impeccable and mark the restaurant as one of the most sophisticated in Copenhagen. Divan II features a great view of Tivoli Lake and offers an incomparable opportunity to explore the history of the park while enjoying spectacular food.

Tivoli. ℂ **33-75-07-50.** www.divan2.dk. Reservations recommended. Main courses 320DKK–500DKK. AE, DC, MC, V. Apr 15–Sept 23 daily noon–10pm.

Færgekroen DANISH   Tivoli is not a place for cheap dining, which makes this affordable lakeside restaurant, housed in a pink half-timbered Danish cottage, all the more delightful. Sit on its outdoor terraces on a sunny day, and enjoy honest, straightforward fare such as fried meatballs, curried chicken, or pork chops with red cabbage. To complement the farm-style food, the owners have recently added a microbrewery, producing two types of wonderfully tasty beer.

Vesterbrogade 3, Tivoli Gardens. ℂ **33-75-06-80.** www.faergekroen.dk. Reservations recommended for outdoor terrace tables. Main courses 175DKK–250DKK, prix-fixe lunch 150DKK. AE, DC, MC, V. Daily 11am–midnight (hot food until 9:45pm).

Pierre André ★★★ FRENCH   A great opportunity to enjoy world-class French cuisine in a relaxed atmosphere. Chef/owner Phillip Houdet's restaurant might no longer be considered cutting edge, but it still puts out a menu that's loaded with creativity and robust flavors. It could easily hold its own against some of the top restaurants in Paris or New York, but the new format means it won't be as hard on your wallet. Don't skip the chocolate cake for dessert!

Ny Ostergarde 21. ℂ **33-16-17-19.** www.pierreandre.dk. Reservations required. Main courses 100DKK–200DKK; fixed menus for groups of 6 or more 350DKK–450DKK. AE, DC, MC, V. Tues-Sat noon–2pm and 6–10pm. Closed 3 weeks July-Aug. Bus: 6, 10, or 14.

Restaurant Els DANISH/FRENCH   With its original 1854 decor intact, this former coffeehouse is now one of Copenhagen's most respected and traditional restaurants. It's certainly the best decorated—just look at the 19th-century murals. Hans Christian Andersen dined here in his day; John Irving stopped by more recently. Pop in at lunch for one of the delectable open-faced Danish sandwiches, or book in the evening for market-fresh food such as grilled scallops with chestnuts or saddle of reindeer with baked apple and cranberries.

Store Strandstraede 3, off Kongens Nytorv. ℂ **33-14-13-41.** Reservations recommended. www. restaurant-els.dk. Main courses 85DKK–265DKK; 4-course prix-fixe dinner from 448DKK. AE, DC, MC, V. Mon-Sat 11am–5pm; daily 5pm–midnight. Kitchen closes at 11pm. Bus: 1, 6, or 10.

Søren K ★ INTERNATIONAL   Named after Denmark's most celebrated philosopher, this minimalist dining room on the ground floor of the Royal Library is decorated in monochromatic tones, with big windows overlooking the canal. The chefs here cook without butter, cream, or high-cholesterol cheese—a heresy in a land known for its "butter-and-egg men"—and consequently some Danes boycott it, though foreign visitors, especially dieters, love it. Try the oyster soup or the roasted venison served with nuts and seasonal berries.

On the ground floor of the Royal Library's Black Diamond Wing, 1 Søren Kierkegaards Plads 1. ℂ **33-47-49-49.** www.soerenk.dk. Reservations recommended. 2-course prix-fixe lunch menu 250DKK, 3-course prix-fixe dinner menu 450DKK. AE, DC, MC, V. Mon–Sat 11am–10:30pm. Bus: 1, 2, 5, 8, or 9.

Shopping

Much of the action takes place on **Strøget,** the pedestrian street in the heart of the capital. Note that *Strøget* is a description, not a place name; it's pronounced "stroll," which is what you do on it. Strøget begins as Frederiksberggade, north of Rådhuspladsen, and winds to Østergade, which opens onto Kongens Nytorv. The jampacked street is lined with stores selling everything from porcelain statues of *Youthful Boldness* to pizza slices. The hurried visitor searching for Danish design might head first for **Illum,** Ostergade 52 (ℂ **33-14-40-02;** www.illum.dk), one of Copenhagen's leading department stores, filled with top-notch Danish designs, as well as those from other Scandinavian countries. Another elegant department store is **Magasin,** Kongens Nytorv (ℂ **33-11-44-33;** www.magasin.dk), which offers the tops in Scandinavia fashion, plus lots of fine glass and porcelain, along with handicrafts.

Georg Jensen, Amagertorv 6 (ℂ **33-11-40-80;** www.georgjensen.com; bus: 1, 6, 8, 9, or 10), in the Royal Copenhagen retail center, is known for its fine silver. The store features jewelry, as well as the largest collection of Jensen hollowware in Europe. It's a must-see for lovers of fine silver, connoisseurs and otherwise.

Those who flock to flea markets will find **Det Blå Pakhus,** Holmbladsgade 113 (ℂ **32-95-17-07**), to their liking. Charging an entrance fee of 15DKK, "The Blue Warehouse" (its English name) is the country's largest indoor market, with 325 vendors hawking everything from antiques and carpets to assorted bric-a-brac.

For Copenhagen's world-renowned porcelain, head to **Royal Copenhagen Porcelain,** in the Royal Scandinavia retail center, Amagertorv 4 (ℂ **33-13-71-81**). Founded in 1775, the company's trademark of three wavy blue lines is now a world-famous symbol, and the showroom attracts some serious collectors.

Nightlife

To find out what's on in Copenhagen when you're there, pick up a free copy of *Copenhagen This Week* at the tourist information center or look online at **www.ctw.dk**.

For the summer visitor, nothing competes with the **Tivoli Gardens** (p. 214) after dark. On an open-air stage in the center of the garden, various acts perform at 10pm on Friday evenings and on an arbitrary, oft-changing schedule varying from week to week and summer to summer. These performances are free and are often a venue for jazz or folkloric entertainment. More than a dozen commedia dell'arte productions are performed at the **Pantomime Theater,** with a Chinese stage and peacock curtain. The free shows are staged Tuesday and Thursday through Sunday in the evening.

Grand concerts, everything from symphony to opera, are presented in the 2,000-seat **Tivolis Koncertsal,** or concert hall; tickets cost from 200DKK to 700DKK when major artists are performing, but most performances are free. Concerts ranging from symphony to opera take place Monday to Saturday at 7:30pm (sometimes at 8pm, depending on the event). For more information and to book tickets, call ℂ **33-15-10-12.**

Copenhagen is also filled with music clubs featuring jazz, rock, and blues, and has many dance clubs. Some of the best jazz artists in the world perform at **Copenhagen JazzHouse,** Niels Hemmingsensgade 10 (② **33-15-26-00;** www.jazzhouse.dk), with shows beginning at 8:30pm nightly and a cover ranging from 75DKK to 300DKK, depending on the artists booked. Small and cozy (60 people max), **La Fontaine,** Kompagnistraede 11 (② **33-11-60-98**), presents jazz artists Friday and Saturday beginning around 11pm until 3am and Sunday from 11pm to 1am. Otherwise, it's a lively bar open daily from 8pm to 6am. There is a cover charge of 60DKK on Friday and Saturday.

Considered the best place for clubbing and concerts in the city, **Rust,** Guldbergsgade 8 (② **35-24-52-00;** www.rust.dk), has made an interesting transition from its first incarnation as a political coffeehouse to two floors of cutting-edge cool and great music, both live and DJ'd. It's in the neighborhood of Norrebro, which can be reached by bus 5A, 69, and 250S, and it's worth the ride, especially as it stays open till 5am from Wednesday to Saturday. Entrance is 60DKK Friday and Saturday, 30DKK Wednesday and 40DKK Thursday, though concerts cost extra. A trendy joint, **Vega,** Enghavevej 40, Vesterbrø (② **33-25-70-11;** www.vega.dk), is the biggest venue in Copenhagen, with three floors of entertainment and three separate venues for concerts, clubbing, and cocktail lounging. International names such as Bjork, Prince, and David Bowie have played here, so keep an eye on the website for info on upcoming events. Opening hours vary, as does the cover, which ranges from free to 60DKK; concert ticket prices depend on who's playing but are usually between 100DKK and 180DKK. For a taste of the homegrown Danish rock scene, stop by **The Rock,** Skindergade 45–47 (② **33-91-39-13;** www.the-rock.dk), located in an old courthouse. Bands usually start up around 9pm, powering through until midnight, when the venue morphs into a "rock club." Cover usually ranges from 55DKK to 225DKK.

Copenhagen also has a number of atmospheric old bars, of which our favorite is **Det Lille Apotek,** Stor Kannikestraede 15 (② **33-12-56-06;** www.detlilleapotek. dk). The Little Pharmacy, Copenhagen's oldest restaurant (dating from 1720), offers an antique atmosphere and is a student favorite. It is open daily from 11am to midnight (except on Sun, when it opens at midday). Prices run from 95DKK to 190DKK for dinner. Although spruced up today, **Nyhavn 17,** Nyhavn 17 (② **33-12-54-19;** www.nyhavn17.dk), is one of the remaining honky-tonks left over from the days when this gentrified quarter was a sailors' haunt. Maintaining a maritime flavor, it mixes up a wide selection of grog with live music most nights of the week. Open Sunday to Thursday 10am to 2am, Friday and Saturday until 3am.

Excursion to Helsingør (Hamlet's Castle) ★

Does it really matter to the pilgrims flocking to this town that Hamlet never existed? Or that William Shakespeare never visited Helsingør? To the pilgrims wanting to see "Hamlet's Castle," the power of legend is what really matters.

After making the 25-mile (40km) journey north from Copenhagen, make your way through the noisy, congested crowds and the fast-food stalls, and move deeper into Helsingør, where you'll find that it has a certain charm, with a market square, medieval lanes, and old half-timbered and brick buildings, many constructed by ships' captains in the heyday of the 19th-century shipping industry.

The Danish Riviera, with its sandy but windy and cold beaches, separates Helsingør from Copenhagen. To the east, a fleet of ferries links Helsingør across a 2½-mile (4km) strait with the town of Helsingborg, Sweden. Helsingør became important to merchants and mariners because of its strategic position at the entrance to the Øresund, a narrow strip of water connecting the Baltic Sea to the North Sea.

GETTING THERE Helsingør lies at the end of the northern line of trains heading from Copenhagen into the final reaches of North Zealand. A one-way trip takes 50 minutes, and trains leave frequently throughout the day from Copenhagen's Central Station.

Ferries, covered by the Eurail Global Pass and Eurail Scandinavia Pass, ply the waters of the narrow channel separating Helsingør (Denmark) from Helsingborg (Sweden) in less than 25 minutes. They're operated around the clock by **Scandlines** (© 33-15-15-15; www.scandlines.dk), which charges 21DKK each way for a pedestrian. Between 6am and 11pm, departures are every 20 minutes; 11pm to 6am, departures are timed at intervals of 40 to 80 minutes. Border formalities during the crossing between Denmark and Sweden are perfunctory, and although you should carry a passport, you might not even be asked for it.

VISITOR INFORMATION The **Helsingør Tourist Office,** Havnepladsen 3 (© 49-21-13-33; www.visitnordsjaelland.com), is open Monday to Friday 10am to 4pm and Saturday 10am to 1pm; June 20 to August 31 Monday to Friday 10am to 5pm, and Saturday 10am to 3pm.

TOP ATTRACTIONS & SPECIAL MOMENTS

For most visitors, there is only one site here worthy of making the trip: **Kronborg Slot ★★★**, Kronborg (© 49-21-30-78; www.ses.dk/en/SlotteOgHaver/Slotte/Kronborg/), a sandstone-and-copper Dutch Renaissance castle known in English as "Elsinore Castle." The most famous castle in Scandinavia lies on a peninsula jutting out into the Øresund, and it's said to be the home of Holger Danske (Holger the Dane), a mythological hero who sleeps beneath the castle. Though he never saw it, literary historians believe that the Bard had heard enough about the castle from some well-traveled friends to use this dank and gloomy place as the setting for his *Hamlet,* repeatedly staged at the castle since 1816. There have been numerous British productions here: Lawrence Olivier, John Gielgud, and Kenneth Branagh are just a few of the Hamlets who've fretted and strutted their hour upon the courtyard of Elsinore. Dating from 1426, the castle was completely rebuilt in 1585 and restored again after a fire gutted it in 1629. Several rooms, including the state apartments, are open to the public, although the place is rather starkly furnished. The **Great Hall** is the largest in Northern Europe, but only 7 of its original 40 tapestries—each commissioned by Frederik II in 1585—remain.

Also on the premises is the **Danish Maritime Museum** (© 49-21-06-85; www.maritime-museum.dk), which explores the history of Danish shipping. Unless you're really nautical, you might skip this, but that would mean missing the world's oldest surviving ship's biscuit, dating from 1852.

The castle is ½ mile (.8km) north of the Helsingør train depot. Admission to the castle and maritime museum is 90DKK for adults, 65DKK for young people between 15 and 18, and 25DKK for children under 15. The castle is open from May to September daily from 10:30am to 5pm, in April and October from Tuesday to Sunday from 11am to 4pm, and from November to March from Tuesday to Sunday from 11am to 3pm. It's closed December 24 and 25.

WHERE TO DINE

Typical Danish hot meals, such as *hakkebof* (hamburger steak), *frikadeller* (Danish rissoles or meatballs), rib roast with red cabbage, cooked or fried flounder or herring, and *æggekage* (egg cake) with bacon, are served in the local restaurants. You'll also find many fast-food places, and you won't want to miss the celebrated ice-cream wafers.

For good value and self-service, try **San Remo,** Stengade 53 (℗ **49-21-00-55**), which dishes out good, hearty Danish food—and plenty of it—in a most un-cafeteria-style dining room with crystal chandeliers. The location is in a shopping mall near the harbor. Main courses cost 32DKK to 95DKK.

An Excursion to Odense ★★

After Helsingør, the second-most-popular rail trip from Copenhagen is to the ancient town of Odense, the third largest in Denmark, situated 97 miles (156km) west of Copenhagen. This was the birthplace of Hans Christian Andersen (1805–75), Scandinavia's most famous storyteller, still as popular today as he was more than a century ago.

Odense lies on the island of Funen, which separates Zealand (site of Copenhagen) from Jutland, attached to the European mainland. Even without the Andersen connection, Odense is a lively little town of quaint charm.

GETTING THERE From Copenhagen's Central Station, dozens of trains per day make the 90-minute trip west to the city of Odense.

Note: Every hotel in Odense is located within a 1-mile (1.6km) radius of the railway station, and even the main shopping streets (Kongensgade and Vestergade) are on the opposite side of a verdant downtown park (Kongens Have) from the railway station.

VISITOR INFORMATION The **Odense Tourist Bureau,** at Rådhuset, Vestergade 2A (℗ **66-75-75-20**; www.visitodense.com), is open mid-June to late August Monday to Friday 9am to 6pm, Saturday and Sunday 10am to 3pm; early September to mid-June Monday to Friday 9:30am to 4:30pm, Saturday 10am to 1pm. Should you wish to stay overnight, the staff here will reserve you a hotel room for 35DKK.

Besides helping arrange excursions, the tourist bureau sells the value-laden **Odense Adventure Pass.** It gives you access to 16 of the city's museums, the Odense Zoo, six indoor swimming pools, and unlimited free travel on the city buses and DSB trains within the municipality. It also entitles you to discounts on river cruises. Passes are valid for 1 day and cost 129DKK.

GETTING AROUND Most Odense buses originate or terminate at the railway station. You can hop aboard a bus at various stops and buy your ticket once you're aboard; you must have exact change. Buses cost 16DKK per ride within Odense city center (on the buses with two-digit numbers) and are each valid for transfers within a 60-minute period of their issue.

You can rent a bike from **Odense Cykler,** Nedergade 36 (℗ **66-75-39-64**; www.odensecykler.dk), for prices ranging from 100DKK to 150DKK per day, depending on the type of cycle. A 500DKK deposit is required.

TOP ATTRACTIONS & SPECIAL MOMENTS

Odense Tourist Bureau (see above) offers 2-hour **walking tours** in July and August every Tuesday and Thursday at 2pm, from a meeting place behind its office. Covering the town's major sites, it costs 50DKK for adults and 25DKK for children. Reservations are recommended.

Other than the Hans Christian Andersen monuments (see below), you can visit the chief attraction, **Funen Village/Den Fynske Landsby ★★**, Sejerkovvej 20 (℗ **65-51-46-01**; www.museum.odense.dk), a large open-air museum of regional artifacts and buildings 1½ miles (2.4km) south of the historic center and reached by bus no. 21 or 22 from Flakhaven, a street in the center of Odense. This is really a living museum to Funen in the 18th and 19th centuries. Old structures from all over Funen were brought here and reassembled, including a village school, vicarage, jail, windmill, farmstead, and weaver's shop. Everything is authentically furnished, and you can visit workshops to see craftspeople at work, and later enjoy plays and folkloric dances at the Greek-style theater. An exhibition in the visitor center helps aid the transition from modern life to Hans Christian Andersen times. Admission to the village is 60DKK for adults and free for children under 18, except from late October to the end of March, when admission drops to 40DKK for adults, as visitors are not allowed inside the individual houses. It's open Mid-June to mid-August daily 10am to 6pm, then April to mid-June and mid-August to mid-October Tuesday to Sunday 10am to 5pm, and mid-October to March Sunday 11am to 3pm.

H.C. Andersen's Hus ★★, Bangs Boder 29 (✆ **65-51-46-01;** http://museum. odense.dk/museums/hans-christian-andersen-museum.aspx), is the goal of most pilgrims to Odense. Popular with children of all ages, this museum is devoted to keeping alive the memory of Andersen, whose centenary in 2005 was honored with a spiffing-up of the museum and yearlong celebrations. Precious memorabilia include his top hat, a battered suitcase, and even his celebrated walking stick. Rare artifacts include letters to fellow writer Charles Dickens in London and to "the Swedish nightingale," Jenny Lind, on whom Andersen had developed a crush. Reprints of his books in countless languages are on view. Admission is 60DKK for adults and free for children under 17. Open mid-June to mid-August daily 9am to 6pm, mid-August to mid-June Tuesday to Sunday 10am to 4pm.

The other site associated with the writer is the **H.C. Andersen's Barndomshjem (Andersen's Childhood Home),** Munkemøllestræde 3–5 (✆ **65-51-46-01**). The house is a grim little place, which no doubt fueled the fairy-tale writer's imagination, as he grew from age 2 to 14 within its tiny confines. He was a gawky boy, a true ugly duckling, made fun of by his schoolmates. Life didn't get better after school, when he went home to a drunken, superstitious mother who worked as a washerwoman. But all is serene at the cottage today, and the "garden still blooms," as it did in *The Snow Queen*. Admission is 25DKK for adults and free for children under 17; hours from mid-June to mid-August are daily 10am to 4pm, January to June Tuesday to Sunday 11am to 3pm, and September to January 10am to 3pm.

Before bidding adieu to Odense, head for **St. Canute's Cathedral ★**, Klosterbakken 2 (✆ **66-12-03-92;** www.odense-domkirke.dk), the most impressive Gothic-style building in Denmark. Work on this cathedral began in the 13th century, but it wasn't completed until the 15th century. Note the gold altar screen with an elegant **triptych ★★★** carved by Claus Berg in 1526 at the request of Queen Christina. The admission-free church stands opposite City Hall. Open April to October Monday to Saturday 10am to 5pm, Sunday and holidays noon to 2pm; and November to March Monday to Saturday 10am to 4pm.

WHERE TO DINE

While you're exploring the historic core of Odense, you'll find a number of atmospheric restaurants serving good food, including **Den Gamle Kro,** Overgade 23 (✆ **66-12-14-33;** www.den-gamle-kro.dk). A refined French and Danish cuisine based on fresh ingredients from the surrounding countryside is served at this old town center inn dating from 1683. Dine in one of two intimate and antique-filled rooms, or have a drink in the cellar bar. Main courses cost 228DKK to 338DKK, with fixed-price meals going for between 298DKK and 418DKK.

The landmark **Under Lindetraeet,** Ramsherred 2 (© **66-12-92-86;** www. underlindetraet.dk), a centuries-old inn across from the much-visited H. C. Andersen's Hus, is noted for its fresh, top-quality ingredients and skillfully prepared Danish dishes. It serves some of the best meat and shellfish dishes in the area—including tender Danish lamb and filet of plaice with butter sauce—while also dishing out *lobscouse,* the fabled sailors' hash. The prix-fixe menus run from 370DKK to 810DKK, depending on the number of courses.

HIGHLIGHTS OF JUTLAND

From the islands of Zealand, on which Copenhagen sits, and Funen, whose heart is Odense, we move to the largest landmass of Denmark: Jutland. It's a peninsula of heather-covered moors, fjords, lakes, sandy dunes, and farmland. For your final look at Denmark, head via fast train to Jutland's major city, Århus.

Århus ★★

The capital of Jutland and Denmark's second-largest city, Århus lies 109 miles (175km) west of Copenhagen. A university town with a lively port, it's the cultural center of Jutland and a major industrial center as well. Pronounced *Ore*-hoos, Århus is self-styled "the world's smallest big city" and has some good museums and historic buildings. But we prefer to amble through the cobblestone streets before people-watching in the city's bars and sidewalk cafes, or picnicking at one of the city parks or sandy beaches.

GETTING THERE   Nearly 40 trains leave Copenhagen's Central Station each day, reaching Århus in 3 to 3½ hours. The city's railway station, Århus Hovedbanegard, lies on the south side of the town center.

VISITOR INFORMATION   Tourist Århus, Banegårdspladsen 20 (© **87-31-50-10;** www.visitaarhus.com), just a few minutes' walk from the train station, is open July to mid-September Monday to Friday 9:30am to 6pm, Saturday 9:30am to 3pm, and Sunday 9:30am to 1pm; mid-September to June Monday to Thursday 9:30am to 5pm, Friday 9:30am to 4pm, Saturday 9:30am to 1pm, closed on Sunday.

GETTING AROUND   A regular bus ticket, to cover a journey in the city center through up to two zones, can be purchased on the rear platform of all city buses for 18DKK.

Or go eco and borrow one of Århus' 250 free city bikes. You'll find them at 30 stands dotted around the city. All you need to liberate a bike is a returnable 20-kroner coin. For more information about where to find a stand, ask at the tourist office (see above).

The value-filled **Århus Pass** allows unlimited travel by public transportation and free admission to many museums and attractions. A 1-day pass costs 119DKK for adults, 59DKK for children 3 to 12; 2-day passes are 149DKK for adults and 69DKK for children under 16. The Århus Pass is sold at the tourist office and many hotels, camping grounds, and kiosks throughout the city.

TOP ATTRACTIONS & SPECIAL MOMENTS

For an introduction to Århus, head to the town hall's tourist office, from which all sorts of different walking tours depart every weekday. Themes range from "Architecture and Art in Århus" to "The Latin Quarter." Each one lasts 2 hours and costs 125DKK for adults or 75DKK for children; if you have the Arhus Pass, tours are

100DKK for adults and 55DKK for kids. Call the tourist office (above) for more information.

The late-Gothic **Cathedral of St. Clemens (Århus Domkirke),** Bispetorvet (© **86-20-54-00**), is the longest in Denmark, with a 315-foot (95m) nave. Begun in the 13th century in the Romanesque style, it was completely overhauled in the 15th century into a rather flamboyant Gothic overlay. Admission is free, and the cathedral is open May to September 9:30am to 4pm, October to April Monday to Saturday 10am to 3pm; it opens 10:30am Tuesday and is closed during church services. Get there on bus no. 3, 11, 54, or 56.

The town's other crowning achievement is its **Rådhuset (Town Hall),** Rådhuspladsen (© **89-40-20-00**), built from 1936 to 1941 to commemorate the 500th anniversary of the town charter. Arne Jacobsen, Denmark's most famous architect, was one of the designers of this marble-plated building. You can either take an elevator or brave 346 steps to get to the top of the 194-foot (58m) tower, which opens onto a panoramic view of Århus and the countryside around it. The building is still in use, so visitors can enter at any time. There is a guided tour every Wednesday in July and August at 2pm. Private tour guides can be booked for just under 600DKK.

The biggest attraction of all, **Den Gamle By ★★★,** an open-air museum, is located 1½ miles (2.4km) west of the train station, just outside of town, at Viborgvej 2 (© **86-12-31-88;** www.dengamleby.dk). The little community of more than 75 buildings lies in a park west of the town center. Re-created in a botanical garden, urban life from the 16th to the 19th centuries comes alive here. You can wander at leisure through workshops watching craftspeople at work, including carpenters, hatters, bookbinders, and so on. You can also explore old-fashioned buildings such as a schoolhouse, pharmacy, or post office, as well as the Burgomaster's House, the half-timbered 16th-century home of a rich merchant. Summer music programs are staged, and on the grounds you'll find a tea garden, bakery, beer cellar, and full-service restaurant. Admission is 100DKK from the end of March until the end of June, 125DKK from the end of June through September, 100DKK weekdays September through December, 125DKK weekends for the same period, and 50DKK January to March. Children under 18 get in free, and students are half-price. Opening hours are mid-September to mid-November and April to June daily 10am to 5pm; mid-November to Christmas weekdays 9am to 7pm, weekends 10am to 7pm; mid-February to March daily 10am to 4pm; January to mid-February daily 11am to 3pm; July to mid-September daily 9am to 6pm. To get here, take bus no. 3, 14, 25, or 55 (trip time: 3–5 min.), or walk (about 15–20 min.) from the train station.

WHERE TO STAY & DINE

With a history dating from 1907, **Teater Bodega,** Skolegade 7 (© **86-12-19-17;** www.teaterbodega.dk), is still going strong, serving excellent Danish meals, including delectable open-faced sandwiches at lunch, across from the Århus Cathedral. Theater buffs and art lovers, among others, are drawn to the atmosphere of thespian memorabilia and the Danish country-style cooking, including hash, Danish roast beef, and freshly caught fish. Lunch *smørrebrød* costs 58DKK to 138DKK, and main courses run 90DKK to 250DKK.

Inside the most exclusive hotel in Arhus lies the **Hotel Philip Restaurant ★★★** (© **87-32-14-44),** which serves high-quality food made from fresh ingredients. Beautiful hardwood floors and brass candelabras set a romantic mood that is more than accentuated by the inventive cuisine. The chefs use a lot of local seafood and regularly adjust the menu to what's in season. Lunch costs between 60DKK and 225DKK; dinner features a three-course prix fixe menu for 354DKK.

Should you wish to stay overnight, the chain-run **Scandic Plaza** ★, Banegård-splads 14, DK-8100 (✆ **87-32-01-00;** www.scandic-hotels.com), is in the center of town, close to the Town Hall and major attractions. A remake of an original 1930s hotel, the 162-room property was vastly renovated and overhauled in 1997 to provide tastefully decorated and comfortably furnished bedrooms. Rates, which include breakfast, are 990DKK to 2,390DKK double.

Frederikshavn

The embarkation ferry departure point for Norway, the coastal town of Frederikshavn, 238 miles (383km) northwest of Copenhagen, is the final stop for rail passengers in North Jutland.

In lieu of major attractions, you get stores loaded with Danish goods. Swedes and Norwegians arrive by sea in droves to shop for Danish food products that are much cheaper than back in their hometowns.

GETTING THERE   Frederikshavn is the northern terminus of the DSB rail line. About 11 direct trains leave daily from Århus to Frederikshavn; travel time is roughly 2¾ hours. Trains leaving out of Copenhagen take 5¼ hours.

VISITOR INFORMATION   The **Frederikshavn Turistbureau, Skandiatorv** 1 (✆ **98-42-32-66;** www.frederikshavn-tourist.dk), near the ferry dock and a short walk down Havnepladsen from the train station, is open in midsummer Monday to Saturday from 9am to 6pm, Sunday from 9am to 2pm. In the off season, hours are Monday to Friday 9am to 4pm, Saturday 11am to 2pm. Staff can recommend and reserve local hotel rooms for you at no charge.

THE TOP ATTRACTIONS & SPECIAL MOMENTS

Worth exploring, the oldest part of Frederikshavn, **Fiskerkylyngen,** lies north of the fishing harbor and is filled with well-preserved homes, many dating from the 1600s. Otherwise, attractions are minor except for the **Bangsbo Museum** ★, Dronning Margrethesvej (✆ **98-42-31-11;** www.bangsbo.com), an open-air museum in the north of Jutland, 1¾ miles (2.8km) south of the town center in a deer park. Several 18th-century buildings lie near the ruins of a 14th-century manor house. Many mementos of Denmark of yesterday are found here, including a barn from 1580 (one of the oldest in Denmark), farm equipment, and a large display of World War II relics. An ancient ship, similar to vessels used by the Vikings, is also displayed. Admission is 40DKK for adults, free for children under 18. It's open May to June and August to December 10am to 4pm weekdays, 11am to 4pm weekends; and July 10am to 5pm weekdays, 11am to 4pm weekends. Closed Mondays year round, weekends October to December.

WHERE TO STAY & DINE

Near the harbor in an 1850s building, **Restaurant Baachus,** Lodsgade 8A (✆ **98-43-29-00**), is an unpretentious bistro serving a mix of Italian and Mexican food at affordable prices. Its 40-seat old-fashioned dining room turns out quick fillers such as pizza, succulent pastas, burritos, and a spicy chili con carne. They have a two-course prix-fixe menu for 119DKK and a three-course menu for 129DKK.

For something a little grander, head to the **Restaurant GråAnden (Gray Duck Restaurant),** in the Radisson SAS Jutlandia Hotel (see below), Havnepladsen

ferries TO SWEDEN & NORWAY

Stena Line (© **96-20-02-00;** www.stenaline.dk), one of Europe's largest and most reliable ferryboat operators, runs the two most popular routes in and out of town. Passengers heading to Norway can take a daily, daytime 9-hour ferryboat between Frederikshavn and Oslo. Foot passengers pay 195DKK. Be warned in advance that southbound boats originating in Oslo depart after dark, and consequently, all passengers are required to rent an overnight cabin for the 9-hour evening transit. Cabins, each suitable for two passengers, rent for between 380DKK and 1,560DKK. Stena also has seven departures daily between the Swedish port of Gothenburg and Frederikshavn. Transit time is between 2 and 3¾ hours, depending on the boat. Passengers pay between 105KK and 255DKK each way, though Eurail passholders get a 30% reduction on this ferry. Stena also operates two catamaran crossings every day that are much faster than the ferries. Stena Line charges 40DKK for phone reservations, but Internet reservations are free.

(© **98-42-42-00;** www.hotel-jutlandia.dk), where you'll be one of a handful of diners eating in a dining room overlooking the blue-gray expanse of the sea. The food is a mix of French and Danish. It might include seafood cocktail followed by lemon sole in a ragout of mussels and curried cream, or quail with foie gras and a red-wine flambé. During July and August, there is a buffet in the evening. Year-round, main courses go from 132DKK to 189DKK, with set meals starting at 178DKK for two courses. The buffet special runs 185DKK per person.

The 95-room **Radisson SAS Jutlandia Hotel,** Havnepladsen, DK-9900 (© **98-42-42-00;** www.hotel-jutlandia.dk), is the best-rated place to stay in town, situated close to the embarkation point for the boats to Gothenburg. Scandinavian design and first-class comfort are found here, especially in the midsize and comfortably furnished bedrooms. Rates, including breakfast, range from 1,150DKK to 2,450DKK for a double.

FINLAND

Finland often gets lumped in with the Scandinavian countries: Norway, Denmark, and Sweden. But it's not actually a Scandinavian country at all. It's a Nordic country. And although it shares many similar traits—stunning wild landscapes and modern urban environments—there's something different about Finland. Maybe it's the Russian influence (Finland was part of the Russian Empire for over a century, and you can still taste the remnants of this in the Helsinki restaurants dishing out bear steaks and caviar), or the fact it's one of the least populated countries in the world (with only 5.3 million people and a density of 14.8 inhabitants per sq. km—Japan has 327), or that its location on the top edge of Europe (it is one of the northernmost countries in the world, with nearly one-third of its land, Lapland, north of the Arctic Circle) has given its residents more mental freedom, more imagination. They are dreamy, outdoor-loving souls, given to escaping off to their ramshackle summerhouses in the warmer months, to spend the season cooking over a campfire, foraging for wild food, and doing what everyone imagines Finnish people should be doing—swimming in cold lakes and taking saunas.

Of the countries sitting on the "roof" of Europe, Finland is the most difficult to reach by rail. But once arriving in Helsinki, the Finnish capital, you'll have access to two unique travel opportunities. From Helsinki, you can take one of four daily high-speed trains to St. Petersburg in Russia, where you can visit the Hermitage, one of the great depositories of world art. You can also take a daily overnight train to Moscow. Helsinki is also the gateway to the newly emerging Baltic countries, especially Estonia, which is only a short boat ride from the Finnish capital.

And even though Finland has the most difficult connections to European rail networks, it nonetheless is an easy ferry trip from Stockholm, which enjoys excellent rail links to other Scandinavian capitals and, consequently, the rest of continental Europe. With a Eurail pass, you can, for example, get on a train in Rome and ride the rails all the way to Stockholm, where you can make the final run by ferry into Helsinki. Once in Helsinki, you can hook up with efficient rail lines in what is increasingly emerging as the "crossroads" between the east and west of Europe.

Finland also possesses a number of other pluses as a rail destination. The Finnish rail system is one of the most modern in the world, linking all the country's major towns and cities, except those in the remote north. Even though Finland is a large country, it's easy to get around by rail. And in what may be the most literate country in the world, there is no language barrier, as almost all Finns speak English—and rather fluently, at that.

FESTIVALS & special events

After a long, cold winter, most Helsinki residents turn out to celebrate the arrival of spring at the **Walpurgis Eve Celebration,** held on April 30. Celebrations are held at Market Square, followed by May Day parades and other activities the next morning.

A major Scandinavian musical event, the **Helsinki Festival** presents orchestral concerts by outstanding soloists and ensembles, chamber music and recitals, exhibitions, ballet, theater, and opera performances, along with jazz, pop, and rock concerts. For complete information about the program, contact the **Helsinki Festival,** Lasipalatsi Mannerheimintie 22–24, Finland–00100, Helsinki (✆ **09/6126-5100;** www.helsinkifestival.fi). The festival takes place from mid-August to early September.

Since the 1700s, the annual **Baltic Herring Market** has taken place along the quays of Market Square in early October. Fishermen continue the centuries-old tradition of bringing their catch into the city to sell from their boats. Prizes and blue ribbons go to the tastiest herring.

Summer is the best season to visit (although it's also when the Finns take their long summer vacations, so prepare for some restaurants and shop closures in Helsinki), when the country's endless scenic vistas of vast green forests and blue lakes can be seen from your train window. Many rail passengers visit in summer just to enjoy the Midnight Sun, best seen from Rovaniemi, the capital of Finnish Lapland.

Highlights of Finland

Of course, an entire book could be written on the lakes and untamed wilderness of Finland, which contrast nicely with the country's small, ultramodern cities. But the remoteness of the country's location means a rail visitor who makes it to this part of the world (mostly by boat or air from Stockholm) usually descends on Helsinki for a visit of only 2 or 3 days before moving on to other points on the Continent.

Now that the Iron Curtain is long gone, many adventurous travelers also stop off in Finland before ferrying over to Tallin, the capital of Estonia, or taking the train to Russia's St. Petersburg (the former Leningrad).

As the capital of Finland, **Helsinki** lies at the crossroads between Eastern and Western Europe. It's also the country's rail hub. You can begin your adventure in this city by heading for **Market Square** to test the pulse of the capital, followed by visits to two of the most important attractions, one of the three museums making up the **Finnish National Gallery** and the **Mannerheim Museum,** the latter the former home of World War II hero and Finnish president Baron Carl Gustaf Mannherheim. The following morning you can spend in the **National Museum of Finland,** followed by an afternoon at the **Seurasaari Open-Air Museum** and **Suomenlinna Fortress,** the "Gibraltar of the North." At some point in your journey, enjoy an authentic Finnish sauna in the land where the institution was invented.

ESSENTIALS

Getting There

With more flights to Helsinki from more parts of the world (including Europe, Asia, and North America) than any other airline, **Finnair** (✆ **800/950-5000** in the U.S.;

www.finnair.com) is the only airline that flies nonstop from North America to Finland (an 8-hr. trip). Departures take place from New York; most flights from major U.S. cities will transfer to a nonstop flight at Kennedy International Airport.

Several other airlines fly from North America to gateway European cities and then connect to Helsinki. Foremost among these is **British Airways (BA; ℰ 800/247-9297** in the U.S., or 0844/493-0787 in London; www.britishairways.com). **Finnair** (**ℰ 0870/241-4411** in London; www.finnair.com) also offers more frequent service to Helsinki from several airports in Britain.

If you're stopping in Finland after traveling by train through the Continent, it's likely you'll head here via modern ferry service from Stockholm on **Silja Line (www.silja.com)** or **Viking Line (www.vikingline.fi)**. Discounts on Viking line come with some restrictions—consult the website. Eurail or Scandinavia passholders get a 50% discount on these routes, and a 50% discount on a bed in a four-berth cabin on the Silja route (passes must be valid in both Sweden and Finland to obtain these discounts). More comfort costs extra and prices depend on the class of cabin, the number of passengers per room, and the line you take.

If you take the ferry from Stockholm to Turku (an 11-hr. journey—also discounted with a Eurail pass), the county's former capital on the west coast of Finland, you can catch one of the seven daily trains (including a high-speed Pendolino) taking passengers across southern Finland to Helsinki. The trip takes 2¼ hours. Most passengers, however, take a ferry directly from Stockholm to Helsinki without any extra rail travel. Ferry service, with Silja Line, is also available from Rostock, Germany, to Hanko, but we do not recommend this option, as it takes over 24 hours to make the crossing. If you do want to go this way, a bus service operated by Silja Line connects Hanko with Helsinki, approximately 90 minutes away. Passengers with a railpass, even if it is just for Finland, get a 30% reduction on this journey.

Finland by Rail
PASSES
For information on the **Eurail Global Pass,** the **Eurail Global Pass Flexi,** the **Eurail Select Pass,** the **Eurail Scandinavia Pass,** and other multicountry options, see chapter 2.

The Eurail Finland Pass entitles holders to unlimited travel for any 3, 5, or 10 days within a 1-month period on all passenger trains of the VR Ltd. Finnish Railways. Travel days may be used either consecutively or nonconsecutively. Prices start at $165 in second class. Children 6 to 16 are charged half the full fare (proof of age required); children 5 and under ride free when accompanied by a full-fare adult (they do not, however, get a seat).

The Eurail Finland Pass should be purchased before you leave home and can be obtained from **Rail Europe (ℰ 888/438-7245** in the United States, ℰ **800/361-7245** in Canada; www.raileurope.com) or through your travel agent.

Note: Second-class trains in Finland are comparable to first-class trains in many other countries, so splurging on a first-class ticket or pass is unnecessary.

FOREIGN TRAIN TERMS
Forget trying to learn Finnish; to speak it, you pretty much need to be born there, as it's one of the world's most difficult languages. The good news for English-speakers is that Finnish "train lingo" is hardly a consideration because school children in Finland start learning English in grade school and you won't have problems finding someone at any of the major stations who speaks English.

Trains & Travel Times for Finland

From	To	Type of Train	# of Trains	Frequency	Travel Time
Stockholm	Helsinki	Ferry	3	Daily	16 hr., 55 min.
Helsinki	St. Petersburg	*Allegro*	4	Daily	3 hr., 36 min.
Helsinki	Moscow	*Tolstoi*	1	Daily	14 hr., 16 min.

PRACTICAL TRAIN INFORMATION

Finland's extensive and reliable rail network is run by VR Ltd. Finnish Railways, and all major Finnish cities are linked by rail to Helsinki. Most trains are new (or close to it) and operate on a timely basis. And Finland's rail engineers now offer some of the most modern and high-speed trains in Europe. For example, the new high-tech Pendolino (they "tilt" as they take corners) trains have cut traveling time between Helsinki, the present capital, and Turku, the ancient capital, to under 2 hours. There are a total of four types of trains that operate in the country: **InterCity (IC)** trains, high-speed **Pendolino (EP)** express trains, regular express trains, and slower local and commuter trains.

The good news for budget travelers: Finnish trains are cheaper than those in the rest of Scandinavia. And if you choose to purchase open round-trip (return) tickets, they are valid for 15 days.

For a Finnish Railways journey planner, check **www.vr.fi**.

RESERVATIONS   Seat reservations are included in the price of an advance ticket on Pendolino, InterCity, and express trains, but not on the regional trains, where seats are unreservable. If you buy your ticket on board a train, you can't reserve a seat, either. We recommend booking in advance, if you can, and getting a reserved seat, as Finnish trains tend to be crowded. If you have a Eurail pass, you can also make a reservation before you leave North America through Rail Europe for $11 or in Finland itself for prices from 6€ on the InterCity trains and from 11€ on the Pendolino trains, with prices getting steeper as the length of the journey increases. **Warning:** Reserved seats are not marked, so you'll never know if you're taking someone's seat unless the passenger shows up to evict you.

SERVICES & AMENITIES   It's not possible to reserve couchettes on Finnish rails, as there are none. You can reserve two- and three-berth compartments, however. Twenty new sleeper cars debuted in late 2006, each with two beds per compartment; some compartments have their own shower and toilet. All sleepers should be reserved as far in advance as possible, especially during the peak times of July, August, Christmas, and the skiing season between February and April. To reserve in advance, contact Rail Europe or your travel agent. Prices for accommodations vary, so ask when you make the reservation.

Most express trains are air-conditioned and offer nonsmoking sections, music channels, and facilities for those with mobility issues. Some Finnish trains, such as the double-decker InterCity2 trains, have outlets peddling snacks and drinks. Prices, however, are lethal. If you're watching your euros, it's far better to pick up a supply of food and drink for your journey at the rail station before boarding the train.

[FastFACTS] FINLAND

Area Code The international country code for Finland is **358.** The city area code for Helsinki is **09.**

Business Hours Most **banks** are open Monday to Friday from 9am to 4:15pm. You can also exchange money at the railway station in Helsinki daily from 8am to 9pm, and at the airport daily from 6:30am to 11pm. **Store** hours vary. Most are open Monday to Friday from 9am to 6pm and Saturday from 9 or 10am to 5 or 6pm. Some department stores and malls stay open until 9pm on weekdays. Shops are allowed to open on Sundays during the summer months and in the run-up to Christmas. Many do, including **R-kiosks,** which sell candy, tobacco, toiletries, cosmetics, and souvenirs all over Helsinki and elsewhere; they're open Monday to Saturday 8am to 9pm and Sunday from 9 or 10am to 9pm.

Climate Spring arrives in May and the summers are short—a standing joke in Helsinki claims summer lasts from Tuesday to Thursday. July is the warmest month, with temperatures averaging around 59°F (15°C). The coldest months are January and February, when the Finnish climate is comparable to that of New England. Snow usually arrives in December and lasts until April.

Currency As part of the European Union, Finland uses the euro as its currency. At press time, 1€ = $1.30, or $1 = 75p.

Documents Required American and Canadian citizens need only a valid **passport** to enter Finland. You need to apply for a visa only if you want to stay more than 3 months.

Electricity Finland operates on 220 volts AC. Plugs are usually of the continental type, with rounded pins. Always ask at your hotel desk before plugging in any electrical appliance. Without an appropriate transformer or adapter, you'll destroy the appliance.

Embassies & Consulates The Embassy of the **United States** is at Itäinen Puistotie 14B, FIN-00140 Helsinki (✆ **09/616-250;** http://finland.usembassy.gov/); and the Embassy of **Canada** is at Pohjoisesplanadi 25B, FIN-00101 Helsinki (✆ **09/228-530;** www.canada.fi). If you're planning to visit Russia after Finland and need information about visas, the **Russian Embassy** is at Tehtaankatu 1B, FIN-00140 Helsinki (✆ **09/661-876**). It's better, however, to make all your travel arrangements to Russia before you leave home. For information on the documents you need to go to Russia, visit **http://moscow.usembassy.gov/russian-visas.html** well

before you travel. There are a number of private companies which offer you help in navigating the entry and exit visa system in Russia.

Health & Safety Finland's national health plan does not cover U.S. or Canadian visitors. Any medical expenses that arise must be paid in cash. (Medical costs in Finland, however, are generally more reasonable than elsewhere in Western Europe.) British and other European Union (E.U.) citizens can get reduced-cost/free medical care in Finland with a European Health Insurance Card, which replaces the E111 form and covers emergencies in Finland and all other E.U. countries.

Finland is one of the safest countries in Europe, although the recent arrival of desperately poor immigrants from former Communist lands to the south means the situation is not as tranquil or as safe as before.

Holidays The following holidays are observed in Finland: January 1 (New Year's Day); Epiphany (Jan 6); Good Friday, Easter Monday; May 1 (May Day); Ascension Day (mid-May); Whitsun (late May/early June); Midsummer Eve and Midsummer Day (Fri and Sat of the weekend closest to June 24); All Saints' Day (Nov 5 in 2011; varies by year); December 6 (Independence Day); and December 25 and 26

(Christmas and Boxing days).

Mail   Airmail letters take about a week to 10 days to reach North America; surface mail—sent by boat—takes 1 to 2 months. Parcels are weighed and registered at the post office, which may ask you to declare the value and contents of the package on a preprinted form. Stamps are sold at post offices in all towns and cities, at most hotels, sometimes at news kiosks, and often by shopkeepers who offer the service for customers' convenience. In Finland, mailboxes are bright yellow with a trumpet embossed on them. Airmail letters cost .65€ for up to 20 grams. For postal information, call ✆ **0200/71-000.**

Police & Emergencies
In Helsinki, for emergencies dial ✆ **112.**

Telephone   To make **international calls** from

Finland, first dial the international prefix of 00, 990, 994, or 999; then the country code; then the area code (without the general prefix 0); and finally the local number. For information on long-distance calls and tariffs, call ✆ **02-02-08.** To place calls to Finland, dial whatever code is needed in your country to reach the international lines (for example, in the United States, dial **011** for international long distance), then the country code for Finland **(358),** then the area code (without the Finnish long-distance prefix 0), and finally the local number. To make long-distance calls within Finland, dial 0 to get a long-distance line (the carrier is chosen at random), the area code, and the local number. (Note that all area codes in this guide are given with the prefix 0.) For phone number information, dial ✆ **02-02-02.** Besides

phone booths and hotels, calls can be made from local post and telephone offices.

Tipping   Tipping is not really part of the culture in Finland, but if you think someone has done something really well, you can show your appreciation with a tip. It's standard for **hotels** and **restaurants** to add a service charge of 15%, and usually no further tipping is necessary, although it's usual to leave the small change in restaurants. **Taxi drivers** don't expect a tip. It is appropriate to tip **doormen** at least 1€, and **bellhops** usually get 1€ per bag (in most Finnish provincial hotels, guests normally carry their own luggage to their room). At railway stations, **porters** are usually tipped 1€ per bag. Hairdressers and barbers don't expect tips. **Coat check charges** are usually posted; there's no need for additional tipping.

HELSINKI ★★★

A rail hub situated at the crossroads of Eastern and Western Europe, Helsinki is the capital of the Independent Republic of Finland and is home to some 560,000 people. Although Helsinki is most often reached by a boat cruise from Stockholm, the city contains a vast network of rail lines coming in from all over Finland, and even extending south to Russia for those who want to go to either Moscow or St. Petersburg. You can visit every major town or city in Finland via Helsinki.

The city was founded in 1550 at the mouth of the Vantaa River by Swedish King Gustav Vasa, when Finland was a part of Sweden, and was later relocated on the Vironniemi peninsula in the place now known as Kruununhaka. It was not the capital of Finland until after the Napoleonic Wars of the early 19th century. Russia, concluding a peace with the French, annexed Finland to its empire and moved the capital from Turku to Helsinki, which was closer to St. Petersburg.

Perhaps the city's greatest allure for the rail traveler is its individuality—it is distinct from all other European capitals and has a flavor all its own. Unlike Athens, you'll find no ancient temples here, for Finland is a decidedly modern nation with granite neoclassical structures. And, unlike Vienna, Helsinki is not full of unicorns, gargoyles, palaces, and tombs that testify to architectural splendor and the glory of empire. All the kings who've ruled the city have been foreigners; instead of glorifying monarchy, the Finns are more likely to honor an athlete or a worker in their sculpture. As proof, just take a look at the figures standing proudly, even defiantly, in front of Stockmann's Department Store: three nude blacksmiths.

Station Information

GETTING FROM THE AIRPORT TO THE TRAIN STATION

Helsinki–Vantaa Airport (© 0200/14-636, .57€ per min.; www.helsinki-vantaa.fi) is 12 miles (19km) north of the center of town, about a 35-minute bus ride from the center of the city. Bus no. 615 goes back and forth from the airport and Railway Square, site of the main train terminal. A bus departs two to three times an hour from 5:30am to 10:20pm, for 4€ one-way. You can also take the Finnair/City Bus to Helsinki for 6€. A taxi from the airport to the rail station in the center of Helsinki costs around 35€ to 40€ one-way.

INSIDE THE STATION

Trains arrive in the center of the city at the **Central Helsinki Railway Station,** Kaivokatu. Designed by Eliel Saarinen (1873–1950) in the early 20th century, the station itself is a national monument and a classic example of the Art Nouveau style. And it's an especially good station for English speakers: All information in the station is posted in both Finnish and English.

Trains heading to St. Petersburg and ultimately to Moscow, the latter a 13-hour journey from Helsinki, depart from here. Trains also leave from this station for all major cities in Finland, including Tampere and Turku (both just 2 hr. away). You can catch a northbound train from here to Rovaniemi, the capital of Finnish Lapland (about three direct trains leave daily). The Lapland trip takes 10 to 13 hours, depending on the train.

If you don't want to go to the tourist office (see below), you'll find a hotel booking service, **Hotellikeskus** (© 09/2288-1400; www.helsinkiexpert.fi), in the main central hall of the station, straight in front of you as you exit from the trains. There's a fee of 8€ per person if you show up and speak to a staff member; the service is free by phone, online, or if you e-mail **hotel@helsinkiexpert.fi.** Here you'll also find a small tourist information point, linked to the larger one (see "Information Elsewhere in the City," below) in the center of town.

You can store your luggage at the office on the far right of the main hall as you emerge from the trains. Lockers cost 3€ per day. A money exchange kiosk is also located in the main hall and is open daily from 7am to 10pm. For rail information, you can visit the **Train Information Center** on the right-hand side of the main hall. It's possible to make seat reservations on Finnish trains at counters 1 through 10 Monday to Friday 8am to 9:30pm and Saturday and Sunday 9:30am to 9:30pm. To validate a railpass, go to counters 14 through 17. For more information or to make train reservations, call © 60-04-19 00.

Information Elsewhere in the City

From the train station, walk 2 blocks down Keskuskatu, make a left onto Pohjoisesplanadi, and you'll arrive at the **Helsinki City Tourist Office,** Pohjoisesplanadi 19 (© 09/3101-3300; www.visithelsinki.fi). The tourist office is open May 2 to September 30 Monday to Friday 9am to 8pm and Saturday and Sunday 9am to 6pm; off season Monday to Friday 9am to 6pm, Saturday and Sunday 10am to 4pm. Staff here hands out free brochures and maps, alongside information on the city and its sights and events.

Helsinki

ACCOMMODATIONS ■
Helka Hotel **7**
Hotel Anna **11**
Hotel Arthur **15**
Hotelli Finn **10**
Rivoli Jardin **12**
Seurahuone Helsinki **9**

DINING ◆
Bellevue **18**
Kellarikrouvi **13**
Ravintola Perho **6**
Ravintola Sipuli **17**
Rivoli Ravintolat **8**
Wellamo **19**

ATTRACTIONS ●
Ateneum Art Museum **14**
Eduskunta (Finnish
  Parliament) **5**
Helsinki City Museum **4**
Kiasma (Museum of
  Contemporary Art) **14**
Lutheran Cathedral
  (Tuomiokirkko) **16**
Mannerheim Museum **20**
National Museum
  of Finland **3**
Olympiastadion
  (Olympic Stadium) **2**
Seurasaari Open-Air
  Museum **1**
Sinebrychoff Art
  Museum (Museum of
  Foreign Art) **14**
Suomenlinna Fortress **21**

Helsinki Expert/Tourshop (✆ **09/2288-1500**), a service offered from the same premises as the Helsinki City Tourist Office, is your best bet for booking tours once you reach Helsinki. The Tour Shop will also make hotel reservations for 8€ and sells bus and cruise tickets, and the money-saving **Helsinki Card** (see below).

Getting Around

Helsinki is small enough to be explored on foot, but some of its best attractions lie outside the city center, and you'll need to take a taxi or public transportation to get to them.

Visitors to Helsinki can buy the **Helsinki Card,** which offers unlimited travel on the city's public buses, trams, subway, and ferries, and a free guided sightseeing bus tour (in summer daily, off season on Sun), as well as free entry to about 50 museums and other sights in Helsinki. The Helsinki Card is available for 1-, 2-, or 3-day periods. The price of the card for adults is 34€ for 1 day, 45€ for 2 days, and 55€ for 3 days. A card for children costs 13€, 16€, and 19€ for 1-, 2-, and 3-day cards. Cards are sold at over 50 sales points in the Helsinki area, including the Helsinki City Tourist Office, Tour Shop, and hotel reception desks. Or you can buy them online at **www.helsinkiexpert.fi**.

You can also buy a **Tourist Ticket** for travel over a 1-, 3-, or 5-day period. This ticket lets you travel as much as you like within the city limits on all forms of public transportation except regional buses. A 1-day ticket costs 6.80€ for adults, 3.40€ for children ages 7 to 16; each additional day costs 3.40€ for adults, 1.70€ for kids. Children under 7 travel free. Tickets can be purchased at many places throughout Helsinki, including the Helsinki City Tourist Office and transportation service depots, such as the Railway Square Metro Station.

A single ticket bought from an automatic machine costs 2€ for adults, 1€ for children. A single ticket is valid for 60 minutes from the moment of purchase and allows passengers to transfer between different lines or types of transport. Tickets bought on public transportation cost 2.50€.

You can order **taxis** by telephone (✆ **0100/0700**), find them at taxi ranks, or hail them on the street. All taxis have an illuminated yellow sign that reads TAKSI/TAXI. The basic fare costs 4.50€ and rises on a per-kilometer basis, as indicated on the meter. In the evening (8pm–6am Mon–Fri and 4–6pm Sat) and on Sunday, the basic fare is 7€.

Where to Stay

Helka Hotel ★★ 🍴   This 1928 hotel is a budget oasis in a sea of expensive hotels close to the train station. This centrally located property is also pretty stylish for the price. Guest rooms are minimalist, spacious, and filled with light-wood Scandinavian furniture. Each has a private bathroom with shower attached. Double windows cut down on the noise. The on-site **Finnish restaurant** is surprisingly hip, and there's free Internet access throughout the building.

Pohjoinen Rautatiekatu 23, Helsinki 00100. ✆ **09/613-580.** Fax 09/441-087. www.helka.fi. 150 units. 122€–185€ double; 150€–290€ suite. Rates include breakfast. AE, DC, MC, V. Tram: 3B or 3T (stop at Kauppakorkeakoulut). Metro: Kamppi. **Amenities:** Restaurant; bar; rooms for those w/limited mobility; smoke-free rooms.

Hotel Anna 🍴   This well-run and affordable hotel was converted from a 1926 apartment building that survived World War II Russian bombardment. It is located in a lovely residential neighborhood, and convenient to shopping and museums. The hotel retains a lot of its original charm, even though it was practically rebuilt in 1985, with additional upgrades completed in 2010. The small to midsize bedrooms are comfortably decorated.

Annankatu 1, FIN-00120 Helsinki. © **09/616-621.** Fax 09/602-664. www.hotelanna.fi. 64 units. 130€–170€ double; 160€–205€ suite. Rates include breakfast buffet. AE, DC, MC, V. Tram: 3B, 3T, or 10. **Amenities:** Breakfast room; smoke-free rooms.

Hotel Arthur 🏅   In high-priced Helsinki, the privately owned Arthur is an affordable stopover for the frugal rail traveler. A 4-minute walk from the rail station, the hotel is in a turn-of-the-20th-century building with an annex dating from 1950. The small rooms and equally cramped bathrooms feature pretty standard motel furnishings. Breakfasts are tasty, and lunch buffets are generous and reasonably priced.

Vuorikatu 19, FIN-00100 Helsinki. © **09/173-441.** Fax 09/626-880. www.hotelarthur.fi. 168 units. 94€–124€ double; 250€ suite. Rates include breakfast. Additional bed 20€. AE, DC, MC, V. Tram: 1, 3, 6, or 7. Metro: Kaisaniemi. **Amenities:** Restaurant; bar; smoke-free rooms.

Hotelli Finn 🏅   This small hotel is less than 1,000 feet (300m) from the rail station, set on the fifth and sixth floors of a dignified but rather austere city office building. It's a welcoming place, however, and has been in the hands of the same family owners since 1960. Rooms can comfortably house two to four guests; furnishings are basic but adequate. The Finn's owners pride themselves on being one of the least expensive hotels in central Helsinki.

Kalevankatu 3B, FIN-00100 Helsinki. © **09/684-4360.** Fax 09/6844-3610. www.hotellifinn.fi. 27 units. 75€ double. AE, DC, MC, V. Tram: 3, 4, 7, or 10. **Amenities:** Lounge.

Rivoli Jardin ★★   This recently renovated and well-managed hotel is one of the best boutique hotels in Helsinki, and is just over ¼ mile (.4km) from the rail stations. Custom-designed as a hotel in 1984, it has stayed abreast of the times with frequent refurbishing, and a warm welcome awaits you in its stone-and-marble-clad lobby. Most of the midsize bedrooms are individually decorated with lovely furniture and exquisite woodcarvings. Rooms have wall-to-wall carpeting or Asian rugs placed on hardwood floors, and each has an attractively tiled bathroom.

Kasarmikatu 40, FIN-00130 Helsinki. © **09/681-500.** Fax 09/656-988. www.rivoli.fi. 55 units. 207€ double; 237€ suite. Rates include breakfast. AE, DC, MC, V. Tram: 10. **Amenities:** 3 restaurants; breakfast room; bar; 1 room for those w/limited mobility; smoke-free rooms.

Seurahuone Helsinki ★   Originally opening in 1833, this hotel moved to its current location in a five-story Art Nouveau town house across from Helsinki's railway station in 1913. Since then, it has been expanded, most recently in 2006, as part of a series of comprehensive upgrades, one of which included a new wing. Rooms are moderate in size, mostly with twin beds, along with combination bathrooms (both showers and tubs). The public rooms are often crowded, as the hotel hosts many public organizations.

Kaivokatu 12. FIN-00100. Helsinki. © **09/691-41.** Fax 09/691-4010. www.hotelliseurahuone.fi. 118 units. 127€–227€ double; 350€–400€ suite. Rates include breakfast. AE, DC, MC, V. Tram: 3B, 3T, or 4. **Amenities:** Restaurant; bar.

Top Attractions & Special Moments

Ateneum Art Museum ★★   Part of The Finnish National Gallery, Finland's largest selection of sculpture, painting, and graphic art is displayed at this museum. The Finnish National Gallery is an umbrella term for three independent museums:

PAYING HOMAGE TO Finlandia & Sibelius

Jean Sibelius (1865–1957), composer of *Finlandia*, lived for more than half a century at **Ainola Ainolantie** (☎ **09/287-322;** www.ainola.fi), in Järvenpää, 24 miles (39km) from Helsinki. Few countries seem as proud of one of their native composers as the Finns are of Jean Sibelius. In 1903, while he was skiing with his brother-in-law, Sibelius discovered a forested hill, which inspired him to commission construction of what would eventually become his family home. He named it after his wife, Aino, and from 1904 maintained a residence there with his children for many years. Today he and his wife are buried on the property, which has become a shrine for music lovers. Some claim that they can hear the first notes of his violin concerto as they approach the house on a still day.

Visitors can tour the interior of the Art Nouveau house, which remains as the maestro left it. There are no great antiques or art—in fact, Ainola is simplicity itself—just as Sibelius preferred. In many places, the log walls remain in their natural state, and traditional tiled heating stoves are visible. The highlight of the exhibits is the grand piano. Some of the walls are decorated with paintings from the composer's private collection.

To get to the house, hop on a train from Central Helsinki Railway Station to Järvenpää. Admission is 5.5€ adults, 3€ students, 1€ children. Open May to September, Tuesday to Sunday 10am to 5pm.

the **Ateneum Art Museum,** the **Kiasma (Museum of Contemporary Art),** and the **Sinebrychoff Art Museum (Museum of Foreign Art).** The first museum is housed in the Ateneum building across from the railway station. More than a century old, it was designed by Theodore Höijer. The Museum of Finnish Art has the largest collection of Finnish artists, from the mid-1700s to 1960, as well as the works of some 19th- and 20th-century international artists. The remaining two museums are listed separately below.

Kaivokatu 2. ☎ **09/173-361.** www.fng.fi. Admission 9€ adults, 7€ students and seniors, free for children 17 and under. Free admission every Wed 5–8pm. Tues and Fri 9am–6pm; Wed–Thurs 9am–8pm; Sat–Sun 11am–5pm. Tram: 3B, 3T, 6, 9.

Eduskunta (Finnish Parliament)   Near the post office and only a few blocks from the rail station, this building of reddish Kavola granite (built in 1931) houses the 200 members of the one-chamber parliament (40% of whose members are women). The building looks austere on the outside, but it's much warmer inside. The goal was to use all Finnish material and artists in its construction, and there are nearly 1,000 art pieces in the collection, including five impressive bronze statues by Wäinö Aaltonen. The architect, J. S. Sirén, who wanted to celebrate the new republic, chose a modernized neoclassic style.

Mannerheimintie 30. ☎ **09/432-21** (switchboard). www.eduskunta.fi. Free admission. Guided tours daily July–Aug 11am (Finnish, Swedish) and 1pm (English); they are given in all three languages year-round Sat at 11am and 1:30pm and Sun at noon and 1:30pm. Tram: 3B, 3T, 4, 7A, 7B, and 10.

Helsinki City Museum   At Villa Hakasalmi, about ¼ mile (.4km) from the railway station, the museum presents the history of Helsinki from its founding up to modern times. A small-scale model of the town in the 1870s is on display. There is also an exhibit of home decorations from the 18th and 19th centuries, glass, porcelain, and toys.

Sofiankatu 4 (by Senate Sq.). © **09/3103-6630.** www.hel.fi/wps/portal/Kaupunginmuseo_en?WCM_ GLOBAL_CONTEXT=/Museo/en/Etusivu. Free admission. Mon–Fri 9am–5pm; Sat–Sun 11am–5pm. Tram: 1, 3B, or 3T.

Kiasma (Museum of Contemporary Art) ★ Part of the Finnish National Gallery (see the Ateneum Art Museum, above), this museum opened in 1998 and houses Finland's finest collection of contemporary art. An American architect, Steven Hall, designed the stunning 14,400-square-foot (1,338-sq.-m) structure, which is ideally lit for displaying modern art. The permanent collection exhibits post-1960 Finnish and international art, but also features changing exhibitions. Based on the word *chiasma,* which refers to crossovers in genetics and rhetoric, the name for the new museum suggests Finland's special ability to achieve crossovers between the worlds of fine art and high technology. A "mediatheque" concentrates on displaying the museum's media collections.

Mannerheiminaukio 2. © **09/1733-6501.** www.kiasma.fi. Admission 8€ adults, 6€ students and seniors, free for those 17 and under. Free admission first Wed of every month 5–8:30pm. Tues 10am–5pm; Wed–Fri 10am–8:30pm; Sat–Sun 10am–6pm. Tram: 3B or 3T.

Lutheran Cathedral (Tuomiokirkko) ★ Dominating the city's skyline is one of the city's most visible symbols, a green-domed cathedral erected between 1830 and 1852. Built during the Russian administration of Finland in a severe, almost stark interpretation of the glory of ancient Greece and Rome, the Lutheran Cathedral was designed by German architect Carl Ludwig Engel. It was inaugurated as part of the 19th-century reconstruction of Helsinki—mostly in the neoclassical style—after a fire had destroyed most of the city. Called St. Nicholas until Finland became independent from Russia in 1917, the church has always been Lutheran and today's services conform to the Evangelical Lutheran denomination. Extensive renovations in 1998, both to the cathedral and to its crypt, brought it back to its original beauty.

Senaatintori. © **09/2340-6120.** www.muuka.com/finnishpumpkin/churches/helsinki/chtuh/church_ chtuh.html. Free admission. June–Aug daily 9am–midnight; Sept–May daily 9am–6pm. No sightseeing access is allowed during services. Tram: 1, 3B, 3T, 4, 7A, or 7B.

Mannerheim Museum ★★ Visit the home of the late Baron Carl Gustaf Mannerheim, Finland's former president and World War II field marshal—he's a sort of George Washington in this country. Now a museum, his former residence houses his collection of European furniture, Asian art and rugs, and personal items (uniforms, swords, decorations, gifts from admirers) that he acquired during his long career as a military man and statesman. The house remains the same as it was when he died in 1951. It's quite a hike from the train station, so take the tram.

Kallionlinnantie 14. © **09/635-443.** www.mannerheim-museo.fi. Admission (including guided tour) 10€ adults; 8€ children 12–16, students, and seniors; free for children 11 and under. Fri–Sun 11am–4pm. Tram: 3B or 3T.

National Museum of Finland ★★ This museum was designed in the style called National Romantic. Opened in 1916, it contains three major sections—prehistoric, historic, and ethnographic. The country's prehistory in the light of archaeological finds may be seen, revealing that after the Ice Age and at the dawn of the Stone Age, humans made their homes in Finland. Of particular interest are the Finno–Ugric collections representing the folk culture of the various peoples of northeastern and Eastern Europe, as well as northwestern Siberia, who speak a language related to Finnish. Church art of the medieval and Lutheran periods, folk culture artifacts, folk costumes and textiles, furniture, and an important coin collection are exhibited.

Mannerheimintie 34. © **09/4050-9544.** www.nba.fi. Admission 7€ adults, 5€ students, free for children 17 and under. Free admission on Tues 5:30-8pm. Tues 11am-8pm; Wed-Sun 11am-6pm. Tram: 4, 7A, 7B, or 10.

Seurasaari Open-Air Museum ★★   In a national park on the island of Seurasaari (a short boat trip from the mainland) is a wondrous re-creation of Old Finland—about 100 buildings (authentically furnished), a 17th-century church, and a gentleman's manor dating from the 18th century and containing period furnishings. In addition, visitors can see one of the "aboriginal" saunas, which resemble a smokehouse. The best time to visit this collection of historic, freestanding buildings is during the summer months, when you can visit the interiors, and when an unpretentious restaurant serves coffee, drinks, and platters of food. Although the buildings are locked during the winter months, you can still view the exteriors and explore the parkland that surrounds them. A wintertime walk through this place is not as far-fetched an idea as you might think—it's a favorite of strollers and joggers, even during snowfalls.

Seurasaari Island. © **09/4050-9660.** www.seurasaari.fi. Admission 6€ adults, 5€ students, free for children 17 and under. Sept 1-15 Mon-Fri 9am-3pm, Sat-Sun 11am-5pm; June 1-Aug 31 daily 11am-5pm. Closed Sept 16-May 31. Bus: 24 from the Erottaja bus stop, near Stockmann Department Store, to the island. The 3-mile (4.8km) ride takes about 15 min. and costs 2€ each way.

Sinebrychoff Art Museum (Museum of Foreign Art) ★ 🏛   Part of the Finnish National Gallery (see Antaneum Art Museum, above), this museum was built in 1840 and still displays its original furnishings. It houses an extensive collection of foreign paintings from the 14th to the 19th centuries and has a stunning collection of foreign miniatures. The collection originated from the wealthy Sinebrychoff dynasty, a family of Russians who owned a local brewery and occupied this yellow-and-white neo-Renaissance mansion. They were great collectors of antiques, with opulent taste in furnishings. Their art collection was wide ranging, especially noted for its Dutch and Swedish portraits from the 17th and 18th centuries. There is also a stunning collection of porcelain. Outdoor concerts in summer are often staged in the formerly private park surrounding the estate.

🅾 Olympic memories **& A FLYING FINN**

Way back in 1952, Helsinki hosted the Olympic Games at its impressive **Olympiastadion,** Paavo Nurmi tie 1 (© **09/436-6010;** www.stadion.fi). You can ascend to the top of a tower by elevator for a panoramic view of the city and the archipelago. The stadium, 1¼ miles (2km) from the city center, was originally built in 1938, but the Olympic Games scheduled for Finland that year were cancelled when World War II broke out. The seating capacity of the stadium is 40,000, larger than any other arena in the country. The stadium was closed and rebuilt between 1992 and 1994, and today is a first-rate sports venue. Outside the stadium is a statue by Wäinö Aaltonen of the great athlete Paavo Nurmi, "The Flying Finn." The runner is depicted in full stride and is completely nude, a fact that caused considerable controversy when the statue was unveiled in 1952. Admission is 2€ adults, 1€ children under 16. Open Monday to Friday 9am to 8pm, Saturday and Sunday 9am to 6pm. Tram: 3B, 3T, 4, or 10.

EXPLORING THE fortress OF FINLAND

The 18th-century **Suomenlinna Fortress ★★** (📞 **09/684-1880;** www.suomenlinna.fi) is known as the "Gibraltar of the North" and lies on the archipelago guarding the approach to Helsinki. With its walks and gardens, cafes, restaurants, museums, shops, and old frame buildings, the island makes for one of the most interesting outings from Helsinki. Originally built in the mid-18th century when Finland was a part of Sweden, the fortress was taken over by the Russians in 1808. After Finland gained independence in 1917, the fortress was given its present name, Suomenlinna, which means "the fortress of Finland." It served as part of the nation's defenses until 1973. The fortification work involved six islands, but today the main attraction is the part of the fortress on **Susisaari** and **Kustaanmiekka** islands, now joined as one land body. Kustaanmiekka is a small, well-preserved fort with defense walls and tunnels. The main fortress is on

Susisaari, which is also home to a number of parks and squares.

You can take a **ferry** from Market Square to Suomenlinna year-round beginning at 6am daily. The boats run about once an hour, and the last one returns from the island at 1:45am. The round-trip ferry ride costs 3.80€ for adults and 1.90€ for children.

The island has no "streets," but individual attractions are signposted. Suomenlinna has a visitor center, situated by the bridge on Tykistölahti Bay (📞 **09/684-1880**), open year-round from January to April and October to December daily from 10:30am to 4:30pm, and May to September daily from 10am to 6pm. The center serves as the starting point for **guided tours**—offered in English—of the fortress, with a focus on its military history. Tours are scheduled between June and August daily at 11am and 2pm, and between September and May on weekends only at 1:30pm. They cost 7€ for adults and 3€ for children.

Bulevardi 40. 📞 **09/1733-6460.** www.sinebrychoffintaidemuseo.fi. Admission 7.50€ adults, 6€ students/seniors, free for children 17 and under. Tues and Fri 10am-6pm; Wed-Thurs 10am-8pm; Sat-Sun 11am-5pm. Free admission first Wed of month. Tram: 6.

Where to Dine

Bellevue RUSSIAN   Immensely popular, this restaurant dates from 1917 and is still serving the time-tested specialties that put it on the Helsinki culinary map in the first place. With Russian wines as a side offering, the menu offers all those favorites that delighted Finland's former czarist rulers, including blinis, caviar, Russian-style herring, stuffed cabbage, and even bear steak. The Bellevue is located in the center of the city, near the Uspenski Orthodox Cathedral.

Rahapajankatu 3. 📞 **09/179-560.** www.restaurantbellevue.com. Reservations required. Main courses 18€-65€. AE, DC, MC, V. Tues-Fri 11am-midnight; Sat 5pm-midnight. Closed Sun-Mon. Tram: 4.

Kellarikrouvi ★ FINNISH/INTERNATIONAL   Built at the turn of the 20th century, this restaurant is installed in a former storage cellar for firewood and "winter potatoes." When it opened in 1965, it became the first restaurant in Helsinki to serve beer from a keg, which it still does today in great abundance. The cuisine is inspired, combining local Finnish recipes with innovative continental influences.

Pohjoinen Makasiinikatu 6. 📞 **09/6128-5100.** www.royalravintolat.com/kellarikrouvi/index_eng.asp. Reservations recommended for dinner. Main courses 15€-30€. AE, DC, MC, V. Mon-Sat 4pm-midnight. Closed June 25-Aug 1. Tram: 3B.

Ravintola Perho ★ FINNISH/CONTINENTAL Owned and managed by the Helsinki Culinary School, this restaurant is staffed by students and trainees. What's on offer depends on the day's cooking lesson but could include smoked whitebait with mustard sauce, a terrine of smoked reindeer, and glow-fried Arctic char with creamed asparagus and herbed potatoes. The youthful enthusiasm of the staff is infectious. Ask them to recommend a beer, as there's a small brewery on-site.

Mechelininkatu 7. ℂ **09/5807-8649.** www.perho.fi. Reservations not accepted. Main courses 10€–20€. AE, DC, MC, V. Mon–Fri 11am–11pm. Closed late June to early Aug. Hours severely reduced in summer; call or consult the website for up-to-date times. Tram: 8.

Ravintola Sipuli ★★ In the 1800s, this was a warehouse, taking its name of *Sipuli* (onion) from the onion-shaped domes of the Orthodox Upenski Cathedral in the vicinity. Architects successfully turned the structure into a restaurant of atmosphere and charm, with thick beams, paneling, and brick walls. Today the chef is known for his robust flavors and clever use of Finnish products, especially reindeer meat shipped down from Lapland.

Kanavaranta 7. ℂ **09/622-9280.** www.royalravintolat.com/sipuli. Reservations recommended. Main courses 26€–32€. AE, DC, MC, V. Tues–Sat 6pm–midnight. Closed late June to early Aug. Tram: 2 or 4.

Rivoli Ravintolat SEAFOOD/FRENCH/FINNISH Visit this Art Nouveau restaurant for some of the best and freshest-tasting Finnish seafood, such as the grilled rainbow trout or freshly caught salmon from very chilly local rivers. Or try something more warming, such as the roasted duck breast with fig sauce and goats cheese polenta. The tasty dishes are prepared with market-fresh ingredients, and some are inspired by French cooking techniques.

Albertinkatu 38. ℂ **09/643-455.** www.rivolirestaurants.fi/rivoli/index.shtml. Reservations recommended. Main courses 14€–29€. AE, DC, MC, V. Mon–Fri 11am–midnight. Tram: 6. Bus: 14.

Wellamo ★ 🍴 FINNISH/FRENCH/RUSSIAN On the residential island of Katajanokka, but easily reached by tram from the heart of the city, this elegant restaurant draws a steady stream of habitués. The menu features many dishes evocative of a Paris bistro, but also heads east to chilly Siberia for such delights as a regional ravioli stuffed with minced lamb, fresh herbs, mushrooms, and sour cream. The chef is also known for his many game dishes.

Vyökatu 9. ℂ **09/663-139.** Reservations recommended. Main courses 12€–24€. AE, MC, V. Tues–Fri 11am–2pm and 5–11pm; Sat 5–11pm; Sun 1–8pm. Closed Mon. Tram: 4.

 The Art of Crayfish Eating

Every Finn looks forward to the crayfish season, which runs between mid-July and mid-September. Some 225,000 pounds of this delicacy are caught yearly in inland waters, and you'll find it in virtually every restaurant in Helsinki. Called *rapu,* the crayfish is usually boiled in salt water and seasoned with dill. For Finns, the eating of crayfish is an art form, and they suck out every morsel of flavor. Of course, with all this slurping and shelling, you'll need a bib. After devouring half a dozen, Finns will down a glass of schnapps, but unless you're accustomed to schnapps, we suggest you order a beer or glass of white wine instead.

TRAVELING ON TO St. Petersburg

Known as Leningrad in its Communist heyday, St. Petersburg is hailed as one of the most beautiful cities on the globe. Home of the famous Hermitage museum, the city is only a little more than 3½ hours by train from Helsinki and is a popular destination with rail travelers. In late 2010, a new high-speed train operated jointly by Finland and Russia, the *Allegro*, began making the run between the two cities, cutting nearly 2 hours off the old travel time. Both the Russian and Finnish trains have first-class restaurant cars. Second-class fares run around 84€ one-way, 134€ in first class; tickets and the mandatory seat reservations can be purchased at major rail stations in Finland.

Border formalities when traveling between the two countries are now at a minimum, and currency exchange and tax-free refunds are all smoothly handled on the trains. You don't even have to clear Customs unless you have something to declare.

Tip: Bring along your own supply of drinking water.

You no longer have to purchase tickets through a designated tourist agency to get to St. Petersburg. Any travel agent in Helsinki can sell you a ticket. Note that reservations are mandatory and must be made at least 48 hours in advance of departure.

Arrivals in St. Petersburg are at the rail station, **Finlandsky Vokzal,** 71 Zanevski Prospekt, where you can catch a taxi to your hotel. You can arrange your hotel through a Helsinki travel agent before leaving Finland. For more information on train service to St. Petersburg, head online to **www. vr.fi**.

Note: You will need a visa to enter Russia and it should be obtained before you leave home. Visas are issued by the nearest Russian embassy or consulate. For information in the United States, contact the Russian Embassy, 2650 Wisconsin Ave. NW, Washington, DC 20007 ((*C* **202/298-5700;** www. russianembassy.org).

Shopping

Most stores are open Monday to Friday 9am to 6 or 7pm (with small shops shutting earlier and department stores and shopping centers staying open until 9pm) and on Saturday 9 or 10am to 5 or 6pm (with small shops opening for fewer hours). A government regulation now allows shopping on Sunday in May, June, July, and August, and in the run-up to Christmas. As a result, many shops will open for sometime between noon and 6pm on Sunday during these months, with some staying open as late as 9pm.

The most important shopping neighborhoods are in the center of the city. They include **Esplanadi,** for those seeking the finest of Finnish design—but at high prices. Even if you don't buy anything, it's a delightful promenade in summer, loaded with shops filled with the best of Finnish crafts, as well as a number of art galleries.

Esplanadi leads from the commercial heart of town all the way to the waterfront. Bordering the water is **Market Square (Kauppatori),** a fresh open-air market that's open Monday to Friday 6:30am to 6pm and Saturday 6:30am to 4pm, and on Sunday in the summer from 10am to 5pm. In winter, turn up early, as the cold sends many of the vendors scurrying back to their homes by 2pm.

In summer, peddlers set up trolleys and tables to display their wares. Most of the goods for sale are produce (some of them ideal for picnic food), but there are souvenir and gift items as well.

The other main shopping section is called simply **Central,** beginning at Esplanadi and extending to the famous Central Helsinki Railway Station. Many of the big names in Finnish shopping are located here. One of the main shopping streets is **Aleksanterinkatu,** which runs parallel to Esplanadi, stretching from the harborfront to Mannerheimintie.

Other shopping streets, all in the center, include **Iso Roobertinkatu** and **Bulevardi,** lying off Esplanadi. Bulevardi starts at the Klaus Kurki Hotel and winds its way to the water.

Helsinki's largest department store, **Stockmann,** Aleksanterinkatu 52B (✆ 09/1211; www.stockmann.fi; tram: 3B), is also Finland's finest and oldest. Stockmann has a little bit of everything, with the most diversified sampling of Finnish and imported merchandise of any store: glassware, stoneware, ceramics, lamps, furniture, furs, contemporary jewelry, clothes and textiles, handmade candles, reindeer hides—everything.

The **Forum Shopping Center,** Mannerheimintie 20 (**09/565-74523;** www.cityforum.fi; tram: 3B, 3T, 7A, or 7B), covering an entire block, houses over 100 shops, a seven-story atrium, restaurants, and service enterprises—making it the number-one shopping center in Finland. You'll find a wide array of merchandise here, including art, gold, jewelry, food, clothing, leather, glasses, rugs, and watches.

Nightlife

The ballet and opera performances of the **Finnish National Opera,** Helsinginkatu 58 (✆ **09/4030-2211;** www.operafin.fi; tram: 3T, 4, 7A/7B, 8 and 10), are internationally acclaimed and the stage was thoroughly renovated in the summer of 2007. The ticket office is open April to May and August to September Monday to Friday 10am to 5pm. On performance nights, the ticket office stays open until the performance begins. The opera and ballet season runs from late August to early June, and tickets are 12€ to 95€. Guided tours of the opera house can be booked; call for more information.

Although it has been reconfigured, redecorated, and reincarnated many times since it was established in 1915, **Baker's,** Mannerheimintie 12 (✆ **0207/701-440;** www.ravintolabakers.com; tram: 3B), is the most deeply entrenched, long-lived drinking and dining complex in Helsinki. It sprawls across three floors (it's got a nightclub, a bar, a pub, and a restaurant) and on a busy night is often crammed with clubbers—many of them single. Most people come for the cafe—open Monday to Friday 7am to 4am, Saturday 10am to 4am, and Sunday 1pm to 4am—or for one of the bars—open Tuesday to Thursday from 4:30pm to 10pm, Friday and Saturday 4:30pm to 4am.

Storyville, Museokatu 8 (✆ **09/408-007;** www.storyville.fi; tram: 4, 7, or 10), is the busiest and most active live music venue in Helsinki and was named after the fabled red-light district of New Orleans. The music offered includes blues, jazz, Dixieland, soul, and funk Monday to Saturday from 8pm to 4am. The cover is 6.50€ to 10€ when there is live music.

FRANCE

Throughout time, France, with its civilization, its history, and its way of life—the savoir-faire of its people—has lured rail travelers from around the world. The fact that it is among the easiest countries to travel by train makes it all the more appealing. Smaller than the state of Texas, France is the global leader of rail technology. Its TGV trains hold the world's friction rail speed record, at 320 mph (515kmph). Rail lines, stretching some 19,188 miles (30,893km), go almost anywhere—and rapidly.

Often referred to as "the garden of Europe," France is a land to be savored, not sped through. Each region is so intriguing and varied that it's easy to immerse yourself in one province for too long. Overall, it's better to get to know a few regions intimately rather than trying to explore them all.

Of course, the primary language of the country is French, which might intimidate nonspeakers, though it shouldn't—most tourism officials and rail personnel speak at least some English. So you should have little trouble riding the rails and getting your questions answered. And, as a final plus, though train travel is not cheap in France when compared to other countries, it's unquestionably the most economical way to see the country.

Highlights of France

On the tightest of schedules, particularly if you're traveling by rail to other European capitals such as London or Rome, you'll need 3 days for Paris—the logical starting point for any journey in France, as it's the country's rail hub. While in Paris, see world-class museums (including the **Musée du Louvre** and **Musée d'Orsay**); tour famous monuments, such as the **Eiffel Tower** and **Arc de Triomphe;** and bask in the glorious architecture of the city's magnificent churches, including **Ste-Chapelle** and, of course, the cathedral of **Notre-Dame.** But the city is also full of marvelous and evocative neighborhoods just waiting to be explored: Like Sartre, have a coffee and croissant on the **Left Bank,** then explore **St-Germain-des-Prés,** the ancient **Ile de la Cité,** the glamorous **Ile St. Louis,** the historic **Le Marais,** and, an absolute must-do, stroll down the famous **Champs-Elysées.**

Set aside a fourth day to journey south by rail to the magnificent palace of **Versailles,** an easy day trip from the French capital.

But don't make the mistake of limiting your visit to Paris, unless you'd call a trip to New York a look at America. France has a number of scenic and sight-filled provinces (enough to fill a whole book—*Frommer's France,* for example) just waiting to be explored. Note, however, that we limit ourselves in this chapter to the most popular regions that are also easily reached by rail out of Paris. So you will find plenty about the Loire Valley, Provence, and the Riviera, but you won't see Brittany or Normandy (including the famous abbey of Mont-St-Michel) because it's very difficult to get to some of those places by train.

About 120 rail miles (193km) southwest of Paris stretches the "green heart of France," the breathtakingly beautiful region of the **Loire Valley.** The towns of this area have magical names, but they also read like Joan of Arc's battle register—Orléans, Blois, Tours. Every hilltop has a castle or palace, there are vineyards as far as your eye can see, the Loire river winds like a silver ribbon, and walled cities cluster around medieval churches. It is estimated that the average visitor spends only 3 nights in the Loire Valley. A week would be better. Even then, you will have only skimmed the surface. If you're severely hampered by lack of time, then try at least to see the following châteaux: **Chenonceau, Amboise, Azay-le-Rideau, Chambord,** and **Blois.**

Regardless, the most central location with the best rail connections is the ancient city of **Tours.** Many visitors also like to pay a rail visit first to the city of **Orléans**—another good base—with its evocative memories of Joan of Arc.

To continue your rail journey through France, head for **Provence,** where you'll need at least 3 days. High-speed TGV trains have put the south of France within an easy commute of Paris, speeding you to where you want to go in record times. The chief centers of the region are **Avignon,** seat of the popes during the 14th century; **Arles,** which once cast a spell over van Gogh and inspired some of his greatest paintings; and **Aix-en-Provence,** home to Provence's most celebrated son, the artist Paul Cézanne.

To conclude your French rail trip, head to France's vacation hot spot par excellence for 2 to 3 days. Known to the world as the **Cote d'Azur** (the French name for its Riviera), this is a short stretch of curving coastline near the Italian border with a veritable bounty of hotels and resorts. It's also a land drenched in sunshine, sprinkled with vineyards and olive groves, and dotted with some of the world's most fascinating tourist meccas.

For the rail traveler, the resort of **Cannes** in the west and the city of **Nice** in the east make the best centers. Both have high-speed train connections to Paris. For a more sophisticated beach-style ambience, head to Cannes for at least 2 days, enjoying its glamour and style. But for a more typically Provençal city, make it Nice, which is also the best for sightseeing, as it has far more museums and monuments, and is the better center for day excursions to hill towns such as **Vence, St-Paul-de-Vence,** and especially **Monaco.**

 Tidbits on French Food Culture

The French know how to enjoy their food, drink, and daily breaks. Embracing this tradition will make your rail-travel experience far more complete. Wherever you stay, take a daily trip to the local *boulangerie* (bakery) for a baguette, sandwich, or pastry; or create a picnic feast of fresh baguette, *du fromage* (cheese), *des tomates* (tomatoes), and *du poulet rotisserie* (roasted chicken) from the local *marché*. Marketplaces are common on different days in every region, but try to find one in Provence (see "Arles," on p. 299) if you travel there. You should also stop for an afternoon *goûter* (snack) on a city square—perhaps a *crêpe avec nutella,* sorbet, or café au lait—where you can relax, people-watch, and soak up the local atmosphere.

ESSENTIALS
Getting There

The French national carrier, **Air France** (© 800/237-2747; www.airfrance.com), offers daily or several-times-a-week flights out of several North American cities to Paris.

Other major carriers offering direct flights to Paris out of North America include **American Airlines** (© 800/433-7300; www.aa.com), **Continental Airlines** (© 800/231-0856; www.continental.com), **Delta Air Lines** (© 800/221-1212; www.delta.com), **US Airways** (© 800/428-4322; www.usairways.com), and **Air Canada** (© 888/247-2262; www.aircanada.ca).

FESTIVALS & special events

Parades, boat races, music, balls, and fireworks are all part of the ancient **Carnival of Nice,** which draws visitors from all over Europe and North America. This "Mardi Gras of the Riviera" begins sometime in February, usually 12 days before Shrove Tuesday, celebrating the return of spring with 3 weeks of parades, *corsi* (floats), and *veglioni* (masked balls). The climax is the century-year-old tradition of burning King Carnival in effigy, after *Les Batailles des Fleurs* (Battles of the Flowers), when teams pelt each other with flowers. Make reservations well in advance. For information, contact the **Nice Convention and Visitors Bureau** (✆ 08-92-70-74-07; fax 04-92-14-46-49; www.nicecarnaval.com).

The world-class **Festival d'Avignon** (last 3 weeks in July) has a reputation for exposing new talent to critical acclaim. The focus is usually on avant-garde works in theater, dance, and music by groups from around the world. Much of the music is presented within the 14th-century courtyard of the Palais de l'Ancien Archeveché (the Old Archbishop's Palace). Other events occur in the medieval cloister of the Cathédral St-Sauveur. Part of the fun is the bacchanalia that takes place nightly in the streets. The prices for rooms and meals skyrocket, so make reservations far in advance. For more information contact the **Bureaux du Festival,** Cloître Saint-Louis, 20 rue du portail Boquier, 84000 Avignon (✆ 04-90-27-66-50; www.festival-avignon.com). Tickets cost 13€ to 38€.

One of France's most famous festivals, the **Festival d'Automne** (mid-Sept to late Dec) in Paris, is one of its most eclectic, focusing mainly on modern music, ballet, theater, and modern art. For more information, contact the Festival d'Automne (✆ 01-53-45-17-00; www.festival-automne.com).

British Airways (✆ 800/247-9297; www.britishairways.com) offers connecting flights to Paris from 18 U.S. cities, with a stop in either Heathrow or Gatwick airport in England where British Airways offers connecting flights. Other carriers offering connecting flights to Paris include **Aer Lingus** (✆ 800/IRISH-AIR [474-7424]; www.aerlingus.com) and **Delta/KLM** (✆ 800/225-2525; www.klm.com or www.delta.com).

Flight time to Paris varies according to the departure city, but it generally takes 7 to 11 hours to get to France's capital from most major North American cities.

France by Rail

The *Société Nationale des Chemins de Fer* (**SNCF**) is the French National Railway, and it runs more than 3,000 train stations, supervises more than 19,188 miles (30,893km) of track, and is fabled for its on-time performance. About 181 of the country's cities are linked by some 665 TGVs (some of the world's fastest trains), and you can get from Paris to just about anywhere in a matter of hours. For information, check out **www.sncf.com** or **www.raileurope.com.**

France is also well connected to the major international rail lines running through Europe. High-speed **Artesia** trains connect Paris to Milan in Italy, with overnight Artesia service as well to Venice, Florence and Rome; the **Eurostar** connects Paris with both London and Brussels; **Thalys** trains link Paris with several cities in Belgium, the Netherlands, and Cologne in Germany; **TGV** trains connect many French cities with Brussels and Switzerland; and **Elipsos** overnight hotel trains connect Paris with Madrid, Barcelona, Switzerland, and Milan. TGV Est connects Paris to eastern France, Luxembourg, Zurich, and a number of German cities. These connections make Paris one of Europe's busiest rail junctions.

PASSES

For information on the **Eurail Global Pass, Eurail Global Pass Flexi,** and other multicountry options, see chapter 2.

The **France Rail Pass** provides unlimited rail transport in France for any 3 days within 1 month, from $291 in first class and from $248 in second. You can purchase up to 6 more days (9 days total) for an extra of about $42 per person per day. Children 4 to 11 get a discounted rate.

The **France Rail 'n Drive Pass** is best used by arriving at a major rail station, then striking out to explore the countryside by car. It includes 2 days' use of France Rail in first class (see above) and 2 days' use of a rental car, only Avis or Hertz (cheapest is economy size with unlimited mileage), within a given month. Three days can be added to your pass. The pass, in economy, starts at $546 per person (based on two people traveling together). Note that second class is not an option for this pass. For more on rail 'n drive passes, see chapter 2.

The railpasses mentioned above, as well as point-to-point rail tickets within France, are available through most travel agencies or through **Rail Europe** (✆ **888/438-7245** in the United States, ✆ **800/361-7245** in Canada; www.raileurope.com).

FOREIGN TRAIN TERMS

Welcome officers (called *Agents d'accueil*) wear electric-blue jackets and caps, and are found at major rail stations to help answer your questions. Most officers speak English (to ask, say, *Parlez vous anglais?*).

Ticket windows are marked *guichets* and generally have signs for *billets* (tickets)—you can ask about your *résa* (reservation); a left-luggage office is called *consigne*. SNCF's time schedules are *horaires*. Sleepers are known as *voitures-lits,* and in second-class sections you can often request *sieges inclinables* (reclining seats) for an extra fee.

A *supplement* is a supplement—they are color coded. SNCF calendars designate days for rail travelers as *période bleue* or *période rouge*. Trips in the blue period get many discounts; trips in the red period are peak periods where you get no discounts. There is also a *période blanche,* or white, when moderate discounts are available. To be eligible for a discount, each leg of your rail trip must begin during a period of the appropriate color. For a complete list of these red, white, and blue periods, request a *Calendrier Voyageurs* at any rail station information office.

PRACTICAL TRAIN INFORMATION

SNCF-operated, the heavily state-subsidized French rail system is one of the world's greatest. Trains radiate out from Paris like the spokes of a wheel, taking you to all parts of France, though service may not be as extensive in some regions as in others.

The country also has **Transilien** trains, servicing the Paris suburban area (Ile-de-France), **T.E.R.** (Train Regional express) trains, and **Corail (TRN)** trains. T.E.R. trains are regional trains that link smaller cities to such transportation hubs as Paris, Nimes, and Toulouse. The Corail Teoz trains offer modern comfort, are air-conditioned, and travel at speeds of about 81 to 93 mph (130–150kmph). These trains are used on many major city routes.

Tickets are most often valid for up to 2 months following purchase. In some very large train stations, such as those in Paris, separate ticket windows are set aside for different types of trains: long haul is *grandes-lignes; banlieue* is for suburban lines. You

Train Schedules & Travel Times in France

From	To	Type of Train	# of Trains	Frequency	Travel Time
Paris	Tours	TRN	13	Daily	2 hr., 30 min.–3 hr., 14 min.
Paris	Tours	TGV	6	Daily	1 hr., 10 min.
Paris	Orléans	TRN	17	Daily	1 hr., 30 min.–1 hr., 42 min.
Paris	Avignon	TGV	14	Daily	2 hr., 30 min.–3 hr., 30 min.
Paris	Arles	TGV	2	Daily	3 hr., 52 min.–4 hr., 3 min.
Paris	Aix-en-Provence	TGV	11	Daily	2 hr., 55 min.–3 hr., 14 min.
Paris	Cannes	TRN	5	Daily	4 hr., 58 min.–5 hr., 41 min.
Paris	Nice	TRN	5	Daily	5 hr., 25 min.–6 hr., 16 min.
Nice	Monaco	TER	43	Daily	16 min.–22 min.

can, of course, purchase tickets on board a train, but you'll be hit with a hefty surcharge, and travel agents will sell you a rail ticket but will charge you a stiff handling fee. Here rail travel can get very expensive, so if you plan to travel quite a bit, a railpass makes sense. Railpasses should be hand-stamped at a designated rail station ticket window before you get on the first leg of your journey.

We admit that there is great freedom in seeing France by car, but the high price of gasoline/petrol, the never-ending high *autoroute* tolls, and the stiff car-rental fees make driving superexpensive. Trains are a whole lot cheaper. If you want to drive even a little, consider the **France Rail 'n Drive Pass** (see above).

For one-way travel, request *un billet aller-simple;* for round-trip journeys, ask for *un billet aller-retour.* In all cases, round-trips are less expensive.

For SNCF routes, timetables, and information, check **www.sncf.com** or **www.raileurope.com**.

RESERVATIONS   Although you can travel on most French trains without reservations, they are compulsory on Eurostar, Thalys, Artesia, Elipsos, TGVs, and Corail Teoz, and are available on regional trains. If you're heading into or out of Paris on an international train, make reservations at least 2 to 3 days in advance. Reservations can be made as early as 90 days in advance of departure online at SNCF's website or through Rail Europe. During holiday periods, ski season, at Easter, and in July and August (especially Aug), reservations should be made as far in advance as possible.

If you're taking an overnight train, be sure to reserve your sleeping accommodations (see "Services & Amenities," below) far in advance. Having a railpass does not exempt you from reservation fees.

SERVICES & AMENITIES   Nearly all the country's trains, including the TGV, offer both first- or second-class seating, the first-class carriages designated by the number 1. Second-class travel on French trains is usually the equivalent of first-class travel in many parts of the world.

On overnight trains, you can reserve a couchette, although you must reserve one in advance (up to 1¼ hr. before departure). The second-class couchette compartments are crowded with six berths, while there are only four in first class. Note that we've had reports of unpleasant experiences (dirty cars, crowding) aboard couchettes in France, so we recommend traveling during the day.

The elegant and expensive (and more comfortable) way to go is with a sleeper (called *voitures-lits*), filled with real beds. Sleepers hold up to four people, and prices run \$80 to \$200 per person. Hotel trains that run in France include the Trenhotel Ellipsos running between Spain and France, the Paris–Germany night train, and the Artesia Nuit trains that run between France and Italy.

Although food and drink are served aboard most French trains, especially long-haul ones, if you want to save money, board a train with enough bottled water and food for the length of your journey, as the prices are very high indeed (equivalent to buying a drink in a New York theater at intermission). Most major rail stations have restaurants and bars, but prices there are also ridiculously high. If you have time, you can often leave the station and find a local *boulangerie* (bakery that usually serves delicious sandwiches) or grocery store where the prices are far more reasonable.

SNCF has services for rail travelers with disabilities who might face accessibility issues. For information, contact **Rail Europe** (© **888/438-7245** in the United States, © **800/361-7245** in Canada; www.raileurope.com).

[FastFACTS] FRANCE

Area Code All French telephone numbers consist of 10 digits, the first two of which are like an area code. If you're calling anywhere in France from within France, just dial all 10 digits—no additional codes are needed. If you're calling from the United States, dial 0-11-33 and then drop the initial zero of the local area code.

Business Hours Business hours are erratic. Most banks are open Monday to Friday 9:30am to 4:30pm. Many, particularly in small towns, take a lunch break. Hours are usually posted on the door. Most museums close 1 day a week (often Tues), and they're generally closed on national holidays. Usually hours are from 9:30am to 5pm. Refer to the individual listings for hours.

Offices tend to be open Monday to Friday 9am to 5pm, but always call first. In Paris and other big French cities, stores are open from 9 or 10am to 6 or 7pm

without a break for lunch. Some shops, particularly those operated by foreigners, open at 8am and close at 8 or 9pm. In some small stores, the lunch break can last 3 hours, but this is more common in the south than in the north.

Climate France's weather varies by region and even sometimes by towns separated by only 12 miles (19km). Despite its northern latitude, Paris never gets very cold—snow is a rarity. Rain usually falls in a kind of steady drizzle and rarely lasts more than a day. May is the driest month. The Mediterranean coast in the south has the driest climate. When it does rain, it's heaviest in spring and autumn. (Cannes sometimes receives more rainfall than Paris.) Summers are comfortably dry. Provence dreads *le mistral* (an unrelenting hot, dusty wind), which most often blows in winter for a few days but can last for up to 2 weeks.

Documents Required All foreign (non-French) nationals need a valid passport to enter France. The French government no longer requires visas for U.S. citizens, providing they're staying in France for less than 90 days. Citizens of Canada do not need visas. *Note:* They are very strict with regard to children (from birth) entering the country; make sure your child has an up-to-date passport.

Electricity In general, expect 220 volts or a 50-cycle AC current, though you'll encounter a 110-volt, 60-cycle current in some older places. Adapters are needed to fit sockets. You may also need a voltage adaptor. It's best to ask your concierge before plugging in any appliance.

Embassies & Consulates If you have a passport, immigration, legal, or other problem, contact your consulate. Call *before* you go, as they often keep odd hours and observe both

French and home-country holidays. The Embassy of the **United States,** at 2 rue Gabriel, 8e (✆ **01-43-12-22-22;** http://france.us embassy.gov; Métro: Concorde), is open Monday to Friday 8:30am to 5pm. The Embassy of **Canada** is at 35 av. Montaigne, 8e (✆ **01-44-43-29-00;** www.international.gc.ca/canada-europa/france/menu-en.asp; Métro: F.D.-Roosevelt or Alma-Marceau), open Monday to Friday 9am to noon and from 2pm to 5pm.

Health & Safety In general, France is viewed as a "safe" destination. You don't need to get shots; most food is safe and the water is potable. For tap water, order *une carafe d'eau,* but if you're concerned, order bottled water *(une bouteille d'eau).* It is easy to get a prescription filled in French towns and cities, and nearly all places have English-speaking doctors at hospitals with well-trained staff. For minor health problems, local pharmacies (marked by a green cross) are extremely helpful.

The most common menace, especially in large cities, is pickpockets and gangs of Gypsy children who surround you, distract you, and steal your purse or wallet (especially in Métro stations). Also protect your valuables on French trains, where most robberies occur while passengers are asleep. Much of the country, particularly central France,

remains relatively safe, though no place in the world is crime-free. Try to carry a backpack or purse that is difficult to get into (with the wallet hidden)—or hold it in front of you when walking in crowded areas.

Holidays In France, holidays are *jours feriés.* The main holidays include New Year's Day (Jan 1), Easter Sunday and Monday, Labor Day (May 1), V-E Day in Europe (May 8), Whitmonday (May 19), Ascension Thursday (40 days after Easter), Bastille Day (July 14), Assumption of the Blessed Virgin (Aug 15), All Saints' Day (Nov 1), Armistice Day (Nov 11), and Christmas (Dec 25). Monaco's National Day is November 19.

Mail Most post offices are open Monday to Friday 8am to 7pm (smaller ones close for lunch) and Saturday 8am to noon. Allow 5 to 8 days to send or receive mail from your home. Airmail letters within Europe cost .85€; to the United States and Canada, .90€. You can exchange money at post offices. Many hotels, post offices, and cafes displaying a red TABAC sign outside sell stamps.

Police & Emergencies If your wallet gets stolen, go to the police station in person (ask at your hotel's front desk for the nearest one). Otherwise, you can get help anywhere in France by calling ✆ **17** for the police, ✆ **18** for the fire department *(pompiers),* or

✆ **15** for medical emergencies.

Telephone The French use a *Télécarte,* a phone debit card, which you can purchase at railway stations, tabacs, and post offices. Sold in two versions, it allows you to use either 50 or 120 charge units (depending on the card) by inserting the card into the slot of most public phones. Depending on the type of card you buy, the cost is 10€ and goes up from there. At some public phones (for a hefty fee), you can insert your credit card and call directly, but the minimum charge is 20€. The phone system gives you 30 days to use up this 20€ credit.

If possible, avoid making calls from your hotel, as some French establishments will double or triple the charges.

Tipping The law requires all bills to say *service compris,* which means the tip has been included. But French diners often leave some small change as an additional tip.

In general, locals tip *only* for exceptional services; the money is assumed to be included in the employee's paycheck. That being said, restroom and cloakroom attendants are usually left a few coins. Taxi drivers, tour guides, and hotel staff is left 1€ to 2€ if the employee has gone out of his or her way for you (with luggage, children, the elderly, and so on).

PARIS ★★★

Paris has been celebrated in such a torrent of media that for millions of people, the capital of France is an abstraction rather than a city. To most North American visitors, the city is still "Gay Paree," the fairy-tale town inviting you for a fling, the hub of everything "European," and the epitome of that nebulous attribute known as "chic." Paris remains the metropolis of pleasure, the picture postcard of blooming chestnut trees and young couples kissing by the Seine.

Paris is the glamour capital of the globe: by day a stone mosaic of delicate gray and green, by night a stunning, unforgettable sea of lights—white, red, orange. Broad, tree-lined boulevards open up before you, the mansions flanking them looming tall, ornate, and graceful. Everywhere you look are trees, squares, and monuments—and train stations. For Paris is also the center of France's extensive web of rail networks and a major international rail hub—a natural spot to begin a multicountry rail tour of Europe.

Station Information
GETTING FROM AIRPORTS TO TRAIN STATIONS

Paris has two international airports: **Aéroport d'Orly,** 8 miles (13km) south of the city, and **Aéroport Roissy–Charles de Gaulle,** 14 miles (23km) northeast of the city. A shuttle (**www.paris-airport-shuttle.com**), costing 19€ per person, makes the 50- to 75-minute journey between the two airports about every 30 minutes from 5am to 8pm. There is an additional fee of 3€ for rides outside of these hours.

At **Charles de Gaulle** (✆ **01-48-62-63-63;** www.paris-cdg.com), foreign carriers use Aérogare (Terminal) 1, while Air France and other airlines flying to European destinations wing into Aérogare 2. From Aérogare 1, you take a moving walkway to the checkpoint and Customs. The two terminals are linked by the CDGVAL (automated light-rail shuttle). The CDGVAL also transports you to the **Roissy rail station** (Terminal 3), from which fast **RER** (Réseau Express Régional) trains leave every 15 minutes heading to such Métro stations as Gare du Nord (see below), Châtelet, Luxembourg, Port-Royal, and Denfert-Rochereau. A typical fare from Roissy to any point in central Paris is 8.20€. From terminals 2 and 3, you can access the RER line B to Paris Gare du Nord (departs every 10–15 min.; trip time: 30 min.) from approximately 5am to midnight.

Note: Underneath Aérogare 2 is a TGV (and RER) rail station. If you're headed for Avignon, Tours, or Brussels, you can catch a train here.

You can also take an **Air France Coach Line 2 or 4** (✆ **08-92-35-08-20;** www.cars-airfrance.com) to central Paris for 15€ or 17€, respectively. It stops at the Palais des Congrès (Port Maillot) and then continues on to place Charles-de-Gaulle-étoile, where subway lines can carry you to any point in Paris. Depending on traffic it takes between 45 and 55 minutes. The shuttle departs about every 20 minutes between 5:40am and 11pm daily.

Another option is the **Roissybus** (✆ **01-58-76-16-16**), departing from the airport daily from 6am to 11:45pm and costing 8.60€ for the 45- to 50-minute ride. Departures are about every 15 to 20 minutes, and the bus will take you near the corner of rue Scribe and place de l'Opéra in the heart of Paris.

A **taxi** from Roissy to the central Paris rail stations will cost about 47€ to 60€, but from 8pm to 7am, the fares are 40% higher. Long lines for taxis form outside each of the airport's terminals and are surprisingly orderly. Be sure to ask for an estimate of the fee *before* you get in the taxi.

Paris

ACCOMMODATIONS ■

Galileo Hôtel **2**
Grand Hôtel
  St-Michel **39**
Hôtel Aviatic **8**
Hôtel Britannique **20**
Hôtel de la Place
  des Vosges **26**
Hôtel de l'Université **10**
Hôtel du Pas-de-
  Calais **9**
Hôtel Thérèse **18**
Hôtel Le Tourville **5**
Hôtel Queen Mary **15**
Hôtel Saint-Merry **21**
Hôtel St-Louis **28**

DINING ◆

Alcazar Bar &
  Restaurant **33**
Allard **34**
Angélina **13**
Aux Charpentiers **35**
Aux Lyonnais **17**
Bofinger **27**
Brasserie Balzar **37**

Crémerie-Restaurant
  Polidor **36**
L'Ambassade
  d'Auvergne **23**
L'Ambroisie **25**
Le Pré Verre **38**
Pinxo **14**
Ze Kitchen
  Galerie **32**

ATTRACTIONS
Arc de Triomphe **1**
Basilique du
  Sacré Cœur **16**
Centre Pompidou **22**
Conciergerie **30**
Eiffel Tower **4**
Hôtel des Invalides **6**
Musée d'Orsay **11**
Musée du Louvre **19**
Musée National
  Auguste Rodin **7**
Musée Picasso **24**
Notre-Dame **29**
Place de la
  Concorde **12**
Ste-Chapelle **31**
The Sewers of Paris
  (Les Egouts) **3**

The Airport Shuttle

Cheaper than a taxi for one or two people but more expensive than airport buses and trains, the **Paris Shuttle** (✆ **01-53-39-18-18**; www.parisshuttle. com) will pick you up in a minivan at Charles de Gaulle or Orly and take you to your hotel or rail station for 25€ for one person or 19€ per person for parties of two or more. It'll take you to the airports from your hotel for the same price. **Blue Vans** (✆ **01-30-11-13-00**; www.paris-blue-airport-shuttle.fr) offers a similar service, charging about 27€ for one passenger and 35€ for two. Both accept major credit cards, but only if you book online. You get a discount if you book online.

Orly Airport (✆ **01-49-75-52-52** or 39-50 from France only) has two terminals—Orly *Sud* (south) for international flights and Orly *Ouest* (west) for domestic flights. They're linked by a free shuttle bus (trip time: 3 min.).

Air France Coaches leave from exit E of Orly Sud and from exit F of Orly Ouest every 12 minutes between 6am and 11:30pm for Gare des Invalides; the fare is 9€ one-way, 14€ round-trip. Returning to the airport, buses leave both the Montparnasse and the Invalides terminals for Orly Sud or Orly Ouest every 15 minutes, taking about 30 minutes.

Another way to get to central Paris is to take the RER from points throughout central Paris to the station at Pont-de-Rungis/Aéroport d'Orly for a per-person one-way fare of 6€ and, from here, take the free shuttle bus that departs every 15 minutes from Pont-de-Rungis to both of Orly's terminals. Combined travel time is about 45 to 55 minutes.

A **taxi** from Orly to central Paris costs about 30€ to 50€, more at night. Don't take a meterless taxi from Orly—it's much safer (and usually cheaper) to hire one of the metered cabs, which are under the scrutiny of a police officer.

INSIDE THE STATIONS

There are six major train stations in Paris and multiple branches of the **Paris Convention and Visitors Bureau** (✆ **08-92-68-30-00**; .35€ per minute; www.paris-info.com), two of which are located in the city's rail stations (**Gare de Lyon** and **Gare de Nord**). They can give you free maps, brochures, and a selection of magazines listing current events and performances, as well as museum passes and hotel reservations. If you need a hotel room and you arrive at another station, visit the city's main tourist office or other Welcome Centers located around the city (see "Information Elsewhere in the City," below).

Paris's North Station, or **Gare du Nord,** 18 rue de Dunkerque, 15e (Métro: Gare du Nord), is a major gateway to France. Passengers from the English Channel ports of Boulogne and Calais arrive here, as do trains from the Netherlands, Belgium, Denmark, and Germany. It is also the termination point for Eurostar trains arriving from London and for Thalys trains from Brussels and Amsterdam. For rail information and tickets, go to the office across from platform #1 daily 6am to 11pm. Seat reservations on TGV trains and sleeping car reservations can be made here. Across from platform #3 is a kiosk that exchanges money, and there are also ATMs scattered throughout the station. **Eurostar** (**www.eurostar.com**) has its own terminal and reservations offices in the building, and there's a special waiting room upstairs from the main terminal. For more on Eurostar, see chapter 10 and check out **www.rail europe.com**.

Daily from 8am to 6pm, a **Paris Convention and Visitors Bureau** located beneath the glass roof in the Ile-de-France zone sells museum passes and will make hotel reservations and bookings for excursions.

Gare de Lyon, 20 bd. Diderot, 12e (Métro: Gare de Lyon), is the best equipped in Paris and is the gateway station for passengers heading southeast for Burgundy, Provence, and the French Riviera, as well as Italy and western Switzerland. Train information and reservations are handled at an office in the center of the station; open Monday to Saturday 8am to 8pm.

The **Paris Convention and Visitors Bureau** here is found in the station's main ticket hall. It's open Monday to Saturday 8am to 6pm. There are no service fees. This station is also the site of **Restaurant Le Train Bleu** (✆ **01-43-43-09-06;** www. le-train-bleu.com), the most elegant train station restaurant in Europe. Open since 1901, the restaurant serves good food in a fanciful Belle Epoque–style dining room.

The East Station, or **Gare de l'Est,** place du 11 Novembre 1918, 10e (Métro: Gare de l'Est), is the main terminal for departures into eastern France, with continuing service to such countries as Switzerland, Austria, Germany, and Luxembourg. The tourist information booth lies in front of platforms #1 and #2 and is open daily 8am to 7pm. You can make seat reservations here, but only from Monday to Saturday. A currency exchange kiosk is located in the main terminal opposite platforms #25 and #26, and ATMs are also available.

Gare d'Austerlitz, 55 quai d'Austerlitz (Métro: Gare d'Austerlitz), is the arrival and departure point for night trains heading into the central and southwestern sections of France and going on to Iberia (Spain and Portugal). The grand Train Hotel Elipsos trains to Madrid (*Francisco de Goya*) and Barcelona (*Joan Miró*) depart from and arrive in this station. In the foyer of the station (not the main hall) is a Train Information Center open Monday to Saturday 7:30am to 7:45pm. Seat reservations can also be made here. There is a currency exchange office in the main hall.

Two other major stations are **Gare St-Lazare,** 13 rue d' Amsterdam, 8e (Métro: Gare St-Lazare), with trains to and from Normandy; and **Gare de Montparnasse** (Métro: Montparnasse-Bienvenue), with trains going to Brittany, and TGV departures to southwestern France, and day trains to Spain. The Artesia de Nuit night trains from Italy pull into **Gare de Bercy** (Métro: Bercy), near Gare de Lyon and Gare d'Austerlitz.

The stations above are not connected to each other by rail, but all are linked by bus, which is preferable to the Métro if you have luggage. All stations have cafes, bars, washing facilities, and waiting rooms. For information and reservations, call ✆ **08-92-35-35-35.** *Warning:* The stations and surrounding areas are usually seedy and frequented by pickpockets, hustlers, hookers, and addicts. Be alert, especially at night.

Information Elsewhere in the City

The main headquarters of the **Paris Convention and Visitors Bureau** is **Pyramides** center, 25 rue des Pyramides, 1er (✆ **08-92-68-30-00;** www.paris-info.com; Métro: Pyramides); it's open from 10am to 7pm from Monday to Saturday (June–Oct from 9am) and from 11am to 7pm on Sundays and holidays.

There are **welcome centers** located outside of the train stations at strategic points around Paris. For general information about them, call the number listed above. The

Anvers Welcome Center, 72 bd. Rochechouart (Métro: Ancers), is open daily year-round from 10am to 6pm. The **Notre-Dame Welcome Center,** Parvis de Notre-Dame (Métro: Cité), is open daily from 10am to 7pm from June 3 to October 29. A less comprehensive branch office is the **Clémenceau Welcome Center,** corner of avenue Champs-Elysées and avenue Marigny, 8e (℃ **08-92-68-31-12;** Métro: Champs-Elysées-Clémenceau), open April 6 to October 20 daily 9am to 7pm.

The City Layout

Paris is surprisingly compact and an excellent city for strollers. Occupying 1,051 square miles (2,723 sq. km), it's home to more than 11 million people. The river Seine divides Paris into the *Rive Droite* **(Right Bank)** to the north and the *Rive Gauche* **(Left Bank)** to the south. These designations make sense when you stand on a bridge and face downstream (west)—to your right is the north bank, to your left the south. A total of 32 bridges link the Right Bank and the Left Bank, some providing access to the two islands at the heart of the city—**Ile de la Cité,** the city's birthplace and site of Notre-Dame; and **Ile St-Louis,** a moat-guarded oasis of 17th-century mansions.

The "main street" on the Right Bank is, of course, **avenue des Champs-Elysées,** beginning at the Arc de Triomphe and running to place de la Concorde. Avenue des Champs-Elysées and 11 other avenues radiate like the arms of an asterisk from the Arc de Triomphe, giving it its original name, place de l'Etoile (*étoile* means "star"). It was renamed place Charles-de-Gaulle following the general's death; today it's often referred to as place Charles-de-Gaulle-Etoile.

ARRONDISSEMENTS IN BRIEF The heart of medieval Paris was the **Ile de la Cité** and the areas immediately surrounding it. As Paris grew, it absorbed many of the once-distant villages, and today each of these *arrondissements* (districts) retains a distinct character. They're numbered 1 to 20 starting at the center and progressing in a clockwise spiral. The key to finding any address in Paris is to look for the arrondissement number rendered as a number followed by either *e* or *er* (1er, 2e, and so on). If the address is written out more formally, you can tell what arrondissement it's in by looking at the postal code. For example, the address may be written with the street name, then "75014 Paris." The last two digits, 14, indicate that the address is in the 14th arrondissement, Montparnasse.

On the Right Bank, the **1er** is home to the Louvre, place Vendôme, rues de Rivoli and St-Honoré, Palais Royal, and Comédie-Française—an area filled with grand institutions and grand stores. At the center of the **2e** is the Bourse (Stock Exchange), making it the city's financial center. The east end of the 2nd is devoted to the garment district (Le Sentier). Most of the **3e** is referred to as the Marais (the Swamp), one of the best loved of the old Right Bank neighborhoods. Kings have called Le Marais home, and its salons have echoed with the remarks of Racine, Voltaire, Molière, and Mme. de Sévigné. The old Jewish quarter from the 17th century is located there. Today it's a trendy area of boutiques and restored mansions as well as the center of Paris's gay and lesbian community. **4e** (Ile de la Cité) has it all, with Notre-Dame, Ste-Chapelle, and the Conciergerie. On the Left Bank, the **5e** is known as the Latin Quarter, home to the Sorbonne and associated with the intellectual life that thrived in the 1920s and 1930s. The **6e,** known as St-Germain-des-Prés, stretches from the Seine to boulevard du Montparnasse and is the most colorful on the Left Bank. It is associated with the 1920s and 1930s and known as a center for art and antiques; it boasts the Palais and Jardin du Luxembourg. The **7e,** containing both the Eiffel

Tower and Hôtel des Invalides, is a residential district for the well heeled. It also houses the Musée d'Orsay, the world's premier showcase of 19th-century French art and culture.

Back on the Right Bank, the **8e** epitomizes monumental Paris, with the triumphal avenue des Champs-Elysées, the Elysées Palace, the Arc de Triomphe and the obelisk on place e la Concorde, and the fashion houses along avenue Montaigne and the Faubourg St-Honoré. The **18e** is home to Sacré-Coeur, the Moulin Rougue, and Montmartre, and all that the name conjures of the bohemian life painted most notably by Toulouse-Lautrec. The **14e** incorporates most of Montparnasse, including its cemetery, whereas the **20e** is where the city's famous lie buried in Père-Lachaise and where today the recent immigrants from North Africa live. Beyond the arrondissements stretch the vast *banlieue,* or suburbs, of Greater Paris, where the majority of Parisians live.

Getting Around

BY METRO (SUBWAY)   The Métro (☏ **32-46** in France, or 08-92-69-32-46 from abroad; www.ratp.fr) is the fastest and most efficient means of transportation in Paris. All lines are numbered, and the final destination of each line is clearly marked on subway maps, in the underground passageways, and on the train cars. The Métro runs daily from 5:30am to around 1:15am. It's reasonably safe at any hour, but beware of pickpockets.

Note: To familiarize yourself with Paris's Métro, check out the **color map** on the inside front cover of this book.

To make sure you catch the correct train, find your destination on the map, then follow the rail line it's on to the end of the route and note the name of the final destination—this final stop is the direction. In the station, follow the signs labeled with your direction in the passageways until you see it labeled on a train.

Transfer stations are *correspondances*—some require long walks; Châtelet is the largest, but most trips require only one transfer. When transferring, follow the orange CORRESPONDANCE signs to the proper platform. Don't follow a SORTIE (EXIT) sign, or you'll have to pay another fare to get back on the train.

---

 saving ON TRAVEL

When purchasing Métro tickets, a *carnet* (book of coupons) is the best buy—10 tickets for 12€. You can also purchase a **Paris-Visite** (**www.ratp.info**), a tourist pass valid for 1, 2, 3, or 5 days on the public transportation system, including the Métro, buses, the funicular ride to Montmartre, and RER (Réseau Express Régional) trains (most not included on a railpass). The RER has both first- and second-class compartments, and the pass lets you travel in first class. The cost ranges from 8.80€ for a 1-day pass to 28€ for 5 days. The card is available at RATP (Régie Autonome des Transports Parisiens), tourist offices, or the main Métro stations (☏ **08-36-68-77-14**). The Paris-Visite is also available in advance from Rail Europe, with prices starting at $27 for a 1-day pass.

Another discount pass is **Carte Mobilis,** which allows unlimited travel on all bus, subway, and RER lines during a 1-day period for 6.10€ within Paris (zones 1–2). The price increases as the zone gets farther from Paris. Ask for it at any Métro station.

The urban lines cost 1.60€. At the turnstile entrances, insert your ticket and pass through. At some exits, on platforms, and on trains, tickets are occasionally checked, so hold on to yours.

BY BUS Buses are much slower than the Métro, and the majority run from 6:30am to 9:30pm (a few operate until 12:30am, and 10 operate during early morning hours). Service is limited on Sunday and holidays. Bus and Métro fares are the same; you can use the same tickets on both. Most bus rides require one ticket, but some destinations require two.

At certain stops, signs list the destinations (listed north to south, east to west) and numbers of the buses serving that point. Most stops are also posted on the sides of the buses. During rush hours, you may have to take a ticket from a dispensing machine, indicating your position in the line at the stop.

If you intend to use the buses a lot, pick up an RATP bus map at the office on place de la Madeleine, 8e, or at the tourist office at RATP headquarters, 54 Quai de la Rapée, 12e. For recorded information in English, call ✆ **32-46,** open Monday to Friday 7am to 9pm.

The RATP also operates the **Balabus,** big-windowed orange-and-white motorcoaches that run only during limited hours: Sunday and national holidays from noon to 8:30pm, from April 15 to the end of September. Itineraries run in both directions between Gare de Lyon and the Grande Arche de La Défense, encompassing some of the city's most beautiful vistas. It's a great deal—three Métro tickets, for 1.60€ each, will carry you the entire route. You'll recognize the bus and the route it follows by the BB symbol emblazoned on each bus's side and on signs posted beside the route it follows.

BY TAXI It's impossible to get one at rush hour, so don't even try. Taxi drivers are organized into a lobby that keeps their number limited to 15,000.

Watch out for common rip-offs. Always check the meter to make sure you're not paying the previous passenger's fare. Beware of cabs without meters, which often wait outside nightclubs for tipsy patrons, or settle the tab in advance. You can hail regular cabs on the street when their signs read LIBRE. Taxis are easier to find at the many stands near Métro stations.

The flag drops at 5.50€, and from 10am to 5pm you pay .89€ per kilometer. From 5pm to 10am, you pay 1.14€ per kilometer. On airport trips, you're not required to pay for the driver's empty return ride.

You're allowed several pieces of luggage free if they're transported inside and are less than 11 pounds (5kg). Heavier suitcases carried in the trunk cost 1€ to 1.50€ apiece. Tip 12% to 15%—the latter usually elicits a *"Merci."* For radio cabs, call **Les Taxis Bleus** (✆ **08-25-16-10-10**) or **Taxi G7** (✆ **01-47-39-47-39**)—note that you'll be charged from the point where the taxi begins the drive to pick you up.

Where to Stay

Although Paris hotels are quite expensive, there is some good news. Scores of lackluster Paris lodgings have been renovated and offer much better value in the moderate-to-inexpensive price range, especially in the 7th arrondissement.

Hot weather doesn't last long in Paris (though it can get brutal every now and then), so many hotels don't have air-conditioning (we note those that don't in the listings below). To avoid a noise problem when you have to open windows, request a room in the back when making a reservation.

Galileo Hotel ★ 🏨 This charming and elegant town house hotel is only a short walk from the Champs-Elysées and the Arc de Triomphe, and close to Gare St-Lazare. Owners Roland and Elisabeth Buffat have built up a good reputation with their attractively furnished and affordable bedrooms, which are filled with modern comforts. Within this hotel, rooms with numbers ending in 3 (for example, nos. 103, 203, 303, 403, and 503) are more spacious than the others. Room nos. 501 and 502 have private glassed-in verandas that you can use even in winter.

54 rue Galilée, 75008 Paris. ✆ **01-47-20-66-06.** Fax 01-47-20-67-17. www.galileo-paris-hotel.com. 27 units. 185€ double. AE, DC, MC, V. Métro: Georges-V or Charles-de-Gaulle–Etoile. RER: Etoile. **Amenities:** Rooms for those w/limited mobility; smoke-free rooms.

Grand Hôtel Saint-Michel Located near the Luxembourg Gardens and a 10-minute walk from Notre-Dame, this 19th-century building is in the heart of the Latin Quarter. The hotel, more businesslike than many town house–style inns nearby, has been tastefully restored and decorated with antique reproductions and elegant fabrics, enlarging some rooms and added amenities. Its sixth-floor bedrooms open onto views over the rooftops of Paris; the most desirable rooms have balconies (on the fifth floor) with views of the Sorbonne and the Pantheon. Most rooms have showers and tubs (the rest have showers only).

19 rue Cujas, 75005 Paris. ✆ **01-46-33-33-02.** Fax 01-40-46-96-33. www.grand-hotel-st-michel.com. 47 units. 290€–350€ double; 400€ suite. AE, DC, MC, V. Métro: Cluny–La Sorbonne or Odéon. RER: Luxembourg or St-Michel. **Amenities:** Breakfast room; bar; rooms for those w/limited mobility; smoke-free rooms.

Hôtel Aviatic Deep in the heart of Montparnasse, this hotel has been completely remodeled. Many of its old architectural touches remain, including an inner courtyard with a vine-covered wall lattice, and a lobby with marble columns, antiques, and crystal chandeliers. Its conservatory is an oasis of plants and natural light, and its Empire Lounge is a relaxing retreat. Run by the same family for over a century, Aviatic offers midsize bedrooms with thoughtful extras such as air-conditioning and good reading lamps. The breakfast buffet is 14€.

105 rue de Vaugirard, 75006 Paris. ✆ **01-53-63-25-50.** Fax 01-53-63-25-55. www.aviatic.fr. 43 units. 235€–285€ double; 490€ suite. AE, DC, MC, V. Métro: Montparnasse-Bienvenue or St-Placide. **Amenities:** Breakfast room; lounge; smoke-free rooms.

Hôtel Britannique This attractive and well-furnished boutique hotel enjoys a privileged position close to the Louvre and Ste-Chapelle. The French call it a *hotel de charme*, and so it is, with an English aura as suggested by its name. The public rooms could be the setting for an Agatha Christie novel, and the immaculate and soundproof bedrooms in this renovated 19th-century town house, though small, are studies in taste and comfort.

20 av. Victoria, 75001 Paris. ✆ **01-42-33-74-59.** Fax 01-42-33-82-65. www.hotel-britannique.fr. 39 units. 190€–221€ double; 279€–325€ suite. AE, DC, MC, V. Métro: Châtelet.

Hôtel de la Place des Vosges ★ 🍴 Built 350 years ago in the Marais district, this hotel is a 2-minute walk from the beautiful city square from which it takes its name. Author Victor Hugo lived around the corner of this well-managed and small-scale property, which was once a stable for the horses of Henri IV. Classified as a historical monument, the hotel offers cozy bedrooms with beamed ceilings and adjoining tile-clad bathrooms (with tub or shower). Breakfast costs 8€.

12 rue de Birague, 75004 Paris. ✆ **01-42-72-60-46.** Fax 01-42-72-02-64. www.hotelplacedesvosges. com. 16 units. 90€ double; 150€ suite. AE, MC, V. Métro: Bastille or St. Paul. **Amenities:** Breakfast room. *In room:* No A/C.

Hôtel de l'Université ★ This *hotel de charme,* a restored 300-year-old town house, is popular with North American visitors. Its Left Bank location (close to the Musée d'Orsay) is much favored by the literati, and it is filled with atmospheric touches such as antiques-filled rooms, splendid staircases and fireplaces (evocative of its status as a former convent), rattan beds, vaulted ceilings, and oak pillars. Try for room no. 35, which has a fireplace and opens onto a courtyard with a fountain. All bedrooms have a private terrace. The hotel offers discounts for last-minute bookings.

22 rue de l'Université, 75007 Paris. ℰ **01-42-61-09-39.** Fax 01-42-60-40-84. www.hoteluniversite. com. 27 units. 140€–175€ double. AE, MC, V. Métro: St-Germain-des-Prés or Rue du Bac. **Amenities:** Breakfast room; lounge.

Hôtel du Pas-de-Calais This hotel is a good choice for those nostalgic for some of that old St-Germain-des-Prés bohemian atmosphere—in fact Jean-Paul Sartre worked on his play *Dirty Hands* in room no. 41. It retains its elegant facade, with wooden doors, but is a bit weak on style, and the rooms are small. The inner bedrooms open onto a secluded courtyard with garden tables set out.

59 rue des Sts-Pères, 75006 Paris. ℰ **01-45-48-78-74.** Fax 01-45-44-94-57. www.hotelpasdecalais. com. 38 units. 185€–315€ double; 300€ suite. AE, DC, MC, V. Métro: St-Germain-des-Prés or Sèvres-Babylone. RER: St. Michel or Luxembourg. **Amenities:** Bar; breakfast room.

Hotel Le Tourville ★ Between the Eiffel Tower and Les Invalides, this small luxe hotel is located in a town house that dates from the Belle Epoque era of the 1890s. Today it's been renovated and tastefully furnished with old paintings, antiques, and contemporary chairs and sofas. The four best accommodations open onto a terrace. The bedrooms are light in color and have such homey touches as quilted bedspreads; the large bathrooms are clad in black marble and white tiles.

16 av. de Tourville, 75007 Paris. ℰ **800/376-7831** in the U.S., or 01-47-05-62-62. Fax 01-47-05-43-90. www.hotelletourville.com. 30 units. 210€ double; 470€ suite. AE, DC, MC, V. Métro: Ecole Militaire. **Amenities:** Bar; breakfast room; lounge; smoke-free rooms.

Hôtel Queen Mary ★ A model of charm and homey comfort, this hotel is housed in a restored turn-of-the-20th-century building with an iron-and-glass canopy. All the midsize bedrooms and spacious suites have deep mahogany furnishings, comfortable beds, and luxurious fabrics. All but five bathrooms have both tubs and showers (others are shower only). Other grace notes include a flowery patio and a liberal sprinkling of antiques. There is a buffet breakfast for 16€.

9 rue Greffulhe, 75008 Paris. ℰ/fax **01-42-66-40-50.** www.hotelqueenmary.com. 36 units. 209€–239€ double; 319€ suite. AE, DC, MC, V. Métro: Madeleine, Saint-Lazare, or Havre-Caumartin. **Amenities:** Bar; breakfast room; rooms for those w/limited mobility; smoke-free rooms.

Hôtel Saint-Merry ★ 📷 This former bordello, with its 18th-century ceiling beams still intact, is today a little boutique hotel that's a choice address for an arts-oriented crowd. Rooms are a bit small but are handsomely furnished and comfortable, with a lot of atmosphere, including neo-Gothic architectural details. Once in total decay, the surrounding Marais quarter has now been completely gentrified and is the center of gay Paris (about half the hotel's clientele consists of gay travelers)—it's a great place for strolling about.

78 rue de la Verrerie, 75004 Paris. ℰ **01-42-78-14-15.** Fax 01-40-29-06-82. www.hotelmarais.com. 12 units. 160€–200€ double; 350€ suite. Métro: Hôtel de Ville or Châtelet. *In room:* No A/C.

Hôtel St-Louis ★ 🔥 This most affordable hotel occupies some of the most expensive real estate in Paris. Filled with antiques and loaded with atmosphere, this restored 17th-century town house lies on the romantic Ile St-Louis, right between the Left and Right banks. The bedrooms are small but charming. If you opt for one of the top-floor rooms, you might get a small balcony opening onto some of the Paris's best cityscapes.

75 rue St-Louis-en-l'Ile, 75004 Paris. © **01-46-34-04-80.** Fax 01-46-34-02-13. www.hotelsaintlouis. com. 19 units. 140€–155€ double; 270€ suite. Breakfast 12€. MC, V. Métro: Pont Marie, St-Michel, or St-Paul. **Amenities:** Breakfast room; smoke-free rooms.

Hôtel Thérèse Close to the Louvre, place Vendôme, and the Tuileries Gardens, this hotel combines French charm with English classicism. For example, the wood library/bar evokes a London club with its wood-paneled walls and plush armchairs, but the lounge is adorned with Parisian art. It's a government-rated three-star hotel but seems more like four stars in ambience, style, and comfort. Owner Sylvia de Lattre, who likes shades of pistachio and royal blue, trolled the flea markets for paintings and prints to personalize each bedroom. The rooms are unpretentious but filled with quality furnishings, from the soft, efficient lighting by Philippe Starck to the natural wool quilts.

5-7 rue Thérèse, Paris 75001. © **01-42-96-10-01.** Fax 01-42-96-15-22. www.hoteltherese.com. 43 units. 185€–320€ double. AE, MC, V. Métro: Musée du Louvre. **Amenities:** Bar; library.

Top Attractions & Special Moments

The French capital is home to some of the world's greatest museums and monuments, but the main attraction of Paris is the city itself. From the moment you start sightseeing, you are liable to become so ensnared by the vistas you find en route to a particular sight that you run the risk of never getting there. The city streets lure you into hours of aimless rambling when you should be steering resolutely toward some three-star edifice.

There are people—and you well might agree with them—who find visiting museums in Paris redundant. Why sacrifice the sunshine to pursue art and culture through dim museum corridors when every Seine-side stroll reflects paintings of the masters and every city square is a model of architectural excellence?

If that is your view, stick with it. Of the almost 100 highly worthy Paris museums, only two or three are "required viewing" for the world traveler: the Louvre, Centre Pompidou, and the Musée d'Orsay. So before we hit the must-see museums, here are the greatest districts for wandering, with monuments galore.

PLACE DE LA CONCORDE ★★★ Regarded by many as the most beautiful urban square in the world, this immense 765,000-square-foot (71,071-sq.-m) expanse is so vast that your eye can't take it in at one glance. The center of the oval is swarming with cars, a motorist's nightmare, but the hugeness of the place seems to swallow them up.

In the middle, looking pencil-small, rises an obelisk from Egypt carved in 1200 B.C., flanked by cascading fountains. Grouped around the outer edges are eight statues, each representing a different French city. Near the statue of Brest was the spot where the guillotine stood during the French Revolution. On Sunday morning January 21, 1793, King Louis XVI lost his royal head there and was followed by 1,343 other victims, including Marie Antoinette and subsequently Danton and Robespierre, the very men who had launched the Reign of Terror.

The square borders the Tuileries Gardens on the east, and on the west is the second great showpiece of Paris, the Champs-Elysées.

CHAMPS-ELYSEES ★★★ This is the world's most famous promenade. Pointing from the place de la Concorde like a broad, straight arrow to the Arc de Triomphe at the far end, this avenue is at its best when lit at night.

Automobile showrooms and gift stores have marred the once-impeccable elegance of this stretch, but this is still the greatest vantage point from which to watch Paris pass you by, preferably while sipping a cold drink at one of the many cafes that line the sidewalk.

TROCADERO This is actually a series of adjoining sights, which a master touch of city planning has telescoped into one (a characteristic Parisian knack). From the place du Trocadéro, you can step between the two curved wings of the **Palais de Chaillot** and gaze out on a view that is nothing short of breathtaking. At your feet lies the **Jardins de Trocadéro,** centered by fountains. Directly in front, pont d'Iéna spans the Seine. Then, on the opposite bank, rises the iron immensity of the **Tour Eiffel.** And beyond is the **Champ de Mars,** once a military parade ground but now a garden landscape with arches, grottoes, lakes, and cascades.

THE SEINE ISLANDS ★★★ Ile de la Cité, the "egg from which Paris was hatched," lies quietly in the shadow of Notre-Dame. The home of French kings until the 14th century, the island still has a curiously medieval air, with massive gray walls rising up all around you, relieved by tiny patches of parkland.

Just behind Notre-Dame, sunken almost to the level of the river, is the **Memorial de la Déportation,** the monument to the thousands of French men, women, and children who perished in Nazi concentration camps from 1940 to 1945. You step down into a series of granite chambers with narrow, iron-barred windows. Hewn into the stone walls are the nightmarish names of the camps.

Back on the ground level, you'll see an iron bridge leading over to **Ile St-Louis**— the smaller and quieter of the river islands. It has remained almost exactly as it was in the 17th century, after it had been divided up into private building lots. Sober patrician houses stand along the four quays, and the fever-beat of the city seems a hundred miles away.

PLACE VENDÔME ★★★ This is *the* textbook example of classical French architecture, a pure gem set in the fashionable heart of the Right Bank. The pillared palaces encircling the square include the Ritz Hotel, as well as the Ministry of Justice. The center is crowned by a 144-foot-high (44m) column, erected to commemorate Napoléon's greatest victory—Austerlitz. The actual column is stone, but the enclosing spiral band of bronze was cast from the 1, 200 cannons captured by the emperor in the battle. The statue on top of the pillar is, of course, Napoléon, restored here after being pulled down twice: once by Royalist reactionaries, the second time by Communard revolutionaries.

A TOUR OF LE MARAIS ★★★ Very few cities on earth boast an entire district that can be labeled a sight. Paris has several. The Marais, or "marshland," is the vaguely defined maze of streets north of the **place de la Bastille.**

During the 17th century, this was a region of the aristocratic. Today Le Marais is increasingly chic, and many artists and craftspeople have moved in and restored once-decaying mansions.

In addition to the galleries, boutiques, and history, this is the old Jewish quarter of Paris. Wander around **rue des Rosiers** and perpendicular streets to find kosher patisseries, grocery stores, bookstores, schools, restaurants (including amazing and inexpensive falafels at **L'As du Fallafel,** 34 rue des Rosiers), commemorative plaques above doorways for lives lost in the Holocaust, and signs to the nearby **Musée Temple d'Art et d'Histoire du Judaisme.** The quarter shuts down on the Sabbath.

Take the Métro to the place de la Bastille to begin your tour of the neighborhood. The actual Bastille no longer exists, but it once housed such illustrious tenants as "The Man in the Iron Mask" and the Marquis de Sade. The mob attack on the fortress on July 14, 1789, touched off the French Revolution and Bastille Day, a major French holiday that commemorates the storming of the prison.

The **Colonne de Juillet,** in the middle of the square, honors the victims of the July Revolution of 1830 that marked the supremacy of Louis-Philippe. The winged god of liberty crowns the column.

From place de la Bastille, head up rue Saint-Antoine, cutting right on rue des Tournelles, with its statue honoring Beaumarchais (*The Barber of Seville*). Take a left again onto the Pas-de-la-Mule, "the footsteps of the mule," which takes you to place des Vosges.

PLACE DES VOSGES ★★★ Charming backstreets from place de la Bastille lead you to the oldest and most entrancing square in Paris.

Laid out in 1605 by order of King Henry IV, it was once called Palais Royale and was the scene of innumerable cavaliers' duels. The Revolutionary government changed its name but—luckily—left its structure intact. In the middle is a tiny park, and on three sides an arcaded walk supported by arches and paved with ancient flagstones. At No. 6 on the square is the **Maison De Victor Hugo.** Victor Hugo, known as a literary great, lived and worked here from 1832 to 1848; today it is a miniature museum full of Hugo's lesser-known drawings, carvings, paintings, and pieces of furniture. The windows of his study overlook the square—it's easy to see where he drew his inspiration.

QUARTIER LATIN ★★★ The Latin Quarter lies in the 5th arrondissement on the Left Bank and consists of the streets winding around the Paris University, of which the **Sorbonne** is only a part.

The logical starting point for touring this area is the **Place Saint-Michel,** right on the river, decorated by an impressive fountain. This was the scene of some of the most savage fighting of the French Resistance in August 1944. Here—as in many, many other spots—you'll see the little name tablets marking the place where a Resistance fighter fell: *"Ici est Tombé . . . le 19 Août 1944. Pour la Libération de Paris."*

Running straight south is the main thoroughfare of the quarter, the wide, pulsating **boulevard St-Michel.** But turn left instead and dive into the warren of dogleg alleys adjoining the river—**rue de la Huchette, rue de la Harpe, rue St-Séverin.** Thronged with students, shoppers, and tourists, the surroundings exude exotic smells of Middle Eastern, African, and Asian cooking. Narrow, twisting, and noisy, the alleys resemble an Oriental bazaar more than a European city. Emerge at the **Church of St-Séverin,** and you're back in Paris again. This flamboyant 13th-century Gothic edifice acts like a sanctuary of serenity away from the crowded streets.

Head down the **rue St-Jacques,** and Paris reasserts herself completely. The next crossing is the **boulevard St-Germain,** lined with sophisticated cafes and some of the most avant-garde fashion shops in town.

MONTMARTRE ★★★ This name has caused confusion in many an unwary visitor. So just to make things clear, there are three of them in Paris.

A Surreal Moment

Hidden around the corner from Montmartre's place de Tertre is **Espace Dalí**, 11 rue Poulbot, 18e (✆ **01-42-64-40-10;** www.daliparis.com; Métro: Anvers, Abbesses), a tribute to surrealist Salvadore Dalí, who made his home in this artistic haven during the 1930s. A rare French collection of over 300 of Dalí's sketches, sculptures, lithographs, and paintings is on display in this modest museum. Admission is 10€ adults, 7€ seniors, 6€ students and children ages 9 to 26, free ages 8 and under. Open daily 10am to 6pm.

The first is the **boulevard Montmartre,** a busy commercial street nowhere near the mountain. The second is the tawdry amusement belt along the **boulevard de Clichy,** culminating at **place Pigalle** (the "Pig Alley" of World War II GIs). The third—*the* Montmartre we're talking about—lies on top, on the slopes of the actual *Mont.*

The best way to get here is to take the Métro to **Anvers,** then walk to the nearby rue de Steinkerque and ride the curious little funicular to the top.

Montmartre used to be the city's artists' village, glorified by masters such as Utrillo, and has been painted, sketched, sculpted, and photographed by 10,000 lesser lights. The tourists, building speculators, and nightclub entrepreneurs came and most of the artists went, but a few still linger. And so does some of the village charm that once drew them.

The center point, **place de Tertre,** is a bustling square filled with terraced restaurants, cafes, and crêpéries. Artists and caricaturists are entertaining to watch as they bargain with tourists tirelessly. Just a few minutes away, the lively atmosphere is quickly contrasted by the peaceful and powerful presence of the **Basilica of Sacré-Coeur.** Behind the church and clinging to the hillside below are steep and crooked little streets that seem—almost—to have survived the relentless march of progress. **Rue des Saules** still has Montmartre's last vineyard. **Rue Lepic** still looks—almost—the way Renoir and the melancholy van Gogh and the dwarfish genius Toulouse-Lautrec saw it. This—almost—makes up for the blitz of portraitists and souvenir stores and postcard vendors up on top.

Arc de Triomphe ★★★ At the western end of the Champs-Elysées, the Arc de Triomphe is the largest triumphal arch in the world, about 161 feet high (48m) and 144 feet wide (4em). Its central location is unequalled in the city, but don't try crossing the busy square to reach it! Take the underground passage.

Commissioned by Napoléon in 1806 to commemorate his Grande Armée's victories, the arch wasn't completed until 1836, under Louis-Philippe. The arch is engraved with the names of the 128 victories of Napoléon and the 600 generals who participated in them. You can take an elevator or stairs to the top, where there are lithographs and photos depicting the arch throughout its history. From the observation deck, you have a panoramic view of the Champs-Elysées, the Louvre, the Eiffel Tower, and Sacré-Coeur.

Underneath the arch burns the Flame of Remembrance that marks the Tomb of France's Unknown Soldier—the effect at night is magical.

Place Charles de Gaulle-Etoile, 8e. ✆ **01-55-37-73-77.** www.monum.fr. Admission 9€ adults, 5.50€ ages 18–25, free for 17 and under. Apr–Sept daily 10am–11pm; Oct–Mar daily 10am–10:30pm. Métro: Charles de Gaulle-Etoile. Bus: 22, 30, 31, 52, 73, or 92.

Basilique du Sacré-Coeur ★★★ Montmartre's crowning achievement is the white church that, along with the Eiffel Tower, dominates the skyline of Paris. Its gleaming white domes and campanile (bell tower) tower over Paris like a Byzantine church of the 12th century. But it's not that old: After France's defeat by the Prussians in 1870, the basilica was planned as an offering to cure the country's misfortunes; rich and poor alike contributed. Construction began in 1873, but the church wasn't consecrated until 1919. The interior is decorated with mosaics, the most striking of which are the ceiling depiction of Christ and the mural of the Passion at the back of the altar. The crypt contains what some believe is a piece of the sacred heart of Christ—hence the church's name.

On a clear day, the vista from the dome can extend for 35 miles (56km). You can also walk around the inner dome of the church, peering down like a pigeon (one is likely to be keeping you company).

Place St-Pierre, 18e. ℂ **01-53-41-89-00.** www.sacre-coeur-montmartre.com/us. Free admission to basilica; joint ticket to dome and crypt 5€ adults. Basilica daily 6am–11pm; dome and crypt daily 9am–6pm. Métro: Abbesses; take the elevator to the surface and follow the signs to the *funiculaire,* which goes up to the church for the price of a Métro ticket (if you don't want to walk).

Centre Pompidou ★★★ Dreamed up in 1969 by then–French president Georges Pompidou, this temple for 20th-century art was designed by Richard Rogers and Renzo Piano, opened in 1977, and became the focus of immediate controversy. Its bold exoskeletal architecture and the brightly painted pipes and ducts crisscrossing its transparent facade (green for water, red for heat, blue for air, and yellow for electricity) created a toy factory–like impression that was jarring in the old Beaubourg neighborhood. Relaunched in 2000, in what has been called "the most avant-garde building in the world," the newly restored Pompidou Center is packing in the art-loving crowds again.

The **Musée National d'Art Moderne ★★★** housed in the center offers a large collection of 20th-century art. With some 40,000 works, only 850 can be displayed at one time. Minor Cubists are represented alongside such giants as Braque and Picasso (many of his harlequins). The permanent collection includes works ranging from the Fauves to Icelandic conceptual art. Among the sculpture, which leans heavily on the use of 20th-century metals, is a walk-through Calder and his ironic wire portrayal of the late Josephine Baker. Other sculpture includes works by Henry Moore and Jacob Epstein. Seasonally, special exhibitions are organized.

Place Georges-Pompidou, 4e. ℂ **01-44-78-12-33.** www.centrepompidou.fr. Admission 12€ adults, 9€ students ages 18–25, free for 17 and under. Special exhibits range in price. Wed–Mon 11am–10pm. Métro: Rambuteau, Hôtel de Ville, or Châtelet–Les Halles.

 Watching Twilight Fall over Paris

Even if you have only 24 hours in Paris and can't explore most of the sights recommended in this chapter, try to make it to Sacré-Coeur at dusk. Here, as you sit on the top steps, the church at your back, the Square Willette in front of you, nighttime Paris comes alive. First, a twinkle like a firefly; then all of the lights go on. One young American got carried away describing it all: "Here, away from the whirling taxis, concierges, crazy elevators, and tipping problems, the sound of Paris permeates by osmosis." Try to see it.

Conciergerie ★★ The most sinister building in France squats on the north bank of the Ile de la Cité (near the Pont au Change) and forms part of the huge Palais de Justice. Its name is derived from the title *concierge* (constable), once held by a high official of the Royal Court, but its reputation stems from the Revolution.

Here, as nowhere else in Paris, you can see the tall, square shadow of the guillotine. For, after the fall of the Bastille, this became the country's chief prison. When the Reign of Terror got under way, the Conciergerie turned into a kind of stopover depot en route to the "National Razor."

The conciergerie has the splendid remnants of a medieval royal palace, complete with refectory and giant kitchen. But most memorable are the rows of cells in which prisoners sat waiting for their ride to the blade. Famous prisoners who had a brief stay here before an even briefer trip to the guillotine include Marie Antoinette (you can visit her cell), Madame du Barry, Danton, and Robespierre. Among the few who stayed here and lived to write about it was America's Thomas Paine, who remembered chatting in English with Danton.

1 quai de l'Horloge, 4e. ✆ **01-53-40-60-80.** www.monum.fr. Admission 7€ adults, 4.50€ ages 18–25, free for children 17 and under. Mar–Oct daily 9:30am–6pm; Nov–Feb daily 9am–5pm. Métro: Cité, Châtelet, or St-Michel. RER: St-Michel.

Eiffel Tower ★★★ Strangely enough, this symbol of Paris wasn't meant to be a permanent structure at all. Gustave-Alexandre Eiffel erected it specifically for the Universal Exhibition of 1889, and it was destined to be pulled down a few years later. But Parisians loved it, and, when wireless telegraphy and radio appeared on the scene, the 985-foot (296m) tower—the tallest on the earth—presented a handy signaling station. During the German advance on Paris in 1914, the powerful beam from the top of the tower effectively jammed the enemy's field radios. Today the tower has a TV antenna tacked on the top and is 1,040 feet (312m) tall.

But forget all of the statistics and just stand underneath the tower and look straight up. If nothing else, it is a fantastic engineering achievement.

The view is the reason most people go to the third landing at the top of the tower, and this extends for 42 miles (68km), theoretically. In practice, weather conditions tend to limit it. Nevertheless, it's fabulous, and the best time for visibility is about an hour before sunset.

Champ de Mars, 7e. ✆ **01-44-11-23-23.** www.tour-eiffel.fr. Admission (elevator) to 2nd landing 8€, 3rd landing 13€. Stairs to 2nd landing 4.50€. Sept–May daily 9:30am–11:45pm; June–Aug daily 9am–12:45am. Oct–June stairs open only to 6:30pm. Métro: Trocadéro, Ecole Militaire, or Bir-Hakeim. RER: Champs de Mars–Tour Eiffel.

Hôtel des Invalides ★★★ This is not a "hotel," but rather a combined palace and church, which today houses a great museum, dozens of military administration offices, and the tomb of Napoléon. The monumental ensemble was originally built by Louis XIV as a stately home for invalid soldiers (hence the name). Most of the enormous space is taken up by the military-themed **Musée de l'Armée,** housing a collection that includes Viking swords, Burgundian basinets, 14th-century blunderbusses, Balkan khandjars, American Browning machine guns, and suits of armor worn by kings and dignitaries. You can gain access to the **Musée des Plans-Reliefs** through the west wing. This collection shows scale models of French towns and monuments (the model of Strasbourg fills an entire room), as well as models of military fortifications since the days of the great Vauban.

Napoléon's Tomb beneath the golden dome is one of Paris's greatest showpieces. Napoléon rests in a sarcophagus of red granite on a pedestal of green granite.

Surrounding the tomb are 12 figures of victories and 6 stands of captured enemy flags. The pavement of the crypt consists of a mosaic of laurel leaves. First buried at St. Helena, Napoléon's remains were returned to Paris in 1840. Also interred here are Napoléon's brothers, Joseph and Jerome; his son (who was never crowned); and Marshal Foch, who led the Allied armies to victory in 1918.

Place des Invalides, 7e. ✆ **01-44-42-37-72.** www.invalides.org. Admission to Musée de l'Armée, Napoléon's Tomb, and Musée des Plans-Reliefs 8.50€ adults, 6.50€ students under 26, free for children 17 and under. Oct–Mar daily 10am–5pm; dome Apr–Sept daily 10am–6pm. Closed New Year's Day, May 1, Nov 1, and Christmas. Métro: Latour-Maubourg, Varenne, St-Francois-Xavier, or Invalides.

Musée d'Orsay ★★★   Rail travelers will feel right at home in the neoclassical Gare d'Orsay train station, which has been transformed into one of the world's greatest art museums. It contains an important collection devoted to the pivotal years from 1848 to 1914. Across the Seine from the Louvre and the Tuileries, it is a repository of works by the Impressionists as well as the Symbolists, Pointillists, Realists, and late Romantics. Artists represented include van Gogh, Manet, Monet, Degas, and Renoir. It houses thousands of sculptures and paintings across 80 galleries, plus Belle Epoque furniture, photographs, objets d'art, architectural models, and a cinema.

One of Renoir's most joyous paintings is here: *Moulin de la Galette* (1876). Another celebrated work is by James McNeill Whistler—*Arrangement in Gray and Black: Portrait of the Painter's Mother.* The most famous piece in the museum is Manet's 1863 *Déjeuner sur l'herbe* (Picnic on the Grass).

1 rue de Bellechasse or 62 rue de Lille, 7e. ✆ **01-40-49-48-14.** www.musee-orsay.fr. Admission 8€ adults, 5.50€ ages 18–24 and seniors, free for children 17 and under. Tues–Wed and Fri–Sun 9:30am–6pm (Thurs until 9:45pm). Closed Christmas and New Year's Day. Métro: Solférino. RER: Musée d'Orsay.

Musée du Louvre ★★★   The largest palace in the world (converted into a museum after the revolution), the Louvre is also one of the world's greatest museums, housing a collection of up to 208,500 works of art. The collection is both impressive and exhausting.

To enter the Louvre, you pass through the 71-foot (21m) **I. M. Pei glass pyramid** in the courtyard (or, to try to avoid lines, enter through the underground shopping mall—a less impressive entrance—off of rue de Rivoli). Commissioned by Francois Mitterrand and completed in 1989, the pyramid received mixed reviews. There's so much to see, so many endless nightmare hallways to get lost in, that—regardless of how much you may enjoy exploring a museum on your own—here we suggest you start with a **guided tour** (in English), which lasts about 90 minutes. These start under the pyramid at the station marked ACCEIL DES GROUPES. Once you've gotten the lay of the land, you can always go back and see what you missed.

The collections are divided into eight departments: Asian antiquities; Egyptian antiquities; Greek, Etruscan, and Roman antiquities; Islamic art; sculpture; paintings; prints and drawings; and objets d'art. Three items are standouts and usually top everybody's must-see list. To the left of the main entrance, at the crest of a graceful flight of stairs, stands *The Winged Victory.* In the Department of Greek Antiquities, on the ground floor, stands the supple statue of *Venus de Milo,* the warm marble subtly tinted by sunlight. Upstairs, in a room of her own, and covered with bulletproof glass and surrounded by art students, photographers, and awe-struck visitors, hangs the gently chiding portrait of the *Mona Lisa.*

Note: Though the $1.2-billion Grand Louvre Project, a 15-year-long project, is officially complete, refurbishment of individual galleries and paintings continues. For up-to-date information, check out **www.louvre.fr**.

34–36 quai du Louvre, 1er. Main entrance in the glass pyramid, Cour Napoléon. ℰ **01-40-20-53-17,** 01-40-20-50-50 for operator, or 08-92-68-46-94 for advance credit card sales. www.louvre.fr. Admission 9€, free for children 17 and under, free for art students with ID, free 1st Sun of every month. Wed and Fri 9am–10pm; Thurs, Sat–Mon 9am–6pm. (Parts of the museum begin to close at 5:30pm.) 1½-hr. English-language tours (Mon and Wed–Sun) 6€, free for children 12 and under with museum ticket. Métro: Palais Royal–Musée du Louvre.

Musée National Auguste Rodin ★★ Auguste Rodin, the man credited with freeing French sculpture of Classicism, once lived and had his studio in the charming 18th-century mansion **Hôtel Biron,** across the boulevard from Napoléon's Tomb in the Hôtel des Invalides. Today the house and garden are filled with his works, a soul-satisfying feast for the Rodin enthusiast. In the cobbled Court of Honor, within the walls as you enter, you'll see *The Thinker* crouched on his pedestal to the right of you; *the Burghers of Calais* grouped off to the left of you; and, to the far left, the writhing *Gates of Hell,* atop which *The Thinker* once more meditates. There's a third *Thinker* inside the museum before the second-floor window. In the almost too-packed rooms, men, women, and angels emerge from blocks of marble, hands twisted in supplication, and the nude torso of Balzac rises up from a tree.

In the Hôtel Biron, 79 rue de Varenne, 7e. ℰ **01-44-18-61-10.** www.musee-rodin.fr. Admission 6€ adults, 5€ ages 18–25; free for children 17 and under, 1€ for garden entry (without museum ticket). Apr–Sept Tues–Sun 10am–5:45pm (gardens open until 6:45pm); Oct–Mar Tues and Thurs–Sun 10am–5:45pm, Wed 10am–8:45pm. Métro: Varenne or Invalides.

Musée Picasso ★★★ When it opened in the beautifully restored Hôtel Salé in the Marais, the press hailed it as a "museum for Picasso's Picassos," meaning those he chose not to sell. The world's greatest Picasso collection, acquired by the state in lieu of $50 million in inheritance taxes, consists of 203 paintings, 158 sculptures, 16 collages, 19 bas-reliefs, 88 ceramics, and more than 1,500 sketches and 1,600 engravings, plus 30 notebooks. These works span some 75 years of Picasso's life and changing styles.

The range of paintings includes a 1901 self-portrait and embraces such masterpieces as *Le Baiser* (The Kiss). Other masterpieces are *Reclining Nude* and *the Man with a Guitar* and the delightfully wicked *Jeune garçon à la langouste (Young Man with a Lobster).* The museum also owns several studies for *Les Demoiselles d'Avignon,* the painting that launched Cubism in 1907.

In the Hôtel Salé, 5 rue de Thorigny, 3e. ℰ **01-42-71-25-21.** www.musee-picasso.fr. Admission 8.50€ adults, 6.50€ ages 18–25, free for children 17 and under. Apr–Sept Wed–Mon 9:30am–6pm; Oct–Mar Wed–Mon 9:30am–5:30pm. Métro: St-Paul, St-Sébastien Froissart, or Chemin Vert.

Notre-Dame ★★★ The Cathedral of Paris and one of civilization's greatest edifices replaced two Romanesque churches (Ste. Mary and St. Stephen), which stood on the spot until 1160. Then Bishop Maurice de Sully, following the example of

The Handy Museum Pass

The **Paris Museum Pass (www.paris museumpass.com)** is available at any branch of the Paris Tourist Office and at some of the included museums. It offers entrance to 70 monuments and museums in Paris and the Ile de France.

The longer you stay in Paris and the more places you plan to visit, the more likely the pass will be a good buy for you. A 2-day pass is 32€, a 4-day pass 48€, and a 6-day pass 64€.

Suger, the abbot of St. Denis, undertook the new structure, and building continued for more than 150 years. The final result was a piece of Gothic perfection. The rose window above the main portal, for instance, forms a halo 31 feet (9.3m) in diameter around the head of the statue of the Virgin. You'll have to walk around the entire structure to appreciate this "vast symphony of stone" with its classic flying buttresses. Better yet, cross the bridge to the Left Bank and view it from the quay.

More than any other building, Notre-Dame is the history of a nation. Here the boy-monarch Henry VI of England was crowned king of France in 1422, during the Hundred Years War, when—but for Joan of Arc—France would have become an English dominion. Here Napoléon took the crown out of the hands of Pope Pius VII, and crowned himself and Josephine emperor and empress. Here General de Gaulle knelt before the altar on August 26, 1944, to give thanks for the liberation of Paris—imperturbably praying while sniper bullets screeched around the choir galleries. Because of the beauty of its ornaments and of its symbolic meaning of redemption of all evil, Notre-Dame is a joyous church—though those devils and gargoyles grinning from its ledges add a genuinely macabre touch. You can almost see Victor Hugo's hunchback peering from behind them. You can climb the 402 steps up the 225-foot (68m) flat-topped twin towers to complete this image—and for a panoramic view of the city.

6 place de Parvis Notre-Dame, 4e. ☎ **01-53-10-07-02.** www.monum.fr. Admission free to cathedral; towers 8€ adults, 5€ ages 18–25 and seniors, free for children 17 and under; treasury 3€ adults, 2€ ages 12–25, 1€ ages 6–12, free for children 5 and under. Cathedral open year-round daily 8am–6:45pm (until 7:15pm Sat–Sun). Towers and crypt year-round Tues–Sun 10am–6pm (until 11pm Sat–Sun June–Aug). Museum Wed and Sat–Sun 2–5pm. Treasury Mon–Fri 9:30am–6pm, Sat 9:30am–6:30pm, Sun 1:30–6:30pm. Métro: Cité or St-Michel. RER: St-Michel.

The Sewers of Paris (Les Egouts) ★ Some say Baron Haussmann will be remembered mainly for erecting this vast, complicated network of Paris sewers. They were made famous by Victor Hugo's *Les Misérables*. "All dripping with slime, his soul filled with a strange light," Jean Valjean in his desperate flight through the sewers of Paris is one of the heroes of narrative drama.

The *égouts* of the city are constructed around a quartet of principal tunnels, one of them 18 feet wide (5.4m) and 15 feet high (4.5m). These underground passages are truly mammoth, containing pipes bringing in drinking water and compressed air, as well as telephone and telegraph lines. Furthermore, each branch pipe bears the number of the building to which it is connected—like an underground city. Tours begin at Pont de l'Alma on the Left Bank. You do, however, often have to wait in line for as much as 30 minutes.

Pont de l'Alma, 7e. ☎ **01-53-68-27-81.** Admission 4.20€ adults; 3.40€ students, seniors, and children 5–16; free for children 4 and under. May–Sept Sat–Wed 11am–5pm; Oct–Apr Sat–Wed 11am–4pm. Last ticket sold 1 hr. before closing. Métro: Alma-Marceau. RER: Pont de l'Alma.

Ste-Chapelle ★★★ One of the oldest, most beautiful medieval churches in the world, Ste-Chapelle was built in 1246 to house the relics of the Crucifixion obtained from Constantinople. But the relics were later transferred to Notre-Dame, leaving Ste-Chapelle as an empty showcase, although a magnificent one.

The church actually has two levels: one humble, the other superb. You enter through the lower chapel (originally for servants), supported by flying buttresses and ornamented with fleurs-de-lis. The upper chapel, reached by a spiral staircase, was used by the royal household. You can still see the small grated window from which Louis XI could participate in services without being noticed.

Fifteen unforgettable stained-glass windows flood the church's interior with sunshine and colored light—deep blue, ruby, and dark green—and depict more than a thousand scenes from the Bible.

Ste-Chapelle stages **concerts** in March to November (daily at 7 and 8:30pm), with tickets running 19€ to 25€. Call ✆ **01-44-07-12-38** from 11am to 6pm daily for details.

Palais de Justice, 6 bd. du Palais, 1er. ✆ **01-53-40-60-80.** www.monum.fr. Admission 8€ adults, 5€ students 18–25, free for children 17 and under. Mar–Oct daily 9:30am–6pm; Nov–Feb daily 9am–5pm. Métro: Cité, St-Michel, or Châtelet–Les Halles. RER: St-Michel.

Boat Tours

A boat tour on the Seine provides vistas of the riverbanks and Notre-Dame. Many boats have sun decks, bars, and restaurants. **Bateaux-Mouche** (✆ **01-42-25-96-10;** www.bateaux-mouches.fr; Métro: Alma-Marceau) cruises depart from the Right Bank of the Seine, adjacent to pont de l'Alma, and last about 75 minutes. Tours leave daily at 20-minute intervals from 10:15am to 11pm between April and September. Between October and March, there are at least five departures daily between 11am and 9pm, with a schedule that changes according to demand and the weather. Fares are 10€ for adults and 5€ for children 4 to 13. Dinner cruises depart daily at 8:30pm, last 2 hours, and cost 95€ to 135€. On dinner cruises, jackets and ties are required for men. There are also lunch cruises Saturday and Sunday departing at 1pm, costing 50€ or else 25€ for kids 11 and under. Paris dinner-cruise tickets can be obtained from Rail Europe.

Where to Dine

Alcazar Bar & Restaurant ★ MODERN FRENCH This is what the French Parisians call a *brasserie de luxe*. The creation of famous British restaurateur Sir Terence Conran, it features an avant-garde decor in its street-level dining room and chic bar upstairs. The menu is personal, creative, perfumed with herbs, and constantly changing with the addition of new taste sensations such as magret of duckling with white radishes and sesame oil.

62 rue Mazarine, 6e. ✆ **01-53-10-19-99.** Reservations recommended. Main courses 17€–33€; fixed-price menu 20€–32€ lunch, 43€ dinner. AE, DC, MC, V. Daily noon–2:30pm and 7pm–1am. Métro: Odéon.

Allard ★ TRADITIONAL FRENCH This is one of the most fashionable Left Bank bistros, with a tradition dating from 1931. Following a long decline, it has bounced back to reclaim its former prestige, when it catered to Left Bank artists and even an occasional French prime minister. Here you can try famous dishes considered typically French: foie gras, escargots, cassoulet Toulousian, and, of course, the inevitable frogs' legs. Many platters, such as roast duck with olives, are served for two.

41 rue St-André-des-Arts, 6e (Entrance on the corner of rue de l'Eperon). ✆ **01-43-26-48-23.** Reservations required. Main courses 19€–39€; fixed-price menu 25€ lunch, 34€ dinner. AE, DC, MC, V. Daily noon–2:30pm and 7:30–11:30pm. Métro: St-Michel or Odéon.

Angélina ★★ TEA/TRADITIONAL FRENCH This *salon de thé*, or tea salon, is well known in Paris for its intensely rich, dark drinking chocolate served with freshly whipped cream—a treat for the true chocolate lover. In an elegant setting of carpets and high ceilings, Angélina also offers a constantly changing plat du jour and serves old French favorites, such as steak tartare or sole meunière, as main courses.

A dessert specialty—designed to go well with tea—is the Mont Blanc, a combination of chestnut cream and meringue.

226 rue de Rivoli, 1er. ℭ **01-42-60-82-00.** www.groupe-bertrand.com. Reservations accepted for lunch, not for teatime. Pot of tea for 1 7€; pot of drinking chocolate for 1 6.90€; sandwiches and salads 10€–15€; main courses 16€–30€. AE, MC, V. Mon–Fri 8am–7pm; Sun 9am–7pm. Métro: Tuileries or Concorde.

Aux Charpentiers ♦ TRADITIONAL FRENCH   In days of yore, it seemed that practically every frugal traveler to Paris made this notation: Visit the Louvre and dine at Aux Charpentiers. This St-Germain-des-Prés bistro (with a patio downstairs), in business for a century and a half, is still going strong serving the *cuisine bourgeoise* that made it such a legend in the '50s and '60s. Feast on one of the plats du jour, invariably an example of French home-style cookery, featuring the likes of stuffed cabbage, or *boudin noire* (black pudding).

10 rue Mabillon, 6e. ℭ **01-43-26-30-05.** Reservations required. Main courses 18€–31€; fixed-price menu 21€ lunch, 28€ dinner. AE, DC, MC, V. Daily noon–3pm and 7–11:30pm. Métro: St-Germain-des-Prés or Mabillon.

Aux Lyonnais ★ LYONNAIS/FRENCH   This 1890 bistro offers the finest Lyonnaise cuisine in Paris—especially the pork dishes. (The menu proclaims that, in Lyon, *"le cochon est roi"*—pig is king.) The *fin de siècle* atmosphere is set by frosted globe chandeliers, floral tiled walls, and stuffed deer and boar heads. Inventiveness and solid technique characterize such dishes as parsleyed calves' liver, pike dumplings (the best in Paris), skate meunière, and peppery coq au vin (chicken stewed in red wine) with *crème fraîche* (fresh cream) macaroni. Save the best for last: a heaven-sent Grand Marnier soufflé.

32 rue St-Marc, 2e. ℭ **01-42-96-65-04.** www.auxlyonnais.com. Reservations required. Main courses 22€–25€; 3-course fixed-price menu 26€–34€. AE, DC, MC, V. Tues–Fri noon–1:30pm; Tues–Sat 7:30–10pm. Métro: Grands-Boulevards.

Bofinger ★ ALSATIAN/FRENCH   The oldest Alsatian brasserie in Paris traces its origins from 1864. It successfully retains the palatial style of that era: lots of leaded glass, creamy macramé curtains, lampshades shaped like tulips, antique mirrors, mahogany pieces, dark-gray benches, a revolving main door, and a central dome of stained glass. In other words, Emile Zola would feel right at home here. At night, many members of the Parisian slumming chic venture into the Bastille district for beer and sauerkraut complete with sausages, smoked bacon, and pork chops. The restaurant has updated its menu, retaining the most popular traditional dishes, such as sauerkraut and sole meunière (sole in lemon-butter sauce).

5-7 rue de la Bastille, 4e. ℭ **01-42-72-87-82.** www.bofingerparis.com. Reservations recommended. Main courses 15€–35€; fixed-price menu 25€–32€. AE, DC, MC, V. Mon–Fri noon–3pm and 6:30pm–1am; Sat–Sun noon–1am. Métro: Bastille.

Brasserie Balzar ★ TRADITIONAL FRENCH   If they visited Paris, chances are, your grandfather (maybe even your great-grandfather), your father, or your ancestors, dined at this 1886 cheerful Left Bank bistro near the Sorbonne that Sartre, Camus, James Thurber, and a host of international journalists called their favorite. Count on the most traditional of French cookery—we're talking onion soup, pepper steak, sole meunière, fried calves' liver, and even pigs' feet.

49 rue des Ecoles, 5e. ℭ **01-43-54-13-67.** www.brasseriebalzar.com. Reservations strongly recommended. Main courses 18€–35€. AE, DC, MC, V. Daily noon–midnight. Métro: Odéon or Cluny–La Sorbonne.

Crémerie–Restaurant Polidor ★ TRADITIONAL FRENCH Along with the previously recommended Aux Charpentiers, this is one of the most famous and traditional of French bistros, serving a *cuisine familiale* (family cuisine) since the early 1900s. Over the years, it has attracted the literati, including Hemingway and Kerouac, but today is likely to be filled with students and area artists. Nothing is as French as their *boeuf bourguignon* or *blanquette de veau*. For dessert, get a chocolate, raspberry, or lemon tart—the best in all of Paris.

39 rue Monsieur-le-Prince, 6e. ✆ **01-43-26-95-34.** www.polidor.com. Main courses 11€–48€; fixed-price menus 22€–32€. No credit cards. Daily noon–2:30pm; Mon–Sat 7pm–12:30am; Sun 7–11pm. Métro: Odéon.

L'Ambassade d'Auvergne ★ AUVERGNAT/FRENCH In an obscure district of Paris, this rustic tavern not only oozes charm, but also dispenses *cuisine bourgeoise* of Auvergne, the heartland of France. You enter through a busy bar, with heavy oak beams, hanging hams, and ceramic plates. At the entrance is a display of the chef's specialties: jellied meats and fowls, pâté cakes, plus an assortment of regional cheese and fresh fruit of the season. Rough wheat bread is stacked in baskets, and rush-seated, ladder-back chairs are placed at tables, along with a jug of mustard to go with all those pork products.

22 rue de Grenier St-Lazare, 3e. ✆ **01-42-72-31-22.** www.ambassade-auvergne.com. Reservations recommended. Main courses 14€–23€; fixed-price menu 28€. AE, MC, V. Daily noon–2pm and 7:30–10:30pm. Métro: Rambuteau.

L'Ambroisie ★★★ MODERN & TRADITIONAL FRENCH One of Paris's most talented chefs, Bernard Pacaud, draws world attention (and three coveted Michelin stars) with his vivid flavors and expert skill, but culinary standards here are declining. Expect a cool reception at this early-17th-century town house in Le Marais, with three high-ceilinged salons whose decor recalls an Italian palazzo. Dishes change seasonally; one of our favorite dishes is the *poulard de Bresse demi-deuil homage à la Mère Brazier* (chicken roasted with black truffles and truffled vegetables in a style invented by a Lyonnais matron after World War II).

9 place des Vosges, 4e. ✆ **01-42-78-51-45.** www.ambroisie-placedesvosges.com. Reservations required far in advance. Main courses 100€–140€. AE, MC, V. Tues–Sat noon–1:30pm and 8–9:30pm. Métro: St-Paul or Chemin Vert.

Le Pré Verre ★ 🍴 ASIAN/TRADITIONAL FRENCH Around the corner from the Sorbonne is this refreshing restaurant where you can get seriously good food—all for an affordable price. Even if this is not an earth-shattering gastronomic experience, it is solid and reliable, with good cooking and market-fresh ingredients. Dishes are firmly based in the French tradition but have innovative modern twists, thanks to extra spicing, many of the flavorings inspired by Asia. In a welcoming, relaxed, and convivial atmosphere, tables are placed so close together that you're literally dining and rubbing elbows with the same people. Main courses might include suckling pig with aromatic spices and crisp-cooked cabbage, or roasted codfish.

8 rue Thenard, 5e. ✆ **01-43-54-59-47.** www.lepreverre.com. Reservations required. Main courses 18€; fixed-price menu at lunch 14€–29€, at dinner 29€. MC, V. Tues–Sat noon–2pm and 7:30–10:30pm. Closed Aug. Métro: Maubert-Mutualité.

Pinxo ★ 🍴 SOUTHWESTERN FRENCH A cost-conscious brasserie associated with megachef Alain Dutournier. The good-looking waitstaff encourages clients to share their starters and platters with their tablemates, which is relatively easy because

THE famous cafes **OF PARIS**

Whatever your pleasure—reading, meeting a lover, writing your memoirs, or drinking yourself into oblivion—you can do it at a French cafe.

On one of the main corners across from the Centre Pompidou, the avant-garde **Café Beaubourg,** 100 rue St-Martin, 4e (☎ **01-48-87-63-96;** Métro: Rambuteau or Hôtel-de-Ville), boasts soaring concrete columns and a minimalist decor by the architect Christian de Portzamparc. In summer, tables are set on the sprawling terrace, providing a panoramic view of the neighborhood's goings-on. Open Sunday through Wednesday from 8am to 1am (Thurs–Sat until 2am).

Jean-Paul Sartre came to **Café de Flore,** 172 bd. St-Germain, 6e (☎ **01-45-48-55-26;** www.cafe-de-flore.com; Métro: St-Germain-des-Prés). It's said he wrote his trilogy, *Les Chemins de la Liberté (The Roads to Freedom),* here. The cafe is still going strong, though the celebrities have moved on. Open daily 7:30am to 1:30am.

Next door, the legendary **Deux Magots,** 6 place St-Germain-des-Prés, 6e (☎ **01-45-48-55-25;** www.lesdeux magots.fr; Métro: St-Germain-des-Prés), is still the hangout for sophisticated residents and a tourist favorite in summer. Inside are two Asian statues that give the cafe its name. Open daily from 7:30am to 1am.

Fouquet's, 99 av. des Champs-Elysées, 8e (☎ **01-47-23-50-00;** www. fouquets-barriere.com; Métro: George-V),

is the premier cafe on the Champs-Elysées. The outside tables are separated from the sidewalk by a barricade of potted flowers. Inside are an elegant grill room, private rooms, and a restaurant. The cafe is open daily 8am to 2am; the restaurant and slightly less formal grill are open daily noon to 3pm and 7pm to 1am.

At **La Coupole,** 102 bd. Montparnasse, 14e (☎ **01-43-20-14-20;** www. lacoupoleparis.com; Métro: Vavin), the crowd ranges from artists' models to young men dressed like Rasputin. Perhaps order a coffee or cognac VSOP at one of the sidewalk tables. People don't come here for the cuisine; it's more on the see-and-be-seen circuit. The dining room serves food that is sometimes good, sometimes indifferent. A buffet breakfast is served Monday to Friday 8:30 to 10:30am. Open daily 8am to 1am, until 1:30am on Friday and Saturday.

Café de la Musique, in the Cité de la Musique, place Fontaine Aux Lions, 213 av. Jean-Jaurès, 19e (☎ **01-48-03-15-91;** Métro: Porte de Pantin), attracts a crowd devoted to music. The recorded sounds in the background are likely to be more diverse and eclectic than in any other cafe in Paris. The red-and-green-velour setting may remind you of a modern opera house. On the menu you'll find pasta with shellfish, pork in cider sauce, and stingray in black-butter sauce. Open daily 8am to 2am (until 1am only Sun–Mon).

anytime something appears on a plate, it's replicated, sometimes with variations, three times. The setting manages to elevate kitchen drudgery to a high, and high-tech, art form. Expect a wooden floor, white walls, and views that extend directly into an all-black open kitchen-cum-theater. Most foods here are grilled or at least prepared with heart-healthy cooking oils. Examples include a mixture of Aquitaine beef on the same plate as a steak, a tartare, and a blood sausage, all of them accompanied by a slice of foie gras.

In the Plaza-Paris-Vendôme Hôtel, 9 rue d'Alger, 1er. ☏ **01-40-20-72-00.** www.pinxo.fr. Reservations recommended. Main courses 13€–28€; fixed-price lunch 21€. AE, MC, V. Daily 12:15–2:30pm and 7:15–11:30pm. Métro: Tuileries.

Ze Kitchen Galerie ★ 📷 FRENCH/INTERNATIONAL   Since William Ledeuil established this place in 2001, he's attracted the likes of First Lady Laura Bush. The setting—a block from the Seine and winding backstreets full of art galleries—is a colorful loft space in an antique building, with an open-to-view showcase kitchen. Menu items change about every 5 weeks; main courses are divided into meats and fish that are usually grilled *"a la plancha"* (on an iron skillet). The best examples include platters of oysters, mussels, and sea urchins served with herb sauce and *crostini,* and grilled shoulder of wild boar with tamarind sauce.

4 rue des Grands-Augustins, 6e. ☏ **01-44-32-00-32.** www.zekitchengalerie.fr. Reservations recommended. Main courses 30€–35€; fixed-price lunch with wine 24€–39€; fixed-price dinner 76€. AE, DC, MC, V. Mon–Fri noon–2:30pm; Mon–Sat 7–11pm. Métro: St-Michel or Pont-Neuf.

Shopping

Perfumes and **cosmetics,** including such famous brands as Guerlain, Chanel, Schiaparelli, and Jean Patou, are almost always cheaper in Paris than in the United States. Paris is also a good place to buy Lalique and Baccarat **crystal.** They're expensive but still priced below international market value. **Lingerie** is another great French export. Top lingerie designers are represented in boutiques and in the major department stores, Galeries Lafayette and Le Printemps.

Directly across from the Louvre, **Le Louvre des Antiquaires,** 2 place du Palais-Royal, 1er (☏ **01-42-97-27-27;** www.louvre-antiquaires.com; Métro: Palais-Royal), is the largest repository of antiques in central Paris. More than 250 dealers display their wares on three floors, specializing in objets d'art and small-scale furniture of the type that might have been favored by Mme. de Pompadour.

Viaduc des Arts, 119 av. Daumesnil (btw. rue de Lyon and av. Diderot), 12e (☏ **01-44-75-80-66;** www.viaducdesarts.fr; Métro: Bastille, Ledru-Rollin, Reuilly-Diderot, or Gare-de-Lyon), occupies the vaulted spaces beneath a 19th-century railway access route into the Gare de Lyon. Around 1990, crafts artists, including furniture makers, potters, glassblowers, and weavers, began occupying the then-empty niches beneath the viaduct, selling their wares to homeowners and members of Paris's decorating trades.

Purveyor to kings and presidents since 1765, **Baccarat** has a central location at 11 place de la Madeleine, 8e (☏ **01-42-65-36-26;** www.baccarat.fr; Métro: Madeleine), and an even larger showroom at 11 place des Etats-Unis, 16e (☏ **01-40-22-11-22;** Métro: Boissière or Iéna)—site of the **Musée du Cristal Baccarat,** a repository of some of the most extravagant crystal items the organization has ever made.

Boutique Lalique, 11 rue Royale, 8e (☏ **01-53-05-12-81;** www.cristallalique. fr; Métro: Concorde), famous for its clear- and frosted-glass sculpture, Art Deco crystal, and perfume bottles, has recently branched out into sales of other types of merchandise, such as silk scarves meant to compete with Hermès and leather belts with Lalique buckles.

One of the few regional handcrafts stores in Paris worth going out of your way to find, **La Tuile à Loup,** 35 rue Daubenton, 5e (☏ **01-47-07-28-90;** www. latuilealoup.com; Métro: Censier-Daubenton), carries beautiful pottery and faïence from many regions of France. Look for figures of Breton folk on the faïence of

Quimper as well as garlands of fruits and flowers from the *terre vernissée* (varnished earth, a charming way to define stoneware) from Normandy, Savoy, Alsace, and Provence.

After you've admired the architecture of one of Europe's most famous department stores, step inside **Au Printemps,** 64 bd. Haussmann, 9e (© **01-42-82-50-00;** www.printemps.com; Métro: Havre-Caumartin; RER: Auber), for a view of all it offers. Inside the main building is **Printemps de la Mode,** which occupies the bulk of the structure, and a housewares shop, **Printemps de la Maison.** Upstairs are wares of every sort, especially clothing. An affiliated store across the street is **Le Printemps de l'Homme,** the menswear division. Behind the main store is a branch of **Prisunic,** Printemps's workaday but serviceable dime store, which contains groceries. At **Galeries Lafayette,** 40 bd. Haussmann, 9e (© **01-42-82-34-56;** www. galerieslafayette.com; Métro: Chaussée-d'Antin; RER: Auber), stand under "the Dome"—a stained-glass cupola that towers above the arcaded store. Built in 1912, Galeries Lafayette is divided into several stores: **Galfa** men's store, **Lafayette Sports,** and two other general-merchandise stores, both known simply as "**GL.**"

Anna Lowe, 104 rue du Faubourg St-Honoré, 8e (© **01-42-66-11-32** or 01-40-06-02-42; www.annalowe.com; Métro: Miromesnil), is one of the premier boutiques for the woman who wishes to purchase a little Chanel or perhaps a Versace at a discount. Many clothes are runway samples; some have been gently worn. The inventory at **Réciproque,** 88–123 rue de la Pompe (btw. av. Victor-Hugo and av. Georges-Mandel), 16e (© **01-47-04-30-28;** Métro: Pompe), is scattered over five buildings. Everything is secondhand, clustered into sections devoted to Chanel, Versace, Lacroix, Hermès, and Mugler. Women will find gowns, suits, sportswear, and shoes.

At the place de la Madeleine stands one of the most popular sights in the city—not La Madeleine church, but **Fauchon,** 26 place de la Madeleine, 8e (© **01-70-39-38-00;** www.fauchon.fr; Métro: Madeleine), which offers a wider choice of upscale gourmet products than any other store in the world. Areas are devoted to candy, pastries, and bread; fresh fruits and veggies; dry and canned goods; fresh fish and meats; awe-inspiring takeout food; and wine.

Almost every working woman around place de la Madeleine shops at **Catherine,** 7 rue Castiglione, 1er (© **01-42-61-02-89;** Métro: Concorde). It resembles a high-volume pharmacy more than a boutique; flacons of perfume move in and out of the premises very fast. You get a 30% discount on most brands of makeup and perfume, and a 20% discount on high-end brands such as Chanel and Dior.

Nightlife

Opéra Garnier ★★★, place de l'Opéra, 9e (© **08-92-89-90-90;** www.operade paris.fr; Métro: Opéra), is the premier stage for dance and opera. Painstaking restorations have returned the Garnier to its former glory: Its boxes and walls are again lined with flowing red and blue damask, the gilt gleams, the ceiling (painted by Marc Chagall) has been cleaned, and air-conditioning has been added. The box office is open Monday through Saturday from 10:30am to 6:30pm. The controversial building known as the **Opéra Bastille ★★★**, place de la Bastille, 120 rue de Lyon (© **08-92-89-90-90** or 01-40-01-17-89; www.operadeparis.fr; Métro: Bastille), was designed by the Canadian architect Carlos Ott, with curtains created by fashion designer Issey Miyake. The main hall is the largest of any French opera house, with 2,700 seats, but music critics have lambasted the acoustics. Both traditional opera performances and symphony concerts are presented here. Tours (75 min.) of the opera house are offered, though the schedule varies, and sometimes there are free concerts on French holidays; call before your visit.

Conceived by the Mitterrand administration, **Cité de la Musique ★★★**, 221 av. Jean-Jaurès, 19e (© **01-44-84-45-00** for tickets and information; www.cite-musique. fr; Métro: Porte-de-Pantin), has been widely applauded. At the city's northeastern edge in what used to be a run-down neighborhood, the $120-million stone-and-glass structure, designed by Christian de Portzamparc, incorporates a network of concert halls, a library, a research center, and a museum. The complex hosts a variety of concerts, ranging from Renaissance to 20th-century programs. As an added convenience, they offer a bus service to various locations within Paris after evening concerts.

Picasso and Utrillo once patronized **Au Lapin Agile,** 22 rue des Saules, 18e (© **01-46-06-85-87;** www.au-lapin-agile.com; Métro: Lamarck-Caulaincourt), formerly known as the Cabaret des Assassins and housed in a cottage near the top of Montmartre. For decades, it has been the heart of French folk music. You'll sit at wooden tables in a dimly lit room with walls covered by bohemian memorabilia, listening to French folk tunes, love ballads, army songs, and sea chanteys. It's open Tuesday through Sunday nights from 9pm to 2am, with a cover charge of 24€ (17€ for students), which includes the first drink.

The **Crazy Horse Saloon,** 12 av. George-V, 8e (© **01-47-23-32-32;** www. lecrazyhorseparis.com; Métro: George-V or Alma-Marceau), a sophisticated strip joint, has thrived for decades, thanks to good choreography and a sly, flirty theme that celebrates and exalts the female form. Shows are Sunday through Friday 8:15 and 10:45pm; Saturday 7, 9:30, and 11:45pm, and last just under 2 hours. The **Folies-Bergère,** 32 rue Richer, 9e (© **01-44-79-98-90;** www.foliesbergere.com; Métro: Grands-Boulevards or Cadet), is a Paris institution; foreign visitors have been flocking here since 1886. Don't expect the naughty permissive skin-and-glitter revue that used to be the trademark of this place—today it's a conventional 1,600-seat theater devoted to a frequently changing roster of big-stage performances, in French, many of which are adaptations of Broadway blockbusters. Hours and days of spectacles vary according to the performance, but shows are usually Tuesday through Saturday at 9pm and Sunday at 3pm.

As it moves deeper into the millennium, **Lido de Paris,** 116 bis av. des Champs-Elysées, 8e (© **01-40-76-56-10;** www.lido.fr; Métro: George-V), has changed its feathers and modernized its shows. Its $15-million production, *C'est Magique,* reflects a dramatic reworking of the classic Parisian cabaret show, with eye-popping special effects, water technology using more than 60,000 gallons per minute, even aerial and aquatic ballet.

Moulin Rouge, 82 bd. de Clichy, 18e (© **01-53-09-82-82;** www.moulinrouge.fr; Métro: Blanche), is a camp classic with a long history of famous performers, events, and visitors—including King Edward VI and Queen Elizabeth II. Try to get a table, as the view is much better on the main floor than from the bar. Handsome men and girls, girls, girls—virtually all topless—keep the place going. Dance finales usually include two dozen belles ripping loose with a topless cancan. Revues are nightly at 9 and 11pm.

Some Paris watchers consider **Nouveau Casino,** 109 rue Oberkamp, 9e (© **01-43-57-57-40;** www.nouveaucasino.net; Métro: Parmentier, or Ménilmontant), the epitome of the counterculture and hyperhip context that blossoms along the rue Oberkampf nightly. Every weeknight live concerts (tickets 16€–27€) take place between 8pm and 1am; and Thursday, Friday, and Saturday, the party continues from 1am till dawn with a DJ who spins out some of the most avant-garde dance music in Paris.

Jazz lovers go to **Baiser Salé,** 58 rue des Lombards, 1er (© **01-42-33-37-71;** www.lebaisersale.com; Métro: Châtelet), a cellar transformed with its jazz-related paintings, large bar, and an ongoing roster of videos that show great jazz players (Charlie Parker, Miles Davis) of the past. Everything is mellow and laid-back, with an emphasis on the music. There's a cover Tuesday through Sunday of 8€ (18€ after 10pm). Sometimes French jazz aficionados refer to the jazz club and restaurant **Le Petit Journal,** 71 bd. St-Michel, 5e (© **01-43-26-28-59;** www.petitjournalsaint michel.com; RER: Luxembourg), by its English name—"The Small Newspaper of Saint-Michel." The club lies in the center of the Latin Quarter, opposite the Garden of Luxembourg. Created in 1971, it is the "high temple" in Paris for the jazz of New Orleans. Some of the country's top artists appear here, including Claude Bolling. The music is downstairs in the cellar. Open Monday to Saturday 9:15pm to 2am. The cover (17€–20€) includes a drink; you can also try dinner and a show here for 48€ to 53€.

If you are in the mood for dancing, go to **Batofar ★,** facing 11 quai François Mauriac, 13e (© **01-53-14-76-59;** www.batofar.org; Métro: Quai de la Gare). Self-consciously proud of its status as a club that virtually everybody views as hip, Batofar is housed in a converted barge that floats on the Seine, sometimes filled with hundreds of gyrating dancers, most of whom are in their 20s and 30s. In the music department, you'll find house, garage, techno, reggae, hip-hop, and live jazz from musicians from around the world. It's generally open Tuesday to Saturday from 10pm to 6am. The cost (always reasonable— beer costs around 8.50€) and hours vary depending on bands, DJs, dance classes, and special events. Call or check out their website in advance. Established in 1936, **La Balajo,** 9 rue de Lappe, 11e (© **01-47-00-07-87;** www.balajo.fr; Métro: Bastille), is the place where Edith Piaf won the hearts of Parisian music lovers. Evenings attract a younger crowd (age 20–35-ish), who groove to a mixture, depending on the DJ, of house, garage, techno, and old-fashioned disco. Open Tuesday to Thursday 7pm to 2am, Friday and Saturday 11pm to 6am, and Sunday 3 to 7pm. **Les Bains Douches,** 7 rue du Bourg-l'Abbé, 3e (© **01-53-01-40-60;** www.lesbainsdouches.net; Métro: Etienne Marcel), got its name thanks to this hot spot's former life as a Turkish bath. Dancing begins at midnight, and a supper club–like restaurant is located upstairs, open Wednesday to Sunday. Meals cost 32€ to 120€. On certain nights, this is the hottest party atmosphere in Paris, and Mondays are increasingly gay. Open from 9pm to 2am.

Many Parisians now prefer the wine bar to the traditional cafe or bistro—the food is often better and the ambience more inviting. **Au Sauvignon,** 80 rue des Sts-Pères, 7e (© **01-45-48-49-02;** Métro: Sèvres-Babylone or Saint Sulpiee), is a tiny corner spot with tables overflowing onto a covered terrace and a decor featuring old ceramic tiles and frescoes done by Left Bank artists. Wines range from the cheapest Beaujolais to the most expensive Puligny-Montrachet. A glass of wine costs 4.50€ to 6€. To go with your wine, choose an Auvergne specialty, such as goat cheese or a terrine. Fresh Poilâne bread is ideal with ham, pâté, or goat cheese. Hours are Monday to Saturday from 8am to 10pm (closed in Aug). Engagingly old-fashioned, with an agreeable staff and food prepared fresh every day, the wine bar **Le Sancerre,** 22 av. Rapp, 7e (© **01-45-51-75-91;** Métro: Alma-Marceau), specializes in vintages from the Loire Valley and Sancerre. The latter, produced in red, rosé, and white, is known for its not-too-dry fruity aroma and legions of fans who believe it should be more celebrated. Other wine choices are from the Loire Valley, Burgundy, the Ardèche Valley in France's southwest, and the Beaujolais. Food items usually include *andouillettes* (chitterling sausages), omelets with flap mushrooms, fresh oysters, and quiche. Glasses of wine cost 3€ to 6€; simple platters of food cost 8€ to 10€ each. Open Monday to Friday 8am to 4pm and 6:30 to

11pm, Saturday 8:30am to 4pm. **Willi's Wine Bar** ★★, 13 rue des Petits-Champs, 1er (✆ **01-42-61-05-09;** www.williswinebar.com; Métro: Bourse, Pyramides, or Palais-Royal), offers about 300 kinds of wine, including a dozen "wine specials" you can taste by the glass for 4€ to 18€. Daily specials are likely to include lamb brochette with cumin or Lyonnais sausage in truffled vinaigrette, plus a spectacular dessert such as chocolate terrine. A fixed-price menu runs 21€ to 27€. The restaurant is open from Monday to Saturday noon to 2:30pm and 7 to 11pm.

Barrio Latino, 46 rue du Faubourg St-Antoine, 12e (✆ **01-55-78-84-75;** www. buddhabar.com; Métro: Bastille), is a multistory emporium of good times, Gallic flair, and Latino charm. Tapas bars, dance floors, and a Latino restaurant each take up a different floor. The restaurant specializes in food that French palates find refreshing: Argentine steaks, Brazilian *feijoada* (a bean-based dish that's similar to cassoulet), and Mexican chili, all of which taste wonderful with beer, caipirinhas, *Cuba libres,* or rum punches. The clientele is mixed, mostly straight, partly gay, and 100% blasé about matters such as an individual's sexuality. Open daily noon to 2am. **Harry's New York Bar** ★, 5 rue Daunou, 2e (✆ **01-42-61-71-14;** www.harrys-bar.fr; Métro: Opéra), was opened on Thanksgiving Day 1911 by an expat named MacElhone. It's the spot where members of the World War I ambulance corps drank themselves silly. In addition to being Hemingway's favorite, Harry's is where the White Lady and sidecar cocktails were invented; it's also the alleged birthplace of the bloody mary and the headquarters of a loosely organized fraternity of drinkers known as the International Bar Flies (IBF). A softer, somewhat less macho ambience reigns in the cellar, where a pianist provides music. Open daily noon to 2am.

An Excursion to Versailles

The town of Versailles, 13 miles (21km) southwest of Paris, is a stodgily formal place, but the palace here is the sight of a lifetime.

GETTING THERE To get to Versailles, catch the **RER** line C1 at the Gare d'Austerlitz, St-Michel, Musée d'Orsay, Invalides, Ponte de l'Alma, Champ de Mars, or Javel stop, and take it to the Versailles-Rive Gauche station, from which the château is a 5-minute walk. The RER departs every 15 minutes, and the trip takes about 35 to 40 minutes. Railpass holders travel free on the RER but need to show their pass at the ticket kiosk near any RER entrance to get an RER ticket. Or you can take one of the regular **SNCF trains** that make frequent runs from Gare St-Lazare and Gare Montparnasse in Paris to Versailles: Trains departing from Gare St-Lazare arrive at the Versailles/Rive Droite railway station; trains departing from Gare Montparnasse arrive at Versailles Chantiers station, a long walk from the château.

VISITOR INFORMATION The **Office de Tourisme** is at 2 bis av. de Paris (✆ **01-39-24-88-88;** fax 01-39-24-88-89; www.versailles-tourisme.com), a short walk from the rail station and close to the main entrance to Versailles. Open April to September Tuesday to Sunday 9am to 7pm, Monday 10am to 6pm; October to March Tuesday to Saturday 9am to 6pm, Sunday and Monday 11am to 5pm.

TOP ATTRACTIONS & SPECIAL MOMENTS

The unbelievably vast **Château de Versailles** ★★★ (✆ **01-30-83-78-00;** www. chateauversailles.fr) is as ornately artificial as a jewel box. Here the kings of France built a whole glittering private world for themselves, as remote from the grime and noise and bustle of Paris as a gilded planet. Begun in 1661, the construction of the château involved 32,000 to 45,000 workmen, some of whom had to drain marshes— often at the cost of their lives—and move forests. Louis XIV set out to create a palace that would awe all Europe, and the result was a symbol of pomp and opulence that was to be copied, yet never quite duplicated.

For viewing purposes, the palace is divided up into sections. The first section features the six magnificent **Grands Appartements ★★★**, done in the Louis XIV style; each takes its name from the allegorical painting on its ceiling. The most famous room in this section is the recently restored 2,323-foot (697m) **Hall of Mirrors ★★★** (where the Treaty of Versailles was signed). Begun by Mansart in 1678, it was decorated by Le Brun with 17 large arched windows matched by beveled mirrors in simulated arcades.

Highlights in other sections include the **Opera House ★★**, designed by Gabriel for Louis XV in 1748, though it wasn't completed until 1770. Also of interest are the **apartments of Mme. de Pompadour,** the queen's private suites, the salons, the **Royal Chapel,** and the **Museum of the History of France.**

The Grands Appartements, the Royal Chapel, and the Hall of Mirrors can be visited without a guide. There are various opening times for other parts of the château. Seeing all of it can take up an entire morning and leave you pretty exhausted.

For a little relaxation, head for the **Gardens of Versailles ★★★**. This park is the ultimate in French landscaping perfection—every tree, shrub, flower, and hedge disciplined into a frozen ballet pattern and blended with soaring fountains, sparkling little lakes, grandiose steps, and hundreds of marble statues. Try to save time to visit the **Grand Trianon ★★**, which is a good walk across the park. The pink-and-white marble structure was designed by Hardouin-Mansart for Louis XIV in 1687. You can also visit the **Petit Trianon ★★**, which was built by Gabriel in 1768 as a retreat for Louis XV and his mistress, Mme. du Barry. Later on, it was the favorite residence of Marie Antoinette, who could escape the rigors of court here.

The latest attraction is the **Grande Ecourie,** the stables of Louis XIV. For 2 centuries, these historic stables have been closed to the public. They once housed more than 600 horses of the king. Today they are home to 20 cream-colored Lusitanian horses from Portugal. Visitors are taken on a brief guided tour and then witness morning dressage demonstrations.

The château is open from April to October Tuesday through Sunday from 9am to 6pm (5pm the rest of the year). It's closed Christmas and New Year's Day. The grounds are open daily from dawn to dusk; the Trianons are open from noon to 6pm Tuesday to Sunday. Individual attractions may have earlier opening and closing times.

Call or visit the website for a complete fee schedule (which varies, depending on which attractions you visit and the time of year). An unguided day pass covering many of the attractions, including an audio guide, costs 15€, free for ages 18 and under. A visit to both Trianons is 10€ for adults and free for anyone 26 and under.

THE LOIRE VALLEY ★★★

Val de Loire, the Loire Valley, is known popularly around the world as "châteaux country." Bordered by vineyards, the winding Loire Valley cuts through the soft contours of the land of castles deep in the heart of France. When royalty and nobility built châteaux throughout this valley during the Renaissance, sumptuousness was uppermost in their minds. An era of excessive pomp reigned here until Henri IV moved his court to Paris.

The Valley of the Loire has also played a major part in the national consciousness. Joan of Arc, the maid of Orléans, came this way looking for her dauphin, finding him at Chinon. A now-legendary list of mistresses, ranging from Agnés Sorel (the mistress of Charles VII) to Diane du Poitiers (the mistress of Henri II), were carried from castle to castle. In his heyday, the Chevalier King brought Leonardo da Vinci from Florence, installing him at Amboise. Catherine de Médici and her "flying squadron" of beauties, Henry III and his handsome minions—these historical figures and events make for a rich tapestry.

The Loire has a fascinating tale to tell. Its sights and curiosities are multifarious, ranging from Renaissance, medieval, and classical châteaux to residences where Balzac wrote or Rabelais lived, to Romanesque and Gothic churches, to Roman ramparts, to art treasures. Attempts to explore the valley in 2 to 3 days are doomed, but that is all the time most rail passengers have to spare. If your schedule can accommodate it, allow at least a week. Autumn or spring is ideal for a visit, though most of the intriguing *son-et-lumiére* (sound-and-light) programs take place in summer when the châteaux are floodlit and their stories are told.

The cities of **Orléans, Tours,** and **Blois,** all within easy rail reach of Paris, are the major transportation hubs for the Loire Valley. Tours makes the best base because it is better connected by rail and public transport to the major châteaux: **Chenonceau, Amboise, Azay-le-Rideau, Chambord,** and **Blois.**

Orléans ★

Orléans suffered heavy damage in World War II, so those hoping to see how it looked when the Maid of Orléans was here are likely to be disappointed. However, the reconstruction of Orléans has been judiciously planned, with many rewarding targets.

Orléans is the chief town of Loiret, on the Loire River, 74 miles (119km) southwest of Paris. Joan of Arc freed the city in 1429 from the attacks of the Burgundians and the English. That deliverance is celebrated every year on May 8, the anniversary of her victory. An equestrian statue of Joan of Arc stands in the **Place du Martroi,** which was created by Foyatier in 1855.

From that square, you can head down the **rue Royale**—rebuilt in the 18th-century style—across the **Pont George V,** erected in 1760. After crossing the bridge, you'll have a good view of the town. A simple cross marks the site of the Fort des Tourelles, which Joan of Arc and her men captured.

GETTING THERE Ten trains per day arrive from Paris's Gare d'Austerlitz (trip time: 1 hr., 15 min.). Make sure it is an express train, as some require a transfer. The ticket can be purchased through Rail Europe. There are also a dozen connections from Tours (trip time: 50 min.). From Tours, it's 17€ to 25€. The Orléans station is about a 10- to 15-minute walk from the town center.

VISITOR INFORMATION The **Office de Tourisme** is at 2 place de l'Etape (② **02-38-24-05-05;** www.tourisme-orleans.com), connected to the town hall, which is across from the cathedral. Hours vary by month, but the office, on average, is open from 10am to 2pm, 3 to 5pm.

TOP ATTRACTIONS & SPECIAL MOMENTS

In the heart of town stands **Cathédrale Ste-Croix ★**, place Ste-Croix (② **02-38-77-87-50**), begun in 1287 in the High Gothic style, although burned by the Huguenots in 1568. The first stone on the present building was laid by Henry IV in 1601, and work continued on the cathedral until 1829. Inside, the church of the Holy Cross contains a gigantic 17th-century organ and some magnificent 18th-century woodwork in the chancel. You'll need a guide to tour the chancel, the crypt, and the treasury, with its Byzantine enamels and textiles, its 15th- and 16th-century goldwork, and its Limoges enamels. Admission is free, but you should tip the tour guide 1€. Visitors are welcome at daily services. Hours from May to September are 9:15am to 6pm. In October to April, the hours are 9:15am to noon and 2:15 to 5pm.

Hôtel Groslot, place de l'Etape (northwest of the cathedral, across from the town hall; © **02-38-79-22-30**), is a Renaissance mansion begun in 1550 and embellished in the 19th century. François II (first husband of Mary, Queen of Scots) lived in it during the fall of 1560 and died on December 5 of the same year. Between the revolution and the mid-1970s, it functioned as the town hall. Marriage ceremonies, performed by the town's magistrates, still occur here. Romance is nothing new to this building: It was here that Charles IX met his lovely Marie Touchet. The statue of Joan of Arc praying (at the foot of the flight of steps) was the work of Louis Phillipe's daughter, Princess Marie d'Orléans. In the charming garden in the back, you can see remains of the 15th-century Chapelle St-Jacques. Admission is free, and guided tours in French and English are offered every hour on the hour. Open July to September Monday to Friday 9am to 6pm, October to June Monday to Friday and Sunday from 10am to noon and 2 to 6pm.

After visiting the Groslot, you can backtrack to the cathedral square and walk down rue Jeanne-d'Arc, across rue Royale, to see a small museum dedicated to Orléans's favorite mademoiselle, the **Maison Jeanne-d'Arc,** 3 place de Gaulle (© **02-38-52-99-89;** www.jeannedarc.com.fr). The house is a 20th-century reproduction of the 15th-century house where Joan of Arc, the liberator and patron of Orléans, stayed during her local heroics. The original house was destroyed by bombing in 1940. The first floor has temporary exhibitions, and the second and third floors contain Joan-related models and memorabilia. Admission is 2€ adults, 1€ seniors and students, free for children under 17. Hours are May 2 to October 31 Tuesday to Sunday 10am to 12:30pm and 1:30 to 6:30pm, November 2 to April 30 Tuesday to Sunday 1:30 to 6pm.

The **Musée des Beaux-Arts ★★**, 1 rue Fernand-Rabier (© **02-38-79-21-55**), occupies the 16th-century town hall, known as Hôtel des Créneaux. It mainly houses French works from the 15th to 19th centuries. Some of the art here once hung in Richelieu's château. Other pieces include busts by Pigalle and a fine array of portraits, including one of Mme. de Pompadour, of whom, when she crossed the Pont George V, the people of the town remarked, "Our bridge has just borne France's heaviest weight." The collection also includes works by Flemish and Dutch artists, as well as a lovely Velásquez. Admission is 3€ adults, 1.50€ students, and free for children 15 and under. Hours are Tuesday to Sunday 10am to 6pm.

WHERE TO STAY & DINE

Hôtel d'Arc, 37 rue de la République, 45000 Orléans (© **02-38-53-10-94;** www. hoteldarc.fr), a 35-room hotel with an Art Deco facade, sits in the middle of the town center and is close to nearly everything, including the train station and the city's pedestrian-only shopping streets. The 1920s structure has been considerably modernized; its average-size bedrooms are tastefully furnished. Avoid rooms facing rue de la République—they tend to be noisy. Rates are 99€ to 163€ double. This hotel does not have a restaurant, but serves breakfast.

If you seek more modern comfort, **Hôtel Mercure Orléans ★**, 44-46 quai Barentin, 45000 Orléans (© **02-38-62-17-39;** www.mercure.com), is the town's finest address. Along the river, adjacent to pont Joffre, this 111-room bandbox structure is within walking distance of place du Martroi and its Joan of Arc statue. The air-conditioned bedrooms are done in an impersonal chain style but are nevertheless comfortable and inviting. Rates are 133€ to 163€ double.

La Vieille Auberge ★, 2 rue du Faubourg St-Vincent (© **02-38-53-55-81;** http://la-vieille-auberge.net), is one of the most dignified-looking and best restaurants in Orléans. Menu items include sophisticated treatments of Loire Valley whitefish, game, and local produce, all accompanied by regional Loire wines that blend well with the cuisine. Main courses cost 18€ to 35€, and a fixed-price menu is offered at 25€ for lunch and 35€ to 49€ for dinner. Closed Sunday nights. Reservations are recommended.

La Mangeoire, 28 rue de Poirier (© **02-38-68-15-38;** www.lamangeoire.fr), is a bistro usually filled with lively locals who are not in a hurry. Owner/chef Florent

Orléans

To Etampes

Gare | To Chartres & Paris

PARC
LOUIS
PASTEUR

place de Gambetta

bd. de Verdun

Bus Station

place Albert-1er

rue E. Vignat

rue du Faubourg St-Vincent

Paris
Orléans
FRANCE

rue Jules Lemaître

bd. de Alexandre Martin

1

rue Bannier

rue de la République

rue d'Alsace-Lorraine

la Bretonnerie

rue R. Chollet

0   200 yds
0   200 m

8

bd. St-Euverte

place de l'Etape

rue du Bourdon Blanc

place du Martroi

rue d'Escures

Hôtel Groslot (i)

rue Dupanloup

place Ste-Croix 7

Cathédrale Ste-Croix

place du Gén de Gaulle

rue Jeanne d'Arc

place Abbé Desnoyes

Musée Historique

Maison Jeanne d'Arc 2

Musée des Beaux-Arts 5

rue de Bourgogne

rue de Bourgogne

To Sens & Gien

rue Royale

4

rue de la Tour Neuve

Eglise St-Aignan

To Blois & Tours

place du Châtelet

Nouvelle Halle

quai Cypierre

quai du Châtelet

quai du Fort-Alleaume

pont George-V

Loire

Church

Information (i)

Post Office

ACCOMMODATIONS ■

Hôtel d'Arc 1

Mercure Orléans Centre 3

DINING ◆

La Vieille Auberge 8

La Mangeoire 4

ATTRACTIONS ●

Cathédrale Ste-Croix 7

Hôtel Groslot 6

Maison Jeanne-d'Arc 2

Musée des Beaux-Arts 5

Dubois uses his American-influenced culinary skills to create plate-sized "tartines," a grilled open-faced sandwich loaded with combinations of melted cheeses, meats, and potatoes. Fish, pasta dishes, and large salads are also popular. Main courses cost 10€ to 16€. Closed Sundays. (Dubois also owns the new **BaraFlor,** quai du Chatelet, on the promenade; it's connected to a 19th-century replica paddleboat, adding a little dash of New Orleans to the original Orléans.)

Tours ★

With a population of 138,000, Tours is known for its fine food and wine. Although without a major château itself, this industrial and residential city is the traditional center for exploring the Loire Valley.

At the heart of the châteaux country, Tours is 144 miles (232km) southwest of Paris and 70 miles (113km) southwest of Orléans. At the junction of the Loire and Cher rivers, it was one of the great pilgrimage sites of Europe in the Middle Ages. The townspeople are fond of pointing out that Tours, not Paris, is actually the logical site for the capital of France. And it virtually *was* the capital in June 1940, when Churchill flew here to meet with Paul Reynaud during World War II.

Because many of the city's buildings were bombed in World War II, 20th-century apartment towers have taken the place of stately châteaux. It is, however, still at the doorstep of some of the most magnificent châteaux in France. And while most Loire Valley towns are rather sleepy, Tours is where the action is, as you'll see by its noisy streets and cafes. A quarter of the residents are students, who add a vibrant touch to the city.

GETTING THERE   **Trains** to Tours/St. Pierre des Corps depart from Paris from two stations, Gare Montparnasse and Gare d'Austerlitz. The quickest transits are usually from Gare Montparnasse, departure point for as many as 14 TGV trains per day, charging 29€ to 49€ one-way for the 70-minute trip. Most of the conventional— slower—trains to Tours depart from the Gare d'Austerlitz. Transit time on these trains is about 2½ hours.

Many, but not all, of the conventional (non-TGV) trains pull into the center of Tours, at the Gare Tours Centre Ville, place du Maréchal-Leclerc, 3 rue Edouard-Vaillant. Some conventional trains and virtually all the TGV trains, however, arrive at the isolated railway station of Tours/St-Pierre-des-Corps, about 3¾ miles (6km) east of the center of Tours. If your train drops you off here, know in advance that at least one (and, during peak hours, several) *navette* (shuttle train) awaits every TGV train for free ongoing transport to the center of Tours.

VISITOR INFORMATION   The **Office de Tourisme** is at 78–82 rue Bernard-Palissy (© **02-47-70-37-37;** www.ligeris.com), just across the place du Géneral-Leclerc from the train station (with the large blue fluorescent lights). Hours April to September are Monday to Friday 8:30am to 7pm, and Sunday 10am to 12:30pm and 2:30 to 5pm. From October to March, hours are Monday to Friday 9am to 12:30pm and 1:30 to 6pm, Sunday 10am to 1pm.

TOP ATTRACTIONS & SPECIAL MOMENTS

Cathédrale St-Gatien, 5 place de la Cathédrale (© **02-47-70-21-00**), the chief attraction of Tours, honors an evangelist of the 3rd century. Its facade is in the flamboyant Gothic style, flanked by two towers, the bases of which date from the 12th century, although the lanterns are Renaissance. The choir was built in the 13th century, with new additions taking place up until the 16th century. Sheltered inside is the handsome 16th-century tomb of the children of Charles VIII. Some of the stained-glass windows, the building's glory, date from the 13th century. Admission is free, and hours are daily 9am to 7pm until 8pm in July and August.

The **Musée des Beaux-Arts,** 18 place François-Sicard (© **02-47-05-68-73**), is housed in an archbishop's palace of the 17th and 18th centuries, complete with Louis XVI woodwork and Tours silk-damask hangings. Among the foreign acquisitions, the most outstanding paintings are Mantegna's *Christ in the Garden of Olives* and *The Resurrection.* Other foreign works include an early Rembrandt (*Flight into Egypt*), plus canvases by Rubens, Luca Giordano, and Mattäus Günther. The French school is represented by Le Sueur, Fouquet, Boucher, Vernet, Vuillard, David, Ingres, Degas (*Calvary*), Delacroix (*Comedians and Buffoons*), and Monet. The most important sculpture is by Houdon and Lemoyne. Free entrance to gardens daily from 7am to 8:30pm. Admission to the museum is 4€ adults, 2€ students and seniors, free for children under 13. Hours are Wednesday to Monday 9am to 12:45pm and 2 to 6pm.

WHERE TO STAY & DINE

The **Best Western Le Central,** 21 rue Berthelot, 37000 Tours (© **800/528-1234** in the U.S. and Canada, or 02-47-05-46-44; www.bestwestern.com), is within walking distance of the river and cathedral, surrounded by gardens, lawns, and trees. Built

Tours

ACCOMMODATIONS ■
Best Western Le Central **1**
Hôtel du Manoir **5**

DINING ◆
La Roche le Roy **6**
Le Petit Patrimoine **2**

ATTRACTIONS ●
Cathédrale St-Gatien **3**
Musée des Beaux-Arts **4**

8

FRANCE | The Loire Valley

in 1850, this 37-room hotel is a modest but economical choice, with homey bed-rooms that come in a variety of shapes and sizes, all of them renovated in 2003. About half the bathrooms have showers only. Rates are 92€ to 152€ double.

The 19th-century **Hôtel du Manoir,** 2 rue Traversière, 37000 Tours (© **02-47-05-37-37;** www.hotel-manoir-tours.federal-hotel.com), is situated on a quiet street near the train station, shops, and restaurants. This 20-room family-run residence provides guests with a comfortable, cheerful place to stay. The midsize bedrooms offer simple furnishings and lots of windows; half the bathrooms have showers only. Rates run 56€ to 70€ double; take bus 3 or 70.

One of the hottest chefs in town, Alain Couturier, blends new and old techniques at **La Roche le Roy ★★**, 55 rte. St-Avertin (© **02-47-27-22-00;** www.rocheleroy. com), in a steep-gabled 18th-century manor south of the town center. Couturier's repertoire includes such delights as scalloped foie gras with lentils, cod with saffron cream, and pan-fried scallops with truffle vinaigrette. Main courses run 28€ to 32€. To get here, follow avenue Grammot south from town center until you pass over a bridge and the street becomes route St-Avertin. Reservations are recommended, and the hours are Tuesday to Saturday noon to 1:30pm and 7:30 to 9:30pm; closed 1 week in February and 3 weeks in August.

Le Petit Patrimoine, 58 rue Colbert (℃ **02-47-66-05-81**), is small, cozy, and extremely popular with locals as well as tourists. Generous-sized regional dishes include *rillons* (similar to bacon) and *chèvre* (goat's cheese)—both of which are in their specialty pie, the *torte Tourangelle aux rillons.* For dessert, try the local *poire tapée de Rivarennes* (reyhdrated pears with red wine). Main courses cost 12€ to 17€; the fixed-price menu is 13€ for lunch and 17€ to 24€ for dinner. Reservations are strongly recommended (at least a day in advance).

Excursions from Tours

If you wish to see at least five or six of the greatest châteaux in Europe (previewed below), Tours is your best choice as a transportation hub, although some connections can be a bit difficult and are not always via a rail line. Once you land on your feet in these Loire towns, you can go immediately to the châteaux without feeling you're missing out on a lot of other attractions.

AZAY-LE-RIDEAU

This sleepy little town is 13 miles (21km) southwest of Tours. Now named after its château, the village was once known as Azay-le-Brûlé, or "Azay the Burnt." Passing through with his court in 1418, the dauphin, later Charles VII, was insulted by the Burgundians. The result: A whole garrison was killed and the village and its fortress razed. Today's château was built upon the ruins of the destroyed structure.

GETTING THERE   To reach Azay-le-Rideau, take the **train** from Tours or Chinon. From either starting point, the trip time is about 30 minutes; the one-way fare is 4.40€ from Chinon, 4.90€ from Tours. Tours has express service to Paris. For SNCF bus and rail schedules to Azay-le-Rideau, call ℃ **36-35.**

Because trains arrive at Azay-le-Rideau's railway station in relatively small numbers (only during the morning and evening rush hours weekdays, all-day Sat, and only evenings on Sun), some visitors prefer to travel to the railway station at nearby Tours, switching to any of the frequent buses between Tours's railway station and Azay. TER, a subsidiary of the SNCF, operates the route and charges 4.50€ each way. For more information, call ℃ **08-92-35-35-35.** There's no public transport, but visitors can call a **taxi** (℃ **02-47-45-26-26**).

VISITOR INFORMATION   The **Office de Tourisme** (in the town center) is on 5 place de l'Europe (℃ **02-47-45-44-40;** www.ot-paysazaylerideau.com). July and August hours are Monday to Saturday 9am to 7pm and Sunday 10am to 6pm. June and September hours are Monday to Saturday 9am to 1pm and 2 to 6pm, and Sunday 10am to 1pm and 2 to 7pm. From October to May, the office is closed on Sundays and bank holidays.

Top Attractions & Special Moments

Château d'Azay-le-Rideau ★★, 19 rue Balzac, Azay-le-Rideau 37190 (℃ **02-47-45-42-04;** www.monum.fr), despite its medieval appearance and defensive architecture, was actually created as a private residence during the Renaissance.

Gilles Berthelot, the financial minister of François I, built the château beginning in 1518. Actually, his big-spending wife, Phillipa, supervised its construction. So elegant and harmonious, so imposing was their creation that the Chevalier King grew immensely jealous. In time, Berthelot fled and the château reverted to the king. François I didn't live there, however, but started the custom of granting it to "friends of the crown." After a brief residency by Prince Frederick of Prussia in 1870, the château became the property of the state in 1905.

In the hills of Vouvray, 8 miles (13km) from Tours and 7 miles (11km) from Amboise, the 15th-century **Château de Jallanges**, 37210 Vouvray (ⓒ **02-47-52-06-66;** www.jallanges.com), is a journey into the past. With seven spacious rooms/suites (including bathrooms) and access to beautiful gardens, an outdoor heated pool (June–Sept), and good access to some of the Loire Valley's most well-known châteaux (they're all within 25 miles/40km), you're certain to feel like royalty if you stay here. Carriage rides through Vouvray vineyards, hot-air balloon and helicopter excursions, and wine tastings of local wines can all be arranged by request.

Rates run 135€ to 190€ double, 170€ to 20€ for a suite (a buffet breakfast is included). The closest train station is St-Pierre-de-Corps (the hotel can arrange taxi pickup for 15€–20€), outside of Tours; your best option, however, would be to rent a car using the **France Rail 'n Drive Pass** (p. 249).

Before you enter, circle the mansion, enjoying its near-perfect proportions, the crowning achievement of the French Renaissance in Touraine. Architecturally, its most fancifully ornate feature is a great bay enclosing a grand stairway with a straight flight of steps.

The largest room, the **Banqueting Hall,** is adorned with four 17th-century Flemish tapestries representing scenes from the life of Constantine (it took a craftsperson 1 year just to weave 4 sq. ft./.35 sq. m). In the kitchen is a collection of utensils, including a wooden mold capable of making 45 designs on cakes.

In the dining room is a trio of 16th-century Flemish tapestries. The fireplace is only a plaster molding of a chimney piece made by Rodin for the Château of Montal. The fireplace masterpiece, however, is in a ground-floor bedroom containing a 16th-century four-poster bed. Over the stone fireplace hovers a salamander, the symbol of François I.

The château is open daily during July and August from 9:30am to 7pm, April to June and September from 9:30am to 6pm, and October to March from 10am to 12:30pm and 2 to 5:30pm. Admission is 8€ for adults and 5€ for ages 18 to 25 and seniors, free for children under 18. Allow 2 hours for a visit. From May to July, *son-et-lumière* (sound and light) performances (1½ hr.), with recorded music and lights beaming on the celebrated exterior of the château, begin at 10:30pm nightly from May to September. Tickets are 9€ for adults, 5€ for ages 12 to 25, and free for those under 12.

AMBOISE

On the banks of the Loire, Amboise is a real Renaissance town in the center of vineyards known as Touraine-Amboise. Leonardo da Vinci spent his last years in this ancient city at **Clos Lucé.** Dominating the town is the **Château of Amboise,** the first in France to reflect the impact of the Italian Renaissance. Amboise is the most important day trip from Tours. *Note:* Because it is so beautiful, tour buses overrun it, especially in summer. The town is 22 miles (35km) east of Tours and 136 miles (219km) southwest of Paris.

GETTING THERE   Amboise lies on the main Paris–Blois–Tours rail line, with about a dozen trains per day arriving from both Tours and Blois (see below). The trip from Tours takes about 20 minutes and costs 4.80€ one-way; the trip from Blois also takes 20 minutes and costs 6€. About five conventional trains per day depart from Paris's Gare d'Austerlitz from Paris (trip time: 3 hr.), and many TGV trains leave from the Gare Montparnasse for St-Pierre-des-Corps (trip time: 1 hr., 15 min.), less than a ½ mile (1km) from Tours. From St-Pierre-des-Corps, you can transfer to a conventional train bound for Amboise. One-way fares from Paris to Amboise cost 27€.

VISITOR INFORMATION The **Office de Tourisme,** quai du Général-de-Gaulle (© **02-47-57-09-28;** www.amboise-valdeloire.com), is open October to June Monday to Saturday 9am to 7pm, Sunday 10am to 1pm and 2 to 5pm; July and August Monday to Saturday 9:30am to 7pm, Sunday 10am to 6pm.To get here from the train station, walk across the bridge over the river and turn right. Be sure to visit the *marché* (marketplace) nearby, if you have time. The château is a short walk away. *Note:* The office sells a discount pass (skip lines!) that includes Château Royal d'Amboise, Clos Lucé, and Château de Chenonceau. Admission runs 29€.

Top Attractions & Special Moments

Château Royal d'Amboise ★★ (© **02-47-57-00-98;** www.chateau-amboise. com) is a combination of Gothic and Renaissance architecture. This 15th-century château suffered during the French Revolution (only about a quarter of the original structure remains) and is mainly associated with Charles VIII, who built it on a rock spur separating the valleys of the Loire and the Amasse. Born at Amboise on June 30, 1470, Charles returned to France at the age of 25 following an Italian campaign. With him, he brought artists, designers, and architects from "that land of enchantment." In a sense, he brought the Italian Renaissance to France.

You visit first the flamboyant Gothic **Chapel of St. Hubert,** distinguished by its lacelike tracery. It allegedly contains the remains of da Vinci. Actually, the great artist was buried in the castle's Collegiate Church, which was destroyed between 1806 and 1810. During the Second Empire, excavations were undertaken on the site of the church, and bones discovered were "identified" as those of Leonardo.

The **Logis du roi (the king's apartment),** its facade, pierced by large double mullioned windows and crowned by towering dormers and sculptured canopies, survived the Revolution intact. Alas, Charles VIII's own apartment caused his death: He died at Amboise on April 8, 1498, after accidentally banging his head against a wall. At the end of the terrace, near the room of his queen, Anne of Brittany, is a low doorway where it is said the mishap took place. These rooms are now open to visitors.

Adjoining the apartment are two squat towers, the Hurtalt and the Minimes, which contain ramps of huge dimensions so that cavaliers on horseback or nobles in horse-drawn chariots could ascend them.

Today the walls of the château are hung with tapestries, the rooms furnished in the style of "La Belle Epoque." From the terraces are panoramic views of the town and the Loire Valley. Admission is 9.70€ adults, 8.30€ students, 6.30€ children ages 7 to 14, free for children 6 and under. Hours are daily as follows: January 2 to 31 9am to 12:30pm and 2 to 4:45pm, February 9am to 12:30pm and 1:30 to 5pm, March 9am to 5:30pm, April to June 9am to 6:30pm, July to August 9am to 7pm, September to November 15 9am to 5:30pm, and November 16 to December 31 9am to 12:30pm and 2 to 4:45pm.

Château du Clos-Lucé ★, 2 rue de Clos-Lucé (© **02-47-57-00-73;** www. vinci-closluce.com), is a 15th-century manor house of brick and stone about a 2-mile (3.2km) walk from the Château d'Amboise. In what had been an oratory for Anne of Brittany, François I installed "the great master in all forms of art and science," Leonardo da Vinci. Loved and venerated by the Chevalier King, da Vinci lived there for

3 years, dying at the manor in 1519. (Incidentally, those deathbed paintings depicting Leonardo in the arms of François I are probably symbolic; the king was supposedly out of town when the artist died.)

From the window of his bedroom, Leonardo liked to look out at the château where François lived. Whenever he was restless, the king would visit Leonardo via an underground tunnel.

Inside, the rooms are well furnished, some containing reproductions from the period of the artist. The downstairs is reserved for da Vinci's designs, models, and inventions, including his plans for a turbine engine, an airplane, and a parachute. From May to October, admission is 13€ adults, 9.50€ students and seniors, 7€ children 6 to 15, 32€ family ticket (2 adults, 2 children), free for children 5 and under; November to March, admission is 9.50€ adults, 6€ students and seniors, 6€ children 6 to 15, 25€ family ticket (2 adults, 2 children), free for children 5 and under. Hours are January daily 10am to 6pm, Feburary to June daily 9am to 7pm, July to August daily 9am to 8pm, September to October daily 9am to 7pm, November to December daily 9am to 6pm. Closed Christmas and New Year's Day.

BLOIS

Just 37 miles (60km) northeast of Tours, the small town of **Blois** ("Blwah") is often called the center of the châteaux country. Although Blois does not have the same liveliness as Tours, it is a convenient base for rail travelers, as it is between Tours and Orléans. It lies on the right bank of the Loire and is often visited by rail passengers in the morning, who then spend the afternoon at the château nearby, Chambord (see below). In 1429, Joan of Arc launched her expeditionary forces from Blois to oust the English from Orléans.

GETTING THERE   The Paris–Austerlitz line via Orléans delivers six **trains** per day from Paris (trip time: 1½ hr.), at a cost of 24€ one-way. From Tours, 8 to 13 trains arrive per day (trip time: 40 min.), at a cost of 10€ one-way. For information and schedules, call ℘ **08-92-35-35-35.**

The train station is at place de la Gare. Once here, you can take the **bus** (℘ **02-54-58-55-44**) to tour various châteaux in the area, including Chambord. One bus a day departs from the train station from June to September only. The Château de Blois and tourist office are an easy 5-minute walk southeast of the rail station.

VISITOR INFORMATION   The **Office de Tourisme** is located at 23 place du Chateau (℘ **02-54-90-41-41;** www.bloispaysdechambord.com). The hours are January to March from 10am to 5pm; April, May, and September from 9am to 6pm; and June to August from 9am to 7pm.

Top Attractions & Special Moments

Château Royal de Blois ★★★ (℘ **02-54-90-33-33**) is forever linked to one of the most famous murders in French history, that of the Duke of Guise, *Balafre* (Scarface), on December 23, 1588. His archrival, Henri III, ordered the murder. The murder of the duc de Guise is only one of the events associated with the Château de Blois, begun in the 13th century by the comte de Blois. Charles d'Orléans, the "poet prince," lived at Blois after his release from 25 years of English captivity. He had married Mary of Cleves and brought a "court of letters" to Blois. In his 70s, Charles became father of the future Louis XII, who was to marry Anne of Brittany, and Blois was launched in its new role as a royal château. In time, it would be called the second capital of France, and Blois itself, the city of kings.

Blois, however, eventually became a palace of banishment. Louis XIII sent his interfering mother, Marie de Médici, here, but the plump matron escaped by sliding on a coat down a mound of dirt left by the builders and into the moat. In 1626, the king sent his conspiring brother, Gaston d'Orléans, here. He actually stayed put.

If you stand in the courtyard of the great château, you'll find it's like an illustrated storybook of French architecture. The **Hall of the Estates-General** is a beautiful work from the 13th century; the so-called **gallery of Charles d'Orléans** was actually built by Louis XII between 1498 and 1501, as was the **Louis XII wing.** The **François I** wing is a masterpiece of the French Renaissance; the **Gaston d'Orléans** wing was constructed by François Mansart between 1635 and 1637. Of them all, the most remarkable is the François I wing, which contains a spiral staircase with elaborately ornamented balustrades and the king's symbol, the salamander. In the Louis XII wing, seek out paintings by Antoine Caron, court painter to Henri III, depicting the persecution of Thomas More.

The château presents a *son-et-lumière* show in French from May to September, beginning at 10:30pm and lasting 45 minutes in English. As a taped lecture is played, colored lights and dramatic readings evoke the age in which the château was built. The show costs 7€ for adults, 3€ for children ages 7 to 15, and free for children 6 and under. Admission to the château is 8€ adults, 6.50€ students, 4€ for children ages 6 to 17, free for children 5 and under. There are also several options for combination tickets (for the château, sound-and-light show, and *maison de la magie*—the magic museum), so be sure to consider these, depending on your interests. Hours are July to August daily 9am to 7pm, April to June and September daily 9am to 5:30pm, October to March daily 9am to 12:30pm and 1:30 to 5:30pm.

WHERE TO STAY

Situated 5 minutes from the train station, the town center, and the Château Royal de Blois, the cozy hotel **Anne de Bretagne,** 31 av. Jean Laigret (© **02-54-78-05-38;** annedebretagne.free.fr), makes rail travel easy (the closest castles are Chambord and Chaumont-sur-Loire). The 27 warmly painted rooms have a Provençal feel, with either a bathtub or shower, and the multilingual staff does everything to make guests comfortable. Rates run about 54€ for a double.

CHAMBORD

In the village of Chambord, 11 miles (18km) east of Blois (see above), and 118 miles (190km) southwest of Paris, stands a château where the French Renaissance in architecture reached its peak.

GETTING THERE This is one place you can't get to by rail alone; you'll need to take a train to Blois (see above), then travel here by other means. From June 15 to September 2, **Transports du Loir et Cher** (© **02-54-58-55-44**) operates bus service to Chambord, leaving Blois at 9am and 1:30pm, with return trips at 1 and 6pm. You can also rent a **bicycle** in Blois and ride the 18km (11 miles) to Chambord, or take a **tour** to Chambord from Blois in summer.

VISITOR INFORMATION The **Office de Tourisme,** on place St-Michel (© **02-54-33-39-16**), is open mid-June to October.

Top Attractions & Special Moments

Work on **Château de Chambord** ★★★, 41250, intersection of route de Bracieux and route de la Commission (© **02-54-50-40-00;** www.chambord.org), was begun in 1519 by 2,000 laborers. After 20 years, the largest château in the Loire Valley

Chinon: For History Buffs

Located between the "chalk cliff" and the river (La Vienne), the 2,000-year-old charming city of **Chinon** (1hr., 10 min. from Tours) should not be missed by historical enthusiasts. Visit the château remains (an uphill trek) that overlook the old city's streets, reflecting a long history marked by battles and such historic residents as Henry II (Middle Ages), Charles VII (Hundred Years War), and Joan of Arc (1429). If you get hungry, have lunch or dinner at **Brasserie le Gandoyau** (connected to **Hostellerie Gargantua**, a cozy place to stay), 73 rue Haute St. Maurice (✆ **02-47-93-04-71**; www.hostelleriegargantua.com), where traditional French food is complemented by a peaceful terrace in the midst of the city walls and rooftops. Main courses run 15€ to 20€; it's closed Wednesday all year and Thursday from September to March 31.

emerged. It was ready for the visit of Charles V of Germany, who was welcomed by nymphets in transparent veils tossing wildflowers in the emperor's path.

French monarchs—Henri II, Catherine de Medici, and Louis XIII—came and went from Chambord, but it was the favorite of François I, the Chevalier King (who is said to have carved the following on one of the window panes with his diamond ring: "A woman is a creature of change; to trust her is to play the fool.").

The château was restored in part by the brother of Louis XIII, Gaston d'Orléans. His daughter, "La Grand Mademoiselle" (Mademoiselle de Montpensier), wrote that she used to force her father to run up and down Chambord's famous double spiral staircase after her. Because of its corkscrew structure, he never caught her (one person may descend at one end and another ascend at the other without ever meeting).

The château is set in a park of more than 13,000 acres (5,260 hectares), enclosed within a wall stretching 20 miles (32km). At its lowest point, the château was used as a munitions factory. The state acquired Chambord in 1932. Its facade is characterized by four monumental towers. The keep contains a spectacular terrace, on which the ladies of the court used to stand to watch the return of their men from the hunt. From that platform, you can inspect the dormer windows and the richly decorated chimneys, some characterized by winged horses. The apartments of **Louis XIV** (the Sun King paid nine visits here), including his redecorated bedchamber, are also in the keep.

The château is open April to September daily 9am to 6:15pm and October to March 9am to 5:15pm. For horse enthusiasts, there are shows presented on the grounds from May to September at 11:45am and/or 4:30pm. Admission is 9.50€ for adults and free for ages 25 and under. At the tourist office, you can pick up tickets for the summer *son-et-lumière* presentation, "Jours et Siècles" ("Days and Centuries"). The price is 10€. Allow 1½ hours to go through the château.

CHENONCEAUX

Only 16 miles (26km) east of Tours is the tiny village of Chenonceaux, home to the fairy-tale-like château Chenonceau (notice the missing *x*).

GETTING THERE There are four daily **trains** (more on Sat, though morning departures require a connection; none on Sun morning) from Tours to Chenonceaux (trip time: 30 min.), costing 5.80€ one-way. The train deposits you at the base of the château; from there, you can walk or take a taxi.

NATURE & ART IN Chaumont-sur-Loire

Travelers interested in nature merged with art should be sure to visit Chaumont-sur-Loire. The rail station for the town is Onzain (© **36-35** or 08-92-35-35-35); it's a 15-minute train ride from Blois and 45 minutes from Tours. On the grounds of the Château de Chaumont is an annual **Festival International des Jardins** (© **02-54-20-99-22;** www.domaine-chaumont.fr; late Apr to mid-Oct), where an average of 30 fabulous outdoor garden exhibits are created by artists, students, architects, engineers, and designers from around the world. Admission is 9.50€ adults, 7.50€ ages 12 to 18, 4.50€ for ages 6 to 11, and free for ages under 6.

The **Château de Chaumont ★★** (© **02-54-51-26-26;** www.domaine-chaumont.fr) was built next to the Loire River during the reign of Louis XII by Charles d'Amboise. The original fortress

was dismantled by Louis XI, and in 1560, Chaumont was acquired by Catherine de Médici and then became the home (by force) of Diane Poitiers, mistress of Henry II. The château was later privately owned until it was taken over by the state in 1938. It is one of the Loire Valley's most well-known castles. The château is open daily (except New Year's Day, May 1, Nov 1 and 11, and Christmas): November 3 to March 31 10am to 5pm, April 1 to June 30 10am to 6:30pm, July 1 to August 31 10am to 7pm, September 10am to 6:30pm, and October 10am to 6pm. Admission is 8€ for adults, 5.50€ for students and children 18 and under. Allow 2 hours to see Chaumont.

The **Office de Tourisme** is located at 24 rue du Maréchal-Leclerc (© **02-54-20-91-73;** www.chaumontsurloire.info). **Note:** It's a long uphill trek to the château from the rail station.

VISITOR INFORMATION The **Syndicat d'Initiative** (tourist office), 1 rue du Dr. Bretonneau (© **02-47-23-94-45**), is open year-round.

Top Attractions & Special Moments

The Renaissance masterpiece **Château de Chenonceau ★★★** (© **02-47-23-90-07;** www.chenonceau.com) is known for the series of famous *dames de Chenonceau* who occupied it. François I seized the château in 1524 from a wealthy Tours family, and in 1547, Henri II gave Chenonceau to his mistress, Diane de Poitiers, who was 20 years his senior. For a time, this remarkable woman was virtually the queen of France. But when Henri died in a jousting tournament in 1559, his jealous wife, Catherine de Médici, became regent of France and immediately forced Diane de Poitiers to abandon her beloved Chenonceau in exchange for Chaumont (see below). Catherine added her own touches to the château, building a two-story gallery across the bridge—obviously inspired by her native Florence. The long gallery running along the Cher River contains a black-and-white diamond floor.

It was at Chenonceau that Catherine received a pair of teenage honeymooners: her son, François II, and his bride, Mary Stuart (aka Mary, Queen of Scots). And it was here, in the 18th century, that Rousseau declared his undying love for the mistress of the château, Madame Dupin, the grandmother of George Sand, and was promptly rebuffed.

Many of the château's walls today are covered with Gobelin tapestries, including one depicting a woman pouring water over the back of an angry dragon, another of a three-headed dog and a seven-headed monster. The chapel contains a delicate marble Virgin and Child, plus portraits of Catherine de Médici in her traditional black and white. There's even a portrait of the stern Catherine in the former bedroom of her rival, Diane de Poitiers. But in the Renaissance-style bedchamber of François I, the most interesting portrait is that of Diane de Poitiers as the huntress Diana, complete with a sling of arrows on her back. *The Three Graces* are by Van Loo. The chateau is open daily 9am to 8pm July and August, 9am to 7pm mid-March to June, 9am to 6:30pm September and October, 9am to 5pm the rest of the year. Admission is 11€ for adults and 8€ for students and children 7 to 15. A *son-et-lumière* show, "The Era of the Ladies of Chenonceau," starts at 10:15pm daily in July and August; admission is 6€ and free for children 6 and under. Allow 2 hours to see this château.

PROVENCE & THE RIVIERA

The French Riviera, known to the world as the fashionable Côte d'Azur, is actually part of the greater region of sunny Provence that sweeps across the southern tier of France—it's an easy train ride from Paris.

Provence has its own language and customs. The region is bounded on the north by the Dauphine, the west by the Rhône, the east by the Alps, and the south by the Mediterranean. In this section, we cover the northern area of this region, what's traditionally thought of as Provence (and whose most evocative cities include **Avignon, Aix-en-Provence,** and **Arles**), and then head down to the French Riviera and its two grandest resorts, **Cannes** and **Nice**—from which you can easily visit the principality of **Monaco.** The good news for rail travelers is that, no matter what section you choose, you'll have very few problems getting around by train.

Of course, easy rail access isn't necessarily the big draw in this region. The weather isn't bad, either. The winter temperature is higher in the Riviera than the rest of France, mainly because of the Alpine chain that protects the Côte d'Azur from cold continental winds. The Riviera's high season used to be winter and spring only. However, with changing tastes, July and August have become the most crowded months, and reservations are imperative. The average summer temperature is 75°F (24°C), the average winter temperature 49°F (10°C). If you can, we recommend coming here in May or October, when crowds thin, prices drop, but the weather remains lovely, giving you exactly what the travel posters promise.

Another compelling trait of the Riviera is the incredible number of artists who are/ were drawn to its shores and hillside villas, leaving behind a rich legacy. At Cagnes, Renoir praised the "light effects" of the region. Matisse chose Nice in which to spend the last years of his life (you can visit his remarkable museum there and his Chapelle du Rosaire in Vence). Cocteau decorated a chapel for the fishermen of Villefranche. Picasso left an art legacy from one end of the Riviera to the other, as did Cezanne in Aix-en-Provence and van Gogh in Arles.

Many visitors come to Provence specifically to dine, so do try some of the region's specialties, especially the *salade niçoise,* which essentially includes fresh vine-ripened tomatoes, small radishes, green peppers, potatoes, and green beans. The thick, saffron-flavored fish soup of the Mediterranean, the *bouillabaisse,* is eagerly ordered by diners, as is *ratatouille* (a mixture of small eggplants, tomatoes, miniature squash, and red peppers simmered in olive oil).

Avignon ★★★

In the 14th century, Avignon was the capital of Christendom; the popes lived here during what the Romans called "the Babylonian Captivity." The legacy left by that "court of splendor and magnificence" makes Avignon one of the most interesting and beautiful of Europe's cities of the Middle Ages.

Today this walled city of some 100,000 residents is a major stopover on the rail route from Paris to the Mediterranean and is the transportation hub for inland Provence. It is increasingly known as a cultural center. Artists and painters have been moving here, especially to rue des Teinturiers. Experimental theaters, galleries, and cinemas have brought diversity to the city. The popes are long gone, but life goes on exceedingly well.

GETTING THERE From Paris, TGV Med trains frequently depart from Gare de Lyon, the trip taking 3 hours and 30 minutes. A one-way fare costs 78€. Trains also arrive frequently from Marseilles (trip time: 70 min.), with a ticket costing 23€; and from Arles, the SNCF runs nine buses (trip time: 1½ hr.), with a fare of 6.60€ one-way. For train information and reservations, check out **www.raileurope.com**. The TGV train station has a shuttle bus, the *navette,* which runs frequently and costs 1.10€ one-way. The 10-minute trip terminates in the city center between the local train station and the Office de Tourisme.

VISITOR INFORMATION The **Office de Tourisme** is at 41 cours Jean-Jaurès (*©* **04-32-74-32-74;** www.ot-avignon.fr), about 600 feet (180m) north of the train station. Off-season (Nov–Mar) hours are Monday to Friday 9am to 6pm, Saturday 9am to 5pm, and Sunday 10am to noon. Summer (Apr 2–Oct 31) hours are Monday to Saturday 9am to 6pm and Sunday 9:45am to 5pm. During the month of July, hours are extended to 6:45pm Monday to Saturday. This office does not reserve hotel rooms. Here you can also pick up "Avignon Passion," a pass that gives you a discounted rate for most of the attractions.

TOP ATTRACTIONS & SPECIAL MOMENTS

Even more famous than the papal residency is the ditty *"Sur le pont d'Avignon, l'on y danse, l'on y danse,"* echoing through every French nursery and around the world. Ironically, **pont St-Bénézet ★★** (*©* **04-90-27-51-16**) was far too narrow for the *danse* of the rhyme. Spanning the Rhône and connecting Avignon with Villeneuve-lèz-Avignon, the bridge is now a ruin, with only 4 of its original 22 arches. According to legend, it was inspired by a vision that a shepherd named Bénézet had while tending his flock. The bridge was built between 1177 and 1185 and suffered various disasters from then on. (In 1669, half the bridge fell into the river.) On one of the piers is the **Chapelle St-Nicolas**—one story in Romanesque style, the other in Gothic. The remains of the bridge are open November through March daily 9:30am to 5:45pm, April to June and October daily 9am to 7pm, July and September daily 9am to 8pm, and August daily 9am to 9pm. Admission is 4.50€ for adults, 3.50€ for seniors and students, and free for children 7 and under. Once you pay to walk on the bridge, the small chapel on the bridge can be visited as part of the overall admission fee.

The **Palais des Papes ★★★**, 6 rue Pente Rapide (*©* **04-90-27-50-00;** www. palais-des-papes.com), dominates Avignon. In 1309, a sick man, nearing the end of his life, arrived in Avignon. His name was Clement V, and he was the leader of the Christian world. Lodged as a guest of the Dominicans, he died in the spring of 1314 and was succeeded by John XXII. The new pope lived modestly in the Episcopal Palace. When Benedict XII took over, he greatly enlarged and rebuilt the palace. Clement VI, who followed, built an even more elaborate extension, the New Palace. After Innocent VI and Urban V, Pope Gregory XI did no building. Inspired by Catherine of Siena, he was intent upon returning the papacy to Rome, and he succeeded. In all, seven popes reigned at Avignon. Under them, art and culture flourished, as did vice. Prostitutes blatantly went about peddling their wares in front of fat cardinals, rich merchants were robbed, and innocent pilgrims from the hinterlands were brutally swindled.

From 1378, during the Great Schism, one pope ruled in Avignon, another in Rome. The reign of the pope and the "anti-pope" continued, one following the other, until both rulers were dismissed by the election of Martin V in 1417. Rome continued to rule Avignon until it was joined to France during the French Revolution.

You're shown through the palace today on a guided 50-minute tour, taking in the **Chapelle St-Jean,** known for its 14th-century frescoes, and the **Grand Tinel,** or banquet hall, about 135 feet long (41km). The **Pope's Bedroom** is on the first floor of the Tour des Anges, and other attractions include the Great Audience Hall, containing frescoes attributed to Giovanetti and painted in 1352.

Admission (including a tour with a guide or cassette recording) is 11€ adults, 8.50€ students and seniors, free for ages 7 and under. It is 12€ for a combination ticket to the palace and the bridge. Hours are daily November to March from 9:30am to 5:45pm, April to June and August to October from 9am to 7pm, July daily. The on-site **Musée du Petit Palais** contains an important collection of paintings from the Italian schools from the 13th through the 16th centuries, including works from Florence, Venice, Sienna, and Lombardy. In addition, salons display Roman and Gothic sculptures and 15th-century paintings created in Avignon.

The ramparts (still standing) around Avignon were built in the 14th century and are characterized by their machicolated battlements, turrets, and old gates. The fortifications were rebuilt in the 19th century by Viollet-le-Duc, the busiest man in France, who also restored Notre-Dame in Paris and the fortified walls at Carcassonne.

Admission is 6€ adults and 2€ for students. Hours are Wednesday to Monday 10am to 1pm and 2 to 6pm. Nearby is **Cathédrale Notre-Dame des Doms,** place du Palais (✆ **04-90-86-81-01;** free admission; daily 8am–6pm), dating from the 12th century and containing the flamboyant Gothic tomb of John XXII, who died at the age of 90. Benedict XII is also buried there. Crowning the top is a gilded statue of the Virgin from the 19th century. From the cathedral, you can enter the **Promenade des Rocher-des-Doms** (✆ **04-90-82-27-96**), strolling through its garden and enjoying the view across the Rhône to Villeneuve-lés-Avignon. Admission is free. Hours vary according to religious ceremonies but are generally daily 9am to noon and 2 to 6pm.

It's been decades since the death of Jacques Doucet (1853–1929), the Belle Epoque dandy, dilettante, and designer of Parisian haute couture, but his magnificent art collection is on view to the general public at **La Fondation Angladon-Dubrujeaud ★★**, 5 rue Laboureur (✆ **04-90-82-29-03;** www.angladon.com). When not designing, Doucet collected the early works of a number of artists, among them Picasso, Max Jacob, and van Gogh. Today you can wander through Doucet's former abode, viewing rare antiques; 16th-century Buddhas; Louis XVI chairs designed by Jacob; and canvases by Cézanne, Sisley, Degas, and Modigliani. Doucet died in 1929 at 76, his fortune so diminished that his nephew paid for his funeral, but his rich legacy lives on here. Admission is 6€ adults, 3€ students and teens 15 to 18, 1.50€ children 7 to 14, free for children under 7. Hours are Tuesday to Sunday 1 to 6pm; it's closed on Tuesday in the winter.

WHERE TO STAY & DINE

Not far from the rail station, the 80-room **Clarion Hotel Cloître St-Louis ★**, 20 rue Portail Boquier, 84000 Avignon (✆ **800/CLARION** [252-7466] in the U.S., or 04-90-27-55-55; www.cloitre-saint-louis.com), is housed in a former Jesuit school built in the 1580s. While public areas retain many original features, the bedrooms are more functional. Their decor is rather dull and severe are renovations; some overlook a patio. Rates are 100€ to 210€ double, 250€ to 350€ suite.

Mercure Pont d'Avignon, quartier de la Balance, rue Ferruce, 84000 Avignon (✆ **04-90-80-93-93;** www.mercure.com), is one of the best in Avignon and is a good value for what it offers. The 88 midsize bedrooms are well maintained, though comfortably furnished, with small bathrooms. It lies within the city walls, at the foot of the Palace of the Popes. Rates are 125€ to 170€ double, 250€ suite. Breakfast is the only meal served.

The three-story Art Deco **Hôtel d'Angleterre,** 29 bd. Raspail (✆ **04-90-86-34-31;** www.hoteldangleterre.fr), in the heart of Avignon, is the city's best budget hotel, with the advantage of being located inside the city ramparts. It was built in 1929 of gray stone, emulating the style that local builders imagined was characteristic of English houses. The air-conditioned rooms are on the small side, but they are comfortably furnished and offer free Wi-Fi; most have compact shower-only bathrooms. Breakfast is the only meal served. Rates run 60€ to 85€ double.

Hiély-Lucullus ★★, 5 rue de la République (✆ **04-90-86-17-07;** www.hielylucullus.com), is a formidable competitor on the Avignon restaurant scene. It offers reasonable fixed-price menus. The *pièce de résistance* is *agneau des Alpilles grillé* (grilled Alpine lamb). Fixed-price menu prices are 35€ to 60€. Reservations are required. It's open Thursday to Tuesday noon to 2pm and 7 to 10pm.

La Fourchette, 17 rue Racine (© **04-90-85-20-93;** bus: 11), offers creative French cooking, although it shuts down on the weekends. The two dining rooms are light and airy, thanks to large windows. For a main course, we recommend monkfish stew with endive or daube of beef with a gratin of macaroni. Fixed-price meals are the best in town and cost 25€ to 31€ for lunch and 31€ for dinner. Hours are Monday to Friday 12:15 to 1:45pm and 7:15 to 9:45pm; closed for 3 weeks in August.

Arles ★★★

It's been called "the soul of Provence," though it was known as "the little Rome of the Gauls" when Constantine the Great named it the second capital in his empire in A.D. 306. Before the Romans, the Greeks founded Arles in the 6th B.C. Julius Caesar established a Roman colony here. Art lovers, archaeologists, and historians have all been attracted to this town on the Rhône. Many of its scenes, painted so luminously by van Gogh in his declining years, remain to delight. The great Dutch painter left Paris for Arles in 1888—same year that he cut off part of his left ear. But here he painted some of his most celebrated works, including *Starry Night, The Bridge at Arles, Sunflowers,* and *L'Arlésienne.*

Befitting its glorious past, Arles is still well connected—by rail, that is. It's linked to both Paris and Avignon (where you usually need to change trains to get here) by high-speed lines and also offers connections to other cities in Provence.

GETTING THERE   **Trains** leave from Paris's Gare de Lyon and arrive at Arles's **Gare SNCF** (av. Paulin-Talabot), a short walk (about 15 min.) from the town center. Two high-speed direct TGV trains travel from Paris to Arles each day (trip time: 4 hr.; about 64€). For other trains, you must change in Avignon. There are about four **bus** connections run by the SNCF between Arles and Avignon from Marseille and Aix-en-Provence. For rail schedules and information, check out **www.raileurope.com**.

VISITOR INFORMATION   The **Office de Tourisme,** where you can buy a *billet global* (see below), is on the boulevard des Lices (© **04-90-18-41-20;** www.arlestourisme.com). Hours vary per month, so call ahead of time. If stuck, you can make a hotel reservation there, but it is much easier to book online to be able to select according to your needs.

TOP ATTRACTIONS & SPECIAL MOMENTS

At the tourist office (see "Essentials," earlier in this chapter), buy a **billet global ★**, a combination pass that admits you to the town's museums, Roman monuments, and major attractions, at a cost of 7€ to 9€.

The town is full of Roman monuments. The general vicinity of the old Roman forum is occupied by **place du Forum,** shaded by plane trees. Once, the Café de Nuit, immortalized by van Gogh, stood on this square. Two Corinthian columns and pediment fragments from a temple can be seen at the corner of the Hôtel Nord-Pinus. South of here is **place de la République** (also known as the place de l'Hôtel de Ville), the principal plaza, dominated by a 50-foot (15m) blue porphyry obelisk. On the north is the impressive **Hôtel-de-Ville** (town hall) from 1673, built to Mansart's plans and surmounted by a Renaissance belfry.

One of the city's great classical monuments is the Roman **Théâtre Antique ★★**, rue de la Calade (© **04-90-49-38-20**). Begun by Augustus in the 1st century, only two Corinthian columns remain. The theater was where the *Venus of Arles* was discovered in 1651. Take rue de la Calade from city hall. The theater is open May to September daily 9am to 6:30pm; March, April, and October daily 9 to 11:30am and 2 to 6pm; and November to February daily 10 to 11:30am and 2 to 4:30pm. Admission costs 3€ for adults, 2.20€ for students and ages 12 to 18. It's free for children under 12.

Nearby is the **Amphithéâtre (Les Arènes Romaines)** ★★, rond-point des Arènes (© **04-90-49-36-86**), also built in the 1st century. It seats almost 25,000 and still hosts bullfights in summer. Be careful, as the stone steps are uneven, and much of the masonry is worn. For a good view, you can climb the three towers that remain from medieval times, when the amphitheater was turned into a fortress. Hours are May through September daily 9am to 6pm; March, April, and October daily 9am to 6pm; and November to February daily 10am to 5pm. Admission costs 6€ for adults, 4.50€ for students and children 18 and under. **Thermes de Constantin,** the roman public baths, are a 10-minute-walk from the amphitheater.

Perhaps the most memorable sight in Arles, **Les Alyscamps** ★, rue Pierre-Renaudel (© **04-90-49-36-87**), was once a necropolis established by the Romans. After being converted into a Christian burial ground in the 4th century, it became a setting for legends and was even mentioned in Dante's *Inferno*. Today it's lined with poplars and the remaining sarcophagi. Admission is 3.50€ adults, 2.60€ ages 12 to 18, free for ages 11 and under. Hours are November to February 10am to noon and 2 to 4:30pm daily; March, April, and October 9:30 to noon and 2 to 5:30pm; and May to September 9am to 6:30pm. It is closed New Year's Day, May 1, November 1, and Christmas.

Half a mile (.8km) south of the town center, you'll find the **Musée de l'Arles et de la Provence antiques** ★★, Presqu'île du Cirque Romain (© **04-90-18-88-88**), with an incredible collection of Roman Christian sarcophagi, plus a rich ensemble of sculptures, mosaics, and inscriptions from the Augustinian period to the 6th century A.D. Eleven detailed models show ancient monuments of the region as they existed in the past. Admission is 6€ adults, 4.50€ students, and free for children 17 and under. Hours are April to October daily 9am to 7pm, November to March daily 10am to 5pm; closed New Year's Day, May 1, November 1, and Christmas.

Musée Réattu ★, 10 rue du Grand-Prieuré (© **04-90-49-37-58**), has been updated recently with works including etchings and drawings by Picasso and local painter Jacques Réattu. Other pieces are by Alechinsky, Dufy, and Zadkine. Note the Arras tapestries from the 16th century. Admission is 7€ for adults, 5€ for students and children 12 to 18, and free for children 11 and under. The hours are May to September 10am to noon and 2 to 6:30pm, March to April and October from 10am to noon and 2 to 5pm, and November to February daily from 1 to 5:30pm.

WHERE TO STAY & DINE

Because of its reasonable rates, **Hôtel Calendal** ★, 5 rue Porte de Laure, 13200 Arles (© **04-90-96-11-89**; www.lecalendal.com; bus: 4), is a bargain hunter's favorite. On a quiet square near the arena, this 38-unit hotel offers rooms with bright colors, high ceilings, and a sense of spaciousness. Most have views of the hotel's peaceful garden. Rates run 79€ to 109€ double.

Hôtel d'Arlatan ★, 26 rue du Sauvage, 13100 Arles (© **04-90-93-56-66;** www.hotel-arlatan.fr), the former residence of the *comtes* d'Arlatan de Beaumont, has been managed by the same family since 1920. It was built in the 15th century on the ruins of an old palace begun by Emperor Constantine. Rooms are furnished with authentic Provençal antiques and walls covered by tapestries. Rates are 85€ to 157€ double, 175€ to 247€ for a suite.

A Trip to the Market

While in Provence, be sure to experience the magic of wandering through a bustling **marché** (market). On certain days (check with the tourism office—it depends on the season) in Arles, the boulevard des Lices is filled with seemingly endless market stalls brimming with fruits, vegetables, cheeses, olives, honey, breads, clothing, antiques, pottery, lavender, flowers, and more. The market can take up an entire morning—and you will end up with enough goodies for a great picnic lunch!

A few steps from the arena, **Le Bout du Monde,** 49 rue des Arènes (*℃* **04-90-96-68-59**), offers unique cuisine and a relaxed setting at reasonable prices. It's outfitted with a decor inspired by India but with a European twist. The seasonally changing menu items include dishes from France, Thailand, Vietnam, and India, with an emphasis on curries and such French staples as a pâté of foie gras (made in-house). Main courses run 12€ to 19€.

Restaurant Lou Marquès ★★, at the Hôtel Jules-César, 9 bd. des Lices (*℃* **04-90-52-52-52**), part of a luxury hotel, has the highest reputation in town for its creative twists on Provençal specialties. As a main course, try *pavé de loup en barigoule d'artichaut et à la sauge* (a thick slice of wolf fish with sage-stuffed artichokes) or *filet mignon de veau et ragoût fin de cèpes et salsifis* (veal with a stew of mushrooms and salsify, a long-forgotten oyster-flavored vegetable). Main courses (change seasonally) run 26€ to 34€; fixed-price menus run 21€ to 28€ at lunch, from 28€ to 60€ at dinner.

Aix-en-Provence ★★★

The celebrated son of this old capital city of Provence, Paul Cézanne, immortalized the countryside nearby. Just as he saw it, Montagne Sainte-Victoire still looms over the town, although a string of high-rises have now cropped up on the landscape. The most charming center in all of Provence, this faded university town was once a seat of the aristocracy, its streets walked by counts and kings. Aix still has much of the atmosphere it acquired in the 17th and 18th centuries before losing its prestige to Marseille, 20 miles (32km) to the south.

GETTING THERE The city is easily accessible. Twenty-seven **trains** arrive daily from Marseille; the trip takes 45 minutes and costs 7€ one-way. Twenty-five trains arrive from Nice; the trip takes 3 to 4 hours and costs 36€ one-way. There are also 25 trains per day from Cannes (3½ hr.), costing 35€ one-way. High-speed TGV trains (including the ones above from Nice and Cannes) arrive at Vitroll, 3½ miles (5.5km) west of Aix. Bus links to the center of Aix cost 4.10€ one-way. For more information, call *℃* **36-35. Buses** from Marseille arrive every 10 minutes; from Avignon, five times a day; and twice a day from Nice. For more information, call *℃* **08-91-02-40-25.**

VISITOR INFORMATION The **Office de Tourisme** is at 2 place du Général-de-Gaulle (*℃* **04-42-16-11-61**; www.aixenprovencetourism.com). To get here from the train station, stroll up avenue Victor-Hugo (bearing left) and you'll eventually see it on your left. The office will reserve hotel rooms and tours, among other services. They are extremely helpful and multilingual. Hours are Monday to Saturday 8:30am to 7pm and Sunday 10am to 1pm and 2 to 6pm. There are extended hours in season.

TOP ATTRACTIONS & SPECIAL MOMENTS

Aix's main street, **cours Mirabeau** ★, is one of Europe's most beautiful. Plane trees stretch their branches across the top like an umbrella, shading it from the hot Provençal sun and filtering the light into shadows that play on the rococo fountains below. Shops and sidewalk cafes line one side of the street; sandstone *hôtels particuliers* (mansions) from the 17th and 18th centuries fill the other. The street begins at the 1860 fountain on place de la Libération, which honors Mirabeau, the revolutionary and statesman.

Cézanne was the major forerunner of Cubism. **Atelier de Cézanne,** 9 av. Paul-Cézanne (outside town; ℂ **04-42-21-06-53**), surrounded by a wall and restored in 1970 by American admirers, is where he worked. Admission is 5.50€ adults, 2€ students and children ages 12 and under. Hours are daily October to March 10am to noon and 2 to 5pm, April to June and September daily 10am to noon and 2 to 6pm, July and August daily 10am to 6pm.

Cathédrale St-Sauveur ★, place des Martyrs de la Résistance (ℂ **04-42-23-45-65**), is dedicated to Christ under the title St-Sauveur (Holy Savior or Redeemer). Its baptistery dates from the 4th and 5th centuries, but the complex as a whole has seen many additions. It contains a 15th-century Nicolas Froment triptych, *The Burning Bush.* Masses are conducted every Sunday at 10am and 7pm. Admission is free, and hours are daily 8am to noon and 2 to 6pm. Mass is held on Sunday at 10:30am and 7pm.

Three series of tapestries from the 17th and 18th centuries line the gilded walls of **Musée des Tapisseries** ★, 28 place des Martyrs de la Résistance (ℂ **04-42-23-09-91**), a former archbishop's palace. *The History of Don Quixote,* by Natoire; *The Russian Games,* by Leprince; and *The Grotesques,* by Monnoyer were paintings collected by archbishops to decorate the palace. Admission is 3€ adults, free for ages 24 and under. Hours are mid-October to mid-April Wednesday to Monday 1:30 to 5pm, mid-April to mid-October Wednesday to Monday 10am to 6pm; closed January, May 1, and December 25 and 26.

WHERE TO STAY & DINE

Grand Hôtel Nègre Coste, 33 cours Mirabeau, 13100 Aix-en-Provence (ℂ **04-42-27-74-22;** www.hotelnegrecoste.com), a former 18th-century town house, is popular with the dozens of musicians who flock to Aix for the summer festivals. The higher floors of this 37-room hotel overlook cours Mirabeau and the old city. The soundproof rooms contain interesting antiques and good bathrooms. Room rates are 90€ to 145€ double.

 Aix Through the Eyes of Cézanne

One of the best experiences in Aix is a walk along the well-marked *route de Cézanne* (D17), which winds eastward through the countryside toward Ste-Victoire. From the east end of cours Mirabeau, take rue du Maréchal-Joffre across boulevard Carnot to boulevard des Poilus, which becomes avenue des Ecoles-Militaires and finally D17. The stretch between Aix and the hamlet of Le Tholonet is full of twists and turns where Cézanne often set up his easel to paint. The entire route is a lovely 3.5-mile (5.5km) stroll. Le Tholonet has a cafe or two where you can refresh yourself while waiting for one of the frequent buses back to Aix.

Aix-en-Provence

ACCOMMODATIONS ■
Grand Hôtel Nègre Coste **5**
Hôtel Cardinal **6**

DINING ◆
Chez Maxime **3**
Le Bistro Latin **4**

ATTRACTIONS ●
Cathédrale St-Sauveur **1**
Musée des Tapisseries **2**

Not everything is state-of-the-art at **Hôtel Cardinal,** 24 rue Cardinale (☎ **04-42-38-32-30;** www.hotel-cardinal-aix.com), but because of the old-fashioned setting (an 18th-c. town house loaded with personalized quirks), a collection of 18th- and 19th-century antiques, and upscale and historically appropriate upholsteries, many clients don't seem to mind. Guests stay in the 29 simply furnished rooms either in the main building or in the high-ceilinged 18th-century annex up the street, site of most of the hotel's suites. Bathrooms tend to be small but good. Rates are 70€ double; suites each have a simple kitchenette and cost 110€.

Le Bistro Latin ★★, 18 rue de la Couronne, (☎ **04-42-38-22-88**), is the best little bistro in Aix-en-Provence for the price. Guests dine in two intimate rooms: a street-level space and a cellar decorated in Greco-Latin style. The staff is young and enthusiastic, taking special pride in their fixed-price menus. Try chartreuse of mussels, a meat dish with spinach-and-saffron cream sauce, scampi risotto, or rack of lamb in an herbed crust. Main courses run from 16€ to 20€, fixed-price lunch is 23€, and fixed-price dinner is 23€ to 45€. Reservations are recommended. Hours are Thursday to Tuesday from noon to 2pm and 7pm to 10:30pm.

Chez Maxime, 12 place Ramus (☎ **04-42-26-28-51;** www.restaurant-chez maxime.com), located in the pedestrian shopping zone, offers an all-Provençal ambience of bordeaux-colored banquettes, salmon-colored walls, and tables, each shaded by an enormous linden tree, that spill out onto the pavement during clement weather. There's a succulent array of a dozen grills, beefsteaks, and fresh fish, as well as a main course laced with saffron and the flavors of the sea, a *marmite* (stewpot) *de la mer.* Also appealing is house-made foie gras of duckling, a kind of pâté made from beef and Provençal herbs known as *caillette de province,* and such desserts as a *fondant au chocolat.* The wine list features dozens of vintages, many of them esoteric bottles from the region. Main courses run 12€ to 20€; fixed-price menus 12€ lunch, 25€ to 30€ dinner.

Cannes ★★★

Popular with celebrities, Cannes is at its most frenzied during the **International Film Festival** at the **Palais des Festivals** on the **promenade de la Croisette.** Held in May, it attracts not only film stars but also those with similar aspirations. On the seafront boulevards, flashbulbs pop as the starlets emerge, pose, and set new trends. International regattas, galas, *concours d'élégance,* even a Mimosa Festival in February—something is always happening at Cannes, except in November, which is traditionally a dead month.

Sixteen miles (26km) southwest of Nice, Cannes is sheltered by hills. It is said that the Prince of Wales (before he became Edward VII) contributed to its original cost. But he was a Johnny-come-lately to Cannes. Setting out for Nice in 1834, Lord Brougham, a lord chancellor of England, was turned away because of an outbreak of cholera. He landed at Cannes and liked it so much he decided to build a villa there. Returning every winter until his death in 1868, he proselytized it in London, drawing a long line of British visitors. In the 1890s, Cannes became popular with Russian grand dukes (it is said more caviar was consumed there than in all of Moscow). One French writer claimed that when the Russians returned as refugees in the 1920s, they were given the garbage-collection franchise.

A port of call for cruise liners, the seafront of Cannes is lined with hotels, apartment houses, and chic boutiques. Many of the bigger hotels, some dating from the 19th century, claim part of the beaches for the private use of their guests, though there are public areas.

GETTING THERE   Cannes is connected to Nice, Paris, and the rest of France by rail. **Trains** arrive frequently throughout the day. Cannes is only 15 minutes by train from Antibes and only 35 minutes from Nice. The TGV from Paris via Marseille makes stops at Cannes, taking 5 hours and costing 50€ to 95€. For rail information, call © **08-92-35-35-35,** or visit **www.voyages-sncf.com** or **www.raileurope. com**.

In case you want to fly into Nice and begin your rail journey on the Riviera, the **Nice International Airport** (© 08-20-42-33-33; www.rca.tm.fr) is a 30-minute drive northeast of Cannes. **Buses** pick up passengers at the airport about every 40 minutes during the day, delivering them in Cannes to the rail station, **Gare Routière,** place de l'Hôtel de Ville (© **04-93-45-20-08**).

VISITOR INFORMATION   The **Office de Tourisme** is in the Palais des Festivals, esplanade Georges-Pompidou (© **04-92-99-84-22;** www.cannes.travel), a short walk along the quays, which parallel the edge of the harbor, from the railway station (there is a smaller office next to the train station). Hours are daily 9am to 7pm (until 8pm July–Aug). The office can reserve a hotel room for you.

Cannes

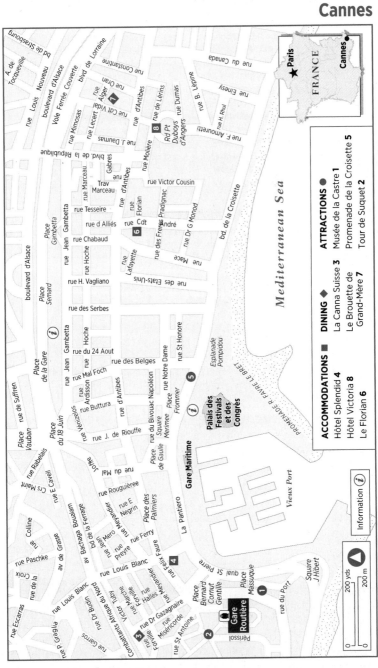

ACCOMMODATIONS ■
Hôtel Splendid **4**
Hôtel Victoria **8**
Le Florian **6**

DINING ◆
La Canna Suisse **3**
Le Brouette de
Grand-Mère **7**

ATTRACTIONS ●
Musée de la Castre **1**
Promenade de la Croisette **5**
Tour de Suquet **2**

Mediterranean Sea

Information ⓘ

305

At the end of May, the **International Film Festival** is held at the Palais des Festivals on promenade de la Croisette. It attracts not only film stars, but also seemingly every photographer in the world. You've got a better chance of being named prime minister of France than you do of attending one of the major screenings. (Hotel rooms and tables at restaurants are equally scarce during the festival.) But the people-watching is fabulous. If you find yourself here at the right time, you can join the thousands of others who line up in front of the Palais des Festivals, aka "the bunker," where the premieres are held. With paparazzi shouting and gendarmes holding back the fans, the guests parade along the red carpet, stopping for a moment to strike a pose and chat with a journalist. *C'est Cannes!*

TOP ATTRACTIONS & SPECIAL MOMENTS

Cannes is sheltered by hills. For many visitors, it might as well consist of only one street, **promenade de la Croisette ★★** (or just La Croisette), curving along the coast and split by islands of palms and flowers.

Above the harbor, the old town of Cannes sits on Suquet Hill, where you'll see the 14th-century **Tour de Suquet,** which the English dubbed the Lord's Tower.

Nearby is the **Musée de la Castre ★**, in the Château de la Castre, Le Suquet (✆ **04-93-38-55-26**), devoted to ethnography that includes objects from all over the world: from the Pacific islands to Southeast Asia; to Peruvian and Mayan pottery; to relics of Mediterranean civilizations, from the Greeks to the Romans, and the Cypriots to the Egyptians. Five rooms display 19th-century paintings. The museum is open daily in July and August 10am to 7pm, September to March Tuesday to Sunday 10am to 1pm and 2 to 5pm, April to June Tuesday to Sunday 10am to 1pm and 2 to 6pm. Admission is 3.20€, 2€ for ages 18 to 25, free for kids 17 and under.

FERRYING TO THE ILES DE LERINS ★★

Across the bay from Cannes, the Lérins Islands are the most interesting excursion from the port. Ferryboats depart at 30-minute intervals throughout the day, beginning at 7:30am to 30 minutes before sundown. Return boats begin at noon and end service at 6pm—make sure you're on time, or you'll be stranded until the next morning. For access to Ile Ste-Marguerite, head for the quai Laubeuf, opposite the Hotel Sofitel, in Cannes, where ferryboats operated by **Trans-Côte d'Azur** (✆ **04-92-98-71-30**) haul passengers back and forth year-round at intervals of between 15 and 75 minutes, depending on the season. For access to Ile St-Honorat, head for the same quai (quai Laubeuf) for the ferryboats operated by **Cie Transports Planaria** (✆ **04-92-98-71-38**). Boats depart daily year-round at intervals of between 30 and 90 minutes, depending on the season. Round-trip transport to both venues costs 11€ per adult, 5.50€ for children 5 to 10, and free for children 4 and under. Ferryboats operated by both of the above-noted companies have a capacity of around 220 passengers.

ILE STE-MARGUERITE   This island was named after St-Honorat's sister, Ste-Marguerite, who lived here with a group of nuns in the 5th century. Today it is a youth center whose members (when they aren't sailing and diving) are dedicated to the restoration of the fort. From the dock, you can stroll along the island (signs point the way) to the Fort de l'Ile, built by Spanish troops from 1635 to 1637. Below is the

1st-century-B.C. Roman town where the "Man in the Iron Mask" was imprisoned. You can visit his cell.

Musée de la Mer, Fort Royal (© **04-93-43-18-17**), traces the history of the island, displaying artifacts of Ligurian, Roman, and Arab civilizations, plus the remains discovered by excavations, including paintings, mosaics, and ceramics. The museum is open April to September Tuesday to Sunday 10:30am to 5:45pm (closing at 4:45pm Oct–Mar). Admission is 3.20€ for adults, free for students and children 17 and under.

ILE ST-HONORAT ★★   Only a mile (1.6km) long, but richer in history than its sibling islands, Ile St-Honorat is the site of a monastery whose origins go back to the 5th century. Today **Abbaye de Notre Dame de Lérins ★**, Les Iles de Lérins, Cannes 06400 (© **04-92-99-54-00**; www.abbayedelerins.com), boasts a combination of medieval ruins and early-20th-century ecclesiastical buildings, and a community of about 30 Cistercian monks. Under controlled circumstances, if space is available, well-intentioned outsiders can visit and spend the night, but only for prayer and meditation. Most visitors opt to avoid the monastery, wandering through the pine forests on the island's western side and sunbathing on its beaches.

WHERE TO STAY & DINE

Note: During major festivals in Cannes, hotels often increase their rates significantly and reservations can be difficult to obtain.

Hôtel Le Florian, 8 rue Commandant-André, 06400 Cannes (© **04-93-39-24-82**; www.hotel-leflorian.com; bus: 1), is on a busy but narrow, densely commercial street that leads directly into La Croisette, near the beach. Three generations of the Giordano family have maintained it since the 1950s. The hotel is basic but comfortable, and most rooms are rather small and Provençal in their styling, with decor that dates from 2004. Breakfast is the only meal available. Rates are 60€ to 80€ for a double. The 64-room **Hotel Splendid ★**, 4–6 rue Félix-Faure, 06400 Cannes (© **04-97-06-22-22**; www.spledid-hotel-cannes.fr), is an ornate white building with wrought-iron accents looking out onto the sea, the old port, and a park. The rooms boast antique furniture and paintings; about 15 have kitchenettes. It's a favorite of actors, musicians, and politicians. Rates are 131€ to 264€ double, including breakfast.

Hôtel Victoria ★, rond-point Duboys-d'Angers (© **04-92-59-40-00**; www.hotel-victoria-cannes.com), a stylish modern hotel in the heart of Cannes, offers accommodations with period reproductions and refrigerators. Nearly half of the 25 rooms have balconies overlooking the small park and the hotel pool (worth the extra cost). Rates are 110€ to 305€ double. Closed 2 weeks in December and 3 weeks in February. No rooms are available to the public during festivals (check website for exact dates).

Two sisters own **La Canna Suisse ★**, 23 rue Forville (le Suquet; © **04-93-99-01-27**; www.cannasuisse.com), a 30-year-old restaurant in Vieux Cannes that's decked out like a Swiss chalet and that specializes in the cheese-based cuisine of Switzerland's Alps. The menu features only two kinds of fondue—a traditional version concocted from six kinds of cheese and served in a bubbling pot with chunks of bread on skewers, plus another that adds either morels or cèpes to the blend, depending on your wishes. Main courses run 17€ to 26€; fixed-price menu 26€ to 27€.

Few other restaurants in Cannes work so successfully at establishing a cozy testimonial to the culinary skills of old-fashioned French cooking as **La Brouette de Grand-Mère,** 9 bis rue d'Oran (© **04-93-39-12-10**). Owner Didier has taken over from father Christian Bruno, who revitalized the recipes that many of the chic and trendy residents of Cannes remember from their childhood (or from an idealized version of their childhood). Memories are evoked in a way that Proust might have appreciated, through seasonally changing dishes that might include *les cailles rôties à la niçoise* (roasted quail served with a niçoise sauce) and *magret de canard aux griottes* (duck filet with morello cherries). A fixed-price menu, including half a bottle of wine, is 35€.

CANNES AFTER DARK

Palm Beach Casino, place F-D-Roosevelt (58 bd. Pointe de la Croisette; ✆ **04-97-06-36-90;** www.lepalmbeach.com), lies on the southeast edge of La Croisette. The casino maintains slot machines that operate daily from 10am to 5am; plus suites of rooms devoted to *les grands jeux* (blackjack, roulette, and baccarat) that are open nightly 8pm to 4am. There is a cover charge for access to *les grands jeux,* where presentation of a passport or an identity card is required.

An English-speaker's oasis is **Morrison's Irish Pub,** 10 rue Teisseire (✆ **04-92-98-16-17;** www.morrisonspub.com), which offers live music on Sunday; an international crowd; and big-screen TVs for soccer, golf, and rugby fans. Prices here are a welcome relief from the usual wallet-emptying costs of Cannes; there's even a happy hour from 5 to 8pm. Sunday is Ladies' Night starting at 10pm. Expect lots of French girls and some American students. Hours are daily from 5pm to 2am.

Nice ★★★

The Victorian upper class and czarist aristocrats loved Nice in the 19th century, but it is solidly middle class today. In fact, of all the major resorts of France, from Deauville to Biarritz to Cannes, Nice is the least expensive. It is also the best excursion center on the Riviera and has the best rail connections.

Nice is the capital of the Riviera, the largest city between Genoa and Marseille (also one of the most ancient, having been founded by the Greeks, who called it Nike, or "Victory"). Because of its brilliant sunshine and relaxed living, artists and writers have been attracted to Nice for years. Among them were Matisse, Dumas, Nietzsche, Appollinaire, Flaubert, Victor Hugo, Guy de Maupassant, George Sand, Stendhal, Chateaubriand, and Mistral.

GETTING THERE   Trains arrive at **Gare Nice-Ville,** avenue Thiers (✆ **08-92-35-35-35;** www.voyages-sncf.com). From here you can ride to Cannes for 5.80€, Monaco for 2.80€, and Antibes for 3.90€, with easy connections to anywhere else along the Mediterranean coast. There's a small-scale tourist center (✆ **08-92-70-74-07**) at the train station, open mid-September to mid-June Monday to Saturday 8am to 7pm and Sunday 9am to 5pm. In the summer, hours are Monday to Saturday 8am to 8pm and Sunday 9am to 6pm. The staff makes hotel reservations at no charge. If you face a long delay, you can eat at the cafeteria and even take showers at the station (or head to the beach—10 min. away).

Transatlantic and intercontinental flights land at **Aéroport Nice–Côte d'Azur** (✆ **08-20-42-33-33**). From here, municipal bus no. 98 departs at 30-minute intervals from the airport for Nice's bus station, Gare Routière, charging 4€ per person (day pass). To return to the airport, the no. 98 leaves at 20 and 40 minutes past the hour from Gare Routière. Bus nos. 23 and 99 go from the airport to the train station; bus no. 23 leaves from Gare Routière every 15 minutes and costs 1.30€, but only goes to/from terminal 1 (there is a free shuttle waiting at terminal 1 to take passengers to

Nice

ACCOMMODATIONS ■
Hôtel du Petit Palais **5**
Hôtel Gounod **8**
Hôtel Windsor **7**

DINING ◆
Brasserie Flo **2**
La Zucca Magica **6**

ATTRACTIONS ●
Cathédrale Orthodoxe
Russe St-Nicolas à Nice **1**
Musée des Beaux-Arts **9**
Musée de Matisse **4**
Musée National Message
Biblique Marc-Chagall **3**

Beach ⚓
ⓘ Information
⊠ Post Office

8

FRANCE | Provence & the Riviera

terminal 2). A **taxi** ride from the airport to the station will cost at least 30€ to 40€ each way (ask the price before getting in the taxi). Trip time is about 30 minutes.

VISITOR INFORMATION   Of the city's three tourist offices, the largest and most central is at 5 promenade des Anglais (✆ **08-92-70-74-07;** www.nicetourism. com), near place Masséna (about a ¾-mile/1.2km walk from the train station). The staff can make a same-day hotel reservation at no charge. Hours are October to May Monday to Saturday 9am to 6pm, and June to September Monday to Saturday 8am to 8pm and Sunday 9am to 6pm.

GETTING AROUND   Most of the local bus routes in Nice connect with one another at their central hub, the **Station Central SNCF,** 10 av. Félix-Faure (✆ **04-93-13-53-13;** www.voyages-sncf.com), a very short walk from place Masséna. Municipal buses each charge 1€ for a ride within Greater Nice. To save money, consider buying a 10-ticket *carnet* for 10€. Bus no. 2 or 12 makes frequent trips to the beach. You can use the **tram system** (✆ **08-11-00-20-06**) to reach popular areas of Nice such as the train station (Gare Thiers), Place Masséna, and the Old town (Vieille Ville); line 1 is from Las Planas to Pont Michel. Each ride is 1€ and includes transfers between tram and bus.

TOP ATTRACTIONS & SPECIAL MOMENTS

There's a higher density of museums in Nice than in many comparable French cities. If you decide to skip the beach and devote your time to touring in the south of France, you can buy the **French Riviera Pass.** The 1-, 2-, or 3-day pass gives you access to museums, guided tours, monuments, and even wine tasting in Nice. The 1-day pass is 24€, 2-day is 36€, and 3-day is 54€. The pass is also accepted in surrounding areas.

If you would prefer to tour on a hop-on, hop-off bus (with an open-air top deck), try **Gray Line's "Nice Le Grand Tour"** (✆ **04-92-29-17-00;** www.grayline.com) around the city sights. Buses depart from the promenade des Anglais (across from Jardin Albert 1er—Albert Gardens) every 30 minutes from 9:30am and cost 20€, 18€ for students, and 5€ children 4 to 11 (free with the French Riviera Pass). The tour is 1½ hours, but you can get on and off at any of the stops all day.

In 1822, the orange crop at Nice was bad and the workers faced a lean time. So the English residents put them to work building the **promenade des Anglais ★★**, a wide boulevard fronting the bay, split by "islands" of palms and flowers and stretching for about 4 miles (6.5km). Fronting the beach are rows of grand cafes, the Musée Masséna, villas, and hotels—some good, others decaying.

Crossing this boulevard in the briefest of bikinis or thongs are some of the world's most attractive bronzed bodies. They're heading for the **beach**—"on the rocks," as it's called here. Tough on tender feet, the beach is made not of sand, but of pebbles (and not-too-small ones). It's one of the least attractive aspects of the cosmopolitan resort city. Many bathhouses provide mattresses for a fee.

In the east, the promenade becomes **quai des Etats-Unis,** the original boulevard, lined with some of the best restaurants in Nice, all specializing in bouillabaisse. Rising sharply on a rock is the site known as **Le Château,** the spot where the ducs de Savoie built their castle, torn down in 1706. The hill has been turned into a garden of pines and exotic flowers. To reach the site for the view, you can take an elevator (many take the elevator up) or walk. The park is open daily from 8am to dusk.

At the north end of Le Château is the famous old **graveyard** of Nice, the largest one in France. It's visited primarily for its lavish monuments, which form their own enduring art statement. To reach it, you can take a small, canopied **Train Touristique** de Nice (© 06-16-39-53-51; fax 04-93-62-85-48), which departs from the Jardin Albert-1er. It makes a 40-minute sightseeing transit past many of Nice's most heralded sites, leaving every 30 to 60 minutes daily from 10am to 5pm (until 6pm Apr–May and Sept, until 7pm June–Aug). There's no service between mid-November and mid-December and during most of January. The price is 7€ for adults and 4€ for children 9 and under.

Continuing east from "the Rock" (the site of Le Château), you reach the **harbor,** where the restaurants are even cheaper and the bouillabaisse is just as good. While lingering over a drink at a sidewalk cafe, you can watch the boats depart for Corsica. The port was excavated between 1750 and 1830. Since then, the port has gained an outer harbor, protected by two jetties.

The "authentic" Niçoise live in **Vieille Ville** ★, the old town, beginning at the foot of the Rock and stretching to place Masséna. Sheltered by sienna-tiled roofs, many of the Italianate facades suggest 17th-century Genoese palaces. The old town is a maze of narrow streets, teeming with local life and studded with the least expensive restaurants in Nice. Buy an onion pizza *(la pissaladière)* from a vendor. Many of the buildings are painted a faded Roman gold, and their banners are laundry flapping in the sea breezes.

While here, try to visit the **Marché aux Fleurs,** the flower market at cours Saleya. A flamboyant array of carnations, violets, jonquils, roses, and birds of paradise, it operates Tuesday to Sunday 8am to 6pm in summer, and 8am until between 2 and 4pm in winter, depending on the vendors' remaining inventory and energy level.

Cathédrale Orthodoxe Russe St-Nicolas à Nice ★, avenue Nicolas-II (off bd. du Tzaréwitch; © 04-93-96-88-02), was ordered built by none other than Czar Nicholas II. This is the most beautiful religious edifice of the Orthodoxy outside Russia. It dates from the Belle Epoque, when some of the Romanovs and their entourage turned the Riviera into their own stomping ground. Admission is 3€ adults, 2€ students, free for children 12 and under. Hours are May to September daily 9am to noon and 2:30 to 6pm, October to April 9:30am to noon and 2:30 to 5pm. Celebration of the Russian Orthodox liturgy occurs every Sunday at 10am (open to public for worship only). From the central rail station, head west along avenue Thiers to boulevard Gambetta; then go north to avenue Nicolas-II.

The villa housing the **Musée des Beaux-Arts** ★★, 33 av. des Baumettes (© 04-92-15-28-28; www.musee-beaux-arts-nice.org; bus: 3, 9, 12, 22, or 60), was built in 1878 for the Ukrainian Princess Kotschoubey. The city of Nice has converted the villa into a museum of local history and decorative art. The first-floor gallery exhibits Niçoise primitives and masterpieces—paintings, sculptures, plates, and jewelry decorated with enamel (Limoges)—from the 15th to the 18th centuries. On the second floor are 19th-century collections devoted to sculptures, portraits, Impressionists, and post-Impressionists, including works by Monet, Rodin, and Viullard, as well as rooms featuring the history of Nice (and local artist Raoul Dufy). Admission is free. Hours are Tuesday to Sunday 10am to 6pm.

In the hills of Cimiez above Nice, the single-story **Musée National Message Biblique Marc-Chagall** ★★, avenue du Dr.-Ménard (© 04-93-53-87-31; www.musee-chagall.fr), cannot be missed! It is devoted to Marc Chagall's treatment of biblical themes. Born in Russia in 1887, Chagall became a French citizen in 1937. The artist and his wife donated the works—the most important collection of Chagall ever assembled—to France in 1966 and 1972. Displayed are 450 of his vibrant oil paintings, gouaches, drawings, pastels, lithographs, sculptures, ceramics, a mosaic, three stained-glass windows, and a tapestry. Admission is 7.50€ adults and 5.50€ students. Hours are Wednesday to Monday 10am to 6pm from May to October and until 5pm November to April. To get to Cimiez, catch bus no. 15 or 22 on rue Gioffredo near to place Masséna to "Museé Chagall" (it costs 1€).

While in Cimiez, visit the charming **Musée de Matisse ★★**, 164 av. des Arènes de Cimiez (📞 **04-93-81-08-08**; www.musee-matisse-nice.org; bus: 15 or 22 to Les Arènes/Musée). The 17th-century Genoese villa is filled with an impressive collection of Henri Matisse's drawings, sculptures, and paintings done from 1890 to 1953 (including sketches/models for his Chapelle du Rosaire in Vence). Admission is free for permanent collections and exhibits. For a guided tour, it is 5€ adults and 2.50€ students. Hours are Wednesday to Monday 10am to 6pm. *Tip:* Across from the museum are the gardens of the Cimiez monastery, which offer a great view of Nice.

WHERE TO STAY & DINE

The 46-room **Hôtel Gounod ★**, 3 rue Gounod, 0600 Nice (📞 **04-93-16-42-00;** www.gounod-nice.com), is situated in the city center, a 5-minute walk from the sea. The high-ceilinged guest rooms are comfortable and quiet, usually overlooking the gardens of private homes. Ornate balconies, a domed roof, and an elaborate canopy of wrought iron and glass embellish the Gounod. The attractive lobby and adjoining lounge are festive and stylish, with old prints, copper flowerpots, and antiques. Guests have free unlimited use of the pool and Jacuzzi at the Hôtel Splendid next door. Rates are 110€ to 160€ double, 150€ to 260€ suite.

The 57-room **Hôtel Windsor,** 11 rue Dalpozzo, 0600 Nice (📞 **04-93-88-59-35;** www.hotelwindsornice.com; bus 10 or 22), one of the most arts-conscious hotels in Provence, is set within a *maison bourgeoise* (near the Negresco and the promenade des Anglais), built by disciples of Gustav Eiffel in 1895. Inside you'll find an artsy ambience and comfortable, individually furnished bedrooms. A one-of-a-kind series of frescoes adorns each of the midsize guest rooms. The fifth floor holds the health club, steam room, and sauna. In the back is a quaint patio with parrots and an abundance of tropical flora. Rates are 90€ to 175€ double.

The 25-room **Hôtel du Petit Palais,** 17 av. Emile-Bieckert, 06000 Nice (📞 **04-93-62-19-11;** www.petitpalaisnice.com), occupies a mansion built around 1890; in the 1970s, it was the home of the actor and writer Sacha Guitry, a name that's instantly recognized in millions of French households. The preferred rooms—the most expensive—have balconies offering sea views during the day and sunset-watching at dusk. Rooms are Art Deco and Italianate in style; bathrooms are small but efficient, and each has a shower and tub. Rates are 90€ to 170€ double.

Housed in a restored turn-of-the-20th-century building near place Masséna, **Brasserie Flo,** 2–4 rue Sacha-Guitry (📞 **04-93-13-38-38**), is brisk, stylish, reasonably priced, and fun. The seasonal menu items might include an array of grilled fish, *choucroute* (sauerkraut) Alsatian style, steak with brandied pepper sauce, and fresh oysters and shellfish. Main courses run 18€ to 40€; fixed-price menus at dinner cost 23€ and 38€.

The chef at **La Zucca Magica (The Magic Pumpkin) ★**, 4 bis quai Papacino (📞 **04-93-56-25-27**), is the best Italian chef in Nice. Chef Marco serves refined vegetarian cuisine at reasonable prices, using recipes from Italy's Piedmont region and updating them with no meat or fish. Be warned that this is not your typical restaurant: There is no written menu, and everything is served here as part of a set-price "menu surprise." Four courses, plus a dessert, will be brought to your table unannounced and unheralded, but because everything is fresh and tasty, nobody leaves disappointed. Set menus cost 17€ at lunch, 29€ at dinner. Closed Sunday and Monday. Credit cards are not accepted.

NICE AFTER DARK

OPERA   The major cultural center on the Riviera is the **Opéra de Nice,** 4 rue St-François-de-Paule (℗ **04-92-17-40-00;** www.opera-nice.org), built in 1885 by Charles Garnier, fabled architect of the Paris Opéra. A full repertoire is presented, with emphasis on serious, often large-scale operas, as well as concerts and recitals. In one season you might see *Tosca, Les Contes de Hoffmann,* Verdi's *Macbeth,* Beethoven's *Fidelio,* and *Carmen,* as well as a *saison symphonique,* dominated by the Orchestre Philharmonique de Nice. Tickets are available up to about a day or two prior to any performance. You can show up at the box office (Mon–Sat 10am–5:30pm; Sun 10am–6pm) or buy tickets in advance by phoning ℗ **04-92-17-40-47.** Tickets run from 10€ for nosebleed (and we mean it) seats to 100€ for front-and-center seats on opening night.

Cabaret du Casino Ruhl, in the Casino Ruhl, 1 promenade des Anglais (℗ **04-97-03-12-22**), is Nice's answer to the cabaret glitter that appears in more ostentatious forms in Monte Carlo and Las Vegas. It includes a medley of cross-cultural jokes and nostalgia for the old days of French *chanson.* The cover of 22€ includes the first drink; dinner and the show (plus a bottle of wine per person) costs 62€. Shows are presented every Friday and Saturday at 10:15pm No jeans or sneakers.

AN EXCURSION TO ST-PAUL-DE-VENCE ★★

Of all the perched hill towns of the Riviera, St-Paul-de-Vence, 19 miles (31km) north of Nice, is the best known. It was popularized in the 1920s, when many noted artists and writers (including Henri Matisse, Marc Chagall—buried in the local cemetery—and expat James Baldwin) lived here, occupying the little 16th-century houses that flank the narrow cobblestone streets. The hill town was originally built to protect its inhabitants from Saracens raiding the coast. The feudal hamlet grew up on a bastion of rock, almost blending into it. Its ramparts (allow 30 min. to encircle them) overlook a peaceful setting of flowers and olive and orange trees. As you make your way through the warren of streets, you'll pass endless souvenir shops, art galleries, a charming old fountain carved in the form of an urn, and a Gothic church from the 13th century.

GETTING THERE   The nearest rail station is in Cagnes-sur-Mer, from which buses depart every 45 minutes for St-Paul-de-Vence. Rail passengers who arrive in Nice usually rent a car or opt for 1 of about 20 buses a day (bus no. 400), departing from Gare Routière, near the Nice railway station (trip time: 1 hr.). For bus information, call **Cie SAP** (℗ **04-93-58-37-60**). Buses stop in St-Paul near the post office, on the route de Vence, about ¼ mile (.4km) from the town center. Bus fare is 1€ one-way.

VISITOR INFORMATION   The **Office de Tourisme,** 2 rue Grande (℗ **04-93-32-86-95;** fax 04-93-32-60-27; www.saint-pauldevence.com), is open June to September daily 10am to 7pm, October to May daily 10am to 6pm. It's closed year-round between 1 and 2pm on the weekends and bank holidays. The local tourist office, if you phone at least a day (and sometimes a few hours) in advance, can arrange any of several distinctly themed walking tours of the town's historic core, as well as to some of the town's outskirts. Most tours last for about an hour and are priced at 5€ each; all of them depart from the tourist office.

TOP ATTRACTIONS & SPECIAL MOMENTS

Foundation Maeght ★★★, outside the town walls (✆ **04-93-32-81-63**), is the most important attraction in St-Paul. On the slope of a hill in pine-studded woods, the Maeght Foundation is like a Shangri-la. Not only is the architecture daringly avant-garde (designed by José Luis Sert), but the building itself houses one of the finest collections of contemporary art on the Riviera.

Calder and Miró's stark sculptures welcome visitors from the grassy lawns. In a courtyard, the elongated bronze works of Giacometti form a surrealistic garden, creating a hallucinatory mood. The museum is built on several levels, its many glass walls providing an indoor-outdoor vista. Everywhere you look, you see 20th-century art: mosaics by Chagall and Braque, Miró ceramics in the "labyrinth," and Ubac and Braque stained glass in the chapel. Bonnard, Kandinsky, Léger, Matisse, Hepworth, and many other artists are well represented. Scattered throughout are cheerful photographs, newspaper clippings, and videos—all reflecting happy times; it feels as if Aimé and Marguerite Maeght and the many artists who touched their lives are still very much present in this peaceful space.

The foundation, a gift "to the people" from the Maeghts, also provides a showcase for new talent. Exhibitions are always changing.

Admission is 11€ adults, 9€ students and ages 10 to 25, free for children ages 9 and under. Hours are July to September daily 10am to 7pm, October to June daily 10am to 6pm.

An Excursion to Vence ★★

Travel up into the hills northwest of Nice—across country studded with cypresses, olive trees, and pines, where bright flowers, especially carnations, roses, and oleanders, grow in profusion—and Vence comes into view. Outside the town, along boulevard Paul-André, two old olive presses carry on with their age-old duties. But the charm lies in the **Vieille Ville (Old Town).**

GETTING THERE   It's easier to reach Vence by bus than by train. Frequent **buses** (no. 94 direct or 200, which stops in St-Paul-de-Vence, 5 min. away) originating in Nice take about an hour to reach Vence and cost 1€ each way. For bus information, contact the **Compagnie SAP** at ✆ **04-93-58-37-60** for schedules. The nearest **rail station** is in Cagnes-sur-Mer, about 4½ miles (7km) from Vence. For rail info, call ✆ **08-92-35-35-35.**

VISITOR INFORMATION   The **Office de Tourisme** is on 8 place Grand-Jardin (✆ **04-93-58-06-38;** www.vence.fr/-Tourism-Office-.html). It's open July and August Monday to Saturday 9am to 7pm and Sunday until 6pm, September to October and March to June Monday to Saturday from 9am to 6pm, November to February Monday to Saturday from 9am to 5pm.

TOP ATTRACTIONS & SPECIAL MOMENTS

Visitors invariably have themselves photographed on **place du Peyra** in front of the urn-shaped **Vieille Fontaine (Old Fountain),** a background shot in several motion pictures. The 15th-century **square tower** is also a curiosity.

If you're wearing the right kind of shoes, the narrow, steep streets of the old town are worth exploring. Dating from the 10th century, the **cathedral** on place Godeau is unremarkable except for some 15th-century Gothic choir stalls. But if it's the right day of the week, most visitors quickly journey 15 minutes north of Vence's city center to the Chapelle du Rosaire.

For Art Lovers

To witness an artist's life and work in process, visit the **N.A.L.L Art Association** (Nature Art and Life League), 232 bd. de Lattre, Vence (℃ **04-93-58-13-26** or 06-19-22-46-01; www.nall.org), a hidden gem. In 1997 American artist Nall, and his wife, Tuscia, purchased 9 acres (3.6 hectares) of land in Vence's serene valley. Today they run a small museum and offer apprenticeships to young artists. Inspired by Dalí, Dures, Bellmer, and Seraphim, Nall's own mosaics combine collected materials from around the world with watercolors, creating vibrant, thought-provoking, and spiritual images. The association is a 10-minute walk from the no. 400 bus stop (follow the signs). Tours last 1 hour and cost 5€ per person on weekends and 10€ per person on weekdays. Reservations are required in advance.

The **Chapelle du Rosaire ★★**, avenue Henri-Matisse (℃ **04-93-58-03-26**), was built by the great Henri Matisse at age 77. After a turbulent personal search, the artist set out to create "the culmination of a whole life dedicated to the search for truth." Just outside Vence, Matisse created a Chapel of the Rosary for the Dominican nuns of Monteils, who continue to administer it today.

Matisse wrote: "What I have done in the chapel is to create a religious space . . . in an enclosed area of very reduced proportions and to give it, solely by the play of colors and lines, the dimensions of infinity." The light picks up the subtle coloring in the simply rendered leaf forms and abstract patterns: sapphire blue, aquamarine, and lemon yellow. In black-and-white ceramics, St. Dominic is depicted in only a few lines. The most remarkable design is the black-and-white-tiled Stations of the Cross, with Matisse's self-styled "tormented and passionate" figures. The bishop of Nice came to bless the chapel in the late spring of 1951, and, his masterpiece completed, Matisse died 3 years later.

Admission is 3€ adults, 1.50€ children 16 and under; contributions to maintain the chapel are welcomed. Hours are Tuesday and Thursday 10 to 11:30am and 2 to 5:30pm; Monday, Wednesday, and Saturday 2 to 5:30pm. Sunday Mass is at 10am, followed by visits at 10:45am. Closed Friday and November 15 to December 15.

WHERE TO DINE

If you, like most rail passengers, visit both St-Paul-De-Vence and Vence in a single day, one of the best and most affordable places for lunch (noon–2pm) in the area is in Vence.

La Farigoule, 15 rue Henri-Isnard (℃ **04-93-58-01-27**), is set within a century-old house in Vence that opens onto a rose garden, where tables are set out during summer. This restaurant specializes in Provençal cuisine, including an array of dishes that feature a *bourride Provençal* (a bouillabaisse with a dollop of cream and lots of garlic), or a shoulder of roasted lamb with a ragout of fresh vegetables, served with fresh thyme. The fixed-price menus run from 30€ to 40€. It's open Wednesday to Monday from noon to 2pm and 7:30 to 10pm; closed November 15 to December 15.

An Excursion to Monaco ★★★

The outspoken Katharine Hepburn called it "a pimple on the chin of the south of France." She wasn't referring to the principality's lack of beauty, but rather to the preposterous idea of having a little country, a feudal anomaly, taking up some of the choicest coastline along the Riviera. Hemmed in by France on three sides and facing the Mediterranean, Monaco staunchly maintains its independence. Even Charles de Gaulle couldn't force the late Prince Rainier to do away with his tax-free policy (Monegasques do not pay taxes).

Monaco, or rather, its capital of Monte Carlo, has for a century been a symbol of glamour. Its legend was further enhanced by the marriage in 1956 of the world's most eligible bachelor, Prince Rainier, to an American film star, Grace Kelly. She met the prince when she attended the Cannes Film Festival to promote the Hitchcock movie she made with Cary Grant, *To Catch a Thief*. Following the death of his father in 2005, Prince Albert II became the ruler of the principality.

Monaco became property of the Grimaldi clan, a Genoese family, as early as 1297. With shifting loyalties, it has maintained something resembling independence ever since. In a fit of impatience, the French annexed it in 1793, but the ruling family recovered it in 1814, although the prince at the time couldn't bear to tear himself away from the pleasures of Paris for "dreary old Monaco."

The second-smallest state in Europe (Vatican City is first), Monaco consists of the old town, **Monaco-Ville,** sitting on a promontory, the Rock, 200 feet high (60m)—the seat of the royal palace and the government building, as well as the famous Oceanographic Museum (see below). On the west of the bay, **La Condamine,** the home of the Monegasques, is at the foot of the old town, forming its harbor and port sector.

Up from the port (walking is steep in Monaco) is **Monte Carlo,** once the playground of European royalty and still the center for the wintering wealthy, the setting for the casino and its gardens and the deluxe hotels, such as the Hôtel de Paris. The fourth part of Monaco, **Fontvieille,** is an industrial suburb, surprisingly neat—but this entire principality is kept tidy.

Ironically, **Monte Carlo Beach,** at the far frontier, is on French soil. It attracts a chic, well-heeled crowd, including movie stars. The resort consists of a freshwater swimming pool, an artificial beach, and a sea-bathing establishment.

GETTING THERE   Monaco has rail connections to other coastal cities. Trains arrive every 30 minutes from Cannes, Nice, Menton, and Antibes. For more rail information and schedules, call ☎ **08-92-35-35-35.** Monaco's railway station (Gare SNCF) is on avenue Prince Pierre. It's a long, steep walk uphill from the train station to Monte Carlo. If you'd rather take a **taxi** but can't find one at the station, call ☎ **08-20-20-98-98;** the ride into town will cost about 10€. There are no border formalities for anyone entering Monaco from mainland France. If there is a train strike at the time of your visit, you can take the no. 100 bus from Nice for 1€.

VISITOR INFORMATION   The **Direction du Tourisme** office is in Monte Carlo at 2A bd. des Moulins (☎ **92-16-61-16;** fax 92-16-60-00; www.visitmonaco. com). They do not reserve rooms for visitors. Hours are Monday to Saturday 9am to 7pm and Sunday 11am to 1pm. *Note:* November 19 is Monaco's National Day, and most museums and attractions are closed.

TOP ATTRACTIONS & SPECIAL MOMENTS

During summer, most day-trippers from Nice head to **Les Grands Appartements du Palais ★**, place du Palais (☎ **93-25-18-31;** www.palais.mc), wanting to see the home of Monaco's royal family, the Palais du Prince, which dominates the principality from "the Rock." A tour of the Grands Appartements allows you a glimpse of the

8

FRANCE | Provence & the Riviera

ATTRACTIONS ●

Jardin Exotique **2**
Les Grand Appartements du Palais **3**
Musée d'Anthropologie
  Préhistorique **1**
Musée de l'Océanographie **4**
Musée du Palais du Prince
  (Souvenirs Napoléoniens
  et Collection d'Archives) **3**
Musée National de Monaco **8**

DINING ◆

Fusion on the Port **6**
Le Café de Paris **7**
Stars 'n' Bars **5**

Information ⓘ
Post Office ✉

Throne Room and some of the art (including works by Bruegel and Holbein), as well as the late Princess Grace's state portrait. The palace was built in the 13th century, and part of it dates from the Renaissance. The ideal time to arrive is 11:55am, to watch the 10-minute **Relève de la Garde (Changing of the Guard).**

In a wing of the palace, the **Musée du Palais du Prince (Souvenirs Napoléoniens et Collection d'Archives),** place du Palais (ⓒ **93-25-18-31**), has a collection of mementos of Napoléon and Monaco itself. When the royal residence is closed, this museum is the only part of the palace the public can visit.

A single ticket to the Grands Apartments costs 7€ for adults, 3.50€ for children aged 8 to 14 and students. A single to the Musée du Palais is 4€ for adults, 2€ for children aged 8 to 14 and students. A combination ticket is 4€ for adults, 2€ children 8 to 14, free for children ages 7 and under. Palace and museum hours are daily January to March 10:30am to 5pm, April 10:30am to 6pm, May to September 9:30am to 6:30pm, October 10am to 5:30pm, December 10:30am to 5pm. Closed in November.

Built on the side of a rock, the **Jardin Exotique ★★**, 62 bd. du Jardin-Exotique (✆ **93-15-29-80;** www.jardineexotique.mc), is known for its cactus collection, which was begun by Prince Albert I, who was a naturalist and scientist, and was great-great-grandfather to the present prince. He spotted some succulents growing in the palace gardens and created this garden from them. You can also explore the grottoes here, as well as the **Musée d'Anthropologie Préhistorique** (✆ 93-15-29-80). The view of the principality is splendid. Admission to garden and museum costs 6.90€, 3.60€ children 6 to 18, free for children under 6. It's open mid-May to mid-September daily 9am to 7pm; mid-September to mid-May daily 9am to 6pm or until sunset, whichever comes first. Closed November 19 to Christmas.

The **Musée de l'Océanographie ★★**, avenue St-Martin (✆ **93-15-36-00;** www.oceano.mc), was founded in 1910 by Albert I. In the main rotunda is a statue of Albert in his favorite costume: that of a sea captain. Displayed are specimens he collected during 30 years of expeditions. The aquarium, one of the finest in Europe, contains more than 90 tanks. Some of the exotic creatures you'll see were unknown before he captured them. Skeletons of specimens are located on the main floor, including a whale that drifted ashore at Pietra Ligure in 1896. The skeleton is remarkable for its healed fractures, sustained when a vessel struck the animal as it was drifting on the surface. Admission is 13€ adults, 6€ children 6 to 18, free for children under 6. Hours are daily October to March 10am to 6pm, April to June and September 9:30am to 7pm, July to August 9:30am to 7:30pm.

In a villa designed by Charles Garnier (architect of Paris's Opéra Garnier), the **Musée National de Monaco ★**, 17 av. Princesse-Grace (✆ **98-98-91-26;** www.monte-carlo.mc/musee-national), stems from an 18th- and 19th-century trend to create magnificent displays of antique mechanical toys and dolls. See the 18th-century Neapolitan crib, which contains some 200 figures. This collection, assembled by Mme. de Galea, was presented to the principality in 1972. Admission is 6€ adults, 3.50€ students and children 6 to 14, free for children under 6. Open daily 10am to 6pm; closed New Year's Day, May 1, May 24 to May 27, November 19, Christmas, and 4 days during Grand Prix.

WHERE TO DINE

Le Café de Paris ★, place du Casino (✆ **92-16-20-20**), provides you with a front-row view of the comings and goings of the nerve center of Monte Carlo. Menu items change frequently. The platters are appreciated by local office workers, especially at lunchtime, because they can be served and consumed relatively quickly. Main courses run 30€ to 50€, and a fixed-price menu costs 35€. Reservations are recommended.

Stars 'n' Bars, 6 quai Antoine-1er (© **97-97-95-95;** http://starsnbars.liferiviera. com), is modeled on the sports bars popular in the U.S. ,with Tex-Mex, steaks, pizza, sandwiches, and salads—and a happy hour (Tues–Fri 5:30–7:30pm). On weekends (11am–3pm), they offer the "Brunch of Champions," a great addition to the all-around American experience at one of Monte Carlo's hot spots. You might even see a celebrity while you're there! Dinner salads and platters cost 10€ to 28€, sandwiches 11€ to 15€, and pizzas 10€ to 15€. Reservations recommended.

Fusion on the Port, 6 quai Antoine-1er (© **97-97-95-90;** http://starsnbars. liferiviera.com), is the chic upstairs addition to Stars 'n' Bars, with an excellent view of Monaco's port. The Pan-Asian menu "fuses" fresh, local products with traditional Japanese, Chinese, Thai, and Indian cooking techniques. On the terrace, diners can opt for the Fusion or Stars menu—plenty of choice for everyone! Main courses run 15€ to 28€.

GERMANY

Although it's only about half the size of Texas, Germany is a large country by European standards. It also has an enviable location smack-dab in the center of the Continent, offering comprehensive rail links to most other major European nations. Within Germany, traveling by train is a snap, due to one of the world's most efficient and speedy—though by no means least expensive—rail networks. These networks crisscross a multitude of inspiring landscapes, from Alpine peaks to low-lying coastal plains, from dense forests to river valleys, passing hillside vineyards, craggy bluffs topped by medieval castles, and other scenes straight from the fairy tales.

Germany's cities beckon, too, even though many of them, on the surface at least, share a similar trait of bland modernity—they were blown to bits during World War II bombings and rebuilt in haste in the postwar period. But throughout Germany, an impressive array of the finest of the lost architectural and cultural treasures has been re-created, and this work continues apace. And in many smaller towns that were spared the hard hand of war, historic cores of astonishing harmony and beauty seduce travelers just as they have for centuries. In short, Germany is both an easy and a fascinating stop on any rail traveler's journey though Europe.

Highlights of Germany

Covering all of the fascinating towns and sights of Germany could easily take an entire book and several months of travel. Because most rail travelers won't have more than a week or so to visit the country, in this chapter we stick to the regions and cities we feel give the visitor a good yet varied look at the best Germany has to offer, from bustling metropolises to quaint villages, from the Bavarian charm of the south to the imposing grandeur of cities that were once part of former East Germany. We also stick to places that can easily be reached by rail. So while many people fly into the commercial hub of Frankfurt, we don't cover it beyond telling you how to board a train out of the city, because there are far better places for travelers on a limited timetable to explore.

To say that Germany's capital, **Berlin,** had its ups and downs during the century just past would be an understatement of monumental proportions. Berlin has seen it all: proud imperial capital through defeat in World War I, 1920s instability and decadence, Hitler and the Holocaust, total destruction and defeat in World War II, occupation, partition by the Cold War "iron curtain" of the Berlin Wall, peaceful reunification, and national capital once again. And guess what? Berlin is back! It boasts the nation's greatest museums, a wealth of other attractions linked to its checkered past, and Germany's hottest nightlife. As the capital city and a major rail junction in the north, it's a natural starting point for many a visitor, and we rank it first on our tour of the country as well. While you can get a quick glimpse of Berlin in a couple of hours from the top deck of an open-top tour bus, as with all the world's great cities, you need to take time to explore, to settle in, and to allow a little of the city's unique atmosphere to seep into your psyche. For those with limited time, we recommend spending 3 days in Berlin before you set out to see more of Germany. On the outskirts of Berlin is **Potsdam,** a charming small town with a quaint historic core and a lovely palace set amid an expansive garden.

Oktoberfest, Germany's most famous festival, takes place in Munich from mid-September to the first Sunday in October. Millions show up, and hotels are packed. Most activities are at Theresienwiese, where local breweries sponsor gigantic tents that can hold up to 6,000 beer drinkers and there are many amusement rides and booths. Contact **Munich Tourist Information** (✆ **089/23396500;** www.muenchen.de) for particulars, or just show up. However, always reserve hotel rooms well in advance. Munich's other big bash is **Fasching** (Carnival), which culminates Shrove Tuesday (Mardi Gras, before Ash Wed) in a parade through town and a festive atmosphere at Viktualienmarkt.

Jazz-Fest Berlin is an annual festival staged in early November at Berlin's Philharmonie and attracts some of the world's finest jazz artists, ranging from traditional to experimental. Contact the **Berlin Festspiele Ticket Office** (✆ **030/254890;** www.berlinerfestspiele.de) for more information.

In Heidelberg, there are fireworks displays and a spectacular illumination of its castle in June, July, and September. For more information, contact **Heidelberg Tourist Bureau,** Willy-Brandt-Platz 1 (✆ **06221/14220;** www.heidelberg-marketing.de).

Down south is another great city, **Munich,** the exuberant capital of the highly independent state of Bavaria. It, too, serves as one of Germany's most important cultural centers and is graced with an impressive architecture that includes royal residences, steepled churches, grand squares, and ornate monuments. A worthy side trip is **Neuschwanstein,** a picture-perfect castle perched on a cliff and famous as the model for Walt Disney's Sleeping Beauty castle at Disneyland.

A good contrast to the bustling cities of Berlin and Munich is **Heidelberg,** a medieval jewel and a thriving university town, famous for its massive castle that looms above the town's narrow, picturesque streets. Just a short train ride from Frankfurt, it's a perfect first-night stopover after a long transatlantic flight. Another great town worthy of a stopover, this time in former East Germany, is **Dresden,** once one of Germany's most important cultural centers and almost completely reconstructed in time for its 800th birthday celebration in 2006. It lies about halfway between Berlin and Prague by rail.

Finally, while Germany may not have a reputation as a land of romance, it does have its own **Romantic Road,** a route that stretches from **Würzburg** south to Füssen, connecting some of Europe's best-preserved medieval towns and monuments along the way.

ESSENTIALS

Getting There

Germany's own **Lufthansa** (✆ **800/645-3880;** www.lufthansa.com) operates the most frequent service from around 23 gateway cities in the U.S. and Canada, and flies to the greatest number of Germany's airports.

Other major North American carriers that fly to Germany include **American Airlines** (✆ 800/443-7300; www.aa.com), **Continental Airlines** (✆ 800/231-0856; www.continental.com), **Delta Airlines** (✆ 800/241-4141; www.delta.com), **United**

Airlines (© 800/241-6522; www.united.com), **US Airways** (© 800/428-4322; www.usairways.com), and **Air Canada** (© 888/247-2262; www.aircanada.com).

Germany's major international gateway—and continental Europe's busiest airport—is **Flughafen Frankfurt/Main** (© 180/53724636; www.airportcity-frankfurt. com), which lies 7 miles (11km) from the city center at the Frankfurter Kreuz, the intersection of two major expressways. The airport consists of two terminals, Terminal 1 and Terminal 2, connected by a people-mover system, Sky Line, which provides quick transfers (the airport's standard connection time is 45 min. maximum). There are connecting flights to all major German airports. Flying time from Frankfurt to either Berlin or Munich is approximately 1 hour.

At the **Airport Train Stations** (Regional and Long-distance) close to Terminal 1, you can connect to German InterCity and S-Bahn commuter trains that go directly to other German cities, such as Munich, and a few other European cities, including Vienna and Basel. Otherwise, local trains link the airport to Frankfurt's main rail station, the **Hauptbahnhof,** in about 15 minutes, with connections to all major German cities.

Germany by Rail

The national rail corporation in Germany, **Deutsche Bahn (German Rail)—DB,** for short—spreads its silvery tentacles into the remotest corners of the land and manages more than 22,320 miles (35,935km) of rail track. The rail system is renowned for its timeliness and reach; German trains even crank their way up more than a few Alpine mountainsides. The busiest stations, in places such as Berlin, Munich, and Frankfurt, see hundreds of arrivals and departures—regional, national, and international—every day. For more information, to order tickets, and for the best European train timetables on the Web, check out DB's website at **www.bahn.de** (click on "Internat. Guests"). From outside Germany, you can obtain train schedules, purchase tickets, and make seat reservations by calling © **49/1805/996633.** Within Germany, dial © **11861.** An automated toll-free service for train schedules is available by calling © **0800/1507090.** Once you begin traveling, you'll find **Travel Centres** in major stations helpful for purchasing tickets and planning routes, while the **ServicePoint,** available in about 90 stations, provides quick answers to questions about connections, rail travel, timetables, and local information (if the local tourist office is closed, you may be able to pick up a city map here).

TICKETS & PASSES

For details on purchasing multicountry options, such as the **Eurail Global Pass,** and for information on the **German Rail Pass,** see chapter 2. In addition to the German Rail Pass, DB offers a **Twinpass** for two adults traveling together that's a real bargain. This pass costs $530 for 4 days in 1 month for first class or $402 for second class (price is for two, not per person). The passes above must be purchased in North America through your travel agent or **Rail Europe** (© **877/272-RAIL** [7245] in North America; www.raileurope.com).

Other discount fares and tickets available in Germany at most rail stations include:

BAHNCARD A range of cards—BahnCard 25, 50, and 100—offer reduced-rate travel for people who intend to do a lot of traveling by train in Germany over an extended period of time. The BahnCard 25, for example, is worth purchasing for rail travel costing more than 228€, the equivalent of traveling round-trip between Hamburg and Munich; it costs 57€ and provides a 25% discount off regular and special train fares.

GRUPPE & SPAR Tickets for groups of up to five people traveling together, offering savings from 50% to 70%, depending on how far in advance you buy them (up to 14 days).

LÄNDER-TICKETS In some of the German *Länder* (states), a range of reduced-rate tickets is offered on particular routes for individuals and groups of up to five people. The Bayern-Ticket, for example, allows nearly unlimited travel on local trains in Bavaria for 20€ for an individual and 28€ for up to five people if bought at a ticket machine; tickets bought at a ticket counter cost 2€ more.

SCHÖNES-WOCHENENDE-TICKET The Beautiful-Weekend-Ticket is valid for up to five people traveling on local trains throughout Germany on a Saturday or Sunday for 37€ if bought from a ticket machine, or 39€ if bought at a ticket window. It is also available for families traveling with children 14 or under.

FOREIGN TRAIN TERMS

The rail network as a whole is known as *Die Bahn*. A *Zug* is a train. A fast regional train is known as a *Schnellzug* or *Eilzuge*. Night trains are known as *Nachtzüge*. A *Zuschlag* is a supplement, which you'll need to pay only on ICE high-speed German trains, if not using a railpass.

Class is *Klasse*. *Zweite (2.) Klasse* is second class, and *Erste (1.) Klasse* is first class. A station is a *Bahnhof*. In towns and cities that have more than one station, the main station is often called the *Hauptbahnhof (Hbf)*. The German term for platform is *Bahnsteig; Gleis* means "track." The bigger stations have separate counters for selling domestic tickets (*Inlandsreisen*) and international tickets (*Auslandsreisen*, or just plain *International*). A *Fahrkarte* or *Fahrschein* is a ticket. A timetable is a *Fahrplan*. Platforms are generally subdivided into sections—A, B, C, D, and so on—and you are often informed of what section (*Abschnitt*) you will board or vacate the train at. If you have baggage you want to store for a time, look for the *Gepäckaufbewahrung*. Arrival and departure are *Ankunft* and *Abfahrt*, respectively. And if you need to change trains, the word for "transfer" is *Umsteigen*.

PRACTICAL TRAIN INFORMATION

As Berlin strengthens its role as capital, increasing numbers of trains are speeding their way into town. All points of the country, especially Frankfurt, Munich, and Bonn, maintain excellent rail connections, with high-tech, high-speed improvements being made to the country's railway system virtually all the time. Unlike many other European countries whose rail service is highly centralized, Germany uses a multihub system, which means you rarely have to wait long for a train.

Germany's high-speed **InterCity Express (ICE)** trains are sleek, comfortable, and among the fastest in Europe, reaching speeds of 174 mph (280kmph). These trains run on most major rail corridors in the country (and a number of international routes as well), with each train making a few stops along the way. There are actually several different types of ICE trains, ranging from the older but incredibly spacious domestic ICE 1 trains to the newer ICE T trains that use tilting technology and travel internationally.

All ICE trains offer state-of-the-art amenities, which may include electronic seat reservation displays, personal audio systems (and even personal video screens in first class), luggage storage lockers, fold-down tabletops, and computer ports. Some ICE trains have panoramic lounges that offer excellent views of the surrounding landscape. The ICE network significantly reduces travel time, making transits north to south or east to west across the country easily in the course of a single day.

Trains & Travel Times in Germany

From	To	Type of Train	# of Trains	Frequency	Travel Time
Frankfurt	Berlin	ICE	18	Daily	4 hr.
Frankfurt	Heidelberg	ICE, IC, RB	34	Daily	1 hr.
Frankfurt	Munich	ICE, IC	18	Daily	3 hr., 45 min.
Berlin	Munich	ICE, IC	13	Daily	6 hr.
Berlin	Potsdam	RE	29	Daily	25 min.
Berlin	Dresden	EC, IC	7	Daily	2 hr.
Munich	Heidelberg	IC	7	Daily	3 hr., 15 min.

Slightly slower are the hundreds of **InterCity (IC)** passenger trains, traveling up to 124 mph (200kmph), with service every hour or two to the centers of some 60 German cities. IC trains have adjustable cushioned seats and individual reading lights. Bars, lounges, and dining rooms are available, too. A network of **EuroCity (EC)** trains connecting Germany with 13 other countries offers the same high standards of service as those of IC.

Interregio-Express (IRE) trains, some with double-decker compartments, handle inter-regional service and stop at more stations than the InterCity trains. *Regionalverkehr* (RV, RB, and RE) trains are local trains that stop at most, if not all, stations on their route.

CityNightLine (CNL) trains are exceptionally comfortable, including some double-decker night trains that run domestically, as well as between Germany and surrounding countries, such as the route from Berlin to Zurich, or Frankfurt to Vienna or Copenhagen. They offer four categories of comfort, from private cabins with bathrooms to reclining seats. Similarly, the **EuroNights** provide night service on major international routes, including Munich to Budapest.

RESERVATIONS German trains are invariably crowded, and even though they aren't required on most IC or ICE routes, many people reserve seats. We strongly recommend that you do, too, if you don't want to end up standing. Reservations cost 1.50€ to 3.50€ extra; reservations for the ICE Sprinters cost 11€ extra. Reservations on all night trains and ICE Sprinters are mandatory and should be made as far in advance as possible, especially if you're traveling on an international route; sleeper reservations are normally included in the price of the ticket or pass supplement that you pay. Seat reservations can be made at all train stations or can be reserved in North America through Rail Europe.

SERVICES & AMENITIES Nearly all German trains, even the smallest, have a first-class section or cars (offering more leg space and comfier seats). Trains are generally clean and comfortable. All trains are nonsmoking.

ICE trains have a buffet or restaurant car (called BordBistro or BordRestaurant) that sells drinks, meals, and snacks. The quality is usually good. IC trains generally have an attendant who pushes around a small cart from which coffee, tea, mineral water, sandwiches, potato chips, and other snack items are dispensed. These are more expensive than the same things bought from a supermarket, so if you're on a tight budget, buy them before boarding the train.

Night trains offer first and tourist class. Sleeping accommodations in first class include single or double compartments with shower and toilet, and are equipped with key cards, phones for wake-up service, luggage storage, and other amenities. Tourist class offers four-bed cabins with shared bathrooms, as well as open seating with *sleeperettes* (reclining seats). Trains are equipped with a restaurant and bistro car, and breakfast is included in the first-class fare.

DB will arrange assistance for travelers with disabilities (getting to and boarding trains, among other things), provided you call their **Mobility Assistance Centre** (✆ **01805/512-512**) at least a day in advance.

[Fast FACTS] GERMANY

Area Codes The country code for Germany is **49.** To call Germany from North America, dial 011 (the international access code), followed by the country code, the local area code minus the first zero (see below), and the telephone number. *Note:* The phone numbers listed in this book are the local numbers within Germany. The area code for Berlin is **030.** Other area codes used in this book include: Munich **089,** Heidelberg **06221,** and Dresden **0351.**

Business Hours Most **banks** are open Monday to Friday 8:30am to 1pm and 2:30 to 4pm (Thurs to 5:30pm), though hours vary from city to city. Money exchanges at airports and major train stations are generally open daily from about 6 or 7am to 10pm. Most **stores** are generally open Monday to Friday 9 or 10am to 6 or 6:30pm (Thurs to 8:30pm). Saturday hours are generally from 9am to 1 or 2pm, except on the first Saturday of the month, when stores may remain open until 4pm. Stores are closed on Sunday, though convenience stores are open at major train stations.

Climate The most popular tourist months are May to October, although winter travel to Germany is becoming increasingly popular, especially to the ski areas in the Bavarian Alps. Germany's climate varies widely. In the north, winters tend to be cold and rainy; summers are most agreeable. In the south and in the Alps, it can be very cold in winter, especially in January, and very warm in summer, but with cool, rainy days even in July and August. Spring and fall are often stretched out.

Documents Required For stays of up to 3 months, citizens of the U.S. and Canada need only to have a valid passport. A visa is required for stays of longer than 3 months.

Electricity Germany operates on 220 volts electricity (North America uses 110 volts). So you'll need a small voltage transformer that plugs into the round-holed European electrical outlet for any small appliance up to 1,500 watts. When in doubt, ask your hotel's front desk for advice before plugging anything in.

Embassies & Consulates The following are in Berlin: **United States:** Pariser Platz 2 (✆ **030/ 83050;** http://germany. usembassy.gov; U-Bahn: Zoologischer Garden), open Monday to Friday 8:30am to 3pm.; **Canada:** Leipziger Platz 17 (✆ **030/203120;** www.canadainternational. gc.ca; U-Bahn: Potsdamer Platz), open Monday to Friday 9am to noon. In Munich, the consulate of the **United States** is at Königstrasse 5 (✆ **089/ 288575;** bus: 53), open Monday, Wednesday, and Friday 1 to 4pm, and Tuesday and Thursday 8:30am to noon; and the consulate of **Canada** is at Tal Strasse 29 (✆ **089/2199570;** S-Bahn: Isartor), open Monday to Friday 9am to noon and Monday to Friday 2 to 4pm by appointment only.

Health & Safety Should you get ill while in Germany, hotels and tourist offices usually keep a list of English-speaking doctors and dentists, and the country's medical system is excellent. At least one pharmacy in every major city is open all night. Water is safe to drink in all major cities, but you should not drink any mountain stream water, no matter how pure it looks.

Germany is a reasonably safe country in which to travel, although neo-Nazi skinheads, especially in the eastern part of the country, have sometimes attacked black or Asian travelers. One of the most dangerous places, especially at night, is around the large railway stations in such cities as Frankfurt, Munich, Berlin, and Hamburg. Some beer halls get especially rowdy late at night.

Holidays January 1 (New Year's Day), Easter (Good Friday and Easter Monday), May 1 (Labor Day), Ascension Day (10 days before Pentecost/Whitsunday, the seventh Sun after Easter), Whitmonday (day after Pentecost/Whitsunday), October 3 (Day of German Unity), November 17 (Day of Prayer and Repentance), and December 25 to 26 (Christmas). In addition, the following holidays are observed in some German states: January 6 (Epiphany), Corpus Christi (10 days after Pentecost), August 15 (Assumption), and November 1 (All Saints' Day).

Mail General delivery—mark it POSTE RESTANTE—can be used in any major town or city in Germany. You can pick up your mail upon presentation of a valid identity card or passport. Street mailboxes are painted yellow. It costs 1.70€ for the first 5 grams (about ⅕ oz.) to send an airmail letter to the United States or Canada, and 1€ for postcards. To mail a package, go to one of the larger post offices, preferably the main branch in the area.

Police & Emergencies Throughout Germany, the emergency number for **police** is ✆ **110;** for fire or to call an ambulance, dial ✆ **112.**

Telephone Local and long-distance calls may be placed from public telephone booths, most of which nowadays require an advance-payment telephone card. **Telekom,** the German telephone company, offers phone cards at post offices in denominations of 6€ to 25€. Otherwise, insert the basic local rate as a deposit. In any

case, don't make phone calls from a hotel, where rates are often quadruple the standard.

German phone numbers are not standard and come in various formats. Hyphens in a telephone number indicate an extension. But because all the area codes are the same, these various configurations should have little effect on your phone usage once you get used to the fact that numbers are inconsistent and vary from place to place.

Tipping If a restaurant bill says *Bedienung,* that means a service charge has already been added, so just round up to the nearest euro.

If not, add 10% to 15%. Round up to the nearest euro for taxis. Bellhops get 1€ per bag, as does the doorperson at your hotel, restaurant, or nightclub. Room-cleaning staff gets small tips in Germany (about 1€ a night), as do concierges who perform some special favors, such as obtaining hard-to-get theater or opera tickets.

BERLIN ★★★

With its field of new skyscrapers, hip clubs, and fashion boutiques, Berlin is positioning itself as the Continent's new capital of cool. As one hip young Berliner, Joachim Stressmann, put it: "We don't know where we're going, but we know where we've been, and no one wants to go back there."

Before World War II, the section of the city that became East Berlin was the cultural and political heart of Germany, where the best museums, the finest churches, and the most important boulevards lay. The walled-in East Berliners turned to restoring their important museums, theaters, and landmarks (especially in the Berlin-Mitte section), while the West Berliners built entirely new museums and cultural centers. Today museum collections either have merged or are in the process of being merged, and it's difficult to see much difference between the former East and West. Former

Western Berlin

ACCOMMODATIONS ■
Art'otel **11**
Hotel Alexander **12**
Hotel Domus **13**
Hotel Hansablick **17**
Savoy Berlin **15**
Tiergarten Berlin **18**

DINING ◆
Brasserie Desbrosses **22**
Calcutta **7**
Le Buffet im KaDaWe **19**
Marjellchen **8**
Restaurant Lubitsch **6**

Restaurant Lutter &
Wegner Seit 1811 **4**
Zwölf Apostel **5**

9

GERMANY | Berlin

GERMANY | Berlin

ATTRACTIONS ●

Brandenburger Tor **21**
Bröhan Museum **3**
Die Sammlung
  Berggruen **2**
Gemäldegalerie **23**
Jüdisches Museum **24**

Kaiser-Wilhelm-
  Gedächtniskirche **14**
Käthe-Kollwitz-Museum **10**
Reichstag **20**
Schloss Charlottenburg **1**
The Story of Berlin **9**
Zoologischer Garten **16**

Information — Post Office — S-Bahn — U-Bahn

Hamburg • Berlin ★ GERMANY • Frankfurt am Main • Munich

East Berlin, in particular, has changed wildly since the reunification, with renovated historic buildings, spanking new ones, and the city's hottest nightlife. If you've never been to Berlin—or even if you have—it will be hard to imagine that the city was ever divided.

Given its history and its wide range of attractions, hotels, and restaurants, the city is a natural starting point for a rail tour of the country, even if you end up flying into a more popular airport such as Frankfurt. Situated in the northeast of Germany, Berlin offers excellent rail connections to all of the major cities of Germany and has direct rail connections to many major cities, including Paris, Warsaw, Vienna, Zurich, Budapest, and Prague.

Station Information
GETTING FROM THE AIRPORT TO THE TRAIN STATION
Note: If you fly into Frankfurt, a popular airport for flights out of North America, follow the directions listed under "Getting There," earlier, for getting to the Frankfurt main train station, and then hop a train to Berlin. It takes approximately 4 hours by train to get to Berlin from Frankfurt's main train station, with trains departing every hour or less.

In 2012, the new **Airport Berlin Brandenburg International (BBI;** www. berlin-airport.de) will open in Schönefeld to replace the east and west sectors' former airports. Until then, **Berlin-Tegel Airport,** 5 miles (8km) northwest of the city center, is the city's busiest. If you're arriving via Lufthansa, Air Berlin, or any other of the other airlines serving Berlin from Frankfurt, Munich, or Western Europe, you'll likely arrive here. The best and easiest way to get into town, particularly if your destination is one of the hotels on or around Kurfürstendamm, is by **city bus 109,** which costs 2.10€ one-way and departs every 10 to 15 minutes from outside the arrivals hall. It travels along Kurfürstendamm, where many hotels are located, to Bahnhof Zoologischer Garten (usually shortened to Bahnhof Zoo) in about 30 minutes. **Bus X9** travels a more direct route, with fewer stops (it does *not* travel along Kurfürstendamm), between Tegel Airport and Bahnhof Zoo in less than 20 minutes for the same fare. If you're staying near Berlin-Mitte, take one of the buses above to Bahnhof Zoo and transfer to the S-Bahn, or take the **JetExpressBus TXL** directly to Berlin-Mitte's Unter den Linden for 2.10€. If you think you'll be using public transportation more than one more time during the rest of the day, consider purchasing a *Tageskarte* (day ticket); see "Getting Around," below. The trip by **taxi** to Bahnhof Zoo is about 16€.

Schönefeld Airport, which once served as East Berlin's major airport, also receives both domestic and international flights, including many from Eastern Europe. The fastest way to get from Schönefeld to the city center is by the Airport-Express train, which delivers you from Schönefeld Station (a 5-min. walk from the airport) to the Hauptbahnhof (main train station) in about 30 minutes or to or Bahnhof Zoo (where many hotels are located) in about 40 minutes. The **S-Bahn S-9** makes the run to Bahnhof Zoo in about 50 minutes. Both trains cost 2.80€.

For information on Berlin's airports, call ✆ **01805/000186** or head online to **www.berlin-airport.de**.

INSIDE THE STATIONS
Berlin is easily reached from Frankfurt (trip time: 4 hr.), Munich (7 hr.), and Dresden (2 hr.). Most arrivals are at Berlin's contemporary **Hauptbahnhof,** which serves some 1,100 long-distance, regional, and rapid-transit trains daily. The S-Bahn train

ACCOMMODATIONS ■
Arcotel Velvet **1**
Art'otel **17**
Hotel Luisenhof **18**
Lux 11 **15**
Riverside Hotel & Spa **3**

DINING ◆
Brasserie Desbrosses **10**
Curry 36 **11**
Dressler Restaurant **9**
Mutter Hoppe **14**
Restaurant Oranium **2**
Zur Letzten Instanz **16**
Zwölf Apostel **4**

ATTRACTIONS ●
Altes Museum **7**
Deutsches Historisches
  Museum **8**
Jüdisches Museum **13**
Mauermuseum-Haus am
  Checkpoint Charlie **12**
Neues Museum **6**
Pergamon Museum **5**

system connects the train station to the rest of the city. A money exchange office, ATMs, lockers for luggage, and restaurants are in the station. For information on Berlin, stop by the **BERLIN infostore** (✆ **030/250025;** http://tourist.visitberlin. de/en), located on the ground floor's north exit (opposite the Service Point) and open daily 8am to 10pm. In addition, **EurAide** (www.euraide.com), in the DB Reisezentrum (Travel Center) on the lower level, is an English-language information counter for train travel and local sightseeing. It's open daily 10am to 7pm in summer (May–Aug) and Monday to Friday 11am to 6pm in winter. It is closed from December 23 to February 15.

Bahnhof Zoologischer Garten, nicknamed "Bahnhof Zoo," is just three stops by S-Bahn from the Hauptbahnhof. It's just a few minutes' walk from the Kurfürstendamm and its many hotels and restaurants.

For information on train services, prices, and reservations, call ✆ **11861** (available from within Germany only) or go to **www.bahn.de**.

Information Elsewhere in the City

In addition to the Hauptbahnhof, there's a **BERLIN infostore** conveniently located at Kurfürstendamm 21, at the Neues Kranzler Eck, where you can obtain a map and get sightseeing advice. It's open Monday to Saturday 10am to 8pm and Sunday 10am to 6pm. Other convenient tourist offices are at **Brandenburg Gate,** Unter den Linden, open daily from 10am to 6pm; and in **ALEXA** shopping center a few blocks down from Alexanderplatz at Grunerstrasse 20, which is open Monday to Saturday 10am to 8pm. The central phone number for all tourist information is ✆ **030/250025** (www.visitberlin.de).

For more information or to book a hotel reservation, call **Berlin Tourismus,** at ✆ **030/250025.** For information online, check out **http://tourist.visitberlin.de/ en**. For the viewpoint of individual travelers, check www.hotelrooms365.com.

City Layout

Berlin consists of 12 precincts. Berlin's greatest concentration of hotels, restaurants, and shops is clustered around the **Kurfürstendamm,** located in former West Berlin and affectionately called the **Ku'damm.** About 2½ miles (4km) long, it starts at the Kaiser-Wilhelm Gedächtniskirche (Memorial Church), a ruin left standing as a reminder of the horrors of war. Near the church are the Bahnhof Zoologischer Garten and a large park called the Tiergarten. To the northwest, easily reached by bus, are Charlottenburg Palace and a cluster of fine museums, including the Berggruen Sammlung, with its Picasso collection, and Bröhan Museum, with its decorative arts.

Berlin's other well-known street—and historically much more significant—is **Unter den Linden,** in a precinct called **Berlin-Mitte** (literally, Central Berlin). This was the heart of Old Berlin before World War II, its most fashionable and lively street, and thereafter was part of East Berlin. Today Mitte has once again become the city center and contains the city's highest concentration of monuments, tourist attractions, and federal government buildings. At the head of the wide, tree-lined Unter den Linden is Berlin's most readily recognized landmark, the Brandenburg Gate. The boulevard leads to **Museum Island (Museum Island),** which boasts the outstanding Pergamon and other museums, and to the drab modern square called **Alexanderplatz,** once the heart of East Berlin and easily found by its tall TV tower. Nearby is the **Nikolai Quarter,** a reconstructed neighborhood of shops, bars, and restaurants built to resemble Old Berlin. Berlin's other important museum district, the **Tiergarten,** is in Mitte near

Potsdamer Platz, which has blossomed into a major business, retail, and entertainment hub.

Getting Around

Berlin has an excellent public transport network, including the U-Bahn (Underground), the S-Bahn (inner-city railway), buses, and trams (in eastern Berlin only). All use the same ticket and fare system and are run by the **Public Transport Company Berlin–Brandenburg** (BVG; ☏ 030/19449; www.bvg.de), which maintains an information booth outside Bahnhof Zoo on Hardenbergplatz, at Alexanderplatz, and many other stations, most open daily 6am to 10pm. They provide details on how to reach destinations and the various ticket options available, and also sell tickets. Public transportation throughout the city operates from about 4:30am to 1:30am daily, with special night buses, marked with an N in front of their numbers (68 buses and trams, U-Bahn lines U-9 and U-12), running throughout the night and supplemented by U-Bahn and S-Bahn lines operating all night on weekends.

Although Greater Berlin is divided into three fare zones, A, B, and C (zone maps are posted at all U-Bahn and S-Bahn stations), most places of interest to you require purchase only of the **AB Einzelfahrausweis** single ticket, at 2.10€. With this ticket, you can travel all of the U-Bahn system, most of the S-Bahn network, and all buses and trams, including travel to Berlin's two airports and its major attractions. The only exception is Potsdam, for which you must buy a three-zone ABC Einzelfahrausweis for 2.80€.

If you're traveling only a short distance (six stops by bus or three by subway), you need buy only a **Kurzstreckenkarte,** for 1.20€.

If you don't want to hassle with individual tickets and plan to travel more than twice on a given day, consider buying a **Tageskarte** (day ticket) for 6.10€. If you're going to Potsdam, buy the 6.50€ Tageskarte valid for all three zones; it's good for local travel within Potsdam as well.

Tickets should be purchased before boarding (though standard single tickets are available on buses) from vending machines and then time-punched by one of the small red boxes found at the entrances to city buses and Underground stations.

Note that railpasses are valid only on Berlin's S-Bahn lines that connect DB city center train stations, such as the S-7 that connects the Hauptbahnhof with the Lichtenberg and Zoo stations; one can, however, ride the RB/RE limited-stop service available on some of the S-Bahn lines.

 The WelcomeCard

If you're going to be in Berlin for a few days and think you'll be traveling a lot by public conveyance, consider purchasing a **Berlin WelcomeCard** for 17€, valid for 2 days, or 23€, valid for 3 days for most areas of Berlin. If you're traveling to Potsdam, get the **Berlin-Potsdam WelcomeCard,** valid for all three zones, for 19€ and 26€, respectively. The card entitles you to 48 or 72 hours of free travel on public transportation, as well as a 25% to 50% reduction on sightseeing tours and a small selection of museums, attractions, and theaters. Be sure to ask for a list of participating establishments, however, to see whether they're attractions you're interested in; the SchauLUST Museen Berlin ticket (described below) may be a better fit for you. The WelcomeCard is valid for one adult and up to three children 13 or younger. It's available at BERLIN infostores, many hotels, and BVG ticket offices.

Berlin U-Bahn & S-Bahn

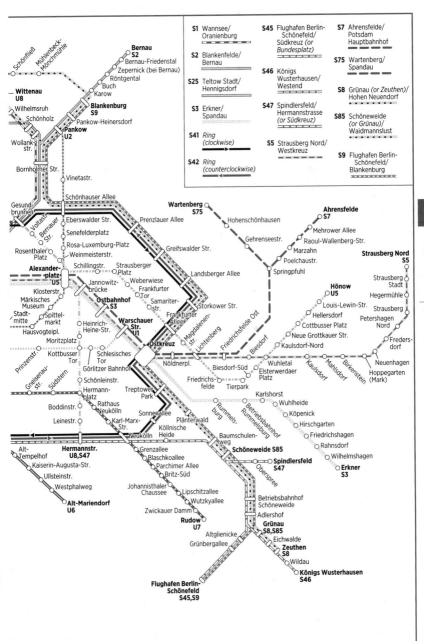

Taxis are available throughout Berlin. The meter starts at 3€, around 2€ per kilometer after that, depending on the time of day. Visitors can flag down taxis that have a T-sign illuminated. For a **taxi**, call ☏ **030/202020.**

Where to Stay

Arcotel Velvet ★ 📖 With its Andy Warhol–inspired decor, this hotel stands in what used to be a Cold War no man's land. Enveloped by a vibrant artist and designer scene, the hotel lies right in the midst of some of Mitte's hippest cafes, bars, and restaurants. Its glass facade conceals a comfortably modern hotel that employs minimalist design and innovative concepts in its use of modern equipment, soft furnishings, and tasteful materials. All the beautifully designed bedrooms are stylish and inviting. **The Velvet Bar** is a Mitte hot spot.

Oranienburger Strasse 52, 10117 Berlin. ☏ **030/2787530.** Fax 030/278753800. www.arcotel.at. 85 units. 95€–230€ double. AE, DC, MC, V. S-Bahn: Oranienburger Strasse. **Amenities:** Restaurant; bar; room service.

Art'otel ★ 📖 Chic, discreet, and avant-garde, this is unlike any other Berlin hotel. The location is ideal, in the heart of cosmopolitan Berlin, with the Ku'Damm action virtually outside the front door. The decor, strictly minimalist, includes touches from top designers like Philippe Starck and Arne Jacobsen. Modernists will be at home here, but traditionalists might not be so pleased. Rooms are all comfortable, with soundproofing, large beds, and tasteful lighting. The service here is among Berlin's finest. On weekends, a minimum stay of 2 nights is required.

Joachimstalerstrasse 29, 10719 Berlin. ☏ **030/884470.** Fax 030/88447700. www.artotels.com. 133 units. 69€–240€ double. Rates include buffet breakfast with champagne. AE, DC, MC, V. U-Bahn: Kurfürstendamm. **Amenities:** Restaurant; bar; concierge.

Hotel Alexander ★ 🍴 Just a few-minutes' walk from the Ku'damm, this hotel combines the patina of age with contemporary furnishings, most which were custom-built by an artist in 1990. Rooms are simple but tastefully decorated, with all the creature comforts you'd expect in medium-range accommodations, including wireless Internet access.

Pariser Strasse 37, 10707 Berlin. ☏ **030/8871650.** Fax 03/88716565. www.hotelalexander.de. 18 units. 79€–149€ double; 99€–189€ suite. Off-season discounts available. Buffet breakfast 13€. MC, V. U-Bahn: Uhlandstrasse. **Amenities:** Restaurant; smoke-free rooms. *In room:* No A/C.

Hotel Domus 🍴 Clean, streamlined, and unpretentious, this government-rated three-star hotel dates from 1975 and lies in one of Berlin's most attractive districts in Wilmersdorf, a short walk from St. Ludwig's Church. Most of the accommodations come with a small private bathroom. As such, it has a high proportion of single rooms. Rooms are well designed, well scrubbed, and, although not particularly large, very comfortable, each with a neat bathroom that is quite spacious. There are virtually no extras on-site, except soundproof windows and a charming breakfast room.

Uhlandstrasse 49, 10719 Berlin. ☏ **030/8803440.** Fax 030/88034444. www.hotel-domus-berlin.de. 70 units. 53€–110€ double. AE, DC, MC, V. U-Bahn: Hohenzollernplatz or Spichernstrasse. **Amenities:** Bar.

Hotel Hansablick ★★ 📖 One S-Bahn station or a 15-minute walk north of Bahnhof Zoo, this hotel is located on a quiet residential street beside the Spree River, lined with willows, and is only a few minutes' walk from the Tiergarten park (and a great weekend flea market). The rooms, in an early 1900s building without an elevator, come in different sizes and are a sophisticated blend of antique and modern, with wood floors, stucco ceilings, high-tech lighting, and modern furniture. The best rooms are those with views of the Spree, the largest (and most expensive) of which even has a balcony.

Flotowstrasse 6, 10555 Berlin. ✆ **030/3904800.** Fax 030/3926937. www.hotel-hansablick.de. 29 units. 85€–145€ double. Rates include buffet breakfast. A 10% reduction for guests who show this Frommer's guide. AE, DC, MC, V. S-Bahn: Tiergarten. U-Bahn: Hansaplatz. **Amenities:** Bar; smoke-free rooms.

Hotel Luisenhof ★   It has an out-of-the-way location, but the Luisenhof, occupying a dignified house built in 1822, is still one of the most desirable small hotels in Berlin's eastern district. Its five floors of high-ceilinged rooms, decorated in a conservative and traditional style, will appeal to those desiring to escape from modern Berlin. Rooms range from small to spacious, but each is equipped with fine beds and offers touches of Renaissance decor. Bathrooms, though small, are nicely appointed.

Köpenicker Strasse 92, 10179 Berlin. ✆ **030/2462810.** Fax 030/24628160. 27 units. 120€–299€ double; 249€–399€ suite. Rates include buffet breakfast. AE, DC, MC, V. U-Bahn: Märkisches Museum. **Amenities:** Restaurant; bar; smoke-free rooms.

Lux 11 ★ 🏨   In the hip central Mitte district, among fashionable art galleries and trendy media firms, this is an oasis of charm, comfort, and style. In a chic minimalist style, its bedrooms occupy a monolithic space, with a modern, glamorous decor. The open bathrooms are furnished in honey-colored wood and concrete. In the basement is an Aveda Spa, and there's even a "micro" department store.

Rosa-Luxemburg-Strasse 9–13, 10178 Berlin. ✆ **030/9362800.** www.lux-eleven.com. 72 units. 149€–205€ double; 230€–295€ suite. AE, MC, V. U-Bahn: Weinmeisterstrasse. **Amenities:** Restaurant; bar.

Riverside Hotel & Spa ★★ 🔥   This boutique hotel is our top choice in fast-changing Berlin-Mitte. Although it's in a nondescript Communist-era building, it has a great location beside the Spree River, near Museum Island and the Oranienburger Strasse nightlife. But what sets it apart is its design concept, from the hand-painted Jugendstil detailing in each room to the comfortable cafe with outdoor seating beside the Spree. A spa offers everything from massages and body treatments to saunas and baths. For individuals who revel in the offbeat, this place is a true find.

Friedrichstrasse 106, 10117 Berlin. ✆ **030/284900.** Fax 03/2849049. www.great-hotel.com. 40 units. 105€–145€ double; 195€–300€ suite. Discounts available for the spa. Buffet breakfast 12€. MC, V. S-/U-Bahn: Friedrichstrasse. **Amenities:** Bar; smoke-free rooms.

Savoy Berlin ★★★   This small, classy hotel, within walking distance of the Ku'damm and Bahnhof Zoo, has been welcoming international guests for more than 70 years. Any writer worth his or her salt has stayed here while in Berlin, including Thomas Mann and Henry Miller. Rooms, most equipped with bidets, are cozy and come in various styles and furnishings, including four-poster beds. Its clubby bar, the venerable **Times Bar,** offers Cuban cigars from its own humidors, and the elegant restaurant offers terrace dining in summer. You can't go wrong here.

Fasanenstrasse 9-10, 10623 Berlin. ✆ **030/311030.** Fax 030/31103333. www.hotel-savoy.com. 125 units. 146€–277€ double. Buffet breakfast 19€. AE, DC, MC, V. S-/U-Bahn: Bahnhof Zoologischer Garten. **Amenities:** Restaurant; bar; rooms for those w/limited mobility; smoke-free rooms.

Tiergarten Berlin ★★ 🏨   This intimate hotel possesses all the makings of a first-rate hotel: a polite and efficient staff; early 1900s charm and elegance; and airy, lightly furnished rooms sporting tall stucco ceilings. The bathrooms are modern and spotless. Even the breakfast room, with its great buffet, is something to write home about.

In short, it's the kind of place that appeals to both business and pleasure travelers, despite its out-of-the way location two subway stops north of Bahnhof Zoo.

Alt-Moabit 89, 10559 Berlin. ℭ **030/39 98 96.** Fax 030/39 98 97 35. www.hotel-tiergarten.de. 60 units. 110€–128€ double. Rates include buffet breakfast. AE, DC, MC, V. U-Bahn: Turmstrasse. **Amenities:** Bar; smoke-free rooms.

Top Attractions & Special Moments

The great art collections of Old Berlin suffered during and after World War II. Although many paintings were saved by being stored in salt mines, many larger works were destroyed by fire. Part of the surviving art stayed in the East, including a wealth of ancient treasures that remind us of the leading role played by German archaeologists during the 19th and early 20th centuries. The paintings that turned up in the West and were passed from nation to nation in the late 1940s have nearly all been returned to Berlin.

Berlin has three major museum centers: **Charlottenburg,** with its palace and two significant museums; **Museum Island (Museumsinsel),** with the world-famous Pergamon Museum; and the **Tiergarten,** a center for European art, including the Gemäldegalerie. It makes sense to cover Berlin section by section—saving time and money on transportation.

CHARLOTTENBURG PALACE & MUSEUMS

Bröhan Museum This wonderful museum specializes in decorative objects of the Art Nouveau (*Jugendstil* in German) and Art Deco periods (1889–1939), with exquisite vases, figurines, glass, furniture, carpets, silver, paintings of artists belonging to the Berlin Secession, and other works of art arranged in drawing-room fashion, including an outstanding porcelain collection. You'll see glassware by Emile Gallé, furniture by Eugene Gaillard and Hector Guimard, and works by Belgian Art Nouveau artist Henry van de Velde and Vienna Secession artist Josef Hommann.

Schlossstrasse 1a. ℭ **030/32690600.** www.broehan-museum.de Admission 6€ adults, 4€ students/children 12 and under. Tues–Sun 10am–6pm. U-Bahn: Sophie-Charlotte-Platz or Richard-Wagner-Platz (then a 10-min. walk). Bus: 109 or 309.

Die Sammlung Berggruen: Picasso und Seine Zeit (The Berggruen Collection: Picasso and His Era) ★

Beside the Bröhan Museum, this outstanding collection of respected art dealer Heinz Berggruen, who fled the Nazis in 1936 but returned to Berlin in 1996, is located in a renovated former barracks built by August Stüler in 1859. It contains an astonishing 100 works by **Picasso,** from his student years in Madrid through his major periods to late in his life. There are also works by contemporaries like **Cézanne, Matisse** (with one room devoted to about 12 of his works), **Braque, van Gogh,** and **Klee.**

Schlossstrasse 1. ⓒ **030/326 958-15.** www.smb.museum. Admission 6€ adults, 3€ students/children. Tues–Sun 10am–6pm. U-Bahn: Sophie-Charlotte-Platz or Richard-Wagner-Platz (then a 10-min. walk). Bus: 109, 309, or M45.

Schloss Charlottenburg (Charlottenburg Palace) ★★★ Berlin's most beautiful baroque building, Charlottenburg Palace was built in 1695 for Sophia Charlotte, the popular wife of the future king of Prussia, Frederick I. Later it was expanded and served as the summer residence of the Prussian kings, the Hohenzollerns. The main wing (**Altes Schloss,** also known as the Nering-Eosander Building) contains the ground-floor **Historical Rooms,** once the quarters of Sophia Charlotte and her husband. Of these, the **Porcelain Cabinet** is the most striking (and kitschy), filled with more than 2,000 pieces of porcelain. Also of note is the baroque chapel. You have to join a 50-minute guided tour to visit these rooms. Alternatively, you can skip the tour and head to the upper floor, where you can wander on your own through rooms containing tapestries; goblets; swords; portraits of Sophie Charlotte, her husband, Frederick, and their son (the so-called Soldier King); and other royal possessions, including the Hohenzollern insignia and a stunning silver place setting. If you join the guided tour, a visit to these rooms is included.

To the right of this building is the **Neuer Flügel** (New Wing), also called the **Knobelsdorff Flügel,** where you can wander with an audio guide through more royal quarters, the state dining hall, and the elaborate Golden Galerie, one of the prettiest rococo ballrooms in Germany. Behind the palace is a beautiful baroque-style park, which contains the **Schinkel Pavilion,** a delightful summer house built in 1825 by Karl Friedrich Schinkel, Berlin's most important early-19th-century architect, and the **Belvedere,** a former teahouse containing 18th- and 19th-century KPM (Königliche Porzellan-Manufaktur) Berlin porcelain.

Luisenplatz. ⓒ **030/32091275.** www.spsg.de. Combined ticket for all buildings and historical rooms 12€ adults, 9€ students and children 13 and under. Palace Tues–Fri 9am–4pm, Sat–Sun 10am–4pm; museum Tues–Fri 10am–6pm; gardens (free admission) daily 6:30am–8pm (Nov–Feb until 6pm). U-Bahn: Richard-Wagner-Platz. Bus: 145 or 204.

BERLIN-MITTE

Start with a stroll down **Unter den Linden,** beginning at the Reichstag and Brandenburg Gate (S-Bahn: Unter den Linden; bus: 100). During the decades of the Wall, the **Brandenburg Gate,** built in the 18th century as the grand entrance to Unter den Linden, stood in no man's land, marking the boundary of East and West Berlin and becoming the symbol of a divided Germany. After the November 1989 revolution and the fall of the Wall, many Berliners gathered here to rejoice and dance on top of the Wall. Near the Brandenburg Gate is the 5-acre (2-hectare) **Holocaust Memorial,** consisting of 2,751 concrete blocks of different sizes and an underground information center dedicated to victims and their families.

Altes Museum Resembling a Greek temple and designed in 1822 by Berlin's greatest architect, Karl Friedrich Schinkel, this is Berlin's oldest museum. On its main floor is the **Antikensammlung,** a collection of ancient arts and crafts, primarily Greek and Roman antiquities, including pottery, figurines, statues, busts, glassware, jewelry, Greek helmets, and wood and stone sarcophagi. Outstanding are the **Attic red-figure vases** of the 5th century B.C. (the best known is a large Athenian wine amphora, or jar, found in Vulci, Etruria, dating from 490 B.C., which shows a satyr with a lyre and the god Hermes). In the Brandenburg–Prussian art collection is an exceptional bronze statue of the goddess Luna descending through an "arch of the sky." The Prussians called it "the pearl of the collection."

On Museum Island. © **030/20905555.** www.smb.museum. Admission 8€ adults, 4€ students/children 16 and under. Daily 10am–6pm. S-Bahn: Hackescher Markt (the closest), or Friedrichstrasse. U-Bahn: Friedrichstrasse. Bus: 100 to Lustgarten, 147, 157, or 358.

Deutsches Historisches Museum (German Historical Museum)

Housed in the oldest building on Unter den Linden, the 1695 Zeughaus (Arsenal), the national museum of German history tackles the ambitious goal of chronicling Germany's tumultuous past from the Middle Ages to the present day, utilizing both historic artifacts and audiovisual displays. Clothing, items used in daily life, photographs, furniture, maps, posters, military uniforms, weapons, and more breathe life into the political events, social upheavals, wars, and cultural blossoming that have shaped German history over the past several centuries. The architectural gem of the museum is the inner courtyard with the masks of dying warriors by Andreas Schlüter, now topped by a glass roof. An addition by I. M. Pei houses special exhibitions.

Unter den Linden 2. © **030/203040.** www.dhm.de. Admission 5€. Daily 10am–6pm. S-Bahn:, Friedrich-strasse, Hackescher Markt. U-Bahn: Hausvogteiplatz, Friedrichstrasse. Bus: 100, 200, or 348 to Staats-oper.

Neues Museum ★★★

When the doors of this museum opened in 2009, it was the first time in 70 years that all five museums on Museum Island could be visited. The museum now contains the collections of the **Egyptian Museum ★★★** and the Papyrus Collection, as well as a part of the collection of the Museum of Prehistory and Early History and the Antiquities Collection. The famous artifact of Berlin is the bust of **Queen Nefertiti ★★★**, which rests in the North Cupola. Of special interest is the **Burial Cult Room ★★**, where coffins, mummies, and grave objects are displayed along with life-size X-ray photographs of the mummies of humans and animals. The **Papyrus Collection ★★** displays about 25,000 documents of papyrus, ostraca, parchment, limestone, wax, and wood in eight different languages.

Museumsinsel. © **030/266424242.** www.neues-museum.de. Admission 10€ adults, 5€ students and children. Sun-Wed 10am–6pm; Fri-Sat 10am–8pm. S-Bahn: Hackescher Markt. U-Bahn: Friedrich-strasse. Bus: 100 or 200 to Lustgarten.

Pergamon Museum ★★★

One of Berlin's most famous museums is named after its most prized possession, the **Pergamon Altar ★★★**, a magnificent master-piece of Hellenistic art of the 2nd century B.C. and certainly one of the wonders of the ancient world. This Greek altar (180–160 B.C.) has a huge room all to itself, with some 27 steps leading up to the colonnade. Most fascinating is the frieze around the base, tediously pieced together over a 20-year period. Depicting the struggle of the Olympian gods against the Titans as told in Hesiod's *Theogony,* the relief is strikingly alive, with figures projecting as much as a foot from the background.

Essentially a museum of architecture and antiquities, the Pergamon also contains the impressive 2nd-century **Roman Market Gate of Miletus ★★★**, as well as the dazzling **Babylonian Processional Way** leading to the **Gate of Ishtar ★★★**, dating from 575 B.C. You can also visit the throne room of Nebuchadnezzar. Greek and Roman sculpture and Islamic art are also on display, including the incredible **facade of Mshatta Palace** from Jordan. If you see only one museum on Museum Island, this should be it.

Bodestrasse 1-3 (entrance on Kupfergraben), Museum Island. © **030/20905577.** www.smb.museum. Admission 10€ adults, 5€ students/children. Daily 10am–6pm (Thurs to 10pm). S-Bahn: Hackescher Markt. S-Bahn/U-Bahn: Friedrichstrasse. Bus: 100, or 20 to Lustgarten.

Strolling the Historic Nikolai Quarter

The historic **Nikolaiviertel** (U-Bahn: Klosterstrasse), a symbol of East Berlin's desire to bounce back after war damage, was restored in time for the city's 750th anniversary in 1987. Here, on the banks of the Spree River, is where Berlin was born. Many of the 16th-century neighborhood's medieval and baroque buildings were completely and authentically reconstructed after World War II. Subsequently, some of the city's old flavor has been recaptured here. Period taverns, cozy restaurants, souvenir shops, and churches make it ideal for a leisurely stroll down narrow streets illuminated by gas lanterns.

Reichstag (Parliament) ★ Completed in 1894 in neo-Renaissance style to serve as the German house of parliament, the Reichstag had its darkest hour on the night of February 17, 1933, when a mysterious fire broke out that was blamed on the German Communist Party and was used as an excuse by the Nazi government to arrest dissidents and abolish basic democratic rights. Heavily damaged in World War II, it was rebuilt with the exception of a glass cupola that had adorned its center.

The Reichstag again became home of German lawmakers after the fall of the Wall and German reunification in 1990. Following a ceremonial wrapping by artist Christo in 1995, it underwent extensive renovation, including a new glass dome by British architect Sir Norman Foster. Today you can enter the main (west) entrance for an elevator ride up to the impressive glass dome and its spiraling ramp, with panoramic views from an observation platform and a rooftop restaurant (the view is better than the food). A photographic display chronicles the Reichstag's history. Try to arrive early in the morning; until every German has visited, you can expect long lines at the entrance.

Platz der Republik 1. © **030/22732152.** www.bundestag.de. Free admission. Daily 8am–midnight (you must enter by 10pm). S-Bahn: Unter den Linden. Bus: 100 to Reichstag.

KREUZBERG

Jüdisches Museum Berlin (Jewish Museum Berlin) ★★ Opened in 2001, this addition to the city's roster of impressive museums was designed by Daniel Libeskind, the son of Holocaust refugees. The zinc-clad building's jagged, zigzagging structure (resembling, perhaps, a deconstructed Star of David, and slashed by hundreds of asymmetrical windows) houses collections chronicling 2,000 years of German-Jewish history, from Roman times to the present. Through photographs, artwork, historic artifacts, religious objects, and audiovisual displays, visitors learn about Jewish emigration to Europe 2,000 years ago; the persecution of Jews in medieval times; the integration of Jews in Germany; Jewish life in Berlin; the development of Jewish community and religious life; and Jewish contributions to German culture, politics, economy, and science. Small rooms scattered throughout the museum are designed especially for children, allowing them to enjoy the museum on a different level. Although the Holocaust is addressed, this is far more than a Holocaust museum.

Lindenstrasse 9–14. © **030/25993300.** www.juedisches-museum-berlin.de. Admission 5€ adults, free for children 6 and under, 10€ families. Daily 10am–8pm (Mon until 10pm). U-Bahn: Hallesches Tor or Kochstrasse. Bus: M29, M41, or 265.

Mauermuseum—Haus am Checkpoint Charlie ★ 📷 This is by far the best museum for gaining an understanding of what life was like before, during, and after

A NEW wall

The hideous 100-mile-long (161km) **Berlin Wall,** built in 1961 to prevent East Germans from fleeing into the sanctity of West Berlin, was reinforced by hundreds of guardhouses, 293 watchtowers, patrol dogs, and a vast swath of no man's land. Today the wall is history, but there are several places that recall its notoriety.

The **Mauermuseum—Haus am Checkpoint Charlie** (p. 341) is the best place to gain an understanding of what life was like during the Cold War. If you have time, there's also the **Berlin Wall Documentation Center,** on Bernauer Strasse (✆ **030/464 10 30;** www. berliner-mauer-dokumentationszentrum. de; U-Bahn: Bernauer Strasse; S-Bahn: Nordbahnhof). Bernauer Strasse was one of Berlin's most notorious streets during the Cold War, divided its entire length into east and west, with buildings on the east empty and boarded up. Here you'll find a chapel (built on the site of a former church blown up by the Communists in 1985), a Berlin Wall memorial, and a Documentation Center

with photographs and other items chronicling in English the historical and political background of the Wall and presenting a personal view of what the Wall meant for Berliners on both sides. The center is open Tuesday to Sunday 10am to 6pm (to 5pm Nov–Mar), and admission is free.

A few sections of the Wall have been left standing, most notably on **Niederkirchnerstrasse** (not far from the Museum Haus am Checkpoint Charlie; S-Bahn/U-Bahn: Potsdamer Platz), where an 820-foot (246m) section remains. But the most colorful remainder of the Wall is in former East Berlin on **Mühlenstrasse** (S-Bahn: Ostbahnhof; U-Bahn: Warschauer Strasse). Called the **East Side Gallery (www.eastsidegallery. com),** this ½-mile-long (1km) section on the banks of the Spree was painted on its east side with more than 100 murals by international artists in 1990. The murals are now a bit faded and chipped, though some artists restored their murals in 2000.

the fall of the Wall—if you have never been to Berlin, don't miss it. Near what was once the most frequently used border crossing into East Berlin, Checkpoint Charlie, this collection documents events that took place around the Berlin Wall, including successful and failed attempts to escape East Berlin. With displays in English, the museum aptly illustrates these years in Berlin's history with photographs, items used in escape attempts (such as cars with hidden compartments), videos, artwork, and newspaper clippings. The fall of the Wall and the demise of Communism in East Germany, Russia, Poland, and Hungary are also documented, and part of the museum is devoted to nonviolent struggles for human rights around the world, including those led by Gandhi, Walesa, and Martin Luther King, Jr.

Friedrichstrasse 43–45. ✆ **030/2537250.** www.mauermuseum.de. Admission 13€ adults, 9.50€ students, free for children 16 and under. Daily 9am–10pm. U-Bahn: Kochstrasse or Stadtmitte. Bus: 129.

TIERGARTEN

Gemäldegalerie (Picture Gallery) ★★★   This is one of Germany's greatest art museums. Several rooms are devoted to early German masters, with panels from altarpieces dating from the 13th to the 15th centuries. Note the panel *The Virgin Enthroned with Child* (1350), surrounded by angels that resemble the demons in the works of Hieronymus Bosch. Eight paintings make up the Dürer collection.

Most of the great European masters are represented. The Italian collection contains five Raphael Madonnas, along with works by Titian, Fra Filippo Lippi, Botticelli, and Correggio *(Leda with the Swan)*. There are early Netherlandish paintings from the 15th and 16th centuries (van Eyck, van der Weyden, Bosch, and Bruegel) as well. Look for Bruegel's ***100 Proverbs (100 Sprichwörter),*** a delight, with peasants engaged in proverbial activities—see how many proverbs you can detect, such as "No use crying over spilled milk." Several galleries are devoted to 17th-century Flemish and Dutch masters, with no fewer than 15 works by Rembrandt, such as his famous ***Head of Christ.***

Matthäiskirchplatz 4. (C) **030/20905555.** www.smb.spk-berlin.de/gg. Admission 8€ adults, 4€ students, free for children 16 and under. Tues–Sun 10am–6pm (to 10pm Thurs). U-/S-Bahn: Potsdamer Platz. Bus: 200 or 347.

NEAR THE KU'DAMM

Kaiser-Wilhelm Gedächtniskirche (Kaiser Wilhelm Memorial Church)
Completed in 1895 as a memorial to Kaiser Wilhelm II, this church was destroyed by bombs during World War II and left in ruins as a reminder of the horrors of war. Today it contains a small museum with displays photos related to war and destruction. Beside the ruined church is a new church designed by Professor Egon Eiermann and finished in 1961; come here for free organ concerts Saturday at 6pm or a daily service conducted in English at 9am.

Breitscheidplatz. (C) **030/2185023.** www.gedaechtniskirche.com. Free admission. Ruined church Mon–Sat 10am–4pm; new church daily 9am–6pm. U-Bahn: Zoologischer Garten or urfürstendamm.

Käthe-Kollwitz Museum ★ 🎁
This small but significant museum shows the powerful drawings, sketches, and sculptures of Käthe Kollwitz (1867–1945), a Berliner who managed to capture human emotions both tender and disturbing in her subjects, mostly the working class. War, poverty, death, hunger, love, grief, and happiness are all deftly rendered with just a few strokes. Who can forget Kollwitz's portrayal of horror on the face of a mother whose child has just been run over, or the wonderment expressed by a young mother and her infant gazing into each other's eyes? Because she routinely took up causes of the suppressed, her work was outlawed by the Nazis.

Fasanenstrasse 24 (just off Ku'damm). (C) **030/8825210.** www.kaethe-kollwitz.de. Admission 6€ adults, 3€ students/children. Daily 11am–6pm. U-Bahn: Kurfürstendamm or Uhlandstrasse. Bus: 109, 110, 204, or 249.

The Story of Berlin
This multimedia extravaganza ambitiously attempts to portray 8 centuries of the city's history through photos, films, sounds, and colorful displays. Beginning with the founding of Berlin in 1237, it chronicles the plague, the Thirty Years' War, Frederick the Great's reign, military life, the Industrial Revolution and the working poor, the Golden 1920s, World War II, divided Berlin during the Cold War, and the fall of the Wall. Hidden loudspeakers heighten the effects: In a 19th-century tenement courtyard, for example, you hear a dog barking, a baby crying, and other sounds of a densely packed neighborhood, while the sound of breaking glass accompanies a display on Nazis and their treatment of Jews. Lights flash in a media blitz as you enter the display on the fall of the Wall, making you feel like one of the first East Berliners to wonderingly cross to the West. Conclude your tour on the 14th floor with a panoramic view over today's Berlin. Be sure, too, to join the 30-minute tour of the underground bunker built in 1974 at the height of the Cold War to house 3,500 people. Although the displays are a bit jarring and the historical

information is too jumbled to be truly educational, the museum does leave a lasting impression.

Ku'damm-Karree, Kurfürstendamm 207-208 (at the corner of Uhlandstrasse). ℭ **030/88720100.** www.story-of-berlin.de. Admission 10€ adults, 8€ students, 5€ children 6-13, 23€ families. Daily 10am-8pm (you must enter by 6pm). U-Bahn: Uhlandstrasse.

Zoologischer Garten (Berlin Zoo) ★ ☺ Founded in 1844 and just a short walk from the Ku'damm and Bahnhof Zoo, the Berlin Zoo is Germany's oldest zoo and one of Europe's most attractive. Until World War II, it boasted thousands of animals of every imaginable species and description—many familiar to Berliners by nicknames. By the end of World War II in 1945, only 91 animals remained. Since the war, the city has been rebuilding its large and unique collection; today more than 13,000 animals are housed here. The zoo has Europe's most modern birdhouse, featuring more than 550 species. The most valuable inhabitants are giant pandas. The **Aquarium** is as impressive as the adjacent zoo, with more than 9,000 fish, reptiles, amphibians, insects, and other creatures, including sharks, crocodiles, and Komodo dragons. The "hippoquarium" is a popular attraction.

Budapester Strasse 32 and Hardenbergplatz 8. ℭ **030/254010.** www.zoo-berlin.de. Combination ticket for zoo and aquarium 18€ adults, 14€ students/seniors, 9€ children 5 to 15; zoo or aquarium only 12€ adults, 9€ students/seniors, 6€ children. Jan 1-Mar 20 and Oct 26-Dec 31 daily 9am-5pm; Mar 21-Sept 14 daily 9am-7pm; Sept 15-Oct 25 daily 9am-6pm.S-/U-Bahn: Zoologischer Garten.

Where to Dine

Brasserie Desbrosses ★ FRENCH   The Ritz-Carlton may be much too ritzy for most budgets, but this classic brasserie—built in 1875 in a French village but dismantled and reassembled here—offers casual dining in a traditional setting, as well as alfresco dining on a terrace. A good choice if you're visiting museums in the Tiergarten or the shops around Potsdamer Platz, it offers a reasonably priced weekday business lunch for 14€, home-baked pastries and breads, seafood and meat dishes, a Sunday champagne brunch for 78€, and more. Keep in mind, however, that even though dining here is casual, the rest of the hotel is so upscale that it's not the kind of place you want to visit on a bad hair day.

The Ritz-Carlton, Potsdamer Platz 3. ℭ **030/337777.** www.desbrosses.de. Main courses 24€-40€; check for fixed-price menu. AE, DC, MC, V. Daily 6:30-10:30am, 11:30am-11:30pm. S-Bahn: Savignyplatz.

Calcutta ★ INDIAN   Berlin's first Indian restaurant has been in business for almost 40 years. This small, cheerful establishment with colorful murals and the obligatory Indian background music offers curries, tandoori from a wood-fired clay oven imported from India, and vegetarian dishes. Just a short walk north of the Ku'damm, it's a good place for a relaxing, unhurried meal.

Bleibtreustrasse 17. ℭ **030/8836293.** www.befo.de/calcutta. Main courses 10€-15€. DC, MC, V. Daily noon-midnight. S-Bahn: Savignyplatz.

Curry 36 BRATWURST   A former mayor of Berlin told us, "You haven't been to Berlin until you've sampled our most famous street food." Basically, it's Currywurst, which is Bratwurst sausage covered in ketchup and seasoned with curry powder. Traditionally, it's served with mayonnaise-topped fries. The most famous Currywurst Imbiss in Berlin is Curry 36. That same mayor told us that the treat (that's debatable) was served to President John F. Kennedy during his visit to the city. After downing it, Kennedy said, "Now I am a true Berliner, but I don't have to eat it ever again, do I?"

36 Mehringdamm. ℂ **030/2517368.** Reservations not needed. Bratwurst 2€–7.50€. No credit cards. Mon–Fri 9am–4pm; Sat 10am–4pm; Sun 11am–3pm.

Dressler Restaurant CONTINENTAL   Resembling an arts-conscious bistro of the sort that might have entertained tuxedo-clad clients in the 1920s, Dressler is set behind a wine-colored facade and outfitted with leather banquettes, black-and-white tile floors, mirrors, and film memorabilia from the great days of early German cinema. Waiters scurry around with vests and aprons, carrying trays of everything from hefty portions of lobster salad to duck. You can always drop in to ogle the racks of elegant pastries, consuming them with steaming pots of tea or coffee. It's located near Brandenburg Gate.

Unter den Linden 39. ℂ **030/2044422.** www.restaurant-dressler.de. Reservations recommended. Meals 15€–28€. AE, DC, V. Daily 8am–midnight. S-Bahn: Unter den Linden or Friedrichstrasse. Bus: 100.

Le Buffet im KaDeWe 🍴 INTERNATIONAL   On the sixth floor of the immense KaDeWe department store (see "Shopping," below), you'll find continental Europe's biggest food emporium. It's so amazing that it alone may be worth a trip to Berlin—more types of sausages than you can count, cheeses, teas, breads, jams, sweets, coffees, and more. Interspersed throughout the floor are small dining counters specializing in specific cuisines, but an even greater selection is available one floor up at a glass-enclosed self-service restaurant reminiscent of a greenhouse. The restaurant offers daily specials of Berlin favorites, pasta, an extensive salad bar, an antipasti buffet, desserts, and more.

In KaDeWe, Wittenbergplatz. ℂ **030/217 77 39.** www.lebuffet.de. Meals 10€–15€. AE, DC, MC, V. Mon–Fri 9:30am–7:30pm; Sat 9am–7:30pm. U-Bahn: Wittenbergplatz.

Marjellchen ★ EAST PRUSSIAN   This is the only restaurant in Berlin specializing in the cuisine of Germany's long-lost province of East Prussia. Amid a Bismarckian ambience of vested waiters and oil lamps, you can enjoy savory old-fashioned fare such as marinated elk, roast filet of hare in a cherry sauce, or *Falscher Gänsebraten* (pork spareribs stuffed with prunes and bread crumbs), of a type that Goethe and Schiller favored. Marjellchen isn't the place to go, however, if you want to keep tabs on your cholesterol intake.

Mommsenstrasse 9. ℂ **030/8832676.** www.marjellchen-berlin.de. Reservations required. Main courses 11€–24€. AE, DC, MC, V. Daily 5pm–midnight. Closed Dec 23, 24, and 31. U-Bahn: Uhlandstrasse or Adenauerplatz. S-Bahn: Savignyplatz. Bus 109,119, or 129.

Mutter Hoppe GERMAN   This cozy, wood-paneled basement restaurant still serves the solid Teutonic cuisine favored by a quasi-legendary matriarch (Mother Hoppe) who used to churn out vast amounts of food to members of her extended family and entourage. Within a quartet of old-fashioned dining rooms, you'll enjoy heaping portions of such rib-sticking fare as *Sauerbraten* (marinated beef in sauce) with roasted potatoes, and braised filet of pork in mushroom-flavored cream sauce. On weekend nights, there's live music from the 1920s and '30s.

Rathausstrasse 21, Nikolaiviertel. ℂ **030/2415625.** www.prostmahlzeit.de/mutterhoppe. Main courses 8€–15€. AE, MC, V. Daily 11:30am–midnight. U-Bahn/S-Bahn: Alexanderplatz.

Restaurant Lubitsch CONTINENTAL/GERMAN/MEDITERRANEAN Deeply entrenched in the consciousness of many local residents, Lubitsch is considered in some quarters to have a degree of conservative chic. Expect platters of chicken curry salad with roasted potatoes, Berlin-style potato soup, braised chicken with salad and fresh vegetables, a roulade of suckling pig, and Nürnberger-style *Wursts*. Count on a not-so-friendly staff, a black-and-white decor with Thonet-style chairs, and a somewhat arrogant environment that, despite its drawbacks, is very, very *Berliner*.

Bleibtreustrasse 47. ℂ **030/8823756.** www.restaurant-lubitsch.de. Main courses lunch 8€–10€, dinner 14€–22€. AE, DC, MC, V. Mon–Sat 10am–midnight; Sun 6pm–1am. U-Bahn: Kurfürstendamm.

Restaurant Lutter & Wegner Seit 1811 ★★ AUSTRIAN/GERMAN This wine bar/restaurant dates from 1811, when it first opened as a wine cellar in East Berlin. With its dark wainscoting, candles on white tablecloths, and changing art exhibits, it still exudes an old-world charm, although tables are too close together in the tiny restaurant for much intimacy. In addition to a standard English menu, there's a more interesting daily menu in German, with offerings of fresh fish, grilled meats, and more, so be sure to ask for a translation.

Schlüterstrasse 55. ℂ **030/881 34 40.** www.restaurantlutterundwegner.de. Reservations recommended. Main courses 13€–20€. AE, MC, V. Tues–Sun 6pm–11:30pm. S-Bahn: Savignyplatz.

Restaurant Oranium ★★ 🏨 INTERNATIONAL A 7-minute walk north of Museum Island in the midst of Mitte's main nightlife scene, this lively bistro offers a varied, intriguing menu that hits the spot for those seeking escape from the heavier German cuisine. Hearty breakfasts (served until 4pm), salads, wraps, sandwiches, tapas, fish, and more are listed on the extensive menu. The business breakfast served from 9am to noon is a steal, at only 3.90€.

Oranienburgerstrasse 33-34. ℂ **030/308 82 967.** www.oranium.de. Main courses 5.60€–20€. AE, MC, V. Sun–Thurs 9am–midnight; Fri–Sat 9am–2am. S-Bahn: Oranienburgerstrasse. U-Bahn: Oranienburger Tor.

Zur Letzten Instanz GERMAN Open since 1621, this tiny restaurant claims to be Berlin's oldest *Gaststätte* (neighborhood pub) and has supposedly been frequented by everybody from Napoleon to Beethoven. Its rooms are rustic, with plank floors, wainscoting, and a few antiques. The English menu offers traditional, hearty Berlin specialties, all served with side dishes like dumplings, potatoes, or red cabbage. Be sure to save room for Berlin's famous dessert, *rote Grütze* (cooked fruits with vanilla sauce). Tables are placed outside in summer.

Waisenstrasse 14-16. ℂ **030/2425528.** www.zurletzteninstanz.de. Reservations recommended. Main courses 12€–20€. AE, DC, MC, V. Mon–Sat noon–1am. U-Bahn: Klosterstrasse.

Zwölf Apostel ★ 🍴 PIZZA/PASTA If you're hungry for pizza or pasta after visiting the Pergamon on Museum Island, there's no more popular (or packed) place than this very successful local chain. Catering to everyone from business types to students and occupying colorfully painted vaulted rooms underneath the S-Bahn tracks (you can hear the trains rumble as they pass overhead), it offers very good pastas and pizzas, with reduced prices available until 4pm. There's also a branch near the Ku'Damm at Bleibtreustrasse 49 (ℂ **030/3121433;** S-Bahn: Savignyplatz).

Georgenstrasse 2 (underneath the S-Bahn tracks near the Pergamon). ℂ **030/2010222.** www.12-apostel.de Reservations recommended. Pizzas and pastas 8€–18€. No credit cards. Sun–Thurs 11am–midnight; Fri–Sat 11am–1am. S-/U-Bahn: Friedrichstrasse.

Shopping

The **Ku'damm** (or Kurfürstendamm) is the Fifth Avenue of Berlin. It's filled with quality stores but also has outlets hustling cheap souvenirs and T-shirts. Although Berliners themselves shop on the Ku'damm, many prefer the specialty stores on the side streets, especially between **Breitscheidplatz** and **Olivaer Platz.** Lovers of porcelain should make a point of visiting the prestigious emporium **KPM (Königliche Porzellan-Manufaktur [Royal Porcelain Factory]),** in the Kempinski Hotel Bristol, Kurfürstendamm 27 (© 030/88627961; http://en.kpm-berlin.com; U-Bahn: Kurfürstendamm). Founded in 1763, KPM has become famous the world over for its exquisite hand-painted, hand-decorated items.

Another major shopping street is nearby **Tauentzienstrasse,** with a wide array of stores that are often cheaper than on the Ku'damm, many specializing in German fashions and accessories for women. Anchoring one end of Tauentzienstrasse is the **Europa Center,** once *the* address for mall shopping in West Berlin but now overshadowed by bigger and better malls. At the other end of the street is the 100-year-old **Kaufhaus des Westens,** Tauentzienstrasse 21 (© 030/21210; www.kadewe.de; U-Bahn: Kurfürstendamm or Wittenbergplatz), a huge luxury department store (the largest in continental Europe), known popularly as **KaDeWe** (pronounced *Kah*-day-vay). It's best known for its food department, where more than 1,000 varieties of German sausages are displayed along with delicacies from all over the world, but there are many equally eye-popping displays on its six floors of merchandise.

If you're looking for serious bargains, head to where the natives shop—**Wilmersdorferstrasse,** with a vast number of discount stores and department stores. Try to avoid Saturday morning, when it's often impossibly overcrowded.

In eastern Berlin, not that long ago, you couldn't find much to buy except a few souvenirs. All that is changed now. The main street, **Friedrichstrasse,** offers some of Berlin's most elegant shopping, including the **Galeries Lafayette** department store and the upscale **Quartier 206** shopping mall. Upmarket boutiques—selling everything from quality women's fashions to Meissen porcelain—are found along **Unter den Linden.** The cheaper stores in eastern Berlin are around the rather bleak-looking **Alexanderplatz.** Many souvenir, specialty, and clothing shops are found in the **Nikolai Quarter.** The largest shopping mall in eastern Berlin, with outlets offering a little bit of everything, is at the **Berliner Markthalle,** at the corner of Rosa-Luxemburg-Strasse and Karl-Liebknecht-Strasse. **Potsdamer Platz,** once Berlin's busiest intersection and a no man's land during the Cold War, is home to the **Arkaden,** an American-style shopping mall with more than 120 stores and restaurants.

Most stores in Berlin are open Monday to Saturday from 9 or 10am to 6pm, though department stores remain open until 8pm.

Berlin's best-known and biggest outdoor market is the **Berliner Trödelmarkt und Kunstmarkt (Art and Junk Market),** on Strasse des 17 Juni, (© 030/26550096; www.berliner-troedelmarkt.de), a minute's walk east of the Tiergarten S-Bahn station. A staggering selection of books, CDs, silverware, coins, stamps, china, glass, original artwork, jewelry, clothing, and junk is sold at this market divided into two parts, one with antiques and junk, the other, across the bridge, with arts and crafts. The market is open Saturday and Sunday 10am to 5pm.

Nightlife

Berlin never sleeps. There are no mandatory closing hours for nightclubs, dance clubs, and bars, so you can stay out all night, if you want. Nightlife in Berlin means everything from far-out bars and dance clubs to world-renowned opera and theater. To find out what's going on in the performing arts, pick up a copy of *The Ex-Berliner* or *New Berlin.*

If you don't mind taking a chance on what's available, the best bargain for last-minute tickets is **Hekticket** (✆ 030/2309930; www.heckticket.de), with outlets at Hardenbergstrasse 29d, across from Bahnhof Zoo on Hardenbergplatz, on the corner of Deutsche Bank (Mon–Sat 10am–8pm, Sun 2–6pm; S-/U-Bahn: Bahnhof Zoologischer Garten), and Karl-Liebknechtstrasse 13, opposite McDonald's near Alexanderplatz (Mon–Sat noon–8pm; S-/U-Bahn: Alexanderplatz). Unsold tickets for that evening's performances are available for more than 200 venues, including the Staatsoper, Komische Oper, classical concerts, pop concerts, and cabaret—most at up to 50% off.

PERFORMING ARTS Performances of the world-renowned Berliner Philharmonisches Orchester (Berlin Philharmonic Orchestra), founded in 1882, take place at the **Philharmonie,** in the Kulturforum, Herbert-von-Karajan-Strasse 1 (✆ 030/254880; www.berlin-philharmonic.com; U-/S-Bahn: Potsdamer Platz). Tickets for most performances cost 14€ to 85€, but those for the Berlin Philharmonic usually sell out months in advance (if you're staying in a first-class hotel, the concierge may be able to get seats for you). The **Konzerthaus Berlin,** on beautiful Gendarmenmarkt in Berlin-Mitte (✆ 030/203092101; www.konzerthaus.de; U-Bahn: Französische Strasse), serves as the venue of the Berlin Symphonic Orchestra, founded in 1952 in the former East Germany, and hosts other musical events. Tickets cost anywhere from 10€ to 99€.

The **Deutsche Oper Berlin** ★, Bismarckstrasse 35, Charlottenburg (✆ 030/34384343; www.deutscheoperberlin.de; U-Bahn: Deutsche Oper; S-Bahn: Charlottenburg), is the largest of Berlin's three opera houses. Works by Mozart, Verdi, and Wagner are perennial favorites, but it also cultivates forgotten operas and works of the 20th century, staging opera virtually every evening except when there's ballet. Tickets for most performances run 12€ to 120€. The **Staatsoper Unter den Linden,** Unter den Linden 7, Berlin-Mitte (✆ 030/20354555 for tickets; www.staatsoper-berlin.de; U-Bahn: Friedrichstrasse or Französische Strasse; bus: 100 or 200), has long been one of Berlin's famous opera houses, featuring opera, ballet, and concerts under the musical direction of conductor Daniel Barenboim. Tickets go for 15€ to 160€ for most performances. The box office is at Bismarckstrasse 110, D, and is open daily from noon to 8pm. The **Komische Oper (Comic Opera),** Behrenstrasse 55–57, Berlin-Mitte (✆ 030/202600; www.komische-oper-berlin.de; S-Bahn: Unter den Linden or Friedrichstrasse; U-Bahn: Französische Strasse; bus: 100), an innovative musical theater company, serves as an alternative to the grander mainstream productions of the two other opera houses, presenting a varied program of opera, operetta, symphony concerts, ballet, and even modern dance. Tickets here cost 8€ to 93€ for most performances.

CLUBS Berlin's oldest jazz club is **Quasimodo** ★, Kantstrasse 12a, Charlottenburg (✆ 030/3180456; www.quasimodo.de; S-/U-Bahn: Zoologischer Garten).

Although many different styles of music are offered here, including rock, Latin, blues, funk, and soul, jazz is the focus. Cover ranges from 12€ to 24€ but it is free to get in on Tuesday and Wednesday. Opening hours depend on the event; call for the schedule. A small and smoky jazz house, **A Trane,** Pestalozzistrasse 105, at the corner of Bleibtreustrasse and Pestalozzistrasse (℗ **030/3132550;** www.a-trane.de; S-Bahn: Savignyplatz), features musicians from around the world performing everything from contemporary and mainstream jazz to bebop and swing. It's open daily from 9pm, and music begins at 10pm; closing times vary. Cover generally ranges from 8€ to 15€.

Hip 20-somethings flock like birds to the Spree riverside bar **Club der Visionaere** (Am Flutgraben 1; ℗ **030/69518944;** www.clubdervisionaere.com; U-Bahn: Warschauer Strasse), in Kreuzberg. Its interior has been compared to a shipwreck. The club has become famous for its Sunday-afternoon parties that virtually last until dawn streaks the sky. House music fills the night in this very Louisiana Bayou–like atmosphere. If you're here at sunrise, take in the concrete watchtower across the street, one of the last surviving towers constructed by the East German police to shoot down "deserters" from the DDR. Open Monday to Friday 2pm to 4am (or beyond), Saturday and Sunday noon to 4am (or beyond). Cover ranges from 1€ to 5€.

BARS & CAFES Those in search of a beer near the Ku'damm might try **Zille-markt,** Bleibtreustrasse 48a (℗ **030/8817040;** www.zillemarkt.de; S-Bahn: Savignyplatz), which dates from the early 1900s and is a popular neighborhood joint for drinks, weekend brunch, and backyard outdoor seating in nice weather. **Zwie-belfisch,** Savignyplatz 7–8 (℗ **030/3127363;** S-Bahn: Savignyplatz), is a neighborhood bar that's been around for more than 30 years and still enjoys great popularity, especially in the wee hours of the night. But on a fine summer's day, nothing beats a beer under the 130-year old chestnut trees at **Zollpackhof,** on Elizabeth-Abegg-Strasse 1 (℗ **030/30099720;** www.zollpackhof.de; S-Bahn: Hauptbahnhof), a beer garden that overlooks Berlin's Chancellery and the Spree River. It is open Tuesday to Saturday from 11am to midnight.

One of our favorite lounge retreats is **Victoria Bar** (Potsdamer Strasse 102; ℗ **030/25759977;** www.victoriabar.de; U-Bahn: Potsdamer Platz), a stylish, retro bar in the heart of Berlin. In sophisticated surroundings, you can enjoy an excellent list of cocktails or order a sandwich if you are hungry. The bartender said, "People come here to get away from the hustle and bustle." There is a happy hour Monday to Saturday 6:30 to 9:30pm or all day Sunday. Hours are Sunday to Thursday 6:30pm to 3am, Friday and Saturday until 4am.

In the eastern part of Berlin, the **Fernsehturm** on Alexanderplatz is a top pick for both the best bird's-eye view of the city and a romantic early evening drink. After paying the 10€ admission fee to the tower, head straight for the revolving **Telecafe** (℗ **030/2423333;** www.berlinerfernsehturm.de; U-/S-Bahn: Alexanderplatz), which, at 669 feet (200m) high, offers a terrific view during its 30-minute spin.

In the heart of the Nikolai Quarter, **Georg Bräu,** Spreeufer 4 (℗ **030/2424244;** S-/U-Bahn: Alexanderplatz), is a popular microbrewery that offers German fare, along with outdoor seating and live music on some weekends. **Joe's Wirthaus zum Löwen,** Hardenbergstrasse 29 (℗ **030/2621020;** www.joes-baerlin.de; U-Bahn: Zoologischer Garten), is a cozy and comfortable pub that is attractively decorated with traditional Teutonic accessories. Even in the winter, when snug and warm inside, you feel like you are sitting out under the chestnut trees.

An Excursion to Potsdam

If you take only one excursion outside Berlin, it should be to the beautiful baroque town of **Potsdam,** 15 miles (24km) southwest of the city. It served as a garrison and residence of Prussia's kings and royal families from the 17th to the 20th centuries. Its most famous resident was Frederick the Great, who succeeded in uniting Germany under his rule and built himself the delightful rococo palace **Schloss Sanssouci** ("without care"), which he used as a place for quiet meditation away from the rigors of war and government. His palace still stands, surrounded by a 750-acre (300-hectare) estate, Park Sanssouci, with several other magnificent structures, including the Neues Palais.

GETTING THERE **Potsdam Hauptbahnhof** is 23 minutes from Bahnhof Zoo via the **RE1** commuter line, with departures every half-hour. For rail information and schedules, call ✆ **01805/996633** or visit www.bahn.de. Otherwise, you can also reach Potsdam by **S-Bahn** lines S1 and S7 from Berlin, connecting at Wannsee station with lines R1, R3, and R4 in about 30 minutes. For more information, call **BVG Berlin** (✆ **030/19449;** www.bvg.de).

VISITOR INFORMATION **Potsdam-Information Centre,** Brandenburger Strasse 3 (✆ **0331/275580;** www.potsdam-tourism.com), at the Brandenburger Gate, is the place to go for information and maps. The office is open April to October Monday to Friday 9:30am to 6pm, and Saturday and Sunday 9:30am to 4pm; from November to March, hours are Monday to Friday 10am to 6pm, Saturday and Sunday 9:30am to 2pm.

GETTING AROUND From Potsdam Hauptbahnhof, you can board **bus no. 695** directly for Schloss Sanssouci or Neues Palais. Otherwise, for the most dramatic approach to the palace, take any **tram** departing from in front of the station going in the direction of *"Zentrum"* and get off at Platz der Einheit. From there, you can walk 30 minutes through the heart of the historic town via the pedestrian Brandenburger Strasse, passing delightful shops, cafes, and restaurants along the way. A day transportation pass for Greater Berlin, including Potsdam, is 6.50€, or ask at the tourism office about a **Potsdam Card,** which allows you to ride the city's public transportation system at a discount. The card costs 9.60€ for 2 days, or 3 days for 12€.

TOP ATTRACTIONS & SPECIAL MOMENTS

Potsdam's star attraction is **Schloss Sanssouci ★★★**, Zur Historischen Mühle (✆ **0331/9694200;** www.spsg.de). Built in the 1740s by Georg von Knobelsdorff, it served as Frederick the Great's summer residence for almost 40 years. (He died here and is buried on the grounds.) With only a dozen rooms, the one-story rococo palace is exceedingly modest compared to most royal residences, yet its rooms are a delight, filled with paintings, marble, and gold leaf, with playful motifs of grapes, wine, and images of Bacchus. The elliptically shaped **Marble Hall** is the largest in the palace, but the **music salon** is the supreme example of the rococo style. A small bust of Voltaire commemorates the writer's sojourns here. Don't miss the most dramatic view of the palace—from its park side, it sits atop six grassy terraces, cut into the side of a hill like steps in a pyramid, created for Frederick's vineyards (if you walk through town to the palace, this is the view you'll be treated to first). The palace is open April to October Tuesday to Sunday 10am to 6pm, and November to March Tuesday to Sunday 10am to 5pm. Guided tours (in English) of the palace cost 8€ to 12€ for adults, 5€ to 8€ for students and children 6 to 18, free for children 5 and under. *Tip:* It is best (especially in summer) to show up before noon to buy your tickets for the palace tour. Slots for the rest of the day can be filled by noon.

At the other end of Sanssouci Park, about a 25-minute walk away, is the estate's largest building, the extravagant **Neues Palais** (© **0331/9694200;** www.spsg.de), built 20 years after Schloss Sanssouci as a show of Prussian strength following the devastation of the Seven Years' War. Also serving as a summer residence for the royal Hohenzollerns, it's much more ostentatious than Schloss Sanssouci and, in comparison, seems grave, solemn, and humorless. Of note is the **Hall of Shells,** its walls and ceiling smothered with shells, mica, minerals, fossils, and semiprecious stones. The Neues Palais is open Tuesday to Sunday: April to October 10am to 6pm, and November to March 10am to 5pm. Admission here is 6€ for adults and 5€ students/children. It is usually less crowded than Sanssouci.

WHERE TO DINE
Friedrish-Wilhelm ★★★, Im Wildpark 1 (© **0331/55050**), is romantically scenic and tranquil—and also serves the city's finest gourmet cuisine. In the winter a fireplace blazes, and in the summer diners enjoy the open-air terrace. The cuisine is market fresh, creative, and wonderfully delicate. The menu frequently changes but is always fresh, offering German and international fare. Main courses range from 28€ to 42€, and the fixed-price menus range from 58€ to 85€. Located in the Hotel Bayrisches, it is open Tuesday to Saturday from 6 to 10pm, and reservations are required.

The most convenient place for a meal, **Specker's Gästästatte zur Ratswaag ★★**, Jägerallee 13 (© **0331/2804311;** www.speckers.de; S-Bahn: Potsdam Hauptbahnhof), is midway between the rail station and the historic center. This is the oldest restaurant in Potsdam, though the continental menu offers inventive cuisine. The menu changes every 2 weeks, depending on what is fresh and the inspiration of the chef. However, expect the ongoing specialties that include breast of guinea fowl with a mango-flavored cream sauce or the wild mushroom soup. Main courses range from 16€ to 35€, and the fixed-price menu is 30€. It is open Tuesday to Saturday from noon to 2pm and 6 to 11pm. Reservations are recommended.

MUNICH ★★

Named after the Munichen monks who settled more than 1,200 years ago on the banks of the Isar River, **Munich** is the capital of the state (or land) of Bavaria and a sprawling city of 1.3 million. Home of industrial giants like BMW and Siemens, it's one of Germany's important cultural capitals, with four symphony orchestras, two opera houses, dozens of world-class museums, more than 50 theaters, and one of Germany's largest universities. The diverse student population and the foreign residents who make up more than 22% of the citizenry ensure an active avant-garde cultural scene and a liberal attitude in an otherwise conservative region.

Munich is striking, largely the product of the exuberant imagination and aspirations of past Bavarian kings and rulers. Royal residences, majestic museums, steepled churches, and ornate monuments celebrate architectural styles from baroque and Gothic to neoclassical and postmodern. Add wide boulevards, spacious parks, thriving nightlife, at least six breweries, and the world's largest beer fest, and you have what amounts to one of Germany's most interesting, exciting, and festive cities.

Munich is a prime rail destination, and though we rate Berlin first in importance, Munich is definitely more picturesque and, in many ways, is more strategically located. Not only are its train connections to the rest of Germany superb, but its link

Munich

ACCOMMODATIONS ■
Eden-Hotel-Wolff **3**
Gästehaus Englischer
  Garten **31**
Hotel Advokat Munich **13**
Hotel an der Oper **25**
Hotel Exquisit **8**
Hotel Jedermann **4**
Hotel Mark **6**
Hotel Schlicker **16**
Hotel Splendid-Dollmann
  im Lehel **28**
Hotel Torbräu **14**
Hotel Uhland **5**

DINING ◆
Alois Dallmayr **23**
Andechser am Dom **22**
Bayerischer Donisl **20**
Bier- und Oktoberfest-
  museum **15**
La Valle **18**
Nürnberger Bratwurst
  Glöckl am Dom **21**
Prinz Myshkin **9**
Ratskeller München **19**
Restaurant Pfistermühle **24**
Spatenhaus an der Oper **26**
Weinhaus Neuner **7**
Weisses Bräuhaus **17**

ATTRACTIONS ●
Alte Pinakothek **2**
Amalienburg **37**
Badenburg **38**
Bayerisches National-
  museum **29**
Deutsches Museum **12**
Englischer Garten **30**
Magdalenenklause **34**
Marstallmuseum **36**
Münchner Stadtmuseum **10**
Neue Pinakothek **1**
Nymphenburg Palace **35**
Pagodenburg **33**
Pinakothek der Moderne **32**
Residenz, Residenzmuseum
  & Schatzkammer **27**
Tierpark Hellabrun **11**

ⓘ Information
✉ Post office
〓Ⓤ〓 U-Bahn
〓Ⓢ〓 S-Bahn

0   1/4 mi
0   0.25 km

Nymphenburg

33 Kleiner See

34

Nymphenburger Kanal

35

SCHLOSSPARK NYMPHENBURG

37

36

Grosser See

38

Zuccalistr.

LUDWIG-MAXIMILIANS-UNIVERSITÄT MÜNCHEN
Geschwister-Scholl-Pl. Ⓤ
Universität

Schellingstrasse

Amalienstr.

Theresien-

Museum Brandhorst

Pinakothek der Moderne
32

strasse

Türkenstrasse

Fürstenstr.

Rheinberger-str.

Ludwigstrasse

Bayerische Staatsbibliothek

Ludwig-Str.

Oskar-Von-Miller-Ring

Kardinal-Döpfner-Str.

Jägerstr.

Von-der-Tann-t Str.

Schönfeld-str.

31

Königinstrasse

ENGLISCHER GARTEN

30

Finkenstr.

Wittelsbacherplatz

Odeonsplatz

Galeriestrasse

Dichtergarten

Hofgarten

Haus der Kunst

Lerchenfeldstrasse

Seeaaustr.

Himbselstr.

Bayerisches Nationalmuseum
29

strasse

Platz der Opfer des Nationalsozialismus

Odeonspl. Ⓤ

Hofgartenstr.

Bayerische Staatskanzlei

Prinzregentenstrasse

Wagmüllerstr.

Alexandrastr.

Oettingenstrasse

platz

Jungfern-turmstr.

Rochusberg

Salvatorstr.

Theatiner-kirche

Residenzstr.

Residenz
27

Hofgartenstr.

Unsöldstrasse

Liebig-strasse

Sankt-Anna-Platz

Bruder-str.

Franz-Josef-Strauss-Ring

Christophstr.

LEHEL

Triftstr.

Barerstr.

Robert-Koch-Str.

Reitmor-

Prannerstr.

Kard-Faulhaber-

Promenade-platz

Maffeistr.

Perusa-str.

Max-Joseph-Platz

National-theater

Marstallplatz

Marstallstr.

Wurzerstr.

Falcken-bergstr.

Herzog-Rudolf-Str.

Karl-Scharnagl-Ring

Seitz-str.

Sankt-

Anna-Str.

Prafrstr.

Lehel Ⓤ

Stern-

Gewürzmühlstr.

Tratten-

Widenmayerstr.

Maximilians-brücke

Löwengrube

Schäfflerstr.

Augustiner-str.

Frauen-kirche
22

Frauen-platz
21

Weinstr.

Marien-hof

Schrammer-str.

Hofgraben

Alter Hof
24

23

25

Pfisterstr.

Neuturmstr.

Münz-str.

Maximilian-

strasse

Neuhauser-

Kaufingerstr.

Neues Rathaus
19

20

Dienerstr.

Burgstr.

Maderbräustr.

Kassenstr.

Platzl

Bräuhaus-str.

Hildegardstr.

Völkerkunde-museum

strasse

Stollbergstr.

Knöbel-

Thomas-Wimmer-Ring

Adelgundenstr.

Steindorfstrasse

PRATER-INSEL

MAXIMILIAN-ANLAGEN

9
Fürstenfelder Str.

Färbergraben

Rosenstr.

Rindermarkt

Marien-platz Ⓢ

Marienplatz

Spar-

Lederer-

Hochbrückenstr.

Hernnstr.

Kanal-str.

Mann-hardtstr.

Am Gasteig

Innere Wiener Str.

9

Peterskirche

Rosental

Heiligeiststr.

18

17

16

Tal

Radlsteg

14

Isartor

Kellerstrasse

Preysingstr.

Stadt-museum
10

Dultstr.

Sack-str.

VIKTUALIEN-MARKT

Westenriederstr.

15

Isartor Ⓢ

Isartor-platz

Thierschstr.

Ludwigs-brücke

Rosenheimer-Str.

Gasteig

Jüdisches Zentrum Jakobsplatz

Schrannenhalle

Frauenstrasse

ford-

strasse

Zweibrückenstr.

Liebherrstr.

Isar

Anger-

Prälat-Zistl-

Am Einlass

Rum-strasse

Blumenstrasse

Corneliusstrasse

Buttermelcherstr.

Aventinstr.

strasse

13

Kohl-

Morassistr.

Thiersch-str.

Kleine Isar

Zeppelinstrasse

Lilienstrasse

Hochstrasse

Auer Mühlbach

Papa-Schmid-Str.

Müllerstrasse

Gärtner-platz

Klenze-

strasse

strasse

Baader-

MUSEUMS-INSEL

Staatstheater am Gärtnerplatz

Fraunhoferstrasse

Cornelius-

str.

Reichenbach-

Erhard-

str.

Isar

12
Deutsches Museum

Jahnstr.

Klenze-

Frauenhoferstr. Ⓤ

11

Rosenheimer Pl. Ⓢ

9

GERMANY | Munich

353

to several high-speed international rail lines makes it an easy stop for anyone on a multicountry tour of Europe. And with an international airport offering direct flight connections with North America, it also makes a good starting or stopping point on a rail trip through Europe.

Station Information

GETTING FROM THE AIRPORT TO THE TRAIN STATION

About 17 miles (27km) northeast of central Munich at Erdinger Moos, the **Munich International Airport** (✆ 089/97500; www.munich-airport.de), inaugurated in 1992, is among the most modern, best-equipped, and most efficient airports in the world. The airport handles more than 400 flights a day, serving at least 65 cities worldwide. Passengers can fly nonstop from several North American gateways, including New York, Atlanta, and Chicago.

The easiest way to get into town is via the **S-Bahn** (✆ 01805/661010; www. s-bahn-muenchen.de), with lines S-8 or S-1 traveling to Marienplatz (the city center) and the Hauptbahnhof (main train station). Trains leave every 20 minutes, and the trip to the Hauptbahnhof takes about 40 minutes. If you have a valid railpass, you can ride for free. Otherwise, a ticket is 12€. Alternatively, you can buy a 10€ **1-day transportation pass (Tageskarte)** for greater Munich, advisable if you plan on using public transportation at least once more the remainder of the day. A taxi to the city center costs 50€ to 60€.

INSIDE THE STATION

Munich's main rail station, the **Hauptbahnhof** (✆ 01805/661010), on Bahnhof-platz near the city center, is one of Europe's largest. It contains a hotel, restaurants, shopping, and banking facilities. All major German cities are connected to this station. Some 20 daily trains connect Munich directly to Frankfurt's main train station or its airport (trip time: 3¾ hr.). In addition, there are a half-dozen direct trains from Heidelberg to Munich (trip time: 3 hr.), and 23 trains depart for Berlin each day (trip time: 6¾ hr.). For information about long-distance trains, call ✆ **11861.** You can also drop by **EurAide,** a special service for English-speaking travelers providing free train and sightseeing info and selling various rail tickets. It's located off the main hall (behind the DB Reisezentrum–travel center). From May to September, the office is open daily from 8am to noon and Monday to Saturday 2 to 5pm; from October to April, open weekdays 8am to noon and 1 to 4pm. The office is closed December 23 to January 1 and January 15 to February 15.

You'll find a branch of Munich's **Tourismus Information** just outside the Haupt-bahnhof's main exit at Bahnhofplatz 2. The staff there will book hotel rooms and dispense information, among other services.

The **Hauptbahnhof** serves as a nucleus for the many tram, bus, U-Bahn (underground subway), and S-Bahn (metropolitan railway) lines.

Information Elsewhere in the City

In addition to the tourist office at the Hauptbahnhof, there's another convenient office in the **Neues Rathaus (New Town Hall),** on Marienplatz, open Monday to Friday 10am to 8pm, Saturday 10am to 4pm, and Sunday 10am to 2pm.

For more information, call ✆ **089/23396500.** You can also get information on the Internet at **www.muenchen.de.**

City Layout

The heart of Munich, the **Altstadt (Old Town)** is east of the Hauptbahnhof. Its very center is **Marienplatz,** a cobblestone plaza a 15-minute walk from the train station and connected to the rest of the city by an extensive subway network. Over the centuries, it has served as a market square, a stage for knightly tournaments, and the site of public executions. Today it's no less important, bordered on one side by the impressive Neues Rathaus (New Town Hall), famous for its chimes and mechanized figures appearing daily at 11am and noon (also 5pm in summer). Much of the Old Town is a **pedestrian zone,** where you'll find the smartest boutiques, most traditional restaurants, and oldest churches, plus the Viktualienmarkt outdoor market. Most of Munich's museums are within an easy walk or short subway ride from the center.

As for other areas worth exploring, the **Englischer Garten,** with its wide green expanses and beer gardens, stretches northeast from the city center. Oktoberfest is held at **Theresienwiese,** just south of the Hauptbahnhof, while **Schwabing,** north of the city center, is home to Munich's university and nightlife. **Schloss Nymphenburg,** once the royal family's summer residence, is northwest of town, accessible by streetcar from the train station.

Getting Around

Munich's wonderful underground network, created in conjunction with the 1972 Summer Olympics, is the ultimate in German efficiency. It's divided into the **U-Bahn** (underground subway) and **S-Bahn** (metropolitan railway), with the most convenient connection between the two at Marienplatz. Buses and trams go everywhere the subway doesn't. Munich's public transport system operates daily about 5am to 1am, with some S-Bahn lines, including one to the airport, operating frequently throughout the night. In addition, a handful of bus and tram lines run nightly about 1:30 to 5am, designated by an N in front of their number.

Because the S-Bahn is part of the German Federal Railroads, you can use a valid railpass on these lines. Otherwise, you'll have to buy a ticket, which is good for all forms of transportation in Munich and includes transfers. Validate the ticket yourself by inserting it into one of the little blue machines at the entrance to the underground track or on board the bus or tram.

A **single journey** to most destinations costs 2.40€. Shorter journeys—trips of, at most, two stops on the subway or four on the tram or bus—require a ticket called a **Kurzstrecke,** at only 1.20€. Slightly more economical is the **Streifenkarte,** a strip ticket allowing multiple journeys and saving the hassle of buying individual tickets each time you travel. It costs 12€. For short journeys (a Kurzstrecke), you use one stripe. Most trips in the city, however, require two stripes (a total of 2.30€ for the ride). Simply fold up two segments of the *Streifenkarte* and insert them into the validating machine.

A simpler solution still is to buy a **Tageskarte** (day ticket), allowing unlimited travel on all modes of transport for 1 day. A 5.20€ *Tageskarte* is valid for most of Munich's inner city and includes the entire U-Bahn network. If you want to travel to the outskirts, buy the 11€ card for the metropolitan area (about a 50-mile/80km) radius, including the airport and Dachau. The Parnter-Tageskarte, valid for up to five adults (two children count as one adult), costs 9.40€ and 19€, respectively.

For more information on Munich's public transportation system (MVV), call **089/41424344** (www.mvv-muenchen.de) or drop by the MVV Kundencenter kiosk inside the Hauptbahnhof or Marientplatz subway station.

Munich U-Bahn & S-Bahn

Cabs begin at 2.90€, plus 1.60€ per kilometer, unless your ride is longer than 6¼ miles (10km), in which event the per-kilometer rate goes down to between 1.25€ and 1.40€, depending on the distance you travel. If you need to call a taxi, phone ✆ **089/ 21610,** and 1€ is added to your fare.

Where to Stay

The area surrounding the Bahnhof doesn't have many recommendable hotels, but hotels in the Altstadt center of town tend to be very expensive. We list the best hotels closest to the train station, as well as some of our favorite value selections for the rest of the city.

Eden-Hotel-Wolff ★ If you must stay in the train station area, this family-owned hotel across from the station's north side is your best bet. Built in 1890, its interior is richly traditional, with chandeliers and dark-wood paneling, and the staff is attentive and efficient. Most rooms are spacious, and all are tastefully furnished in a decor that runs the gamut from extremely modern to rustic. After sightseeing, guests can use an exercise room, sauna, solarium, steam room, and rooftop terrace. Ask whether they have special weekend rates.

Arnulfstrasse 4-8, 80335 München. ✆ **089/551150.** Fax 089/55115555. www.ehw.de. 210 units. 184€– 325€ double; 295€-400€ suite. Rates include buffet breakfast. AE, DC, MC, V. S-/U-Bahn: Hauptbahnhof. **Amenities:** Restaurant; bar; smoke-free rooms.

Gästehaus Englischer Garten ★★ 🎁 This is an oasis of charm and tranquillity, separated from the Englischer Garten only by a bubbling brook, yet just a short walk away from Schwabing's nightlife. A dozen rooms (half without private bathroom) are located in a 130-year-old converted mill, where breakfast is served outside in fair weather and where small to medium rooms offer "Bavarian grandmotherly" furnishings, including genuine antiques, old-fashioned but comfortable beds, and Oriental rugs. The rest of the units are located in an apartment complex down the street, complete with kitchenettes. Ask for room no. 10, 20, 30, or 90—these are bigger and have better views. There are rental bikes for 12€ a day to explore the expansive English Gardens.

Liebergesellstrasse 8, 80802 München. ✆ **089/3839410.** Fax 089/38394133. www.hotelenglischer garten.de. 25 units, 16 with bathroom. 75€–109€ double without bathroom; 129€–169€ double with bathroom; 110€–163€ apt. AE, DC, MC, V. U-Bahn: Münchener Freiheit. *In room:* No A/C.

Hotel Advokat Munich This hotel occupies a six-story apartment house originally constructed in the 1930s. Although its curbside appeal is nil, its stripped-down, streamlined interior borrows in discreet ways from Bauhaus and minimalist models. The result is an aggressively simple, clean-lined, and artfully spartan hotel, with a rooftop terrace great for summer evenings. Half the rooms have balconies, the staff is helpful, and prices are reasonable.

Baaderstrasse 1, 80469 München. ✆ **089/216310.** Fax 089/2163190. www.hotel-advokat.de. 50 units. 165€–285€ double. Rates include buffet breakfast. AE, DC, MC, V. S-Bahn: Isartor. **Amenities:** Smoke-free rooms. *In room:* No A/C.

Hotel an der Oper This five-floor hotel, just steps from the Bavarian National Theater in the Altstadt, but tucked away on an overlooked side street, is superbly located for sightseeing and shopping. In spite of its basic decor, there are touches of elegance. Rooms, bathed in white and a bit kitschy with overstated chandeliers, range from small to medium and have a small sitting area with armchairs. Bathrooms tend to be small, but are well organized and come mainly with just a shower. What you're paying for here is location.

Falkenturmstrasse 11 (just off Maximilianstrasse, near Marienplatz), 80331 München. © **089/2900270.** Fax 089/29002729. www.hotelanderoper.com. 68 units. 180€–270€ double; 246€–390€ apt. Rates include buffet breakfast. AE, MC, V. Tram: 19. **Amenities:** Restaurant, smoke-free rooms.

Hotel Exquisit ★   One of the most appealing hotels in this quiet residential neighborhood, the Exquisit lies behind a wine-colored facade only a 10-minute walk from the Hauptbahnhof and Marienplatz. It has a paneled lobby whose focal point is a lounge that gets busy around 6 or 7pm, as well as a sauna and solarium. Rooms are spacious and comfortably furnished, with about half overlooking an ivy-draped garden. The shower-only bathrooms have adequate shelf space, and some have double basins.

Pettenkoferstrasse 3, 80336 München. © **089/5519900.** Fax 089/55199499. www.hotel-exquisit.com. 50 units. 185€–295€ double; 239€–355€ suite. Rates include buffet breakfast. AE, DC, MC, V. U-Bahn: Sendlinger Tor. **Amenities:** Restaurant; bar; rooms for those w/limited mobility; smoke-free rooms. *In room:* No A/C.

Hotel Jedermann ☺ ⚐   Those in awe of the high prices of Munich hotels find comfort at this pleasant and deftly run hotel, just a 10-minute walk from the Hauptbahnhof and owned by the English-speaking Jenke family since 1962. The old-fashioned Bavarian rooms are generally small but cozy and comfortable; nice touches include flowers, antiques, traditional Bavarian furniture, and chocolates left on the pillows. A computer in the lobby offers free Internet access. Staff attitude here, however, needs a major overhaul.

Bayerstrasse 95, 80335 München. © **089/543240.** Fax 089/5432 4111. www.hotel-jedermann.de. 55 units. 75€–189€ double; 90€–219€ triple. Rates include buffet breakfast. MC, V. 10-min. walk from Hauptbahnhof (turn right on Bayerstrasse from south exit). **Amenities:** Bar.

Hotel Mark ⚐   This hotel near the Hauptbahnhof's south exit is known for comfort and moderate prices. The rooms are functionally furnished, although a bit cramped, but you should sleep in peace. All rooms have soundproof windows.

Senefelderstrasse 12, 80336 München. © **089/559820.** Fax 089/55982333. www.hotel-mark.de. 95 units. 82€–262€ double. Rates include buffet breakfast. AE, DC, MC, V. U-Bahn or S-Bahn: Hauptbahnhof.

Hotel Schlicker ☺ ⚔   In spite of its location between a McDonald's and a Burger King, this hotel exudes a certain kind of charm. Its pedigree dates from 1544, and the same family has managed it for five generations. Due to extensive renovation, however, only the breakfast room suggests that this was once an ancient inn. The midsize bedrooms are comfortable and traditional, but the hotel's main selling point is its location, in the heart of Munich just steps away from the Marienplatz.

Tal 8, 80331 München. © **089/2428870.** Fax 089/296059. www.hotel-schlicker.de. 69 units. 145€–185€ double; 260€ suite. Rates include continental breakfast. AE, DC, MC, V. S-/U-Bahn: Marienplatz. *In room:* No A/C.

Hotel Splendid-Dollmann im Lehel ★ ⚔   Check in here if you want a hotel that's up-to-date yet replete with antiques, fine paintings, quality Oriental carpets, and a sense of Munich's sometimes gracious 18th- and 19th-century past. The venue is an elegant 19th-century town house in the upscale Lehel district. Inside, an attentive staff welcomes you into a small, boutique-style hotel replete with a library-style bar and many of the decorative accessories of an upscale private home. Bedrooms are cozy, colorful, and well maintained, each with a different theme and reproductions of antique furniture.

Thierschstrasse 49, 80538 München. © **089/238080.** Fax 089/23808365. www.hotel-splendid-dollmann.de. 37 units. 160€–200€ double; 230€–270€ suite. AE, DC, MC, V. U-Bahn: Lehel. **Amenities:** Bar.

Hotel Torbräu ★   The foundations of this hotel in the heart of historic Munich date from the 15th century. Although many vestiges of its folkloric exterior attest to the hotel's distinguished past, the bedrooms are modern and are reasonably comfortable. In all, the place is a lot more charming than many of its bandbox-modern competitors.

Tal 41, 80331 München. © **089/242340.** Fax 089/24234235. www.torbraeu.de. 92 units. 189€–276€ double; 275€–397€ suite. Rates include buffet breakfast. AE, MC, V. Closed 1 week at Christmas. U-Bahn: Isartor. **Amenities:** 2 restaurants; bar.

Hotel Uhland   Located in a residential area, just a 10-minute walk from the Hauptbahnhof, the Uhland could easily become your home in Munich. The stately town mansion, built in Art Nouveau style, stands in its own small garden. The hotel offers friendly, personal service; and the individually decorated rooms are soundproof, snug, traditional, and cozy.

Uhlandstrasse 1, 80336 München. © **089/543350.** Fax 089/54335250. www.hotel-uhland.de. 30 units. 82€–199€ double. Rates include buffet breakfast. AE, DC, MC, V. S-/U-Bahn: Theresienwiese. Bus: 58 from Hauptbahnhof to Georg-Hirth-Platz. **Amenities:** Smoke-free rooms. *In room:* No A/C.

Top Attractions & Special Moments

Munich is stocked with so many treasures that any visitor who plans to "do" the city in a day or two not only will miss out on many major sights but also will fail to grasp the city's spirit and absorb its special flavor. Below, you'll find a few vital highlights to help you make the best of your time in the city.

MUSEUMS

Alte Pinakothek ★★★   If you visit only one art museum in Munich, this should be it. Begun as the collection of the royal Wittelsbach family in the early 1500s, it ranks as one of Europe's most important galleries and contains virtually all European schools of painting from the Middle Ages to the early 19th century, with one of the world's largest collections of Rubens, plus galleries filled with German, Dutch, Flemish, Italian, Spanish, and French masterpieces. You'll also find galleries of religious allegorical paintings, portraits of peasants and patricians, Romantic landscapes, still lifes, and scenes of war and hunting.

Although it's difficult to pick the collection's stars, **Dürer** is well represented with *Four Apostles, The Baumgartner Altar, Lamentation for the Dead Christ,* and, probably most famous, his *Self-Portrait (Selbstbildnis im Pelzrock).* Watch for **Titian's** *Crowning with Thorns (Die Dornenkrönung);* **Rembrandt's** *Birth of Christ,* with his remarkable use of light and shadows; and **Bruegel's** *Land of Cockaigne.* Among the many **Rubens** are the rather frightening *Last Judgment (Das Grosse Jüngste Gericht)* and *The Damned's Descent into Hell (Der Höllensturz der Verdammten),* sure to make a convert of the most avowed sinner. In **Albrecht Altdorfer's** *Battle of Alexander,* which took him 12 years to complete, notice the painstaking detail of the thousands of lances and all the men on horseback. Another favorite is **Adriaen Brouwer,** of the Netherlands, one of the best painters of the peasant genre. The Alte Pinakothek has 17 of his paintings in Room 11, the largest collection in the world. Brouwer's skill at capturing the life of his subjects as they drink at an inn, play cards, or engage in a brawl is delightful.

On Sundays, several of Munich's major museums, including all the Pinakothek museums and the Bayerishes Nationalmuseum, charge an admission of only 1€ to their permanent exhibitions, while the Münchener Stadtmuseum is absolutely free.

Barer Strasse 27 (entrance on Theresienstrasse). ℂ **089/23805216.** www.pinakothek.de/alte-pinakothek. Admission 7€ adults, 5€ seniors and students, free for children 14 and under. Tues 10am–8pm; Wed–Sun 10am–6pm. U-Bahn: Theresienstrasse. Tram: 27 to Pinakotheken. Bus: 100.

Bayerisches Nationalmuseum ★★ The Bavarian National Museum emphasizes the historical and cultural development of Bavaria, as well as the rest of Europe, from the Middle Ages to the early 19th century. It complements the Alte Pinakothek, showing what was happening in other genres of art and crafts at the same time that painters were producing their masterpieces. Glass, miniatures, musical instruments, wood and ivory carvings, jewelry, clothing, textiles and tapestries, porcelain, medieval armor and weaponry, furniture, stained-glass windows, sculpture, and religious artifacts and altars are some of the 20,000 items. Outstanding are the **wood sculptures** from the Gothic through rococo periods, especially carvings by **Tilman Riemenschneider** (notice the facial expressions of the 12 Apostles in Room 16), as well as works by **Erasmus Grasser, Michael Pacher, Johann Baptist Staub,** and **Ignaz Günther.**

One delightful thing about this museum is that the architecture complements the objects. The Late Gothic Church Art Room (Room 15), for example, is modeled after a church in Augsburg, providing a perfect background for the religious art it displays. The basement, partly devoted to folk art, includes furniture and complete rooms showing how people lived long ago. Notice the wooden floors and low ceiling (to save heat). The other half of the museum houses an incredible collection of **nativity scenes (Krippe) ★★** from the Alpine region and Italy. Some of the displays are made of paper, but most are amazingly elaborate and lifelike; it's worth visiting the museum for them alone.

Prinzregentenstrasse 3. ℂ **089/2112401.** www.bayerisches-nationalmuseum.de. Admission 5€ adults, 4€ seniors and students, free for children 14 and under. Tues–Sun 10am–5pm (to 8pm Thurs). U-Bahn: Lehel. Tram: 17 to Nationalmuseum. Bus: 100.

Deutsches Museum von Meisterwerken der Naturwissenschaft und Technik ★★★ ☺ The world's largest and oldest technological museum of its kind, the Deutsches Museum contains a huge collection of artifacts and historic originals, divided into 50-some exhibits relating to physics, navigation, mining, vehicle engineering, musical instruments, glass technology, writing and printing, photography, textiles, and weights and measures. There's also a planetarium. You can see a replica of the **Gutenberg press,** and **musical instruments** from electronic drums to a glass harmonica. Its huge collection of priceless artifacts and historic originals includes the first electric dynamo (Siemens, 1866), the first automobile (Benz, 1886), and the laboratory bench at which the atom was first split (Hahn, Strassmann, 1938). For one of the most popular exhibits, you can descend into the bowels of a **coal** and a **salt mine**—it takes the better part of an hour just to walk through. Would you like to ponder the meaning behind the prehistoric drawings of the **Altamira Cave?** What makes the museum fascinating for adults and children alike is that there are buttons to push, gears to crank, and levers to pull. There's also a children's section, the **Kinderreich,** geared toward youngsters 8 and younger. In any case, you could easily spend a half-day here.

Museumsinsel 1 (Ludwigsbrücke). ℭ **089/21791.** www.deutsches-museum.de Admission 8.50€ adults, 7€ seniors, 3€ students, free for children 6 and under. Daily 9am–5pm. Closed major holidays. U-Bahn: Fraunhoferstrasse. S-Bahn: Isartor. Tram: 18.

Münchner Stadtmuseum ★ Centrally located in the Altstadt (Old Town) and often overlooked, the eclectic Munich City Museum is a great repository of the city's history—but that's not all. The **Puppet Theater Collection** is outstanding, with puppets and theater stages from around the world, as well as fairground art (including the Oktoberfest), while the **Musical Instrument Collection** displays European instruments from the 16th to the 20th centuries and primitive instruments from around the world. There's also a section devoted to the **history of photography,** with original photographs and cameras from 1839 to 1919. The exhibits on Munich cover the history of the city from the late 15th century to the present day, with maps, models, paintings, photographs, and furniture (unfortunately, only in German). But the most valuable pieces are **Erasmus Grasser's 10 Morris Dancers,** carved in 1480 for display in Munich's old town hall. The morris (or morrice) dance, popular in the 15th century, was a rustic ambulatory dance performed by companies of actors at festivals. Daily at 6:30 and 9pm, the film museum shows two films from its extensive archives.

St. Jakobs-Platz 1. ℭ **089/23322370.** www.stadtmuseum-online.de. Admission 4€ adults, 2€ students and children 6–15, 6€ families, free for children 5 and under, more for special exhibits. Sun free for everyone. Tues–Sun 10am–6pm. S-/U-Bahn: Marienplatz.

Neue Pinakothek ★ Across from the Alte Pinakothek is the Neue Pinakothek, with its comprehensive view of European painting in the late 18th and 19th centuries. It begins with art from around 1800 (**Goya, Turner,** and **Gainsborough**) and works through early romantic landscape painters **Caspar David Friedrich** and **Leo von Klenze,** then continues with works of the Biedermeier era (**Waldmüller's** romanticized renditions of peasant life are wonderful), German and French Impressionism, Symbolism, and Art Nouveau. **Corinth, Courbet, Delacroix, Liebermann, Menzel, Cézanne, Gauguin, Rodin, van Gogh, Degas, Manet, Monet,** and **Renoir** all have canvases here. Note particularly the genre works by Carl Spitzweg, whose paintings poke gentle fun at everyday life in Munich. The building itself is a delight, designed by Alexander von Branca and opened in 1981 to replace the old museum destroyed in World War II. Using the natural lighting of skylights and windows, it's the perfect setting for the paintings it displays, and perimeter ramps make the works accessible by wheelchair or stroller.

Barer Strasse 29 (entrance on Theresienstrasse). ℭ **089/23805195.** www.pinakothek.de. Admission 7€ adults, 5€ seniors and students, free for children 15 and under. Wed 10am–8pm; Thurs–Mon 10am–6pm. U-Bahn: Theresienstrasse. Tram: 27 to Pinakotheken. Bus: 100.

Pinakothek der Moderne ★★ This spacious, modern museum brings together four major collections under one roof—art, graphics, architecture, and design—making it Germany's largest museum of art from the 20th and 21st centuries. Foremost is the art collection, which features changing exhibitions that might include German expressionists such as Ernst Ludwig Kirchner and Max Beckmann (the museum possesses Europe's largest collection of his works); surrealists like René Magritte and Dalí; and some of the most important names in modern art, including Picasso, Warhol,

Beuys, Rauschenberg, Jasper Johns, and Bruce Nauman. The **Architecture Museum** displays temporary exhibits on the history of architecture and current developments, while the **State Graphic Art Collection** stages temporary displays from the beginning of classical modernism to the present. The **New Collection** is always interesting for its visually pleasing displays of industrial design and applied arts, which can run the gamut from automobiles and computers to teapots and chairs.

Barerstrasse 40. © **089/23805360.** www.pinakothek.de. Admission 10€ adults; 7€ seniors, students, and children 16 and under. Sun admission for all 1€. Wed–Sun 10am–6pm (to 8pm Thurs). U-Bahn: Odeonsplatz or Theresienstrasse. Tram: 27 to Pinakotheken.

PALACES

Nymphenburg Palace ★★ The former summer residence of the Wittelsbach family, who ruled over Bavaria, Nymphenburg is Germany's largest baroque palace. Construction began in 1664 but took more than 150 years to complete. The first room you'll see is the **great hall,** decorated in rococo colors and stuccoes. The frescoes by Zimmermann (1756) depict incidents from mythology, especially those dealing with Flora, goddess of nymphs, for whom the palace was named. Concerts are still presented here in summer. Probably the most interesting room is Ludwig I's **Gallery of Beauties:** The 36 portraits, commissioned by Ludwig, represent the most beautiful women in Munich in his time. Among them are Queen Marie of Bavaria (mother of Ludwig II), Helene Sedlmayr (daughter of a shoemaker, who later married a footman and had 10 children), and Lola Montez (a dancer whose scandalous relations with Ludwig prompted an 1848 revolt by a disgruntled people who forced his abdication).

To the south of the palace buildings is the **Marstallmuseum,** with a splendid collection of state coaches, carriages, and sleds used for weddings, coronations, and special events. Housed in what used to be the royal stables, the museum culminates in the fantastic fairy-tale carriages of Ludwig II, which are no less extravagant than his castles. In the first hall, look for the glass coronation coach of Elector Karl Albrecht, built in Paris in 1740. On the floor above the Marstallmuseum is the **Porzellansammlung (Porcelain Collection),** with a fine collection of delicate figurines, tea services, plates, and bowls from the mid–18th century through the 1920s.

Nymphenburg's park ★, first laid out as a geometrical baroque garden but transformed into an English landscape garden in the early 19th century, contains statues, artificial hills, lakes, canals, botanical gardens, and a number of pavilions. **Amalienburg** ★★, a small pink hunting lodge unlike anything you've ever seen, is one of the world's great masterpieces of rococo art. Though the first couple of rooms are simple enough, the rest take off in a flight of fantasy, with an amazing amount of decorative silver covering almost every inch of the walls with vines, grapes, and cherubs. Its **Hall of Mirrors** is as splendid a room as you're likely to find anywhere, far surpassing anything in the main palace. In the park are three other pavilions (closed in winter): the **Magdalenenklause (Hermitage),** a meditation retreat, complete with artificial cracks in the walls to make it look like a ruin; the **Pagodenburg,** an elegant two-story tea pavilion; and **Badenburg,** a bathhouse with Europe's first heated indoor pool.

Schloss Nymphenburg 1. © **089/179080.** www.schloss-nymphenburg.de. Admission to all attractions: 10€ adults, 8€ seniors, free for students and children 17 and under. Admission to Schloss Nymphenburg only: 5€ adults, 4€ seniors, free for students and children 17 and under. Admission to Marstallmuseum, Amalienburg, or Porzellansammlung only: 4€ adults, 3€ seniors, free for students and children 17 and under. Oct–Mar daily 10am–4pm; Apr–Sept daily 9am–6pm. Free parking beside the Marstallmuseum. U-Bahn: Rotkreuzplatz, then tram 17 to Botanischergarten. Bus: 51.

The World's Greatest Beer Fest

Munich's most famous event is **Oktoberfest (www.muenchen.de)**, held from mid-September to the first Sunday in October. The celebration began in 1810 to honor Ludwig I's marriage, when the main event was a horse race in a field called the Thereisenwiese. Everyone had so much fun that the celebration was held again the following year, and then again and again. Today Oktoberfest is among the largest fairs in the world. Every year the festivities get underway with a parade on the first Oktoberfest Sunday, with almost 7,000 participants marching through the streets in folk costumes. Most activities, however, are at the Theresienwiese, where huge beer tents sponsored by local breweries dispense both beer and merriment, complete with Bavarian bands and singing. Each tent holds up to 6,000, which gives you some idea of how rowdy things can get. During the 16-day period, an estimated six million visitors guzzle more than a million gallons of beer and eat 700,000 broiled chickens! In addition to the beer tents, there are carnival attractions and amusement rides. Entry to the fairgrounds is free, but rides cost extra.

Residenz, Residenzmuseum & Schatzkammer ★ While Nymphenburg Palace was the Wittelsbach summer home, the Residenz was the Bavarian rulers' official town residence for 4 centuries until 1918. The **Residenz Museum,** comprises the southwestern section of the palace, some 120 rooms of art and furnishings collected by centuries of Wittelsbachs. The stunning **Antiquarium** is possibly the finest example of interior Renaissance secular styling in Germany; in the **Silver Chamber** is the complete table silver of the House of Wittelsbach—some 3,500 pieces. The **Ancestors Hall** contains the portraits of 121 members of the family—eerie because of the way their eyes seem to follow you as you walk down the hall. Be sure to see the **Emperor's Hall,** the **Ornate Chapel,** the **Green Gallery,** and the **Ornate Rooms** by François de Cuvilliés the Elder, one of the best examples of South German rococo. On the second floor of the palace, directly over the Antiquarium, is an enormous collection of Far Eastern porcelain. Note also the fine assemblage of Oriental rugs in the long, narrow **Porcelain Gallery.**

In the Residenz is also the **Schatzkammer (Treasury)** ★★, housing an amazing collection of jewelry, gold, silver, insignia, and religious items belonging to the Bavarian royalty and collected over 1,000 years, including the royal crown, swords, scepters, goblets, bowls, toiletry objects, serving platters, treasures from other countries, and more. The highlight is the 1586 jewel-studded statue of *St. George Slaying the Dragon* on his horse.

Max-Joseph-Platz 3. ☎ **089/290671.** www.residenz-muenchen.de. Combination ticket for Residenzmuseum and Schatzkammer 9€ adults, 8€ seniors, free for students and children 17 and under. Ticket for either Residenzmuseum or Schatzkammer 6€ adults, 5€ seniors, free for students and children 17 and under. Apr to mid-Oct daily 9am–6pm; mid-Oct to Mar daily 10am–5pm. U-Bahn: Odeonsplatz.

A PARK & A ZOO

The **Englischer Garten** ★ is one of the largest and most beautiful city parks in Germany. It was the brainchild of Sir Benjamin Thompson, the English scientist who spent most of his life in the service of the Bavarian government. Stretching 3 miles (4.8km) along the Isar in the heart of the city, it offers beer gardens, sunbathing (including nude sunbathing, a surprise to quite a few unsuspecting visitors—some claim these areas are Munich's most popular tourist attraction), and recreation. For a break, stop for tea on the plaza near the Chinese pagoda or have a beer at the nearby beer garden. You might also take along a picnic.

Hellabrunn Zoo (Munich Zoo) stands in Tierpark Hellabrunn, about 4 miles (6.4km) south of the city center, at Tierparkstrasse 30 (ℂ **089/625080;** www.zoo-munich.de; U-Bahn: Thalkirchen; bus: 52). It's one of the largest zoos in the world and includes the Elephant House (built in 1913); Europe's largest walk-through aviary; an aquarium; the Tropical House for gorillas and chimps; and all the usual inhabitants, including penguins, rhinos, polar bears, and lions, in environments that mimic native habitats. It also has a petting zoo and playgrounds. You can visit the zoo daily 8am to 6pm (in winter 9am–5pm); admission is 9€ for adults, 6€ for students and seniors, 4.50€ for children ages 4 to 14, and free for children 3 and under.

Where to Dine

Alois Dallmayr ★★ CONTINENTAL   Alois Dallmayr, which traces its history from 1700, is the most famous delicatessen in Germany, sampled by many royal courts. The upstairs dining room, seating only 42 and with views of the Frauenkirche's towers, offers a subtle German version of Continental cuisine (owing a heavy debt to France), served on Nymphenburg porcelain and best enjoyed with wine from the very ample cellar. The famous French *poulet de Bresse* (this Bresse chicken is identified throughout Europe as the most flavorful and tender chicken anywhere) is shipped in. The smoked fish is fabulous, and the soups are superbly flavored, especially the one made with shrimp.

Dienerstrasse 14-15. ℂ **089/2135100.** www.dallmayr.de. Reservations recommended. Main courses 35€-46€; fixed-price 4-course lunch 72€, 7-course dinner 128€. AE, DC, MC, V. Tues–Sat noon–2pm and 7–10pm. S-/U-Bahn: Marienplatz. Tram: 19.

Andechser am Dom GERMAN/BAVARIAN   This restaurant and beer hall is in a building adjacent to the rear of the Frauenkirche. It serves beer brewed in a monastery near Munich (Andechser) and generous portions of German food. You're welcome to order a snack, a full meal, or just a beer. Menu items are often accompanied by German-style potato salad and green salad. The chef's specialties are *Schweinebraten* (pork roast); *Tafelspitz* (boiled veal with horseradish); and *Sülze,* a local dish of pink meat in gelatin. In clement weather, tables are set up on the roof and on the sidewalk.

Weinstrasse 7A. ℂ **089/298481.** www.andechser-am-dom.de. Reservations recommended. Main courses 8.50€–18€. AE, DC, MC, V. Daily 10am–1am. U-Bahn or S-Bahn: Marienplatz.

Bayerischer Donisl BAVARIAN/INTERNATIONAL   Open since 1715, Donisl is popular with visitors because of its convenient location near the Neues Rathaus, comfortable (and cozy) atmosphere, typical Bavarian decor, live music every evening, local specialties, English menu, and meals that are all bargain priced. Try the *Weisswurst,* the little white sausage that has been a decades-long tradition of this place, and wash it down with beers from Munich's own Hacker-Pschorr Brewery. There is dining in the garden during the summer.

Weinstrasse 1 (off Marienplatz). ℂ **089/220184.** www.bayerischer-donisl.de. Main courses 6€–8€. AE, DC, MC, V. Daily 9am–midnight. S-/U-Bahn: Marienplatz.

Bier- und Oktoberfest Museum ★ 🏛 BAVARIAN   Nothing else in Munich is this authentically Bavarian. The Augustiner Brewery operates this museum and restaurant in a building that dates from 1327. You can first visit the museum and learn a lot about beer and even the famous Oktoberfest festival. After the tour, you're given a voucher for a Bavarian snack and a glass of brew for only 4€. The snack includes the famous Camembert-like cheese of Munich, *Obatzda,* along with *Leberwurst* (liver sausage). Go Bavarian all the way and spread *Schmalz* (chicken fat) over your freshly baked rye bread.

After 6pm you can stick around for the regional Bavarian fare, starting perhaps with a beer-infused goulash and noodles, and following with sausage salads or *Schnitzels* and the like. Naturally, everything is washed down with the Augustiner brew.

Sterneckstrasse 2. © **089/24231607.** www.bier-und-oktoberfestmuseum.de. Reservations not needed. Main courses 4€–14€. No credit cards. Museum Tues–Sat 1–5pm; beer hall Tues–Sat 6pm–midnight. U-Bahn or S-Bahn: Isartor.

Nürnberger Bratwurst Glöckl am Dom ★ ☺ 🍴 BAVARIAN The homesick Nürnberger comes here just for one dish: *Nürnberger Schweinwurst mit Kraut,* with those delectable little sausages. You can also find such items as crispy roast pork with bread dumplings and cabbage salad, veal breast stuffed with a potato-and-cucumber salad, or breaded veal escalopes topped with a cream sauce. This old restaurant is the coziest and warmest of all the local restaurants. Tables are shared, and food is served on tin plates. Last food orders go in at midnight. A short walk from Marienplatz, the restaurant faces the Frauenkirche.

Frauenplatz 9. © **089/2919450.** www.bratwurst-gloeckl.de. Reservations recommended. Main courses 10€–22€. MC, V. Daily 10am–1am. U-Bahn: U2 or U3 to Marienplatz.

Prinz Myshkin ★ VEGETARIAN This trendy restaurant serves vegetarian dishes in a refined setting. You'll find a variety of changing salads, soups, pizza, vegetarian *involtini* (stuffed roll-ups), and innovative dishes inspired by the cuisines of Asia, Italy, India, and beyond, ranging from baked zucchini blossoms in Japanese tempura dough filled with a vegetable ricotta cream to Swiss chard with roasted nuts, fresh mushrooms, and tofu in an herb-flavored cream sauce to tofu stroganoff. It's a great alternative to heavier Bavarian food.

Hackenstrasse 2 (off Sendlinger Strasse, a few minutes' walk from Marienplatz). © **089/265596.** www.prinzmyshkin.com. Reservations recommended. Main courses 12€–16€. AE, MC, V. Daily 11am–12:30am. S-/U-Bahn: Marienplatz.

Ratskeller München BAVARIAN Throughout Germany, you'll find *Ratskellers,* traditional cellar restaurants in Rathaus (city hall) basements, but this cavernous restaurant with its low, vaulted, painted ceilings is one of the best. Besides Bavarian and Franconian specialties such as roast Bavarian duckling with mustard-seed gravy, roast pork shank with potato dumplings, and Munich white sausages, it has vegetarian dishes, sandwiches, and salads, as well as changing specials featuring national dishes from other countries. This is also a good choice for an afternoon coffee and dessert, or a glass of Franconian wine in the adjoining wine cellar.

In Town Hall's cellar, Marienplatz 8. © **089/2199890.** www.ratskeller.com. Reservations required. Main courses 13€–27€. AE, MC, V. Daily 10am–midnight. S-/U-Bahn: Marienplatz.

Restaurant La Valle ★ ITALIAN Right off the Marienplatz, this is one of the best restaurants and pizzerias in town. The interior is decorated in a classic Italian style, and there's an elegant bar for a predinner drink. For starters, the minestrone is about the best in Munich, as are the pastas, especially the rich spaghetti carbonara. Pizzas come with toppings ranging from cheese and mushrooms to salami. There's

always a grilled fish of the day, and the best meat dish is the tender veal in a white wine–and-lemon sauce.

Sparkassenstrasse 5. ☎ **089/29160676.** www.ristorante-lavalle.com. Reservations recommended. Small main courses and pizzas 8€–13€; main courses 17€–26€. AE, MC, V. Daily 11am–12:30am. U-Bahn or S-Bahn: Marienplatz.

Restaurant Pfistermühle BAVARIAN   The country comes right into the heart of Munich at this authentic and old-fashioned restaurant, a series of charmingly decorated dining rooms in a converted 1573 mill. Add outdoor seating in summer, and this ranks as one of the prettiest spots in the Altstadt, just a block from the Hofbräuhaus. Many of the perfectly prepared roasts and fresh fish from the lakes and rivers of Bavaria would be familiar to your Bavarian grandmother, and portions are generous.

In the Platz Hotel, Pfistermühle 4. ☎ **089/23703865.** www.platzl.de. Reservations recommended. Main courses 24€–27€. AE, DC, MC, V. Mon–Sat 11:30am–11pm. U-Bahn: Marienplatz.

Spatenhaus an der Oper GERMAN/INTERNATIONAL   One of Munich's best-known beer restaurants, across from the Residenz and Nationaltheater, Spatenhaus offers typical rustic Bavarian atmosphere, regional specialties, and generous portions at reasonable prices. If you want to know what this fabled Bavarian gluttony is all about, order the "Bavarian plate" (Schmankerlplatte), which is loaded down with various meats, including pork and sausages. Top it off with the restaurant's own beer, Spaten-Franziskaner-Bier.

Residenzstrasse 12. ☎ **089/2907060.** www.kuffler-gastronomie.de/en/muenchen/spatenhaus/index. php. Reservations recommended. Main courses 10€–29€. AE, MC, V. Daily 9:30am–12:30am. U-Bahn: Marienplatz or Odeonsplatz.

Weinhaus Neuner BAVARIAN/INTERNATIONAL   This is an *Ältestes Weinhaus Münchens* (Old Munich Wine House), one of the city's landmark taverns. Dating from

---

 Beer Gardens

The city's beer gardens (biergarten) are as fickle as the weather—if the weather's bad, the beer gardens don't open. By the same token, if the weather suddenly turns gloriously warm in the middle of February, the beer gardens start turning on the taps. Generally speaking, beer gardens are open on sunny days from spring through autumn, usually 10am to 11pm. Ranging from tiny neighborhood gardens accommodating a few hundred to those seating several thousand, they number about 30 in and around Munich, making it the world's beer garden capital. There are self-serve counters for food, or you can bring your own food with you.

These are some of Munich's most famous beer gardens: **Augustiner Biergarten,** Arnulfstrasse 52 (☎ **089/594393**), about a 10-minute walk northwest of the Hauptbahnhof; **Gaststätte zum Flaucher,** Isarauen 8 (☎ **089/7232677;** www.zum-flaucher.de; bus: 52), near the zoo, which is traditional and mellow; **Chinesischer Turm,** with a lovely location in the Englischer Garten (☎ **089/3838730;** www.chinaturm.de; U-Bahn: Universität); and **Hirschgarten,** Hirschgartenstrasse 1 (☎ **089/17999199;** www.hirschgarten.de; S-Bahn: Laim; tram: 17 to Romanplatz), one of Europe's largest, near Nymphenburg Palace. In the Old Town, the famous **Hofbräuhaus am Platzl ★,** Platzl 9 (☎ **089/221676;** www.hofbrauhaus.de; U-/S-Bahn: Marienplatz), also has a beer garden.

the late 15th century, it's the only building in Munich with its original Tyrolean vaults. The place brims with warmth and charm. The casual *Weinstube* is the less formal section and has lots of local atmosphere. You'll relish such dishes as medallions of monkfish with a crust of chanterelles with a champagne sauce, or the roast gray partridge in a port-wine sauce, or perhaps saddle of wild pig with a juniper cream sauce.

Herzogspitalstrasse 8. (℃ **089/2603954.** www.weinhaus-neuner.de. Reservations recommended. Main courses 19€–26€; fixed-price lunch 18€–23€, dinner 45€. AE, MC, V. Mon–Sat 11:30am–3pm and 5:30pm–midnight. U-Bahn or S-Bahn: Karlsplatz/Stachus.

Weisses Bräuhaus GERMAN   This boisterous place is famous for its wheat beer (*Bräuhaus* means "brewery"), which Bavarians will drink even for breakfast. With an informal, smoke-blackened front room outfitted with long wooden tables (you'll have to share your table, but that's part of the fun) and a more formal back dining room with white tablecloths, it serves typical Bavarian fare from a lengthy menu. If you're hungry, go for the Bavarian Farmer's Feast (Bayrischer Bauernschmaus)—roast and smoked pork, pork sausage, dumplings, and sauerkraut. It's a less touristy choice than the Hofbräuhaus.

Tal 7. (℃ **089/299875.** www.weisses-brauhaus.de. Reservations recommended, especially for the back room. Main courses 8€–20€. MC, V. Daily 7am–1am. S-/U-Bahn: Marienplatz.

Shopping

As Germany's fashion center, Munich boasts upscale boutiques, department stores, and designer names, primarily in the pedestrian-zoned Altstadt (all the following shops are near the S-/U-Bahn Marienplatz station). For traditional Bavarian clothing, the outlet **Wies'n Tracht & Mehr,** Tal 19 (www.wiesn-tracht-mehr.de), has the best selection of both new and vintage dirndls. The very upscale **Loden-Frey,** Maffeistrasse 7 (℃ **089/210390**), offers the world's largest selection of *Loden* clothing and traditional Bavarian costumes, along with Armani and other modern designer fashions.

If you're looking for German and Bavarian souvenirs, a good place to hunt is **Orlandostrasse,** about a 5-minute walk from Marienplatz, near the Hofbräuhaus. This small pedestrian lane is lined with shops selling T-shirts, beer steins, dolls in Bavarian costume, pipes, postcards, Christmas tree ornaments, and nutcrackers. Other specialty shops, all in the Altstadtalt, include **Max Krug,** Neuhauser Strasse 2 (℃ **089/224501;** www.max-krug.com), which has been selling beer mugs, nutcrackers, and cuckoo clocks since 1926; and **Leute,** Viktualienmarkt 2 (℃ **089/ 268248;** www.holz-leute.de), with a wide selection of bowls, trays, boxes, toys, and other finely crafted items made from wood. Germany's oldest miniature pewter foundry, the **Münchner Puppenstuben und Zinnfiguren-Kabinett,** Maxburgstrasse 4 (℃ **089/293797;** www.mini-kabi.net), dates from 1796 and is a great source for miniature houses, furniture, and people, all cunningly crafted from pewter or carved wood. Some of the figures are made from 150-year-old molds that are collector's items in their own right.

Since the early 1800s, Munich's most famous market has been **Viktualienmarkt,** in the Altstadt, where you can buy bread, cheese, honey, cakes, fruit, wine, vegetables, flowers, and much more.

Store hours in Munich are generally Monday to Saturday from 9 or 10am to 6pm, though department stores stay open until 8pm. In addition, some specialty stores close at 2pm on Saturday.

Nightlife

To find out what's happening in Munich, go to one of the two tourist offices and get a copy of the monthly *Monatsprogramm* for 1.80€, a complete cultural guide that tells you not only what's being presented—including concerts, opera, special exhibits, and museum hours—but also how to purchase tickets. In addition, *Munich Found,* an English-language publication selling for 3€, lists operas, plays, classical concerts, rock and jazz concerts, movies, and more. You can also view it online for free at **www. munichfound.com**.

THE PERFORMING ARTS   Nowhere else in Europe, other than London and Paris, will you find so many musical and theatrical events. The good news is that seats don't cost a fortune. Tickets for most productions range from about 10€ to 45€. The neoclassical-style **Nationaltheater,** on Max-Joseph-Platz (✆ 089/21851920; S-/U-Bahn: Marienplatz), is Germany's largest opera house. The Nationaltheater's **Bavarian State Opera** (www.bayerische.staatsoper.de) performs mostly Mozart, Wagner, Verdi, and Strauss, though it also stages works from the baroque period (all operas are performed in their original language, though some have German subtitles). The Nationaltheater also stages ballets. Box office hours are Monday to Saturday 10am to 7pm.

The **Gasteig,** Rosenheimer Strasse 5 (✆ 089/480 98-0; S-Bahn: Rosenheimer Platz; tram: 18 to Gasteig), serves as the stage for major concerts. Its largest concert hall, the Philharmonie, seats 2,400 and features performances of the **Munich Philharmonic Orchestra** (✆ 089/480985500; www.mphil.de; S-Bahn: Rosenheimer-platz; tram: 18 to Gasteig; bus: 51) and guest orchestras and ensembles. The Kleiner Konzertsaal (Small Concert Hall) features a wide range of musical talent, from flamenco guitar or piano recitals to concerts of Renaissance and baroque music. Tickets for the Munich Philharmonic Orchestra are 15€ to 64€.

BEER HALLS   A *Bierhalle* (beer hall) is a traditional Munich institution, offering food, entertainment, and, of course, beer. This brewery, **Max Emanuel Brauerei** (Adalbertstrasse 33; ✆ 089/2715158; www.max-emanuel-brauerei.de; U-Bahn: Universität), turned into a beer hall in the 1920s. It still serves steins of beer and platters of filling German grub. On Wednesday and Friday, the second floor plays host to a popular salsa dance club. In the summer they feature a beer garden. The hall is open in the winter daily 5pm to 1am and during the summer daily 11am to 1am. Cover on Wednesday is 8€ and on Friday and Saturday 10€.

The **Augustinerbräu,** Neuhauser Strasse 27, on the main pedestrian lane in the Old Town (✆ 089/23183257; www.augustiner-restaurant.com; S-/U-Bahn: Karls-platz/Stachus or Marienplatz), is much smaller than the Hofbräuhaus, with correspondingly lower prices. It still, however, has typical Bavarian decor, with dark paneled walls and wooden tables. They claim beer was first brewed here in 1328. It's open daily 11am to 11pm.

CLUBS & BARS   Munich's premier spot for serious jazz is **Jazzclub Unterfahrt,** Einsteinstrasse 42 (✆ 089/4482794; www.unterfahrt.de; U-Bahn: Max-Weber-Platz), with a varied program featuring traditional jazz international acts and other genres of crossover jazz. Reaching it requires wandering down a labyrinth of underground cement-sided corridors that might remind you of a bomb shelter during the Cold War. Once inside, the space opens to reveal flickering candles, a convivial bar, high ceilings, and clusters of smallish tables facing the stage. It opens daily at 7:30pm, with live music Tuesday to Sunday from 8:30pm to 1am. Admission ranges from 5€ to 32€ for most performances.

Nachtgalerie, The "Night Gallery," contains two dance halls rocking to party music and hip-hop, along with house, electronica, or even rhythm 'n' blues. The club attracts largely intoxicated crowds in their 20s and 30s. International student parties are often staged here. Expect various theme nights. It is a very mixed crowd. There is a cover, but once inside, drinks are cheap—beginning at 2€. It is open Friday and Saturday 10pm to 5am, and cover is 10€.

Schumann's Bar am Hofgarten, at Odeonsplatz 6–7, at the corner of Galerie Strasse (⌀ **089/229060;** www.schumanns.de; U-Bahn: Odeonsplatz), is Munich's most legendary bar. It has an international fan club, lots of pizazz, a history that goes back forever, and new premises that have been the subject of many architectural reviews because of the ample use of green marble and the wooden paneling evocative of a church. All of that changes, however, when the drinks begin to flow and the crowd gets animated. This bar is a grand-slam rip-roaring affair that gets very crowded. There's a simple roster of menu items that changes with the season and the outside temperature. Schumann's is open Monday to Friday 5pm to 3am, Saturday and Sunday 6pm to 3am. In the Aldstadt, the sophisticated **Vinorant Alter Hof,** Alterhof 3 (⌀ **089/24 24 37 33;** www.alter-hof-muenchen.de; S-/U-Bahn: Marien-platz), is primarily a restaurant, with vaulted ceilings, candles, and jazz playing softly in the background. In the basement is a wine bar where you can enjoy inexpensive snacks and the best of regional wines. It's open daily 3 to 11:30pm.

An Excursion to Mad King Ludwig's Neuschwanstein

Of the dozens of castles dotting the Bavarian countryside, none is as famous as **Neuschwanstein ★★★**), created by the extravagant Bavarian King Ludwig II. No doubt you've seen pictures of this fairy-tale castle, perched on a cliff above the town of Hohenschwangau, but even if you haven't, it'll seem familiar, for this is the castle that served as the model for Walt Disney's Sleeping Beauty Castle at Disneyland.

Construction on Ludwig II's most famous castle began in 1869, but only a third of the original plans had been completed at the time of his mysterious death in 1886 (his body, as well as the body of his doctor, was found floating in a lake, but no one has ever proved whether he was murdered or committed suicide). Neuschwanstein, one of several overly ornate castles Ludwig left to the world, is a lesson in extrava-gance and fantasy, with almost every inch covered in gilt, stucco, woodcarvings, and marble mosaics. Swans are used as a motif throughout, and Ludwig's admiration of Richard Wagner is expressed in operatic themes virtually everywhere, including murals illustrating *Tristan and Isolde* in his bedroom, the most opulent room in the palace—it took 14 artisans more than 4 years to produce the elaborate woodcarvings.

You can see the castle by joining a 35-minute guided tour, available in English, but be aware that the tour requires climbing 165 stairs and descending 181 stairs. This is in addition to the 35 minutes it takes to walk up the steep hill to even reach the castle.

Although overshadowed by Neuschwanstein and not quite as fanciful, there's another worthwhile castle here offering 35-minute tours: **Hohenschwangau Cas-tle ★**, built in the 1830s by Ludwig II's father, Maximilian II. Young Ludwig spent much of his childhood here, where he was greatly influenced by the castle's many murals depicting the saga of the Swan Knight Lohengrin, immortalized in an opera by Wagner.

To reach Neuschwanstein, take the **train** from Munich's Hauptbahnhof to Füssen, a 2-hour trip costing 19€ one-way. Better yet, if you don't have a railpass, buy a **Bayern Ticket,** allowing travel on local trains throughout Bavaria after 9am. It costs 19€ for one person or 27€ for up to five people traveling together. Inquire at **EurAide** at the Hauptbahnhof for more information.

In Füssen, you must take a **bus** from in front of the train station 15 minutes onward to the town of Hohenschwangau. Tickets for Neuschwanstein and Hohenschwangau castles must be purchased at the **Hohenschwangau Ticket-Center,** Alpseestrasse 12 (*©* **08362/93 08 30;** www.hohenschangau.de), which you'll see upon disembarking from the bus. Tours of either Neuschwanstein or Hohenschwangau are 9€ for adults and 8€ for seniors and students; children under 18 are free. Combination tickets to both cost 17€ and 15€, respectively. Tours are for a specific time (avoid weekends in summer, when the wait for a tour can be as long as 3 hr., or book online to avoid the wait). Both castles are open daily April to September 9am to 6pm (last tour), and October to March 10am to 4pm.

An Excursion to Dachau

About 10 miles (15km) from Munich is **Dachau,** site of Germany's first concentration camp under the Hitler regime and now a memorial to those who died under the Nazis. Some 206,000 prisoners from 30 countries—primarily political and religious dissidents, Jews, Gypsies, and other "undesirables"—passed through Dachau's gates between 1933 and 1945, of whom at least 30,000 were registered as dead. However, there are many other thousands who were also murdered there, even if their deaths weren't officially logged.

At the **KZ-Gedenkstätte Dachau (Concentration Camp Memorial) ★★**, Alte-Roemer-Strasse 75 (*©* **08131/669970;** www.kz-gedenkstaette-dachau.de), two of the camp's original buildings have been preserved or reconstructed, and you can also tour a model barrack, a bunker, and the crematorium—all set in a landscape that's bleak and desolate. But what really makes a visit here a sobering experience is the museum, with photograph after photograph illustrating the rise of the Nazi Regime and the SS, the horrors of the Holocaust, and detailed explanation as to how such atrocities came to pass. Photographs show bodies piled high on top of one another and prisoners so malnourished they can't walk. Every effort has been made to present the facts, and a tour of Dachau is a truly moving experience. Be sure to see the museum's 22-minute English documentary, shown at 11:30am, 2 and 3:30pm. In addition, 2½-hour guided tours in English for 3€ (Tues–Sat 11am and 1pm), and audio guides are available for 3.50€ (2.50€ for students), but the museum provides so much information and everything is so well documented, we don't think they're necessary unless you want more detailed information.

Visiting the Dachau concentration camp, which takes about 3 hours, isn't pleasant, but perhaps it's necessary: A plaque near the museum exit reminds us that those who forget the past are destined to repeat it. Note that the memorial isn't recommended for children under 12.

Admission to the Dachau memorial is free, and it's open Tuesday to Sunday 9am to 5pm. To get there, take **S-Bahn S2** going in the direction of Petershausen to Dachau (about a 20-min. ride). In Dachau, transfer to **bus no. 726** to the KZ-Gedenkstätte stop, or **bus no. 724** to the K-Z Gedenkstätte-Parkplatz, both a 10-minute ride.

MORE HIGHLIGHTS
OF GERMANY

Heidelberg ★★★

Heidelberg, 55 miles (89km) south of Frankfurt, has an idyllic location on the Neckar River and rates as one of Germany's most romantic cities. One of the few German cities not leveled by air raids in World War II, it boasts a historic, picturesque Altstadt (Old Town), with winding, narrow cobblestone streets lined with medieval and early Renaissance buildings. Above the town looms Heidelberg Castle, while across the Neckar is the Philosophers Pathway, with its panoramic views of the city. Above all, however, Heidelberg is a university town and has been since 1386 (the oldest such municipality in Germany). Students make up much of the city's population, imparting a vibrancy that's especially apparent in the Altstadt's colorful student quarter, with its narrow streets and lively inns. Finally, Heidelberg's proximity to Frankfurt's international airport, together with its small-town atmosphere, makes it an ideal first or final stop on a rail tour of Europe. *Note:* Summertime in Heidelberg, according to the song from *The Student Prince,* is a time for music and romance. Today, it's also a time when droves of visitors invade this beautiful city.

ESSENTIALS

GETTING THERE Heidelberg's nearest international airport is Frankfurt (see "Essentials," at the beginning of this chapter). Trains from Frankfurt Hauptbahnhof reach **Heidelberg Hauptbahnhof** (✆ **06221/52 53 41**) in about 1 hour. About 55 trains depart here from Frankfurt each day. Heidelberg Hauptbahnhof is an important railroad station, lying on the Mannheim line, with frequent service to both regional towns and major cities. Travel time to and from Munich is about 3½ hours. For information, call ✆ **01805/996633** or visit www.bahn.de. The station is 1¾ miles (2.7km) southwest of the Altstadt; take the bus to get to the town center (see "Getting Around," below).

VISITOR INFORMATION Heidelberg's **Tourist Information** is located just outside the Hauptbahnhof, in a pavilion at Willy-Brandt-Platz 1 (✆ **06221/19433;** www.heidelberg-marketing.de). It's open April through October Monday to Saturday 9am to 7pm, and Sunday and holidays 10am to 6pm; November through March Monday to Saturday 9am to 6pm.

GETTING AROUND Heidelberg is crisscrossed by a network of trams and buses, many of which intersect at Bismarckplatz in the town center. Although you can walk to the Altstadt (Old Town) in about 30 minutes, bus nos. 41 and 42 travel at frequent intervals between the railway station and Universitätsplatz in the Altstadt. To gain a better appreciation for the town's atmosphere, however, consider disembarking earlier at Bismarckplatz and walking along the pedestrian Hauptstrasse (Main St.). Bus nos. 11 and 33 go directly from the Hauptbahnhof to the castle (bus stop: Rathaus/Bergbahn). Bus or tram fares cost 2.20€ for a single ride, or purchase a **Ticket 24,** good for 24 hours on public transportation and costing 5€ for one person and 8.50€ for up to five persons traveling within a group. Otherwise, consider purchasing the **Heidelberg Card,** which provides unlimited travel on public transportation; free admission to various attractions (including the castle); and a reduction in prices on other attractions, tours, shopping, restaurants, hotels, museums and more. Available at Tourist Information, it costs 11€ for 1 day, 17€ for 2 days; a family card for 2 days costs 30€.

TOP ATTRACTIONS & SPECIAL MOMENTS

Heidelberg's most famous landmark is the hard-to-miss **Heidelberg Castle ★★★** (*©* **06221/538421;** www.heidelberg-schloss.de), a huge red-stone structure that spreads along the top of a ridge directly above the Altstadt. A 17th-century fire destroyed much of the castle, and even though parts of it remain a dignified ruin, it's still one of the finest Gothic-Renaissance castles in Germany.

You can reach the castle, set amid woodlands and terraced gardens, by taking bus 33 to Konmarkt/Bergbahn (Funicular). You take the Funicular to the castle from there. More rewarding, however, is the journey by foot (it's a very steep climb if you come up the Burgweg from Kornmarkt, though) for the views it affords of the town along the way. From Klingentor, the much easier walk with a gradual slope takes about 20 minutes. From Kornmarkt in the center of town, it can take a good 30 to 40 minutes, depending on your stamina.

The castle is a dignified ruin, but even in its deteriorated state, it's one of the finest Gothic-Renaissance castles in Germany. Entering at the main gate, the huge **Gun Park** is to your left, from which you can gaze down upon Heidelberg and the Neckar Valley. Straight ahead is the **Thick Tower,** or what remains of it, after its 26-ft. (7.8m) walls were blown up by the French in the late 17th century. Leaving Gun Park via Elizabeth's Gate (erected by Friedrich V in 1615 for his Scottish wife, the daughter of James I), you come to the Bridge House and the bridge crossing the site of the former moat.

Along the north side of the courtyard stretches the stern **palace of Friedrich IV ★★**, erected 1601 to 1607. The palace is less damaged than other parts of the castle, and its rooms are almost completely restored, including the gallery of princes and kings of the German empire from the time of Charlemagne. The ancient bell tower, at the northeast end of the Altan, dates from the early 1500s.

Afterward, stop by the late-16th-century **Wine Vat Building,** worth a visit for a look at the **Great Cask.** This huge barrel-like monstrosity, built in 1751 and thought to be the world's largest wine vat, is capable of holding more than 55,000 gallons (208,000 liters) of wine. To the east, connecting the palace of Friedrich IV to the **Ottheinrich Building,** itself an outstanding example of German Renaissance architecture, is the **Hall of Mirrors Building,** constructed in 1549—a Renaissance masterpiece. Only the shell of the original building remains, enough to give you an idea of its former glory, with arcades and steep gables decorated with cherubs and sirens. Be sure, too, to tour the **Deutsches Apotheken-Museum ★** (**Germany Pharmaceutical Museum;** *©* **06221/25880;** www.deutsches-apotheken-museum.de). It describes the history of medicine and treatments, contains four reconstructed pharmacies, and displays various plants, minerals, spices, and other materials (including animal and human body parts) that have served as treatments for various ailments through the ages.

Admission to castle grounds, including the Wine Vat Building, Deutsches Apotheken-Museum, and the Funicular, costs 5€ for adults and 3€ for children. Cost of the audio tour is 4€ extra. The castle grounds are open daily 8am to 6pm. A 1-hour guided tour of the castle costs 5€ for adults and 3€ for children. Tours are frequent, especially in summer, and some are conducted in English. The castle is open April to October daily 10am to 6pm, November to March daily 10am to 5:30pm. The Pharmacy Museum is open daily 10am to 5:30pm.

In the town itself, a tour of the main attractions begins at the **Marktplatz** in front of the Rathaus. On market days, the square is filled with stalls of fresh flowers, fish,

Boating in the Neckar

Heidelberg is an ideal point from which to explore the romantic Neckar Valley. From April to early October, you can take a boat tour along the river as far as Neckarsteinach. There are usually four or five round-trips daily, and you need not return on the same boat. Boats are operated by the **Rhein-Neckar-Fahrgastschiffahrt GmbH** (✆ **06221/20181; www.rnf-schifffahrt. de).** Trips between Heidelberg and Neckarsteinach cost 20€ round-trip. You can order drinks or snacks on the boat. Some of the people operating the boats are descended from the Neckar fishers, and the same families have been working the Neckar since the early 1600s. The boat dock, just a short walk from the Altstadt, can also be reached by taking bus nos. 12, 35, 41, or 42 to Kongresshaus/Stadthalle.

and vegetables. At the opposite end of the square is the late Gothic **Heiliggeist-kirche,** built around 1400, the largest Gothic church in the Palatinate.

If you have time, consider swinging by the **Kurpfälzisches Museum (Museum of the Palatinate)** ★, Hauptstrasse 97 (✆ **06221/5834020;** www.museum-heidelberg.de; bus: 11, 12, 35, 41, or 42), which is housed in a baroque palace. It contains items pertaining to Heidelberg's long history, finds from the time of Heidelberg's important status as a Roman military outpost; medieval objects; and paintings and sculptures from the late 15th to 20th centuries. The most significant work of art is Tilman Riemenschneider's late-Gothic **Altar from Windsheim** (1509), depicting Christ and the 12 Apostles, with amazing details in their facial expressions. Another section of the museum features period rooms as they might have appeared in the 18th and 19th centuries, complete with furniture and decorative arts. There's also an archaeological collection with a cast of the jawbone of the 500,000-year-old Heidelberg Man and a section on the history of the Palatinate. The restaurant is a great lunch stop. Unfortunately, explanations in the museum are only in German. The museum is open Tuesday to Sunday 10am to 6pm. Admission is 3€ adults, 1.80€ students and children under 18.

Also of interest is the **Studentenkarzer (Student Prison)** in the Old University off Universitätsplatz, Augustinergasse 2 (✆ **06221/543554),** where students were held in detention from 1712 to 1914. In those days, students could be punished only by the university, not town officials, so those caught disturbing the peace through drunkenness or misbehavior, chasing citizens' pigs through the alleys, or fighting against members of other student fraternities were incarcerated here. Most students, who were allowed to attend classes and receive outside visitors, considered it an honor to be imprisoned at least once during their studies. The walls and ceilings are covered with graffiti, drawings, portraits, engraved names, dates, and funny verses. It's open October Tuesday to Sunday 10am to 4pm, November to March Tuesday to Saturday 10am to 4pm. Admission is 3€ for adults, 2.50€ students and children under 15.

All the important sights of Heidelberg lie on or near the south bank of the Neckar. However, you should cross to the north side of the river (via the ornately decorated 18th-c. Karl Theodore Bridge) for the best overall view, especially from the **Philoso-phenweg (Philosophers' Way),** a footpath halfway up Heilegenberg hill.

SHOPPING

The main shopping street is the traffic-free **Hauptstrasse,** which is filled with stores selling glass, crystal, handcrafts, and other items. For leather items, stop by **Leder-Meid,** Hauptstrasse 88 (✆ **06221/22570;** tram: 1 or 3; bus: 35 or 41), which sells the crafts of German and other manufacturers.

Heidelberg is also known for its **markets,** including the one held on Wednesday and Saturday mornings at Marktplatz and another held Tuesday and Friday mornings at Friedrich-Ebert-Platz.

WHERE TO STAY & DINE

A glorious old inn right out of the German Renaissance, the **Romantik Hotel Zum Ritter St. Georg** ★, Hauptstrasse 178 (✆ **06221/1350;** www.ritter-heidelberg.de; bus: 11, 12, 41, or 42), is a well-preserved rarity just a stone's throw from the colorful Marktplatz. Built in 1592 by a French merchant, the gabled house is considered a major sightseeing attraction due to its ornately decorated facade. Many rooms are somewhat cramped, but beds are comfortable and the bathrooms have been renewed. See our review of one of their restaurants below. Better are the deluxe rooms facing the main street and the beautiful Heiliggeistkirche. Rates are 118€ to 176€ for a double.

On the other side of the Neckar, **Hotel Hirschgasse** ★★, Hirschgasse 3 (✆ **06221/4540;** www.hirschgasse.de; bus: 34), is tops in Heidelberg for its tranquil and romantic setting, nestled on the hillside of a lane adjoining Philosophers' Way. Heidelberg's oldest inn, the historic country-style home dates from 1472 and counts Mark Twain and Otto van Bismarck among its distinguished guests. Its 20 rooms (all nonsmoking) are all suites, each different in Laura Ashley designs and some boasting four-poster beds, whirlpool baths, or a balcony. Its two **restaurants** are considered among the best in town. Rates are 195€ to 245€ for two people.

Hotel Anlage, Friedrich-Ebert-Anlage 32 (✆ **06221/5850960;** www.hotel-anlage.de; bus: 11 or 33), is one of Heidelberg's best affordable hotels, located in the heart of the city, on the street leading up to the castle. It occupies one wing of a lavishly built, late-19th-century palace. Rooms are cozy and have well-kept bathrooms. A double costs 84€ to 104€, and rates include a continental breakfast.

When visiting Heidelberg Castle, there's no better place for dinner than in the castle itself, at **Schlossweinstube** ★ (✆ **06221/97970;** http://www.schoenmehl. de/gastro/sw_info.html). An elegant venue, it is the most dramatic place to dine, with Heidelberg laid out below. The seasonal menu always offers the freshest of fish, meat, and poultry. The chefs have made their reputation on *Ente von Heidelberg* (roast duck), a savory platter that is the most-ordered dish. Main courses run 15€ to 27€, a three-course menu is 49€, a four-course menu is 62€, and reservations are required. It's open Tuesday to Saturday from 5pm to midnight. The neighboring Bistro offers reasonably priced traditional German fare where you can stop for coffee and cake.

The **Ritterstube** ★, Hauptstrasse 178 (✆ **06221/1350;** bus: 10, 11, or 12), is located in one of Heidelberg's most famous Renaissance buildings—Romantik Hotel Zum Ritter St. Georg—with vaulted ceilings, wainscoting, and Oriental rugs. It's popular among locals for its good German cooking, as well as the wonderful Dortmunder Actien-Bräuerei beer. The menu is seasonal, but when saddle of Odenwald venison for two is offered, locals flock here. Also try the salmon with a garlic-laced chili mousse, or fried filet of pikeperch with a Martini lime sauce. Main courses cost 10€ to 23€. It's open daily noon to 2pm and 6 to 10pm; reservations are recommended.

The family-owned **Zur Herrenmühle ★**, Hauptstrasse 239 (*© 06221/602909;* www.herrenmuehle-heidelberg.de; bus: 33), occupies a 17th-century house, with thick walls and antique paneling. The sophisticated maitre d' adds both glamour and an appropriate theatricality. The classical German cuisine is based on fresh ingredients, offering good quality at reasonable prices. Try the rack of lamb with herbs and homemade green noodles, or the roast roebuck with a vinegar-and-honey sauce and ranging from 15€ to 25€ for most meals. There is a fixed-price menu for 25€. It's open Monday to Saturday from 6pm to 11pm; reservations are recommended.

No other place in Heidelberg captures bygone days quite like the **Mensurstube ★**, in the Hotel Hirschgasse, Hirschgasse 3 (*© 06221/4540;* www. hirschgasse.de; bus: 34). In this rustic and cozy spot, you sit at tables more than 2 centuries old—you can still see where Bismarck and others carved their names. Swords hang from the ceiling—in the past, when dueling was the regular sport of the student fraternities, duels were fought in what is now the dining room. Traditional recipes are served from a limited menu. Main courses run 12€ to 29€. Open hours are Monday to Saturday 6 to 10pm.

NIGHTLIFE

Nights here are alive with the youthful enthusiasm of Heidelberg's students. Nowhere is that more apparent than at Heidelberg's many student taverns. Most famous is **Zum Roten Ochsen (Red Ox Inn) ★**, Hauptstrasse 217 (*© 06221/ 20977;* www.roterochsen.de; bus: 33), opened in 1703. It's been in the Spengel family for six generations, and they've welcomed everybody from Bismarck to Mark Twain. It seems that every student who has attended the university has left his or her mark (or initials) on the walls. There's live piano music nightly, and as the evening progresses, the songs become louder and louder. Hearty German meals are also available. A mug of beer costs 3€, and wine is 4€ by the glass. The tavern is open from April to October Monday to Friday 11am to 2:30pm and 5pm to midnight, Saturday 11am to midnight, and Sunday 11am to 2:30pm; and from November to March Monday to Friday 5pm to midnight, and Saturday 11:30am to 2:30pm.

Next door is Heidelberg's oldest student pub, **Zum Sepp'l,** open since 1634, Hauptstrasse 213 (*© 06221/23085;* www.zum-seppl.de; bus: 11 or 33). It's also filled with photographs and carved initials of former students, along with memorabilia that ranges from old Berlin street signs to Alabama license plates. There's live piano music Monday, Tuesday, Friday, and Saturday from 7 to midnight, and a menu offers traditional German pub grub. A mug of beer goes for 3€. It's open Monday to Friday noon to 11pm, and Saturday and Sunday 11:30am to 3:30pm and 5pm to midnight.

Dresden ★★★

Dresden, once known as the "Florence on the Elbe," was celebrated throughout Europe for its impressive baroque architecture and stunning art treasures. Then came the night of February 13, 1945, when Allied bombers rained down phosphorus and high-explosive bombs on the city. By morning, the Dresden of legend was only a memory. After the war, when Germany was divided by the victors, Dresden landed in the Soviet sector and languished under Communist rule. Today the capital of Saxony is experiencing a renaissance, after a painstaking reconstruction of its beautiful historic core just in time for the city's 800th birthday bash in 2006. While Dresden is hardly undiscovered, especially among Germans, it lies off the beaten path of most traveling North Americans, despite its convenient location approximately halfway between Prague and Berlin.

ESSENTIALS

GETTING THERE   The **Dresden-Klotsche Airport** (© 0351/8813360; www.
dresden-airport.de) lies 6 miles (9.6km) north of the city center. A suburban rail line
that's linked to Dresden's S-Bahn network stretches from the airport to the city's main
train station, the Hauptbahnhof, with a stop also at the Bahnhof Neustadt train station. The trip takes about 13 minutes to Neustadt and 20 minutes to the Hauptbahnhof, and costs 1.90€ one-way. A taxi from the airport to the center of Dresden costs
about 25€.

Dresden has two main rail stations, the **Hauptbahnhof** main station on Wiener
Platz, which is on the Berlin–Prague line, and **Dresden-Neustadt,** at Schlesischer
Park. Some trains stop at both stations—frequent regional trains do—but otherwise
tram 3 connects the two. About nine trains depart Frankfurt Hauptbahnhof directly
for Dresden (trip time: 5 hr.). From Berlin and Prague, direct trains depart approximately every 2 hours (trip time: 2–2½ hr. from Berlin, 3 hr. from Prague). For rail
information and schedules, call © 01805/996633 or visit www.bahn.de.

VISITOR INFORMATION   Dresden's **Tourist Information Center** is located
in the Kulturpalast, on Wilsdrufferstrasse (© 0351/50160160; www.dresden.de).
Open April to December Monday to Friday 10am to 7pm, Saturday 10am to 6pm,
and Sunday 10am to 3pm. Off-season hours are Monday to Friday 10am to 6pm,
Saturday 10am to 4pm, and Sunday 10am to 2pm. Here you can book accommodations, get information booklets in English, and obtain tickets for theater, opera, and
concerts. There's a branch tourist office in the Altstadt at the Schinkelwache, Theaterplatz, and has the same hours as the main office. For more information, call
© 0351/50160160 or search the website at **www.dresden.de.**

GETTING AROUND   Dresden's Altstadt and attractions can be reached on foot
from either the Hauptbahnhof or Bahnhof Neustadt in about 20 minutes. Otherwise,
both trams and buses are available. A single ride, good for 1 hour, costs 1.90€, or you
can purchase a 24-hour pass for 5€. Maps and tickets are sold at automated dispens-
ers outside the main rail station. Most major lines operate every hour, though service
is curtailed between midnight and 5am. Dresden's S-Bahn reaches the suburbs. If
you're in town longer than a day, another option is the **Dresden City-Card** for 21€,
available at the Tourist Information Center and good for 48 hours of unlimited travel,
plus free access to 12 of the city's best museums. There are also reductions on
charges for certain sightseeing tours and some cultural events.

TOP ATTRACTIONS & SPECIAL MOMENTS

Dresden's major attractions are concentrated in two famous buildings in the Altstadt.
Foremost is the newly restored **Residenzschloss (Royal Palace),** a stately building
with an imposing neo-Renaissance facade. First erected some 700 years ago and
rebuilt and enlarged over the centuries, it contains the magnificent **Grünes
Gewölbe (Green Vault)** ★★★, Sophienstrasse 1 (© 0351/49142000; www.
skd-dresden.de; tram: 2, 4, or 8 to Theaterplatz). Although there are royal treasuries
throughout Europe, this may well be the most stunning and is the most important
thing to see in Dresden. Many pieces were created by the craftspeople of local guilds;
others were acquired from the far corners of the earth. The collection is divided into
two parts, each with its own admission. The Neues Grünes Gewölbe, which costs 6€
for adults and 3.50€ for students and children, contains an amazing collection of
gem-encrusted bowls and dishes, an incredibly ornate coffee set, a fantastic ivory-
carved sailing ship, stone-inlaid pictures, ivory goblets, etched glass, ornamental

Dresden

ACCOMMODATIONS ■
Art'otel dresden **4**
Hotel Bayerischer Hof **2**
Hotel Kipping **13**
Raskolnikoff Pension **3**
Rothenburger Hof **3**

DINING ◆
Altmarkt Keller **12**
Brauhaus Watzke **1**
Pulverturm **10**
Sophienkeller im
 Taschenbergpalais **6**

ATTRACTIONS ●
Brühlsche Terrasse **9**
Frauenkirche **11**
Fürstenzug **8**
Gemäldegalerie
 Alte Meister **5**
Grünes Gewölbe **7**
Kupferstich-Kabinett **7**
Porzellansammlung **5**
Residenzschloss **7**
Rüstkammer **5**
Zwinger **5**

clocks, game sets, and much, much more. The Historic Green Vault, consisting of historic rooms restored to their baroque splendor, houses more treasures, including items made of silver, gold, and bronze, and jewelry dripping with precious stones, all displayed out in the open rather than behind glass cases. For this reason, admission here is restricted to 100 persons per hour, with tickets issued for a specific time (you can reserve in advance by phone or online). The cost here, including audio guide, is 10€, 12€ if purchased in advance. The New Green Vault is open Wednesday to Monday 10am to 6pm, while the Historic Green Vault is open Wednesday to Monday 10am to 7pm.

Also in the Royal Palace is the **Kupferstich-Kabinett (Collection of Prints and Drawings;** ℭ **0351/491 42 11;** www.skd-dresden.de), with changing exhibitions drawn from its collection of more than 500,000 drawings, watercolors, lithographs, etchings, illustrated books, and photographs dating from the 15th century to the present and created by more than 11,000 artists. Admission is usually 3€ for adults and 2€ for students and children. It's open Wednesday to Monday 10am to 6pm.

Just a stone's throw away is Dresden's other imposing building, the **Zwinger.** Augustus the Strong built this baroque masterpiece, modeled after Versailles, in 1719, and it's where he staged tournaments and kept dozens of concubines. His physique was called Herculean, his temperament Rabelaisian, but the king was also a lover of the arts. Today this artfully symmetrical complex of buildings holds a collection of museums and, in its center courtyard, a formal garden of fountains and promenades.

The most important museum in the Zwinger is the **Gemäldegalerie Alte Meister (Old Masters Picture Gallery)** ★★★, located in the Semperbau part of the complex, with an entrance at Theaterplatz 1 (ℭ **0351/49142000;** www.skd-dresden.de; tram: 1, 2, 4, 7, 8, 11, 12, or 14 to Theaterplatz; bus: 82 or 94 to Postplatz). This gallery, one of the best on the Continent, concentrates on great masterpieces of the 16th to 18th centuries. Italian Renaissance and baroque art is strongly represented, with works by Raphael (look for Raphael's showpiece, *Sistine Madonna*), Giorgione *(Sleeping Venus),* Titian, Correggio, and others. Of equal significance are Dutch and Flemish paintings of the 17th century, with works by Rembrandt, Vermeer, Van Dyck, and Rubens (the Rubens collection includes his spectacular *Neptune,* full of rearing horses, and an exquisite *St. Jerome*), and old German masterpieces by such artists as Albrecht Dürer.

It's open Tuesday to Sunday 10am to 6pm and charges an admission of 10€ for adults, free for children under 16. The **Rüstkammer (Armory;** same telephone and website as above), with a vast collection of decorative weapons and costumes, including suits of armor, shields, swords, sabers, rifles, jousting sticks, and more. Admission is 3€ for adults and free for children under 16.

Finally, one more museum worth seeing in Zwinger is the sumptuous **Porzellansammlung (Porcelain Collection;** same contact details as above), which also owes its existence to Augustus the Strong. It boasts an outstanding collection of Chinese, Japanese, and early Meissen porcelain, including Chinese burial objects from the 3rd century B.C., Chinese pieces from the Song and Ming dynasties, and a very valuable collection of Japanese Imari ware. Its Meissen collection, beginning at the time of its invention in 1708, is unparalleled. It's open Tuesday to Sunday 10am to 6pm. Admission is 6€ for adults, 3.50€ for students, and free for children under 18.

Admission to the whole Royal Place complex is 12€ for adults, 7.50€ students, and free for children 16 and under.

📷 A cruise ON THE ELBE

You can take a cruise on the historic Elbe River from central moorings below the Brühlsche Terrasse, aboard the oldest and largest paddle-steamer fleet in the world. Throughout the year, there are 2¾-hour round-trip cruises that pass several imposing castles along the way, including Pillnitz Castle, a former baroque summer residence of Saxon kings. These depart most days of the week every 30 to 90 minutes (times are subject to change per season). It costs 21€ for adults and 11€ for children. While you're cruising, look for the **Blaues Wunder (Blue Wonder),** one of Dresden's most celebrated bridges, completed in 1893. It is a beautiful expression of the bridge-building genius that flourished here at the turn of the 20th century.

From the end of March through October, there are longer cruises along the Elbe from Dresden to Rathen, a German village at the border of the Czech Republic, and beyond, with several departures daily. These trips take you through some of the finest river scenery in eastern Germany, including an area known as **"Swiss Saxony,"** one of Germany's most popular natural wonders. It's a land of table-shaped outcrops, isolated pillars, deep gorges, and sheer sandstone cliffs. Because each leg of this waterborne journey to Rathen requires 4½ hours, you'll have to block out an entire day for this experience if you opt for round-trip transport by boat. Alternatively, you can opt for one-way transit by boat, with a return back to Dresden from Rathen by train, a 40-minute ride, with trains departing every 30 minutes or so. The boat passage to Rathen costs 21€ each way. Rail transport costs 10€ each way. Tickets are available at the kiosk on the bank of the Elbe below the Altstadt, or contact the **Sächsische Dampfschiffahrt** (✆ **0351/866090;** www.saechsische-dampfschiffahrt.de).

Any stroll of Dresden should also take in the **Frauenkirche ★★** (**Church of Our Lady;** ✆ **0351/65606100;** www.frauenkirche-dresden.org; tram: 1, 2, or 4 to Altmarkt), dedicated to Jesus' mother. Although a church has stood on this spot since the 11th century, the church in its present form was first erected in the early 1700s as one of Germany's most important Protestant churches, destroyed during World War II, left as a ruined shell by the East German government as a reminder of the war, and then painstakingly restored, including the famous dome, in celebration of Dresden's 800th birthday. Admission is free, and hours are daily from 10am to noon and 1 to 6pm.

Nearby, on a narrow lane linking the Frauenkirche with Schlossplatz, is the **Fürstenzug (Procession of Princes),** one of the world's longest friezes, at 101 meters long, composed of 25,000 Meissen porcelain tiles depicting the rulers of the local dynasty over 800 years. On the banks of the Elbe is the **Brühlsche Terrasse,** a promenade celebrated as the "Balcony of Europe" for its views over the valley. On the other side of the Elbe is the picturesque **Neustadt,** popular for shopping and dining.

SHOPPING

After gaining an appreciation of Meissen porcelain at the Porcelain Collection, you might be drawn to the **Meissener Porzellan am Fürstenzug,** Kalkberg 15, D (✆ **0351/732613;** www.meissener-bleikristall.de), to start your own collection. The largest shopping center in the Altstadt is the **Altmarkt Galerie Dresden,** located on the Altmarkt at Webergasse 1 (© **0351/482040**), which boasts more than 100 shops. The Altmarkt is best known, however, for **Striezelmarkt** (© **0351/1608652;** www.striezel-markt.de), Germany's oldest Christmas market and a great place to find handmade regional crafts and food. If you miss the market, console yourself at **Weihnachtsland am Zwinger,** Kleine Brüdergasse 5 (© **0351/8621230;** www.weihnachtsland-dresden.com), which stocks Christmas gifts, decorations, and ornaments year-round.

On the other side of the Elbe, in Neustadt, the most fashionable shopping mecca is the elegant **Königstrasse,** lined with unbroken rows of baroque patrician houses that give an inkling of how Dresden used to look prior to 1945. Tony boutiques and restaurants now occupy the houses.

WHERE TO STAY & DINE

If you are really on a budget or staying for a short period of time, **Raskolnikoff Pension,** Böhmische Strasse 34 (© **0351/8045706;** www.raskolnikoff.de), is your choice. It is one of the better *pensiones* (boardinghouses) in town, lying across the river in Neustadt (New Town). It is in a restored building dating from 1732 and is an artsy choice, with a modern gallery on-site. Special features include a courtyard garden and a cozy restaurant serving regional specialties of Saxony. All the bedrooms have been renovated and are done in an extreme modern style, though private bathrooms have been installed in only two rooms. Doubles without a bathroom go for 52€; with a bathroom, they're 55€. Rates include a continental breakfast. The pension does not accept credit cards.

On the other side of the Hauptbahnhof (and also just a 3-min. walk away) is **Hotel Kipping ★**, Antonstrasse 33–35 (© **0351/829370;** www.hotel-kipping.de). This 20-room find was built in neo-Renaissance style in 1884 by a local businessman and was one of the few neighborhood buildings left standing after 1945. It offers attractive, high-ceilinged rooms and a restaurant serving local Saxon cuisine. Doubles here cost 95€ to 120€, including buffet breakfast.

Just a 2-minute walk from the Bahnhof Neustadt, the city's other train station, is the **Hotel Bayerischer Hof,** Antonstrasse 33–35 (© **0351/82 93 70;** www.bayerischer-hof-dresden.de). Set in a stately 1864 building, it offers 50 spacious rooms, simple but with modern furnishings. Its public spaces, including a restaurant and a bar, are elegant with a bit of flair, leading one to assume the hotel would be more expensive than the 95€ to 138€ cost of a double room, including buffet breakfast. Check the website for offers and deals.

Beautifully renovated, **Rothenburger Hof ★★**, Rothenburger Strasse 15–17 (© **0351/81260;** www.rothenburger-hof.de; tram: 11), is a time-honored and traditional hotel that first opened its doors in 1685 and is once again claiming its regal position as a small luxury hotel. A family-run hotel, it is in Neustadt. It's within an easy walk of the historical monuments of the Old City. It's much more comfortable today than when it first opened because so many modern improvements were made. The midsize rooms are traditionally furnished and comfortable, with freshly renovated tiled bathrooms. Double rooms cost from 99€ to 160€ and include a buffet breakfast.

In between the two train stations, near the Altstadt, **Art'otel dresden,** Ostra-Allee 33 (© **0351/49220;** www.artotels.com; tram: 11 to Haus der Presse), is the most self-consciously "arty" hotel in Dresden. The 174 stylish rooms, which eschew the usual box shape in favor of sensuous curves, are full of design surprises, from chairs that can be pulled up to form bar stools to voyeuristic bathroom windows that become opaque when the light is turned on. Naturally, artwork fills the white walls and the in-house art gallery, all by cutting-edge native artist A. R. Penck. Doubles cost from 160€, and rates include a buffet breakfast.

Theme restaurants are big in Dresden, but few carry it off as well as **Sophienkeller im Taschenbergpalais ★**, Taschenberg 3 (© 0351/497260; www.sophienkeller-dresden.de; tram: 4 or 11), near the Zwinger and Residenzschloss. Located in the vaulted cellars of a historic palace, it offers medieval hearty feasts that might have been served in the Royal Saxon Court. There are four distinct dining areas, including one outfitted like a medieval torture chamber. Waitresses in traditional dirndl haul steaming platters of suckling pig fresh off the spit, venison goulash, or juicy chicken filet, with most meals costing 8€ to 15€. It's open daily 11am to 1am.

Sister restaurant to the Sophienkeller, **Pulverturm,** An der Frauenkirche 12 (© 0351/262600; www.pulverturm-dresden.de; tram: 1, 2, or 4), is also based on a medieval theme and is located in the vaulted cellar of a former tower used to store gunpowder. It offers many of the similar dishes as above and is open the same hours. Main dishes cost 11€ to 17€.

Less touristy but very popular is the **Altmarkt Keller,** Altmarkt 4 (© 0351/4818130; www.altmarktkeller-dresden.de; tram: 4), located on the east side of the old market square. This huge, historic cellar with a vaulted ceiling and cozy side rooms is a boisterous venue for Saxon and Bohemian (Czech) cuisine, with platters going for 7.80€ to 16€. Can't decide? How about a unique beer and onion soup, followed by pork goulash with Bohemian dumplings and braised cabbage? There's also an extensive salad menu. It's open daily 11am to midnight. In summer, tables are set up in the historic square.

Brauhaus Watzke, Kötzschenbroder Strasse 1 (© 0351/852920; www.watzke.de; tram: 4 or 13), one of Dresden's most famous and atmospheric beer halls, is located west of the city center, on a site overlooking the Elbe. There is a sprawling garden. Inside, the venue—established in 1898—is appropriately woodsy looking and *gemütlich* (cozy). Anything you drink here will have been brewed on the premises. Regardless of which kind of beer you pick, a half-liter costs 2.70€. It's offered only in kegs, and it's almost never available anywhere else. Menu items are appropriately hearty and include *Meltzer Schnitzel,* a filet of veal dredged in malt and fried, and *Watzke Bierfleische,* a ragout of beef stewed in dark aromatic beer. Salads, soups, and fish dishes are just as tasty. Main courses cost 8.50€ to 15€. and it is open daily from 11am to midnight.

NIGHTLIFE

Between the Elbe River and the Zwinger, on the west side of grand Theaterplatz, stands **Semper Opera House ★★★**, Theaterplatz 2 (© 0351/4911705; www.semperoper.de; tram: 1, 2, 4, 7, 8, 11, 12, 14, or 17). Gottfried Semper, the same architect who mapped out the famous picture gallery in the Zwinger, designed the Renaissance-style building, known for its fine acoustics. Opera seats range from 20€ to 120€. The opera company takes a vacation mid-July to mid-August.

A once run-down but now gentrified nightlife destination that assembles about 20 different bars, art galleries, and restaurants into one historic site is **Kunsthof,** Alaunstrasse 70 (© 0351/8106617; www.kunsthof-dresden.de), where a series of hip cafes, art galleries, and affordable restaurants line the edges of an interior courtyard. A particularly appealing bar, tapas bar, and restaurant within the complex is the Spain-inspired **El Perro** (© 0351/8036723; www.elperro.de).

TRAVELING THE romantic road BY BUS

If you have only a limited amount of vacation time allotted for your rail trip to Germany, have a railpass, and would like to see the Romantic Road in a more convenient fashion than that afforded by public transportation (some of the smallest towns do not have train stations and can be reached only by bus), the best option for traveling the route is aboard the comfortable and modern **Romantic Road Europabus** (www. romantischestrasse.de), which links all towns and cities along the route daily in both directions from April through October. Travelers who arrive by air can join the Europabus easily at Frankfurt, Munich, or Augsburg, but the most scenic part of the trip is from Würzburg to Füssen, passing through many of the route's charming villages and towns. In fact, it's probably one of the most scenic bus rides on the planet.

The trip between Würzburg and Füssen takes about 9 hours and costs 59€ one-way, but if you have a railpass, you'll get a 20% discount off the fare on the "Romantic Road" route (Frankfurt am Main-Wurburg-Augsburg-Munich-Fussen). From Frankfurt to Füssen one-way costs 99€. If you travel the entire distance of the Europabus, which departs daily at around 8am from both Frankfurt and Munich train stations, the trip will take roughly 13 hours from start to finish and costs 75€ one-way, 60€ if you have a railpass. However, we suggest you break up your trip with an overnight stay, in, say, Rothenburg (for 85€) or Augsburg. Seats should be reserved at least 2 working days in advance through **Deutsche Touring GmbH** (© 069/ 79030). For timetables, fare information, and further route details, see the company's website at **www.touring.de**.

Highlights of the Romantic Road

The aptly named Romantic Road, or *Romantische Strasse,* is one of Germany's most popular tourist routes. Stretching 180 miles (290km) between Würzburg in the north and Füssen in the foothills of the Bavarian Alps, it links a series of medieval villages and 2,000-year-old towns. The entire length of the Romantic Road is best done by car or bus and could take days to see in its entirety. That said, several of the top cities along the route can easily be reached by rail, and we highlight the best of those cities in this section (for a description of Neuschwanstein castle near Füssen, see the section on Munich, earlier). Both Frankfurt and Munich are convenient gateways for exploring the road by rail.

Note: The Romantic Road Association will provide information on sights and attractions and mail information packs in English. Contact the **Romantische Strasse Arbeitsgemeinschaft,** Segringer Strasse 19, DE-19550 Dinkelsbühl (© 09851/551387; www.romantischestrasse.de).

WÜRZBURG ★★

For Germans, the south begins at Würzburg, one of the loveliest baroque cities in the country and the best starting point for the Romantic Road. About 174 miles (280km) northwest of Munich, it not only has excellent rail connections to most of Germany's major cities and to major cities along the Romantic Road route, but also is an interesting town in and of itself. A lively university town, Würzburg, known for its baroque architecture and its Franconian wine, has a 1,300-year history and occupies an idyllic setting surrounded by vineyards. Although 86% of the city's center was destroyed on

March 16, 1945, by bombs of the Royal Air Force, the old town has been lovingly restored.

The **Würzburg Hauptbahnhof** is connected to several major and regional rail lines. From Frankfurt, 30 trains arrive per day (trip time: 1½ hr.); from Munich, 20 trains (2½ hr.); from Nürnberg, 30 trains (1 hr., 10 min.); and several trains from Berlin (5 hr., 50 min.). For rail information and schedules, call ✆ **01805/996633** or visit www.bahn.de.

Contact the **Tourist Information Office,** Zeppelinstrasse (✆ **0931/372335**). It's open April to December Monday to Friday 10am to 6pm, Saturday 10am to 2pm (May–Oct also open Sun 10am–2pm); hours January to March are Monday to Friday 10am to 4pm, Saturday 10am to 1pm.

Top Attractions & Special Moments

In spring and summer, the liveliest place in town is the **Marktplatz (central marketplace),** where street performers entertain and vendors hawk their wares, ranging from fresh fruit to souvenir trinkets. You can also stroll down the traffic-free **Schönbornstrasse,** with its modern boutiques, wine merchants, and cafes.

Würzburg's cathedral, **Dom St. Kilian,** Domstrasse (✆ **0931/3211830**), begun in 1040 and dedicated to a 7th-century Irish missionary to Franconia, is the fourth-largest Romanesque church in Germany. The high-baroque stucco work was done after 1700. The imposing row of bishops' tombs begins with that of Gottfried von Spitzenberg (ca. 1190), who was one of the first prince-bishops to rule over the town. Look for three sandstone tombstones by Riemenschneider, constructed between 1502 and 1506. The Dom is dedicated to St. Kilian, an Irish missionary to Franconia in the 7th century. The Dom is open Easter to October Monday to Saturday from 10am to 5pm, and Sunday from 1 to 6pm; November to the day before Easter Monday to Saturday from 10am to noon and 2 to 4:30pm, and Sunday from 12:30 to 1:30pm and 2:30 to 6pm. Admission is free.

The most important thing to see in Würzburg is the **Residenz ★★,** Residenzplatz 2, Tor B (✆ **0931/3211830;** www.residenz-wuerzburg.de; tram: 1, 3, 4, or 5), one of Germany's most important baroque palaces and a UNESCO World Heritage Site. Seat of Würzburg's prince-bishops, it was begun in 1720 to satisfy Prince-Bishop Johann Philipp Franz von Schönborn's passion for elegance and splendor. At its center is the masterful **Treppenhaus (staircase),** above which a high, unsupported vaulted ceiling is decorated with one of the world's largest contiguous ceiling frescos, painted by Tiepolo. It represents the four known continents of the world, with North America depicted by a crocodile and Indian. Beyond the staircase are the palace rooms containing furniture, tapestries, paintings, and other treasures, as well as the Court Gardens. Time your visit to coincide with one of the English tours (given at 11am and 3pm), which allows you to see seven extra rooms (including the famous Mirror Cabinet) and is included in the price of admission (otherwise, you can join a German tour every 15–30 min.). Be sure to see the **court chapel,** a rectangular room divided into five oval sections, three with domed ceilings; window arches are placed at oblique angles to coordinate the windows with the oval sections. Colored marble columns define the sections, their gilded capitals enriching the ceiling frescoes by Johann Rudolf Byss. At the side altars, Tiepolo painted two important works: *The Fall of the Angels* on the left and *The Assumption of the Virgin* on the right. During the summer, a **Mozart festival** is held in the upper halls of the Residenz. The castle is open Easter to October Monday to Saturday 10am to 5pm, Sunday 1 to 6pm; November to the day before Easter

Monday to Saturday 10am to noon and 2 to 4:30pm, Sunday 12:30 to 1:30pm and 2:30 to 6pm. Admission is free.

Finally, another sight worth seeing if there's time is the city's landmark, **Festung Marienberg (Fortress Marienberg)** ★ (℃ **0931/3551750;** www.schloesser. bayern.de; bus: 9 Apr–Oct only), located across from the Altstadt over the Alte Mainbrücke stone bridge (which is adorned with statues of saints). This imposing fortress, almost completely destroyed in 1945 and completely restored in 1990, served as the residence of the local prince-bishops from 1253 to 1719. Admission is 4€ for adults, 3€ for a reduced rate. Within its walls is the 8th-century **Marienkirche,** one of the oldest churches in Germany. In the former baroque armory is the **Mainfränkisches Museum** (℃ **0931/205940;** www.mainfraenkisches-museum.de), with the world's largest collection of sculptures by the great flamboyant Gothic master, Tilman Riemenschneider (1460–1531), called "the master of Würzburg." The sculptor came to live here in 1483 and was the town's mayor in 1520 and 1521. Never a totally decorative artist, Riemenschneider concentrated on the reality of people's appearance, highlighting their hands, faces, and clothing. After siding with the farmers in a 1525 uprising, Riemenschneider was imprisoned for 2 months and, after his release, never received another large commission. The museum also displays paintings by Tiepolo and Lucas Cranach, and sandstone figures from the rococo gardens of the prince-bishops' summer palace. A tribute to one of the few industries of the city, winemaking, is paid in the press house, which contains historic casks and carved cask bases, and a large collection of glasses and goblets. It's open Tuesday through Sunday 10am to 5pm (to 4pm in winter).

Fürstenbaumuseum (℃ **0931/43838**), situated in the restored princes' wing of the fortress, illustrates the history of Würzburg and the prince-bishops. The urban history section offers a stroll through 1,300 eventful years of Würzburg's history, including an exhibit relating to the discovery of X-rays by Wilhelm Conrad Röntgen in 1895. A model of the town shows its appearance in 1525, and another shows the destruction after the bombing of 1945. It is open April to October Tuesday to Sunday 10am to 5pm.

Admission to both museums is 4€ adults, 2€ for students, and free for children 13 and under.

Where to Stay & Dine

A 10-minute walk from the train station, **Hotel-Restaurant St. Josef** ★, Semmelstrasse 28–30 (℃ **0931/308680;** www.hotel-st-josef.de; tram: 1, 2, 3, or 5), has the best inexpensive accommodations in the Altstadt. Its owner has been successful in bringing it up-to-date. Rooms, though small, are pleasantly furnished and well maintained, each equipped with an efficiently organized bathroom. Fresh flowers add a personalized touch to this well-run establishment. Doubles range from 89€ to 95€, and a triple is 124€. Rates include a continental breakfast.

The 500-year-old **Ratskeller Würzburg,** Langgasse 1 (℃ **0931/13021;** www. wuerzburger-ratskeller.de; tram: 1, 2, 3, or 5), in the town hall, not only is an interesting place to visit, but also serves tasty Franconian and international fare at reasonable prices. Country cookery is an art here, as you'll discover if you order the boiled breast of beef with horseradish sauce and noodles. Other specialties include marinated salmon with potato pancakes, pikeperch in a white-wine sauce, and medallions of pork gratin with cheese. They also specialize in local beer and Franconian white wines. Main courses are 12€ to 25€. It's open daily 11:30am to 10:30pm. Reservations are required on Saturday and Sunday.

ROTHENBURG OB DER TAUBER ★★★

If you have time for only one town on the Romantic Road, make it Rothenburg, the best-preserved medieval city in Germany. Contemporary life and industry have made an impact, and as you leave the station, you'll initially see factories and office buildings. Inside its undamaged 13th-century city walls, however, the old town center seems untouched by the passage of time from its heyday as a free imperial city in the 14th century. The only drawback is that Rothenburg, about 32 miles (52km) southeast of Würzburg, suffers from serious overcrowding, especially in summer.

You can reach Rothenburg via train from Frankfurt (trip time: 3 hr.), from Hamburg (trip time: 5½ hr.), or from Berlin (trip time: 7 hr.). Rothenburg lies on the Steinach–Rothenburg branch line, with frequent connections to all major German cities, including Nürnberg and Stuttgart. From the train station, it's about a 10-minute walk to the old town center. For tourist information, contact **Rothenburg Tourismus Service,** Marktplatz (✆ **09861/404800;** www.rothenburg.de). It's open November to April Monday to Friday 9am to 5pm, and Saturday 10am to 5pm; May to October, it's open Monday to Friday 9am to 7pm, Saturday and Sunday 10am to 5pm.

Top Attractions & Special Moments

For an excellent view, take a walk on the **town ramparts ★**. This pleasant walk, from the massive 16th-century Spitaltor (at the end of the Spitalgasse) to the Klingentor, takes about a half-hour, with panoramic views over the city along the way. You might stop at one of the many kiosks in town selling the local pastry called *Schneeballen* (snowballs), a round, sugarcoated pastry that's fattening but delicious.

Rothenburg's **Rathaus (Town Hall) ★**, Marktplatz (✆ **09861/40492**), consists of an older Gothic section from 1240 and a newer Renaissance structure facing the square, built in 1572 to replace a portion destroyed in a fire. It's decorated with intricate friezes and a large stone portico opening onto the square. From the 160-foot (50m) tower of the Gothic hall, the highest spot in town, you get a great **view ★** of the town below. The Rathaus is open Monday to Friday 8am to 6pm. The tower is open April to October daily 9:30am to 12:30pm and 1 to 5pm; December daily noon to 3pm; November and January to March Saturday to Sunday, and holidays noon to 3pm. It will cost you 1.50€ to climb to the top; children pay 1€.

The most important church in town, the Gothic **St. Jakobskirche (Church of St. Jacob),** Klostergasse 15 (✆ **09861/700620**), dates from 1336. In the west gallery is the **Altar of the Holy Blood ★★**, a masterpiece by the famous Würzburg sculptor Tilman Riemenschneider (ca. 1460–1531). The work was executed between 1499 and 1505 to provide a worthy setting for its Reliquary of the Holy Blood. This relic, venerated in the Middle Ages, is contained in a rock-crystal capsule set in the reliquary cross (ca. 1270) in the center of the shrine. The scene on the altar beneath *The Last Supper* immediately makes a strong impact on the viewer. The church is open April to October Monday through Saturday 9am to 5:30pm, Sunday 11am to 5:30pm; December daily from 10am to 5pm; November and January to March, daily from 10am to noon and 2 to 4pm. Admission is 1.50€ for adults and .50€ for children.

The historical collection of Rothenburg is housed at the **Reichsstadtmuseum (Imperial City Museum),** Klosterhof 5 (✆ **09861/939043;** www.reichsstadt museum.rothenburg.de), in a 13th-century Dominican nunnery. The cloisters are well preserved, and you can visit the convent hall, kitchen, and apothecary. The museum collection includes period furniture and art from Rothenburg's more prosperous periods, including the original glazed elector's tankard, and a new section of archaeological objects from prehistoric times up to the Middle Ages. Among the artistic exhibits is the 1494 *Rothenburg Passion* series, 12 pictures by Martinus Schwartz that depict scenes from the suffering of Christ. An interesting object is a historic tankard that holds more than 6 pints. The museum is open April to October daily from 10am to 5pm, November to March daily from 1 to 4pm. Admission is 3.50€ for adults, 2.50€ for students and children 6 to 18. A family ticket is available for 7€.

An unusual museum is the **Kriminalmuseum (Medieval Crime Museum),** Burggasse 3–5 (© **09861/5359;** www.kriminalmuseum.rothenburg.de). The only museum of its kind in Europe, it is housed in a structure built in 1395 for the Order of the Johanniter, who cared for the sick. The building was redone in 1718 in the baroque style; it's the only example of baroque architecture in town. The museum's four floors provide an insight into the life, laws, and punishments of medieval days. You'll see chastity belts, shame masks, a shame flute for bad musicians, and a cage for bakers who baked bread too small or too light. It's open January to Feburary and November daily 2 to 4pm, March and December 1 to 4pm, April daily 11am to 5pm; May to October daily 10am to 6pm. Admission is 4€ for adults, 2.80€ for students, and 2.40€ for children 6 to 17.

Where to Stay & Dine

The 45-room **Flair-Hotel Reichs-Küchenmeister ★**, Kircheplatz 8 (© **09861/ 9700;** www.reichskuechenmeister.com), is one of the town's oldest structures and was salvaged from a World War II firestorm through a massive, thoroughly sensitive restoration has rendered it both stylish and well equipped. Rooms are furnished with regional wooden furniture; some contain minibars. Bathrooms are a bit small, but maintenance is tidy. Seventeen less expensive rooms are in a less desirable annex across the street. Rates include a buffet breakfast and cost 75€ to 120€ double.

Hotel Mittermeier Restaurant ★★★, Vorm Würzburger Tor 7–9. (© **09861/ 94540;** www.villamittermeier.de), is one of the great restaurants along the Romantic Road. The chef has an inventive and original take on Franconian cuisine. It has a garden terrace and near-faultless cuisine. On offer are such lunch dishes as slices of bison rib-eye on wild garlic with risotto or "on the skin" roast pikeperch with a potato-and-poppy-seed roulade. Dinner is even more elaborate. Main dishes tend to be sublime, including a roasted ridge of suckling pig on leaf spinach or else truffled filet of salmon with crayfish in puff pastry. Main courses range from 18€ to 34€; a 4-course fixed-price menu is 88€. It's open Tuesday to Saturday noon to 2pm and 7 to 9:30pm. Reservations are required.

AUGSBURG

Augsburg's 2,000 years of history (it's Germany's second-oldest city and was founded by the Roman emperor Augustus in 15 B.C.) have made it one of southern Germany's major sightseeing attractions. The city is especially noteworthy for its picture-perfect Renaissance and baroque architecture. About 42 miles (68km) northwest of Munich, it's the Romantic Road's largest town and serves also as a gateway to the Alps and the south. It's well connected to area rail lines and has especially good connections to Munich, so if you can't travel the entire Romantic Road, you can do it as an easy day trip out of Munich.

There are more than 60 trains a day from Munich (trip time: 30–50 min.); 35 trains depart from Frankfurt (trip time: 3–4½ hr.) and every hour from Würzburg (trip time: 2 hr.). For information, call © **01805/996633** or visit www.bahn.de. The main station is ½ mile (1km) west of the center of town, about a 15-minute walk away or a short ride by tram. It's quite easy to get around on foot. For visitor information, contact **Tourist-Information,** Schiessgrabenstrasse 14 (*C* **0821/502070;** www.regio-augsburg.de), open Monday to Friday 9am to 6pm.

Top Attractions & Special Moments

Extending southward from the Rathaus is the wide **Maximilianstrasse ★**, lined with shops and old burghers' houses, and studded with fountains by the Renaissance Dutch sculptor Adrien de Vries.

One of the most famous buildings here is the **Schaezlerpalais,** Maximilianstrasse 46 (*C* **0821/3244102;** tram: 1), a 60-room rococo mansion facing the Hercules Fountain and constructed between 1765 and 1770. It contains an amazing art collection, mostly by regional German artists of the Renaissance and baroque periods, including Hans Holbein the Elder and Hans Burgkmair. Albrecht Dürer's famous portrait of Jakob Fugger is here. Rubens, Veronese, Tiepolo, Cranach, and others are also represented. The palace contains a rococo ballroom, with gilded and mirrored wall panels and a ceiling fresco, *The Four Continents,* as well as a period garden. It's open Tuesday 10am to 8pm and Wednesday to Sunday 10am to 5pm. Admission is 9€ for adults and 3€ for children.

Anchoring the northern end of the historic old town is the Romanesque and Gothic cathedral of Augsburg, **Dom St. Maria,** Hoher Weg (*C* **0821/3166353;** tram: 1), with records dating from 823. It's famous for four stained-glass windows, the oldest in Germany, dating from the 12th century. They're located at the top of the nave and depict Old Testament prophets in a severe but colorful style. The south bronze door, dating from the 14th century, features 25 bas-reliefs of a mixture of biblical and mythological characters. The Dom is open Monday to Saturday from 7am to 5pm, Sunday from noon to 5pm. Admission is free.

About a 10-minute walk east of the city center, the **Fuggerei ★**, Vorderer Lech (*C* **0821/3198810;** www.fuggerei.de; tram: 1), was founded in 1521 to house Augsburg's needy citizens. It was established by Jakob Fugger, one of the most powerful bankers, merchants, and businessmen of his time. Surviving today as the world's oldest social settlement, the Fuggerei is a miniature, self-contained town, enclosed by its own wall and with entry gates. Since its founding, residents have had to pay a nominal rent of only 1€ (formerly a Rhenish guilder) per year. The only obligation is that tenants pray daily for the souls of their founders. A house at Mittlere Gasse 13, next to the one once occupied by Mozart's ancestor, is now the Fuggerei's **museum.** The rough 16th- and 17th-century furniture, wood-paneled ceilings and walls, and cast-iron stove, as well as other objects of everyday life, show what it was like to live here in earlier times. The museum is open April to September daily 8am to 8pm and October to March daily 9am to 6pm. Admission to the Fuggerei, including the museum, is 4€ for adults and 2€ for students and children.

Where to Stay & Dine

The Steigenberger Drei Mohren ★★, Maximilianstrasse 40 (*C* **0821/5036-0** or 800/223-5652 in the U.S. and Canada; www.augsburg.steigenberger.de; tram: 1), is Augsburg's most famous hotel, with a history stretching back several centuries and counting Mozart, Goethe, Napoleon, and various royalty among its guests. Its 105 rooms are comfortable and spacious, but the real draws here are the hotel's prime location, its elegant lobby, and its two restaurants, one decked out like a French bistro and the other serving Mediterranean cuisine. Rooms cost 110€ to 181€ double, with weekend discounts available.

Also with an enviable location, **Privat Hotel Riegele,** Viktoriastrasse 4 (© **0821/ 509000;** www.hotel-riegele.de), is a little hotel opposite the Hauptbahnhof (main rail station). The owners run a neat, tidy hotel with midsize to spacious bedrooms, each with comfortably modern furnishings that are renewed as needed, along with highly polished, tiled private bathrooms. Doubles range 89€ to 130€. On-site is the **Braus Bräustüble,** a tavern patronized by locals as well as visitors for its hearty regional dishes. The breakfast buffet, which is included, is one of the most generous in town.

Haupt im Prinz Karl Palais ★★, Theaterstrasse 8 (© **0821/9076464;** www. papageno-restaurant.de), is one of the grandest restaurants in the Augsburg area. Under vaulted ceilings, with alfresco dining in midsummer, the restaurant is only deceptively rustic. Its market-fresh cuisine strives for perfection and is backed up by a sound technique. For flavor, the chefs roam the world, borrowing a teriyaki sauce from Asia, mangoes from tropical countries, or truffles from Italy. One dish combines *Fisch und Fleisch* (fish and meat) with fresh asparagus. Some of their veal and beef dishes are worthy of a prize. Main courses range from 9.50€ to 14€; fixed-price menus are 47€ for three-course, 55€ for five-course, 59€ for six-course, and 65€ for seven-course. Reservations are required.

The affordable **Fuggerei Stube,** Jakoberstrasse 26 (© **0821/30870;** www. fuggerei-stube.de; tram: 1), can fit 60 people at a time into its large, *gemütlich* dining room. Expect generous portions of well-prepared food such as *Sauerbraten,* pork *Schnitzel,* game, and fish dishes. The beer foaming out of the taps here is Storchen-bräu; most visitors find that it goes wonderfully with the conservative German specialties that are this establishment's forte. Main courses range from 10€ to 21€. It is open from Tuesday to Saturday 11:30am to 2pm and 6 to 11pm, Sunday and public holidays 11:30am to 3pm. Reservations are recommended.

Nearby, the lively **König von Flandern,** Karolinenstrasse 12 (© **0821/158050;** www.koenigvonflandern.de; tram: 2), is a basement brewery, serving wurst, roast pork, and other hearty fare in addition to its own brews. You can dine here for 5.50€ to 14€, and it's open daily 11am to 1am. Hot food is served until 12:30am.

GREAT BRITAIN & IRELAND

G reat Britain is made up of England, Scotland, and Wales, three ancient kingdoms that are today part of the United Kingdom (Northern Ireland is the final member of the U.K.). It might be small—just 88,150 square miles (228,300 sq. km)—but thanks to its history and landscape, it consistently ranks among the top destinations for travelers across the globe. Yes, the weather can be a little damp, but the summer brings with it sunshine and long evenings. And the food is really rather good now, with gastropubs and delis sprouting up everywhere from villages to cities. Speaking of which, London is still Europe's center of cool, and the once-grim industrial cities up north—such as Leeds and Newcastle—have been reborn as buzzing cultural hubs. Even farther up, Edinburgh remains Scotland's capital, both politically and artistically, while Ireland is an altogether separate nation—with a different currency, laws, and even its own Gaelic language—but is still a destination easily added to a rail tour of the British Isles.

10

Highlights of Great Britain

You could spend weeks exploring this fascinating country and still have plenty more to see. Mighty castles, stately homes, magnificent gardens, soaring cathedrals, romantic landscapes, and historic cities are flung across the far corners of Great Britain like so many jewels. But if time is an issue, you couldn't do any better than to limit yourself to London, Edinburgh, and Dublin, the great capital cities of England, Scotland, and the Republic of Ireland. **London** is a dizzying delight, full of pomp and pedigree, a place where high culture and cutting-edge trends feed off one another. London is sedate and raucous, a time-tested background for legendary sites harking back to the earliest days of the kingdom. **Edinburgh,** crowned by its famous castle, is almost as royal as London and far more dramatically situated, but it's much smaller and easier to digest in a short period. With its unique combination of medieval and neoclassical districts, Edinburgh invites exploration. Scotland's greatest national museums and art collections are concentrated here. The town is suffused with creative energy that blossoms during the famed Edinburgh International Festival. With 40% of the Republic of Ireland's population living within 61 miles (98km) of **Dublin,** this capital is by far the largest and most workaday of all Irish cities. And though the city (along with all of Ireland) took a beating during the global recession, the decades-long boom before the

On the Saturday closest to her official birthday in mid-June (her real birthday is Apr 21 and is celebrated with gun salutes in Hyde Park), Elizabeth II inspects her regiments from an open carriage and receives the salute during the **Trooping the Colour.** The event dates back to the 1600s, when a regiment's colors or flag were trooped in front of the infantry soldiers so they would recognize them on the battlefield. Now it is an opportunity for certain regiments to pay tribute to the queen. With huge military bands, its quintessential English pageantry draws big crowds— many of them waiting to see a wretched young soldier faint in the heat under his ridiculous bearskin hat. Tickets for the parade and two reviews, held on preceding Saturdays, are allocated by ballot. Applicants must write between January 1 and the end of February, enclosing a self-addressed stamped envelope or International Reply Coupon to the Ticket Office, HQ Household Division, Horse Guards, Whitehall, London SW1X 6AA. Tickets are free. The ballot is held in mid-March, and only successful applicants are informed in April. Call ℂ **020/7414-2479** for more details or look online at **www.trooping-the-colour.co.uk**.

The thrilling **Wimbledon Lawn Tennis Championships,** just outside London, is the event where the posh and the people rub shoulders, and you can get right up close to the world's top tennis players. Savor the strawberries and cream that are part of the experience. Tickets for Centre and Number One courts are obtainable through a lottery. Write in from August to December to **All England Lawn Tennis Club,** P.O. Box 98, Church Road, Wimbledon, London S W19 5AE (ℂ **020/8944-1066;** www. wimbledon.org). Outside court tickets are available daily, but be prepared to wait in line.

The Henry Wood Promenade Concerts—aka "The Proms"— attract music aficionados from around the world. Staged daily, the concerts were launched in 1895 and are the principal summer venue for the BBC Symphony Orchestra. Banners, balloons, and Union Jacks on parade contribute to the festive summer atmosphere. Visit **www. bbc.co.uk/proms** for more information and for tickets. Tickets should be bought in advance. The season runs from mid-July to mid-September.

The Edinburgh International Festival and **Festival Fringe** are the highlight of the Edinburgh year and turn the city into a nonstop celebration. The festivals attract artists and companies of the highest international standard in all fields of the arts. Around the same time, the city also runs the exciting spectacle of the **Military Tattoo** on the floodlit esplanade in front of Edinburgh Castle, high on its rock above the city. The city is jammed during this period, and it's essential to book a hotel in advance. For more details on the festival, see "The Edinburgh Festival: Art & Tattoos," on p. 432.

bust ensured Dublin's permanent transformation into a modern European capital, packed with great shopping; wonderful restaurants and pubs; historic treasures such as the Book of Kells, the National Museum, and Dublin Castle; and the bucolic pleasures of St. Stephen's Green and Phoenix Park.

ESSENTIALS

Getting There

The main international airports serving the U.K. are Heathrow and Gatwick, both near London.

HEATHROW Heathrow (© 0844/335-1801; www.baa.co.uk and www.heathrow airport.com), the main international airport, is 15 miles (24km) west of Central London. It's served by **Air Canada** (© 888/247-2262; www.aircanada.ca), **American Airlines** (© 800/433-7300; www.aa.com), **British Airways** (© 800/247-9297; www.britishairways.com), **Continental Airlines** (© 800/231-0856; www.continental.com), **United Airlines** (© 800/864-8331; www.united.com), and **Virgin Atlantic Airways** (© 800/821-5438; www.virgin-atlantic.com).

The majority of flights from North America arrive at Terminals 3 and 4, with flights from some U.S. destinations touching down at Terminal 5. There is a **Tourist Information Centre** in the Tube station concourse that connects with **Terminals 1, 2, and 3,** open daily from 7:15am to 9pm. You can find **British Hotel Reservation Centre** desks (© 020/7592-3055; www.bhronline.com) in the arrivals area of every terminal, open daily.

GATWICK Gatwick (© 0870/574-7777; www.baa.co.uk) is a smaller airport about 25 miles (40km) south of London. It's served by American Airlines, British Airways, Delta, Continental, Northwest, and Virgin Atlantic.

Britain by Train

Getting to London from the Continent by train used to involve at least one ferry transfer. Not anymore. With the 1994 opening of the Chunnel, running underneath the English Channel between England and France, one can now travel between London and Paris with relative ease. The **Eurostar** (**www.eurostar.com**) train offers direct service from Paris's Gare du Nord and Brussels' Gare du Midi to St. Pancras in London in about 2 hours, making London (or Paris) a day-trip destination. More than a dozen Eurostar trains travel both to and from the Continent daily. **Rail Europe** (© 888/438-7245 in the United States, © 800/361-7245 in Canada; www.rail europe.com) sells Eurostar tickets, allowing you to combine a trip to London with a rail tour of the Continent. Eurail passholders do get a discount when purchasing a Eurostar ticket.

Should you wish to go the slow train route from the Continent to London, you'll need to get off your train in France near the English Channel and take a ferry or hovercraft across the water (up until the 1980s, certain trains would board a ferry, but this seamless travel route has now been replaced by the Eurotunnel). You'll disembark at one of the U.K. channel ports—those closest to London are Dover, Ramsgate, and Folkestone to the east, and Southhampton, Portsmouth, and Newhaven to the south—and from there, you'll board a British train for the journey onward to London. This can actually end up costing more than some of the supersaver round-trip Eurostar fares and is a lot more of a hassle, but some people may just want to see the fabled white cliffs of Dover from the English Channel.

PASSES

The **Eurail Global Pass** is not accepted on British trains. If you're going to be traveling by train around England, Wales, and Scotland—perhaps taking a few train excursions out of London—then consider buying a **BritRail Pass.** If you're going to Great

Britain in winter, this may be a very economical option, as the pass is often discounted for January and February travel. For information on the various BritRail pass options available, including the **BritRail Pass,** the **BritRail Flexipass,** and the **Britrail Plus Ireland Pass,** see chapter 2.

Note that BritRail passes are not for sale in the U.K., so you must obtain them before you leave home. You can purchase BritRail passes on the phone or online through **Rail Europe** (✆ **888/438-7245** in the United States, ✆ **800/361-7245** in Canada; www.raileurope.com) or your travel agent.

Note: If you plan to travel for only a day or two to Edinburgh out of London, it may be more economical to purchase Rail Europe's Edinburgh Overnight or Day Trip to Edinburgh excursion packages instead of a pass. For more information on these, call Rail Europe or check their website.

TICKET TYPES

You won't encounter any incomprehensible train terms in England (although it might help to remember that the U.K. uses the terms *return* rather than *round-trip* and *single* rather than *one-way*), but there are several ticket types you might be unfamiliar with. Broadly speaking, ticket types divide into three groups: **Advance** (booked ahead with restrictions), **Cheap Day/Saver** (bought same day and has restrictions), and **Open** (bought same day, but doesn't have restrictions). Within these groups are various subcategories. It's ridiculous to try to memorize them all. Instead, let the ticket seller know your travel plans in detail (especially which parts are flexible and which parts are not) and question him closely to determine your best option. If you can plan your travel in advance and stick to set times, it can often be cheaper to buy two advance, single tickets than to buy a return ticket. If you input your journey details into **www.nationalrail.co.uk**, the website will tell you which tickets are still available for your desired route. For a list of all available ticket types, go to **www.nationalrail. co.uk/times_fares/purchasing_tickets/ticket_types.htm**. The above-mentioned ticket types are also available from the Rail Europe call center.

PRACTICAL TRAIN INFORMATION

The entire British railway system was privatized under Margaret Thatcher, so there are now a number of different companies operating trains to specific parts of the country. Virgin, First, and East Coast are three of the major names you might encounter.

The sleek high-speed InterCity trains running between London and heavily traveled main-line routes (such as Edinburgh) are the most dependable and the most comfortable. For shorter trips (to Brighton or Cambridge, for example) commuter trains are used. In some cases, you might need to transfer to a local train to reach your destination. The local trains connect small towns between larger towns and are very basic. Local stations are small, and sometimes (particularly on Sun) there's no one to help with information or ticket sales. You will always find train schedules posted in local stations, and if there is no window service, you can buy your ticket on the train. There is no smoking on British trains; even the tobacco-friendly French have forbidden smoking on the Eurostar.

An announcement is (usually) made before a train arrives at each station; some trains will have a digital sign in each car announcing the stop. Station stops are short, so be ready to disembark when the train comes to a halt. In newer trains, there will be a well-marked push button that will open the door automatically. In older trains, you'll need to open the door yourself. It may open from the inside, or you may have to open the window and reach outside to turn the door handle.

Trains have a two-tiered ticket system: first class and standard (second) class. First-class tickets cost about one-third more than standard class. The first-class cars have roomier seats and fewer people, but you can travel quite comfortably in standard class. There is no first-class service on local trains. There are toilets on board all but local trains.

First-class service on InterCity trains (such as those btw. London and Edinburgh) includes free coffee, tea, beverages, and snacks served at your seat; some trains offer a free newspaper and a higher standard of personal service. Standard-class passengers can buy sandwiches and drinks in a cafe car. On most lines, an employee comes through with a food and beverage cart. There is no food service on local trains.

TICKETS & RESERVATIONS You can purchase your ticket with cash or a credit card at a ticket window in any British train station, and you can get your BritRail passes validated there as well. You can also buy a ticket on a train (cash only) if there is not a staffed ticket office or a Permit to Travel machine (these enable you to pay some money toward your fare, avoid a penalty fare, and then upgrade to a full ticket on board the train) at your departure station. If you have a validated BritRail Pass (see "Passes," above), just board your train. Seat reservations are not required on most trains, but they are a good idea on some InterCity trains, especially if you're traveling on a weekend or on journeys longer than 3 hours. They are pretty much a must on the night and weekend trains between Edinburgh and London in the summer. Reservations can be purchased (usually for about £3, though they are often free if you have a BritRail Pass) at the same time you buy your ticket, or you can make them inside the train station up to a couple of hours before departure. Should you wish to reserve a seat on a British train before arriving in the U.K., you can do so through Rail Europe (see "Passes," above) for around $11.

[FastFACTS] GREAT BRITAIN

Area Codes Every telephone number in England and Scotland is prefaced by an area code that must be used if you are dialing long distance (London's area code, for example, is **20;** Edinburgh's is **131**). If you're calling long distance but within the United Kingdom, preface the area code with a zero (in other words, London would be 020), followed by the number. See "Telephone," below.

Business Hours Banks are usually open Monday through Friday 9:30am to 3:30pm. Business offices are open Monday through Friday 9am to 5pm. English

pubs used to be allowed to stay open only Monday through Saturday 11am to 11pm and Sunday noon to 10:30pm, but since 2005, drinking establishments can apply for a license to serve alcohol longer—and many do, especially in the cities, where many bars go on until midnight or 1 am and clubs often stay open until 4 or 6am. Scottish licensing laws have always been more flexible, with many pubs and bars staying open until midnight, but most closing at 11pm. Stores generally open at 10am and close at 6pm Monday through Saturday, staying open until 7 or 8pm on

Wednesday or Thursday. Outside of the large cities, shops may be open for only a half-day on Saturday and shut one afternoon a week, often Wednesdays. Nowadays, more stores open on Sunday in London and Edinburgh.

Climate Unpredictable is the best that can be said about the weather in England and Scotland. Great Britain is an island, and its climate is influenced by the often-stormy North Atlantic. Precipitation is frequent; so are gray skies. Year-round, it tends to be wetter, windier, and colder in Edinburgh than in London. Without question, the best times to visit the U.K. are late spring, early autumn, and summer.

Currency Britain's decimal monetary system is based on the pound (£), which is made up of 100 pence (written as "p"). Scotland has its own notes, which can legally be used in England, though some smaller storekeepers may be suspicious of them. (Note, however, that Ireland uses the euro and not the pound.) The exchange rate used in this chapter is £1=$1.60, though fluctuations are constant. Currency exchange services can be found in railway stations, some banks, most post offices, and many tourist information centers.

Documents Required All U.S. citizens and Canadians must have a passport with at least 2 months' validity remaining. No visa is required. The immigration officer may also want proof of your intention to return to your point of origin (usually a round-trip ticket) and visible means of support while in Britain.

Electricity Britain uses 240 volts AC (50 cycles), roughly twice the voltage in North America, which is 115 to 120 volts AC (60 cycles). American plugs don't fit British wall outlets. Always bring suitable transformers and/or adapters. Most laptops and some cellphone and digital camera chargers come with transformers built in, but always check carefully before plugging anything in.

Embassies & High Commissions All embassies, consulates, and high commissions are located in London, the capital of the U.K. The **U.S. Embassy** is at 24 Grosvenor Sq., W1 (☎ **020/7499-9000;** www.usembassy.org. uk; Tube: Bond St.). The **Canadian High Commission** is at MacDonald House, 38 Grosvenor Sq., W1 (☎ **020/ 7258-6600;** www.canada. org.uk; Tube: Bond St.).

Health & Safety There are no major health risks associated with traveling in Britain. Pharmacies are called chemists in the United Kingdom; **Boots** is a chain with outlets all over the country. Any prescriptions you bring with you should use generic names, not brand names. England and Scotland are generally safe countries, although London is a teeming metropolis subject to petty crimes such as pickpocketing and con games, and more serious offenses such as mugging and rape. Be cautious at night; don't carry all your valuables on you when you go out, and be alert when taking money from ATMs. For police, fire, or an ambulance, dial ☎ **999.**

Holidays **Bank Holidays** (there are two in May and one in Aug) celebrate various events, and fall on a Monday, making for a nice long weekend. All banks and many shops, museums, historic houses, and other places of interest are closed, and public transport is radically reduced. The same holds true for other holidays:

New Year's Day, Good Friday, Easter Monday, Christmas, and Boxing Day (Dec 26). Crowds swell during school holidays: mid-July to early September, 3 weeks at Christmas and at Easter, and a week in mid-October and in mid-February.

Legal Aid Your consulate, embassy, or high commission (see above) will give you advice if you run into trouble. They can advise you of your rights and even provide a list of attorneys (for which you'll have to pay if services are used), but they can't interfere on your behalf in the legal processes of Great Britain. For questions about American citizens who are arrested abroad, including ways of getting money to them, telephone the **Citizens Emergency Center** of the Office of Special Consulate Services, in Washington, D.C. (☎ **202/ 647-5225**). Canadians should consult their London-based consulate (see above) for advice.

Mail Post offices and sub-post offices throughout England and Scotland are open Monday through Friday 9am to 5pm and Saturday 9am to noon. Many sub-post offices and some main post offices close for an hour at lunchtime. Post offices are identified by a big red sign and may be tucked inside office supply or souvenir shops. At press time, an airmail letter to North America costs 56p for 10 grams; postcards also require a

56p stamp. Letters generally take 7 to 10 days to arrive in the United States. The British postal system is among the most reliable in the world, so you don't need to depend on Federal Express or some other carrier unless you're in a great hurry.

Police & Emergencies The best source of help and advice in emergencies is the police; dial ☎ **999** for emergencies only (no coin required). If the local police can't assist, they'll have the address of a person who can. Losses, thefts, and other crimes should be reported immediately; just don't expect to retrieve your stolen goods.

Telephone The country code for the United Kingdom is **44.** To call England or Scotland from the United States, dial **011-44,** then the area or city code, and then the six-, seven-, or eight-digit phone number. (Drop the first zero.) If you're in England or Scotland and dialing a number within the same area code, put the zero back on (that is, ☎ 020/7123-1234). For **directory assistance** in London, dial ☎ **142;** for the rest of Britain, ☎ **192.**

Within the U.K., despite the growing prevalence of mobile phones, you'll still find at least three kinds of **public pay phones:** those relatively old-fashioned models that accept only coins, those accepting only prepaid phone cards, and those accepting both phone cards and credit cards. **Note:** The "old-fashioned"

phone boxes with the royal coat of arms and the bright red coat of paint tend to be maintained by British Telecom and fall into the latter of these three categories. Telephones that accept such credit cards as Access/MasterCard, Visa, American Express, and Diners Club tend to be most common at airports and large railway stations.

In a "confrontation" with a coin-operated phone, insert your (British) coins before dialing, with the understanding that the minimum charge these days even for calls placed to destinations within the same neighborhood will begin at 30p—more, prorated per call, than equivalent calls paid for with a phone card.

Phone cards are issued throughout the U.K. by a wide variety of corporate issuers, and with a wide variety of denominations that begin at £2.50 and go up to as much as £50 or higher. Each is reusable until the card's total value has been electronically depleted. Phone cards are sold in post offices, at newsstands, and within large retail supermarkets, including branches of Tesco and Sainsbury's.

To make an **international call** from Britain, dial the international access code **(00),** then the country code, then the area code, and finally the local number. Or call through one of the following long-distance access codes: **AT&T USA Direct** (☎ 800/CALL-ATT [225-5288]) or **Canada Direct** (☎ 0800/890016).

The country code for the U.S. and Canada is **1.** To make a **collect call,** or if you need an international operator, dial ☎ **155.**

Tipping In hotels, tip **porters** or **bellhops** 75p per bag, even if you have only one small suitcase. Hall porters are tipped only for special services. Tip **chamber staff** £1 per day. In top-ranking hotels, the **concierge** will often submit a separate bill showing charges for newspapers and other items; if he or she has been particularly helpful, tip extra. In restaurants and nightclubs, a 15% service charge is added to the bill, which is distributed among all the staff. To that, add another 3% to 5%, depending on the service. **Waiters** in deluxe restaurants and nightclubs are accustomed to the extra 5%. **Sommeliers** (wine stewards) get about £1 per bottle of wine served. Tipping in pubs isn't common, but in wine bars, the server usually gets about 75p per round of drinks.

Tip **cab drivers** 10% to 15% of the fare on the meter. If the driver loads or unloads your luggage, add something extra. Tip **barbers** and **hairdressers** 10% to 15%. It's not mandatory, but **tour guides** expect £2.

Note: Try not to tip by credit card in England, as—thanks to a 2002 court ruling—this money can then be used by the owner to make up serving staff's pay. Instead, tip with cash to ensure that your money rewards the right people.

LONDON

London is one of the world's great cities, with attractions for visitors of every age. It has a 2,000-year-old history and yet is as culturally cutting edge as tomorrow. There's no end of things to do and ways to enjoy the pulsating capital of the United Kingdom. Famous monuments such as the Tower of London and Westminster Abbey draw flocks of visitors every day, as they have for centuries. Pomp and ceremony still define Royal London, with its palaces and protocols. London's museums, nothing short of fabulous, are unrivaled in the scope and quality of their collections. And when it comes to nightlife, London has got it all: theater, dance, music of every kind, pubs, and late-night clubs—take your pick. Most important of all for the rail traveler, London's the major transit point to and from the Continent, and Great Britain's largest rail hub.

Station Information

GETTING FROM THE AIRPORT INTO TOWN

The odds are that you will arrive in London at either Heathrow or Gatwick, London's two main international airports (though it's possible that you'll land at Stansted, which now has some transatlantic flights). The other airports—Luton and London City—generally do not service scheduled international flights, only charters and European destinations.

FROM HEATHROW To get from Heathrow to the center of London, it takes 45 to 50 minutes via the **Underground (Tube)** and costs £4 to make the 15-mile (24km) trip. For more information about Tube or bus connections, call © **020/7222-1234** or go to www.tfl.gov.uk.

The quickest and most comfortable way into town is via **Heathrow Express** (© **0845/600-1515;** www.heathrowexpress.com), a 161kmph (100-mph) train service running every 15 minutes daily from 5:10am until 11:40pm between Heathrow and Paddington Station in the center of London. Trips cost £18 one-way in economy class, rising to £26 one-way in first class. Children 14 and younger pay £9 in economy, £13 in first class. (You can save £1.50 by booking online or by phone.) Tickets are sold at self-service machines at Heathrow Airport; if you purchase them on the train, you'll pay a surcharge of up to £5. BritRail Passes may be used on the Heathrow Express. Simply go to the ticket office to have your pass validated before boarding the train. The trip takes 15 minutes each way between Paddington and Terminals 1 and 3, and 23 minutes from Terminal 4. The trains have special areas for wheelchairs. From Paddington, you can connect to other trains and the Underground, or you can hail a taxi.

If you take a **taxi** to central London, the fare is likely to range from £50 to £80.

FROM GATWICK From Gatwick, the fastest way to get to London is via the **Gatwick Express** (© **0845/850-1530;** www.gatwickexpress.com). These trains depart approximately every 15 minutes daily between 4:35am and 1:35am. The one-way fare between Gatwick and Victoria Station in central London is £17 for adults and £8.45 for children. The travel time each way is 30 minutes Monday to Saturday, 35 minutes on Sunday. A Britrail Pass can be used on this train. It is cheaper to purchase a day travel card for £7, which is good for travel into London on the Southern route and on the Tube for the rest of the day.

A **taxi** from Gatwick to central London costs from £77 to £100. Fares vary according to a printed price list that defines the price from Gatwick to whichever neighborhood

London

ACCOMMODATIONS ■
Draycott Hotel **11**
Durrants Hotel **16**
Harlingford Hotel **26**
Hart House Hotel **14**
The Jenkins Hotel **21**
Malmaison London **34**
Mint Hotel
  Westminster **5**
Park Plaza Sherlock
  Holmes Hotel **15**
Rhodes Hotel **6**
The Rubens at
  the Palace **17**

10

GREAT BRITAIN & IRELAND | London

DINING ◆

The Criterion
Brasserie **24**
Gordon Ramsay **10**
Mela **23**
Mildreds **22**
Royal China **4**
Rules **28**
Salt Yard **20**
Scott's **13**
The Stockpot **25**
Zafferano **12**

ATTRACTIONS ●

Big Ben **31**
British Airways London Eye **30**
British Museum **27**
Buckingham Palace **19**
Houses of Parliament **31**
Kensington Palace **3**
National Gallery **29**
National History Museum **2**
Queen's Gallery **18**
St. Paul's Cathedral **35**
Science Museum **8**
Tate Britain **33**
Tate Modern **36**
Tower Bridge **38**
The Tower of London **37**
Victoria and Albert Museum **9**
Westminster Abbey **32**

of London you're traveling to. Meters, in this case, don't apply because Gatwick lies outside the Metropolitan Police District. For further transportation information, call ℂ 020/7222-1234.

INSIDE THE STATIONS

The British Rail train network connects London to all the major cities and most towns within the U.K. (and some European destinations; see "Britain by Train," earlier in this chapter). There are a number of major British Rail train stations in London, each serving different parts of the U.K. Each of these train stations is connected to the city's vast bus and Underground network, and each has phones, restaurants, pubs, luggage storage areas, and Transport for London Travel Information Centres. Tickets can be purchased at each station (ticket desks and machines) before boarding the train. For more information on the destinations each station serves, see "London's Major Train Stations," below. The station you travel to or from will be determined by where you're coming from or where you want to go. You can obtain 24-hour train information by calling **National Rail Enquiries**, at ℂ **0845/748-4950.**

If there's one station to keep in mind, especially if you plan on tackling the Continent as well as Britain, it's **St. Pancras International (www.stpancras.com),** which is the London hub for Eurostar. Restored and opened in 2007, it is the point where the high-speed Eurostar pulls into London, connecting England with Belgium and France through the Channel Tunnel.

The station boasts Europe's longest champagne bar, a daily farmers' market, all the Wi-Fi you'll ever need, plus dozens of boutiques—and some of the world's fastest trains. It is also served by six underground Tubes, including Victoria, Northern, Piccadilly, Circle, Hammersmith & City, and Metropolitan, as well as seven other rail companies. With such a vast network of transport, you can head virtually anywhere in greater London.

London's Major Train Stations*

Station	Destinations Served
Charing Cross	Trains travel southeast to Canterbury, Hastings, Dover, and English Channel ports that connect with ferry service to the Continent.
Euston	Trains head northwest to the Lake District, up to Scotland (overnight service to Scotland), and to Holyhead for ferries to Ireland.
Kings Cross	Trains travel to destinations in the east and north of England, including York, and up to Edinburgh.
Liverpool Street	Trains head east to English Channel ports, with connecting ferry service to the Netherlands and Denmark.
Paddington	Trains travel to Heathrow airport and southwest to Bath, the West Country, and South Wales.
St. Pancras	Handles Eurostar trains to Paris and Brussels, as well as trains to the midlands and high-speed regional trains to the Southeast.
Victoria	Trains head for Gatwick airport and the southeast, including Canterbury and Brighton.
Waterloo	Trains go primarily to the south of England.

* In addition to the mainline stations, there are numerous regional stations, including Blackfriars, Charing Cross, London Bridge, Marylebone, Stratford, and Clapham Junction.

If all you need is a hotel room, the simplest way to get one is to call the reliable **British Hotel Reservation Centre** (☏ 020/7592-3055; www.bhrc.co.uk); they book hotel rooms in all price categories and offer some very attractive discounts.

Information Elsewhere in the City

Visit London, the official tourism organization for London, operates the **Britain and London Visitor Centre (BLVC),** 1 Lower Regent St., London SW1Y 4XT (☏ 8701/566-366; www.visitlondon.com; Tube: Piccadilly Circus), which can help you with almost anything, from the most superficial to the most serious. Located within a 10-minute walk from Piccadilly Circus, it deals chiefly with booking accommodations in all price categories through an on-site travel agency (www.lastminute.com), which can also book transit on British Rail or with bus carriers throughout the U.K. There's a kiosk for procuring theater or group tour tickets, a bookshop loaded with titles dealing with travel in the British Isles, a souvenir shop, and a staff that's pleasant, helpful, and friendly. It's open year-round Monday 9:30am to 6:30pm, Tuesday through Friday 9am to 6:30pm, and Sunday 9am to 5pm. Between October and May, Saturday hours are 10am to 4pm, and between June and September, Saturday hours are 9am to 5pm.

Getting Around

London's a great walking city, but distances are simply too large to make getting everywhere on your own two feet a viable option. Without question, public transportation is the way to go. Tube and bus maps are available at all Underground stations, or you can download them before your trip from the excellent Transport for London (TfL) website, at **www.tfl.gov.uk/tfl**. You can also call the 24-hour **travel hot line** (☏ 020/7222-1234) for information on how to get from one point to another. TfL also runs **Travel Information Centres** at several major Tube stations (Kings Cross, Liverpool Street, and Piccadilly Circus), at the rail stations at Euston and Victoria, and at Heathrow Airport's Terminal 123 Tube station. Most of them are open daily from at least 9am to 5pm.

BY UNDERGROUND

The Underground, or Tube, is the fastest and easiest way to get around. All Tube stations are clearly marked with a red circle and blue crossbar. Routes are conveniently color-coded. Route maps are posted everywhere, and signs above the tracks will let you know how long you'll need to wait before your train arrives.

If you have British coins or a credit card, you can get your ticket at a vending machine. Otherwise, buy it at the ticket office. You can transfer as many times as you like, as long as you stay in the Underground. Children 4 and younger travel free if accompanied by an adult.

Slide your ticket into the slot at the gate and pick it up as it comes through on the other side, and hold on to it—it must be presented when you exit the station at your destination. If you're caught without a valid ticket, you'll be fined £20 on the spot. If you owe extra money, you'll be asked to pay the difference by the attendant at the exit. The Tube runs roughly from 5am to 12:30am Monday to Saturday and 7:30am to 10:30pm Sunday. Outside those hours, you must take a taxi or night bus to your destination. For information on the London Tube system, call the **London Underground** at ☏ 020/7222-1234, but expect to stay on hold for a good while before a live person comes on the line. Information is also available online at **www.tfl.gov.uk**.

discount TRANSPORTATION PASSES

If you plan to use public transportation a lot, investigate the range of fare discounts available. **Travelcards** offer unlimited use of buses, Underground, Docklands Light Railway, and National Rail services in Greater London for any period ranging from a day to a year. Travelcards are available from Underground ticket offices, TfL Travel Information Centres, main post offices in the London area, many newsagents, and some newsstands. Children 10 and younger generally travel free on the Tube and buses when accompanied by an adult.

The **1-Day Travelcard** allows you to go anywhere throughout greater London. For travel within zones 1 and 2, the cost is £7.20 for adults, £3.60 for children 5 to 15. The **Off-Peak 1-Day Travelcard,** which is valid after 9:30am on weekdays, is even cheaper. For two zones, the cost is £5.60 for adults and £2 for children 5 to 15. The **1-Week Travelcard** for zones 1 and 2 costs £26 for adults and £13 for children 5 to 15.

Consider purchasing the **Oyster Card** (www.oystercard.com), a travel discount card that's all the rage. You can prepay for single fares, which cost considerably less than a paper ticket—usually about half the price. Oysters are valid on the Tube, DLR, tram, and National Rail services within your chosen zones and across the entire London bus network. For 24-hour information, call the Oyster hot line at ✆ **0871/2301100.** The card has a daily price cap, meaning you never pay more than £7.20, regardless of how many trips you make in 1 day. You can buy an Oyster Card at any ticket office.

The Jubilee Line Extension has been extended eastward to serve the growing suburbs of the southeast and the Docklands area. This east-west axis helps ease traffic on some of London's most hard-pressed Underground lines. The line also makes it much easier to reach Greenwich.

BY BUS

The comparably priced bus system is almost as good as the Underground and gives you better views of the city. To find out about current routes, pick up a free bus map at one of Transport for London's Travel Information Centres, listed above. You can also obtain a map at **www.tfl.gov.uk**.

As with the Underground, fares vary according to distance traveled. Generally, bus fares are £1.20 to £3.80. If you want your stop called out, simply ask the conductor or driver. To speed up bus travel, passengers have to purchase tickets before boarding; drivers no longer collect fares on board. Some 300 roadside ticket machines serve stops in central London—in other words, it's "pay as you board." You'll need the exact fare, however, as ticket machines don't make change.

Buses generally run 24 hours a day. A few night buses have special routes, running once an hour or so; most pass through Trafalgar Square. Keep in mind that night buses are often so crowded (especially on weekends) that they are unable to pick up passengers after a few stops. If you find yourself waiting a long time, you may want to take a taxi instead. Call the 24-hour **hot line** (✆ **020/7222-1234**) for bus schedule and fare information.

Where to Stay

Draycott Hotel ★★★ Everything about this radically upgraded hotel reeks of British gentility, style, and charm. Past clients are greeted like old friends by a staff that manages to be both hip and cordial. The Draycott took its present-day form when a third brick-fronted town house was added to a pair of interconnected town houses that had been functioning as a five-star hotel since the 1980s. That—coupled with tons of money spent on English antiques, rich draperies, and an upgrade of those expensive infrastructures you'll never see, including security—has transformed this place into a gem. Bedrooms are outfitted uniquely, each with haute English style and plenty of fashion chic. As a special feature, the hotel serves complimentary drinks— tea at 4pm, champagne at 6pm, and hot chocolate at 9:30pm.

26 Cadogan Gardens, London SW3 2RP. © **800/747-4942** or 020/7730-6466. Fax 020/7730-0236. www.draycotthotel.com. 35 units. £260–£315 double; £385 suite. AE, DC, MC, V. Tube: Sloane Sq. **Amenities:** Lounge.

Durrants Hotel ★ This historic hotel off Manchester Square (established in 1789), with its Georgian-detailed facade, is snug, cozy, and traditional. We find it to be one of the most quintessentially English of all London hotels—you could invite the queen to Durrants for tea. A walk through the pine-and-mahogany-paneled public rooms is like stepping back in time: You'll even find an 18th-century letter-writing room. The guest rooms are rather bland except for elaborate cove moldings and comfortable furnishings, and bathrooms are tiny. It's an ideal location for the shopping of Oxford Street and for taking quick nips across the street to the Wallace Collection, a jewel of a small museum.

26–32 George St., London W1H 5BJ. © **020/7935-8131.** Fax 020/7487-3510. www.durrantshotel.co.uk. 92 units. £250 double; £265 family room for 3; £295–£425 suite. AE, MC, V. Tube: Bond St. or Baker St. **Amenities:** Restaurant; bar; lounge. *In room:* No A/C (in some).

Harlingford Hotel   This hotel comprises three town houses built in the 1820s and joined around 1900 with a bewildering array of staircases and meandering hallways. Set in the heart of Bloomsbury, it's run by folks who seem genuinely concerned about the welfare of their guests, unlike the management at many of the neighboring hotel rivals. Double-glazed windows cut down on the street noise, and all rooms are inviting. The most comfortable units are on the second and third levels (avoid rooms on the ground level), but expect to climb some steep English stairs (there's no elevator).

A Stroll Through the City

You may not be able to get around the city by shoe leather alone, but London's still a great walking town when taken in small doses. Stroll in London's great parks: Kensington Gardens, Hyde Park, Green Park, St. James's Park, and Regent's Park offer beautiful paths, fountains, trees, flowers, and meadows. Or pick a neighborhood and stroll down its historic streets, admiring the architecture, the hidden mews, and the garden squares. One of the most pleasant London walks is along the Thames on the South Bank: Starting at the south side of Westminster Bridge, you can follow a riverside path all the way down to Tower Bridge, or cut over the Thames to St. Paul's Cathedral on the Millennium footbridge.

61-63 Cartwright Gardens, London WC1H 9EL. © **020/7387-1551.** Fax 020/7387-4616. www.harlingfordhotel.com. 43 units. £110 double; £125 triple; £135 quad. Rates include English breakfast. AE, MC, V. Tube: Russell Sq., Kings Cross, or Euston. **Amenities:** Lounge. *In room:* No A/C.

Hart House Hotel ★   A long-enduring favorite with Frommer's readers, and popular with families, this well-preserved historic building—one of a group of Georgian mansions occupied by exiled French nobles during the French Revolution—lies within easy walking distance of many West End theaters. The comfortably appointed rooms are spick-and-span, each one with a different character. They're decorated with a combination of furnishings, ranging from Portobello antique to modern. Favorites include no. 7, a triple with a big bathroom and shower, and no. 11, on the top floor, for a brightly lit aerie.

51 Gloucester Place, Portman Sq., London W1U 8JF. © **020/7935-2288.** Fax 020/7935-8516. www.harthouse.co.uk. 15 units. £110–£150 double; £130–£175 triple; £155–£185 quad. Rates include English breakfast. MC, V. Tube: Marble Arch or Baker St. **Amenities:** Smoke-free rooms. *In room:* No A/C.

The Jenkins Hotel ★ ✦   Followers of the Agatha Christie TV series *Poirot* will recognize this residence—it was featured in the series. The antiques are gone and the rooms are small, but some of the original charm of the Georgian house remains—enough so that the *London Mail* proclaimed it one of the "10 best hotel values" in the city. All the rooms have been redecorated in traditional Georgian style and have fridges and free Wi-Fi. The location is great, near Euston Station and the British Museum. There are some drawbacks: no elevator and no reception or sitting room. But this is a place where you can settle in and feel at home.

45 Cartwright Gardens, London WC1H 9EH. © **020/7387-2067.** Fax 020/7383-3139. www.jenkinshotel.demon.co.uk. 14 units. £95 double; £110 triple. Rates include English breakfast. MC, V. Tube: Russell Sq., Kings Cross, or Euston. *In room:* No A/C.

Malmaison London ★★   Who could imagine that this used to be a dreary nursing home? Talk about recycling. The Victorian mansion block overlooks a green cobbled square and is the London showcase for the U.K.-only hotel chain that is known for opening up winning hotels with clever contemporary designs, state-of-the-art facilities, and, as always, a chic little brasserie serving French classics. On the southern rim of now trendy Clerkenwell, Malmaison is awash in dark teakwood; tall, glowing floor lamps; a highly polished European staff; and tasteful fabrics in neutral shades. The dark-wood guest rooms are individually designed and larger than average for central London.

18-21 Charterhouse Sq., London EC1M 6AH. © **020/7012-3700.** Fax 020/7012-3702. www.malmaison.com. 97 units. £225–£295 double; £315–£520 suite. AE, MC, V. Tube: Barbican or Farringdon. **Amenities:** Bar; restaurant; smoke-free rooms.

Mint Hotel Westminster ★   This elegant Victorian town house is ideally situated, overlooking Hyde Park and a short walk from Paddington Station. Amid the buzz and excitement of central London, the hotel's atmosphere is an oasis of charm and refinement. Individually decorated rooms remind us of staying in an English country house and offer free Wi-Fi. Deluxe rooms are fully air-conditioned, and some contain four-poster beds; executive units usually contain one double or twin bed. Some rooms have special features such as Victorian antique fireplaces.

30 John Islip St., London SW1P 4DD. © **020/7630-1000.** Fax 020/7233-7575. www.cityinn.com. 460 units. £119–£159 double; £139–£179 city club room; £219–£259 suite. AE, DC, MC, V. Tube: Pimlico or Westminster. **Amenities:** Restaurant; 2 bars.

Park Plaza Sherlock Holmes Hotel   It's not located at that legendary address, 221B Baker St., but it is within walking distance of Marylebone Station. The converted boutique hotel was once part of Bedford College for Women and later the YWCA. Former tenants wouldn't know the place today. Modern portraits of the world's most famous detective are on display, but the decor is contemporary. Bedrooms come in a wide range of sizes and styles, ranked superior, executive, or studio. Most preferred, at least by us, is a trio of loft suites. Guests gather in **Sherlock's Bar & Grill** for good British beer and food.

108 Baker St., London W1U 6LJ. ⓒ **888/201-1803** or 020/7486-6161. Fax 020/7958-5211. www.park plazasherlockholmes.com. 119 units. £109–£144 double; £139–£485 studio/loft-suite. AE, MC, V. Tube: Baker St. **Amenities:** Restaurant; bar.

Rhodes Hotel ★   This elegant late-Georgian house, just a short stroll from Paddington Station, is decorated with a certain theatrical flair. The owners, Chris and Maria Crias, have poured many pounds into their hotel to give it a cozy charm, with a Victorian curtained lounge, Greek murals, lacquered walls, and *trompe l'oeil* bambini on puffy clouds. Creature comforts weren't ignored, either. You'll find air-conditioning—a bit of a rarity in the neighborhood, especially at these prices—plus Asian rugs, fridges, and up-to-date bathrooms. The superior accommodations have Jacuzzi baths and private terraces, and there's a good bunkroom for families.

195 Sussex Gardens, London W2 2RJ. ⓒ **020/7262-0537.** Fax 020/7723-4054. www.rhodeshotel.com. 36 units. £90–£110 double; £105–£115 triple; £125–£145 family. Rates include buffet breakfast. MC, V. Tube: Paddington or Lancaster Gate. **Amenities:** Breakfast room; lounge.

The Rubens at the Palace ★★ ✦   The very British Rubens is popular with Americans and Europeans seeking traditional English hospitality while enjoying the latest creature comforts. And its location is one of the best in town directly across the street from Buckingham Palace and only a 2-minute walk from Victoria Station. The public rooms are lavishly decorated with antiques, fabric wallcoverings, and fresh flowers. The size and decor of the guest rooms vary, but all feature grand comfort. Housed in a private wing, each of the eight "Royal Rooms" is named for an English monarch and is decorated in the style of that ruler's period.

39 Buckingham Palace Rd., London SW1W 0PS. ⓒ **877/955-1515** in the U.S. and Canada, or 020/7834-6600. Fax 020/7828-5401. www.rubenshotel.com. 161 units. £139–£169 double; £189 Royal Room; £279–£579 suite. AE, DC, MC, V. Tube: Victoria. **Amenities:** 2 restaurants; bar.

Top Attractions & Special Moments

British Airways London Eye ★   Located on the south bank of the Thames, across from the Houses of Parliament, this 443-foot-high (133m) structure is the world's largest observation wheel and offers panoramic views extending for some 25 miles (40km) when the weather's clear. Passengers are carried in 32 "pods," each making a complete revolution every half-hour (a pod holds about 25 passengers and is large enough for everyone to move around in). Along the way, you'll see some of London's most famous landmarks from a bird's-eye view. The wheel uses a timed-entry system; book your "boarding ticket" in advance to avoid standing in line.

Jubilee Gardens, SE1. ⓒ **0870/500-0600.** www.ba-londoneye.com. Admission £18 adults, £14 seniors and students, £9.50 children 4–15, children 3 and under free. Book online for 10% discount. Daily 10am–8pm (until 9pm June–Sept). Tube: Waterloo, Westminster. River services: Festival Pier.

British Museum ★★★   Set in scholarly Bloomsbury, this immense museum grew out of a private collection of manuscripts purchased in 1753 with the proceeds of a lottery. It grew and grew, fed by legacies, discoveries, and purchases, until it became one of the most comprehensive collections of art and artifacts in the world. It's impossible to take in this museum in a day.

The museum is divided basically into the national collections of antiquities; prints and drawings; coins, medals, and banknotes; and ethnography. Even on a cursory first visit, be sure to see the Asian collections (the finest assembly of Islamic pottery outside the Islamic world), the Chinese porcelain, the Indian sculpture, and the prehistoric and Romano-British collections. Special treasures you might want to seek out on your first visit include the **Rosetta Stone,** in the Egyptian Room, the discovery of which led to the deciphering of hieroglyphics; the **Parthenon Sculptures,** a series of pediments, metopes, and friezes from the Parthenon in Athens, in the Duveen Gallery; and the legendary **Black Obelisk,** dating from around 860 B.C., in the Nimrud Gallery. Other treasures include the contents of Egyptian royal tombs (including mummies); fabulous arrays of 2,000-year-old jewelry, cosmetics, weapons, furniture, and tools; Babylonian astronomical instruments; and winged lion statues (in the Assyrian Transept) that guarded Ashurnasirpal's palace at Nimrud. The exhibits change throughout the year, so if your heart is set on seeing a specific treasure, call to make sure it's on display.

Insider's tip: If you're a first-time visitor, you will, of course, want to concentrate on some of the fabled treasures previewed above. But what we do is duck into the British Museum several times on our visits to London, even if we have only an hour or two, to see the less heralded but equally fascinating exhibits. We recommend wandering rooms 33 and 34, and 91 to 94, to take in the glory of the Orient, covering Taoism, Confucianism, and Buddhism. The Chinese collection is particularly strong. Sculpture from India is as fine as anything at the Victoria and Albert. The Mexican Gallery in room 33C traces that country's art from the 2nd millennium B.C. to the 16th century A.D. A gallery for the North American collection is also nearby. Another section of the museum is devoted to the **Sainsbury African Galleries ★**, one of the finest collections of African art and artifacts in the world, featuring changing displays selected from more than 200,000 objects. Finally, the Money Gallery in room 68 traces the story of (what else?) money. You'll learn that, around 2000 B.C. in Mesopotamia, grain was used as currency, and that printed money came into being in the 10th century in China.

The museum's inner courtyard is now canopied by a lightweight, transparent roof, transforming the area into a covered square that houses a Centre for Education, exhibition space, bookshops, and restaurants. The center of the Great Court features the Round Reading Room, which is famous as the place where Karl Marx hung out while writing *Das Kapital.*

Warning: Watch your wallets when you're standing in crowds, particularly in front of the Rosetta Stone. The museum is free and tends to attract a few grab-happy drifters.

Great Russell St., WC1. ℂ **020/7323-8299** or 020/7636-1555 for recorded information. www.british museum.org. Free admission. Sat–Wed 10am–5:30pm; Thurs–Fri 10am–8:30pm. Tube: Holborn, Tottenham Court Rd., Goodge St., or Russell Sq.

Buckingham Palace ★★   This massive, graceful building is the official residence of the Queen. The redbrick palace was built as a country house for the notoriously rakish Duke of Buckingham. In 1762, King George III, who needed room for his 15 children, bought it. It didn't become the official royal residence, though, until Queen Victoria took the throne; she preferred it to St. James's Palace. From George III's time,

Changing of the Guard

Buckingham Palace's most famous spectacle is the vastly overrated **Changing of the Guard** (daily Apr–July and on alternating days for the rest of the year). The new guard, marching behind a band, comes from either the Wellington or Chelsea barracks and takes over from the old guard in the forecourt of the palace. The ceremony begins at 11:30am, although it's frequently canceled because of bad weather, state events, and other, harder-to-fathom reasons. If you insist on checking it out, arrive as early as 10:30am and claim territorial rights to a space in front of the palace. If you're not firmly anchored here, you'll miss much of the ceremony.

the building was continuously expanded and remodeled, faced with Portland stone, and twice bombed (during the Blitz). Located in a 40-acre (16-hectare) garden, it's 354 feet (106m) long and contains 600 rooms. You can tell whether the Queen is at home by checking to see if the Royal Standard is flying from the mast outside. For most of the year, you can't visit the palace without an official invitation. Since 1993, though, much of it has been open for tours during an 8-week period in August and September, when the royal family is usually vacationing outside London. Elizabeth II agreed to allow visitors to tour the State Room, the Grand Staircase, the Throne Room, and other areas designed by John Nash for George IV, as well as the Picture Gallery, which displays masterpieces by Van Dyck, Rembrandt, Rubens, and others. You have to buy a timed-entrance ticket the same day you plan to tour the palace. Tickets go on sale at 9am, but rather than lining up at sunrise with all the other tourists—this is one of London's most popular attractions—book by phone with a credit card and give yourself a few more hours of sleep.

At end of the Mall (on the road running from Trafalgar Sq.). © **020/7766-7300.** www.royalcollection. org.uk. Palace tours £17 adults, £16 61 and older and students, £9.75 16 and younger, family ticket £45, free for ages 4 and younger; Changing of the Guard free. Aug 1–Sept 27 (dates can vary), and additional dates may be added. Daily 9:45am–6pm. Changing of the Guard daily Apr–July at 11:30am and alternating days for the rest of the year at 11am. Tube: St. James's Park, Green Park, or Victoria.

Houses of Parliament & Big Ben ★★ The Houses of Parliament, along with their trademark clock tower, Big Ben, are the ultimate symbols of London. They're the strongholds of Britain's democracy, the assemblies that effectively trimmed the sails of royal power. Both the House of Commons and the House of Lords are in the former royal Palace of Westminster, which was the king's residence until Henry VIII moved to Whitehall. The current Gothic Revival buildings date from 1840 and were designed by Charles Barry. (The earlier buildings were destroyed by fire in 1834.) Assisting Barry was Augustus Welby Pugin, who designed the paneled ceilings, tiled floors, stained glass, clocks, fireplaces, umbrella stands, and even inkwells. There are more than 1,000 rooms and 1¾ miles (2.8km) of corridors. The clock tower at the eastern end houses the world's most famous timepiece. **"Big Ben"** refers not to the clock tower itself, but to the largest bell in the chime, which weighs close to 14 tons and is named for the first commissioner of works, Sir Benjamin Hall.

You may observe debates for free from the **Stranger's Galleries** in both houses. Sessions usually begin in mid-October and run to the end of July, with recesses at Christmas and Easter. The chances of getting into the House of Lords when it's in session are generally better than for the more popular House of Commons. Although we can't promise you the oratory of a Charles James Fox or a William Pitt the Elder, the debates in the House of Commons are often lively and controversial (seats are at a premium during crises). You'll need a card of introduction to observe a session. Foreign and Commonwealth visitors should apply to their embassy or High Commission in the U.K. for a card of introduction, which will normally permit entry during the early afternoon. Embassies and High Commissions may issue no more than four cards on any day, so visitors from certain countries may find cards are booked for several weeks ahead. Please note that such cards do not guarantee entry. British embassies abroad do not issue such cards.

With your card of introduction in hand, you line up at Stephen's Gate, heading to your left for the entrance into the Commons or to the right for the Lords. The London daily newspapers announce sessions of Parliament.

Insider's tip: The hottest ticket and the most exciting time to visit is during Prime Minister's Question Time on Wednesdays, which is only from noon to 12:30pm, but which must seem like hours to Gordon Brown, who is on the hot seat.

Westminster Palace, Old Palace Yard, SW1. House of Commons © **020/7219-4272;** House of Lords © **020/7219-3107.** www.parliament.uk. Free admission. Mid-Oct to Aug Mon–Tues 9am–noon; Wed 9–9:20am; Fri 3:30–5pm. Join line at St. Stephen's entrance. Tube: Westminster.

Kensington Palace ★   Located at the western edge of Kensington Gardens, Kensington Palace was acquired by William and Mary in 1689 and remodeled by Sir Christopher Wren. George II, who died in 1760, was the last king to use it as a royal residence. Princess Diana lived here when in London; the area in front of the palace drew tens of thousands of mourners after her death, a sea of flowers and tributes testifying to a nation's grief.

You can tour the main **State Apartments** of the palace, but many rooms are private and still lived in by lesser Royals, whose "grace and favour" flats are soon to be a thing of the past as the monarchy tries to modernize its operations and trim its expenses. One of the more interesting chambers to visit is Queen Victoria's bedroom, where, on the morning of June 20, 1837, the 18-year-old was roused from her sleep with the news that she was now queen. As you wander through the apartments, you'll see many fine paintings from the Royal Collection. A special attraction is the **Royal Ceremonial Dress Collection,** set in several restored rooms from the 19th century, where you'll find a series of settings with the appropriate court dress of the day and some of Diana's famous frocks. The former apartment of the late Princess Margaret—a fashion icon in her time—is also open to the public.

The Broad Walk, Kensington Gardens, W8. © **0844/482-7777.** www.hrp.org.uk. Admission £13 adults, £11 seniors and students, £6.25 children 5-15, £34 family ticket. Mar–Oct daily 10am–6pm; Nov–Feb daily 10am–5pm. Tube: Queensway or Notting Hill Gate; High St. Kensington on south side.

National Gallery ★★★   One of the finest art museums in the world, Britain's national art collection comprises more than 2,300 paintings dating from 1260 to 1900, supplemented by masterpieces on loan from private collectors. The gallery is arranged in four time bands. The **Sainsbury Wing** shows work from 1260 to 1510 by such artists as Giotto, Botticelli, Leonardo da Vinci, and Raphael. The **West Wing** takes on the next 90 years, with El Greco, Holbein, Bruegel, Michelangelo, Titian, and Veronese. The **North Wing** holds the 17th-century masters, including Rubens, Poussin, Velázquez, Rembrandt, and Vermeer. Works by Stubbs, Gainsborough, Constable, Turner, Canaletto, van Gogh, Corot, Monet, Manet, Renoir, and Cézanne can all be found in the **East Wing.** Very famous works in the museum's collection include Leonardo's *Virgin of the Rocks*, Titian's *Bacchus and Ariadne*, van Eyck's *Arnolfini Portrait*, and El Greco's *Agony in the Garden*.

There's a free (donation invited) audio guide to every painting on the main floor, and free guided tours start at 11:30am and 2:30pm every day. Most of the gallery talks are also free. The National Gallery also has a computer information center, located in the Micro Gallery, where you can design your own personal tour map for free.

North side of Trafalgar Sq., WC2. © **020/7747-2885**. www.nationalgallery.org.uk. Free admission. Thurs–Tues 10am–6pm; Wed 10am–9pm. Tube: Charing Cross or Leicester Sq.

Natural History Museum ★★ This is the home of the national collections of living and fossil plants, animals, and minerals, with many magnificent specimens on display. The zoological displays are quite wonderful. Exciting exhibits designed to encourage people of all ages to learn about natural history include "Human Biology—An Exhibition of Ourselves," "Our Place in Evolution," "Origin of the Species," "Creepy Crawlies," and "Discovering Mammals." The Mineral Gallery displays marvelous examples of crystals and gemstones. Visit the Meteorite Pavilion, which exhibits fragments of rocks that have crashed into the earth, some from the farthest reaches of the galaxy. The dinosaur exhibit attracts the most attention, displaying 14 complete skeletons. "Earth Galleries" is an exhibition outlining humankind's relationship with planet Earth. Here, in the section "Earth Today and Tomorrow," visitors are invited to explore the planet's dramatic history, from the big bang to its inevitable death. The latest development here is the new Darwin Centre. Dedicated to the great naturalist Charles Darwin, the center reveals the museum's scientific research and outreach facilities and activities. You're given an insider look at the storage facilities—including 22 million preserved specimens—and the laboratories of the museum. Fourteen behind-the-scenes free tours (ages 10 and up only) are given daily; you should book immediately upon entering the museum if you're interested.

Cromwell Rd., SW7. © **020/7942-5000**. www.nhm.ac.uk. Free admission. Mon–Sat 10am–5:50pm; Sun 11am–5:50pm. Tube: S. Kensington.

The Queen's Gallery ★★ The refurbished gallery on the grounds of Buckingham Palace reopened to the public in 2002 in time for the Golden Jubilee celebration of Queen Elizabeth II. The 1831 building by John Nash was converted to a chapel for Queen Victoria in 1843 and later destroyed in an air raid in 1940. Today the gallery is dedicated to changing exhibitions of the wide-ranging treasure-trove that forms the Royal Collection. You'll find special showings of paintings, prints, drawings, watercolors, furniture, porcelain, miniatures, enamels, jewelry, and other works of art. At any given time, you may see such artistic peaks as Van Dyck's equestrian portrait of Charles I; the world-famous *Lady at the Virginal*, by Vermeer; a dazzling array of gold snuffboxes; paintings by Monet from the collection of the late Queen Mother; personal jewelry; studies by Leonardo da Vinci; and even the very controversial portrait of the current queen by Lucian Freud.

Buckingham Palace, Buckingham Palace Rd., SW1. © **020/7766-7301**. www.royalcollection.org.uk. Admission £5 adults, £4.50 students and seniors, £3 children 5–16, free for children 4 and under. Daily 10am–5:30pm. Tube: Hyde Park Corner, Green Park, or Victoria.

Science Museum ★★★ This museum traces the development of science and industry and their influence on everyday life. These scientific collections are among the largest and most significant anywhere. On display is Stephenson's original rocket and the tiny prototype railroad engine; you can also see Whittle's original jet engine and the *Apollo 10* space module. The King George III Collection of scientific instruments is the highlight of a gallery on 18th-century science. The museum has two hands-on galleries, as well as working models and video displays.

Insider's tip: A large addition to this museum explores such topics as genetics, digital technology, and artificial intelligence. Four floors of a new Welcome Wing shelter half a dozen exhibition areas and a 450-seat IMAX theater. On an upper floor, visitors can learn how DNA was used to identify living relatives of the Bleadon Man, a 2,000-year-old Iron Age man. On the third floor is the computer that Tim Berners-Lee used to design the World Wide Web outside Geneva, writing the first software for it in 1990.

Note also the marvelous interactive consoles placed strategically in locations throughout the museum. These display special itineraries, including directions to the various galleries for families, teens, adults, and those with special interests.

Exhibition Rd., SW7. ℂ **087/0870-4868.** www.sciencemuseum.org.uk. Free admission. Daily 10am–6pm. Closed Dec 24–26. Tube: S. Kensington.

St. Paul's Cathedral ★★★ During World War II, newsreel footage reaching America showed St. Paul's Cathedral standing virtually alone among the rubble of the City, its dome lit by fires caused by bombings all around it. That the cathedral survived at all is a miracle, since it was badly hit twice during the early years of the bombardment of London. But St. Paul's is accustomed to calamity, having been burned down three times and destroyed by invading Norsemen. The old St. Paul's was razed during the Great Fire of 1666, making way for a new structure designed by Sir Christopher Wren and built between 1675 and 1710. The cathedral is architectural genius Wren's ultimate masterpiece.

The classical dome of St. Paul's dominates the City's square mile. The golden cross surmounting it is 361 feet (108m) above the ground; the golden ball on which the cross rests measures 6½ feet (2m) in diameter, though it looks like a marble from below. In the interior of the dome is the **Whispering Gallery,** an acoustic marvel in which the faintest whisper can be heard clearly on the opposite side. Sit on one side, have your traveling companions sit on the other, and whisper away. You can climb to the top of the dome for a 360-degree view of London. A second steep climb leads from the Whispering Gallery to the **Stone Gallery,** which opens onto a panoramic view of London. Another 153 steps take you to the **Inner Golden Gallery,** situated at the top of the inner dome. Here an even more panoramic view of London unfolds.

St. Paul's Churchyard, EC4. ℂ **020/7246-8350.** www.stpauls.co.uk. Cathedral and galleries £13 adults, £12 seniors and students, £4.50 children 6–16, £30 family ticket, free for children 5 and younger; guided tours £3 adults, £2.50 students and seniors, £1 children; recorded tours £4, free for children 5 and younger. Cathedral (excluding galleries) Mon–Sat 8:30am–4pm; galleries Mon–Sat 9:30am–4pm. No sightseeing Sun (services only). Tube: St. Paul's, Mansion House, Cannon St., or Blackfriars.

Tate Britain ★★★ Founded in 1897, the most prestigious gallery in Britain houses the national collections, covering British art from the 16th century to the present day, as well as an array of international works. The older works include some of the best of Gainsborough, Reynolds, Stubbs, Blake, and Constable. William Hogarth is well represented, particularly by his satirical *O the Roast Beef of Old England* (known as *The Gate of Calais*). You'll find the illustrations of William Blake, the incomparable mystical poet, including such works as *The Book of Job, The Divine Comedy,* and *Paradise Lost.* The collection of works by J. M. W. Turner is the Tate's largest collection of works by a single artist—Turner himself willed most of his paintings and watercolors to the nation.

Also on display are the works of many major 19th- and 20th-century painters, including Paul Nash, Matisse, Dalí, Modigliani, Munch, Bonnard, and Picasso. Truly remarkable are the several enormous abstract canvases by Mark Rothko, the group of paintings and sculptures by Giacometti, and the paintings by one of England's best-known modern artists, Francis Bacon.

Millbank, SW1. © **020/7887-8008.** www.tate.org.uk. Free admission; special exhibitions sometimes incur a charge of £5–£15. Daily 10:30am–5:50pm. Tube: Pimlico.

Tate Modern ★★★ The Tate Modern, London's wildly popular cathedral of modern art, occupies the defunct Bankside Power Station on the South Bank of the Thames opposite St. Paul's Cathedral. Instead of exhibiting art chronologically and by school, the Tate Modern, in a radical break from tradition, takes a thematic approach. This allows displays to cut across movements. All the big painting stars are here—a whole galaxy ranging from Dalí to Duchamp, from Giacometti to Matisse and Mondrian, from Picasso and Pollock to Rothko and Warhol. The Modern is also a gallery of 21st-century art, displaying new and exciting works.

Bankside, SE1. © **020/7887-8888.** www.tate.org.uk. Free admission. Sun–Thurs 10am–6pm; Fri–Sat 10am–10pm. Tube: Southwark or Blackfriars.

Tower Bridge ★★ This is one of the world's most celebrated landmarks and possibly the most photographed and painted bridge on earth. Despite its medieval appearance, Tower Bridge was built in 1894. In 1993, the Tower Bridge Exhibition opened inside the bridge to commemorate its century-old history; it takes you up the north tower to high-level walkways between the two towers with spectacular views of St. Paul's, the Tower of London, and the Houses of Parliament. You're then led down the south tower and into the bridge's original engine room, containing the Victorian boilers and steam engines that used to raise and lower the bridge for ships to pass. Exhibits in the towers use animatronic characters, video, and computers to illustrate the history of the bridge.

Tower Bridge Rd., SE1. © **020/7403-3761.** www.towerbridge.org.uk. Tower Bridge Exhibition £7 adults, £5 students and seniors, £3 children 5–15, £14 family ticket, free for children 4 and younger. Tower Bridge Exhibition Apr–Sept daily 10am–6:30pm; off season daily 9:30am–6pm. Closed Dec 24–26. Tube: Tower Hill, London Bridge, or Fenchurch St.

The Tower of London ★★★ 📷 This is the most perfectly preserved medieval fortress in Britain, and you'll need at least 2 or 3 hours for your visit. Over the centuries, the Tower has served as a palace and royal refuge; a prison, military base, and supplies depot; home to the Royal Mint and the Royal Observatory; and finally a national monument. The oldest part is the massive **White Tower,** built in 1078 by the Norman king, William the Conqueror, to protect London and discourage rebellion among his new Saxon subjects. Every king after him added to the main structure, so when Edward I completed the outer walls in the late 13th century, they enclosed an 18-acre (7.2-hectare) square.

The **Crown Jewels** are hugely popular, with people queuing to gape at the glorious gems, which include the Imperial State Crown, encrusted with 3,200 precious stones and one gob-smacking 317-carat diamond. **The Chapel Royal of St. Peter ad Vincula** contains the graves of all the unfortunates executed at the Tower. The Scaffold Site, where the axe man dispatched seven of the highest-ranking victims, including two of Henry VIII's six wives, Anne Boleyn and Catherine Howard, is just outside.

Everyone else met his or her end on **Tower Green** after arriving by boat at **Traitors' Gate.** The **Bloody Tower** was, according to Shakespeare, where Richard III's henchmen murdered the two little princes (the young sons of his brother, Edward IV). Richard knew his position as king could not be secure as long as his nephews were alive, and there seems no reasonable doubt that the princes were killed on his orders.

One-hour guided tours of the entire compound are given by the Yeoman Warders (also known as "Beefeaters") every half-hour, starting at 9:30am, from the Middle Tower near the main entrance. The last guided walk starts about 3:30pm in summer, 2:30pm in winter—weather permitting, of course. Costumed guides also re-create historic happenings or simply chat you up without breaking character. Booking tickets prior to your visit is a great time-saver.

Tower Hill, EC3. © **0844/482-7777.** www.hrp.org.uk. Admission £17 adults, £15 students and seniors, £9.50 children ages 5–15, family ticket £47, free for children 4 and under. Mar–Oct Tues–Sat 9am–5:30pm, Sun–Mon 10am–5:30pm; Nov–Feb Tues–Sat 9am–4:30pm, Sun–Mon 10am–4:30pm. Tube: Tower Hill.

Victoria and Albert Museum ★★★ 📷 The Victoria and Albert (V&A) is *the* greatest museum in the world devoted to the decorative arts. Its medieval holdings include such treasures as the early English Gloucester Candlestick; the Byzantine Veroli Casket, with its ivory panels based on Greek plays; and the Syon Cope, a highly valued embroidery made in England in the early 14th century. An area devoted to Islamic art houses the Ardabil Carpet from 16th-century Persia. The V&A houses the largest collection of **Renaissance sculpture** outside Italy and the greatest collection of **Indian art** outside India. One room displays Raphael's giant cartoons for tapestries for the Sistine Chapel. There are suites of furniture, metalwork, and ceramics, and a superb collection of portrait miniatures, including the one Hans Holbein the Younger made of Anne of Cleves for the wife-hunting Henry VIII. The **Dress Collection** includes a collection of corsetry through the ages that's sure to make you wince, and is regularly updated with exhibits from various eras or designers. The exceptional **British Galleries ★★★** are dedicated to British design from 1500 to 1900, with exhibits ranging from Chippendale to Mackintosh, as well as the "Great Bed of Ware," mentioned in Shakespeare's *Twelfth Night.*

In 2009, the **Gilbert Collection ★★★**, among the most distinguished decorative arts collections in the world, was moved to a suite of galleries in the V&A. Consisting of some 800 objects in three fields, the collection encompasses one of the world's most comprehensive arrays of mosaics, a stunning collection of some 200 gold snuff boxes, and an exceptional selection of gold and silver objects. Such exhibits as the Maharajah pieces, the "Gold Crown," and Catherine the Great's Royal Gates are fabulous.

Cromwell Rd., SW7. © **020/7942-2000.** www.vam.ac.uk. Free admission. Temporary exhibitions often £12. Daily 10am–5:45pm (until 10pm every Wed and the last Fri of each month). Tube: South Kensington.

Westminster Abbey ★★★ With its identical square towers and superb archways, this early-English Gothic abbey is one of the greatest examples of ecclesiastical architecture on earth. But it's far more than that: It's the shrine of a nation, the symbol of everything Britain has stood for and stands for, and the place in which most of its rulers were crowned and where many lie buried. The ancient building is neither a cathedral nor a parish church, but a "royal peculiar," under the jurisdiction of the Dean and Chapter of Westminster, and subject only to the Sovereign. Mostly dating from the 13th to 16th centuries, Westminster Abbey has played a prominent part in British history, most recently with the funeral of Princess Diana and, in 2002, of the Queen Mother. All but two coronations since 1066 have taken place here. The oak **Coronation Chair,** made in 1308 for Edward I, can be seen in the **Chapel of Edward the Confessor.** Five kings and four queens are buried in the beautiful, fan-vaulted **Chapel of Henry VII.** In 1400, Geoffrey Chaucer became the first literary celebrity to be buried in **Poets' Corner,** followed by Ben Jonson, Dryden, Samuel Johnson, Sheridan, Browning, and Tennyson. Statesmen and men of science—Disraeli, Newton, Charles Darwin—are also interred in the abbey or honored by monuments.

Broad Sanctuary, SW1. ℂ **020/7222-5152.** www.westminster-abbey.org. Admission £15 adults, £12 students and seniors, £6 children 11-18, £32 family ticket, free for children 10 and younger. Mon-Tues and Thurs-Fri 9:30am-3:45pm; Wed 9:30am-6pm; Sat 9:30am-2:45pm. Tube: Westminster or St. James's Park.

Where to Dine

The Criterion Brasserie ★ FRENCH/MODERN BRITISH Designed by Thomas Verity in the 1870s, this palatial neo-Byzantine mirrored marble hall is a glamorous backdrop for a superb cuisine, served under a golden ceiling, with theatrical peacock-blue draperies. The menu is wide ranging, offering everything from Paris brasserie food to "nouvelle-classical," a combination of classic French cooking techniques with some of the lighter, more experimental leanings of modern French cuisine. The food is excellent but falls short of sublime.

224 Piccadilly, W1. ℂ **020/7930-0488.** www.criterionrestaurant.com. Main courses £16-£26; 2- to 3-course lunch special £16-£19. AE, MC, V. Mon-Sat noon-2:30pm and 5:30-11:30pm; Sun noon-3:30pm and 5:30-6:30pm. Tube: Piccadilly Circus.

Gordon Ramsay ★★★ 🍴 FRENCH North Americans may know him best as the demanding host on the reality TV series *Hell's Kitchen,* but Gordon Ramsay is one of the city's most innovative and talented chefs in London. Every dish from this kitchen is gratifying, reflecting subtlety and delicacy without any sacrifice to the food's natural essence. The appetizers are dazzling (try the celebrated cappuccino of white beans with grated truffles), and the main courses, such as oven-roasted pigeon from Anjou wrapped in Parma ham with foie gras, are equally fabulous.

68 Royal Hospital Rd., SW3. ℂ **020/7352-4441.** www.gordonramsay.com. Reservations essential (1 month in advance). Fixed-price 3-course lunch £45, 3-course dinner £90, 7-course dinner £120. AE, DC, MC, V. Mon-Fri noon-2:30pm and 6:30-11pm. Tube: Sloane Sq.

 Eating at an Authentic Chippy

Déclassé or not, Britain's national dish of fish and chips was called "the good companions" by Sir Winston Churchill. Britons consume some 300 million fish-and-chips meals per year. We always head for London's oldest chippy (open since 1871), **Rock & Sole Plaice,** 47 Endell St., WC2 (ℂ **0871/426-3380;** Tube: Covent Garden), for our fish-and-chips fix.

The cooks here prefer to fry the fish, such as sweet, delicate lemon sole, in clean peanut oil instead of the traditional beef drippings. Fish here is cooked in a puffy, ale-colored batter. Count on spending from £10 to £15 for a dinner, served Monday to Saturday 11:30am to 10:30pm and Sunday noon to 10pm.

Mela ★ 🍴 INDIAN Serious foodies know you'll likely be served some of London's finest Indian cuisine at this address. This festive restaurant—its name means "fair"—is a huge hit with Indian expats and visiting Bollywood stars. It claims to take its inspiration from Wali Gali, where Delhi's workers go to refuel at midday from a food stall on the street. Tawa cookery (which in India is street food, cooked on a hot plate) is a specialty. At Mela, the fresh meats and other ingredients are cooked straight on a hot plate. Look for the chef's special Tawa dish of the day, perhaps queen prawns cooked with onions and fresh tomatoes. Save room for one of their special desserts.

152–156 Shaftesbury Ave., WC2. ✆ 020/7836-8635. www.melarestaurant.co.uk. Reservations required. Main courses £5.95–£22; 3-course fixed-price meal (available before 7pm) £11. AE, MC, V. Mon–Thurs noon–11:30pm; Fri noon–11:45pm; Sat 1–11:45pm; Sun noon–10:30pm. Tube: Tottenham Court Rd. or Leicester Sq.

Mildreds ★ 🍴 VEGETARIAN One of London's most enduring vegetarian and vegan dining spots is a busy, bustling diner with casual, friendly service. Sometimes it's a bit crowded and tables are shared. They do a mean series of delectable stir-fries. The ingredients in their dishes are organically grown, and they strongly emphasize the best seasonal produce. The menu changes daily but always features an array of homemade soups, casseroles, and salads. Organic wines are served, and portions are very large.

45 Lexington St., W1. ✆ 020/7494-1634. www.mildreds.co.uk. Reservations not accepted. Main courses £7–£9.25. No credit cards. Mon–Sat noon–11pm. Tube: Tottenham Court Rd.

Royal China ★ CANTONESE/SZECHUAN Unexpectedly delightful Cantonese and Szechuan specialties are available at this popular eatery, a family favorite. Come here for the best dim sum in London. We noticed a table of London Chinese raving about the jellyfish with sesame oil, although we opted for the sautéed prawns with fresh mango. Forget the garish decor and concentrate on what's on your plate—you'd probably have to go to Hong Kong to find Chinese cooking as authentic as this.

13 Queensway, W2. ✆ 020/7221-2535. Reservations recommended. Main courses £8–£55; fixed-price dinner £30–£38. AE, DC, MC, V. Mon–Thurs noon–11pm; Fri–Sat noon–11:30pm; Sun 11am–10pm. Tube: Bayswater or Queensway.

Rules ★ TRADITIONAL BRITISH If you're looking for London's most quintessentially British restaurant, eat here. London's oldest restaurant (Lillie Langtry and Edward VII used to tryst here) was established in 1798 as an oyster bar; today the antler-filled Edwardian dining rooms exude nostalgia. You can order such classic dishes as Irish or Scottish oysters, jugged hare, and mussels. Game and fish dishes are offered from mid-August to February or March, including wild Scottish salmon; wild sea trout; wild Highland red deer; and game birds such as grouse, snipe, partridge, pheasant, and woodcock. As a finale, the "great puddings" continue to impress.

35 Maiden Lane, WC2. ✆ 020/7836-5314. www.rules.co.uk. Reservations recommended. Main courses £17–£28. AE, DC, MC, V. Mon–Sat noon–11:30pm; Sun noon–10:30pm. Tube: Covent Garden.

Salt Yard ★ SPANISH/ITALIAN Calling itself a "charcuterie bar and restaurant," this is a fashionable choice with a bustling downstairs. The chefs here specialize in affordable plates of tasty Spanish and Italian dishes that are often shared. This joint is far superior to most tapas houses. How many places do you know that serve truffle-laced honey? Its Serrano ham, 18 months in "curing," is arguably the finest in London. Braised beef cheek comes with broad beans, and zucchini flowers are stuffed with Monte Enebro cheese and drizzled with honey. Fresh squid arrives with aioli, and bar snacks are also served.

The French had to show them how to do it, but Londoners have taken to sweet flaky pastries, tarts, and cakes with a vengeance. There are patisseries all over the city, but it's most fun to go to Soho and people-watch while you eat. The most venerable patisserie is **Maison Bertaux**, 28 Greek St., W1 (*℃* **020/7437-6007**), and we defy you to pass by its delectable window without wanting to dunk a brioche in a cup of coffee.

Patisserie Valerie has several branches in London, including one at 44 Old Compton St., W1 (*℃* **020/7437-3466; www.patisserie-valerie.co.uk**), in Soho. It's *the* place to gawk at greedy film and theater types who've fallen for its chocolate truffle cake.

54 Goodge St., W1. *℃* **020/7637-0657.** www.saltyard.co.uk. Reservations recommended. Tapas £3.50–£7.50; charcuterie platters £7.60–£13. AE, MC, V. Mon–Fri noon–11pm (3–6pm bar snacks only); Sat 5–11pm. Tube: Goodge St.

Scott's ★★ SEAFOOD   Opened as an oyster warehouse in 1851 by a young fishmonger, John Scott, this great restaurant first earned its fame at its Haymarket site where it resided until 1968. Now filled with cosmopolitan glitter in Mayfair, it doesn't rest on its long-ago fame but has made its reputation anew. Once a favorite of Ian Fleming, creator of the James Bond character, it was the setting in the '50s and '60s where he discovered the dry martini—"shaken, not stirred." It is dear to the seafood lover's heart, from market-fresh Dover sole to "cockles and mussels." Always ask about the fresh catch of the day, or else order filet of halibut with chervil butter or Scottish lobster thermidor.

20 Mount St., W1. *℃* **020/7495-7309.** www.scotts-restaurant.com. Reservations required. Main courses £16–£40. AE, DC, MC, V. Mon–Sat noon–10:30pm; Sun noon–10pm. Tube: Green Park or Bond St.

The Stockpot *♦* CONTINENTAL/TRADITIONAL BRITISH   Pound for pound (British pounds, that is), we'd hazard a guess that this cozy little restaurant offers one of the best dining bargains in London. Mains include such familiar favorites as beef Stroganoff or penne with ham and broccoli. You might also opt for the fish cakes with chips and salad or else a vegetable moussaka. Desserts include Jell-O and ice cream (if you're feeling nostalgic for childhood) or else a rhubarb crumble with vanilla custard. At these prices, the food is hardly refined, but it's filling and satisfying nonetheless. During peak hours, the Stockpot has a share-the-table policy in its dining room.

38 Panton St. (off Haymarket, opposite the Comedy Theatre), SW1. *℃* **020/7839-5142.** Reservations accepted for groups for dinner. Main courses £3.50–£6.95; fixed-price 2-course meal £6.50, 3-course meal £8.60. No credit cards. Mon–Tues 11:30am–11:30pm; Wed–Sat 11:30am–midnight; Sun noon–11:30pm. Tube: Piccadilly Circus or Leicester Sq.

Zafferano ★★ ITALIAN   There's something honest and satisfying about this restaurant, where decor consists of little more than ochre-colored walls, immaculate linens, and a bevy of diligent staff members. The modernized interpretation of Italian cuisine features such dishes as ravioli of pheasant with black truffles, wild pigeon with garlic purée, and monkfish with almonds. The owners pride themselves on one of the most esoteric and well-rounded collections of Italian wine in London: You'll find as many as 20 different vintages each of Brunello and Barolo, and about a dozen vintages of Sassecaia.

15 Lowndes St., SW1. ℂ **020/7235-5800.** www.zafferanorestaurant.com. Reservations required. Main courses £17–£25; set-price dinner menu £35–£55. AE, MC, V. Mon–Fri noon–2:30pm; Sat–Sun 12:30–3pm; daily 7–11pm (until 10:30pm Sun). Tube: Knightsbridge.

Shopping

London is one of the world's great shopping cities, with a vast and enticing array of department stores, boutiques, small shops, and markets. Major shopping areas are found in the West End, Knightsbridge, and Chelsea. Most stores are open Monday through Saturday from 10am to 6pm, and stay open until 8 or 9pm at least one night a week. Sunday shopping is now legal. Stores are allowed to be open for 6 hours; usually they choose 11am to 5pm. Major sales are held in January and June/July. Bargains you will probably not find, given the current murderous dollar-to-pound exchange rate, but there are some things here you won't necessarily find for less money (or even at all) anywhere else, such as antiques, some stationery, and British and European designer goods.

WEST END SHOPPING   Most of the department stores, designer shops, and chain stores have their flagships in the West End. **Oxford Street** is home to many large stores with prices that are more affordable than in other areas in the West End. Two of the department stores you might want to check out are **Marks & Spencer,** 458 Oxford St. (ℂ **020/7935-7954;** www.marksandspencer.com; Tube: Marble Arch), where you find well-made, if dull, basics of all kinds and styles; and the much more upscale **Selfridges,** 400 Oxford St. (ℂ **0800/123-400;** Tube: Marble Arch), one of the largest department stores in Europe. For affordable, hip clothing—supermodel Kate Moss designed a line here in 2007—brave the teen herds at **Top Shop,** 216 Oxford St. (ℂ **0844/848-7487;** www.topshop.com; Tube: Tottenham Court Rd.).

   Bond Street (Tube: Bond St.) is the address for the luxury trade and hot international designers. Here and on adjacent streets, you'll find a large selection of very expensive fashion boutiques and jewelry stores (think Chanel, Ferragamo, and Versace). For books, head to **Charing Cross Road,** where, among other booksellers, you'll find **Foyles,** 113–119 Charing Cross Rd., WC2 (ℂ **020/7437-5660;** Tube: Tottenham Court Rd.), which claims to be the largest bookshop in the world and carries an impressive array of hardcovers and paperbacks, as well as travel maps, records, and sheet music.

   The **Covent Garden Market** (ℂ **020/7836-9136;** www.coventgardenlondon uk.com; Tube: Covent Garden), in the restored Covent Garden fruit and vegetable market, offers several markets Monday to Saturday 10am to 6pm (we think it's most fun to come on Sun 11am–6pm). It can be a little confusing until you dive in and explore. **Apple Market** is the bustling market in the courtyard, where traders sell—well, everything. Out back is **Jubilee Market** (ℂ **020/7836-2139**), also an antiques market, which takes place on Monday; the rest of the week, it's sort of a fancy hippie market with cheap clothes and books. At the indoor market section of Covent Garden Market (in a superbly restored hall), specialty shops sell fashions and herbs, gifts and toys, books and dollhouses, cigars, and much more.

   Penhaligon's, 41 Wellington St., WC2 (ℂ **020/7836-2150;** www.penhaligons. co.uk; Tube: Covent Garden), has its own line of ladylike and light perfumes, as well as a large selection of after-shaves, soaps, candles, and bath oils.

   Curving **Regent Street,** just off Piccadilly Circus, is a major shopping street for all sorts of goods. **Liberty,** 214–220 Regent St., W1 (ℂ **020/7734-1234;** www. liberty.co.uk; Tube: Oxford Circus), is a six-floor emporium famous for its fine-quality fabrics. That old Brit institution **Burberry** is so much more than well-made raincoats these days; check out the currently cutting-edge designer digs at 157–167 Regent St., W1 (✆ **020/7806-1328;** www.burberry.com; Tube: Piccadilly). If you're looking for toys or children's gifts, check out **Hamleys,** 188–196 Regent St., W1 (✆ **0800/280-2444;** www.hamleys.com; Tube: Piccadilly Circus), which stocks more than 35,000 toys and games on seven floors. *Be warned:* It gets quite scary pre-Christmas.

KNIGHTSBRIDGE SHOPPING It's not nearly as cutting edge as it used to be (even a bit dowdy), but **Harrods,** 87–135 Brompton Rd., SW1 (✆ **020/8479-5100;** www.harrods.com; Tube: Knightsbridge), is still the most famous department store in London. As firmly entrenched in the city as Buckingham Palace, this enormous store has some 300 departments, delectable Food Halls, and several cafes and eateries. Nearby **Sloane Street** is chockablock with designer shops.

CHELSEA SHOPPING Chelsea's **King's Road** (Tube: Sloane Sq.) will forever remain a symbol of the Swinging '60s. It's still popular with the young crowd, but more and more, King's Road is a lineup of markets and "multistores," conglomerations of indoor stands, stalls, and booths within one building or enclosure. About a third of King's Road is devoted to "multistore" antiques markets, another third houses design-trade showrooms and stores of household wares, and the remaining third is faithful to the area's teenybopper roots.

PORTOBELLO ROAD MARKET Portobello Road in Notting Hill (Tube: Notting Hill Gate) is London's most famous street market. The market, held on Saturdays from 6am to 5pm, is a magnet for collectors of everything from overpriced junk to valuable antiques. If you're a serious collector, get here before 9am. Find out more at **www.portobelloroad.co.uk**. *Note:* Some 90 antiques and art shops along Portobello Road are open during the week when the street market is closed. This is actually a better time for the serious collector to shop because you'll get more attention from dealers, and you won't be distracted by the organ grinder.

Nightlife

London is one of the world's great cultural capitals and is renowned for its nightlife. Theater, music, and dance performances of all kinds take place every night. You can also spend an evening in a pub or dancing at one of London's many clubs. Weekly publications such as *Time Out* and *Where* carry full entertainment listings, including information on restaurants and nightclubs. You'll also find listings in daily newspapers, notably the *Times* and the *Telegraph*. Online, you'll find extensive listings at www.whatsonwhen.com.

To see specific shows, especially hits, purchase your tickets in advance. The best method is to buy your tickets from the theater's box office, which you can do over the phone using a credit card. You'll pay the theater price and pick up the tickets at the box office on the day of the show. You can also go to a ticket agent, especially for discount tickets such as those sold by the **Society of London Theatre,** on the southwest corner of Leicester Square (✆ **020/7557-6700;** www.officiallondontheatre.co.uk), open Monday to Saturday 10am to 7pm and Sunday noon to 3pm. A £2 service fee is charged. You can purchase all tickets here, although the booth specializes in half-price sales for shows that are undersold. These tickets must be purchased in person—not over the phone. For phone or online orders, you have to contact **Ticketmaster** (✆ **0870/060-2340;** www.ticketmaster.co.uk).

THEATER   Plays and musicals are staged all over the city in approximately 100 theaters, but the commercial hits are centered in the **West End.** The West End theater district is concentrated in the area around Piccadilly Circus, Leicester Square, and Covent Garden. Elsewhere, on the south bank of the Thames, is the **Royal National Theatre** (✆ 020/7452-3000; www.nationaltheatre.org.uk), offering a mix of contemporary and classic plays spread over three theaters. A choice of at least six plays is offered at any one time. One of the world's finest theater companies, the **Royal Shakespeare Company** performs at various theaters throughout London. Check its website at **www.rsc.org.uk** for current shows and venues, or call ✆ 0844/800-1110 Monday to Saturday 9am to 8pm. The theater troupe performs in London during the winter months, specializing in the plays of the Bard. If you want to see the Shakespeare's work performed in a truly authentic setting, opt to see a play at **Shakespeare's Globe Theatre** (✆ 020/7902-1400; www.shakespeares-globe. org), on the South Bank.

BALLET, OPERA & CLASSICAL MUSIC   London is home base to two major opera and dance companies. The **Royal Opera** and **Royal Ballet** perform at the **Royal Opera House** (Covent Garden, WC2E; ✆ 020/7304-4000; www.royal opera.org; Tube: Covent Garden). The **English National Opera** and occasionally the **English National Ballet** perform at the **London Coliseum** (St. Martin's Lane, WC2; ✆ 0871/911-0200; www.eno.org; Tube: Leicester Sq.).

The home base for the **London Symphony Orchestra** (www.lso.co.uk) is **Barbican Hall,** at the Barbican Centre, Silk Street, EC2 (✆ 020/7638-8891; Tube: Barbican). You may also catch a performance there by the **Royal Philharmonic Orchestra** (www.rpo.co.uk), which plays concerts at the Barbican and at the **Royal Albert Hall,** Kensington Gore SW7 (✆ 020/7589-8212; www.royalalbert hall.com; Tube: High St. Kensington), an enormous circular domed concert hall that has been a landmark in South Kensington since 1871. The **Southbank Centre** (South Bank, SE1; ✆ 0844/875-0073; www.southbankcentre.co.uk; Tube: Waterloo) is made up of The Royal Festival Hall (reopened in June 2007), The Hayward, The Queen Elizabeth Hall, and The Saison Poetry Library. Together they put on a diverse program encompassing world music, classical concerts, homegrown literature, and contemporary dance.

PUBS   The general opening hours for pubs are noon to 11pm. *Americans, take note:* In a pub, you don't tip the bartender, but you can offer to buy him or her a drink. Ten minutes before closing, a bell rings, signaling it's time to order your last round. There are hundreds of pubs in London; the following is a very selective list.

Cittie of Yorke, 22 High Holborn, WC1 (✆ 020/7242-7670; Tube: Holborn or Chancery Lane), is a wonderfully atmospheric pub with a number of rooms, one of which looks like a great medieval hall—an appropriate appearance, because a pub has existed at this location since 1430. The tiny and modest **Seven Stars,** 53 Carey St., WC2 (© 020/7242-8521; Tube: Holborn), dates back to 1602 and has a collection of old Toby mugs and law-related art. One can linger over pub food and real ales behind Irish-linen lace curtains with litigants, barristers, reporters, and pit musicians from West End shows. **Black Friar,** 174 Queen Victoria St., EC4 (© 020/7236-5474; Tube: Blackfriars), is an Edwardian wonder made of marble and bronze Art Nouveau designs. The interior features bas-reliefs of mad monks, a low-vaulted mosaic ceiling, and seating carved out of gold marble recesses. **Churchill Arms,** 119 Kensington Church St., W8 (© 020/7727-4242; Tube: Notting Hill Gate or High St. Kensington), is a nod to the Empire's end and loaded with Churchill memorabilia. The pub hosts an entire week of celebration leading up to Sir Winston's birthday on November 30. Visitors will find the overall ambience to be down-to-earth and homey.

DANCE CLUBS   Cover charges vary according to day of the week and/or what band is playing. For more options, check out the music and clubs listings in *Time Out.* The big dance clubs don't really start hopping until after 10pm and typically stay open until 3 or 4am on weekends.

A classic (but still incredibly hip) option is **Fabric,** 77a Charterhouse St., EC1 (© 020/7336-8898; www.fabriclondon.com; Tube: Farringdon), located in a refurbished Victorian meat storage unit opposite London's historic Smithfield market. Big-name DJs and super-cool unknowns frequently keep the party going until dawn (or even later). For gay action, **Heaven,** Under-the-Arches, Villiers St., WC2 (© 020/7930-2020; www.heaven-london.com; Tube: Embankment), is a London landmark with great DJs, live bands, and acres of dance floors. The Latin bar and music club **Bar Rumba,** 36 Shaftesbury Ave., W1 (© 020/7287-6933; www.bar rumba.co.uk; Tube: Piccadilly Circus), is all over the map musically, featuring a different theme every night, including jazz fusion, phat funk, hip-hop, soul, R&B, and swing. Vibe-wise, it's small but easygoing. Meanwhile, **Ronnie Scott's,** 47 Frith St. W1 (© 020/7439-0747; www.ronniescotts.co.uk: Tube: Tottenham Court Rd.), is a must-go for jazz aficionados, who will be entertained every night of the week by the coolest musicians in the universe.

BARS   If you want to slip into an elegant mode and mood, head for one of these classy hotel bars for your favorite cocktail.

Check out the dramatic visuals at **Axis & the Lobby Bar,** in the One Aldwych hotel, 1 Aldwych, WC2 (© 020/7300-1000; www.campbellgrayhotels.com; Tube: Covent Garden), then decide which bar appeals the most and park yourself there for the evening. The Lobby Bar occupies what was built in 1907 as the grand, high-ceilinged reception area for one of London's premier newspapers. Many under-40 fashionistas frequent the travertine, hardwood, and leather-sheathed bar in the Axis restaurant. **Artesian,** in the Langham Hotel, 1C Portland Place, W1 (© 020/7636-1000; www. artesian-bar.co.uk; Tube: Oxford Circus), is a chic rendezvous with pricey cocktails. It boasts more than 50 types of rum, and the bartender's specialty is hot buttered rum.

EDINBURGH

Edinburgh (pronounced *Edin-*burra) is one of the most beautiful and fascinating cities in Europe. Located near the Firth of Forth (try saying that four times fast), an inlet from the North Sea, and surrounded by rolling hills, lakes, and forests, Scotland's capital enjoys an unparalleled setting with panoramic views from every hilltop.

Edinburgh

ACCOMMODATIONS ■
Bank Hotel **22**
The Bonham **4**
Channings **2**
The Howard **11**
Macdonald Roxburghe
 Hotel **3**
Mercure Point Hotel **6**
Sheraton Grand
 Hotel & Spa **5**
The Walton **10**

DINING ◆
Atrium **7**
Café Royal Oyster Bar **20**
David Bann **24**
Dusit **9**
Forth Floor Restaurant
 & Brasserie **19**
Haldanes Restaurant **12**
La Garrigue **21**
Oloroso **8**
Spoon Café Bistro **23**
The Witchery by the Castle
 and The Secret Garden **16**

To Leith 27

To the
Brittania

Brunswick Road

Annandale St.

Elm Row

Montgomery Street

Montgomery St.

0   200 yds
0   200 m

✝ Church
(i) Information

Union Street

Broughton Street

Hillside

Crescent

London Road

Union Place

Albany Street

Royal Terrace

York Place

Elder St.

CALTON
HILL

REGENT
GARDENS

19

Lincoln
Monument

Nelson
Monument

Regent Terrace

Abbey Hill

20

W. Register St.

Leith Street

Waterloo Place

Regent Road

Regent Terrace

(i)

Burns
Monument

Palace of
Holyroodhouse

26

North Bridge

Calton Road

Waverley Bridge

WAVERLEY
STATION

Jeffrey
Street

Canongate
Church

25

Market St.

Market St.

The Royal Mile

21

Canongate

John Knox House

High Street

St. Mary's St.

CANONGATE

Huntly
House

The Queen's Drive

Lawnmarket

22

18

South Bridge

Museum
of Childhood

23

24

Holyrood Road

HOLYROOD
PARK

Cowgate

National Library

George IV Bridge

Chambers St.

National Museum
of Scotland

Drummond St.

Pleasance

Bristo Place

Row

College St.

Potterrow

Nicolson St.

West Richmond

McEwan
Hall

Buccleuch Street

Crosscauseway

St. Leonard's St.

ATTRACTIONS ●

George
Square

Middle Meadow Walk

Buccleuch Place

Clerk St.

Melville Drive

THE MEADOWS

Meadow Lane

Dalkeith Road

S. Clerk St.

Edinburgh Castle **15**
National Gallery of
   Scotland **14**
National Museum of
   Scotland **17**
Our Dynamic Earth **25**
Palace of Holyrood-
   house **26**
Royal Botanic Garden **1**
The Royal Yacht
   Britannia **27**
St. Giles Cathedral **18**
Scott Monument **13**

The looming presence of Edinburgh Castle lends a romantic, historic air to this fair city, but Edinburgh is also very much an international city of today, where you'll find chic cafes and modern architecture within the city's quaint core. Edinburgh is divided into two distinct areas: **Old Town,** where the medieval fortress city began, and **New Town,** an elegant example of 18th-century urban planning. It's a wonderfully strollable city full of fine museums, galleries, historic attractions, and real character.

Getting There

BY PLANE **Edinburgh Airport** (© 0844/481-8989; www.edinburghairport. com), 7 miles (11km) west of the city center, receives flights from within the British Isles, the rest of Europe, and some flights from locations in America and Canada. A double-decker Airlink bus makes the trip from the airport to the city center every 10 minutes, letting you off near Waverley Bridge, between the Old Town and the New Town; the fare is £3.50 one-way or £6 round-trip, and the trip takes about 25 minutes. For more information, search www.flybybus.com. A **taxi** (© **0131/344-3344**) into the city will cost £20 or more, depending on traffic, and the ride will be about 25 minutes.

BY RAIL Fast trains operated by **East Coast** (www.eastcoast.co.uk) link London with Edinburgh's **Waverley Station,** at the east end of Princes Street, right in the middle of the city. The station is the central rail hub for all of Scotland and has a train information center, a couple of restaurants, and a luggage storage facility. All fast trains to Waverley provide restaurant, buffet, and trolley service; complimentary beverages and snacks are available in first class. BritRail Passes (but not Eurail passes) may be used for the trip between London and Edinburgh.

Nearly all trains depart from London **Kings Cross** Station, except for the **overnight train,** which departs from London **Euston** and an earlier afternoon service also leaving from Euston. Fares vary quite widely, but advance reservations for nonflexible tickets are the cheapest and as low as about £10 each way. Bought on the day or for a ticket offering travel any time with no restrictions, the price will be considerably more expensive. **East Coast** (www.eastcoast.co.uk) runs the service from Kings Cross. Overnight trains are run by **First Scot Rail** (© **0845/601-5929;** www.firstgroup.com), take 7¼ hours, and have sleeper berths you can reserve from £52 one-way Seat reservations are strongly recommended but not required on all London–Edinburgh trains. If you're traveling around the same time as the Edinburgh Festival or on a summer weekend, we advise getting a seat reservation well in advance. Reservations are obtainable through Rail Europe.

Visitor InformatIon & Room Reservations

Edinburgh Information Centre, atop the Princes Mall near Waverley Station (VisitScotland; © **0131/473-3800** or 0845/225-5121; fax 0131/473-3881; www. edinburgh.org; bus: 3, 8, 22, 25, or 31), can give you sightseeing information and also arrange lodgings. The center sells bus tours, theater tickets, and souvenirs of Edinburgh. It also has racks and racks of free brochures. It's open year-round; typically, the hours are Monday through Saturday from 9am to 7pm and Sunday from 10am to 7pm, though it is open later during the Festival and closes earlier in the winter months.

Getting Around

ON FOOT Edinburgh is divided into a New Town and an Old Town, and walking is the best way to see both. Most of the city's major attractions lie along or near the

Royal Mile, the main thoroughfare of the **Old Town,** which begins at Edinburgh Castle and runs all the way to the Palace of Holyroodhouse. Because of its narrow lanes and passageways, you can explore the Old Town in any depth only on foot. Lying below the Old Town and separated from it by a deep leafy ravine is the **New Town,** an extraordinary adventure in urban planning built between 1766 and 1840. It takes in most of the northern half of the heart of the city and is made up of a network of squares, streets, terraces, and circuses, reaching from Haymarket in the west to Abbeyhill in the east. **Princes Street,** famed for its shopping, is the New Town's main artery. Expect to do some climbing, because parts of Edinburgh are quite hilly.

BY BUS   Edinburgh is in the process of installing a tram system that won't be operational until sometime in 2011, and until it is completed, buses remain the main and least expensive mode of travel in the city. **Lothian Buses** (⊘ **0131/555-6363;** www.lothianbuses.co.uk) operates a comprehensive system of buses throughout Edinburgh. Fares depend on the distance traveled, with the adult one-way (single) **minimum fare** of £1.20 covering the principal Edinburgh districts. The **Day Ticket** allows 1-day unlimited travel on city buses for £3 and can be purchased from the bus driver. Be advised that bus drivers will not give change, so carry the correct amount in coins or purchase a pack of 20 tear-off tickets (called "City Singles") for £24. At Travelshops, 1-week **Ridacard** passes, which allow unlimited travel on buses, can be purchased for £13 for adults or £9 for kids.

For an introduction to the principal attractions in and around Edinburgh, consider the **Edinburgh Tour** (**www.edinburghtour.com**), which allows you to hop on and off at any of 15 stops. Buses start from the Waverley Bridge near the Scott Monument daily at 9:15am, departing every 15 minutes in summer and about every 30 minutes in winter. If you remain on the bus without getting off, the trip will take about 2 hours. The cost is £12 for adults, £11 for seniors/students, £5 for kids 5 to 15, and £28 for a family ticket. Visitors can find advance tickets and further information in the city center at the **Waverley Bridge Travelshop,** Waverley Bridge, open Monday to Saturday 8:15am to 6pm and Sunday 9:30am to 5:15pm, or at **27 Hanover Street Travelshop,** open Monday to Saturday 8:15am to 6pm.

BY TAXI   You can hail a "black" taxi similar to those in London, or pick one up at a taxi stand. Fares start at around £1.50 in the day, and a typical trek across town might cost about £7. Taxi ranks are at High Street near North Bridge, Waverley and Haymarket stations, Hanover Street, North Street, Andrew Street, and Lauriston Place. Fares are displayed in the front of the taxi, and charges are posted, including extra fees for night drivers or destinations outside the city limits. You can also call a taxi. Try **City Cabs** at ⊘ **0131/228-1211,** or **Central Taxis** at ⊘ **0131/229-2468.**

Where to Stay

Edinburgh offers a full range of accommodations throughout the year. Hotels fill up during the 3-week period of the Edinburgh International Festival in August, so if you're coming then, be sure to reserve far in advance.

Bank Hotel ⚓   This hotel on the Royal Mile offers good value. You enter the hotel via the informal Bank Bar, and once inside, you'll discover high ceilings, well-chosen furnishings, and king-size beds; all but one of the guest rooms have both a shower and a tub.

1 South Bridge St., Edinburgh EH1 1LL. ⊘ **0131/556-9940.** Fax 0131/558-1362. www.festival-inns.co.uk. 9 units. £100–£150 double with breakfast. AE, MC, V. Bus: 35. **Amenities:** Bar. *In room:* No A/C.

The Bonham ★★★ One of Edinburgh's most stylish hotels, The Bonham is arguably the jewel in the shimmering crown of the Townhouse Group of hotels in Edinburgh (which also includes The Howard, described below). Its rooms have individual themes with plush contemporary furniture and upholsteries. Bathrooms are state-of-the-art, with expensive toiletries. The Restaurant at the Bonham is elegant yet modern.

35 Drumsheugh Gardens, Edinburgh EH3 7RN. © **0131/226-6050.** Fax 0131/226-6080. www.the bonham.com. 48 units. £100–£250 small double with breakfast. AE, DC, MC, V. Free parking. Bus: 19 or 37. **Amenities:** Restaurant; bar; smoke-free rooms. *In room:* No A/C.

Channings ★ Five Edwardian town houses were knocked together in this tranquil residential area on the edge of the city center to create this hotel, which maintains the atmosphere of a Scottish country house. Most of the furniture has been personally collected by the company's owner over the years. Guest rooms are modern in style; the front units get the views of the neighboring Georgian architecture, while the rear ones offer vistas toward the Firth of Forth and have a more secluded feel.

12–16 S. Learmonth Gardens, Edinburgh EH4 1EZ. © **0131/623-9302.** Fax 0131/332-9631. www. channings.co.uk. 46 units. £99–£139 double with breakfast. AE, DC, MC, V. Bus: 37. **Amenities:** Restaurant; bar. *In room:* No A/C.

The Howard ★★ One of the most discreet luxury hotels in the city, the Howard links a set of Georgian terraced houses in northern New Town, and is sister hotel to the highly desirable the Bonham (above). Rooms here are individually and elegantly decorated, and some feature a Jacuzzi. Excellent service is a hallmark of the Howard—a group of butlers tend to your individual needs, from parking your car to unpacking your luggage, should you so desire.

34 Great King St., Edinburgh EH3 6QH. © **0131/557-3500.** Fax 0131/557-6515. www.thehoward.com. 18 units. £190–£275 double with breakfast. AE, DC, MC, V. Free parking. Bus: 23 or 27. **Amenities:** Restaurant. *In room:* No A/C.

Macdonald Roxburghe Hotel ★ Housed in Georgian buildings designed by the great 18th-century architect Robert Adam just adjacent to Charlotte Square, the Roxburghe creates a classy atmosphere—reflected in the elegant drawing room, with its ornate ceiling and woodwork, antique furnishings, and tall arched windows. The largest guest rooms have traditional features such as imposing fireplaces. Notable amenities include an indoor pool and a spa.

38 Charlotte St. (at George St.), Edinburgh EH2 4HG. © **0870/194-2108** or 888/892-0038 (U.S. only). Fax 0131/240-5555. www.macdonaldhotels.co.uk/roxburghe. 198 units. From £115 double with breakfast. AE, DC, MC, V. Bus: 13, 19, or 41. **Amenities:** Restaurant; bar. *In room:* No A/C.

Mercure Point Hotel The Point has been listed among the 50 premier hotel designs in the world. The guest rooms are equally attractive. Standard ones may feel a bit small, but the premium units are spacious. Many units have views of the castle, but those at the rear do not. If you like stainless steel and brushed chrome instead of Scottish tartan and antiques, this might be the place for you.

34 Bread St., Edinburgh EH3 9AF. © **0131/221-5555.** Fax 0131/221-9929. www.accorhotels.com. 139 units. From £105 double with breakfast. AE, DC, MC, V. Bus: 2 or 28. **Amenities:** Restaurant; bar. *In room:* No A/C.

Sheraton Grand Hotel & Spa ★ The modern exterior of the Sheraton Grand belies the elegant, even a bit old-fashioned, interior—think soaring public rooms and rich carpeting. With a good location and state-of-the-art spa and leisure facilities (including a rooftop indoor/outdoor pool), this hotel pretty much has it all. The castle-view rooms on the top floors are the best (and most expensive). The main restaurant, with views of Festival Square, presents well-prepared meals and a lavish Sunday buffet.

1 Festival Sq., Edinburgh EH3 9SR. © **800/325-3535** in the U.S. and Canada, or 0131/229-9131. Fax 0131/228-4510. www.sheratonedinburgh.co.uk. 260 units. £180–£360 double with breakfast. AE, DC, MC, V. Parking nearby. Bus: 10, 22, or 30. **Amenities:** 3 restaurants; bar; smoke-free rooms.

The Walton   This guesthouse with Georgian character and elegant features sits at the heart of Edinburgh's less frenetic northern New Town—a short walk up the hill to the busy streets of New Town proper. There are limited hotel amenities, so if you require an in-house restaurant or a full-service desk 24/7, look elsewhere. A sister hotel, The Glenora, offers alternative rooms on Rosebery Crescent, near the Haymarket railway station.

79 Dundas St., Edinburgh EH3 6SD. © **0131/556-1137.** Fax 0131/557-8367. www.waltonhotel.com. 10 units. £85–£140 double with breakfast. MC, V. Bus: 23 or 27. *In room:* No A/C.

The Top Attractions & Special Moments

Old Town's **Royal Mile ★★★** stretches from Edinburgh Castle all the way to the Palace of Holyroodhouse and bears four names along its length: Castlehill, Lawnmarket, High Street, and Canongate. Walking along it, you'll see some of the most interesting old structures in the city, with turrets, gables, and towering chimneys.

Edinburgh Castle ★   Few locations in Scotland have lore equal to that of Edinburgh Castle. The very early history is somewhat vague, but in the 11th century, Malcolm III and his Saxon queen, later venerated as St. Margaret, founded a building on this spot. There's only a fragment of their original pile in St. Margaret's Chapel, which dates principally to the 1100s. After centuries of destruction, demolitions, and upheavals, the buildings that stand today are basically those that resulted from the castle's role as a military garrison over the past 300-odd years. It still barracks soldiers, and many of the displays are devoted to military history, which might limit the place's appeal for some. The castle vaults served as prisons for foreign soldiers in the 18th century, and these great storerooms held hundreds of Napoleonic soldiers in the early 19th century. Some prisoners made wall carvings still seen today.

However, it is not all about war. Visitors can see where Mary, Queen of Scots gave birth to James VI of Scotland (later James I of England) in 1566. Scottish Parliaments used to convene in the Great Hall of the castle. Another highlight for visitors is the

Great Scott!

Looking more like a neo-Gothic church spire than a monument to a famous writer, the **Scott Monument,** in the East Princes Street Gardens (© 0131/529-4068), is secretly a super place to get some of the best views in the city. In the center of this 200-foot (60m) spire completed in the mid-19th century is a large seated statue of novelist Sir Walter Scott and his dog, Maida. Some of Scott's characters are carved as small figures in the monument. Climb the 287 steps to the top to see the views. Admission to the Scott Monument is £3. It's an easy walk from Waverley station, or take any city center bus along Princes Street.

Scottish Crown Jewels, used at the coronations, along with the scepter and sword of state of Scotland and the infamous Stone of Scone. Note that last entry is 45 minutes before closing, and buying tickets online in advance will save time during busy periods.

Castlehill. ✆ **0131/225-9846.** www.edinburghcastle.gov.uk. Admission £13 adults, £10 seniors, £7 children 5–15. MC, V. Apr–Sept daily 9:30am–6pm; Oct–Mar daily 9:30am–5pm. Bus: 23, 27, 41, or 45.

National Gallery of Scotland ★★ Although the fine-art collection held by Scotland is small by the standards of larger countries, it has been chosen with great care and expanded by bequests, gifts, loans, and purchases. There's only enough space to display part of the entire collected works. One recent major acquisition was Botticelli's *The Virgin Adoring the Sleeping Christ Child.* The Duke of Sutherland has lent the museum two Raphaels, two of Titian's *Diana* canvases, and *Venus Rising from the Sea.* The gallery also has works by El Greco and Velázquez, and Dutch art by Rembrandt and van Dyck.

Impressionism and post-Impressionism are represented by Cézanne, Degas, van Gogh, Monet, Renoir, Gauguin, and Seurat. In a basement wing (opened in 1978), Scottish art is highlighted. Henry Raeburn is at his best in the whimsical *Rev. Robert Walker Skating on Duddingston Loch,* while the late-19th-century Glasgow School is represented by artists such as Sir James Guthrie.

Next door on the Mound is the **Royal Scottish Academy** (✆ **0131/624-6200**), now connected by the Weston Link, which opened in summer 2004. The RSA was renovated and now hosts blockbuster exhibitions, such as works by Monet, Titian, or the 20th-century virtuoso Joan Eardley.

2 The Mound. ✆ **0131/624-6200.** www.nationalgalleries.org. Free admission, except for some temporary exhibits. Fri–Wed 10am–5pm (till 6pm Aug); Thurs 10am–7pm. Closed Dec 25–26. Bus: 23, 27, 41, 42, 45, or National Galleries shuttle.

National Museum of Scotland ★★ Opened in 1998, this impressive museum housed in an effective, modern sandstone building not far from the Royal Mile follows the story of Scotland with exhibits on archaeology, technology, science, the decorative arts, royalty, and geology. Hundreds of millions of years of Scottish history are distilled in this collection of some 12,000 items, which range from 2.9-billion-year-old rocks found on the island of South Uist to a cute Hillman Imp, one of the last 500 automobiles manufactured in Scotland. One gallery is devoted to Scotland's centuries as an independent nation. Another gallery, devoted to industry and empire from 1707 to 1914, includes exhibits on shipbuilding, whisky distilling, and the railways. The adjacent **Royal Museum** (whose 3-year upgrade ends sometime in 2011) includes a well-preserved and airy Victorian-era Main Hall and some 36 more galleries.

Chambers St. ✆ **0131/247-4422.** www.nms.ac.uk. Free admission. Daily 10am–5pm. Bus: 2, 7, 23, 31, 35, 41, or 42.

Our Dynamic Earth A former brewery was converted into this multimedia amphitheater capped by a translucent tentlike roof. Its galleries explain the natural diversity of the earth, elaborating on the seismological and biological processes that led from the Big Bang to the world we know today. The presentation features audio and video clips; buttons you can push to simulate earthquakes, meteor showers, and views of outer space; time capsules winding their way back through the eons; and a series of specialized aquariums, some with replicas of primordial life forms, some with living sharks, dolphins, and coral. Also on the premises are a restaurant, a cafe, and a gift shop.

Holyrood Rd. ℂ **0131/550-7800.** www.dynamicearth.co.uk. Admission £11 adults, £9 seniors and students, £7 children 3-15. July and Aug daily 10am–6pm; Sept–June daily 10am–5pm. Bus: 35 or 36.

Palace of Holyroodhouse ★★ Early in the 16th century, this palace was built by James IV adjacent to a 12th-century Augustinian abbey; now it's the Queen's official residence in Edinburgh and used for state entertaining. The nave of the abbey church still remains, but only the north tower of James's palace is left. Most of what you see today was built by Charles II after Scotland and England were united in the 17th century.

One of the more dramatic incidents at Holyroodhouse occurred in 1566 when David Rizzio, the Italian secretary of Mary Queen of Scots, was stabbed 56 times in front of her by her jealous husband, Lord Darnley, and his accomplices. A plaque marks the spot. And one of the more curious exhibits is a piece of needlework done by Mary depicting a cat-and-mouse scene—her cousin, Elizabeth I, happens to be the cat. Some of the rich tapestries, paneling, massive fireplaces, and antiques from the 1700s are still in place.

Today the royal family stays here whenever they visit Edinburgh. When they're not in residence, the palace is open to visitors, and you see the various reception rooms where the queen dines, entertains, and meets Scottish government leaders. Some of the rich tapestries, paneling, massive fireplaces, and antiques from the 1700s are still in place. More recently, the modern **Queen's Gallery** (additional admission) opened to display works from the royal collection, whether Mughal art or Dutch paintings.

Behind Holyroodhouse begins **Holyrood Park,** Edinburgh's largest. With rocky crags, a loch, sweeping meadows, and the ruins of a chapel, it's a wee bit of the Scottish countryside in the city, and a great place for a picnic. From the park, you can climb up a treeless, heather-covered crag called **Arthur's Seat** ★★★ for breathtaking panoramas of the city and the Firth of Forth.

Canongate, at the eastern end of the Royal Mile. ℂ **0131/556-5100.** www.royalcollection.org.uk. Admission (includes audio tour) £10 adults, £9.30 seniors and students, £6.20 children 5-17, £27 families. MC, V. Apr–Oct daily 9:30am–6pm; Nov–Mar 9:30am–4:30pm. Closed when Royal Family is in residence, typically a few weeks from mid-May to late June, mid-July, and Christmas. Bus: 35, 36, or open-top tours.

Royal Botanic Garden ★★★ One of the grandest gardens in Great Britain, the Royal Botanic Garden sprawls across 70 acres (28 hectares) on the north side of the Water of Leith. It dates from the late 17th century, when it was originally used to grow and study medicinal plants. The collection grew dramatically between 1904 and 1932 with plants collected in southwestern China and brought to Edinburgh by George Forrest. In spring, the various rhododendrons, from low ground cover to towering shrubs, are reason alone to visit the Royal Botanic Garden in Edinburgh. But the planting in various areas ensures year-round interest, whether in the rock garden or in the wide and long "herbaceous" borders elsewhere. The grounds include numerous glass houses, the Palm House (Britain's tallest) being foremost among them. Inverleith House is a venue for art exhibitions.

20A Inverleith Row. ℂ **0131/552-7171.** www.rbge.org.uk. Free admission to garden; glass houses £3.50 adults, £3 children. Daily Apr–Sept 10am–7pm; Oct 10am–6pm; Nov–Feb 10am–4pm; Mar 10am–6pm (glass houses close 30 min. earlier). Bus: 8, 17, 23, or 27.

The Royal Yacht *Britannia* ★★★ Used by Queen Elizabeth II and the royal family since 1952, this luxurious 412-foot (124m) yacht was decommissioned in 1997, berthed in Leith (2 miles/3.2km from Edinburgh's center), and opened to the public. You reach the famous vessel by going through a rather dreary shopping mall to a visitor center, where you collect a portable audio guide keyed to the major state-rooms and working areas on all five decks. You can visit the drawing room and the little-changed Royal Apartments, and explore the engine room, the galleys, and the captain's cabin. An air of the 1950s still permeates the vessel.

Ocean Terminal, Leith. ℭ **0131/555-5566.** www.royalyachtbritannia.co.uk. £11 adults, £9 seniors/students, £6.75 kids 5-17, free for 4 and under, £31 family. Apr–Oct daily 9:30am–4:30pm (last admission); Nov–Mar 10:30am–3:30pm (last admission). Bus: 1, 11, 22, 34, or 35.

St. Giles Cathedral ★ A brief walk downhill from Edinburgh Castle, this church—and its steeple, in particular—is one of the most important architectural landmarks along the Royal Mile. Here is where Scotland's equal to Martin Luther, John Knox, preached his sermons on the Reformation. Also known as the High Kirk of St. Giles, the building combines a dark and brooding stone exterior (the result of a Victorian-era restoration) with surprisingly graceful buttresses. Only the tower represents the medieval era of the church. One of its outstanding features is the Thistle Chapel, housing beautiful stalls and notable heraldic stained-glass windows.

High St. ℭ **0131/225-9442.** www.stgilescathedral.org.uk. Free admission, but £3 donation suggested. May–Sept Mon–Fri 9am–7pm, Sat 9am–5pm, Sun 1–5pm (and for services); Oct–Apr Mon–Sat 9am–5pm, Sun 1–5pm (and for services). Bus: 23, 27, 28, 35, 41, or 42.

Where to Dine

Edinburgh boasts the finest restaurants in Scotland and a wide variety of available cuisines, including Scottish, French, Asian, Italian, and modern European. Scotland's reputation for excellent fresh produce is growing, so look out for the following in season: shellfish such as langoustines (aka Dublin Bay Prawns), oysters, mussels, and exquisite hand-dived scallops; locally landed finned fish (such as halibut, bream, and sea bass); heather-fed lamb; and Aberdeen Angus beef.

Note: A lot of restaurants still close for a few hours every afternoon, but bistro-style operations and pubs often serve food right through the day. The hours given in the information below reflect when food may be ordered; bars on the premises may keep longer hours.

Atrium ★ MODERN SCOTTISH/INTERNATIONAL Since 1993, this has been one of the most acclaimed and stylish restaurants in Edinburgh. Dishes often feature local and organic ingredients, displaying flair but not excessive amounts of fuss or fancy presentation. Main courses might include Perthshire lamb cooked pink with an accompanying mini shepherd's pie, or Gressingham duck with roast squash. Or how about seared scallops served with chilies and garlic on lemon linguini? Desserts are equally superb.

10 Cambridge St. (adjacent to the Traverse Theatre). ℭ **0131/228-8882.** www.atriumrestaurant.co.uk. Reservations recommended. Fixed-price lunch £15; main courses £18–£22. AE, MC, V. Mon–Fri noon–2pm and 5:30–10pm; Sat 5:30–10pm. Bus: 1, 10, 15, or 24.

Café Royal Oyster Bar ★ SEAFOOD/FISH The Café Royal first opened in 1862, and after some 140 years, its splendorous Victorian touches remain intact. The main menu offers more than just oysters: Salmon, langoustines, and lobsters—as well as beef and rabbit—might feature. If the restaurant's dining room is closed (btw. lunch and dinner), head for the neighboring Circle Bar, which serves food and beverages throughout the day. Its menu is more limited but also less pricey. A highlight of the bar is the collection of tile pictures of notable inventors.

17a W. Register St. © **0131/556-1884.** Reservations recommended. Main courses £14–£22. AE, MC, V. Daily noon–2pm and 6–10pm (bar daily 11am–11pm). Bus: 8 or 29.

David Bann ★★ 🏦 VEGETARIAN   Chef David Bann has been at the forefront of meat-free cooking in Edinburgh for more than a decade. He comes from the school of thought that insists (and proves) that vegetarian meals can be *both* tasty and healthy: No need to sacrifice the former for the latter. The menu at his eponymous restaurant (located just a short stroll south of Royal Mile) is internationally eclectic: from Mexico to Thailand, India to the Med. The dining room is as stylish as the cooking, and to top it off, the prices are very reasonable.

56–58 St. Mary's St. © **0131/556-5888.** www.davidbann.com. Reservations recommended. Main courses £7.50–£12. AE, MC, V. Daily noon–10pm. Bus: 36.

Dusit ★ 🏦 THAI   Thistle Street, although little more than a slender lane with narrow sidewalks, has become something of a hot bed for restaurants. This rather unassuming restaurant has a reputation for being one of the best in the city for Thai cuisine—some say the best in Scotland for any style of cuisine. The menu is not typical and has a tendency toward modern dishes—many of which incorporate Scottish produce, such as venison and Jerusalem artichokes. Recommended are *hoi yang* scallops or stir-fried guinea fowl. The wines are plentiful and matched to the cuisine.

49a Thistle St. © **0131/220-6846.** www.dusit.co.uk. Reservations recommended. Fixed-price lunch £11; main courses £12–£18. AE, MC, V. Mon–Sat noon–3pm and 6–11pm; Sun noon–11pm. Bus: 24, 29, or 42.

Forth Floor Restaurant & Brasserie ★★ SCOTTISH/MODERN BRITISH   At the top of the Harvey Nichols boutique department store, this restaurant has excellent views of the Firth of Forth. It matches the commanding vistas with excellent contemporary Scottish cooking. While you do feel a little like you're dining in a department store annex (despite the slick, minimalist decor), the food can be phenomenal, whether it's roast monkfish with chorizo and red-wine butter or a light salad with endive and seasonal truffles. The produce used by the kitchen is notably well sourced and fresh, such as West Coast langoustines as an *amuse-bouche* to start your meal or beef certified by the Scottish Beef Club. The brasserie menu, while less extensive than the restaurant's selections, offers good value, especially on the fixed-price lunch.

Harvey Nichols, 30–34 St. Andrew Sq. © **0131/524-8350.** www.harveynichols.com. Reservations recommended for restaurant. Fixed-price lunch £15; main courses £16–£22. AE, DC, MC, V. Tues–Sat noon–10pm; Sun and Mon lunch only. Bus: 8, 10, 12, or 45.

Haldanes Restaurant 🏦 SCOTTISH   Haldanes serves dinners conducted like meals in a private country house, with polite and deferential service. Run by chef George Kelso and wife Michelle, the restaurant offers cooking with a light touch, despite using robust and mostly traditional ingredients, whether venison, wood pigeon, or salmon. The dining room's layout and candlelit decor with deep carpets and wood paneling are excellent for a romantic meal, even if the location underneath the Albany Hotel is a little unprepossessing.

39a Albany St. © **0131/556-8407.** www.haldanesrestaurant.com. Reservations recommended. Main courses £16–£20. MC, V. Daily 5:30–9pm (9:30pm Fri–Sat). Bus: 23 or 27.

La Garrigue ★ 🏦 FRENCH   The chef and proprietor of La Garrigue, Jean Michel Gauffre, hails from the southern French region of Languedoc and he effectively re-creates the fresh and rustic cooking of his birthplace. The feeling of the

The much-misunderstood traditional dish of Scotland, haggis may be an acquired taste, but a well-made one is delicious with mashed potatoes and swede. **Macsween of Edinburgh** (www.macsween.co.uk) is a long-established family business specializing in Robert Burn's "King o' the Puddin' Race." Macsween haggis includes lamb, beef, oatmeal, onions, and a special blend of seasonings and spices cooked together and stuffed into a natural casing. They also make a popular vegetarian version. Both are sold in vacuum-packed plastic bags and require only reheating in a microwave or simmering pot of water. You can find this company's product at a range of food stores and supermarkets throughout Edinburgh.

dining room is informal but still smart, with some stylish hand-crafted timber furniture. The menu can feature a hearty roast or cassoulet (stew) with beans, confit duck, Toulouse sausage, pork, or lamb. In addition to such hearty dishes, expect something more delicate, such as pan-fried filet of bream. The wines are from southern France, too. Often chef Gauffre will come in the dining room to see how it is going and have a friendly chat—he knows that small touches go a long way. La Garrigue is well worth a detour off the Royal Mile.

31 Jeffrey St. ✆ **0131/557-3032.** www.lagarrigue.co.uk. Reservations recommended. Fixed-price lunch £14; fixed-price dinner £26. AE, MC, V. Mon–Sat noon–2:30pm and 6:30–10:30pm. Bus: 36.

Oloroso INTERNATIONAL   Though they're fantastic, it's not all about the vistas from this restaurant in the heart of Old Town. Oloroso's chef and owner, Tony Singh, is a Scottish-born Sikh with an imaginative approach to cooking Scottish produce. Here, in his rooftop restaurant with an ample veranda and excellent panoramic views, the feeling is contemporary and swanky. Frequently changing menus include dishes such as veal T-bones or fresh fish from the grill menu, or pan-fried breast of duck with puy lentils and black pudding. The bar, which mixes some mean cocktails, is usually open until 1am.

33 Castle St. ✆ **0131/226-7614.** www.oloroso.co.uk. Reservations recommended. Fixed-price lunch £19; main courses £15–£25. MC, V. Daily noon–2:30pm and 7–10pm. Bus: 24, 29, or 42.

Spoon Café Bistro ★★ CAFE   This particular "spoon" is far from greasy. Owner Richard Alexander could cook at the best restaurants in town—instead, he's opted for his own operation, which combines a relaxed ambience, first-rate espresso-based coffees, and the sure hand of a classically trained chef. The soups are always superb. Sandwiches are prepared freshly, and now you can get more elaborate dishes like crispy pan-seared trout fillet with a cider vinegar dressing or braised beef with baby potatoes. Alternatively, you can still simply drop in for a piece of homemade cake: moist carrot or rich chocolate.

6a Nicolson St. ✆ **0131/557-4567.** www.spooncafe.co.uk. Soups from £3; sandwiches and salads from £4.50; main courses £10. MC, V. Mon–Sat 10am–10pm; Sun noon–6pm. Bus: 3, 5, 29, 31, or 35.

The Witchery by the Castle ★★ SCOTTISH/FRENCH   The restaurant, so named because of historical connections to medieval executions nearby and rumors of lingering ghosts, serves classy Scottish food in classier still surroundings, with dishes that feature ingredients such as Angus beef, Scottish lobster, and Loch Fyne oysters. Well-prepared old-time British favorites, such as beef Wellington for two (with accompanying jug of red wine *jus*), contrast with a list of more contemporary specials—a starter of hot-smoked salmon with beetroot purée, for example. Atmospheric and good for special occasions, the Witchery is also ideal for a sumptuous late meal and then lingering over a postprandial drink until midnight or so. In addition to the dark and lavish dining room near the street, there is also the "Secret Garden" farther down the narrow close.

Boswell Court, Castlehill, Royal Mile. ✆ **0131/225-5613.** www.thewitchery.com. Reservations required. Fixed-price 2-course lunch and pre- and post-theater dinner £13; main courses £18–£25. AE, DC, MC, V. Daily noon–4pm and 5:30–11:30pm. Bus: 23, 27, 41, or 45.

Shopping

New Town's **Princes Street** is the main shopping artery. **George Street** and Old Town's **Royal Mile** are also major shopping areas. The best buys are in tartans and woolens, along with bone china and Scottish crystal. Shopping hours in central Edinburgh are generally from 9 or 10am to 6pm Monday through Wednesday and on Friday and Saturday. On Sunday, shops open at 11am or noon and close around 5pm. On Thursdays, many shops remain open until 7 or 8pm.

James Pringle Woolen Mill, 70–74 Bangor Rd., Leith (✆ **0131/553-5161**), produces a large variety of top-quality wool items, including cashmere sweaters, tartan and tweed ties, blankets, and tam-o'-shanters. In addition, it boasts one of Scotland's best Clan Tartan Centres, with more than 5,000 tartans accessible. **Bill Baber,** 66 Grassmarket (✆ **0131/225-3249;** www.billbaber.com), turns out artfully modernized adaptations of traditional Scottish patterns for both men and women. Expect to find traditional knits spiced up with strands of Caribbean-inspired turquoise or aqua, or rugged-looking blazers or sweaters suitable for treks or bike rides through the moors.

Geoffrey (Tailor) Highland Crafts, 57–61 High St. (✆ **0131/557-0256;** www.geoffreykilts.co.uk), is the most famous kilt maker in the Scottish capital. It stocks 200 of Scotland's best-known clan patterns and is revolutionizing the kilt by creating so-called "21st-century kilts" in different patterns, such as pinstripe. Some of the most stylish tartans are found at **Anta,** 91–93 West Bow, Victoria Street (✆ **0131/225-4616;** www.anta.co.uk), especially cool minikilts and silk *earasaids* (oversize scarves) for women. The woolen blankets with hand-purled fringe are woven on old-style looms. **Tartan Gift Shop,** 54 High St. (✆ **0131/558-3187**), has a chart indicating the Scottish origin of family names, and offers a bewildering array of hunt and dress tartans, sold by the yard. There's also a line of lambs' wool and cashmere sweaters.

Nightlife

For 3 weeks in August, the **Edinburgh International Festival** brings world-class cultural offerings to the city, but there are plenty of choices year-round, whether you prefer theater, opera, ballet, symphony concerts, or other diversions. The waterfront district, featuring many jazz clubs and restaurants, is especially lively in summer, and students flock to the pubs and clubs around Grassmarket. Dance clubs are found off High and Princes streets, and in the city's numerous pubs you can often hear live traditional Scottish folk music for the price of a pint. For a complete rundown of what is happening in Edinburgh, pick up a copy of ***The List,*** a biweekly magazine available at all major newsstands and bookshops, or visit its website, **www.list.co.uk.**

THE EDINBURGH FESTIVAL: art & tattoos

The brightest highlight of Edinburgh's year comes in August during the **Edinburgh International Festival** ★★★. Since 1947, the festival has attracted artists and companies of the highest international standard in all fields of the arts, including music, opera, dance, and theater. These days, however, it's been somewhat eclipsed by the **Festival Fringe** ★★★, which presents some 2,000 shows at nearly 250 venues. It provides an opportunity for almost anybody—professional or nonprofessional, an individual, a group of friends, or a whole company—to put on a show wherever they can find an empty stage or street corner. The range is mind-boggling: a gospel choir from Soweto, penis puppetry, or avant-garde theater. The International Festival box office is at the Hub, Castle Hill (✆ **0131/473-2000;** www.eif.co.uk). The Fringe is based in 180 High St. (✆ **0131/226-0000;**

www.edfringe.com). Information on all the festivals is found at **www.edinburgh festivals.co.uk.** Ticket prices vary from £5 to £15 for Fringe performances, to £10 to £50 for the International Festival.

And the August fun doesn't stop there. Happening around the same time as the festivals is another exciting event: the **Military Tattoo,** taking place on the floodlit esplanade in front of Edinburgh Castle, high on its rock above the city. The Tattoo features precision marching of not only Scottish regiments, but also soldiers and performers (including bands, drill teams, and gymnasts) from dozens of countries. Schedules are released each year about 6 months before the festival. Tickets are available from the **Edinburgh Military Tattoo Office,** 32 Market St., Edinburgh EH1 1QB (✆ **0870/225-1188;** www.edintattoo.co. uk), and run about £13 to £44. Advance reservations are essential.

THE PERFORMING ARTS

THEATER Edinburgh has a lively theater scene. In 1994, the **Edinburgh Festival Theatre,** 13–29 Nicolson St. (✆ **0131/529-6000;** www.eft.co.uk; bus: 5 or 22), opened on the eastern edge of Edinburgh. It boasts the largest stage in Britain and is used for theater, dance, opera, and presentations of all kinds. Tickets are £6 to £45. The **King's Theatre,** 2 Leven St. (✆ **0131/529-6000;** www.eft.co.uk; bus: 11 or 15), is a 1,600-seat Victorian venue offering a wide repertoire of classical entertainment, including ballet, opera, and productions from London's West End. Tickets run £5 to £25. The resident company of the **Royal Lyceum Theatre,** Grindlay Street (✆ **0131/248-4848;** www.lyceum.org; bus: 1, 10, 15, or 34), presents everything from Shakespeare to new Scottish playwrights. Tickets run £8 to £30. The **Traverse Theatre,** 10 Cambridge St. (✆ **0131/228-1404;** www.traverse.co.uk; bus: 1, 10, 15, or 34), is one of the few theaters in Britain funded solely to present new plays by British writers and first translations into English of international works. Tickets run £5 to £16.

BALLET, OPERA & CLASSICAL MUSIC The **Scottish Ballet** (www.scottish ballet.co.uk) and the **Scottish Opera** (www.scottishopera.org.uk) perform at the **Edinburgh Festival Theatre** (see "Theater," above). The **Scottish Chamber Orchestra** (www.sco.org.uk) makes its home at the **Queen's Hall,** Clerk Street (✆ **0131/668-2019;** www.thequeenshall.net; bus: 5, 7, 8, or 29), also a major venue for the Edinburgh International Festival. Another major player on the classical music scene is **Usher Hall,** 71 Lothian Rd. (✆ **0131/228-1155;** www.usherhall.co. uk;bus: 1, 10, 15, or 34), the Edinburgh equivalent of New York's Carnegie Hall.

IRISH RAIL ESSENTIALS

Highlights of Ireland

Traveling in Ireland by train is a breeze. It takes you to many of Ireland's top towns and cities (Cork, Belfast, Galway), as well as some of the lesser-known gems (Athlone, Portrush), and getting train information is easy for English speakers (although watch out for the accent and slang). On the downside, the ferry journey to (or from) the U.K. or France can take the best part of the day (once you've added in the journey to the ferry port), and the Irish Sea is known for setting stomachs a-jumbling. But brave these minor irritations, and you'll be rewarded with stunning rural scenery and a lively cultural welcome.

Ireland is a separate nation from the United Kingdom, and you'll find they do things differently here. All the public notices are written in English and Gaelic, the euro is the currency, the Irish have no problem electing a female president or allowing gay marriage, and Ireland was the first country in Europe to ban smoking in public places. Add to that the astonishing number of great writers, playwrights, and musicians produced here, and you've got yourself an interesting foreign climate. But don't come expecting a nation of farming folk sipping Guinness in the afternoons. Yes, there are places where this happens, but Ireland has undergone massive economic expansion in the past few years and is now a young, wealthy nation, with hip Dublin at the center of the action.

Getting There

BY PLANE

About half of all visitors from North America arrive in Ireland on direct transatlantic flights to Dublin Airport. The other half fly first into Britain or Europe, then "backtrack" into Ireland by air or sea. **Dublin Airport** lies about 6½ miles (10km) to the north of the city (**01/814-1111**; www.dublinairport.com). It's a small and very busy airport offering all the usual comforts and services of an international hub. Other airports include **Shannon Airport** (**SNN;** ℂ **061/471369;** www.shannonairport. com) and **Belfast International Airport** (**BFS;** ℂ **028/9448-4848;** www. belfastairport.com). There are seven smaller regional airports.

FROM NORTH AMERICA The Irish national carrier, **Aer Lingus** (ℂ **800/474-7424;** www.aerlingus.com), is the traditional leader in providing transatlantic flights to Ireland. Other carriers flying directly to Ireland from the U.S. are **American**

FESTIVALS & special events

The most up-to-date listings of events in Ireland can be found at **www.ireland.ie** and **www.entertainment.ie**.

St. Patrick's Dublin Festival is a massive 4-day fest (Mar 15–18) that's open, free, and accessible to everyone. Street theater, carnival acts, sports, music, fireworks, and other festivities culminate in Ireland's grandest parade, with marching bands, drill teams, floats, and delegations from around the world. For information, call ℂ **01/676-3205** or surf the Web to **www.stpatricksday.ie**. *Warning:* The popular hotels in Dublin often fill up a year in advance of the festival. Book a long way ahead to get a good room.

Airlines (© 800/433-7300; www.aa.com), **Delta Airlines** (© 800/241-4141; www.delta.com), and **Continental Airlines** (© 800/231-0856; www.continental.com).

FROM BRITAIN The following carriers offer direct flights from London to Ireland: **Aer Lingus** (© 800/474-7424 in the U.S., or 0871/1718-5000 in Britain; www.aerlingus.com); **British Airways** (© 800/AIRWAYS [247-9297] in the U.S., or 0870/ 850-9850 in Britain; www.ba.com), **Lufthansa** (© 800/645-3880 in the U.S., or 0871/945-9747 in Britain; www.lufthansa.com), and **British Midland** (© 800/788-0555 in the U.S., or 0844/8484-888 in Britain; www.flybmi.com).

Two low-cost airlines making the London–Dublin hop are **CityJet** (© 0871/666-50-50 in Britain; www.cityjet.com) and **Ryanair,** for which Dublin is the hub city (© 0871/246-0000 in Britain; www.ryanair.com).

FROM THE CONTINENT Major direct flights into Dublin from the Continent include service from Amsterdam on **KLM** (© 800/447-4747 in the U.S.; www.klm.com), Madrid and Barcelona on **Iberia** (© 800/772-4642 in the U.S.; www.iberia.com), Copenhagen on **Aer Lingus** and **SAS** (© 800/221-2350 in the U.S.; www.scandinavian.net), Frankfurt on **Aer Lingus** and **Lufthansa** (© 800/645-3880 in the U.S.; www.lufthansa.com), Paris on **Aer Lingus** and **Air France** (© 800/237-2747 in the U.S.; www.airfrance.com), and Rome on **Aer Lingus.**

BY FERRY

10

The Irish Sea has a reputation for making seafarers woozy, so it's always a good idea to consider an over-the-counter pill or patch to guard against seasickness if you choose to take this route.

FROM BRITAIN There are two ports for the Dublin-bound sea craft: **Dun Laoghaire,** pronounced "dun lehry," is used exclusively by the Stena Line (see info below), and **Dublin Port** (© 01/887-6000; www.dublinport.ie), which is about 2 miles (3.2km) outside of Dublin. The following ferries have a wildly varying number of ticket prices, discounts, packages, and special offers, so always check the websites for the most up-to-date information.

Irish Ferries (© 8717/300-400 in the U.K., or 818/300-400 in Ireland; www.irishferries.ie) sails between Dublin and Holyhead in North Wales. Travel time is 2 hours on a fast boat, and close to 4 hours on a more sedate ship, with foot-passenger round-trip tickets starting from 26€. Their other route connects Rosslare in southern Ireland to Pembroke in southern Wales, takes 3 hours and 45 minutes, and costs the same as the Dublin–Holyhead route. The Eurail Global Pass gives holders a 30% discount on standard passenger fares on both routes. Book online to save €6 on handling charges.

Stena Line (© 0870/570-7070 in the U.K., or 01/204-7777 in Ireland; www.stenaline.com) travels between Holyhead in Wales and Dun Laorghaire, which is just south of Dublin. The trip takes about 99 minutes. Another route connects Rosslare (in southern Ireland) to Fishguard (in southern Wales). It takes 2 hours and 15 minutes. The Eurail Global Pass entitles holders to a 30% discount on standard passenger fares on both routes. Call for prices.

FROM THE CONTINENT Irish Ferries (**www.irishferries.ie**) sails from Roscoff and Cherbourg, France, to Rosslare, which is about 60 miles (97km) south of Dublin. Transit time between the two ports is 18 hours. For reservations, call **Scots-American Travel** (© 561/563-2856 in the U.S.; info@scotsamerican.com)

Ireland

or **Irish Ferries** (☏ **0870/517-1717** in the U.K., or 818/300-400 in Ireland). Call for prices. Eurail Global Pass holders get a 30% discount on this ferry trip.

Brittany Ferries (☏ **021/427-7801** in Cork; www.brittany-ferries.com) connects Roscoff, France, to Cork (crossing time is about 14 hr.). A ship sails only once each week. For prices and information on these ferries, see the "Major European Ferry Lines" chart on p. 66.

IRELAND RAILPASSES

The **Eurail Ireland Pass** is valid for 5 days of second-class travel in a period of 1 month and costs $352 for first class and $281 for second class. It can be purchased in advance from **Rail Europe** (✆ **877/272-RAIL** [7245] in North America; www.raileurope.com) or your travel agent.

The Ireland-only passes listed below are available from booking offices of **Iarnród Éireann** (✆ **1850/366-222;** www.irishrail.com) and the Dublin Tourism office on Suffolk Street (p. 442). *Note:* Discounted passes are available for children.

READY-MADE RAIL GETAWAYS

Iarnrod Eireann (✆ **01/856-0045;** www.railtours.ie), the Irish rail network, also offers a variety of ready-made day tours and getaways departing by train from Dublin. They can be purchased at booking offices of Iarnrod Eireann and at the Dublin Tourism office on Suffolk Street (see "Information Elsewhere in the City," later).

RAILTOURS   These 1-day or half-day tours are a convenient way to see a hefty portion of the country. The fare includes reserved seats on InterCity rail services with full dining facilities. For some itineraries, special coaches with qualified driver/guides take you where rail lines don't. There are various itineraries available, including: Connemara and Galway Bay for €89; The Ring of Kerry for €99; The Cliffs of Moher, Burren, and Galway Bay for €99; and The Aran Islands for €119, including flights.

RAILBREAKS   These ready-made 2- or 3-day vacations include train travel and accommodations and let you take in a specific region. There are various options to choose from, with rates starting as low as €219 per person for a 2-day break covering Cork, The Ring of Kerry, Blarney Castle, and Killarney including rail travel, B&B accommodations, and breakfast daily. A 5-day Royal Atlantic Tour taking in Cork, Cobh, Blarney Castle, Cliffs of Moher, Galway Bay, Connemara, and The Aran Islands (including rail travel, flights, and hotel accommodations) costs €569 per person.

Foreign Train Terms

Booking tickets in Ireland is self-explanatory for English speakers, aside from the occasional variance in vocabulary. ***One piece of useful information:*** The Irish, like the British, use the term *return* instead of *round-trip,* and *single* instead of *one-way.*

Practical Train Information

Iarnrod Eireann (✆ **1890/778899;** www.irishrail.com), aka Irish Railways, runs all of the train routes in the Republic of Ireland. The company's website is loaded with valuable information and has timetables, route maps, station information, and tips for rail travelers with disabilities.

RESERVATIONS   Holders of Eurail, BritRail + Ireland, Emerald Card, and Irish Explorer passes do not need to make reservations on trains. Ireland is a small country, and there are no overnight trains or sleeper coaches. Be aware, however, that trains on the more popular routes can be very crowded, with standing room only, especially on Bank Holiday weekends. It's a good idea to arrive at least 45 minutes before departure time to ensure that you get a seat.

Note: Don't worry if a station's booking office is closed or unstaffed as your train readies for departure, should you decide to make a spur-of-the-moment trip and haven't got a pass; you can always buy your ticket on board the train.

SERVICES & AMENITIES   All InterCity train stations are staffed during rush hours and during the day Monday through Saturday; Dublin city stations are staffed around the clock daily, and stations in larger cities, such as Cork and Limerick, are staffed virtually around the clock. Tickets can be purchased during booking hours

Trains & Travel Times in Ireland

From	To	Type of Train	# of Trains	Frequency	Travel Time
Dublin Heuston	Cork	IC	16	Mon–Sat	2 hr., 50 min.
Dublin Heuston	Cork	IC	10	Sun	2 hr., 50 min.
Dublin Heuston	Killarney	IC	7	Mon–Sat	3 hr., 30 min.
Dublin Heuston	Killarney	IC	5	Sun	3 hr., 30 min.
Dublin Heuston	Galway	IC	7	Mon–Sat	2 hr., 42 min.
Dublin Heuston	Galway	IC	6	Sun	2 hr., 42 min.
Dublin Connolly	Rosslare Europort	IC	3	Daily	3 hr.
Dublin Connolly	Wexford	IC	3	Daily	2 hr., 30 min.

using cash or major credit cards. Stations in cities and larger towns have public restrooms, shops, telephones, lockers, luggage carts, and taxi stands. Stations in smaller suburbs and small towns have public restrooms, telephones, and taxi stands. You can view the list of amenities offered in each station on **www.irishrail.com**.

Most InterCity trains offer some kind of food service, be it a restaurant car or a snack cart. If you're traveling first class, you may even be able to get tableside meal service (albeit for a high price) on some routes.

[Fast FACTS] IRELAND

Area Codes The country code for Ireland is **353.** The area code for Dublin is **01.**

Business Hours **Banks** are open 10am to 4pm Monday to Wednesday and Friday, and 10 am to 5pm on Thursday.

Post offices (known as **An Post**) in city centers are open from 9am to 5:30pm Monday to Friday and 9am to 1pm Saturday. Post offices in smaller towns often close for lunch between 1 and 2:30pm.

Museums and sights are generally open 10am to 5pm Tuesday to Saturday, and 2 to 5pm Sunday.

Shops are generally open 9am to 6pm Monday to Friday, with late opening on Thursdays until 7 or 8pm, or Saturday from

10am to 5pm. In Dublin's city center, most department stores and many shops are open noon to 6pm Sunday.

Currency The Republic of Ireland has adopted the single European currency, the **euro,** symbolized in this chapter by the € sign.

Electricity The Irish electric system operates on 220 volts, with a plug bearing three rectangular prongs. To use standard North American 110-volt appliances without destroying them or causing a fire, you'll need both a transformer and a plug adapter. Most laptops have built-in transformers and require only a plug adaptor, available at travel and electronic shops.

Embassies/Consulates The **American Embassy** is at 42 Elgin Rd., Ballsbridge, Dublin 4 (☎ **01/668-8777;** http://dublin.usembassy.gov); the **Canadian Embassy** is at 7–8 Wilton Terrace, 3rd Floor, Dublin 2 (☎ **01/417-4100;** www.canadainternational.gc.ca).

Health & Safety The Republic of Ireland has enjoyed a traditionally low crime rate, particularly when it comes to violent crime. Those days do regrettably seem to be passing, especially in the cities. By U.S. standards, Ireland is still very safe, but not safe enough to warrant carelessness. Travelers should take normal precautions to protect their belongings from theft and themselves from harm.

In recent years, the larger cities have been prey to pickpockets, purse-snatchers, car thieves, and drug traffickers. Some neighborhoods that are mild mannered by day change character at night, especially if they are home to pubs and nightclubs. Ask at your hotel about which areas are dodgy and when. After midnight, you're best off using a taxi for transport.

Ireland poses no major health risks to the rail traveler.

Mail   In Ireland, mailboxes are painted green with the word POST on top. From the Republic, an airmail letter or postcard to the United States or Canada not exceeding 25 grams costs €.85 and takes 5 to 7 days to arrive.

Police   In the Republic of Ireland, a law enforcement officer is called a **Garda**, a member of the *Garda Síochána* ("Guardian of the Peace"); in the plural, it's **Gardaí** (pronounced *Gar*dee), or simply "the Guards." Dial ℭ **999** to reach the Gardaí in an emergency.

Telephone   In the Republic, the telephone system is known as Eircom. Phone numbers in Ireland are currently in flux, as digits are added to accommodate expanded service. Every effort has been made to ensure that the numbers and information in this guide are accurate at the time of writing. To dial a local number within an area code, drop the initial 0. To dial a number within Ireland, but in a different area code, use the initial 0. If you have difficulty reaching a party, the Irish toll-free number for directory assistance is ℭ **11811** (www.11811.ie).

Local calls from a phone booth in the Republic require a **Callcard,** a prepaid computerized card that you insert into the phone instead of coins. They can be purchased in a range of denominations at phone company offices, post offices, and many retail outlets (such as newsstands). There's a local and international phone center at the General Post Office on O'Connell Street.

To place a call from your home country to Ireland, dial the international access code (**011** in the U.S.), plus the country code (**353** for the Republic), and finally the number, remembering to omit the initial 0, which is for use only within Ireland (for example, to call Dublin Castle from the United States, you'd dial 011-353-1/677-7129).

To place a direct international call from Ireland, dial the international access code **(00),** plus the country code (U.S. and Canada 1), the area or city code, and the number.

Tipping   Most hotels and guesthouses add a service charge to the bill, usually 12.5% to 15%, although some smaller places add only 10% or nothing at all. Always check to see what amount, if any, has been added to your bill. If it is 12.5% to 15%, and you feel this is sufficient, then there is no need for further gratuities. If a smaller amount has been added, however, or if staff members have provided exceptional service, it is appropriate to give an additional tip. For porters or bellhops, tip 1€ per piece of luggage. For taxi drivers, hairdressers, and other providers of service, tip as you would at home, an average of 10% to 15%.

For restaurants, the policy is usually printed on the menu—either a gratuity of 10% to 15% is automatically added to your bill or it's left up to you ("service not included" may be written on the bill). Always ask if you are in doubt. As a rule, bartenders do not expect a tip, except when table service is provided.

DUBLIN

Dublin isn't an immediate beauty. Compared to cities such as Edinburgh and Paris, it seems rather squat and lacking in oh-wow architecture. But the inhabitants—the city is home to more than a third of the entire population of Ireland—are the real reason to visit this city. They have a knack for making even everyday living seem poetic, and excel in storytelling and music-making. And Dublin offers far more than just old-style hospitality; it's also packed with young people, with an estimated 50% of its population under 30 years old.

Dublin was shaken in 2008, however, when the Irish economy took a nosedive—unemployment shot up and the property market collapsed. The long-expected end to the Irish economic bubble had begun. The downward trend continued in 2009, and in 2010, the country instituted deep cuts to its spending in an attempt to staunch the bleeding. As this book was being written, the situation in Ireland was still quite serious. The Irish boom days are over, at least for now. Still, in the face of endless bad news, Dublin retained its irrepressible enthusiasm and vigor. This is an exciting city to explore. A weekend in Dublin is one of the hottest city breaks in Europe, for good reason.

It's also the rail hub of the Republic and home to a major international airport, making it the logical first stop for rail travelers touring the country. Another bonus: Compared to other European capitals, Dublin is a relatively small metropolis and easily traversed. The city center—identified in Irish on bus destination signs as AN LAR—is bisected by the River Liffey, flowing west to east into Dublin Bay. Canals ring the city center: The Royal Canal forms a skirt through the north half, and the Grand Canal the southern half. The buzzing, prosperous hub of Dublin lies mostly south of the Liffey. The area containing most of the best hotels, restaurants, shops, and sights is a small, well-defined compound easily walked in a half-hour.

On the downside, Dublin's an expensive place to visit, but it's still cheaper than some other cities in Europe.

Station Information
GETTING FROM THE AIRPORT TO THE TRAIN STATION
Dublin International Airport (℡ 01/814-1111; www.dublinairport.com) is 6.2 miles (10km) north of the city center. A tourist information office located in the Arrivals Concourse provides information on public bus and rail services throughout the country.

If you need to connect immediately with the Irish rail service, the **Airlink Express Coach** (℡ 01/844-4265; www.dublinbus.ie) provides express bus service (nos. 747 and 748) from the airport to the two main rail stations, **Connolly** and **Heuston.** Service runs daily from 5:45am until 11:30pm (Sun 7:15am–11:30pm), with departures every 20 to 30 minutes. One-way fare is €6 for adults and €3 for children 11 and under. Buy a ticket before boarding the bus from the pay machine just on your left as you exit the airport. The buses leave from the lay-by opposite the pay machine. The journey takes 30 to 35 minutes.

An excellent airport-to-city bus service called **AirCoach** operates 24 hours a day, making runs at 15-minute intervals. AirCoach runs direct from the airport to Dublin's city center and south side, serving all the key hotel and business districts. The one-way fare is €7 or €12 round-trip, €1.50 for children aged 5 to 12. You buy your ticket from the driver. Although AirCoach is slightly more expensive than the **Express Coach** (above), it is faster because it makes fewer intermediary stops and it brings you right into the hotel districts. To confirm AirCoach departures and arrivals, call ℡ 01/844-7118 or find it on the Web at **www.aircoach.ie.**

Dublin Bus (℡ 01/873-4222; www.dublinbus.ie) runs daily connections between the airport and the city center from 6am to 11:30pm. The one-way trip takes about 30 minutes, and the fare is €6. Bus nos. 16a, 41, 41b, 46x, 230, 746, 747, and

Dublin

ACCOMMODATIONS ■

Avalon House **15**
Buswells Hotel **24**
Butlers Town House **26**
Eliza Lodge **9**
The Fitzwilliam Hotel **22**

Isaac's Hotel **6**
Number 31 **31**
Premier Suites
  Stephen's Hall **30**
Trinity Lodge **23**
Waterloo House **26**

DINING ◆

Café Mao **21**
Epicurean Food Hall **7**
Irish Film Centre
  Café Bar **19**
Leo Burdock's **13**

Mermaid Café **18**
Nude **20**
Roly's Bistro **27**
The Tea Room **10**
Winding Stair **8**
Yamamori Noodles **16**

CONNOLLY

CONNOLLY
STATION

Central
Bus
Station

Inner
Dock

George's
Dock

Custom
House

Custom House Quay

Talbot
Memorial
Bridge

City Quay

TARA ST.

DART

Hanover St.

Four
Courts

Trinity
College

PEARSE ST.

Dublin
Castle

College
Green

Leinster
House

Merrion
Square

St. Stephen's
Green

Fitzwilliam
Square

ATTRACTIONS
The Book of Kells **25**
Christ Church Cathedral **11**
Collins Barracks **3**
Dublin Castle **17**
Dublinia **12**

Dublin Writers Museum **5**
Hugh Lane Municipal Gallery of
  Modern Art **4**
Kilmainham Gaol
  Historical Museum **1**
National Gallery of Ireland **28**

National Museum
  of Ireland **29**
Phoenix Park **2**
St. Patrick's
  Cathedral **14**

748 all serve the city center from Dublin Airport. Consult the travel information desk in the arrivals concourse to figure out which bus takes you closest to your hotel.

If you have a lot of luggage, a **taxi** is the best way to get directly to your hotel or guesthouse. Depending on your destination in Dublin, fares average between €20 and €30. Each additional passenger is charged €.50 for each piece of luggage. Depending on traffic (which can be horrendous), a cab should take 20 to 45 minutes to get into the city center. Taxis are lined up on a first-come, first-served taxi stand outside the arrivals terminal.

Passenger and car ferries from Britain arrive at the **Dublin Ferryport** (✆ **01/855-2222**), on the eastern end of the North Docks, and at the **Dún Laoghaire Ferryport** (✆ **01/842-8864**). Call **Irish Ferries** (✆ **0818/300-400**; www.irishferries. ie), **P&O Irish Sea** (✆ **01/407-3434**; www.poirishsea.com), or **Stena Line** (✆ **01/204-7777**; www.stenaline.com) for bookings and information. There is bus and taxi service from both ports.

INSIDE THE STATIONS

Dublin has two major train stations—**Heuston Station,** Kingsbridge, off St. John's Road, and **Connolly Station,** Amiens Street—and an additional two minor ones. To determine which station works best for your rail itinerary, see "Which Dublin Station?" below. Both stations are staffed 24 hours daily, and Connolly Station will book tickets Monday through Saturday 7am to 10:20pm and Sunday 8:30am to 11:30pm. At Heuston Station, hours are Monday through Saturday 6:30am to 7:15pm and 7:35 to 11pm, Sunday 7:30am to 7:25pm and 10 to 11:35pm.

CONNOLLY STATION   The major train station for points north of Dublin, Connolly is on the eastern side of Dublin, just a block away from the city's Central Bus Station. Station facilities include lockers, fast-food restaurants and cafes, a taxi stand, ATMs, public restrooms, news agents, and ticket-vending machines. A visitor information desk is located at track level in the station. There are maps, brochures and a booking office. For more information about this station, call ✆ **01/703-2132** or see **www.irishrail.ie.**

HEUSTON STATION   On the western side of the Dublin, Heuston appropriately handles a lot of the trains heading west out of the city. A visitor information desk is located at track level in the station. Station facilities include fast-food restaurants and cafes, a taxi stand, ATMs, public restrooms, newsagents, and ticket-vending machines. There are maps, brochures, and a booking office. For more information about this station, call ✆ **01/703-2132** or see **www.irishrail.com.**

Information Elsewhere in the City

Dublin Tourism (✆ **01/605-7700**; www.visitdublin.com) operates six walk-in visitor centers in greater Dublin. The principal center is in the wonderfully restored

WHICH DUBLIN station?

Connolly Station InterCity routes to Sligo, Belfast; Rosslare; Longford; DART service to Malahide/Howth, County Dublin (north) and Greystones, County Wicklow (south).	**Heuston Station** InterCity routes to Cork, Tralee, Limerick, Waterford, Ballina/Westport, Galway, Kildare, Clonmel; No DART service.

Late-Night Crime

Dublin is a booze-fueled city. This is particularly noticeable on weekends around the Temple Bar/Grafton Street/O'Connell Street areas. The Gardai do their best to keep the public order incidents under control, but rowdy herds of men can turn nasty and have been known to attack passersby without any provocation. Although there are no official police warnings about walking back to your hotel alone at certain times of night, we get a taxi if we're arriving at the train station after 10pm (if nothing else, it avoids the possibility of inadvertently stepping in vomit), and make sure we don't walk back home alone around pub/club closing time (anywhere btw. 11pm and dawn).

Church of St. Andrew on Suffolk Street, Dublin 2, open from June to August Monday to Saturday from 9am to 8:30pm, Sunday and bank holidays 10:30am to 3pm; and the rest of the year Monday to Saturday 9am to 5:30pm, Sunday and bank holidays 10:30am to 3pm. The Suffolk Street office is about ½ mile (.8km) from Connolly Station and includes a currency exchange counter, a car-rental counter, an accommodations reservation service, bus and rail information desks, a gift shop, and a cafe.

The other centers are in the **arrivals concourse** of Dublin Airport; **O'Connell Street,** 14 Upper O'Connell St., Dublin 1; **Baggot Street Bridge,** Baggot Street, Dublin 2; the **Square Towncentre,** Tallaght, Dublin 24; and the ferry terminal at **Dun Laoghaire Harbor** (© 01/605-7700 or www.visitdublin.com). All centers are open year-round (except Christmas) for at least the following hours: Monday to Friday 9am to 5:30pm and Saturday 9am to 5pm.

For information on Ireland outside of Dublin, call **Bord Fáilte** (© 1850/230330 in Ireland; www.discoverireland.com).

For accommodations reservations throughout Ireland by credit card (including some good last-minute deals on Dublin hotels), contact Dublin Tourism at the phone number and website listed above. For individual research and bookings, go to **www. hotelrooms365.com**.

Getting Around

Getting around Dublin is a breeze. Public transportation is good and getting better, taxis are plentiful and reasonably priced, and walking is a pleasure. In fact, with its current traffic and parking problems, it's a city where the foot is mightier than the wheel.

ON FOOT   Small and compact, Dublin is ideal for walking, as long as you remember to look right and then left (in the direction opposite your instincts) for oncoming traffic before crossing the street, and to obey traffic signals. Each traffic light has timed "walk–don't walk" signals for pedestrians. Pedestrians have the right of way at specially marked, zebra-striped crossings; as a warning, there are usually two flashing lights at these intersections.

BY BUS   Dublin Bus operates a fleet of green double-decker buses, single-deck buses, and minibuses (called "imps") throughout the city and its suburbs. Most buses originate on or near O'Connell Street, Abbey Street, and Eden Quay on the north side, and at Aston Quay, College Street, and Fleet Street on the south side. Bus stops are located every few blocks. Destinations and bus numbers are posted above the front windows; buses destined for the city center are marked with the Irish Gaelic words VIA AN LAR.

Bus service runs daily throughout the city, starting at 6am (10am on Sun), with the last bus at 11:30pm. On Thursday, Friday, and Saturday nights, **Nitelink** service runs from the city center to the suburbs from midnight to 3am. Buses operate every 10 to 15 minutes for most runs; schedules are posted on revolving notice boards at each bus stop.

Inner-city fares are calculated based on distances traveled. The minimum fare is €1.15 (unless you're only going a very short distance within the city center, in which case it's €.50); the maximum fare for journeys in the city center is €2.20, rising to €4.50 if you go as far as the outer suburbs. Children under 16 pay between €.65 and €1. The Nitelink fare is a flat €5. Buy your tickets from the driver as you enter the bus. Following a rise in robberies of bus drivers in Dublin, all buses now use an "Autofare" machine. This means that fares must be paid with coins directly into a fare box next to the driver's cab. Bills are not accepted, and no change is given. If you have to pay more than the cost of the ticket, the driver will issue you a refund ticket, which must be presented along with your travel ticket at the Dublin Bus office on Upper O'Connell Street to claim a refund for the difference. Inevitably, this is rarely worth the effort.

You can also get 1-day, 3-day, 5-day, and 7-day **bus passes** or a **Rambler** ticket. The 1-day bus-only pass costs €6; the 3-day pass costs €14; the 5-day pass goes for €20; and the 7-day pass costs €21. For more information, contact **Dublin Bus,** 59 Upper O'Connell St., Dublin 1 (© **01/872-0000;** www.dublinbus.ie). Another option worth considering is the **freedom ticket.** Specially designed for tourists, it works like a standard 3-day bus pass, but also includes unlimited travel on the Airlink, Nitelink, and Dublin City Tour buses. The cost is €25 adults and €16 children under 14. These can be purchased from most major stores in the city center and any Dublin Tourist Information Office.

BY DART   While Dublin has no subway in the strict sense, there is an electric rapid-transit train, known as the **DART (Dublin Area Rapid Transit).** It travels mostly at ground level or on elevated tracks, linking the city-center stations at **Connolly Station, Tara Street,** and **Pearse Street** with suburbs and seaside communities as far as Malahide to the north and Greystones to the south. Trains run roughly every 10 to 20 minutes Monday to Saturday from around 6am to midnight and Sunday from 9:30am to 11pm. Typical adult fares cost around €1.60 for a short single journey; combination rail-and-bus tickets, valid all day within the "short hop" zone of the city center, start from €9 adults. One-day, 3-day, and 10-trip passes, as well as student and family tickets, are available at reduced rates from ticket windows in stations. For further information, contact DART, Dublin Pearse Station (© **01/703-3592;** www.dart.ie).

BY TRAM   The newest addition to Dublin's public transportation network is the sleek, modern (and wheelchair-accessible) light-rail tram known as **LUAS,** which means "speed" in Gaelic. Traveling at a maximum speed of 45 mph (72kmph) and departing every 5 minutes in peak hours, LUAS has helped ease Dublin's congestion problems; an estimated 120,000 people use it each day. There are two lines: The **St. Stephen's Green** line goes from Sandyford in the southeast to St. Stephen's Green; the red line starts at the southwest suburb of Tallaght and terminates at **Connolly Station.** Fares are calculated by length of trip, starting at €1.60 for a single central

Dublin trip; round-trip is €2.90. Your best bet is a 1-day travel card that is good for all zones and costs €6 adults and €2.50 kids. The cards are slightly more expensive if bought direct from LUAS at the tram stops, so you'll save if you buy from one of the agents (usually convenience stores such as Spar and Centra located near the tram stops). Whichever way you go, be sure to have a valid ticket when you board, or you could be fined €45. For further information, contact **LUAS** at ✆ **01/800-300-604** (in Ireland only) or visit **www.luas.ie**.

BY TAXI   Taxis don't usually respond to being hailed on the street; instead, they line up at stands called "ranks." Stands are located outside all of the leading hotels, at bus and train stations, and on prime thoroughfares such as Upper O'Connell Street, College Green, and the north side of St. Stephen's Green near the Shelbourne Hotel. You can also phone for a taxi. Here are some companies: **Co-Op** (✆ **01/676-6666**), **National Radio Cabs** (✆ **01/677-2222**), and **VIP/ACE Taxis** (✆ **01/ 478-3333**). If you need a wake-up call, VIP offers that service, along with especially courteous dependability.

Taxi rates are fixed by law and posted in each vehicle. The following are typical travel costs in the city center: The starting fare for the first kilometer (½ mile) is €4.10 by day and €4.45 at night. For the next 8¾₃ miles (14km), the fare is €1.05 per kilometer by day, €1.35 by night, rising to a maximum of €1.75 per kilometer thereafter. You may instead be charged an equivalent price per minute (which runs a minimum €.35 during the day, up to a maximum of €.65 at night). It costs an extra €2 if you order a cab by phone, with €1 extra per passenger. *Be warned:* At some hotels, staff members will tack on as much as €5 for calling you a cab, although this practice violates city taxi regulations. Ask before you request a taxi whether you'll be charged. Complaints can be registered at the **Garda Siochana,** at ✆ **01/659-3800.**

Where to Stay

Avalon House 🗲   This warm and friendly hostel in a beautiful old redbrick building is well among those who travel to Dublin on a budget. Its pine floors, high ceilings, and open fireplace make it a pleasant place in which to relax, and its cafe is a popular hangout for international travelers. Most accommodations are in dorms of varying sizes, with a few single and twin-bedded rooms available, too. It's clean, cheerful rooms in a safe location at a cheap price. This is one of the best budget options in town.

55 Aungier St., Dublin 2. ✆ **01/475-0001.** Fax 01/475-0303. www.avalon-house.ie. 12 units. €27–€45 per person double with private bathroom. Rates include light continental breakfast. AE, MC, V. Bus: 16, 16A, 19, 22, or 155. No curfew, but passes must be shown on entry after 9pm. **Amenities:** Cafe; smoke-free rooms.

Buswells Hotel ★   This traditional hotel has a wonderful sense of class but isn't stuffy. The spacious, slightly masculine rooms are spread throughout three Georgian buildings. The fact that the hotel is so sprawling can make it feel a bit idiosyncratic, and finding your room can be a challenge after a few pints of Guinness. But it's worth the wandering, as it has great style and a unique ambience, in part because its location near the Irish government buildings.

23–25 Molesworth St., Dublin 2. ✆ **01/614-6500.** Fax 01/676-2090. www.buswellshotel.com. 69 units. €140–€290 double. AE, DC, MC, V. DART: Pearse. Bus: 10, 11, 13, or 46A. **Amenities:** Restaurant; bar; smoke-free floors.

Butlers Town House ★   This beautifully restored and expanded Victorian town house B&B feels like a gracious family home. The atmosphere is elegant, but comfortable rooms are richly furnished with four-poster or half-tester beds, and draped in luxurious fabrics in rich colors. The gem here is the Glendalough Room, with a lovely bay window and small library (you have to request it when you book your room). Still, prices here are rather high, given the lack of amenities (there's no restaurant or bar, for example), so consider that before you book.

44 Lansdowne Rd., Ballsbridge, Dublin 4. ℂ **800/44-UTELL** [448-8355] in the U.S., or 01/667-4022. Fax 01/667-3960. www.butlers-hotel.com. 20 units. €240 double. Rates include full breakfast. AE, DC, MC, V. Closed Dec 23–Jan 10. DART: Lansdowne Rd. Bus: 7, 7A, 8, or 45. **Amenities:** Breakfast room.

Eliza Lodge ★   This hotel, beside the Liffey, embodies all the exuberance and zest of Temple Bar. The reception rooms aren't impressive, but guest rooms are simple and attractive, done in neutral creams, with big floor-to-ceiling windows to take in the riverside vistas. *Note:* The windows are not soundproof, and rooms on the lower floors can get a lot of street noise. Take your breakfast (included in the room rate) in the Liffey-view **Italian Corner** restaurant.

23–24 Wellington Quay, Dublin 2. ℂ **01/671-8044.** Fax 01/671-8362. www.elizalodge.com. 18 units. €100–€170 double. AE, MC, V. Bus: 51B, 51C, 68, 69, or 79. **Amenities:** Restaurant; bar.

The Fitzwilliam Hotel ★★★   With sweeping views over St. Stephen's Green, this hotel has an unbeatable location and a contemporary design. The Fitzwilliam has an easygoing sophistication, with clean lines and only a few neutral colors throughout guest rooms. The beauty is in the detail here—attentive staff; big, comfortable beds; and stripped-down furniture. **Thornton's,** the Michelin-starred hotel restaurant, is very good, or you could try the more casual **Citron,** or linger over canapés and mojitos at the **Inn on the Green** bar.

109 St. Stephen's Green, Dublin 2. ℂ **01/478-7000.** Fax 01/478-7878. www.fitzwilliamhotel.com. 130 units. €165–€290 double. Breakfast €22. AE, DC, MC, V. DART: Pearse. Bus: 10, 11A, 11B, 13, or 20B. **Amenities:** 2 restaurants; bar; smoke-free rooms.

Isaac's Hotel   This friendly guesthouse has had something of an upgrade recently; rooms are now basic and cheap (by Irish standards). Bedrooms are clean and comfortable, with polished pine furniture. Rooms in the more expensive "Georgian wing" are more elegantly designed, and with fancier furnishings. On the downside, the super-central location means that it can get quite noisy on weekends, and management charges for each additional amenity. We recommend this hotel if you're traveling in the high season and can't get a good advance-booking bargain at a better hotel.

2–5 Frenchman's Lane, Dublin 1. ℂ **01/855-6215.** Fax 01/855-6524. www.isaacs.ie. 54 units. €80–€140. Room upgrades €25–€50. Rates include breakfast. MC, V. DART: Connolly. All cross-city buses. **Amenities:** Restaurant; cafe/bar.

Number 31 ★   This award-winning town house B&B, discretely located in the heart of Georgian Dublin, is actually two beautifully renovated architectural show houses: one a Georgian town house, the other a modern coach house. Features include a fabulous sunken fireside seating area with mosaic tiles in the main lounge. In the main house, rooms are large and simply decorated, while in the coach house, rooms are elegant and modern. All the rooms are a triumph of quiet good taste. Breakfast is cooked to order and delicious.

31 Leeson Close, Lower Leeson St., Dublin 2. ℂ **01/676-5011.** Fax 01/676-29-29. www.number31.ie. 21 units. €150–€320 double. Rates include breakfast. AE, MC, V. Bus: 11, 11A, 11B, 13, 13A, or 13B.

Premier Suites Stephen's Hall ⚓ How suite it is. Well located on the southeast corner of St. Stephen's Green in a handsome Georgian town house, this all-suite hotel appeals to visitors who want to save on food or folks who want to do their own cooking. The building recently underwent a full renovation, which renewed each large suite in tasteful modern style. Each apartment contains a sitting room, dining area, fully equipped kitchenette, tiled bathroom, and bedroom.

14-17 Lower Leeson St., Dublin 2. ℗ **01/638-1111.** Fax 01/638-1122. www.stephens-hall.com. 30 units. €95–€175 studio and 1-bedroom suite; €153–€242 2-bedroom suite. AE, DC, MC, V. DART: Pearse. Bus: 11, 11A, 11B, 13, 13A, or 13B. **Amenities:** Concierge; smoke-free floor.

Trinity Lodge Feeling miles away from the anonymous chain hotels, the Trinity is a classy option a few blocks off Grafton Street. The gray stone building dates from 1785, and its 10 large guest rooms are brightly decorated in keeping with that period, some with paintings by the respected Irish artists. The breakfast room downstairs is warmly designed in country-house style. A second building across the street houses six large rooms with a more contemporary edge. The buildings are protected historical structures, so there's no elevator access to their four levels—ask for a ground-floor room if you have mobility problems. The room prices include both breakfast and a nightly cocktail hour.

12 S. Frederick St., Dublin 2. ℗ **01/617-0900.** Fax 01/617-0999. www.trinitylodge.com. 16 units. €195–€250 double. Rates include breakfast. MC, V. Bus: All An Lar (cross-city) buses. **Amenities:** Restaurant; bar; room service; smoke-free rooms. *In room:* A/C (in some), TV, Wi-Fi.

Waterloo House ★ This classy and peaceful guesthouse is charming in an old-world kind of way, with classical music wafting through the lobby, and the elegant, high-ceilinged drawing room looking like a parlor out of an Agatha Christie novel. Guest rooms are comfortable and large (some have two double beds), and breakfast goes beyond the usual Irish fried eggs and bacon.

8-10 Waterloo Rd., Ballsbridge, Dublin 4. ℗ **01/660-1888.** www.waterloohouse.ie. 17 units. €130–€175 double. Rates include full breakfast. MC, V. Closed Christmas week. DART: Lansdowne Rd. Bus: 5, 7, or 8. **Amenities:** Breakfast room; all rooms smoke-free.

Top Attractions & Special Moments

The Book of Kells ★★★ 👋 The jewel in Ireland's tourism crown is the Book of Kells, a magnificent 9th-century manuscript of the four Gospels, painstakingly scripted and illuminated by talented monks. It's the most majestic work of art to survive from the early centuries of Celtic Christianity, and has often been described as "the most beautiful book in the world." Its fascination derives from the astonishing variety and complexity of the linear ornamentation that adorns every one of its 680 pages. This famous treasure and other early Christian manuscripts are on permanent public view at Trinity College. *Note:* Only 2 pages at a time are displayed behind bulletproof glass. An exhibition area on the ground floor of the Library's Long Room contains rare works on Irish history. The oldest university in Ireland, Trinity was founded in 1592 by Queen Elizabeth I. It occupies a beautiful 40-acre (16-hectare) site just south of the River Liffey, with cobbled squares, gardens, a picturesque quadrangle, and buildings dating from the 17th to the 20th centuries. This is one of Dublin's busiest visitor attractions, meaning it can be heaving in summer months. The quietest times are from October to April; if you have to go during the summer, get here as soon as it opens, to avoid the crowds.

College Green, Dublin 2. © **01/608-2320.** www.tcd.ie/about/trinity/bookofkells. Free admission to college grounds. €9 adults, €8 seniors/students, €18 families, free for children 11 and under. Combination ticket for the Library and Dublin Experience also available. Mon–Sat 9:30am–5pm; Sun 9:30am–4:30pm (opens noon Oct–Apr). Bus: Any An Lar (cross-city) bus.

Christ Church Cathedral ★   Standing on high ground in the oldest part of the city, this cathedral is one of Dublin's finest historic buildings, and the best way to approach it is to walk from the riverside in order to truly appreciate its size. It dates from 1038, when Sitric, Danish king of Dublin, built the first wooden Christ Church here. The present structure dates mainly from 1871 to 1878, when a huge restoration took place and much of the old detail was destroyed. Highlights of the interior include magnificent stonework and graceful pointed arches, with delicately chiseled supporting columns. The best way to get a glimpse of what the original building must have been like is to visit the crypt, which is original to the 12th-century structure.

Christ Church Place, Dublin 8. © **01/677-8099.** www.cccdub.ie. Admission €6 adults, €4 seniors, €3 students and children 14 and under. June to mid-July Mon, Tues, and Fri 9:45am–6:15pm; Wed, Thurs, and Sat 9:45am–4:15pm, Sun 12:30–2:30pm and 4:30–6:15pm. Mid-July to Aug Mon–Sat 9:45am–4:15pm, Sun 12:30–2:30pm and 4:30–6:15pm; Sept–May Mon–Sat 9:45am–6:15pm, 12:30–2:30pm. Bus: 21A, 50, 50A, 78, 78A, or 78B.

Collins Barracks   Collins Barracks is a splendidly restored early-18th-century military building, but worth visiting only if you're a fan of the decorative arts, as it's been converted into part of the National Museum of Ireland. Until the acquisition of this vast space, only a fraction of the National Museum's collection could be displayed, but more and more treasures have found their way here. Notable collections include a huge display of Irish silver and furniture; a magnificent collection of rare 19th-century art from Tibet, China, and Japan; and an exhibition devoted to the work of the influential Irish designer and architect Eileen Gray (1878–1976).

Benburb St., Dublin 7. © **01/677-7444.** Free admission. Tours (hours vary) €2 adults; free for seniors and children. Tues–Sat 10am–5pm; Sun 2–5pm. Bus: 34, 70, or 80.

Dublin Castle ★★   Built between 1208 and 1220, this complex displays some of the oldest surviving architecture in the city. It was the center of British power in Ireland for more than 7 centuries, until the new Irish government took it over in 1922. Highlights, which you can see only if you are on a tour, include the 13th-century record tower; the state apartments, once the residence of English viceroys; and the Chapel Royal, a 19th-century Gothic building with particularly fine plaster decoration and carved oak gallery fronts and fittings. The atmospheric and ancient Undercroft (if it's open) is an excavated site on the grounds where an early Viking fortress stood, and the Treasury, built between 1712 and 1715, is believed to be the oldest surviving office building in Ireland. There are also a vaguely interesting on-site craft shop, heritage center, and restaurant. *Be warned:* Much of this area is now office space and parking lots.

Palace St. (off Dame St.), Dublin 2. © **01/677-7129.** www.dublincastle.ie. Admission €4.50 adults, €3.50 students/seniors, €2 children 11 and under. €1 discount when state apts. aren't available (children enter free). Mon–Fri 10am–4:45pm; Sat–Sun and holidays 2–4:45pm. Guided tours every 20–25 min. Bus: 50, 50A, 54, 56A, 77, 77A, or 77B.

Dublinia ☺   This museum aims to teach the little ones about the Viking and medieval history of Dublin through a series of interactive exhibits. With visual effects, background sounds (some on an annoying loop seem to follow you around repeating the same phrase over and over, until you can still hear it in your sleep weeks later), and aromas ostensibly from that time, it's designed to stimulate, but will probably bore anybody over the age of 14. Still, you and the kids can dress up in medieval garb, be chained up as Viking slaves, and put yourselves in the town stocks. If you plan to visit Dublinia and Christ Church Cathedral on the same day, keep hold of your ticket to claim reduced-price admission.

St. Michael's Hill, Christ Church, Dublin 8. © **01/679-4611.** www.dublinia.ie. Admission €6.25 adults, €5 seniors, €5.25 students, €3.75 children, €17 families. Daily 10am–5pm (last admission 4:15pm, Oct–Mar last admission 4pm). Closed Dec 23–26 and Mar 17. Bus: 50, 78A, or 123.

Dublin Writers Museum ★★ 📷 Housed in a stunning 18th-century Georgian mansion with splendid plasterwork and stained glass, the museum is itself an impressive reminder of the grandeur of the Irish literary tradition. A fine collection of personal manuscripts and mementos that belonged to Yeats, Joyce, Beckett, Behan, Shaw, Wilde, Swift, and Sheridan are among the items that celebrate the written word. This museum opens a window and lets in light on Ireland's rich literary heritage, and it is wonderful to walk in that glow. There's a good gift shop with writing-related souvenirs and a selection of books by many classic and modern Irish writers. The museum also hosts occasional literary readings and lectures.

18-19 Parnell Sq. N., Dublin 1. © **01/872-2077.** www.writersmuseum.com. Admission €7.50 adults, €6.30 seniors and students, €4.70 children, €20 families. Combined ticket with James Joyce Museum or Shaw Birthplace, plus Malahide Castle €12 adults, €9.50 seniors and students, €7.50 children, €31 families. Mon–Sat 10am–5pm (until 6pm June–Aug); Sun and holidays 11am–5pm. Last admission 45 min. before closing. DART: Connolly Station. Bus: 11, 13, 16, 16A, 22, or 22A.

Hugh Lane Municipal Gallery of Modern Art ★ Housed in a finely restored 18th-century building known as Charlemont House, this gallery is situated next to the Dublin Writers Museum. This little gallery, which celebrated its 100-year anniversary in 2008, has a strong collection of Impressionist works led by Degas's *Sur la Plage* and Manet's *La Musique aux Tuileries,* and also holds sculptures by Rodin, a marvelous collection of Harry Clarke stained glass, and numerous works by modern Irish artists. One room holds the maddeningly cluttered studio of the Irish painter Francis Bacon, which the gallery purchased from London and moved to Dublin piece by piece, where it was reconstructed behind glass. Everything was moved, right down to the dust. It's an excellent, compact art museum, and a great place to spend an afternoon.

Parnell Sq. N., Dublin 1. © **01/222-5550.** www.hughlane.ie. Free admission. Tues–Thurs 10am–6pm; Fri–Sat 10am–5pm; Sun 11am–5pm. DART: Connolly or Tara stations. Bus: 3, 10, 11, 13, 16, or 19.

Kilmainham Gaol Historical Museum ★★★ This is a key sight for anyone interested in Ireland's struggle for independence from British rule. Within these walls, political prisoners were incarcerated, tortured, and killed from 1796 until 1924, when President Éamon de Valera left as its final prisoner. To walk along these corridors, through the grim exercise yard, or into the main compound is a moving experience that lingers hauntingly in the memory.

Kilmainham, Dublin 8. © **01/453-5984.** www.heritageireland.ie. Guided tour €6 adults, €4 seniors, €2 children, €14 family. Apr–Sept daily 9:30am–6pm (last admission 5pm); Oct–Mar Mon–Sat 9:30am–5:30pm (last admission 4pm), Sun 10am–6pm (last admission 5pm). Bus: 51B, 78A, or 79.

National Gallery of Ireland ★ This museum houses Ireland's national art collection, as well as a European collection of art spanning the 14th to the 20th centuries. Every major European school of painting is represented, including fine selections by Italian Renaissance artists (especially Caravaggio's *The Taking of Christ*), French

Impressionists, and Dutch 17th-century masters. In 2007 the gallery gained its first van Gogh, *Rooftops of Paris*. The highlight of the Irish collection is the room dedicated to the witty and shimmering works of Jack B. Yeats, brother of the poet W. B. Yeats. The museum has a shop and an excellent self-service restaurant.

Merrion Sq. W., Dublin 2. ℂ **01/661-5133.** www.nationalgallery.ie. Free admission. Mon–Sat 9:30am–5:30pm (Thurs until 8:30pm); Sun noon–5:30pm. Closed Dec 24–26 and Good Friday. Free guided tours (meet in the Shaw Room) Sat 3pm and Sun 2, 3, and 4pm. DART: Pearse. Bus: 5, 6, 7, 7A, 8, 10, 44, 47, 47B, 48A, or 62.

National Museum of Ireland ★★   Established in 1890, this museum is a reflection of Ireland's heritage from 2000 B.C. to the present, with sections devoted to archaeology, decorative arts, and natural history. The institution spans four sites and is the home of many of the country's greatest historical finds, including the Treasury exhibit, which features the Ardagh Chalice, Tara Brooch, and Cross of Cong. Other highlights include the artifacts from the Wood Quay excavations of the Old Dublin Settlements, and an exhibition of Irish Bronze Age gold ornaments dating from 2200 to 700 B.C. *Note:* The National Museum's other sites are the Museum of Decorative Arts and History at Collins Barracks (p. 448), the newly renovated Natural History Museum on Merrion Street, and the Museum of Country Life in Castlebar, County Mayo.

Kildare St. and Merrion St., Dublin 2. ℂ **01/677-7444.** www.museum.ie. Free admission. Tues–Sat 10am–5pm; Sun 2–5pm. Closed Christmas and Good Friday. DART: Pearse. Bus: 7, 7A, 8, 10, 11, or 13.

Phoenix Park ★ ☺   Just 2 miles (3.2km) west of the city center, Phoenix Park, the largest urban park in Europe, is the playground of Dublin. A network of roads and quiet pedestrian walkways traverses its 1,739 acres (696 hectares), which are informally landscaped with ornamental gardens and nature trails. Avenues of trees, including oak, beech, pine, chestnut, and lime, separate broad expanses of grassland. The homes of the Irish president and the U.S. ambassador are on the grounds, as is the Dublin Zoo. Livestock graze peacefully on pasturelands, deer roam the forested areas, and horses romp on polo fields. The **Phoenix Park Visitor Centre,** adjacent to Ashtown Castle, has information about all the park has to offer. The cafe/restaurant is open 10am to 5pm weekdays, 10am to 6pm weekends.

Phoenix Park, Dublin 8. ℂ **01/677-0095.** www.heritageireland.ie. Free admission. Apr–Sept daily 10am–6pm; Jan–Mar and Nov–Dec daily 10am–5pm; Oct daily 10am–5:30pm. Bus: 37, 38, or 39.

St. Patrick's Cathedral ★   It is said that St. Patrick baptized converts on this site, and consequently a church has stood here since A.D. 450, making it the oldest Christian site in Dublin. The present cathedral dates from 1190, but because of a fire and 14th-century rebuilding, not much of the original foundation remains. It is mainly early English in style, with a square medieval tower that houses the largest ringing peal bells in Ireland, and an 18th-century spire. The plaques, monuments, and sarcophagi throughout its 300-foot (90m) interior make it as fascinating a church as any in Europe. St. Patrick's is closely associated with Jonathan Swift, who was dean from 1713 to 1745 and whose tomb lies in the south aisle. Patrick's is the national cathedral of the Church of Ireland. Look for special, changing exhibits of an architectural, fine art, or religious nature.

21–50 Patrick's Close, Patrick St., Dublin 8. ℂ **01/475-4817.** Fax 01/454-6374. www.stpatrickscathedral. ie. Admission €5.50 adults, €4.50 seniors and students, €15 families. Mar–Oct Mon–Fri 9am–5:30pm; Sat 9am–6:30pm; Sun 9–11am, 12:30–3pm and 4:30–6:30pm; Nov–Feb Mon–Sat 9am–5:30pm, Sun 9–11am and 12:30–3pm. Last admission 30 min. before closing. Closed Dec 24–26, except for services. Bus: 50, 50A, 54, 54A, 56A, 65, 65B, or 77.

Where to Dine

Café Mao ★ ASIAN   This is where to go when you feel like some Asian cooking with an exhilarating attitude. The exposed kitchen lines one entire wall, and the rest of the space is wide open—great for people-watching. The menu reads like a Best of Asia list: Thai fish cakes, *nasi goreng*, chicken hoisin, salmon ramen. Everything is delicious—you can't go wrong. There are also branches in the Pavilion in Dún Laoghaire (✆ **01/214-8090**), and in Civic Square, Dundrum, Dublin 16 (✆ **01/296/2802.**

2 Chatham Row, Dublin 2. ✆ **01/670-4899.** www.cafemao.com. Reservations recommended. Main courses €10–€18. AE, MC, V. Mon–Wed noon–10:30pm; Thurs noon–11pm; Fri–Sat noon–11:30pm; Sun noon–10pm. DART: Pearse. Bus: 10, 11A, 11B, 13, or 20B.

Epicurean Food Hall FOOD COURT   This wonderful food hall houses a wide variety of artisan produce, delicious local Irish meats, and regional specialties. Favorites include **Caviston's,** Dublin's premier deli, for smoked salmon and seafood; **Itsabagel,** for its delicious bagels, imported from H&H Bagels in New York City; **Crème de la Crème,** for its French-style pastries and cakes; **Missy and Mandy's,** for its American-style ice cream; **Nectar,** for its plethora of healthy juice drinks; **Christophe's Café,** for its delicious gourmet sandwiches, wraps, and panini; and **Layden's Fine Wines,** which sells wine by the bottle or glass, if you want to make your foraged meal just that little bit fancier. There is some seating in the hall, but it gets packed during lunch hour on weekdays, so visit at off-peak times, if possible.

Middle Abbey St., Dublin 1. ✆ **01/878-7016.** All items around €3–€15. No credit cards. Mon–Sat 10am–6pm. Bus: 70 or 80.

Irish Film Centre Cafe Bar INTERNATIONAL   A trendy drinking spot in Temple Bar, the hip Cafe Bar (in the lobby of the city's coolest place to watch a movie) features an excellent, affordable menu that changes daily. Dishes are simple and well prepared; deli sandwiches are available at lunchtime, alongside a small selection of burgers, fish cakes, salads, and the like, which later form the backbone of the dinner menu. A vegetarian menu is available for both lunch and dinner. The weekend entertainment usually includes music or comedy.

6 Eustace St., Temple Bar, Dublin 2. ✆ **01/677-8788.** www.irishfilm.ie. Lunch and dinner €7–€10. MC, V. Mon–Fri 12:30–3pm; Sat–Sun 1–3pm; daily 6–9pm. Bus: 21A, 78A, or 78B.

Leo Burdock's FISH AND CHIPS   Established in 1913, this quintessential Irish takeout shop across from Christ Church Cathedral is a cherished Dublin institution. Cabinet ministers, university students, and Hollywood stars alike (Tom Cruise and Liam Neeson are both fans) can be found at the counter waiting for fish bought fresh that morning and good Irish potatoes, both cooked in "drippings" (none of that modern cooking oil!). There's no seating, but you can sit on a nearby bench or stroll down to the park at St. Patrick's Cathedral.

2 Werburgh St., Dublin 8. ✆ **01/454-0306.** www.leoburdocks.com. Main courses €6–€8. No credit cards. Mon–Sat noon–midnight; Sun 4pm–midnight. Bus: 21A, 50, 50A, 78, 78A, or 78B.

Mermaid Café ★★ MODERN   Owned by a chef and an artist, this popular eatery is a mixture of good restaurant and classy hangout. It's a lunchtime favorite of local professionals and a good place to take a date in the evening. Dishes often found on the frequently changing menu range from the likes of slow-roasted pork belly to an array of excellent seafood dishes, including a rich seafood casserole. The popular weekend brunch can give you a good idea of the menu at a less wallet-denting price than going for an evening meal.

69-70 Dame St., Dublin 2. ✆ **01/670-8236.** www.mermaid.ie. Reservations required. Main courses €11-€16 lunch, €18-€26 dinner; Sun brunch €11-€17. MC, V. Mon-Sat 12:30-2:30pm and 6-11pm; Sun noon-3:30pm (brunch) and 6-9pm. Bus: 50, 50A, 54, 56A, 77, 77A, or 77B.

Nude 🖋 MODERN CAFE This small chain with sleek little outlets all around town is an excellent (and decidedly trendy) place to grab lunch or a snack without blowing your diet. The emphasis here is on healthy and organic, from the freshly squeezed juices down to the wraps (chickpea and chili is a longtime favorite), sandwiches, soups, salads, and sweets. Dedicated U2 fans will want to know that Nude is run by Norman Hewson, Bono's older brother. Other branches are at 103 Lower Leeson St., 38 Upper Baggot St., and 28 Grafton St.

21 Suffolk St., Trinity College, Dublin 2. ✆ **01/677-4804.** www.nude.ie. Main courses €3.50-€7. No credit cards. Mon-Sat 7:30am-9pm; Sun 9:30am-7pm. Bus: 50, 54, or 56.

Roly's Bistro ★ IRISH/INTERNATIONAL This two-story, shop-front restaurant is a local institution, beloved for providing the kind of reliably good, tummy-warming food you never tire of: roasted breast of chicken with orzo pasta and wild mushrooms, or braised shank of lamb with root vegetable purée and rosemary *jus*, to name just two. The bright and airy main dining room can be noisy when the house is full, but there's also an enclave of booths for those who prefer a quiet tête-à-tête.

7 Ballsbridge Terrace, Dublin 4. ✆ **01/668-2611.** www.rolysbistro.ie. Reservations required. Dinner main courses €24-€36; fixed-price 3-course lunch €23, dinner €42. AE, DC, MC, V. Daily noon-3pm and 6-9:45pm. DART: Lansdowne Rd. Station. Bus: 5, 6, 7, 8, 18, or 45.

The Tea Room ★★★ INTERNATIONAL This ultrasmart restaurant, ensconced in the U2-owned Clarence hotel, is guaranteed to deliver one of your most memorable meals in Ireland. This gorgeous room's soaring yet understated lines are the perfect backdrop for the complex but controlled cooking that takes form in dishes such as filet of John Dory with wild mushroom and razor clams, or red-leg partridge with juniper-flavored *jus*. A fixed-price Market Dinner menu offering more straightforward fare is available during all dinner hours Sunday through Thursday, and from 7 to 8pm on Friday and Saturday.

In the Clarence, 6-8 Wellington Quay, Dublin 2. ✆ **01/407-0813.** www.theclarence.ie. Reservations required. Main courses €14-€28; Market Menu 3-course fixed-price dinner Sun-Thurs €26. AE, MC, V. Mon-Fri 12:30-2pm; daily 6:30-9:45pm. Bus: 51B, 51C, 68, 69, or 79.

Winding Stair ★★ MODERN IRISH This long-beloved bookstore cafe was recently reworked into a sleek, gorgeous restaurant with wood floors, big windows, and stunning river views. It's still in a lovely old bookstore (you can pick up some Joyce on your way to dinner), but it's definitively modern in its cooking style. Dishes are clever interpretations of Irish favorites: steamed mussels and homemade fries with aioli; boiled Irish bacon collar (shoulder) with buttered organic cabbage and mashed potatoes; or seafood chowder with chorizo and treacle bread. The wine list is brilliantly chosen; the atmosphere is pure elegant sophistication. This place isn't trendy, it's classic.

40 Lower Ormond Quay, Dublin 1. ✆ **01/872-7320.** www.winding-stair.com. Reservations recommended. Fixed-price lunch menus: 2 courses €16, 3 courses €21. Main courses €21-€27. AE, DC, MC, V. Daily noon-3pm; Mon-Sat 5:30-10:30pm; Sun 6-9:30pm. Bus: 90, 92, or 151.

Yamamori Noodles ★ JAPANESE If you're skeptical about Japanese cuisine, Yamamori will make you an instant believer. In a pop, casual, and exuberant atmosphere, you may just be startled by how good the food is here. The splendid menu is a who's who of Japanese cuisine, and the prices range from budget to splurge. On a raw, drizzly Dublin day, the chili chicken ramen is a pot of bliss, while the *yamamori yaki soba* offers—in a mound of wok-fried noodles—a well-rewarded treasure hunt for prawns, squid, chicken, and roast pork.

71–72 S. Great George's St., Dublin 2. ☏ **01/475-5001.** www.yamamorinoodles.ie. Reservations only for parties of 4 or more. Dinner main courses €16–€20; sushi and sashimi €4–€6 per piece. MC, V. Sun–Wed 12:15–11pm; Thurs–Sat 12:15–11:30pm. Bus: 50, 50A, 54, 56, or 77.

Shopping

Ireland is known the world over for its handmade products and fine craftsmanship, and Dublin sells the country's best wares. **Tower Craft Design Centre,** Pearse St., off Grand Canal Quay (☏ **01/677-5655;** DART: Pearse; bus: 2 or 3), is a beautifully restored 1862 sugar refinery that houses a nest of craft workshops where you can watch the artisans at work. Merchandise ranges from hand-marbled stationery and Celtic jewelry to all-wool wall hangings and heraldic gifts.

There are many good shopping malls in Dublin, but our favorite is the **Powerscourt Townhouse Centre,** 59 S. William St. (☏ **01/679-4144;** www.powerscourtcentre.com), housed in a restored Georgian town house. This four-story complex consists of a central skylit courtyard and more than 60 boutiques, craft shops, art galleries, cafes, and restaurants. The wares include all kinds of crafts, antiques, paintings, prints, ceramics, leather goods, jewelry, clothing, hand-dipped chocolates, and farmhouse cheeses.

The Temple Bar area has three excellent weekend markets. **Temple Bar Book Market** is held every Saturday and Sunday from 11am to 6pm in Temple Bar Square and has enough of everything to make for some great browsing—old and new titles, classics and contemporary novels, science fiction and mysteries, serious biographies, and pulp fiction. **Temple Bar Food Market** is held every Saturday on Meeting House Square from 10am to 4:30pm and is a great picnic-shopping spot. Everything here is organic, from fruits and veggies to a delicious selection of homemade cheeses, chutneys, breads, and jams. And then there's the **Cow's Lane Fashion and Design Market,** a fashionista's delight, held every Saturday on Cow's Lane, Old City Temple Bar, from 10am to 5pm, and packed with jewelry and clothes from up-and-coming Irish designers.

Nightlife

One general fact to keep in mind concerning Dublin's nightlife is that there are very few fixed points. Apart from a handful of established institutions, venues come and go, change character, open their doors to ballet one night and cabaret the next. Pick up a copy of *InDublin* and the *Event Guide* at local cafes and shops if you're looking for the latest club scene. Both have good listings.

The award-winning website of the *Irish Times* (**www.ireland.com**) offers a "what's on" daily guide to cinema, theater, music, and whatever else you're up for. The **Dublin Events Guide,** at **www.dublinevents.com**, also provides a comprehensive listing of the week's entertainment possibilities.

PUBS The mainstay of Dublin social life is unquestionably the pub. In January 2004, Ireland banned smoking in most public places, a move smokers darkly predicted would kill pub life. It didn't. Below we list a few the city's most distinctive pubs.

For conversation and atmosphere, head to the **Brazen Head,** 20 Bridge St. (✆ **01/679-9549;** www.brazenhead.com). This brass-filled, lantern-lit pub claims to be the city's oldest, and it might very well be, considering that it was originally opened as a coaching inn back in 1668 and occupies the site of an even earlier tavern dating from 1198. Nestled on the south bank of the River Liffey, it is at the end of a cobblestone courtyard with castellated ramparts and was once the meeting place of Irish freedom fighters such as Robert Emmet and Wolfe Tone. **The Long Hall,** 51 S. Great George's St. (✆ **01/475-1590**), is one of the city's most photographed pubs, with a beautiful Victorian decor of filigree-edged mirrors, polished dark woods, and traditional snugs (private rooms). The hand-carved bar is a wonder in itself. For a laid-back evening, try **The Market Bar,** Fade Street (off South Great George's St.), Dublin 2 (✆ **01/613-9094;** www.marketbar.ie). This is what they call around here a "superpub," though it's really just a big bar, with a soaring ceiling, gorgeous design, a good beer and wine list, and friendly bar staff. It's the kind of place where you could sit in the late afternoon and have a solitary pint, and nobody would bother you. Its no-music policy means that it's quiet enough to hear yourself drink.

If you like live Irish traditional music, **Oliver St. John Gogarty,** 58–59 Fleet St. (✆ **01/671-1822;** www.gogartys.ie), in the heart of Temple Bar, has an inviting and quirky old-world atmosphere, and offers hostel quarters on the upper floors, where you would need to be stone deaf, very drunk, or otherwise noise-resistant to fall asleep. There are traditional music sessions every day from 3pm until 2:30am, and it serves oysters and mussels to go with the Guinness.

THEATER Dublin has a venerable and vital theatrical tradition, which has lately seen a renaissance erupting (along with gentrification and cost-of-living expenses). The new playwrights must wrestle with the titanic Irish ghosts of G. B. Shaw, Beckett, W. B. Yeats, J. M. Synge, Sean O'Casey, and Oscar Wilde, but they manage to hold their own. Advance bookings for most large concerts, plays, and so forth can be made through **Ticketmaster Ireland** (✆ **081/871-9300** in Ireland, or 353/1485-8010 internationally; www.ticketmaster.ie), with ticket centers in most HMV music stores, as well as at the Dublin Tourism Centre, Suffolk Street, Dublin 2.

The **Abbey Theatre,** 26 Lower Abbey St. (✆ **01/878-7222;** www.abbeytheatre. ie), has been the national theater of Ireland since 1904. The original theater, destroyed by fire in 1951, was replaced in 1966 by the current uninspired 600-seat house. The box office is open Monday to Saturday 10:30am to 7pm; shows run Monday to Saturday at 8pm, and also at 2:30pm on Saturday. Tickets cost €15 to €40. There are senior, student, and children's discounts available Monday to Thursday evening and for the Saturday matinee.

Just north of O'Connell Street off Parnell Square, the restored 370-seat **Gate Theatre,** 1 Cavendish Row (✆ **01/874-4045;** www.gate-theatre.ie), was founded in 1928 to provide a venue for a broad range of plays. That policy prevails today, with a program that includes a blend of modern works and the classics. The box office is open Monday to Saturday 10am to 7:30pm; shows run Monday to Thursday at 8pm. Tickets cost €15 to €35.

HUNGARY

Hungary has a long, rich history that includes membership in the Roman, Turkish, and Austro-Hungarian empires, and a gloomy spell trapped behind the Iron Curtain. Today Hungary has once again regained its position as a vibrant Eastern European country and is one of the Continent's hottest travel destinations. Though the Lake Balaton region has lost much of its allure in recent years, Hungary's infrastructure as a whole has developed measurably. The country's geographic placement makes it a perfect stopover for the train traveler crisscrossing the Continent. For visitors looking for more bang for their buck, the country is still a little cheaper than most of its Western counterparts, though it is not the true budget destination it once was. Still, in a land of expensive gasoline and hefty highway tolls, trains are the principal means of long-distance travel for most of the population; the best way to see this remarkable little country is by rail.

Highlights of Hungary

All rails in Hungary lead into and out of **Budapest,** lively capital and undisputed transportation hub, a proud city sitting astride the Danube River in the middle of the country. Savor Budapest, one of Europe's most appealing cities. But you should also go beyond the capital and explore the smaller cities and the countryside. Hop a train up the Danube to the "Danube Bend" towns of Szentendre, Esztergom, or Visegrád. In the artists' village of **Szentendre,** wander the winding streets and visit some interesting museums or galleries; in **Visegrád,** don't miss the ruins of King Matthias's Renaissance Palace; ascend the steep stairs to the cupola at **Esztergom**'s cathedral, from where you can see deep into the Slovak countryside across the Danube. Ride to Lake Tisza, where you will find beautiful fauna and flora. Explore the little villages around the lake, tucked away in the rolling countryside, grapes of the popular Balaton wines ripening.

ESSENTIALS

Getting There

BY PLANE   The Hungarian airline **Malév** (✆ 1/235-3888; www.malev.hu) is the local flagship carrier from North America to Budapest. Other airlines offering service to the area include Delta, Lufthansa, and British Airways.

All flights that originate in North America arrive at **Ferihegy II Airport** (✆ 1/296-7000), located in the XVIII district in southeastern Pest.

Both the 2-week **Budapest Spring Festival** and **Autumn Festival** feature opera, ballet, classical music, and drama performances in all the major halls and theaters of Budapest. It's advisable to purchase tickets for the performances months in advance, when they are listed. Simultaneous to each festival's performing arts events, temporary exhibitions are also open in many of Budapest's museums. You can buy tickets at the **Budapest Festival Center,** V. Szervita tér 5 (© **1/486-3311;** www.festival city.hu), at the individual venues, or online. The action happens in mid- to late March and mid- to late October.

Every year on the second weekend in July, the ancient town of **Visegrád,** on the Danube, hosts the **International Palace Tournament,** an authentic medieval festival replete with dueling knights on horseback, early music, and dance.

On **King St. Stephen's Day,** August 20, the country's first king and patron saint is celebrated nationwide with cultural events and a display of fireworks over the Danube. Hungarians also celebrate their constitution on this day, as well as ceremoniously welcome the first new bread from the recent crop of July wheat.

The **Budapest Summer Music Festival** starts in July and runs through mid-August. Celebrating the opening of the fall season, special classical music and dance performances are held for 3 weeks starting in late September and going through October, in all the city's major halls during **Music Weeks in Budapest.** For information on the summer and autumn programs, contact the **Hungarian Arts Festivals Federation** (© **36/1-202-1095;** www.artsfestivals.hu). The latter festival's traditional start is September 25, the day of Béla Bartók's death.

A decreasing number of low-cost European airlines (now six at press time) has made Hungary less accessible by air from the rest of the Continent—though if you can fly cheaply to, say, London, you might find a bargain fare to hop over to Budapest. Book early for the best-priced tickets. Be prepared for delays, however, and be sure to check which airport your carrier flies out of—it may be on the outskirts of town. Budget airlines that offer flights to Hungary out of many European countries now fly into **Ferihegy I,** also in district XVIII (© **1/296-9696**). These include **Wizzair** (© **1/470-9499;** www.wizzair.com), **easyJet** (© **0871/244-2366;** www.easyjet. com), and **Air Berlin** (© **80/017110;** www.airberlin.com), as well as a few others. Due to continual changes, for the most current information on budget airlines within Europe, visit **www.skyscanner.com**.

Hungary by Rail

PASSES

For information on the **Eurail Global Pass, Eurail Global Pass Flexi, European East Pass,** and other multicountry options, see chapter 2.

The **Eurail Hungary Pass** offers first-class travel within Hungary for either 5 nonconsecutive days in a 15-day period or 10 nonconsecutive days in a 1-month period. The 5-day pass costs $95; the 10-day pass is $129. The pass is best obtained in North America before departing for your trip. You can buy it from **Rail Europe** (© **888/438-7245** in the United States, © **800/361-7245** in Canada; www.rail europe.com) or your travel agent. Pass discounts for travelers under 26 and those traveling in groups of five or more are available.

Foreign Train Terms

Hungarian ticket agents generally speak little English, so you will need to know some basic terminology in Hungarian. For a list of the most words for train travelers, see "Useful Hungarian Train Terms," above.

PRACTICAL TRAIN INFORMATION

Timetables for arrivals are displayed in stations on big white posters, while departures are on yellow posters in glass cases.

Train service in Hungary is generally reliable and usually runs according to schedule, though it's somewhat slower than in Western Europe. Its rail network is extensive, totaling more than 4,800 miles (7,728km), but you should keep in mind that the network is oriented on Budapest, so that city will almost always be both your arrival and your departure point from Hungary or within it. Numerous international trains stop in Budapest, and several daily trains arrive in the city from Vienna, Prague, Warsaw, Zagreb, Bratislava, and Berlin.

Aside from international express trains, the best choices within Hungary are the **InterCity (IC)** express trains, which stop less often en route between major cities. These modern trains are clean and the only trains in Hungary with air-conditioning.

USEFUL HUNGARIAN train terms

Indul	departure	*Jegy*	ticket
Érkezik	arrival	*Oda*	one-way
Honnan	from where	*Oda-vissza*	round-trip
Hová	to where	*Helyjegy*	reservation
Vágány	platform	*Első Osztály*	first class
Munkanap	weekdays	*Másodosztály*	second class
Hétvége	weekend	*Nem Dohányzó*	nonsmoking
Szombat	Saturday	*Ma*	today
Ünnepnap	legal holiday	*Holnap*	tomorrow
Gyors	fast train or express		

After the InterCity trains come the *gyors* fast trains, which are almost as fast as the IC trains but are older and grittier. Avoid the slow *személy* and *sebes* trains, as they stop at all local stations, making a ride seem interminable.

Unfortunately, the Hungarian railway authority **MÁV Hungarian Railways** is poorly run and outdated. After consulting computers for information, ticket agents at the stations still rely on handwriting most tickets purchased. Ticket information is in Hungarian only; the destination is not even indicated—simply the number of kilometers you're authorized to travel. The ticketing service people are surly at times; don't be surprised if you are faced with an unfriendly, unilingual, grumpy Hungarian, though they have improved over the years. If you know the language, you can purchase and print inter-Hungary tickets online. They need to be printed and validated at the stations in specific machines. You can access a timetable on the Web at **www.mav-start.hu**, which can be searched in English.

RESERVATIONS   You must reserve a seat on some international express trains and on all InterCity trains. You should ask if a reservation is needed when buying a ticket, but if you want to be guaranteed a seat, spend the extra money. Note that Hungarian trains are often crowded during the summer high season and weekends, so lines for reservations can get very long. You might want to reserve a seat several days in advance (the inefficient pricing and reservations system is currently so complicated that you'll need to head to the ticket office to sort out your options).

SERVICES & AMENITIES   Generally speaking, most trains in Hungary do not have as many amenities as their Western European counterparts, and other than the new InterCity trains, they can be downright dirty (and covered in graffiti). You will find a snack bar and eatery on IC and international express trains, but not on other

---

 Service Outages

MÁV, the government-owned train service, continually seems to be in bankruptcy. The company cuts back services and then reinstitutes them. Generally, these cuts are only to smaller towns and, for the most part, don't affect the cities where tourists are likely to travel. It is always best to check train schedules and routes online at **www.mav-start.hu**.

Trains & Travel Times in Hungary

From	To	Train Type	# of Trains	Frequency	Travel Time
Budapest	Esztergom	Reg.	26	Daily	1 hr., 35 min.
Budapest	Nagymaros-Visegrád	Reg	29	Daily	50 min.

* *Reservations compulsory on InterCity trains between Budapest and both Veszprém and Keszthely. Numerous regional trains also travel these routes, but the travel time is longer.*

trains in Hungary. Occasionally, on trains other than IC trains, you will encounter a snack cart. Note also that trains do not have potable water, so you'll need to bring your own. Eating on trains is customary, so don't hesitate to bring food along. Load up on drinks and eats before you depart on your trip; every station has snack bars. Bear in mind that, on many local trains, the restrooms are kept locked if they are out of order, so you may have to walk through a few cars to find one available.

Some international trains that pass through Hungary have sleeping cars, but none of the local trains or regional trains have sleeper options of any sort.

[FastFACTS] HUNGARY

Area Codes See "Telephone," below.

Business Hours Banks are usually open from Monday to Thursday 8am to 5pm and Friday 8am to 1pm. Most **stores** are open Monday to Friday 10am to 6pm, and Saturday 9 or 10am to 1 or 2pm (except many shopping malls, which keep later hours). As a rule, only stores in central tourist areas are open Sunday. Many shops and restaurants close for 2 weeks in August.

Climate Hungary's climate is fairly mild—the annual mean temperature is 50°F (10°C). That said, summers can get swelteringly hot and humid, especially in July and August (when flash storms are possible), and winters can be damp and chilly, especially December and January. Fall and spring are generally pleasant and mild, though it can get wet in May and June.

Currency The basic unit of currency in Hungary is the **forint (Ft).** Hungary won't adopt the euro before 2014, but many Hungarian hotels and restaurants started quoting their rates in euros as soon as Hungary joined the E.U., to try to hedge against inflation. The restaurant menu rates are never to your advantage.

Documents Required A valid passport is the only document required for citizens of the U.S., Canada, Australia, and New Zealand.

Electricity Most hotels use 220 volts AC (50 cycles) and a European two-prong plug. Electrical equipment operating on 110 volts AC requires the use of an adapter and/or voltage converter.

Embassies & Consulates The embassy of the **United States** is at V. Szabadság tér 12 (© **1/475-4400;** http://hungary.

usembassy.gov; Metro: Kossuth tér); the embassy of **Canada** is at II. Ganz u. 12–14 (© **1/392-3360;** www.canadainternational. gc.ca/hungary-hongrie/ index.aspx?lang=eng; Metro: Moszkva tér); the **United Kingdom** embassy is at V. Harmincad u. 6 (© **1/266-2888;** http:// ukinhungary.fco.gov.uk/en).

Health & Safety For medical treatment, try the **First Med Center,** across from the Mammut shopping center, at I. Hattyu u. 14 (© **1/224-9090;** www. firstmedcenters.com; Metro: Moszkva tér).

By U.S. standards, Hungary is a relatively safe country—muggings and violent attacks are rare. Nevertheless, foreigners are always prime targets. Beware of pickpockets, especially on crowded trams, Metros, and buses. Avoid being victimized by wearing a money belt under your clothes instead of wearing a fanny pack or carrying a wallet or purse. No valuables should ever be kept in the outer pockets of a backpack.

Holidays   National holidays include: January 1, March 15 (National Day), Easter Sunday and Monday, May 1 (May Day), Pentecost (Whitsun), August 20 (St. Stephen's Day), October 23 (1956 Remembrance Day), November 1 (All Saints' Day), December 25 (Christmas), and December 26 (Boxing Day).

Legal Aid   Contact your embassy for legal assistance.

Mail   If you need to receive or send mail, it's best to arrange it with your hotel.

Police & Emergencies   Call ✆ **1/438-8080** to reach a 24-hour hot line service in English, or call ✆ **104** for an ambulance, ✆ **105** for the fire

department, or ✆ **107** or 112 for the police.

Telephone   The **country code** for Hungary is **36.** The **city code** for Budapest is **1;** use this code when you're calling from outside Hungary. If you're within Hungary but not in Budapest, first dial **06;** when you hear a tone, dial the city code and phone number. If you're calling within Budapest, simply leave off the code and dial only the regular seven-digit phone number. Dial ✆ **198** for domestic directory assistance and ✆ **199** for international queries.

Numbers beginning with **06-20, 06-30,** or **06-70** followed by a seven-digit number are **mobile phone numbers.** The number **06-80** is toll-free. Public **pay phones** charge varying amounts for local calls, depending on the time of

day you place your call; it's cheapest in the evenings and on weekends. Most public phones are now operated by the T Com phone company and operate with coins or, more commonly, phone cards that you can buy from post offices, newsstands, and convenience stores. Note that many pay phones are not maintained well and often do not work, so we caution against using them unless it is necessary.

You can reach the **AT&T** operator at ✆ **06/800-01111,** the **MCI Worldphone** operator at ✆ **06/800-01411,** and the **Sprint** operator at ✆ **06/800-01877.**

Tipping   The general tipping rate is usually 15%. Among those who welcome tips are waiters, taxi drivers, hotel employees, barbers, cloakroom attendants, toilet attendants, masseuses, and tour guides.

BUDAPEST

Budapest came of age in the 19th century, when the two towns of Buda and Pest were little more than provincial outposts on the Danube. Indeed, Budapest, notwithstanding its long and tattered history of Roman, Mongol, and Turkish conquest, is very much a late-19th-century city, with its characteristic coffeehouse and music hall culture. But along with its extraordinary ambience, the city has most of the modern conveniences one expects of a European capital.

As the central rail hub of Hungary and the home of the region's major airport, this remarkably unpretentious city is a must-stop location on any rail tour of the country. On a rail journey that spans Europe's eastern and western halves, Budapest is an ideal stopover—a city that combines the best of both worlds. *Note:* Many businesses and attractions have jumped on the bandwidth wagon creating websites for marketing their presence only to then let their websites sit forgotten. For the most reliable information, always call, e-mail, or (when feasible) stop in at a location. The exception to this rule is hotels, which maintain accurate websites.

Station Information

GETTING FROM THE AIRPORT TO THE TRAIN STATIONS

The **Airport Minibus** (✆ **1/296-8555;** www.bud.hu), a service of the Budapest Airport Authority, leaves **Ferihegy 2** (✆ **1/296-7000** for general info; for arrivals or departures, use the website), located in the XVIII district in southeastern Pest, every 10 or 15 minutes throughout the day. It will take you directly to any city address and costs 2,990Ft one-way, or 4,960Ft round-trip. Multiple persons traveling together are discounted. For more information, see **www.airportshuttle.hu/en**.

The airport has authorized **Zóna Taxi** (*℃* **1/365-5555**) as the official airport taxi service, which has a kiosk by the curb as you exit the airport. They charge using a zone system, and the fixed rates range from 3,600Ft for zone 1 to 5,800Ft for zone 4. If you want to use a different service, phone from the terminal (see "By Taxi," on p. 466), and a cab will be there in a matter of minutes. There is a separate pickup area for other taxis, so look for the posted sign. For two people traveling together, a taxi from a recommended fleet to the city will be comparable in price to the combined minibus fares, at about 4,500Ft. The ride should take 30 to 40 minutes, depending on traffic.

There is a rail link from **Ferihegy I** to **Nyugati** train station. Travel time is 30 minutes, and the cost is 300Ft; trains depart regularly. **Bus 200E** can be used to get from **Ferihegy II** to **I** to connect with the train. This bus requires a regular transport ticket of 320Ft.

Another cheap way into the city is by public transportation; the bus-to-Metro-to-town trip takes about an hour's time in total. Take **bus 200E** from either airport or bus 93 from **Ferihegy I** to the last stop, Kobánya-Kispest. From there, the Blue Metro line runs to the Inner City of Pest and Nyugati pályaudvar, one of the city's major train stations. The bus trip takes a transit ticket, which costs 340Ft when bought from the driver. News kiosks in the airport lobby also sell tickets for 320Ft. You will need a new ticket for the Metro ride and one for each successive mode of transport thereafter. A public transportation pass is the most convenient option (see "Getting Around," below).

INSIDE THE STATIONS

Budapest has three major train stations: Keleti pályaudvar (Eastern Station), Nyugati (Western Station), and Déli (Southern Station), though there is no actual correlation between their names and their geographic locations. Each has a Metro station beneath it and an array of accommodations booking offices (see "Information Elsewhere in the City," below), currency exchange booths, and other services. We would avoid most of them, as they prey on tourists.

Most international express trains pull into and depart from bustling **Keleti Station** (*℃* **1/313-6835;** Metro: Keleti pu.), a lovely, classic, steel-girdered structure built in the eclectic style between 1881 and 1884 that's unfortunately located in Pest's run-down Baross tér. In addition to the Metro (the Red line), numerous bus, tram, and trolleybus lines serve Baross tér. Digital information boards will keep you apprised of arrivals and departures at the platforms at the main entrance and in the international ticketing area. Note that international tickets sales are to the left side of the station on the main floor; domestic tickets for north and northeastern destinations are sold on the main floor on the right side, and also on the lower level. Some international trains call at **Nyugati Station** (*℃* **1/461-5400** for domestic routes, or 1/461-5500 for international routes; Metro: Nyugati pu.), another classic designed by the Eiffel company and built in the 1870s. Numerous tram and bus lines serve busy Nyugati tér, and the Blue Metro line stops underneath the station.

Different hotel reservation services come and go, opening and closing their offices here. Whichever one is operating at the time, you can be assured they are going to

ACCOMMODATIONS ■

Andrássy Hotel **34**
Art'Otel Budapest **2**
Atrium Hotel **23**
Baross Hotel **24**
BudaBaB **21**
City Hotel Mátyás **16**
City Ring Hotel **31**
Ibis Budapest Centrum **13**
Leo Panzio **18**
NH Hotel **32**

DINING ◆

Café New York **22**
Central Kávéház **15**
Frici Papa Kifőzés **27**
Gerbeaud **7**
Gerlóczy Kávéház **19**
Govinda Vegetariánus
  Étterem **4**
Hemingway **11**
Kossuth Museum
  Vénhajó Étterem **6**
M **25**
Mátyás Pince **17**
Mosselen Belgium
  Beer Café **33**
Művész Kávéház **28**
Paprika Vendéglő **35**
Tabáni Terasz **9**
Trófea Grill Étterem **39**

ATTRACTIONS ●

Budapesti Történeti
  Múzeum (Budapest
  History Museum) **8**
Chain Bridge **5**
City Park **36**
Dohány Synagogue **20**
Gellért Hegy **10**
Hungarian State
  Opera House **29**
Mátyás Templom **3**
Nemzeti Múzeum
  (Hungarian National
  Museum) **14**
Palace of Arts **12**
Parliament **1**
Szent István Bazilika **30**
Széchenyi Baths **38**
Szépművészeti Múzeum
  (Museum of Fine Arts) **37**
Zeneakademia (Ferenc Liszt
  Academy of Music) **26**

direct you only to the hotels they own or a limited number of contracted properties not necessarily in your favor. It is best to arrange your accommodations ahead of time.

A few international trains arrive at **Déli Station** (𝄢 1/375-6293; Metro: Déli pu.), an ugly modern building in central Buda. The Red Metro line terminates just beneath the station. Besides the usual tourist amenities, the station has a number of kiosks where you can stock up on snacks before your train journey.

The train station phone numbers listed above are good for Hungarian speakers from 8pm to 6am. During the day, MÁV operates a ticket center called **MÁVDI-REKT** at V. József Attila utca 16 (no phone calls), where they can provide you with information about timetables, prices, reductions, and offers in English, as well as sell you tickets. They are open weekdays 9am to 6pm.

Information Elsewhere in the City

The city's best source of visitor information is **TourInform,** the official Budapest Tourism offices. They have a booth at each of the airports, plus three offices in the city: V. Liszt Ferenc tér 11, in Pest (𝄢 1/322-4098; www.tourinform.hu; Metro: Opera, Yellow line; tram: Oktogon, no. 4–6), open daily from 10am to 6pm; V. Sütő Street 2 (Deák sq.; Metro: Deák tér), with hours from 8am to 8pm daily, with these exceptions: December 24 8am to 1pm, December 25, December 26, and January 1 10am to 6pm; and at the Castle (Var bus), where hours are daily 9am to 8pm May 5 to October 31 and daily 9am to 6pm November 2 to April 30, but closed May 1 to 4 and November 1. Hours change often and without prior notice due to budget allowances at any given time. The Sütő Street 2 is the most stable for hours.

The most established and still solvent hotel reservation agency is the former state-owned travel agent **Ibusz.** They tend to have the greatest number of rooms and apartments listed and have offices in the airport. The main **Ibusz reservations office** is at Ferenciek tere 10 (𝄢 1/485-2767; fax 1/337-1205; www.ibusz.hu. Metro: Ferenciek tere), open year-round from Monday to Friday 9am to 5pm. All major credit cards are accepted.

It's a good idea before you even arrive in Budapest to consult one of the many websites that offer tourist information in English. The site **www.gotohungary.com** has a wealth of tourist information, as does **www.hungarytourism.hu**. Local news, entertainment listings, and the like can be found at **www.funzine.com** and **www. budapestinfo.hu/en**.

Getting Around

Budapest has an extensive and inexpensive public transportation system; it's the best way to get around town. The Metros and trams start at 4:30am, but all three Metros stop running at 11pm and most of the trams cease around 11:30pm. Night buses substitute for the major tram lines. All night buses start with a 9; hence, the 906 bus is the night replacement for the number 6 tram. There are 34 night bus routes, but they are limited compared to daytime transport. Note that the 4 and 6 tram lines undergo periodic reconstruction, causing the routes to be replaced with buses for stretches of up to 8 weeks (often during very inconvenient times, such as the holiday season). Closure notices are posted in Metro cars and at tram stations. Adding to the public transportation chaos is the never-ending construction of a new fourth Metro line; buses replace trams on routes that have been disrupted because of the ongoing work (signs are posted in English where substitutions have been made).

All forms of public transportation require the self-validation of prepurchased **tickets** (*vonaljegy*), costing 320Ft apiece (children under 6 travel free). Purchase single tickets at Metro ticket windows and newspaper kiosks, and at major transportation hubs. We never recommend using the machines at tram stops or on buses, for they rarely work. You can buy a 10-pack (*tizes csomag*) for 2,800Ft. During the process of validating tickets, you must keep the pack intact. The covers are the control ID for that pack. Do not tear individual tickets off as you use them until you are away from the transport. Inspectors can check tickets upon exiting Metros.

If you will be here for a day or more, the best and least expensive choice is a pass. A **1-day pass** is 1,550Ft and is valid for 24 hours from the time the clerk writes down as the validated issue date/time. Passes are available at any Metro ticket window. After the clerk validates the pass, you don't need to validate it again. You only need to show it to inspectors when asked; other times, keep it tucked away. A **3-day pass** (*turistajegy*) costs 3,850Ft and a **7-day pass** (*hetibérlet*) costs 4,600Ft.

Uniformed inspectors, generally wearing a blue armband, will frequently be checking for valid tickets, particularly at the top or bottom of the escalators to Metro platforms. Fare dodgers face on-the-spot fines of 6,000Ft. Inspectors have a reputation for being abusive to tourists, but employees are being trained to be more tourist-friendly. All public transport operates on rough schedules, posted at bus and tram shelters and in Metro stations.

BY METRO The Metro is clean and efficient, with trains running every 3 to 5 minutes from about 4:30am until about 11:30pm. The three lines are known by color—Yellow, Red, and Blue. Officially, they have numbers as well, but all signs are color-coded. All three lines converge at **Deák tér.** This is the only station where all lines are available.

The **Yellow (1) line,** the oldest Metro on the European continent, lies just a few steps underground and runs from Vörösmarty tér in the heart of central Pest, under the length of Andrássy út, and past the Városliget (City Park). Tickets for the Yellow line are validated in red or orange machines as you enter the station. The **Red (2)** and **Blue (3) lines** are modern subways, set deep underground, and most stations are accessible by escalator. The Red line runs from eastern Pest, through the city center, and across the Danube to Déli Station. The Blue line runs from southeastern Pest, through the city center, to northern Pest. Tickets must be validated at the automated time-stamp boxes before you descend the escalator. When changing lines at Deák tér, you must validate a new ticket at the orange machines in the hallway between lines. A fourth Metro line is under construction, but all estimates of completion have passed, so it is anyone's guess.

BY BUS Many parts of the city, most notably the Buda Hills, are best accessed by bus (*busz*). Most lines are in service from about 4:30am to about 11:30pm, with less frequent weekend or holiday service on some. You must validate your bus ticket on board at the red box found by each door. Tickets for Budapest buses cannot be purchased from the driver. You can board the bus by any door.

Black-numbered local buses constitute the majority of bus lines. Red-numbered buses are express. If an *E* follows the red number on a bus, the bus runs nonstop between terminals. All night buses start with a 9 followed by two more digits. A few buses are labeled by something other than a number; one you may need to use are buses labeled *V* (for *villamos*/tram) when they occasionally run in place of a tram that is down.

BY TRAM   You'll find Budapest's bright-yellow trams (*villamos* in Hungarian) very useful, particularly the **4** and **6,** which travel along the city's Outer Ring (Nagykörút) section. You must validate your ticket on board in the red box. As with buses, tickets are valid for one ride, not for the line itself. Trams stop at every station. *The red buttons near the tram doors are for emergency stops, not stop requests.* Some of the tram lines commonly used by tourists (2, 2A, 4, 6, 47, and 49) may have buses running in their place at various times due to the ongoing construction of the fourth Metro line.

BY HÉV   The HÉV is a suburban railway network that connects Budapest to various points along the city's outskirts. There are four HÉV lines; only one, the **Szentendre line,** is of serious interest to tourists. The terminus for the Szentendre HÉV line is Buda's Batthyány tér, also a station on the Red Metro line. On the Pest side, you can catch the HÉV from the Margit Híd, Budai Híd Fő. To reach Óbuda's Fő tér (Main Sq.), get off at the Árpád híd (Árpád Bridge) stop. The HÉV runs regularly between 4am and 11:30pm. If you have a valid day pass, you do not need to buy a ticket for trips within the city limits; otherwise, a single ticket is needed. For Szentendre, you will need to buy a supplemental ticket for the portion beyond the Budapest boundary only. Show the cashier your transportation pass, if you have one, when asking for the tickets. The supplemental tickets are 285Ft each way and will be checked and punched by a conductor after you pass the city limits. You may be asked to show your pass again to prove you needed only the supplemental ticket. A full-price ticket is 650Ft each way.

BY TAXI   Budapest taxis have become better regulated, but there are still rogue taxis roaming, especially at the train stations. Never take a taxi from a driver who approaches you in the station. Many drivers are experts at fleecing foreigners. Fares can vary tremendously, but there are two legal pricing schemes, for the reliable services. If you hail a taxi or take one from the curb, the rate is higher than if you were to call the dispatcher. You may be standing in front of it when you call, but the rate will be cheaper. They will often ask for your name, and you need to tell the driver. It is illegal for a driver to pick up the wrong customer if you have called in. The law dictates that you be provided with a paper receipt; ask for it if the driver does not offer one, making the driver accountable. Several fleet companies have good reputations, honest drivers, and competitive rates. There is no standard rate across the various companies, but each should have its own rates displayed on the meter. So take the front seat (which is the standard practice in Hungary) and check the rates before you start your journey. We particularly recommend **Fő Taxi** (② 1/222-2222). Other reliable fleets are **Volántaxi** (② 1/466-6666), **City Taxi** (② 1/211-1111), **Tele5** (② 1/355-5555), and **6×6** (② 1/266-6666).

Where to Stay

Budapest has seen a proliferation of new accommodations for various budgets. The better choices among these used to be outside the city center, but as tourism has risen, so have the prices of the outer accommodations; we have chosen those places that are near or easily accessible to train stations, by public transportation. In high season, it used to be difficult to secure a room, but with the global economy, it is never certain, so make reservations and get a written confirmation well ahead, if possible, just to be safe.

   Note that most hotels and pensions in Budapest divide the year into three seasons. **High season** is roughly from March or April to September or October and New

Year's. **Low season** is roughly from November to February, except the days before New Year's. **Special season** includes the Hungarian Formula One race and Sziget Festival in August. Most hotels offer discounts and special package deals on their website if you book early, so be sure to check it.

Andrássy Hotel ★★★ 🏨 This luxury boutique hotel (one of only two in Hungary that merit Small Luxury Hotels of the World membership) is just a few minutes' walk from Heroes' Square and the City Park, and 1 minute from the Metro. The rooms have been redecorated and have an eclectic Asian scheme. Double rooms are generous, but the suites are grandly spacious, some with artificial fireplaces in the living room. The holistic atmosphere lends itself to a Zen feel, making this the perfect place to relax after a long train journey.

VI. Andrássy út 111. ✆ **1/462-2100.** Fax 1/322-9445. www.andrassyhotel.com. 70 units. High season 129€–179€ classic, 149€–219€ superior, 169€–239€ deluxe, 229€–299€ junior suite, 319€–399€ ambassador suite; low season 109€–159€ classic, 129€–179€ superior, 149€–199€ deluxe, 209€–259€ junior suite, 299€–349€ ambassador suite. No special season rates. AE, DC, MC, V. Metro: Bajza u. (Yellow line). **Amenities:** Restaurant; lounge.

Art'Otel Budapest ★★★ This is the first branch of a German lifestyle hotel chain to be situated outside of that country, and it's a successful one, especially for art lovers. Each of the chain's properties highlights the work of one particular artist, enabling guests to stay in a virtual gallery of modern art. At this hotel, the artist is Donald Sultan, an American modernist. More than 600 pieces of his work grace the hotel's walls, from the lobby to the hallways, to the well-equipped guest rooms. Sultan also designed everything from the carpets to the dinnerware.

I. Bem Rakpart 16–19, Budapest. ✆ **800/814-7000** or 1/487-9487. Fax 1/487-9488. www.artotels.com. 165 units. High season 139€ double non-Danube view, 20€ Danube view supplement, 30€ executive room supplement, 60€ art suite supplement; low season 99€ double non-Danube view, supplement as for high season above. No special season rates. Children 12 and under stay free in parent's room. Breakfast 12€ per person. AE, DC, MC, V. Metro: Batthyány tér (Red line). **Amenities:** Restaurant; bar.

Atrium Hotel ★★ Opened in March 2007, this ultramodern hotel is a breath of fresh air and great for travelers of all ages. The greenish-gray walls mix with blues in the carpet to make the rooms feel airy and roomy, yet they exude a warmth that will welcome even finicky guests. Soundproof windows guard against noise. Attention to detail was taken when converting this former post office to its current incarnation, and it's completely smoke free. It's a block from the Red Metro, close to Keleti station.

VIII. Csokonai u.14. ✆ **1/299-0777.** Fax 1/215-6090. www.hotelatrium.hu. 57 units (22 with double beds, 35 with twin beds). High and special season 122€ double, 162€ triple; low season 84€ double, 104€ triple. Rates include full breakfast. AE, MC, V. Parking 5,000Ft per day. Metro: Keleti (Red line). **Amenities:** Bar.

Baross Hotel ★ For rail travel convenience, you couldn't ask for a better location than this hotel, right across the street from Keleti train station. The hotel is located on different floors of an otherwise residential building. In addition to the regular rooms, there are eight apartments, whose different configurations can accommodate two to three adults with a double bed and a couch; each has a fully equipped kitchen. On the negative side, Baross tér is where one of the Metro 4 stations is being built, causing construction confusion. This hotel is a little diamond; all rooms were redecorated in 2008, giving them a fresher and roomier feeling. We suggest requesting a room with a courtyard view, for plenty of natural light. Flower pots hanging on the railings give a minigarden effect. The apartments have kitchenettes.

Throwing humility to the wind, my partner and I are the owners of **Bud-aBaB,** VII. Akácfa u. 18 (☏ 1/267-5240; www.budabab.com), a small, smoke-free B&B. We have been open for 8 years and have had guests from 19 countries. We thrive on the interaction with guests, which was the motivating reason for opening our home. Being small (just two units) allows us to give individualized attention to meet guests' needs. Plus, you can tell your friends you stayed with the author of this chapter. Situated at the edge of the historic Jewish ghetto, we are only 2 blocks from two tram lines, the red Metro, and two bus lines. Keleti and Nyugati train stations are less than a mile on foot, and it's about 5 minutes via public transit (take the Red line to Blaha Lujza). Rates include breakfast and run 45€ to 55€ double, 55€ to 70€ triple, and 85€ quad. It's closed December 15 to January 15.

VII.-Baross tér 15. ☏ **1/461-3010.** Fax 1/343-2770. www.barosshotel.hu. 49 units. High season 108€ double, 126€ triple, 152€ quad; low season 80€ double, 99€ triple, 110€ quad. Rates include breakfast. AE, MC, V. Metro: Keleti (Red line). **Amenities:** Smoke-free rooms.

City Hotel Mátyás ★   Flowing with simple, old-world charm, this hotel caters to guests 40 and older. The comfortable rooms have plain white walls (all repainted in 2008) and minimal decor, but there's adequate space for two people. Some rooms have a fantastic view of the Buda castle district. Note that the hotel's apartments do not have kitchens. In 2008, the hotel was sold to the Taverna Hotel chain. Breakfast is served in the adjoining famous Mátyás Pince Restaurant.

V. Marcius 15 tér. ☏ **1/338-4711.** Fax 1/317-9086. www.cityhotel.hu. 85 units. High season 88€ double; low season 60€ double; special season 146€ double with 3-night minimum. Extra bed 20€ all seasons. Rates include full breakfast. AE, MC, V. Metro: Ferenciek tere (Blue line). **Amenities:** Restaurant; bar; smoke-free rooms.

City Ring Hotel ★★   Perfectly located for the train traveler, this hotel is only 1 block from Nyugati train station, making it an ultraconvenient base with easy access to transportation, shopping, and restaurants. The rooms will comfortably fit two people but are not overly spacious. They are modestly decorated, with an emphasis on functionality, but are tasteful. You stay here for the location and cleanliness, not the decor. One nitpick: The showers in the bathrooms are on the small side. The staff is incredibly helpful and friendly.

XIII. Szent István krt. 22. ☏ **1/340-5450.** Fax 1/340-4884. www.cityhotel.hu. 39 units. High season 78€ double; low season 51€ double; special season (3-night minimum) 115€ double. Deluxe double add 15€ per night to double room rate and 20€ per night to double room rate for all seasons. Rates include full breakfast. AE, MC, V. Metro: Nyugati (Blue line). Tram: 4 or 6. **Amenities:** Smoke-free rooms.

Ibis Budapest Centrum ★★   The location of this hotel is top-notch; it's at the foot of Ráday u., one of the major dining streets in the city and a cultural hot spot. Museums and shopping are also within easy walking distance. Rooms are basic, adequately sized, and impeccably clean. There is a peaceful garden terrace on the first floor where you can sit and relax. Light sleepers should request a room overlooking the terrace rather than Ráday.

IX. Ráday u. 6. ☏ **1/456-4100.** Fax 1/456-4116. www.ibishotel.com. 126 units. High season 63€ double; low season 52€ double; special season 75€-125€ double. VAT is not included in rates. Breakfast 7.60€ per person. AE, DC, MC, V. Metro: Kálvin tér (Blue line). **Amenities:** Bar; smoke-free rooms.

Leo Panzio ★★ 🏠 This small pension sports a fantastic location in the down-town area of Budapest, just minutes from Váci utca's shopping opportunities and a stone's throw from the Metro. Rooms are comfortable but not spacious, decorated in dark woods and with framed antique postcards on the walls. If charm and location are more important than living space, this is the place to stay.

V. Kossuth Lajos u. 2/A. ✆ **1/266-9041.** Fax 1/266-9042. www.leopanzio.hu. 14 units. High season 99€ double, 118€ triple; low season 76€ double,; 99€ triple; special season 119€ double, 148€ triple. No Internet deals. Rates include breakfast. DC, MC, V. Metro: Ferenciek tere (Blue line).

NH Hotel ★★★ We don't usually associate modern elegance with a homey atmo-sphere, but this hotel near Nyugati station has it. Built from the ground up in 2003 directly behind the Vigszinház Theater, this hotel has taken a modern, minimalist approach but still has a warm, welcoming feeling. This is one of the most eco-friendly hotels in the city.

XIII. Vigszinház 3. ✆ **1/814-0000.** Fax 1/814-0100. www.nh-hotels.com. 160 units. High season 196€ double; low season 99€ double. No special season rates. Rates include VAT. Breakfast 17€ per person. AE, DC, MC, V. Metro: Nyugati (Blue line). Tram: 4 or 6. **Amenities:** Restaurant; bar.

Top Attractions & Special Moments

Note: Almost all museums and attractions allow photography and video recording without a flash, but most museums require that you purchase a photo ticket for still photography or video, with videotaping costing much more. Keep your ticket visible, and the guards will not continually ask you to produce it. Photo ticket prices are listed in each entry below.

Budapesti Történeti Múzeum (Budapest History Museum) ★★ This museum, also known as the Castle Museum, is the best place to get a sense of once-great medieval Buda. Many of the museum's descriptions are written in English, but not throughout, so it's probably worth splurging for an audio tour. The history of the palace's repeated cycles of destruction and reconstruction is so arcane that it's difficult to understand what you're really seeing, but it is worth it for those who have the time.

I. In Buda Palace, Wing E., on Castle Hill. ✆ **1/487-8887.** www.btm.hu. Admission 1,200Ft adults, 600Ft students and seniors. Photo 600Ft; video 1,600Ft. Audio-guided tours 850Ft. Mar 20–Sept 15 daily 10am–6pm; Sept 16–Oct 31 closed Tues; Nov 1–Mar 19 10am–4pm, closed Tues. Bus: 16A from Moszkva tér or 16 from Deák tér to Castle Hill. Funicular: From Clark Ádám tér to Castle Hill.

Nemzeti Múzeum (Hungarian National Museum) ★★ This enormous neo-classical structure, built from 1837 to 1847, played a major role in the beginning of the Hungarian Revolution of 1848 and 1849; on its wide steps on March 15, 1848, poet Sándor Petőfi and other young radicals are said to have exhorted the people of Pest to revolt against the Habsburgs. The two main museum exhibits on view are "The History of the Peoples of Hungary from the Paleolithic Age to the Magyar Conquest" and "The History of the Hungarian People from the Magyar Conquest to 1989."

VIII. Múzeum krt. 14. ✆ **1/327-7700.** www.hnm.hu. Admission for permanent exhibits 1,040Ft, children and seniors 520Ft, temporary exhibits vary. Free admission Mar 15, Aug 20, and Oct 23. Photo ticket 3,000Ft, video 5,000Ft. ✆ 1/327-7773 for guided tours; book a week in advance. Tues–Sun 10am–6pm. Metro: Kálvin tér (Blue line) or Astoria (Red line).

Széchenyi Baths ★★★ Part of an immense health spa located in the City Park, the Széchenyi Baths are second to none in terms of facilities and popular appeal. On a nice day, crowds of bathers, including many families and tourists, visit the palatial unisex outdoor swimming pool. Look for older gentlemen, concentrating intently on their floating chess boards as they play half immersed in the steaming pool. Turkish-style thermal baths are segregated and located off to the sides of the pool. In warm weather, there is segregated nude sunbathing on the roof. Massages are available at a rate of 3,500Ft for 30 minutes.

XIV. Állatkerti út 11–14, in City Park. ⓒ 1/363-3210. Day ticket with cabin 3,400Ft or 3,000Ft with locker; massage 3,500Ft for 30 min. Daily 6am–10pm, some pools close earlier on Sat–Sun. Metro: Széchenyi fürdő (Yellow line).

Szépművészeti Múzeum (Museum of Fine Arts) ★★★   Opened in 1906, this neoclassical behemoth is situated on the left side of huge Heroes' Square. A significant part of the collection was acquired in 1871 from the Esterházys, an enormously wealthy noble family that spent centuries amassing great art. The museum's holdings consist of more than 15,000 works, including the largest number of Spanish paintings in Europe outside of Madrid. Trained docents offer daily (and free upon admission) 1-hour tours in English of one gallery at 11am and 2pm; the featured gallery is changed on a rotating basis.

XIV. Hősök tere. ⓒ 1/469-7100. www.szepmuveszeti.hu. Admission 1,400Ft for permanent collection; temporary exhibits are in addition and vary. Photography permitted only in the permanent collection. Photo 300Ft; video 1,500Ft. Tues–Sun 10am–5pm. Every 2nd Thurs on odd weeks until 10pm. Metro: Hősök tere (Yellow line).

HISTORIC BUILDINGS

Magyar Állami Operaház (Hungarian State Opera House) ★★★   Designed by Miklós Ybl in the neo-Renaissance style, Budapest's Opera House was completed in 1884 and boasts an ornate interior featuring frescoes by two of the best-known Hungarian artists of the day, Bertalan Székely and Károly Lotz. Considered one of the most beautiful in Europe, with a rich and evocative history, it is home to both the State Opera and the State Ballet. Tickets can still be purchased here for as little as 800Ft for some performances. If you are not attending a performance, a tour is highly recommended.

VI. Andrássy út 22. ⓒ 1/332-8197. www.opera.hu. Guided tour 2,800Ft adults, 1,400Ft students with international ID. Photo 500Ft, video (with small camera) 500Ft. Tours daily 3 and 4pm. Metro: Opera (Yellow line).

Parliament ★★★   Budapest's great Parliament building, the second largest in Europe after London's, is an eclectic design mixing the predominant Gothic revival style with a neo-Renaissance dome. It was completed in 1902. Standing proudly on the Danube bank, visible from almost any riverside point, it has been one of Budapest's symbols from the outset, though until 1989 a democratically elected government convened here only once (just after World War II, before the Communist takeover). The Parliament is home to the "legendary" jeweled crown of King St. Stephen. Historical records have shown that the crown is constructed of two parts and from two different eras—neither from King St. Stephen's time—but Hungarians want to believe it was Stephen's.

V. Kossuth tér. ⓒ 1/441-4415. Tourist.office@parliament.hu. Admission (by guided tour only) 50 min. tour in English 2,640Ft adults, 1,320Ft students, free admission for E.U. Passport holders with passport. Photos free. Tickets available at gate X for individuals; prebooking for large groups mandatory by e-mail or phone at ⓒ 1/441-4904 or 1/441-4415. English tours year-round daily 10am, noon, and 2pm. Ticket office Mon–Fri 8am–6pm, Sat 8am–4pm, Sun 8am–2pm. Closed to tours when Parliament is in session, usually Mon and Thurs. Metro: Kossuth tér (Red line). Tram 2 or 2A Szalay u.

CHURCHES & SYNAGOGUES

Dohány Synagogue ★★★   Built in 1859, this is the second-largest working synagogue in the world (the oldest is in New York). The architect was non-Jewish Lajos Förster, who designed it using Romantic, Moorish, and Byzantine elements. The synagogue's interior pulls its inspiration from a mix of Orthodox and Reformed Judaism. It has a rich but tragic history. There's a Jewish museum next door that traces the origins of Hungarian Judaism and features exhibits of ceremonial Judaica throughout the centuries. The museum periodically puts on excellent temporary exhibitions. The Holocaust Memorial and Heroes' Temple in the courtyard are well worth visiting.

VII. Dohány u. 2–8. ✆ **1/413–5500.** Admission 1,600Ft adults, 750Ft students. Photo 500Ft synagogue, free for museum. Mar 1–Oct 31 Sun–Thurs 10am–5:30pm, Fri 10am–2:30pm; Nov 1–Feb 28 Sun–Thurs 10am–3:30pm, Fri 10am–1:30pm. Closed national holidays and Jewish holidays, except for services. Metro: Astoria (Red line) or Deák tér (all lines). Bus: 74.

Mátyás Templom (Matthias Church) ★★   Originally founded by King Béla IV in the 13th century, this symbol of Buda's Castle District is officially named the Church of Our Lady. It is popularly referred to as Matthias Church, after the 15th-century King Matthias Corvinus, who added a royal oratory and who was twice married here. Like other old churches in Budapest, it has an interesting history of destruction and reconstruction, always being refashioned in the architectural style of the time. Renovation has been an ongoing process continuing at least through 2012. If possible, do not miss the museum upstairs, often overlooked by travelers who do not realize it is there; it has an interesting history of the royal crown and a wonderful view of the church. It has been closed at times due to the renovations.

I. Szentháromság tér 2. ✆ **1/355-5657.** www.matyas-templom.hu. Admission 750Ft adults, 500Ft students. Photos free. Mon–Fri 9am–5pm; Sat 9am–2:30pm, but depends on weddings; Sun 1–5pm. Metro: Moszkva tér, then bus no. 16A; or Deák tér, then bus 16. Funicular: From Clark Ádám tér to Castle Hill.

Szent István Bazilika (St. Stephen's Church) ★★   The country's largest church, this basilica took more than 50 years to build (the 1868 collapse of the dome caused significant delay) and was finally completed in 1906. Szent István Square, a once-sleepy square in front of the church, was elegantly renovated in the autumn of 2002, converted along with several neighboring streets into a pedestrian-only zone. If you wander to the left of the church into the back chapel and spring for 100Ft, you can view St. Stephen's mummified hand, or you can wait until August 20, his feast day, and see it for free when it is paraded around the city.

V. Szent István tér 33. ✆ **1/318-9159.** www.basilica.hu. Church free admission; treasury 400Ft; panorama tower 500Ft, students and seniors 400Ft. Photos free. Tour 12,000Ft. Church Mon–Fri 9am–5:15pm, Sat 9am–1pm, Sun 1–5pm. Services at 8, 10am, noon, 6, 7:30pm; treasury daily 9am–5pm; Szent Jobb Chapel Mon–Sat 9am–5pm, Sun 1–5pm; panorama tower daily 10am–6pm. Metro: Arany János u. (Blue line) or Bajcsy-Zsilinszky út (Yellow line).

PARKS & PANORAMAS

Gellért Hegy (Gellért Hill) ★★, towering 750 feet (225m) above the Danube, offers a city panorama (bus: 27 from Móricz Zsigmond körtér). It's named after the Italian Bishop Gellért, who assisted Hungary's first Christian king, Stephen I, in converting the Magyars. He was killed by pagans where his enormous statue now stands. On top of Gellért Hill is the **Liberation Monument,** built in 1947 to commemorate the Red Army's liberation of Budapest from Nazi occupation. Also atop the

Quick Picnic

For great picnic fare (perfect for your next train excursion or park visit), head over to the **Spar Grocery** store at the Wesselényi u. tram stop (4 or 6 tram). Inside the door to your right, they sell delicious oven-roasted whole chickens for 1,090 Ft. If you want only half, ask for fél (pronounced *fail*). To the left of the chicken stand, the deli sells an assortment of salads, and they will give you plastic utensils. On the other side of the lobby is a bakery where you can pick up dessert, and the grocery section sells drinks.

hill is the **Citadella,** built by the Austrians shortly after they crushed the Hungarian uprising of 1848–49. Views of the city from both vistas are excellent, but the Citadella is spectacular. Don't bother paying extra to get into the upper part; the view is not that much higher, so it is a waste of money.

City Park (Városliget) ★★★ is an equally popular place to spend a summer day (Metro: Hósök tere/Heroes' Sq. or Széchenyi Fürdó). Heroes' Square, at the end of Andrássy út, is the most logical starting point for a walk in City Park. The lake behind the square is used for boating in summer and ice-skating in winter. **Gundel,** Budapest's most famous restaurant, is also here, as are the immense Habsburg-style **Széchenyi Baths.** One highlight is the **Vajdahunyad Castle** (Vajdahunyad vára), which is in part a replica of a Transylvania castle on **Széchenyi Island.** It is now home to the **Agricultural Museum.** Admission is 600Ft adults, 300Ft students; photos are free.

Where to Dine

Étterem is the most common Hungarian word for "restaurant" and is used for everything from cafeteria-style eateries to first-class restaurants. A *vendéglő,* or guesthouse, is a smaller, more intimate restaurant, often with a Hungarian folk motif; *café* has blurred meanings, with some serving full meals, while others serving only snacks. An *önkiszolgáló* is a self-service cafeteria, typically open only for lunch. Stand-up *bufes* are often found in transport hubs. A *cukrászda* or *kávéház* is a Central European coffeehouse, where coffee and sweets are served. A *borozó* is a wine bar, a *söröző* a beer bar; sandwiches are usually available at both. Unless stated otherwise, all restaurants listed have menus in English, and all are required to have nonsmoking areas.

Frici Papa Kifőzés ★ 🍴 HUNGARIAN   The staff can be downright surly, but customers keep coming anyway; we think the attitude actually makes for entertainment with your meal if you're prepared for it. This is a plain, homey place with no frills, and its prices reflect that. The daily offerings are posted with signs hanging on a Pegboard near the front windows, and everything is a la carte, even the ketchup. For the best selections, go for lunch or an early dinner; after 7pm, you are taking your chances.

VI. Király u. 55. No phone. Reservations not accepted. Main courses 649Ft–699Ft. Cash only. Mon–Sat 11am–9pm. Tram: 4 or 6 to Király u.

Gerlóczy Kávéház ★★★ HUNGARIAN MODERN   The romantic ambiance of this venue is worth a visit for the tree that shades the outdoor eating area or the live music most evenings. Lunch specials are ubiquitous these days, but here they do it right. A choice of the two- or three-course special will be positively delightful for both your taste buds and your stomach—and will also cost less than preparing a meal at home. We have fond memories of great dinners here in the past and anticipate having more in the future.

V. Gerlóczy u. 1. ✆ **1/501-4000.** www.gerloczy.hu. Reservations recommended. Cold main courses 900Ft-2,750Ft; hot main courses 1,350Ft-4,900Ft. MC. Daily 7am-11pm. Metro: Deák tér (all lines).

Govinda Vegetariánus Étterem ★★★ INDIAN/VEGETARIAN This self-serve restaurant serves delicious vegetarian food in a tranquil, smoke-free environment. Seating is plentiful, but this place can be packed at lunchtime on weekdays, so you may have to wait in line. The staff speaks English and will explain each dish. Another plus: Proceeds from the restaurant help to support efforts to feed the homeless of the city in the form of monthly food giveaways.

V. Vigyázó Ferenc u. 4. ✆ **1/269-1625.** www.govinda.hu. Reservations not accepted. Main courses 220Ft-650Ft; small sampler meal 1,550Ft; large sampler meal 1,850Ft; student menu 760Ft. No credit cards. Mon-Fri 11:30am-8pm; Sat noon-8pm. Metro: Kossuth Lajos tér (Red line).

Hemingway ★★★ 📷 HUNGARIAN You will feel like you've escaped the city when visiting this restaurant, situated next to a small lake surrounded by plenty of trees. The open and airy interior makes us feel like we've joined Hemingway inside one of his favorite getaways. The piano and bass duo adds to the relaxing Casablanca atmosphere. The food and service are superb. In good weather, eat outside on the terrace overlooking the water for a romantic meal.

XI. Kosztolányi D. tér 2, Feneketlen tó. ✆ **1/381-0522.** www.hemingway-etterem.hu. Reservations recommended. Main courses 1,980Ft-8,900Ft. AE, DC, MC, V. Mon-Sat noon-midnight. Bus: 7 to Buda from Ferenciek tér to Feneketlen tó, a small "lake." Trams: 19 or 49 to Kosztolányi Dezső tér.

Kossuth Museum Vénhajó Étterem (Old Ship Museum Restaurant) ★★★ 📷 HUNGARIAN Romance and a delicious dinner are perfectly blended on this ship, docked at the port closest to the Chain Bridge. Request a table outside, and in the evening you will have the best view of the castle district and of the Chain Bridge, all sparkling with lights. The boat itself is a still-working paddle boat and a museum. The service is attentive and the food is excellent. *Note:* The boat does leave port for dinner cruises, so call ahead.

V. Vigadó 2. ✆ **1/411-0942.** www.europahajo.hu. Reservations recommended. Main courses 1,450Ft-4,950Ft. MC, V. Daily 11am-11pm. Tram: 2 to Eötvös.

M ★★ HUNGARIAN This quiet and unassuming restaurant might easily be overlooked, but it shouldn't be. There are only three tables inside the entrance, but there's more seating upstairs. The menu, an eclectic mix of Hungarian and international influences, is left to the whims of the chef, who changes the menu (available on the website) every Tuesday but always gets rave reviews. The decor is notable: Every inch of the walls and ceiling is covered in brown wrapping paper with black line drawings of furnishings found in a home. Reserve an outside table or one on the main level in warm weather.

VII. Kertész 48. ✆ **1/322-3108.** www.metterem.hu. Reservations recommended. Main courses 1,600Ft-2,900Ft. No credit cards. Daily 6pm-midnight; Sat-Sun menu noon-4pm. Tram: 4 or 6, Király u.

Mátyás Pince ★★★ 📷 HUNGARIAN Art, history, and music buffs will love this restaurant, established in 1904 and named for King Matyás; the myths and legends of his reign grace the walls in magnificent style. The frescoes and stained glass decorating the dining areas were registered as national monuments in 1973. Music is provided by the Lakatos gypsy music dynasty every night but Mondays from 7pm until closing, creating an all-around romantic experience. The combination of excellent Hungarian cuisine (the menu's extensive), entertainment, and service makes for a wonderful evening out.

V. Március 15 tér 7-8. © **1/266-8008.** www.cityhotels.hu. Reservations recommended. Main courses 3,500Ft–10,900Ft. AE, MC, V. Daily 11am–midnight. Metro: Ferenciek tere (Blue line).

Mosselen Belgian Beer Café ★★★ 🍴 FLEMISH *Mosselen* means "mussels" in Flemish, but this L-shaped restaurant is best known as a beer lovers' paradise; if you love beer, this is the only bar with such a wide selection. There are 10 different beers on tap, plus a further selection of over 50 other brews to choose from, each served in a distinctive glass. The wainscoted walls of deep, rich wood help instill a Belgium country atmosphere. The menu has an interesting selection of fish dishes, ranging from tuna steak to prawns, but meat and vegetarian options are available. Thanks to its combination of excellent food and beer choices, this is a favorite spot.

XIII. Pannónia u. 14. © **1/452-0535.** Reservations recommended. Main courses 2,390Ft–4,890Ft; beer 790Ft–5,900Ft. AE, DC, MC, V. Daily noon–midnight. Tram: 4 or 6 to Jászai Mari tér.

Paprika Vendéglő ★★★ 🍴 HUNGARIAN   If you want to sample the cuisine of the Hungarian countryside without leaving the city, this is the place. Of all of the restaurants in the city, this is our absolute favorite. The old-fashioned earthen oven, oversized cooking utensils, and log cabin interior will envelop you in rustic comfort. Let yourself go hog wild, and try the roasted wild boar with brandy or the saddle of deer. No matter what you order, the portions will be generous.

VII. Dozsa Gyorgy 72. © **06/70-574-6508** (mobile phone). Reservations recommended. Main courses 1,550Ft–3,900Ft. AE, MC, V. Daily 11am–11pm. Metro: Hősök tere (Yellow line), 4½ blocks from Heroes' Square.

Tabáni Terasz ★★ HUNGARIAN   The dishes here are all prepared with a nice variety of vegetables, which is unusual for traditional Hungarian cuisine, which uses vegetables sparingly. The portions are substantial. The interior is made up of small rooms with tables and chairs—a layout that makes you feel like you're entering someone's home—and is decorated with wall hangings, paintings, and other regional touches. It is a bit difficult to get to from the Pest side of the city, but worth the effort. In summer, dine on the lovely terrace.

I. Apród utca 10. © **1/201-1086.** www.tabaniterasz.hu. Main courses 2,500Ft–4,700Ft. MC, V. Daily noon–midnight. Bus: 86. Tram: 18 to Döbrentei tér.

Trófea Grill Étterem ★★★ 🍴 HUNGARIAN   This is the best all-you-can-eat restaurant in the city, and you get to select from a daily-changing menu of over 100 different dishes and drinks. The hot entrees are Hungarian favorites and usually include some version of beef, chicken, or venison in a hearty sauce. You can also take marinated chicken or pork to the grill to be prepared for you. Everything is included in one price if you don't order wine off of the wine list. *Note:* There are five restaurants by this name in the city, but they are owned by different companies; this location is the only one we highly recommend.

XIV. Erzsébet Királyné útja 5. © **1/251-6377.** www.trofeagrill.com. Reservations recommended. Lunch Mon–Fri 2,999Ft; dinner Mon–Thurs 3,999Ft; dinner Fri and all day Sat–Sun or holidays 4,599Ft. Half-price for children up to 150cm (59 in.). No credit cards. Mon–Fri noon–midnight; Sat 11:30am–midnight; Sun 11:30am–8:30pm. Playroom Sun 11:30am–5pm. Metro: Mexikói (Yellow line).

coffeehouse CULTURE

Budapest, like Vienna, was famous for its coffeehouse culture. Coffeehouses have housed the literary movements and political circles of many a revolution, with their members identified in large part by which coffeehouse they met in. You can still go to several classic coffeehouse-style venues today that more or less resemble their historic counterparts. All offer delicious pastries, coffee, and more in an atmosphere of splendor.

The **Gerbeaud** ★★ is a classic, but it's overrated, overpriced, and frequented mostly by tourists. It's located in the Inner City at V. Vörösmarty tér 7 (✆ **1/429-9000**). The **Central Kávéház** ★★★ is one of the noblest and most beautifully renovated establishments, and to this day is a haunt for

many a writer or thinker. It's at V. Károlyi Mihály u. 9. (✆ **1/266-2110;** www. centralkavehaz.hu; Metro: Ferenciek tere). **Művész Kávéház** ★★, another historic coffeehouse frequented by the artistic community for decades, is across the street from the Opera House, at VI. Andrássy út 29 (✆ **1/352-1337;** Metro: Opera). They remodeled in 2009, but it's still charming and historic.

Of major historical importance is the reopened (2006) **Café New York** ★★ in the New York Palace Hotel, located at VII. Erzsébet Krt 9-11 (✆ **1/886-6167**). The building was built by the New York Life Insurance Company in 1894; the cafe was the meeting place of many of Hungary's famous writers, poets, and artists. It is worth a look but is overpriced.

Shopping

Shoppers fill the pedestrian-only **Váci utca,** from the stately Vörösmarty tér, the center of Pest, across the roaring Kossuth Lajos utca, all the way to Vámház krt. Prices in this area reflect the touristy feel, so if you are looking for bargains, look here but shop elsewhere.

The **Castle District** in Buda, with many folk-art boutiques and galleries, is another popular but overpriced area for souvenir hunters. Locals (and careful travelers) might window-shop in these two neighborhoods but do their buying elsewhere. One popular street is Pest's **Outer Ring** (Nagykörút); another bustling street is Pest's **Kossuth Lajos utca,** off the Erzsébet Bridge, and its continuation of **Rákóczi út,** extending all the way out to Keleti Station.

Hungary's famous folkloric objects are the most popular souvenirs among foreign visitors. The mushrooming number of folk-art shops (*Népművészeti Háziipar*) has a diverse selection of handmade goods. Popular items include pillowcases, embroidered tablecloths, runners, wine cozies, pottery, porcelain, dolls, intricately painted or carved eggs, dresses, skirts, and sheepskin vests. One shop that has a wide selection and helpful staff is **Folkart Craftman's House** (✆ 1/318-5143), on the side street, at Régiposta u. 12, right off of Váci utca and open daily 10am to 7pm. One outstanding private shop on Váci utca is **Vali Folklór,** in the courtyard of Váci u. 23 (✆ 1/337-6301), open Monday through Saturday 10am to 8pm and Sunday noon to 8pm. A soft-spoken man named Bálint Ács runs this cluttered shop and travels the villages of Hungary and neighboring countries in search of authentic folk items, Communist-era badges, pins, and medals. His sales staff does not speak English, so don't try to ask questions.

Another popular Hungarian item is **porcelain,** particularly from the country's two best-known producers, Herend and Zsolnay. Although both brands are available in the West, here you'll find a better selection and perhaps lower prices. At the **Herend Shops,** V. József nádor tér 11 (© 1/317-2622) or VI. Andrássy út 16 (© 1/374-0006), you'll find the widest Herend selection in the capital. Delightfully gaudy Zsolnay porcelain from the southern city of Pécs is Hungary's second-most-celebrated brand, found in almost all shopping centers and in numerous porcelain shops; one to visit is **Zsolnay,** XIII. Pozsonyi út 11 (no phone). Take note if you are a collector that the company has gone bankrupt and is in receivership, which may cause dramatic changes in prices. The factory will still operate under government ownership until a buyer is found. This store is open Monday to Saturday from 10am to 6pm.

Budapest also has five **vintage market halls** (*vásárcsarnok*) of historic importance, wonders of steel and glass, built in the 1890s in the ambitious grandiose style of the time. Specifically built to bring food merchants indoors to improve sanitary conditions, they are still in use. They provide a measure of local color you won't find in the grocery store. The **Központi Vásárcsarnok** (Central Market Hall), on IX. Vámház körút (on the Pest side of the Szabadság Bridge), is the largest and most spectacular market hall. Visit the second floor for a large selection of common souvenirs at better prices than elsewhere in the city.

Nightlife

The weekly English-language newspaper *The Budapest Times* (**www.budapest times.hu**) is a good all-round resource that can be found at newsstands and sometimes at TourInform. The free *Funzine* (**www.funzine.hu**) magazine comes out every 2 weeks and can be found just about everywhere in the city; it has the latest info on youthful entertainment.

The **Cultur-Comfort Ticket Office** (Cultur-Comfort Központi Jegyiroda; www. cultur-comfort.hu), VI. Paulay Ede u. 31 (© 1/322-0000; Metro: Opera), sells tickets to just about everything, from theater and operetta to sports events and rock concerts. It's open from Monday to Friday 9am to 6pm. For **opera and ballet,** go to the **Hungarian State Opera Ticket Office** (Magyar Állami Opera Jegyiroda), VI. Andrássy út 22 (© 1/353-0170; Metro: Opera). For **rock, pop, and jazz concert** tickets, try Ticket Express, VI. Andrássy út 18 (© 30/303-0999 mobile only; www.tex.hu; Metro: Opera), as well as **Concert & Media,** ticket counters in most Libri Bookstores, but check the website for other locations (© 1/222-1313; www. jegyelado.hu).

THE PERFORMING ARTS   Many of the city's indoor venues do not offer regular programming during the summer because they are not air-conditioned; the newer **Palace of Arts** is the exception. When these venues do have special summer events, keep the cooling situation in mind.

Completed in 1884, the **Magyar Állami Operaház** (Hungarian State Opera House), VI. Andrássy út 22 (© 1/332-8197; Metro: Opera), is Budapest's most famous performance hall. Hungarians adore opera, and a large percentage of seats are sold on a subscription basis; buy your tickets a few days or weeks ahead, if possible. If a performance is sold out, go to the box office an hour before the opening curtain to obtain "no-show" tickets. The box office is open from Monday to Friday 11am to 6pm. Ticket prices range from 300Ft to 16,900Ft.

The **Palace of Arts,** Budapest, Komor Marcell u. 1 (© 1/555-3001; http:// mupa.hu; tram 2: Közvágóhíd station), is a place where the classical music tradition

During the hot, hazy, lazy days of summer, you'll find special venues for classical music. **St. Stephen's Church (Bazilika) Plaza** hosts outdoor symphony concerts. The **Hungarian State Opera House** hosts opera and symphony performances, usually in August, but the schedule is limited due to the lack air-conditioning.

Margaret Island is also the scene of many musical events, but they change from year to year. Check *Funzine* or *The Budapest Times* for a current schedule.

and the avant-garde (in the form of contemporary dance and art) coexist. Adjacent to Hungary's National Theater, the building is home to the elegant **National Concert Hall** and the **Festival Theater.** The **Ludwig Museum,** home to a mix of period and contemporary pop art from geographic regions ranging from the U.S. to Central Europe, is also housed here. You can buy tickets to concerts or to the museum on the first floor in the Palace of Arts.

The Great Hall (Nagyterem) of the **Zeneakadémia** (Ferenc Liszt Academy of Music), VI. Liszt Ferenc tér 8 (© 1/341-4788, ext. 179; Metro: Oktogon), is the city's premier music hall. The academy is closed until late in 2012 for extensive renovations, but some performances will be offered at different venues, so it's best to check with TourInform for current details.

LIVE-MUSIC CLUBS   **Fat Mo's Music Club,** always a hot place, is at V. Nyári Pál u. 11 (© 1/267-3199; Metro: Kálvin tér [Blue line]). There's no cover charge. The live jazz concerts start at 9pm and dancing starts at 11pm. The best night is definitely Sunday, with *Hot Jazz Band* performing in the style of the '20s and '30s. Make sure you book a table if you wish to enjoy their superb food as well. **TRAFO,** XI. Liliom u. 41 (© 1/456-2040; tram: 4 or 6 to Üllöi út), is an old electric power station that was transformed into a cultural center. It has modern dance performances and hosts a hip disco for 20- and 30-somethings. *The* nights are Wednesday and Sunday, with the party starting at 10pm, but on Fridays dance to the '60s and '70s greatest hits; Trafo is closed during summers. **Old Man's Pub,** VIII. Akácfa u. 13 (© 1/322-7645; Metro: Blaha Luzja tér), is the place to take in the best jazz and blues in Hungary. This very hip spot is open daily from 3pm to 4am but closed in August. The **Columbus Pub,** opposite the Intercontinental Hotel (© 1/266–9013), is a docked boat restaurant/nightclub on the Pest side of the Danube; the best of local jazz musicians play nightly.

Excursions to the Danube Bend

The delightful towns along the Danube Bend—Szentendre, Esztergom, and Visegrád—are easy day trips from Budapest. The great natural beauty of the area, where forested hills loom over the river, makes it a welcome departure for the city weary.

SZENTENDRE

Szentendre (pronounced *Sen*-ten-dreh), 13 miles (21km) north of Budapest, has been populated since the Stone Age by Illyrians, the Celtic Eraviscus tribe, Romans, Lombards, Avars, and, naturally, Hungarians. Serbians settled here in the 17th century, embellishing the town with their unique characteristics. **Szentendre** counts half a dozen Serbian churches among its rich collection of historical buildings. Since the turn of the 20th century, Szentendre has been home to an artist's colony. Museums here do not have stable hours, even when posted on their door. Think of a museum as icing on the cake, if it is open. The town is an extremely popular tourist destination, which is sometimes a turn-off for visitors, but it really is a treasure. To appreciate the rich flavor of the town, look beyond the touristy shops and wander the streets looking at the architecture, the galleries, and the churches. Don't miss walking along the river for a lovely and relaxing view. Almost all of the streets are cobblestone, so choose comfortable footwear.

GETTING THERE   The HÉV suburban railroad connects Budapest's Batthyány tér with Szentendre. On the Pest side, you can catch the HÉV from the Margit Híd, Budai Híd Fő. Trains leave daily, year-round, every 20 minutes or so from 4am to 11:30pm (trip time: 45 min.). The one-way fare is 650Ft; subtract 285Ft if you have a valid Budapest public transportation pass. The trip takes 45 minutes.

VISITOR INFORMATION   The information office **Tourinform** is at Dumtsa Jenő u. 22 (© **26/317-965;** www.szentendre.hu). Published open dates and times are April through October Monday to Wednesday from 9:30am to 6pm and Thursday to Sunday 9:30am to 7:30pm; in the off season, it's open Monday to Friday from 9:30am to 5pm. In reality, they march to the beat of their own drummer, so they may or may not be open. To get here, just follow the flow of pedestrian traffic into town on Kossuth Lajos utca.

Top Attractions & Special Moments

If you want to visit a unique shop, make it **Handpets ★★★**, Dumsta Jeno u. 15 (© **26/ 373-746;** www.handpets.hu). Made for three or five fingers and designed by Kati Szili, Handpets are the most creative hand puppets we have ever seen. The handmade puppets are of high quality, sure to delight children of all ages, us included. This is the only shop where the entire collection is available, though there are poor imitations sold elsewhere.

The most widely known museum in this village is the **Szabó Marzipan Museum ★★**, Dumsta Jeno u. 12 (© **26/311-931**). Here's your chance to see a 5¼-foot-long (1.6m) reproduction of the Hungarian Parliament made entirely in marzipan. Kids will love the Disney characters. From May to September, it is open daily from 10am to 7pm; October to April, the hours are daily 10am to 6pm Admission is 400Ft. The **Margit Kovács Museum ★★★**, Vastagh György u. 1 (© **26/ 310-244**), is a must-see, displaying the exceptional and highly original work of Hungary's best-known ceramic artist. Her sculptures of elderly women and friezes of village life are particularly moving. The museum is open March to September Tuesday to Sunday from 9am to 6pm. Admission is 1,000Ft.

The **Serbian Orthodox Blagovestenska Church,** at Fo tér 4, is a fine example of an orthodox church built in the 1700s. It is open October to April Tuesday through Sunday from 10am to 5pm. The rest of the year, it closes at 6pm. Admission is 600Ft; an extensive collection of Serbian icons is housed in a nearby hilltop museum. **Szántó Jewish Memorial House and Temple ★★★**, Albotmány u. 4, is the first temple built in Hungary after World War II and is probably the smallest synagogue in the world. It was dedicated on May 17, 1998, by the Chief Rabbi of Hungary. Men are given a yarmulke to wear when entering. It's open Tuesday to Sunday from 11am to 5pm. Donations are accepted.

Where to Dine

For a full sit-down meal, try **Chez Nicolas Restaurant** ★★★, Kígyó utca 10 (© **26/311-288**; www.cheznicolas.hu). It offers intimate, romantic dining with an outdoor terrace looking out on the river. You can choose from Hungarian or French dishes. Main courses vary from 1,790Ft to 3,800Ft. Open Tuesday through Sunday from noon to 10pm.

Aranysárkány Vendéglő (Golden Dragon Inn) ★★, Alkotmány u. 1/a (© **26/ 301-479**; www.aranysarkany.hu), just east of Fő tér on Hunyadi utca, is always crowded. Choose from such enticing offerings as spicy leg of lamb, roast leg of goose, and venison ragout. A tasty vegetarian plate is also offered. Various traditional Hungarian beers are on tap. Main courses are 2,400Ft to 4,000Ft, with special tourist menus for 3,300Ft. It's open daily from noon to 10pm.

An elegant restaurant in a former private home, **Régimódi** ★★, Futó u. 3 (© **26/ 311-105**), is furnished with antique Hungarian carpets and chandeliers. Original artwork decorates the walls. Limited terrace dining is available, and in the summer, you will appreciate the outside seating. If you walk directly south from Fő tér, you'll find this excellent choice for dining. The menu offers a wide range of Hungarian specialties, with an emphasis on game dishes. It does get crowded with tour groups. Main dish dinner options range from 2,000Ft to 4,550Ft, but there are also three set menus from 2,200Ft to 2,800Ft. They serve daily from 9am to 10pm.

ESZTERGOM

Formerly a Roman settlement, **Esztergom** (pronounced *Ess*-tair-gome), 29 miles (47km) northwest of Budapest, was the seat of the Hungarian kingdom for 300 years. Hungary's first king, István I (Stephen I), received the crown from the pope in A.D. 1000. He converted Hungary to Catholicism, and Esztergom became the country's center of the early church. Although its glory days are long gone, this quiet town remains the seat of the archbishop-primate—the "Hungarian Rome."

GETTING THERE   One train every hour makes the run daily between Budapest's Nyugati Station and Esztergom (trip time: 1½ hr.); IC trains are not available on this route. Train tickets cost 955Ft each way.

VISITOR INFORMATION   **Gran Tours,** Széchenyi tér 25 (© **33/502-001**), is the best source of information. Summer hours are from Monday to Friday 8am to 4pm and Saturday 9am to noon; winter hours are from Monday to Friday 8am to 4pm. The station is on the outskirts of town, while the tourist info center is in the city center. Take bus no. 1 or 6 to Széchenyi tér. Local buses depart from outside the train station. You can buy a ticket from the driver. Tickets vary from 100Ft to 165Ft, depending on your destination.

Top Attractions & Special Moments

The massive, neoclassical **Esztergom Cathedral** ★★★ (© **33/402-354**), in Szent István tér on Castle Hill, is the largest church in Hungary. It is Esztergom's most popular attraction and one of Hungary's most impressive buildings. Built in the last century, it was to replace the cathedral ruined during the Turkish occupation. It claims the world's largest altarpiece painted on one continuous piece of canvas. The cathedral **Treasury** *(Kincstár)* ★ contains a stunning array of ecclesiastical jewels and gold works. The cupola provides unparalleled views of Esztergom and the surrounding Hungarian and Slovak countryside. The cathedral is open daily in summer from 8am to 7pm, winter from 8am to 4pm. The treasury and crypt are open daily in summer from 9am to 4pm, winter Tuesday to Sunday noon to 4pm. The cupola is open in the summer only daily 9am to 4pm. Admission to the cathedral is free, but to see the crypt costs 200Ft. The Treasury is 700Ft, and to see the view from the cupola costs 400Ft. To get here, take bus no. 6 from the train station and get off at the cathedral or in good weather, it is a nice walk.

Where to Dine

Creative specialties abound at **Padlizsán Étterem ★★★**, Pazmány Peter u. 21 (© **33/311-212**), a homey restaurant housed behind the basilica. In warm weather, there is a great view of the basilica above the hill. Four of us dined here, and each was impressed and with our selection, enchanted by the flavors. At the time, the service was scattered, but most likely due to a wedding inside. The main offerings run 1,850Ft to 3,800Ft. They do not take credit cards. Serving hours are Monday to Thursday noon to 10pm, Friday to Sunday noon to 11pm.

VISEGRÁD

Halfway between Szentendre and Esztergom, **Visegrád** (pronounced *Vee*-sheh-grod) is the smallest town in the country, making it historically fascinating. The Romans built a fort here, which was still extant when Slovak settlers gave the town its present name (meaning "High Castle") in the 9th or 10th century. After the Mongol invasion (1241–42), construction began on both the present ruined hilltop citadel and the former riverside palace. Visegrád boasted one of the finest royal palaces ever built in Hungary. Only one king, Charles Robert (1307–42), actually used it as his primary residence, but monarchs from Béla IV, in the 13th century, through Matthias Corvinus, in the late 15th century, spent time in Visegrád and contributed to its development, the latter expanding the palace into a great Renaissance center known throughout Europe.

GETTING THERE   There's no direct train service to Visegrád. Instead, take 1 of 20 daily trains departing from Nyugati Station for Nagymaros (trip time: 45 min.–1 hr.). From Nagymaros, take a ferry across the river to Visegrád. The ferry dock (RÉV; © **26/398-344**) is a 5-minute walk from the train station. A ferry leaves every hour throughout the day. The train ticket to Nagymaros costs 955Ft; the ferryboat ticket to Visegrád costs 250Ft for adults and 125Ft for students.

VISITOR INFORMATION   **Visegrád Tours,** RÉV u. 15 (© **26/398-160**), is located across the road from the RÉV ferry boat landing. It is open daily 8am to 5:30pm; from November to March, they are open, but they use the hotel next door as their winter office.

Top Attractions & Special Moments

Once covering much of the area where the boat landing and Fő utca (Main St.) are now found, the ruins of the Royal Palace and the Salamon tower are all that remain today for visitors to explore. The entrance to the open-air ruins of the **King Matthias Museum ★★** is at Fő u. 27 (© **26/398-026**). Entrance to the palace is 1,040Ft and 620Ft for the tower; students receive a 50% discount. Both locations are open Tuesday to Sunday from 9am to 5pm, but the tower is closed from October 1 to April 30. The buried ruins of the palace, having achieved a near-mythical status, were not discovered until the 21st century.

The **Cloud Castle (Fellegvár) ★★★** (© **26/598-082**), a mountaintop citadel above Visegrád, affords one of the finest views you'll find over the Danube. Admission to the citadel is 900Ft. It is open daily from 9:30am to 5:30pm from March 15 to October 14. The "City Bus," a van taxi that awaits passengers outside Visegrád Tours, takes people up the steep hill for a steep fare of 2,500Ft apiece for the ride up or 4,000Ft for a round-trip, if you stay a maximum of 30 minutes (otherwise, it is again 2,500Ft). Note that it is not a casual walk to the citadel; consider it a day hike and pack bottled water accordingly.

Where to Dine

In keeping with its name, **Renaissance Restaurant,** at Fő u. 11, across the street from the MAHART boat landing (© **26/398-081**), specializes in authentic medieval cuisine. Food is served in clay crockery without silverware (only a wooden spoon), and guests are offered paper crowns to wear. A meal is 4,500Ft per person. If you're big on the medieval theme, come for dinner (July–Aug only), when a six-course "Royal Feast" is celebrated following a 45-minute duel between knights. It's is available only to groups of not less than 30 people, but if you call, they will include you in a group if one is scheduled. It's open daily from noon to 10pm. Tickets for this special evening are handled by the restaurant directly or Visegrád Tours (see above).

ITALY

12

This boot-shaped peninsula is called *La Bell'Italia* (Beautiful Italy), and so it is, stretching from the Alpine peaks in its north to the offshore island of Sicily. The works left by Leonardo da Vinci, Raphael, Michelangelo, and all the gang are waiting to dazzle you, along with the ruins of Rome, the decaying but still magnificent palazzi of Venice, and the Renaissance treasures of Florence. You'll find enough Duomos, Madonnas, masterpieces, and scenery to dazzle the eye. And that's not all: Italy is a citadel of style and fashion and serves, at least in the view of Italians, the world's greatest cuisine. Each of the country's 20 regions has its own distinctive kitchen.

In our very limited space, we can only preview some of the highlights of this vast, diversified land, with its more than 5,000 miles (8,050km) of coastline, from the Ligurian Sea in the northwest to the Adriatic Sea washing eastward. The most hurried visitor with a railpass usually confines his or her itinerary to Rome, Florence, and Venice, and that's not a bad idea, as this trio of cities ranks among the top 10 in the world for attractions. Just seeing those cities will easily eat up a week's vacation. And if you have extra time, you can venture into other major cities, such as Milan or Naples, or explore some of Italy's charming towns, such as Pisa and Turin, or the scenic Lake Como. The good news is that visiting these cities by rail is a breeze, thanks to a thoroughly improved rail network. And though the cities themselves may not be cheap, rail travel in Italy is relatively inexpensive, making it a good destination for travelers trying to conserve their euros.

Highlights of Italy

On international flights, chances are, you'll fly into **Rome** to begin your rail journey through Italy, though some people will find themselves flying into Milan (from which you can easily connect to Rome by train or plane). Rome deserves as much of your time as your schedule allows. It is one of the planet's great historical cities and is filled with museums, monuments, and a *joie de vivre* unlike any other city in Italy.

Allow at least 3 or 4 days to skim the highlights. You can divide your time among the ancient, papal, and modern attractions the city has to offer. Visit the Colosseum, the Roman Forum, and Palatine Hill; then take in St. Peter's Basilica and the Sistine Chapel before tossing in a few coins at the Trevi Fountain. And these are just a tiny few of the sights the city has to offer.

After Rome, if you have time for the south, you can take the train to Naples for a day of exploring. If you can spare an extra day, stay overnight and spend the following day wandering around the ruins of **Pompeii** or **Herculaneum**.

Italy

Once back in Rome, grab a train north to **Florence,** where a minimum of 3 days is needed to explore the glories of the city of the Renaissance. Here are all the churches, museums, historic squares, panoramic views, and galleries you would ever want to see, beginning with the masterpieces of the Uffizi Gallery, one of the world's largest and greatest repositories of art. Other highlights include the multicolored Duomo (cathedral), Giotto's bell tower, the Palazzo Pitti, Michelangelo's *David* in the Galleria dell'Accademia, the massive Palazzo Vecchio (another Medici residence) opening onto Piazza della Signoria (where you'll want to have a coffee in a cafe), and the Medici Chapels. Walk the Ponte Vecchio, shop at San Lorenzo Market, and look into some of the world's greatest churches to occupy your final day or hours.

FESTIVALS & special events

At the riotous **Carnevale,** theatrical presentations and masked balls take place throughout Venice and on the islands in the lagoon. The balls are by invitation only (except the Doge's Ball), but the street events and fireworks are open to everyone. The festivities take place the week before Ash Wednesday, the beginning of Lent. Contact the **Venice Tourist Office,** APT Venezia, Castello 5050, 30122 Venezia (© **041/5298711;** www.turismo.venezia.it).

Processions and age-old ceremonies—some from pagan days, some from the Middle Ages—are staged during the **Holy Week observances** held nationwide. The most notable procession is led by the pope, passing the Colosseum and the Roman Forum up to Palatine Hill; a torch-lit parade caps the observance. The events kick off 4 days before Easter Sunday, sometimes at the end of March but often in April.

Palio fever grips the Tuscan hill town of Siena from early July to mid-August for a wild and exciting horse race that originated in the Middle Ages. Pageantry, costumes, and the celebrations of the victorious *contrada* (sort of a neighborhood social club) mark the spectacle. It's a "no rules" event: Even a horse without a rider can win the race. For details on Il Palio, contact the **Azienda di Promozione Turistica,** Piazza del Campo 56, 53100 Siena (© **0577/280551;** www.terresiena.it).

From Florence, head northeast by train to **Venice,** the queen of the Veneto and one of the world's most dazzling cities, built on 118 islets linked by 400 bridges with 150 canals cut through the maze. Venice is filled with attractions, including *palazzi* and churches, but it is the glorious city itself that is its major allure. It shouldn't exist but does, like a preposterous dream.

After Venice, your rail journey takes you northwest to the sprawling metropolis of **Milan.** You'll need a full day for Milan, capital of Lombardy and a city of glitz and glamour. It doesn't have the attractions of the "royal trio" but is rich in sights nonetheless, highlighted by its Gothic Duomo, its famous opera house of La Scala; Leonardo's masterpiece, *The Last Supper,* in Santa Maria delle Grazie; and the Brera Palace and Art Gallery, one of northern Italy's greatest showcases of art.

After Milan, all of Italy's lake district, especially Como, is at your doorstep. You can also take the train northwest to the Piedmontese city of **Turin,** famous as the resting place of the controversial Holy Shroud, or else go to the port city of **Genoa,** birthplace of Columbus, to survey its many monuments and to tour its port facilities.

ESSENTIALS

Getting There

High season on most airlines' routes to Italy is usually June to the beginning of September. This is the most expensive and most crowded time to travel. **Shoulder season** is April to May, early September to October, and December 15 to 24. **Low season** is November 1 to December 14, and December 25 to March 31.

Alitalia (© **800/223-5730;** www.alitalia.com) is the Italian national airline, with nonstop flights to Rome from a number of North American cities. Most flights arrive in either Milan or Rome.

Major North American carriers offering direct flights to Italy inclu/
Airlines (✆ 800/433-7300; www.aa.com), **Delta** (✆ 800/221-1212;
com), **United** (✆ 800/538-2929; www.united.com), **US Airways/Americ.**
(✆ 800/622-1015; www.usairways.com), **Continental** (✆ 800/231-0856; www.
continental.com), and **Air Canada** (✆ 888/247-2262; www.aircanada.ca). **British
Airways** (✆ 800/AIRWAYS [247-9297]; www.britishairways.com), **Virgin Atlantic
Airways** (✆ 800/821-5438; www.virgin-atlantic.com), **Air France** (✆ 800/237-
2747; www.airfrance.com), **Northwest/KLM** (✆ 800/225-2525; www.nwa.com),
and **Lufthansa** (✆ 800/645-3880; www.lufthansa-usa.com) offer some attractive
deals for anyone interested in combining a trip to Italy with a stopover in, say, Britain,
Paris, Amsterdam, or Germany.

Depending on your departure city, flying time to Italy ranges from 8 to 12 hours.

Italy by Rail
PASSES

For information on the **Eurail Global Pass, Eurail Select Pass,** and other multicountry options, see chapter 2. Information on the **Eurail Italy Pass** and **Eurail Italy Rail
'n Drive** options is also available in chapter 2. All of these passes should be purchased
in North America and are available through **Rail Europe** (✆ **888/438-7245** in the
United States, ✆ **800/361-7245** in Canada; www.raileurope.com) or your travel agent.

FOREIGN TRAIN TERMS

A station is a *stazione,* and trains are *Espresso,* meaning an express, or *Diretto,* meaning direct. Additional charges are referred to as *supplemento.* These *Diretto* and
Espresso trains can also be called *Regionali* or *Interregionali.* The train to avoid, especially on long-distance journeys, is a *locali,* which stops at all stations.

Tickets are called *biglietti,* with a single ticket labeled an *andata* or a round-trip
andata e ritorno. First class is *prima;* second class is *seconda classe.* Ticket offices are
called *la biglietteria.* For journeys up to 155 miles (250km), you can often make ticket
purchases at newsstands or even a station tobacconist. Such a ticket is called *un
biglietto a fascia chilometrica.*

PRACTICAL TRAIN INFORMATION

The train is the way to go in Italy. Train travel is midpriced, service is frequent, and
the trains among the most modern in Europe. Most of Italian trains have been integrated into the state system and are operated by **Trenitalia.** Information on the rail
network is available online at **www.trenitalia.it** in Italian and English. Most trains,
except in deep rural areas of the south, are modern and air-conditioned.

Trains provide an excellent means of transport, even if you don't buy a railpass or
one of the special Italian railway tickets (see above). As a rule of thumb, second-class
travel usually costs about two-thirds the price of an equivalent first-class trip. The
relatively new **InterCity (IC)** trains are modern, air-conditioned trains that make
limited stops; compared to the slower direct or regional trains, the supplement can be
steep, but a second-class IC ticket will provide a first-class experience. Eurostar City
trains (reservations a must) run the fastest schedules with conventional equipment.
The best of the Italian trains are unquestionably the high-speed **Eurostar Italia (ES)**
trains (don't confuse these with the Eurostar trains that run from Britain to France—
they aren't the same!). Using the same tilting technology as the German ICE T and
Pendolino trains, these trains are modern and exceptionally comfortable, and though
passholders pay a supplement to ride them, they are definitely the way to go in Italy.

Children 4 to 11 receive a discount of 50% off the adult fare, and children 3 and under travel free with their parents. Seniors and travelers under age 26 can also purchase discount cards.

Artesia (electric trains) have made travel between France and Italy faster and more comfortable than ever. **France**'s **TGVs** travel at speeds of up to 185 mph (297kmph) and have cut travel time between Paris and Turin from 7 to 5½ hours and between Paris and Milan (express routes only) from 7½ to 6¾ hours.

Tilting EC trains, formerly called **Cisalpino** (*Chee*-sahl-peeno) trains, are some of the world's most advanced and speed from northern Italy (primarily Venice and Milan) to major cities in Switzerland. Though aimed mostly at business travelers, they're a great way to get from Italy to Switzerland. To ride these trains, passholders must buy a Passholder Ticket that includes a seat reservation (mandatory).

A luxurious overnight train (the *Salvador Dalí*) connects Milan and Turin with Barcelona in Spain. **Artesia de Nuit** trains connect Paris to various cities in Italy. **InterCity Night (ICN)** trains essentially offer the same services as EuroNight trains but travel only within Italy's borders.

RESERVATIONS   When you purchase either a single or a round-trip ticket, the validity is for a period of 2 months from the date you bought the ticket. The date you want to travel is stamped on the ticket at the time of purchase, providing you make a seat reservation. Undated tickets purchased at newsstands or from tobacconists need to be validated on the day you plan to take the journey.

It's still wise to book a ticket and a seat on runs between such major cities as Florence and Venice, Rome and Naples, or Rome and either Florence or Milan. Italian trains are very crowded on public holidays, and reservations should be obtained in advance during these peak periods. A regular seat reservation is about $15, depending on the train and class you've selected. Big rail depots, such as the Stazione Termini in Rome, often have separate windows for making reservations—labeled *prenotazioni*. Reservations are mandatory on all ES, Artesia, EC/Cisalpino, IC, ES City, and night trains.

If you're traveling at night, it's wise to reserve a *couchette* (foldaway bed) or sleeper (private sleeping cabin), especially for long distances, such as the train that goes from Paris to Rome, or vice versa. A wide variety of sleeping accommodations are available depending on the night trains that you choose. If you ask for *Superiore* or *Finestrino* when booking, you'll get a top bunk, giving you more legroom and greater privacy. When reserving, try not to get a seat next to the corridor, as passengers here are the most likely to get robbed.

The supplement you'll pay for access to a couchette aboard an Italian night train varies considerably depending on how many others you'll be sharing a compartment with. For a couchette within a compartment shared by six, you'll pay a supplement of $35 per person. For a couchette within a compartment shared by four (and these are available only on an increasingly limited number of trains), you'll pay a supplement of $45 per person. And for a sleeper shared with only one other person, you'll pay a supplement of between $56 and $68 per person, depending on the train and the itinerary (single sleepers are available on Ellipsos night trains—the supplement varies). You can and should prereserve sleeper options (and pay the supplement) through Rail Europe as soon as you have your trip dates figured out, especially if you're traveling during in high season. If you're already within Italy, you can reserve these in advance by heading for the ticket window of any railway station.

Trains & Travel Times in Italy

From	To	Type of Train	# of Trains	Frequency	Travel Time
Rome	Bari	Eurostar Italia	4	Daily	4 hr., 43 min.
Rome	Ancona	Eurostar Italia	4	Daily	3 hr., 20 min.
Rome	Florence	Eurostar Italia	38	Daily	1 hr., 35 min.
Rome	Milan	Eurostar Italia	30	Daily	3 hr., 30 min.
Rome	Naples	Eurostar Italia	20	Daily	1 hr., 10 min.
Rome	Palermo	InterCity	2	Daily	11 hr., 50 min.
Rome	Salerno	Eurostar Italia	11	Daily	2 hr., 31 min.
Rome	Salerno	InterCity	5	Daily	2 hr., 42 min.
Rome	Venice	Eurostar Italia	14	Daily	3 hr., 40 min.
Milan	Venice	Eurostar City	18	Daily	2 hr., 30 min.

Note: Seat reservations are not always marked on seats and some people may try to claim your reserved seat as their own. Firmly but politely insist they vacate (and if you haven't reserved and sit in an apparently unreserved seat, be advised that you may actually be sitting in someone else's seat).

SERVICES & AMENITIES Most InterCity trains have facilities for persons with limited mobility. There are dining facilities on all major trains, though prices are lethal. If you're on a strict budget, do as the Italians do and pack your own picnic for consumption while riding the rails and taking in the scenery. It's a great way to travel. ES trains offer better seating and are one of the only domestic trains in Italy where second-class travel won't be a less grand experience than first class. First-class passengers on ES trains get a free drink and snack served at their seats.

Overnight accommodations on Italian trains range from "Gran Class" single-sleeper cabins with private bathrooms and showers on the Ellipsos hotel train from Milan to Barcelona, to six-berth economy couchettes on the Artesia de Nuit trains from Paris to Rome, to reclining sleeperette seats on ICN trains from Rome to Venice. Note that although sleeper cabins are segregated by sex (except for families taking a whole cabin), couchettes are not segregated by sex. First-class sleeper cabins usually include a continental breakfast in their rates. All sleeping accommodations require the payment of a supplement in addition to your railpass—and must be reserved well in advance. We recommend reserving through Rail Europe (© **888/438-7245** in the United States, © **800/361-7245** in Canada; www.raileurope.com) before you leave home. Note that to reserve some classes of sleeper cabins, you'll need to have a first-class railpass.

Warning: Theft on some Italian trains is a problem. If you opt for a couchette or sleeper on an Italian train, make sure your belongings are well secured.

[FastFACTS] ITALY

Area Code The country code for Italy is **39.** Today city codes (or area codes for cities) have been folded into each phone number.

Therefore, you must dial the whole number, whether you're calling from outside or inside Italy, or even within a city such as Rome itself.

Climate It's warm all over Italy in summer; it can be very hot in the south, especially inland. The high temperatures (measured in

Italy in degrees Celsius) begin in Rome in May, often lasting until sometime in October. Winters in the north of Italy are cold, with rain and snow, but in the south the weather is warm all year, averaging 50°F (10°C) in winter. For the most part, it's drier in Italy than in North America, so high temperatures don't seem as bad because the humidity is lower. In Rome, Naples, and the south, temperatures can stay in the 90s for days, but nights are most often comfortably cooler.

Documents Required

U.S. and Canadian citizens with a **valid passport** don't need a visa to enter Italy if they don't expect to stay more than 90 days and don't expect to work there. If after entering Italy you want to stay more than 90 days, a visa is a must. For information on obtaining a visa, visit the Ministry of Foreign Affairs website (**www.esteri.it**).

Electricity   The electricity in Italy varies considerably. It's usually alternating current (AC), varying from 42 to 50 cycles. The voltage can be anywhere from 115 to 220. It's recommended that any visitor carrying electrical appliances obtain a transformer. Check the exact local current at the hotel where you're staying. Plugs have prongs that are round, not flat; therefore, an adapter plug is also needed.

Embassies/Consulates

In case of an emergency, embassies have a 24-hour referral service.

The **U.S. Embassy** is in Rome at Via Vittorio Veneto 121 (✆ **06/46741;** fax 06/46742244; http://italy.us embassy.gov). **U.S. consulates** are in Florence, at Lungarno Amerigo Vespucci 38 (✆ **055/266951;** fax 055/215550), and in Milan, at Via Principe Amedeo 2–10 (✆ **02/290351;** fax 02/29035273). There's also a consulate in Naples on Piazza della Repubblica 1 (✆ **081/5838111**). For consulate hours, see individual city listings.

The **Canadian Embassy** in Rome is at Via Salaria 243 (✆ **06-85444-2911;** fax 06-445-982912; www.canadainternational.gc.ca/italy-italie). The **Canadian Consulate** and passport service is in Rome at Via Zara 30 (✆ **06-854441**). The **Canadian Consulate** in Naples is at Via Carducci 29 (✆ **081-401338;** fax 081-410210).

Health & Safety   Italy has a low rate of violent crime, little of which is directed at tourists. Petty crimes such as pickpocketing, theft from parked cars, and purse-snatching, however, are serious problems, especially in large cities. Most reported thefts occur at crowded tourist sites, on public buses or trains, or at the major railway stations: Rome's Termini, Milan's Centrale, Florence's Santa Maria Novella, and Naples's Centrale. Clients of Internet cafes in major cities have been targeted. Elderly tourists who have tried to resist petty thieves on motor scooters have suffered broken arms and collarbones.

On trains, a commonly reported trick involves one or more persons who pretend to befriend a traveler and offer drugged food or drink. Also, thieves have been known to impersonate police officers to gain the confidence of tourists. The thief shows the prospective victim a circular plastic sign with the words "police" or "international police." If this happens, the tourist should insist on seeing the officer's identification card (documento), as impersonators tend not to carry forged documents. Tourists should immediately report thefts or other crimes to the local police.

Medical facilities are available but may be limited outside urban areas. Public hospitals sometimes do not maintain the same standards as hospitals in the United States, so travelers are encouraged to obtain insurance that would cover a stay in a private Italian hospital or clinic. It is almost impossible to obtain an itemized hospital bill from public hospitals, as required by many U.S. insurance companies, because the Italian National Health Service charges one inclusive rate (care services, bed, and board).

Holidays   Offices and shops in Italy are closed on the following **national holidays:** January 1 (New Year's Day), Easter Monday, April

25 (Liberation Day), May 1 (Labor Day), June 2 (Anniversary of the Republic), August 15 (Assumption of the Virgin), November 1 (All Saints' Day), December 8 (Feast of the Immaculate Conception), December 25 (Christmas Day), and December 26 (Santo Stefano).

Closings are also observed in the following cities on **feast days** honoring their patron saints: Venice, April 25 (St. Mark); Florence, Genoa, and Turin, June 24 (St. John the Baptist); Rome, June 29 (Sts. Peter and Paul); Palermo, July 15 (St. Rosalia); Naples, September 19 (St. Gennaro); Bologna, October 4 (St. Petronio); Cagliari, October 30 (St. Saturnino); Trieste, November 3 (St. Giusto); Bari, December 6 (St. Nicola); and Milan, December 7 (St. Ambrose).

Legal Aid   The consulate of your country is the place to turn for legal aid, although offices can't interfere in the Italian legal process. They can, however, inform you of your rights and provide a list of attorneys. You'll have to pay for the attorney out of your pocket—there's no free legal assistance. If you're arrested for a drug offense, about all the consulate will do is notify a lawyer about your case and perhaps inform your family.

Mail   Mail delivery in Italy is notoriously bad. Your family and friends back home might receive your postcards in 1 week, or it might take 2

weeks (sometimes longer). Postcards, aerogrammes, and letters weighing up to 20 grams sent to the United States and Canada cost .85€. Stamps (francobolli) can be bought at tabacchi (tobacco stores). You can buy special stamps at the **Vatican City Post Office,** adjacent to the information office in St. Peter's Square; it's open Monday to Friday 8:30am to 7pm and Saturday 8:30am to 6pm. Letters mailed at Vatican City reach North America far more quickly than mail sent from elsewhere for the same cost.

Police & Emergencies   Dial 🕿 **113** for the police, 118 for an ambulance, or 115 in case of fire. In case of a breakdown on an Italian road, dial 🕿 **803116** at the nearest telephone box; the nearest Automobile Club of Italy (ACI) will be notified to come to your aid.

Telephone   To call Italy from the United States, dial the **international prefix, 011;** then Italy's **country code, 39;** and then the actual **phone number** (which has a city code built in).

A **local phone call** in Italy costs around .10€. **Public phones** accept coins, precharged phone cards (scheda or carta telefonica), or both. You can buy a carta telefonica at any tabacchi (most display a sign with a white T on a blue or black background) in increments of 5€, 10€, and 20€. To make a call, pick up the receiver and

insert .10€ or (break off the Most phones h display that'll te much money you ve inserted (or how much is left on the card). Dial the number, and don't forget to take the card with you after you hang up.

To call the free **national telephone information** (in Italian) in Italy, dial 🕿 **12. International information** is available at 🕿 **176** but costs .60€ a shot.

Tipping   In **hotels,** a service charge of 15% to 19% is already added to a bill. In addition, it's customary to tip the chambermaid .50€ per day, the doorman (for calling a cab) 1€, and the bellhop or porter 1.50€ to 1.95€ for carrying your bags to your room. A concierge expects about 15% of his or her bill, as well as tips for extra services performed, which could include help with long-distance calls.

In **restaurants and cafes,** 15% is usually added to your bill to cover most charges. If you're not sure whether this has been done, ask, "È incluso il servizio?" (ay een-cloo-soh eel sair-vee-tsoh?). An additional tip isn't expected, but it's nice to leave the equivalent of an extra couple of dollars if you've been pleased with the service. Checkroom attendants expect 1€, and washroom attendants should get the same. Restaurants are required by law to give customers official receipts. Taxi drivers expect at least 15% of the fare.

ROME

The city of Rome is simultaneously strident, romantic, and sensual. And although the romantic poets would probably be horrified at today's traffic, pollution, overcrowding, crime, political discontent, and barely controlled chaos of modern Rome, the city endures and thrives in a way that is called "eternal."

It would take a lifetime to know a city filled with 27 centuries of artistic achievement. A cradle of Western civilization, timeless Rome is home to more treasures of ancient history, art, and architecture per square foot than any other city in the world. Caesar was assassinated here, Charlemagne crowned, and the list of the major events goes on and on.

In between all that absorption of culture and history, take time to relax and meet the Romans. Savor their succulent pastas while enjoying a fine glass of wine on one of the city's splendid squares where one of the reigning Caesars might have gone before you, or perhaps Michelangelo or Raphael.

For the rail traveler, Rome, though too far south to be considered truly central, is easily reached by rail, and its ultra modern **Stazione Termini** is well connected to most other Italian cities, as well as several major European destinations. It's unquestionably the best starting point for a rail trip of Italy and it makes an excellent starting or termination point for a rail tour of Europe.

Station Information

GETTING FROM THE AIRPORT TO THE TRAIN STATION

The gateway for most visitors beginning a rail journey of Italy is **Leonardo da Vinci Airport** (✆ **06/65951**), also called Fiumicino.

After you leave Passport Control, you'll see two **information desks** (one for Rome, one for Italy). At the Rome desk, you can pick up a general map and some pamphlets daily from 9am to 6:30pm. At both desks, the staff can help you find a hotel room if you haven't reserved ahead. A *cambio* (money exchange) operates daily 8am to 9pm, offering surprisingly good rates.

There's a **train station** in the airport. To get into the city, follow the signs marked TRENI for the 30-minute shuttle to Rome's main station, **Stazione Termini** (arriving on Track 22). The shuttle (the Leonardo Express) runs 6:37am to 11:37pm for 11€ one-way. On the way, you'll pass a machine dispensing tickets, or you can buy them in person near the tracks if you don't have small bills on you. When you arrive at Termini, get out of the train quickly and grab a baggage cart. (It's a long schlep from the track to the exit or to the other train connections, and baggage carts can be scarce.)

A **taxi** from Da Vinci airport to the city costs 40€ and up for the 1-hour trip, depending on traffic. The expense might be worth it if you have a lot of luggage or just don't want to be bothered with the train trip. Call ✆ **06/6645,** 06/3570, or 06/4994 for information.

INSIDE THE STATION

Trains and buses (including trains from the airport) arrive in the center of old Rome at the silver **Stazione Termini,** Piazza dei Cinquecento (✆ **892021**); this is the train, bus, and subway transportation hub for all Rome and is surrounded by many hotels (especially cheaper ones). If you're taking the **Metropolitana (subway),** follow the illuminated red-and-white M signs. To catch a bus, go straight through the outer hall and enter the sprawling bus lot of **Piazza dei Cinquecento.** You'll also find **taxis** there.

The Roma Termini is a virtual city within a city. On the lower level of the two-level station is a vast array of services such as a drugstore, ATMs, clothing shops, fast food, lounges, hairdressers, a bookstore, and barbershops. On-site is a **tourist office** (no phone), open daily 8am to 9pm. You can get minor information here, but for hotel reservations, go to desk no. 6 (① **06/4821888**) on the ground floor of the Ala Termini section. It is open daily from 7am to 10pm.There's always a line, but you can pick up one of the nearby phones and make a reservation for free by dialing ① **06/97745496.**

A **luggage storage** office (① **06/4744777**) is located on the underground floor of the Termini wing. It is open daily from 6am to midnight and it costs 4€ to store your luggage for the first 5 hours. **Train information** is available from three computer touch screens at tracks 1, 9, and 22 in the center of the station. Train reservations are made at ticket windows no. 30 to no. 45. Windows no. 30 to no. 38—*Prenotazioni Posti–WL–Cuccette–Pendolino*—make reservations, and also arrange sleeper and couchette reservations. Windows no. 7 to no. 29—*biglietti Ordinari e Ridotti*—actually sell tickets. **Informazioni ferroviarie** (in the outer hall) dispenses information on rail travel to other parts of Italy. For more information about Stazione Termini, check out **www.grandistazioni.it.**

Information Elsewhere in the City

The chief tourist office is the **Azienda Provinciale di Turismo (APT)** at Via XX Settembre 26 (① **06/421381;** www.aptprovroma.it). The headquarters is open Monday to Saturday 9am to 7pm.

More helpful are the offices maintained by the **Comune di Roma** at various sites around the city. Hours are from 9:30am to 7pm, except the one at Termini (daily 8am–8:30pm). Here are the addresses: on Via Nazionale 183, near the Palazzo delle Esposizioni; on Piazza Sonnino in Trastevere; on Piazza delle Cinque Lune, near Piazza Navona; and on Via dell'Olmata. All phone calls for Comune di Roma are directed through a centralized number: ① **06/0608.** Call daily 9am to 7pm.

Enjoy Rome, Via Marghera 8A (① **06/4451843;** www.enjoyrome.com), was begun by an English-speaking couple, Fulvia and Pierluigi. They dispense information about almost everything in Rome and are far more pleasant and organized than the Board of Tourism. They'll also help you find a hotel room, with no service charge (in anything from a hostel to a three-star hotel). Hours are Monday to Friday 8:30am to 5pm and Saturday 8:30am to 2pm.

Getting Around

BY PUBLIC TRANSPORTATION The **Metropolitana,** or **Metro,** for short, is the fastest means of transportation, operating daily 5:30am to 11:30pm (until 12:30am Sat). A big red M indicates the entrance to the subway. Tickets are 1€ and are available from *tabacchi,* many newsstands, and vending machines at all stations. Some stations have managers, but they won't make change. Booklets of tickets are available at *tabacchi* and in some terminals. *Tip:* Avoid riding the trains when the Romans are going to or from work or you'll be mashed flatter than fettuccine.

Roman buses are operated by **ATAC (Agenzia del Trasporto Autoferrotranviario del Comune di Roma),** Via Ostiense 131L (① **800/431784;** www.atac.roma.it). For 1€, you can ride to most parts of Rome, although it can be slow going in all that traffic and the buses are often very crowded. Your ticket is valid for 75 minutes, and

Rome

ACCOMMODATIONS ■
Albergo Santa Chiara **8**
Casa Howard **17**
Hotel Adriano **10**
Hotel Columbia **25**
Hotel dei Mellini **11**

Hotel La Residenza **18**
Hotel Morgana **33**
Royal Court **23**
Villa delle Rose **24**

DINING ◆
Cesare **3**
Césarina **15**
Colline Emiliane **20**
Dal Bolognese **12**
La Cisterna **5**

Monte Arci **22**
Piperno Restaurant **6**
Ristorante del Pallaro **7**
Trattoria San Teodoro **29**
Trimani Wine Bar **21**
Tuna **19**

ATTRACTIONS ●

Arch of Constantine **31**
Basilica di San Giovanni in Laterano **34**
Basilica di San Pietro **2**
Campidoglio, Palazzo dei Conservatori and Museo Capitolino **27**

Castel Sant' Angelo **4**
The Colosseum **32**
Foro Imperiali (Imperial Forum) **28**
Foro Romano (Roman Forum) and Palatine Hill **30**
Galleria Borghese **14**
Museo Nazionale di Villa Giulia **13**

Musei Vaticani (Vatican Museums) and Sistine Chapel **1**
Pantheon **9**
Spanish Steps **16**
Trevi Fountain **26**

you can get on many buses and trams during that time by using the same ticket. Buy bus tickets in *tabacchi* or bus terminals. You must have your ticket before boarding because there are no ticket-issuing machines on the vehicles.

Buses and trams stop at areas marked FERMATA. At most of these, a yellow sign will display the numbers of the buses that stop there and a list of all the stops along each bus's route in order, so you can easily search out your destination. Bus service runs from 6am to midnight, and the night service is from 12:10 to 5:30am; an N after the line number defines buses running at night. It's best, however, to take a taxi in the wee hours—if you can find one. At the **bus information booth** at Piazza dei Cinquecento, in front of the Stazione Termini, you can purchase a directory complete with maps summarizing the routes.

Although routes change often, a few old reliable routes have remained valid for years, such as **no. 75** from Stazione Termini to the Colosseum, **H** from Stazione Termini to Trastevere, and **no. 40** from Stazione Termini to the Vatican. But if you're going somewhere and are dependent on the bus, be sure to carefully check where the bus stop is and exactly which bus goes there—don't assume that it'll be the same bus the next day.

BY TAXI   Don't count on hailing a taxi on the street or even getting one at a stand. If you're going out, have your hotel call one. At a restaurant, ask the waiter or cashier to dial for you. If you want to phone for yourself, try one of these numbers: ℂ **06/6645,** 06/3570, or 06/4994. The meter begins at 2.80€ for the first 2 miles (3.2km) and then rises .92€ per kilometer. Every suitcase costs 1€, and on Sunday a 4€ supplement is assessed. There's another 5.80€ supplement 10pm to 7am.

Where to Stay

Albergo Santa Chiara   This is one of the best-located hotels in the inner core of historic Rome, right in back of the Pantheon and opening onto the Piazza della Minerva. The Corteggiani family has been welcoming visitors to this hotel since 1838. Marble columns evoke the elegance of yesterday. The comfortable and well-maintained bedrooms are furnished with classic simplicity and range in size from the very small to the very large, the latter spacious enough to be classified as Roman apartments. If you face Piazza della Minerva, you'll have a grand view but can also anticipate noise late at night.

Via Santa Chiara 21, 00186 Roma. ℂ **06/6872979.** Fax 06/6873144. www.albergosantachiara.com. 98 units. 225€–280€ double; 460€–550€ suite. Rates include buffet breakfast. AE, DC, MC, V. Metro: Piazza di Spagna. **Amenities:** Bar; 1 room for those w/limited mobility.

Casa Howard ★ 🏠   It's rare to make a discovery in the tourist-trodden Spanish Steps area, which is why Casa Howard comes as a pleasant surprise. The little B&B occupies about two-thirds of the second floor of a historic structure in an ideal location for shoppers. The welcoming family owners maintain beautifully furnished guest rooms, each with its own private bathroom (although some bathrooms lie outside the bedrooms in the hallway). The Green Room is the most spacious, with its own en suite bathroom. The house's private Turkish *hammam* (steam bath) needs to be booked and costs 25€. Breakfast is brought to your room and costs 10€ per person.

Via Capo le Case 18, 00187 Roma. ☏ **06/69924555.** Fax 06/6794644. www.casahoward.com. 5 units. 170€–250€ double. MC, V. Metro: Piazza di Spagna. **Amenities:** All rooms smoke-free.

Hotel Adriano This hotel is housed within the original walls of a 15th-century *palazzo* and is close to the Spanish Steps, the Piazza Navona, and the Pantheon. It's been converted into a well-run and government-rated three-star hotel to welcome guests and house them comfortably. Bedrooms are simply furnished but tasteful, with excellent beds usually resting on hardwood floors. You can enjoy breakfast on the hotel's roof terrace.

Via di Pallacorda 2, 00186 Roma. ☏ **06/68802451.** Fax 06/68803926. www.hoteladriano.com. 80 units. 95€–265€ double; 350€–500€ suite. Rates include buffet breakfast. AE, DC, MC, V. Bus: 95 or 175. **Amenities:** Bar; 1 room for those w/limited mobility.

Hotel Columbia ★★ 🛉 This is one of the most modern hotels in the neighborhood, with a hardworking multilingual staff. Originally built around 1900, the hotel keeps up-to-date with the times. The interior contains Murano chandeliers and conservatively modern furniture. The compact and cozy guest rooms have shower-only bathrooms and compare well against the accommodations in the best hotels nearby. The appealing roof garden has a view over the surrounding rooftops.

Via del Viminale 15, 00184 Roma. ☏ **06/4883509.** Fax 06/4740209. www.hotelcolumbia.com. 45 units. 85€–239€ double; 249€ triple. Rates include buffet breakfast. AE, DC, MC, V. Metro: Repubblica. **Amenities:** Bar; smoke-free rooms.

Hotel dei Mellini ★ Pilgrims planning to explore the Vatican area can splurge on this hotel, situated on the right bank of the Tiber between the Spanish Steps and St. Peter's Basilica. The handsome public rooms are tastefully elegant. Guest rooms are spacious and have a classic Art Deco styling in their choice of furnishings and fixtures, including beautiful private bathrooms. Its roof terrace opens onto panoramic nighttime views of the floodlit city.

Via Muzio Clementi 81, 00193 Roma. ☏ **06/324771.** Fax 06/32477801. www.hotelmellini.com. 80 units. 153€–289€ double; from 219€ suite. Rates include buffet breakfast. AE, DC, MC, V. Metro: Lepanto. **Amenities:** Restaurant; bar; cafe; rooms for those w/limited mobility; smoke-free rooms.

Hotel Morgana Between Santa Maria Maggiore and Stazione Termini, the completely up-to-date Morgana is a hotel of style and substance. Bedrooms are most comfortable and furnished in a sleek modern styling based on traditional designs. The rooms have all the modern amenities and a vaguely English-style decor. The English-speaking staff is pleasant and will help guide you to some of the city's most important attractions, many of which are only a short walk from the hotel. Because this hotel lies in a noisy section of Rome, all of the bedrooms are soundproof. The hotel offers pickup and transfer services to and from the Leonardo da Vinci Airport.

Via F. Turati 33–37, 00185 Roma. ☏ **06/4467230.** Fax 06/4469142. www.hotelmorgana.com. 106 units. 100€–235€ double; 165€–250€ suite. Rates include buffet breakfast. AE, DC, MC, V. Parking 15€. Metro: Termini. **Amenities:** Bar; airport transfer (58€).

Hotel La Residenza ★★ In a glamorous location (admittedly far from the Termini area) 10 minutes from the Spanish Steps, this little hotel successfully combines intimacy and elegance. A bit old-fashioned and homelike, the converted villa has an ivy-covered courtyard and a series of grand public rooms with Empire divans, oil portraits, and rattan chairs. Terraces are scattered throughout. The guest rooms are generally spacious, containing bentwood chairs and built-in furniture, including beds. The dozen or so junior suites boast balconies. The bathrooms have robes and even come equipped with ice machines.

Via Emilia 22-24, 00187 Roma. © **06/4880789.** Fax 06/485721. www.hotel-la-residenza.com/eng/ laresidenza/home.asp. 29 units. 250€–300€ double; 300€–330€ suite. Rates include buffet breakfast. AE, MC, V. Metro: Piazza Barberini. **Amenities:** Bar.

Royal Court ★ 🛏️ This winner lies in a restored Liberty-style palace a short walk from the Termini. The hotel evokes a tranquil, elegantly decorated private town house. All units feature well-maintained and -designed bathrooms with tub/showers. The superior rooms also come with small balconies opening onto cityscapes. Even the standard doubles are comfortable, but if you're willing to pay the price, you can stay in the deluxe doubles, which are like junior suites in most Rome hotels. Some of the bedrooms are large enough to sleep three or four guests comfortably.

Via Marghera 51, 00185 Roma. © **06/44340364.** Fax 06/4469121. www.morganaroyalcourt.com. 24 units. 130€–250€ double. Rates include buffet breakfast. AE, DC, MC, V. Metro: Termini. **Amenities:** Bar.

Villa delle Rose Long a favorite with rail passengers, this hotel is only 2 blocks from Termini Station and is an acceptable, if not exciting, choice. In the late 19th century, it was a private villa, but it has been much altered and modified over the years to receive guests. Much of its old architectural allure is still in evidence, including the Corinthian-capped marble columns in the lobby and the luxuriant garden in back. Redecorating and upgrading of the bedrooms and the tiled bathrooms has made them more comfortable than ever, though the overall look is still one of faded grandeur. Breakfasts in the garden do a lot to add country flavor to an otherwise very urban setting.

Via Vicenza 5, 00185 Roma. © **06/4451788.** Fax 06/4451639. www.villadellerose.it. 38 units. 90€–160€ double. Rates include buffet breakfast. AE, DC, MC, V. Metro: Termini or Castro Pretorio. **Amenities:** Breakfast garden; bar; all smoke-free rooms. *In room:* A/C (only in some rooms).

Top Attractions & Special Moments

Basilica di San Giovanni in Laterano ★ This church—not St. Peter's—is the cathedral of the diocese of Rome. Catholics all over the world refer to it as their "mother church." Originally built in A.D. 314 by Constantine, the cathedral has suffered many vicissitudes and was forced to rebuild many times. The present building is characterized by its 18th-century facade by Alessandro Galilei (statues of Christ and the Apostles ring the top). Borromini gets the credit—some say blame—for the interior, built for Innocent X.

The most unusual sight is across the street at the "Palace of the Holy Steps," called the **Santuario della Scala Santa**, Piazza San Giovanni in Laterano (© **06/ 7726641**). It's alleged that these were the actual steps that Christ climbed when he was brought before Pontius Pilate. These steps are supposed to be climbed only on your knees, which you're likely to see the faithful doing throughout the day. Visiting hours are daily from 6:15am to noon and 3:30 to 6:30pm. Admission is free. *Note:* **Santuario della Scala Santa** is open daily from 6:15am to noon and 3:30 to 6:30pm.

Piazza San Giovanni in Laterano 4. © **06/69886452.** Basilica free; cloisters 2€. Summer daily 9am–6:45pm (off season to 6pm). Metro: San Giovanni. Bus: 16, 81, 85, 87, 186, 218, or 650.

Basilica di San Pietro (St. Peter's Basilica) ★★★ As you stand in Bernini's **Piazza San Pietro (St. Peter's Sq.),** you'll be in the arms of an ellipse; like a loving parent, the Doric-pillared colonnade reaches out to embrace the faithful. Holding 300,000 is no problem for this square. Inside, the size of this famous church is awe-inspiring—though its dimensions (about two football fields long) are not apparent at first. St. Peter's is said to have been built over the tomb of the crucified saint. The original church was erected on the order of Constantine, but it threatened to collapse and the present structure is 17th-century Renaissance and baroque; it showcases the talents of some of Italy's greatest artists—Michelangelo and Raphael, among others.

In such a grand church, don't expect subtlety. But the basilica is rich in art. Under Michelangelo's dome is the celebrated **baldacchino ★★** by Bernini. In the nave on the right (the 1st chapel) is the best-known piece of sculpture, the *Pietà* **★★★** that Michelangelo sculpted while still in his early twenties. Just before the altar, and on the right, you'll see **a bronze statue of St. Peter ★**. It has been the custom for centuries for the faithful to kiss the saint's right foot, which today has literally been kissed smooth. You can visit the **treasury ★**, filled with jewel-studded chalices, reliquaries, and copes. One robe worn by Pius XII strikes a simple note in these halls of elegance. The sacristy now contains a **Museo Storico (Historical Museum) ★** displaying Vatican treasures, including the large 1400s bronze tomb of Pope Sixtus V by Antonio Pollaiuolo and several antique chalices. In addition, you can visit the **Vatican grottoes ★★**, with their tombs, both ancient and modern (Pope John XXII gets the most adulation).

The grandest sight is yet to come: the climb to **Michelangelo's dome ★★★**, which towers about 375 feet high (113m). Although you can walk up the steps, we recommend the elevator as far as it'll carry you (you'll still face 320 steps). You can walk along the roof, from which you'll be rewarded with a panoramic view of Rome and the Vatican.

To tour the **Necropolis Vaticana,** the area around **St. Peter's tomb,** you must send a fax 3 weeks beforehand to the *Ufficio Scavi,* or excavations office (© **06/69885318;** fax 06/69873017), open Monday to Saturday from 9am to 5pm. Pass under the arch to the left of the facade of St. Peter's to find it.

Piazza San Pietro. © **06/69881662** (for information on celebrations). Basilica (including grottoes) free. Guided tour of excavations around St. Peter's tomb 10€; children younger than 15 are not admitted. Stairs to the dome 5€; elevator to the dome 7€; Sacristy (with Historical Museum) free. Basilica (including the sacristy and treasury) daily 9am–6pm. Grottoes daily 8am–5pm. Dome Oct–Mar daily 8am–5pm; Apr–Sept 8am–6pm. Bus: 49. Metro: Ottaviano/San Pietro, then a long stroll.

Campidoglio ★★★, Palazzo dei Conservatori ★★, and Museo Capitolino ★★ The summit of the Capitoline Hill, the most sacred of ancient Rome, is where the Temples of Jupiter and Juno once stood. This was the spiritual heart of Rome, where triumphant generals made sacrifices to the gods who had given them their victories, and where the earthly homes of the king and queen of heaven stood.

One side of the piazza is open; the others are bounded by the **Senatorium (Town Council),** the statuary-filled **Palace of the Conservatori (Curators),** and the **Capitoline Museum.** These museums house some of the greatest pieces of classical sculpture in the world.

On the left is the **Capitoline Museum,** based on an architectural plan by Michelangelo, with an enormous collection of marble carvings from the ancient world. Many of them are just statues—notable for their age, but that's about it. In the first room is *The Dying Gaul* **★★**, a work of majestic skill; in a special gallery all her own is **The Capitoline Venus** ★★, who demurely covers herself—this statue (a Roman copy of the Greek original) has been a symbol of feminine beauty and charm through the centuries. The famous statue of **Marcus Aurelius** ★★ is kept in the museum to protect it from pollution. This is the only bronze equestrian statue to have survived from ancient Rome, mainly because it was thought for centuries that the statue was that of Constantine the Great, and papal Rome respected the memory of the first Christian emperor.

The Palace of the Conservatori ★★, across the way, is rich in classical sculpture and paintings. One of the most notable bronzes is **Lo Spinario** ★★★ (little boy picking a thorn from his foot), a Greek classic from the 1st century B.C. In addition, you'll find **Lupa Capitolina** ★★★ (Capitoline Wolf), a rare Etruscan bronze possibly from the 5th century B.C. (Romulus and Remus, the legendary twins that the she-wolf suckled, were added at a later date.) The entrance to the courtyard is lined with the remains (head, hands, a foot, and a kneecap) of an ancient colossal statue of Constantine the Great.

Piazza del Campidoglio 1. ⓒ **06/82059127.** www.museicapitolini.org. Admission (to both museums) 6.50€. Tues–Sun 9am–8pm. Bus: 44, 81, 95, 160, 170, 715, or 780.

Castel Sant'Angelo ★   This overpowering castle on the Tiber was built in the 2nd century as a tomb for Emperor Hadrian; it continued as an imperial mausoleum until the time of Caracalla. If it looks like a fortress, it should—that was its function in the Middle Ages. It was built over the Roman walls and linked to the Vatican by an underground passage that was much used by the fleeing pontiff, Pope Clement VII, who escaped from unwanted visitors such as Charles V during his 1527 sack of the city. In the 14th century, it became a papal residence, enjoying various connections with Boniface IX, Nicholas V, and Julius II, patron of Michelangelo and Raphael.

But its legend rests largely on its link with Pope Alexander VI, whose mistress bore him two children (those darlings of debauchery, Cesare and Lucrezia Borgia). Even those on a rushed visit might want to budget time for a stopover here because it's a most intriguing sight, an imposing fortress that has seen more blood, treachery, and turmoil than any other left in Rome. It is Rome's chief citadel and dungeon. An audio guide is available to help you understand what you're seeing.

The highlight here is a trip through the Renaissance apartments, with their coffered ceilings and lush decoration. Their walls have witnessed some of the most diabolical plots and intrigues of the High Renaissance. Later, you can go through the dank cells that once echoed with the screams of Cesare's victims of torture. The most famous figure imprisoned here was Benvenuto Cellini, the eminent sculptor/goldsmith, remembered chiefly for his *Autobiography.* Now an art museum, the castle halls display the history of the Roman mausoleum, along with a wide-ranging selection of ancient arms and armor. You can climb to the top terrace for another one of those dazzling views of the Eternal City.

Lungotevere Castello 50. ☎ **06/39967600.** www.castelsantangelo.com. Admission 5€. Tues–Sun 9am–7pm. Bus: 23, 40, 46, 49, 62, 80, 87, 280, 492, or 910. Metro: Ottaviano, then a long stroll.

Colosseo (Colosseum) ★★★ In spite of the fact that it's a mere shell, the Colosseum remains the greatest architectural inheritance from ancient Rome. The completed stadium, called the Amphitheatrum Flavirum, was dedicated by Titus in A.D. 80 with a weeks-long bloody combat between gladiators and wild beasts. At its peak, the Colosseum could seat 50,000 spectators; exotic animals—humans also— were shipped in from the far corners of the empire to satisfy their jaded tastes. The games were quite an event, and everybody went. A day at the Colosseum was rather formal—the toga was de rigueur dress for men, even though many resented it much the way modern suburbanites hate to put on a tie on Saturday. The seating arrangement was a strictly social arrangement. The higher you were in society, the lower your seat was—even if you had the money, it was out of the question to "buy" a better seat if your birth didn't warrant it.

Next to the Colosseum is the intricately carved **Arch of Constantine** ★★, erected in honor of Constantine's defeat of the pagan Maxentius (A.D. 306). Many of the reliefs have nothing whatsoever to do with Constantine or his works, but tell of the victories of earlier Antonine rulers—they were apparently lifted from other, long-forgotten memorials.

Piazzale del Colosseo, Via dei Fori Imperiali. ☎ **06/39967700.** Admission 9€ all levels (includes Palatine Hill). Nov–Feb 15 daily 8:30am–4:30pm; Feb 16–Mar 15 daily 8:30am–5pm; Mar 16–Mar 27 daily 8:30am–5:30pm; Mar 28–Aug daily 8:30am–7:15pm; Sept daily 9am–7pm; Oct daily 8:30am–7pm. Guided tours in English with an archaeologist Nov 1–Mar 15 daily at 9:45, 10:15, 11:15, and 11:45am, and 12:30, 1:45, and 3pm; Mar–Oct daily at 9:45, 10:15, 11:15, and 11:45am, and 12:30, 1:45, 3, 4:15, 4:45, 5:15, and 5:45pm. Tours 4€.

Fontana di Trevi (Trevi Fountain) ★★ As you elbow your way through the summertime crowds around the Trevi Fountain, it's hard to believe that this little piazza was nearly always deserted before the film *Three Coins in the Fountain* brought the tour buses. Today it's a must on everybody's itinerary. The fountain is an 18th-century extravaganza of baroque stonework ruled over by a large statue of Neptune. While some of the statuary is the work of other artists, the man who gets the credit for the entire project is Nicola Salvi. The tradition of throwing coins into the fountain is an evolution of earlier customs. At one time, visitors drank water from the fountain; later they combined that with an offering to the spirits of the place. In our inflationary world, all we get to do is make the offering.

Piazza di Trevi. Metro: Barberini.

Fori Imperiali (Imperial Forums) ★★ The Imperial Forums were constructed by a succession of emperors to make commerce more comfortable for the merchants of Rome and to provide new libraries and more room for assembly, since the original Roman Forum had become too small.

With your back to the Colosseum, begin walking up the Via dei Fori Imperiali (built by the Fascists in the '30s), keeping to the right side of the street. Those ruins across the street are what's left of the colonnade that once surrounded the **Temple of Venus and Roma.** Next to it, you'll recognize the back wall of the Basilica of Constantine. Shortly, you'll come to a large outdoor restaurant, where Via Cavour joins the boulevard you're on. Just beyond the small park across Via Cavour are the

I LEFT MY HEART ON THE Piazza Navona

One of the most beautifully baroque sites in all of Rome, **Piazza Navona** ★★★ is like an ocher-colored gem, unspoiled by new buildings, or even by traffic. The shape results from the Stadium of Domitian, whose ruins lie underneath the present constructions. Great chariot races were once held here (some rather unusual, such as the one in which the head of the winning horse was lopped off as it crossed the finish line and was then carried by runners to be offered as a sacrifice by the Vestal Virgins atop the Capitoline). In medieval times, the popes used to flood the piazza to stage mock naval encounters. Today the piazza is packed with vendors and street performers, and lined with pricey cafes where you can enjoy a cappuccino or gelato and indulge in unparalleled people-watching.

Besides the twin-towered facade of 17th-century Santa Agnes, the piazza boasts several baroque masterpieces. The best known, in the center, is Bernini's **Fountain of the Four Rivers (Fontana dei Quattro Fiumi)** ★★★, whose four stone personifications symbolize the world's greatest rivers: the Ganges, Danube, della Plata, and Nile. It's fun to try to figure out which is which. (**Hint:** The figure with the shroud on its head is the Nile, so represented because the river's source was unknown at the time.) At the south end is the **Fountain of the Moor (Fontana del Moro),** also by Bernini. The **Fountain of Neptune (Fontana di Nettuno),** which balances that of the Moor, is a 19th-century addition.

remains of the **Forum of Nerva,** built by the emperor whose 2-year reign (A.D. 96–98) followed that of the paranoid Domitian. Nerva's Forum is best observed from the railing that skirts it on the Via dei Fori Imperiali. The only really intelligible remnant is a wall of the Temple of Minerva, with two fine Corinthian columns.

The next forum up was that of **Augustus** ★★ and was built before the birth of Christ to commemorate the emperor's victory over the assassins Cassius and Brutus in the Battle of Filippi (42 B.C.).

You can enter the **Forum of Trajan** ★★ on Via Quattro Novembre near the steps of Via Magnanapoli. Once through the tunnel, you'll emerge into the newest and most beautiful of the Imperial Forums, built between A.D. 107 and 113. There are many statue fragments and pedestals bearing still-legible inscriptions, but more interesting is the great Basilica Ulpia, whose gray marble columns rise roofless into the sky. This forum was once regarded as one of the architectural wonders of the world.

Beyond the Basilica Ulpia is **Trajan's Column** ★★★, in magnificent condition, with intricate bas-relief sculpture depicting Trajan's victorious campaign (though, from your vantage point, you'll be able to see only the earliest stages). The next stop is the **Forum of Julius Caesar** ★★, the first of the Imperial Forums. It lies on the opposite side of Via dei Fori Imperiali. This was the site of the Roman stock exchange, as well as the Temple of Venus; restored columns stand cinematically in the middle of the excavations.

Via de Fori Imperiali. Free admission. Metro: Colosseo. On view 24 hr.

Foro Romano (Roman Forum) ★★★ The Roman Forum was built in the marshy land between the Palatine and the Capitoline hills (where legend has it that Romulus and Remus were suckled by the she-wolf). It flourished as the center of

Roman life in the days of the Republic, before it gradually lost prestige to the Imperial Forum. By day the columns of now-vanished temples and the stones from which long-forgotten orators spoke are mere shells. But at night, when the Forum is silent in the moonlight, it isn't difficult to imagine that Vestal Virgins still guard the sacred temple fire.

If you want the stones to have some meaning, you'll have to purchase a detailed plan, as the temples can be hard to locate. Arm yourself with a good map sold at the entrance and allow at least 3 hours for wandering about. The best of the lot is the handsomely adorned **Temple of the Dioscuri ★★★**, erected in the 5th century B.C. in honor of a battle triumph and dedicated to the Gemini twins, Castor and Pollux. The **House of the Vestal Virgins ★★** is a popular attraction; some of the statuary, mostly headless, remains. Head toward the Colosseum and you'll encounter the **Arch of Titus ★★**, which depicts Rome's sacking of Jerusalem's temple—look closely and you'll see a menorah among the booty.

From the arch it's a long walk up to the **Palatine Hill ★**, one of the seven hills of Rome; your ticket from the Forum will admit you to this attraction (it's open the same hours). The Palatine, tradition tells us, was the spot on which the first settlers built their huts, under the direction of Romulus. In later years, the hill became a patrician residential district that attracted citizens such as Cicero. It's worth the climb for the panoramic, sweeping view of both the Roman and Imperial forums, as well as the Capitoline Hill and the Colosseum. Of the ruins that remain, none is finer than the so-called **House of Livia ★★**, whose frescoes are in miraculous condition.

When the glory that was Rome has completely overwhelmed you, you can enjoy a respite in the cooling **Farnese Gardens ★**, laid out in the 16th century, which incorporate some of Michelangelo's designs.

Largo Romolo e Remo. ⓒ **06/39967700**. Forum free admission; Palatine Hill 9€. Oct 30–Dec and Jan 2–Feb 15 daily 8:30am–4:30pm; Feb 16–Mar 15 daily 8:30am–5pm; Mar 16–24 daily 8:30am–5:30pm; Mar 25–Aug daily 8:30am–7:15pm; Sept daily 8:30am–7pm; Oct 1–29 daily 8:30am–6:30pm. Last admission 1 hr. before closing. Guided tours are given daily at 11am, lasting 1 hr., costing 4€. Last admission 1 hr. before closing. Closed holidays. Metro: Colosseo. Bus: 75 or 84.

Galleria Borghese ★★★ Most visitors come here to see Canova's famous **statue of Pauline Bonaparte Borghese ★★★**, the sister of Napoleon. But there are numerous other works of art worth seeing here. This treasure-trove of art, housed in an opulent 17th-century palace, includes such masterpieces as Bernini's *David*, *The Rape of Persephone*, and his *Apollo and Daphne*. Also on the ground floor of the palace are interesting 17th-century busts of Roman emperors, and a few pieces of

A Lazy Afternoon at the Villa Borghese

The **Borghese Gardens** (encompassing the Galeria Borghese), now a perfectly exquisite 17th-century estate, were developed by Cardinal Scipio Borghese, a high churchman belonging to another of Rome's mighty families. The most striking feature of the Borghese Gardens is its trees—stark and eerie looking, their trunks rising some 50 feet (15m) into the air without a single branch, only to burst forth in an evergreen canopy high above. Few activities are quite as pleasant as a slow stroll through the Villa Borghese on a sunny afternoon, pausing to admire carefully planned 17th-century vistas, ornamental fountains, and the magnificent trees.

Roman statuary from antiquity. Upstairs is a treasure house of painting, including works of Raphael (*Young Woman with a Unicorn* and a famous **Deposition from the Cross ★★★**), Pinturicchio, Botticelli, Correggio, Titian, Veronese, Bellini, and even some non-Italians, such as Bruegel and Albrecht Dürer. Two of the greatest paintings in all of Rome are showcased here—**Madonna del Palafrenieri ★★★** by the "divine" Caravaggio, showing the Virgin, Jesus, and St. Anne; and Domenichino's **Diana the Huntress ★★★**, with its rich, lush detail.

Important information: No more than 360 visitors at a time are allowed on the ground floor, and no more than 90 are allowed on the upper floor. Reservations are essential, so call ℂ **06/32810** (Mon–Fri 9am–6pm; Sat 9am–1pm). However, the number always seems to be busy. If you'll be in Rome for a few days, try stopping by in person on your first day to reserve tickets for a later day. Better yet, before you leave home, contact **Select Italy** (ℂ **800/877-1755;** www.selectitaly.com).

Piazza Scipione Borghese 5 (off Via Pinciano). ℂ **06/32810** for information. www.galleriaborghese.it. Admission 8.50€. Tues–Sun 9am–7pm. Bus: 5, 19, 52, 116, 204, 490, or 910.

Musei Vaticani (Vatican Museums) ★★★ This is a repository of one of the world's greatest art collections, especially rich in treasures from antiquity and the Renaissance. Too many visitors try to squeeze the Vatican Museums into a day's itinerary that includes a half-dozen other sights. This is utter foolishness. There are many museums in the Vatican, in addition to Michelangelo's Sistine Chapel and several papal apartments you'll want to see. It would require much more time than a day to examine all that's here, so if all you have is a day, pick a few spots to concentrate on.

The art collection of the **Pinacoteca ★★★**, or picture gallery, includes paintings and tapestries from the 11th to the 19th centuries. As you pass through room 1, note the oldest picture at the Vatican, a keyhole-shaped wood panel of the *Last Judgment* from the 11th century. In room 2 is one of the finest pieces—the *Stefaneschi Triptych* (six panels), by Giotto and his assistants. Bernardo Daddi's masterpiece of early Italian Renaissance art, *Madonna del Magnificat,* is also here. And you'll see works by Fra Angelico, the 15th-century Dominican monk who distinguished himself as a miniaturist (his *Virgin with Child* is justly praised—check out the Madonna's microscopic eyes).

The handsomely decorated rooms of the **Pio Clementino Museum ★★★** contain a vast collection of Greek and Roman sculpture. Of particular note is a sculpture from the 1st century B.C. of **Laocoön ★★★** and his two sons locked in an eternal struggle with serpents *Hercules* (a gilded bronze of the 1st c.; note also the magnificent room it's in), the **Apollo Belvedere ★★★** (a Roman copy of a 4th-c. B.C. Greek original), mosaics from the floor of the Villa Hadrian outside Tivoli, and the **Belvedere Torso ★★★** (a fragment of a Greek statue from the 1st c. B.C. that was carefully studied by Michelangelo). There are literally hundreds of other statues lounging in the halls.

The **Raphael Rooms ★★** are one of the highlights of the museums. While still a young man, Raphael was given one of the greatest assignments of his short life: to decorate a series of rooms in the apartments of Pope Julius II. The decoration was carried out by Raphael and his workshop from 1508 to 1524. In these works, Raphael achieves the Renaissance aim of blending classic beauty with realism. In the important Stanza della Segnatura, the first room decorated by the artist, you'll find the majestic **School of Athens ★★★**, one of his best-known works, depicting such philosophers from the ages as Aristotle, Plato, and Socrates.

Michelangelo devoted 4½ years to painting the beautiful ceiling frescoes of the majestic **Sistine Chapel ★★★** for Pope Sistus IX. The epic work was so physically taxing that it permanently damaged his eyesight. Glorifying the human body as only a sculptor could, Michelangelo painted nine panels taken from the pages of Genesis and surrounded them with prophets and sibyls. Today throngs of visitors walk around bumping into one another, faces pointed ceiling-ward, admiring the frescoes at the expense of a crick in the neck. Michelangelo did not only the ceiling but also the monumental fresco of *The Last Judgment* **★★★** on the altar wall. The chapel, in danger of collapse, underwent a controversial restoration in the 1990s that some purists say altered Michelangelo's original figures.

Vatican City, Viale Vaticano (a long walk around the Vatican walls from St. Peter's Sq.).℃ **06/69883332.** Admission is 14€ adults, 8€ children 6-13, free for ages 5 and under. Mon–Sat 9am–4pm. Closed Jan 1 and 6, Easter, May 1 and 17, June 7 and 29, Aug 15–16, Nov 1, and Dec 8 and 25–26. Reservations for guided tours 30€ per person through Vatican website at www.vatican.va. Metro: Cipro–Musei Vaticani.

Museo Nazionale di Villa Giulia (Etruscan) ★★★

Like the Palazzo Borghese, the 16th-century Villa Giulia was built as a country house and today houses a priceless collection of art and artifacts left by the mysterious Etruscans, who predated the Romans in Italy (arriving around 800 B.C.).

If you have time only for the masterpieces, head for Sala 7, which has a remarkable *Apollo from Veio* from the end of the 6th century B.C. (clothed, for a change). Two other widely acclaimed pieces of statuary in this gallery are *Dea con Bambino* (*Goddess with a Baby*) and a greatly mutilated but still powerful *Hercules* with a stag. In the adjoining Sala 8, you'll see the lions' sarcophagus from he mid–6th century B.C., which was excavated at Cerveteri, north of Rome. Finally, in Sala 9, is one of the world's most important Etruscan art treasures, the bride and bridegroom coffin from the 6th century B.C., also from Cerveteri. Near the end of your tour, another masterpiece of Etruscan art awaits you in room 33: the *Cista Ficoroni*, a bronze urn with paw feet, mounted by three figures, dating from the 4th century B.C.

Piazzale di Villa Giulia 9. ℃ **06/3226571.** Admission 4€. Tues–Sun 8:30am–7:30pm. Metro: Flaminio.

Pantheon ★★★

Of all the great buildings of ancient Rome, only the Pantheon ("All the Gods") remains intact today. It was built in 27 B.C. by Marcus Agrippa and later reconstructed by the emperor Hadrian in the first part of the 2nd century A.D. This remarkable building is among the architectural wonders of the world because of its dome and its concept of space. The Pantheon was once ringed with niches containing white marble statues of Roman gods. Animals were sacrificed and burned in the center, and the smoke escaped through the only means of light, the oculus, an opening at the top 18 feet (5.4m) in diameter. Michelangelo came here to study the dome before designing the cupola of St. Peter's, whose dome is only 2 feet (.6m) smaller than the Pantheon's.

Piazza della Rotonda. ℃ **06/68300230.** Free admission. Mon–Sat 9am–7:30pm; Sun 9am–1pm. Bus: 30, 40, 62, 64, 81, or 492 to Largo di Torre.

Scalinata di Spagna (Spanish Steps) ★★

The Spanish Steps and the adjoining Piazza di Spagna both take their name from the Spanish embassy, which was housed in a palace here during the 19th century. The Spanish, however, had nothing to do with the construction of the steps. Designed by Italian architect Francesco de Sanctis and built from 1723 to 1725, they were funded almost entirely by the French. They lead to the French church in Rome, Trinita' dei Monti. The twin-towered church behind the obelisk at the top of the steps is early 16th century. The steps themselves are early 18th century.

Piazza di Spagna. Metro: Spagna.

Where to Dine

Cesare ROMAN/TUSCAN   The area around the Vatican is not the place to look for great restaurants, but Cesare is a fine old-world dining room known for its deft handling of fresh ingredients. You can select your fresh fish from the refrigerated glass case at the entrance. We come here for the fresh and tender seafood salad, brimming with cuttlefish, shrimp, squid, mussels, and octopus, and dressed with olive oil, fresh parsley, and lemon. The *saltimbocca alla romana,* that classic Roman dish, is a masterpiece as served here—butter-tender veal slices topped with prosciutto and fresh sage and sautéed in white wine. The cooks also keep the wood-fired pizza ovens hot.

Via Crescenzio 13, near Piazza Cavour. (✆ **06/6861227.** www.ristorantecesare.com. Reservations recommended. Main courses 10€–28€; fixed-price Tuscan menu 38€. AE, DC, MC, V. Daily 12:30–3pm; Mon–Sat 7:30pm–midnight. Closed in Aug. Bus: 23, 34, or 49. Metro: Lepanto or Ottaviano.

Césarina EMILIANA-ROMAGNOLA/ROMAN   This restaurant, specializing in the cuisines of Rome and the region of Bologna, perpetuates the culinary traditions of the late Césarina Masi in a newer manifestation of her famous original hole-in-the-wall, which catered to Rome's fashionable set in the 1960s. Today this favorite of Roman families serves excellent versions of *bollito misto* (an array of well-seasoned boiled meats), rolled from table to table on a cart; and *misto Césarina*—three kinds of pasta, each handmade and served with a different sauce. A dessert specialty is *semifreddo Cesarina* (ice cream with whipped cream) with hot chocolate, which is meltingly good.

Via Piemonte 109. (✆ **06/4880828.** Reservations recommended. Main courses 15€–24€. AE, DC, MC, V. Mon–Sat 12:30–3pm and 7:30–11pm. Metro: Barberini. Bus: 910.

Colline Emiliane ★★ 🍴 EMILIANA-ROMAGNOLA   This small local favorite right off Piazza Barberini serves *classica cucina Bolognese* in a bustling, trattoria setting. It's a family-run place where everybody helps out. The owner is the cook and his wife makes the pasta, which, incidentally, is about the best you'll find in Rome. The enticing menu is loaded with old favorites and delicacies—none finer than an inspired *tortellini alla panna* (cream sauce) with truffles.

Via Avignonesi 22 (off Piazza Barberini). (✆ **06/4817538.** Reservations highly recommended. Main courses 12€–22€. MC, V. Tues–Sun 12:45–2:45pm; Tues–Sat 7:45–10:45pm. Closed Aug. Metro: Barberini.

Dal Bolognese ★ BOLOGNESE   If *La Dolce Vita* were being filmed now, this restaurant would be used as a backdrop, its patrons photographed in their latest Fendi drag. It's one of those rare dining spots that's chic but actually lives up to the hype with noteworthy Bolognese cuisine. To begin your meal, we suggest *misto di pasta*—four pastas, each flavored with a different sauce, arranged on the same plate. The chefs also turn out the town's best veal cutlets Bolognese topped with cheese—simply superb.

Piazza del Popolo 1–2. (✆ **06/3611426.** Reservations required. Main courses 10€–20€. AE, DC, MC, V. Tues–Sun 1–3pm and 8:15pm–midnight (last dinner order at 11:15pm). Closed 20 days in Aug. Metro: Flaminio.

La Cisterna ROMAN   Consider having at least one meal in the ancient district of Trastevere across the Tiber, as it's the most typical and atmospheric of all Roman districts. For more than 75 years, the Simmi family has been turning out real Roman cookery—and serving it fresh from the ovens. In summer, guests like to sit at the restaurant's sidewalk tables as they devour fresh fish and other delectable dishes, including homemade pastas and well-flavored meats.

Via della Cisterna 13. (*C*) **06/5812543.** www.lacisterna.com. Reservations recommended. Main courses 15€–30€. AE, MC, V. Mon–Sat 7pm–1am. Bus: H, 75, 170, 280, or 710.

Monte Arci ROMAN/SARDINIAN   This restaurant is set behind a sienna-colored facade on a cobblestone street near Piazza Indipendenza. It features Roman and Sardinian specialties (you'll spend even less for pizza) such as *nialoreddus* (a regional form of gnocchetti); pasta with clams, lobster, or the musky-earthy notes of porcini mushrooms; and delicious lamb sausage flavored with herbs and pecorino cheese. The best pasta dish we sampled was *paglia e fieno al Monte Arci* (homemade pasta with pancetta, spinach, cream, and Parmesan). It's all home cooking—hearty but not that creative.

Via Castelfirdardo 33. (*C*) **06/4941220.** www.ristorantemontearci.com. Reservations recommended. Main courses 8€–15€. AE, DC, MC, V. Mon–Fri 12:30–3pm; Mon–Sat 7–11:30pm. Closed Aug. Metro: Stazione Termini or Repubblica.

Piperno Restaurant ★ ROMAN/JEWISH   In the heart of the old Jewish ghetto, this trattoria has been open and running since 1856, and every year it makes new fans of visitors to this historic part of old Rome. Its celebrated Jerusalem artichokes (which isn't really an artichoke) are deep-fried but appear on your plate flaky and dry—not greasy. The time-tested recipes are prepared with market-fresh ingredients—count yourself lucky if the stuffed squash blossoms appear on the menu. You'll be served by a uniformed crew of hardworking waiters, whose advice and suggestions are worth considering.

Via Monte de' Cenci 9. (*C*) **06/68806629.** www.ristorantepiperno.com. Reservations recommended. Main courses 18€–25€. MC, V. Tues–Sat 12:45–2:20pm and 7:45–10:20pm; Sun 12:45–2:20pm. Closed Mon. Bus: 64.

Ristorante del Pallaro ★★ 🍴 ROMAN   The cheerful woman in white who emerges with clouds of steam from the bustling kitchen is owner Paola Fazi, who runs two dining rooms where value-conscious Romans go for good food at bargain prices. (She also claims—though others dispute it—that Julius Caesar was assassinated on this site.) The fixed-price menu is the only choice and has made the place famous. Ms. Fazi prepares everything with love, as if she were feeding her extended family. As you sit down, your antipasto, the first of eight courses, appears. Then comes the pasta of the day, followed by such main dishes as roast veal with broad beans and homemade potato chips, or roast pork cutlets, tender and flavorful. For your final courses, you're served mozzarella, cake with custard, and fruit in season.

Largo del Pallaro 15. (*C*) **06/68801488.** Reservations recommended. Fixed-price menu 25€. No credit cards. Tues–Sun noon–3:30pm and 7pm–12:30am. Closed Aug 12–25. Bus: 40, 46, 60, 62, or 64.

Trattoria San Teodoro ★ ROMAN   At last there's a good place to eat in the former gastronomic wasteland near the Roman Forum and Palatine Hill. The helpful staff at this top-rated trattoria welcomes visitors and locals to a shady terrace or a dimly lit dining room. The market-fresh menu includes succulent homemade pastas, some excellent seafood (try the carpaccio made with tuna, turbot, or sea bass), and any number of well-flavored and tender meat dishes.

Via dei Fienili 49–51. (*C*) **06/6780933.** www.st-teodoro.it. Reservations recommended. Main courses 23€–29€. MC, V. Mon–Sat 12:30–3:30pm and 7:30pm–midnight. Closed 2 weeks at Christmas. Metro: Circo Massimo.

Trimani Wine Bar ★ CONTINENTAL   Opened as a tasting center for French and Italian wines, spumantis, and liqueurs, this is an elegant wine bar with a lovely decor (stylish but informal) near Stazione Termini. More than 30 wines are available by the glass. To accompany them, you can choose from a bistro-style menu, with dishes such as salad niçoise, vegetarian pastas, herb-laden bean soups (*fagiole*), and quiche. Also available is a wider menu, including meat and fish courses. The specialty is the large choice of little "bruschette" with cheese and radicchio—the chef orders every kind of prosciutto and cheese from all over Italy. The dishes are matched with the appropriate wines.

Via Cernaia 37B. ✆ **06/4469630.** www.trimani.com. Reservations recommended. Main courses 10€– 18€; glass of wine (depending on vintage) 3€–18€. AE, DC, MC, V. Daily 11:30am–3pm and 5:30pm– 12:30am. Closed 2 weeks in Aug. Metro: Repubblica or Castro Pretorio.

Tuna ★ SEAFOOD   This seafood emporium in the center of Rome, overlooking the via Veneto, is dedicated to serving some of the freshest fish in the capital. From crayfish to sea truffles, from oysters to sea urchins, the fish is turned into platters of delight with perfect seasonings and preparation. Start with the midget mussels or the octopus salad or else calamari and artichoke tempura. For a main course, the catch

ANCONA & BARI: gateways TO GREECE

The port cities of Ancona (190 miles/306km northeast of Rome) and Bari (284 miles/457km southeast of Rome) are the two major embarkation points for passholders crossing the Adriatic to Greece. Ferries from both these cities run to Patras in Greece (usually via Igoumenitsa); rail travel from Patras to other cities in Greece, however, is problematic (p. 806).

For trains running between Rome and Bari or Ancona, refer to "Trains & Travel Times in Italy," earlier. If you don't want to use a day on your pass, one-way rail fares from Rome to Bari cost $98 to $140 when bought in advance through Rail Europe; fares to Ancona run $37 to $53. Ferries generally depart in the afternoon and arrive on the afternoon of the following day in Greece; when planning your schedule, be sure to leave plenty of time to catch the ferry.

Ferry routes are operated by **Superfast Ferries/Blue Star Lines** (**www. superfast.com**) and **Minoan Lines** (**www.minoan.gr**). Transit aboard one of these ferries costs 77€ to 90€ (depending on the season) one-way

in an airline-style seat. If you want a private cabin, it'll cost you approximately 188€ for a double, or 133€ in a quad. Ask about family discounts if you're traveling with children. **Warning:** Snack bars aboard these ferries charge outrageous prices, so cost-conscious travelers should purchase their own food in Ancona or Bari and bring it aboard.

Note: The Eurail Global Pass and the Eurail Greece–Italy Pass are accepted on these ferries for deck passage only (cabins cost extra), though a supplement of 15€ to 30€ is assessed during the summer high season. Port taxes and fuel surcharges may also be assessed. If you have a Flexi version of a pass, you will lose 1 day on the pass (either at arrival or departure) to cover the ferry trip. For more on ferries covered by the Eurail Global Pass, see chapter 2.

Bookings need to be made with an agent for the Superfast/Blue Star lines. Fill out the form on the website and an agent will contact you. You can book your ticket for Minoan Lines on the company's website.

of the day is in general the best choice, or else you may order sliced sea bass with chives and fresh thyme.

11 via Veneto. ☎ **06/42016531.** www.tunaroma.it. Reservations required. Main courses 15€–30€. AE, DC, MC, V. Mon–Fri 12:30–3pm; daily 7:30pm–midnight. Closed 2 weeks in Aug. Metro: Barberini.

Shopping

We won't pretend that Rome is Italy's finest shopping center (Florence and Venice are), or that its shops are unusually inexpensive—many of them aren't. But even on the most elegant of Rome's thoroughfares, there are values mixed in with the costly boutiques. On a short visit, the best method is to stroll the major shopping streets (see below), ferreting out the best values.

The posh shopping streets **Via Borgognona** and **Via Condotti** begin near Piazza di Spagna. For the most part, the merchandise on both is chic and very, very expensive. Wise shoppers are advised to take a look at the goods displayed on the Spanish Steps before a tour of Via Condotti. Here, craftspeople good and bad lay out their wares on old velvet cloths—usually paintings, beads, silver and turquoise jewelry, some of it quite good—and bargain for the best offer. **Via Frattina** runs parallel to Via Condotti, its more famous sibling, and is the hippest and busiest shopping street in town. You'll frequently find it closed to traffic, converted into a pedestrian mall thronged with shoppers moving from boutique to boutique.

Beginning at the top of the Spanish Steps, **Via Sistina** runs to Piazza Barberini. It houses the city's densest concentration of boutiques and expensive dress shops. It's good for browsing, and women visitors will occasionally find exciting items on sale. Most shoppers reach **Via Francesco Crispi** by following Via Sistina 1 long block from the top of the Spanish Steps. Near the intersection of these streets are several shops full of unusual and not overly expensive gifts. Evocative of *La Dolce Vita,* **Via Veneto** is filled these days with expensive hotels and cafes, and an array of relatively expensive stores selling shoes, gloves, and leather goods.

Traffic-clogged **Via Nazionale**—just crossing the street is no small feat—begins at Piazza della Repubblica and runs down almost to Piazza Venezia. Here you'll find an abundance of leather stores—more reasonable in price than those in many other parts of Rome—and a welcome handful of stylish boutiques.

Via dei Coronari should be seen whether or not you buy. Buried in a colorful section of the Campus Martius (Renaissance Rome), Via dei Coronari is an antiquer's dream, literally lined with magnificent vases, urns, chandeliers, breakfronts, chaises, refectory tables, candelabra, you name it. You'll find the entrance to the street just north of the Piazza Navona.

Nightlife

Evenings in Rome always begin at one of the cafes, the most famous of which line the **Via Veneto.** Two other popular gathering places for cafe-sitting are **Piazza della Rotonda** and **Piazza del Popolo.** For the cost of an espresso, the people-watching is free.

There are few evening diversions quite as pleasurable as a stroll past the solemn pillars of old temples or the cascading torrents of Renaissance fountains glowing under a blue-black sky. Of the **fountains,** the Naiads (Piazza della Repubblica), the Tortoises (Piazza Mattei), and, of course, the Trevi are particularly beautiful at night. The **Capitoline Hill** is magnificently lit after dark, with its Renaissance facades glowing like jewel boxes. Behind the Senatorial Palace is a fine view of the **Roman Forum.** If you're staying across the Tiber, **Piazza San Pietro,** in front of St. Peter's Basilica, is impressive at night without tour buses and crowds. And a combination of illuminated architecture, Renaissance fountains, and frequent sidewalk shows and art expositions is at **Piazza Navona.** If you're ambitious and have a good sense of direction, try exploring the streets to the west of Piazza Navona, which look like a stage set when lit at night.

The minimagazine *Wanted in Rome* has listings of jazz, rock, and such, and gives an interesting look at expatriate Rome. The daily *Il Messaggero* lists current cultural news. And *Un Ospite a Roma,* available free from the concierge desks of top hotels, is full of details on what's happening. Even if you don't speak Italian, you can generally follow the listings of special events and evening entertainment in *La Repubblica,* one of the leading Italian newspapers.

THE PERFORMING ARTS If you're in the capital for the opera season, usually late December to June, you might want to attend the historic **Teatro dell'Opera (Rome Opera House),** Piazza Beniamino Gigli 1, off Via Nazionale (© 06/481601; www.operaroma.it; Metro: Repubblica). Tickets cost 11€ to 130€. In summer, opera switches to the Baths of Caracalla. Call ahead or ask your concierge before you go. Tickets are 25€ to 110€. The **Rome Opera Ballet** also performs at the Teatro dell'Opera. Look for announcements of classical concerts that take place in churches and other venues.

CAFES & BARS Along the Via Veneto, **Harry's Bar,** at #150 (© 06/484643; www.harrysbar.it; Metro: Piazza di Spagna or Barberini), is the choicest watering hole. It has no connection with other famous Harry's bars, such as the one in Venice, and in many respects, the Roman Harry's is the most elegant of them all. **Cafè de Paris,** Via Vittorio Veneto 90 (© 06/4815631), is a local landmark and a good place to get the night started. Tables spill out onto the sidewalk in summer, and the passing crowd walks through the maze.

The fashion-conscious descend on the Piazza de Popolo, where there is always an aura of excitement, especially after midnight. The best place for a drink here is **Café Rosati** ★, Piazza del Popolo 5A (© 06/3225859; www.rosatibar.it; Metro: Piazzale Flaminio; bus: 117), in business since 1923. The preferred tables are out front, where growling Maseratis cruise by while young Italian men in silk shirts hang from the car windows. Its rival, **Canova Café,** Piazza del Popolo 16 (© 06/3612231; bus: 117), is another great place for people-watching. We also gravitate to the Piazza della Rotonda, across from the Pantheon, which is dramatically lit at night. The top cafe here is **Di Rienzo,** Piazza della Rotonda 8–9 (© 06/6869097; Metro: Piazza di Spagna; bus: 62, 65, or 95). The best coffee in Rome is brewed at **Caffè Sant'Eustachio** ★, Piazza Sant'Eustachio 82 (© 06/68802048; www.santeustachioilcaffe.it; bus: 116), where the water supply is funneled into the city by an aqueduct built in 19 B.C.

Alternately, you could try **Antico Caffè Greco,** 86 Via Condotti (© 06/6791700), which has been serving drinks since 1760. Over the years it has attracted such habitués as Goethe, Stendhal, Keats, and D'Annunzio. Half a block from the foot of the Spanish Steps, it still retains a 19th-century atmosphere. The waiters wear morning coats—most effective looking—and seat you at small marble tables. Beyond the carved wooden bar are a series of small elegant rooms hung with oil paintings in gilded frames.

CLUBS **Arciliuto,** Piazza Monte Vecchio 5 (℡ **06/6879419;** www.arciliuto.it; bus: 42, 62, or 64), is a romantic candlelit spot within walking distance of the Piazza Navona that was reputedly once the studio of Raphael. From 10pm to 1:30am, Monday through Saturday, guests enjoy a musical-salon ambience, listening to a guitarist, a pianist, and a violinist. The evening's presentation also includes live Neapolitan songs and new Italian madrigals, even current hits from Broadway or London's West End. There is no cover, but there's a one-drink minimum, with beverages starting at 10€. It's closed July 15 to September 5.

In a high-tech, futuristic setting, **Alien,** Via Velletri 13–19 (℡ **06/8412212;** www.aliendisco.it; bus: 38, 63, 80, or 92), provides a bizarre space-age dance floor, bathed in strobe lights and rocking to the sounds of house/techno music. The crowd is young. It's open Tuesday to Sunday 11pm to 5am, with a cover of 16€ to 18€ that includes the first drink. It's closed from mid-June to early September.

Piper, Via Tagliamento 9 (℡ **06/8555398;** www.piperclub.it; bus: 63), opened in 1965 in a former cinema and became the first modern disco of its kind in Italy. Many dances such as "the shake" were first introduced to Italy at this club. No longer what it was in those *La Dolce Vita* years, the Piper is still going strong. Today it lures with fashion shows, screenings, some of the hottest parties in town, and various gigs, drawing a casual and mixed-age crowd. The pickup scene here is hot and heavy. The kind of music you'll hear depends on the night. Open Monday to Saturday 11pm to 4am, charging a cover of 20€ to 26€, including one drink.

Big Mama, Vicolo San Francesco a Ripa 18 (℡ **06/5812551;** www.bigmama.it; Metro: Piramide; bus: 75 or 170), is a hangout for jazz and blues musicians where you're likely to meet the up-and-coming stars of tomorrow and sometimes even the big names. For big acts, the cover is 12€ to 30€, plus 14€ for a seasonal membership fee.

An Excursion to Tivoli ★★

An ancient town 20 miles (32km) east of Rome, Tivoli, known as Tibur to the ancient Romans, was the playground of emperors, who maintained lavish villas here near the famous woods and waterfalls. Today its reputation continues unabated: It's the most popular half-day jaunt from Rome.

GETTING THERE From Rome, take Metro Line B to Ponte Mammolo. After exiting the station, board a COTRAL bus for the rest of the way to Tivoli (it will drop you off in front of the tourist information office). A bus marked TIVOLI also leaves every 20 minutes during the day from Via Gaeta (west of Via Volturno), near the Stazione Termini. Both buses are part of the regular public transportation system. A one-way fare from Rome to Tivoli costs 2.50€.

VISITOR INFORMATION For information about the town and its attractions, go to **Azienda Autonoma di Turismo,** Vicolo Barchetto (℡ **0774/334522;** www. aptprovroma.it), open Monday to Friday 9am to 1pm and 3 to 5pm, and Saturday 9am to 7pm.

TOP ATTRACTIONS & SPECIAL MOMENTS

Four miles (6.4km) from the foothills on which Tivoli is built lies a gently sloping plain, the site of **Villa Adriana,** or **Hadrian's Villa ★★★**, Via di Villa Adriana (℡ **0774/530203;** www.villa-adriana.net.). Of all the Roman emperors dedicated to *la dolce vita*, the globetrotting Hadrian spent the last 3 years of his life in the grandest style. Today the ruins of his estate cover 180 acres of rolling terrain. The estate was built as a heaven on earth in which to spend a long and luxurious retirement. Hadrian himself designed a self-contained world for a vast royal entourage, the guards required to protect them, and the hundreds of servants needed to bathe them, feed them, and satisfy their libidos. On the estate were theaters, baths, temples, fountains, gardens, and canals bordered with statuary. Much of the ruin is readily recognizable, and it's easy to wander around the hot and cold baths and experience a real sense of the villa as it once was (though if you wish to see what it looked like during its heyday, see the plastic reconstruction at the entrance). Admission is 6.50€. It's open daily 9am to sunset (about 7:30pm in summer, 5:30pm Nov–Mar). To get here, take bus no. 4 from the center of Tivoli.

At Tivoli itself, the clutter and clamor of 21st-century Italy is forgotten in a perfect gem from the Renaissance: **Villa d'Este ★★**, Piazza Trento, Viale delle Centro Fontane (© **0774/312070**; www.villadestetivoli.info; bus: Roma-Tivoli), so named after the 16th-century cardinal who transformed it from a government palace (it had been built in the 13th c. as a Benedictine convent) into a princely residence, which remained in the cardinal's family until 1918. The 16th-century frescoes and decorations of the place itself are attractive but unexceptional. The **garden** on the sloping hill beneath is another story—a perfect fairy tale of the Renaissance, using water as a medium of sculpture, much the way the ancients used marble. Pathways are lined with 100 fountains of every imaginable size and shape. The most spectacular achievement: the **Fountain of the Hydraulic Organ (Fontana dell'Organo Idraulico),** dazzling with its water jets in front of a baroque chapel, with four maidens who look tipsy. The work represents the genius of Frenchman Claude Veanard. The moss-covered **Fountain of the Dragons (Fontana dei Draghi),** also by Ligorio, and the so-called **Fountain of Glass (Fontana di Vetro),** by Bernini, are the most intriguing. Admission is 6.50€. It's open Tuesday to Sunday at 8:30am; closing times vary according to the season (1 hr. before sunset).

NAPLES

Nestled by a blue bay in the shadow of Mount Vesuvius, Naples, just 136 miles (219km) southeast of Rome, has been known to seafarers since the 6th century B.C. It remains one of the Mediterranean's foremost port cities to this day, its streets teeming with life—shirtless dockworkers, prostitutes, scampering children, throngs of pedestrians, huge open markets, and apartment houses whose facades are all but obscured with laundry. It has its towering castles and elegant palaces, too, as befits a town whose past enthusiasts have included the Emperor Nero and the poet Virgil.

Naples is also an ideal jumping-off point for some of the most popular vacation and sightseeing attractions in southern Italy. From here you can explore the ruins of Pompeii and Herculaneum, or sail to the fabled Isle of Capri. But the city itself has its own impressive sights, including some excellent museums. We rank it behind Florence and Venice, but if you're in the area and can spare a day or two, Naples has excellent rail connections to Rome and makes for a good 1- or 2-day rail excursion out of the capital city.

GETTING THERE   The rail lines between Rome and Naples are among the most frequently used in Italy. You can take either a regular train or a Eurostar Italia train to go from Rome to Naples. Some 20 express trains run daily from Rome's Stazione Termini to the **Stazione Centrale** in Naples, the trip taking only 1 hour and 10 minutes and costing about 50€ one-way. Tickets may be booked through Rail Europe or by calling 🕿 **892021.** Regular train service is slower but cheaper, taking about 2½ hours and costing about 28€ one-way.

Trains from Rome usually pull into Stazione Centrale in the heart of Naples. Here you will find many services, including a 24-hour pharmacy, plus a train information and reservations office right off the main hall that's open daily from 7am to 11pm. There is also a money exchange kiosk here (charging very expensive rates) and various food services. The office for storing luggage is open daily from 7am to 11pm and charges 4€ per bag for the first 5 hours, .60€ for the following 6 hours, and .20€ per hour onward.

Some 656 feet (197m) outside the station is the **Ente Provinciale per il Turismo,** the local tourist office at Piazza Garibaldi (🕿 **081/268779**), open Monday to Saturday 8:30am to 8pm, Sunday 8:30am to 2pm. It does not make hotel reservations.

VISITOR INFORMATION   The main tourist office, **Ente Provinciale per il Turismo,** is at Piazza dei Martiri 58 (🕿 **081/413788;** bus: C25), open Monday to Friday 9am to 2pm. The staff does not make hotel reservations, which you'll need to make by yourself or through a travel agency.

GETTING AROUND   The **Metropolitana** line will deliver you from Stazione Centrale in the east all the way to the suburb of Pozzuoli. Get off at Piazza Piedigrotta if you want to take the funicular to Vomero. The Metro uses the same tickets as buses and trams. It's dangerous to ride **buses** at rush hours—never have we seen such pushing and shoving. Many people prefer to leave the buses to the battle-hardened Neapolitans and take the subway or **tram** 1 or 4, running from Stazione Centrale to Stazione Mergellina. For a ticket valid for 90 minutes with unlimited transfers during that time, the cost is 1.10€. A ticket for a full day of unlimited travel costs 3.10€.

If you survive the **taxi** driver's reckless driving, you'll have to do battle over the bill. Many cab drivers claim that the meter is broken and assess the cost of the ride, always to your disadvantage. Some legitimate surcharges are imposed, such as night drives and extra luggage. Many drivers, however, deliberately take the scenic route to run up costs. You can call a radio taxi at 🕿 **081/5520399** or 081/5707070.

Funiculars take passengers up and down the steep hills of Naples. **Funicolare Centrale** (🕿 **800/568866**), for example, connects the lower part of the city to Vomero. Departures, daily 6:30am to 12:30am, are from Piazzetta Duca d'Aosta, just off Via Roma. The same tickets valid for buses and the Metro are good for the funicular.

Top Attractions & Special Moments

Charles III of Spain took over a 16th-century building and turned it into **Museo Archeologico Nazionale (National Archaeological Museum)** ★★★, Piazza Museo Nazionale 18–19 (🕿 **081/4422149;** Metro: Piazza Cavour or Museo), when he became king of Naples in the mid–18th century. Installed in the mansion was his exquisite Farnese collection. Since that time, the museum has added art and artifacts from the excavations at Pompeii and Herculaneum as well as the Borgia collection of Etruscan and Egyptian antiquities, making its contents the most valuable archaeological collection in Europe.

Among the outstanding works in the Farnese collection are the gigantic marble *Farnese Hercules,* dating from the 1st century B.C., and the *Group of Farnese Bull,* a sculptured group from the Greek Apollonius of Tralles. The original dates from the 2nd century B.C., and this work, a copy, once stood in the Baths of Caracalla in Rome. Also from the collection is a bas-relief of Orpheus and Eurydice, whose original dates from the 5th century B.C.

Several galleries on the mezzanine level are given over to mosaics recovered from Pompeii and Herculaneum, the most magnificent of which depicts Alexander battling with the Persian forces. Admission is 6.50€, and hours are Monday and Wednesday to Sunday 9am to 7pm, Sunday from 9am to 8pm.

Museo e Gallerie Nazionale di Capodimonte (National Museum & Gallery of the Capodimonte) ★★★, in the Palazzo Capodimonte, Parco di Capodimonte lying off Amedeo di Savoia and entered at Via Miano 2 (**✆ 081/7499111**), stands near the outskirts of the city. The Capodimonte Galleries are housed in an 18th-century palace, surrounded by its own attractive gardens. The State Apartments contain a rich collection of ivories, porcelains, glass, and china, as well as the **Farnese Armory.** The real attraction of the palace, however, is the National Gallery, which occupies the top floor. One of the finest galleries in Italy, it is especially rich in paintings of the 14th century and the early Italian Renaissance.

One of the best of the 14th-century group is a coronation scene painted by Simone Martini, a leader of the Sienese School. The Renaissance is well represented by the greatest artists of that period: Raphael with *The Holy Family and Saint John,* Filippino Lippi with *Annunciation and Saints,* and Michelangelo, Botticelli, Titian, and Mantegna. Hours are Thursday to Tuesday 8:30am to 7:30pm, and you take bus 24 or R4. Admission is 7.50€.

Museo Nazionale di San Martino (National Museum of San Martino) ★★, Largo San Martino 5 (**✆ 081/5781769;** funicular: Stazione Centrale from Via Toledo or Montesanto; Metro: Vanvitelli), in the Vomero district, is worth the trip if you do nothing more than stand on the balcony overlooking the Bay of Naples and gaze in awe at the panorama that includes Vesuvius and Capri. Reconstructed in the 17th century in a Neapolitan baroque style on the site of a 14th-century monastery, the museum is on the grounds of the Castel Sant'Elmo and houses a broad collection of costumes, armor, carriages, documents, and 19th-century Campania paintings. Of special interest is the elaborately decorated nativity scene by Curiniello. Admission is 6€; it's open Monday, Tuesday and Thursday to Saturday 8:30am to 7:30pm; Sunday 9am to 7:30pm.

Castel Nuovo (New Castle) ★★, Piazza del Municipio (**✆ 081/4201241;** tram: 1 or 4; bus: R2), is marked by three massive turrets towering above the square. Although it was begun in 1279 by Charles of Anjou, most of what you see today dates from its mid-15th-century restoration (after Alfonso the Magnanimous drove the House of Anjou from its premises). The castle's most celebrated feature is the Arch of Triumph, by Francesco Laurana, commemorating Alfonso's victory. Among the rooms you can visit are the massive Hall of the Barons, now used by the Naples City Commission, and the 14th-century Palatine Chapel, at the core of the castle. Admission is 5€. Hours are Monday to Saturday 9am to 7pm.

Where to Stay & Dine

Hotel Britannique ★, Corso Vittorio Emanuele 133, 80121 Napoli (**✆ 081/7614145;** www.hotelbritannique.it; Metro: Piazza Amedeo; bus: C24 or C27), is known for its central location close to the satellite rail station of Mergellina and for its attractive bedrooms overlooking the Bay of Naples. Personally managed by the owners, it remains charmingly old-fashioned, although it has been modernized. An oasis is the hotel's flower-filled garden. Many guest rooms, ranging from small to large, have some antiques, although most of the furnishings are functional. Doubles cost 130€ to 190€, with a junior suite going for 220€; rates include buffet breakfast.

The boutique hotel **Art Resort Galleria Umberto** ★★, Piazza Plebiscito 83, 80132 Napoli (✆/fax **081/4976224;** www.artresortgalleriaumberto.it; bus: R2 or R3), lies within the landmark Galleria Umberto, making it unique in Naples. Rooms, each named after a different artist, are done in a classic romantic style, some with fabric-draped four-poster beds. Accommodations are decorated in tasteful and harmonious colors; the windows are soundproof, and each unit has a large wardrobe, along with luxurious bathrooms with hydroshowers or bathtubs. Rooms with balconies are reserved for smokers. Opera singers and musicians from the nearby opera house often stay here. Doubles cost 150€ to 160€, with a junior suite from 160€ to 180€.

L'Alloggio dei Vassalli ★, Via Donnalbina 56, 80134 Napoli (✆ **081/5515118;** www.bandbnapoli.it; Metro: Montesanto), is small but one of the best and most upscale of Naples' B&Bs. It's set on the second floor of the historic 18th-century Palazzo Donnalbina. In the heart of Naples, the B&B is imbued with some of the building's original architectural details, including ceilings of antique wooden rafters and decorative stucco work. Bedrooms are spacious and bright, each tastefully and comfortably furnished. Doubles cost 79€ to 99€, with triples going for 105€ to 125€.

Near the seafront, **Don Salvatore** ★, Strada Mergellina 4A (✆ **081/681817;** www.donsalvatore.it; Metro: Mergellina), naturally specializes in seafood and does so exceedingly well. The fish, which comes from the Bay of Naples, is then either grilled or shaped into an array of dishes, including linguine with shrimp or squid. The wine cellar is said to be the finest in Campania, as well as reasonably priced. Main courses cost 10€ to 24€. Another favorite for seafood, **Giuseppone a Mare** ★★, Via Ferdinando Russo 13 (✆ **081/5756002;** bus: C3 or 140), is known for serving some of the best and freshest seafood in Campania. Diners make their fishy choices—ranging from fresh crabs to eels—from a trolley wheeled by each table. Often the day's catch is deep-fried, as many locals like it that way. Main courses cost 10€ to 22€. The grilled seafood is even better at the more highly rated **La Cantinella** ★★, Via Cuma 42 (✆ **081/7648684;** www.lacantinella.it; bus: C25 or 140), on a bustling street opening onto the bay in the romantic Santa Lucia area. The chefs have a deft way of turning out both Neapolitan classics and more imaginative dishes. The *antipasti* table is one of the most alluring in town, and you can include all sorts of other dishes—not just fish. Main courses cost 20€ to 30€. Open daily from 12:30 to 3pm and 7:30pm to midnight (closed Aug 9–27 and Sun Apr–Nov), and reservations are required.

1-Day Excursions from Naples

The most exciting sightseeing attractions in southern Italy lie within a 15-mile (24km) radius of Naples, making that city an ideal home base for many excursions into the surrounding countryside. We list the three most compelling places to visit below in order of their importance.

POMPEII ★★★

Buried in its heyday in A.D. 79 by the eruption of Mount Vesuvius, the city of Pompeii, 15 miles (24km) south of Naples, offers visitors a glimpse of life as it was lived 2,000 years ago. The volcanic ash and lava that destroyed the city also helped to preserve the ruins until their rediscovery in 1748.

GETTING THERE The **Circumvesuviana Railway** (✆ **800/053939**) departs Naples every half-hour from Piazza Garibaldi. However, be sure you get on the train headed toward Sorrento and get off at Pompeii/Scavi (*scavi* means "archaeological

Sicily: LAND OF MYTH & LEGEND

Sicily is the largest of Mediterranean islands, 110 miles (178km) north to south and 175 miles (282km) wide, and a land of dramatic intensity. For centuries, its beauty and charm have attracted the greedy eye of foreign invaders: the Greeks, Romans, Vandals, Arabs, Normans, Swabians, and Houses of Bourbon and Aragon. Luigi Barzini wrote: "Sicily is the schoolroom model of Italy for beginners, with every Italian quality and defect magnified, exasperated and brightly colored." Of course, it is the people themselves—bound by tradition and local customs—that provide the greatest interest. Most rail travelers on their first journey to Italy won't have time to visit Sicily, but it's well worth exploring on subsequent excursions.

The best centers for touring are Palermo, Syracuse, and Taormina. If you're considering anchoring into Sicily for a holiday, then Taormina is the best site, with the finest choice of hotels in all price ranges. If you stick to the main road that skirts the coast, encircling the island, you'll get to see most of the major sights, veering inland for such attractions as the active volcano of Mount Etna.

Trains from all over Italy arrive at the port at Villa San Giovanni, near Reggio di Calabria on the Italian mainland, and roll onto enormous barges for the 1-hour crossing to Sicily. Passengers remain in their seats during the short voyage across the Strait of Messina, eventually rolling back onto the rail tracks at Messina, Sicily. From Rome, the trip to Palermo takes 11 to 12 hours, depending on the speed of the train; the rail route from Naples takes 9 hours. Aboard any of the night trains pulling into Palermo, you can book a couchette or sleeper. For fares and information, call ✆ **892021.**

Palermo, the capital of Sicily and also its largest port, lies 447 miles (720km) south of Naples and 579 miles (932km) south of Rome, and is reached by rail, part of it involving a sea crossing, as mentioned above. Its major attractions include the **Cathedral of Palermo ★★**, on the Corso Vittorio Emanuele (✆ **091/334373**), built in the 12th century on the foundation of an earlier basilica that had been converted by the Arabs into a mosque. The **Palace of the Normanni (Palace of the Normans) ★★**, at the Piazza Parlamento (✆ **091/7051111**), contains one of the greatest art treasures in Sicily, the **Cappella**

excavation"). Beware of pickpockets on the circumvesuviana platforms! If you get on the Pompeii train, you'll end up in the town of Pompeii and will have to transfer there to the other train to get to the ruins. A round-trip ticket costs 5€; trip time is 35 minutes each way. Circumvesuviana trains leave Sorrento for Pompeii every half-hour, costing 1.90€ one-way. There's an entrance about 150 feet (45m) from the rail station at the Villa dei Misteri. At the rail station in the town of Pompeii, **bus** connections take you to the entrance to the excavations.

VISITOR INFORMATION The **tourist office** is at Via Sacra 1 (✆ **081/8507255**). It's open Monday to Friday 8am to 3:30pm (until 7pm Apr–Oct) and Saturday 8am to 2pm.

Top Attractions & Special Moments

Most people visit the **Ufficio Scavi di Pompeii,** Via Villa dei Misteri 1, Piazza Esedra (✆ **081/8610744**), the best-preserved 2,000-year-old ruins in Europe, on a

Palatina (Palatine Chapel) ★★★. Erected at the request of Roger II in the 1130s, it is the finest example of the Arabic-Norman style of design and building. In a former convent, **Museo Archeologico Regionale** ★★★, Via Bara all'Olivella 24 (✆ **091/6116805**), houses one of the greatest archaeological collections in southern Italy. Many works displayed here were excavated from Selinunte, once one of the major towns in *Magna Graecia* (Greater Greece).

Taormina, 155 miles (250km) east of Palermo, is the greatest holiday resort south of Capri. Dating from the 4th century B.C., Taormina hugs the edge of a cliff overlooking the Ionian Sea. The sea—and the railroad track—is down below, connected to the town by bus routes. Looming in the background is Mount Etna, the active volcano. Noted for its mild climate, the town enjoys a year-round season. The **Taormina Tourist Office** is in the Palazzo Corvaja, Piazza Santa Caterina (✆ **0942/23243**), open Monday to Thursday 8:30am to 2pm and 4 to 7pm, and Friday 8:30am to 2pm.

Syracuse is 35 miles (56km) southeast of Catania, the leading city along the coast of eastern Sicily and a transportation hub for rail lines in the area. From other major cities in Sicily, Syracuse is best reached by **train.** It's 1½ hours from Catania, 2 hours from Taormina, and 5 hours from Palermo. Usually you must transfer trains in Catania. For information, call ✆ **892021.** Trains arrive in Syracuse at the station on Via Francesco Crispi, centrally located midway between the archaeological park and Ortygia.

The main **tourist office** is at Via San Sebastiano 43A (✆ **0931/481211**), with a branch office at Via della Maestranza 33 (✆ **0931/464255**). Both are open Monday to Friday 8:15am to 2pm and 2:30 to 5:30pm, and Saturday 8:15am to 2pm.

Syracuse's **Archaeological Park** ★★★ lies west of the modern town reached along Viale Rizzo. It is peppered with the most important attractions, beginning with **Teatro Greco** ★★★, or the Greek Theater, on Temenite Hill. Although in ruins, this is one of the great Greek theaters remaining from the classical era. The **Roman Amphitheater** ★ nearby was erected at the time of Augustus. It ranks among the top live amphitheaters left by the Romans in Italy.

day trip from Naples (allow at least 4 hr. for even a superficial look at the archaeological site). The ruins are open November to March daily from 8:30am to 5pm (last admission at 3:30pm), April to October daily 8:30am to 7:30pm (last admission at 6pm). Admission is 11€ for adults but free for ages 17 and under.

Of particular interest are the elegant patrician villas, some of which are in an amazing state of preservation. The finest of these is the **House of the Vettii (Casa dei Vettii)** ★★★, built around an attractive Etruscan courtyard and adorned with handsome statuary. The dining room, frescoed with cupids, is decorated in the traditional Pompeiian black and red. Among the statues still remaining in the villa is a sculpture of Janus, the two-faced household god. The **House of the Mysteries (Villa dei Misteri)** ★★, near the Porto Ercolano, just outside the city walls, is an unusual villa—in appearance and purpose. As a cult center for the mysterious sect of Dionysus, it is decorated with murals and frescoes depicting some of the sacred—and very secret—initiation rites of this popular but strange religion.

The **Stabian Thermae (baths)** ★★★, near the center of town, are a surprisingly intact example of public baths in an early Roman town. If you miss seeing the small household accessories in the Pompeiian homes, you'll find them on display in the **Antiquarium,** where pottery, utensils, sculptures, and kitchen equipment are exhibited. Flanked by the Temples of Jupiter and Apollo and the huge basilica is the physical and political core of Pompeii, the **Forum** ★. Damaged in the earthquake that crippled the city 16 years before Mount Vesuvius finished the job, this important edifice was never completely restored. As you wander through the ruins, you can try your hand at translating the graffiti and campaign slogans immortalized on the walls and columns.

VESUVIUS ★★★

It may not look as sinister as it did in A.D. 79 when it buried Pompeii, Herculaneum, and Stabiae in a flood of lava and volcanic ash, but Vesuvius is still an active volcano. It has erupted more than once since the dawn of the Christian era, including a tragic spouting of lava in 1631 that killed thousands, and a less fatal explosion in 1906 when it simply blew the ring off its crater. The last spectacular eruption was on March 31, 1944.

It might sound like a dubious invitation, but it's possible to visit the rim of the crater's mouth. As you look down into its smoldering core, you might recall that Spartacus, a century before the eruption that buried Pompeii, hid in the hollow of the crater, which was then covered with vines.

To reach Vesuvius from Naples, take the Circumvesuviana Railway from Piazza Garibaldi to Ercolano (Herculaneum), the 10th stop. The Vesuvio Express at the Ercolano stop leaves for the top of the crater daily from 9am to 4:30pm, with service about every half-hour. The cost is 17€. For more information, call ✆ **081/7393666;** www.vesuvioexpress.it. Once at the top, you must be accompanied by a guide, which will cost 8€. Assorted tour guides are found in the bus parking lot; they are available daily from 9am to about 4pm.

HERCULANEUM ★★

If you've a yen to explore more ruins, you can head for this seaside resort buried in the same eruption that doomed Pompeii. The site of Herculaneum is much smaller—only about one-fourth the size of Pompeii—and a portion of it remains unexcavated because it is covered by the sprawling slums of Resina. According to legend, Hercules himself founded the city, which was covered in A.D. 79 by much thicker volcanic mud than the lava layer that buried Pompeii. This mud acted as an excellent preservative until 1709 when Prince Elbeuf began "mining" the town for all the treasures he could carry away. In spite of the harm caused by this destructive looting, subsequent excavations have revealed a remarkably well preserved town, whose buildings are frequently of a higher quality than those found in Pompeii.

Casa dei Cervi (House of the Stags) ★, the finest house in Herculaneum, was named for the sculpture found inside it. Important private homes to seek out are the **House of the Bicentenary (Casa del Bicentenario)** ★; the **House of the Wooden Cabinet (Casa a Graticcio)** ★★; the **House of the Wooden Partition (Casa del Tramezzo di Legno)** ★; and the **House of Poseidon (Casa di Poseidon);** as well as the **Amphitheater (Anfiteatro),** containing the best-known mosaic discovered in the ruins.

In addition to the private homes and villas, Herculaneum contains some fascinating public buildings, including the large **Municipal Baths (*terme*)** ★★★ and the more lavish **Suburban Baths (Terme Suburbane) ★**, built near the elegant villas at the outskirts of the city.

From April to October, the ruins are open daily 8:30am to 7:30pm (last admission at 6pm). Off-season hours are daily 8:30am to 5pm (last admission at 3:30pm). Admission is 11€. To reach the archaeological zone, take the regular train service from Naples on the Circumvesuviana Railway, a 20-minute ride that leaves about every half-hour from Corso Garibaldi 387, just south of the main train station (you can also catch Circumvesuviana trains underneath the main Stazione Centrale itself; follow the signs). This train will get you to Vesuvius (same stop), Pompeii, and Sorrento. *Note:* A cumulative ticket for Herculaneum and Pompeii costs 20€, which is a good buy. You can purchase it at the Circumvesuviana Railway Station at Piazza Garibaldi in Naples.

FLORENCE & TUSCANY

On the banks of the Arno, Florence had been a Roman stronghold since the 1st century B.C., but it was not until after A.D. 1200 that it began to come into its own as a commercial and cultural center. During the 13th century, the merchants and tradesmen organized the guilds, which were to control the economy and government of Florence for nearly 150 years. These guilds supervised the construction of several important buildings of the city and, with their newfound wealth, commissioned works of art that were to adorn the churches and palaces.

This revival of interest in art and architecture brought about the Italian Renaissance, an amazing outburst of activity between the 14th and 16th centuries that completely changed the face of the Tuscan town. During its heyday under the benevolent eye (and purse) of the Medicis, the city was lavishly decorated with churches, palaces, galleries, and monuments, making it the world's greatest repository of art treasures. The list of geniuses who lived or worked here reads like a who's who in the world of art and literature: Dante (he "invented" the Italian language here), Boccaccio, Fra Angelico, Brunelleschi, Donatello, da Vinci, Raphael, Cellini, Michelangelo, Ghiberti, Giotto, and Pisano.

Smack in the middle of the country, Florence sits on one of the country's major high-speed rail lines and offers good connections to Rome, Milan, and Venice, as well as several foreign cities (Artesia de Nuit trains, for example, connect the city to Paris). It's the best spot to explore the Tuscany region by rail. Aside from its good train links, the city is a fabulous destination for rail travelers because of its compact nature— nearly everything, from the city's attractions to its hotels, is within walking distance of the city's train station.

Station Information
GETTING FROM THE AIRPORT TO THE TRAIN STATION
If you fly into the Tuscany region (usually through a connection from another Italian city), you can take an express train into the city from **Galileo Galilei Airport** at Pisa (ⓒ **050/849111;** www.pisa-airport.com), 58 miles (93km) west of Florence. It costs 5.70€ one-way into Florence.

There's also a small domestic airport, **Amerigo Vespucci,** on Via del Termine, near A-11 (ⓒ **055/3061300;** www.aeroporto.firenze.it), 3½ miles (5.6km) northwest of Florence, a 15-minute drive. From the airport, you can reach Florence by the ATAF shuttle bus ("Vola in Bus"), which stops at the main Santa Maria Novella rail terminal. The fare is 5€.

Florence

ACCOMMODATIONS ■
Grand Hotel Cavour **23**
Hotel Albion **8**
Hotel Bellettini **3**
Hotel Monna Lisa **26**
Hotel Tornabuoni Beacci **7**
Hotel Torre Guelfa **11**
Hotel Vasari **1**
Relais Uffizi **15**

DINING ◆
Buca dell'Orafo **14**
Cantinetta Antinori **6**
Il Pennello Ristorante **20**
La Carabuccia **9**
La Cucina Garga **10**
Paoli **19**
Ristorante Don Chisciotte **1**
Ristorante Sabatini **4**
Trattoria Le Mossacce **24**
Vecchia Firenze **22**

ATTRACTIONS ●
Basilica di San Lorenzo **30**
Basilica di Santa Maria
  Novella **5**
Battistero San Giovanni **29**
Cappelle dei Medici **2**
Galleria degli Uffizi **16**
Galleria dell'Accademia **31**
Giardini di Boboli **13**
Giotto's Bell Tower
  (Campanile di Giotto) **25**
Il Duomo (Cattedrale di
  Santa Maria del Fiore) **28**
Museo dell'Opera
  del Duomo **27**
Museo di San Marco **32**
Museo Nazionale
  del Bargello **21**
Palazzo Pitti **12**
Palazzo Vecchio **17**
Piazza della Signoria **18**

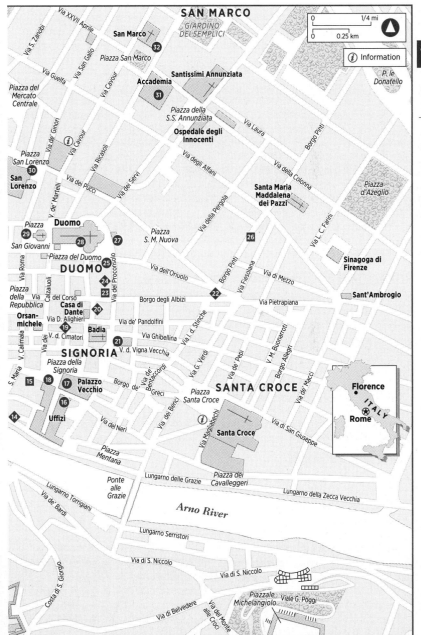

SAN MARCO

GIARDINO
DEI SEMPLICI

Via XXVII Aprile

Via S. Zanobi

San Marco

Piazza San Marco

Via San Gallo

Via Guelfa

Via Cavour

Santissimi Annunziata

Accademia

Piazza del
Mercato
Centrale

Piazza della
S.S. Annunziata

Via Laura

Borgo Pinti

P. le
Donatello

Ospedale degli
Innocenti

Piazza del
Mercato
Centrale

Via de' Ginori

Via Cavour

Via Ricasoli

Via dei Pucci

Via dei Servi

Via degli Alfani

Via della Colonna

Santa Maria
Maddalena
dei Pazzi

Piazza
d'Azeglio

Piazza
San Lorenzo

San
Lorenzo

V. de' Martelli

Via della Pergola

Via L. C. Farini

Piazza
San Giovanni

Duomo

Piazza
S. M. Nuova

Piazza del Duomo

Via dell'Oriuolo

Borgo Pinti

Via Fiesolana

Via di Mezzo

Sinagoga di
Firenze

DUOMO

Via Proconsolo

Via Roma

Calzaiuoli

Piazza
della
Repubblica

del Corso

Borgo degli Albizi

Via Pietrapiana

Sant'Ambrogio

Casa di
Dante

Via D. Alighieri

Via de' Pandolfini

Orsan-
michele

V. dei

V. de' Cimatori

Badia

Via Ghibellina

V. d. Vigna Vecchia

SIGNORIA

Piazza della
Signoria

Palazzo
Vecchio

Borgo de'

Via de'
Bentaccordi

Greci

Via G. Verdi

Via d. Stinche

Via de' Pepi

V. M. Buonarroti

Borgo Allegri

SANTA CROCE

Via de' Macci

Florence

ITALY

Rome

S. Maria

V. Calimala

Uffizi

Via del Neri

Via dei Benci

Piazza
Santa Croce

Via Magliabechi

Santa Croce

Via di San Giuseppe

Piazza
Mentana

Ponte
alle
Grazie

Lungarno delle Grazie

Piazza dei
Cavalleggeri

Lungarno della Zecca Vecchia

Via de Torrigiani

Via de Bardi

Arno River

Lungarno Serristori

Costa di S. Giorgio

Via di S. Niccolo

Via di S. Niccolo

Via di Belvedere

Via del Monte
alle Croci

Piazzale
Michelangiolo

Viale G. Poggi

(i) Information

INSIDE THE STATION

If you're coming north by train from Rome, count on a trip time of 1 to 2 hours, depending on your connections. In Florence, **Santa Maria Novella rail station,** Piazza della Stazione, adjoins Piazza Santa Maria Novella. For railway information, call ✆ **892021.** Some trains into Florence stop at the **Stazione Campo di Marte,** on the eastern side of Florence. A 24-hour bus service (no. 12) runs between the two rail terminals and costs 1.20€.

Santa Maria Novella station has all the usual amenities. A train reservation office on-site is open daily from 6am to 11pm, and a money exchange center (Mon–Sat 8:45am–7:20pm) is right inside the main station hall. A luggage storage facility is located at track #16 and charges 4€ per bag for the first 5 hours, .60€ per bag for the next 6 hours, and .20€ per bag for the remaining hours; it's open daily 6am to midnight. A 24-hour pharmacy, **Farmacia Comunale** (✆ **055/216761**), lies just outside the station opening onto Piazza della Stazione on the ground floor.

A small **Ufficio Informazioni Turistiche** (✆ **055/212245**) at the station is located directly across the square from the main exit. It dispenses free maps and a listing of the hours for city attractions but doesn't make hotel reservations. It's open Monday to Saturday 8:30am to 7pm and Sunday 8:30am to 2pm.

For hotel reservations, visit **Imprese Alberghiere** (✆ **055/2381885**), in the train station, open from 8am to 7:30pm daily. There is also a travel agency called **365** (✆ **055/284201**), located on the ground floor, open daily from 8am to 11pm.

Information Elsewhere in the City

The main tourist office is the **Azienda Promozione Turistica** at Via Manzoni 16 (✆ **055/23320;** www.firenzeturismo.it), near the Uffizi galleries; it's open Monday to Friday 9am to 1pm. There is another branch at Via Cavour 1R (✆ **055/290832**), open Monday to Saturday 8:30am to 6:30pm and Sunday 8:30am to 1:30pm. There are also information offices maintained by the **Comune di Firenze.** One is just south of Piazza Santa Croce, at Borgo Santa Croce 29R (✆ **055/2340444**), open March to October Monday to Saturday 9am to 7pm and Sunday 9am to 2pm. From November to February, it's open Monday to Saturday 9am to 5pm and Sunday 9am to 2pm.

Two useful websites with information about Florence include **www.mega.it** and **http://english.firenze.net.**

Getting Around

Florence is a city designed for walking, with all the major sights in a compact area. The only problem is that the sidewalks are almost unbearably crowded in summer.

If you plan to use **public buses,** you must buy your ticket before boarding, but for 1.20€ you can ride on any public bus for a total of 90 minutes. A 24-hour ticket costs 5€. You can buy bus tickets at *tabacchi* and newsstands. Once on board, you must validate your ticket in the box near the rear door, or you stand to be fined 40€—no excuses accepted. The local **bus station** (which serves as the terminal for ATAF city buses) is at Piazza della Stazione (✆ **055/56501**), behind the train station.

Bus routes are posted at bus stops, but the numbers of routes can change overnight because of sudden repair work going on at one of the ancient streets—perhaps a water main broke overnight and caused flooding. We recently found that a bus route map printed only 1 week beforehand was already outdated. Therefore, if you're dependent on bus transport, you'll need to inquire that day for the exact number of the vehicle you want to board.

You can find **taxis** at stands at nearly all the major squares. Rates are a bit expensive: The charge is .90€ per kilometer (½ mile), with a 3.30€ minimum, 6.60€ between 10pm and 6am. If you need a **radio taxi,** call ✆ **055/4390** or 055/4798.

Where to Stay

Grand Hotel Cavour ★ Opposite the Bargello Museum, this hotel was converted from a private mansion and has retained much of the original pristine beauty, such as frescoed and coved ceilings. The hotel is known for its atmospherically decorated wine bar and restaurant, and for its roof terrace, "Michelangelo," which offers a panoramic sweep over the Duomo, Palazzo Vecchio, and more. The rooms are traditional in styling and comfortable, although a bit small. Regrettably, this hotel lies in a particularly noisy part of town, and even the soundproofed windows can't quite block out the sounds.

Via del Proconsolo 3, 50122 Firenze. ✆ **055/266271.** Fax 055/218955. www.albergocavour.it. 105 units. 250€–400€ double; 450€ triple. Rates include buffet breakfast. AE, DC, MC, V. Bus: 14, 23, or 71. **Amenities:** Restaurant; rooms for those w/limited mobility, smoke-free rooms.

Hotel Albion ★★ 📖 A true gem. Housed in a lovely 19th-century English neo-classical *palazzo,* the family-owned Hotel Albion is the sort of place you'll come back to again and again. The rooms, some of which have balconies, are charmingly simple and spotless, and the hallways, reception area, and breakfast room are decorated with the family's eclectic art collection. The location, a short walk from the train station at Santa Maria Novella, the Duomo, and other major attractions, is ideal. But the big draw here is the service. Owner Massimo and his daughter Sara will happily reserve museum tickets for you long before you arrive and provide outstanding restaurant advice (and take care of the reservations).

Via il Prato 22R, 50123 Firenze. ✆ **055/214171.** www.hotelalbion.it. 85€–166€ double. Rates include continental breakfast. AE, MC, V.

Hotel Bellettini 🍃 Midway between the Duomo (cathedral) and the rail station, this 32-room hotel was carved out of a 14th-century palace with a history of innkeeping going back 3 centuries. Run by two Tuscan-born sisters, it's one of the more traditional choices in the center of Florence, and filled with atmospheric trappings such as carved wood, wrought-iron beds, stained-glass windows, antiques, and terra-cotta tiles. The small to midsize bedrooms are furnished minimally but comfortably. Many have sweeping views of Florence. Only two rooms per floor share the corridor bathrooms, so you'll rarely have to wait in line.

Via De' Conti 7, 50123 Firenze. ✆ **055/213561.** Fax 055/283551. www.hotelbellettini.com. 32 units, 28 with bathroom (shower only). 40€–72€ double without bathroom; 45€–65€ double with bathroom. Rates include buffet breakfast. AE, DC, MC, V. Bus: 1, 9, 14, 17, 23, 36, or 37. **Amenities:** Smoke-free rooms.

Hotel Monna Lisa ★ This privately owned Renaissance palazzo has been well preserved and tastefully furnished, and it's exceptionally located—just 4 blocks east of the Duomo. Most of the great old rooms (some are spacious, others cramped) overlook either an inner patio or a modest rear garden. Each room is handsomely furnished with antiques and artwork; many have their original painted wooden ceilings. Some of the tiled bathrooms have Jacuzzi tubs.

Borgo Pinti 27, 50121 Firenze. ✆ **055/2479751.** Fax 055/2479755. www.monnalisa.it. 45 units. 140€–180€ double; 199€–299€ suite. Rates include buffet breakfast. AE, DC, MC, V. Bus: A, 6, 31, or 32. **Amenities:** Bar; rooms for those w/limited mobility; smoke-free rooms.

Hotel Tornabuoni Beacci ★   Near the Arno and Piazza S. Trinità, on the principal shopping street, this near-century-old pensione occupies the top three floors of a 16th-century *palazzo*. The hotel still bears an air of old-fashioned gentility and a lot of atmosphere. The rooms are moderately well furnished with period pieces in an old Florentine style. Rooms at the top are smaller but have better views. The roof terrace for breakfast or drinks is a delight, opening onto scenic vistas of the skyline of Florence. Dinner is served here in the summer, except in August, when it is closed.

Via Tornabuoni 3, 50123 Firenze. ℂ **055/212645.** Fax 055/283594. www.tornabuonihotels.com. 28 units. 220€–280€ double; 300€–350€ suite. Rates include buffet breakfast. AE, DC, MC, V. Bus: C1, C2, 6, 11, or 36. **Amenities:** Restaurant; bar.

Hotel Torre Guelfa ★★   Only 164 feet (49m) from the Ponte Vecchio, this hotel is crowned with a 13th-century tower offering panoramic views of the city. The structure dates from 1280, although there have been many alterations over the years. Although you're just two steps from the Ponte Vecchio (and equidistant from the Duomo), you'll want to put sightseeing on hold and linger in your comfy canopied iron bed; your room is made even more inviting by pastel-washed walls and paisley carpeting. (For a view similar to the medieval tower's, ask for room no. 15, with its huge private terrace.)

Borgo SS. Apostoli 8 (btw. Via dei Tornabuoni and Via Per Santa Maria), 50123 Firenze. ℂ **055/2396338.** Fax 055/2398577. www.hoteltorreguelfa.com. 22 units. 110€–250€ double; 160€–260€ suite. Rates include buffet breakfast. AE, MC, V. Bus: C1, C2, 6, 11, 36, or 37. **Amenities:** Bar; smoke-free rooms.

Hotel Vasari ★ 🍴   Before it was completely revamped into an excellent hotel in 1993, this inn enjoyed a long history, having served as a monastery in the 16th century and as the town house of 19th-century French poet Alfonse de Lamartine. Much of the old charm remains, including ceiling frescoes and an original stone fireplace in the breakfast room. Bedrooms are small to midsize and are comfortably but minimally furnished. The tiled bathrooms are small but immaculate. The central location, just 1,000 feet (300m) from the Duomo, is a plus.

Via B. Cennini 9-11, 50123 Firenze. ℂ **055/212753.** Fax 055/294246. www.hotelvasari.com. 27 units (shower only). 155€ double; 210€ triple. Rates include buffet breakfast. AE, DC, MC, V. Bus: 4, 7, 10, 13, 14, 23, or 71. **Amenities:** Bar; rooms for those w/limited mobility.

Relais Uffizi ★ 🎎   Next door to the Uffizi, this appropriately named inn is a real find and an unbeatable value. The restored 15th-century villa is imbued with homelike comfort and old-fashioned style, with antiques used liberally throughout the hotel. Attractively furnished midsize to spacious bedrooms open onto the landmark Piazza della Signoria, and the entrance is through the charming little walking lane, Chiasso del Buco. Bedrooms all contain marble bathrooms, and the most preferred rooms contain canopied beds. Considering its location, it's amazing that the Relais Uffizi isn't better known.

Chiasso del Buco 16, 50122 Firenze. ℂ **055/2676239.** Fax 055/2657909. www.relaisuffizi.it. 10 units. 100€–220€ double; 180€–260€ suite. Rates include buffet breakfast. AE, DC, MC, V. Parking 30€. Bus: C1, C2, 23, or 71. **Amenities:** Bar; smoke-free rooms.

Top Attractions & Special Moments

To truly see the city at less than a breakneck pace, you need at least 3 days in Florence. If you have less time than that, make sure to see the **Uffizi** and the **Galleria dell'Accademia.** Don't forget to have a meal in one of the city's excellent Tuscan restaurants, and try to make time to view the city (especially the Ponte Vecchio) at sunset—it's a truly memorable experience.

One other noteworthy spot worth your attention is the **Piazza della Signoria** ★★. As the "front yard" of Florence's city hall, Palazzo Vecchio, Piazza della Signoria was the center of the city's political life from around A.D. 1300. Today the square is a favorite attraction, not only because of its historical significance, but for its wealth of artistic sights as well. On the piazza itself is the **Fountain of Neptune** ★, a massively detailed work by Ammannati. Created in the 16th century, it portrays the sea god surrounded by his following of water creatures and woodland nymphs. Also on the plaza is a copy of Michelangelo's *David,* substituted for the original after it was removed to the safety of the Academy Gallery in 1873. Opening onto the square is the **Loggia dei Lanzi** ★★, a spacious open hallway dating from the 14th century. It is lined with several important sculptures, all of them outshined by Cellini's brilliant masterpiece of *Perseus* ★★★ holding the head of Medusa.

Baptistery (Battistero San Giovanni) ★★★   Facing the Duomo, the octagonal Baptistery is a splendid example of Romanesque architecture as only the Florentines could interpret it. Dating from the 5th century, it was virtually rebuilt in the 11th and 12th centuries with particularly Florentine innovations. The facade is covered with green and white marble, and set into three sides are magnificent bronze doors decorated with gilded bas-reliefs. The greatest treasures here are the reproductions of the **East and North Doors** ★★★, artistically created by Lorenzo Ghiberti under a commission awarded him by the cloth guild of Florence. They took Ghiberti a total of 52 years to complete. After the second door was unveiled in 1452, Michelangelo is said to have exclaimed, "These doors are fit to stand at the gates of Paradise," and so they've been nicknamed the *Gates of Paradise* ever since.

Piazza San Giovanni. ⓒ **055/2302885.** www.operaduomo.firenze.it. Admission 4€. Mon–Sat noon–7pm; Sun 8:30am–2pm. Last admission 30 min. before closing. Bus: C1 or C2.

Bargello Museum (Museo Nazionale del Bargello) ★★   Begun in 1254, this medieval palace was once a powerful military fortress. Today, as a museum, it exhibits the arms and armor used during the more violent periods of its history, along with a fine collection of decorative art. But the real attraction at the Bargello is the splendid array of medieval and Renaissance sculpture. There's another *David* by Michelangelo here, though not nearly as virile as the famous one in the Accademia. Nor does it stand up to the most famous *David* ★★ here—Donatello's free-standing bronze creation, nude (except for boots and bonnet) atop the severed head of Goliath. Also by Donatello is his heroic and extremely lifelike interpretation of *St. George* ★. Michelangelo is represented in several works, including his *Bacchus,* a bust of *Brutus,* and a bas-relief of *Madonna and Child with John the Baptist.*

Via del Proconsolo 4. ⓒ **055/2388606.** www.firenzemusei.it. Admission 4€. Daily 8:15am–1:50pm. Closed 2nd and 4th Mon and 1st, 3rd, and 5th Sun of each month; Jan 1; May 1; and Christmas. Bus: C1, C2, 14, or 23.

Basilica di San Lorenzo ★★   This is Brunelleschi's 1426 Renaissance church. Shaped like a Latin cross, the church was the favorite of the Medicis (the adjoining New Sacristy contains the tombs of the clan), so a great deal of money and artistic effort went into decorating it. The **Old Sacristy (Vecchia Sacrestia),** at the left of the nave, was partially decorated by Donatello, including some terra-cotta reliefs. The adjoining **Medici Laurentian Library (Biblioteca Medicea Laurenziana;** ⓒ **055/210760)** ★★ was designed by Michelangelo to contain the huge Medici collection of manuscripts. It boasts an unusual staircase and an intricately carved and paneled reading room.

Piazza San Lorenzo. ℂ **055/210760.** Free admission. Mon, Wed, and Fri 8am–5:30pm. Bus: 1, 6, 7, 11, 17, 33, 67, or 68.

Basilica di Santa Maria Novella ★★

Right near the rail station, on the Piazza Santa Maria Novella, this landmark is a large Dominican edifice built between 1278 and 1350. Its geometric facade, made of inlaid marble, was added in the 15th century by Alberti. The church is especially interesting for its frescoes by Masaccio, Ghirlandaio, Orcagna, and Filippo Lippi. The adjoining cloisters are also worth a visit, especially the Spanish Chapel with frescoes by Andrea di Bonaiuto and his assistants.

Piazza Santa Maria Novella. ℂ **055/282187.** Church free; Spanish Chapel and cloisters 2.75€. Church Mon–Thurs 9:30am–5pm. Spanish Chapel and cloisters Sat and Mon–Thurs 9am–5pm. Bus: C1, C2, 6, 9, 11, 36, 37, or 68.

Duomo Museum (Museo dell'Opera del Duomo) ★★

Across the street from the Duomo, but facing the apse of Santa Maria del Fiore, is the museum beloved by connoisseurs of Renaissance sculptural works. It shelters the sculpture removed from the campanile and the Duomo. A major reason for visiting the museum is to see the world-famous **marble choirs ★★**—*cantorie*—of **Donatello** and **Luca della Robbia** (both works face each other and are housed in the first room you enter after climbing the stairs). One of Donatello's most celebrated works, *Magdalene* ★★, is in the room with the *cantorie*. A major attraction is an **unfinished** *Pietà* ★★, **by Michelangelo,** in the middle of the stairs. It was carved between 1548 and 1555, when the artist was in his 70s. The premier attraction, however, is the **restored panels of Ghiberti's** *Gates of Paradise* ★★★, which were removed from the baptistery. In gilded bronze, each is a masterpiece of Renaissance sculpture, perhaps the finest low-relief perspective in all Italian art.

Piazza del Duomo 9. ℂ **055/2302885.** www.operaduomo.firenze.it. Admission 6€. Mon–Sat 9am–7:30pm; Sun 9am–1:30pm. Last admission 40 min. before closing. Closed Jan 1, Easter, Sept 8, and Christmas. Bus: C1 or C2.

Galleria degli Uffizi ★★★

Few art museums in the world can compare with the Uffizi, home to Italy's finest collection of art. The 16th-century building stretches from the Palazzo Vecchio to the Arno. In spite of its size and multitudinous works of

---

How to Avoid Those Endless Lines

Select Italy offers the possibility to reserve your tickets for the Uffizi, Boboli Gardens, Galleria dell'Accademia, and many other attractions in Florence (plus Rome and Venice). The cost varies from 13€ to 33€, depending on the museum, and several combination passes are available. Contact **Select Italy** at ℂ **800/877-1755,** or buy online at **www.selectitaly.com.**

If you're already in Florence and don't want to waste half a day waiting to enter the Galleria degli Uffizi, Galleria dell'Accademia, Boboli Gardens,

Pitti Palace, and many others, call **Firenze Musei** (ℂ **055/2654321;** www.firenzemusei.it). The service operates Monday to Friday from 8:30am to 6:30pm, and Saturday to 12:30pm. Requests must be made a minimum of 5 days in advance; you pick up the tickets at the museum booth on the day your visit has been approved. There's a service charge of 3€, plus, of course, the regular price of the museum admission. If your hotel has a concierge, don't be shy about asking what he can do to get you tickets.

Miraculously spared by the Nazis in their bitter retreat from the Allied advance in 1944, the **Ponte Vecchio (Old Bridge)** ★★ is the last remaining medieval *ponte* that once spanned the Arno (the Germans blew up the rest). The existence of the Ponte Vecchio was again threatened in the flood of 1966—in fact, the waters of the Arno swept over it, washing away a fortune in jewelry from the famous goldsmiths' shops that flank the bridge.

Today the Ponte Vecchio is back in business, closed to traffic except the *pedoni,* or foot passenger type. The little shops continue to sell everything from the most expensive of Florentine gold to something simple—say, a Lucrezia Borgia poison ring.

art (about 2,500 paintings alone, plus miniatures, statues, and more than 100,000 drawings and prints), the museum is easily navigated because the galleries are grouped by periods and schools. But don't expect to see everything in 1 day. Laid out progressively, the galleries begin with Room 1 (classical sculptures) and extend through Room 42 (Italian and French paintings of the 18th c.). The largest concentration of paintings is on Italian works of the 15th and 16th centuries (more than 400 of these alone). Room 10 is the most popular in the entire gallery. Here you'll find the works of Botticelli, including his ***Birth of Venus*** ★★★ and ***Allegory of Spring,*** or ***Primavera*** ★★, two of the most famous paintings in the world.

In room 15, you'll come across one of Leonardo da Vinci's unfinished paintings, the brilliant ***Adoration of the Magi*** ★★. Also here hangs Leonardo's *Annunciation,* reflecting the early years of his genius. Located in room 25 is Michelangelo's magnificent ***Holy Family*** ★★ (1506–08). This is one of the few panel paintings by the great artist, still glowing with color. Michelangelo also designed the elaborate frame.

Piazzale degli Uffizi 6. ℰ **055/2388651.** www.uffizi.firenze.it. Admission 6.50€. Tues–Sun 8:15am–7pm (last entrance 45 min. before closing). Advance booking necessary. Bus: C1, C2, 14, or 23.

Galleria dell'Accademia ★★ This museum is visited mainly for one exhibit: Michelangelo's awesome statue of ***David*** ★★★. For years the 17-foot (5.1m) statue weathered the elements on the Piazza della Signoria, but it was finally moved to the Accademia in 1873 and placed beneath the rotunda of a room built exclusively for its display. When he began work, Michelangelo was just 29. In the connecting picture gallery is a collection of Tuscan masters, such as Botticelli, and Umbrian works by Perugino (teacher of Raphael).

Via Ricasoli 60. ℰ **055/2388612.** www.firenzemusei.it. Admission 6.50€. Tues–Sun 8:15am–7pm. Bus: C1, C2, D, or 12.

Giotto's Bell Tower (Campanile di Giotto) ★★ Although better known for his great skill in fresco painting, Giotto left to posterity the most beautiful campanile (bell tower) in Europe, rhythmic in line and form. The 274-foot (82m) tower, a "Tuscanized" Gothic, with bands of colored marble, can be scaled for a truly memorable **panoramic view** ★★★ of the sienna-colored city and the blue-green Tuscan hills in the distance.

Piazza del Duomo. ℰ **055/2302885.** www.operaduomo.firenze.it. Admission 6€. Daily 8:30am–7:30pm. Last admission 40 min. before closing. Closed Jan 1, Easter, Sept 8, and Christmas. Bus: C1 or C2.

Il Duomo (Cattedrale di Santa Maria del Fiore) ★★★   The cathedral of Florence, called simply the *Duomo,* is the crowning glory of Florence. But don't rush inside too quickly, as the view of the exterior, with its geometrically patterned bands of white, pink, and green marble, is, along with **Brunelleschi's dome** ★★★, the best feature. One of the world's largest churches, the Duomo represents the flowering of the "Florentine Gothic" style. Begun in 1296, it was finally consecrated in 1436, yet finishing touches on the facade were applied as late as the 19th century. Inside, the overall effect is bleak, except when you stand under the cupola, frescoed in part by Vasari. Some of the stained-glass windows in the dome were based on designs by Donatello (Brunelleschi's friend) and Ghiberti (Brunelleschi's rival). The overall effect of the cathedral's famous dome atop its octagonal drum is one of the most striking sights of the city—and its most famous landmark. If you resist scaling Giotto's bell tower, you may want to climb Brunelleschi's ribbed dome. The view is well worth the trek.

Piazza del Duomo. ⓒ **055/2302885.** www.operaduomo.firenze.it. Cathedral free; excavations 3€; cupola 8€. Duomo Mon–Wed and Fri 10am–5pm; Thurs 10am–3:30pm; Sat 10am–4:45pm (1st Sat of each month 10am–3:30pm); Sun 1:30–4:45pm. Cupola Mon–Fri 8:30am–7pm; Sat 8:30am–5:30pm. Bus: C1 or C2.

Medici Chapels (Cappelle Medicee) ★★   Michelangelo left his mark on Florence in many places, but nowhere can you feel so completely surrounded by his works as in the Medici Chapels, adjoining the Basilica di San Lorenzo (see above). Working from 1521 to 1534, Michelangelo created the Medici tomb in a style that foreshadowed the baroque. Lorenzo the Magnificent was buried in the **New Sacristy** ★★★ near Michelangelo's uncompleted *Madonna and Child* group. Ironically, the finest groups of sculpture were reserved for two of the lesser Medicis, who are represented as armored, idealized princes. The other two figures on Lorenzo's tomb are most often called *Dawn* (represented as woman) and *Dusk* (as man). The best-known figures are *Night* ★★★ (chiseled as a woman in troubled sleep) and *Day* ★★★ (a man of strength awakening to a foreboding world) at the feet of Giuliano, the duke of Nemours.

Piazza Madonna degli Aldobrandini 6. ⓒ **055/2388602.** www.polomuseale.firenze.it. Admission 6€. Daily 8:15am–1:50pm. Closed 2nd and 4th Sun, and 1st, 3rd, and 5th Mon of each month. Bus: 1, 6, 7, 11, 17, 33, 67, or 68.

Palazzo Pitti and the Giardini di Boboli (Boboli Gardens) ★★   Just 5 minutes from the Ponte Vecchio, the Pitti, built in the mid–15th century (Brunelleschi was the original architect), was once the residence of the powerful Medici family. Today it contains several museums, the most important of which is the **Galleria Palatina** ★★, a repository of old masters. Devoted mainly to Renaissance works, the Palatine is especially rich in Raphaels, including his world-famous *Madonna of the Chair.* Other works by Titian, Botticelli, Fra Bartolomeo, Filippo Lippi, Tintoretto, Rubens, Van Dyck, and Velázquez round out the collection.

The **Royal Apartments (Appartamenti Reali)** ★ boast lavish reminders of the time when the Pitti was the home of the kings of Savoy. These apartments, in all their baroque sumptuousness, including a flamboyant decor and works of art by del Sarto and Caravaggio, can be viewed only on a guided tour, usually Tuesday and Saturday (also on an occasional Thurs) 9 to 11am and 3 to 5pm. Tours leave every hour. Reservations are needed, so call ⓒ **051/2388614.**

A Garden Stroll

Behind the Pitti Palace are the extensive **Boboli Gardens** ★, Piazza de'Pitti 1 (☎ **055/2388786**), designed and executed by Triboli, a landscape artist (on canvas and in real life), in the 16th century. Studded with fountains and statues, it provides an ideal setting for a relaxing break between museum visits. The gardens are also the setting for Fort Belvedere, an imposing structure that dominates the hillside and offers a spectacular view of Florence. For opening times, see above.

Other museums are the **Museo degli Argenti (Museum of Silver)** ★ (☎ **055/2388786**), 16 rooms devoted to displays of the "loot" acquired by the Medici dukes; and the **Galleria d'Arte Moderna** (☎ **055/2388616**).

Piazza Pitti, across the Arno. ☎ **055/2388614.** www.firenzemusei.it. Palatina and Modern Art Gallery 8.50€; 6€ for both Argenti and Boboli Gardens. Galleria Palatina, Appartamenti Reali, and Modern Art Gallery Tues–Sun 8:15am–6:45pm. Boboli Gardens and Museo degli Argenti June–Aug daily 8:30am–7:45pm; Apr–May and Sept–Oct daily 8:30am–6:30pm; Nov–Feb daily 8:15am–4:30pm. Ticket office closes 1 hr. before the gardens. Bus: C1, C2, 11, 36, 37, or 68.

St. Mark's Museum (Museo di San Marco) ★★   This state museum is a handsome Renaissance palace whose cell walls are decorated with magnificent 15th-century **frescoes** ★★★ by the mystical Fra Angelico. In the days of Cosimo dei Medici, San Marco was built as a Dominican convent. It originally contained bleak, bare cells, which Angelico and his students then brightened considerably. One of his better-known paintings here is *The Last Judgment* ★★, contrasting the beautiful angels and saints on the left with the demons and tortured sinners of hell on the right. Among his other works are a masterful *Annunciation* ★★★ and *Crucifixion and Saints,* painted in 1442.

Piazza San Marco 1. ☎ **055/2388608.** www.firenzemusei.it. Admission 4€. Mon–Fri 8:30am–1:50pm; Sat 8:15am–6:50pm; Sun 8:15am–7pm. Ticket office closes 30 min. before the museum. Closed 2nd and 4th Mon of the month; 1st, 3rd, and 5th Sun of the month; Jan 1, May 1, and Christmas. Bus: 7, 10, 11, 17, or 33.

Where to Dine

Buca dell'Orafo ★★★ 🍴 FLORENTINE   This authentic neighborhood restaurant's cuisine is firmly rooted in Tuscan traditions and inspired by whatever happens to be in season. Accessible via an alley beneath a vaulted arcade adjacent to Piazza del Pesce, the place is usually stuffed with regulars, who appreciate that the chef has made almost no concessions to international palates. Pastas are homemade, a specialty being *maltagliati* with a tomato-and-beef sauce and a serving of pecorino cheese.

Via dei Girolami 28R. ☎ **055/213619.** Main courses 8€–23€. MC, V. Tues–Sat 12:30–2:30pm and 7:30–10:30pm. Closed Aug and 2 weeks in Dec. Bus: C1 or C2.

Cantinetta Antinori ★ 🍴 FLORENTINE/TUSCAN   The menu at one of Florence's most highly rated wine bars changes with the seasons, and is it ever good. You can visit this 15th-century palazzo for complete meals or else snacks. Regardless of what you order, your food is most often accompanied by one of the best-stocked cellars in town from a company—the most distinguished in Tuscany, Umbria, and

Piedmont—that has been hawking wines for 6 centuries. The food is standard but satisfying, and many of the ingredients come directly from the Antinori farms.

Piazza Antinori 3. ⓒ **055/292234.** www.cantinetta-antinori.com. Reservations recommended. Main courses 12€–27€. AE, DC, MC, V. Mon–Fri 12:30–2:30pm and 7–10:30pm. Closed Aug and Dec 24–25. Bus: 6, 11, 14, 36, 37, or 68.

Il Pennello Ristorante ♦ FLORENTINE/ITALIAN   This informal trattoria—also called Casa di Dante—offers many Florentine specialties on its a la carte menu and is known for its wide selection of antipasti; you can make a meal out of these delectable hors d'oeuvres. The ravioli is homemade, and one pasta specialty (loved by locals) is *spaghetti carrettiera,* with tomatoes and pepperoni. Sometimes it's best to order the daily specials, which are made with food bought fresh that day at the market. Da Pennello is on a narrow street near Dante's house, about a 5-minute walk from the Duomo. Called "The Painter" in English, its walls are hung with art.

Via Dante Alighieri 4R. ⓒ **055/294848.** Fax 055/21455. www.ristoranteilpennello.it. Main courses 7€–18€; fixed-price menus from 25€. AE, DC, MC, V. Tues–Sat noon–3pm and 7–10pm and Sun noon–3pm. Closed 1st 3 weeks in Aug and Dec 24–Jan 2. Bus: 14, 22, or 23.

La Cucina del Garga ★★ TUSCAN/FLORENTINE   Some of the most creative cuisine in Florence is served at this restaurant, set midway between the Ponte Vecchio and Santa Maria Novella. This local favorite's postage-size kitchen turns out dishes based on old Tuscan recipes that have been given a new twist. The walls are from the days of the Renaissance, and they are decorated with contemporary paintings. One dish has earned a lot of publicity: *tagliolini magnifico,* made with angel-hair pasta, orange and lemon rind, mint-flavored cream, and Parmigiano-Reggiano. One of the most delectable pastas is spaghetti cooked with fresh tomatoes, shrimp, oranges, and chili peppers.

Via del Moro 48R. ⓒ **055/2398898.** www.garga.it. Reservations required. Main courses 13€–30€. AE, MC, V. Tues–Sun 7:30–11pm. Bus: C1, C2, 11, 36, 37, or 68.

Paoli ★★ TUSCAN/ITALIAN   Paoli, between the Duomo and Piazza della Signoria, is one of Florence's finest restaurants. It turns out a host of specialties but could be recommended almost solely for its atmospheric medieval-tavern atmosphere. All pastas are homemade, including a house specialty, green handmade gnocchi with Gorgonzola cheese. The chef does a superb chicken breast with curry and rice pilaf,

 One of the World's Greatest Views

The best overall view of the city is from the **Piazzale Michelangelo** (bus 13 from the Central Station), an elevated plaza on the south side of the river. If you can ignore the milling crowds and souvenir peddlers who flood the square, you can enjoy a **spectacular view ★★★** of old Florence, circled by the hazy hills of Tuscany. It's like looking at a Renaissance painting. We prefer the view at dusk, when the purple-fringed Tuscan hills form a frame for Giotto's bell tower, Brunelleschi's dome, and the towering hunk of stones that stick up from the Palazzo Vecchio. If you look up into the hills, you can also see the ancient town of Fiesole, with its Roman ruins and cathedral. Another copy of Michelangelo's famous statue *David* dominates Piazzale Michelangelo, giving the wide square its name. Crown your view with some of the delectable ice cream served on the square at **Gelateria Michelangelo** (ⓒ 055/2342705), open daily 7am to 2am.

or else veal piccata with lemon zest. It's worth saving room for one of the yummy desserts.

Via dei Tavolini 12R. ✆ **055/216215.** Reservations required. Main courses 8€–20€. AE, DC, MC, V. Wed-Mon noon–3pm and 7–11pm. Closed 3 weeks in Aug. Bus: 16 or 17.

Ristorante Don Chisciotte ★★ ITALIAN/SEAFOOD   One floor above street level in a Florentine *palazzo*, this soft-pink dining room is known for its creative cuisine and a changing array of fresh fish that emerges with a flourish from the kitchens. Flavors are often enhanced by an unusual assortment of fresh herbs, vegetables, and fish stocks. Some of the best items on the menu include squid filled with ricotta, Saridnian cheese, and truffles served with a cream of artichoke sauce, or *cappellacci di branzino* (a kind of ravioli filled with sea bass) served on an asparagus purée. One especially delectable dish is scampi with truffles.

Via Ridolfi 4R. ✆ **055/475430.** www.ristorantedonchisciotte.it. Reservations recommended. Main courses 15€–30€. AE, DC, MC, V. Tues-Sat 1-2:30pm; Mon-Sat 8-10:30pm. Closed Aug. Bus: 20.

Ristorante Sabatini ★★ FLORENTINE/INTERNATIONAL   Locals and visitors alike extol this restaurant's classic Tuscan cuisine, served in an antique house only 600 feet (180m) from the Duomo. Understated and traditional, it offers all the old-time favorites Florentines have grown to love, including *bistecca alla fiorentina* and classics such as boiled Valdarno chicken in a savory green sauce. The wine cellar is particularly notable here for both its Tuscan and Umbrian vintages—one habitué called it "seductive."

Via de'Panzani 9A. ✆ **055/211559.** www.ristorantesabatini.it. Reservations recommended. Main courses 15€–30€. AE, DC, MC, V. Tues-Sun 12:30-2:30pm and 7:30-11pm. Bus: C1 or C2.

Trattoria La Carabaccia ★ 🍴 FLORENTINE   Two hundred years ago, a *carabaccia* was a workaday boat. This restaurant still features the Medicis' favorite *zuppa carabaccia,* a creamy white-onion soup with croutons. You can sample such specialties as paper-thin slices of beef on a nest of radicchio and Parmesan. You might choose the soup of the day, followed by one of four or five pastas, such as green gnocchi with Parmesan zabalone and truffle slices, or *bavette* (a pasta) served with broccoli and a sea bass ragout. Two recommendable specialties include pork filets with sweet-and-sour onions, and prime sirloin with porcini mushrooms. The homemade breads are irresistible.

Via Palazzuolo 190R. ✆ **055/214782.** www.trattorialacarabaccia.com. Reservations recommended. Main courses 9€–22€. AE, DC, MC, V. Daily noon–3pm and 7–11pm. Bus: C1, C2, 11, 36, 37, or 68.

Trattoria Le Mossacce 🍴 TUSCAN/FLORENTINE   Near the Duomo, or cathedral, this small *osteria* is known for serving tasty, affordable home cooking in generous portions to hungry Florentines. Many of the delights of the Florentine menu appear here, including such classics as *ribollita* (a thick vegetable soup) and those justly celebrated slices of *bistecca* (beefsteak) *alla fiorentina*. A tradition since 1942, Le Mossacce hires waiters who prefer to tantalize you with the offerings of the day instead of presenting you with a menu—we had a great meal following their advice.

Via del Proconsolo 55R. ✆ **055/294361.** www.trattorialemossacce.it. Main courses 7€–18€. AE, DC, MC, V. Mon-Fri noon-2:30pm and 7-9:30pm. Closed Aug. Bus: 14.

Vecchia Firenze FLORENTINE/TUSCAN   Housed in a 14th-century palace with an elegant entrance, this trattoria combines atmosphere and budget meals. The place caters to those who eat here regularly and never tire of its simple but hearty offerings such as a creamy risotto with mushrooms, and large-size ravioli flavored with butter and fresh sage. With a minimum of artifice, chefs regale you with such dishes as grilled sea bass with tartare sauce, grilled sirloin steak with pepper sauce, and tenderloin of beef Rossini in a gooseliver sauce. Almost any kind of meat you select can be grilled on a barbecue.

Borgo degli Albizi 18. (✆ **055/2340361.** www.vecchiafirenze.eu. Main courses 7€–18€; pizzas 7€–11€. AE, DC, MC, V. Tues–Sun noon–3pm and 7–10pm. Bus: 14, 23, or 71.

Shopping

Florence is a city of high fashion, and it's also known for its leather goods, straw products, and magnificently crafted gold jewelry, much of the latter sold at the pint-sized shops along the Ponte Vecchio. Note, however, that it's not a city for bargains—prices are almost always appropriately up there.

Befani e Tai, Via Vacchereccia 13R (✆ **055/287825**), is one of the most unusual jewelry stores in Florence; some of its pieces date from the 19th century. The store was opened after World War II by expert goldsmiths who were childhood friends. Some of their clients even design their own jewelry for special orders.

Intrepid shoppers head for the **Mercato della Paglia** or **Mercato Nuovo** (**Straw Market** or **New Market**), 2 blocks south of Piazza della Repubblica. (It's called Il Porcellino by the Italians because of the bronze statue of a reclining wild boar, a copy of the one in the Uffizi.) Tourists pet its snout (which is well worn) for good luck. The market stands in the monumental heart of Florence, an easy stroll from the Palazzo Vecchio. It sells not only straw items, but also leather goods (not the best quality), along with typical Florentine merchandise: frames, trays, hand embroidery, table linens, and hand-sprayed and -painted boxes in traditional designs.

Even better bargains await those who make their way through the pushcarts to the stalls of the open-air **Mercato Centrale (Mercato San Lorenzo),** in and around Borgo San Lorenzo, near the rail station. If you don't mind bargaining, which is imperative, you'll find an array of merchandise such as raffia bags, Florentine leather purses, sweaters, gloves, salt and pepper shakers, straw handbags, and art reproductions.

For one-stop shopping, the best outlet is **La Rinascente,** Piazza della Repubblica 2 (✆ **055/219113;** www.rinascente.it), right in the heart of Florence. This is where frugal but taste-conscious Florentines go to shop. Their clothing for men and women features some of the big names but also talented and lesser-known Italian designers. You'll also find good buys in china, perfumes, and jewelry, along with a "made in Tuscany" department that sells everything from terra-cotta vases to the finest virgin olive oils.

Nightlife

For theatrical and concert listings, check at the tourist office.

THE PERFORMING ARTS   From late April or early May to mid-June, the city welcomes classical musicians for its **Maggio Musicale** festival of cantatas, madrigals, concertos, operas, and ballets, many of which are presented in Renaissance buildings. The main venue for the festival is the **Teatro Comunale di Firenze/ Maggio Musicale Fiorentino ★★★**, Corso Italia 16 (✆ **055/27791**), which also presents opera and ballet from September to December and a concert season from January to April. Schedule and ticket information for the festival is available from the box office at Corso Italia 16, or by phone at ✆ **055/2779350.** Tickets to theatrical productions and the festival cost 20€ to 85€. For further information, visit the theater's website, at **www.maggiofiorentino.com**.

CAFES & CLUBS   **Café Rivoire** ★, Piazza della Signoria 4R (✆ **055/214412;** www.rivoire.it), offers a classy and amusing old-world ambience with a direct view of the statues on one of our favorite squares in the world. You can sit at one of the metal tables on the flagstones outside or at one of the wooden tables in a choice of inner rooms filled with marble detailing and unusual oil renderings of the piazza outside.

The oldest and most beautiful cafe in Florence, **Gilli's,** Via Roma 1, adjacent to Piazza Repubblica 39R, Via Roma 1 (✆ **055/213896**), is a few minutes' walk from the Duomo. It was founded in 1789, when Piazza della Repubblica had a different name. You can sit at a brightly lit table near the bar or retreat to an intricately paneled pair of rooms to the side and enjoy the flattering light from the Venetian-glass chandeliers.

At **Space Electronic,** Via Palazzuolo 37 (✆ **055/293082;** www.spaceelectronic. net), the decor consists of wall-to-wall mirrors and an imitation space capsule that goes back and forth across the dance floor. If karaoke doesn't thrill you, head to the ground-floor pub, which stocks an ample supply of imported beers. On the upper level is a large dance floor with a wide choice of music and a high-energy row of laser beams. This place attracts a lot of foreign students who want to hook up with Florentine men and women on the prowl. The disco opens Tuesday to Sunday at 10pm and usually goes until 3am. The 15€ cover includes the first drink.

An Excursion to Pisa ★★

No longer the powerful port it was in the western Mediterranean in the 12th century, Pisa is still visited for its magnificent buildings, especially the Leaning Tower of Pisa, a building that is one of the most recognizable on earth. The silting up of its harbor marked Pisa's decline in 1284, and it suffered even greater devastation in the Allied bombings of 1944. Nonetheless, there is much here to celebrate at a point lying 47 miles (76km) west of Florence and easily visited on a day trip from that city.

A 6€ **combination ticket** (you can buy it at any of the included attractions) allows you to visit two of these three sights: the baptistery, the cemetery, and the Duomo Museum. For 10€, you can visit the five major attractions: the baptistery, the Duomo, the cemetery, the Duomo Museum, and the Museum of Preliminary Frescoes.

GETTING THERE   Chances are, you might land in Pisa to begin your descent on Florence. Both domestic and international flights land at Pisa's **Galileo Galilei Airport** (✆ **050/849111;** www.pisa-airport.com). From the airport, trains depart every 15 to 30 minutes, depending on the time of day, for the 5-minute ride into Pisa, costing 1.10€ each way. As an alternative, bus no. 3 leaves the airport every 20 minutes heading for Pisa, costing 1€ one-way.

Frequent trains make the 1-hour journey between Pisa and Florence; the ride costs 5.90€ one-way. Trains running along the coast link Pisa with Rome, a trip of 3 hours. Depending on the time of day and the speed of the train, one-way fares are 17€ to 53€. In Pisa, trains arrive at the **Stazione Pisa Centrale** (✆ **892021** for information in Italy), about a 30-minute walk from the Leaning Tower. Otherwise, you can take bus LAM rossa, which runs every 20 minutes, from the station to the heart of the city. A ticket costs 1€ and is valid for 60 minutes, 1.50€ if you buy it on board.

TOURIST INFORMATION The **tourist office** at Piazza Vittorio Emanuele II, next to the train station (✆ **050/42291;** www.pisaturismo.it), is open Monday to Friday 9am to 7pm and Saturday 9am to 4pm. A second branch is at Piazza Arcivescovado 8 (✆ **334/6419408**), near the Leaning Tower, open daily 9:30am to 7:30pm.

TOP ATTRACTIONS & SPECIAL MOMENTS

Seemingly every visitor heads first for the **Leaning Tower of Pisa (Campanile)** ★★★, Piazza del Duomo 17 (✆ **050/3872210;** www.opapisa.it). Construction began on the eight-story campanile in 1174 by Bonanno, and there has been a persistent legend that the architect deliberately intended that the bell tower lean (that claim is undocumented). Another legend is that Galileo let objects of different weights fall from the tower, timing their descent to prove his theories of bodies in motion. The real story is that the tower began to tilt sometime after the completion of the first three stories; only then did its builders discover that the foundation wasn't rock solid, but water-soaked clay. If it stood up straight, the tower would measure about 180 feet (54m). Admission is 15€; hours November to February daily 10am to 5pm, October and March daily 9am to 7pm, April to June and September daily 8:30am to 8:30pm, July to August daily 8:30am to 11pm. Only 40 people are admitted at one time, and children 7 and under are not admitted. Reservations are a necessity; you can call for one or reserve online at **www.opapisa.it**.

Also at the Piazza del Duomo, the **Baptistery (Battistero; ★★★**; ✆ **050/ 3872210;** www.opapisa.it) is circular in shape, dating from 1153, when it was constructed along Romanesque lines, the work taking 100 years. It was finished in a more ornate Gothic style by Nicola and Giovanni Pisano. Its greatest treasure is the **hexagonal pulpit ★★**, designed by Nicola Pisano. Supported by pillars, it rests on the backs of a trio of marble lions, containing bas-reliefs of the *Crucifixion,* the *Adoration of the Magi,* the *Presentation of the Christ Child at the Temple,* and *The Last Judgment.* Admission is 5€, and it is open November to February daily from 10am to 5pm, March and October daily from 9am to 7pm, and April to September daily from 8am to 8pm.

The **Duomo ★★** (✆ **050/3872210;** www.opapisa.it) itself, dominating the so-called Campo dei Miracoli (Field of Miracles), was begun by Buscheto in 1063 and is today one of the finest Pisan-Romanesque buildings in Tuscany, with a **west front ★★★** that is light and graceful with three tiers of marble columns. The south transept door has impressive Romanesque **bronze panels ★★** from the late 12th century, the work of Bonanno Pisano. Yet another **impressive pulpit ★★★** found here was the creation of Giovanni Pisano, who worked on it from 1302 to 1310. Admission is 2€ but free from November to March. It's open April to September daily 10am to 8pm, March and October daily 10am to 7pm, and November to February daily 10am to 1pm and 2 to 5pm. Sightseeing visits are discouraged during Mass and religious rites.

Camposanto ★★, Piazza del Duomo (✆ **050/3872210;** www.opapisa.it), is a cemetery that was begun in 1278 by Giovanni di Simone, one of the architects of the Leaning Tower. Called the Holy Field, the vast marble arcades of this long building, or so legend has it, contain soil brought back from the Holy Land. Allied bombings in 1944 destroyed most of its once-lavish frescoes, although scenes depicting *The Triumph of Death* remain (1350–80). Admission costs 5€. Hours are April to September daily 8am to 8pm, March and October daily 9am to 7pm, and November to February daily 10am to 5pm.

WHERE TO DINE

Because of its well-prepared food and its proximity to Piazza del Duomo, **Emilio,** Via Cammeo 44 (✆ **050/562141**), is always packed. Inside, a large, high window, similar to what you'd find in a church, filters light down upon the brick-walled interior. The menu (it serves lunch only) features a fresh assortment of antipasti, spaghetti with clams, risotto with mushrooms, perfectly prepared grilled fish, and Florentine beefsteaks. In season, try one of the game dishes with polenta. The chef's dessert specialty is *crema di limoncello,* a mousse prepared with limoncello liqueur. Main courses cost 8€ to 18€, with fixed-price menus going for 15€ to 25€. Open Saturday to Thursday noon to 3:30pm.

Another good choice for Pisan cuisine is **Antica Trattoria Da Bruno,** Via Luigi Bianchi 12 (✆ **050/560818**), which has been in business for some 50 years at its location close to the Leaning Tower. The recipes may be old-fashioned, but the food is completely fresh and well prepared. Local favorites include *zuppa pisana,* a minestrone made with black cabbage, or wild boar with olives and polenta. Main courses cost 12€ to 23€. It's open Monday noon to 3pm, Wednesday to Sunday noon to 3pm and 7 to 10:30pm. Reservations are recommended for dinner.

An Excursion to Siena

Although such a point of view may be heretical, one can almost be grateful that Siena lost its medieval battles with Florence. Had it continued to expand and change after reaching the zenith of its power in the 14th century, chances are, it would be remarkably different today, influenced by the rising tides of the Renaissance and the baroque (represented today only in a small degree). But Siena retained its uniqueness (certain Sienese painters were still showing the influence of Byzantium in the late 15th c.) and is a showplace of the Italian Gothic.

GETTING THERE   The rail link between Florence and Siena is sometimes inconvenient because you sometimes have to change trains and wait at other stations, such as the one at the town of Empoli. Trains arrive every hour from Florence, however, costing 6.20€ one-way. Trains pull in at Siena's station at Piazza Carlo Rosselli (✆ **892021**), a difficult 30-minute climb uphill to the monumental center unless you take bus no. 10, which deposits you at Piazza Gramsci in the heart of Siena.

TOURIST INFORMATION   The **Siena Tourist Office,** at Piazza del Campo 56 (✆ **0577/280551;** www.terresiena.it), is open daily 9am to 7pm, and dispenses information and good, free maps.

TOP ATTRACTIONS & SPECIAL MOMENTS

The Town Hall of Siena, **Palazzo Comunale,** stands in the virtual heart of Siena at the shell-shaped **Piazza del Campo ★★★**, described by Montaigne as "the finest of any city in the world." Pause to enjoy **Fonte Gaia,** which locals sometimes call the Fountain of Joy because it was inaugurated to great jubilation throughout the city, with embellishments by Jacopo della Quercia (the present sculptured works are reproductions—the badly beaten-up original ones are found in the town hall). The square is truly stunning, designed like a sloping scalloped shell; you'll want to linger in one of the cafes along its edge. You'll hardly be able to miss the lithe **Torre (tower) del Mangia ★★★**, dating from the 14th century, which soars to a height of 335 feet (101m) over the skyline of the city.

The brick-built **Palazzo Pubblico** (1288–1309) on the square is filled with important artworks by some of the leaders of the Sienese school of painting and sculpture. Upstairs in a museum is the *Sala della Pace,* frescoed from 1337 to 1339 by Ambrogio Lorenzetti, and showing the **Allegory of Good and Bad Government and Their Effects on the Town and Countryside ★★★**. In this depiction, the most notable figure of the Virtues surrounding the King is *La Pace* (Peace). To the right of the King and the Virtues is a representation of Siena in peaceful times. The museum at Piazza del Campo (*✆* **0577/226230**) is open mid-March to October daily 10am to 7pm, November to mid-March daily 10am to 6pm. The tower is open mid-October to February daily from 10am to 6pm, March to mid-October daily from 10am to 7pm. Admission to both is 7€.

Southwest of Piazza del Campo stands **Il Duomo ★★★**, Piazza del Duomo (*✆* **0577/283048;** www.operaduomo.siena.it), built from 1136 to 1382; it's one of the great cathedrals of Italy, with a Pisan-influenced Romanesque-Gothic architecture. The impressive facade is from the 13th century, as is the Romanesque campanile, or bell tower. The interior is a series of black-and-white zebralike striped designs. Black-and-white marble pillars support the vault. The chief treasure is the **octagonal pulpit ★★★** of the 13th century, the work of Nicola Pisano (Giovanni's father). The pillars of the pulpit are held up by a quartet of marble lions, evocative of the Pisano pulpit at Pisa.

On Piazza San Giovanni, the **Battistero (Baptistery) ★** (*✆* **0577/283048;** www.operaduomo.siena.it) lies behind the Duomo. Its Gothic facade left unfinished by Domenico di Agostino, it is nonetheless an impressive site. Inside, its chief attraction is the **baptismal font ★★**, from 1417 to 1430, the work of Jacopo della Quercia, containing some bas-reliefs by such Tuscan masters as Donatello and Lorenzo Ghiberti. It is a Renaissance work of superb design and craftsmanship. Admission is 3€. It's open March to May, September, and October daily 9:30am to 7pm; June to August daily 9:30am to 8pm; November to February daily from 10am to 5pm.

Pinacoteca Nazionale ★★, in the Palazzo Buonsignori, Via San Pietro 29 (*✆* **0577/281161**), displays an amazing and extensive collection from the Sienese school, ranging from the late 12th to the mid–16th century, everything housed in a 14th-century *palazzo.* Displayed here are many of the Italian masters of the pre-Renaissance era. The principal treasures are found on the second floor, where you'll contemplate the artistry of Duccio in rooms 3 and 4. The gallery is rich in the art of the two Lorenzetti brothers, Ambrogio and Pietro, who painted in the 14th century (rooms 5 to 8). Ambrogio is represented by an *Annunciation* and a *Crucifix.* But one of his most celebrated works, carried out with consummate skill, is an almond-eyed *Madonna and Bambino* surrounded by saints and angels. Pietro's most important entry here is an altarpiece—*Madonna of the Carmine*—made for a church in Siena in the 1329. There is also Simone Martini's *Madonna and Child,* damaged, but one of the most famous paintings in the entire collection. Admission is 4€. It's open Monday from 8:30am to 1:30pm, Tuesday to Saturday from 8:30am to 7pm, and Sunday from 8:30am to 1:30pm.

WHERE TO DINE

On Siena's most historic square stands **Al Mangia,** Piazza del Campo 43 (*✆* **0577/281121;** www.almangia.it), which serves seasonally adjusted menus of refined Tuscan and international cuisine, and offers outside tables opening onto the landmark town hall. In a building from the 12th century, you are served artfully prepared food. Look for *pici alla Sienese* (thick noodles made only with flour and water) with a sauce of fresh tomatoes, tarragon, and cheese, or *filetto alla terra di Siena* (grilled steak with a chianti-and-tarragon sauce). The service and the cooking are first rate, with main courses costing 14€ to 28€. It's open daily from noon to 3:30pm and 7 to 10pm, but is closed Thursdays in the winter.

Equally good is **Ristorante Al Marsili,** Via del Castoro 3 (© **0577/47154;** www.ristorantealmarsili.it; bus: 1, 2, or 5), serving a Sienese and Italian cuisine in its atmospheric setting between the cathedral and Via di Città. Some of the best antipasti in town is offered here, and you get such unusual but tasty dishes as smoked venison or wild boar. Their risottos—such as one made with four different cheeses—are superb, as are the tender and well-flavored meat and poultry dishes. Main courses cost 13€ to 20€. It's open Tuesday to Sunday 12:30 to 2:30pm and 7:30 to 10:30pm.

VENICE & THE NORTHEAST

Venice is a fairy-tale city of islands and gondolas, where the canals are lined with wedding cake palaces. The "Serene Republic" of Venice had a turbulent and fascinating history. As Attila the Hun swept through 5th-century Italy toward trembling Rome, he spread proverbial death and destruction in his path. Attila was on his way to claim the emperor's stepsister, Honoria, as his "bride," and though his ultimate sack of Rome was averted, the swath of desolation he left in his wake was real enough. One particularly unfortunate town was razed to the ground, and its terrified inhabitants fled into the marshes on the shores of the Adriatic. The political climate of the times was so insecure that the population deemed it wisest to remain in the swamps and build their houses on stilts in the water, and so Venice got her start.

The Venice we know today is from a much later era, though, an era rich with the accumulated spoils of Crusaders and merchantmen. The wizardlike rulers of Renaissance Venice shrewdly—sometimes unscrupulously—parlayed Venice into mistress of the Adriatic, and the many monuments and palaces erected in those days attest to the profit inherent in such a position.

The city is an excellent rail destination, though you'll naturally have to take to the water once you get to the city proper. Venice is easily reached by train from all parts of Italy (it's the northeast rail hub for Italy) and several other European countries. And rail travelers actually have the easiest time getting into the city, as the main railway station on the Grand Canal is right in the thick of things.

Station Information
GETTING FROM THE AIRPORT TO THE TRAIN STATION
You can fly nonstop from North America to Venice on Delta. You'll land at the **Aeroporto Marco Polo** (© **041/2606111;** www.veniceairport.it), at Mestre, north of the city on the mainland. The **Consorzio Motoscafi** (© **041/5222303;** www.motoscafivenezia.it) operates a *motoscafo* (shuttle boat) service that can deliver you from the airport directly to the center of Venice at Piazza San Marco in about 30 minutes. The boats wait just outside the main entrance, and the fare begins at 98€ for up to six passengers (if there are only two of you, find some fellow travelers to share the ride and split the fare with you). If you've got some extra euros to spend, you can arrange for a **private water taxi** by calling © **041/5222303.** The cost of the ride to the heart of Venice is 98€.

Buses from the airport are less expensive, though they can take you only as far as Piazzale Roma; from here you will need to take a *vaporetto* to reach your hotel. The **Azienda Trasporti Veneto Orientale** (© **041/383672**) shuttle bus links the airport with Piazzale Roma (where the main train station is located) for 3€. The trip

Venice

ACCOMMODATIONS ■
Hotel Abbazia **1**
Hotel ai do Mori **22**
Hotel do Pozzi **17**
Hotel Marconi **11**
Hotel Mantecarlo **21**
Hotel San Cassiano
   Ca' Favretto **8**
Hotel Savoia & Jolanda **28**
La Residenza **28**
Residenza Goldoni **12**

DINING ◆
Al Covo **28**
Do Leoni **26**
Fiaschetteria Toscana **10**
Osteria alle Testiere **14**
Ristorante Corte Sconta **13**
Ristorante da Raffaele **16**
Ristorante Noemi **15**
Trattoria da Fiore **5**

ATTRACTIONS ●
Basilica di San Marco **23**
Bridge of Sighs **25**
Campanile di San Marco **20**
Ca' d'Oro **9**
Ca' Rezzonico **4**
Collezione Peggy
   Guggenheim **7**
Ducale Palace **24**
Galleria dell'Accademia **6**
The Grand Canal **3**
Museo Civico Correr **18**
Piazza San Marco **19**
Scuola di San Giorgio
   degli Schiavoni **26**
Scuola di San Rocco **2**

Pal. Flangini
S. Marcuola
Riva da Biásio
Riva da Biásio
Palazzo Giovanelli
Canàl Grande
Fónd. d. Turchi
Ca' Tron
S. Stae
Palazzo Donà-Balbi
S. Zan Degolà
S. Stae
Ca' Pesaro
Staz. Venezia-Santa Lucia
S. Simeòn Grande
Calle d. Tintòr
Pal. Mocenigo
Ca' Cassiano
S. Simeòn Piccolo
Palazzo Gradenigo
Campo N. Sáuro
S. Giacomo dell'Orio
Campo S. Giacomo dell'Oro
S. Maria Máter Dòmini
Ferrovia
Fónd. Rio Marin
SANTA CROCE
Pal. Zàne
Rio d. S.
Palazzo Soranzo-Cappello
Pal. Grioni
S. Cassiano
Rio di S. Agostino
Pal. Muti Baglioni
Giardino Pápadòpoli
Scuola Grande di S. Giovanni
Pal. Zàne Collalto
Pal. Molin
Palazzo Albrizzi
Pal. Molin-Cappello
S. Giovanni Evangelista
Pal. Donà d. Rose
Calle d. Chiesa
SAN POLO
Ex Convento dei Frari
Palazzo Zen
Pal. Corner
Campo S. Polo
Pal. Soranzo
S. Rocco
Campo d. Frari
Frari
San Polo
Scuola Grande di San Rocco
Palazzo Centani (Museo Goldoni)
Pal. Papadòpoli
S. Pantalòn
Rio d. Frescada
S. Tomà
Rio di San Polo
Pal. Layard
Pal. Grimani
Pal. Dona
Palazzo Barbarigo
Pal. Civràn-Grimani
S. Tomà
S. Àngelo
Rio Ca' Foscari
Calle Foscari
Pal. Balbi
Palazzo Mocenigo
Pal. Cornèr Spinelli
Pal. Fortuny
Ca' Foscari
Pal. Contarini d. Figure
Oratorio dell'Annunciata
Palazzo Grassi
Pal. Moro-Lin
Saliz S. Samuele
Campo S. Àngelo
Pal. Nani
Ca' Rezzonico
S. Samuele
San Samuele
San Stefano
S. Bárnaba
Pal. Stern
Ca' Rezzonico
Palazzo Malipiero
Campo S. Stefano
S. Maurízio
Rio Malpaga
Ca' del Duca
C. Vettur
S. Vidal
Pal. Falier
Pal. Morosini
S. Maria d. Giglio
DORSODURO
Pal. Loredan
Pal. Contarini degli Scrigni
Pal. Bárbaro
Pal. Pisani
Palazzo Cornèr d. Ca' Granda
Accademia
Ponte dell'Accademia
Canàl Grande
S. Maria d. Giglio
S. Trovaso
Gallerie dell' Accademia
Palazzo Contarini dal Zaffo
Pal. Centani
Rio di S. Vio
Pal. Nani
Pal. Giustiniàn
S. Maria d. Visitaz.
S. Agnese
Gesuati
Pal. Venièr dei Leoni (Guggenheim)
Zàttere

CANNAREGIO

Pal. Giovanelli
S. Felice
Pal. Zen
Palazzo Seriman
Pal. Fontana
Ca' d'Oro **9**
8
S. Sofia
Calle d. Vele
Calle d'Oro
Pal. Sagredo
Ca' d'Oro
Pal. Brandolin
Pescaria
Pal. Mangilli
Pal. Falier
Ss. Apóstoli
Pal. Widman
Pal. Grifalconi
Calle d. Fumo
Calle d. Squero
H
Ospedale Civile
Fond. Nove
Canale Fondamente Nuove
Fábbriche Nuove
Ca' da Mosto
Rio di
S. Giovanni Crisostomo
S. Canciano
C. larga G. Gallina
S. Maria d. Miracoli
Pal. Soranzo-Van Axel
Ss. Giovanni e Paolo (S. Zanipolo)
Palazzo Dieci Savi **10**
Teatro Málibran
Pal. Pisani
S. Aponàl **11**
Fóndaco d. Tedeschi
Pal. Cavazza-Foscari
Campo S. Marina
Rio di S. Marina
Pal. Morosini
Pal. Muazzo
S. Bartolomeo **13**
S. Lio
Palazzo Ruzzini
Pal. Donà
Pal. Cavignis
Palazzo Cappello
Riva del Vin
Riva del Carbon
S. Silvestro
Palazzo Dolfin-Manin **12**
Pal. Bembo
C. Stagneri
S. Salvador
S. Maria della Fava
Campo S. Maria Formosa **14**
S. Maria Formosa
Pal. Donà
Palazzo Grimani
Ca' Farsetti
Pal. Tasca Papafáva
Questura
CASTELLO
S. Luca
Cínema Rossini
Campo Manin
Palazzo Contarini d. Bovolo **15**
SAN MARCO
S. Zuliàn **21**
Palazzo Querini Stampalia
Ruga Giuffa
Palazzo Soranzo
S. Giovanni Novo
Pal. Priuli
Pal. Zorzi
Ateneo Véneto
22
Palazzo Trevisan-Cappello
S. Zaccaria
S. Giorgio dei Greci
Pisc. di Frezzeria
Torre d. Orologio
C. Canonica
Basilica di San Marco **23**
Pal. d. Prigioni
Convento
La Pietà
Teatro La Fénice
S. Fantin
18
Museo Corrèr
19
Piazza San Marco **20**
Campanile
24
26 **27**
28
28
S. Moisè
SS. Moisè
Palazzo Ducale (Doge's Palace) **25**
Riva d. Schiavoni
S. Zaccaria
16
C. Larga XXII Marzo
17
Palazzo Tiépolo
Palazzi Contarini
Pal. Gritti
Palazzo Treves d. Bonfili
Giardini ex Reali
Capo di Porto
S. Marco
Ponte d. Sospiri (Bridge of Sighs)
Pal. Genovese
Salute
S. Maria d. Salute
Dogana da Mar
Seminario Patriarcale
Ex Ospízio
Punta d. Dogana
Bacino di San Marco

ITALY
Venice
Florence
Rome
Naples

Isola di S. Giorgio Maggiore

0   200 yds
0   200 m

537

takes about 20 minutes, and departures are about every 30 minutes daily 8:20am to 12:10pm. Even cheaper is a local bus company, **ACTV** (✆ **041/2424**), whose bus no. 5 makes the run for 2€. The ACTV buses depart every half-hour and take about a half-hour to reach Piazzale Roma.

INSIDE THE STATION

Trains pull into the **Stazione di Santa Lucia,** at Piazzale Roma, from Rome (trip time: 5 hr.), Milan (3½ hr.), Florence (4 hr.), and Bologna (2 hr.). For information and timetables, contact **FS** (✆ **892021;** www.trenitalia.it) or Rail Europe. The best and least expensive way to get from the station to the rest of town is to take a *vaporetto,* which departs near the main entrance to the station.

The station has all the expected amenities, including a currency exchange desk, luggage storage, restaurants, and ATMs. The *vaporetto* departs near the station's main entrance.

A **tourist office** (✆ **041/5298711**), located just off the station's main hall, dispenses information and maps but does not make hotel reservations. It's open 8am to 6:30pm daily.

Anyone between the ages of 14 and 29 is eligible for a **Rolling Venice pass,** entitling you to discounts for museums, restaurants, stores, language courses, hotels, and bars. Valid for 1 year, it costs 4€ and can be picked up at any tourist office in Venice.

Information Elsewhere in the City

From spring to autumn, hotel reservations in overcrowded Venice should be made as far in advance as possible, either through a travel agent or independently. The tourist office (see above) does not make reservations. **Azienda di Promozione Turistica,** San Marco 71/F (✆ **041/5298711;** www.turismovenezia.it), is open daily 9am to 3:30pm. Posters around town with exhibit and concert schedules are more helpful. Ask for a schedule of the month's special events and an updated list of museum and church hours, because these can change erratically and often.

Getting Around

BY VAPORETTO   Much to the chagrin of the once-ubiquitous gondoliers, Venice's **motorboats** *(vaporetti)* provide inexpensive and frequent, if not always fast, transportation in this canal city. The *vaporetti* are called "water buses," and they are indeed the "buses" of Venice because traveling by water is usually faster than traveling by land. The service is operated by **ACTV (Azienda del Consorzio Trasporti Veneziano),** Isola Nova del Tronchetto 32 (✆ **041/2424;** www.actv.it). An *accelerato* is a vessel that makes every stop; a *diretto* makes only express stops. The average fare is 6.50€. ACTV also sells a ticket valid for 1 hour on all *vaporetti,* costing 6€. Note that, in summer, the *vaporetti* are often fiercely crowded. Pick up a map of the system at the tourist office. They run daily up and down the Grand Canal, with frequent service 7am to midnight and then hourly midnight to 7am. To save money, you can buy a 24-hour ticket for 18€ or a 3-day ticket for 33€.

BY MOTOR LAUNCH (WATER TAXI)   Motor launches *(taxi acquei)* cost more than public *vaporetti,* but you won't be hassled as much when you arrive with your luggage if you hire one of the many private ones. You might or might not have the cabin of one of these sleek vessels to yourself, because the captains fill their boats with as many passengers as the law allows before taking off. Your porter's uncanny radar will guide you to one of the inconspicuous piers where a water taxi waits. The price of a transit by water taxi from the train station to Piazza San Marco begins at 98€ for up to four passengers and 90€ for more than four. The captains adroitly deliver you, with luggage, to the canal-side entrance of your hotel or on one of the smaller waterways within a short walking distance of your destination. You can also call for a water taxi; try the **Consorzio Motoscafi**, at ✆ **041/5222303.**

Where to Stay

Hotel Abbazia   The benefit of staying here is that there's no need to transfer to any *vaporetto*—you can walk here from the rail station, about 10 minutes away. This hotel was built in 1889 as a monastery for barefooted Carmelite monks, who established a verdant garden in what's now the courtyard; it's planted with subtropical plants that thrive, sheltered as they are from the cold Adriatic winds. You'll find a highly accommodating staff and comfortable but very plain guest rooms with well-kept bathrooms. Twenty-five rooms overlook the courtyard, ensuring quiet in an otherwise noisy neighborhood.

Calle Priuli ai Cavaletti, Cannaregio 68, 30121 Venezia. ✆ **041/717333.** Fax 041/717949. www.abbazia hotel.com. 49 units (some with shower only). 95€–270€ double; 200€–300€ junior suite. Rates include buffet breakfast. AE, DC, MC, V. *Vaporetto*: Ferrovia. **Amenities:** Smoke-free rooms.

Hotel ai do Mori ★ ✦   Since Venice is one of the globe's most expensive cities, many visitors put up with some inconveniences to stay at this affordable choice in the central tourist zone near Piazza San Marco. The town house dates from the mid–15th century, and you'll have to balance your need for space with your desire for a view (and your willingness to climb stairs, because there's no elevator): The lower-level rooms are larger but don't have views; the third- and fourth-floor rooms are cramped but have sweeping views over the basilica's domes. Furnishings are in a simple, modern style, and bathrooms are well maintained. In lieu of any food service here, numerous cafes and trattorie lie outside your door.

Calle Larga San Marco, San Marco 658, 30124 Venezia. ✆ **041/5204817.** Fax 041/5205328. www.hotel aidomori.com. 11 units, 9 with private bathroom (shower only). 85€–95€ double without bathroom; 130€–150€ double with bathroom. MC, V. *Vaporetto*: San Marco. **Amenities:** All rooms smoke-free.

Hotel do Pozzi ★   This antique building, just a short walk from Piazza San Marco and its basilica, feels more like a country tavern than a hotel. It's more than 2 centuries old but has been modernized. The hotel is really old Venice, with lots of atmosphere, and in summer breakfast is served out on a characteristic little square surrounded by flowers. Antiques are mixed with functional modern furniture in the small to midsize bedrooms, some of which have showers in the bathrooms, others a tub/shower. A major refurbishment has given a fresh touch to the bathrooms.

Via XXII Marzo, San Marco 2373, 30124 Venezia. ✆ **041/5207855.** Fax 041/5229413. www.hoteldopozzi. it. 35 units. 135€–280€ double. Rates include buffet breakfast. AE, DC, MC, V. *Vaporetto*: Santa Maria del Giglio. **Amenities:** Bar; smoke-free rooms.

Hotel Marconi   Just 50 feet (15m) from the Rialto Bridge, this old relic is still going strong, though its heyday was in the 1930s. When Venice is in high season and overcrowded, it's very expensive—otherwise, it's one of the bargains in town. The building itself was constructed at the beginning of the 16th century, and the drawing room still evokes that era. The four most desirable rooms (and the most expensive) open onto dramatic views of the Grand Canal. Bedrooms range from small to medium, each with a comfortable bed and a tiled shower-only bathroom. Sidewalk tables are placed outside in fair weather to take in a lovely view of the Grand Canal.

Riva del Vin, San Polo 729, 30125 Venezia. ✆ **041/5222068.** Fax 041/5229700. www.hotelmarconi.it. 26 units. 90€–340€ double; 180€–500€ triple. Rates include buffet breakfast. AE, DC, MC, V. *Vaporetto*: Rialto. **Amenities:** All rooms smoke-free.

Hotel Montecarlo   Just a 2-minute walk from Piazza San Marco, this Best Western hotel is installed in a much-upgraded 17th-century town house. The owners have given it Venetian flair, lining its upper halls with the work of some of the city's most outstanding old masters and decorating the small guest rooms with Venetian-styled antique reproductions and glass chandeliers from the neighboring island of Murano. Some are quite dark, the curse of many Venetian hotels. All have well-kept bathrooms.

Calle dei Specchieri, San Marco 463, 30124 Venezia. ✆ **800/780-7234** in the U.S. and Canada, or 041/5207144. Fax 041/5207789. www.venicehotelmontecarlo.com. 48 units. 89€–225€ double. Children 12 and under stay free in parent's room. Rates include buffet breakfast. AE, DC, MC, V. *Vaporetto*: San Marco. **Amenities:** Restaurant; bar; smoke-free rooms.

Hotel San Cassiano Ca'Favretto ★   San Cassiano Ca'Favretto was once the studio of 19th-century painter Giacomo Favretto. The views from the hotel's gondola pier and from the dining room's porch encompass the lacy facade of the Ca' d'Oro. The hotel is a 16th-century palace, and many of its architectural details, including 20-foot (6m) ceilings, have been retained. There's no elevator, but the Murano chandeliers, the rooms filled with antique reproductions, the 18th-century stucco work in the breakfast room, and a wood-beamed bar with a canal view do much to compensate.

Calle della Rosa, Santa Croce 2232, 30135 Venezia. ✆ **041/5241768.** Fax 041/721033. www.san cassiano.it. 35 units. 90€–430€ double. Rates include buffet breakfast. AE, DC, MC, V. *Vaporetto*: San Stae. **Amenities:** Bar; rooms for those w/limited mobility; smoke-free rooms.

Hotel Savoia & Jolanda ★   Better-heeled rail passengers seeking a taste of the Venetian luxury for which the city is renowned will find solace in this hotel, just a few minutes' walk from Piazza San Marco, right off a Venetian lagoon. It's truly a special place for lodgings and very romantic. Try for one of the midsize and well-furnished guest rooms opening onto a view of the lagoon. Well-chosen fabrics, paintings, and Venetian glass from the island of Murano add to the luster of the hotel, as do the old wooden beams and the flower-bedecked terraces. The suites have panoramic balconies and terraces.

Riva degli Schiavoni, Castello 4187, 30122 Venezia. ✆ **041/5206644.** Fax 041/5207494. www.hotel savoiajolanda.com. 51 units. 208€–312€ double; from 330€ suite. Rates include buffet breakfast. AE, DC, MC, V. *Vaporetto*: San Zaccaria. **Amenities:** Restaurant.

La Residenza ★★   One of our all-time favorite nests in Venice occupies a 14th-century palazzo overlooking an evocative square of old Venice a few steps from Piazza San Marco. The legend and lore of old Venice is kept alive in this palace, which has also been kept abreast of the times. The guest rooms are far less opulent, with contemporary pieces and good beds. There's no elevator, so be prepared. Because the address is known by some of the world's most discerning hotel shoppers, book well in advance if arriving in season.

Campo Bandiera e Moro, Castello 3608, 30122 Venezia. ✆ **041/5285315.** Fax 041/5238859. www. vencelaresidenza.com. 15 units (shower only). 80€–200€ double. Rates include continental breakfast. MC, V. *Vaporetto*: Arsenale. **Amenities:** Smoke-free rooms.

Residenza Goldoni ★ 🎁   Near Ponte di Rialto, this small, charming, and much-renovated inn is one of the gems of the area. Although in a noisy part of the city, all the bedrooms are soundproof. The interior is intimate and inviting, with a touch of elegance. Breakfast is served in your room. Each guest room comes with a small private bathroom—some with shower, others with tub. The furnishings are in the Louis Philippe style. If you can get them, go for the two rooms on the fourth floor, one resting in wooden beams and the other opening onto a terrace.

San Marco 5234, 30124 Venezia. ✆ **041/2410086.** Fax 041/2774728. www.residenzagoldoni.com. 12 units. 65€–250€ double; 140€–320€ suite. Rates include breakfast in room. AE, DC, MC, V. *Vaporetto:* Rialto. **Amenities:** Room service.

Top Attractions & Special Moments

You really need 2 to 3 days to properly take in the city, but if you have only 1 day, be sure to watch the sun rise over **Piazzetta San Marco** ★. Adjacent to the Palace of the Doges is this landmark little square, noted for its fabulous statue of the winged lion of St. Mark. It stands atop a granite column (which was also ripped off from Constantinople) and is flanked by a similar column, on whose capital stands St. Theodore, patron of Venice until he was supplanted by St. Mark.

In what has been called the "antechamber" of Venice, you have the best view of the southern facade of St. Mark's Basilica. Embedded in the facade is a *Virgin and Bambino* in mosaics, honoring a poor baker—that is, Pietro Fasiol, who was unjustly accused and executed on a false charge of murder. At the left of the entrance to the Palace of the Doges stands a world-famous collection of four porphyry figures called *The Moors.* Naturally puce colored, they are huddled together in fear.

Ca' d'Oro ★★★   The grandest setting for any art gallery is Ca' d'Oro, formerly a private palace, donated to the Italian state after World War I by the owner, Baron Franchetti. The collection ranges from Van Dyck to Carpaccio, and the lush appointments of the palace itself compete with the works of art on the walls.

The "House of Gold" was so named because it was once gilded (imagine what that would cost today). Today the pink-and-white stone exterior has a lacy Gothic look, making it almost appear like a candy box. Opposite the entrance door, you can go into a salon to see Titian's voluptuous *Venus.* The masterpiece on this floor is Andrea Mantegna's *St. Sebastian.* Another equally renowned work of art is Anthony Van Dyck's *Portrait of a Gentleman.* At some point, you emerge onto a loggia where you can enjoy a panoramic view of the Grand Canal.

Cannaregio 3931-3932. ✆ **041/5238790.** www.cadoro.org. Admission 5€. Mon 8:15am–2pm; Tues–Sun 8:15am–7:15pm. Closed Jan 1, May 1, and Dec 25. *Vaporetto:* Ca' d'Oro.

Campanile di San Marco ★★   The bell tower of St. Mark's Basilica is a reconstruction of the original, which dramatically collapsed into the Piazza in the summer of 1902. No one was hurt because, the night before the fall, the tower had emitted a telltale groan that sent everyone within earshot racing to safety. It collapsed the next day, when the populace was kept at a safe distance. The Venetians rebuilt their belfry, and it's now safe to ascend. A modern elevator takes you up for a splendid view of the city.

Piazza San Marco. ✆ **041/5224064.** www.basilicasanmarco.it. Admission 8€. Oct–Mar daily 9:30am–4pm; Apr–June daily 9am–7pm; July–Sept daily 9am–9pm. *Vaporetto:* San Marco.

Ca' Rezzonico ★★   At this 17th- and 18th-century palace along the Grand Canal, Robert Browning lived as a widower in rooms once occupied by Clement XII.

Nowadays, it's a museum of baroque furnishings and paintings. A **Throne Room** contains an allegorical ceiling by Tiepolo. Here are all the rich props that characterized Venice in the 18th century, including elaborate chandeliers, gilded furniture, and the inevitable chinoiserie. The best paintings are by Pietro Longhi, including his well-known work *The Lady and the Hairdresser*. Majolica and Venetian costumes are exhibited on the top floor.

Fondamenta Rezzonico, Dorsoduro 3136. ✆ **041/2410100.** www.museicivicivenziani.it. Admission 6.50€ adults. Nov–Mar Wed–Mon 10am–5pm; Apr–Oct Wed–Mon 10am–6pm. Closed Jan 1, May 1, and Dec 25. *Vaporetto*: Ca' Rezzonico.

Collezione Peggy Guggenheim ★★★ This is one of the most comprehensive and brilliant modern art collections in the Western world, and it reveals the foresight and critical judgment of its founder. The collection is housed in an unfinished palazzo, the former home of Peggy Guggenheim. In the tradition of her family, Guggenheim was a lifelong patron of contemporary painters and sculptors. As her private collection increased, she decided to find a larger showcase and selected Venice. Displayed here are works not only by Pollock and Ernst, but also by Picasso (see his cubist *The Poet* of 1911), Duchamp, Chagall, Mondrian, Brancusi, Delvaux, and Dalí, plus a garden of modern sculpture that includes works by Giacometti.

In the Palazzo Venier dei Leoni, Calle Venier dei Leoni, Dorsoduro 701. ✆ **041/2405411.** www.guggenheim-venice.it. Admission 12€; 6.50€ for children and students. Free for children 11 and under. Wed–Mon 10am–6pm. *Vaporetto*: Accademia.

Ducal Palace & Bridge of Sighs (Palazzo Ducale & Ponte dei Sospiri) ★★★
This Venetian landmark is around the corner from the Basilica of St. Mark. It is a 16th-century reconstruction of the original 14th-century palace, which was gutted by a great fire. Here sat the Council of Ten, that rather arbitrary administrative body of Renaissance Venice that meted out justice at the height of the republic. Justice was unfortunately characterized largely by torture and execution, and not always for the best of reasons. The room in which the old men sat is a great gloomy chamber, decorated with somber oil paintings, and reached via an antechamber with a lion's mouth, into which letters of accusation were dropped. The famous resident of the place was the Doge himself, whose private apartments are aglow with frescoed walls and ceilings with magnificent paintings.

Dungeons are connected to the palace by the Bridge of Sighs, or **Ponte dei Sospiri ★★**. The bridge was named because of the sad laments of the prisoners led across to torture and even death. Casanova was imprisoned here in 1775, but he managed to escape.

Piazzetta San Marco. ✆ **041/2715911.** Admission 12€. Apr–Oct daily 9am–7pm; Nov–Mar daily 9am–6pm. Closed Dec 25 and Jan 1. *Vaporetto*: San Marco.

Galleria dell'Accademia ★★★ The pomp and circumstance, the glory that was Venice, lives on in this remarkable collection of paintings spanning the 14th century to the 18th century. The hallmark of the Venetian school is color and more color. From Giorgione to Veronese, from Titian to Tintoretto, with a Carpaccio cycle thrown in, the Accademia has samples—often their best—of its most famous sons.

You'll first see works by such 14th-century artists as Paolo and Lorenzo Veneziano, who bridged the gap from Byzantine art to Gothic (see the latter's *Annunciation*). Next, you'll view Giovanni Bellini's *Madonna and Saint* (poor Sebastian, not another arrow), and Carpaccio's fascinating yet gruesome work of mass crucifixion. Two of the most important works with secular themes are Mantegna's armored *St. George*, with the dragon slain at his feet, and Hans Memling's 15th-century portrait of a young man. Giorgione's *Tempest* is the most famous painting at the Accademia. Lastly, seek out the cycle of narrative paintings that Vittore Carpaccio did of St. Ursula.

Campo della Carità, Dorsoduro. (℃) **041/5222247.** www.gallerieaccademia.org. Admission 8.50€. Mon 8:15am–2pm; Tues–Sun 8:15am–7:15pm. Closed Jan 1, May 1, and Dec 25. *Vaporetto*: Accademia.

Museo Civico Correr ★★   This museum traces the development of Venetian painting from the 14th century to the 16th century. On the second floor are the red and maroon robes once worn by the doges, plus some fabulous street lanterns. There's also an illustrated copy of *Marco Polo in Tartaria*. You can see Cosmé Tura's *La Pietà*, a miniature of renown from the genius in the Ferrara School. This is one of his more gruesome works, depicting a bony, gnarled Christ sprawled on the lap of the Madonna. Farther on, search out a Schiavone *Madonna and Child* (no. 545), our candidate for ugliest bambino ever depicted on canvas (no wonder the mother looks askance). One of the most important rooms at the Correr is filled with three masterpieces: Antonello da Messina's *Pietà*, Hugo van der Goes's *Crucifixion*, and Dieric Bouts's *Madonna and Child*. The star attraction of the Correr is the Bellini salon, which includes works by founding padre Jacopo and his son, Gentile. But the real master of the household was the other son, Giovanni, the major painter of the 15th-century Venetian school (see his *Crucifixion* and compare it with his father's treatment of the same subject).

In the Procuratie Nuove, Piazza San Marco. (℃) **041/2405211.** www.museicivicivenezia.it. Admission (including admission to the Ducale Palace, above) 12€. Apr–Oct daily 10am–7pm; Nov–Mar daily 10am–5pm. Closed Dec 25 and Jan 1. *Vaporetto*: San Marco.

Scuola di San Giorgio degli Schiavoni ★★   At St. Antonino Bridge (Fondamenta dei Furlani), off the Riva degli Schiavoni, is the second important school to visit in Venice. Between 1507 and 1509, Vittore Carpaccio painted a pictorial cycle here of exceptional merit and interest. Of enduring fame are his works of **St. George and the Dragon ★**, our favorite art in Venice—certainly the most delightful. In one frame, St. George charges the dragon on a field littered with half-eaten bodies and skulls. Gruesome? Not at all. Any moment you expect the director to call "Cut!"

Calle dei Furiani, Castello. (℃) **041/5228828.** Admission 3€. Nov–Mar Tues–Sat 10am–12:30pm and 3–6pm, Sun 10am–12:30pm; Apr–Oct Tues–Sat 9:30am–12:30pm and 3:30–6:30pm, Sun 9:30am–12:30pm. Last entrance 30 min. before closing. *Vaporetto*: San Zaccaria.

Scuola di San Rocco ★★★   This dark, early-16th-century "school" was richly decorated by the great Tintoretto. *Scuole* were Venetian institutions throughout the

---

  A Ride Along the Grand Canal

The main street of town is the **Grand Canal ★★★**, thronged with gondolas and *vaporetti* (those motorized boatbuses), spanned by graceful bridges, and lined with palaces. Many of those palaces house fabulous museums, with collections encompassing art from the Renaissance to the present.

The best way to see the Grand Canal is to board *vaporetto* no. 1 (push and shove until you secure a seat at the front of the vessel). Settle yourself in, make sure that you have your long-distance viewing glasses, and prepare yourself for a view that can thrill even the most experienced world traveler.

A RIDE IN A gondola

In *Death in Venice,* Thomas Mann wrote: "Is there anyone but must repress a secret thrill, on arriving in Venice for the first time—or returning thither after long absence—and stepping into a Venetian gondola? That singular conveyance, come down unchanged from ballad times, black as nothing else on earth except a coffin—what pictures it calls up of lawless, silent adventures in the plashing night; or even more, what visions of death itself, the bier and solemn rites and last soundless voyage!"

Mann reflected the point of view of German romanticism, but he didn't tell the whole story. The voyage on a gondola isn't likely to be so soundless—at least not when the time comes to pay the bill. When riding in a gondola, two major agreements have to be reached—one, the price of the ride; two, the length of the trip.

The official rate is 80€ for 40 minutes, but we've never known anyone to honor it. The actual fare depends on how well you stand up to the gondolier, *beginning* at 110€ for up to 50 minutes. Most gondoliers will ask at least double the official rate and reduce your trip to 30 to 40 minutes or even less. Prices go up after 8pm. Two major stations where you can hire gondolas are **Piazza San Marco** (✆ **041/5200685**) and **Ponte di Rialto** (✆ **041/5224904**).

various quarters in which the patricians met. The best-known one is San Rocco, in which Tintoretto won a commission to do 56 canvases, a task that took 18 years. Paintings cover the Upper and Lower Halls, including the well-known *Flight into Egypt.* The school owns Tintoretto's masterpiece, his huge *Crucifixion.* Other scenes also illustrate episodes from the life of Christ.

Campo San Rocco, San Polo. ✆ 041/5234864. www.scuolagrandesanrocco.it. Admission 7€ adults, free for children up to 18 years old. Mar 28–Nov 2 daily 9am–5:30pm; Nov 3–30 and Mar 1–27 daily 10am–4pm; Dec–Feb Mon–Sat 7:30am–12:30pm, Sun 7:30am–12:30pm and 2–4pm. Closed Easter, Dec 25, and Jan 1. Ticket office closes 30 min. before last entrance. *Vaporetto:* San Tomà.

St. Mark's Basilica (Basilica di San Marco) ★★★ Dominating Piazza San Marco is the **Basilica of St. Mark,** named for the patron saint of the city, whose body was carried here from Alexandria in A.D. 828. It is called the "Church of Gold" and is one of the most fabulously embellished structures in Europe. A great central dome and satellite cupolas form the silhouette, and inside is a profusion of mosaics depicting biblical scenes.

The **Presbytery** is said to contain the sarcophagus of St. Mark under a green marble "blanket." Here you'll find the *Pala d'Oro* ★★★, a fabulous altar screen made of beaten gold and liberally encrusted with diamonds, rubies, emeralds, and pearls. You're also admitted to the **Treasury (*tesoro*) ★,** filled with some of the loot the Crusaders brought back from Constantinople.

After leaving the basilica, head up the stairs in the atrium to the **Marciano Museum** and the **Loggia dei Cavalli.** The star of the museum is the world-famous *Triumphal Quadriga* ★★, four horses looted from Constantinople by Venetian crusaders during the sack of that city in 1204. These horses once surmounted the basilica but were removed because of pollution damage and were subsequently restored. The museum, with its mosaics and tapestries, is especially interesting, but also be sure to walk out onto the loggia for a view of Piazza San Marco.

Piazza San Marco. ℂ **041/5225205.** www.basilicasanmarco.it. Basilica free; treasury 3€; presbytery 2€; Marciano Museum 4€. Basilica and presbytery Apr–Sept Mon–Sat 10am–5pm, Sun 2–5pm; Oct–Mar Mon–Sat 10am–4:30pm, Sun 2–4pm. Marciano Museum Apr–Oct Mon–Sat 10am–5pm, Sun 2–4pm; Nov–Mar Mon–Sat 10am–4pm, Sun 2–4pm. *Vaporetto:* San Marco.

Where to Dine

Al Covo ★★ VENETIAN/SEAFOOD   Al Covo has a special charm because of its atmospheric setting, sophisticated service, and the fine cooking of Cesare Benelli and his Texas-born wife, Diane. Look for a reinvention of a medieval version of fish soup, roast lamb chops with mint sauce and lentils, roast codfish with prunes and fresh rosemary, soft-shell crabs fried with potatoes and onion rings, and homemade potato gnocchi with baby calamari and spider crab roe. Al Covo prides itself on not having any freezers, guaranteeing that all food is prepared fresh every day.

Campiello della Pescaria, Castello 3968. ℂ **041/5223812.** www.ristorantealcovo.com. Reservations recommended for dinner. Main courses 23€–35€; fixed-price menus 49€. MC, V. Fri–Tues 12:45–2:15pm and 7:30–10pm. *Vaporetto:* Arsenale.

Do Leoni ★★ VENETIAN/INTERNATIONAL   This restaurant offers a view of a 19th-century equestrian statue ringed with heroic women taming (you guessed it) lions. The menu is something to savor. The chef isn't afraid to dip into Venice's culinary attic at times for inspiration—take the boneless sardines fried and left to marinate in onions before being served with fresh pine nuts and Cyprus sultanas. The risottos and pastas are delectable. Savor such main dishes as roast saddle of lamb with eggplant (*aubergine*) or filet of grouper with Swiss chard and an orange hollandaise mousse. If weather permits, you can dine out on the piazza.

In the Londra Palace, Riva degli Schiavoni, Castello 4171. ℂ **041/5200533.** Reservations required. Main courses 16€–38€. AE, DC, MC, V. Restaurant daily 12:30–2:30pm and 7:30–11pm. Bar daily 11am–12:30am. *Vaporetto:* San Zaccaria.

Fiaschetteria Toscana ★ 🍴 VENETIAN   The service at this hip restaurant might be uneven and the staff might be frantic, but lots of local foodies come here. The dining rooms are on two levels, the upstairs of which is somewhat more claustrophobic. In the evening, the downstairs is especially appealing, with its romantic candlelit ambience. Menu items include *frittura della Serenissima* (a mixed platter of fried seafood with vegetables), a succulent ravioli filled with lobster and broccoli, and freshly caught fish from the North Adriatic, along with tender and well-flavored Tuscan beefsteak.

Campo San Giovanni Crisostomo, Cannaregio 5719. ℂ **041/5285281.** www.fiaschetteriatoscana.it. Reservations required. Main courses 15€–35€; fixed-price menus 26€–50€. MC, V. Wed 7:30–10:30pm; Thurs–Mon 12:30–2:30pm and 7:30–10:30pm. Closed July 25–Aug 20. *Vaporetto:* Rialto.

Osteria alle Testiere ★ 🎒 VENETIAN/ITALIAN   A restaurant for the young at heart, this 24-seat trattoria seats you at tables covered with butcher paper and feeds you well at affordable prices. Beefed up by a wine list of some 100 selections, you can enjoy well-prepared dishes in a tavernlike setting. When you ask for a recipe here— the food is that good—you're often told it's a secret. Among the menu temptations, tuna steak flavored with juniper berries is a delight, as is a savory Gnocchetti with baby squid.

Castello 5801 (on Calle del Mondo Novo). ℂ **041/5227220.** www.osteriatestiere.it. Reservations recommended. Main courses 16€–24€. MC, V. Tues–Sat noon–2pm and 7–10pm. Closed Aug and Dec 20–Jan 15. *Vaporetto:* San Marco or Rialto.

Ristorante Corte Sconta VENETIAN/SEAFOOD   This restaurant lies on a narrow alley, whose name is shared by at least three other streets in Venice (this is near Campo Bandiere Moro and San Giovanni in Bragora). The modest restaurant's plain wooden tables are often filled with artists, writers, and filmmakers who come here for one of the most varied selection of freshly caught seafood in Venice. The fish is flawlessly fresh, including, for example, *gamberi*—tiny baby shrimp placed live on the grill. A great starter is the marinated salmon with arugula and pomegranate seeds in olive oil.

Calle del Pestrin, Castello 3886. (*c*) **041/5227024.** Reservations required. Main courses 16€–28€. MC, V. Tues–Sat 12:30–2pm and 7:30–9:30pm. Closed Jan 7–Feb 7 and July 20–Aug 18. *Vaporetto:* Arsenale or San Zaccaria.

Ristorante da Raffaele ★ ITALIAN/VENETIAN   One of our favorite canal-side restaurants, named for the famous artist, is a 5-minute stroll from Piazza San Marco. It's often overrun with tourists, though the veteran kitchen staff handles the onslaught well. Against an atmospheric backdrop of Old Venice (high-beamed ceilings, wrought-iron chandeliers, and hundreds of copper pots), you can feast on such treats as deep-fried fish from the Adriatic, wonderful grilled meats, and the city's best bean soup.

Calle Larga XXII Marzo (Fondamenta delle Ostreghe), San Marco 2347. (*c*) **041/5232317.** Reservations recommended Sat–Sun. Main courses 13€–24€. AE, DC, MC, V. Fri–Wed noon–3pm and 7–10:30pm. Closed Dec 10–Feb. *Vaporetto:* San Marco or Santa Maria del Giglio.

Ristorante Noemi VENETIAN   Since 1927, discerning Venetian foodies have been making their way to this simple trattoria for its friendly service, affordable mid-range prices, and market-fresh ingredients. Some of its dishes are inspired by *nuova cucina,* but many rely on old-fashioned recipes known to everybody's mamma mia. The cooks are known for their infallible skill in the kitchen and marvelous fish dishes such as "black" spaghetti with cuttlefish in its own sauce or a filet of sole Casanova (a white wine sauce, fresh mushrooms, and Adriatic shrimp).

Calle dei Fabbri, San Marco 912. (*c*) **041/5225238.** www.ristorantenoemi.com. Reservations recommended. Main courses 19€–30€. AE, DC, MC, V. Tues–Sun 11:30am–1am. *Vaporetto:* San Marco.

Trattroria da Fiore ★ 🌿 VENETIAN   This affordable place is an eagerly sought-out address because of its take on really typical local cookery, including some of the best regional fare served in the Accademia area. The house specialty is *pennette all Fiore,* which is served with seven fresh vegetables in season, a hearty, filling pasta dish. If you have more room, you can taste some very fresh and well-prepared fish dishes from the Adriatic, including a savory kettle of fish soup.

Calle delle Botteghe, San Marco 3461. (*c*) **041/5235310.** www.dafiore.it. Reservations suggested. Pastas 11€–18€; main courses 18€–29€. MC, V. Wed–Mon noon–3pm and 7–10pm. Closed Jan 15–30 and Aug 1–15. *Vaporetto:* Accademia.

Shopping

There's virtually a shop—or shops—in every block, selling Venetian crafts such as glass and lace, and oh, so much more. Most of the shopping is concentrated around **Piazza San Marco** or **Ponte Rialto.**

The best place to buy Carnevale masks is **Mondonovo,** Rio Terrà Canal, Dorsoduro 3063 (*c* **041/5287344;** www.mondonovomaschere.it), where talented artisans labor to produce copies of both traditional and more modern masks, each of which is one-of-a-kind and richly nuanced with references to Venetian lore and traditions. Prices start at 40€ for a fairly basic model. Most lace vendors center on Piazza San Marco. Although the price of handmade Venetian lace is high, it's still reasonable, considering the painstaking work that goes into the real thing. Authentic hand-tatted lace is cheaper in Venice than it is elsewhere, and it's even cheaper on the island of Burano. Regardless of where you buy lace, however, make sure it's the real thing. **Norelene,** Calle della Chiesa, Dorsoduro 727 (© **041/5237605**), features lustrous hand-printed silks, velvets, and cottons, plus wall hangings and clothing.

One of the oldest (founded in 1866) and largest purveyors of traditional Venetian glass is **Pauly & Co. ★★★**, Ponte Consorzi, San Marco 4391 (© **041/5209899**), with more than two dozen showrooms. Part of the premises is devoted to something akin to a museum, where past successes (now antiques) are displayed. Antique items are only rarely offered for sale, but they can be copied and shipped anywhere, and chandeliers can be electrified to match your standards. They begin at about 1,000€.

The art glass sold by **Venini ★★★**, Piazzetta Leoncini, San Marco 314 (© **041/5224045;** www.venini.com), has caught the attention of collectors from all over the world. Its best-known glass has a distinctive swirl pattern in several colors, called a *venature*. This shop is known for the refined quality of its glass, some of which appears almost transparent. Much of it is very fragile, but the shop learned long ago how to ship it anywhere safely. To visit the furnace, call © **041/2737211.**

Nightlife

The tourist office distributes a free pamphlet (part in English, part in Italian), called *Un Ospite di Venezia.* A section of this useful publication lists events, including any music and opera or theatrical presentations, along with art exhibitions and local special events.

Teatro La Fenice ★★★ (© **041/786511;** www.teatrolafenice.it) reopened in 2004 after renovations in the wake of a 1996 fire. New seating gives the renovated hall a total of 1,076 seats, and the stage curtain was donated by Italian fashion designer Laura Biagiotti. Tickets and subscriptions can be purchased in person from the Ve.La box offices at Piazzale Roma and Ferrovia Scalzi, both of which are open daily 8:30am to 6:30pm. For further information call Ve.La (© **041/2424**).

The **Teatro Goldoni ★**, Calle Goldoni, near Campo San Luca, San Marco 4650B (© **041/2402011**), honors Carlo Goldoni (1707–93), the most prolific and one of the best of the Italian playwrights. The theater presents a changing repertoire of productions, often plays in Italian, but musical presentations as well. The box office is open Monday to Saturday 10am to 1pm and 4:30 to 7pm, and tickets cost 15€ to 30€.

In olden days, wealthy Venetians were rowed down the Grand Canal while being serenaded by gondoliers. To date, no one has improved on that age-old but now very expensive custom. Strolling through St. Mark's Square, having a cup of espresso at one of the two famous cafes (see below), and listening to a band concert may be even better.

CAFES & BARS Venice's most famous spot is **Caffè Florian ★★★**, Piazza San Marco, San Marco 56–59 (© **041/5205641;** www.caffeflorian.com), built in 1720 and elaborately decorated with plush red banquettes, elaborate murals under glass, and Art Nouveau lighting. The Florian has hosted everyone from Casanova to Lord Byron and Goethe. Light lunch is served noon to 3pm, and an English tea is offered 3 to 6pm, when you can select from a choice of pastries, ice creams, and cakes. It's open Thursday to Tuesday 10am to midnight; it's closed the week before Christmas and January 7 to January 13.

Its rival, **Quadri ★★★**, Piazza San Marco, San Marco 120–124 (© **041/5289299;** www.quadrivenice.com), stands on the opposite side of the square from Florian's and is as elegantly decorated in antique style. It should be: It was founded in 1638. Wagner used to drop in for a drink when he was working on *Tristan und Isolde.* The bar was a favorite with the Austrians during their long-ago occupation. From April to October, it's open daily 9am to 11:30pm; in the off season, it is closed on Mondays, as well as the first week of December and the first week of January.

The single most famous of all the watering holes of Ernest Hemingway is **Harry's Bar,** Calle Vallaresso, San Marco 1323 (© 041/5285777; www.cipriani.com). Harry's is known for inventing its own drinks and exporting them around the world, and it's said that *carpaccio,* the delicate raw-beef dish, was invented here. Fans say that Harry's makes the best Bellini in the world, although many old-time visitors still prefer a vodka martini. Harry's Bar is now found around the world, but this is the original (the others are unauthorized knockoffs). Celebrities frequent the place during the various film and art festivals. Harry's is open daily 10:30am to 11pm.

The hippest cafe in Venice today is funky little **Cip's ★**, on Isola della Giudecca, within the Cipriani Hotel (© **041/5207744**). Pronounced *chips* (as in potato), this cafe with its summer terrace frames one of the grandest views of Piazza San Marco. If you arrive between May and August, ask for a Bellini, made from prosecco and white-peach purée. You can also order the best bitter chocolate gelato in Venice here. Cip's also serves terrific international and Venetian dishes. It closes from November 8 to March 31. To reach the place, take the *vaporetto* to Zittelle.

At **Vino Vino,** Ponte della Veste, San Marco 2007A (© **041/2417688**), you can choose from more than 350 Italian and imported wines (available by the glass or by the bottle). This place is loved by everyone from snobs to young people, to almostbroke tourists. Popular and supercheap Venetian dishes are served. Main dishes range from 10€ to 22€. It's open daily 11:30am to 11:30pm.

CLUBS   Near the Accademia, **Il Piccolo Mondo,** Calle Contarini Corfu, Dorsoduro 1056A (© **041/5200371;** www.piccolomondo.biz), is open during the day but comes alive with dance music at night. The crowd is often young. It's open daily 10pm to 4am, but the action actually doesn't begin until after midnight. Cover, including the first drink, is 10€ Thursday and Friday, and 15€ Saturday.

An Excursion to Padua

The most popular day trip out of Venice, and a spot easily reached by rail, is the ancient university city of Padua, 25 miles (40km) west of Venice. Padua remains a major art center of the Venetia region. A university that grew to fame throughout Europe was founded here as early as 1222 (in time, Galileo and the Poet Tasso were to attend).

Padua itself is sometimes known as *La Città del Santo* (City of the Saint), the reference being to St. Anthony of Padua, who is buried at a basilica the city dedicated to him. *Il Santo* was an itinerant Franciscan monk (who is not to be confused with St. Anthony of Egypt, the monastic hermit who could resist all temptations of the Devil).

GETTING THERE   Padua-bound trains depart for and arrive from Venice once every 30 minutes (trip time: about 30 min.), costing 2.90€ to 18€ depending on the train, for a one-way ticket. For information and schedules, call © **892021.** Padua's main rail terminus is at the **Piazza Stazione,** north of the historic core and outside the 16th-century walls. Frequent buses run to the center from the station.

TOURIST INFORMATION The **Padua Tourist Office** is at Galleria Pedrocchi (✆ **049/8767927;** www.turismopadova.it), and open Monday to Saturday from 9am to 12:30pm and 3 to 7pm. There's another tourist office at the train station (✆ **049-8752077**), open Monday to Saturday 9am to 7pm and Sunday 9:15am to noon.

TOP ATTRACTIONS & SPECIAL MOMENTS

Many visitors arrive just to visit **Cappella degli Scrovegni,** Piazza Eremitani 8, off Corso Garibaldi (✆ **049/2010020;** www.cappelladegliscrovegni.it; bus: 3, 8, 12, or 18), to see the celebrated *Giotto frescoes* ★★★. Sometime around 1305 and 1306, Giotto did a cycle of more than 35 (remarkably well-preserved) frescoes inside, which (along with those at Assisi) form the basis of his claim to fame. Like an illustrated storybook, the frescoes unfold biblical scenes. The third bottom panel (lower level on the right) depicts Judas kissing a most skeptical Christ, perhaps the most reproduced and widely known panel in the cycle. On the entrance wall is Giotto's *Last Judgment,* with Hell winning out for sheer fascination. The chapel is open daily from 9am to 9:30pm, and charges an admission fee of 12€ for adults and 5€ for ages 6 to 17. The fee includes entrance to the nearby **Museo Civico di Padova** ★, Piazza Eremitani 8 (✆ **049/8204551**), open Tuesday to Sunday from 9am to 7pm. Of the museums sheltered in this building, the picture gallery is the most important—filled with minor works by major Venetian artists, dating from the 14th century.

The art world lost heavily on March 11, 1944, when Allied bombs rained down on **Chiesa degli Eremitani** ★, Piazza Eremitani 9 (✆ **049/8756410;** bus: 3, 8, 12, or 18). Before that time, it housed one of the greatest art treasures in Italy, the **Ovetari Chapel,** frescoed by Andrea Mantegna. The cycle of frescoes ★ was the first significant work by Mantegna (1431–1506). The church was rebuilt, but you can't resurrect 15th-century frescoes, of course. Inside, in the chapel to the right of the main altar, are fragments left after the bombing, a preview of what we missed in Mantegna's work. The most interesting fresco saved is a panel depicting the dragging of St. Christopher's body through the streets. Note also the *Assumption of the Virgin.* Mantegna is recommended even to those who don't like "religious painting." In the chancel chapel are some **splendid frescoes** ★★ attributed to Guarineto, a Venetian student of the great Giotto. The chapel is admission free and open Monday to Saturday from 8am to 6pm, Sunday from 10am to 1pm and 4 to 7pm.

At Piazza del Santo, **Basilica di Sant'Antonio** ★★ (✆ **049/8242811;** www.basilicadelsanto.org; bus: 3, 8, 12, or 18) dates from the 13th century, when it was dedicated to St. Anthony of Padua, interred inside. The basilica is a hodgepodge of styles, with mainly Romanesque and Gothic features. It has as many cupolas as Salome had veils. *Campanili* and minarets combine to give it a curious Eastern appearance. Inside, the **interior** ★★ is richly frescoed and decorated—and usually swarming with pilgrims devoutly ritualistic to the point of paganism, touching "holy" marble supposed to have divine power. The greatest art treasures are the **Donatello bronzes** ★★ at the main altar, with a realistic *Crucifix* (fluid, lyrical line) towering over the rest. Seek out, too, the Donatello relief depicting the removal of Christ from the cross, a unified composition expressing in simple lines the tragedy of Christ and the sadness of the mourners—an unromantic approach.

WHERE TO DINE

At some point, head for **Caffè Pedrocchi** ★★, Piazzetta Pedrocchi 15 (✆ **049/8781231;** www.caffepedrocchi.it), off Piazza Cavour in a neoclassical landmark hailed as the most elegant coffeehouse in Europe when it opened its doors in 1831. It's open Tuesday through Sunday from 8am to midnight.

For a special lunch, visit **Antico Brolo ★★**, Corso Milano 22 (© **049/664555**), across from the town's Civic Theater. Installed in a Renaissance-style dining room, with tables on its garden terrace, this restaurant serves the best food in town, a combination of the Veneto and Italian in general. Seasonal ingredients are used to shape the changing menu of classic dishes, many given a modern twist. Main courses cost 16€ to 39€, and hours are Tuesday to Sunday from 12:30 to 2:30pm and 7:30 to midnight (closed Aug 10–20).

An Excursion to Verona

The fictional home of Shakespeare's "pair of star-cross'd lovers," Romeo and Juliet, Verona is 71 miles (114km) west of Venice. In the city's medieval "age of flowering" under the despotic, often cruel Scaligeri princes, Verona reached the pinnacle of its influence and prestige, developing into a town that even today is among the great art cities of Italy. The best-known member of the ruling Della Scala family, Can Grande I, was a patron of Dante. His sway over Verona has often been compared to that of Lorenzo the Magnificent over Florence.

GETTING THERE   A total of 36 trains a day make the 2-hour run between Venice and Verona, charging 6.15€ to 28€ depending on the train, for a one-way ticket. From Milan and points west, there are many trains a day that make the 2-hour journey to Verona. Tickets cost 8€ to 24€ one-way. Four daily trains come up from Rome, the 5-hour journey costing 40€ one-way.

Trains arrive at Verona's **Stazione Porta Nuova,** Piazza XXV Aprile, south of the centrally located arena and Piazza Brà; call © **892021** for schedules and information. A branch of the **Verona Tourist Office** (© **045/8000861**) is located at the rail station. It's open Monday to Saturday from 8am to 7pm and Sunday 9am to 2pm and 3 to 5pm.

TOURIST INFORMATION   The **Verona Tourist Office** is at Via Degli Alpini 9, at Piazza Brà (© **045/8068680**; www.tourism.verona.it). Hours are Monday to Saturday 8:30am to 7pm and Sunday 9am to 1pm and 2 to 5pm. The tourist office and its railway branch don't make hotel reservations.

TOP ATTRACTIONS & SPECIAL MOMENTS

The most famous and most beautiful square in Verona is **Piazza dei Signori ★★**, dominated by the **Palazzo del Governo,** where Cangrande extended the shelter of his "hearth and home" to that fleeing Florentine Dante Alighieri. The marble statue in the center of the square is of the "divine poet." Facing Dante's back is the later 15th-century **Loggia del Consiglio,** surmounted by five statues. The most attractive building on the square, the loggia is frescoed. Five different arches lead into the Piazza dei Signori, the innermost chamber of the heart of Verona.

The **Arche Scaligere** are outdoor tombs surrounded by wrought-iron gates that form a kind of open-air pantheon of the Scaligeri princes. One tomb, that of Cangrande della Scala, rests directly over the door of the 12th-century **Santa Maria Antica.**

Basilica San Zeno Maggiore ★★, Piazza San Zeno (© **045/8006120**), is a near-perfect Romanesque church and *campanile,* graced with a stunning entrance— two pillars supported by puce-colored marble lions and surmounted with a rose window called the **Ruota della Fortuna (Wheel of Fortune).** On either side of the portal are bas-reliefs depicting scenes from the Old and New Testaments, as well as a mythological story portraying Theodoric as a huntsman lured to hell (the king of the Goths defeated Odoacer in Verona). The panels on the bronze doors—nearly 50 in all—are truly a remarkable achievement of medieval art, sculpted perhaps in the 12th century. Admission is 3€, and hours are April to October Monday to Saturday 8:30am to 6pm, Sunday 1 to 6pm; November to March Tuesday to Saturday 10am to 1pm, Sunday 1 to 5pm.

Arena di Verona ★★, Piazza Brà (© **045/8005151;** www.arena.it), evoking the Colosseum in Rome, is an elliptically shaped amphitheater dating from the 1st century A.D. Four arches of the "outer circle" and a complete "inner ring" still stand, which is rather remarkable because an earthquake hit this area in the 12th century. For nearly half a century, it's been the setting of a summer opera house, usually from mid-July to mid-August. More than 20,000 people are treated to Verdi, Mascagni, or a performance of *Aïda,* the latter considered by some to be "the greatest operatic spectacle in the world." Admission is 4.50€ for adults and 1€ for children ages 8 to 13. It's open Tuesday to Sunday from 8:30am to 7:30pm (on performance days 9am–3pm), Monday 1:45 to 7:30pm.

The 14th-century **Castelvecchio (Old Castle) ★★**, Corso Castelvecchio 2 (© **045/8062611**), is situated alongside the Adige River (and reached by heading out the Via Roma). It stands near the Ponte Scaligera, the famous bridge bombed by the Nazis in World War II and subsequently reconstructed. The former seat of the Della Scala family, the restored castle has now been turned into an **Art Museum,** with important paintings from the Veronese school. Admission is 6€, and hours are Monday 1:30 to 7:30pm, Tuesday to Sunday 8:30am to 7:30pm; last admission is at 6:30pm.

WHERE TO DINE

While not the gourmet citadel of Italy, Verona is blessed with a series of good restaurants, notably **Ristorante 12 Apostoli ★★**, Vicolo Corticella San Marco 3 (© **045/596999;** www.12apostoli.it), which, at 250 years old, is the city's oldest. The present owners, the Gioco brothers, keep it humming, with Giorgio being the culinary whiz in the kitchen and Franco welcoming you to the table. This is Italian cookery with a flair prepared with market-fresh ingredients; main courses cost 18€ to 28€. Open Tuesday to Sunday 12:30 to 2:30pm and Tuesday to Saturday 7 to 10pm. Closed the first week in January and June 15 to July 5.

Another choice, almost as good, is **Ristorante Re Teodorico ★**, Piazzale Castel San Pietro 1 (© **045/8349990;** www.ristorantereteodorico.com), serving a finely honed regional and international cuisine at a site on the edge of town, opening onto vistas of Verona and the Adige. At a table under an arbor, you can partake of some of the finest and most imaginative dishes in Verona, featuring the freshest of fish and meat dishes, with main courses costing 17€ to 28€. A special delight is ravioli filled with fresh asparagus and served in a mushroom-cream sauce. It's open Thursday to Tuesday (closed Sun night) from noon to 3pm and 7 to 10pm. It's closed January 1 to January 24.

Rewriting its Italian and international menu every 6 months, **Brunello,** in the Due Torri Hotel Baglioni, Piazza Sant'Anastasia 4 (© **045/595044**), serves impeccably fresh ingredients fashioned into a series of palate-pleasing dishes that transcend the ordinary. Spicings and flavorings are subtle, and sometimes seemingly ill-matched ingredients are cooked into harmonious platters of delight. Main courses cost 19€ to 35€, and hours are daily from 12:30 to 2:30pm and 7 to 10:30pm. Reservations are recommended.

MILAN & THE NORTHWEST

Busy Milan is a commercial powerhouse and, partly because of its banks and major industrial companies, Italy's most influential city. It's the center of publishing, silk production, TV and advertising, and fashion design; it's also close to Italy's densest collection of automobile-assembly plants, rubber and textile factories, and chemical plants. The industry and prosperity of the capital of the Lombardy region have imbued it with a 21st-century commercial atmosphere unlike Italy's other large cities, where the past is so tangible.

The city's commercialism, combined with World War II bombings, has spared very few of the city's oldest buildings, but those that do remain are definitely worth visiting. And Milan also boasts La Scala, one of Europe's most prestigious opera houses.

For the rail traveler, Milan is an ideal stopover during a grand tour of Europe, as several of Europe's most strategic rail lines converge here and most international trains heading into Italy stop in the city. It's also home to one of the major airports welcoming arriving traffic from North America, so many people start off their Italian rail journeys in this metropolis. From Milan, you can make connections (many of them high speed) to all of the major cities in Italy. Though we rank this the fourth-best city in the Italian scheme of things, Milan is definitely the busiest and best of Italy's rail hubs.

Station Information

GETTING FROM THE AIRPORT TO THE TRAIN STATION

Milan has two airports: **Aeroporto di Linate,** 4¼ miles (6.8km) east of the inner city, and the **Aeroporto Malpensa,** 27 miles (43km) northwest. Malpensa is used for most transatlantic flights, whereas Linate is used for flights within Italy and Europe. For general airport and flight information, call ✆ **02/74852200.**

Malpensa Express (www.malpensaexpress.it) trains connect Malpensa airport with the minor rail station, Stazione Cadorna, in the center of Milan. The trip takes about 45 minutes; trains generally leave every 30 minutes, but for an up-to-date schedule between the airport and the city, check the website. A one-way fare costs 11€ for adults and 6€ for children 4 to 12. The trip is not covered by a railpass. For more information, call ✆ **199/151152.**

Buses run between Linate and Milan's Centrale station every 30 minutes daily from 6am to 11:45pm. A bus (no. 73) also runs between Piazza San Babila and Linate airport every 20 minutes daily from 6am to 12:30am. Buses run from Malpensa to Stazione Centrale daily every 30 to 45 minutes, costing 7€ one-way. Buses from Linate to Milan's Centrale Station cost 5€ one-way. Bus no. 73, from Linate to Piazza San Babila, costs only 1€ one-way. For information about buses from Linate to Milan, call ✆ **800/808181.** For information about buses from Malpensa to Milan and vice versa, call ✆ **0331/519000.** This is much cheaper than taking a taxi, which could run you a whopping 70€.

INSIDE THE STATION

Milan has the finest rail connections in Italy. The main rail station for arrivals is Mussolini's mammoth **Stazione Centrale,** Piazza Duca d'Aosta (✆ **892021**), where you'll find the National Railways information office open daily from 7am to 9pm.

One train per hour arrives from Genoa (trip time: 1½ hr.), costing 15€ one-way. Trains from Turin to Milan take 1 hour, 55 minutes, costing 9.20€ to 15€ one-way.

The new high-speed train (Frecciarossa) from Turin takes only 1 hour, costing 31€ to 44€ one-way. Twenty-five trains arrive daily from Venice (trip time: 3 hr.), costing 30€ to 42€ one-way. Trains from Florence to Milan take 3½ hours, costing 28€ to 38€ one-way. The new high-speed train (Frecciarossa) from Florence takes only 1 hour and 45 minutes, costing 52€ to 67€ one-way. Trains from Rome to Milan take 6 hours and 35 minutes, with the high-speed train (Frecciarossa) taking 3½ hours. A one-way ticket costs 46€ to 109€, depending on the train. Artesia trains arrive daily from Paris. Contact Rail Europe for more information.

The station is directly northeast of the heart of town; trams, buses, and the Metro link the station to Piazza del Duomo in the very center.

At the train station, you can arrange for luggage storage daily from 6am to midnight; the cost is 4€ for the first 5 hours, .60€ for the following 6 hours, and .20€ per hour for the remaining time. Baggage-check facilities are labeled *Deposito Bagagli* and are on the ground floor in the internal walking path (side piazza Luigi di Savoia). The lost property office, **Ufficio Oggetti Smarriti Comune** (© 02/63712027), is open Monday to Friday from 8:30am to 4pm. There are also a pharmacy, currency exchange, and ATMs.

For train information, look for a black I sign. The office is located at the extreme right end of the station as you enter from the tracks on the ground floor. The British flag indicates that an English-speaking clerk is there to help you daily from 7am to 9pm. Note, however, that this is not the office at which to make reservations for EuroCity, InterCity, Rapido Express, or Eurostar Italia trains. To reach that office, go through the main station hall and down the stairs to the foyer on the lower street level. Look for a door marked *Biglietteria Est,* meaning Ticket Office East, and go through that entrance, then take a number from the machine and wait your turn. This reservation office—counters no. 49 and 53—is called *Prenotazioni,* and the hours are daily from 5:45am to 11:45pm. For railpass validation, you must go to another office at the station's street level. It's marked *Biglietteria Ovest;* reservations are processed at windows no. 20 and 22. These windows are marked INTERNATIONAL TICKETS (yes, in English).

A branch of the **Milan Tourist Office** at Stazione Central (© 02/77404318) is open Monday through Saturday from 9am to 6pm, and Sunday from 9am to 1pm and 2 to 5pm. The staff here will give you a list of hotels but will not make reservations. Because Milan is a city of commerce that's often filled with business clients or hosting conventions, a hotel reservation should be made before you ever get to the city.

Note: The area surrounding the train station is not the safest after dark; caution should be used when leaving or arriving here at night.

Information Elsewhere in the City

The main tourist office, **Azienda di Promozione Turistica del Milanese,** is at Piazza del Duomo (the very heart of Milan), at Via Marconi 1 (© 02/77404343). It's open Monday to Saturday 8:45am to 1pm and 2 to 6pm, and Sunday 9am to 1pm and 2 to 5pm. The staff will provide a listing of hotels but won't make reservations.

Getting Around

The **Metro subway** system is extensive and efficient, covering most of Milan; in addition, there are buses and trams, making it fairly easy to navigate. Regular tickets cost 1€ and are sold at Metro stations and newsstands. Some subway tickets are good for continuing trips on city buses at no extra charge, but they must be used within 75

Milan

Milan ○ Venice

Florence

Rome

ITALY

ACCOMMODATIONS ■

Antica Locanda dei Mercanti **4**
Antica Locanda Leonardo **2**
Casa Mia **14**
Hotel Gran Duca di York **6**
Hotel Rovello **3**

DINING ◆

A Santa Lucia **12**
Boeucc Antico Ristorante **11**
Cracco **9**
Trattoria Bagutta **13**
Trattoria Milanese **8**

ATTRACTIONS ●

Ambrosiana Library
 & Picture Gallery **7**
Brera Picture Gallery **5**
Il Duomo & Baptistery **10**
Santa Maria delle Grazie
 (*The Last Supper*) **1**

Information *i*
Metro — Ⓜ

0   1/4 mi
0   0.25 km

12

ITALY | Milan & the Northwest

minutes of purchase. You must stamp your ticket when you board a bus or tram, or risk incurring a fine. The tourist office and all subway ticket offices sell a **travel pass** for 3€ for 1 day, or 5.50€ for 2 days, good for unlimited use on the city's tram, bus, and subway network. For information on transportation in Milan, call A.T.M. (© **800/808181** toll-free in Italy, daily 7:30am–7:30pm).

To phone a **taxi,** dial © **02/4040,** 02/8585, or 02/8383; fares start at 3€, with a nighttime surcharge of 6.10€.

Where to Stay

Antica Locanda dei Mercanti   In the historic district, this eccentric choice won't please everybody, but it has its devotees. This sophisticated and reasonably priced hotel is a favorite with many movers and shakers in Milan's fashion industry. Former model Paolo Ora gutted the second floor of a building from the 1800s and turned it into this little charmer in 1996. Each midsize room comes with a marble-clad shower-only bathroom, and the design lines are sleek and contemporary, with fine use of fabrics. Some rooms have canopied beds, and all feature fresh flowers, books, and magazines.

Via San Tommaso 6, 20123 Milano. © **02/8054080.** Fax 02/8054090. www.locanda.it. 14 units (showers only). 185€–275€ double. MC, V. Tram: 1, 14, or 24. Metro: Cairoli, Cordusio, or Duomo. **Amenities:** Smoke-free rooms. *In room:* A/C (in some).

Antica Locanda Leonardo ★ 🎁   If you're seeking both atmosphere and comfort, this undiscovered gem is a worthy choice. A restored 19th-century building houses the hotel, whose chief grace note is an inner courtyard and garden that features wildly blooming wisteria in summer. Even though it's in the city center, it enjoys a very tranquil location. Many of the bedrooms open onto small balconies, and the mostly midsize rooms are individually decorated in styles ranging from Liberty to rococo, to very modern. Half of the bathrooms come with a shower, the rest with a tub.

Corso Magenta 78, 20123 Milano. © **02/463317.** Fax 02/48019012. www.leoloc.com. 20 units. 165€–245€ double; 285€ triple. Rates include continental breakfast. AE, DC, MC, V. **Amenities:** Bar; 1 room for those w/limited mobility.

Casa Mia 🔱   This small, attentive hotel is one of the best maintained and comfortable (for the price) in the area of Central Station, and it lies within easy access to all of Milan. The small, family-run hotel is on the second floor of a modern building. Bedrooms are simply furnished, ranging from small to midsize, with tiny bathrooms. The staff is welcoming and helpful.

Viale Vittorio Veneto 30, 20124 Milano. © **02/6575249.** Fax 02/92877803. www.casamiahotel.it. 15 units. 55€–150€ double; 75€–200€ triple. Rates include continental breakfast. AE, MC, V. Parking 23€. Metro: Repubblica. **Amenities:** Bar.

Hotel Gran Duca di York ★★   This Liberty-style *palazzo* dates from the 1890s, when it was constructed by the Catholic Church to shelter the clergy from the nearby Duomo. Among them was the cardinal of Milan, who later became Pope Pius XI. Today anyone can rent one of the pleasantly furnished and well-kept rooms. They range in size from small to medium in size, and each has a tiled bathroom.

Via Moneta 1A (Piazza Cordusio), 20123 Milano. © **02/874863.** Fax 02/8690344. www.ducadiyork.com. 33 units. 208€–248€ double. Rates include buffet breakfast. AE, MC, V. Closed Aug. Metro: Cordusio or Duomo. **Amenities:** Bar.

Hotel Rovello This affordable hotel's location is ideal, close to the Santa Maria delle Grazie, between Castello Sforzesco and Piazza Duomo. Renovations added soundproofing to the windows and improved the hotel's guest rooms, which are furnished in a minimalist yet comfortable style, but many original details have been retained. Hardwood floors, orthopedic mattresses, and small dressing areas in some units add to this hotel's charm, along with the immaculately kept shower-only bathrooms. The place is not luxurious but is highly commendable.

Via Rovello 18, 20121 Milano. ⓒ **02/86464654.** Fax 02/72023656. www.hotel-rovello.it. 10 units. 120€–220€ double; 150€–260€ triple. Rates include continental breakfast. AE, DC, MC, V. Bus: 1, 2, 3, 4, 12, 14, 18, 19, 20, 24, or 27. Metro: Cordusio. **Amenities:** Bar.

Top Attractions & Special Moments

Ambrosiana Library & Picture Gallery (Biblioteca–Pinacoteca Ambrosiana) ★★ Near the Duomo, this museum houses one of the leading art galleries in the north of Italy, primarily featuring paintings from the 15th through the 17th centuries. Among its most famous works are *Madonna and Angels,* by Botticelli; works by Bruegel; paintings by Lombard artists, including Bramantino's *Presepe;* a curious miniature *St. Jerome with Crucifix,* by Andrea Solario; and works by Bernardino Luini. One of the museum's highlights is room 10, with 10 magnificent **cartoons by Raphael** ★★★, which he prepared for the frescoes of the School of Athens in the Vatican. Another room contains a collection of reproductions from the drawings of Leonardo da Vinci's *Codex Atlanticus.* The **Ambrosiana Library** contains many medieval manuscripts that are shown for scholarly examination only.

Piazza Pio XI 2. ⓒ **02/806921.** www.ambrosiana.eu. Admission 10€ adults; seniors and children 17 and under 5€. Tues–Sun 10am–5:30pm. Metro: Duomo or Cordusio.

Brera Picture Gallery (Pinacoteca di Brera) ★★★ A 17th-century palace houses one of the finest collections of paintings in Italy. Most of the paintings are religious works, especially by Lombard and other northern Italian painters, but you'll also find representative paintings by El Greco, Rubens, Rembrandt, and Van Dyck. One of the gallery's prize possessions is the *Urbino Altarpiece,* by Piero della Francesca, depicting the Virgin and Child surrounded by a number of saints with the Duke of Urbino kneeling in the foreground. Also on display are Mantegna's ***Dead Christ*** ★★★, Giovanni Bellini's ***La Pietà*** ★★, Carpaccio's ***St. Stephen Debating*** ★★, and Bernardino's ***Virgin of the Rose Bush.*** Another masterpiece is Raphael's ***Bethrothal of the Virgin*** ★★. The Venetian School is well represented in the works of Titian, Tintoretto, and Veronese.

Via Brera 28. ⓒ **02/722631.** www.brera.beniculturali.it. Admission 10€. Tues–Sun 8:30am–7:30pm. Metro: Lanza or Montenapoleone.

Il Duomo & Baptistery ★★★ Dominating the Piazza del Duomo, Milan's cathedral is the largest Gothic structure in Italy. Begun in 1386, it took nearly 500 years to complete. Work was carried on during this period by architects and master masons from France and Germany, as well as all parts of Italy, giving the Duomo a flamboyant Gothic **exterior** ★★★ more reminiscent of the cathedrals north of the Alps than of its sister churches in Italy. With a floor plan in the shape of a Latin cross and five naves, the cathedral is supported by 40 exterior buttresses and 50 interior columns. Its height, including the spire topped by a gilded statue of the Virgin (added in 1859), is 367 feet (110m). More than 3,000 statues decorate the inside and outside.

To experience the Duomo at its most majestic, you must take the elevator to the **roof** or **visita ai terrazzo** ★★★, where you can walk through a forest of pinnacles, turrets, and marble statuary.

Piazza del Duomo. ⓒ **02/86463456.** www.duomomilano.it. Cathedral free; roof via stairs 5€, roof via elevator 7€; crypt free; baptistery 1.50€. Cathedral daily 7am-7pm. Roof daily 9am-5:30pm. Crypt daily 9am-noon and 2:30-6pm. Baptistery Tues-Sun 9:30am-5pm. Metro: Duomo.

Santa Maria delle Grazie & *The Last Supper* ★★ At the same time that Bramante was adding the purely Renaissance dome to the transitional Gothic church on the Piazza Santa Maria delle Grazie, his friend Leonardo da Vinci was working on his great fresco, ***The Last Supper (Il Cenacolo Vinciano)*** ★★★, in the adjoining refectory of the Dominican convent. Bramante's vast domed crossing with its apsed transepts and choir struck an entirely original note in Milanese architecture. Visitors today often ignore the main church, however, and go directly to the simple refectory next door to gaze in awe at what is the best-known and most frequently copied religious painting in the world. Although Leonardo's *The Last Supper* miraculously survived such threats as a bombing attack in World War II, it is barely holding its own against the ravages of time. The painting depicts Christ at the moment when he announces that 1 of the 12 will betray him. Only 25 people are admitted at one time, and for a timed 15 minutes, so be prepared to wait in line.

Piazza Santa Maria delle Grazie (off Corso Magenta). ⓒ **02/4987588.** Free admission to church; 6.50€, plus 3.50€ for reservation to see *The Last Supper.* Church Mon-Sat 7:30am-noon and 3-7pm; Sun 3:30-6:30pm. *The Last Supper* viewings Tues-Sun 8:15am-6:45pm. Reservations required for *The Last Supper;* call Mon-Sat 8am-7pm and leave your name. Metro: Cadorna or Conciliazione.

Where to Dine

A Santa Lucia ★ MEDITERRANEAN/SEAFOOD   This festive place is decked out with photographs of pleased celebs, who attest to the skill of the kitchen. You can order such specialties as savory fish soup (a meal in itself), fried baby squid, or well-prepared sole. *Spaghetti alla vongole* evokes the tang of the sea with its succulent clam sauce. A signature pasta is *rigatoni strascicati* (pasta with tomatoes, fresh basil, and hot chili peppers). Pizza also reigns supreme: Try either the calzone or the traditional pie, both *alla napoletana.*

Via San Pietro all'Orto 3. ⓒ **02/76023155.** www.asantalucia.it. Reservations recommended. Main courses 12€-30€. AE, DC, MC, V. Daily noon-3pm and 7pm-1am. Closed Aug. Metro: San Babila.

Boeucc Antico Ristorante INTERNATIONAL/MILANESE   This longtime favorite, opened in 1696, features a trio of rooms in an antique *palazzo* that's within walking distance of the Duomo and the major shopping arteries. In summer, guests gravitate to a terrace for open-air dining. You might enjoy ravioli with lobster and scampi, salmon steak flavored with green peppercorns, or swordfish in a sauce made of capers and white wine.

Piazza Belgioioso 2. ⓒ **02/76020224.** www.boeucc.it. Reservations required. Main courses 13€-28€. AE. Mon-Fri 12:40-2:30pm; Sun-Fri 7:40-10:30pm. Closed Dec 25-Jan 4, Easter, and Aug. Metro: Duomo, Montenapoleone, or San Babila.

Cracco ★ MILANESE/ITALIAN   Some of the freshest and tastiest dishes in Milan are served by an efficient staff, including a classic version of risotto Milanese (with his own imaginative twist), amid shimmering marble and modern Italian paintings. A sea urchin salad is a specialty, as is a concoction of layers of marinated egg yolk with smoked sea bass. The wine cellar features 1,800 kinds of wine from around the world.

Via Victor Hugo 4. ✆ **02/876774.** www.ristorantecracco.it. Reservations required. Main courses 32€–48€. AE, DC, MC, V. Mon–Fri 12:30–2pm and 7:30–10pm; Sat 7:30–10pm. Closed Dec 23–Jan 11 and 3 weeks starting Aug 15. Metro: Duomo.

Trattoria Bagutta ★ INTERNATIONAL   Dating from 1927, this bustling trattoria has long been our favorite in Milan, and we always have at least one or two meals here on every visit. The cuisine is not just from Lombardy, but also borrows heavily from the kitchens of Tuscany and Bologna. This is generous, home-style cooking, and the interior is cozy and comfortable, amusingly decorated with caricatures of famous Italians (the rear dining room is the most enticing). Main-dish specialties include fried squid and scampi; rigatoni with cream, peas, and a beef ragout; linguine with shrimp in tomato-cream sauce; and *scaloppine alla Bagutta* (veal baked with fresh tomatoes, mozzarella, and lettuce).

Via Bagutta 14. ✆ **02/76002767.** Reservations required. Main courses 15€–30€. AE, DC, MC, V. Mon–Sat 12:30–2:30pm and 7:30–10:30pm. Closed Dec 24, Jan 6, and Aug. Metro: San Babila.

Trattoria Milanese ★ 🍴 MILANESE/LOMBARD   West of the Duomo, this traditional trattoria has been a local favorite since 1933. In a narrow lane in a historic district of Milan, it is most convenient for dining as you tour the sights of the historic core. Begin with the *minestrone alla Milanese.* The *risotto alla milanese* is classic, simple, and good. Two classic dishes are the *osso buco alla milanese* (on-the-bone shin of veal cooked slowly with wine and vegetables) and their *cotoletta alla milanese* (breaded veal sautéed to a golden brown).

Via Santa Marta 11. ✆ **02/86451991.** Reservations required. Main courses 8€–19€. AE, DC, MC, V. Wed–Mon noon–3pm and 7pm–1am. Closed July 18–Aug and Dec 25–Jan 7. Metro: Cordusio.

Shopping

London has Harrods, Paris has all the big-name boutiques you can think of, and Rome and Florence instill an acquisitional fever in the eyes of anyone who even window-gazes. Milan, however, is blessed with one of the most unusual concentrations of shopping possibilities in Europe. Most of the boutiques are infused with the style, humor, and sophistication that has made Milan the dynamo of the Italian fashion industry, a place where the sidewalks sizzle with the hard-driving entrepreneurial spirit that has been part of the northern Italian textile industry for centuries.

A walk on the fashion subculture's focal point, **via Montenapoleone**—heart of the Golden Triangle and one of Italy's great shopping streets—a mile-long (1.6km) strip that has become a showcase for famous (and high-priced) makers of clothes and shoes, with excursions into the side streets, will quickly confirm that Milan is home to what one shopper we met deemed, "the most unbelievable variety of shoes, clothes, and accessories in the world."

Early-morning risers will be welcomed only by silent streets and closed gates. Most shops are closed all day Sunday and Monday (although some open on Mon afternoon). Some stores open at 9am unless they're very chic, and then they're not likely to open until 10:30am. They remain open, for the most part, until 1pm, reopening again between 3:30 and 7:30pm.

Bargain hunters leave the Golden Triangle and head for a mile-long (1.6km) stretch of **Corso Buenos Aires,** where you can find style at more affordable prices. Start off at **Piazza Oberdan,** the square closest to the heart of Milan. Clothing abounds on Corso Buenos Aires, especially casual wear and knockoffs of designer goods. But you'll also find a vast array of merchandise, from scuba-diving equipment to soft luggage. Saturdays are unbelievably crowded here. You'll find more bargains in the **Brera,** the name given to a sprawling shopping district around the Brera Museum. This area is far more attractive than Corso Buenos Aires and has often been compared to New York's Greenwich Village because of its cafes, shops, antiques stores, and art students. Skip the main street, **Via Brera,** and concentrate on the side streets, especially **Via Solferino, Via Madonnina,** and **Via Fiori Chiari.**

Nightlife

THE PERFORMING ARTS   The most complete list of cultural events appears in the large Milan newspaper, the left-wing *La Repubblica.* Try for a Thursday edition, which usually has the most complete listings.

The world's most famous opera house is **La Scala ★★★**, Piazza della Scala (Metro: Duomo). Reopening before Christmas in 2004, after 3 years of renovation, producers presented Mozart's envious antagonist Antonio Salieri's long-forgotten opera *Europe Riconosciuta,* which was an opera commissioned for the house's original opening in 1778. The opera had gone unproduced since that time—many critics felt with good reason. La Scala is fully restored, with a technologically advanced stage and a splendid auditorium. Critics raved about the new acoustics. There are now three movable stages and 200 added seats. Tickets are hard to come by for La Scala and should be arranged as far in advance as possible. Costing 10€ to 187€, tickets can be purchased at **Biglietteria Centrale** (② **02/72003744**), in the Galleria del Sagrato (Piazza Duomo), open daily noon to 6pm. Metro: Duomo. For more information, check out **www.teatroallascala.org**.

LIVE-MUSIC CLUBS   At **Le Scimmie,** Via Ascanio Sforza 49 (② **02/89402874;** www.scimmie.it; bus: 59), bands play everything from funk to blues to creative jazz. Doors open Tuesday to Sunday around 8pm, and music is presented 9:30pm to around 3am.

Rolling Stone, Corso XXII Marzo 32 (② **02/733172;** www.rollingstone.it; tram: 27), features head-banging rock bands. It's open every night, usually 10:30pm to 4am, but things don't get going until at least midnight. It's closed in August. Cover ranges from 13€ to 30€.

CAFES   **Sant'Ambroeus,** Corso Matteotti 7 (② **02/76000540;** www. santambroeusmilano.it; Metro: Montenapoleone), is the best pastry and coffee shop in Milan. The espresso will give you a jolt even if you've stayed up all night. Designers from the Dolce & Gabbana firm often hang out here. For the very best taste sensation, opt for the cafe's Ambrogetto chocolate. The cafe opens early for breakfast and serves until 8pm daily.

Boasting a chic crowd of garment-district workers and shoppers, **Café Cova ★**, Via Montenapoleone 8 (② **02/76000578;** www.pasticceriacova.it; Metro: Montenapoleone), has been around since 1817, serving pralines, chocolates, brioches, and sandwiches. The more elegant sandwiches contain smoked salmon and truffles. Sip your espresso from fragile gold-rimmed cups at one of the small tables in an elegant inner room or while standing at the prominent bar. It's closed in August and on Sunday year-round. Closing time is in the early evening.

An Excursion to Lake Como ★★★

Flower-bedecked promenades, lemon trees, romantic villas, parks and gardens, and crystal-clear blue waters welcome you to Lake Como, 30 miles (48km) north of Milan and stretching 2½ miles (4km) at its widest point. "Everything noble, everything evoking love"—that's how Stendhal characterized fork-tongued Lake Como. Others have called it "the looking glass of Venus."

GETTING THERE At the southern tip of the lake, the town of **Como,** known for its silk industry, makes a good base for exploring. Trains arrive daily at Como from Milan (trip time: 40 min.) every hour; fares cost 3.60€ one-way. **Stazione San Giovanni,** Piazzale San Gottardo (© **892021**), is at the end of Viale Gallio, a 15-minute walk from the center of Como (Piazza Cavour).

VISITOR INFORMATION In the exact center of town, at Piazza Cavour (#17), you'll find the **tourist office** (© **031/269712;** www.lakecomo.org). It's open Monday to Saturday from 9am to 1pm and 2:30 to 6pm. From June to September, it is open on Sunday 9am to 1pm. The staff doesn't make hotel reservations.

TOP ATTRACTIONS & SPECIAL MOMENTS

Touring **Lake Como** by boat is the main reason to visit the town of Como. It's easy to take a cruise around the lake; boats departing from the town's piers make calls at every significant settlement along its shores. Stroll down to the **Lungo Lario,** adjacent to Piazza Cavour, and head to the ticket windows of the **Società Navigazione Lago di Como** (© **031/304060;** www.navigazionelaghi.it). Half a dozen ferries and almost as many high-speed hydrofoils embark on circumnavigations of the lake. One-way transit from Como to Colico at the northern end of the lake takes 4 hours by ferry and 90 minutes by hydrofoil, and includes stops at each of the towns or major villages en route. Transit each way costs 10€ to 14€, depending on which boat you take. One-way transit between Como and Bellagio takes 2 hours by ferry and 45 minutes by hydrofoil, and costs 8.20€ to 12€ per person. There's no service from Como between October and Easter.

To get an overview of the lake area, take the funicular at Lungolario Trieste (near the main beach at Villa Genio) to the top of **Brunate,** a hill overlooking Como and providing a panoramic view. Departures are every 30 minutes daily, and the trip costs 4.50€ round-trip. For information, call © **031/303608.**

Before rushing off on a boat for a tour of the lake, you might want to visit the **Cattedrale di Como ★**, Piazza del Duomo (© **031/265244**). Construction on the cathedral began in the 14th century in the Lombard Gothic style and continued on through the Renaissance until the 1700s. Frankly, the exterior is more interesting than the interior. Dating from 1487, the exterior is lavishly decorated with statues, including those of Pliny the Elder (A.D. 23–79) and the Younger (A.D. 62–113), who one writer once called "the beautiful people of ancient Rome." Inside, look for the 16th-century tapestries depicting scenes from the Bible. The cathedral is open Monday to Saturday 7am to noon and 3 to 7pm.

WHERE TO DINE

Close to the cathedral, **Ristorante Imbarcadero ★**, in the Metropole & Suisse hotel, Piazza Cavour 20, 22100 Como (© **031/270166;** www.ristoranteimbarcadero. it), serves an enticing Lombard and Italian cuisine on tables placed near the edge of the lake. All the food, including the pastas, is homemade, and much of the fresh fish served here comes from the lake itself. Main courses cost 11€ to 24€, with a fixed-price menu at 25€. It's open daily from 12:30 to 2:30pm and 7:30 to 10:30pm, but is closed January 2 to January 6.

An Excursion to Turin ★★

Also known as Torino, Turin is one of Italy's richest cities and the automobile capital of the country. It was also the host city for the 2006 Olympic Winter Games. The capital of Piedmont, Turin became the first capital of a united Italy, and much of its history is linked to the House of Savoy. Its chief treasure is the Shroud of Turin, whose mysterious origins have been the subject of much controversy. Was it really the shroud that Joseph of Arimathea wrapped about the body of Christ when his body was removed from the cross?

In addition to being an economic powerhouse, Turin is a city of grace and elegance, known for its baroque architecture, its bevy of first-rate museums, its Fiat cars, its Juventus soccer team, and its scenic location at the foothills of the Alps.

GETTING THERE   Turin is a major **rail** terminus, with arrivals at **Stazione di Porta Nuova,** Corso Vittorio Emanuele (© **892021;** www.trenitalia.com), in the heart of the city. It takes 1 to 2 hours to reach Turin by train from Milan, but it takes anywhere from 4½ to 8 hours to reach Turin from Rome, depending on the connection. The one-way fare from Milan is 9.20€; from Rome, fares start at 45€. Direct trains also arrive here from Paris; for more information, contact Rail Europe.

TOURIST INFORMATION   Go to the office of **APT,** Piazza Castello (© 011/ 535181; www.turismotorino.org), which is open daily 9am to 7pm. There's another office at the Porta Nuova train station (same phone), open daily 9:30am to 7pm. These offices will make "last-minute" hotel reservations for free if you call 48 hours in advance—no sooner than that.

TOP ATTRACTIONS & SPECIAL MOMENTS

To begin your exploration, head first for the **Piazza San Carlo ★★**, the loveliest and most unified square in the city, covering about 3½ acres (1.4 hectares). Heavily bombed in the last war, it dates from the 17th century and was built to the design of Carlo di Castellamonte. In the heart of the piazza is an equestrian statue of Emanuele Filiberto (1528–80), Duke of Savoy and the only child of Charles III, who is known chiefly today for replacing Latin with Italian as the official language of the kingdom. The two churches are those of **Santa Cristina** and **San Carlo.** On the square, some of the most prestigious names in Italy have sat sipping coffee and plotting the unification of Italy. The most popular coffee house is the **Caffè Torino,** 204 Piazza San Carlo (© **011/545118;** www.caffe-torino.it), where, under the arcade, you'll often see elegant Turinese who turn up for pastries, Campari, and much talk.

The city's most interesting museums are located in the Guarini-designed, 17th-century **Science Academy Building,** 6 Via Accademia delle Scienze (www.museo egizio.it), whose ground floor houses an **Egyptian Museum ★★★** (011/5617776) with a collection so vast that it's surpassed only by the ones at Cairo and the British Museum in London. Of the statuary, that of **Ramses II** is the best known, though there is one of **Amenhotel II** as well. In the rather crowded wings upstairs, the world of the pharaohs lives on (one of the prized exhibits is the "Royal Papyrus," with its valuable chronicling of the Egyptian monarchs from the 1st through the 17th dynasties). The funereal art is exceptionally rare and valuable, especially the chapel built for Merie and his young wife, and an entirely reassembled tomb (that of Chaie and Merie, 18th dynasty), discovered in an amazingly well-preserved condition at the turn of the 20th century.

In the same building, you can visit the **Sabauda (Savoy) Gallery ★★** (011/ 547440), one of the richest in Italy, whose collection was acquired over a period of centuries by the House of Savoy. The Academy has the largest exhibit of the Piedmontese masters but is well endowed in Flemish art as well. Of the latter, the most celebrated painting is Sir Anthony Van Dyck's *Three Children of Charles I* (England).

Other important works include Botticelli's *Venus,* Memling's *Passion of Christ,* Rembrandt's *Sleeping Old Man,* Mantegna's *Holy Conversation,* Jan van Eyck's *The Stigmata of Francis of Assisi,* Veronese's *Dinner in the House of the Pharisee,* Bellotto's *Views of Turin,* and intriguing paintings by the Bruegels. Admission to the Egyptian Museum is 7.50€; to the Galleria Sabauda, it's 4.50€. Admission to both museums is 8€. Egyptian Museum Tuesday to Sunday 9:30am to 8:30pm in summer, Tuesday to Sunday 8:30am to 7:30pm off season. Galleria Tuesday and Friday to Sunday 8:30am to 2pm, Wednesday to Thursday 2 to 7:30pm. To get here, take tram 18 from the train station.

Cattedrale di San Giovanni ★, Piazza San Giovanni (*☎* **011/4361540**), is a Renaissance cathedral dedicated to John the Baptist. A tragic fire swept across the cathedral in the spring of 1997, but its major treasure, the **Holy Shroud ★★★**, was not damaged. Acquired by Emanuele Filiberto (whose equestrian statue you saw in the Piazza San Carlo), the shroud is purported to be the one that Joseph of Arimathea wrapped around the body of Christ when he was removed from the cross. Detailed charts in front of the holy relic claim to show evidence of a hemorrhage produced by the crown of thorns. The shroud is rarely on view, but you can see dramatically lit photographs of the amazing relic. The shroud is contained in the **Museo della Santissima Sindone,** Via San Domenico 28 (*☎* **011/4365832**), which is open daily from 9am to noon and 3 to 7pm, and charges an admission of 6€. Entrance to the cathedral is free daily from 7am to noon and 3 to 7pm. To get here from the train station, take bus no. 63.

WHERE TO DINE

Turin is home to some of the best restaurants in northwest Italy, notably **Del Cambio ★★**, Piazza Carignano 2 (*☎* **011/543760;** bus: 13, 15, or 55), where you dine in a setting of white-and-gilt walls, crystal chandeliers, and gilt mirrors. Opened in 1757, it's the oldest restaurant in Turin. The chef, who has received many culinary honors, features white truffles in many of his specialties. The assorted fresh antipasti are excellent; the best pasta dish is the regional *agnolotti piemontesi.* Among the main dishes, the *agnolotti* with truffles and the beef braised in Barolo wine deserve special praise. Main courses cost 15€ to 28€, and reservations are required. It is open September to June Monday to Saturday 12:30 to 2:30pm and 8 to 10:30pm, July to August Monday to Friday 12:30 to 2:30pm and 8 to 10:30pm; closed August 3 to August 25.

Surpassed only by Del Cambio (see above) is **Vintage 1997 ★★**, Piazza Solferino 16 (*☎* **011/535948;** tram: 4 or 10; bus: 5 or 67), which specializes in regional, mainly meat-based Piedmontese fare along with a nightly offering of fresh seafood from the coast. We enjoyed some of our best meals in the region here, including tuna in a delectable starring role in chateaubriand of tuna with fresh spinach, and the rack of lamb in an almond crust. Main courses cost 18€ to 36€, and hours are Monday to Friday noon to 3pm and Monday to Saturday 8pm to 11pm; closed August and the first week in January.

THE NETHERLANDS

13

Exploring the Netherlands by train is a snap. In a country barely half the size of Maine and with 16 million inhabitants, few are the towns and places of interest that can't be reached directly by train (or require only a minimal amount of additional traveling by bus or bicycle). Dutch trains are frequent and invariably both punctual and clean, so traveling from one end of the realm to another, and to points in between, is no great trial.

Not needing to spend too much time riding the rails means you can stay focused on getting the most out of your time in Amsterdam, The Hague, Haarlem, and other historic Dutch towns and cities. Each of these cities is no more than a short train ride away from the other. Even places in relatively remote Zeeland, Friesland, and Limburg provinces are within easy reach, enabling you to get close to a slower-paced rural way of life in a land that has been wrested acre by acre from the sea.

Highlights of the Netherlands

The principal highlight of the Netherlands—the city of **Amsterdam**—also happens to be one of the great cities of the world. That's why it's as much a fixture on any well-conceived European rail tour as London, Paris, and Rome. Just 20 minutes by train from Schiphol Airport, Holland's capital is a high-energy metropolis with a multiethnic population of 750,000 (and 600,000 bicycles), and runs the cultural gamut from the heights of the Van Gogh Museum to legal prostitution and officially tolerated dope dens.

Some visitors to Holland make the mistake of thinking there's no more to the country than Amsterdam. Not so. Just 15 minutes away by train is **Haarlem,** a graceful and historic small city that's well worth a side trip. Your next stop could well be **The Hague,** sophisticated, a little stuffy, and the seat of the Dutch government and royal family. Nearby **Delft**—ancient seat of Dutch royalty and the hometown of Dutch master Vermeer—is smaller and easier to get to grips with.

Should you feel the need to stretch your legs, metaphorically speaking, head down to handsome **Maastricht,** at the country's borders with Germany and Belgium. A different kind of Dutch spirit, full of southern charm, and some of the best eating and drinking in the land will be your rewards.

ESSENTIALS

Getting There

Carriers with flights into Amsterdam from North America include **Continental Airlines** (✆ 800/231-0856; www.continental.com), **Delta** (✆ 800/241-4141; www.delta.com), **KLM** (✆ 800/225-2525; www.klm.com), **United** (✆ 800/538-2929; www.united.com), and **US Airways** (✆ 800/428-4322; www.usairways.com).

Amsterdam Airport Schiphol (✆ 0900/0141, or 31-20/794-0800 from outside Holland; www.schiphol.nl), 8 miles (13km) southwest of the city center, is the principal airport in the Netherlands and handles virtually all of the country's international flights. Schiphol has quick, direct rail links to Amsterdam Centraal Station and to many more Dutch cities. There's a desk of **Holland Tourist Information** (✆ 0900/400-4040, or 31-20/201-8800 outside the Netherlands; www.iamsterdam.nl) at the airport, in Schiphol Plaza.

The Netherlands by Rail

High-speed **Thalys** trains from France and Belgium, and high-speed **ICE** trains from Germany serve Amsterdam and other Dutch cities. The Thalys travel time from Paris is 3 hours and 18 minutes, and Brussels 1 hour and 45 minutes; the ICE travel time from Frankfurt is just under 4 hours. In addition, Amsterdam is linked to many cities around Europe by slower **EuroCity (EC), CityNightLine (CNL),** and other international trains.

All major Dutch tourist destinations are within 2½ hours of Amsterdam on **Nederlandse Spoorwegen** (**Netherlands Railways/NS;** ✆ 0900/9292; www.ns.nl), Holland's national rail system. NS trains are a good way to travel with the Dutch, who use them even for short journeys to the next town up the line. In addition to

 FESTIVALS & special events

Koninginnedag (Queen's Day), April 30, a nationwide holiday for the House of Orange, is vigorously celebrated in Amsterdam. So jampacked with people are the city center's streets that it's virtually impossible to move. A street market held all over town features masses of stalls, run by everybody from kids selling old toys to professional market folk. Dutch flags and orange ribbons, orange-dyed hair, and orange-painted faces are everywhere. Street music and theater combine with too much drinking, but Koninginnedag remains good-natured, if boisterous. For more information, contact **VVV Amsterdam** (✆ 0900/400-4040, or 31-20/201-8800 from outside Holland; www.iamsterdam.nl).

Among the world's leading gatherings of top international jazz and blues musicians, the **North Sea Jazz Festival** unfolds over 3 concert-packed days in early July at Rotterdam's giant Ahoy venue. Last-minute tickets are scarce, so book as far ahead as you can. Contact **North Sea Jazz Festival** (✆ 0900/300-1250, or 31-10/591-9000 outside Holland; www.northseajazz.nl) for more information.

Lastly, the **Grachtenfestival Canals Festival,** a 5-day festival of classical music, plays at various intimate and atmospheric venues along Amsterdam's canals in mid-August. Part of the festival is the exuberant Prinsengracht Concert. Contact **Stichting Grachtenfestival** (✆ 020/421-4542; www.grachtenfestival.nl) for details.

Amsterdam, other destinations easily reached by train from Schiphol Airport include The Hague (32 min.), Rotterdam (48 min.), and Utrecht (33 min.)—these are travel times by the fastest available option, generally Thalys, NS Hispeed, or InterCity train. The trains run so often you can usually just go to a Dutch station and wait for the next one—your wait will be short. At even the smallest stations, there is half-hour or hourly service in both directions, and major destinations have between four and eight trains an hour. Service begins as early as 5am (slightly later on Sun and holidays) and runs until around 1am. A special **Night Train** runs between Utrecht and Rotterdam, via Amsterdam, Schiphol Airport, Leiden, and The Hague; on the weekends this service is extended from both ends to Eindhoven.

There are three kinds of national train service in Holland: NS Hispeed, for high-speed trains on main national and international lines (some services are operated by Thalys); **InterCity** express trains connecting the main towns and cities; and the *stoptrein* (stop train), a slow train that stops at every station on the line—for some services, a *stoptrein* is called, counter-intuitively, a **Sprinter,** which travels faster between stations, yet still stops at all of them.

Note: Should you wish to bike some of your travel route—and Holland is Europe's bicycling country par excellence—Netherlands Railways has some handy arrangements whereby you can rent a bicycle at one station and drop it off at another.

PASSES

For details on purchasing multicountry options, such as the **Eurail Pass,** see chapter 2. The **Benelux Pass** allows 5 days of unlimited travel in 1 month in Belgium, the Netherlands, and Luxembourg for $221 in second class and $325 in first class. Two to five adults traveling together should purchase instead the **Benelux Saverpass,** to benefit from a discount of around 18%. For passengers ages 12 to 25, the **Benelux Youth Pass** (available in second class only) costs $148. Children ages 4 to 11 pay around half the adult fare, and children ages 3 and under 4 ride free, as long as they share a seat or berth with an adult. These passes must be purchased in North America and can be obtained from **Rail Europe** (𝄐 **888/438-7245** in the United States, 𝄐 **800/361-7245** in Canada; www.raileurope.com) or through your travel agent.

In addition to Netherlands Railways's regular one-way (*enkele reis*), day round-trip (*dagretour*), and weekend round-trip (*weekendretour*) tickets (note that a round-trip ticket costs less than two one-way tickets), look for the discounted *dagkaart* (day card) and *5-dagkaart* (5-day card)—both passes have extra-cost **OV** options that include additional public transportation. Locally, a 1-day *Railrunner* unlimited travel pass can be purchased for children ages 4 to 11 (up to a maximum three children per adult over 19) for 2.50€ per child (children ages 3 and under ride free). These various tickets and passes are valid only in the Netherlands and can be purchased only at train stations in Holland. You can purchase most tickets from in-station automats (ticket machines); tickets purchased from the station ticket counters cost .50€ per ticket over the automat price.

Note: Tickets cannot be purchased onboard Dutch trains. The fine for riding a train without a valid ticket is 35€, plus the fare.

FOREIGN TRAIN TERMS

A train is a *trein* in Dutch. Class is *klas*; second class is *tweede klas*, and first class is *eerste klas*. A station is, easily enough, a *station*. In big cities such as Amsterdam, Rotterdam, and Den Haag (The Hague), which have more than one station, the main station is generally called Centraal Station (Central Station). The Dutch word for "platform" is *spoor* (it rhymes with "boar"). The bigger stations have separate

The Netherlands

counters for selling domestic tickets *(Binnenland)* and international tickets *(Buiten-land* or just plain *International).*

Departure and arrival are *vertrek* and *aankomst* in Dutch (announcements are also made in English in the most important stations). Information is *Informatie.*

PRACTICAL TRAIN INFORMATION

Dutch trains are often crowded, and since reservations are not available (except for international trains), it makes sense not to travel during peak hours, when you may need to stand. On the other hand, distances between stations are short and a bunch of people are sure to get out at whatever the next one is.

All trains, even the smallest, have a first-class section or cars. Smoking is forbidden both on trains and on station platforms.

Due to the country's small size, no Dutch trains have restaurant cars (some international trains do), but on long-distance InterCity trains, an attendant pushes around a small cart, from which coffee, tea, mineral water, sandwiches, potato chips, and other snack items are dispensed. These are more expensive than the same things bought from a supermarket, so if you are on a tight budget, buy them before boarding the train. Similarly, a lack of long distances means there are no sleeper cars on trains traveling within the Netherlands.

Train Frequency & Travel Times in the Netherlands

	Amsterdam	Haarlem	The Hague	Delft	Rotterdam	Maastricht
Travel Time		15 min.	51 min.	57 min.	1 hr.	2 hr., 35 min.
Frequency*		6	6	5	6	2

Frequency is average number of trains per hour during daytime.

Some trains, employed most often during rush hours in urban areas, are double-deckers; these often get very crowded, but an upstairs window seat affords a great view of whatever there is to be seen.

[FastFACTS]
THE NETHERLANDS

Area Codes When making local calls in Amsterdam, you won't need to use the area codes shown in this chapter. You do need to use an area code between towns and cities. The area code for Amsterdam is **020.** Other area codes are: Haarlem **023,** The Hague and Scheveningen **070,** Delft **015,** Maastricht **043.**

Business Hours **Banks** are open Monday to Friday from 9am to 4pm (some stay open until 5pm). Some banks also open on late-hour shopping nights and Saturdays. **Stores** generally are open Monday from 10 or 11am to 6pm, and Tuesday to Saturday from 8:30 or 9am to 6pm. Some stores close for lunch, and nearly all have 1 full closing day or 1 morning or afternoon when they're closed. Many stores, especially in the larger towns, have late hours on Thursday and/or Friday evening, and in the cities some main-street stores are open on Sundays.

Climate Holland has a maritime climate, with few temperature extremes in either summer or winter. Summer temperatures average 67°F (19°C); the winter average is 35°F (2°C). Winters, moderated by the North Sea and the fading glow of the Gulf Stream, most often are rainy (it's driest Feb–May). July and August are the best months for soaking up rays at sidewalk cafes, in the park, and on the beach, and for dining at an outdoor restaurant in the evening. September usually has a few weeks of fine weather. There are even sunny spells in winter, when brilliant, crisp weather alternates with clouded skies.

Documents Required For stays of up to 3 months, citizens of the U.S. and Canada need only a valid passport. A visa is required for stays of longer than 3 months.

Electricity The Netherlands runs on 230 (220–240) volts electricity (North America uses 110 volts). To use appliances from home without burning them out, you'll need a small voltage transformer (available at your local hardware store) that plugs into the round-holed European electrical outlet and converts the Dutch voltage for any small appliance up to 1,500 watts.

Embassies & Consulates **U.S. Embassy:** Lange Voorhout 102, Den Haag (✆ **070/310-2209;** http://thehague.usembassy. gov); **U.S. Consulate** in Amsterdam: Museumplein 19 (✆ **020/575-5309;** http://amsterdam.us consulate.gov; tram: 3, 5, 12, or 16). **Canadian Embassy:** Sophialaan 7, Den Haag (✆ **070/311-1600;** www. canada.nl).

Health & Safety In the event of a medical emergency, call the national emergency number: ✆ **112.** For 24-hour nonurgent doctor referral and urgent dentist referral in Amsterdam, call the **Central Doctors Service** (✆ **020/ 592-3434**). During regular office hours you will probably be better off checking with your hotel reception desk—most hotels either have an arrangement with or can point you to a nearby practice.

Holidays   January 1 (New Year's Day), Good Friday, Easter Sunday and Monday, April 30 (Queen's Day/*Koninginnedag*), Ascension Day, Pentecost Sunday and Monday, December 25 (Christmas) and December 26. The dates for Easter, Ascension, and Pentecost change each year.

Mail   Postage for a postcard or ordinary letter to the U.S. and Canada is .95€.

Police & Emergencies   Holland's emergency number to call for the police *(politie)*, fire department, and ambulance is $\textcircled{C}$ **112.** For routine matters, call the general police number ($\textcircled{C}$ **0900/8844**) or visit a district police office; in Amsterdam; a centrally located one is at Lijnbaansgracht 219 (tram: 1, 2, 5, 7, or 10), just off Leidseplein.

Telephone   The international access code for the Netherlands is **011** and the country code is **31.** To call the Netherlands from the United States, dial 011, then 31, then the area code of the city you'd like to reach (20 in Amsterdam, for example), followed by the telephone number. So the whole number you'd dial would be 011-31-20-000-0000.

To make international calls from the Netherlands, first dial 00 and then the country code for the U.S. or Canada: 1. Next you dial the area code and number.

For directory assistance: Dial $\textcircled{C}$ **0900/8418** for international information. Dial $\textcircled{C}$ **0900/8008** for multiple numbers inside Holland and $\textcircled{C}$ **118** for a maximum of one number per call. **For operator assistance:** To make an international collect call, dial $\textcircled{C}$ **0800/0410.**

Toll-free numbers: Numbers beginning with 0800 within Holland are toll-free, but calling a 1-800 number in the States from Holland is not toll-free. In fact, it is the same as an overseas call. Watch out for special Dutch numbers that begin with 0900. Calls to these numbers are charged at a higher rate than ordinary local calls and can cost up to .90€ a minute.

You can use pay phones with either a KPN or a Telfort *telekaart* (phone card). KPN cards cost 5€, 10€, 20€, and 50€ from post offices, and Telfort cards 8€, from train ticket counters, and some tobacconists and newsstands. Some pay phones take credit cards, and some take coins.

To charge a call to your calling card, call **AT&T** ($\textcircled{C}$ **0800/022-9111**), **MCI** ($\textcircled{C}$ **0800/022-9122**), **Sprint** ($\textcircled{C}$ **0800/022-9119**), or **Canada Direct** ($\textcircled{C}$ **0800/022-9116**).

Tipping   All taxes and service charges are supposed to be included in the prices of hotels, restaurants, cafes, nightclubs, salons, and sightseeing companies. Even taxi fare includes taxes and a standard 15% service charge. To be absolutely sure in a restaurant that tax and service are included, look for the words *inclusief BTW en service* (BTW is the abbreviation for the Dutch words that mean value-added tax), or ask the waiter. The Dutch are so accustomed to having these charges included that many restaurants have stopped spelling it out.

To tip like the Dutch (no, seriously!), in a cafe or snack bar, leave some small change; in a standard restaurant, leave 2€ to 3€, and up to a generous 5€ if you think the service was particularly good; for expensive tabs, you may want to leave more—or maybe less! It's enough to round up taxi fares.

AMSTERDAM ★★★

Old Amsterdam's graceful cityscape recalls its 17th-century golden age as the heart of a global trading network and colonial empire, when wealthy merchants constructed gabled residences along neatly laid-out canals. A delicious irony is that today these placid old structures also host brothels, smoke shops, and some extravagant nightlife.

Amsterdam

ACCOMMODATIONS ■ **ATTRACTIONS** ●

Agora **14**
Amstel Botel **23**
Amsterdam
 Wiechmann **10**
Bilderberg Hotel
 Jan Luyken **19**
De Filosoof **15**
Hotel Amsterdam–
 De Roode Leeuw **22**
Park Plaza Victoria
 Amsterdam **25**
Prinsenhof **32**
Seven Bridges **30**
Sint Nicolaas **24**

DINING ◆
Bolhoed **3**
Café Luxembourg **13**
Christophe **4**
De Belhamel **2**
De Prins **6**
Kantjil & de Tijger **11**
Lof **1**
Spanjer & Van Twist **5**
Tempo Doeloe **31**
Wilhelmina-Dok **33**

Amsterdams Historisch
 Museum **12**
Amsterdamse Bos **21**
Anne Frankhuis **7**
Hash Marihuana &
 Hemp Museum **28**
Koninklijk Paleis **9**
Museum Het
 Rembrandthuis **29**
Ons' Lieve Heer op
 Solder **26**
Oude Kerk **27**
Rijksmuseum **20**
Stedelijk Museum **17**
Van Gogh Museum **18**
Vondelpark **16**
Westerkerk **8**

NETHERLANDS

★ Amsterdam

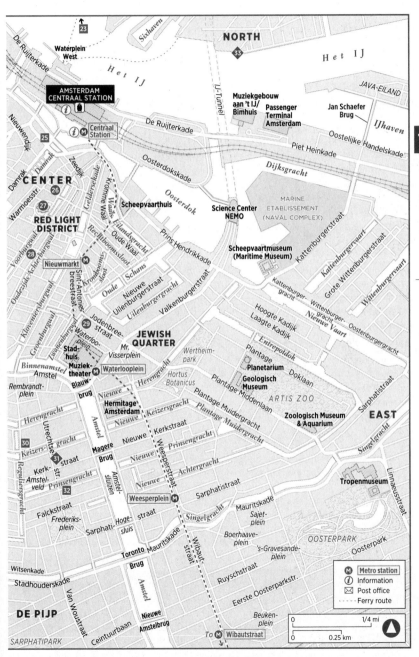

The city's inhabitants, proud of their live-and-let-live attitude, which is based on pragmatism as much as on a long history of tolerance, have decided to control what they cannot effectively outlaw. They permit licensed prostitution in the Red Light District, and the sale of hashish and marijuana in designated "coffee shops."

Don't think most Amsterdammers are late-model hippies, though, drifting around town in a drug-induced haze. They are too busy whizzing around on bicycles, jogging through Vondelpark, feasting on arrays of ethnic dishes, or simply watching the parade of street life from a sidewalk cafe. A new generation of entrepreneurs has revitalized old neighborhoods such as the Jordaan, turning some of the distinctive houses into offbeat stores and bustling cafes, hotels, and restaurants. And along the waterfront, old harbor installations have been put to bold new uses or swept away entirely in favor of large-scale modern cultural, business, and residential developments.

Between dips into Amsterdam's artistic and historical treasures, be sure to take time out to absorb the freewheeling spirit of Europe's most vibrant city.

Station Information

GETTING FROM THE AIRPORT TO THE TRAIN STATION

Netherlands Railways **trains** from Amsterdam Airport Schiphol (see "Getting There," earlier in this chapter) for Amsterdam Centraal Station depart from Schiphol Station, downstairs from Schiphol Plaza, attached to the airport. Frequency ranges from eight trains an hour at peak times to one an hour at night. The fare is 3.80€ one-way in second class and 6.50€ in first class (or free if you hold a valid train pass), and the ride takes 20 minutes.

You'll find **taxi** stands in front of Schiphol Plaza. All taxis from the airport are metered. Expect to pay around 40€ to the center of town.

INSIDE THE STATION

Amsterdam Centraal Station is the mammoth hub for all rail travel and public transportation in the city. An office of **VVV Amsterdam** tourist information (© **0900/400-4040,** or 31-20/201-8800 from outside the Netherlands; www. iamsterdam.nl) is inside the station on platform 2B, open Monday to Saturday from 8am to 8pm, and Sunday and holidays from 9am to 5pm; it can make last-minute hotel reservations. Another office is right in front of the station on Stationsplein, open daily from 9am to 5pm. In addition, you'll find currency exchange at GWK Travelex; a Netherlands Railways office for tickets, reservations, and information, with separate desks for international and national trains; ticket machines; restaurants and snack bars; and a host of small stores.

The station, a Dutch neo-Renaissance architectural monument dating from 1889, is currently—and for some years to come—a confusing construction site. A new Metro station, set to be the hub of the Noord–Zuid line (due to enter service in 2015) is being dug at the front; a new main entrance for the train station and generally improved passenger facilities are being tackled at the same time; and the waterfront zone at the rear is being completely revamped.

When you emerge at the front of the station, you will find a taxi stand; a bunch of stops for trams (streetcars) and buses; the entrance to the existing Metro station; and docks for tour boats, the Water Taxi, the Canal Bus, and the Museum Quarter Line. At the rear of the station are docks for the ferryboats that shuttle passengers across to the north shore of the city's fast-developing waterfront.

Beware: The station is a pickpocket convention that's in full swing at all times.

Information Elsewhere in the City

VVV Amsterdam has an agency office in a white kiosk facing Stadhouderskade 1, at Leidseplein (tram: 1, 2, 5, 7, or 10); it's open daily from 9am to 6pm.

Getting Around

The city center is small enough that the best way to get around Amsterdam is on your own two feet. Be sure to wear good walking shoes, as those charming cobblestones will get under your soles and on your nerves after a while. When crossing the street, watch out for trams and bikes.

Of the city's 16 **tram** (streetcar) lines, 10 begin and end at Centraal Station, and one passes through. An extensive **bus** network complements the trams. The current four **Metro** lines—50, 51, 53, and 54—are mainly useful for getting to and from the suburbs, but from Centraal Station, you can use Metro trains to reach both Nieuwmarkt and Waterlooplein in the central zone. Most tram/bus shelters and all Metro stations have maps that show the entire transit network. A detailed map is available from VVV tourist information offices and from the GVB Tickets & Info office outside Centraal Station on Stationsplein.

Note: By the start of 2011, virtually all public transportation in the Netherlands will be using an electronic card, the **OV-chipkaart,** in place of tickets. Three main types of OV-chipkaart are available, valid for travel on buses, trams, Metro trains, and some trains: a reloadable "personal" card that can be used only by its pictured owner; a reloadable "anonymous" card that can be used by anyone; and a nonreloadable "throwaway" card that can be used by anyone. Electronic readers automatically deduct the correct fare when you ride. The personal and anonymous reusable cards, both valid for 5 years, cost 7.50€ and can be loaded and reloaded with up to 30€; the throwaway card costs 2.50€ for one ride and 4.80€ for two rides. Reduced-rate cards are available for seniors and children. Cards are available from the **GVB Tickets & Info** office on Stationsplein, in front of Centraal Station, and from Metro station ticket counters.

A **day ticket** (*dagkaart*), valid for the entire day of purchase and the following night, can be purchased from any bus or tram driver, conductor, or ticket dispenser for 7.50€. Tickets for **2, 3, 4, 5, 6,** and **7 days** (for 12€, 15€, 18€, 23€, 26€, and 29€, respectively) can be purchased from the GVB Tickets & Info office.

Officially, you can't hail a **taxi** from the street, but taxis will often stop anyway if you do. Otherwise, find one of the strategically located taxi stands sprinkled around town, marked by distinctive yellow phone boxes, or call **Taxi Centrale Amsterdam** (✆ **020/677-7777**). Taxis are metered. Fares—which include a service charge—begin at 7.50€ when the meter starts and, after 2km (1¼ miles), run up at 2.20€ a kilometer; after 25km, at 1.75€ a kilometer; and after 50km, at 1.45€ a kilometer.

Two waterbus services travel to many of the city's top museums and other attractions. Day tickets for the **Canal Bus** (✆ **0900/333-4442**) allow you to hop on and off as many times as you like on the three lines. These cost 22€ for 24 hours, 33€ for 48 hours, and 44€ for 72 hours; children ages 4 to 12 travel for half the adult price; and children 3 and under are free. It's also available through Rail Europe. The **Hop On Hop Off Museum Line** (✆ **020/530-5412**) operates a scheduled service every 30 to 45 minutes from Centraal Station to Prinsengracht, Leidseplein, Museumplein, Herengracht, the Muziektheater, and the Eastern Dock. A day ticket is 20€ for adults, 10€ for children ages 4 to 12, and free for children 3 and under. Special tickets are available that include discounted admission to some museums and attractions.

You can also follow the Dutch example and travel around by bicycle. Bike-rental rates are around 12€ a day or 50€ a week; a deposit of 50€ is generally required. You can rent bikes from Centraal Station when you arrive and from many rental stores, all of which have similar rates. **MacBike** (*✆* **020/620-0985;** www.macbike.nl) rents a range of bikes, including tandems and six-speed touring bikes; it has branches at Centraal Station; Mr. Visserplein 2, close to the Muziektheater; and Marnixstraat 220, close to Rozengracht. **Rent-a-Bike** is at Damstraat 20–22 (*✆* **020/625-5029;** www.rentabike.nl), close to the Dam.

Where to Stay

Agora   Old-fashioned friendliness is the keynote at this efficiently run and well-maintained lodging, a block from the Flower Market, in a fully restored canal house from 1735. Furniture from the 1930s and 1940s mixes with fine mahogany antiques and an abundance of overstuffed furniture. Those rooms that don't have a canal view look out on a pretty garden at the back. There's no elevator.

Singel 462, 1017 AW Amsterdam. *✆* **020/627-2200.** Fax 020/627-2202. www.hotelagora.nl. 16 units. 75€–159€ double; add 5% city tax. Rates include buffet breakfast. AE, DC, MC, V. Tram: 1, 2, or 5 to Koningsplein. **Amenities:** Lounge; smoke-free rooms. *In room:* No A/C.

Amstel Botel ☺   Where better to experience a city on the water than by lodging in a boat-hotel, a short ferry ride from Centraal Station? Its cabins are spread out over four decks connected by elevator. The bright, modern rooms are no-nonsense but comfortable, and the showers small. Be sure to ask for a room with a view on the water, not on the uninspiring quay side.

NDSM-Werf 3, 1033 RG Amsterdam. *✆* **020/626-4247.** Fax 020/639-1952. www.amstelbotel.com. 175 units. 69€–94€ double. AE, DC, MC, V. Boat: NDSM Ferry from Centraal Station. **Amenities:** Bar; smoke-free rooms. *In room:* No A/C.

Amsterdam Wiechmann ★   It takes only a moment to feel at home in the antique-adorned Wiechmann, a classic, comfortable, casual place beside Looiersgracht. Besides, the location is one of the best you'll find in this or any price range. Most of the rooms are standard, with good-size twin or double beds, and some have big bay windows. Furnishings are elegant. The higher-priced doubles, with a view on the canal, have antique furnishings.

Prinsengracht 328–332, 1016 HX Amsterdam. *✆* **020/626-3321.** Fax 020/626-8962. www.hotel wiechmann.nl. 37 units. 90€–165€ double. Rates include continental breakfast. MC, V. Tram: 1, 2, or 5 to Prinsengracht. **Amenities:** Lounge; smoke-free rooms. *In room:* No A/C.

Bilderberg Hotel Jan Luyken ★   Close to the Rijksmuseum, this is a medium-size hotel with some of the amenities and facilities of a large one—though without the large rooms. Everything here is done to maintain a balance between a sophisticated lineup of facilities and an intimate and personalized approach appropriate to a 19th-century residential neighborhood. That feel extends to the guest rooms, which look more like those in a well-designed home than in a standard hotel room.

Jan Luijkenstraat 58, 1071 CS Amsterdam. *✆* **020/573-0730.** Fax 020/676-3841. www.janluyken.nl. 62 units. 99€–159€ double. AE, DC, MC, V. Tram: 2 or 5 to Hobbemastraat. **Amenities:** Wine bar; smoke-free rooms.

De Filosoof ★ 🏠   On a quiet street facing Vondelpark, this might be the very place if you fancy yourself as something of a philosopher. Each room is dedicated to a mental maestro—Aristotle, Plato, Goethe, Wittgenstein, Nietzsche, Marx, and Einstein are among those who get a look-in—or are based on motifs like Eros, the Renaissance, and astrology. Regular all-around improvements keep the service and amenities up-to-date.

Anna van den Vondelstraat 6, 1054 GZ Amsterdam. ✆ **020/683-3013.** Fax 020/685-3750. www.sandton.eu/en/amsterdam. 38 units. 105€–180€ double. Rates include buffet breakfast. AE, MC, V. Tram: 1 to Jan Pieter Heijestraat. **Amenities:** Bar; smoke-free rooms. *In room:* No A/C.

Hotel Amsterdam–De Roode Leeuw ★★
Close to Centraal Station and right next to the Dam, this family hotel, housed in a 1911 building, is still owned by descendants of the original proprietors. Its rooms are supermodern, though, with thick carpets, air-conditioning, and ample wardrobe space. Rooms at the front get more light but are also subjected to more street noise; some have balconies. The award-winning **De Roode Leeuw** restaurant serves classic Dutch cuisine.

Damrak 93–94, 1012 LP Amsterdam. ✆ **800/44-UTELL** [448-8355] in the U.S. and Canada, or 020/555-0666. Fax 020/620-4716. www.hotelamsterdam.nl. 79 units. 110€–325€ double. AE, DC, MC, V. Tram: 4, 9, 14, 16, 24, or 25 to the Dam. **Amenities:** Restaurant; cafe; smoke-free rooms.

Park Plaza Victoria Amsterdam ★
Since 1890, the elegant Victoria has been a turreted landmark at the head of Damrak, overlooking Centraal Station and the canal-boat piers. It can be noisy and tacky out on the busy street below, but you won't notice that once you get inside the hushed, plush interiors. You can survive quite nicely without taking taxis if you stay here, about as close as you can get to Centraal Station. Guest rooms in an adjacent new block lack some of the atmosphere of the old wing.

Damrak 1–5, 1012 LG Amsterdam. ✆ **888/201-1803** in the U.S. and Canada, or 020/623-4255. Fax 020/625-2997. www.parkplaza.com. 306 units. 160€–360€ double; from 500€ suite. Add 5% city tax. AE, DC, MC, V. Tram: 1, 2, 4, 5, 9, 13, 16, 17, 24, 25, or 26 to Centraal Station. **Amenities:** Restaurant; bar; cafe; smoke-free rooms.

Prinsenhof 🏷
A modernized canal house close to the Amstel River, this hotel has rooms (two with bathroom) with beamed ceilings and basic yet tolerably comfortable beds. Front rooms look out onto Prinsengracht, where houseboats are moored. The proprietors, Rik and André van Houten, take pride in their hotel and make you feel welcome (check out the hotel's website for a good dose of their humor). There's no elevator, but a pulley hauls your luggage up and down the stairs.

Prinsengracht 810, 1017 JL Amsterdam. ✆ **020/623-1772.** Fax 020/638-3368. www.hotelprinsenhof.com. 10 units. 95€ double with bathroom; 65€ double without bathroom. Rates include continental breakfast. AE, MC, V. Tram: 4 to Prinsengracht. *In room:* No A/C, no TV.

Seven Bridges ★★ 🏨
One of Amsterdam's canal-house gems, not far from Rembrandtplein, gets its name from its view of seven arched bridges. There are antique furnishings, handmade Italian drapes, hand-painted tiles and wood-tiled floors, and Impressionist art posters on the walls. The biggest room, on the first landing, can accommodate up to four and has a huge bathroom with marble floor and double sinks. Attic rooms have sloped ceilings and exposed wood beams, and there are big, bright basement rooms done almost entirely in white.

Reguliersgracht 31, 1017 LK Amsterdam. ✆ **020/623-1329.** Fax 020/624-7652. www.sevenbridgeshotel.nl. 11 units. 90€–250€ double. Rates include full breakfast. AE, MC, V. Tram: 16, 24, or 25 to Keizersgracht. **Amenities:** Smoke-free rooms. *In room:* No A/C.

Sint Nicolaas ★★ 🏷
New owners have upgraded the interior of this onetime rope and carpet factory near Centraal Station to near-boutique status, affording a level of comfort that's rarely achieved by Amsterdam hotels in this price range. This

applies especially if you score a rate at the lower end of what is a wide scale, though you should bear in mind that the entire hotel has a thin amenities roster. Each room has a different character, with the regular ones emphasizing classic comforts, warm colors, prints, and exposed wood beams; and the deluxe doubles all cool blacks, grays, and whites.

Spuistraat 1A, 1012 SP Amsterdam. ✆ **020/626-1384.** Fax 020/623-0979. www.centrehotels.nl. 27 units. 95€–250€ double. Rates include continental breakfast. AE, DC, MC, V. Tram: 1, 2, 5, 13, or 17 to Martelaarsgracht. **Amenities:** Lounge; bar.

Top Attractions & Special Moments

For sightseers in Amsterdam, the question is not simply what to see and do, but rather how much of this intriguing city's marvelous sights you can fit into the time you have. There are miles and miles of canals to cruise, hundreds of narrow streets to wander, countless historic buildings to visit, more than 40 museums holding collections of everything from artistic wonders to obscure curiosities, not to mention diamond cutters and craftspeople to watch as they practice generations-old skills . . . the list is as long as every visitor's individual interests.

Amsterdams Historisch Museum (Amsterdam Historical Museum) ★★

Housed in the rambling 17th-century Burger Weeshuis, the former City Orphanage next to the Begijnhof, this fascinating museum gives you a better understanding of everything you'll see when you go out to explore the city on your own. Gallery by gallery, century by century, you learn how a small fishing village founded around 1200 became a major sea power and trading center. The main focus is on Holland's *Gouden Eeuw* (Golden Age), a period when Amsterdam was the world's wealthiest city, and some of the most interesting exhibits are of the trades that made it rich in the 17th century. You can also view some famous paintings by the Old Dutch masters in the context of their time and place in history.

When you leave the museum, cut through the **Schuttersgalerij (Civic Guards Gallery),** a covered passageway that leads to the Begijnhof and is bedecked with 15 enormous 17th-century paintings of the Amsterdam Civic Guards. The open hours are the same as for the museum, and admission is free.

Kalverstraat 92, Nieuwezijds Voorburgwal 357, and Sint-Luciënsteeg 27. ✆ **020/523-1822.** www.ahm. nl. Admission 10€ adults, 7.50€ seniors, 5€ children 6–18, free for children 5 and under. Mon–Fri 10am–5pm; Sat–Sun 11am–5pm. Tram: 1, 2, 4, 5, 9, 14, 16, 24, or 25 to Spui.

Anne Frankhuis ★★★

In summer, you may have to wait an hour or more to get in, but no one should miss experiencing this house, where eight people from three separate Jewish families lived together in near total silence for more than 2 years during World War II. The hiding place Otto Frank found for his family and friends, next to Westermarkt, kept them safe until it was raided by Nazi forces and its occupants were deported to concentration camps. Anne, whose ambition was to be a writer, kept her famous diary here as a way to deal with both the boredom and her youthful jumble of thoughts, which had as much to do with personal growth as with the war and the Nazi terror raging outside her hiding place. Visiting the rooms where she hid is a moving and eerily real experience.

The rooms of the building, which was an office and warehouse at that time, are still as bare as they were when Anne's father returned, the only survivor of the eight *onderduikers* (divers, or hiders). Nothing has been changed, except that protective Plexiglas panels have been placed over the wall where Anne pinned up photos of her favorite actress, Deanna Durbin, and of the little English princesses Elizabeth and Margaret. As you tour the building, it's easy to imagine Anne's experience growing up in this place, awakening as a young woman, and writing down her secret thoughts in a diary.

Prinsengracht 263. Ⓒ **020/556-7105.** www.annefrank.org. Admission 8.50€ adults, 4€ children 10–17, free for children 9 and under. Mid-Mar to June and 1st 2 weeks Sept Mon–Fri 9am–9pm, Sat 9am–10pm; July–Aug daily 9am–10pm; mid-Sept to mid-Mar daily 9am–7pm; Jan 1 noon–7pm; Dec 25 noon–5pm, Dec 31 9am–5pm. Tram: 13, 14, or 17 to Westermarkt.

Hash Marihuana & Hemp Museum   It wouldn't really be Amsterdam without its fascination with intoxicating weeds, would it? This museum in the Red Light District will teach you everything you ever wanted to know, and much you maybe didn't, about hash, marijuana, and related products. It does not promote drug use, but aims to make you better informed before deciding whether to light up and, of course, whether to inhale. One way it does this is by having a cannabis garden in the joint—sorry—on the premises. Hemp plants fill the air with a heady, resinous fragrance, and hemp fiber could be the material of the future if the exhibit on its multifarious uses is anything to go by. Among several artworks in the museum's collection is David Teniers the Younger's painting *Hemp-Smoking Peasants in a Smoke House* (1660).

Oudezijds Achterburgwal 148. Ⓒ **020/624-8926.** www.hashmuseum.com. Admission 9€ adults, children 12 and under (accompanied by an adult) free. Daily 10am–11pm. Tram: 4, 9, 14, 16, 24, or 25 to the Dam.

Koninklijk Paleis (Royal Palace) ★   One of the Dam's heavier features is the solid, neoclassical facade of the Royal Palace (1648–55), designed by Jacob van Campen—the Thomas Jefferson of the Dutch Republic—as the city's Stadhuis (Town Hall). Its interior is replete with white Italian marble, sculptures, and painted ceilings. Poet Constantijn Huygens called the then-new Town Hall the "Eighth Wonder of the World." It was built on a foundation of a precisely tabulated 13,659 timber piles—a figure all Dutch schoolchildren are taught.

Dam. Ⓒ **020/620-4060.** www.paleisamsterdam.nl. Admission 7.50€ adults; 6.50€ seniors, students, and children 5–16; children 4 and under free. Generally July–Aug Tues–Sun 11am–5pm; Sept–June Tues–Sun noon–5pm (days and hours vary; check before going). Tram: 1, 2, 4, 5, 9, 13, 14, 16, 17, 24, or 25 to the Dam.

Museum Het Rembrandthuis ★   Bought by Rembrandt in 1639 when he was Amsterdam's most fashionable portrait painter, the house, behind Waterlooplein, is a shrine to one of the greatest artists the world has ever known. In this house, Rembrandt's son, Titus, was born and his wife, Saskia, died. The artist was bankrupt when he left in 1658. Not until 1906 was the building rescued from a succession of subsequent owners and restored as a museum. In 1998, a modern wing for temporary exhibits was added. Restoration has returned the old house to the way it looked when Rembrandt lived and worked here, complete with his combined living room and bedroom, the studio he and his pupils used, the artist's cabinet of art and curiosities, a ground-floor kitchen, and the maid's bedroom. The rooms are furnished with 17th-century objects and furniture that, as far as possible, match the descriptions in Rembrandt's 1656 bankruptcy petition. His printing press is back in place, and you can view 250 of his etchings and drawings hanging on the walls. These include self-portraits and landscapes, and several relate to the traditionally Jewish character of the neighborhood. In addition, there are works by contemporaries like Jan Lievens.

Jodenbreestraat 4–6. Ⓒ **020/520-0400.** www.rembrandthuis.nl. Admission 9€ adults, 6€ students, 2.50€ children 6–17, free for children 5 and under. Daily 10am–5pm. Tram: 9 or 14 to Waterlooplein.

Ons' Lieve Heer op Solder (Our Lord in the Attic) ★   After the 1578 Protestant *Alteratie* (Changeover), Catholics fell into disfavor and were forced to worship in secret. This museum in the heart of the Red Light District incorporates a clandestine church in the attic of one of the oldest canal houses you can visit, which was transformed in 1661–63 by wealthy Catholic merchant Jan Hartman. Worshipers climbed a narrow flight of stairs to the hidden third-floor church. An 18th-century redecoration created the chapel-size church you see now, with its large baroque altar, religious statuary, pews to seat 150, a spinet-size pipe organ, vaulted ceiling, two narrow upper balconies, and a side chapel dedicated to the Virgin Mary. It's still used for services and concerts. The chance to see a rambling old canal house furnished much as it would have been in the mid–18th century, with heavy oak furniture, Delft tiles, and period paintings, makes a visit here worthwhile by itself.

Oudezijds Voorburgwal 40. ✆ **020/624-6604.** www.opsolder.nl. Admission 7€ adults, 5€ students, 1€ children 5-18, free for children 4 and under. Mon-Sat 10am–5pm; Sun and holidays 1–5pm. Closed Jan 1 and Apr 30. Tram: 1, 2, 4, 5, 9, 13, 16, 17, 24, 25, or 26 to Centraal Station.

Oude Kerk (Old Church) ★   This late-Gothic church at Oudezijds Voorburgwal—its official name is the Sint-Nicolaaskerk (St. Nicholas's Church), but nobody ever calls it that—was begun in 1250 and essentially completed with the construction of the bell tower in 1566. On its southern porch, to the right of the sexton's house, is a coat of arms belonging to Maximilian of Austria, who, with his son Philip, contributed to the porch's construction. Rembrandt's wife is buried in vault 28K, which bears the simple inscription "Saskia Juni 1642." The church contains a magnificent Christian Müller organ from 1728 that is regularly used for recitals. On hourly guided tours, you can climb the church tower for an outstanding view of Old Amsterdam. Nowadays, the pretty gabled almshouses around the church feature red-fringed windows through which can be seen the scantily dressed ladies of the Red Light District.

Oudekerksplein. ✆ **020/625-8284.** www.oudekerk.nl. Church: Admission 7.50€ adults; 5.50€ seniors, students, and children 5-13; children 12 and under free. Mon-Sat 11am–5pm; Sun 1–5:30pm; Tower: Admission 6€ (minimum age 12). Sat-Sun 1–5pm; guided tours every 30 min. Metro: Nieuwmarkt.

Rijksmuseum ★★★   Most of Holland's premier museum is closed during a decade-long refurbishment that's due to end in 2013. During this time, under the heading "The Masterpieces," key paintings and other stellar works from the magnificent 17th-century Dutch Golden Age collections can be viewed in the Philips Wing. The three-star rating given here is justified even for the truncated highlights alone, but you need to remember that most of the collections, which total seven million individual objects (only a fraction of which would be displayed at any given time), will be "invisible" to visitors for some time to come.

Petrus Josephus Hubertus Cuypers (1827–1921), the "grandfather of modern Dutch architecture," designed the brick and gabled museum in a monumental Dutch neo-Renaissance style. Cuypers, a Catholic, slipped in more than a dab of neo-Gothic, too, causing the country's thoroughly Protestant King William III to scorn what he called "that cathedral"; the museum opened in 1885 to a less than enthusiastic public reception. Since then, many additions have been made to both the collections and the building.

The Rijksmuseum contains the world's largest collection of paintings by the Dutch masters, including the most famous of all, a single work that all but defines the Golden Age. The painting is Rembrandt's *The Shooting Company of Captain Frans*

Banning Cocq and Lieutenant Willem van Ruytenburch, better known as *The Night Watch* (1642). The scene so dramatically depicted is surely alien to most of the people who flock to see it: gaily uniformed militiamen checking their weapons and accouterments before moving out on patrol. Works by Jacob van Ruisdael, Maerten van Heemskerck, Frans Hals, Paulus Potter, Jan Steen, Jan Vermeer, Pieter de Hooch, Gerard Terborch, Gerard Dou, and others also grace the walls. The range is impressive—individual portraits, guild paintings, landscapes, seascapes, domestic scenes, medieval religious subjects, allegories, and the incredible (and nearly photographic) Dutch still lifes.

Jan Luijkenstraat 1. © **020/674-7000.** www.rijksmuseum.nl. Admission 13€ adults, children 18 and under free. Daily 9am–6pm. Tram: 2 or 5 to Hobbemastraat.

Stedelijk Museum ★   This is the place to see works by such Dutch painters as Karel Appel, Willem de Kooning, and Piet Mondrian, alongside works by the French artists Chagall, Cézanne, Picasso, Renoir, Monet, and Manet, and by the Americans Calder, Oldenburg, Rosenquist, and Warhol. The Stedelijk centers its collection around the De Stijl, Cobra, post-Cobra, Nouveau Réalisme, pop art, color-field painting, zero, minimalist, and conceptual schools of modern art, and it houses the largest collection outside Russia of Kasimir Malevich's abstract paintings. *Note:* After a years' long renovation, the museum, now billing itself "The Temporary Stedelijk," reopened on March 3, 2011, with exhibitions featuring items from its permanent collection, which will allow visitors to see the work while construction continues.

Paulus Potterstraat 13. © **020/573-2911.** www.stedelijk.nl. Admission 9€ adults; 4.50€ seniors, students, children 7–16; children 6 and under free. Daily 10am–6pm. Tram: 1, 2, 4, 5, 9, 13, 16, 17, 24, 25, or 26 to Centraal Station.

Van Gogh Museum ★★★   More than 200 paintings by Vincent van Gogh (1853–90), along with nearly every sketch, print, etching, and piece of correspondence the artist ever produced, are housed here. Van Gogh painted for only 10 years, sold only one painting in his lifetime, and was on the threshold of success when he committed suicide at age 37. You can trace this great artist's artistic development and psychological decline by viewing the paintings displayed in chronological order according to the seven distinct periods that defined his short career.

One particularly splendid wall, on the second floor, has a progression of 18 paintings produced during the 2-year period when Vincent lived in the south of France, generally considered to be his artistic high point. It's a symphony of colors and color contrasts that includes *Gauguin's Chair; The Yellow House; Self-Portrait with Pipe and Straw Hat; Vincent's Bedroom at Arles; Wheatfield with Reaper; Bugler of the Zouave Regiment;* and one of the most famous paintings of modern times, *Still Life Vase with Fourteen Sunflowers,* best known simply as *Sunflowers.*

Paulus Potterstraat 7. © **020/570-5200.** www.vangoghmuseum.nl. Admission 13€ adults, 2.50€ children 13–17, children 12 and under free. Daily 10am–6pm (Fri 10pm). Tram: 2, 3, 5, or 12 to Van Baerlestraat.

Westerkerk (West Church)   The Dutch Renaissance–style Westerkerk (1631) is where Rembrandt and his son, Titus, were buried, and where in 1966 Queen (then Princess) Beatrix and Prince Claus said their marriage vows. Architect Pieter de Keyser took over the design work from his father, Hendrick, who died in 1621. The light, spacious interior has a fine organ. The 277-foot-high (83m) tower, the Westertoren, is Amsterdam's tallest and affords spectacular city views; at its top is the blue, red, and gold imperial crown of the Holy Roman Empire, a symbol bestowed by the Habsburg Emperor Maximilian. You can climb the tower on a guided tour.

SPECIAL Amsterdam EXPERIENCES

- **For outdoors types:** Rent a bicycle and join the flow of bikers for one of Amsterdam's classic experiences—but go carefully.
- **For shoppers:** Pick up a bunch of tulips from the Flower Market on Singel, even if they're just to brighten up your hotel room.
- **For night owls:** Stroll through the Red Light District, to examine the quaint gabled architecture along its narrow canals—oh, yes, and you might also notice certain ladies watching the world go by through their red-fringed windows.
- **For bar flies:** Spend a leisurely evening in a *bruine kroeg* (brown cafe), the traditional Amsterdam watering hole.

Westermarkt. Church: ✆ **020/624-7766.** www.westerkerk.nl. Free admission. Apr–Sept Mon–Fri 11am–3pm. Tower: ✆ **020/689-2565.** Admission 6€. Apr–Oct Mon–Sat 10am–5:30pm; guided tours every 30 min. Tram: 13, 14, or 17 to Westermarkt.

THE RED LIGHT DISTRICT

The warren of streets and old canals of the **Rosse Buurt (Red Light District),** around Oudezijds Achterburgwal and Oudezijds Voorburgwal—also known as **De Wallen (the Walls)** or **De Walletjes (the Little Walls)**—is on most people's sightseeing agenda for its open attitude to the world's oldest profession. This is one of the few traditional Amsterdam "industries" still practiced in its original setting, and the first guide to the district's peculiar attractions dates from the 17th century.

Plenty of tourists visit the Rosse Buurt and suffer nothing more serious than a come-on from one of the prostitutes. Stick to busy streets and be leery of pickpockets at all times. Do not take photographs of the women in the windows. Large, observant men are on the lookout, and they won't hesitate to throw your camera (and maybe your person) into the canal.

Still, it's extraordinary to view the prostitutes in leather and lace sitting in storefronts listening to their iPods as they knit or adjust their makeup, waiting patiently for customers. The district seems to reflect Dutch pragmatism; if you can't stop prostitution, you can at least confine it to a particular area and impose health, tax, and other regulations on it.

Underneath its tacky glitter, the Red Light District contains some of Amsterdam's prettiest canals and loveliest old architecture, plus some excellent bars and restaurants, secondhand bookstores, and other specialty stores (not all of which aim at erogenous zones).

PARKS

When the sun shines in Amsterdam, people head for the city's parks. The most popular and centrally located is the 122-acre (49-hectare) **Vondelpark ★★** (tram: 1, 2, 3, 5, 7, 10, or 12). Vondelpark lies generally southwest of Leidseplein, with the main entrance adjacent to Leidseplein, on Stadhouderskade. A pattern of ponds and streams surrounded by meadows, trees, and colorful flowers, it hosts skateboarding; Frisbee-flipping; in-line skating; model-boat sailing; pickup soccer, softball, and basketball; open-air concerts and theater; smooching in the undergrowth; parties; picnics; and crafts stalls.

To enjoy scenery and fresh air, head out to the giant **Amsterdamse Bos** (bus: 170 or 172 from outside Centraal Station), in the Amstelveen southern suburb. Nature on the city's doorstep, the park was laid out during the Depression years as a public works project. At the main entrance on Amstelveenseweg, stop by the **Bezoeker-scentrum (Visitor Center),** Bosbaanweg 5 (✆ **020/545-6100;** www.amsterdamse bos.nl), where you can trace the park's history, learn about its wildlife, and pick up a plan of the park. The center is open daily from noon to 5pm, and admission is free. Across the way is a bicycle rental shop (✆ **020/644-5473**), where bikes are available for from 10€ a day. Then follow the path to a long stretch of water called the **Bosbaan,** a 1¼-mile (2km) competition-rowing course. Beyond the course's western end are a pond, the **Grote Vijver,** where you can rent boats, and the **Openlucht-theater (Open-Air Theater),** which often has performances on summer evenings.

CANAL-BOAT TOURS

The canals are the best starting point to Amsterdam. Tours last approximately an hour and leave at regular intervals from *rondvaart* (excursion) piers in key locations around town. Most launches are docked along Prins Hendrikkade and Damrak near Centraal Station, on Rokin near Muntplein, and at Leidseplein. Tours leave every 15 to 30 minutes during the summer season (9am–9:30pm), every 45 minutes in winter (10am–4pm). Prices vary, but a basic 1-hour tour costs around 10€ to 13€ for adults, 5€ to 7€ for children 4 to 12, and free for children 3 and under. Tickets are also available from Rail Europe.

Where to Dine

Bolhoed ★ VEGETARIAN   Forget the corn-sheaf 'n' brown-rice image affected by so many vegetarian restaurants. Instead, garnish your healthful habits with tangy flavors and a dash of zest. Latin style, aboriginal art, world music, evening candlelight, and a fine view of the canal from each of the "Bowler Hat's" two plant-bedecked, cheerful rooms near Noordermarkt distinguish a restaurant for which *vegetarian* is a tad too wholesome-sounding. For outdoors dining in summer, there are a few canal-side tables.

Prinsengracht 60-62. ✆ **020/626-1803.** Main courses 13€–17€; fixed-price menus 13€–19€. No credit cards. Sun–Fri noon–11pm; Sat 11am–11pm. Tram: 13, 14, or 17 to Westermarkt.

Café Luxembourg ★ INTERNATIONAL   "One of the world's great cafes," wrote the *New York Times* about this relaxed grand cafe, at Spui, which draws all kinds of people to its large portions of food at reasonable prices. Soups, sandwiches, and such dishes as meatloaf are available. Special attractions are choices like Chinese dim sum and *satay ajam* (Indonesian grilled chicken in a peanut sauce). Sunday, in particular, but also on other days, it's a good place to do breakfast over the morning papers and a cup of strong coffee. You're encouraged to linger, and in summer there's sidewalk dining.

Spui 24. ✆ **020/620-6264.** www.cafeluxembourg.nl. Salads and specials 7.50€–13€; lunch 4.90€–9.90€; main courses 9.50€–16€. AE, DC, MC, V. Sun–Thurs 9am–1am; Fri–Sat 9am–2am. Tram: 1, 2, or 5 to Spui.

Christophe ★★★ MODERN FRENCH/MEDITERRANEAN   French chef Jean-Joel Bonsens has a penchant for wielding tangy Mediterranean flourishes to create a version of classic French cuisine. His ultrarefined food, served in a main dining room of modern flair, employs traditional Mediterranean ingredients—figs, truffles, olives, anchovies, peppers, saffron, and more—in exciting new ways. North

African *tajine* and Italian *pata negra* ham have a place on the menu, alongside French "staples" like roast Vendée duck. Bonsen rings the changes seasonally, so what you might get depends on when you visit.

Leliegracht 46. © **020/625-0807.** www.restaurantchristophe.nl. Main courses 29€–36€; fixed-price menus 36€–66€. AE, DC, MC, V. Tues-Sat 6:30-10:30pm. Tram: 13, 14, or 17 to Westermarkt.

De Belhamel ★ ▮▮ CONTINENTAL   Soft classical music complements a graceful Art Nouveau setting at this split-level restaurant overlooking the photogenic junction of the Herengracht and Brouwersgracht canals. The tables fill up quickly on most evenings, so make reservations or go early. Try for a window table and take in the superb canal views. Although generally excellent, De Belhamel does have two minor flaws: The waitstaff is occasionally a bit too laid-back, and it can get noisy when it's busy.

Brouwersgracht 60. © **020/622-1095.** www.belhamel.nl. Main courses 11€–27€; fixed-price menu 34€–45€. AE, MC, V. Sun-Thurs 6-10pm; Fri-Sat 6-10:30pm. Tram: 1, 2, 5, 13, or 17 to Martelaarsgracht.

De Prins ★★ 🍴 DUTCH/FRENCH   This companionable restaurant in a 17th-century canal house across the canal from the Anne Frank House has a smoke-stained, brown-cafe style and food that could easily grace a much more expensive place. This is a quiet neighborhood place—nothing fancy or trendy, and the relatively few tables fill up fast. There's a bar area on a slightly lower level than the restaurant. From March to September, De Prins spreads a sidewalk terrace out onto the canal side.

Prinsengracht 124. © **020/624-9382.** www.deprins.nl. Main courses 11€–17€; *dagschotel* 12€. AE, DC, MC, V. Daily 10am-1 or 2am (kitchen to 10pm). Tram: 13, 14, or 17 to Westermarkt.

Kantjil & de Tijger ★ INDONESIAN   Unlike the many Indonesian restaurants in Holland that wear their ethnic origins on their sleeves, with waitstaff decked out in traditional costume, the "Antelope and the Tiger" is chic, modern, and cool. Moreover, this eatery near Spui attracts customers who like their Indonesian food not only chic, modern, and cool—but good as well. The 20-item *rijsttafel* (rice table) for two is deservedly a bestseller.

Spuistraat 291-293. © **020/620-0994.** www.kantjil.nl. Reservations recommended on weekends. Main courses 11€–16€; rijsttafels 40€–50€ for 2. AE, DC, MC, V. Mon-Fri 4:30-11pm; Sat-Sun noon-11pm. Tram: 1, 2, or 5 to Spui.

Lof ★ ▮▮ CONTINENTAL   It's hard to pin down this fashionable, vaguely French-Italian eatery. For one thing, there's no menu. Its youthful chefs describe their creations as *cuisine spontane*—they go to the markets, spontaneously pick out whatever's fresh and catches their fancy, and equally spontaneously figure out what to do with it back at base. But *lof* means "praise" in Dutch, and it's an apt name, since the results are invariably admirable, though the choice is deliberately limited. You dine on one of two levels, at plain tables in a cozy setting with bare brick walls, or with a view of proceedings in the open kitchen.

Haarlemmerstraat 62. © **020/620-2997.** Main course 23€; fixed-price menu 35€. AE, DC, MC, V. Tues-Sat 7-11pm. Tram: 1, 2, 5, 13, or 17 to Maartelaarsgracht.

Spanjer & Van Twist ★ ▮▮ CONTINENTAL   This place just off Keizersgracht would almost be worth the visit for its name alone, so it's doubly gratifying to find the food good, too. The interior is typical *eetcafé*-style, with the day's specials chalked on a blackboard, a long table with newspapers at the front, and the kitchen visible in

Even if you're on a tight budget, aim to eat at least one Indonesian *rijsttafel.* This traditional "rice table" banquet of as many as 25 succulent and spicy foods, served in tiny bowls, usually costs around 15€ to 30€. Pick and choose from among the bowls and add your choice to the pile of rice on your plate. It's a delicious and true taste of multicultural Amsterdam. For an abbreviated version served on one plate, try *nasi rames.* At lunch, the standard Indonesian fare is *nasi goreng* (fried rice with meat and vegetables) or *bami goreng* (fried noodles prepared in a similar way). A great place to eat rijsttafel is Tempo Doeloe (see above).

back. In fine weather, you can eat on an outdoor terrace next to the tranquil Leliegracht canal.

Leliegracht 60. ℂ **020/639-0109.** www.spanjerenvantwist.nl. Reservations not accepted. Main courses 14€–17€. MC, V. Sun–Thurs 10am–1am; Fri–Sat 10am–2am (only light snacks after 10pm). Tram: 13, 14, or 17 to Westermarkt.

Tempo Doeloe ★★ INDONESIAN   For authentic Indonesian cuisine, from Java, Sumatra, and Bali—which doesn't leave out much—this place between Prinsengracht and Keizersgracht is hard to beat. You dine in a *batik* ambience that's Indonesian but restrained. Try out one of the many little meat, fish, and vegetable dishes of the three different rijsttafel options, from the 15-plate vegetarian rijsttafel *sayoeran* and the 15-plate rijsttafel *stimoelan,* to the sumptuous 25-plate rijsttafel *istemewa.*

Utrechtsestraat 75. ℂ **020/625-6718.** www.tempodoeloerestaurant.nl. Reservations required. Main courses 15€–26€; rijsttafel 28€–36€; fixed-price menu 27€–45€. AE, DC, MC, V. Daily 6–11:30pm. Tram: 4 to Keizersgracht.

Wilhelmina-Dok ★ CONTINENTAL   Across the IJ waterway from Centraal Station, this fine waterfront eatery more than justifies a short, free ferryboat ride across the IJ followed by a 5-minute walk. Plain wood, candlelit tables, wood floors, and oak cabinets give the interior an old-fashioned maritime look, and large windows serve up views across the narrow, boat-speckled channel. Tables on the terrace are sheltered from the wind in a glass-walled enclosure.

Nordwal 1. ℂ **020/632-3701.** www.wilhelmina-dok.nl. Main courses 18€–21€; chef's menu 28€. AE, DC, MC, V. Daily 11am–midnight. Ferry: IJveer from Waterplein West behind Centraal Station to the dock at IJplein, then walk or bike east along the dike-top path.

Shopping

Bargain-hunters won't have much luck (except maybe at the flea markets), but shopping in Amsterdam definitely has its rewards. Best buys include diamonds and traditional Dutch products such as Delftware, pewter, crystal, and old-fashioned clocks. Modern Dutch fashion and interior designers have a deserved reputation for innovation, and maintain many outlets in the city. No matter what you're looking for, you're sure to be impressed with the range of possibilities.

By far the most ubiquitous items you'll see will be those in the familiar blue-and-white "Delft" colors that have almost become synonymous with Holland. Souvenir stores, specialty stores, and department stores feature Delftware earthenware products in the widest variety of forms imaginable. Be aware that unless it meets certain specifications, that souvenir you bring home with you won't be an authentic piece of the hand-painted earthenware pottery that has made the Delft name famous. A wide selection of Delftware can be found at **Galeria d'Arte Rinascimento,** Prinsengracht 170 (© **020/622-7509;** www.delft-art-gallery.com), across the canal from the Anne Frank House, and at the two branches of **Jorritt Heinen,** Prinsengracht 440 (© **020/627-8299;** www.jorritheinen.com), and Muntplein 12 (© 020/623-2271).

De Bijenkorf ★, Dam 1 (© **0900/0919;** www.debijenkorf.nl), Amsterdam's premier department store, has a vast array of goods in all price ranges.

Amsterdam diamond cutters have an international reputation for high standards. When you buy from them, you'll be given a certificate listing the weight, color, cut, and identifying marks of the gem you purchase. The following stores offer diamond cutting and polishing tours, as well as sales of the finished product: **Amsterdam Diamond Center,** Rokin 1–5 (© **020/624-5787;** www.amsterdamdiamondcenter. nl); **Coster Diamonds,** Paulus Potterstraat 2–8 (© **020/305-5555;** www.coster diamonds.com); and **Gassan Diamonds,** Nieuwe Uilenburgerstraat 173–175 (© **020/622-5333;** www.gassandiamonds.nl/en).

MARKETS

You find just about anything your imagination can dream up, at the **Albert Cuyp Markt,** Albert Cuypstraat. It's open Monday to Saturday from 9am to 6pm. From March to December, Thorbeckeplein hosts a **Sunday Art Market** where local artists show off their wares. **Waterlooplein Flea Market** ★ is the city's classic market, offering everything from cooking pots to mariners' telescopes, to decent prints of Dutch cities; it's open Monday to Saturday from 10am to 5pm. And gardeners will find it well-nigh impossible to leave Amsterdam without at least one purchase from the floating **Flower Market,** on Singel at Muntplein, open daily year-round. Just be certain the bulbs you buy bear the obligatory certificate clearing them for entry into the United States and Canada.

Nightlife

Like an Indonesian rijsttafel, nightlife in Amsterdam is a bit of this and a bit of that. There's a strong jazz scene, good music clubs, and some enjoyable English-language shows at the little cabarets and theaters along the canals. The club and bar scene can be entertaining, if not outrageous; the dance clubs may indeed seem quiet and small to anyone used to the flash of New York, L.A., or London. However, the brown cafes—the typical Amsterdam pubs—have never been better.

Amsterdam's top orchestra is the famed **Royal Concertgebouw Orchestra,** whose home is the **Concertgebouw** ★★, Concertgebouwplein 2–6 (© 0900/671-8345; www.concertgebouworkest.nl/en). World-class orchestras and soloists are only too happy to appear at the Concertgebouw's Grote Zaal (Great Hall) because of its perfect acoustics. Chamber and solo recitals are given in the Kleine Zaal (Little Hall). Tickets cost from 17€ to 100€. The main concert season is September to mid-June, and during July and August there are summer concerts, also world class but with a listener-friendly price tag—all seats are just 25€.

The **Netherlands Opera** has established an international reputation for mounting daring productions. The company performs at the **Muziektheater** ★, Waterlooplein 22 (© **020/625-5455;** www.dno.nl). This theater is also used by the **National Ballet,** which performs large-scale classical ballet repertoire as well as contemporary work, and by the **Netherlands Dance Theater,** which is based in The Hague and is famous for its groundbreaking contemporary repertoire. Most performances begin at 8:15pm, with opera tickets selling for 25€ to 100€ and ballet tickets for 15€ to 150€.

In a spectacular piece of modern architecture that debuted in 2005 on the IJ waterfront just east of Centraal Station, the **Muziekgebouw aan 't IJ,** Piet Heinkade 1 (✆ **020/788-2000;** www.muziekgebouw.nl), is the city's home for avant-garde and experimental music. Look for concerts of modern, old, jazz, electronic, and non-Western music, along with small-scale musical theater, opera, and dance. Tickets are 10€ to 65€. In a kind of annex is the equally new home of the jazz and improvised music club **Bimhuis,** Piet Heinkade 3 (✆ **020/788-2188;** http://bimhuis.nl/home). Tickets here are 10€ to 30€.

Boom Chicago, Leidsepleintheater, Leidseplein 12 (✆ **020/423-0101;** www.boomchicago.nl/en), brings delightful English-language improvisational comedy to Amsterdam. Dutch audiences don't have much of a problem with the English sketches; they often seem to get the point ahead of the native English speakers in attendance. Tickets are 15€ to 35€. Spectators are seated around candlelit tables for eight people and can have dinner and a drink while they enjoy the show. The restaurant is open at 7pm, and meals cost 30€.

In Amsterdam, jazz and blues groups hold forth in bars, and the joints start jumping at around 11pm. You'll find listings in *Time Out Amsterdam.* **Bourbon Street,** Leidsekruisstraat 6–8 (✆ **020/623-3440;** www.bourbonstreet.nl), hosts a mix of local and traveling jazz and blues talent. **Bluescafe Maloe Melo,** Lijnbaansgracht 163 (✆ **020/420-4592;** www.maloemelo.com), Amsterdam's "home of the blues," features live blues most nights, interspersed with jazz and country evenings, and jams on Tuesday and Thursday nights. It's generally packed every night.

Amsterdam's dance-club scene embraces every type of ambience and clientele, from the sophisticated rooms in large hotels to underground alternative spots. The scene isn't wildly volatile, but places do come and go. Leading clubs include **Akhnaton,** Nieuwezijds Kolk 25 (✆ **020/624-3396;** www.akhnaton.nl), for African music and salsa; **Melkweg,** Lijnbaansgracht 234A (✆ **020/531-8181;** www.melkweg.nl), for a variety of live music plus dance events; and **Paradiso,** Weteringschans 6–8 (✆ **020/626-4521;** www.paradiso.nl), which has live music followed by dance parties. At **Odeon,** Singel 460 (✆ **020/521-8555;** www.odeontheater.nl), set in a 17th-century canal house, you can dance to jazz, funk, house, techno, R&B, and classic disco—all at the same time, since there are three different floors. A waterfront building from 1899 that used to be a power station houses hip **Panama,** Oostelijke Handelskade 4 (✆ **020/311-8689;** www.panama.nl), a see-and-be-seen place for 30- to 40-something professionals, which hosts big-name DJs and special events, depending on the day and seasons.

BROWN CAFES

You'll find *bruine kroegen* (brown cafes) everywhere: on street corners, at the canal intersections, and down narrow little lanes. They look as if they've been there forever, and they have, practically. These neighborhood bars are the favorite local haunts. Brown cafes will typically sport lace half-curtains at the front window and ancient Oriental rugs on tabletops (to sop up any spills from your beer). Wooden floors, overhead beams, and plastered walls blend into a murky brown background, darkened by the centuries of smoke from Dutch pipes and cigars. Frequently, there's a wall rack with newspapers and magazines, but they get little attention in the evening, when conversation flows as readily as *pils* (beer). *Jenever,* the potent Dutch gin, is on hand in several different flavors, some served ice cold—but never on the rocks.

smoking COFFEE SHOPS

Visitors often get confused about "smoking" coffee shops and how they differ from "no-smoking" ones. Well, to begin with, "smoking" and "no-smoking" don't refer to cigarettes—they refer to hashish and marijuana. The use of narcotic drugs is officially illegal in the Netherlands, but Amsterdam and some other local authorities permit the sale in licensed premises of up to 5 grams (.2 oz.) of hashish or marijuana for personal consumption.

Smoking coffee shops not only sell cannabis, most commonly in the form of hashish, but also provide a place where patrons can sit and smoke it all day long if they so choose. Generally, these smoking coffee shops are the only places in Amsterdam called "coffee shops"—regular cafes are called cafes or *eetcafes*—so chances are, whether or not you want to smoke, you'll be able to find what you're looking for without too much difficulty.

Your hotel neighborhood is sure to have at least one brown cafe close at hand. Far be it for us to set any sort of rigid itinerary for a brown-cafe *kroegentocht* ("pub crawl"), but you just might want to look into the following: **Cafe Hoppe,** Spui 18–20 (© **020/623-7849;** www.cafe-hoppe.nl), a student and journalist hangout since 1670, which has sawdust on the floor and is always packed; **'t Smalle,** Egelantiersgracht 12 (© **020/623-9617;** www.t-smalle.nl), in the Jordaan district on the canal side, a bar in a former distillery and tasting house that dates from 1786; **Café Chris,** Bloemstraat 42 (© **020/624-5942;** www.cafechris.nl), a tap house since 1624; **De Karpershoek,** Martelaarsgracht 2 (© **020/624-7886**), which dates from 1629 and was once a favorite hangout of sailors; and **Cafe het Papeneiland,** Prinsengracht 2 (© **020/624-1989;** www.papeneiland.nl), a 300-year-old establishment filled with character and with a secret tunnel used by 17th-century Catholics.

An Excursion to Haarlem ★

Traditionally the little sister city of Amsterdam, this handsome small city has a similar 17th-century ambience but gets by fine without the hassles that go with the capital's famously tolerant and often eccentric lifestyle.

ESSENTIALS

GETTING THERE **Trains** depart at least every 15 minutes from Amsterdam Centraal Station for Haarlem; the trip takes around 15 minutes. The historic center is a 5- to 10-minute walk from the graceful 1908 Art Nouveau train station (which is decorated with painted tiles and has a fine station restaurant).

VISITOR INFORMATION City Marketing Haarlem/VVV Informatiecentrum, Verwulft 11, 2011 GJ Haarlem (© **0900/616-1600;** www.vvvhaarlem.nl) is in the center of town, at the intersection of Grote Houtstraat and Gedempte Oude Gracht.

TOP ATTRACTIONS & SPECIAL MOMENTS

First-time visitors generally head straight for the **Grote Markt ★★★**, the handsome central market square. Most points of interest in Haarlem are within easy walking distance of the Grote Markt. The monumental buildings around the square date from the 15th to the 19th centuries and are a visual mini course in the development of Dutch architecture. Here stands Haarlem's 14th-century **Stadhuis (Town Hall),** a former hunting lodge of the counts of Holland rebuilt in the 17th century.

Adjacent to the Grote Markt, the splendid **Sint-Bavokerk (Church of St. Bavo),** also known as the **Grote Kerk (Great Church)** ★, Oude Groenmarkt 23 (② **023/ 532-4399;** www.bavo.nl), soars into the sky. Finished by 1520 after a relatively short building period, it has a rare unity of structure and proportion. Mozart, Handel, Mendelssohn, Schubert, and Liszt all made special visits to Haarlem to play the church's magnificent **Christian Müller Organ** (1738). It has 5,068 pipes and is nearly 98 feet (29m) tall, and when it's going flat out, it's loud enough to blow your socks off. You can hear it played at one of the free concerts on Tuesday evening and Thursday afternoon from April to October. St. Bavo's is open Monday to Saturday from 10am to 4pm. Admission is 2€ for adults, 1.25€ for children ages 12 to 16, and free for children 11 and under.

The city's finest attraction is the **Frans Hals Museum ★★**, Groot Heiligland 62 (② **023/511-5775;** www.franshalsmuseum.nl). In the galleries, halls, and furnished chambers of a 1608 home for retired gentlemen, the famous paintings by Frans Hals (ca. 1580–1686) and other masters of the Haarlem school hang in settings that look like the 17th-century houses they were intended to adorn. The museum is open Tuesday to Saturday from 11am to 5pm, and Sunday and holidays from noon to 5pm. Admission is 7.50€ for adults, 3.75€ for visitors ages 19 to 24, and free for children 18 and under.

An ideal way to view the town is by canal boat. Tours by **Post Verkade Cruises** (② **023/535-7723;** www.postverkadecruises.nl) depart from a jetty on the Spaarne River next to the Gravenstenenbrug, a handsome lift bridge. May to September, cruises are daily every hour from 11am to 6pm (the first and last cruises depart only if the number of passengers is sufficient); October to April, Tuesday to Saturday at the same times. Tickets are 9.50€ for adults, 4.50€ for children ages 3 to 11, and free for children 2 and under.

WHERE TO DINE

A popular cafe-restaurant, **Jacobus Pieck,** Warmoesstraat 18 (② **023/532-6144;** www.jacobuspieck.nl), has a lovely shaded terrace in the garden for fine-weather days, and inside it's bustling and stylish. Outside or in, you'll find excellent food and friendly, efficient service. At lunchtime they serve generous sandwiches and burgers, and their salads are particularly good. Main dinner courses range from pastas and Middle Eastern dishes to wholesome Dutch standards. Main courses are 13€ to 18€.

THE HAGUE ★★

Amsterdam is the national capital, but The Hague (or more commonly Den Haag, in Dutch) is the seat of government and the official residence of the Dutch monarchs. This tradition began in 1248, when Count Willem II of Holland was crowned king of the Romans in the German city of Aachen but chose to live at the Binnenhof Palace in what is now The Hague. Sophisticated, full of parks and elegant homes, the city has an 18th-century French look that suits its role as the diplomatic center of the Dutch nation.

GETTING THERE The Hague is an easy day trip from Amsterdam, with frequent **train** service—including the Thalys international high-speed train—from Amsterdam Centraal Station. Note that The Hague has two main train stations, Den Haag Centraal Station and Den Haag HS; most of the sights are closer to Centraal Station, but some trains stop only at HS station (in 2010, a complete refurbishment of this old station began and is due to be completed sometime in 2011). Neither station has a tourist information office, but just outside both are tram and bus stops, and taxi stands.

TOURIST INFORMATION VVV Den Haag, Hofweg 1 (mailing address: Postbus 85456, 2500 CD Den Haag; © **0900/340-3505**; www.denhaag.com; tram: 1 or 16), is across the street from the Binnenhof (Parliament). The office is open Monday to Friday from 9:30am to 6pm, Saturday from 9:30am to 5pm, and Sunday from 11am to 5pm.

Top Attractions & Special Moments

The Hague's most notable attraction is the impressive **Binnenhof (Inner Court)** ★ complex of Parliament buildings, in the center city. Join a tour, to visit the medieval **Ridderzaal (Hall of the Knights).** The queen delivers a speech from the throne here each year on the 3rd Tuesday in September, arriving and departing in her golden coach—like Cinderella—drawn by high-stepping royal horses. Depending on government business, you can tour one or the other of the two chambers of the **Staten-Generaal (States General),** the Dutch Parliament, which is open for guided tours Monday to Saturday from 10am to 4pm. Tours are 6€ or 4€ for adults, depending on the tour being offered at the time. It's requested you book ahead by telephone (© **070/364-6144;** www.binnenhofbezoek.nl) for the guided tour, and that you call ahead to confirm that tours are going on the day you intend to visit. Admission to the Parliament exhibit in the reception room of the Hall of Knights is free.

Adjacent to the Binnenhof is the Italian Renaissance–style **Mauritshuis,** Korte Vijverberg 8 (© **070/302-3435;** www.mauritshuis.nl), built in 1644 as the home of a young court dandy and cousin of the Orange-Nassaus. Today this small palace houses the **Koninklijk Kabinet van Schilderijen (Royal Cabinet of Paintings)** ★★ and is the permanent home of an impressive art collection given to the Dutch nation by King Willem I in 1816. Highlights include 13 Rembrandts, 3 Frans Hals, and 3 Vermeers (including the famous *View of Delft*), plus hundreds of other famous works by such painters as Bruegel, Rubens, Steen, and Holbein (including his portrait of Jane Seymour, third wife of King Henry VIII of England). The gallery is open April to September Monday to Saturday from 10am to 5pm, and Sunday from 11am to 5pm; October to March Tuesday to Saturday from 10am to 5pm, and Sunday from 11am to 5pm. Admission is 12€ for adults and free for visitors 18 and under.

The **Gemeentemuseum Den Haag (The Hague Municipal Museum)** ★, Stadhouderslaan 41 (© **070/338-1111;** www.gemeentemuseum.nl), possesses a world-famous collection of works by Piet Mondrian (1872–1944), including his last work, *Victory Boogie Woogie* (1943), inspired by New York. The museum is open Tuesday to Sunday from 11am to 5pm. Admission is 10€ for adults, 6.50€ for seniors and students, and free for children 18 and under.

Not far away, in the Scheveningen Woods, is enchanting **Madurodam** ★, George Maduroplein 1 (© **070/416-2400;** www.madurodam.nl; tram: 9), a miniature village in 1-to-25 scale that represents the Dutch nation in actual proportions of farmland to urban areas. It presents many of the country's most historic buildings in miniature, with lights that actually work, bells that ring, and trains that run efficiently—as trains do in Holland. It's open April to June daily from 9am to 8pm, July to August daily from 9am to 11pm, and September to March daily from 9am to 6pm. Admission is 15€ for adults, 14€ for seniors, 11€ for children ages 3 to 11, and free for children 2 and under.

SCHEVENINGEN ★

So close to The Hague is the beach resort and fishing port of **Scheveningen**—just 3 miles (5km)—that it seems part of the same city. This is probably Holland's most chic

The Hague & Scheveningen

ACCOMMODATIONS ■
Corona **8**
Het Boulevard **1**
Paleishotel **6**

DINING ◆
Ducdalf **3**
Le Bistroquet **11**
Stadsherberg
't Goude Hooft **7**

ATTRACTIONS ●
Binnenhof (Parliament) **9**
Gemeentemuseum
Den Haag **4**
Holland Casino
Scheveningen **2**
Madurodam **5**
Mauritshuis/Koninklijk
Kabinet van Schilderijen **10**

NETHERLANDS

The Hague &
Scheveningen   ✹ Amsterdam

seacoast resort and contains an array of international-name boutiques and upscale restaurants. Yet you can still catch a sight of costumed fishermen's wives near the harbor—they dress up in their traditional Dutch garb for special events, like *Vlaggetjes-dag* (Flag Day) in June, when the first of the new season's herring are landed.

To get there from The Hague, take tram 1 or 9 from Den Haag Centraal Station to Gevers Deynootplein in Scheveningen (tram nos. 10, 11, and 17 from The Hague stop close to Scheveningen's fishing harbor). Tourist information is available from VVV Den Haag's **Informatiepunt Scheveningen** on the Pier (tram: 1 or 9), open mid-May to August daily from 11am to 5pm. For mail, phone, and website details, see "Visitor Information" for The Hague, above.

Among Scheveningen's attractions are biking, strolling on the dunes, fishing in the North Sea, and splashing in the waves at the beach or in a heated wave pool. The beach and bathing zone is called Scheveningen Bad—but it looks pretty good to the Dutch.

Tuxedoed croupiers provide blackjack and roulette at **Holland Casino Scheveningen,** Kurhausweg 1 (✆ **070/306-7777**), across from the beautifully restored 19th-century Kurhaus Hotel. The dress code is "correct" (collar and tie for men), and the minimum age is 18. You need your passport to get in. The casino is open daily from 10am to 3am. Admission is 5€.

Where to Stay

Boulevard Hotel ★ ☺ Perched atop the sea dunes at Scheveningen within walking distance of the Palace Promenade, this hotel has a commanding sea view from its sun lounge/restaurant and from some of the guest rooms, which all are plainly furnished in a clean-cut, modern style. The Boulevard has special family rooms for those with young children.

Seinpostduin 1, 2586 EA Scheveningen. ✆ **070/354-0067.** Fax 070/355-2574. www.boulevard-hotel. nl. 30 units. 85€–150€ double. Rates include buffet breakfast. AE, DC, MC, V. Tram: 1 or 9 to Keizerstraat; or 11 to Scheveningen Haven. *In room:* No A/C.

Corona Hotel ★ Centrally located opposite the Parliament, this charming, small hotel is housed in three 17th-century buildings, graced with touches of handsome marble and mahogany. The guest rooms are done in soft pastel colors with graceful window drapes. The elegant main restaurant, full of French provincial furnishings, is a favorite retreat for the good and the great in government circles. On balmy days, part of the restaurant becomes a sidewalk terrace.

Buitenhof 39–42, 2513 AH Den Haag. ✆ **070/363-7930.** Fax 070/361-5785. www.corona.nl. 36 units. 110€–175€ double. Rates include buffet breakfast on weekends. AE, DC, MC, V. Tram: 10, 16, or 17 to Buitenhof. **Amenities:** 2 restaurants; bar. *In room:* No A/C.

Paleis Hotel ★★ Behind the royal family's Noordeinde Palace, this intimate hotel has spacious and elegant guest rooms furnished with soft chairs and settees, in a quiet city-center setting. Bathrooms are a bit small but fitted out beautifully. Some rooms are air-conditioned. The location is excellent both for shopping (the pedestrian shopping promenade is nearby) and for sightseeing.

Molenstraat 26, 2513 BL Den Haag. ✆ **070/362-4621.** Fax 070/361-4533. www.paleishotel.nl. 20 units. 185€–295€ double. AE, DC, MC, V. Tram: 17 to Gravenstraat. **Amenities:** Bar. *In room:* No A/C (in some).

Where to Dine

The Harbour Club ★ SEAFOOD While some seafoodies mourned the passing of the traditional old restaurant Ducdalf from this spot on Scheveningen's yacht harbor, others liked the cut of its successor's jib. You dine amid a thoroughly modern *joie de vivre* in a trendily rambling interior of bare brick walls, or outside by the water's edge. The kitchen can handle everything from sushi through *nouvelle*-style grilled North Sea fish, and oyster or mixed-shellfish platters, to surf-and-organic turf.

Dr. Lelykade 5–13, Scheveningen. ✆ **070/891-3224.** www.theharbourclub.nl. Main courses 20€–45€; fixed-price menus 25€–45€. AE, DC, MC, V. Daily 11am–1am. Tram: 11 to Dr. Lelykade.

Le Bistroquet ★ CONTINENTAL   This small, popular restaurant in the center city is one of The Hague's finest, its quietly elegant dining room featuring lovely table settings. The menu, though short, is to the point and covers lamb, fish, and poultry dishes. A fine Dutch menu choice is the three variations of Texel lamb with roasted garlic and a basil sauce.

Lange Voorhout 98. ✆ **070/360-1170.** www.bistroquet.nl. Reservations recommended on weekends. Main courses 25€–38€; fixed-price menus 39€–49€. AE, DC, MC, V. Mon–Fri noon–2pm and 6–10pm; Sat 6–10pm. Tram: 10, 16, or 17 to Kneuterdijk.

Stadsherberg 't Goude Hooft ★★ DUTCH/CONTINENTAL   There's a definite old Dutch flavor to this wonderful, large restaurant overlooking the city's old market square, yet its 1600s exterior cloaks a 1939 interior installed after a disastrous fire. The wooden beams, brass chandeliers, and rustic chairs and tables blend harmoniously with the stained-glass windows, medieval banners, and wall murals. There's a large sidewalk cafe on the "Green Market" square. An extensive menu covers everything from snacks to light lunches to full dinners.

Dagelijkse Groenmarkt 13. ✆070/346-9713. www.tgoudehooft.nl. Main courses 22€–30€. AE, DC, MC, V. Mon noon–6pm; Tues–Wed and Fri–Sat 10am–7pm; Thurs 10am–9:30pm, Sun 11am–6pm. Tram: 17 to Gravenstraat.

An Excursion to Delft ★★

Yes, this is the home of the famous blue-and-white porcelain, and you can visit the factory where it is produced. This small, handsome city is also the cradle of the Dutch Republic and the burial place of the royal family, and was the birthplace and inspiration of artist Jan Vermeer, the 17th-century master of light and subtle emotion.

GETTING THERE   There's frequent **train** service from Amsterdam; the ride takes just under 1 hour. The train station in Delft is only a short walk from the center of town, or you can take one of the buses, trams, or taxis that stop right outside the station.

VISITOR INFORMATION   Touristen Informatie Punt (TIP), Hippolytusbuurt 4, 2611 HN Delft (✆ **0900/515-1555** from inside Holland, 31-15/215-4051 from abroad; www.delft.nl), is located in the center of town. The office is open April to September Sunday and Monday from 10am to 4pm, Tuesday to Friday from 9am to 6pm, and Saturday from 10am to 5pm; October to March Sunday from 10am to 3pm, Monday from 11am to 4pm, and Tuesday to Saturday from 10am to 4pm.

TOP ATTRACTIONS & SPECIAL MOMENTS

The house where Vermeer was born, lived, and painted is long gone from Delft, as are his paintings. The artist's burial place, the **Oude Kerk (Old Church),** Roland Holstlaan 753 (✆ **015/212-3015**), is noted for its 27 stained-glass windows by Joep Nicolas. You should also visit the **Nieuwe Kerk (New Church)** ★, Markt (✆ **015/212-3025**), where Prince William of Orange and other members of the House of Orange-Nassau are buried. Both churches are open April to October Monday to Saturday from 9am to 6pm; November to January Monday to Friday from 11am to

4pm, and Saturday from 11am to 5pm; and February to March Monday to Saturday from 10am to 5pm. Combined admission is 3.50€ for adults, 3€ for seniors, 1.50€ for children ages 6 to 12, and free for children 5 and under. Admission to the Nieuwe Kerk tower is 3€ for adults, 2.50€ for seniors, 1.50€ for children ages 6 to 12, and free for children 5 and under.

The **Stedelijk Museum Het Prinsenhof ★**, St. Agathaplein 1 (© **015/260-2358;** www.prinsenhof-delft.nl), on nearby Oude Delft, is where William I of Orange (William the Silent) lived and had his headquarters in the years when he helped found the Dutch Republic. He was assassinated here in 1584, and you can see the bullet holes in the stairwell. Today the Prinsenhof is a museum of paintings, tapestries, silverware, and pottery. The museum is open Tuesday to Sunday from 11am to 5pm. Admission is 7.50€ for adults, 4€ for students and children ages 12 to 16, and free for children 11 and under.

In the same neighborhood, you can view a fine collection of old Delft tiles displayed in the wood-paneled setting of a 19th-century mansion museum called **Lambert van Meerten,** Oude Delft 199 (© **015/260-2358;** www.lambertvanmeerten-delft.nl). The museum is open Tuesday to Sunday from 11am to 5pm. Admission is 3.50€ for adults; 1.50€ for students and children ages 12 to 16; and free for children 11 and under.

To view a demonstration of the traditional art of making and hand-painting Delftware, visit the factory and showroom of **Koninklijke Porceleyne Fles,** Rotterdamseweg 196 (© **015/251-2030;** www.royaldelft.com), founded in 1653. It's open from the third week in March to October daily from 9am to 5pm, November to the third week in March Monday to Saturday from 9am to 5pm. Admission is 8€ for adults, and free for children 12 and under.

WHERE TO DINE

The skillfully prepared dishes at **Le Vieux Jean,** Heilige Geestkerkhof 3 (© **015/213-0433;** www.levieuxjean.nl), draw from the provincial French tradition, using the freshest of top-quality ingredients. The setting is an old churchyard just across from the Oude Kerk, and you receive a warm and friendly welcome. Main courses cost 22€ to 34€, fixed-price menus 34€ to 57€.

Some of the best Dutch cooking in the country is dished up at the atmospheric **Spijshuis de Dis ★**, Beestenmarkt 36 (© **015/213-1782;** www.spijshuisdedis.com), east of the market. Look out for traditional plates presented in modern variations. A good example is the *Bakke pot*—a stew made from three kinds of meat (beef, chicken, and rabbit) in a beer sauce, served in the pan. An entree will set you back 18€ to 23€, a fixed-price menu 30€.

MAASTRICHT ★

A riverside city of cafes and churches, Maastricht (pop. 120,000) is a seductive mixture of historic buildings and monuments, a lighthearted carnival, and some of the finest restaurants to be found in any Dutch city of its size. Somehow—in between eating, drinking, church-going, stepping out for Carnival, and hanging on to their heritage—the people of Maastricht are building a modern, prosperous, and vibrant city. Discovering how they do it all can be quite an education.

GETTING THERE **Trains** depart twice hourly from Amsterdam, Rotterdam, and The Hague for the approximately 2½-hour journey to Maastricht (trains from

Amsterdam are direct; those from Rotterdam and The Hague require a transfer in Eindhoven). Maastricht station is a 15- to 20-minute walk from the Vrijthof square in the center of town. Outside the station are bus stops and a taxi stand.

VISITOR INFORMATION VVV Maastricht, Kleine Staat 1 (✆ 043/325-2121; www.vvv-maastricht.eu), is off Grote Staat, a 15-minute walk from the train station, across the Maas River. It's open May to October Monday to Saturday from 9am to 6pm, and Sunday from 11am to 3pm; November to April Monday to Friday from 9am to 6pm, and Saturday from 9am to 5pm.

Top Attractions & Special Moments

Walking from the train station to the center of town, you head down Stationstraat, cross the Maas on the **Sint-Servaasbrug (St. Servatius Bridge),** which dates from 1280 to 1289 and is one of the oldest bridges in the Netherlands. The **Vrijthof ★★,** the city's most glorious square, is a vast open space bordered on three sides by restaurants and cafes with sidewalk terraces, and on the fourth by the Romanesque Sint-Servaas Basilica and the Gothic Sint-Jan's Church with its soaring red belfry. This is Maastricht's forum, especially in good weather, when the cafe terraces are filled with people soaking up the atmosphere and watching the world go by.

The oldest parts of the majestic cruciform **Sint-Servaasbasiliek (Basilica of St. Servatius),** Keizer Karelplein (✆ 043/325-2121; www.sintservaas.nl), date from the year 1000, though the church was considerably enlarged in the 14th and 15th centuries. St. Servatius, Maastricht's first bishop, is buried in the crypt. Over the centuries, people have honored the saint with gifts, so the treasury has a collection of incredible richness and beauty that includes two superb 12th-century reliquaries fashioned by Maastricht goldsmiths. The basilica is open Monday to Saturday from 10am to 5pm, and Sunday from 12:30 to 5pm. Admission is 3.80€ for adults, 2.30€ for seniors and students, and free for children 17 and under.

Next door, the sober, whitewashed interior of the city's main Dutch Reformed (Protestant) church, **Sint-Janskerk (St. John's Church),** dating from the 14th century and given to the Protestants in 1633, makes a study in contrasts with the lavish Catholic decoration at St. Servatius's. But there are murals, sculpted corbels of the 12 Apostles, and grave monuments of local dignitaries and wealthy individuals. Most visitors come here, though, to climb the 218 narrow, winding steps to the 230-foot-high (69m) belfry's windy viewing platform, 141 feet (42m) above the streets, and the fine city views it affords. The church is open Easter to mid-October Monday to Saturday from 11am to 4pm. Admission to the church is free, and to the tower is 1.50€ for adults and .50€ for children 12 and under.

The west wing and crypts of the Romanesque cruciform **Onze-Lieve-Vrouwbasiliek (Basilica of Our Lady) ★,** Onze-Lieve-Vrouweplein (✆ 043/325-1851; www.sterre-der-zee.nl), date from the 11th century, and there's evidence of an even earlier church and a pagan place of worship on the site. But the side chapel sheltering a statue of Our Lady Star of the Sea is the focus for most pilgrims. The richly robed statue, fronted by a blaze of candles, is credited with many miracles, even during long years when it was hidden away because of religious persecution. The church treasury contains a rich collection of tapestries, reliquaries, church silver, and other religious objects. The basilica is open daily from 11am to 5pm, except during services; the treasury is open Easter to mid-October Monday to Saturday from 11am to 5pm, and Sunday from 1 to 5pm. Admission to the basilica is free and to the treasury is 3€ for adults, 2€ for seniors, and 1€ for children 12 and under.

Designed by Italian architect Aldo Rossi and opened in 1995, the riverside **Bon-nefanten Museum ★**, av. Céramique 250 (*✆* **043/329-0190;** www.bonnefanten.nl), is instantly recognizable from its striking, bullet-shaped dome. Works of art within include pieces from the Maasland School, such as sculpture, silverwork, and wood-carvings produced along the Maas Valley in Limburg and Belgium. This art dates from as far back as the 13th century and had its apogee during the 15th and 16th centuries. Internationalism is illustrated in the museum's collection of Italian and Flemish masters. These include works by Filippo Lippi and Bellini, and Pieter Brue-gel the Younger's *Wedding in Front of a Farm* and *Census at Bethlehem*. The museum is open Tuesday to Sunday from 11am to 5pm. Admission is 8€ for adults, 4€ for children ages 13 to 18, and free for children 12 and under.

For centuries, marlstone has been extracted from **Sint-Pietersberg (Mount St. Peter) ★★** (*✆* **043/325-2121;** www.pietersberg.nl), on the city's southwestern edge, leaving the hill's interior honeycombed with 20,000 passages. From Roman times to the days of medieval sieges, to the 4 years of Nazi occupation during World War II, these passages have served as a place of refuge. The temperature under-ground is about 50°F (10°C), and it's damp, so bring a cardigan or a coat to protect against the chill. The caves are open July to September daily at 2:45pm. Guided tours are 5€ for adults and 3€ for children 12 and under.

Where to Stay & Dine

There's been an inn on the site of the **Amrâth Hotel DuCasque ★**, Helmstraat 14 (*✆* **043/321-4343;** www.amrathhotels.nl), since the 15th century. The present family-run hotel carries on the proud tradition, with contemporary facilities, comfort-able rooms, and good old-fashioned friendliness. It faces the lively Vrijthof square; those rooms overlooking the Vrijthof have the finest view in town. Doubles cost 120€ to 190€.

The **Botel Maastricht,** Maasboulevard 95 (*✆* **043/321-9023;** www.botel maastricht.nl), a floating hotel, has 28 small and sparsely furnished cabins, a ship-board ambience, and a nautically themed bar. Try for a cabin on the river side, and then make due allowance for the fact that the Maas River is not the Seine. Doubles with bathroom cost 48€; those without bathroom cost 44€.

One of the city's top restaurants, **Toine Hermsen ★★**, Sint Bernardusstraat 2–4 (*✆* **043/325-8400;** www.toinehermsen.com), on the corner of Onze-Lieve-Vrouwe-plein, is the proud possessor of a Michelin star. The chef creates French cuisine classics and exploits regional seasonal ingredients such as Limburg's asparagus and chicory. You can expect good portions of impeccable food and superb but relaxed service. Reservations are required. Main courses cost 25€ to 55€; fixed-price menus are 25€ to 65€.

Local favorite **Restaurant 't Plenkske ★**, Plankstraat 6 (*✆* **043/321-8456;** www.hetplenkske.nl), is a fine restaurant in the Stokstraat Quarter, with a light, airy decor and an outdoor patio overlooking the site of the city's ancient Roman baths. Regional specialties from both Maastricht and Liège are prominent on the menu, along with a number of French classics thrown in for good measure. Main courses cost 20€ to 26€; fixed-price menus are 30€ to 43€.

NORWAY

For the rail traveler, the mountainous and elongated country of Norway is the crown jewel of Scandinavia. From its snowcapped mountains to its scenic fjords warmed by the Gulf Stream, much of the country's varied land- and seascapes can be seen from your train window. The rail ride between the eastern capital city of Oslo and its western outpost of historic Bergen (gateway to the fjord district) is one of the most scenic in Europe, vying with some of the dramatic mountain rail journeys in alpine Switzerland. See "Highlights of Norway," below, for more details on this 7-hour trip.

14

Norwegian rail engineers have defied nature and laid tracks through dizzying, difficult terrain that was once accessible only to mountain goats and spry adventurers. You are carried quickly and efficiently across the often breathtaking terrain of this beautiful land. Routes are not comprehensive, especially as you go into the far north toward Lapland and the Midnight Sun, but rail lines are gloriously scenic, and the major towns and their myriad attractions are easily reached by train.

Norway has dramatic scenery in abundance, but do bear in mind that it comes at a price; what Norway doesn't have is cheap living. In fact, in 2009, a UBS analysis of the world's most expensive cities placed Oslo as *the* most expensive city in the world. High prices, however, shouldn't deter the value-minded rail traveler. In this chapter, we provide some budget-saving tips along with recommendations of moderately priced hotels and restaurants.

Note: A map detailing Norway's rail routes as well as the rail lines of the major Scandinavian countries can be found on p. 199.

Highlights of Norway

With a very small window of opportunity for warm and sunny days, a key factor in timing your rail visit to Norway is, of course, the weather. The summer season is very short, beginning in June (May is still quite cold) and ending by late August, when it's often possible to see snow flurries whirling about your head. Summer days are long; in fact, north of the Arctic Circle, the Midnight Sun is clearly visible. Once September arrives, days quickly grow cold; open-air museums close down; attractions, including tourist offices, go on reduced hours; and—most important for the rail traveler—trains begin running on less frequent schedules. Winter sports continue under dark, foreboding skies, including dog-sledding, ice-fishing, and cross-country and alpine skiing, but these attract only the most hearty (and warmly dressed) travelers.

Norway's cities and towns stage numerous festivals and special events throughout the year (check with the local tourist office to see what's going on during your visit), but the following three are definitely worth a look if you're in town for them:

The **Holmenkollen Ski Festival,** held on the outskirts of Oslo in early March, is one of Europe's largest ski festivals, with World Cup Nordic skiing and biathlons, international ski-jumping competitions, and Norway's largest cross-country race for amateurs. For more information, contact **Skiforeningen,** Kongeveien 5, Holmenkollen, 0787 Oslo (✆ **22-92-32-00;** www. skiforeningen.no).

From mid-May to early June, the world-class **Bergen International Festival (Bergen Festspill)** features musical artists from Norway and around the world. It's one of the largest annual musical events in Scandinavia. For information, contact the Bergen International Festival, P.O. Box 183, Sentrum, N-5804 Bergen (✆ **55-21-06-30;** www.fib.no).

The major event on the Oslo calendar, the **Nobel Peace Prize Ceremony** is held annually at Oslo City Hall on December 10. Attendance is by invitation only. For information, contact the **Nobel Institute,** Henrik Ibsens gate 51, N-0255 Oslo (✆ **22-12-93-00;** www.nobelpeaceprize. org).

Average rail passengers will not have much time for exploring the northern reaches of this ancient land of the Vikings and can happily confine themselves to the two greatest cities in Norway: Oslo, the capital, and the "second city" of Bergen. Oslo, one of the world's most beautifully sited capitals, deserves at least 2 or 3 days of your time, as does Bergen, whose charm and history are as compelling as its excellent accessibility to the western fjord district. Both cities are located in the south, where this spoon-shaped country rounds out into a bowl, with Oslo on the east and Bergen on the west.

Most flights to the country land in Oslo, making it the obvious starting point for a rail trip in Norway. A number of world-class attractions await you: **Akershus Castle,** one of the oldest historical monuments in Oslo; the 17th-century **Oslo Cathedral; Vigelandsparken** (a field of sculpture by Norway's greatest, Gustav Vigeland); the **Kon-Tiki Museum,** housing the world-famous balsa log raft from 1947; the open-air **Norwegian Folk Museum;** the **Viking Ship Museum** (with a trio of Viking burial vessels); and, outside of town, the **Henie Onstad Kunstsenter,** a treasure-trove of art acquired by former movie star and skating champion Sonja Henie.

One of the great adventures of Norway is to make the 7-hour, 305-mile (491km) rail journey from Oslo to Bergen, one of the most startlingly beautiful in all of Europe. The train after leaving Oslo climbs to the little town of **Gol** at 679 feet (204m) before beginning a much steeper ascent. It reaches the winter resort of **Geilo** at 2,605 feet (782m) and continues to climb until it approaches the village of **Ustaoset,** at 3,248 feet (974m). After that, the train crosses a foreboding landscape of icy mountain lakes and rock-strewn ridges wearing "snow bonnets." Tickets for this journey are available from **Rail Europe** (✆ **888/438-7245** in the United States, ✆ **800/361-7245** in Canada; www.raileurope.com).

At the tiny mountain village of **Finse,** in the vicinity of the **Hardangerjøkulen Glacier,** you are virtually in polar conditions. At 4,009 feet (1,203m), Finse is the highest station in Norway.

Leaving Finse, the Oslo–Bergen line goes through a 6¼-mile (10km) tunnel emerging near **Hallingskeid** before going on to its next stop at **Myrdal.** The descent then is to the lake town of **Voss,** only 184 feet (55m) above sea level and both a winter and a summer sports resort. The scenery grows tamer as the train begins its descent into Bergen, the last lap of this journey taking about an hour.

The final destination of **Bergen** is one of the great historic centers of Scandinavia, and had been the capital of Norway until it was unseated by Oslo. As the gateway to the fjords, its port was once the source of great power, ruled over by the Hanseatic League, a medieval mercantile guild. Situated on a peninsula, this UNESCO World Heritage Site is surrounded by towering mountains (which can be ascended by funicular) and filled with old cobblestone streets flanked by weather-beaten clapboard houses in various hues; one of these old (17th-c.) neighborhoods is called Chaos City because of its crazy mazes and unplanned buildings (go ahead, get lost in its atmosphere). Be sure to see the city's aquarium (one of the largest and best in Scandinavia) and tour old Bryggen, a district of Hanseatic timbered houses along the waterfront. You also may want to tour the marketplace, which offers the best fresh seafood you can imagine.

ESSENTIALS

Getting There

All transatlantic flights from North America land at **Oslo Airport, Gardermoen** (✆ 64-81-20-00; www.osl.no), 31 miles (48km) north of Oslo. **Continental** (✆ 800/231-0856; www.continental.com) flies direct from Newark, New Jersey, to Oslo, taking 7 hours and 35 minutes.

Other airlines flying to Norway through a gateway city in Europe include **British Airways** (✆ 800/AIRWAYS [247-9297] in the U.S.; www.britishairways.com), **SAS** (✆ 800/221-2350 in the U.S.; www.flysas.com), **Icelandair** (✆ 800/223-5500 in the U.S.; www.icelandair.com), and **KLM** (✆ 800/241-4141 in the U.S.; www.klm.com).

Norway by Rail

PASSES

For information on the **Eurail Global Pass, Eurail Global Pass Flexi, Eurail Select Pass, Eurail Scandinavia Pass,** and other multicountry options, see chapter 2.

In addition to the multicountry passes, there is the **Eurail Norway Rail Pass.** The pass offers 3 to 8 days of unlimited second-class train travel in a 1-month period, starting at $239 for adults. Don't worry about it being a second-class pass, as the comfort level of second class on Norwegian trains is equal to first class in many other European countries. Similar passes for travelers under 26 and for seniors (over 60) start at $179. The pass must be purchased before leaving North America. You can buy the pass through **Rail Europe** (✆ 888/438-7245 in the United States, ✆ 800/361-7245 in Canada; www.raileurope.com) or your travel agent.

FOREIGN TRAIN TERMS

Don't bother learning a lot of train terms in difficult-to-pronounce Norwegian. Norwegians start learning English while in grade school, and you can usually learn what you need to know by asking train personnel for help in English. That said, here are a

The must-do rail experience in this country is the trip from Oslo to Bergen, but those with more time—a total of 24 hours—will find another wonderful option that cuts through the heart of Norway on a northward trek: **a train trip from Oslo to Bodø** that captures what local tourist promoters accurately bill as "the essence" of Norway.

As the train heads north from Oslo, the scenery is bucolic, with rolling hills, farmlands, and small villages. The farther north you go, the more dramatic the scenery becomes, especially as you continue north from the resort of Lillehammer, famed for hosting the 1992 Winter Olympics. When you reach Dombås—instead of going to Trondheim—you can detour to the northwest and the town of Åndalsnes. This leg is one of the grandest of all rail journeys in Scandinavia: Your train will plunge through tunnels carved through foreboding mountains, and whiz over bridges and past waterfalls and the highest vertical canyon in Norway.

After arriving in Åndalsnes, you can return to Dombås for a final journey to the north. If possible, plan an overnight stopover in the medieval city of Trondheim, one of the most historic and beautiful in Scandinavia and the ancient capital of Norway.

From Trondheim, you can travel to the northern terminus of the rail line at Bodø, a city that lies north of the Arctic Circle. Many rail passengers in summer take this journey to Bodø just to bask in the Midnight Sun.

At Bodø, you can return on the same train to Oslo, or, as an alternative, you can take a bus northeast from Bodø to the city of Narvik. After a stopover in Narvik, you can once again board a train, the Ofoten Line, for a journey eastward into Sweden, where most passengers head southeast to the capital city of Stockholm.

few common terms you may find helpful to know: *Avgaende tog* means "departure," and *Ankommende tog* means "arrival." *Billetter* are tickets.

PRACTICAL TRAIN INFORMATION

The **Norwegian State Railways (NSB)** operates the major rail lines of Norway. Call ✆ **47/81-50-08-88** (press 4 for English) for timetable info and bookings. For info on the Web, log on to **www.nsb.no**.

Norway's 2,500-mile (4,025km) network of electric and diesel-electric trains runs as far as Bodø, 62 miles (100km) north of the Arctic Circle. (Beyond that, visitors must take a coastal steamer, plane, or bus to Tromsø and the North Cape.) The fastest express trains, called NSB Regiontog, crisscross the mountainous terrain between Oslo, Stavanger, Bergen, and Trondheim, using a tilting technology to help with the corners. Holders of first-class railpasses don't get to travel first class, as this option doesn't exist in Norway, but they do get access to an upgraded second-class compartment, which is just fine on these trains.

The most popular and most scenic run in the country covers the 305 miles (491km) between Oslo and Bergen. Visitors with limited time often choose this route for its fabled mountains, gorges, white-water rivers, and fjords. The trains often stop for passengers to enjoy breathtaking views. The one-way second-class fare from Oslo to Bergen is 775NOK. Seat reservations cost 50NOK (90NOK for Komfort class) with the Eurail pass and are recommended in the summer season. Another popular run, from Oslo to Trondheim, costs 852NOK one-way in second class.

One of the country's obviously scenic trips, from Bergen to Bodø, is not possible by train because of the rough terrain. Trains to Bodø leave from Oslo (see "The Essence of Norway," above).

If you're traveling direct between cities separated by a long distance and don't have a railpass, a **Minipris Ticket** (available in Norway only) might be a good option. With this ticket, you can travel in second class for 199NOK to 399NOK one-way, but only on routes that take you more than 93 miles (150km) from your point of origin. No stopovers are allowed except for a change of trains. Tickets are valid only on select trains, for boarding that begins during designated off-peak hours. You can buy Minipris Tickets at any railway station in Norway, by calling **Customer Service** at ℭ **47/81-50-08-88** (and paying a supplement of 50NOK), or online at **www.nsb. no**. The Minipris ticket has some restrictions, and seats sell out quickly.

Travelers over age 67 are entitled to a 50% discount, called an **Honnorrabatt,** on Norwegian train trips of more than 31 miles (50km). Regardless of age, the spouse of someone over 67 can also receive the 50% discount.

RESERVATIONS   Reservations are recommended on most InterCity and NSB Regiontog trains and on all overnight and international services. A reservation costs 50NOK above the price of your railpass if made in Norway. Reservations are included if you purchase a ticket without a railpass. Sleepers on overnight trains should also be reserved (see below). It's not always necessary to make a reservation on secondary trains, but it's always advised in the summer season, as trains are likely to be filled to capacity.

Timetables are distributed free at all rail stations under the name of *NSB Togruter*. On the more scenic routes, you can often get data in English describing the highlights of the trip.

SERVICES & AMENITIES   Second-class travel on Norwegian trains is highly recommended. In fact, second class in Norway is as good as or better than first-class travel anywhere else in Europe, with reclining seats and various comforts.

The sleepers on night trains (called **InterNordNight**) are a good investment because you'll be saving on a regular hotel accommodation. They have recently been refurbished and can now be booked only by the compartment. Each compartment contains two beds and costs 850NOK for a one-way journey, regardless of whether it is occupied by one or two people. Breakfast is extra. Passengers can choose to travel in an ordinary seat instead, where they'll be given a pillow, blanket, eye mask, and earplugs. Sleepers can be booked through Rail Europe in North America. Children 4 to 15 years of age and senior citizens pay 50% of the regular adult fare. Group and midweek tickets are also available.

There are special compartments for persons with disabilities on most medium- and long-distance trains. People in wheelchairs and others with physical disabilities, as well as their companions, may use the compartments. Some long-distance trains offer special playrooms ("Kiddie-Wagons") for children, complete with toys and educational items.

The express trains running between Oslo and Bergen (or vice versa) have excellent dining cars, some of the best in Northern Europe, but meals are terribly expensive. The secondary express trains have buffets, serving both hot meals and snacks. On the smaller regional trains, expect food wheeled through the cabin on a cart.

Trains & Travel Times in Norway

From	To	Type of Train	# of Trains	Frequency	Travel Time
Oslo	Bergen	Regiontog	4	Daily	6 hr., 40 min.–7 hr., 47 min.
Oslo	Trondheim	Regiontog	4	Daily	7 hr., 46 min.
Trondheim	Bodø	InterCity	2	Daily	9 hr., 48 min.

[FastFACTS] NORWAY

Area Code   The international country code for Norway is **47.** If you're calling from outside the country, the city code is **22** for Oslo and **55** for Bergen. Inside Norway, no area or city codes are needed. Phone numbers have eight digits.

Business Hours   Most **banks** are open Monday to Friday from 8:30am to 3:30pm (Thurs to 5pm) and are closed Saturday and Sunday. Most **businesses** are open Monday to Friday from 9am to 4pm. **Stores** are generally open Monday to Friday from 10am to 5pm (many stay open Thurs until 6 or 7pm) and Saturday 10am to 1 or 2pm. Shopping malls will often open later; until 8pm on weekdays and 1 or 2pm on Saturday. Most shops close on Sunday.

Climate   In summer, the average temperature in Norway ranges from 57° to 65°F (14°–18°C). In January, it hovers around 27°F (-3°C), ideal for winter sports. The Gulf Stream warms the west coast, where winters tend to be temperate. Rainfall, however, is heavy.

Above the Arctic Circle, the sun shines night and day from mid-May until late July. For about 2 months every winter, the North Cape is plunged into darkness.

Currency   The basic unit of currency is the Norwegian krone (crown), or NOK, made up of 100 øre. At this writing, $1 = 6.2NOK. £1 = 9.5NOK.

Documents Required   Citizens of the United States and Canada need a valid **passport** to enter Norway. You need to apply for a visa only if you want to stay more than 3 months.

Electricity   Norway uses 220 volts, 30 to 50 cycles, AC, and standard continental two-pin plugs. Transformers and adapters are needed to use Canadian and American equipment. Always inquire at your hotel before plugging in any electrical equipment.

Embassies & Consulates   In case you lose your passport or have some other emergency, contact your embassy in Oslo. The Embassy of the **United States** is at Henrik Ibsens gate 48, N-0244 Oslo (✆ **21-30-85-40;** http://norway.usembassy.gov), and **Canada**'s is at Wergelandsveien 7, N-0244 Oslo (✆ **22-99-53-00;** www.canada.no).

Health & Safety   Norway offers some of the best medical facilities in Europe, with well-trained, English-speaking doctors. Norway's national health plan does not cover American or Canadian visitors; medical expenses must be paid in cash, but costs are generally more reasonable than elsewhere in Western Europe.

You're probably safer in Norway than in your home country; however, you should take the usual precautions you would when traveling anywhere. Guard your possessions (particularly around Oslo's Gardermoen airport and Central Railway Station), and don't become blasé about security. One of the least safe places at night is east Oslo, which has a growing drug problem, but even there, it's reasonably safe to walk around at night, though you may encounter some hassle from drug addicts, alcoholics, or beggars.

Holidays   Norway celebrates the following public holidays: New year's Day (Jan 1), Maundy Thursday, Good Friday, Easter, Labor Day (May 1), Ascension Day (mid-May), Independence/

Constitution Day (May 17), Whitmonday (late May), Christmas (Dec 25), and Boxing Day (Dec 26).

Legal Aid   If arrested or charged with a crime in Norway, you can obtain a list of private lawyers from the U.S. Embassy to represent you.

Mail   Airmail letters or postcards to the United States and Canada cost 13NOK for up to 20 grams (⁷⁄₁₀ oz.). Airmail letters take 7 to 10 days to reach North America. The principal post office in Norway is **Oslo Central Post Office,** Dronningensgate 15, N-0101 www.posten.no/en. Mailboxes are vibrant red, embossed with the trumpet symbol of the postal service. They're found on walls, at chest level, throughout

cities and towns. Stamps can be bought at the post office, at magazine kiosks, or at some stores. The post office can weigh, evaluate, and inform you of the options for delivery time and regulations for sending parcels. Shipments to places outside Norway require a declaration on a printed form stating the contents and value of the package.

Police & Emergencies   Call ℂ **112** for the **police,** ℂ **110** to report a **fire,** or ℂ **113** to request an **ambulance** throughout Norway.

Telephone   Direct-dial long-distance calls can be made to the United States and Canada from most phones in Norway by dialing ℂ **00** (double zero),

then the country code (**1** for the U.S. and Canada), followed by the area code and phone number. Norwegian coins of 1NOK, 5NOK, and 10NOK are used in the increasingly rare pay phones.

Tipping   Hotels add a 10% to 15% service charge to your bill, which is sufficient unless someone has performed a special service. Most bellhops get at least 10NOK per suitcase. Nearly all restaurants add a service charge of up to 15% to your bill. Barbers and hairdressers usually aren't tipped, but toilet attendants and hat check people expect at least 3NOK. Don't tip theater ushers. Taxi drivers don't expect tips unless they handle heavy luggage.

OSLO

The oldest Scandinavian capital, founded by the Viking king Harald (also known as Harold Fairhair) in 1048, Oslo is renowned for its spectacular natural beauty, with urban subways connecting you to mountain lakes, evergreen forests, and hiking trails—all within the city limits. Oil rich, it is no longer a provincial capital but has risen to become a metropolis and one of the most cosmopolitan cities of Europe, with a vibrant nightlife and an attitude of tolerance.

At the top of the 60-mile (97km) Oslofjord, Norway encompasses 175 square miles (453 sq. km), although its urban growth covers only about a 10th of that. The rest is a vast outdoor playground.

More and more of Oslo's old wooden structures have given way to tall modern buildings and glass-roofed atriums. It's a great city for wandering, as it has incorporated art to decorate both its public and private buildings, with sculpture integral to its public squares and parks, especially the Vigeland Sculpture Park.

Station Information
GETTING FROM THE AIRPORT TO THE TRAIN STATION

Most international flights land at **Oslo Airport** in Gardermoen (ℂ **64-81-20-00;** www.osl.no), about 31 miles (50km) north of Oslo.

High-speed trains (ℂ **81-50-07-77;** www.flytoget.no) run between the airport's train station (right at the air terminal) and Oslo's Central Station. The trip takes a

Oslo

ATTRACTIONS ⬤

Akershus Festning og Slott
 (Akershus Castle and Fortress) **7**
Edvard Munch Museum **19**
Henie Onstad Kunstsenter **1**
Ibsen Apartment **4**
Nasjonalgalleriet **16**
Vigelandsparken **2**

BYGDØY PENINSULA ⬤

Frammuseet **23**
Kon-Tiki Museum **22**
Norsk Folkemuseum **20**
Norsk Sjøfartsmuseum **24**
Vikingskiphuset
 (Viking Ship Museum) **21**

maximum 22 minutes and costs 170NOK per person each way. Trains depart the airport between 5:36 and 12:36am, every 10 minutes. **Note:** A railpass does not cover this train, but does cover the hourly IC trains, which take 26 minutes.

There's also frequent bus service, departing every 20 minutes throughout the day, for downtown Oslo (trip time: 35–40 min.). It's maintained by both **SAS** (whose buses deliver passengers to the Central Station and to most of the SAS hotels within Oslo) and **Norwegian Bus Express** (② **81-54-44-44;** www.nor-way.no) and costs between 135NOK and 230NOK one-way per person.

If you want to take a taxi (and we don't recommend it unless you're traveling in a large group), be prepared for a lethally high charge of around 600NOK to 1,060NOK for up to four passengers plus their luggage. If you need a "maxi-taxi," a minivan suitable for between 5 and 15 passengers, plus luggage, you will pay from 800NOK.

INSIDE THE STATION

Trains from Sweden arrive at **Oslo Sentralstasjon,** Jernbanetorget 1 (② **81-50-08-88** for train information). At the beginning of Karl Johans Gate (the main street of Oslo), the terminal is in the center of the city. From the Central Station, trains leave for Stockholm, Bergen, Stavanger, Trondheim, and Gothenburg. You can also catch trams here to all major sections of Oslo (see "Getting Around," below).

In 2006, a new **Tourist Information Office** (② **81-53-05-55;** www.visitoslo. com) opened at Trafikanten Service Centre, next to the train station, and the old one inside the station closed down. The new center is open Monday to Friday 7am to 8pm, Saturday and Sunday 8am to 6pm (until 8pm May–Sept), and 10am to 4pm on public holidays. Staff can exchange money and make hotel reservations at a cost of 55NOK.

Oslo Central Station is open from 4:30am to 1:20am. Arrival and departure times for trains are displayed on digital bulletin boards inside the station. For train reservations—or to validate a railpass—go to the area marked *Billetter.* Here you can make sleeping car reservations, too, and buy both domestic and international tickets. Opening hours for the ticket office are 6am to 11:15pm Monday to Friday, 6:30am to 11:15pm Saturday, and 7am to 11:15pm Sunday and holidays.

Baggage storage lockers are located on a balcony (follow the signs inside the station). They cost 20NOK to 50NOK, depending on the size of the bag, for 24 hours, with a 7-day maximum. One other amenity of note inside the station is free Internet access.

There are two **currency exchange offices** (**www.forex.no**) in the station: one in the Airport Express Train Terminal (open 7am–7pm Mon–Fri and 9am–4pm Sat) and one in the main hall (8am–8pm Mon–Fri and 9am–5pm Sat). There are also a post office, a bank, and several ATMs.

Information Elsewhere in the City

The **Oslo Tourist Information Office,** Fridtjof Nansens plass 5, entered on Roald Amundsen Street (② **81-53-05-55;** www.visitoslo.com), is open April and May Monday to Saturday 9am to 5pm, June to August daily 9am to 7pm, September Monday to Saturday 9am to 5pm; and October to March Monday to Friday 9am to 4pm. The staff will give you free maps and brochures, and make hotel reservations for a fee of 55NOK. Sightseeing tickets can be purchased and guided tours can also be arranged.

Getting Around

Oslo has an efficient citywide network of buses, trams (streetcars), and subways. Buses and electric trains take passengers to the suburbs. From mid-April to October, ferries to the attraction-filled peninsula of Bygdøy depart from the harbor in front of the Oslo Rådhuset (City Hall).

The **Oslo Pass** (also called the Oslo Card) can help you become acquainted with the city at a fraction of the usual price. It allows free travel on public transportation, free admission to museums and other top sights, discounts on sightseeing buses and boats, and special treats in some restaurants. You can purchase the card at hotels, many shops, tourist information offices, travel agents, and the branches of Sparebanken Oslo Akershus. Adults pay 230NOK for a 1-day card, 340NOK for 2 days, and 430NOK for 3 days. Children's cards cost 100NOK, 120NOK, and 160NOK.

Jernbanetorget is Oslo's major **bus and tram** terminal stop and is located right in front of the train station. Most buses and trams passing through the heart of town stop at Wessels Plass, next to the Parliament, or at Stortorget, the main marketplace. Many also stop at the National Theater or University Square on Karl Johans Gate.

The **T-banen** (subway) has five main lines running to the east of Oslo and four lines running to the west. The most heavily traveled routes by tourists are the eastern lines. The western lines take in Holmenkollen and residential and recreational areas west and north of the city.

For schedule and fare information, call **Trafikanten** (© **81-50-01-76;** www. trafikanten.no). Single-trip tickets cost 26NOK to 40NOK; children 4 to 15 travel for half fare; children 3 and under are free. An eight-coupon Maxi card costs 190NOK and is half-price for children.

From April 1 to September 30, ferries depart for Bygdøy from Pier 3 in front of the Oslo Rådhuset. For schedules, call **Båtservice Sightseeing** (© **23-35-68-90;** www.boatservicesightseeing.com). The ferry or bus to Bygdøy is a good choice because parking there is limited. Other ferries leave for various parts of the Oslofjord. Tickets on the ferry cost 40NOK, half-price for children. The Båtservice also runs excellent sightseeing cruises beginning the end of April, with prices from 170NOK to 620NOK. Inquire at the **Tourist Information Office** or directly through the Båtservice (see above).

Where to Stay

Best Western Hotel Bondeheimen   This restored 1913 building is today an affordable hotel within walking distance of many of Oslo's attractions and transportation hubs. In spite of modernization, it maintains a pleasing old-fashioned Norwegian charm mixed with modern conveniences and comfort. The rooms are a bit small, but space is well used. The rooms are furnished with lovely pinewood pieces. Most bathrooms have showers only (some with tubs). Ask about discount rates and upgrades. The staff aims to please.

Rosenkrantz gate 8 (entrance on Kristian IV's Gate), N-0159 Oslo. © **800/633-6548** in the U.S., or 23-21-41-00. www.bondeheimen.com. 127 units. 850NOK–2,000NOK standard double; discounts usually available on weekends. Rates include breakfast. Tram: 7 or 11. **Amenities:** Restaurant; bar; rooms for those w/limited mobility; smoke-free rooms.

Cochs Pensjonat ✦   Launched in 1927 by the Coch sisters, this is the most famous and enduring boarding house in Oslo. The building's ornate facade curves around a bend in a boulevard banking on the northern edge of the Royal Palace. It's been greatly expanded over the years and is now a clean, well-conceived, inexpensive hotel representing excellent value. Expect very few, if any, amenities (even the kitchenettes have only a hot plate and sink) and services at this hotel—rooms don't have telephones.

Parkveien 25, N-0350 Oslo. ☎ **23-33-24-00.** Fax 23-33-24-10. www.cochspensjonat.no. 88 units, 78 with bathroom. Rooms with bathroom, TV, and kitchenette 840NOK double; rooms without kitchenette and private bathroom 480NOK double. MC, V. Tram: 11, 17, or 18. *In room:* TV (in some), kitchenette (in some), no phone.

First Hotel Millennium ★ 🏩 Created in 1998 out of a 1930s Art Deco office building, this hotel is both minimalist and stylish, and is hailed for its atmosphere and character. At ¼ mile (.4km) from Central Station, it's close to most of central Oslo's major attractions. Bedrooms are generally spacious, with good-size bathrooms, and combine Art Deco touches with Nordic modern decor. The 10 rooms on the top floor have balconies.

Tollbugata 25, N-0157 Oslo. ☎21-02-28-00. Fax 21-02-28-30. www.firsthotels.no. 112 units 1,295NOK-1,695NOK double. AE, DC, MC, V. Tram: 12, 15 or 19. **Amenities:** Restaurant, bar; nonsmoking rooms; room for those w/limited mobility.

Hotel Gabelshus ★ 🏩 Built in 1912, this old-time favorite attracts discerning travelers who know of its relatively secluded location. It's a schlep from the train station, but a worthwhile one. Part of the Choice Hotel Group since 2004, it's been totally remodeled and enlarged while maintaining an old-fashioned charm. The aura of an English manor house is evoked by public lounges filled with art and antiques, along with burnished copper and working fireplaces. Both antique reproductions and Nordic design dominate the midsize to spacious bedrooms, some of which have terraces.

Gabels Gate 16, N-0272 Oslo 2. ☎ **23-27-65-00.** Fax 23-27-65-60. www.choicehotels.no. 114 units. 1,500NOK double; 2,500NOK suite. Rates include breakfast and a light supper. AE, DC, MC, V. Tram: 13. **Amenities:** Breakfast room; smoke-free rooms.

Norlandia Karl Johan ★ Renovations made in the last few years have made this hotel—a 10-minute walk from Central Station—better, brighter, and more welcoming than ever. Norwegian folk art, Oriental carpets, antiques, and reproductions fill each room. The medium-size bedrooms have double-glazed windows and comfortable furnishings, along with marble bathrooms. The best rooms sit in the front of the hotel and feature large French windows that open onto a panorama of the city.

Karl Johans Gate 33, N-0162 Oslo. ☎ **23-16-17-00.** Fax 22-42-05-19. www.norlandia.no/karljohan. 111 units. Mon–Fri 1,595NOK double; Sat–Sun 1,195NOK double; from 1,500-2,000NOK suite. Rates include breakfast. AE, DC, MC, V. T-banen: Stortinget. **Amenities:** Bar; rooms for those w/limited mobility; smoke-free rooms.

Thon Hotel Cecil ★ The Thon chain combines comfort with affordability. This contemporary hotel enjoys a central location, with many restaurants, sights, and shops lying within easy walking distance. The well-maintained rooms are bright yet cozy. Expect relatively simple styling and none of the trappings of more expensive nearby competitors—there's no health club, sauna, or full-fledged room service. For peace and quiet, make sure you don't get one of the street-facing rooms.

Stortingsgata 8 (entrance on Rosenkrantzgate), N-0130 Oslo. ☎23-31-48-00. Fax 23-31-48-50. www.thonhotels.no. 111 units. 1,095NOK-1,545NOK double. AE, DC, MC, V. T-banen: Stortinget. **Amenities:** Breakfast room; rooms for those w/limited mobility; smoke-free rooms.

Top Attractions & Special Moments

There are those who say a visit to Oslo would be worthwhile if you came just to see the harbor and take a boat ride along the Oslofjord. Because this is the most scenically located capital of Europe, panoramic views are important, especially the one from **Tryvannstårnet,** a 390-foot (117m) observation tower atop 1,900-foot (570m) Tryvann Hill.

On even the most cursory visit, you should see the **Viking ships** on Bygdøy peninsula; explore such famous vessels as the polar ship, *Fram,* or the balsa raft, *Kon-Tiki;* and take in the Norwegian Maritime Museum and the Folk Museum. If you're an art lover, visit the **Munch Museum** and go to the outskirts of town to see the famous **Henie Onstad Art Center.**

Akershus Festning og Slott (Akershus Castle and Fortress)   Built by King Haakon V about 1300, Akershus Castle and Fortress is one of the most important relics of Norway in the Middle Ages, though what you'll see when you visit is mostly a Renaissance palace. A fire in 1527 devastated the northern wing, and the castle was rebuilt and transformed under the Danish-Norwegian king Christian IV in the 1600s. The castle is infamous for having served as a prison during the Nazi regime.

 SCANDINAVIA'S greatest painter

Oslo is the city of the great artist Edvard Munch (1863–1944), and many aficionados make a special pilgrimage here to see his finest works. Although he would grow up to become hailed as "the handsomest man in Norway," he suffered through many childhood illnesses and tragic deaths (such as the early death of his mother). Much of that grief later found expression in his works, such as the world-famous *The Scream.*

Heavily influenced by French Realism, Munch studied in Paris in 1885. In time he would reject that movement, succumbing to Impressionism and later Symbolism. His first exhibition in Berlin in 1892 touched off a nationwide scandal. Critics screamed "anarchistic provocation," and the show was forced to close. But Munch was not deterred. He was on a roll in the 1890s, creating some of his most memorable works, including the cycle *The Frieze of Life,* dedicated to love, death, anxiety, and darkness.

Returning to Norway in 1908, he fell in love with the Oslofjord and painted many memorable seascapes. After a love affair went sour, he suffered a nervous breakdown. Although he helped decorate the auditorium of Oslo University, by 1916 he'd turned inward and led the life of a hermit in a home outside Oslo. He continued to paint, however, often landscapes hailed by critics as "sensuous," and always in bold colors.

The best showcase of Munch's paintings is found at **Edvard Munch Museum ★★**, Tøyengata 53, 0578 Oslo (✆ **23-49-35-00;** www.munch.museum.no). The museum traces Munch's works from early Realism to latter-day Expressionism. The rotating collection features 1,100 paintings, some 4,500 drawings, and around 18,000 prints, numerous graphic plates, and 6 sculptures.

Admission to the museum is free from October to March. From April to September, the cost is 75NOK adults; 40NOK students, seniors, and children 7 and over; children under 7 are free. The museum is free with the Oslo pass. It is open June to August daily 10am to 6pm; September to May Tuesday to Friday 10am to 4pm, Saturday and Sunday 11am to 5pm (T-banen: Tøyen).

14

NORWAY | Oslo

607

Commemorating those dreadful years is the on-site Norwegian Resistance Museum, showing underground printing presses and radio transmitters among other illegal artifacts that trace the German attack on Norway in 1940 until that country's liberation in 1945. In summer season, 40-minute English-language guided tours are offered Monday to Saturday at 11am, 1, and 3pm, and on Sunday at 1 and 3pm.

Akershus Festning. © **23-09-56-71.** Admission 65NOK adults, 25NOK children. May-Aug Mon-Sat 10am-4pm, Sun noon-5pm; Sept-Apr Thurs only noon-2pm. Closed for special events. Tram: 15 or 20. Bus: 60.

Henie Onstad Kunstsenter ★★   On a site beside the Oslofjord, 7 miles (11km) west of Oslo, ex–movie star and skating champion Sonja Henie and her husband, Niels Onstad, a shipping tycoon, opened this museum in 1968 to display their prodigious art collection. The center's especially good 20th-century collection includes some 1,800 works by Munch, Picasso, Matisse, Léger, Bonnard, and Miró. Henie's Trophy Room is impressive, with 600 trophies and medals, including 3 Olympic gold medals and 10 world skating championships. In addition to its permanent exhibition, the foundation presents cultural activities—music, theater, film, dance, and poetry readings. There are free tours on Sunday at 2pm.

Høkvikodden, Sonja Henies Vei 31. © **67-80-48-80.** www.hok.no. Admission 80NOK adults, 60NOK seniors, 50NOK students, 30NOK children 6-16, free for children 5 and under. Tues-Fri 11am-7pm; Sat-Sun 11am-5pm. Bus: 151.

Nasjonalgalleriet ★★★   Situated behind Oslo University, this is Norway's greatest art gallery and one of the finest in Northern Europe. It specializes in Norwegian artists, though there is a noteworthy collection of old European masters, including works by van Gogh, Gauguin, Cézanne, and Degas. Norwegian artists whose work is on display include Johan Christian Dahl, Harriet Backer, and Christian Krohg, the latter earning his fame by painting everyone from mariners to prostitutes. The two most notable homegrown artists featured in the collection are Gustav Vigeland, Norway's greatest sculptor, and Edvard Munch, Scandinavia's greatest painter. Munch's iconic *The Scream,* one of the world's most reproduced paintings, can be seen here, as can his *Madonna* and *Melancholy.* Alongside the permanent exhibitions, you'll also often find some more contemporary art in the temporary exhibition space on the first floor and in the Art Hall behind the main building.

Universitetsgata 13. © **22-20-04-04.** www.nationalmuseum.no. Free admission. Tues-Wed and Fri 10am-5pm; Thurs 11am-7pm; Sat-Sun noon-5pm. Closed Mon. Tram: 10, 12, 13, 19.

Vigelandsparken and Museum ★★★   The work of Norway's greatest sculptor, Gustav Vigeland (1869–1943), is spread across the 75-acre (30-hectare) Frogner Park, whose main entrance is on Kirkeveien. Vigeland died a year before the park was completed but left behind a total of 227 monumental sculptures, of which the most celebrated work is the 52-foot (16m) monolith composed of 121 colossal figures, all carved into one piece of stone. The most photographed sculpture, however, is *The Angry Boy.*

Also at the park is the **Vigeland-museet,** to the south in Nobelsgate. Vigeland's former studio, where he lived and worked from 1924 until his death, features his drawings, plaster casts, and woodcuts among other memorabilia.

Frogner Park, Nobelsgate 32. © **23-49-37-00.** www.vigeland.museum.no. Free admission to park. Museum: 50NOK adults; 25NOK children 16 and under, seniors, and students. Park daily 24 hr. Museum June-Aug Tues-Sun 10am-5pm; Sept-May Tues-Sun noon-4pm. Closed Mon. Tram: 12.

RINGING THE DOORBELL AT Ibsen's apartment

Although he sometimes had a troubled relationship with his native country of Norway, **Henrik Ibsen** (1828–1906) today is duly honored as the country's foremost dramatist. Since 1993, it's been possible to visit his **apartment,** just a short walk from the National Theater in Stortingsgate, where so many of his greatest plays—including the 1879 *A Doll's House* and the 1881 *Ghosts*—are still performed with a certain devotion.

A blue plaque on the building at the corner of Arbinsgate and Drammensveien marks the apartment where Ibsen lived from 1895 until his death. He often sat in the window, with a light casting a glow over his white hair. People lined up in the street below to look up at him, and he seemed to take delight in the adulation—so long overdue, as far as he was concerned. Italy's greatest actress, Eleanora Duse, came here to bid him a final adieu, but he was too ill to receive her. She stood outside in the snow, blowing him kisses.

The only time Ibsen broke with Norway was when his country did not come to the aid of Denmark in its war with Prussia. Outraged, Ibsen went into a self-imposed exile in 1864 and stayed away in protest for 27 years, returning to settle in Christiania (the old name for Oslo) when memories of his resentment had faded. All is forgiven now, and his memorable *Peer Gynt* is hailed around the world as a forerunner of contemporary drama.

It's an amazing moment to wander through the apartment, which still has its original furniture. It's as if Ibsen still resides in this "living museum." The entrance is at Henrik Ibsens gate 26 (© **22-12-35-50;** www.ibsen.net), and admission is 85NOK for adults, 60NOK students/seniors, 25NOK for children, and 170NOK for families. The apartment is open mid-May to mid-September Tuesday to Sunday 11am to 6pm, and from mid-September to mid-May from Tuesday to Sunday 11am to 4pm (to 6pm Thurs). Guided tours are given year-round in English. T-banen: Nationaltheatret.

MUSEUMS ON THE BYGDØY PENINSULA

Located south of the city, the peninsula is reached by commuter ferry (summer only) leaving from Pier 3, facing the Rådhuset (Town Hall). Departures during the day are every 40 minutes before 11am and every 20 minutes after 11am, and a one-way fare costs 40NOK, half-price for children. Bus no. 30 from the National Theater also runs to Bygdøy; the museums are only a short walk from the bus stops on Bygdøy.

Frammuseet ★ There's only one exhibit here, but it's world famous: the polar ship *Fram*. The sturdy exploration ship was the vessel Fridtjof Nansen used to sail across the Arctic Ocean (1893–96) at the age of 27. The vessel was later used in the Antarctic by Norwegian explorer Roald Amundsen when he became the first man to reach the South Pole in 1911.

Bygdøynesveien. © **23-28-29-50.** www.fram.museum.no. Admission 60NOK adults, 25NOK students and children 7-16, free for children 6 and under. Nov-Feb Mon-Fri 10am-3pm, Sat-Sun 10am-4pm; Mar-Apr and Oct daily 10am-4pm; May and Sept daily 10am-5pm; June-Aug daily 9am-6pm. Bus: 30 or 3. Ferryboat Pier 3 (summer only).

Kon-Tiki Museum ★★ *Kon-Tiki* is the world-famous balsa-log raft that the young Norwegian scientist Thor Heyerdahl and his five comrades sailed in for 4,300 miles

(7,000km) in 1947—all the way from Callao, Peru, to Raroia, Polynesia. The museum also houses the papyrus *Ra II,* which Heyerdahl and his comrades used in 1970 to cross the Atlantic from Safi in Morocco to Barbados in the southern Caribbean.

Bygdøynesveien 36. ℭ **23-08-67-67.** www.kon-tiki.no. Admission 60NOK adults, 25NOK children, 120NOK family ticket. Mar and Oct daily 10:30am–4pm; Apr–May and Sept daily 10am–5pm; June–Aug 9:30am–5:30pm; Nov–Feb daily 10:30am–3:30pm. Bus 30. Ferryboat Pier 3 (summer only).

Norsk Folkemuseum ★★★ In a beautiful 35-acre (14-hectare) park, this 110-year-old museum traces Norwegian cultural history with both indoor and out-door exhibitions and activities. Preservation-minded Norwegians scoured the coun-tryside, finding more than 150 old buildings, mostly from the 1600s and 1700s, and moved them to Oslo, where they are arranged in an evocative and informative display that's as good as a time-travel machine. Of special note is the museum's **Gamlebyen** (old town), the reproduction of an early-20th-century small village, and a medieval wooden stave church built in 1200. In 2004, the museum merged with the Bygo Royal Farm, enabling visitors to walk through scenic acres of fields and grazing land.

Museumsveien 10. ℭ **22-12-37-00.** www.norskfolke.museum.no. Admission mid-Sept to mid-May 100NOK adults, 75NOK seniors/students, 25NOK children 6–16, free for children 5 and under, 200NOK family ticket; mid-May to mid-Sept. Discounts available in off-season. Mid-Sept to mid-May Mon–Fri 11am–3pm, Sat–Sun 11am–4pm; mid-May to mid-Sept daily 10am–6pm. Bus 30. Ferryboat Pier 3 (summer only).

Norsk Sjøfartsmuseum ★★ This museum, which contains a complete ship's deck with helm and chart house, and a three-deck-high section of the passenger steamer *Sandnaes,* chronicles the maritime history and culture of Norway. The Boat Hall features a fine collection of original small craft. Especially intriguing are the sailing ships used in 18th- and 19th-century polar expeditions, including the vessel *Gjøa,* which Roald Amundsen used to sail through the Northwest Passage from 1903 to 1906.

Bygdøynesveien 37. ℭ **24-11-41-50.** www.norsk-sjofartsmuseum.no/. Admission to museum and boat hall 40NOK adults; 25NOK students and seniors; free for kids 15 and under. Mid-May to Aug daily 10am–6pm; Sept to mid-May Mon–Wed, Fri–Sun 10:30am–4pm, Thurs 10:30am–6pm. Bus 30. Ferryboat Pier 3 (summer only).

Vikingskiphuset (Viking Ship Museum) ★★★ This museum is devoted to one of the rarest finds in the world: three Viking burial vessels that were excavated on the shores of the Oslofjord and preserved in clay. The most spectacular find is the 9th-century *Oseberg ★,* discovered near Norway's oldest town. This 64-foot (19m)

Down by the Old Waterfront

On the waterfront near Rådhusplassen, the town hall, Oslo's Fishermen's Wharf—called **Aker Brygge**—is a favor-ite rendezvous point for visitors and Oslovians alike. One of our favorite pastimes is to head down here and approach one of the shrimp boats, where you can purchase a bag of freshly caught and cooked shellfish from a fisherman. Buy a beer at one of the harbor-fronting cafes, and find a scenic spot where you can shell your feast and eat while taking in a view of the harbor.

After your snack, wander among the little shops, the ethnic food joints, and the fast-food stands, or see what's playing in the on-site theater or the multicinema complex. Jazz concerts are often staged outdoors in summer.

dragon ship features a wealth of ornaments and is the burial chamber of a Viking queen and her slave. The *Gokstad* find is an outstanding example of Viking vessels because it's so well preserved. The smaller *Tune* ship was never restored.

Huk Aveny 35, Bygdøy. ✆ **22-13-52-80.** www.khm.uio.no/vikingskipshuset. Admission 60NOK adults, 35NOK seniors, 30NOK students and children 7–16, free for children 6 and under. May–Sept daily 9am–6pm; Oct–Apr daily 10am–4pm. Bus 30. Ferryboat Pier 3 (summer only).

Where to Dine

Bristol Grill ★★ CONTINENTAL   Located in the prestigious Hotel Bristol and open since 1924, this grill has attracted its fair share of celebrities. It's one of the last bastions of courtly formal service in Oslo, with excellent food served in a dining room resembling an elegant hunting lodge from the 1920s. The best Nordic version of bouillabaisse is served here, along with time-tested favorites such as medallions of venison.

In the Hotel Bristol, Kristian IV's Gate 7. ✆ **22-82-60-20.** www.thonhotels.com/show/bristol-grill/. Reservations recommended. 3-course prix-fixe menu 410NOK. AE, DC, MC, V. Daily 5–11:30pm (kitchen closes at 10:30pm). Tram: 10, 11, 17, or 18.

Frognerseteren Hoved-Restaurant NORWEGIAN   This longtime favorite is on the mountain plateau of Holmenkollen, with a view of the famous ski jump, as well as a sweeping panorama of the city and the Oslofjord. In a landmark Viking-Revival lodge constructed in 1896, guests can choose between an affordable cafe and a more formal restaurant, or else opt for beer and snacks on the breezy terrace outside. Specialties, served 1,600 feet (480m) above sea level and 1,000 feet (300m) downhill from the Holmenkollen railway stop, include such country favorites as filet of elk and smoked Norwegian salmon.

Holmenkollveien 200. ✆ **22-92-40-40.** www.frognerseteren.no. Reservations recommended. Cafe platters 60NOK–210NOK; main courses 240NOK–350NOK. Traditional Norwegian buffet every Wed 495NOK. DC, MC, V. Restaurant Mon–Fri noon–10pm; Sat 1–10pm; Sun noon–9pm. Cafe Mon–Sat 11am–10pm; Sun 11am–9pm. Bus: 1b.

Grand Café ★★ NORWEGIAN   This is the most famous cafe in Oslo, once patronized by Edvard Munch and Henrik Ibsen, the latter a devotee of whale steak. Installed on the ground floor of Oslo's grandest hotel, the restaurant serves tasty traditional Norwegian country cuisine with a modern twist (where else could you get reindeer with polenta?) in a quietly swanky setting. The fish dishes are numerous and delicious, and the desserts divine. If the prices are too steep, stop in for breakfast, between 6:30 and 10am, Monday through Friday (from 7am on weekends).

In the Grand Hotel, Karl Johans Gate 31. ✆ **23-21-20-00.** www.grand.no/en/Restaurants--Bars/Grand-Cafe/. Reservations recommended. Main courses 225NOK–355NOK; 3-course prix-fixe menu 420NOK; 4-course menu 580NOK. AE, DC, MC, V. Mon–Fri 11am–11pm; Sat noon–11pm; Sun noon–10pm. T-banen: Stortinget.

Kristiania Bar & Cafe CONTINENTAL   If you want historical grandeur but don't want to pay the steep prices of the Grand Café, this is the place for you. It serves simple, unpretentious food, such as burgers, sandwiches, pastas, and salads, in a building that evokes a more gracious era, when train stations were temples to progressiveness. It still feels like a station, albeit one of exceptional beauty. The magnificent Victorian-era bar serves reasonably priced drinks and attracts a big after-work crowd. You won't get any surprises in the food department (except for a couple of Tex-Mex starters), but neither will you go into shock over the bill.

Østbanen, Jernbanetorget 1. ✆ **22-17-50-30.** www.kristianiabar.no. Reservations recommended. Main courses 80NOK–250NOK. AE, DC, MC, V. Mon–Thurs and Sat 11am–1am; Fri 11am–3am; Sun 11am–midnight.

Lofoten Fiskerestaurant ★ SEAFOOD   Located in the Aker Brygge complex, this restaurant is one of the best choices for dining along the Oslo waterfront, combining a top-notch seafood dinner with one of the most panoramic views of the city's seascape. Nautical accessories decorate the interior, and when the weather's fair, guests may dine on the outdoor terrace. Scrupulously seasonal and rigorously precise, the cuisine is based on the favorite fish of the Norwegian palate: lobster, oysters, salmon, halibut, and trout.

Stranden 75, Aker Brygge. ✆ **22-83-08-08.** www.fiskerestaurant.no. Reservations recommended. Lunch main courses 220NOK–245NOK; dinner main courses 285NOK–300NOK. AE, DC, MC, V. Mon–Sat 11am–11pm; Sun noon–10pm. Bus: 27.

Stortorvets Gjaestgiveri ★ NORWEGIAN   The oldest restaurant in Oslo, this is one of the city's most atmospheric dining spots. Many of its dining rooms haven't changed much since the early 18th century, when this was an inn for wayfarers, offering both food and lodging. The venue remains a top choice for traditional Norwegian cuisine served in either the cafe up front, a more formal restaurant in the rear, or a secluded courtyard garden during the summer months. To illustrate just how authentic the food is, *Lutefisk*—aged, air-dried cod—a dish abandoned by most chefs as too time-consuming, is still prepared here, as is an equally rare *cassoulet* (bean pot stew). Look for live jazz on weekends.

Grensen 1. ✆ **23-35-63-60.** www.stortorvets-gjestgiveri.no. Small platters and snacks in cafe 70NOK–135NOK. Main courses 195NOK–325NOK. AE, DC, MC, V. Mon–Sat 11am–11pm.

Theatercafeen ★★ INTERNATIONAL   This Vienna-style eatery captures the opulence of its *fin-de-siècle* heyday, having been meticulously re-created from photographs and the memories of its many devotees. The gorgeous dining room was being renovated as we write this, but it should still be decorated with portraits of Norwegian artists, actors, painters, and composers, when you visit. But food is the real star here: Options on the huge menu range from humble smørbrød to a five-course dinner that might include Swedish caviar, beef tartar, reindeer steak, or fjord trout. Follow up your meal with a delectable dessert from the in-house patisserie.

In the Hotel Continental, Stortingsgaten 24/26. ✆ **22-82-40-50.** www.hotel-continental.no/Theater caféen.aspx?ID=236. Reservations recommended. Small dishes and sandwiches (served until 5pm or after 9:30pm) 130NOK–245NOK; main courses 200NOK–318NOK. AE, DC, MC, V. Mon–Sat 11am–11pm; Sun 3–10pm. Closed July. T-banen: Nationaltheatret.

Shopping

Many of the leading stores are found along **Karl Johans Gate,** the main street of Oslo, and its many side streets. In the core of the city, there are many other shops ringing **Stortovet,** the main square of town. These shops tend to specialize in local goods, such as enameled silver jewelry and handicrafts. If you're interested in Norwegian crafts, check out **Baerum Verk,** Verksgata 15, Baerum Verk (✆ **67-13-00-18;** www.baerumsverk.no), where you'll find some 65 different shops hawking handicrafts on-site, especially jewelry and woolens. Some of the best crafts are on display at **Den Norske Husfliden,** Møllergata 4 (✆ **22-42-10-75;** www.dennorskehusfliden.no), near the marketplace and the cathedral. This is the retail outlet of the Norwegian Association of Home Arts and Crafts, an organization founded in 1891 and devoted to quality work. Here you'll find the finest in Norwegian designs, including furnishings, woodworking, gifts, textiles, glassware, ceramics, embroidery, and wrought iron. Another fine showcase of crafts is **Norway Designs,** Stortingsgaten 28 (© **23-11-45-10;** www.norwaydesigns.no), with its mostly upmarket merchandise with good buys in pewter, jewelry, crystal, and knitwear.

Folk costumes often interest those with Norwegian ancestors, and the best purveyor is **Heimen Husflid,** Rosenkrantzgate 8 (© **23-21-42-00;** www.heimen.net), which offers folkloric clothing from all the different regions of the nation, both north and south. The hand-knit sweaters in traditional Norwegian patterns are an especially good buy.

Norway's largest department store, **Steen & Strøm,** Kongensgate 23 (© **22-00-40-01;** www.steenstrom.no; T-banen: Stortinget), is a great stop for anyone looking for quality Nordic goods. It contains 58 individual departments selling items like hand-knit wool sweaters and wood plates.

Nightlife

With more than 100 cafes, restaurants, and clubs, Oslo rocks around the clock. From the tourist office or your hotel reception desk, pick up a copy of *What's On in Oslo* to see what's happening at the time of your visit, or take a look at the entertainments listings on **www.visitoslo.com**. Note that from June 20 to the middle of August, Oslo goes into a cultural slumber—Oslovians are too busy enjoying their natural surroundings while the summer sun shines to go to the theater.

Their city's **Nationaltheatret,** Johanne Dybwads Plass 1 (© **81-50-08-11;** www.nationaltheatret.no), is world famous but it's only for theater buffs who want to see Ibsen or Bjørnson performed in the original Norwegian language. There are no performances in July and August; otherwise, tickets range from 150NOK to 400NOK for adults or 85NOK to 170NOK for students and seniors. A guided tour of the theater is also available for 70NOK.

Even if you don't speak Norwegian, you might want to attend a performance of **Den Norske Opera,** the Norwegian National Opera Company at Kirsten Flagstads plass 1 (© **21-42-21-21;** www.operaen.no), the leading venue for ballet and opera, although there are no performances from mid-June to mid-August. Tickets cost 200NOK to 600NOK except for galas.

Although not the equal of Stockholm or Copenhagen, Oslo has its fair share of dance clubs, including the hottest ticket, **Smuget,** Rosenkrantzgate 22 (© **22-42-52-62;** www.smuget.no), behind the Grand Hotel in the center of town. It offers the liveliest dance floor in town and a stage where bands perform. It is open from 7pm to 4am Monday to Saturday. Cover ranges from 75NOK to 100NOK.

A conventional pub most evenings, **Herr Nilsen,** C. J. Hambros Plass 5 (© **22-33-54-05;** www.herrnilsen.no), also hosts some of the world's best jazz musicians—playing everything from prospective to Dixieland. The cover is 150NOK. It's open Monday to Saturday 2pm to 3am, Sunday 3pm to 3am. One of the largest venues for jazz and rock is the **Rockefeller Music Hall,** Torggata 16 (© **22-20-32-32;** www.rockefeller.no), where tickets for live concerts range from 100NOK to as much as 700NOK. Performances are Sunday to Thursday 8pm, Friday and Saturday 9pm. The bar can stay open until 3am but usually shuts down after the show.

Our favorite Oslovian night cafe is **Lorry,** Parkveien 12 (© **22-69-69-04;** www.lorry.no/), a suds-drenched cafe/restaurant established 120 years ago and still going strong at its location across the street from a park flanking the Royal Palace. An outdoor terrace is a magnet in summer, or else you can retreat inside to enjoy 130 different kinds of beer and a young convivial crowd of both locals and visitors. Open Monday to Saturday 11am to 3am, Sunday noon to 1am.

BERGEN

Many rail passengers bypass Oslo altogether for Norway's second city of Bergen because it's the gateway to the glorious western fjord district. In spite of the fact that it swarms with thousands of visitors and cruise-ship passengers during its short summer, the city at its core manages to retain the feeling of a large country town.

In history, it was the former capital of Norway, having been founded in 1170, and Bergen enjoyed its heyday as the most important trading center for the powerful Hanseatic League of the Middle Ages. Like Oslo, Bergen is scenically located in a sheltered position between a string of islands to the west and the famous silhouette of seven mountains to the east.

Still a maritime city, it is known even today for its fishing industries and shipbuilding. Bergen's unique harborfront, with its old Hanseatic buildings, is today one of UNESCO's World Heritage Sites. Increasingly cosmopolitan in spite of its villagelike center, Bergen is more and more becoming a city of culture—in fact, it launched the new millennium as the "European City of Culture" in 2000.

Station Information

GETTING FROM THE AIRPORT TO THE TRAIN STATION

Should you opt to fly into Bergen, say, from London or Copenhagen, you'll land at the **Bergen Airport** (© 47-67-03-15-55; www.avinor.no/en/airport/bergen), in Flesland, 12 miles (19km) south of the city. Planes operated by **SAS** (© 91-50-54-00 or 800/221-2350; www.scandinavian.net) service Bergen.

Frequent buses connect the airport to the center of town, departing every 15 minutes; a one-way ticket costs 85NOK and takes around 45 minutes to the city center. A taxi from the airport to the city center, including the rail station, costs from 450NOK to 500NOK. Chances are, however, you will not be flying into Bergen and quickly boarding a train for some other destination in Norway, as most visitors head to Bergen and the fjord country as a destination unto itself and not necessarily a stopover en route to somewhere else.

INSIDE THE STATION

The stone-constructed **Bergen Train Station** (© 81-50-01-82) is a 7- to 10-minute walk south of the harbor, along the street from the entrance to the Bergen Storsenter Shopping Mall, which also houses the city's bus station. Trains from Oslo pull in here. On-site is a luggage storage facility, open daily 5:30am to 12:30am, which charges 20NOK to 50NOK per 24 hours, depending on size of items. Because the station is so close to the city center, services such as ATMs, restaurants, currency exchange, pharmacies, and so forth are in the immediate vicinity of the station.

There is no tourist office within the station itself, but the city's visitor information center is just a 10-minute walk away (see below).

Information Elsewhere in the City

The **Bergen Tourist Office,** Vågsallmenningen 1 (© 55-55-20-00; www.visit bergen.com), in the center of town, provides information, maps, and brochures about Bergen and the fjord district. It also makes hotel reservations for 30NOK. You can

ACCOMMODATIONS ■
Augustin Hotel **7**
Comfort Hotel Holberg **6**
Grand Hotel Terminus **21**
Hotel Park **22**
Steens Hotel **13**
Thon Hotel
Rosenkrantz **11**

DINING ◆
Bryggeloftet & Stuene **12**
Enhjørningen **10**
Ned's **16**
Restaurant Potekjeller **15**
To Kokker **9**
Wessel-Stuen **19**

ATTRACTIONS ●
Bergen Aquarium **1**
Bergen Kunstmuseum **20**
Bryggen **8**
Bryggens Museum **5**
Det Hanseatiske
Museum **14**
Gamle Bergen **2**
Mariakirke **4**
Rosenkrantztårnet **3**
Torget **17**
Troldhaugen **18**

Store
Lungegårds-
vann

Nordnes
parken

By-
fjorden

① Information

0   1/4 mi
0 0.25 km

exchange foreign currency and cash traveler's checks here when the banks are closed. You can also purchase city sightseeing tickets here or book tours of the fjords. Open June to August daily from 8:30am to 10pm, May and September daily from 9am to 8pm, October to April Monday to Saturday from 9am to 4pm. *Note:* They stop taking phone calls at 4pm daily year-round.

Getting Around

The **Bergen Card** entitles you to free bus transportation and (usually) free museum admission throughout Bergen, plus discounts on car rentals, parking, and some cultural and leisure activities. It's a good value. Ask for it at the tourist office (see above). A 24-hour card costs 190NOK for adults, 75NOK for children aged 3 to 15. A 48-hour card is 250NOK or 100NOK. Children under 3 generally travel or enter free.

The **Central Bus Station** (Bystasjonen), Strømgaten 8 (✆ **55-31-44-30**), is the terminal for all buses serving the Bergen and Hardanger areas, as well as the airport bus. The station has luggage storage, shops, and a restaurant. City buses are marked with their destination and route number. For **bus information** in the Bergen area, call ✆ **177.** A network of yellow-sided city buses serves the city center only.

You can call a **taxi** by dialing ✆ **55-99-70-10.** Sightseeing by taxi—a bit of a luxury—costs 600NOK for the first hour and 400NOK for each additional hour.

You can take a ferry across the harbor Monday to Friday from 7am to 4:15pm; they don't run on Saturday or Sunday. One-way fares are 40NOK for adults, 20NOK for children. Ferries arrive and depart from either side of the harbor at Dreggekaien and Munkebryggen. For information, call ✆ **55-55-20-00.**

Where to Stay

Augustin Hotel ★ 🛏 Right on the harborfront, this well-run hotel enjoys some of the best scenic views in the city. Owned by the same family for three generations, it was built in 1909 in the Art Nouveau style but added a new wing in 1995. For tradition and old-fashioned comfort, book one of the rooms in the old section; for the latest in amenities, opt for the new wing.

Carl Sundts Gate 22, N-5004 Bergen. ✆ **55-30-40-00.** Fax 55-30-40-10. www.augustin.no. 109 units. July–Aug 1,390NOK–1,590NOK double, 1,790NOK suite; Sept–June 2,050NOK–2,250NOK double, 2,450NOK suite. AE, DC, MC, V. Bus: 2 or 4. **Amenities:** Restaurant; bar; rooms for those w/limited mobility; smoke-free rooms.

Comfort Hotel Holberg ★ This hotel, a 15-minute walk from Bergen's fish market, is named for Holberg, the famous 18th-century Norwegian writer and dramatist, and the lobby is a virtual shrine to the author. The midsize bedrooms are decorated in a modernized Norwegian farmhouse style, with wooden floors, half-paneling stained in forest green, and large windows. Half the tiled bathrooms have tubs and showers; the rest have showers only.

Strandgaten 190, Nordnes, N-5817 Bergen. ✆ **55-30-42-00.** Fax 55-23-18-20. www.choicehotels.no. 140 units. Mon–Thurs 790NOK–1,560NOK double; Fri–Sat 890NOK double. Rates include breakfast. AE, DC, MC, V. **Amenities:** Restaurant; bar; rooms for those w/limited mobility; smoke-free rooms.

Grand Hotel Terminus Opposite the rail station, this enduring favorite and Bergen landmark opened in 1928 as the city's first luxury hotel. It has attracted many interesting guests over the years, including the great explorer of the Arctic wastelands, Roald Amundsen and playwright Henrik Ibsen. In 2006, it was taken over by the Augustin Hotel (see above), and in 2007, it underwent a major overhaul, but the classically elegant atmosphere of the old days remains.

Zander Kaaesgate 6, N-5001 Bergen. ☎ **55-21-25-00.** Fax 55-21-25-01. www.ght.no. 131 units. 1,590NOK double. Rates include breakfast. AE, DC, MC, V. Bus: 2 or 4. **Amenities:** Bar; rooms for those w/limited mobility; smoke-free rooms.

Hotel Park ★ A 10-minute walk from the rail station, this family-run hotel is set in a converted 1890s town house. The spacious to midsize rooms are traditionally furnished and feature some attractive antique pieces. Bathrooms are tiny, but the Norwegian breakfasts are huge. The Park often has rooms when other central hotels are fully booked. *Note:* In summer, the Park uses a nearby building (furnished in the same style) to accommodate its overflow.

Harald Hårfagresgaten 35 and Allegaten 20, N-5007 Bergen. ☎ **55-54-44-00.** Fax 55-54-44-44. www.parkhotel.no. 33 units. 1,250NOK double. Rates include breakfast. **Amenities:** Breakfast room; lounge; smoke-free rooms; Wi-Fi.

Steens Hotel 🍴 This stylish town house, built in 1890, has been owned by the same family since 1950. The B&B's modern and affordable guest rooms are beautifully maintained and quite comfortable; rooms at the front of the hotel open out onto a park and provide a nice glimpse at the natural beauty of Bergen. The public rooms have a lot of atmosphere, and the hotel's location—bus and railway stations are only a short walk away—is super convenient. An added plus: Coffee is served to guests throughout the day.

22 Parkveien, N-5007 Bergen. ☎ **55-30-88-88.** Fax 55-30-88-89. www.steenshotel.no. 21 units. 1,340NOK double. Extra bed 250NOK. Rates include Norwegian breakfast. AE, MC, V. Free parking. Bus: 1 or 5. **Amenities:** Breakfast room.

Thon Hotel Rosenkrantz ★ Near Bryggen, the historic Hanseatic port, this restored 1921 hotel enjoys a bull's-eye central location. It is a small place but offers a nice lobby bar and quality food service. The midsize bedrooms have recently been refurbished and are pleasantly and comfortably furnished, each with a good-size bathroom. Laptop owners will find Wi-Fi access in the public areas but not in all the rooms; ask ahead if it matters to you.

Rosenkrantzgate 7, N-5003 Bergen. ☎ **55-30-14-00.** www.thonhotels.com/rosenkrantz. 129 units. 1,695NOK double. Rates include breakfast and dinner (Mon–Thurs). AE, DC, MC, V. Bus: 1, 5, or 9. **Amenities:** Restaurant; bar (closes for summer holidays); rooms for those w/limited mobility; smoke-free rooms.

Top Attractions & Special Moments

On your first day, explore the top attractions of Bergen, including the old Hanseatic Bryggen and its museums, and discover the shops and artisans' workshops along the harborfront. End your day by taking the funicular to Fløien for a panoramic view of Bergen and its waterfront, and have a fish dinner in an old tavern. On day two, head out to Troldhaugen, the summer villa of the fabled composer, Edvard Grieg, and return to Bergen in time to walk through Gamle Bergen, a re-created old town from the 18th and 19th centuries.

For orientation purposes and to gain a convenient overview of the attractions of Bergen, on Saturdays and Sundays you can take a 1½-hour walking tour of the city at 3pm from late June to late August. Tickets cost 95NOK, and the route passes through Bryggen and the fish market. Tickets can be bought from the tourist office at Vågsalmenningen 1 (☎ **55-55-20-00**), which is also where the tours start.

Akvariet (Bergen Aquarium) ★★ One of the biggest and most impressive aquariums in Scandinavia is only a 15-minute walk from the historic center. If it

STROLLING medieval Bergen

Bryggen ★★★, a row of Hanseatic timbered houses rebuilt along the waterfront after the disastrous fire of 1702, is all that remains of medieval Bergen. Fires have damaged this area repeatedly over the centuries (last in 1955) because of the wooden structures, but much has been restored, enough so that the site has been added to UNESCO's World Heritage list. It's now a center for arts and crafts, where painters, weavers, and craftspeople have their workshops. You'll need at least 2 hours to walk and explore the old wharf.

To see what Bergen was like in the Middle Ages, enter **Det Hanseatiske Museum ★**, Finnegårdsgaten 1A, Bryggen (*C* **55-54- 46-90**), the best preserved of the wooden buildings of old Bryggen. Today the building is furnished with authentic artifacts from the early 18th century. Living conditions, as you can clearly see, were spartan. No heating or lighting was allowed because of

the danger of fire. Hours mid-May to mid-September are daily 9am to 5pm; mid-September to mid-May Tuesday to Saturday 11am to 2pm, Sunday 11am to 4pm. Admission is 50NOK for adults mid-May to mid-September and 30NOK mid-September to mid-May, free for children year-round. Bus: 1, 5, or 9.

Also at Bryggen, you can visit the **Bryggens Museum** (*C* **55-58-80-10;** www.uib.no/bmu), displaying artifacts uncovered in excavations from 1955 to 1972. This museum illustrates the daily life of Bergensers in medieval times. Foundations more than 8 centuries old have been incorporated into today's exhibits. Admission is 60NOK for adults, 30NOK for students, free for children under 16. Open May to August daily 10am to 4pm; September to April Monday to Friday 11am to 3pm, Saturday noon to 3pm, Sunday noon to 4pm. Bus: 1, 5, or 9.

swims off the coast of Bergen, it's swimming here. The aquarium's mammoth outdoor tank holds seals and penguins, and some 70 indoor tanks are home to a host of colorful sea life. It's mesmerizing to watch the schools of herring and anglerfish glide by in complete synchronization. Most popular are the penguin feedings, scheduled at noon and 3pm (and also 6pm May–Sept).

Nordnesbakken 4. *C* **40-10-24-20.** www.akvariet.no. Sept–May 100NOK adults, 75NOK children 3-13, 400NOK family ticket; May 1–June 15 and Aug 16–Sept 150NOK adults, 100NOK children 3-13, 500NOK family; June 16–Aug 15 200NOK adults, 150NOK children 3-13, 600NOK family. May–Aug daily 9am–7pm; Sept–Apr daily 10am–6pm. Bus: 11 from the fish market.

Bergen Kunstmuseum (Bergen Art Museum)   This museum is composed of three galleries situated in three separate buildings overlooking the lake, Lille Lungegardsvann. The Lysverket collection houses the bulk of the museum's treasures, displaying some of its 9,000 pieces, which run the gamut from 13th-century Russian icons to works by Yoko Ono. However, we think the Rasmus Meyers collection, housing a parade of **Edvard Munch masterpieces ★★**, is the main attraction. The Stenersen collection—usually housed in the building of the same name, but currently in the Lysverket while the Stenersen is given over to temporary exhibitions—is a close second, with a collection of 20th-century art that includes a fine assemblage of **works by Paul Klee ★★**.

Rasmus Meyers allé 3, 7, and 9. *C* **55-56-80-00.** www.bergenartmuseum.no. Admission 60NOK adults, 40NOK students, free for children 16 and under. 11am–5pm Daily. Closed Mon Sept 15–May 14.

Gamle Bergen ★ North of the city center, this open-air museum is one of the finest along the western coast of Norway, re-creating life as lived in the 18th and 19th centuries in a parklike setting. More than 40 wooden buildings were moved here from western Norway and reassembled. This Old Town comes with old-fashioned streets and narrow cobblestone alleyways, all converging on an open square. The houses are furnished with pieces authentic to the era. You can visit such sites as a photographer's studio from the turn of the 20th century, a merchant's living room in the style of the 1870s, a baker's house and shop, and even the abode of a poor seamstress from around 1860.

Elsesro and Sandviken. *℃*55-39-43-00. Admission 70NOK adults, 35NOK students/seniors, free for children. Houses mid-May to mid-Sept only, guided tours daily on the hour 10am–5pm. Park and on-site restaurant daily noon–6pm. Bus: 9, 20, 21, 22, or 50.

Mariakirke (St. Mary's Church) ★★ The oldest building in Bergen (its exact date is unknown, but it was built sometime in the 12th c.), this Romanesque church is one of the most beautiful in Norway. It's been in continuous use since the day it opened, having been spared destruction from the numerous fires that swept over this largely wooden city. The oldest artifact is an impressive 15th-century triptych behind the altar, and there's a baroque pulpit, donated by Hanseatic merchants, with carved figures depicting everything from Chastity to Naked Truth.

Dreggen. *℃*55-31-59-60. Admission 10NOK for adults, free for children 6 and under. May–Sept Mon–Fri 11am–4pm; Oct–Apr Tues–Fri noon–1:30pm. Bus: 5, 9, 20, 21, or 22.

Rosenkrantztårnet ★ Scottish masons, who incorporated a mammoth keep from 1270, designed this tower in the 1560s as both a defensive tower and a residence. The tower was named for Erik Rosenkrantz, the governor of Bergen Castle. In 1560, the tower and residence were reconstructed and enlarged. A small octagonal tower, crowned by a cupola, surmounts the Renaissance facade of this five-floor building. Although heavily damaged in an explosion in the harbor during the Nazi era, the tower was reconstructed. From the battlements, a panoramic view of Bergen can be enjoyed.

Bergenhus Bradbenken. *℃* 55-31-43-80. www.bymuseet.no/?vis=202. Admission 50NOK adults, 25NOK students, free for children. May 15–Aug 31 daily 10am–4pm; Sept 1–May 14 Sun noon–3pm. Bus: 1, 5, or 9.

Troldhaugen ★★ This Victorian house, high on a hill overlooking Lake Nordås just outside of Bergen, was the summer villa of composer Edvard Grieg. The house contains Grieg's own furniture, paintings, and other mementos. His Steinway grand piano is frequently used at concerts given in the house during the annual Bergen festival, as well as at Troldhaugen's own summer concerts. Grieg and his wife, Nina, are buried in a cliff grotto on the estate—follow the marked pathway across the wooded grounds.

Troldhaugveien 65, Hop. *℃*55-92-29-92. www.troldhaugen.com. Admission 60NOK adults, 30NOK students, free for children. May–Sept daily 9am–6pm; Oct–Apr Mon–Fri 10am–4pm, Sat–Sun noon–4pm; closed Dec 19–Jan 4. Bus: 23 or 24 to Hop from the Bergen bus station, Platform 20; when you reach Hop exit, turn right, walk about 600 ft. (180m), turn left at Hopsvegen, and follow signs (15-min. walk). Hop is 3 miles (4.8km) from Bergen.

Where to Dine

Bryggeloftet & Stuene ◢ NORWEGIAN One of the town's better bargains, this harborfront restaurant is an atmospheric choice, with a street-level bar and eating

NORWAY'S MOST DRAMATIC train ride

The train ride from Bergen to the little resort of Flåm has been called "Norway in a Nutshell." This **12-hour tour ★★★** is the most scenically captivating in the entire country, the breadth and diversity of its landscapes encapsulating the majesty of the country's fjords and mountains.

Several different transit options operate throughout the day. The one most aggressively recommended by Bergen's tourist office operates year-round. It starts at 8:40am at **Bergen's** railway station. After a 2-hour train ride, you'll disembark in the mountaintop hamlet of **Myrdal,** where you can take in the natural wonders for about 24 minutes. In Myrdal you'll board a cog railway for one of the world's most dramatically inclined train rides. The trip down to the village of **Flåm,** a drop of 2,900 feet (870m), takes an hour and passes roaring streams and seemingly endless waterfalls.

After a 3-hour stopover in Flåm, where you can have lunch or take a brief hike, you'll board a fjord steamer for a ride along the Sognefjord. You'll reach the fjord-side town of Gudvangen after a 2-hour ride. After a quick change in Gudvangen, you'll board a bus for the 75-minute ride to Voss. Here you'll spend 1 hour before boarding a train for the 75-minute ride back to Bergen. Arrival is scheduled for 8:34pm.

Expect only a rushed overview of each town, as there is more scenery than you can digest in a 12-hour day. The round-trip fare, excluding meals, costs 975NOK for adults, 500NOK for children 4 to 15, and free for accompanied children under 4. There are discounts for holders of Eurail passes or Scandinavia passes and a wide availability of options that, for extra fees, allow you to prolong the experience for up to an additional 2 days, thanks to supplemental overnights at panoramic hotels en route. We strongly recommend that you try the more prolonged experience instead of a "quickie." For more information, contact Bergen's **tourist office** (p. 614), call ℂ **81-56-82-22,** or go to **www.norwaynutshell.com.**

area evoking 19th-century Bergen, and a more formal restaurant upstairs resting under high ceilings and paneled in wood. Meals here are quintessentially Norwegian—try the grilled filet of reindeer with a creamy wild game sauce.

Bryggen 11. ℂ **55-30-20-70.** www.bryggeloftet.no. Reservations recommended. Main courses 199NOK–380NOK; lunch *smørbrød* 99NOK–180NOK AE, DC, MC, V. Mon–Fri 11am–11:30pm; Sat 11am–midnight; Sun 1–11:30pm. Bus: 1, 5, or 9.

Enhjørningen (The Unicorn) ★★ SEAFOOD/CONTINENTAL   This is one of the best restaurants in town and one of the most distinctive. You'll dine in one of several old-fashioned rooms set end-to-end railroad-car style in an old Hanseatic clapboard structure on the Bryggen harborfront. The lunchtime buffet is one of the best dining bargains in town, loaded with meat and fish dishes. The seafood and continental menu in the evening is more refined, offering such delights as a cognac-marinated Norwegian salmon.

Enhjørningsgården 29. ℂ **55-30-69-50.** www.enhjorningen.no. Reservations required. Main courses 295NOK–330NOK; set-price menus 530NOK–595NOK. AE, DC, MC, V. Daily 4–11pm; closed Sun Sept–May.

Restaurant Potetkjelleren ★ NORWEGIAN/ITALIAN   For deluxe dining, Bergen style, this citadel of fine food and formal service is worth every krone. Set inside an antique wood building just steps from the Fish Market, this is one of the city's oldest restaurants, its foundations dating from the mid–15th century. Guests, dining in either the ancient cellar or the more formal dining room upstairs, can partake of an unusual yet excellent cuisine that combines some of the best dishes from both the Norwegian and Italian kitchens. Light, inventive cookery is the rule of the day.

Kong Oscargate 1A. © **55-32-00-70.** www.potetkjelleren.no. Reservations required. Set menus 495NOK-685NOK. AE, DC, MC, V. Mon-Sat 4-10pm; bar Mon-Sat till 1am. Bus: 1, 5, or 9.

Smauet Mat & Vinhus ★ CONTINENTAL/FRENCH/ITALIAN   Decorated in the style of a Norwegian farmhouse, this restaurant combines a romantic atmosphere with high-quality cooking. Dine in a candle-lit room on a tempting array of Continental cuisine. Subtly intermingled flavors emerge in the rack of lamb with creamed artichokes and a shallot confit demi-glace. Other standouts include the monkfish studded with lardoons and served with braised Savoy cabbage, and the cinnamon-scented, pan-fried breast of chicken with pancetta.

Vaskerelvsmauet 1-3. © **55-21-07-10.** Reservations recommended, especially on weekends. Main courses 275NOK-295NOK; 6-course menu 695NOK. Daily 5-10pm. AE, MC, V. Closed btw. Christmas and New Year's. Bus: 2, 3, or 4.

To Kokker (Two Cooks) ★ FRENCH/NORWEGIAN   Visiting celebrities and savvy local foodies frequent this bastion of good eating, set in a 1703 building adjacent to the old piers and wharves along the harborfront. Start, perhaps, with the velvety smooth lobster soup before going on to, say, reindeer with lingonberry sauce. The chefs here know their craft well, and the solid staff offers delightful service in a lovely antique setting.

Enhjørninggården. © **55-30-69-55.** www.tokokker.no. Reservations required. Main courses 265NOK-315NOK. AE, DC, MC, V. Mon-Sat 5-11pm. Bus: 1, 5, or 9.

Wessel-Stuen NORWEGIAN   Named for the 18th-century humorist Johan Herman Wessel, this local favorite evokes a wine cellar from the 1700s and is decorated in an old tavern style, with beamed ceilings and an adjoining pub. We are impressed with the recent menu changes, noting that the chefs are becoming more inventive and more attuned to modern taste. You'll still find the classic sirloin steak with béarnaise sauce, but also a pesto-gratinéed filet of lamb with ratatouille.

Something Fishy

There is no livelier place in Bergen than the open-air **Fisketorget (Fish Market)**, held every Monday to Saturday 7am to 3pm at the **Torget** ★★ along the harborfront. You can wander at will through the crowds drawn to the colorful stands where a wide variety of fresh fish is hawked, especially kippers, smoked salmon, and shellfish. We prefer to feast here at lunch on freshly made smoked salmon sandwiches. In addition to fish, there are hawkers peddling flowers, vegetables, fruit, and even handicrafts and souvenirs. You can also pick up the makings of a picnic lunch here. And bring your camera—the sight of the vendors in their bright orange rubber overalls makes a great photo op.

Øvre Ole Bulls pl 6. ⓒ **55-55-49-49.** www.wesselstuen.no. Reservations recommended. Dinner main courses 219NOK–279NOK; lunch main courses 109NOK–159NOK. AE, DC, MC, V. Mon–Sat 11am–12:30am; Sun 2–11:30pm. Bus: 2, 3, or 4.

Shopping

One of the best displays of handicrafts from the western fjord district is the **Torget,** or marketplace (p. 621), along the waterfront, the site of a lively fishing market Monday to Saturday. Good buys here include rugs, handmade tablecloths, and woodcarvings.

For one-stop shopping, head to **Galleriet,** Torgalmenningen 8 (ⓒ **55-30-05-00;** www.galleriet.com), the largest shopping complex in western Norway, with some 70 different shops.

For good buys in local clothing, head for **Berle Bryggen,** Bryggen 5 (ⓒ **55-33-68-50**), along the harbor at the historic core of the old waterfront. The well-stocked emporium offers great buys in sweaters for men and women as well as souvenirs such as troll dolls, pewter, and other gift items.

Close to the fish market and harbor, the four-story **Kloverhuset,** Strandgaten 13–15 (ⓒ **55-31-37-90;** www.kloverhuset.com), offers the biggest inventory of fashion, including gloves, wool sweaters, and Sami jackets from the north of Norway. Opposite the Flower Market, **Oleana,** Strandkaien 2A (ⓒ **55-31-05-20**), specializes in locally produced clothes for women.

The best outlet for handicrafts is in and around **Bryggen Brukskunst,** the Old Town near the wharf. Here local craftspeople have taken over the old buildings and ply their trades in the colorful atmosphere. Some of the items being crafted are based on designs that might go back 3 centuries, even as much as 1,500 years, the latter exemplified by a Romanesque cruciform pilgrim's badge.

The leading purveyor of glassware and ceramics is **Hjertholm,** Galleriet 6 etg. Torgallmenningen 8 (ⓒ **55-31-70-27** www.hjertholm.no). Much of the merchandise comes directly from artisans' studios, including textiles, pewter, and wood items, along with gifts and souvenirs.

Nightlife

From mid-June to mid-August, **Bergen Folklore** performs at Schøtstuene (The Hanseatic Assembly Rooms), Øvregaten 50, at 9pm daily. Tickets cost 100NOK for adults (free for children) and can be bought from the tourist office (p. 614). The performance lasts 1 hour and consists of traditional folk dances and music from rural Norway. Bergen's major cultural venue is **Grieghallen,** Lars Hillesgate 3A (ⓒ **55-21-61-50;** www.grieghallen.no), the 1978 performance hall that is the most prestigious venue in western Norway for music, drama, and other cultural events. Tickets cost 100NOK to 465NOK.

Rick's Café, Veiten 3 (ⓒ **55-55-31-31;** www.7nights.no; bus: 1, 5, or 9), is also popular locally, with its rooms devoted to cabaret, comedy, or just drinking. Open daily 10pm to 3am; no one under 24 permitted.

The biggest sports pub in Bergen is **Fotballpuben (Football Pub),** Vestre Torggate 9 (ⓒ **55-33-66-61;** www.fotballpuben.no; bus: 1 or 9), a sudsy joint where soccer and rugby ignite passions. Its inner rooms are crowded with a heavy-drinking, sports-loving crowd who watch games on the TV screens up above. Known for its inexpensive beer, the club is open Monday to Thursday 9am to 3am, Friday and

Saturday 9am to 3am, and Sunday noon to 3am. The town's most frequented pub is **Kontoret Pub,** Kong Olav Vs Plass 4 (© **55-36-31-30;** www.dickensbergen.no; bus: 2, 3, or 4), next to the Dickens Restaurant and Pub. You can order the same food at the Kontoret as in the Dickens, though most people come here to drink. It's open Sunday to Thursday 4pm to 12:30am, Friday and Saturday 4pm to 2am.

PORTUGAL

Occupying the Iberian Peninsula with the much larger country of Spain, Portugal is a world unto itself, lying in one of the most remote and least explored corners of Western Europe. In no way are you visiting a "suburb of Spain," as Portugal's harshest critics charge. In history, language, culture, and cuisine, Portugal, in spite of its diminutive size, is very much a nation with a distinctive and remarkable heritage and identity.

For such a small country, the regional diversity is immensely varied and of compelling interest, from the beach resorts of the Algarve to the historic capital of Lisbon and onward into the north, embracing not only the city of Porto, but also the rural Minho, where old traditions still prevail, and even the most remote province, Trás-os-Montes, where country life goes on much as it has for decades.

Of all the Western European countries reviewed in this book, Portugal has the least developed rail system, though it is making a concerted effort to upgrade its service, especially on the main lines between Lisbon, Faro, and Porto. And even its conventional service will easily, quickly, conveniently—and cheaply—get the train traveler to the country's scenic highlights. Portugal's rail system, **Caminhos de Ferro Portugueses (CP),** runs InterCidade trains that link a total of 60 Portuguese cities to Lisbon. To rush you to the north, the high-speed Alfa train connects Lisbon, Porto, and the far northern city of Braga and offers both first- and second-class seating. If there is a real downside to the country for the international rail traveler, it's that Portugal has few major international train links. You can travel by rail between Lisbon and Madrid via the Lusitânia Comboio Hotel train, and from Lisbon to the French/Spanish border city Irun (where you can connect to a TGV to Paris) on the Sud-Expresso sleeper train. The only other links are from Lisbon to Badajoz, Spain, and Porto and the northwestern Galician city of Vigo, Spain. Because the number of rail connections is limited, it's best to make Portugal either your first or last stop on a train tour of Europe.

Highlights of Portugal

The areas of Portugal most easily reached by rail, and most likely to leave lasting and evocative memories, are the capital city of **Lisbon** (of course), situated on the western coast of the country; the sun belt southern coast of the **Algarve;** the enchanting medieval walled town of **Óbidos;** the university city of **Coimbra,** seat of one of the oldest universities in the

15

world and the center of the Portuguese Renaissance; and **Porto,** at the mouth of the River Douro, whose vineyards in the hinterlands beyond support the country's thriving port wine trade.

In Portugal, your choice of rail itineraries is more limited: From Lisbon, you can go south to the Algarve or north (the more scenic route) to Óbidos, Coimbra, Porto, and beyond, unless you plan to visit the remote provinces in the eastern plains. No matter which route you choose to take, you won't feel deprived.

The journey south from Lisbon to the Algarve doesn't go through the lush green countryside of Portugal the way the trip north does. It takes you across the country's drier but dramatic plains in a land that its former Moorish rulers called *Al-Gharb.* Much of the terrain you'll see outside your train window evokes the northern tier of the African coastline. You'll pass a countryside fabled for its rice paddies, wheat fields, Arabian horses, and black bulls, and can often gaze upon *campinos,* the region's sturdy horsemen dressed in regional garb.

The capital city of Lisbon, even though not central to Portugal the way Madrid is to Spain, is nonetheless the hub of its vast rail networks. Regardless of where you're going in Portugal by rail, you can reach the destination from Lisbon. When the rail lines run out, buses take over to carry you the rest of the way, but that holds true only for the remotest towns and villages.

To make the most of your trip, it's best to spend 3 days in Lisbon. Most of the first day will be used up merely getting to Lisbon. If you arrive in time, you can walk around the **Alfama** (the oldest and most historic district) and end your tour seeing

FESTIVALS & special events

The **Festas dos Santos Populares** is celebrated throughout Lisbon. Celebrations begin on June 13 and 14 in the Alfama, with feasts honoring Saint Anthony. Parades commemorating the city's patron saint feature *marchas* (parading groups of singers and musicians) along Avenida da Liberdade, singing, dancing, drinking wine, and eating grilled sardines. On June 23 and 24, for the Feast of St. John the Baptist, bonfires brighten the night and participants jump over them. The night of the final celebration is the Feast of St. Peter, on June 29. The **Lisbon Tourist Office** (*Ⓒ* **808/781-212**) supplies details about where some of the events are staged, although much of the action is spontaneous. Mid-June to June 30.

On the first weekend in July, the **Colete Encarnado ("Red Waistcoat")** takes place at Vila Franca de Xira, north of Lisbon on the River Tagus. Like the more famous feria in Pamplona, Spain, this festival involves bulls running through narrow streets, followed by sensational bullfights in what aficionados consider the best bullring in Portugal. Fandango dancing and rodeo-style competition among the Ribatejo *campinos* (cowboys) mark the event. For more information, call *Ⓒ* **26/328-56-05.**

The **Estoril Festival,** at the seaside resort outside of Lisbon, is a festival of classical music usually run from mid-July to the first week in August (dates vary), which occupies two concert halls that were built for the 500th anniversary of Columbus's first voyage to the New World. For information, call the **Associação International de Música da Costa do Estoril** (*Ⓒ* **21/468-5199;** www. estorilfestival.net).

the fantastic panorama afforded by a sunset visit to Castel de São Jorge (St. George's Castle). Start off your next day with a tour of Belém, a suburb of Lisbon, and view the famous Mosteiro dos Jerónimos (Jerónimos Monastery). Toss in some artistic highlights in the afternoon, including the must-see **Museu da Fundacão Calouste Gulbenkian,** one of Europe's artistic treasure-troves. Your third day can be spent exploring the satellite town of **Sintra,** Lord Byron's "glorious Eden," and visiting its two national palaces.

For many rail travelers, that will be all the time allotted for Portugal. Those with another 3 days usually explore the history-rich **Algarve** coast, which stretches for some 100 miles (160km) from Henry the Navigator's Cape St. Vincent to the border town of Vila Real de Santo Antonio, adjacent to Spain. This is the region we focus on most in this chapter. To reach the Algarve, take a train from Lisbon to either **Lagos** or **Faro** (from which you can take buses to all the major resorts). Both of these cities make logical bases because of their convenient rail links to Lisbon, and you can spend some time exploring remote coastal villages to the east and west of either city. A distinct Arabic flavor still prevails in the region, with its fret-cut chimneys, mosquelike cupolas, and cubist houses.

If you seek culture more than time at a beach, you can spend 3 days taking in the major sightseeing targets north of Lisbon—Óbidos, Coimbra, and Porto. If you have only 1 day, we cast our vote for Coimbra. The rail connections from Coimbra and Porto are easy, but less so for Óbidos, although the latter is worth the effort to reach it if you have the time. See "Northward Ho!" on p. 648 for more information on Portugal's northern highlights.

ESSENTIALS
Getting There

Lisbon, the country's capitol, is the major gateway city for flights into Portugal. International flights land at **Aeroporto de Lisboa** (© 21/841-3500; www.ana.pt/portal/page/portal/ANA/AEROPORTO_LISBOA), on the northern edge of Lisbon, 4 miles (6.4km) from the heart of the city. (Instead of flying, however, many rail passengers prefer to get to Lisbon by taking the train west from Madrid after their visit to Spain.)

When it was established in 1946, **TAP** (© 800/221-7890; www.tap-airportugal.pt), the national airline of Portugal, flew only between Lisbon and Angola and Mozambique (then Portuguese colonies). Today TAP flies to four continents and has one of the youngest fleets in the airline industry—its aircraft have an average age of only 4 years. Its U.S. gateway is Newark, New Jersey. In Portugal, it flies to three destinations, the most popular of which are Lisbon, Porto, and Faro, the capital of the Algarve along Portugal's southern coast.

Continental Airlines (© 800/525-0280; www.continental.com) flies direct to Lisbon out of Newark International Airport.

Air Canada (© 800/247-2262; www.aircanada.ca) no longer offers direct flights to Lisbon, but it does offer daily flights from Toronto and Montréal to Paris, London, Munich, Frankfurt, or New York, where you can transfer to another carrier to reach Lisbon.

A lot of passengers fly into London and then head to Portugal from there. For flights from the U.K., contact **British Airways** (© 800/247-9297 in the U.S., or 80/820-0125 in Portugal) or **TAP,** Chapter House, 22 Chapter St., London SW1P 4NP (© 0845/601-0932).

Portugal

TAP also has frequent flights on popular routes from major cities in Western Europe. Its flights to Lisbon from London are an especially good deal; sometimes they're priced so attractively that one might combine a trip to England with an inexpensive rail vacation in Portugal.

Portugal by Rail
PASSES
Both the **Eurail Global Pass** and **Eurail Select Pass** are good for use on Portuguese trains; the **Eurail Spain–Portugal Pass** is good on both Spanish and Portuguese trains. See chapter 2 for more details on these passes.

Portugal also has its own railpass: The **Eurail Portugal Pass** allows 3, 4, or 6 days (consecutively or nonconsecutively) of unlimited first-class train travel in a 1-month period, costing from $134 to $228 per person. Children ages 4 to 11 pay a discounted fare. Kids under 4 ride free.

Note: All of the passes we mention above should be purchased in North America prior to your departure. Passes can be ordered through **Rail Europe**

(© **888/438-7245** in the United States, © **800/361-7245** in Canada; www.rail
europe.com) or your travel agent.

FOREIGN TRAIN TERMS

Posted schedules—called *horarios* in Portuguese—aren't always accurate, so you
should go to the station ticket booths, called *bilheteiras,* instead.

Suburbano trains, as you might have guessed, run to the environs of any city,
such as Lisbon. On timetables, the rail line's long-distance international links are
marked *IN.*

If you prefer to purchase your rail tickets abroad, the words *Bilhetes turisticos* indicate a tourist ticket, which invariably offers a discount. Families should ask about a
cartão de família, which offers good discounts to families traveling together.

The complete rail timetable in Portugal, available at train stations, is called *Guia
Horario a Oficial.* In larger stations, you'll see ticket windows divided between *Cam-
boios de amanhã e doas segiomtes,* meaning ticket offices for purchasing advance
tickets, and *Só para comboios de hoje,* meaning offices in which you buy tickets on the
day of travel. Travelers 65 and over should inquire about a *cartão dourado,* or senior
citizen's card. At rail stations, know that *partida* indicates a departure gate and that
chegada means "arrival."

PRACTICAL TRAIN INFORMATION

Portuguese trains are run by **Caminhos de Ferro Portugueses** (**CP;** © **808/208-
208;** www.cp.pt), the national railway. Originally built by the British, the country's
network of rail lines consists mostly of wide-gauge lines for more comfort, and much
of the 2,236-mile (3,600km) network is electrified. In some of the more remote parts
of Portugal, however, the rail lines are narrow gauge, resulting in slow travel times.

Whenever possible, board an **Alfa** train. These high-speed carriers run between
the most important cities in the north and make only major stops. The best of these
trains are the **Alfa Pendular** express trains racing between Lisbon and Porto/Faro;
these trains are as good as any competitor in Europe, with air-conditioning, fine food
service, and airline-type seating. The Alpha Pendular trains also offer special sections
equipped for the mobility impaired. Far less luxurious and much slower are the **Inter-
Cidade (IC)** trains linking most major towns and cities of Portugal. The air-conditioned IC trains offer dining and drinking facilities, but passengers for years have
complained about the poor quality of the cuisine. The fastest trains that carry no
supplements are the **Regionals (R).** On less popular routes, you'll likely find yourself
aboard one of the slow-moving **Suburbanos** trains, which stop at every hamlet—
travel aboard these lines is spartan, at best.

There are two main sleeper trains that service Portugal. The **Lusitânia Hotel
train** runs from Lisbon to Madrid and costs 105€ per person, one-way in first class.
Your reservation is included in your ticket, and passes are accepted on these trains.
The second sleeper train, the **Sud-Expresso,** runs between Lisbon and the Spanish/
French border, and costs 138€ per person, one-way in first class (the Portuguese refer
to the ticket as "preference," which includes a sink and toiletries) for a double, 188€
for a single. Breakfast is included with both tickets, as is an international phone. The
basic sleeper, 94€, is a compartment for four with a sink. ***Note:*** All prices for sleepers
are based on availability. The Sud-Expresso connects with the Paris TGV train at the
border station at Hendaye/Irún. There are no direct trains to Paris.

Second-class travel is jokingly referred to in Portugal as "an experience, but I'll go
by car next time." Because second-class service tends to be spartan on most trains,

Trains & Travel Times in Portugal

From	To	Type of Train	# of Trains	Frequency	Travel Time
Madrid	Lisbon	Tren	1	Daily	9 hr., 15 min.
Lisbon	Faro	ALFA	1	Daily	3 hr.
Lisbon	Faro	IC	3	Daily	3 hr., 50 min.
Lisbon	Óbidos	Regional	1	Daily	2 hr., 10 min.
Lisbon	Óbidos	Urbano (Regional)	5	Daily	2 hr., 30 min.
Lisbon*	Coimbra	ALFA/Urbano	10	Daily	1 hr., 51 min.–2 hr., 30 min.
Lisbon*	Coimbra	IC/Urbano	3	Daily	2 hr., 3 min.–2 hr., 15 min.
Lisbon*	Porto	ALFA	2	Daily	2 hr., 47 min.
Lisbon*	Porto	ALFA/Urbano	9	Daily	2 hr., 56 min.–3 hr., 5 min.
Lisbon	Porto	IC/Urbano	8	Daily	3 hr., 21 min.
Coimbra	Porto	ALFA	7	Daily	58 min.
Coimbra*	Porto	IC/Urbano	7	Daily	1 hr., 14 min.–1 hr., 30 min.

Train transfer required. Trains schedules and travel times in Portugal are constantly in flux. This chart's info was correct at press time, but you should always confirm travel times for your dates of travel before finalizing any plans.

most passengers opt to spend 40% more per ticket and travel first class, where they get better service and more legroom. We highly recommend that you do the same.

RESERVATIONS   These are mandatory on most Portuguese trains and should be made as far in advance as possible. Likewise, railpass validation should be made at designated windows at rail stations. Tickets for IC or Alfa trains can often be booked up to 20 days ahead; in some cases, only 10-day bookings are allowed. You can make reservations through travel agents or else go to the station, where you'll often have to wait in long lines. If you don't have a ticket before boarding, the conductor may fine you. Riding without a ticket *(sem bilhete)* can lead to exorbitant fines in some cases. Reservations are essential on international and express trains, but on many trains they are optional; nevertheless, because all Portuguese trains are likely to be crowded, reservations are advised. They are free if made on the day before departure. There is no travel supplement fee on any IC or Regional train travel within Portugal.

SERVICES & AMENITIES   Sleepers are rented on the Sud Expresso from Paris to Lisbon and the Lusitania Express from Madrid to Lisbon (the Portugal Pass is not valid on these trains, so if you want to travel on them, you need a regional railpass or must purchase a ticket for them through CP or Rail Europe). On average, a sleeper supplement fee is $46 per person for a four-bed and $77 to $103 per person for a double. You'll also encounter *wagons-lit,* or sleepers—compartments with one to two beds with or without private washroom facilities. Most night trains offer full restaurant service, and stewards provide drinks and snacks around the clock. If you need food and drink, always inquire before boarding a train, because there's no guarantee they will be available on Portuguese trains. If services aren't available, carry the food and drink you'll need for the journey. Most trains in Portugal are air-conditioned and have adequate restroom facilities.

[FastFACTS] PORTUGAL

Area Codes The most-used area code in Portugal is **21,** in Lisbon. Other area codes include **28** for both Lagos and Faro (the capital of the Algarve).

Business Hours Hours vary throughout the country, but there is a set pattern. Banks are generally open Monday to Friday from 8:30am to 3pm. Currency exchange offices at airports and rail terminals are open longer hours, and the office at Portela Airport outside Lisbon is open 24 hours a day. Most museums open at 10am, close at 5pm, and often close for lunch between 12:30 and 2pm. Larger museums with bigger staffs often remain open at midday. Shops are open, in general, Monday to Friday from 9am to 1pm and from 3 to 7pm, and Saturday from 9am to 1pm. Most restaurants serve lunch from noon until 3pm and dinner from 7:30 to 11pm; many close on Sunday. Many nightclubs open at 10pm, but the action doesn't really begin until after midnight and often lasts until the wee hours of the morning.

Climate Summer may be the most popular time to visit Portugal, but for the traveler who can chart his or her own course, spring and autumn are the best seasons. To use a North American analogy, the climate of Portugal most closely parallels that of California. There are only slight fluctuations in temperature between summer and winter; the overall mean ranges from 77°F (25°C) in summer to about 58°F (14°C) in winter. In July and August, however, the temperature is hot and humid, intensified by the crowds of people. The rainy season begins in November and usually lasts through January. Because of the Gulf Stream, Portugal's northernmost area, Minho, enjoys mild (albeit very rainy) winters, even though it's at approximately the same latitude as New York City.

Snow brings many skiing enthusiasts to the Serra de Estrêla in north central Portugal. For the most part, however, winter means only some rain and lower temperatures in other regions. The Algarve enjoys temperate winters and is somewhat of a winter Riviera, attracting sun worshippers from North America and Europe. Summers everywhere tend to be long, hot, clear, and dry.

Lisbon and its satellite resort of Estoril enjoy 46° to 65°F (8°–18°C) temperatures in winter and temperatures between 60° and 82°F (16°–28°C) in summer.

Documents Required If you have a valid passport from the U.S. or Canada and plan to stay no more than 90 days, you do not need a visa to enter Portugal. If you'd like to stay more than 90 days, you can apply for an additional stay at the nearest Portuguese embassy. As a rule, the extension is granted immediately.

Electricity Voltage is 230 volts AC (50 cycles), so you'll need a transformer and an adapter plug—available at most hardware stores in North America—to use electrical appliances from the U.S. and Canada in Portugal. The concierge desks at most large hotels can often lend you a transformer and plug adapters, or tell you where you can buy them nearby. To be on the safe side, ask at your hotel before plugging in anything.

Embassies & Consulates If you lose your passport or have some other pressing problem, you'll need to get in touch with your embassy. The Embassy of the **United States,** on Avenida das Forças Armadas (Sete Rios), 1600 Lisboa (✆ **21/727-3300;** http://portugal.usembassy.gov), is open Monday to Friday from 8am to 12:30 and from 1:30 to 5pm. The Embassy of **Canada** is at Avenida da Liberdade 200, 4th Floor, 1269 Lisboa (✆ **21/316-4600;** www.canadainternational.gc.ca/portugal). It's open Monday to Friday from 9am to noon and from 2 to 4pm (embassy closes at 1pm on Fri July–Aug).

Health & Safety Portugal does not offer free

medical treatment to visitors except for citizens of certain countries, such as Great Britain, which have reciprocal health agreements. Nationals from such countries as Canada and the United States have to pay for medical services rendered.

You should encounter few health problems traveling in Portugal. The tap water is generally safe to drink, the milk is pasteurized, and health services are good. Occasionally, the change in diet may cause some minor diarrhea, so you may want to take some antidiarrhea medicine along.

Limit your exposure to the sun, especially during the first few days of your trip and, thereafter, from 11am to 2pm. Use a sunscreen with a high protection factor and apply it liberally. Remember that children need more protection than adults do and should wear a hat.

Though Portugal has a relatively low rate of violent crime, petty crime against tourists is on the rise in continental Portugal. Travelers may become targets of pickpockets and purse-snatchers, particularly at popular tourist sites, in restaurants, and on public transportation such as trains. Travelers should also avoid using ATMs in isolated or poorly lit areas. In general, visitors to Portugal should carry limited cash and credit cards, and leave extra cash, credit cards, and

personal documents at home or in a hotel safe.

Lisbon used to be one of the safest capitals of Europe, but that hasn't been true for a long time. It's now quite dangerous to walk around at night. Many travelers report being held up at knifepoint. Some bandits operate in pairs or in trios. Not only do they take your money, but they also demand your ATM code. One of the robbers holds a victim captive while another withdraws money. (If the number proves to be fake, the robber might return and harm the victim.)

Pickpocketing and purse-snatching in the Lisbon area occur in buses, restaurants, the airport, trains, train stations, and trams, *especially tram 28 to the Castle of São Jorge.* Gangs of youths have robbed passengers on the Lisbon–Cascais train. At restaurants, thieves snatch items hung over the backs of chairs or placed on the floor, so keep a careful eye on your belongings. There have been reports of theft of unattended luggage at the Lisbon Airport. Special care should also be taken at the Santa Apolónia and Rossio train stations, the Alfama and Bairro Alto districts, the Castle of São Jorge, and Belém.

Holidays Watch for these public holidays, and adjust your banking needs accordingly: January 1 (New Year's Day and Universal Brotherhood Day); Carnaval, early March (dates

vary); Good Friday, March or April (dates vary); April 25 (Liberty Day, anniversary of the revolution); May 1 (Labor Day); Corpus Christi, June (dates vary); June 10 (Portugal Day); August 15 (Feast of the Assumption); October 5 (Proclamation of the Republic); November 1 (All Saints' Day); December 1 (Restoration of Independence); December 8 (Feast of the Immaculate Conception); and December 25 (Christmas Day). June 13 (Feast Day of St. Anthony) is a public holiday in Lisbon, and June 24 (Feast Day of St. John the Baptist) is a public holiday in Porto.

Legal Aid Contact your local consulate for a list of English-speaking lawyers if you run into trouble with the law. After that, you're at the mercy of the local courts.

Mail While in Portugal, you may have your mail directed to your hotel (or hotels), to the American Express representative, or to General Delivery *(Poste Restante)* in Lisbon. You must present your passport to pick up mail. The general post office, Correio Geral, in Lisbon, is at Praça dos Restauradores, 1100 Lisboa (② **21/323-89-71**); it's open Monday to Friday from 8am to 10pm; Saturday, Sunday, and holidays 9am to 6pm.

Police & Emergencies For the police or an ambulance, call ② **112.**

Telephone Public telephones accept phone cards as well as coins. Phone cards can be purchased in

Portugal Telecom shops and kiosks. For most long-distance telephone calls, particularly transatlantic calls, go to the central post office (see "Mail," above). Give an assistant the number, and he or she will make the call for you, billing you at the end. Some phones are equipped for using calling cards, including American Express and Visa. You can also purchase phone cards.

International calls are made by dialing **00** (double zero), followed by the country code, the area code (not prefaced by 0), and then the local phone number. The country code for the United States and Canada is **1**. The country code for Portugal is **351**, and the **city code** for Lisbon is **21**.

Tipping   Most service personnel in Portugal expect a good tip rather than a small one, as in the past. Hotels add a service charge (known as *serviço*), which is divided among the entire staff, but individual tipping is also the rule. Tip 1€ to the bellhop for running an errand, 1€ to the doorman who hails you a cab, 1€ to the porter for each piece of luggage carried, and 1.50€ to the chambermaid.

Figure on tipping about 20% of your taxi fare for short runs. For longer treks—for example, from the airport to Cascais—15% is adequate. Restaurants and nightclubs include a service charge and government taxes. As in hotels, this money is distributed among the entire staff, so extra tipping is customary. Add about 5% to the bill in a moderately priced restaurant, up to 10% in a deluxe or first-class establishment.

LISBON

This capital city's greatest glory came in the 15th and 16th centuries, during Portugal's age of discovery, when mariners such as Vasco da Gama sailed from here to explore the uncharted seas of the world. Those discoveries, such as the first sea route from Western Europe around Africa to the Indies, launched the spice trade and brought great wealth to the city, ushering in the golden age of Lisbon, when it became known as the "Queen of the Tagus River."

Trouble was on the way in the centuries ahead, including a devastating earthquake in 1755, but Lisbon has bounced back from its many disasters and is waiting to greet you today. In spite of extensive rebuilding and modernization, the old charm of Lisbon still remains, especially in its most traditional quarter, the Alfama.

Lisbon is growing and evolving, and the city is considerably more sophisticated than it once was, no doubt due in part to Portugal's joining the European Union (E.U.).

Allow at least 3 days to skim the highlights of Portugal's capital, sitting on the north bank of the Tagus estuary, some 10 miles (16km) from the Atlantic. With a population of some 1.8 million, it is a busy, bustling metropolis and port, noted for its cuisine (especially seafood), monuments, great art, fado music cafes, fashionable bars and clubs, and great shops. It is also the best center for touring Portugal by rail, including spectacular Sintra, located in the immediate environs of Lisbon.

Station Information
GETTING FROM THE AIRPORT TO THE TRAIN STATIONS
There is no direct rail service from Portugal's airport. After a long flight, many passengers arriving at the Aeroporto de Lisboa prefer to take a taxi to meet a connecting train. The average taxi fare to one of the city's main train stations ranges from 12€ to 20€, depending on how heavy traffic is; an additional charge of 1.60€ is leveled for each piece of luggage. Less expensive is the AERO-BUS that takes passengers

Lisbon

ACCOMMODATIONS ■

Albergaria Senhora
e Monte **22**
Dom Carlos Park **9**
Hotel Britânia **12**
Hotel Lisboa Plaza **7**
Hotel Tivoli Lisboa **8**
Hotel Villa Rica **23**
Janelas Verdes Inn **5**
VIP Inn Veneza Hotel **11**
York House **2**

ATTRACTIONS ●

Alfama **20**
Belém **4**
Castelo de São Jorge **21**
Mosteiro dos Jerónimos **4**
Museu Antóniano **18**
Museu Calouste
Gulbenkian **10**
Museu de Marinha **4**
Museu Nacional
de Arte Antiga **3**
Museu Nacional
dos Coches **4**
Oceanário de Lisboa **23**
Sé de Lisboa
(Cathedral) **19**
Torre de Belém **4**

DINING ◆

António Clara **10**
Bachus **15**
Cervejaria Brilhante **14**
Clara Restaurante **13**
Conventual **6**
Kais **23**
Martinho da Arcada **16**
Restaurant/Cafeteria
Teatro de São Carlos **17**
Tasquinha d'Adelaide **1**

15

PORTUGAL | **Lisbon**

between the airport and the Cais do Sodré train station, departing every 20 minutes from 7:45am to 8:15pm. The cost is 3.50€ one-way. At night, bus no. 208 stops at Cais do Sodré. Tickets are 1.40€ one-way and can be purchased on board the bus.

INSIDE THE STATIONS

Lisbon has a confusing number of rail stations—some with a full range of services, such as Estação Rossio or Estação Santa Apolónia, and others with more meager offerings.

Estação Rossio lies between Praça Restauradores and Praça Dom Pedro IV (Metro: Rossio or Restauradores; bus: 759). Trains from here mostly service day-trippers and commuters from the bedroom communities around Lisbon, including the former royal palaces at Quéluz and Sintra. Rossio is the smallest, oldest, and most lavishly decorated of the stations in Lisbon, and is also the site of the grand dowager hotel Avenida Palace. It's set in the heart of the city, so you don't need to worry about public transport links to it.

Rossio remains a vintage, somewhat outmoded piece of architecture, evoking the Manueline style of the great Portuguese kings, and is a sightseeing attraction in its own right. On the ground floor is a small information office dispensing routine advice daily from 10am to 1pm and 2:30 to 6pm. For domestic travel, a window is open daily from 7am to 3:30pm, with an international window open daily from 9am to noon and 1 to 5:30pm. Both of these are staffed by English-speaking attendants. There is a tourist office located nearby (see below), in addition to money exchange kiosks, restaurants, and bars. Most visitors to Lisbon pass through here to catch a train to Sintra. Trains depart on tracks 4 and 5 every 15 to 30 minutes from 6:30am to 1am daily, the trip taking 40 minutes and costing 1.75€ for a one-way ticket. Luggage storage is available here daily from 8:30am to 11:30pm; a locker costs 3€ for 48 hours.

Estação Santa Apolónia, Avenida Infante Dom Henrique (Metro: Sta. Apolónia; tram: 28), lies east of the Alfama on the banks of the Tagus River, and 2 miles (3.2km) east of the center of Lisbon. Depending on traffic, it takes a taxi from 5 to 10 minutes to reach the center of town from this station, with an average fare costing about 6€. It's also possible to go by bus nos. 12, 34, 706, and 759, with a one-way fare going for 1.45€. Major national and international trains pull in here, including those from France and Madrid. Major cities of Lisbon are also served, including Coimbra (the university city) and Porto (home of port wine). Facilities include ATMs, restaurants, bars, and money exchange kiosks. Luggage storage is also available daily from 8:30am to 11:30pm, and costs 3€ for 48 hours. You can get both rail and tourist information at offices to the right as you exit from the trains and walk past ticket window no. 1. These offices are open daily from 9am to 10pm. Hotel reservations can be made here, and there is no commission charged.

Estação Oriente (Metro: Oriente; bus: 204 or 759) is Lisbon's newest and most modern railway station. Designed by a Spanish architect in 1998 as part of the city's Expo 98 improvements, it links railway spurs and railway lines that were previously never connected. Set in the Olivais neighborhood, near Lisbon's southern edge within the showplace park, Parque das Naçaos, it's an industrial-looking structure made of white-painted steel that looks both stylish and post-modern. Prior to its construction, passengers arriving in Rossio had to take a bus, tram, or taxi, with their luggage, if they wanted to continue their rail journey from the north to the south of the country. Today some long-distance and suburban trains stop here. For example, all trains heading for Santa Apolónia make a brief stop here. Trains leave from here to such northern destinations as Porto, the Beiras (Central Portugal), the Minho (in the north), and the Douro of port wine fame. This is also a departure point for Sintra. This railway station's opening coincided with the construction of 10 additional subway stations, and Oriente Station is interconnected with the entire subway system. Oriente also now hosts trains bound for the deep south, the Algarve.

Estação Cais do Sodré (Metro: Cais do Sodré) lies just beyond the end of Rua Alecrim, to the west of Praça Comércio. The station, a 5-minute walk from the Baixa district, is so small in scale that it's easy to mistake it for a tram station. To reach the center, such as the landmark Praça dos Restauradores, take the Metro or bus nos. 1, 36, or 44. If you're connecting with trains at the Estação Santa Apolónia, take bus no. 28. Most passengers exploring Lisbon stop off here to reach the many attractions of Belém, including Mosteiro dos Jerónimos. Trains depart for Belém every 15 minutes during the day, costing 1.20€ for the one-way, 10-minute trip. It's also possible to get trains here for the country's two most famous resorts along the Costa do Sol, Estoril and Cascais, both directly west of Lisbon.

Estação Entrecampos (Metro: Entrecampos; bus: 36, 44, or 54) is an intermediate railway station, a sort of "way station" that's set strategically on a spur line emanating outward from the city's newest, blockbuster railway station, Estação Oriente (see above). Passengers departing from Lisbon for points south of the Tagus, including Faro and Lagos, can board their trains here. They are routed on the lower level of the older of the two bridges traversing the Tagus, Ponte XXV Abrile (locals also refer to this bridge as the "Ponte Sobre Tejo"; its upper level is reserved for cars). Trains from this station go to various nearby points on the south bank of the Tagus as well as to the Algarve.

For rail information at any of these terminals, call ✆ **808/208-208.**

Information Elsewhere in the City

Hotel reservations, for which no commission is levied, can be made at all local tourist offices. The main office is at Palacio da Foz, Praça dos Restauradores (✆ **21/346-3314;** www.visitportugal.com), at the Baixa end of Avenida da Liberdade. The office dispenses information about Lisbon, as well as Portugal in general, and is open daily from 9am to 8pm (Metro: Restauradores; bus: 36). Among several other tourism information sites scattered throughout the city is a **Welcome Center** at Loja 1–r/c, Praça do Comércio (✆ **21/031-2810;** www.visitlisboa.com). Hours are daily 9am to 8pm. At most tourism information locations, you can purchase the **Lisbon Card,** which provides free city transportation and entrance fees to many museums and attractions, plus discounts to certain events. For adults, a 1-day pass costs 16€, 2 days 27€, 3 days 34€. Children 5 to 11 pay 9.50€, 14€, and 17€, respectively. You can purchase the **Lisbon Card** at a discounted price online at **www.askmelisboa.com** and get a wealth of information about the all things Lisbon.

Getting Around

Lisbon is a vast urban sprawl, with many of its most-visited attractions, including Belém and Sintra, lying in the environs. You'll need to rely on public transportation, which more or less runs pretty well. In the heart of town, the best way to cover Lisbon, especially the ancient districts of the Alfama and Baixa, is on foot. Wear sturdy walking shoes along these often cobbled and narrow streets, which haven't changed much from the days when donkeys walked them.

The public transportation system is operated by **CARRIS** (𝓒 **21/361-3000;** www. carris.pt), which supervises the network of funiculars, trains, subways (the Metro), and buses. Consider buying a *bilhete de assinature turistico,* which covers all forms of transportation. A 1-day pass sells for 3.70€, and discounted passes are available for longer periods of time as well. Fares must be loaded onto a 7 Colinas Card, which costs .50€ and can be purchased at CARRIS booths in terminals and transportation hubs, which are open daily from 8am to 8pm, and at most Metro stations.

The Metro subway system's stations are designated by large M signs. A single ticket costs .85€; a day pass goes for 3.70€. Service is daily from 6:30am to 1am. For more information, call 𝓒 **21/350-01-15** or visit **www.metrolisboa.pt**.

Lisbon still operates an old-fashioned tram system, with trolley cars called *eléctricos* making the steep run from the heart of town up to the Bairro Alto section. Buses or tram tickets cost from 1.40€ if you purchase a ticket from the driver. The fare depends on how far you're traveling, as Lisbon is divided into five different zones. At the foot of the Santa Justa Elevator, on Rua Áurea, there's a stand with schedules pinpointing the zigzagging tram and bus routes. Buses and *eléctricos* run daily from 6am to 1am.

The city is linked to its Riviera by a smooth-running, electric train system that will take you from Lisbon to such resorts as Estoril and Cascais. The electric train does not run to Sintra. For Sintra, you must go to the Estação do Rossio station, opening onto Praça de Dom Pedro IV, or the Rossio, where frequent connections can be made. There's only one class of seat, with a one-way fare ranging from 1.80€ to 4€.

There is also a trio of funiculars, including the **Glória,** which goes from Praça dos Restauradores to Rua São Pedro de Alcântara; the **Bica,** from Calçada do Combro to Rua do Boavista; and the **Lavra,** from the eastern side of Avenida da Liberdade to Campo Martires de Pátria. A one-way ticket on any of these funiculars costs 1.40€.

Finally, taxis are often the preferred means of transport, as fares are reasonable, beginning with a basic charge of 2.50€ for the first 502 feet (151m), .10€ for each extra 531 feet (159m). Between 10pm to 6am daily, fares go up by 20%. For a **Radio Taxi,** call 𝓒 **21/811-9000** or visit **www.retalis.pt**.

Where to Stay

Albergaria Senhora do Monte ★ 🏨   Near St. George's Castle, in the oldest part of Lisbon, this inn is welcoming and unpretentious. It's a hidden gem perched on a hilltop near a belvedere, opening onto panoramic views in all directions. The junior suites all have terraces, though all the bedrooms are comfortable and inviting. The restored accommodations are imbued with decorator's touches such as gilt-edged door panels and bronze fixtures.

Calçada do Monte 39, 1170-250 Lisboa.𝓒 **21/886-6002.** Fax 21/887-7783. www.albergariasenhorado monte.com. 28 units. 110€ double; 140€ suite. Rates include continental breakfast. AE, DC, MC, V. Metro: Socorro. **Amenities:** Breakfast room; bar.

Dom Carlos Park 🍴   Just off the landmark Praça do Marquês de Pombal, this hotel is known for its central location and affordable prices. The midsize bedrooms are more functional than stylish, all of them paneled in Portuguese redwood. Facing a little park, the hotel is well run, with a friendly, accommodating staff who will direct you to all the points of interest and tell you the best way to get to where you're going.

Av. Duque de Loulé 121, 1050-089 Lisboa.𝓒 **21/351-2590.** Fax 21/352-0728. www.domcarlospark.com. 76 units. 138€–170€ double; from 196€ junior suite. Rates include buffet breakfast. AE, DC, MC, V. Metro: Marquês de Pombal. **Amenities:** Restaurant; bar.

Hotel Britânia ★ ✦ Only 1,640 feet (492m) from the Rossio, a block from Avenida da Liberdade (the main boulevard), this long-time favorite was carved out of a 1942 Art Deco office building. The six-story hotel hasn't been renovated in quite a while, but there is yearly maintenance and upgrading on an as-needed basis, although many of its vintage architectural features are retained. The property features high ceilings, tasteful carpeting, comfortable furnishings, and carved headboards on twin- or king-size beds. The hotel's service is like that provided by a small, well-run inn.

Rua Rodrigues Sampaio 17, 1150-278 Lisboa. ⓒ **21/315-5016.** Fax 21/315-5021. www.heritage.pt. 32 units. 130€–245€ double. AE, DC, MC, V. Metro: Avenida. **Amenities:** Bar; smoke-free rooms.

Hotel Lisboa Plaza ★★ In the heart of the city, this seven-floor, family-owned hotel sits on a quiet side street ½ mile (1km) north of Rossio. Built in 1953, the hotel was extensively restored by top designers in the '90s, and much of its charm, evoking Edwardian elegance, was retained and touched up. The traditionally styled accommodations range from standard rooms, to much larger superior units, to roomy and tastefully furnished suites (try for one at the rear overlooking botanical gardens). All rooms feature double-glazed windows and marble bathrooms.

Travessa do Salitre 7, Avenida da Liberdade, 1269-066 Lisboa. ⓒ **21/321-8218.** Fax 21/347-1630. www. heritage.pt. 106 units. 99€–235€ double; 203€–450€ suite. Children 11 and under stay free in parent's room. AE, DC, MC, V. Metro: Avenida. **Amenities:** Restaurant; bar; smoke-free rooms.

Hotel Tivoli Lisboa ★★ Located in a prime spot about ¾ mile (1.1km) north of Rossio, this hotel, opened in 1933, is a conservative, cosmopolitan, and enduring favorite of both vacationers and business travelers thanks to such enticing features as the only hotel pool in central Lisbon. A large, dramatically decorated two-floor lobby sets a welcoming tone, and a top-floor restaurant opens onto a terrace for panoramic dining. Tasteful carpeting, stylish chintz, and comfortable furnishings decorate the spacious, bright, and inviting bedrooms, which offer many amenities, including marble bathrooms.

Ave. da Liberdade 185, 1269-050 Lisboa. ⓒ **21/319-8900.** Fax 21/319-8950. www.tivolihotels.com. 329 units. From 200€ double; from 350€ suite. Rates include continental breakfast. AE, DC, MC, V. Metro: Avenida. **Amenities:** 2 restaurants; 2 bars; rooms for those w/limited mobility; smoke-free rooms.

Hotel Villa Rica ★★ Located in Entrecampos, the city's new financial district, this supremely modern property caters to the business set. The midsize bedrooms are decorated in a sleek, contemporary style and are exceedingly comfortable. The dining options in its restaurant cater to a wide range of tastes and pocketbooks. Facilities are strictly deluxe, ranging from a health club with Turkish bath and indoor swimming pool to a piano bar.

Ave. 5 de Outubro, 301-319, 1600-035 Lisboa. ⓒ **21/0043-000.** Fax 21/004-43-33. www.hotelvillarica lisboa.com. 171 units. 79€–100€ double. AE, DC, MC, V. Metro: Entrecampos. **Amenities:** Restaurant; 2 bars; smoke-free rooms.

Janelas Verdes Inn ★★ 🏨 Set 1¼ miles (2km) from Rossio, between the harbor and Bairro Alto, this is one of Lisbon's most atmospheric and charming hotels. It's installed in an 18th-century town house that was once home to Eca de Queiroz, the Portuguese novelist. Rooms are spacious and elegantly furnished with a combination of antiques and reproductions. The best rooms are in the rear and on the upper levels, as they open onto sweeping views of the Tagus River.

Rua das Janelas Verdes 47, 1200-690 Lisboa. ✆ **21/396-8143.** Fax 21/396-8144. 29 units. www.
heritage.pt. 180€–230€ double. AE, DC, MC, V. Bus: 727 R. Janelas Verdes. **Amenities:** Bar; rooms for
those w/limited mobility; smoke-free rooms. *In room:* Hair dryer.

VIP Inn Veneza Hotel ★ 🎁 Housed in one of the few remaining old palaces that
once lined Avenida da Liberdade (it's a splendid structure that dates from 1886), this
hotel opened in 1990 and is a real discovery. A grand staircase leads to a trio of upper
floors where you'll find handsomely furnished and up-to-date guest bedrooms. The
service and friendly welcome are top rate.

Ave. da Liberdade 189, 1250-141 Lisboa. ✆ **21/352-2618.** Fax 21/352-6678. www.viphotels.com. 37 units.
60€–90€ double. Rates include continental breakfast. AE, DC, MC, V. Metro: Avenida. **Amenities:** Bar.

York House ★★ An even more atmospheric choice than the Janelas Verdes Inn
(see above), the York House was carved out of a 17th-century convent and is filled
with more charm and character than any other hotel in Lisbon. Long a celebrity
favorite, it lies on a cobbled street between Bairro Alto and the waterfront 1¼ miles
(2km) west of the Rossio. Mazelike public rooms, filled with antiques, lead to bedrooms that vary in size, although each is beautifully furnished, often with a four-
poster bed and antiques. Breakfast is 15€ per person.

Rua das Janelas Verdes 32, 1200-691 Lisboa. ✆ **21/396-2435.** Fax 21/397-2793. www.yorkhouselisboa.
com. 32 units. 60€–250€ double. AE, DC, MC, V. Bus: 727 R. Janelas Verdes. **Amenities:** Restaurant; bar.

Top Attractions & Special Moments

If you have only a day in Lisbon, take a stroll through the Alfama, the city's most
interesting district. Visit the 12th-century **Sé** (cathedral), and take in a view of the
city and the River Tagus from the **Miradouro Santa Luzia Belvedere.** Climb up
to the **Castelo de São Jorge (St. George's Castle).** Take a taxi or bus to Belém to
see the **Mosteiro dos Jerónimos (Jerónimos Monastery)** and the **Torre de
Belém.** While at Belém, explore one of the major sights of Lisbon, the **Museu
Nacional dos Coches (National Coach Museum).**

IN THE ALFAMA

Castelo de São Jorge ★★ This hilltop fortress, a former citadel of Portuguese
kings, towers over Lisbon. It became a royal abode when Afonso Henriques chased
out the Moors in 1147, and remained so until 1511, when Manuel I constructed a
more lavish palace closer to the harbor. The 1755 earthquake struck it badly, but in
1938, the dictator Salazar ordered the old walls rebuilt and gardens added.

Today's visitors can climb the towers and walk along the **battlements ★**, the reconstructed ramparts, later taking in the **view from the Observation Platform ★★**, a
large, shaded square opening onto Lisbon and the river beyond. You can stroll the
grounds, taking in the landscaping of olive, pine, and cork trees, all graced by elegant
peacocks strutting their feathers or white-bodied swans gliding by.

Rua da Costa do Castelo. ✆ **21/880-0620.** www.castelodesaojorge.pt. Admission 7€ adults, free for
children 9 and under, students 50% discount. Mar–Oct daily 9am–9pm; Nov–Feb daily 9am–6pm.
Metro: Rossio. Bus: 737 Castelo. Tram: 12E or 28E Pç. Figueira.

Museu de Santo Antóniano This Alfama church, so it is said, stands on the spot
where St. Anthony of Padua, an itinerant Franciscan monk who became the patron
saint of Portugal, was born in 1195. Only the crypt remains from the original church.
The present structure dates from 1757 and was based on the design of the architect

STROLLING THE Alfama

It's old and decaying, but the **Alfama ★★** is one of the most history-rich and evocative old quarters of any European capital. Give it at least a morning or an afternoon. Now mired in large part in poverty, the Alfama used to be the toniest neighborhood in Lisbon, inhabited in part by the aristocracy, its closely knit alleyways built around a fortified castle on the hilltop.

The rich fled after Lisbon's 1755 earthquake, leaving the district to the families of fishermen and paupers. The Alfama was allowed to decay gracefully, and it is because of this poverty that its casbah-like layout remains intact today.

Balconies are strung with laundry; music emanates from tavernas filled with immigrants from such former colonies as Mozambique or Cape Verde; crumbling churches have terraces with panoramic views; hidden restaurants spill out onto open-air courtyards; and black-shawled widows grill sardines on open braziers, tossing a fish head to a passing cat.

One of the best views is from **Largo das Portas do Sol ★**, one of the gates to the old city. A lively fish market takes place every morning at Rua de São Pedro.

Another great panoramic sweep is possible from **Miradouro de Santa Luzia ★★**, whose bougainvillea-clad terrace spans the tiled roofs of the Alfama toward the Tagus River.

Mateus Vicente. The church is a medley of styles, including baroque overtones and neoclassical Ionic columns standing on each side of the principal portal. Married couples visit the church on their wedding day, leaving flowers for St. Anthony. The saint was born and reared in Lisbon but spent the last months of his life in Padua. Next to the church, the museum displays ancient manuscripts, ex-votos, and images, all related to St. Anthony.

Largo de Santo António de Sé 24. ℭ **21/886-0447.** Free admission. Tues–Sun 10am–1pm and 2–6pm. Metro: Rossio. Bus: 737 to Sé. Tram: 28 to Sé.

Sé de Lisboa (Cathedral) ★ It's not one of the grand cathedrals of Europe, but this blend of Romanesque and Gothic architecture, characterized by twin towers flanking its entrance, merits 30 or so minutes of your time if you're exploring the Alfama. The cathedral was begun in 1147, when Afonso Henriques ordered it built for the first bishop of Lisbon after he'd kicked out the Moors. Over the years, the cathedral has had a rough time of it. It was devastated by a series of earth tremors in the 14th century. It also shook at its foundations during the earthquake of 1755. The austere interior is a bit gloomy, but there are treasures here, including the font where St. Anthony of Padua is said to have been christened in 1195. Other notable features include the Gothic chapel of Bartholomeu Joanes, plus a crib by Machado de Castro. If time remains, visit the cloister, built on the orders of King Dinis in the 14th century. It's of ogival construction, with garlands and a Romanesque **wrought-iron grille ★**. The sacristy contains valuable images, relics, and other treasures from the 15th and 16th centuries.

Largo de Sé. ℭ **21/886-6752.** Cathedral entrance free; cloister 2.50€. Daily 9am–7pm; holidays 9am–5pm. Bus: 37. Tram: 28 (Graça).

BELÉM

At the mouth of the Tagus River, Portuguese caravels set sail on their voyages of discovery, changing the maps of the world and even the world itself. These voyages led to trade with India and the East, the capture of Goa, the colonization of Brazil, and the granting of Macao as a trading post with China, among other adventures. Portugal was indeed launched upon its golden age.

You can journey to the suburb of Belém in the southwestern district to see where Portuguese mariners such as Ferdinand Magellan, Vasco de Gama, and Barolomeu Dias set out on their voyages across the Sea of Darkness.

Belém is easily reached by public transportation. Take tram 15E for the 20-minute ride from Praça do Comércio in the center of Lisbon to Belém; or else bus nos. 714 or 727, also to Belém, which leave from Marquês Pombal. The slow trains from Cais do Sodré marked CASCAIS also stop at Belém.

You can spend an entire day at Belém enjoying its monuments, parks, and gardens, as well as strolling its setting along the Tagus. If your time is very limited, try to see at least Mosteiro dos Jerónimos, Museu Nacional dos Coches, and Museu de Marinha—all reviewed below, along with some more minor attractions.

Mosteiro dos Jerónimos ★★

This is the jewel of the age of Manueline art. Manuel I, called "The Fortunate," launched this monastery to commemorate the success of Vasco da Gama's voyage to India. Bearing the king's name, Manueline architecture blends the most flamboyant Gothic aspects with Moorish influences. "Pepper money," meaning profits from the spice trade with India, helped finance this magnificent monument.

A former small chapel built by Henry the Navigator is today **Ingreja de Santa Maria ★★**, with one of the most beautiful interiors of any of Lisbon's churches, particularly evocative for its **network vaulting ★** over the aisles and naves. The pinnacle of Manueline expression is achieved in the **cloisters ★★★**, reached through the west door. Completed in 1544, these cloisters are filled with delicate tracery and lushly carved images adorning their arches and balustrades. The church boasts three naves noted for their delicate columns; several of the ceilings are graced with ribbed barrel vaulting. Many of Portugal's greatest national heroes are entombed here, including Vasco da Gama and the land's national poet, Luís Vas de Camões, author of the epic *Os Lusíadas* (The Lusiads), in which he glorified the triumphs of his compatriots.

Praça do Império. ⓒ **21/362-0034.** www.mosteirojeronimos.pt. Church entrance free; cloisters 6€ adults 26 and older, 3€ 15-25 years old, free for seniors 65 and over and children 14 and under. May-Sept Tues-Sun 10am-6pm; Oct-Apr Tues-Sun 10am-5pm. Bus: 201, 727, or 729 to Mosteiro dos Jerónimos. Tram: 15 Mosteiro Jerónimos.

Museu de Marinha ★★

One of Europe's greatest maritime museums depicts Portugal's seafaring past and is installed in the west wing of Mosteiro dos Jerónimos. It was in the chapel here that mariners took Mass before embarking on their fabled voyages, including Vasco da Gama's sail around the Cape of Good Hope to open the sea route to India. Navigational instruments, replicas of maps from the 1500s, and astrolabes evoke the mariners' past and what was known at the time of their discoveries. Royal galleys re-create an age of opulence, with depictions of everything from the heads of dragons to sea monsters. The most elaborate of these galleys was the one ordered built by Queen Maria I in honor of her son's marriage in 1785 to a Spanish princess—the crew consisted of 80 oarsmen. On display are many models of sailing ships ranging from the 15th to the 19th centuries, including pleasure boats and river

TO MARKET, to market . . .

The big market of **Ribeira Nova** ★★ is as close as you can get to the heart of Lisbon. Behind the Cais do Sodré train station, an enormous roof shelters a collection of stalls offering the produce used in Lisbon's finest restaurants. Foodstuffs arrive each morning in wicker baskets bulging with oversize carrots, cabbages big enough to be shrubbery, and stalks of bananas. Some of the freshly plucked produce arrives by donkey, some by truck, some balanced Mediterranean fashion on the heads of Lisboan women. The country's rich soil produces the juiciest peaches and the most aromatic tomatoes.

At the market, women festively clad in voluminous skirts and calico aprons preside over mounds of vegetables, fruit, and fish. On cue, the vendors begin howling about the value of their wares, stopping only to pose for an occasional snapshot. Fishing boats dock at dawn with their catch. The fishermen deposit the cod, squid, bass, hake, and swordfish on long marble counters. The *varinas* (fishwives) balance wicker baskets of the fresh catch on their heads as they climb the cobblestone streets of the Alfama or the Bairro Alto to sell fish from door to door.

crafts. Of special interest is a model of the queen's stateroom on the royal yacht of Carlos I, the Bragança king assassinated at Praça do Comércio in 1908. It was on this craft that the queen mother, Amélia, and her son, Manuel II, escaped to Gibraltar.

Praça do Império. ✆ **21/362-0019.** http://museu.marinha.pt. Admission 4€ adults, 2€ students and children 6–17, free for children 5 and under. Apr–Sept Tues–Sun 10am–6pm; Oct–Mar Tues–Sun 10am–5pm; closed holidays. Train: Belém. Bus: 201, 727, or 729 Mosteiro dos Jerónimos. Tram: 15 Mosteiro dos Jerónimos.

Museu Nacional dos Coches ★★ This is the world's greatest coach museum and is one of the most visited attractions in Lisbon. Founded by Amélia, wife of Carlos I, it's installed in a riding academy built in the 1700s. Gilded coaches, four-wheelers, litters—they are all found here. The most ancient is the splendidly painted **four-wheeler** ★ that Philip of Spain brought to Portugal in the late 16th century. The coaches range from the very simple to the most ostentatious, the latter being the three outrageously adorned coaches built in 1716 for the Marquês de Abrantes, Portugal's ambassador to Pope Clement XI. Their interiors are lined with gold and red velvet, and the coaches are carved and decorated with royal coats-of-arms along with allegories.

Praça de Afonso de Albuquerque. ✆ **21/361-0850.** Admission 4€ adults, 1.60€ ages 14–25, free for children 13 and under. Tues–Sun 10am–6pm; closed holidays. Bus: 28, 201, 714, 727, or 729 Belém. Train: Belém. Tram: 15 Belém.

Torre de Belém ★★ This quadrangular tower is one of Portugal's greatest monuments to its Age of Discovery. Built by Manuel I, the tower was a fortress in the early 16th century and the starting point for the famous Portuguese mariners. The **decoration** ★★ of the tower's exterior is magnificent, adorned with rope carved of stone and balconies. Moorish-styled watchtowers guard it, and the battlements appear in the shape of shields. A monument to Portugal's great naval past, the tower is often used to symbolize Portugal itself. Along the balustrade of the loggias, stone crosses represent the Portuguese crusaders. From the ramparts, you're rewarded with a **panorama** ★★

15

PORTUGAL | Lisbon

of the Tagus and its vessels. In the center of the square on which the tower sits is the **Fonte Luminosa ★**, or Luminous Fountain, whose water jets strike up some 70 original patterns every evening, creating a show that lasts for about an hour.

Praça do Império, Avenida de Brasília. *(₵* **21/362-0034.** www.mosteirojeronimos.pt. Admission 4€ adults, 1.60€ 15–25 years old, free for children 14 and under. Sun free until 2pm. May–Sept Tues–Sun 10am–6pm; Oct–Apr Tues–Sun 10am–5pm. Bus: 729 Centro Cultural Belém. Tram: 15.

OTHER GREAT MUSEUMS

Museu Calouste Gulbenkian ★★★   Hailed by art critics as one of the world's finest private art collections, this magnificent treasure-trove was formed from a nucleus of art acquired by Calouste Gulbenkian, an oil magnate with an eye for art, who died in 1955 and willed his collection to the state. The modern museum was constructed on a former private estate that once belonged to the Count of Vilalva and opened in 1969. Allow at least 3 hours for a romp through this varied collection, which covers Egyptian, Greek, and Roman antiquities among other treasures, even a rare (for Europe) assemblage of Islamic art, including Syrian glass and ceramics and textiles from Turkey and old Persia. The **medieval illuminated manuscripts and ivories ★** form a stunning display, as do the French Impressionist paintings, 18th-century decorative works, antiques, silverware, and jewelry.

In a move requiring great skill in negotiation, Gulbenkian managed to buy art from the Hermitage in St. Petersburg. Among his most notable acquisitions are two Rembrandts: *Portrait of an Old Man* and *Alexander the Great.* Two other well-known paintings are *Portrait of Hélène Fourment,* by Peter Paul Rubens, and *Portrait of Madame Claude Monet,* by Pierre-August Renoir. In addition, we suggest that you seek out Mary Cassatt's *The Stocking.* The French sculptor Jean-Antoine Houdon is represented by a statue of Diana. Silver made by François-Thomas Germain, once used by Catherine the Great, is here, as well as a piece by Thomas Germain, the artist's father.

IF IT swims, IT'S HERE

A legacy left by Expo '98, the second-biggest aquarium in the world (the largest is in Osaka, Japan), **Oceanario de Lisboa ★★** *(₵* **21/891-7002;** www.oceanario.pt), helps you realize what a seafaring nation Portugal was and still is. The centerpiece of this amazing glass-and-stone building is a 1.3-million-gallon (5-million-liter) holding tank. That's about the equivalent of four Olympic swimming pools strung together. From shoals of sardines to menacing sharks, the displays consist of four distinct ecosystems that replicate the Atlantic, Pacific, Indian, and Antarctic oceans. Each is supplemented with aboveground portions on which birds, amphibians, and reptiles flourish. Look for otters in the Pacific waters; penguins in the Antarctic section; trees and flowers that might remind you of Polynesia in the Indian Ocean section; and puffins, terns, and sea gulls in the Atlantic division.

Don't underestimate the national pride associated with this huge facility. Most Portuguese view it as a latter-day reminder of their former mastery of the seas. Admission is 11€ adults, 5.50€ students and children under 13. Summer daily 10am to 8pm (closes at 7pm in winter). Metro: Estaçao do Oriente. Pedestrians should turn right after leaving the Metro station and go along Avenue Dom João II, where you'll see a signpost directing you left and to the water for the attraction itself.

As a cultural center, the Gulbenkian Foundation sponsors plays, films, ballets, and concerts, as well as a rotating exhibition of works by leading modern Portuguese and foreign artists.

Av. de Berna 45. ✆ **21/782-3000.** www.museu.gulbenkian.pt. Admission 4€; free for seniors (65 and over), students, and teachers. Free to all Sun. Tues–Sun 10am–5:45pm. Metro: Sebastião or Praça de Espanha. Bus: 726 or 756 Pç. Espanha/Av. Berna.

Museu Nacional de Arte Antiga ★★★ Set inside the 17th-century palace of the Counts of Alvor, this great museum, one of the finest in Iberia, was founded in part from rare collections taken from monasteries that were suppressed in 1833. The greatest paintings to be found in Portugal are displayed here in a carefully laid-out collection, with the major European paintings from the 14th to the 19th centuries on the ground floor. On the top floor is one of the country's finest displays of Portuguese art and sculpture. The gallery has some celebrated works, including a **polyptych ★★★** from St. Vincent's monastery, a work attributed to Nuno Gonçalves between 1460 and 1470. A triptych, *The Temptation of St. Anthony* ★★★, is the gallery's other celebrated treasure. Other notable works include the portrait of St. Jerome in his old age by Albrecht Dürer, a great work of Renaissance humanism, from 1521. Hans Holbein the Elder weighs in with his masterly *Mother and Child* from 1519. Especially noteworthy is the *12 Apostles,* by Zurbarán. A series of 16th-century **Namban screens ★** form one of the museum's other treasures, as does a ceramics collection and many decorative items made for the royal family, including a strikingly unusual faience violin.

Rua das Janelas Verdes 95. ✆ **21/391-2800.** www.mnarteantiga-ipmuseus.pt. Admission 4€ adults, 2€ students, free for children 13 and under. Tues 2–6pm; Wed–Sun 10am–6pm. Bus: 727 Rua das Janelas Verdes; 28, 201, or 714 Av 24 Julho. Train: Santos. Tram: 15 or 18 Av 24 Julho.

Where to Dine

António Clara ★★ PORTUGUESE/INTERNATIONAL   One of the most celebrated restaurants in Lisbon is located just off the Praça do Marquês de Pompal. This upmarket establishment occupies a late-19th-century villa that was the home of the famous architect Miguel Ventura Terra (1866–1918). In one of the most beautiful dining rooms of the city, you can enjoy top-notch cooking that is a modern and inspired rendition of classic recipes. Meals include such specialties as paella for two, monkfish rice, codfish *Margarida da Praça,* and beef Wellington. The dishes might be familiar, but only the highest-quality ingredients are used. The seafood is especially good here.

Ave. da República 38. ✆ **21/799-4280.** Reservations recommended. Main courses 15€–36€. AE, DC, MC, V. Mon–Sat 12:30–3pm and 7:30–10:30pm. Metro: Saldanha. Bus: 44 Av. República.

Bachus ★★ INTERNATIONAL/PORTUGUESE   In Bairro Alto, a short distance south of Rossio station, this amusing and sophisticated restaurant has an ambience evocative of a turn-of-the-20th-century British club. Classic favorites are dished up by classy waiters who service their tables well. The menu is adjusted to take advantage of seasonal produce, and old and new influences are combined to produce appetizing fare that might range from shrimp Bachus to mountain goat.

Largo da Trindade 8–9. ✆ **21/342-2828.** Reservations recommended. Main courses 17€–26€. AE, DC, MC, V. Tues–Fri noon–2pm and 7pm–midnight; Sat–Sun 6pm–2am. Metro: Chiado. Bus: 758 or 790 Lg. Trindade Coelho.

Cervejaria Brilhante PORTUGUESE/SEAFOOD   Lisboans from every walk of life stop here for a stein of beer and *mariscos* (seafood). The tavern is decorated with stone arches, wood-paneled walls, and pictorial tiles of sea life. The front window is packed with an appetizing array of king crabs, oysters, lobsters, baby clams, shrimp, and even barnacles. The price changes every day, depending on the market, and you pay by the kilo. This is hearty, robust eating, although attracting a waiter's attention is a challenge.

Rua das Portas de Santo Antão 105 (opposite the Coliseu). © **21/346-14-07.** Main courses 12€–22€. AE, DC, MC, V. Daily noon–midnight. Metro: Rossio or Restauradores. Bus: 1, 2, 36, 44, or 45.

Clara Restaurante ★★ INTERNATIONAL/PORTUGUESE On a hillside amid decaying villas and city squares, this green-tile house owned by Célia Pimpista contains an elegant restaurant with a number of different seating areas. You can enjoy a drink under the ornate ceiling of the bar or grab a seat in the indoor dining room—perhaps near the large marble fireplace, in range of the soft music played during dinner; during lunch, you can sit near the garden terrace's plants and fountain. Specialties include tournedos Clara, stuffed rabbit with red-wine sauce, and Valencian paella. As in many of Lisbon's top-rated restaurants, these dishes aren't innovative in any way, but they're often prepared flawlessly.

Campo dos Mártires da Pátria 49. © **21/885-30-53.** www.lisboa-clara.pt. Reservations required. Main courses 25€–45€. AE, DC, MC, V. Mon–Fri 12:30–3pm; Mon–Sat 7:30–11:30pm. Closed Aug 1–15. Metro: Avenida.

Conventual ★★ 🎀 PORTUGUESE One of Lisbon's finest restaurants (the prime minister of Portugal is a fan) is west of Rossio Station, off Praça de Principe Real. This exemplary dining room is comfortably spaced with white-clothed tables evoking a 1930s style and is overseen by a graceful, welcoming staff. The menu is beautifully balanced between rich game favorites such as stewed partridge in port and fish dishes such as grilled monkfish in an herb-flavor cream sauce.

Praça das Flores 45. © **21/390-9246.** Reservations required. Main courses 20€–30€. AE, DC, MC, V. Mon–Fri 12:30–3:30pm; Mon–Sat 7:30–11pm. Closed Aug. Metro: Rato; Bus: 790 Praça Das Flores.

Kais ★ INTERNATIONAL Located at the docks, this bar and restaurant opens onto an esplanade by the river. It's installed in a late-19th-century warehouse that has been amazingly converted into one of the most beautiful restaurants in Lisbon. Against a backdrop of Frank Lloyd Wright–inspired furniture, you can select from a dazzling array of fresh foodstuffs deftly handled by the skilled chefs in the kitchen. Shrimp in champagne sauce is just one of the many tempting dishes that await you.

Cais da Viscondessa-Rua da Cintura-Santos. © **21/393-2930.** Reservations recommended. www.kais-k.com Main courses 25€–35€; prix-fixe menus 80€–125€. Tues–Sat 8pm–midnight; Fri–Sat 8pm–12am. Closed first 2 weeks in Aug. Metro: Cais do Sodré. Bus: 758 or 790 Príncipe Real.

Martinho da Arcada PORTUGUESE It's one of the city's most famous restaurants, thanks to its age (it was established in 1782) and its association with Portugal's beloved poet, Fernando Pessoa, whose photos hang on the wall. There are three distinct sections to this place. There's a cafe section for drinks and sandwiches; an outdoor terrace, where the menu is less complete than what you'll find inside; and an inside dining room, with antecedents that go back more than 225 years. The menu here is long and varied, but if you ask for what the kitchen is the most proud of, a staff member will talk abut the house-style cod (a thick "tenderloin" of cod served with twice-cooked onions and fried potatoes) and house-style filet steak with coffee sauce and fresh vegetables.

Praça di Comercio 3. ⓒ **21/887-9259.** Reservations recommended for dinner. Main courses 14€–18€. AE, DC, MC, V. Mon–Sat 8am–11pm. Metro: Terreiro do Paço. Bus: 28 or 44 Praça Do Comércio. Tram: 15 Praça Do Comércio.

Restaurant/Cafeteria Teatro Nacional de São Carlos CONTINENTAL Just after the turn of the millennium, one of the formal "showcase" salons within Lisbon's Opera House, originally built in 1765, was transformed into a restaurant, the kind of airy, appealingly formal venue where sparkling wine might be served with fresh fish and a rundown on the plot of an upcoming or past opera performance. It's made even more appealing by the tables set up under parasols within the traffic-free square outside. The best menu items include cod with pesto sauce and red cabbage risotto, magret of duck with green peppers, tournedos with three kinds of mushrooms and cream sauce, and grilled beef with three different kinds of Portuguese cheese.

Largo São Carlos. ⓒ **21/346/8082.** Salads, pastas, and risottos 10€–14€; main courses 13€–18€. Mon–Sat 9am–midnight. AE, DC, MC, V. Metro: Baixo/Chiado; Tram: 28 Chiado; Bus: 758 or 790 Pç. Luis Camões.

Tasquinha d'Adelaide ★ 🍴 PORTUGUESE   This unusual restaurant is known for serving the culinary specialties of Trás-os-Montes, the most rugged and remote province of Portugal. The restaurant itself is on the western edge of the Bairro Alto, and a table here is a coveted commodity among Lisboan foodies who appreciate its homelike atmosphere and unpretentious but good-tasting cuisine. This food is not for the faint of heart and attracts those who deliberately seek out its hearty regional fare, which includes such daunting courses as tripe with collard greens and rice. There are options for less adventurous palates as well.

Rua do Patrocinio 70–74. ⓒ **21/396-2239.** Reservations recommended. Complete meal 35€. AE, DC, MC, V. Mon–Sat 12:30–4pm and 8pm–2am. Tram: 25E to R. Saraiva Carvalho. Bus: 74 Rato.

Shopping

Portugal is known for its handicrafts, including exquisite embroideries, decorative glazed tiles, china, fishermen's sweaters, fado recordings, lightweight baskets—and the best buys of all, regional pottery in all types, shapes, and forms. The single best buy in the country is gold, as jewelers are required by law to put in a minimum of 19.2 karats into each piece of jewelry. Many of the ornamental designs of fine gold or silver pieces date from ancient times.

Run by the same family for more than a century, the leading center for silver, gold, and filigree is **W. A. Sarmento,** Rua Aurea 251 (ⓒ **21/347-0783** or 21/342-6774; Metro: Chiado), at the foot of the Santa Justa elevator. The most distinguished silver- and goldsmiths in Portugal, they specialize in lacy filigree jewelry. Also worthy is **Joalharia do Carmo,** Rua do Carmo 87B (ⓒ **21/342-4200**), which sells hand-made silver pieces and even platinum jewelry in stunning designs.

Just for fun, even if you don't buy anything, head for the open-air street market **Feira da Ladra ★★**, the sprawling flea market where Portuguese vendors peddle their wares on Tuesday and Saturday. It's best to go in the morning. One of the best selections of Portuguese baskets and one of the widest displays of regional handcrafts are sold here. The market activity begins about a 5-minute stroll from the Lisbon waterfront as you head into the Alfama sector, beginning your search at Campo de Santa Clara and following your instinctive shopping nose up and down the hilly streets, or take bus no. 12 from the Santa Apolónia station to Campo Sta. Clara.

Unless you have experienced the nostalgic sounds of **fado**, the songs of sorrow, you do not know Portugal—certainly not its soul. Fado is Portugal's most vivid art form; no visit to the country should be planned without at least 1 night spent in a local tavern where this traditional folk music is heard.

A rough translation of *fado* is "fate," from the Latin *fatum*, meaning "prophecy." Fado usually tells of unrequited love, jealousy, and a longing for days gone by. As one expert put it, it speaks of "life commanded by the Oracle, which nothing can change." It's usually sung by females but is also performed by male singers, both known as *fadistas*.

Fado found its earliest fame in the 19th century when Maria Severa, the beautiful daughter of a gypsy, took Lisbon by storm, singing her way into the hearts of the people—and especially the heart of the count of Vimioso, an outstanding bullfighter of his day. Legend has it that she is honored by present-day fadistas, who wear a black-fringed shawl in her memory.

In this century, the most famous exponent of fado has been Amália Rodrigues, who was introduced to American audiences in the 1950s at the New York club La Vie en Rose. She was discovered while walking barefoot and selling flowers on the Lisbon docks, near the Alfama.

Clutching black shawls around themselves, the female *fadistas* pour out their emotions, from the tenderest whisper of hope to a wailing lament of life's tragedies. As they sing, accompanied by a guitar and a viola, standing against a black gas street lamp, without benefit of backdrops or makeup, they seem to lose all contact with the surrounding world—they just stand there, seemingly outdoing the Rhine's Lorelei in drawing you into their world of tenderness and fire. Though much enjoyment can be derived from understanding the poetic imagery, a knowledge of Portuguese is not essential. The power of the lyrics, the warmth of the voices, and the personalities of the singers communicate a great deal.

Fado is sung all over Lisbon and its environs, but the best clubs for this art form include **Adega Machado,** Rua do Norte 91 (© **21/322-4640;** Metro: Est. Carnide; bus: 202 or 726 Carnide Metro), the city's most beloved fado club, where some of the greatest of today's *fadistas* appear. A dinner show starts at 8pm, with music beginning at 9:15pm. Open Tuesday to Sunday; expect to pay 25€ to 30€ for a complete meal.

Another cherished favorite is **A Severa,** Rua das Gaveas 51 (© **21/346-1204;** bus: 1 for night service, 758, or 790 Largo Trindade Coelho), featuring top-notch male and female *fadistas* alternating with folk dancers. You can also dine here on fine regional dishes. Expect to spend at least 36€ per person for a meal with wine. It's open daily from 9pm to 2am.

One of the most famous and enduring clubs in Bairro Alto is **Luso,** Travessa de Queimada 10 (© **21/342-2281**), converted from a vaulted network of 17th-century stables. Great fado shows and good regional food is served, with dinners costing 39€. Dinner (includes a show) is served at 8:30pm daily. For a cover of 25€, including two drinks, you can come just for the second show (10:30pm).

Close to the waterfront and the Alfama, **Parreirinha de Alfama,** Beco do Espirito Santo 1 (© **21/886-8209;** bus: 28 or 745 to Casa Conto), is an old-time cafe that offers one of the purest forms of fado (no folkloric shows here). A favorite since the 1950s, it presents classic fado and serves a good regional dinner for 40€. If you don't want to dine, you pay a modest cover of 15€, which is credited toward your drink bill. Open daily from 8pm to 1am, with music beginning at 9:30pm.

Founded in 1824, **Vista Alegre,** Largo do Chiado 18, in the Chiado district (② **21/ 346-1401;** www.vistaalegreatlantis.com), is the most famous porcelain producer in the country. If you don't see what you want in the main showcase, know that there is a large inventory warehouse at the rear of this two-floor outlet. **Ana Salazar,** Rua do Carmo 87, also in the Chiado district (② **21/347-2289;** www.anasalazar.pt), is the most avant-garde designer of women's clothing in Portugal. Known for her "stretch fabrics," Salazar designs clothes that critics have called "body conscious yet wearable."

Fábrica Viuva Lamego, Largo do Intendente 25, in the Graça district (② **21/ 885-2408;** www.viuvalamego.com), founded in 1879, sells the largest and best selection of tiles and pottery in Lisbon. The tiles are contemporary but based on old Portuguese motifs.

Nightlife

What's On in Lisbon, available at most newsstands, is your best companion for an up-to-the-minute preview of what's going on in the Portuguese capital.

Cultural Lisbon is best showcased at **Teatro Nacional São Carlos,** Rua Serpa Pinto 9 (② **21/325-3045;** www.saocarlos.pt; Metro: Baixa/Chiado; tram: 28 Rua Vítor Cordon), attracting opera and ballet lovers from across the country, its season lasting from mid-September through July. The box office is open Monday to Friday 1 to 7pm; and Saturday, Sunday, and holidays from 1pm to 30 minutes after a show begins. From October to June, concerts and recitals are presented at **Museo da Fundacão Calouste Gulbenkian,** Ave. De Berna 45 (② **21/782-3000;** www. museu.gulbenkian.pt; Metro: Sebastião; bus: 726 or 756 Pç. Espanha/Av. Berna), which stages occasional ballets or jazz concerts as well. Ticket prices vary widely.

To get your evening in Lisbon going, you can head for one of two evocative institutions. **A Brasileira,** Rua Garrett 120 (② **21/346-9541;** Metro: Baixa/Chiado; tram: 28 Chiado; bus: 758 Pç. Luis Camões), in the Chiado district, is the oldest surviving coffeehouse in Lisbon and a tradition since 1905, when it was the gathering place for the city's literati. Sitting here having a demitasse of strong coffee is like wandering back in a time capsule to Lisbon's yesterday. Other than coffee, the most typical drink of Lisbon is port wine, and **Solar do Vinho do Porto,** Rua de São Pedro de Alcântâra 45 (② **21/347-5707;** Metro: Rossio; bus: 758 Elevador Glória), is devoted just to this enticing drink. In a setting from 3 centuries ago, you can peruse the menu of 200 types of port wine—sweet or dry, red or white. It is open daily from 11am to 11:45pm.

If you like a drink with a view, there is no better spot than the aptly named **Panorama Bar,** in the Lisboa Sheraton Hotel, Rua Latino Coelho 1 (② **21/312-0000;** www.sheratonlisboa.com; Metro: Picoas; bus: 30 or 38 Picoas), on the 30th floor. Against the backdrop of a cosmopolitan decor, you can enjoy views over the city and the Tagus. The bar stays open Sunday to Wednesday 12:30pm to 2am, Thursday and Friday from 12:30pm to 3am, Saturday from 6pm to 3am, and Sunday from 6pm to 2am.

The most charming bar of Lisbon is **Procópio,** Alto de São Francisco 21 (② **21/ 385-2851;** www.barprocopio.com; Metro: Rato; bus: 28E Largo Belas Artes), the tired-and-true staple among Lisbon's watering holes, which attracts actors, journalists, and politicos. It's open Monday to Saturday 6pm to 3am.

Lisbon abounds with bars and dance clubs, many offering live music. Another cafe, **Blues Café,** Rua Cintura do Puerto do Lisboa 3–4 (② **21/395-7085;** www.blues cafe.pt; Metro: Alcântara-Mar; bus: 12 Alcântara Mar/Museu Oriente), is also by the

Although we focus more on Portugal's southern region in this chapter (its northern region is really more suited to a driving tour than a rail trip), if you have 3 extra days on your itinerary, you can ride the rails north from Lisbon to experience three widely different jewels in the Portuguese crown: the walled medieval city of **Óbidos,** followed by the ancient university city of **Coimbra,** and topped by several glasses of port wine drunk on home turf in the old city of **Porto** (second largest in Portugal). Unlike the arid but historical plains to the south, these towns and cities lie in lush "Atlantic green" Portugal.

ÓBIDOS

Dominated by the keep and towers of its ancient castle, the walled city of **Óbidos ★★** is only 58 miles (93km) north of Lisbon, but it's a comparatively long train ride away. From the Estaçao do Rossio in Lisbon, frequent daily commuter trains run to the rail junction at Cacém, where you can change trains to Mira Sintra-Melecas (a 5-min. trip) and, from there, head on your final lap into Óbidos. The entire trip takes 2 to 3 hours and costs 8.40€ one-way. The tourist office is located on Rua Direita 87, Aprtado 42 (✆ **262/955-060;** www.rt-oeste.pt).

Óbidos so captivated Queen Isabella in 1228 that her husband, King Denis, presented it to her as a gift, a token of his devotion. You can spend 3 or 4 hours wandering behind its 14th-century castellated walls, viewing the whitewashed houses and old churches, and finding good food and overnight lodging at its converted stone castle, now the

Pousada do Castelo, Paço Real (✆ **28/224-0001;** www.pousadas.pt), which offers 12 air-conditioned rooms and suites. Rates range from 175€ to 275€ double, 257€ to 405€ suite.

COIMBRA

Most rail passengers skip Óbidos and head straight from Lisbon to the romantic city of **Coimbra ★★★**, 123 miles (198km) to the north. Some nine Alfa Pendular high-speed trains per day make the trek of 1 hour and 35 minutes north from Lisbon to Coimbra, at a cost of 22€ to 31€. Urban (2€ one-way) and IC (16€–20€) trains also run from Lisbon to Coimbra.

The birthplace of six kings and the seat of Portugal's oldest university, Coimbra, on the right bank of the Mondego River, is a city rich in attractions—not only its university, but one of the country's greatest Romanesque cathedrals, **Sé Velha,** and a 12th-century Gothic monastery. The renowned 18th-century **Quinta das Lagrimas** (Estate of Tears), or "Garden of Tears," was the former abode of the ill-fated Inês de Castro, mistress of Pedro the Cruel, who was murdered here on order of Pedro's father, King Alfonso IV. The gardens are a favorite pilgrimage spot for romantics, and the house is now the best hotel in the region (see below). The cathedral, a mix of styles ranging from Islamic, Renaissance, and Gothic, is open from 10am to 6pm except Friday when it closes at 4pm. Admission into the cathedral is free, but it costs 1.50€ to visit the cloisters and garden

Stop in at the **Coimbra Tourist Office,** Largo da Portagem (✆ **239/834-158;**

river, with an eagle's nest balcony encircling one floor. The latest hip-hop and garage music is played here every night Tuesday through Saturday.

A two-story warehouse near the Apolónia has been converted into **Lux,** Avenida Infante Don Henrique, Armazém (Warehouse) A, Cais da Pedra a Santa Apolónia (✆ **21/882-08-90;** www.luxfragil.com; bus: 39 or 793 to Azinhaga Das Veigas), on www.turismo-centro.pt), a 5-minute walk from the train station. (**Note:** Many streets are very steep. The bus may be a better option.) You'll be given a map of the town, a list of the monuments with opening hours, and the names of the leading hotels and restaurants. Our favorite place to stay in town is the luxurious and romantic 35-room manor **Quinta das Lagrimas,** Rue Antonio Agusto Gonçalves (✆ **23/980-2380;** www.quintadaslagrimas.pt). The rooms are decorated in traditional Portuguese style but offer every modern comfort. Rates are 169€ to 215€ double, 345€ to 389€ suite.

PORTO

The final stop on your rail journey north is **Porto** ★★, 195 miles (314km) north of Lisbon. A settlement known as Portucale since the 8th century B.C., the town eventually lent its name to the whole country. Once the base of the Portuguese shipping fleet, Porto (literally, "the port") helped Portugal evolve into a great maritime power. Today, however, the city on the Douro River is known mainly for housing the lodges or wine storehouses of the world-famous port wine made across Ponte Dom Luis in the satellite suburb of Vila Nova de Gaia.

The rail traveler can explore some of Porto's notable tourist highlights, including its Romanesque **Sé (Cathedral;** Metro: Linha Amarela D-Sau Bento); its 15th-century church, **Igreja de Santa Clara** (Funicular dos Guindais); its even more impressive 14th-century Gothic **Igreja de São Francisco** (Funicular dos Guindais-Ribeira); and its **Fundaçao de**

Serralves museum (www.serralves.pt; Metro: Casa da Música; connect to buses 201, 203, 502, and 504 in Boavista Rotunda), devoted to modern art. Later in the day, you can take a boat trip up the Douro to sail by the vineyards where the grapes used to make the port are grown.

From Estaçao Santa Apolónia in Lisbon, 11 daily Alfa trains make the trip to Porto. The journey takes about 3 hours and costs 29€ for a one-way ticket. You can also take Urban, Regional, and IC trains. If you spend the night in Coimbra (see above), you can take one of several high-speed trains to Porto (trip time: 1 hr., 10 min.); a one-way ticket costs 16€. Be sure to take a train to the **Estação de Sãu Bento** station (✆ **808/208-208**), which is in the center of town, and not Porto's other rail station, which is south of the city. You may have to transfer to an Urban train to get from Campanha station in Porto to Sãu Bento, which costs 1.50€ and is a 5-minute trip.

For a list of hotels, restaurants, and attractions, stop in at the **Porto Tourist Board,** Rua Clube dos Fenianos 25 (✆ **22/339-3472;** www.portoturismo. pt), just a few minutes' walk from the train station. One good hotel within 5 or 10 minutes' walk of the station is the 149-room **Mercure Batalha Hotel,** Porto Praca da Batalha (✆ **22/204-3300;** www.mercure.com; Metro: Linha Amarela D-Sau Bento). It offers traditional and tastefully decorated rooms. Rates run 67€ to 120€ double, but the hotel often discounts its prices.

the banks of the Tagus. This counterculture joint is filled with hip patrons and cutting-edge music, including both a disco and a bar, with the dance club charging a 15€ cover after midnight. The upstairs bar, where a DJ spins records, is open daily from 10pm to 6am. The more manic, street-level dance floor is open Thursday to Saturday 1 to 7am.

If you'd like to see Sintra the way Lord Byron did when working on his autobiographical *Childe Harold's Pilgrimage*, you can rent a horse-drawn carriage (www.sintratur.com) in front of the National Palace of Sintra at Largo da Rainha Dona Amélia. Carrying up to four passengers, these romantic tours last from 25 minutes to 1½ hours but are worth the price. You'll be following trails blazed by Moorish sultans centuries ago along bougainvillea-lined streets, and can look up at little balconies aflame with red geraniums. Once you've gotten the view the carriage ride has shown you, you can wander about making your own discoveries. Prices have fixed rates, ranging from 30€ to 90€.

One of the most popular watering holes is **Frágil,** Rua da Atalaia 126–128 (© 21/346-95-78; www.fragil.com.pt; Metro: Chiado; bus: 1 for night service or 758 Largo Trindade Coelho). All you'll see are some blue neon lights and a vigilant doorman. Frágil devotes itself to counterculture music, gay men and women, and a scattering of heterosexuals who appreciate the cutting-edge music and permissive atmosphere. Technically, the place opens Tuesday to Saturday at 11:30pm, but don't expect a crowd until at least midnight—and a mob by around 2am. Closing is around 4am the following morning.

In a former factory and warehouse beside the river, **Bar of the Café Alcántara,** Rua Maria Luisa Holstein 15 (© 21/362-1226; www.alcantaracafe.com; bus: 1 or 28 Alcântara Mar), evokes a railway car in turn-of-the-20th-century Paris. The club is a lot of fun and caters to gay, straight, and everything in between.

An Excursion to Sintra

To Lord Byron, it was a "glorious Eden." To today's visitor, it is the single most rewarding day trip from any city within Portugal. Once a favorite summer retreat of Portuguese kings, Sintra is set among freshwater springs, wooded ravines, and lush vegetation of exotic trees and shrubs. In the blistering summer months, Sintra is a cool mountain retreat, especially in the evening.

The natural beauty of this land, located 18 miles (29km) northwest of Lisbon, is enhanced by country manor houses, cobbled streets, horse-drawn carriages, and national palaces. In 1995, UNESCO recognized its charm by naming it a World Heritage Site.

GETTING THERE   Urban trains (Urbanos de Lisboa–Linha de Sintra) depart from Estação do Rossio (p. 634) from tracks 4 and 5, leaving every 15 to 30 minutes daily from 6am to 11pm. The trip time is 45 minutes, and a one-way ticket costs 1.75€. Trains arrive in Sintra (last stop) at **Estação de Caminhos de Ferro,** Avenida Dr. Miguel Bombarda (© 808/208-208). The station is ¾ mile (1.1km) downhill from the center of town. Buses run frequently back and forth; the fare is 2.10€. A taxi into town costs 6€ for up to four passengers. For more information, call © 808/208-208.

TOURIST INFORMATION   The **Sintra Tourist Office** is at Praça da República 23 (© 21/923-1157), in the center of town. From June to September, it is open daily 9am to 8pm, October to May daily 9am to 7pm.

TOP ATTRACTIONS & SPECIAL MOMENTS

Even those on the most rushed of schedules try to budget time to see two of Portugal's greatest palaces. **Palacio Nacional de Sintra ★★★**, Largo da Rainha Dona Amélia (***C*** **21/910-6840** or 21/910-6841; http://pnsintra.imc-ip.pt/), was a royal palace until 1910, when the Portuguese monarchy fled town in the face of revolution. In the heart of *Sintra Vila*, the Old Town, the landmark structure is dominated by a pair of conical chimneys rising above it. Much of it was constructed by João I in the late 1300s and built upon the site of a palace constructed by Moorish sultans that had been torn down. A favorite summer retreat of Portuguese royalty, it has seen much rebuilding and enlarging over the years, and the building is now an interesting conglomeration of architectural styles. Inside, the domed ceiling of **Sala does Brasões (Stag Room) ★** makes for a splendid salon. Stags hold the coats-of-arms of nearly 75 Portuguese noble families, and the lower walls are lined with Delft-like tiled panels from the 1700s. The other splendid chamber is the **Sala dos Cisnes (Swan Room) ★** of the former banquet hall, painted in the 17th century. This room was a favorite of King João I, the father of Prince Henry the Navigator. The ceiling was covered with magpies, a reference to the gossipy ladies of the courts. The Room of the Sirens or Mermaids is one of the most elegant in the palace. It's decorated with intricate Arabesque designs. Admission is 7€ for adults, 3€ for children 15 to 25 and seniors over 65, free for kids under 14. Open Thursday to Tuesday 10am to 1pm and 2 to 5pm. Free admission on Sunday and holidays.

The other great palace in Sintra is **Palacio Nacional de Pena ★★**, Estrada de Pena (***C*** **21/910-5340;** www.parquesdesintra.pt), standing on a plateau of 1,476 feet (443m) above sea level on one of the loftiest peaks in the Serra de Sintra mountain chain. Built in the 19th century, the palace is a blend of various architectural styles and was the royal abode of the young queen Maria II and her husband, Ferdinand Saxe-Coburg-Gotha. Ferdinand took charge of the building, appointing Baron Von Eschwege, a German architect, to construct this cool summer place for the royal family. It's set on parklike grounds and is a monument to a faded royal life. Allow 2 hours to tour the whole place, including the oval-shaped bedroom (adorned with bright red walls) of Manuel II, the last king of Portugal. Decorated with German stained-glass windows, the elegant **Ballroom ★** is a major highlight, with its Asian porcelain and life-size torchbearers supporting a mammoth candelabra. The **Arab Room ★** is a stunner, with its magnificent *trompe l'oeil* frescoes.

The notable **Chapel Altarpiece ★** is from the 16th century and is made of alabaster and marble, each niche depicting a scene from the life of Christ. If time remains, explore the gardens.

Admission is 11€ for adults, 9€ children 6 to 17 years old, 9€ adults 65 and older, and free for children 5 and under. The palace is open June to September Tuesday to Sunday from 10am to 6:30pm, October to May Tuesday to Sunday 10am to 4:30pm.

WHERE TO DINE

In the hillside village right below Sintra, **Cantinho de São Pedro,** Praça Dom Fernando II 18 (***C*** **21/923-0267**), is known for its savory French- and Portuguese-inspired cuisine, and is found right off the main square of this little satellite to Sintra. Daily specials, *pratos do dia,* are some of the finest fare in the area, and the menu always offers something enticing, perhaps salmon and shrimp au gratin or pork with an unusual mixture of clams. Main courses cost about 20€ per person, with a fixed-price three-course meal going for 60€. Open daily noon to 3pm and 7:30 to 10pm.

Uphill from the Praça de República in Sintra, **Tacho Real ★★**, Rua da Ferraria 4 (℃ **21/923-5277**), serves well-prepared Portuguese and French meals in a stylish setting reached after climbing some steep steps. Both meat and fish dishes are handled equally well by a well-trained staff. The fish stew is the best in the area, and the fixed-price menu is one of Sintra's dining bargains. Main courses cost 13€ to 30€. Open Thursday to Tuesday noon to 3pm and 7:30 to 10:30pm.

THE ALGARVE

This strip of beachfront property is a great amphitheater facing the sea, stretching for 100 miles (160km) from Cape St. Vincent of Prince Henry the Navigator fame to the border town of Vila Real de Santo António overlooking the Spanish frontier. Called *Al-Gharb* by the Moorish conquerors, the Algarve is celebrated for the pink blossoms of its almond trees in bloom from the middle of January until the end of February.

Fishing is still a buoyant source of income for this region, although nearly all the coast has been given over to tourism. Those lonely beaches backed up by tiny, whitewashed fishing hamlets are getting harder and harder to find as developers take over. The Algarve consists of two sections. The *barlavento* lying to the west of Portimão is a coastal strip—mainly a rock-strewn coast—that is humid and has cliffs rising 246 feet (74m), with sandy shores and hidden coves often separated by strange grottoes. East of Faro (the capital), the *sotavento* is riddled with salty lagoons, sandy dunes, and broken spits of beaches filled mainly with European sunbathers from June to October.

Lagos and Faro are the best base cities in the Algarve for train travelers because both offer easy rail access to Lisbon.

Getting There

Faro, 192 miles (309km) southeast of Lisbon, is the rail hub of the Algarve, with IC and AP trains departing daily from Lisbon. The trip takes 3 hours, and a one-way ticket costs from 19€ to 21€, depending on whether you take an IC or AP train. If you're connecting with Lagos in the west, trains make the 2-hour journey out of Faro each day. Only Regional trains make the trip, and fares cost 5.90€ one-way.

Estación Faro, Largo da Estaçao (℃ **808/208-208**), lies near the town center, adjacent to the bus station and close to the intersection of Avenida de República and Praça de Estação. Built as an architectural showcase in the 1890s, but dimmed by age, it is the most important and strategic rail junction in the south of Portugal, thanks to its position astride lines that interconnect it to the north-south lines from Lisbon and the east-west lines from Vila Real in the east and Lagos in the west. Faro is Portugal's second-most-used railway transfer point after Lisbon.

There are no tourist offices within the station, but the **Faro Tourist Office,** Rua da Misericórdia 8–12 (℃ **28/980-3604**; www.visitalgarve.pt), is just a few minutes' walk away. It's open June to August daily 9:30am to 7pm, September to May daily 9:30am to 5:30pm. The staff does not make hotel reservations but will provide data about what lodging is available (what's cheap, what's luxurious, and so on). Although there is no ATM at the station, there are banks along Avenida de Rua de Santo António and Avenida de República, all a short walk from the station. For luggage storage, you'll have to go next door to the bus station, which doesn't store bags for more than 24 hours. Depending on size, the cost is from 2€ to 4€ per bag. Note that the kiosk here isn't staffed on Saturday and Sunday. Taxis line up outside the rail station, with fares to most points within the environs of Faro ranging from 6.50€ to 21€.

The Algarve

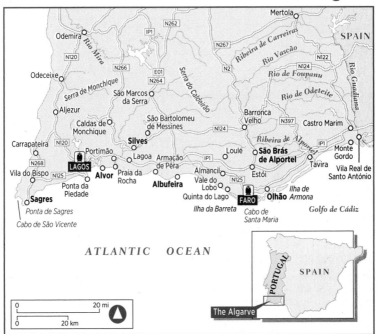

Caminho Ferro Portugues, Largo da Estação (© 808/208-208; www.cp.pt), is the second major rail hub for the Algarve. It's in Lagos, 43 miles (69km) west of Faro and 164 miles (264km) south of Lisbon. The station, in the eastern part of Lagos, is reached via a pedestrian suspension bridge, and is about 2,100 feet (630m) from the town's main square at Praça Gil Eanes. From Lisbon, take an Algarve-bound train to the junction at Tunes, where a change of trains will take you south all the way to Lagos. Three IC trains run from Lisbon to Lagos, taking 4 hours and costing 21€ one-way. There are also two daily ALFA trains going from Lisbon to Lagos in 3 hours and 40 minutes, costing 25€ one-way. From Faro, only Regional trains run to Lagos, taking 1½ hours and costing 5.90€. Faro is the westernmost terminus of rail lines that stretch east to west across the Algarve. Points farther west, including Sagres, require access by bus from either Lagos or Faro.

There are no ATMs within the station, but there are a number of them along Avenida dos Descobrimentos, one of the city's busiest and most visible avenues, just a short walk away. The bus station is directly across the street; neither station offers luggage storage. Taxis are available at the entrance to the station; it will cost about 5€ to 17€ to go virtually anywhere within Lagos.

There is no tourist office within the station. The **Lagos Tourist Office,** Rua Belchior Moreira de Barbudo, Sítio de São João, Lagos (© 28/276-30-31; www.visit algarve.pt), is open daily 9:30am to 1pm and 2 to 5:30pm. If you need to book a hotel, try **PDM Travel,** Rua Victor Costa e Silva, 15–Loja F (© 28/278-2078; www.pdm travel.net); fees are based on the type of booking you make, and the staff speaks English.

Top Attractions & Special Moments

Other than the beaches, the chief man-made attractions in the Algarve lie within the towns of Faro and Lagos. The exception to this is **Sagres** ★, or "The End of the World," lying 21 miles (34km) west of Lagos and 71 miles (114km) west of Faro. At the extreme southwestern corner of Europe, it is a rocky escarpment jutting into the Atlantic Ocean. It was from this remote point that Prince Henry the Navigator launched Portugal onto the seas of exploration, establishing a school where mariners such as Vasco da Gama, Magellan, Diaz, and Cabral apprenticed. We find the sunsets here among the most dramatic in Europe. Ancient mariners thought that when the sun sank from here beyond the cape, it plunged over the edge of the world.

Henry's windswept fortress, **Fortaleza de Sagres,** Ponte de Sagres (✆ **28/262-0140**), has been reconstructed and turned into a small museum documenting the area's naval history. It's open May to September daily from 9:30am to 8pm; October to April daily from 9:30am to 5:30pm. Admission is 3€ for adults, 1.50€ for ages 15 to 25, and free for children 14 and under. Far more dramatic than this man-made attraction are the surrounding pathways that open onto vertigo-inducing panoramas of the turbulent sea and towering cliffs.

Lying 3 miles (4.8km) to the west is the lonely **Cabo de São Vicente,** with the second-most-powerful lighthouse in Europe. This lighthouse beams illumination 62 miles (100km) across the ocean. Tours of the actual lighthouse are not generally available. To reach the cape, you can take a bus Monday through Friday, leaving from Rua Comandante Matos near the tourist office. Trip time is 10 minutes, and departures are at 11:15am, 12:30, and 6pm; a one-way ticket costs 2€.

Lagos ★, your rail hub for the western Algarve, is also the principal resort of the western Algarve, opening onto Baia de Lagos, one of the widest bays of the Portuguese coast. You can spend a morning or an afternoon exploring its attractions, including **Antigo Mercado de Escravos,** Praça do Infante Dom Henríques, an arcaded slave market, the only one of its kind in Europe. Captives were once sold here to the highest bidder. It can be viewed at any time, and admission is free.

Sitting just off the waterfront is the 18-century church, **Igreja de Santo António** ★, Rua General Alberto Carlos Silveira (✆ **28/276-2301**). This church is a real Algarvian gem, its lower part covered with the blue-and-white tiles, or *azulejos,* of Portugal. The rest is in carved, painted, or gilded wood. A series of eight paneled paintings depict so-called miracles performed by Saint Anthony. At the altar are impressive **gilt carvings** ★ created with gold imported from Brazil. Admission is 2€

adults, 1€ students and seniors 65 and older; children 11 and under are free. Hours are Tuesday to Sunday 9:30am to 12:30pm and 2 to 5pm.

Next door to the church of Saint Anthony stands the **Museu Municipal Dr. José Formosinho,** Rua General Alberto Carlos Silveira (② **28/276-2301**), the regional museum of the western Algarve. Of particular interest here are the replicas of the fret-cut chimneys of the Algarve, with exhibitions of various regional handcrafts and artifacts ranging from ecclesiastical sculpture to a numismatic collection. Pickled freak animals are among its more exotic attractions, and there's even a funky pair of 19th-century sunglasses. Admission is 3€ for adults, 2€ for students (not college age), and free for children under 12. Hours are Tuesday to Sunday 9:30am to 12:30pm and 2 to 5pm, and it is closed on holidays.

The capital city of **Faro** is a bit lean on man-made attractions. If you're caught between trains, you can occupy 2 to 3 hours of time by visiting such sights as **Igreja de Nossa Senhora do Monte do Carmo do Faro,** Largo do Carmo (② **28/982-4490**), erected in the 19th century. The church could be easily skipped were it not for its bizarre **Capela d'Ossos,** or "Chapel of Bones." The chapel is lined with an estimated 1,245 human skulls and bones. These bones were dug up from graves around the church in 1816. Entrance to the chapel costs 1€. It's open 10am to 2pm and 3 to 5:30pm.

The **Sé (Cathedral),** Largo da Sé (② **28/989-8300**), the major cathedral for the Algarve, should be more impressive than it is. Nonetheless, it merits 30 minutes or so of your time. This Renaissance cathedral took the tower of its Gothic predecessor, and its wide nave is flanked by *azulejos* from the 18th-century. Its chief attraction is its Capela do Rosário, which is loaded with *azulejos* from the 17th-century. Admission is 2€, and the building is open daily 10am to 5:30pm.

Infante Dom Henrique Archaeological Museum/Monastery of Nossa Senhora da Assunção, Largo Dom Afonso III 14 (② **28/989-7400**), is housed in the 16th-century edifice of the former Convento de Nossa Senhora da Assuncão (Our Lady of the Assumption). Artifacts recovered from the Algarve are on display in the cloister galleries, with some intriguing sights—including a tomb—excavated at nearby Milreu, where the Romans built a temple dedicated to Ossonoba in the 1st century A.D. Other displays include Mudéjar tiles from the Muslim era, ancient weapons and coins, and a 16th-century bishop's throne. Admission is 2€ adults, 3€ for children ages 13 to 18, and free for 12 and under. Students, seniors 65 and older, and ages 26 and under cost 1€. Open in winter Tuesday to Friday 11:30am to 6pm, summer daily 10am to 7pm.

Where to Stay & Dine

A good choice for Lagos-bound travelers is the 324-room **Tivoli Lagos ★**, Rua António Crisógano dos Santos, Lagos 8600-678 (② **28/279-0079;** http://tivoli hotels.com), the town's leading hostelry, housed in a 20th-century castle of Moorish and Portuguese design that's set within its own ramparts and moats. Removed from the beach, the hotel lies at the eastern side of town and has its own pool, all on 3 acres (1.2 hectares) of prime hilltop real estate. Both standard and deluxe rooms are rented, and each is well maintained and attractively furnished. Doubles range from 57€ to 150€, depending on the season, with suites going for 81€ to 200€. All rates include breakfast.

Down the scale a bit, but still very inviting, is the 36-room **Albergaria Marina Rio,** Avenida dos Descobrimentos, Lagos 8600-645 (② **28/278-0830;** www. marinario.com), in the very heart of Lagos opposite the marina. Its most dramatic feature is a panoramic top-floor swimming pool with a broad sun terrace. A courtesy bus takes guests to the beaches. Bedrooms are neatly kept and range in size from small to medium, with doubles averaging 75€ without a harbor view and 85€ with a harbor view; rates include a buffet breakfast.

For the finest lodgings in the Lagos area, head over to **Romantik Hotel Vivenda Miranda ★★★**, Porto de Mos, Lagos 8600-282 (*C* **28/276-3222;** www.vivenda miranda.com), a Moorish-inspired hotel standing on a cliff that opens onto the rugged coastline, 1¾ miles (2.8km) south of Lagos, close to a good sandy beach at Praia do Porto de Mos. The hotel offers well-furnished and somewhat stylish bedrooms ranging from midsize to spacious, and its outdoor pool opens onto lush gardens and sun terraces. Doubles rent for 150€ to 200€, with a suite costing 1160€ to 240€, depending on the time of year you go.

Even though it's a bit uninspired, **Eva Hotel ★**, Avenida da República, Faro 8000-078 (*C* **28/900-1000;** www.tdhotels.pt), is the best of the lodgings in the capital city of Faro. This modern eight-floor, 148-room hotel stands at the harborfront, not at the beach, but offers a rooftop swimming pool. Bedrooms are furnished in a restrained style, the finer accommodations containing balconies opening onto the water. Doubles range from 102€ to 165€, with suites from 145€ to 225€; all rates include buffet breakfast. The best overnight value in town is found at **Hotel Sol Algarve ★**, Rua Infante Dom Henrique 62, Faro 8000-363 (*C* **28/989-5700;** www.hotelsolalgarve. com), which opened in 1999, having been created out of an 1880s private home that was once owned by a local mariner. Before it became a hotel, it had to be practically demolished but was reconstructed in the original style. The hotel, only a short walk from the center of town, offers midsize to spacious bedrooms, each well furnished. Rates range from 45€ to 75€ for a double and 60€ to 90€ for a triple.

In the very heart of Lagos, the undiscovered **A Lagosteira,** Rua do 1 de Maio 20 (*C* **28/276-2486**), is one of the best restaurants in town, serving seafood and regional Portuguese cuisine with an Algarvian slant. We always gravitate to this place for our first meal in town, devouring the fish soup and the savory clams—lobster is also a specialty. Main courses cost from 10€ to 25€. Another local favorite is **Ristorante Don Sebastião ★**, Rua do 25 de Abril 20–22 (*C* **28/278-0480;** www. restaurantedonsebastiao.com), which serves savory Portuguese and Algarvian cuisine that's an equal match for the food dished out at A Lagosteira. It, too, is in the heart of town, lying to the west of the main waterfront, bordering Avenida dos Descobrimentos on the opposite bank from the rail station. The menu is varied and tasty, with a good selection of local wines. In summer, there's outdoor dining. Main courses cost from 16€ to 90€, and it is open daily from noon to 10pm.

The greatest restaurants in the Algarve are not found in Faro, but you are likely to find yourself here because it's a rail hub. Don't despair, as you can order hearty, typical Algarvian cuisine at **Adega Nortenha,** Praça Ferreira de Almeida 25 (*C* **28/982-2709;** www.adeganortenha.pt), in the heart of the city and convenient to bus and rail connections. The restaurant's regional dishes, such as bits of seafood cooked with chunks of pork in a casserole, also make it one of the most affordable bargains in town, with main courses costing 10€ to 12€. It is open daily from noon to 3pm and 7 to 10pm. A tradition since 1925, **Restaurante Marisqueira "Dois Irmãos,"** Largo do Terreiro do Bispo 13–15 (*C* **28/982-3337**), is a modest but a good choice for its Algarvian cuisine of freshly grilled fish and shellfish dishes—most likely the catch was harvested that morning. Service is slow, but it's worth the wait. Main courses cost about 15€.

SPAIN

Riding the rails in Spain is a grand adventure that offers travelers an ideal way to see one of the most diverse landscapes in Europe—from the snowcapped peaks surrounding Granada and the rivers enveloping Toledo to the Moorish-flavored Andalusia to the modern artistry of Catalonia. Traveling through Spain by rail is the cheapest way to see the country—especially if you opt for a railpass—and a relatively inexpensive venture when compared to train travel in other Western European countries. Value-conscious travelers looking for a diverse destination without sacrificing comfort will be hard-pressed to find a better choice on the Continent.

The most economical way to travel in Spain is on Spanish State Railways (RENFE), the national railway of Spain. Most main long-distance connections are served with night express trains, having first- or second-class seats as well as beds and bunks. There are also comfortable high-speed daytime trains of the Euromed, Altaria, and AVE types. You pay a general fare for these trains; bunks, beds, and certain superior-quality trains cost extra. Spain is crisscrossed with a comprehensive network of rail lines. Hundreds of trains depart every day for points around the country, including the newer, faster AVE trains, which reduced rail time between Madrid and Barcelona to only 3 hours or less.

Highlights of Spain

Every major region of Spain, from the Basque country in the northeast to the southern cities of Andalusia, such as Granada and Seville, is within hours of **Madrid** by rail. The capital of Spain is at the geographical center of the country and is the hub of all its major rail networks. Madrid makes the best base for a rail tour of Spain because you can branch out to virtually anywhere in the country.

The country's second major rail transportation hub, **Barcelona,** is in the remote northeast of the country and is a long way from some of Spain's frequently visited cities, such as Toledo. Barcelona is a good launching pad for rail travelers only if they are coming from the east, through the south of France, or are flying first into Barcelona to begin their rail journey.

Madrid's attractions are year-round, including three internationally famous art galleries—**the Prado, Centro de Arte Reina Sofia,** and **Museo Thyssen–Bornemisza**—along with a royal palace, grand public squares, and museum after museum stuffed with treasures. Its 17th-century square, **Plaza Mayor,** lies at the focal point of Madrid's historic core. While in Madrid, be sure to budget a 1-day trip by rail to **Toledo,** the capital of old Castile and one of the five most fascinating cities of Spain.

After seeing Madrid, most rail passengers head south to Andalusia, specifically Seville. Those with an extra 2 or 3 days to spare, however, can continue to take train rides from Madrid to several art cities that lie on its doorstep. In just 2 hours (or less on a high-speed train) you can travel 54 miles (87km) northwest of Madrid to **Segovia.** If you leave early enough from Madrid, you can visit Segovia's Cabildo Catédral de Segovia, the last Gothic cathedral built in Spain (1515), and its fabled Alcázar, dating from the 12th century. Although it would be a long day, you can return to Madrid by nightfall. Another long day trip from Madrid is to the walled city of **Avila,** 68 miles (109km) northwest of Madrid. Some two dozen trains leave daily from Madrid for Avila, taking 1½ to 2 hours each way. The main attraction in this city forever linked to St. Teresa, born here in 1515, are the medieval walls, averaging 33 feet (9.9m) tall.

An even longer day trip out of Madrid (2½ hr.) is an excursion to the ancient university city of **Salamanca,** 127 miles (204km) northwest of Madrid. Labeled a World Heritage City by UNESCO, Salamanca's major attractions, including its Plaza Mayor (the most beautiful in Spain) and both its old and new cathedrals, can be visited in 3 hours.

Although the city of **Bilbao,** capital of the Basque country, is a popular tourist destination now that its Guggenheim Museum has opened, a train ride here from Madrid takes 5 hours, making it somewhat inconvenient for rail travelers with limited time on their hands. The same goes for the sea resort of San Sebastian and for the medieval city of Pamplona, made famous by its running of the bulls.

It's far easier for rail travelers to head south, and we concentrate on options in that area of the country. From Madrid, high-speed trains rush you south to the vast sprawling lands of Andalusia, which takes up the southern tip of Spain, opening onto the Mediterranean. This once-great stronghold of Muslim Spain is rich in history and tradition, containing some of the country's most celebrated treasures: the world-famous Mezquita (mosque) in Córdoba, the Alhambra in Granada, and the great Gothic cathedral in Seville. It also has many smaller towns just waiting to be discovered—Ubeda, Jaén, gorge-split Ronda, Jerez de la Frontera, and the gleaming white port city of Cádiz. Give Andalusia at least a week, and you'll still have only skimmed the surface.

This dry, mountainous region also embraces the overbuilt and often tacky Costa del Sol (Málaga, Marbella, and Torremolinos), or Sun Coast, a strip of beach resorts that's popular with Europeans, but one that we suggest skipping.

Seville, the capital of Andalusia, is of major interest to the rail traveler, as this city ranks along with Madrid, Barcelona, and Toledo as one of the five most visited—and justifiably so—cities of Spain.

On the banks of Río Guadalquivir, Seville flourished under Muslim rule and again in the 16th century. Many architectural treasures remain from those epochs, including a celebrated cathedral, which contains the tomb of Columbus, and **La Giralda,** the minaret of a mosque constructed from 1184 to 1198. This is Spain's most perfect Islamic building. Seville's **Barrio de Santa Cruz,** or medieval Jewish quarter, is alone worth the train ride from Madrid, with its tangle of quaint and winding streets. Because of the sultry climate, July and August are the worst months to visit here.

AVE trains leave anywhere from every 15 minutes to every hour to make the 45-minute trip from Seville to the historic city of **Córdoba** each day. A visit to the city's famous mosque is one no traveler will likely forget.

After a visit to Seville, passengers wanting to see the world-famous **Alhambra,** a palace left over from the days of Moorish occupation, can take one of four trains heading east from Seville. The journey takes you along one of Andalusia's most scenic train rides into the snowcapped Sierra Nevada mountains before reaching the palace's home, the city of **Granada.** After Granada, a traditional rail tour of Spain heads northeast to **Barcelona,** although this is a long journey that will take 11 to 13 hours, depending on the train. If you leave from Seville, AVE trains cut down the journey to 5½ hours.

Barcelona, the capital of Catalonia, is one of the busiest ports in the Mediterranean. In culture, business, and sports, it rivals Madrid and is on par with many of the distinguished capitals of Europe. Barcelona is known for its **Las Ramblas,** the most famous street in Spain, alive at all hours, and for the architecture of Gaudí, best represented by his unfinished masterpiece, **Sagrada Familia,** a cathedral. In the heart of town, the evocative **Barri Gotic,** or Gothic quarter, is reason enough to visit the city, crowned by the 14th-century **Barcelona Cathedral.** Historical monuments and museums, including one dedicated to Picasso, abound here, but the city is celebrated for the scores of structures in its Eixample District, left over from the artistic explosion of *modernista.*

One of the biggest draws on Spain's cultural calendar, **ARCO** (Madrid's International Contemporary Art Fair) showcases the best in contemporary art from Europe and America. At the Nuevo Recinto Ferial Juan Carlos I, the exhibition brings together galleries from throughout Europe, the Americas, Australia, and Asia, who showcase the works of regional and internationally known artists. To buy tickets, contact Parque Ferial Juan Carlos I at ☎ **90-222-15-15.** The cost is between 32€ and 63€. You can get schedules from the tourist office closer to the event. Dates vary, but it's usually held mid-February. For more information, call ☎ **91-722-3000,** or visit **www.ifema.es**.

The **Feria de Sevilla (Seville Fair)** is the most celebrated week of revelry in all of Spain, with all-night flamenco dancing, entertainment booths, bullfights, horseback riding, flower-decked coaches, and dancing in the streets. The action takes place the second week after Easter, and you'll need to reserve a hotel well in advance. For general information and exact festival dates, contact the Office of Tourism in Seville (☎ **95-421-00-05**).

Madrileños run wild during the 10-day **Fiesta de San Isidro** celebration honoring their city's patron saint. Food fairs, Castilian folkloric events, street parades, parties, music, dances, bullfights, and other festivities mark the occasion, which starts the second week of May. Make hotel reservations early. Expect crowds and traffic (and beware of pickpockets). For information, contact the **Oficina Municipal de Información y Turismo,** Plaza Mayor 3, 28014 Madrid (☎ **91-366-54-77;** www.munimadrid.es).

After Barcelona, rail passengers can either fly out of the city or continue by train up the rugged coastline, **Costa Brava,** and into France.

ESSENTIALS

Getting There

The major gateway cities for international and domestic flights into Spain are Barcelona and Madrid. Madrid's international airport, **Barajas** (☎ **91-305-8343**), lies 9 miles (14km) east of the center and has two terminals—one for international flights, the other for domestic traffic. The airport for Barcelona is **El Prat de Llobregat,** Prat de Llobregat (☎ **93-298-3838**), about 7½ miles (12km) southwest of the city. The official website for all of Spain's airports is www.aena.es.

Iberia Airlines (☎ **800/772-4642;** www.iberia.com) offers more routes into and within Spain than any other airline. It features daily nonstop service to Madrid from such North American cities as New York, Chicago, and Miami. **Air Europa** (☎ **011-34-902-401-501;** www.aireuropa.com) is Iberia's chief Spanish-based competitor, serving Madrid from New Jersey's Newark Airport, with continuing service to major cities in Spain.

Note: Barcelona-bound passengers often land in Madrid, which is linked by Iberia flights departing at frequent intervals during peak hours on weekdays. Iberia flights also leave Madrid frequently for Seville, which is the gateway air city to Andalusia.

Other North American carriers with direct service to Spain include **American Airlines** (© 800/433-7300; www.aa.com), **Delta** (© 800/211-1212; www.delta.com), **Continental Airlines** (© 800/231-0856; www.continental.com), and **AmericaWest/US Airways** (© 800/622-1015; www.usairways.com).

United Airlines (© 800/241-6522; www.ual.com) does not fly into Spain directly, but offers airfares from the United States to Spain in conjunction with a host of European airlines.

Spain by Rail

PASSES

Both the **Eurail Global Pass** and **Eurail Global Pass Flexi** are good for use on Spanish trains. See chapter 2 for more details on these and other multicountry passes.

Spain also has its own national railpasses, all issued by **RENFE.** For information on train fares, schedules, and destinations, contact RENFE (© **90-224-02-02;** www.renfe.es) or Rail Europe (© **877/272-RAIL** [7245] in North America; www.raileurope.com). Children 4 to 11 pay approximately half the adult fare, and tots under 4 ride free. For train tickets, go to the principal office of RENFE in Madrid at Alcalá 44 (© **90-224-02-02** or 90-224-34-02; Metro: Banco de España), open Monday to Friday 9:30am to 11:30pm.

Warning: If you purchase a round-trip ticket in Spain, you must hang on to both parts of the ticket until you've completed your entire journey, or you might be fined severely when the conductor comes around to check tickets on your return leg.

The only trains in Spain not run by RENFE are a few narrow-gauge lines, such as the one from Barcelona to Montserrat and the lines along the north coast of Spain; these do not accept railpasses.

The **Eurail Spain Pass** offers 3 to 10 days of unlimited train travel within a 2-month period, with a choice of both first- and second-class travel. First-class travel costs $248 for 3 days or $505 for 10 days; second class, $198 for 3 days or $404 for 10 days. The **Eurail Spain–Portugal Pass** also allows 3 to 10 days of unlimited first-class travel in both Spain and Portugal. In first class, the cost is $284 for 3 days or $548 for 10 days.

The **Eurail Spain Rail 'n Drive** pass combines 3 to 10 days of unlimited first- or second-class train travel and 2 days in your own rental car, costing $387 to $576 per person, depending on the car. Reductions are granted if two adults travel together.

The two most popular countries in Europe with American travelers, Spain and France, are combined in the **Eurail France 'n Spain Pass,** offering 4 to 10 days of unlimited train travel in a 2-month period, with a choice of first- or second-class seats. For 4 days, the cost is $335 per person in first class or $286 in second class. Discounts apply when two or more adults travel together.

All railpasses should be purchased in North America before you depart for Europe. Passes can be ordered in North America through **Rail Europe** (© **877/272-RAIL** [7245]; www.raileurope.com) or your travel agent.

FOREIGN TRAIN TERMS

All stations in Spain post train timetables, *llegadas* indicating arrivals and *salidas* designating departures. For other information, ask at a ticket window, or *taquilla.* Nearly all long-distance trains *(largo recorrido)* offer first- and second-class tickets, the slowest (also the least expensive) of these being the *regionales.*

Regular long-distance interregional trains are known as *diurnos*. When these trains travel at night, they become *estrellas*. Talgos (Tren Articulado Ligero Giocoechea Oriol) are the fastest, most expensive, and also the most comfortable trains in Spain. Talgos stop only at major cities, not outposts. The classic and best version is a **Talgo 200,** featuring both a standard *turista* class and a luxurious *preferente* class. The high-speed train between Madrid and Seville/Barcelona is called AVE. Other high-speed trains include the Alvia, Alaria, Altaria, Avant, and Euromed. Bigger cities such as Madrid have trains making short runs, and these local networks are called *cercanias*.

PRACTICAL TRAIN INFORMATION

The most comfortable and the fastest trains in Spain are the **Euromed, AVE, Alaris, Altaria, Alvia,** and **Avant** trains.

For speed, style, and a flexible schedule, stick to the fast AVE trains linking Barcelona with Madrid. The two most important cities of Andalusia, Seville and Granada, are linked by TRD trains (Regional Diesel Trains), incorporating the latest technology in the field of diesel engines. TRD trains require reservations.

If you're on a strict budget, opt for second-class seats on trains; they are reasonably comfortable and usually well maintained.

RESERVATIONS Reservations are a very good idea in Spain if you're traveling on holidays, on Friday afternoons, or on Sunday nights. Reservations are required for all fast and long-distance trains, and are required for passengers who book couchettes or sleeper accommodations. Only slow regional and local trains do not require reservations. All reservations should be made as far in advance as possible. Unless you're fluent in Spanish and can navigate RENFE's website, the best way to make reservations in advance of your trip is through Rail Europe. The cost of these advance reservations is built into the ticket price. Prices also vary depending on whether you pay by cash or credit card and whether you have a railpass. It's a confusing situation, best discussed on an individual basis with a Rail Europe reservations agent.

If you're traveling on the same day you purchase your ticket and need a reservation, go to the window marked VENTA IMMEDIATA. For future travel, head for the window called VENTA ANTICIPADA. Expect long lines at either window. Sometimes you'll have to take a number from a vending machine and watch for that number to appear on a digital display board. Before leaving the window, be certain that the *fecha* (date) and the *hora salida* (departure time) are correct on your reservation. Railpass validation can also be made at any of these designated windows. For both regular ticket holders and passholders, standard seat reservations start at 9.55€ per passenger for both adults and children and are nonrefundable. Reservation prices for more luxurious trains can be higher, beginning at 14€ per passenger.

SERVICES & AMENITIES If you're taking a long-distance night train—called an *estrella*—you can see if a *Trenhotel* (train hotel) option is available for you. These are clean sleeping compartments with their own shower and toilet. Advance reservations are absolutely essential for one of these compartments.

Based on distance, sleeper fares—in addition to the regular ticket—cost a minimum of $40 and a maximum of $200 for a one-person compartment; it's 19€ to 175€ per passenger for double accommodations; and couchette reservations cost a flat 24€ per person. Reservations can be confirmed up to 2 months prior to the date of travel, but are nonrefundable and nonexchangeable.

Trains & Travel Times in Spain

From	To	Type of Train	# of Trains	Frequency	Travel Time
Madrid	Barcelona	AVE	25	Daily	2 hr., 35 min.
Madrid	Córdoba	AVE	21	Daily	1 hr., 42 min.
Madrid	Córdoba	Altaria	5	Daily	2 hr., 5 min.–2 hr., 9 min.
Madrid	Seville	AVE	19	Daily	2 hr., 30 min.
Madrid	Seville	Altaria	2	Daily	3 hr., 12 min.
Madrid	Algeciras	Altaria	2	Daily	5 hr., 50 min.
Madrid	Malaga	AVE	12	Daily	2 hr., 30 min.
Madrid	Granada	Altaria	2	Daily	4 hr., 32 min.
Seville	Granada	T.R.D.	4	Daily	3 hr.–4 hr.
Seville	Córdoba	AVE	18	Daily	40 min.
Granada	Barcelona	Trenhotel	1	Daily	11 hr., 40 min.

Most night trains have full restaurant service, and stewards also provide drinks and snacks at all hours. Inquire in advance about dining facilities or services. If they don't exist, bring your own food and drink, to be on the safe side.

Most Spanish trains are air-conditioned with adequate toilet facilities. Tickets for *gran clase* (*preferente* on the Talgo) feature sleeping cars with private showers and toilets. In *turista*-class cars, you'll find berths that sleep four. In economy class, expect a "sleeperette" seat.

[FastFACTS] SPAIN

Area Codes In Spain, you must always dial the entire phone number, including the area code, no matter where you are located. Area codes are as follows: **91** for Madrid; **93** for Barcelona; **95** for Seville, Córdoba, Marbella, and Málaga.

Business Hours Banks are open Monday to Friday 9:30am to 2pm and Saturday 9:30am to 1pm. Most offices are open Monday to Friday 9am to 5 or 5:30pm; the longtime practice of early closings in summer seems to be dying out. In restaurants, lunch is usually from 1 to 4pm and dinner from 9 to 11:30pm or midnight. There are no set rules for the opening of bars and taverns, many opening at 8am, others at noon; most stay open until 1:30am or later. Major stores are open Monday to Saturday 9:30am to 8pm; smaller establishments, however, often take a siesta, doing business from 9:30am to 1:30pm and 4:30 to 8pm. Hours can vary from store to store.

Climate Spring and fall are ideal times to visit nearly all of Spain, with the possible exception of the Atlantic coast, which experiences heavy rains in October and November. May and October are the best months in terms of both weather and crowds. In summer, it's hot, hot, and hotter still, with the cities in Castile (Madrid) and Andalusia (Seville and Córdoba) heating up the most. Madrid has dry heat; the average temperature can hover around 84°F (29°C) in July and 75°F (24°C) in September. Seville has the dubious reputation of being about the hottest part of Spain in July and August, often baking under average temperatures of 93°F (34°C). Barcelona, cooler in temperature, is very humid in July and August.

Documents Required Visas are not needed by U.S. and Canadian citizens for visits of less than 3 months.

Electricity Most hotels use 220 volts AC (50 cycles). Some older places have 110 or 125 volts AC. Carry an adapter with you, and always check at your hotel desk before plugging in any electrical appliance.

Embassies & Consulates If you lose your passport, fall seriously ill, get into legal trouble, or have some other serious problem, your embassy or consulate can help. These are the Madrid addresses and hours: The **United States Embassy,** Calle de Serrano 75 (© **91-587-22-00;** http://madrid.us embassy.gov; Metro: Núñez de Balboa), is open Monday to Friday 9am to 6pm. The **Canadian Embassy,** Núñez de Balboa 35 (© **91-423-32-50;** http://canadaonline. about.com/od/travel/a/ embspain.htm; Metro: Velázquez), is open Monday to Thursday 8:30am to 5:30pm, Friday 8:30am to 2:30pm.

Health & Safety Spain should not pose any major health hazards. The rich cuisine—garlic, olive oil, and wine—may give some travelers mild diarrhea, so take along some anti-diarrhea medicine, moderate your eating habits, and, even though the water is generally safe, drink mineral water only. Fish and shellfish from the horrendously polluted Mediterranean should be eaten only cooked.

If you are traveling around Spain (particularly southern Spain) over the summer, limit your exposure to the sun, especially during the first few days of your trip and, thereafter, from 11am to 2pm. Wearing a hat is a good idea. You should also use a sunscreen with an SPF rating of at least 25, and apply it liberally and often. Remember, if you're traveling with kids, they need more protection than adults do.

Water is safe to drink throughout Spain, though you should not drink the water in mountain streams, regardless of how clear and pure it looks.

While most of Spain has a moderate rate of crime, and most of the North American tourists who visit it each year have trouble-free visits, the principal tourist areas have been experiencing an increase in violent crime. Madrid and Barcelona, in particular, have reported growing incidents of muggings and violent attacks, and older tourists and Asian Americans seem to be particularly at risk. Criminals frequent tourist areas and major attractions such as museums, monuments, restaurants, hotels, beach resorts, trains, train stations, airports, subways, and ATMs. In Barcelona, violent attacks have occurred near the Picasso Museum and in the Gothic Quarter, Parc Güell, Plaza Real, and Mont Juic. In Madrid, reported incidents occurred in key tourist areas, including the area near the Prado Museum and Atocha train station,

and areas of old Madrid such as Sol, the El Rastro flea market, and Plaza Mayor. Travelers should exercise caution both day and night, carry limited cash and credit cards, and leave extra cash, credit cards, passports, and personal documents in a safe location. Remember that thieves often work in teams or pairs, and, in most cases, one person is trying to distract you.

Holidays These include January 1 (New Year's Day), January 6 (Feast of the Epiphany), March 19 (Feast of St. Joseph), Good Friday, Easter Monday, May 1 (May Day), June 10 (Corpus Christi), June 29 (Feast of St. Peter and St. Paul), July 25 (Feast of St. James), August 15 (Feast of the Assumption), October 12 (Spain's National Day), November 1 (All Saints' Day), December 8 (Immaculate Conception), and December 25 (Christmas).

Legal Aid If you're in trouble with the law, contact your embassy or consulate (see "Embassies & Consulates," above) for a list of English-speaking lawyers in your area.

Mail Airmail letters to the United States and Canada cost .78€ up to 15 grams; letters within Spain .29€. Postcards have the same rates as letters. Allow about 8 days for delivery to North America; in some cases, letters take 2 weeks to reach North America. Rates change frequently, so check at your local hotel before mailing anything. As for surface mail to North America, forget it. Chances are, you'll be home long before your letter arrives.

Police & Emergencies The national emergency number is ℂ **006** throughout Spain, except in the Basque Country, where it is ℂ **088**.

Telephones If you don't speak Spanish, you'll find it easier to telephone from your hotel, but remember that this is often very expensive because hotels impose a surcharge on every operator-assisted call. In some cases, it can be as high as 40% or more. On the street, phone booths (known as *cabinas*) have dialing instructions in English; you can make local calls by inserting a .25€ coin for 3 minutes.

For directory assistance: Dial ℂ **1003** in Spain.

For operator assistance: If you need operator assistance in making an international call, dial ℂ **025**.

Toll-free numbers: Numbers beginning with **900** in Spain are toll-free, but calling an 800-number in the States from Spain is not toll-free. In fact, it costs the same as an overseas call.

Each number is preceded by its provincial code for local, national, and international calls. For example, when calling to Madrid from Madrid or another province within Spain, telephone customers must dial **91-123-45-67.** Similarly, when calling Valladolid from within or outside the province, dial **979-123-45-67.**

When in Spain, the access number for an **AT&T** calling card is ℂ **900/99-0011.** The access number for **Sprint** is ℂ **900/99-0013.**

More information is also available on the Telefónica website, at **www. telefonica.es**.

To call Spain: If you're calling Spain from the United States, dial the international access code **(011),** then the country code for Spain **(34),** followed by the city code and the telephone number. So the whole number you'd dial would be **011-34-00-000-0000.**

To make international calls: To make international calls from Spain, first dial **00** and then the country code (U.S. or Canada **1**), followed by the city area code and number.

Tipping The government requires restaurants and hotels to include their service charges—usually 15% of the bill. That does not, however, mean that you should skip out of a place without dispensing an extra euro or two. The following are some guidelines:

Your hotel porter should get .80€ per bag. Maids should be given 1€ per day, more if you're generous. Tip doormen .75€ for assisting with baggage and .50€ for calling a cab. In top-ranking hotels, the concierge will often submit a separate bill, showing charges for newspapers and other services; if he or she has been particularly helpful, tip extra. For cab drivers, add about 10% to the fare as shown on the meter. At airports, such as Barajas in Madrid and major terminals, the porter who handles your luggage will present you with a fixed-charge bill.

In both restaurants and nightclubs, a 15% service charge is added to the bill. To that, add another 3% to 5% tip, depending on the quality of the service. Waiters in deluxe restaurants and nightclubs are accustomed to the extra 5%, which means you'll end up tipping 20%. If that seems excessive, you must remember that the initial service charge reflected in the fixed price is distributed among all the help.

Barbers and hairdressers expect a 10% to 15% tip. Tour guides expect 2€, although a tip is not mandatory. Theater and bullfight ushers get .50€.

MADRID

At an altitude of 2,165 feet (650m), lofty Madrid is the geographical center of Spain and the hub of both its rail and highway networks. Since 1561, the city has presided over one of the most volatile and fast-changing countries in the world, going from kingdom to dictatorship to democracy.

ACCOMMODATIONS ■
Casón del Tormes **1**
Hotel A. Gaudí **16**
Hotel Cortezo **12**
Hotel Meninas **6**
Hotel Preciados **9**
Hotel Santo Domingo **5**
Jardín de Recoletos **20**
Mario **8**
NH Nacional **26**

DINING ◆
El Amparo **21**
El Espejo **17**
La Biotika **24**
La Bola **4**
La Gamella **22**
La Terraza del Casino **15**
Lhardy **13**
La Paloma **21**
Pan de Lujo **21**
Taberna del Alabardero **7**

ATTRACTIONS ●
Monasterio de las
   Descalzas Reales **10**
Museo Arqueológico
   Nacional **18**
Museo de la Real Academia
   de Bellas Artes de San
   Fernando **14**
Museo del Prado **25**

C/ Augusto Figueroa
Pl. de Chueca
C/ Gravina
C/ Almirante
Estación Chamartín
C/ Villanueva
C/ Gil de Santivañes
C/ Pelayo
Chueca
C/ Prim
Paseo de Recoletos
C/ Recoletos
C/ Serrano
CHUECA
C/ Hortaleza
C/ San Marcos
C/ Barbieri
C/ Libertad
Palacio de Buenavista
Palacio del Marqués de Salamanca
C/ Villalar
Pl. de Vázquez de Mella
Ministerio de Cultura
Plaza del Rey
C/ Reina
C/ Infantas
Banco de España
Palacio de Linares
Puerta de Alcalá
Independencia
Gran Vía
16
de Gracia
C/ Caballero
Plaza de Cibeles
C/ Alcalá
Pl. de la
Palacio de Comunicaciones
C/ Valenzuela
C/ Alcalá
Banco de España
Paseo del Prado
C/ Marqués de Cubas
C/ Montalbán
C/ Alfonso XI
Sevilla
C/ Sevilla
C/ Madrazo
C/ Cadaceros
C/ Jovellanos
Teatro de la Zarzuela
Museo Naval
C/ Arlabán
Zorrilla
C/ Juan de Mena
Bolsa de Madrid
Pso. de Argentina
Plaza de Canalejas
Carrera de San Jerónimo
C/ Ventura de la Vega
Palacio de Congresos
Museo Thyssen-Bornemisza
Pl. de la Lealtad
C/ A. Maura
Parque
C/ Príncipe
C/ Echegaray
Plaza Cortes
Plaza Cortes
Salón de Reinos
del
Plaza Santa Ana
C/ Prado
C/ Sta. Catalina
C/ Duque de Medinaceli
Pl. de Cánovas del Castillo
C/ Felipe IV
Casón del Buen Retiro
Buen
LAS LETRAS
C/ San Agustín
Cervantes
C/ Moreto
Retiro
Pl. de Matute
C/ León
C/ Lope de Vega
C/ Huertas
C/ Jesús
Museo del Prado
C/ Alfonso XII
C/ Amor de Dios
Sta. María
C/ Magdalena
Antón Martín
Cost. de los Desamparados
C/ Moratín
C/ Olmo
C/ Verónica
Gobernador
C/ Fúcar
C/ Ave María
C/ Santa Isabel
CaixaForum
C/ Almadén
Real Jardín Botánico
LAVAPIÉS
C/ Atocha
Paseo del Prado

Museo Lázaro Galdiano **19**
Museo Nacional Centre de Arte Reina Sofía **27**
Museo Thyssen-Bornemisza **23**
Palacio Real (Royal Palace) **3**
Panteón de Goya **2**
Plaza Mayor **11**

Atocha
Cuesta de Moyano
Reina Sofía
Pl. del Emperador Carlos V
Estación de Atocha (Old station)
Paseo de la Infanta Isabel
Estación de Atocha

Madrid Metro

Madrid is not the most beautiful or charming of European capitals, but it is home to some of the greatest art museums in the world and is also a good base for exploring some of the finest art cities of antiquity, especially Toledo, to its immediate south.

Even more than museums, it is the spirit and lifestyle of the Castilians that provoke interest, even passion, in those who view the city as a grand place to visit. Once night falls, *la movida* (roughly, "the movement") flows until dawn in more bars, cafes, *tascas,* and clubs than there would seem to be stars in heaven.

For the train traveler, Madrid is Valhalla, the "center of the universe" for riding the rails. Trains fan out from Madrid to all the major cities, regions, and provinces of Spain. There are good connections to the "cities of the heartland," such as Segovia and Toledo, and express links to such major cities and attractions as Seville or Barcelona.

Station Information
GETTING FROM THE AIRPORT TO THE TRAIN STATIONS

In lieu of adequate bus connections, many passengers arriving in Madrid at its Barajas airport rely on a taxi to take them to the two major rail terminals, which will cost 25€ and up (trip time: 15–40 min., depending on which station you're going to and traffic). A supplement is charged for trips to the railway station or the bullring, as well as on Sundays and holidays. The ride to Barajas Airport carries a 5.50€ surcharge, and there is a 2.95€ supplement from railway stations. In addition, a 1.15€ supplement is charged on Sundays and holidays, plus a 1.18€ supplement is tacked on at night.

If you are traveling light and want to save money, you can take a subway from Barajas into central Madrid. Take line 8 to Nuevos Ministerios and switch to line 4; a one-way trip costs 3€. Air-conditioned airport buses also take you from the arrivals terminal to the bus depot under Plaza de Colón, a central point. The fare is 2€, and buses leave every 10 to 15 minutes daily from 6am to 10pm. From Plaza de Colón, you can take one of the frequent *cercanias* trains (railpasses are valid) for the short hop to either Atocha or Chamartín station.

INSIDE THE STATIONS

Madrid has two major rail stations, Atocha and Chamartín.

At **Estación Atocha,** Glorieta Carlos V (© 90-24-02-02-902; Metro: Atocha RENFE), high-speed Talgo 200 and AVE trains link Madrid with major points in Andalusia (Córdoba, Seville, and the Costa del Sol, for example), as well as AVE trains to Barcelona. Atocha is linked to the city's second major station, Chamartín (see below), by *cercanias* trains.

The local **RENFE ticket office** (© 90-232-0320) in the station is open daily from 6am to 1am. Go here for train information, seat reservations, and railpass validation. For money exchange, use the on-site offices of **Caja Madrid** (© 91-506-28-00), open Monday to Friday 8am to 2pm; Thursday it reopens from 5 to 7:30pm.

A branch of the **Madrid Tourist Office** (© 902-243-402) is also found here and is open daily from 9am to 9pm. This office doesn't make hotel reservations. For that, go to the on-site travel agency **Viajes El Corte Inglés** (© 91-528-4408), open daily from 7am to 10pm. You pay your hotel bill on the spot and are issued a voucher. There is no charge for hotels booked within Madrid; outside of the city, the cost is 15€ per booking. **Luggage lockers** *(consignas automáticas),* operated by RENFE, are also at the station. Luggage can be stored daily from 6:30am to 10:30pm at a cost of 2.40€ to 4.50€ per day, depending on the space you need.

During the deadliest terrorist attack in recent European history, on March 11, 2004, Islamic extremists bombed four commuter trains entering Madrid, causing 191 deaths and more than 1,400 injuries. The Spanish government continues to investigate the attacks and to arrest suspects.

Despite the publicity generated by the Madrid attacks (and the subsequent London Tube bombings in 2005), by and large, chances are, there's no need to worry about day-to-day safety on Spain's trains. Up-to-date information on safety and security can be obtained by calling ℭ 888/407-4747 toll-free in the U.S. and Canada. Outside the U.S. and Canada, call ℭ 202/501-4444. Both numbers operate from 8am to 8pm Eastern Standard Time Monday to Friday, except on U.S. federal holidays. You can also go online to http://travel.state.gov.

Atocha is a virtual tourist attraction in itself, a 19th-century palace built of iron and glass, with a restaurant, a botanical garden, and numerous cafes and bars. Signs are clearly marked throughout the station, and there are excellent links to public transport such as the Metro. Atocha is far more central than Chamartín, lying directly south of the famous Parque del Buen Retiro and within walking distance of such attractions as Museo del Prado.

Estación Chamartín, San Agustin de Foxá (ℭ **902-24-0202;** Metro: Chamartín), is the international rail station for Madrid. Major destinations reachable from here include Lisbon and Paris. Chamartín is also the depot for domestic destinations in the northwest and parts of southern Spain. For **train information,** seat reservations, and railpass validation, go to the local RENFE office (ℭ **902-32-0320**), in the center of the station between tracks 11 and 12. Hours are daily from 5:30am to midnight.

Opposite track 19 is the **tourist information office** (ℭ **91-315-9976**), open Monday to Friday 8:30am to 9:30pm, Saturday and Sunday 9am to 1pm. Next to the tourist office is **Viajes Brujula** (ℭ **91-315-7894**), a travel agency that will make reservations in Madrid hotels for 2.50€ per person. It's open daily 7:30am to 9:30pm. You can also visit the **Oficina Municipal de Información y Turismo,** Plaza Mayor 3 (ℭ **91-588-16-36**). It's open Monday to Saturday 10am to 8pm, and Sunday 10am to 3pm. For **money exchange,** go to Caja Madrid (ℭ **91-732-0285**), opposite tracks no. 17 and 18, open Monday to Friday 8:30am to 2pm.

Chamartín lies in the north of Madrid, a 15- to 20-minute ride from the center (longer if traffic is bad).

Information Elsewhere in the City

The most convenient **tourist office** in Madrid is on Duque de Medinaceli 2 Banco de España (ℭ **91-429-49-51;** www.turismomadrid.es; Metro: Antón Martín; bus 9, 27, 34, or 37); it's open Monday to Saturday 9am to 7pm, and Sunday and holidays 9am to 3pm. Ask for a street map of the next town on your itinerary, especially if you're driving. The staff here can give you a list of hotels and *hostales*. The Tourist Office of Spain (**www.spain.info**) can help you plan your trip with listings of lodging options, attractions, tour operators, and packages, plus handy tips on getting around. For the viewpoint of individual travelers, check **www.hotelrooms365.com**.

Getting Around

Madrid is a vast urban sprawl. To get around, you'll need to rely on public transportation. The good news is that many of the city's major tourist sights lie in the historic core, which can be covered on foot. In fact, the only way to explore the narrow cobblestone streets of old Madrid is by walking (wear sturdy shoes).

For most attractions, the Metro (or subway) system is the way to go. It's safe, speedy, well maintained, and also inexpensive. Fares and schedules are posted at every one of Madrid's 158 subway stations. Eleven lines, totaling 106 miles (171km), service Greater Madrid, with individual Metro tickets costing 1€.

It's cheaper to purchase a *bonotransporte,* known as *bonos,* at any station, giving you 10 rides on the Metro at a cost of 7.40€. Trains run daily from 6am to 2am. Violent crime is almost unheard of in the subway, but pickpocketing is common. For **Metro information,** call ✆ **90-244-4403** or go online to **www.metromadrid.es**.

Buses pick up the slack caused by gaps in the Metro system, and these vehicles are usually fast and efficient, traveling in special lanes. Both red and blue buses charge 1€ per ride. For 7.40€, you can purchase a 10-trip *bonos* ticket (but without transfers) for Madrid's bus system. Buses run daily from 6am to 11:30pm. Late-night revelers rely on the *Búho,* or "Owl," a late-night bus service. For schedules and information about Madrid buses, call **Empresa Municipal de Transportes** (✆ **91-406-8800**) or go to the office at Calle Cerro de Plata 4 (✆ or 90-250-78-50; www.emtmadrid.es), where you can buy a guide to the bus routes and the *bonos* ticket. The office is open Monday to Friday from 8am to 2pm.

Taxis operate around the clock. The base fare is 2.05€; for every kilometer thereafter, the fare increases by .98€ to 1.15€. Supplements are charged: 2.95€ to a bus or train station, or 5.50€ to the airport. There is also a 1.15€ supplement on Sundays and holidays, and 1.18€ is tacked on at night. Taxis are most often hailed in the street; otherwise, to call a taxi, dial ✆ **90-250-11-30** or 90-247-82-00. *Warning:* Make sure the meter is turned on.

Where to Stay

Casón del Tormes This attractive hotel is around the corner from the Royal Palace and Plaza de España. Behind a four-story red-brick facade with stone-trimmed windows, it overlooks a quiet one-way street. Guest rooms are generally spacious and comfortable, with color-coordinated fabrics and dark wood, including mahogany headboards.

Calle del Río 7, 28013 Madrid. ✆ **91-541-97-46.** Fax 91-541-18-52. www.hotelcasondeltormes.com. 63 units. 60€–121€ double; 156€ triple. AE, DC, MC, V. Metro: Plaza de España. **Amenities:** Restaurant; bar; smoke-free rooms.

Hotel A. Gaudí ★ In the heart of Madrid, this hotel is located in a beautifully restored turn-of-the-20th-century building that's a modernist landmark. It was constructed by Emilio Salas y Cortés, one of the teachers of the great Barcelona architect Gaudí. Some of the most important attractions of Madrid are within an easy walk, including the Prado, Thyssen-Bornemisza Museum, and Plaza Mayor, with its rustic taverns. The guest rooms come in different sizes, each comfortably furnished and beautifully maintained.

Gran Vía 9, 28013 Madrid. ✆ **91-531-22-22.** Fax 91-531-54-69. www.hoteles-catalonia.es. 185 units. 80€–197€ double; from 300€ suite. AE, DC, MC, V. Metro: Gran Vía. **Amenities:** Restaurant; bar.

Hotel Cortezo Just off Calle de Atocha, which leads to the railroad station of the same name, the Cortezo is a short walk from Plaza Mayor and Puerta del Sol. Although it has been renovated many times since, it still has a lingering aura of the 1950s, when it was built. The accommodations are comfortable but simply furnished, with contemporary bathrooms containing tub/showers. Beds are springy and the furniture is pleasantly modern; many rooms have sitting areas with a desk and armchair. The public rooms match the guest rooms in freshness.

Doctor Cortezo 3, 28012 Madrid. (✆ **91-369-01-01.** Fax 91-369-37-74. www.mediumhoteles.com. 88 units. 50€–190€ double. AE, DC, MC, V. Metro: Tirso de Molina. **Amenities:** Restaurant.

Hotel Meninas ★ 🏊 In the very center of Madrid, this little hotel was created out of a 19th-century building that was transformed into one of the better bargains in the area. During the restoration, many amenities were added, such as soundproof rooms—a good thing, because the hotel lies in the center of a traffic-clogged area. The structure may be antique, but not the improvements. The bedrooms come in a range of sizes and styles, from singles to triples, to suites. The little hotel offers a buffet breakfast in a vaulted dining room that also has a welcoming bar with lounge.

Calle Campomanes 7, 28013 Madrid. (✆ **91-541-28-05.** Fax 91-541-28-06. www.hotelmeninas.com. 37 units. 109€–185€ double; 189€ triple; 210€ suite. AE, MC, V. Metro: Opera. **Amenities:** Rooms for those w/limited mobility; smoke-free rooms.

Hotel Preciados ★ 😊 Only a 10-minute taxi ride from Atocha Station, this centrally located hotel is one of the city's less discovered. Housed in a converted 1881 building, the hotel retains much of its architectural past but was completely overhauled to include all the requisite modern comforts. Children are catered to here (even the restaurant offers a kid's menu). The midsize to spacious bedrooms with shiny new bathrooms and double-glazed windows make this one a winner.

Preciados 37, 28013 Madrid. (✆ **91-454-44-00.** Fax 91-454-44-01. www.preciadoshotel.com. 73 units. 90€–203€ double; 208€–350€ suite. MC, V. Metro: Puerta del Sol or Santo Domingo/Callao. **Amenities:** Restaurant; bar; rooms for those w/limited mobility; smoke-free rooms.

Hotel Santo Domingo ★ A 2-minute walk from the Plaza de España, this five-story hotel opened in 1994 and has been overhauled several times since. The atmospheric yet modern public rooms feature lots of antiques and artwork. The soundproof units are individually decorated in pastel-derived shades. Some contain gold damask wall coverings, faux-tortoiseshell desks, and striped satin bedspreads. The best units are the fifth-floor doubles, especially those with furnished balconies and views over the tile roofs of Old Madrid.

Plaza Santo Domingo 13, 28013 Madrid. (✆ **91-547-98-00.** Fax 91-547-59-95. www.hotelsantodomingo. com. 120 units. 75€–180€ double. AE, DC, MC, V. Metro: Santo Domingo. **Amenities:** Restaurant; bar; smoke-free rooms.

Jardín de Recoletos ★ 🏊 This Salamanca District hotel, known for its affordable prices, is close to the Plaza Colón, one of Madrid's major traffic arteries. Rooms are rather spacious and are attractively and comfortably decorated. All have a well-equipped kitchenette, an advantage that makes this hotel popular with families.

Gil de Santivañes 6, 28001 Madrid. (✆ **91-781-16-40.** Fax 91-781-16-41. www.vphoteles.com. 43 units. 148€–209€ double; 200€–261€ suite. Rates include buffet breakfast. AE, DC, MC, V. Metro: Serrano. **Amenities:** Restaurant; cafe.

Mario 🏊 Near the opera house and the Palacio Real, this is one of the most affordable choices in the area, despite its central location. The hotel doesn't have a lot of extras, but if you're seeking a clean, decent, cheap choice, consider this option. The guest rooms, though small, have modern decor along with well-maintained private bathrooms. The best and most requested room is the more spacious no. 201. If you don't plan to spend a lot of time in your room—preferring instead to dine out and experience the city's throbbing nightlife—consider booking here.

Calle Campomanes 4, 28013 Madrid. ℂ **91-548-85-48.** Fax 91-559-12-88. www.room-matehotels.com. 54 units. 134€–192€ double; 173€–214€ suite. Rates include continental breakfast. AE, DC, MC, V. Metro: Opera. **Amenities:** Rooms for those w/limited mobility.

NH Nacional ★   At the turn of the 20th century, this stately hotel was built to service overnight passengers arriving at the nearby Atocha rail station. The restored hotel continues to serve travelers but now has a smooth, seamless decor that takes maximum advantage of the building's tall ceilings and large spaces. Guest rooms feature modern designer decor (including avant-garde art), giving the units a welcoming ambience.

Paseo del Prado 48, 28014 Madrid. ℂ **91-429-66-29.** Fax 91-369-15-64. www.nh-hotels.com. 214 units. 139€–212€ double; 194€–268€ suite. AE, DC, MC, V. Metro: Atocha. **Amenities:** Restaurant; bar-cafeteria; rooms for those w/limited mobility.

Top Attractions & Special Moments

Monasterio de las Descalzas Reales ★★   This magnificent building was once a royal palace. In 1559, Juana of Austria, sister of Felipe II, converted the building into a convent where aristocratic women could retreat to become "the bride of Christ." When the pope learned that the sisters in the convent were starving, he allowed them to open the monastery to visitors wanting to see its rich treasure-trove of art. Each noblewoman who entered the convent brought a dowry, and those precious relics form the nucleus of the collection today. The most valuable painting is Titian's *Caesar's Money*, along with artworks from old masters such as Bruegel the Elder sheltered in The Flemish Hall. Tapestries on display are from Ruben's cartoons with his chubby matrons. A small cloister on the second floor is ringed with chapels containing artwork and precious objects, including bits of wood said to be from the cross on which Christ was crucified.

Plaza de las Descalzas Reales s/n. ℂ **91-454-88-00.** www.patrimonionacional.es. Admission 5€ adults, 2.50€ children 5–16, free for children 4 and under. Tues–Thurs and Sat 10:30am–12:45pm and 4–5:45pm; Fri 10:30am–12:45pm; Sun 11am–1:45pm. Metro: Opera. Bus: 3, 25, 39, or 148. From Plaza del Callao, off Gran Vía, walk down Postigo de San Martín to Plaza de las Descalzas Reales; the convent is on the left.

Museo Arqueológico Nacional ★★   This stately mansion houses one of Iberia's great archaeological museums. Founded by Queen Isabella II in 1867, the museum features exhibits spanning history from unrecorded times to the 19th century. The Iberian artifacts are supplemented by finds at digs from Ancient Greece, Italy at the time of the Etruscans, and Egypt.

The most notable and impressive sculpture is *La Dama de Elche,* a primitive carving from the 4th century B.C. discovered along the southeastern coast of Spain. The austere beauty of the statue reveals traces of Greek influence. Another notable sculpture is *La Dama de Baza.* The museum is especially rich in artifacts in the epoch between Roman and Mudéjar Spain.

The mosaics from the Roman period are notable, especially *Monks and Seasons,* from the Albacete period, with outstanding pieces from the Visigothic era also on display. Outside the museum is an exact reproduction of the Altamira cave paintings discovered near Santander in northern Spain in 1868.

Blood sports may not be your thing, but the art of bullfighting is as old as pagan Spain and reveals much about the character of the Spaniard. Bullfighting's most avid aficionados claim it is a "microcosm of death, catharsis, and rebirth." It remains one of the most evocative and memorable events in Spain, although the action at the *corrida* may horrify the faint of heart.

Madrid draws the finest matadors in Spain. If a matador hasn't proved his worth in the **Plaza Monumental de Toros de las Ventas,** Alcalá 237 (*C* **91-356-22-00;** www.las-ventas.com; Metro: Ventas), he won't be recognized as a top-flight artist. The major season begins during the Fiestas de San Isidro, patron saint of Madrid, on May 15. This is the occasion for a series of fights, with talent scouts in the audience. Matadors who distinguish themselves in the ring are signed up for Majorca, Málaga, and other places.

The best way to get tickets to the bullfights is at the stadium's box office (Fri–Sun 10am–2pm and 5–8pm). Alternatively, you can contact one of Madrid's most competent ticket agents, **Localidades Galicia,** Plaza del Carmen 1 (*C* **91-531-91-31;** www.bullfighttickets madrid.com; Metro: Puerta del Sol). It's open Tuesday through Saturday from 9:30am to 1:30pm and 4:30 to 7pm, Sunday from 10am to 1pm. Regardless of where you buy them, tickets to bullfights range from 16€ to 174€, depending on the event and the position of your seat within the stadium. Concierges for virtually every upper-bracket hotel in Madrid can acquire tickets, through inner channels of their own, to bullfights and other sought-after entertainment. Front-row seats at the bullfights are known as *barreras. Delanteras* (third-row seats) are available in both the *alta* (high) and the *baja* (low) sections. The cheapest seats sold, *filas,* afford the worst view and are in the sun *(sol)* during the entire performance. The best seats are in the shade *(sombra).*

Bullfights are held on Sunday and holidays throughout most of the year, and every day during certain festivals, which tend to last around 3 weeks, usually in the late spring. Starting times are adjusted according to the anticipated hour of sundown on the day of a performance. Late-night fights by neophyte matadors are sometimes staged under spotlights on Saturday around 11pm.

Serrano 13. *C* **91-577-79-12.** http://man.mcu.es. Free admission. Tues–Sat 9:30am–8pm; Sun and holidays 9:30am–3pm. Metro: Serrano or Colón. Bus: 1, 9, 19, 51, or 74.

Museo de la Real Academia de Bellas Artes de San Fernando ★   A short stroll from the Puerta del Sol (the exact center of Madrid), this leading Iberian fine arts museum is set in a 17th-century baroque palace. When the building was an art academy, its alumni included the likes of Salvador Dalí and Picasso. This is hardly the grandest art museum in Madrid, but there are superb works, including a collection of old master paintings ranging from Rubens to Van Dyck, plus excellent drawings by Titian and Raphael. The best selection is the array of Spanish paintings from the 1500s to the 1800s, including works by Velázquez, El Greco, Ribera, and Murillo. Also here is one of the best monk paintings Zurbarán ever did, *Fray Pedro Machado.* A former director of the academy, Goya has a room devoted entirely to his art. Our favorite is his *Burial of a Sardine.*

Alcalá 13.(C) **91-524-08-64.** http://rabasf.insde.es. Admission 3€ adults, 1.50€ students, free for children 17 and under; free for all visitors Wed. Tues-Fri 9am-7pm; Sat-Mon and holidays 9am-2:30pm.
Metro: Puerta del Sol or Sevilla. Bus: 3, 5, 15, 20, 51, 52, 53, or 150.

Museo del Prado ★★★   This museum, one of the world's greatest repositories
of art, began as a royal collection and was later beefed up by the Habsburgs. The
range of art is mainly from the 12th to the 19th centuries, and the collection quite
naturally features the greatest assembly of Spanish paintings in the world, notably the
impressive works by the great Velázquez and Goya. The annex of the Prado, Cason
del Buen Retiro, contains late-19th-century and 20th-century sculpture and painting.

Those who can't see everything might want to enter through the Puerta de Goya,
opening onto Calle Felipe IV. This leads to the second floor (called the first floor in
Spain). The artwork is arranged by school, with the oldest works displayed on the
lower floors. Especially notable is the Goya Collection featuring both his *Clothed
Maja* and *Naked Maja* (both ca. 1800). The artist who depicted "blatant" nudity was
charged with obscenity.

You'll find a splendid array of works by the incomparable Diego Velázquez (1599–
1660). The museum's most famous painting, in fact, is his *Las Meninas,* a triumph for
its use of light effects and perspective. The faces of the queen and king are reflected
in the mirror in the painting itself. The artist in the foreground is Velázquez, of course.

The Prado is a trove of the work of El Greco (ca. 1541–1614), the Crete-born artist who lived much of his life in Toledo. You can see a parade of "The Greek's" saints,
Madonnas, and Holy Families—even a ghostly *John the Baptist.*

The Flemish painter Peter Paul Rubens (1577–1640), who met Velázquez while in
Spain, is represented by the peacock-blue *Garden of Love* and by the *Three Graces.*
Also worthy is the work of José Ribera (1591–1652), a Valencia-born artist and con-
temporary of Velázquez whose best painting is the *Martyrdom of St. Philip.* Seville-
born Bartolomé Murillo (1617–82)—often referred to as the "painter of
Madonnas"—is represented by three versions of the Immaculate Conception.

The Prado has an outstanding collection of the work of Hieronymus Bosch (ca.
1450–1516), the Flemish genius. *The Garden of Earthly Delights,* the best-known
work of "El Bosco," is here. You'll also see his *Seven Deadly Sins* and his triptych *The
Hay Wagon. The Triumph of Death* is by another Flemish painter, Pieter Bruegel the
Elder (ca. 1525–69), who carried on Bosch's ghoulish vision.

Major Italian works are exhibited on the ground floor. You'll see art by Italian masters—Raphael, Botticelli, Mantegna, Andrea del Sarto, Fra Angelico, and Correggio.
The most celebrated Italian painting here is Titian's voluptuous Venus being watched
by a musician who can't keep his eyes on his work.

Thanks to a massive $92-million expansion, the once-stuffy museum has doubled
its floor space and is even making room for children's workshops. Much of the expansion—designed by Rafael Moneo—is found below ground level and includes several
galleries, a restaurant, a lecture hall, and a gift shop. The main structure from 1785
is linked underground to the Prado's modern annex; the passageway runs beneath a
garden and a plaza. The expansion, among other exhibits, allows the Prado to display
1,000 Goya prints that had been in storage. The Prado has also branched out to
incorporate surrounding buildings, including the Casón del Buen Retiro overlooking
Retiro Park. It is filled with the work of 19th-century Spanish painters. Give yourself
at least 3 hours to explore the museum.

Paseo del Prado.© **91-330-28-00**. www.museoprado.es. Admission 8€ adults, 4€ students; free on Sun and for kids 17 and under. Tues–Sun 9am–8pm; holidays 9am–2pm. Call for info on guided tours. Closed Jan 1, Good Friday, May 1, and Dec 25. Metro: Atocha or Banco de España. Bus: 9, 10, 14, 19, 27, 34, 37, or 45.

Museo Lázaro Galdiano ★ 🏛 Bequeathed to the nation in 1947 and often compared to New York's Frick Museum, this is one of the grandest collections of art in Castile, housed in the former manse of the author José Lázaro Galdiano. The original museum, added to over the years, began from the writer's own impressive collection of fine and applied art. Imagine 37 rooms bulging with art, including many of the most famous and reproduced masters of Europe.

We like to take the elevator to the top floor and work our way down, taking in, at our leisure, everything from Goya portraits to a cross-shaped pocket watch worn by Charles V. The *Saviour* is a portrait attributed to Leonardo da Vinci. Surprisingly, the collection is rich in English landscapes, notably by Turner, Gainsborough, and Constable, and also contains paintings from Spain's greatest masters, including El Greco, Murillo, Velázquez, and Zubarán. Of macabre interest is Salon 30, devoted to Goya, including some notorious paintings from his "black period."

Calle Serrano 122.© **91-561-60-84**. www.flg.es. Admission 4€ adults, 3€ students, free 12 and under. Wed–Mon 10am–4:30pm. Metro: Ruben Dario. Bus: 9, 12, 16, 19, 27, 45, 51, or 150.

Museo Nacional Centro de Arte Reina Sofia ★ A former 18th-century general hospital, once called "the ugliest building in Spain," is today a repository of modern art in Spain. The museum has completed a $95-million expansion, creating far more exhibition space and installing everything from an art bookstore to a cafeteria offering reasonably priced meals and snacks, to a 450-seat auditorium for concerts. A third building contains two mammoth galleries for large-scale exhibitions. It's worth the trip alone just to see Picasso's *Guernica* ★★★, the single most famous work of the 20th century. Taking his inspiration from the German attack on the Basque town of Guernica in 1937, this masterpiece represents Picasso's glaring indictment of the destruction of war.

Picasso is also represented by other works, including one of our all-time favorites, *Woman in Blue,* painted in 1901. When it failed to win in a national competition, Picasso disowned the painting. The permanent collection is housed on the second and fourth floors, featuring works by such famous Spanish artists as Dalí and Miró. Sometimes the temporary exhibits are even more stunning than the permanent collection.

Santa Isabel 52.© **91-774-10-00**. www.museoreinasofia.es. Admission 6€ adults, 3€ students, free for children 17 and under. Mon–Sat 10am–9pm; Sun 10am–2:30pm. Free guided tours Mon and Wed 5pm, Sat 11am. Metro: Atocha. Bus: 6, 10, 14, 19, 26, 27, 32, 34, 36, or 37.

Museo Thyssen-Bornemisza ★★★ Installed in Madrid's 18th-century Villahermosa Palace in 1992, this collection grew from one of the greatest private art collections in the world—the assemblage of the late Baron Heinrich Thyssen-Bornemisza and his son, Hans Heinrich. Beginning in the 1920s, the collection was intended to illustrate the history of Western art, and in that, it succeeds brilliantly with some 800 representative works of art, including masterpieces by the likes of Picasso, Goya, van Gogh, and Titian.

As a privately owned collection, the Thyssen museum's treasure-trove was rivaled only by that of Queen Elizabeth II. Spain acquired the collection for $350 million. Rooms are arranged numerically so that by following the order of the rooms (nos. 1–48, spread out over three floors), a logical sequence of European painting can be traced from the 13th to the 20th century. The nucleus of the collection consists of

700 world-class paintings. They include works by, among others, El Greco, Velázquez, Dürer, Rembrandt, Watteau, Canaletto, Caravaggio, Hals, Memling, and Goya.

Unusual among the world's great art collections because of its eclecticism, the walls are rich with the work of notable French Impressionists, including major American works by such artists as Thomas Cole, Winslow Homer, Jackson Pollock, and Edward Hopper.

Like the Prado and the Reina Sofia, the museum expanded into two adjoining buildings, which allows more of the permanent collection to be shown, while also providing new space for temporary exhibitions.

Palacio de Villahermosa, Paseo del Prado 8. ℂ **91-369-01-51.** www.museothyssen.org. Admission 8€ adults, 5.50€ students and seniors, free for children 11 and under. Tues–Sun 10am–7pm. Metro: Banco de España. Bus: 1, 2, 5, 9, 10, 14, 15, 20, 27, 34, 45, 51, 52, 53, 74, 146, or 150.

Palacio Real (Royal Palace) ★★   During the reign of the dictator Franco, this palace was just a monument, but it now has taken on more meaning after the restoration of the monarchy. The lavishly decorated complex is vast, constructed high on a bluff opening onto Río Manzanares. For centuries the site was a royal fortress, but following a fire in 1734, the present palace was built on orders of Felipe V.

Today's royal family resides elsewhere, but this palace was occupied until 1931, when Alfonso XIII abdicated. King Juan Carlos comes here only for state occasions.

Highlights of a visit include the Reception Room, State Apartments, Armory, and Royal Pharmacy. The **Reception Room** and **State Apartments** should get priority here if you're rushed. They embrace a rococo room with a diamond clock; a porcelain salon; the Royal Chapel; the Banquet Room, where receptions for heads of state are still held; and the Throne Room. The rooms are literally stuffed with art treasures and antiques.

If your visit falls on the first Wednesday of the month, look for the changing of the guard ceremony, which occurs at noon and is free to the public.

In the Armory, you'll see the finest collection of weaponry in Spain. From here, the comprehensive tour takes you into the Royal Pharmacy. Afterward, stroll through the **Campo del Moro,** the palace gardens. Plan to spend about 1½ hours here.

Plaza de Oriente, Calle de Bailén 2. ℂ **91-454-88-00.** www.patrimonionacional.es. Admission 10€ adults, 3.50€ students and children 16 and under. Oct–Mar Mon–Sat 9:30am–5pm; Sun 9am–2pm; Apr–Sept Mon–Sat 9am–6pm, Sun 9am–3pm. Metro: Opera or Plaza de España. Bus: 3, 25, 39, or 148.

Panteón de Goya ★★   Outside the city center, Goya's Tomb contains one of his masterpieces, an elaborate **fresco** ★★★ depicting the miracles of St. Anthony on the dome and cupola of the little hermitage of San Antonio de la Florida. Critics have hailed the work as "Goya's Sistine Chapel." Built in the reign of Carlos IV in the neoclassical style, the hermitage is dedicated to St. Anthony. Goya labored dawn to dusk for 16 weeks, painting with sponges rather than with brushes. In the background, the artist depicted common street life—stonemasons, prostitutes, and beggars. In the chapel rests the tomb of the artist, his remains shipped here from Bordeau, where he died as an expatriate in 1828. In 1799, Goya became court painter to Carlos IV but pictured the royal family with grotesque accuracy.

Glorieta de San Antonio de la Florida 5. ℂ **91-542-07-22.** Free admission. Tues–Fri 9:30am–8pm; Sat–Sun 10am–2pm. Metro: Principe Pio. Bus: 41, 46, 75, or C.

Plaza Mayor ★★★   This is the most famous and most historic square in Spain. The plaza is enveloped by 17th-century, three-story buildings with arcades at their base. These arcades are filled with cafes and craft shops. Some of the building facades are graced with allegorical paintings, as well as balconies, pinnacles, and dormer windows. The square was the center of life in old Madrid, staging everything from bullfights and executions to pageants and trials by the Inquisition. In 1621, the square was the venue for the beautification of St. Isidore, Madrid's patron saint. In the center of the plaza stands a statue of Felipe III, who is responsible for the construction of the square. A coin and stamp market is held every Sunday morning, along with stalls hawking used books, old badges, and other collectibles.

In the southwest corner of the square, you can take a flight of steps leading down to the Calle de Cuchilleros, site of a bevy of *mesones* (traditional restaurants). The most famous of these is **Sobrino de Botín ★★**, Calle de Cuchilleros 17 (*©* **91-366-42-17;** www.botin.es), which Hemingway made famous in the pages of *The Sun Also Rises*. Also, painter Francisco Goya was once a dishwasher here. Dating from 1725, the kitchen specializes in roast suckling pig and roast Segovian lamb.

Plaza Mayor. Daily 24 hr. Metro: La Latina or Opera.

Where to Dine

El Amparo ★★ BASQUE   A former carriage house was converted into this elegant enclave of refined Basque cuisine. The cuisine has a real modern accent, made with top-notch ingredients that are fashioned into imaginative and flavorful platters. Under rough-hewn wooden beams, you can partake of such specialties as ravioli with crayfish or roulades of lobster flavored with soy sauce.

Callejón de Puigcerdà 8. *©* **91-431-64-56.** Reservations required. Main courses 24€–40€. AE, DC, MC, V. Mon–Fri 1:45–3:30pm; Mon–Sat 9–11:30pm. Closed Easter week. Metro: Serrano. Bus: 19, 21, or 53.

El Espejo ★ 🐟 INTERNATIONAL   Located near Plaza de las Cortés, this restaurant features one of the best menu values in town, the list of international specialties changing daily. The chefs enhance the pristine flavors of food with skill and restraint, and dish after dish. Some tasty dishes that appear with regularity are lasagna with prawns and fresh vegetables; baked hake with seafood cream; and succulent sirloin steaks grilled as you like. The setting is a beautiful Art Nouveau dining room, with outdoor tables available during most months of the year.

Paseo de Recoletos 31. *©* **91-308-23-47.** www.restauranteelespejo.com. Reservations required. Main courses 14€–23€; fixed-price menus 37€–79€. AE, DC, MC, V. Daily 1–4pm and 9pm–midnight. Metro: Colón. Bus: 5, 27, 45, or 150.

La Biotika ★ 🍴 VEGETARIAN   Vegetarian cuisine doesn't get a lot of attention in most Madrid restaurants, but this discovery is a rare exception. Opening east of the landmark Plaza Santa Ana, La Biotika is intimate and charming. It serves the capital's best macrobiotic vegetarian cuisine, and does so exceedingly well. We always begin with one of the homemade soups, which are made fresh daily, then have one of the large, fresh salads. One specialty is a "meatball without meat" (made with vegetables but shaped like a meatball).

Amor de Dios 3. *©* **91-429-07-80.** www.labiotika.es. *Menú del día* 9.90€. MC, V. Daily 1–5pm. Metro: Antón Martín.

La Bola MADRILEÑA   This is *the* taberna in which to savor the 19th century. Just north of the Teatro Real, it's one of the few restaurants (if not the only one) left in Madrid with a blood-red facade; at one time, nearly all fashionable restaurants were so coated. Time stands still inside this restaurant, with its traditional atmosphere, gently polite waiters, Venetian crystal, and aging velvet. Grilled sole,

Madrid's equivalent of London's pub-crawl is *tasca*-hopping. *Tascas* are local taverns serving tapas along with beer and wine (the hard stuff, too). Many *tascas* specialize in one dish, perhaps mushrooms or else shrimp, although most of them serve a wide array of tasty appetizers. Since the dining hour is late in Madrid, often around 10pm, Madrileños patronize these *tascas* and satisfy their predinner appetites with one "small plate" after another. It's amazing they are still hungry when it's time for dinner.

Our favorite *tascas* include **Casa Mingo,** Paseo de la Florida 34 (✆ **91-547-79-18**), where you can pair the best cider in town with a piece of *cabrales* or goat cheese from the northwestern province of Asturias. Roast chicken, served at communal tables, is the other specialty of the kitchen. Prices range from 2€ to 8€. Service is daily 11am to midnight. No credit cards. Metro: Principe Pio, then a 5-minute walk. Bus: 41, 46, or 75.

One of the most patronized *tascas* in Old Madrid is **Taberna Toscana,** Manuel Fernández y Gonzáles 10 (✆ **91-429-60-31;** www.tabernatoscana.es), where you sit on country stools and order some of the best tapas in town. These include *chorizo* (the spicy Spanish sausage), *lacón y cecina* (boiled ham), and tasty *habas,* or broad beans. The

kidneys in sherry sauce and the snails in hot sauce are also delectable. A glass of wine starts at 1.50€, and tapas range from 4€ to 18€. MasterCard and Visa are accepted, and hours are Tuesday to Saturday noon to 4pm and 8pm to midnight. Metro: Puerta del Sol or Sevilla.

Cervecería Santa Bárbara, Plaza de Santa Barbara 8 (✆ **91-319-04-49;** www.cerveceriasantabarbara.com), set in one of old Madrid's most colorful squares, is the outlet for a beer factory. The two most popular brews are *cerveza negra* (black beer) and *cerveza dorada* (golden beer). This *cerveza* is consumed with homemade potato chips and such seafood delights as barnacles, fresh lobster or shrimp, or crabmeat. Tapas cost 2.50€ to 14€, with a beer going for 1.50€ to 3.50€. MasterCard and Visa are accepted. Open daily 8am to midnight. Metro: Alonzo Martínez. Bus: 3, 7, or 21.

Another well-patronized tapas outlet, **Cervecería La Alemana,** Plaza de Santa Ana 6 (✆ **91-429-70-33**), opens onto an even more colorful square. Evocative of the turn of the 20th century, it offers little tables that are jampacked nightly with locals sampling the fried sardines or a Spanish omelet. A beer costs 2.50€, with tapas going from 4€ to 10€. MasterCard and Visa are accepted. Open Wednesday to Monday 10am to 2am. Metro: Tirso de Molina or Puerta del Sol. Bus: 6, 17, or 56.

filet of veal, and roast veal are regularly featured. Basque-style hake and grilled salmon are well recommended.

Calle de la Bola 5. (✆ **91-547-69-30.** www.labola.es. Reservations required. Main courses 18€–36€. No credit cards. Mon–Sat 1–4pm and 8:30–11pm. Metro: Opera or Santo Domingo. Bus: 25 or 39.

La Gamella ★★ INTERNATIONAL   The russet-colored, high-ceilinged design invites customers to relax. The founder has prepared his delicate and light-textured specialties for the king and queen of Spain, as well as for Madrid's most talked-about artists and merchants, many of whom he knows and greets personally between sessions in his kitchen. Try such temptations as ravioli filled with pumpkin and almonds with a creamy herb sauce, or pan-seared fresh codfish in a mushroom sauce. Another specialty is baby squid stuffed with caramelized onions and served with black pasta.

Alfonso XII no. 4. ☏ **91-532-45-09.** www.lagamella.com. Reservations required. Main courses 17€–25€. *Menú de degustación* 36€. AE, DC, MC, V. Mon–Fri 1:30–4pm and 9pm–midnight; Sat 9pm–midnight. Closed 4 days around Easter. Metro: Retiro. Bus: 19.

La Paloma ★ BASQUE/FRENCH   Two of Europe's greatest cuisines—French and Basque—are wed harmoniously at this exclusive retreat in the elegant Salamanca district. The chef and owner, Segundo Alonso, is known for his perfectly prepared and "robust" dishes, specializing in various meats, such as pigs' trotters, which he fashions into divine concoctions, or you could settle instead for the equally celebrated wood pigeon stuffed with foie gras. The welcome and the service are flawless.

Jorge Juan 39. ☏ **91-576-86-92.** www.rtelapaloma.com. Reservations recommended. Main courses 20€–60€; tasting menu 60€. AE, DC, MC, V. Mon–Sat 1:30–4pm and 9pm–midnight. Metro: Velázquez or Vergara.

La Terraza del Casino ★★★ SPANISH/INTERNATIONAL   The city's most imaginative chef, Ferran Adrià, isn't in Madrid. But the innovative master of cuisine created all the dishes on the menu and flies in regularly to oversee his cooks. This dining hot spot provides a panoramic view of the heart of Madrid and can be reached by an elevator or by a sweeping 19th-century staircase. The exquisite food prepared with fresh seasonal ingredients reinterprets Spanish dishes. An example is *raya* (skate) in oil and saffron with parsley purée and nuts on a bed of finely diced fries. A more traditional dish is the succulent *merluza a la gallega* (Galician hake).

Alcalá 15. ☏ **91-532-12-75.** www.casinodemadrid.es. Main courses 25€–33€. AE, DC, MC, V. Mon–Fri 1:30–4pm and 9–11:45pm; Sat 9–11:45pm. Closed Aug. Metro: Sevilla or Puerta del Sol.

Lhardy ★★ SPANISH/INTERNATIONAL   A Madrid legend since its opening in 1839, this was once the preferred dining choice of the capital's cognoscenti, especially its literary and political leaders. In an antique setting of marble and hardwood, a ground-floor deli still dispenses cups of steaming consommé from silver samovars into little porcelain cups. On the second floor, in an ornate Belle Epoque–styled restaurant, specialties that might have been known to Queen Isabella II are still prepared—and done so exceedingly well. Specialties of the house include monkfish in lobster sauce, partridge stew with French onions, and duck breast in a green pepper sauce.

Carrera de San Jerónimo 8. ☏ **91-521-33-85.** www.lhardy.com. Reservations recommended for the upstairs dining room. Main courses 32€–39€. AE, DC, MC, V. Mon–Sat 1–3:30pm and 8:30–11pm. Closed Aug. Metro: Puerta del Sol.

Pan de Lujo ★★ MEDITERRANEAN/ASIAN   Artful and elegant, with a battery of lights that subtly change, this big-windowed restaurant near Parque del Retiro has earned rave reviews for its interior design and its cuisine. Alberto Chicote, one of the city's most famous chefs, mixes Asian and Mediterranean ideas in ways that have pleased late-night Madrileños. Some of the finest of Spain's regional produce goes into the imaginative, creative dishes served here. Begin perhaps with an appetizer of paper-thin eggplant in delicate virgin olive oil resting on hummus, followed by poached red snapper with crisp baby vegetables.

Calle Jorge Juan 20. ☏ **91-436-11-00.** www.pandelujo.es. Reservations required. Main courses 18€–42€. AE, DC, MC, V. Daily 1:30–4pm and 9pm–midnight. Metro: Serrano or Retiro.

Taberna del Alabardero BASQUE/SPANISH   In proximity to the Royal Palace, this little Spanish classic is known for its selection of tasty tapas, ranging from squid cooked in wine to fried potatoes dipped in hot sauce. Photographs of famous former patrons, including Nelson Rockefeller, line the walls. The restaurant in the rear is said to be another of the city's best-kept secrets. Decorated in typical tavern style, it serves a savory Spanish and Basque cuisine made with market-fresh ingredients.

Felipe V no. 6. ✆ **91-547-25-77.** www.alabardero.eu. Reservations required for restaurant only. Bar: Tapas 3€–12€; glass of house wine 4€. Restaurant: Main courses 17€–25€; *menú degustación* 51€. AE, DC, MC, V. Daily 1–4pm and 9pm–midnight. Metro: Opera.

Shopping

Some call it Madrid's **El Rastro** ★, or flea market. Other, more discerning critics refer to it as the thieves market. It's said that virtually everything stolen in Madrid turns up here at some point. Set in a triangle of streets a few minutes' walk south of Plaza Mayor, this flea market dates from the Middle Ages and is centered around Plaza de Cascorro. The main action takes place along Calle Ribera de Curtidores, or "tanner's riverbank," once the headquarters of the tanning industry and the slaughter-house district. The other major street of vendors hawking their wares is along Calle de Embajadores. The time to go is after 8am on a Sunday morning. What's for sale? Everything from an "original" El Greco to antiques, bric-a-brac, and a vast array of fascinating junk. Plaza de Cascorro and Ribera de Curtidores. Metro: La Latina; bus: 3 or 17.

The leading department store of Madrid—in fact, the flagship of the largest department store chain—is **El Corte Inglés** ★★, Preciados 3 (✆ **91-379-80-00;** www.elcorteingles.es). A lot of the merchandise here is of interest mainly to locals, but you'll also find a large selection of Spanish handcrafts, including damascene steelwork from Toledo, embroidered shawls, and flamenco dolls. You can also preview a wide selection of Spanish fashion for both women and men. Open Monday to Saturday 10am to 10pm; Metro: Puerta del Sol.

An excellent center for crafts is **El Arco de los Cuchilleros Artesania de Hoy,** Plaza Mayor 9, Basement Level (✆ **91-365-26-80**), set within one of the 17th-century vaulted cellars off the historic Plaza Mayor. An unusual and varied collection of one-of-a-kind merchandise from all over Spain has been assembled here, including everything from textiles to pottery and leather items. Daily 11am to 8pm; Metro: Puerta del Sol or Opera. Devotees of antiques, Iberian style, gravitate to **Centro de Anticuarios Lagasca,** Lagasca 36 (✆ **91-577-3752**), where they discover about a dozen different outlets under one arcade. The attics of Spain were raided for this assemblage of furnishings, porcelain, and bric-a-brac. Open Monday to Friday 11am to 2pm and 5 to 8:30pm, Saturday 11am to 2pm; Metro: Serrano or Velázquez.

The quality leather products at **Loewe** ★★★, Serrano 26 (✆ **91-577-60-56;** www.loewe.com), have made this exclusive outlet a Madrid legend since 1846. Its designers have won many gold medals for their tasteful, chic leather designs. The store carries a deluxe assortment of luggage and handbags, along with both leather and suede jackets for men and women. Open Monday to Saturday 9:30am to 8:30pm; Metro: Banco de España or Gran Vía.

Nightlife

Following a $160-million renovation in the late 1990s, **Teatro Real,** Plaza Isabel II (✆ **91-516-06-60;** www.teatro-real.es), is the showcase for cultural Madrid. It first opened in 1850 under the reign of Queen Isabel II, and its acoustics are the best in Iberia. The building is the home for Compañía del Teatro Real, which specializes in

THE EXOTIC SOUND OF flamenco

No art form, other than bullfighting, is more evocative of Spain than flamenco dancing. Although it may have been created by "lowlife roots," including taverns catering to hoodlums, brothels, gypsies, and what one critic called "whoopee hedonism," flamenco has long grown respectable and is heard in the most elegant of clubs today.

The finest flamenco singers and dancers appear in Madrid, accompanied by the guitar music, castanets, and ritualized clapping of the audience. The earliest performers might have been dancer-prostitutes, but today some of the finest talent in all the land, both female and male, pursue the art of flamenco. If you have only 1 night in Madrid, try to take in a flamenco show, notably at the sizzling **Corral de la Morería,** Morería 17 (✆ **91-365-8446**), charging a 32€ cover, including one drink. The show with dinner costs 75€ to 85€. Although it's touristy, some of the best flamenco performers in Spain appear here nightly in colorful costumes. Open daily 8:30pm to 2:30am; Metro: La Latina or Opera.

If you prefer a less touristy atmosphere, check out the scene at **Casa Patas,** Cañizares 10 (✆ **91-369-0496**), which is also a bar and restaurant. Perhaps the best flamenco shows in Madrid are presented here daily. The cover ranges from 25€ to 30€. Two shows are presented Friday and Saturday at 9pm and midnight, with one show Monday to Thursday at 10:30pm. Metro: Tirso de Molina or Anton Martín.

Should you become crazed for flamenco during your stay in Madrid, you might also head for **Café de Chinitas,** Torija 7 (✆ **91-547-1502**), a club of long-enduring popularity. One of Madrid's best flamenco clubs, the cafe lies in an old structure set at midpoint between the Gran Vía (the main drag) and the Opera. Some of the best gypsy flamenco dancers from Andalusia appear here. A dinner and show costs 75€; the cover for the show without dinner, but with one drink included, is 34€. Shows are presented Monday to Saturday from 10:30pm to 2am. Metro: Santo Domingo or Opera; bus: 1 or 2.

opera but is also a major venue for classical music, with tickets ranging from 8€ to 25€. Metro: Opera.

The mammoth **Kapital,** Atocha 125 (✆ **91-420-29-06;** www.grupo-kapital. com), contains seven different levels, each sporting at least one bar and an ambience that's often radically different from that of the previous floor. Voyeurs of any age, take heart—there's a lot to see at the Kapital, with a mixed crowd that pursues whatever form of sexuality seems appropriate at the moment. The action doesn't really get going until 2am. Open Thursday to Sunday midnight to 6am. Admission ranges from 12€ to 15€, including the first drink. Metro: Atocha.

Pachá, Barceló 11 (✆ **91-447-01-28;** www.pacha-madrid.com), another late-night club, attracts the 20-to-40 age group and has long been a fixture on the Madrid nightlife scene. In the 1930s, it was a movie theater, but by the 1980s, it had become a "dance cathedral." As the night grows late, milling crowds pack the precincts and the noise level becomes deafening. Dancing to loud music and hard drinking rule the night. Open Tuesday to Sunday 11pm to 5am, and cover is 12€ to 15€, including the first drink. Metro: Tribunal.

Jazz aficionados flock to **Café Central,** Plaza del Angel 10, off Plaza de Santa Ana (© **91-369-41-43;** www.cafecentralmadrid.com), which has a turn-of-the-20th-century Art Deco decor. Some of the country's leading jazz performers entertain you at their nightly sessions. Open Sunday to Thursday 1:30pm to 2:30am, Friday and Saturday 1:30pm to 3:30am. Live jazz is featured daily from 10pm to midnight. Beer costs 1.80€ to 2.25€, and cover ranges from 7€ to 15€, depending on the show. Metro: Antón Martín or Puerto del Sol. Those seeking jazz also descend on **Clamores ★**, Albuquerque 14 (© **91-445-79-38;** www.salaclamores.com), with its dark and smoky interior. Dating from the 1980s, this is one of the biggest and most frequented jazz clubs in Iberia. Spanish jazz bands appear regularly, in addition to some excellent artists from the United States. The place is open daily from 6:30pm to around 3am, plus Friday and holiday evenings from 6:30pm until 4am. Daily performances are at 10pm and again at 1am. There are jam sessions Friday and Saturday night from 12:30 to 2:30am. Drinks start at around 5€ each. A cover of 6€ to 27€ is imposed Tuesday to Saturday, but varies with act. Metro: Bilbao.

Casino action is found at **Casino Gran Madrid,** Km29 Carretera La Coruña, Apartado 62, the A-6 highway running between Madrid and La Coruña (© **91-856-11-00** or 90-090-08-10; www.casinogranmadrid.es). The largest casino in Madrid, it also attracts nongamblers to its restaurant and entertainment facilities, featuring everything from four bars to a disco. Games of chance include both French and American roulette, blackjack, *punto y banco,* baccarat, and chemin de fer. Entrance costs 3€, and you must present a passport. Open daily 4pm to 5am.

An Excursion to Toledo ★★★

Reached by train in only 35 minutes from Madrid (it's about 42 miles/68km to the south of the capital), this is Iberia's greatest imperial city. Toledo stands atop a hill enveloped on three sides by a bend in the River Tagus, a scene immortalized by the city's most famous painter, El Greco, in his *View of Toledo,* currently hanging in New York's Metropolitan Museum of Art.

Toledo's history is ancient. The Visigoths made it their capital in the 6th century A.D., leaving behind churches extant even today. In medieval times, Toledo was a melting pot of Muslim, Jewish, and, of course, Christian cultures. The Toledo cathedral, one of the greatest in Europe, dates from those times. Even on the most rushed of schedules, try to visit this cathedral, along with the Iglesia de Santo Tomé (with El Greco's masterpiece) and, most definitely, Charles V's fortified palace, the Alcázar. With time remaining, you can see El Greco's house in the old Jewish Quarter.

GETTING THERE

RENFE **trains** run here frequently every day. Those departing Madrid's Atocha railway station for Toledo run daily from 6:50am to 9:50pm; those leaving Toledo for Madrid run daily from 6:50am to 9:30pm. Traveling time is approximately 35 minutes on an *alta velocidad* (high-speed) train. The fare one-way is 9.50€. For train information in Madrid, call © **90-224-02-02** or 90-224-34-02 (www.renfe.es).

Arrivals are at **Estación Toledo,** Paseo de la Rosa 2 (© **90-232-0320**), a beautiful neo-Mudéjar station lying just over the bridge Puente de Azarquiel from the center of town. From the station, bus nos. 5 and 6 run into the center. Buses depart every 15 minutes from the station during the day, taking you to the main square of town, Plaza de Zocodover, the ancient marketplace. A one-way fare costs 1€; the ride is only 5 minutes. The train station has drinking and dining facilities but no tourist information office.

TOURIST INFORMATION

The **Toledo tourist information office,** Plaza del Consistorio 1 (© **92-525-40-30;** www.toledo-turismo.com), is open daily 10am to 6pm.

TOP ATTRACTIONS & SPECIAL MOMENTS

One of the great Gothic structures of the world, the **Catedral de Toledo ★★★,** Cardenal Cisneros 1 (© **92-522-2241**), dates from 1226, when King Ferdinand III laid the first stone. Today the cathedral is renowned for its art and architecture, along with its five naves and stunning stained glass. Among its art treasures, the **transparente** stands out—a wall of marble and florid baroque alabaster sculpture overlooked for years because the cathedral was too poorly lit. Now sunlight touches the high-rising angels, a *Last Supper* in alabaster, and a Virgin in ascension. Other highlights of the cathedral include **El Greco's** *Twelve Apostles* and *Spoliation of Christ,* and **Goya's** *Arrest of Christ on the Mount of Olives.* A splendid 16th-century **silver gilt monstrance ★★,** allegedly made of gold brought back by Christopher Columbus, is found beneath a Mudéjar ceiling in the Treasury. Admission to the cathedral is free, but if you visit its treasury, the cost is 7€. Open Monday to Saturday 10:30am to 6:30pm and Sunday 2 to 6pm.

The second great edifice of Toledo is the **Alcázar ★★★,** Cuesta de Carlos V no. 2, near Plaza de Zocodover (© **92-523-88-00**), close to the eastern edge of the old city, its architectural line dominating the skyline. Charles V ordered this fortified palace built on the site of Roman, Visigoth, and even Muslim fortifications. The Alcázar became world famous in 1936 when it was practically destroyed by Republicans. Holding down the fortress, the Nationalists survived a 70-day siege. Today the Alcázar houses an army museum, with interesting artifacts from varying times in Spanish history. Note that, at press time, the museum was closed for renovations (it may reopen in late 2011); check its status before setting out.

In a 16th-century hospital founded by Cardinal Mendoza, **Museo-Hospital de Santa Cruz ★★,** Calle Miguel de Cervantes 3 (© **92-522-14-02**), is a museum of art and sculpture. The museum is celebrated for its **collection of 16th and 17th century paintings ★,** 18 of which are by El Greco himself. *The Assumption of the Virgin ★* is El Greco's last known work. Paintings by Ribera, Goya, and other great Spanish artists are also on display, along with medieval and Renaissance tapestries and masterful sculptures. During exhibitions, a guided tour costs 4€. Admission is free, and the museum is open Monday to Saturday 10am to 6:30pm, Sunday 10am to 2pm. Bus 5 or 6.

At the modest 14th-century chapel **Iglesia de Santo Tomé,** Plaza del Conde 4, Via Santo Tomé (© **92-525-60-98**), you can gaze upon El Greco's masterpiece, *The Burial of the Count of Orgaz ★★★,* painted in 1586. Admission is 2.30€, and hours are daily 10am to 6:45pm (closes at 5:45pm in winter). *Tip:* To avoid the hordes, go when it first opens.

Founded by Queen Isabella and King Ferdinand in 1477, **Monasterio de San Juan de los Reyes ★,** Calle Reyes Católicos 17 (© **92-522-38-02;** www.sanjuande losreyes.org), is in the Isabelline style, with flamboyant Gothic, traces of Mudéjar, and even Renaissance influences. The church is noted for its **sculptured decoration ★** by Juan Guas, the Flemish architect who designed the church. Its Gothic cloister from 1510 is stunningly beautiful, with a multicolored Mudéjar ceiling. Admission is 2.30€ adults, 1.80€ seniors, and free for children under 9. Hours are winter daily 10am to 6pm and summer daily 10am to 7pm.

It's not known for sure if El Greco actually lived at this address, but even so, **Casa y Museo de El Greco ★**, Calle Samuel Leví 3 (🕿 92-522-40-46), remains one of the most enduring attractions of Toledo. In the old Jewish Quarter, the house is a museum sheltering a collection of the Crete-born artist's works, including his magnificent series *Christ and the Apostles ★*. The museum also displays a copy of his famous *A View of Toledo,* plus three portraits and many other works of art. At press time, this attraction was closed for renovations. It may reopen in 2010; check its status at the time of your visit.

The oldest and largest of Toledo's eight original synagogues, **Sinagoga de Santa Maria la Blanca,** Calle Reyes Católicos 4 (🕿 92-522-72-57), dates from the 12th century. By 1405, it was taken over by the Catholic Church, but in modern times it has been restored, as much as possible, to its pristine beauty, with carved stone capitals and white horseshoe arches, along with ornamental, horizontal moldings. Its five naves and much of its elaborate Mudéjar decorations remain. Admission is 2.30€. Hours April to September are daily 10am to 6:45pm (otherwise daily 10am–5:45pm).

WHERE TO DINE

Just a minute's walk north of the cathedral, **Adolfo Restaurante ★**, Calle Hombre de Palo 7 (🕿 **92-522-73-21;** www.adolforestaurante.com; bus: 5 or 6), is one of the finest in town and serves typical Toledan cuisine. In a building dating in part from the Middle Ages, chefs turn out savory meals, including some of the province's best game dishes, such as roast suckling pig with green apples or roast lamb with white truffles and rosemary flowers. Reservations are recommended, the tasting menu costs 75€ to 96€, and main courses range from 25€ to 43€. Open Tuesday to Saturday 1 to 4pm and 8pm to midnight, Sunday 1 to 4pm.

As you're in the heart of old Castile, you might want to sample some of that province's fabled fare. It doesn't get any better than **Casón de los López ★★**, Sillería 3 (🕿 **90-219-83-44;** www.casontoledo.com). A short walk from the Plaza de Zocodover in the center of town, this restaurant serves the lightest and most sophisticated cuisine in Toledo. The building itself is a virtual antiques museum, but it's the fresh food from the bounty of the agricultural countryside that keeps this place packed. A specialty is loin of venison with fresh, garlic-flecked spinach in a velvety-smooth mushroom cream sauce. Reservations are required. Main courses cost 15€ to 24€, with a set-price menu costing 39€ and a tasting menu costing 52€. Open daily 1:30 to 4pm and Monday to Saturday 8:30 to 11:30pm.

SHOPPING

Toledo is known for its *damasquinado,* or damascene, work—that is, the Moorish art of inlaying gold, and even copper or silver threads, against a matte black steel backdrop. Stores all over town hawk these objects, including **Damasquinados Suarez,** Circo Romano 8 (🕿 **92-528-00-27**), in business since 1920s. It produces quality damascene work, including some objects of rare beauty. Open daily 9:30am to 7pm.

SEVILLE ★★★

The capital of Andalusia, Seville launched itself into greatness after the Christian conquest of the south in the 13th century. The most exciting times to visit are during *Semana Santa* (Holy Week, which leads up to Easter) and for the *Feria de Abril* (April Fair). The religious processions at Holy Week, when sacred images are paraded through the streets, are world famous.

ACCOMMODATIONS ■
Hotel Murillo **6**
La Casa de la Judería **7**

DINING ◆
El Fogon de Leña **8**
Rio Grande **9**
Taberna del
Alabardero **2**

ATTRACTIONS ●
Catedral de Sevilla **4**
Hospital de la
Santa Caridad **3**
Museo de Bellas Artes
de Sevilla **1**
Real Alcázar **5**

Visitors flock to Seville to see its *Catedral* (third largest in the world) and its Alcázar complex, the Moorish fortress enlarged by the Christians in the 14th century to resemble the Alhambra in Granada. The maze of streets east of the cathedral and the Alcázar is called the Barrio de Santa Cruz, the old Jewish Quarter. It's Seville at its most romantic, filled with strolling guitarists, secret plazas, flower-bedecked patios, and tapas bars. This old ghetto is reason enough to visit here.

GETTING THERE   Located to the north of the city, **Estación Santa Justa,** Avenida Kansas City s/n (© 90-224-02-02 for information and reservations; www.renfe.es), is the major transportation hub of Andalusia, with trains, including AVE and regional runs, arriving from all over Spain. It offers especially good connections to Córdoba, Madrid, Barcelona, and Málaga, even Valencia and Granada. For a preview of trains serving the area, refer to the "Trains & Travel Times in Spain" chart on p. 663.

The tourist information office at the train station (© 95-478-2003) is open daily from 8am to 8pm. The staff provides information about hotels available in the area but do not make reservations themselves. The station is easy to navigate, with ATMs available as well as a money exchange kiosk. There are bars and a cafe, plus a restaurant. Bus no. 32 runs to the center, costing 1€. You can also take **Tele Taxi** (© 95-462-22-22) or **Radio Taxi** (© 95-458-36-05); the base rate for a taxi is 1€ per kilometer at night and .85€ during the day. There is a luggage storage facility at the station that charges 2.40€ for a small bag, 3€ for a medium bag, and 4.50€ for a large bag per day.

VISITOR INFORMATION   The tourist office, **Oficina de Información del Turismo,** at Av. de la Constitución 21B (© 95-478-75-78; www.andalucia.org), is open Monday to Friday 9am to 7:30pm, Saturday and Sunday 9:30am to 3pm.

Top Attractions & Special Moments

Catedral de Sevilla ★★★, Plaza del Triunfo, Avenida de la Constitución (© 95-421-49-71; www.catedraldesevilla.es), was constructed in the 12th century on the site of the great mosque of the Almohads. The celebrated cathedral is the largest Gothic building in the world and the third-largest church in Europe. Construction began in the late 1400s and lasted for a century. The stated goal of its architects was simply this: "Those who come after us will take us for madmen." The towering edifice claims to shelter the Tomb of Columbus, his coffin held up by bearers evoking the kings of Navarra, Aragón, Castile, and León. The towering monument to Christian beliefs is filled with objets d'art and architectural monuments, including the *Capilla Mayor* ★, with its huge iron screens *(rejas)* forged in the 16th century. At the Retablo Mayor, a statue of Santa Maria de la Sede, the patron saint of the cathedral, sits at the main altar before a "waterfall" of gold brought back from the New World. Other treasures include **15th-century stained-glass windows** ★; elaborate choir stalls from the same century; and paintings by Murillo, Goya, and Zurbarán, among other Spanish artists. After touring the dark cathedral, you can take delight in the **Patio de los Naranjos** ★, or the Patio of Orange Trees, with its fresh citrus scent of orange blossoms and sound of chirping birds.

The major landmark on the Seville skyline is **La Giralda ★★★,** the bell tower that adjoins the cathedral. Visitors climb this tower for one of Andalusia's most panoramic city views. The Arabs built the tower as a minaret in 1198, crowning it with bronze spheres. Instead of tearing the tower down as a pagan monument, the Catholic conquerors removed these spheres and crowned La Giralda with Christian symbols, such as a bronze weathervane (called *giraldillo*) portraying Faith. The tower has seen other additions over the centuries, including the addition of bells in the 1500s. To ascend it, you walk a seemingly endless ramp, because there are no stairs.

Admission to the tower and cathedral is 8€ for adults, 2€ for students 25 and under, and free for children 11 and under. On Sunday, admission is free for everyone. Hours in July to August are Monday to Saturday 9:30am to 4pm; September to June Monday to Saturday 11am to 5pm, Sunday 2:30 to 6pm.

Hospital de Santa Caridad ★, Calle Temprado 3 (*©* **95-422-32-32;** www. santa-caridad.es), is intricately linked to the legend of Miguel Manara, portrayed by Dumas and Mérimée as the scandalous Don Juan. The death of Manara's beautiful young wife in 1661 caused him such grief that he retired from society and entered the "Charity Brotherhood," burying corpses of the sick and diseased, as well as condemned and executed criminals. The brotherhood still cares for the invalid. The general public come here to delight in the glory of the building's baroque Sevillana style. Nuns will show you through two festive orange-and-sienna courtyards. In the church itself are many old masters–type paintings by some of the leading artists of the 17th century. Especially ghoulish is the *End of the World's Glory,* by Valdés Leal, picturing an archbishop being devoured by maggots. Admission is 5€ for adults, free for children under 12. Open Monday to Saturday 9am to 1:30pm and 3:30 to 7:30pm, Sunday 9am to 1pm.

Museo de Bellas Artes de Sevilla ★★, Plaza del Museo 9 (*©* **95-478-65-00;** www.museosdeandalucia.es; bus: C3 or C4), lies off a main artery, Calle de Alfonso XII, and is a former convent. Today it shelters a gallery devoted to some of the most important works of art in Seville. One gallery showcases two paintings by El Greco, and many other leading Spanish painters are on parade, including Zurbarán. Note especially Zurbarán's *San Hugo en el Refectorio* (1655), painted for the monastery at La Cartuja. The most fascinating of these is by the artist Valdés-Leal, a 17th-century painter with a macabre style, as exemplified by his painting of John the Baptist's head. More contemporary, and less interesting, paintings are displayed on the top floor. Admission is 1.50€. Open Tuesday 2:30 to 8pm, Wednesday to Saturday 9am to 8:30pm, Sunday 9am to 2:30pm.

Real Alcázar ★★★, Plaza del Triunfo s/n (*©* **95-450-23-23;** www.patronato-alcazarsevilla.es), is a complex of magnificent buildings that has been the home of Spanish royalty for almost 7 centuries. The palace was the sometimes residence of Ferdinand and Queen Isabella I, who sent navigators from Seville to the New World in search of gold and other treasures. Mudéjar courtyards and elegantly decorated corridors remain from the Alcázar's imperial heyday. Over the years, subsequent monarchs have added their own architectural touches, including the lavishly decorated **state apartments ★** ordered built by Charles V. Beautiful 16th-century tiles and elaborate tapestries decorated the halls where Charles once trod. The palace contains many notable features, such as the **Patio de las Doncellas ★**, or maidens, with its elaborate plasterwork by the top artisans brought in from Granada, and the **Salon de Embajadores ★**, dating from 1427. This salon is celebrated for its splendid dome of carved and gilded, interlaced wood. In many ways, it evokes the Alhambra at Granada. Wind down in the sumptuous **gardens ★**, with their Moorish fountains, pavilions, and terraces. Admission is 7.50€. Open April to September Tuesday to Sunday 9:30am to 7pm, October to March Tuesday to Sunday 9:30am to 5pm.

Shopping

One of the best selections of Andalusian ceramics is found at **El Postigo,** Calle Arfe s/n (📞 **95-456-00-13**), near the cathedral. The display of hand-painted tiles is exceptional. Open Monday to Saturday 10am to 2pm and Monday to Friday 5 to 8:30pm.

For general merchandise, head for **El Corte Inglés,** Plaza Duque de la Victoria 13B (📞 **95-459-70-00;** www.elcorteingles.es), in the commercial center of town. In addition to its regular line of clothes and items for the home, it sells brightly colored *feria* costumes worn by young girls during Seville's holidays and traditional regional fashion. Open Monday to Saturday 10am to 8pm.

Works by some of the best of the southern Spanish contemporary artists are on display at **Rafael Ortiz,** Marmolles 12 (📞 **95-421-48-74;** www.galeriarafaelortiz. com), where exhibitions are frequently changed. It's open Monday to Saturday 10am to 1:30pm and 4:30 to 8pm.

The fashions of southern Spain are showcased at **Iconos,** Ave. de la Constitución 21A (📞 **95-422-14-08**), a boutique appealing to a wide age group of women, with an array of items from costume jewelry to silk scarves. Open Monday to Saturday 10am to 9pm and Sunday noon to 5pm.

Near the town hall, **Martian,** Calle Sierpes 74 (📞 **95-421-34-13**), sells a wide array of painted tiles and ceramics, all made in or near Seville. Many of the pieces use ancient Andalusian geometric patterns. Other floral motifs are rooted in Spanish traditions of the 18th century. Martian is open Monday to Saturday 10am to 2pm and 5 to 8:30pm.

Nightlife

The people of Seville begin their evening early by touring all the tapas bars. The most typical of the old-fashioned tapas joints is **Casa Ramón,** Plaza de los Venerables 1 (📞 **95-422-84-83**), in Barrio de Santa Cruz. Since 1934, this landmark bar has served delectable tapas along with local wine. Try *pata negra,* a ham from the fabled black-hoofed Iberian breed of pig, celebrated for its sweet flavor caused by a diet of acorns. It's open Monday to Friday 9:30am to 4pm and 7pm to midnight, Saturday and Sunday 11am to 4pm and 7:30pm to midnight. Tapas are priced from 3.50€. On the northern edge of Barrio de Santa Cruz stands **El Rinconcillo,** Gerona 42 (📞 **95-422-31-83;** www.elrinconcillo.es), a *tasca* dating from 1670, making it the oldest bar in town. The selection of cheeses here is especially tempting, and they serve full meals. It's open Thursday to Tuesday from 1pm to 1:30am. A complete meal will cost around 30€. For the best seafood tapas, head over to **La Alicantina,** Plaza del Salvador 2 (📞 **95-422-61-22**), lying 5 blocks north of the cathedral. We can personally vouch for the fried calamari, the clams marinara, and the garlic-flavored grilled shrimp. It is open September to June daily noon to midnight, July and August daily 10:30am to 4pm and 8pm to 1am. Tapas range upward from 3.50€.

If you like bars instead of *tascas,* head for **Abades,** Calle Pío 42–43 (📞 **95-571-8279**), set in a mansion in the Santa Cruz barrio that dates from the 1800s. It is an architectural jewel box from the Spanish *Romantico* era, with classical music playing in the background. Later you can enjoy authentic Andalusian flamenco at **Tablao Los Gallos,** Plaza de Santa Cruz 11 (📞 **95-421-69-81**), which is one of the most reputable of the joints, attracting top talent for its impassioned performances. The cover charge of 30€ includes the first drink. Two shows are presented nightly, the first from 8 to 10pm, the second from 10:30pm to 12:30am.

Its major competition, with shows almost equally good, is **El Arenal,** Calle Rodó 7 (📞 **95-421-64-92;** www.tablaoelarenal.com). Showtimes are usually nightly at 7 and 10pm, but call to confirm that. For a fiesta every night, head for **El Patio Sevillano,** Paseo de Cristobal Colón 11 (📞 **95-421-41-20;** www.elpatiosevillano.com), where exotically costumed Andalusian dancers entertain you with flamenco songs and dance, Andalusian folk songs and dance, and occasional classical pieces by such composers as Chueca or de Falla. Two shows nightly begin at 7 and 9:30pm, and the cover of 37€ includes your first drink.

There's something really special about attending operas inspired by Seville, especially Mozart's *Marriage of Figaro* or Verdi's *La Forza del Destino,* in Seville itself. Since the 1990s, the city has boasted its **Teatro de la Maestranza,** Paseo de Colón 22 (📞 **95-422-33-44;** www.teatromaestranza.com), which is also the setting for other musical presentations ranging from jazz to classical. Spanish *zarzuelas* (operettas) are also performed here. Tickets depend on the event and can be purchased at the box office, open daily from 10am to 2pm and 6 to 9pm.

Where to Stay & Dine

In the heart of the Santa Cruz district, the 57-room **Hotel Murillo,** Calle Lope de Rueda 7–9 (📞 **95-421-60-95;** www.hotelmurillo.com; bus: 21 or 23), is easy on the purse. Named for the artist who used to live in the district, this *residencia* lies near the gardens of the Alcázar. Many of the rooms are cheerless and gloomy, so have a look before checking in. Rates range from 75€ to 100€ double, 93€ to 125€ in a triple.

La Casa de la Judería ★★, Plaza Santa Maria la Blanca, Callejón de dos Hermanos 7 (📞 **95-441-51-50;** www.casasypalacios.com; bus: 21 or 23), is installed inside a 17th-century palace, the former abode of the duke of Beja, and is within easy walking distance of the cathedral and Seville's other major attractions. The 119 bedrooms are medium in size and individually decorated, most often with antiques or reproductions, and some have four-poster beds. All the units have balconies; some of the better units also have whirlpool tubs, and many units have living rooms. Doubles cost 128€ to 265€, with junior suites going for 385€.

Río Grande, in the Hesperia Sevilla, Eduardo Dato 49 (📞 **95-454-83-00;** bus: 23), is a classic Sevillian restaurant named for the Guadalquivir River, which its panoramic windows overlook. It sits near the Plaza de Cuba, in front of the Torre del Oro. Most dishes are priced at the lower end of the scale. A meal might include stuffed sweet-pepper *flamenca,* salmon, chicken-and-shellfish paella, bull's tail Andalusian-style, or garlic chicken. A selection of fresh shellfish is brought in daily. You can often watch sports events such as soccer on the river in this pleasant (and English-speaking) spot. Main dishes cost 12€ to 32€, and hours are Monday to Saturday 1:30 to 4pm and 9pm to midnight (closed Aug).

An unusual blend of Argentine and Andalusian cuisine is served at the relatively unknown **El Fogón de Leña ★**, Santo Domingo de la Calzeda 13 (📞 **95-453-17-10;** www.elfogon.com; bus: 24, 27, or 32), located near the old town. The setting of antique tiles and regional artifacts forms an appropriate backdrop to the skilled cooking of the talented chefs, who turn out savory dishes night after night. Inside the two-story interior, you can stop at the entrance and pay your respects to the mounted head of the last bull killed in the ring by José Luís Vasquez, the celebrated bullfighter. The meat dishes, such as the *chuletón de buey* (ox steak), are especially succulent.

Main courses cost 12€ to 20€, and hours are daily 1 to 4:30pm and 8:30pm to midnight (closed the last 2 weeks in Aug).

Three blocks from the cathedral, **Taberna del Alabardero ★★**, Calle Zaragoza 20 (📞 **95-450-2721;** www.tabernadelalabardero.es), is one of the city's most prestigious restaurants. Set in a 19th-century town house, the restaurant serves refined Andalusian cuisine to politicians, diplomats, and royalty. Against a backdrop of art and antiques, formalized service takes place in two main salons, with additional seating in the rear garden. Devotees of fine food in Seville swear by this place. Main courses cost 20€ to 30€. Hours are daily 1 to 4:30pm and 8pm to midnight.

An Excursion to Córdoba ★★★

Julius Caesar, Pompey, and Agrippa used to stop off in Córdoba when it was the capital of a Roman province called Baetica, established in 151 b.c. But it was under the Moors in the 8th century that the city reached the apex of its power, second only to glittering Constantinople. A visit to its Mezquita (Great Mosque)—still standing today—was said to have been comparable to a pilgrimage to Mecca. Don't forget to bring a good pair of walking shoes, as the only way to explore the monumental heart of the city is on foot.

GETTING THERE   Because the city is a rail junction for routes to the rest of Andalusia, Córdoba is on the vital rail link between Madrid and Seville/Malaga; trains run daily and frequently. The most-used line is the **AVE high-speed train** racing between Córdoba and Seville. Train travel between Seville and Córdoba has been cut to just 25 minutes, and a one-way ticket between Córdoba and Seville sells for 29€. For more information and schedules, contact RENFE (📞 **90-224-0202;** www.renfe.es).

Trains arrive at Estación Córdoba, Glorieta de las Tres Culturas, on the town's northern periphery. Also inside the station is a restaurant and a tourist information office.

The train station is a 10-minute walk from the city center. If you don't want to walk, you can head into town by taxi for about 7€ to 15€. Taxis usually meet arriving trains, or you can call **Radio Taxi** (📞 **95-776-44-44**).

Bus no. 3 makes the run from the train station through Plaza Tendillas and along the river up Calle Doctor Fleming. A one-way ticket costs .80€.

TOURIST INFORMATION   The **Córdoba Tourist Office** is at Calle Torrijos 10 (📞 **95-735-51-79;** www.andalusia.org), open Monday to Friday from 9am to 7:30pm, Saturday and Sunday 9:30am to 3pm.

TOP ATTRACTIONS & SPECIAL MOMENTS

It's worth the train trip to Andalusia to visit the **Mezquita-Catedral de Córdoba ★★★**, Calles Torrijos and Cardenal Herrero s/n (📞 **95-822-52-45;** bus: 3). This magnificent edifice was the Arabs' crowning architectural achievement in the West during their 8th-century heyday. The original mosque, built between 785 and 787, changed and evolved over the centuries using many different styles. The field of more than **850 columns ★★★** was crafted mainly from jasper, granite, and marble, often taken from Roman and Visigothic structures. The richly ornamented prayer niche, the *mihrab* **★★**, is a stunning work. This domed shrine of Byzantine mosaics once housed the Koran.

In the 16th century, a cathedral was placed awkwardly in the middle of this mosque. Highlights of the cathedral include **two pulpits ★★** of mahogany, jasper, and marble, and the **baroque choir stalls** ★★ of Pedro Duque Cornejo from the mid–18th century. Not quite as impressive is the **Capilla de Villaviciosa** ★, the first Christian chapel constructed in the mosque, in 1371, with magnificent multi-lobed arches. For a charming walk, head through the Patio de los Naranjos, a court-yard of orange trees where the faithful once washed before prayer. The hardy can climb a 16th-century tower to catch a panoramic view of Córdoba and its environs. Admission is 8€ adults, 4€ children under 14. Open Monday to Saturday 8:30am to 6pm; Sunday 8:30 to 10:15am and 2 to 6pm.

The second great edifice of Córdoba is the **Alcázar de los Reyes Cristianos** ★, Caballerizas Reales (ⓒ **95-742-01-51**; bus: 3 or 12), 2 blocks southwest of the Mezquita. This fortress was commissioned in 1328 by Alfonso XI and remains a fine example of military architecture. This quadrangular building is notable for powerful walls and a trio of towers—the Tower of the Lions, the Tower of Allegiance, and the Tower of the River. It became the palace-fortress of the Catholic monarchs, its sever-ity softened by its beautiful gardens, fountains, and water terraces. Wander at leisure across the Moorish patios, taking in salons with **Roman mosaics** ★ and an impres-sive **sarcophagus** ★ from the 3rd century A.D. Admission to the Alcázar is 4€ adults (2€ for gardens), free for children 17 and under with parent. The hours are May to June Tuesday to Saturday 10am to 2pm and 5:30 to 7:30pm, Sunday 9:30am to 2:30pm; July to September Tuesday to Saturday 8:30am to 2:30pm; October to April Tuesday to Saturday 10am to 2pm and 4:30 to 6:30pm, Sunday 9:30am to 2:30pm. Gardens are illuminated July to September from 10pm to noon. After seeing the city's two major edifices, you will have viewed the best of Córdoba. If you still have some time remaining before you have to head back to Seville, check out the narrow streets of the old **Judería** ★★, the former Jewish Quarter. This ancient barrio lies directly north of the Mezquita and is filled with 18th-century whitewashed houses with deli-cate window grilles.

Of the private palaces of Córdoba, one is open to the public. **Palacio Museo de Viana** ★★, Plaza de Don Gome 2 (ⓒ **95-749-67-41**), is an impressive example of the civil architecture of Córdoba in the 15th century. With its beautiful garden and a dozen courtyards, it's a stunner outside and in, as it's filled with opulently rich furnish-ings and objets d'art. Note especially the stunning **Mudéjar *artesonado* ceiling** ★, constructed of cedar. The tapestry collection is rich and evocative—many of the hang-ings were made in royal workshops based on cartoons by Goya. Admission is 6€ for the palace and 3€ for the patios. It's open October to May Monday to Friday 10am to 1pm and 4 to 6pm, Saturday 10am to 1pm; June 16 to September Monday to Saturday 9am to 2pm (closed June 1–15).

The **Museo Arqueológico y Etnológico de Córdoba** ★, Plaza Jerónimo Páez 7, Judería (ⓒ **95-735-55-17**), 2 blocks northeast of the Mezquita, is one of the most important archeological museums in Spain. In a palace from 1505, it displays arti-facts, many from Paleolithic and Neolithic times, along with Roman sculptures, bronzes, mosaics, and ceramics, even some Visigothic finds. The most outstanding collection, however, is devoted to Arabic art and spans the entire Muslim occupation. Admission is 1.50€. Open Tuesday 2:30 to 8:30pm, Wednesday to Saturday 9am to 8:30pm, and Sunday and public holidays 9am to 2:30pm.

Another distinguished museum is **Museo de Bellas Artes de Córdoba** ★★, Plaza del Potro 1 (ⓒ **95-735-55-50**), housed in an old hospital. This is an impres-sive regional fine arts museum, housing some outstanding examples of Spanish baroque art, sculpture, and other art objects. There are works by El Greco, Murillo, and Zurbarán, and Juan de Valdés Leal's **macabre paintings ★★**. The museum lies to the immediate east of the Mezquita. Admission is 1.50€. Open Tuesday 2:30 to 8:30pm, Wednesday to Saturday 9am to 8:30pm, and Sunday 9am to 2:30pm.

WHERE TO DINE

Just a 10-minute walk from the Mezquita, **Bodegas Campos ★★**, Calle de los Lineros 32 (© **95-749-75-00;** www.bodegascampos.com; bus: 1, 3, 4, or 7), is a wine cellar (*bodega*) and top-notch restaurant that's been around since 1908. The tapas bar in front is filled with wine drinkers, and you can retreat to the rear, following in the footsteps of numerous celebrities, to dine on fresh and well-prepared Spanish and Andalusian cuisine, such as salt cod salad with orange dressing and *frituritas de la casa con salmorejo* (tiny fried fish served with thick Andalusian gazpacho). Main courses cost 17€ to 28€, and reservations are recommended. Open Monday to Sunday from 11am to midnight, and Sunday until 5pm (closed Dec 25 and Dec 31).

Serving even better is **La Almudaina ★★★**, Plaza Campos de los Santos Mártires 1 (© **95-747-43-42;** www.restaurantealmudaina.com; bus: 3 or 16), set in a 15th-century palace near the Alcázar. Fronting the river in the former Jewish barrio, this is one of Andalusia's finest restaurants. Fresh Spanish and French dishes served in generous portions are the hallmarks of the place. Anglerfish filets with a frothy seafood-brandy sauce taste ultrafresh, and tenderloin of pork is cooked to perfection and served with a delicate wine sauce. Reservations are required, with main courses costing 15€ to 20€ and a fixed-price menu going for 35€. Hours are Monday to Saturday from 12:30 to 4pm and 8:30 to midnight. Only lunch is served on Sundays. It is closed Sundays July 15 to September 1.

Around the corner from the Mezquita, **Taberna Casa Pepe de la Judería ★**, Calle Romero 1 (© **95-720-0744;** bus: 3), is a typical Andalusian restaurant that serves Córdoban recipes of exceptional merit. Spread across three floors, it also offers rooftop dining from May to October. The fare is hearty and regional, and includes combinations such as cod cooked with raisins, pine nuts, and mussels; all dishes use first-rate ingredients. Try the Andalusian gazpacho to start and the *merluza* (hake), prepared Cordovan style with sweet peppers, garlic, and onions. Reservations are recommended, and the fixed-price menu is 28€. Open Sunday to Thursday 1 to 4pm and 8:30 to 11:30pm, Friday to Saturday 1 to 4pm and 8:30pm to midnight.

GRANADA ★★★

In the foothills of the snowcapped Sierra Nevada, Granada, at 2,200 feet (660m), sprawls over two main hills, the Alhambra and the Albaicín, and is crossed by two rivers, the Genil and the Darro. The location is 258 miles (415km) south of Madrid, 164 miles (264km) east of Córdoba, and 155 miles (250km) southeast of Seville. This former stronghold of Moorish Spain is full of folklore. Washington Irving (*Tales of the Alhambra*) used the symbol of this city, the pomegranate (*granada*), to conjure up a spirit of romance.

Most visitors head to this city with one goal in mind—to see the famous Alhambra Palace. Though the palace is the city's must-see attraction, visitors should definitely take the time to soak up the Moorish atmosphere in the old Arab Quarter and take in the other top sites. *Tip:* A good way to tour the city for the rail traveler heading here from Seville (the most popular departure point for Granada) is to schedule one's arrival in the city for late afternoon, overnight in Granada, and then spend the next day touring the wonders of the city before departing on the overnight *Trenhotel* to

Granada

To Sacromonte ↑

To Generalife →

Jardines del Partal

ALHAMBRA (See map below)

San Nicolás

Mirador de San Nicolás

Museo Arqueológico

Torre de Comares

Palacio de Carlos V

ALBAICÍN

Baños Árabes

Patio de los Aljibes

Puerta de la Justicia

Auditorio Manuel de Falla

C/ Antequeru Baja

Alcazaba

Santa Isabel la Real

Plaza San Miguel Bajo

Torre de la Vela

Puerta de las Granadas

C/ Molinos

San Miguel Bajo

Iglesia de Santa Ana

Plaza Sta. Ana

Puerta de las Granadas

REALEJO

0   100 yds
0   100 m

Plaza Nueva

Convento de las Carmelitas

Casa Tiros

Casa Árabe Girones

Convento de Santiago

Santo Domingo

C/ Paco Seco de Lucena

Antigua Capitanía

Capilla Real

Plaza Isabel La Católica

Convento de Carmelitas Descalzas

SAN MATÍAS

Cuarto Real de Santo Domingo

Catedral

Plaza de las Pasiegas

Plaza Carmen

Plaza del Campillo

Palacio de Bibataubin

Plaza Bib-Rambla

Carrera del Genil

ACCOMMODATIONS ■
Casa del Capitel Nazarí **6**
Casa Morisca **1**
Hotel Palacio Santa Inés **5**
Parador de Granada **2**

DINING ◆
Albahaca **8**
Carmen de San Miguel **7**
Cunini **10**

ATTRACTIONS ●
Albaicín **4**
Alhambra and Generalife **3**
Catedral and Capilla Real **9**

Parador de Granada

The Alhambra

Torre de la Vela

Torre de las Armas (Tower of Arms)

Casas Reales

Patio de Comares (Court of the Myrtles)

Palacio Árabe

Alcazaba

Sala de las Dos Hermanas (Hall of the Two Sisters)

Patio de la Acequia (Court of the Water Channel)

Palacio de Carlos V

Sala de los Reyes

Jardines del Partal

GENERALIFE

Patio de los Leones (Court of the Lions)

Torre de la Justicia

ALHAMBRA

Parador de Granada

Teatro

Torre del Cabo de la Carrera (Tower at the End of the Track)

Secano

FRANCE

Madrid ✴

SPAIN

PORTUGAL

Granada ●

0   100 yds
0   100 m

Entrance to Generalife

Barcelona. Be sure to reserve a spot on the overnight train well in advance (see "Practical Train Information," at the beginning of this chapter).

GETTING THERE Most rail passengers head east to Granada after a visit to Seville (see earlier section). Four TRD trains run from Seville to Granada daily, taking between 4 and 5 hours, depending on the train. Instead of launching your Andalusian rail adventure in Seville, you can also take one of two daily Altaria trains leaving from Madrid's Atocha Rail Station and heading south to Granada; the trip takes around 4½ hours.

The **train station** in Granada, **Estación de RENFE de Granada,** is at Avenida de Los Andaluces s/n (© **90-243-23-43;** www.renfe.es), in the southwesterly part of the city, away from the city center. A taxi from the train station to the center of Granada costs 5€ to 10€, but a one-way bus fare is only 1.20€. A stop for bus lines 1, 3, 4, 5, 6, 7, 9, 11, 23, and 33 is about 330 feet (99m) from the entrance to the train station.

The station is open daily from 6:15am to 11:30pm. Immediate tickets can be purchased daily from 6:30am to 11:45pm, and advance tickets from 8:30am to 11:30pm. There is no tourist office, but ATMs are available inside the station.

VISITOR INFORMATION The **Patronato Provincial de Turismo de Granada,** Plaza de Mariana Pineda 10 bajo (© **95-824-71-46;** www.turgranada. es), is open Monday to Friday 9am to 8pm, Saturday 10am to 7pm, and Sunday 10am to 3pm. The staff here will supply you with a list of hotels. Another tourist office, **Tourist Information Office of Junta de Andalucía,** is located at Calle de Santa Ana 4 (© **95-857-52-02;** www.andalucia.org). Open Monday to Friday 9am to 7:30pm, Saturday and Sunday 9:30am to 3pm. It's a 20-minute walk from the train station, or you can take bus no. 3, 9, or 11 from the station.

Getting Around

Walking is a viable option once you arrive in the center of town, and this is the preferred method for exploring Old Granada and the Arab Quarter, *morería.* Cuesta de Gómerez is one of the most important streets in Granada. It climbs uphill from the Plaza Nueva, the center of the modern city, to the Alhambra. At the east-west artery of Plaza Nueva, Calle de los Reyes Católicos goes to the heart of the 19th-century city and the towers of the cathedral. The main street of Granada is the Gran Vía de Colón, the principal north-south artery. One of the most fascinating streets is Calle de Elvira; west of it, the Albaicín, or old Arab Quarter, rises on a hill.

The most-walked street in Granada is **Carrera del Darro,** running north along the Darro River. It was discovered by the Romantic artists of the 19th century; many of their etchings (subsequently engraved) of scenes along this street were widely circulated, doing much to spread the fame of Granada throughout Europe.

Calle de los Reyes Católicos and the Gran Vía de Colón meet at the circular Plaza de Isabel la Católica, graced by a bronze statue of the queen offering Columbus the Santa Fe agreement, which granted the rights to the epochal voyage to the New World. Going west, Calle de los Reyes Católicos passes near the cathedral and other major sights in the downtown section of Granada. The street runs to Puerta Real, the commercial hub of Granada, with many stores, hotels, cafes, and restaurants.

Taxis can be summoned by calling © **95-813-23-23** or © **95-840-01-99.** Otherwise, you can rely on **public buses** (© **95-881-37-11**). The most useful bus is Bus Alhambra, going from Plaza Nueva in the center to the Alhambra (which is a steep climb of almost ¾ mile/1.2km from the city center). Rides cost 1.20€, or you can purchase a packet of 10 tickets costing 11€.

Top Attractions & Special Moments

Later enriched by Moorish occupants into a lavish palace, the **Alhambra and Generalife ★★★**, Palacio de Carlos V (ⓒ **90-244-12-21**; www.alhambra-patronato. es), was originally constructed for defensive purposes on a rocky hilltop outcropping above the Darro River. The modern city of Granada was built across the river from the Alhambra, about half a mile (.8km) from its western foundations.

When you first see the Alhambra, you may be surprised by its somewhat somber exterior. You have to walk across the threshold to discover the true delights of this Moorish palace. Tickets are sold in the office at the Entrada del Generalife y de la Alhambra. Enter through the incongruous 14th-century **Gateway of Justice ★**. Most visitors don't need an expensive guide but will be content to stroll through the richly ornamented open-air rooms, with their lacelike walls and courtyards with fountains.

The tour begins in the **Mexuar,** also known as the Palace of the Nasrids, which is the first of the trio of palaces that compose the Alhambra. This was the main council chamber where the sultan's chief ministers met. From this chapel, a panoramic view spreads over the rooftops of the Albaicín.

The most-photographed part of the palace is the **Court of Lions ★★★**, named after its highly stylized fountain, which rests on 12 marble lions. This was the heart of the palace, the most private section and the royal residence, where the sultan enjoyed his harem. The **Court of the Myrtles** contains a narrow reflecting pool banked by myrtle trees. Note the decorative and rather rare tiles, which are arguably the finest in the Alhambra. Behind it is the **Salón de Embajadores (Hall of the Ambassadors),** with an elaborately carved throne room. Here bay windows open onto **panoramic vistas ★★** of the enveloping countryside. The nearby **Sala de los Reyes (Hall of Kings)** was the great banquet hall of the Alhambra, site of parties, orgies, and feasts.

Charles V built a Renaissance palace at the Alhambra—which, although quite beautiful, is terribly out of place in such a medieval Moorish setting. Today it houses the **Museo Bellas Artes en la Alhambra** (ⓒ **95-822-14-49**), open Tuesday to Saturday 9am to 8pm and Sunday 9am to noon. Of minor interest, it displays mostly religious paintings and sculpture from the 16th to 18th centuries. It also shelters the **Museo de la Alhambra** (ⓒ **95-822-75-27**), devoted to Hispano-Muslim art and open Tuesday to Saturday 9am to 7:15pm and Sunday 9am to 5:45pm.

Before leaving the Alhambra precincts, try to see the **Alcazaba,** which is the oldest part of the complex. This rugged fortress has a spectacular **view ★★** when you climb the **Torre de la Vela (Watchtower).** You look into the lower town onto Plaza Nueva, and you can also see the snowcapped Sierra Nevada in the distance.

Exit from the Alhambra via the Puerta de la Justicia, then circumnavigate the Alhambra's southern foundations until you reach the gardens of the summer palace, where Paseo de los Cipreses quickly leads you to the main building of the **Generalife ★★**, built in the 13th century to overlook the Alhambra. The sultans used to spend their summers in this palace (pronounced Heh-neh-rah-lee-feh), safely locked away with their harems. The Generalife's glory is its gardens and courtyards. Don't expect an Alhambra in miniature: The Generalife was always meant to be a retreat, even from the splendors of the Alhambra. The highlight is its **gardens ★★★**. Much modified, originally, they contained orchards and pastures for domestic animals. Of

Because of the overwhelming crowds, the government limits the number of people who can enter the Alhambra. Go as early as possible, but even if you get here at 10am, you may not be admitted until 1:30pm. If you arrive after 4pm, it's unlikely you'll get in at all. Your best bet is to make arrangements for tickets before you arrive by calling ⓒ **90-288-80001** within Spain. Tickets can also be reserved online at www.alhambra-tickets.es. Tickets carry a 1€ surcharge. Tickets bought on the Internet or by phone can be picked up in the automatic machines of La Caixa, at the entrance to the Alhambra. (You'll need the same credit card that you used to pay for the tickets.) These automatic machines are in the Access Pavilion at the Alhambra. The ticket is valid only for the day you specified.

special note is **Escalera del Agua (the Water Staircase),** with water flowing gently down. Comprehensive tickets, including Alhambra and Generalife, are 12€; Museo Bellas Artes 1.50€; Museo de la Alhambra free; garden visits 6€; illuminated visits 12€. Open March to October daily 8:30am to 8pm, floodlit visits Tuesday to Saturday 10pm to midnight; November to February daily 8:30am to 6pm, floodlit visits Friday and Saturday 8 to 10pm (bus: 30 or 32).

Once you've finished touring the Alhambra, head for the **Albaicín ★★**. The city's old Arab Quarter is on one of the two main hills of Granada and stands in marked contrast to the city center's 19th-century buildings and wide boulevards. It and the surrounding gypsy caves of Sacromonte are holdovers from an older past. The Albaicín once flourished as the residential section of the Moors, even after the city's reconquest, but it fell into decline when the Christians drove them out. This narrow labyrinth of crooked streets escaped the fate of much of Granada, which was torn down in the name of progress. Fortunately, it has been preserved, as have its cisterns, fountains, plazas, whitewashed houses, and villas, and the decaying remnants of the old city gate. To begin your tour of the Albaicín, take bus no. 31 or 32.

In the center of town, **Catedral and Capilla Real ★★**, Plaza de la Lonja, Gran Vía de Colón 5 (ⓒ **95-822-29-59;** www.capillarealgranada.com; bus: 6, 9, or 11), is a richly ornate Renaissance cathedral begun in 1521 and completed in 1714. Its **spectacular altar ★★** is one of the country's architectural highlights, acclaimed for its beautiful facade and gold-and-white interior. Behind the cathedral (entered separately) is the Flamboyant Gothic **Royal Chapel ★★**, where the remains of Queen Isabella and her husband Ferdinand lie. It was their wish to be buried in recaptured Granada, not Castile or Aragón. Accenting the tombs is a wrought-iron grille, itself a masterpiece. In the sacristy, you can view Isabella's personal **art collection ★★**, including works by Rogier Van der Weyden and various Spanish and Italian masters such as Botticelli. Admission to the cathedral is 3.50€, as is admission to the chapel. Both are open daily 10:30am to 1:30pm and 3:30 to 6:30pm (4–8pm in summer).

Where to Stay & Dine

Because the rail station is inconveniently located with respect to the center of the city, all of the following hotels and restaurants are about a 10- to 12-minute taxi or bus ride from the train depot.

Parador de Granada ★★★, Real Alhambra s/n, 18009 Granada (© **95-822-14-40;** www.parador.es; bus: 30), is the most famous *parador* (special state-owned inn) in Spain—and the hardest to get into—set on the grounds of the Alhambra. The decor is tasteful, and the place evokes a lot of history with its rich Andalusian ambience. The 36-room *parador* offer views of the Generalife gardens and the Sacromonte caves from the terrace. The guest rooms are generally roomy and comfortable. Rooms in the older section are furnished with antiques; units in the more modern wing are less inspired. Rates for a double vary from 249€ to 349€.

A real find, the 14-room **Casa Morisca Hotel** ★★, Cuesta de la Victoria 9, 18010 Granada (© **95-822-11-00;** www.hotelcasamorisca.com; bus: 31 or 32), is in the historic lower district of Albaicín, at the foot of the Alhambra. The house dates from the end of the 15th century, and the original interior has been kept and restored, although the facade was given a 17th-century overlay. Bedrooms are individually decorated in an old style, but with all modern comforts. Rates are 90€ to 148€ double, 150€ to 198€ suite.

Hotel Casa del Capitel Nazarí ★ Cuesta Aceituneros 6, 18010 Granada (© **95-821-52-60;** www.hotelcasacapitel.com; bus: 31 or 32), is one of at least four boutique hotels that opened during the early millennium within the cramped but evocative medieval neighborhood known as the Albaicín, a few steps uphill from the Plaza Nueva. Situated within a private, patio-centered home built at least 400 years ago, it's a cozy, appealing mixture of antique and modern. The well-furnished and rather small bedrooms are accented with hand-hewn antiques, including wooden beams in the old Spanish style. Doubles cost 68€ to 110€.

Hotel Palacio Santa Inés ★★, Cuesta de Santa Inés 9, 18010 Granada (© **95-822-23-62;** www.palaciosantaines.com; bus: 30 or 32), in the colorful Albaicín district, is one of the most enchanting places to stay in Granada and about a 5-minute walk from the Alhambra. The painstakingly restored little palace was in complete ruins until the mid-1990s. Now it's a lovely, graceful inn that's even a bit luxe. The 35 medium-size rooms have air-conditioning and lots of antique furniture; some are duplexes and have small sitting rooms, and several open onto views of Granada. The suites have full kitchens. Rates are 80€ to 170€ for a double, 150€ to 250€ for a suite.

Albahaca ★, Calle Varela 17 (© **95-822-49-23;** bus: C, 8 or 13), is a locally beloved bistro housed in a century-old building. Owner Javier Jiménez seats 28 diners at eight tables in this old-fashioned restaurant, decorated in a rustic style. The traditional dishes served are unpretentious and tasty, especially the *salmorejo* (creamy tomato gazpacho) and the *pastel de berenjena con salmón marinado* (layered pastry with eggplant and marinated salmon). Main courses run 9€ to 16€, and reservations are recommended on the weekends. It's open Tuesday to Saturday 1:30 to 4pm and 8:30 to 11pm, and Sunday 1 to 4pm; it's closed in August.

On the sloping incline leading up to the Alhambra, **Carmen de San Miguel,** Plaza de Torres Bermejas 3 (© **95-822-67-23;** www.carmensanmiguel.com; bus: 30 or 32), offers spectacular views of the city center. The restaurant is proud of its glassed-in dining room and patio-style terrace. Specialties include grilled hake, and Iberian ham with Manchego cheese. The food, although good, doesn't quite match the view. Main courses are 10€ to 24€, *menú degustación* 55€. It's open Monday to Saturday 1:30 to 4pm and 8:30 to 11:30pm, winter Sunday 1:30 to 4pm; reservations are recommended.

The array of seafood served at **Cunini,** Plaza de la Pescadería 14 (© **95-826-75-87;** http://cuninigranada.iespana.es; bus: 5 or 11), perhaps 100 selections, extends even to the tapas offered at the long stand-up bar. Even though Granada is inland, it's not that far from the Mediterranean, and some of the freshest and best fish in town is served here. Specialties include a *zarauela* (seafood stew), smoked salmon, and grilled shrimp. Main courses cost 14€ to 32€, and the fixed-priced menu is 20€. Most dishes are reasonably priced except for the very expensive shellfish platters. It is open Tuesday to Saturday noon to 4pm and 8pm to midnight, Sunday noon to 4pm; reservations are recommended.

Nightlife

A good place to begin your night is along the **Campo del Príncipe,** where at least seven old-fashioned tapas bars do a rollicking business during the cool of the evening. One of the most popular tapas bars in Granada (at least, with us) is **El Agua Casa de Vinos,** Calle Algibe de Trillo 7 (© **95-822-43-56**), a well-maintained bar with an adjoining restaurant in a small garden in the heart of the Albaicín. Everyone agrees that the cooling nighttime breezes show off this convivial spot to its best advantage. Its strength is small-scale portions of cheeses, pâtés, and salads, which go especially well with glasses of wine and beer. An equally historic spot with a verdant patio loaded with plants and shrubs is **Bar Pilar del Toro,** Calle Hospital de Santa Ana 12 (© **95-822-54-70;** www.pilardeltoro.es), near the cathedral and the Plaza Nueva. An even larger competitor, **La Gran Taberna,** Plaza Nueva 12 (© **95-822-88-46**), is a modern and irreverent site that attracts coffee and wine tasters, as well as lovers of sliced Serrano ham, fondues, and liqueurs.

BARCELONA

One of the Mediterranean's busiest and most bustling ports, Barcelona is the capital of Catalonia, a province that fiercely clings to its own rich language and culture, both of which Franco systematically tried to eradicate. It lies in the northeast of Spain and leans more to continental Europe in spirit than it does to the peninsula of Iberia.

If your schedule is so rushed that you have to choose either Barcelona or Madrid, that's a tough call. It's like someone saying you can visit either London or Paris. When it comes to sights, food, monuments, and shopping, the rival cities are in a neck-and-neck race. If you want to see the traditional land of bullfights and flamenco, make it Madrid. For wild nightlife, bronzed nude beaches, whimsical and daring *modernista* architecture, and the work of Surrealistic painters such as Dalí or Joan Miró, make it Barcelona. The city, which was revitalized in 1992 when it hosted the Summer Olympics, is fast emerging as one of continental Europe's hottest tourist destinations.

Barcelona is also the gateway to Catalonia; the eastern coast Spanish ports along the Mediterranean, such as Valencia; and the Pyrenees, which are not that distant.

It is not, however, a good center for touring much of Spain. Madrid is in the exact center and is a much better rail hub. Keep that in mind if you prefer to base yourself in a place that offers easy access to day excursions by rail.

Note: Barcelona grapples with problems common to many major cities—the increasing polarization of rich and poor, rising drug abuse, and an escalating crime rate, mostly theft. City authorities have, with some degree of success, brought crime under control in the tourist zones, but do take the usual precautions.

Station Information

GETTING FROM THE AIRPORT TO THE TRAIN STATIONS

You can reach Estaçio Barcelona-Sants by a local train. A train runs between the airport and Barcelona's Estació Central de Barcelona-Sants every day from 6:10am (the first airport departure) to 10:45pm (from Sants) or 11:50pm (the last city departure). The 20-minute trip costs 3.50€. The **Aerobús** (℡ **93-415-60-20**) runs daily every 12 minutes between 6am and 1am from the airport, and till 12:30am from the Plaça de Catalunya. The fare is 5€ one-way, 8.65€ round-trip. To get to the station by taxi, expect a fare ranging from 20€ to 30€.

There is no Metro line that runs to the Estaçio de França station and no Aérobus. Taxis meet all arriving flights at the Barcelona airport, and a trip to Estaçio de França by taxi costs 20€ to 27€. You can, of course, reach Plaça de Catalunya by bus or Metro. From this transportation hub, bus no. 17 runs out to the Estaçio França. If you're carrying heavy luggage, however, it will be a difficult jaunt.

INSIDE THE STATIONS

Like Madrid, Barcelona has two major rail stations: Estaçio Barcelona-Sants and Estaçio França.

Estaçio Barcelona-Sants, in Plaça Paisos Catalans (℡ **90-224-0202;** Metro: Sants-Estaçio), is Barcelona's public transportation hub, with most bus lines, all Metro lines, and both long-distance and regional trains converging here. Direct trains link you to Montpellier, France, with ongoing connections to Paris and Geneva on TGV (high-speed) trains.

You can also catch trains here for Valencia and the Levante, Zaragoza, Madrid, and Seville. For general rail information, call ℡ **90-224-0202,** or visit **www.renfe.es**.

It is linked by frequent buses to the Plaça de Catalunya. Take bus no. 17, which costs 1.35€ for a one-way fare. There is a tourist office here (℡ **90-224-02-02;** Metro: Sants-Estaçió), hotel information, banks, ATMs, a restaurant, a cafe, a book-and-record store, a jazz club, and even a disco at this two-level station. The station's 12 tracks lie beneath the main floor of the station and are accessible by both elevators and escalators.

Estacio de França, Avenida Marqués de l'Argentera (℡ **90-224-0202;** Metro: Barceloneta, L3), is southeast of the center of Barcelona, close to Ciutadella Park, the zoo, the port, and Vila Olímpica. Overnight Elipsos hotel trains arrive from such international destinations as Zurich, Geneva, Paris, and Milan. There are also regional trains to locations west and south of Barcelona. There is no tourist information desk or hotel information, but there are a cafe, restaurant, and bookshop.

Information Elsewhere in the City

There is a large office in the center of Barcelona at the **Palau de Rubert,** Passeig de Gràcia 107 (℡ **93-238-80-91;** www.gencat.net), where there are often exhibitions. It's open Monday to Saturday 10am to 7pm, Sunday and holidays 10am to 2pm.The other organization, **Oficina de Informació de Turisme de Barcelona,** Plaça de Catalunya 17-S (℡ **93-285-38-34;** www.barcelonaturisme.com), deals exclusively with the city of Barcelona. This is also where you can get detailed information about the city and the Barcelona Card for tourist discounts. The office is open daily 9am to 9pm.

Barcelona

ACCOMMODATIONS ■
Banys Orientals **29**
Duques de Bergara **15**
Gat Xino Hotel **4**
Hotel Colón **18**
Hotel 54 **30**
Hotel Omn **10**
HUSA Oriente **20**
Mesón Castilla **14**
Pulitzer **16**
Wilson Boutique
 Hotel **7**

DINING ◆
Café de L'Academia **22**
Can Ravell **12**
Casa Leopoldo **5**
Comerç 24 **26**
Cuines Santa Caterina **24**
Els Quatre Gats **17**
La Gardunya **19**
L'Olive **13**
Los Caracoles **21**
Pla de la Garsa **25**
Restaurant Hoffman **8**

ATTRACTIONS ●
Catedral de Barcelona **23**
Fundació Joan Miró **3**
La Sagrada Família **11**
Museu Barbier-Mueller
 Art Precolombí **28**
Museu d'Art Contemporani
 de Barcelona **6**
Museu Nacional d'Art
 de Catalunya **2**
Museu Picasso **27**
Parc Güell **9**
Poble Espanyol **1**

Getting Around

To save money on public transportation, a *carte* good for 10 trips, the *Tarjeta T-10,* sells for 7.70€ and is good for the Metro and the bus. This pass is available at **Transports Metropolita de Barcelona,** Plaça de la Universitat (☎ **93-138-70-74;** www.tmb.net), open Monday to Friday 8am to 8pm, Saturday 8am to 1pm.

Another money-saver is a ride on *Bus Turistic,* which travels by 24 of the city's most visited attractions. You can get on and off the bus as you please, and your single ticket also covers the Montjuïch cable car and Tibidabo funicular. The *Bus Turistic* can be purchased on the bus or at the tourist office at Plaça de Catalunya, and costs 21€ for 1 day or 27€ for 2 days. Children pay 17€ for 1 day or 21€ for 2 days.

Six **Metro** lines service greater Barcelona Sunday to Thursday from 5am to midnight and Friday to Saturday 5am to 2am. A one-way fare is 1.35€, and all major Metro lines converge at Plaça de Catalunya.

Barcelona also has daily bus service from 5:30am to 10pm, with some night buses running between 11pm and 4am. The one-way fare is 1.35€.

Look for the letters SP (meaning *servicio público*), the designation for taxis, which charge a basic rate of 2€, with each additional kilometer costing 1€, depending on traffic. Supplements are assessed for certain items, including rides to the airport and extra-large pieces of luggage. Most taxis can be hailed on the street, or you can contact **Radio Taxi** (☎ **93-303-30-33;** www.radiotaxi033.com).

Where to Stay

Banys Orientals ★ 🎁   This hotel, off the Vía Laietana in the heart of the city, is in the most historic part of Barcelona. For quality and comfort at an affordable price, it's a feverishly cool choice preferred by hipsters and fashionistas. An 1800s once-private mansion has been given a radical modernist makeover, with dark hardwood floors, shiny marble bathrooms, and some high-ceilinged suites with their private patios. On the ground level is **Senyor Parellada,** a classic Barcelona restaurant serving Catalán cuisine.

Argentería 37, 08003 Barcelona. ☎ **93-268-84-60.** Fax 93-268-84-61. www.hotelbanysorientals.com. 43 units. 100€ double; 130€ suite. AE, DC, MC, V. Metro: Jaume I. **Amenities:** 1 room for those w/limited mobility; all smoke-free rooms.

Duques de Bergara ★   This town house, built for the Duke of Bergara in 1898, has been successfully transformed into an inviting five-story hotel with a modern seven-story tower. All of the bedrooms are generally large and sport elegant fabrics and traditional comforts, including some especially inviting marble bathrooms. The public rooms are dramatically furnished, with stained glass, in a decorative *modernismo* style. This is that rare Barcelona hotel that has a pool.

Bergata 11, 08002 Barcelona. ☎ **93-301-51-51.** Fax 93-317-34-42. www.hoteles-catalonia.com. 151 units. 109€–245€ double; 146€–295€ triple. AE, DC, MC, V. Metro: Plaça de Catalunya. **Amenities:** Restaurant; bar; rooms for those w/limited mobility.

Gat Xino Hotel ★ 🍃   This budget hotel is a comfortable hotel that has affordable prices. One of the chic color schemes involves acid apple greens combined with black trim, and the overall look is modern and inviting. There's a roof terrace, for siestas in the sun and for the daily Mediterranean-style buffet at lunchtime. The Gat is just a 2-minute walk from La Rambla.

Calle Hospital 149–155, 08001 Barcelona. ☎ **93-324-88-33.** Fax 93-324-88-34. www.gatrooms.com. 35 units. 75€–90€ double; 95€–130€ suite. AE, DC, MC, V. Metro: Liceu. **Amenities:** Restaurant.

Hotel Colón ★★ If you want to stay in the heart of Gothic Barcelona, there is no better location than this hotel opposite the main entrance to the cathedral. You parade through old-fashioned public rooms to modernized and good-size bedrooms that are comfortably and traditionally furnished. The sixth-floor rooms with balconies overlooking the square are the most sought after; rooms on the lower floors can be rather dark.

Avinguda de la Catedral 7, 08002 Barcelona. ✆ **800/845-0636** in the U.S., or 93-301-14-04. Fax 93-317-29-15. www.hotelcolon.es. 145 units. 118€–245€ double; from 230€ suite. AE, DC, MC, V. Metro: Urquinaona. Bus: 17, 19, or 45. **Amenities:** Restaurant; bar.

Hotel 54 ★ In the increasingly fashionable fishing quarter of Barceloneta, this boutique hotel has been installed in an old building, offering panoramic views of the harbor and skyline. It stands in front of Port Vell, close to Playa San Sebastián and within an easy walk of La Rambla. After a major restoration, the hotel is now elegantly modern. There are such trendy decorative touches as neon mood lighting and green-glass sinks in the bathrooms. Bedrooms have a lighting system allowing you to "personalize" your choice of color.

Passeig Joan de Borbó 54, 08003 Barcelona. ✆ **93-225-00-54.** Fax 93-225-00-80. www.bestwestern hotel54.com/eng. 28 units. 135€–150€ double. MC, V. Metro: Barceloneta. **Amenities:** Bar.

Hotel Omm In the fashionable Passeig de Gràcia district, Grupo Tragaluz, owner of some of Barcelona's finest gourmet restaurants, operates this nugget of a hotel. The Omm features one of the most sophisticated modern designs in the city, the work of some of Spain's best architects and interior designers. The hotel was designed so that guests could enjoy the view of Gaudí's La Pedrera, opposite the hotel, one of his most celebrated masterpieces. The smooth textures and light tones of the hotel rooms create a tranquil, comfortable, and relaxing atmosphere. As part of the trendy design, bathrooms are open to sunlight. Special features include a rooftop pool and **Moo,** one of Barcelona's finest hotel dining rooms.

Rosello 265, 08008 Barcelona. ✆ **93-445-40-00.** Fax 93-445-40-04. www.hotelomm.es. 59 units. 215€–400€ double; 515€–700€ suite. AE, DC, MC, V. Metro: Diagonal. **Amenities:** Restaurant; bar.

HUSA Oriente If you want to find lodgings on Barcelona's colorful and most famous boulevard, La Rambla, consider this hotel. It dates from 1842 and, in its heyday, was one of the grand hotels of the city (celeb guests included Errol Flynn and Maria Callas). Renovations have improved the hotel, but it lacks the character of its former glory, today attracting mainly frugal travelers. Rooms are simply though comfortably furnished. You get the basics with relatively modern pieces, but little more.

La Rambla 45, 08002 Barcelona. ✆ **93-302-25-58.** Fax 93-412-38-19. www.hotelhusaoriente.com. 142 units. 96€–246€ double. AE, MC, V. Metro: Liceu. **Amenities:** Restaurant; bar.

Mesón Castilla ★ 🖉 Operated by the Spanish hotel chain HUSA, this hotel, a real bargain, was carved out of a former apartment building near the center of La Rambla, Barcelona's main boulevard. The antiques-stuffed hotel features a wealth of Art Nouveau detailing, in both the facade and the interior. Bedrooms are medium in size and quite comfortable, furnished with tasteful pieces such as Catalán-style headboards. The best accommodations open onto private terraces.

Valldoncella 5, 08001 Barcelona. ✆ **93-318-21-82.** Fax 93-412-40-20. www.mesoncastilla.com. 56 units. 107€–165€ double. Rates include continental breakfast. AE, DC, MC, V. Metro: Plaça de Catalunya or Universitat. **Amenities:** Breakfast room; lounge.

Pulitzer ★★ 🏨 With its high-concept modern design, attractive guest rooms, and immensely welcoming sense of comfort, this fashionable boutique hotel is our favorite hotel in an area with many commercial lodging with no heart. Pulitzer, located right off the heartbeat Plaça de Catalunya, boasts a rooftop bar with panoramic views. The bedrooms are decorated in tones gray, black, and white, and some of them are a bit cramped. But even the humblest abode here has a bit of flair, with leather, silk, glamorous fabrics, and state-of-the-art bathrooms.

Bergata 8, 08002 Barcelona. ℂ **93-481-67-67.** Fax 93-481-64-64. www.hotelpulitzer.es. 91 units. 109€–250€ standard double; 139€–275€ superior double. AE, DC, MC, V. Metro: Plaça de Catalunya. **Amenities:** Restaurant; bar.

Wilson Boutique Hotel This comfortable hotel stands in an architecturally rich neighborhood. The small lobby isn't indicative of the rest of the building; the second floor opens into a large, sunny lounge. The guest rooms are well kept, generally spacious, and furnished in a modern minimalist style with parquet floors.

Av. Diagonal 568, 08021 Barcelona. ℂ**93-209-25-11.** Fax 93-200-83-70. www.wilsonbcn.com. 53 units. 95€–100€ double; 150€–200€ suite. AE, DC, MC, V. Metro: Diagonal. **Amenities:** Bar.

Top Attractions & Special Moments

Before wandering the narrow, labyrinthine streets of old Barcelona, consider a panoramic view of it first to get your bearings. That's possible from **Tibidabo Mountain ★**, just north of the port, and reached by a funicular taking you up to 1,600 feet (487m). **Mirador Torre de Collserola** (ℂ **93-406-93-54;** www.torredecollserola.com) was built at the time of the 1992 Barcelona Olympics, and from it the most stunning vistas unfold. It costs 5€ to climb the tower. From Plaça de Catalunya, take bus no. 73 to Avinguda del Tibidabo, where you can board a special bus to take you to the funicular. The funicular runs daily and costs 2€ one-way, 3€ round-trip.

Catedral de Barcelona ★★★ The most acclaimed example of Catalán architecture and one of the great Gothic cathedrals of Europe, construction began in 1298 under the reign of Jaime II but was not completed until 1889. Called "the loveliest oasis in Barcelona" by historian Cirici, it is distinguished by a Gothic interior with a single wide nave, with 28 side chapels branching off of it. Among the most distinguished of these is **Capella de Sant Benet,** dedicated to the patron saint of Europe and housing a splendid altarpiece depicting the *Transfiguration* by Bernat Martorell in 1452. The **choir stalls ★** are especially notable, the top tier of this 15th-century art displaying the coats-of-arms of the 12 knights of the Order of Toisón del Oro. The **cloisters ★** are another notable feature; they're in the Gothic style and decorated with a statue of St. George slaying the dragon. Vaulted galleries in the cloister, enhanced by forged iron grilles, surround a garden of magnolias, medlars, and palm trees. The cloister contains a museum of medieval art. Its most notable work is the 15th-century *La Pietat* of Bartolomé Bermejo. Beneath the main altar is the impressive **crypt ★**, with its alabaster sarcophagus (1339) of the martyred St. Eulalia. The twin octagonal bell towers date from 1386, although the bells were installed in 1545. You can take an elevator to the roof for one of the grand panoramic views of Barcelona's Gothic barrio. At noon on Sunday, the most typical folkloric dance of Catalonia, the *sardana,* is performed in front of this edifice.

Plaça de la Seu s/n. ℂ**93-315-15-54.** www.catedralbcn.org. Admission free to the cathedral; museum 1€; global ticket to museum, choir, rooftop terraces, and towers 5€. Cathedral daily 8am–12:45pm and 5:15–7:30pm. Cloister museum daily 10am–12:30pm and 5:15–7pm. Metro: Jaume I.

Barcelona's **Barri Gòtic** ★★★, or Gothic Quarter, is filled with narrow, winding streets that take you back to the Middle Ages. Every street offers something of interest, a historic sight, and most definitely dozens of shops, restaurants, and cafes, some of which may have been patronized by Picasso. The chief attraction is the **Cathedral of Barcelona** (p. 707), but there are dozens of other historic buildings as well, along with countless squares to discover on your own. None is more notable than Plaça de Sant Jaume, which has been the city's political center since Roman times. Today this square is dominated by the **Palau de la Generalitat,** headquarters of the autonomous government of Catalonia; and by the **Ajuntament,** the Barcelona city hall. If you need guidance in approaching this warren of fascinating old streets, the tourist office leads popular walking tours of the barrio in summer. Tours in English are conducted daily at 10am; the cost is 9€ for adults, 3€ for ages 4 to 12, kids 3 and under are free. For more information, call © **93-285-3832.**

Fundació Joan Miró ★ One of Spain's greatest artists, Joan Miró (1893–1983), was from Catalonia. Some 10,000 works by the Catalán surrealist, including paintings, graphics, and sculptures, are collected here. The building has been greatly expanded in recent years following the design of Catalán architect Josep Lluís Sert, a close friend of Miró's. Trained in Paris and an admirer of Gaudí's *modernista,* Miró is known for his whimsical abstract forms, brilliant colors, and Surrealism. Using multimedia, one wing charts the evolution of Miró's art from the age of 8 until his final works in the 1970s.

Plaça de Neptú, Parc de Montjuïc. © **93-443-94-70.** www.bcn.fjmiro.es. Admission 8€ adults, 6€ students, free for children 14 and under. July–Sept Tues–Wed and Fri–Sat 10am–8pm, Thurs 10am–9:30pm, Sun 10am–2:30pm; Oct–June Tues–Wed and Fri–Sat 10am–7pm, Thurs 10am–9:30pm, Sun 10am–2:30pm. Bus: 50 (at Plaça d'Espanya) or 55.

La Sagrada Família ★★ This, the symbol of Barcelona, is Antoni Gaudí's unfinished masterpiece and the most unconventional church in Europe. The languid, amorphous structure embodies the essence of Gaudí's style, which some have described as "Art Nouveau run wild." The architect lived like a recluse at the site for 16 years and is buried in the **crypt** ★, which was actually constructed by the cathedral's original architect, Francesc de Paula Villar I Lozano. Those who have seen Gaudí's finished plan for Sagrada Família can only lament that the architect died before carrying out his final dream. At the time of his death, only one tower on the Nativity Facade had been completed. Financed by public contributions, work continues to this day. The apse remains the first part of the church completed by Gaudí. The controversial **Passion Façade** ★ was finished in the late 1980s by Josep María Subirach. It is often criticized because of its "sinister" figures. Finished in 1904, the **Nativity Façade** ★ is the most complete part of the church, its doorways representing faith, hope, and charity. A steep climb, 400 steps lead to the towers and upper galleries, opening onto **panoramic views of Barcelona** ★★. There's an elevator for those unable to make the climb. Admission includes a 20-minute video presentation.

Majorca 401 (entrance from Carrer de Sardenya or Carrer de la Marina). © **93-207-30-31.** www.sagradafamilia.org. Admission 11€. Elevator 3€. Oct–Mar daily 9am–6pm; Apr–Sept daily 9am–8pm. Closed Christmas, Dec 26, New Year's Day, and Jan 6. Metro: Sagrada Família.

Museo Barbier-Mueller Art Precolombí ★★   In the medieval Palacio Nadal, this 1997 museum showcases one of the most important collections of pre-Columbian art. On display are some 6,000 exhibitions of tribal art, the first pieces acquired by the museum's namesake, Josef Mueller (1887–1977), in 1908. Of much interest are the artifacts left over from the Mayan culture, dating from 1000 B.C. A vast array is on display, including stone sculpture, ceramic and ornamental objects of great style, and funerary artifacts. Seek out, in particular, the artifacts of the Olmecs, a tribe that settled on the Gulf of Mexico in the 1st millennium B.C. and was known for its impressive stone sculpture and figures carved out of jade.

Carrer de Montcada 12–14. ✆ **93-310-45-16.** www.barbier-mueller.ch. Admission 3€ adults, 1.50€ students, free for children 14 and under and to all the first Sun of every month. Tues–Fri 11am–7pm; Sat 10am–7pm; Sun and holidays 10am–3pm. Metro: Jaume I. Bus: 14, 17, 19, 39, 40, 45, or 51. Tourist bus: Ruta Sur (Azul).

Museu d'Art Contemporani de Barcelona ★   One of the leading showcases of modern art in eastern Spain, this museum houses masterpieces from a wide range of artists, including Tàpies, Paul Klee, and Catalán painter Joan Miró, who was known for his surrealistic style, vivid colors, and fantastical forms. Designed by the American architect Richard Meier, the building is a work of art itself, manipulating sunlight to offer brilliant, natural interior lighting.

Plaça dels Angels 1. ✆ **93-412-08-10.** Admission 3€ adults, 2€ students, free for children 14 and under and seniors over 65. Mon and Wed–Fri 11am–7:30pm; Sat 10am–8pm; Sun 10am–3pm. Metro: Plaça de Catalunya.

Museo Nacional d'Art de Catalunya ★★★   Built for the 1929 World's Fair in Montjuïc Park, this museum, one of Spain's major art showcases, not only is the major repository of Catalán art, but also displays the most significant collection of Romanesque art in the world. Some 100 Romanesque pieces range from icons to sculptures, and also include some splendid frescoes from the 12th century. To round out the collection, churches, monasteries, and other centers were "raided" throughout Catalonia for their treasures. One of the most remarkable exhibitions here features wall paintings from Sant Climent de Taüll and Santa Maria de Taüll. The museum is also rich in Gothic art, especially from Catalonia. Paintings by many great Spanish masters, from Velázquez to Zurbarán, are featured.

Palau Nacional, Parc de Montjuïc. ✆ **93-622-03-76.** Admission 8.50€ adults, 6€ youth 15–20, free for children 14 and under. Tues–Sat 10am–7pm; Sun 10am–2:30pm. Metro: Espanya, line 1 or 3.

Museu Picasso ★★   Pablo Picasso (1881–1973) was born in Málaga but arrived in Barcelona at the age of 14. He fell in love with the city and, in time, donated some 2,500 of his paintings, drawings, and engravings. They are now housed in this museum carved out of several old mansions on this street from the Middle Ages. The greatest attractions here are the early drawings of the teenage Picasso, including *The First Communion,* painted in 1896, and *Science and Charity.* A few paintings from his Blue and Rose periods are displayed, but his most celebrated work is the series *Las Meninas,* based on the Velázquez masterpiece hanging in Madrid's Prado (p. 676). Scenes from Picasso's old notebooks depict street life in Barcelona. It is said that Picasso found inspiration among Barcelona's prostitutes for his *Les Demoiselles d'Avignon,* which some art historians view as the wellspring of modern art. Because the works are arranged in rough chronological order, you can get a wonderful sense of Picasso's development and watch as he discovered a trend or had a new idea, mastered it, grew bored with it, and then moved on to something new.

Montcada 15-19. © **93-256-30-00.** www.museupicasso.bcn.es. Admission to permanent exhibits 9€ adults, 6€ students and ages 16-25, free for children 15 and under. Tues-Sun 10am-8pm. Metro: Jaume I (line 4).

Parc Güell ★★   Like Sagrada Família, Gaudí's eccentric park was never completed. Even so, UNESCO has designated it as a World Heritage Site. The park was commissioned in the 1890s by Count Eusebi Güell and set on 50 acres (20 hectares) as a "garden city." Even though the park opened in 1922, little of Gaudí's grand design had been realized. On-site today is **Casa-Museu Gaudí,** Carrer del Carmel 23 (© **93-219-3811**), designed by the architect Ramon Berenguer. The museum contains drawings and furnishings by Gaudí. Admission to the museum is 4€, and it's open October to March daily 10am to 6:45pm, April to September daily 10am to 8:45pm. Gaudí did complete several of the public areas in the park, which evoke a surrealist Disney World, complete with a mosaic pagoda and a lizard fountain spitting water. A mosaic-encrusted chimney by Gaudí can be seen at the entrance to the park, and the **Room of a Hundred Columns,** with 84 crooked pillars, is the most atmospheric attraction.

Carrer de Olot. © **93-219-38-11.** www.casamuseugaudi.org. Free admission. May-Sept daily 10am-9pm; Oct-Apr daily 10am-6pm. Bus: 24, 25, 31, 74, 92, or 116. Metro: Lesseps.

Poble Espanyol ★   This re-created Spanish village was originally constructed for the 1929 World's Fair. A total of 115 houses illustrate architectural styles from all the Spanish provinces, ranging from Galicia in the northwest to Valencia along the southeastern coast (known as the Levante). Some of these life-size reproductions of typical buildings date in style from the 10th century. The living museum is an entertainment complex with more than a dozen restaurants, "musical" bars, and even a dance club, along with numerous shops selling typical Spanish handicrafts. In some of these artisan havens, you can see craftspeople at work, perhaps blowing glass or printing colorful fabrics. Toledo damascene work along with sculpture and even Catalán canvas sandals are made here. There's also a children's theater. It's a matter of personal taste. Some find it a bit of a tourist trap—overly commercialized and somewhat cheesy.

Av. Marqués de Comillas 13, Parc de Montjuïc. © **93-325-7866.** www.poble-espanyol.com. Admission 8.50€ adults, 5.50€ children 7-12, free for children 6 and under. Mon 9am-8pm; Tues-Thurs 9am-2pm; Fri 9am-4am; Sat 9am-5pm; Sun 9am-midnight. Metro: Espanya. Bus: 13 or 50.

 RAMBLING La Rambla

Commonly called **La Rambla ★★★**, this winding street is the most famous promenade in Spain. It actually consists of five different sections—each a rambla—Rambla de Canaletes, Rambla dels Estudis, Rambla de Sant Josep, Rambla dels Caputxins, and Rambla de Santa Mónica. It begins in the north at the transportation hub, Plaça de Catalunya, and runs all the way to the port and the monument to Columbus. Day and night, this is the most active street in Barcelona. It can be walked at any time, and you'll always see something new, as the street is forever changing. Caged birds and flower stalls greet you, as do street musicians and mime *artistes* and tarot card readers. Hotels, town houses, endless shops, and many cafes and restaurants also flank this fabled boulevard. The most famous building you'll pass along the 1-mile (1.6km) boulevard is Gran Teatre del Liceu, on Rambla dels Caputxins.

Where to Dine

Café de L'Academia ★ 🍴 CATALAN/MEDITERRANEAN   A short walk from Plaça Sant Jaume, one of the most famous squares in the Gothic quarter, this affordable restaurant is housed in an elegant 15th-century building. The chef serves succulent Catalán and Mediterranean dishes and terms his cuisine "kitchen of the market," an accurate appraisal of his use of the freshest of ingredients gathered early in the morning. Recipes are imaginative and nearly always palate pleasing. Try such delights as *lassanye de butifarra i ceps* (lasagna with Catalán sausage and flap mushrooms), *bacalla gratinado i musselina de carofes* (salt cod gratiné with an artichoke mousse), or *terrina d'berengeras amb fortmage de cabra* (terrine of eggplant with goat cheese).

Carrer Lledó 1. ✆ **93-319-82-53.** Reservations required. Main courses 10€–18€; fixed-price menu (lunch only) 14€. AE, MC, V. Mon–Fri 1:30–5pm and 8:30pm–1am. Closed last 2 weeks of Aug. Metro: Jaume I.

Can Ravell ★ 🍴 CATALÁN   There's a good reason that the most serious Barcelona foodies covet this secret address. Founded in 1929, it started as a food store and still is, more or less. Tucked away on the second floor of a deli, you reach it by going through a kitchen and shimmying up a spiral staircase. Some of the freshest food in the city is served here, and the menu takes advantage of the best on the market. Look for the roast lamb with pearl onions, pigs' trotters stuffed with shrimp, and veal steak with foie gras. The restaurant also boasts a fine wine collection, including cavas and champagnes.

Aragó 313. ✆ **93-457-51-14.** www.ravell.com. Reservations required. Main courses 15€–50€. AE, DC, MC, V. Tues–Wed 10am–9pm; Thurs–Sat 10am–11pm. Metro: Gerona.

Casa Leopoldo ★ 🍴 SEAFOOD/MEDITERRANEAN   An excursion through the somewhat seedy streets of the Barri Xinés is part of the Casa Leopoldo experience. At night, it's safer to come by taxi. This colorful restaurant, founded in 1929, serves some of the freshest seafood in town to a loyal clientele. There's a popular stand-up tapas bar in front. Some serious foodies, who have been dining here for decades, launch their repast with scrambled eggs with young garlic and meaty prawns. Our favorite dishes over the years have remained more or less the same: perfectly grilled turbot, small Norwegian lobsters sautéed with clams, and truly savory oxtail stew.

Sant Rafael 24. ✆ **93-441-30-14.** www.casaleopoldo.com. Reservations required. Main courses 45€–70€; tasting menu 50€. AE, DC, MC, V. Tues–Sun 1:30–4pm; Tues–Sat 9–11pm. Closed 1 week in Jan, 1 week at Easter, and Aug 4–Sept 4. Metro: Liceu or Parallel.

Comerç 24 ★ 🍴 CATALÁN/ASIAN/INTERNATIONAL   Chef Carles Abellan earns culinary laurels with his light, imaginative, and original renderings of old-time Catalonia favorites. Set in a renovated salting house along the Barceloneta waterfront, the restaurant features an attractive minimalist and modern decor. Dishes are cooked to order, as the chef believes in "split-second" timing. Try the fresh salmon perfumed with vanilla and served with yogurt. Other vibrant, earthy dishes include a veal entrecote with wasabi sauce, or ravioli with cuttlefish and fresh morels.

Carrer Comerç 24, La Ribera. ✆ **93-319-21-02.** www.comerc24.com. Reservations required. Main courses 12€–36€; tasting menu 62€. MC, V. Tues–Sat 1:30–3:30pm and 8:30–11:30pm. Closed 10 days in Dec, 10 days in Aug. Metro: Arco de Triompho, Estacion de Francia.

Barcelona

SPAIN

Catalonia is famous for its *cava,* the local name for champagne. Throughout Barcelona, champagne bars are called *xampanyerías.* For a fun night on the town, go on a champagne bar crawl, sampling the local bubbly. Our favorites include **El Xampanyet,** Carrer Montcada 22 (✆ **93-319-70-03;** Metro: Jaume I), close to the Picasso Museum in the old town on an ancient street. Revelers go here to drink the champagne at marble tables and to feast on tapas. Open Tuesday to Saturday noon to 4pm and 6 to 11:30pm, Sunday 11am to 4pm. At the corner of Plaça de Tetuan is **Xampú Xampany,** Gran Vía de les Corts Catalanes 702 (✆ **93-265-04-83;** Metro: Girona or Tetuan). Against a backdrop of abstract paintings, you can enjoy hors d'oeuvres and glass after glass of the bubbly Monday to Saturday 8pm to 1:30am.

Cuines Santa Caterina ★ 🍴 ASIAN/MEDITERRANEAN/ITALIAN In the Santa Caterina market, top architects Enric Miralles and Benedetta Tagliabue created this soaring space with an open kitchen, a tapas bar, and chunky wooden tables. It's especially lively at lunchtime, when locals shout their orders after reading the scrawls on a chalkboard. The food comes directly from the market and is suitable for vegetarians. The sushi tastes fresh and is prepared in the best tradition of Japan. A juice bar hawks vegetable and fruit drinks. From Thai green curry to grilled goat kid chops, the dishes are tasty and appealing.

Mercado de Santa Caterina, Av. Francesc Cambó 17, La Ribera. ✆ **93-268-99-18.** www.cuinessanta caterina.com. Reservations not required. Main courses 8€–22€. MC, V. Daily 1–4pm and 8–11:30pm. Metro: Jaume I.

Els Quatre Gats 🍷 CATALÁN Since 1897, this former gathering place of the literati and artistic elite (Picasso was a regular) has been a favorite for drinking and dining in the Gothic barrio close to the cathedral. Today the restored *fin-de-siècle* cafe is visited for its atmosphere, good food, and reasonable prices. The cookery is unpretentious but prepared from fresh ingredients, and the menu is seasonally adjusted. We recommend such specialties as artichoke hearts sautéed with bacon and pork sausage, or Mediterranean sea bass stuffed with red pepper and served with a garlic vinaigrette. Inquire about a fixed-price menu.

Montsió 3. ✆ **93-302-41-40.** www.4gats.com. Reservations required Sat–Sun. Main courses 12€–28€. AE, DC, MC. Daily 10am–1am. Metro: Plaça de Catalunya.

La Gardunya 🍷 CATALÁN In the rear of Catalonia's most famous food market, La Boquería, is battered, somewhat ramshackle, and a bit claustrophobic, but it is fashionable with an artistic set that might have been designated as bohemian in an earlier era. Food here is superfresh—you'll likely pass some of the produce stalls that provided the ingredients for your meal when you walk through the market. The restaurant offers you a choice of dining downstairs at a bustling bar or more formally in the room upstairs. You might try "hors d'oeuvres of the sea," cannelloni Rossini, *rape marinera,* paella, brochettes of veal, or *zarzuela* (stew) of fresh fish with spices.

Carrer Jerusalem 18. ✆ **93-302-43-23.** www.lagardunya.com. Reservations recommended. Main courses 13€–30€; fixed-price menu lunch 15€, dinner 22€. AE, DC, MC, V. Mon–Sat noon–5pm and 8pm–midnight. Metro: Liceu.

L'Olive ★ CATALÁN/MEDITERRANEAN You assume that this two-floor restaurant is named for the olive that figures so prominently in its Mediterranean cuisine, but it's actually named for the owner, Josep Olive. The dining room is designed in a modern Catalán style, and the overall feeling is one of elegance with a touch of intimacy. You won't be disappointed by anything on the menu, especially the *salsa maigret* of duck with strawberry sauce. Monkfish flavored with roasted garlic is always a palate pleaser, and you can finish with a *crema catalán* (a flan) or one of the delicious Catalán pastries.

Calle Balmes 47 (corner of Concéjo de Ciento). ℂ **93-452-19-90.** www.rte-olive.com. Reservations recommended. Main courses 15€–29€. AE, DC, MC, V. Daily 1-4pm; Mon-Sat 8:30pm-midnight. Metro: Passeig de Gràcia.

Los Caracoles CATALÁN "The Snails" (as it translates into English) was founded back in 1835 in the heart of the Gothic Quarter near the Ramble, and the tantalizing aroma of roasting chicken still wafts through this seedy street after all these years. The founding Bofarull family is still in charge of this time-mellowed favorite, which is seemingly visited by every tourist in town. Even though Los Caracoles hasn't been acclaimed the best restaurant in Barcelona since the time of the American Civil War, it remains a bastion of local culture and a favorite of old-time locals who mingle with diners from Japan to the Yukon territories. The food on the menu at this old favorite—which was featured in the inaugural edition of *Spain on $5 a Day* and recommended for many years—has never been altered. Try such dishes as grilled langoustines, fried small squid, or else chicken and ham croquettes. For longtime visitors to Barcelona, the memories might be an important lure.

Escudellers 14. ℂ **93-301-20-41.** www.loscaracoles.es. Main courses 8€–30€. AE, DC, MC, V. Daily 1:15pm-midnight. Metro: Drassanes.

Pla de la Garsa ★ 🦪 SPANISH/FRENCH/CATALÁN Close to the cathedral in the Gothic Quarter, Ignacio Sulle, an antiques seller, has assembled an intriguing collection of furnishings and objets d'art to serve as a backdrop for his succulent menu of old-time Mediterranean and Catalán favorites. Backed up by one of the best wine lists in Barcelona, Sulle searches far and wide for choice ingredients, which his chefs concoct into a series of imaginative dishes, starting with marvelous terrines and the fish and meat pâtés. For a main course, you can order perfectly seasoned beef bourguignon or confit leg of duck with kidney beans. The cheese selection is one of the finest we've found in town.

Assaonadors 13. ℂ **93-315-2413.** Reservations recommended Sat-Sun. Main courses 6€–15€. AE, MC, V. Daily 8pm-1am. Metro: Jaume I.

Restaurant Hofmann ★★ CATALÁN/FRENCH/INTERNATIONAL This restaurant is one of the most famous in Barcelona because of its creative cuisine. Menu items change every 2 months and often include French ingredients. Some of the chef's most notable dishes, which frequently turn up on the menu, include turbot stuffed with mushrooms, lobster-studded risotto, and duck liver with grapes. A marvelous dessert is caramel-coated nut ice cream.

Granada del Penedes 14. ℂ **93-218-71-65.** www.hofmann-bcn.com. Reservations recommended. Main courses 23€–45€. AE, DC, MC, V. Mon-Fri 1:30–3:15pm and 9-11:15pm. Metro: Diagonale.

Shopping

The best one-stop shopping is at **El Corte Inglés**, at Avinguda Diagonal 617–619 (ℂ **93-366-71-00;** www.elcorteingles.es; Metro: María Cristina), one of the finest department stores along the eastern Spanish seaboard, selling everything from high fashion to regional handcrafts. Enjoy food and drink in a rooftop cafe. Open Monday to Saturday 10am to 10pm. There's a branch at Avinguda Diagonal 471 (© **93-493-48-00;** Metro: Hospital Clinic), which keeps the same hours.

As a city of art, Barcelona is known for its galleries. Especially interesting for visitors is **Art Picasso,** Tapinería 10 (© **93-268-32-40;** Metro: Jaume I), which has excellent lithographic reproductions of works by Joan Miró, Dalí, and Picasso, all the homegrown artists. Open daily from 10am to 8pm; summer hours 9:30am to 8pm. The best artwork by Catalonia's living artists and sculptors is sold at **Sala Parés ★★,** Petritxol 5 (© **93-318-70-08;** www.salapares.com; Metro: Placa de Catalunya), established in 1840. Artwork is shown in a two-floor amphitheater, and exhibitions of contemporary works change every 3 weeks. Open Monday to Saturday 10:30am to 2pm and 4:30 to 8:30pm. Antique collectors head for **Antiguedades Artur Ramón,** Palla 23 (© **93-302-59-70;** www.arturamon.com; Metro: Jaume I), a three-story emporium filled with rare pieces from the attics of Catalonia, and also 19th- and 20th-century artwork and sculpture, including many decorative objects and rare ceramics. Open Tuesday to Friday 10am to 1:30pm and 5 to 8pm, Saturday 10am to 1:30pm.

Barcelona is not Milan or Paris, but is increasingly known for its fashion, best represented by **Adolfo Domínguez ★,** Passeig de Gràcia 32 (© **93-487-41-70;** www.adolfo-dominguez.com; Metro: Passeig de Gràcia), an outlet celebrated as the Spanish Armani. Their style, as summed up by one local fashion critic: "Austere but not strict, forgivingly cut in urbane earth tones." Open Monday to Saturday 10am to 8:30pm. One of the most stylish shops in Barcelona, **Groc,** Rambla de Catalunya 100 (© **93-215-77-78;** Metro: Diagona), is expensive but filled with high-quality men's and women's apparel made from the finest natural fibers. The men's store is downstairs, the women's store one flight up. Open Monday to Saturday from 10am to 2pm and 4:30 to 8:30pm.

Catalonia has long been celebrated for its handmade pottery, which is showcased best at **Itaca,** Carrer Ferran 26 (© **93-301-30-44;** Metro: Liceu), which has a wide array of ceramics and other works. Open Monday to Saturday 10am to 8:30pm. The best center for designer housewares is **Vinçón ★★,** Passeig de Gràcia 96 (© **93-215-60-50;** Metro: Diagonal), selling some 10,000 different wares, including beautifully designed household items, along with sleekly designed modern furnishings. Open Monday to Saturday 10am to 8:30pm.

The hurried rail passenger on a tight schedule may have time to visit only the pick of the city's malls, which house a wide variety of Catalonian merchandise under one roof. The best of these includes **Maremagnum,** Moll d'Espanya s/n (© **93-225-81-00;** www.maremagnum.es; Metro: Drassanes or Barceloneta), near the Columbus Monument. In addition to its many shops, there are a dozen theaters, an IMAX theater, and many restaurants, pubs, and dance clubs. Open daily 10am to 10pm. The largest shopping center in Barcelona is **Centre Comercial Barcelona Glòries,** Avinguda Diagonal 208 (© **93-486-04-04;** www.lesglories.com; Metro: Glòries), a three-story emporium with some 100 shops, some posh, some less so. This mall is filled with some treasures, but also lots of lesser merchandise. Open Monday to Saturday 10am to 10pm.

Nightlife

Begin your *tasca* crawl of the Gothic barrio by sitting on the terrace of **La Vinya del Senyor,** Plaça Santa María 5 (© **93-310-33-79),** enjoying the magnificent facade of Santa María del Mar. There are some 300 selections of wine here (many sold by the glass), along with select *cavas* (Catalán sparkling wine), *moscatells,* and sherries. Tantalizing tapas are served, costing 2€ to 9€. Hours are Sunday to Thursday from noon to 1:30am, and Friday and Saturday until 2am (Metro: Jaume I or Barceloneta).

Before attending the theater, head for **Café de la Opera,** La Rambla 74 ((C) **93-317-75-85;** www.cafeoperabcn.com; Metro: Liceu); the city's most fabled cafe has been in business since the beginning of the 20th century. Operagoers flock here, as does one of the widest cross-sections of people. It's open daily from 8:30am until the early morning hours. After a drink, head for the **Gran Teatre del Liceu,** La Rambla dels Caputxins 51–54 ((C) **93-485-99-13;** www.liceubarcelona.com; Metro: Liceu), a Belle Epoque–style, 2,700-seat opera house, one of the greatest theaters in the world. It was rebuilt following a devastating fire in 1994. Today it's the venue for the major cultural events of Catalonia.

At the top of La Rambla, you can patronize **Café Zurich,** Plaça de Catalunya 1 ((C) **93-317-91-53;** Metro: Plaça de Catalunya), another traditional meeting point and one of the best places in the old city for people-watching. Going strong since the early 1920s, it's known for its *bocadillos,* or little sandwiches.

An English-style pub, **Dirty Dick's,** Taberna Inglesa, Carrer Marc Aureli 2 ((C) **93-200-89-52;** Metro: Muntaner), has lots of dark paneling and exposed brick, with banquettes for quiet conversation. The pub is at the crossing of Vía Augusta, a main thoroughfare through the district, and offers tasty sandwiches. Open daily 6pm to 2:30am. For a typical old-town bar, head for **El Born,** Passeig del Born 26 ((C) **93-319-53-33;** Metro: Jaume I or Barceloneta), a converted former fish shop. You can also enjoy an inexpensive dinner; meals cost around 18€ to 25€. Open Monday to Saturday 6pm to 2am (until 3am Fri–Sat). Near Plaça Reial, **Schilling,** Carrer Ferran 23 ((C) **93-317-67-87;** www.cafeschilling.com; Metro: Liceu), attracts a young and stylish crowd to this old cafe that looks like something from Gaudí's era, with its iron columns and marble tables, to sample its drinks, succulent pastas, and savory tapas. Gays and straights mix harmoniously here. Open Monday to Thursday 10am to 2:30am, Friday and Saturday 10am to 3am, and Sunday noon to 2am.

As the evening progresses, the cabarets and jazz clubs start to fill up. One of the oldest and best jazz clubs is **Harlem Jazz Club,** Comtessa de Sobradiel 8 ((C) **93-310-07-55;** www.harlemjazzclub.es; Metro: Jaume I or Liceu). Small and intimate, the club often attracts top jazz artists from Europe and America. Live music begins at 10:30pm Tuesday to Thursday and Sunday, and at 11:30pm on Friday and Saturday. The second set is at midnight (1am Fri–Sat). Open Tuesday to Thursday and Sunday 8pm to 4am, until 5am Friday and Saturday. There's a one-drink minimum but no cover. Closed 2 weeks in August. Another premier venue for good blues and jazz is **Jamboree,** Plaça Reial 17 ((C) **93-314-17-89;** www.masimas.com; Metro: Liceu), in the heart of the Gothic old city. Jazz is not always scheduled here; sometimes a Latin dance band will perform. The crowd demands only the best talent. Cover is 10€ to 12€, and it's open daily from 8:30pm to 5am; shows are at 9 and 11pm.

In the showplace rooms of the Palau Dalmases, **Espai Barroc,** Carrer Montcada 20 ((C) **93-310-0673;** Metro: Jaume I), holds forth in the Barri Gòtic. It's one of the most elegant venues on the after-dark circuit. The best night is Thursday at 11pm, when nearly a dozen singers perform songs from assorted operas. For the opera aficionado, this is a grand evening out. Cover is charged only on Thursday, costing 20€

and including a drink. Open Tuesday to Thursday 8pm to 2am, Friday and Saturday 10pm to 2am, and Sunday 6 to 9pm.

Luz de Gas, Carrer de Muntaner 246 (© **93-209-77-11;** www.luzdegas.com), is a theater and cabaret with some of the best jazz in Barcelona on weekends. Weekdays at this Art Nouveau club are given over to cabaret. A wide range of music is presented here weekly, including pop, soul, jazz, rhythm and blues, and salsa. The cover of 15€ includes the first drink. Open Sunday and Monday 11pm to 4am, Tuesday 11pm to 4:30am, Wednesday 11pm to 5am, Thursday 11pm to 5:30am, Friday and Saturday 11pm to 5:45am. **Barcelona Pipa Club,** Plaça Reial 3 (© **93-301-11-65;** www.bpipaclub.com; Metro: Liceu), is a final venue for jazz devotees. You ring the buzzer as if being admitted to an old speakeasy, and inside the music ranges from Brazilian rhythms to New Orleans jazz. There's no cover, and hours are daily 6pm to 3am.

Barcelona is not associated with flamenco the way Madrid or Andalusia are, but there are some excellent clubs, including a highly rated flamenco cabaret at **El Tablao de Carmen,** Poble Espanyol de Montjuïc (© **93-325-68-95;** www.tablao decarmen.com; Metro: Espanya). You can go early and explore this re-created Spanish village. The first show (Tues–Sun) is always at 7:45pm; the second show is at 10pm. A dinner and show costs 69€. The oldest flamenco club in Barcelona is **Los Tarantos,** Plaça Reial 17 (© **93-319-17-89**), which presents the best of Andalusian flamenco. Each show lasts around an hour, beginning at 8:30, 9:30, and 10:30pm Monday to Saturday. The cover is 6€.

Late at night, especially into the early hours, dance clubs prevail, including **La Paloma,** Tigre 27 (© **93-301-68-97;** Metro: Universitat), the most famous dance hall in Barcelona. It's for an older crowd and those who remember the mambo or the fox trot. The hall is open Thursday to Sunday with matinees lasting from 6 to 9:30pm, and night dances taking place from 11:30pm to 5am. **Razzmatazz,** Carrer Pamplona 88 (© **93-320-82-00;** www.salarazzmatazz.com; Metro: Bogatell), a multilevel club in a converted warehouse, is actually five clubs in one. Each club within the club has its own music. A large crowd of university students favors the place. One entrance fee, which ranges from 8€ to 30€, covers admission to all clubs, but mixed cocktails are expensive, hovering around 8€. Open Friday and Saturday 1pm to 5am.

An Excursion to Montserrat

At a point 35 miles (56km) northwest of Barcelona, the monastery of Montserrat is the most-visited attraction outside Barcelona. One of the major pilgrimage centers in Spain, it sits atop a 3,937-foot-high (1,181m) mountain that's 7 miles (11km) long and 3½ miles (5.6km) wide. A popular venue for weddings, the site possesses the medieval statue of the Black Virgin *(La Moreneta),* the patron saint of Catalonia. Thousands upon thousands of the faithful flock here annually to touch the statue.

GETTING THERE   From Barcelona, Montserrat is reached via the Manresa line of **Ferrocarrils de la Generealitat de Catalunya,** with 12 trains leaving daily from Plaça d'Espanya in Barcelona (trip time: 1 hr.). The central office at Plaça de Catalunya (© **93-205-15-15;** www.fgc.es) sells tickets for 18€ round-trip. The train connects with the aerial cable car, Aeri de Montserrat, whose fare is included in the round-trip. *Note:* Railpasses are not accepted for this journey, so passholders will have to purchase a ticket (though they will receive a discount on the fare).

VISITOR INFORMATION   The visitor information center, at Plaça de la Creu (© 93-877-77-01; www.montserratvisita.com), is open daily from 9am to 5:30pm.

TOP ATTRACTIONS & SPECIAL MOMENTS

Consecrated in 1592, the Montserrat Monastery is entered at Plaça Santa María. Although the French destroyed the monastery in 1811 during their attack on Catalonia, it was reconstructed and repopulated in 1844. During the Franco regime, when the dictator tried to obliterate Catalán culture, the monastery remained a beacon of enlightenment.

One of its noted attractions is the 50-member **Escolanía ★★**, one of the oldest and most renowned boys' choirs in Europe, having been founded in the 13th century. Crowds flock here at 1pm daily to hear the choir sing "Salve Regina" and "Virolai" in the basilica. Hours are daily 8 to 10:30am and noon to 6:30pm, charging no admission. For a view of the **Black Virgin,** a statue from the 12th or 13th century, enter the church through a side door to the right.

Museu de Montserrat stands at Plaça de Santa María (© **93-877-77-77;** www.montserratvisita.com). It contains important works of art, including paintings by old masters such as El Greco and Caravaggio. Even more modern painters such as Picasso are shown here, and you'll also find pieces by French Impressionists, including Monet and Degas. Many ancient artifacts are also shown. The museum is open Monday to Friday from 10am to 5:45pm, charging 6.50€ adults, 5.50€ seniors, free for students and children 17 and under.

A funicular takes you in just 9 minutes to the peak, **Sant Joan,** at 4,005 feet (1,236m); it operates every 20 minutes daily from 9am to 5:30pm in low season and to 7pm in summer. The cost is 8.50€ round-trip. One of the **greatest panoramas in all of Spain ★★★** can be seen from this point—from the distant Pyrenees to the Balearic Islands.

SWEDEN

Clean and fresh are useful adjectives when describing Sweden's cities, furniture, trains, politics, and huge expanse of wilderness groaning with dark pine forests and gleaming blue lakes.

Twice the size of Britain, this large country sits on the northern edge of Europe, and although it requires some effort for the rail traveler to get here (though easier now, thanks to the Oresund Bridge linking Denmark and Sweden), it's definitely worth the trip. Stockholm and Gothenburg are increasingly fashionable, offering up plenty of urban delights—bars, galleries, first-class restaurants, clubs, and so on. But urban areas take up only a little more than 1% of the country, and beyond that is a wonderfully varied landscape featuring everything from the mountainous Arctic reaches of northern Lapland to the sandy white beaches of Skåne in the south. And wherever you go, you'll meet the friendly and efficient residents of Sweden, and get an inspiring thrill from traveling through one of the most modern, liberal, and eco-friendly countries in the world.

Plus, the good news for rail travelers is that Sweden's trains are among the most efficient and high-tech in Europe, with easy rail access to all the top sights, along mostly scenic routes in a country that is relatively underpopulated compared to the rest of Europe. English speakers will have no trouble finding someone to help them out—nearly the whole country speaks English—making this a trouble-free destination in the language department. And to ease the eco-guilt of traveling, most of Sweden's trains are run on electric power, all of which is harvested from renewable resources.

The bad news: Its trains run on time with utter efficiency, and the natural sights are great, but the prices in Scandinavia are a killer. To travel deluxe or first class in Sweden is a costly undertaking (though cheaper than in other Scandinavian countries). We do, of course, recommend a number of moderate choices in this chapter, but one should keep in mind that Sweden's not the best place for a rail trip on a strict budget.

If you have a choice, come here in summer, when the Midnight Sun extends the days in June and July. The climate is generally cool during this brief summer period, except on the southern coast, which, thanks to the effects of the Gulf Stream, can heat up like the Mediterranean. Winter, on the other hand, when the days are gray and too short, can be a horrible experience, and even Stockholm can feel like the deep freeze. On the positive side, the air is clean, crisp, and fresh.

Note: For a detailed look at Sweden's rail routes, as well as the rail lines in all of the major Scandinavian countries, see the map on p. 199.

Highlights of Sweden

The average rail traveler usually allots 3 to 5 days for Sweden. If all you have is 3 days and Sweden's the first stop on your rail itinerary, we recommend you fly to Stockholm. You can also travel into Stockholm by rail from Copenhagen, but you'll lose an extra day in transit. If you have 5 days, we suggest you spend your extra time on the country's west coast in Gothenburg. The rail journey from Gothenburg to Stockholm takes slightly more than 3 hours, and you'll cut through the heartland of the country, passing some of its most soul-stirring landscapes, including rich forestland and glistening blue lakes.

Even those doing a cursory tour of Northern Europe are wise to include **Stockholm,** the capital of Sweden, on their rail itineraries. The city is the rail hub of Sweden, with high-speed trains branching out to the south, north, and west.

Though a city of 1.5 million—Ingmar Bergman called it "simply a rather large village"—Stockholm is filled with wide, open spaces and expanses of water. The city spreads across 14 islands in Lake Mälaren, marking the beginning of a mammoth archipelago taking in 24,000 islands, skerries, and islets stretching all the way to the Baltic Sea. Founded more than 7 centuries ago, it didn't become the official capital until the mid-1600s.

As cities go, Stockholm is one of the most beautiful in Europe, and you can easily budget 3 days to take in the highlights, especially if you include a side trip to Uppsala. Walk the streets of its Old Town, **Gamla Stan,** visit one of the city's many fine museums, and tour the must-see royal warship *Vasa,* a 17th-century man-of-war pulled from the sea and arguably Scandinavia's top attraction. The open-air park, **Skansen,** filled with some 150 historical dwellings, is another attraction well worth your time.

And when you need a change of scenery, take a day trip from Stockholm to the ancient city of **Uppsala,** Sweden's major university town, easily reached by train. It has not only a great university but also a celebrated 15th-century cathedral that is still the seat of the archbishop. Nearby is **Gamla Uppsala,** the capital of the Svea kingdom about 15 centuries ago.

If you have the time and you've finished touring the east coast of Sweden, hop on a train and head west to the city of **Gothenburg** (Göteborg in Sweden), the best center for exploring the western coast of Sweden, and the country's major port. Stockholm, of course, is the far greater attraction, but Gothenburg is not without its charm. Like Stockholm, it is a lively, bustling place riddled with canals, parks, and gardens; a wealth of museums; and the largest amusement park in Scandinavia. And from here, you can easily catch a train to whisk you off to your next international destination.

ESSENTIALS

Getting There

SAS (℃ **800/221-2350** in the U.S.; www.flysas.com) flies direct to Stockholm from Chicago and New York daily. **Continental** (℃ **800/231-0856;** www.continental. com) also flies direct between New York and Stockholm.

Other airlines fly to gateway European cities and then connect to flights into Stockholm. **British Airways** (℃ **800/AIRWAYS** [247-9297] in the U.S.; www.british airways.com) flies to London and offers connecting flights to Sweden. **Icelandair**

FESTIVALS & special events

Some 30 operas and ballets, from the baroque to early romantic eras, are presented in Stockholm's unique 1766 **Drottningholm Court Theater,** with original decorative paintings, stage sets, and machinery. Call ✆ **08/635-62-00** for tickets or go to **www.dtm.se**. The season runs from late May to late September. Take the T-bana to Brommaplan, and then bus no. 301, 323, 176, or 177. A steamboat runs here from Stockholm in the summer; call ✆ **08/1200-4000** for information.

Swedes celebrate **Midsummer Eve** all over the country with maypole dancing to fiddle and accordion music, among other events. It's celebrated on the Saturday falling between June 20 and June 26.

Another of the city's top summer festivals is **The Stockholm Jazz Festival** (✆ **08/440-30-90;** www.stockholm jazz.com). Taking place annually, in the middle of July, the lineup is usually bulging with emerging Scandinavian talent and big names such as Stevie Wonder and Lauryn Hill. The setting is the romantic downtown island of Skeppsholmen. Tickets cost between 430SEK and 660SEK.

(✆ **800/223-5500** in the U.S.; www.icelandair.com) is an excellent choice for travel to Stockholm, thanks to connections through Reykjavik, and usually offers good deals.

To reach Stockholm or Gothenburg by rail, you'll likely pass through Copenhagen, which is the main rail hub connecting Scandinavia to the rest of Europe. There are several daily trains from Copenhagen to both Stockholm and Gothenburg.

If you're traveling out of Norway, there are at least three trains a day between Oslo and Stockholm. Travel time is about 6½ hours. There are also several trains a day from Oslo to Gothenburg. Travel time is about 4 hours.

Sweden by Rail

PASSES

For information on the **Eurail Global Pass,** the **Eurail Global Pass Flexi,** the **Eurail Scandinavia Pass,** and other multicountry options, see chapter 2. The **Eurail Sweden Pass** offers 3 to 8 days of unlimited first- or second-class travel within a 1-month period. Adult prices start at $239 for 3 days of second-class travel; discounts are available for children. Passes should be purchased in North America through your travel agent or **Rail Europe** (✆ **888/438-7245** in the United States, ✆ **800/361-7245** in Canada; www.raileurope.com).

FOREIGN TRAIN TERMS

The Swedish word for train is *tåg*. Beyond that one word, don't bother learning a lot of train terms in difficult-to-pronounce Swedish. Swedes start learning English at a young age, and you can usually find out what you need to know by asking train personnel for help.

PRACTICAL TRAIN INFORMATION

Swedish trains follow tight schedules and travel often—usually every hour, or every other hour—between most of the big Swedish towns. Trains leave Malmö, Uppsala, and Gothenburg for Stockholm every hour throughout the day, Monday through Friday, with slightly restricted services at the weekend.

Swedish trains are among the most modern and efficient in Europe, and the network spans the entire country. The Swedish high-speed train is called the **X2000** and travels at speeds of 125 mph (200kmph) on all major routes. The fleet has recently been refurbished, with new trains offering Wi-Fi access and electrical sockets at every seat. Modern and comfortable overnight trains operate on the longer routes going from north to south (some even have onboard cinemas), or to international destinations such as Oslo and Berlin.

Trains are operated by **Swedish State Railways (Statens Järnvagär).** For train information, call ✆ **0771/75-75-75** or visit **www.sj.se**.

RESERVATIONS At train stations in Sweden, ask for a free copy of *SJ Tagtider,* the rail timetable. Unlike many of its fellow European countries, Swedish trains are generally devoid of surcharges and reservations are not mandatory except on the high-speed X2000 train and the night trains. If you purchase a regular rail ticket on the X2000, a seat reservation will be included in the price, as it will on the night trains. On other trains, a seat reservation costs extra.

For those with a railpass, typical reservations cost around 35SEK for a seat on an InterCity train, 65SEK on an X2000, and 150SEK for a couchette. Railpass holders don't have to pay a supplement on regional trains and often aren't charged on IC trains, either.

Policies may differ slightly on non-SJ trains in Sweden. More than two dozen regional train services are called *Länstrafik* and are run by the various provinces of Sweden, though these are run in close cooperation with SJ. Your international railpass should be valid on most regional trains.

SERVICES & AMENITIES In first-class compartments, passengers are served hot meals in their seats (and on the X2000, a light meal comes as part of the seat price). In second-class cars, meals are served in a bistro coach. All InterCity trains sell meals and refreshments such as snacks and drinks, and many have family cars with play facilities for kids. The X2000 trains offer audio channels and computer outlets, as well as a wireless network for those who have a laptop and want to access the Internet.

Overnight accommodations, where available, range from clean and comfortable couchettes to exclusive two-bed compartments with a shower and toilet. Generally speaking, sleepers in Scandinavia aren't a particularly expensive venture and cost less than in other European countries.

Note: Second class on Swedish trains is the same as first class in many countries to the south, so you may want to save the extra kronor.

Trains & Travel Times in Sweden

From	To	Type of Train	# of Trains	Frequency	Travel Time
Stockholm	Uppsala	SJ Reg/IC	33	Mon–Fri	40 min.
Stockholm	Uppsala	SJ Reg/IC	24–26	Sat–Sun	40 min.
Stockholm	Gothenberg	X2000	8	Mon–Fri	3 hr., 7 min.
Stockholm	Gothenberg	X2000	7	Sat–Sun	3 hr., 7 min.
Stockholm	Gothenberg	InterCity	6	Daily	4 hr., 51 min.

SWEDEN'S MOST FAMOUS rail journey

The most famous rail route in Sweden during summer is the 621-mile (1,000km) run from Mora to Gallivare—called *Inlandsbanan* (✆ **0771/53-53-53;** www.inlandsbanan.se), or "Inland Railway." It crawls along at a speed of 30 mph (48kmph) through unspoiled Swedish landscapes of blue lakes and deep green forests. From your window, you can often see bear, reindeer, and elk. The train makes several stops along the way for photo ops. Passengers can sometimes get off and pick wild berries or take a quick dip in a mountain lake (take care to avoid hungry bears!). You can reach Mora from Stockholm by

train in about 4 hours. If you figure in a return trip to Stockholm, the whole journey takes about a week. From mid-June through the end of August, you can buy an Inland Railway Card valid for 14 days for the entire railway for 1,550SEK, plus an optional 50SEK for each seat reservation, but all the extras will add up. One-week packages are available that include rail fare, hotels, and breakfast, and start at 4,965SEK per person double, with a 1,550SEK single supplement, and go as high as 11,250SEK. The final return to Stockholm is on an overnight train in a two-bed sleeping compartment.

[Fast FACTS] SWEDEN

Area Code The international country code for Sweden is **46.** The local city code for Stockholm is **08;** for Uppsala, it's **18;** and for Gothenberg, it's **31.**

Business Hours Generally, **banks** are open Monday through Friday from 10am to 3pm (Thurs until 4:30 or 5pm). In some larger cities banks extend their hours, usually on Thursday or Friday, until 5:30 or 6pm. Most **offices** are open Monday through Friday from 8:30 or 9am to 5pm (sometimes to 3 or 4pm in the summer); on Saturday, offices and factories are closed, or open for only a half-day. Most **stores and shops** are open Monday through Friday between 9:30am and 6pm, and on Saturday from 9:30am to somewhere

between 1 and 4pm. Once a week, usually on Monday or Friday, some of the larger stores are open from 9:30am to 7pm (July–Aug to 6pm). Some city stores also open on a Sunday between noon and 4pm.

Climate It's hard to generalize Sweden's climate. The country as a whole has many sunny summer days, but it's not super hot. July is the warmest month, with temperatures in Stockholm and Gothenburg averaging around 64°F (17°C). February is the coldest month, when the temperature in Stockholm averages around 26°F (–3°C), and Gothenburg is a few degrees warmer. It's not always true that the farther north you go, the cooler it becomes. During the summer, the northern parts of the

country (Halsingland to northern Lapland) may suddenly have the warmest weather and bluest skies. The southern coast, warmed by the Gulf Stream, can be pleasantly hot in the summer, but don't count on it.

Currency The country's currency is the Swedish krona (SEK), which has 100 ore to the krona (plural form is *kronor*). The exchange rate in this book is calculated at 7.31SEK = $1 and 11.39SEK = £1.

Documents Required U.S. and Canadian citizens with a **valid passport** don't need a visa to enter Sweden if they don't expect to stay more than 90 days and don't expect to work there.

Electricity In Sweden, the electricity is 220 volts AC (50 cycles). To operate North American hair dryers and other electrical appliances, you'll need an electrical transformer or converter, and adaptor plugs that fit the two-pin round continental electrical outlets that are standard in Sweden. Transformers and adaptors can be bought at hardware stores or travel shops.

Embassies & Consulates   All embassies are in Stockholm. The Embassy of the **United States** is at Dag Hammarskjölds Väg 31, S-115 89 Stockholm (© **08/783-53-00;** www.stockholm.usembassy.gov); the **Canadian Embassy** is at Tegelbacken 4, S-103 23 Stockholm (© **08/453-30-00;** www.canadaemb.se).

Health & Safety   Sweden is viewed as a "safe" destination, although problems, of course, can and do occur anywhere. You don't need to get shots, the produce is safe, and the water in cities and towns potable. It is easy to get a prescription filled in towns and cities, and nearly all cities and towns throughout Sweden have hospitals with

English-speaking doctors and well-trained medical staffs. Watch out for pickpockets in the cities where travelers are targeted for their passports and cash.

Holidays   Sweden celebrates the following public holidays: New Year's Day (Jan 1); Epiphany (Jan 6); Good Friday; Easter Sunday; Easter Monday; Labor Day (May 1); Ascension Day (mid-May); Whitsunday (late May); National Day (June 6); Midsummer Eve and Day (late June); All Saints' Day (late Oct/early Nov); Christmas Eve, Christmas Day, and Boxing Day (Dec 24–26); and New Year's Eve (Dec 31). Inquire at a tourist bureau for the dates of the holidays that vary.

Legal Aid   While traveling in Sweden, you are, of course, subject to that country's laws. If arrested or charged, you can obtain a list of private lawyers from the U.S. Embassy to represent you.

Mail   Post office services are now incorporated in

shops and kiosks, so their hours vary. To send a postcard or letter not weighing more than 20 grams (.7oz.) to North America costs 8.10SEK by airmail, which takes about 5 days. Mailboxes carry a yellow post horn on a blue background. You also can buy stamps in most tobacco shops and stationers.

Police & Emergencies   In an emergency, dial © **112** anywhere in the country. These calls are free from pay phones.

Telephone   Instructions in English are posted in public phone boxes, which can be found on street corners. Pay phones in Sweden take credit cards or phone cards, which can be purchased at most newspaper stands and tobacco shops.

Tipping   Hotels include a 15% service charge in your bill. Restaurants, depending on their class, add 13% to 15% to your tab. Taxi drivers are entitled to 10% of the fare, and cloakroom attendants usually get 7SEK.

STOCKHOLM

Stockholm has the biggest airport in the country, so many rail passengers fly into Stockholm and then use the time saved to explore not only Sweden's capital, but also other major rail destinations in the country, including Gothenburg. And, as the country's rail hub, Stockholm also has the best rail connections in Sweden; all of the major tourist destinations are within easy reach, many no more than 3 hours or so away. And thanks to the natural beauty of the country, every major train journey out of the capital is scenic.

Stockholm effortlessly combines more than 7 centuries' worth of beautiful architecture, from the crazy cobblestone streets of its medieval old town to the clean lines of the granite, marble, and glass towers of its modern new town. It's located at a point where the waters of Lake Mälaren join the Baltic Sea, right on the doorstep of an

Stockholm

ATTRACTIONS ●

Drottningholm Palace
and Theater **1**

Hallwyiska Museet
(Hallwyl Museum) **19**

Historiska Museet (Museum
of National Antiquities) **23**

Kungliga Slottet (Royal
Palace) & Museums **15**

Moderna Museet (Museum
of Modern Art) **16**

Nationaluseum (National
Museum of Art) **17**

Nordiska Museet **25**

Prins Eugens
Waldemarsudde **28**

Riddarholm Church **11**

Skansen **27**

Vasamuseet (Royal
Warship Vasa) **26**

Church
Information
Subway

ACCOMMODATIONS ■
Adlon Hotell & Kontor **7**
Best Western
  Hotel Kom **3**
Elite Hotel Stockholm
  Plaza **5**
Hotel Örnsköld **22**

Hotel Rival **13**
Hotel Tegnérlunden **2**
Rica Hotel Stockholm **6**
Sheraton Stockholm
  Hotel and Towers **9**

DINING ◆
Bakfickan **8**
Berns Asian **20**
Cattelin's **14**
Divino **4**
Eriks Bakfica **24**
Grand Veranda **18**

Mälardrottningen **10**
Prinsens **21**
Roxy **12**

archipelago of 24,000 islands, skerries, and islets. But even more than its well-tended past and forward-looking present, Stockholm is most famously a world showcase of democratic socialism. It is a city that is both clean and well planned, a savvy and sophisticated metropolis whose cultural attractions and entertainment venues rival those of Europe's other great capitals.

Give it at least 3 days, and know that you will have scratched only the surface of its allure. Note, however, that rail passengers should avoid a winter visit, when many of Stockholm's major attractions, including all the outdoor ones, close down. The cold weather sets in by October, and you'll need to keep heavily wrapped up well past April.

Station Information

GETTING FROM THE AIRPORT TO THE TRAIN STATION

You'll wing your way into Stockholm's **Arlanda Airport** (✆ **08/797-60-00;** www.lfv. se), approximately 28 miles (45km) north of the city center on the E4 highway. A long covered walkway connects the international and domestic terminals, should you be flying in from Gothenburg or some other Swedish city.

For rail travelers, the fastest and cheapest way to go from the airport to the Central Station within Stockholm is on the high-speed **Arlanda Express** train (trip time: 20 min.), which is covered by the Eurail Pass. Trains run every 15 to 30 minutes daily from 5am to 1am. If you don't have a railpass, the cost of a one-way ticket is 240SEK for adults, 120SEK for seniors and students (kids under 7 travel free), although there are often deals during the summer. For more information, call **020/22-22-24** or go online to **www.arlandaexpress.com**.

Another option is to take the **Flygbussarna Bus** (**www.flygbussarna.se**) outside the airport entrance to Central Station. A round-trip ticket costs 198SEK; one-way fare is 99SEK. Buses run from 4:50am to 1am. The trip takes 40 minutes or so, depending on traffic. A taxi from the airport costs 450SEK to 550SEK; a 10% tip is standard. Always ask about the fare in advance, as some cab companies will try to overcharge.

At the **Centralstationen** (Central Station; ✆ **0771/75-75-75**), you can connect with Stockholm's efficient subway system, called the T-bana. The Central Station is directly across from the bus station, **Cityterminalen (City Terminal),** at Klarabergsviadukten 72. The bus and train stations are serviced by the T-bana Centralen stop.

INSIDE THE STATION

The Central Station is convenient to any number of affordable hotels in the area and is one of the better-equipped stations in the north of Europe, featuring a number of shops on its lower level, and kiosks selling everything from food and beverage to tobacco and newspapers—there's even a casino. There are also cafes, pubs, restaurants, and fast-food chains, plus a **Konsum,** evocative of an American supermarket. The food service ranges from a cafeteria to a first-class restaurant.

Train information is prominently displayed on bulletin boards in several key places just inside the main entrance to the Central Station. In the main hall is a large ticket office where train reservations can be made, including reservations for sleeper-car accommodations. Hours are Monday to Sunday 5am to 12:30am.

Also at the station is a currency exchange kiosk, **Forex** (✆ **08/587-60-700;** www.forex.se), open daily 7am to 9pm. Lockers at the station cost 30SEK to 60SEK per day.

Information Elsewhere in the City

The **Tourist Center** is at Sverigehuset (Sweden House), Hamngatan 27 (✆ **08/50-82-85-08;** www.stockholmtown.com). It's open Monday to Friday 9am to 7pm, Saturday 10am to 5pm, and Sunday 10am to 4pm. Maps and other free tourist materials are available, and the staff can help you find the perfect hotel for your budget. If done in person, this service costs 75SEK, but it is free via phone or e-mail.

Getting Around

You can travel throughout Stockholm by bus, local train, subway (T-bana), and tram, going from Singö in the north to Nynäshamn in the south. Routes are divided into zones, and one ticket is valid for all types of public transportation in the number of zones you have paid to travel in within an hour of being stamped. Subway entrances are marked with a blue T on a white background.

The basic fare for public transportation (subway, tram, streetcar, or bus) is 25SEK per coupon, and you will need a minimum of two for most of Stockholm; the farther you go, the more coupons you need. To travel in all three zones, you will need four units. Purchase a ticket for a tram or streetcar at the tollbooth found at every stop. You can transfer for free (or double back and return to your starting point) within an hour of your departure.

For information on all services, including buses, subways *(Tunnelbana),* and suburban trains *(pendeltåg),* call ✆ **08/600-10-00** or head online to **www.sl.se/English**.

The SL Center, on the lower level of Sergels Torg (east of Central Station), provides transportation information. It also sells a map of the city's system, including suburban trains, and day and discount passes for public transportation. It's open Monday to Friday from 7am to 6:30pm, and Saturday and Sunday 10am to 5pm. In 2008, a new office was opened in the lower hall of Central Station and is open from Monday to Saturday 6:30am to 11:15pm and Sunday 7am to 11:15pm.

Your best transportation bet is to get a **travelcard.** A 1-day card costs 100SEK and is valid for 24 hours of unlimited travel by T-bana, bus, and commuter trains within Stockholm. Most visitors will probably prefer the 3-day card for 200SEK, valid for 72 hours in Stockholm and the adjacent county. The 3-day card is also valid for reduced admission to the Skansen Museum, and free entry to the Kaknäs Tower and Gröna Lunds (Fun Fair). A card for a child 7 to 17 costs 60SEK for 1 day. Kids under 7 travel free with an adult. Tickets are available at tourist information offices, in subway stations, and from most news vendors. Call ✆ **08/689-10-00** for more information.

Stockholmskortet (Stockholm Card) is a discount card allowing unlimited travel by bus (except airport buses), subway, and local trains throughout the city and the surrounding county. Admission to 75 attractions is included in the package, as is a 1-hour sightseeing boat tour exploring either the royal or historical canals. The card is also good for ferry travel to Djurgården, a recreation area packed with museums and cafes. The card is an excellent buy, especially if you plan to do a lot of traveling by public transport around Stockholm to visit a lot of attractions.

You can buy the card at several places in the city, including the Tourist Center in Sweden House. The cards are stamped with the date and time of the first use. For a 24-hour card, adults pay 395SEK; for 48 hours, 525SEK; and for 72 hours, 625SEK, with children paying 195SEK, 225SEK, and 245SEK, respectively.

Taxis in Stockholm are expensive, with fares varying between different firms. Meters start at around 45SEK, and even a short ride within the city can cost as much as 200SEK. You can hail cabs displaying the sign LEDIG, or you can order one by phone. **Taxi Stockholm** (✆ 08/15-00-00; www.taxistockholm.se) is a large, reputable company.

17 Where to Stay

By the standards of U.S. and Canadian cities, hotels in Stockholm are very expensive. But dozens of hotels in Stockholm offer reduced rates on weekends all year, and daily from around mid-June to mid-August. And, conveniently, many of the least expensive lodgings in the city are located near the Central Station.

Adlon Hotell & Kontor This 1880s structure has seen many improvements and changes over the years, but much of the old architecture has been retained. It's a little short on style but big on comfort. The small to midsize bedrooms sport tiny bathrooms but have been modernized with functional Nordic furnishings. The hotel is just a few blocks away from Central Station and is convenient to public transportation. There's also free broadband Internet in every room.

Vasagatan 42, S-111 20 Stockholm. ✆ **08/4026-500.** Fax 08/20-86-10. www.adlon.se. 94 units. 1,500SEK–2,295SEK double. Rates include breakfast. T-bana: Centralen. **Amenities:** Bar; lounge; rooms for those w/limited mobility; smoke-free rooms. *In room:* No A/C.

Best Western Hotel Kom ⚜ In the city center, about a 20-minute walk to Central Station, this hotel was carved out of a modernized hostel built in 1972, and it's still owned by the YMCA and YWCA. In May 2003, the hotel added 29 new rooms located in a nearby building equipped with its own breakfast room. Reflecting their hostel backgrounds, many rooms are quite small, but they are nicely furnished with a host of modern amenities and immaculate shower-only bathrooms.

17 Döbelnsgatan, S-111 40 Stockholm. ✆ **08/412-23-00.** Fax 08/412-23-10. www.komhotel.se. 128 units. 1,300SEK–2,000SEK double. Rates include breakfast. Hostel-type shared rooms cost 600SEK–900SEK, without breakfast (75SEK extra). **Amenities:** Breakfast room; bar; rooms for those w/limited mobility; smoke-free rooms. *In room:* No A/C.

Elite Hotel Stockholm Plaza ★ This top-rated and well-run hotel is set on a triangular piece of land about a 15-minute walk northeast of Central Station. The building is more than a century old but has kept abreast of the times with frequent modernizations. Since 1984, it's been one of the most respectable midrange hotels of central Stockholm. The renovated bedrooms are small to midsize and furnished functionally but comfortably, each with a tiled bathroom. The hotel has a sauna available for private use.

Birger Jarlsgatan 29, S-103 95 Stockholm. ✆ **08/566-22-000.** Fax 08/566-22-020. www.elite.se. 143 units. 1,550SEK–2,700SEK double; 2,650SEK–5,200SEK suite. Rates include breakfast. AE, DC, MC, V. T-bana: Hötorget or Östermalmstorg. **Amenities:** Restaurant; bar; smoke-free rooms. *In room:* No A/C.

Hotel Örnsköld ⚜ Near the Royal Dramatic Theatre (it attracts an artistic crowd), this hotel is east of Central Station but still convenient to the city center. Built in 1910, it's undergone frequent renovations but nevertheless retains a slightly old-fashioned appeal. The high-ceilinged rooms on the floor above street level have modern furnishings, some a little worn, but all immaculately kept. Some of the larger rooms have space for extra beds, and each room comes with a neat little shower-only bathroom.

Nybrogatan 6, S-114 34 Stockholm. ✆ **08/667-02-85.** Fax 08/667-69-91. www.hotelornskold.se. 27 units. 1,495SEK–2,195SEK double. Rates include breakfast. AE, MC, V. T-bana: Östermalmstorg. **Amenities:** Smoke-free rooms. *In room:* No A/C.

Hotel Rival   This charming boutique hotel—once the grand Aston Hotel, which had its heyday in the 1930s—was opened in 2003 by Benny Anderson of ABBA. The decor is first class, elegant, and modern. Rooms sport high-tech conveniences such as plasma-screen TVs and DVD players (there's an ever-changing and up-to-date library of free English-language DVDs downstairs), along with marble bathrooms and Egyptian cotton linens. Other alluring extras include a comfortable movie theater. It's just south of the Old Town.

Mariatorget 3, SE-118 91 Stockholm. ✆ **08/54-57-89-00.** Fax 08/754-57-89-24. www.rival.se. 99 units. Mon–Thurs 2,495SEK–2,995SEK double; Fri–Sun 1,595SEK–2,195SEK. Weekend rates include breakfast. AE, DC, MC, V. **Amenities:** Restaurant; bar; bistro; cafe; lounge; rooms for those w/limited mobility; smoke-free rooms.

Hotel Tegnérlunden ★   Like a London town house hotel, this hidden gem lies next to a leafy park, which is unusual for Stockholm. It features an airy rooftop breakfast room and, despite a big expansion, retains a personal atmosphere. Rooms are tasteful and functionally furnished, but a long way from cutting edge. Those we saw were well maintained and blissfully quiet, especially those opening out onto the rear. The bathrooms, equipped with shower units, are small but beautifully kept.

Tegnérlunden 8, S-113 59 Stockholm. ✆ **08/5454-5550.** Fax 08/5454-5551. www.hoteltegnerlunden. se. 102 units. 1,090SEK–2,690SEK double; 1,690SEK–3,290SEK junior suite. Rates include buffet breakfast. Parking: 250SEK. AE, DC, MC. Bus: 47, 53, or 69. **Amenities:** Breakfast room; bar; smoke-free rooms. *In room:* No A/C.

Rica Hotel Stockholm   This first-class hotel is just 1,290 feet (387m), and an easy walk, from Central Station. Built in the early 1980s, it offers rooms large on international style and comfort but short on local charm. The midsize bedrooms are tasteful and functionally furnished. The large, bountiful breakfast buffet is served in a lovely winter garden.

Slöjdgatan 7, S-111 57 Stockholm. ✆ **08/723-72-72.** Fax 08/723-72-09. www.rica.se. 292 units. 1,220SEK–2,245SEK double, with the cheaper prices on the weekend. Rates include breakfast. AE, DC, MC, V. **Amenities:** Lunch restaurant; bar; lounge; rooms for those w/limited mobility; smoke-free rooms. *In room:* No A/C.

Sheraton Stockholm Hotel and Towers   Just a 2-minute walk from the Central Station, this eight-story hotel looks out on the Old Town, Lake Mälaren, and City Hall. It went through a total renovation in 2007, and what it lacks in old-fashioned Swedish charm, it makes up for with strikingly modern facilities, including a new fitness center. Bedrooms are spacious and luxuriously furnished; all the important amenities—and then some—are here. Because it has lots of rooms to fill, rates here can vary wildly.

Tegelbacken 6, S-101 23 Stockholm. ✆ **800/325-3535** in the U.S., or 08/412-34-00. Fax 08/12-34-09. www.sheraton.com/stockholm. 464 units. 1,500SEK–2000SEK double; from 3000SEK suite. AE, DC, MC, V. T-bana: Centralen. **Amenities:** Restaurant; bar; rooms for those w/limited mobility; smoke-free rooms. *In room:* No A/C.

Top Attractions & Special Moments

Even on the most cursory visit to the city, take the ferry to **Djurgården** to visit the **Vasa Ship Museum,** the city's most celebrated attraction, and the open-air

Skansen Folk Museum. In the afternoon, take a walking tour of **Gamla Stan (Old Town)** and perhaps have dinner here. On the second day, get up early and go for a boat cruise of the archipelago and catch such cultural highlights as **Kungliga Slottet (Royal Palace)** or the **National Museum of Art.** If you have a third day, prepare to descend on the **Drottningholm Palace and Theater** or take a day tour to the ancient university city of **Uppsala.**

Drottningholm Palace and Theater ★★★ On an island in Lake Mälaren, Drottningholm (Queen's Island) has been dubbed the Versailles of Sweden. The majesty of this 17th-century Renaissance palace was enlivened by additional elements of the French baroque and rococo trends of later years. It is about 7 miles (11km) from Stockholm and is easily reached by boat (the best method), bus, or subway. The palace—loaded with courtly art and furnishings—is surrounded by fountains and parks, and still functions as one of the official residences of the country's royal family.

Nearby is the **Drottningholm Slottsteater (Drottningholm Court Theater),** which grew to fame under Gustavus III, himself an accomplished playwright and actor. The best-preserved 18th-century theater in the world, it still uses its original stage, sets, and machinery. Each summer, between May and September, operas and ballets are staged in full 18th-century regalia, complete with period costumes and wigs. In addition to touring the stage, auditorium, and dressing rooms, visitors can pop into the gift shop.

One other item of interest: The **Chinese Pavilion** is located on the palace grounds and must not be missed. It was built during the rococo conquest of Europe, when everything Oriental came into fashion, and rivals the Brighton Pavilion for its whimsical splendor.

Ekerö, Drottningholm. Palace: ✆ **08/402-62-80.** www.royalcourt.se. 100SEK adults, 50SEK students and children under 25, free for children 6 and under; Chinese Pavilion 70SEK adults, 35SEK students and children 7-18, free for children 6 and under. Pavilion and Palace combo ticket 120SEK adults, 60SEK children 7-18. Theater: ✆ **08/759-0406.** www.dtm.se. 70SEK adults, 50SEK students, free for children 15 and under. Palace and Chinese Pavilion Oct-Apr Sat-Sun noon-3pm; May-Aug daily 10am-5pm; Sept daily 11am-3:30pm. Theater, guided tours in English every hour on the hour, May daily noon-4:30pm; June-Aug daily 11am-4:30pm; Sept daily 1-3:30pm. Oct-Apr Sat-Sun noon-2pm. T-bana: Brommaplan, then bus no. 301 or 323 to Drottningholm. Ferry from the dock near City Hall.

Hallwylska Museet (Hallwyl Museum) ★ 🎁 To visit the former home of Countess Wilhelmina von Hallwyl is to wander back into a time capsule of the Belle Epoque. The countess was a world-class collector of art and objets d'art, and she spent the better part of 7 decades acquiring an astonishing collection of priceless paintings, silver, armor, weapons, rare tapestries, glass, and more—she collected virtually anything, even buttons and umbrellas. The house was built to Wilhelmina's specifications in the 1890s, and despite its Renaissance- and Gothic-inspired design, it had all the mod conveniences of the day: indoor plumbing, electricity, telephone, even an elevator. It was donated to the state in 1920, and that is precisely when the clock stopped running inside this fascinating, eccentric museum.

Hamngatan 4. ✆ **08/5402-30-99.** www.lsh.se. Guided tours 80SEK adults, free for children 18 and under. Guided tours in English 3pm daily, museum closed Mon. T-bana: Östermalmstorg.

Historiska Museet (Museum of National Antiquities) ★★ Among other allures, this museum boasts one of the most precious collections of gold in the world. The *Guldrummet*, or **Gold Room ★★★**, is an underground vault accessed to the right of the main entrance. In all, there are 3,000 gold and silver objects displayed in this room, dating from about 2,000 B.C. to A.D. 1520. The room also displays Viking silver and gold jewelry and other precious items, many unearthed from ancient burial sites. Collections include Viking stone inscriptions and coins minted in the 10th century.

Narvavägen 13-17. ⓒ **08/519-556-00.** www.historiska.se. 70SEK adults, 50SEK students and seniors, free for anyone 17 and under. May–Sept daily 10am–5pm; Oct–Apr Tues–Sun 11am–5pm (late viewing Thurs till 8pm). T-bana: Karlaplan or Östermalmstorg. Bus: 44, 47, 56, 69, or 76.

Kungliga Slottet (Royal Palace) & Museums ★★ The pride of Gamla Stan (Old Town), this 608-room showcase is one of the few palaces in Europe still in use as the official home for a monarch (though the king and queen prefer Drottningholm) that may be visited by the general public. Built principally in the Italian baroque style, between 1691 and 1754, it can easily take up to 3 hours to tour.

The highlights here are the **Royal Apartments ★★**, with their magnificent baroque ceilings and fine tapestries. The State Apartments have the oldest palace interiors, having been decorated in 1690 by French artists; look for at least three magnificent baroque ceiling frescoes and fine tapestries.

Nearly all visitors head for the **Royal Armoury (*Livrustkammaren*) ★★**, in the cellars of the palace. Here you can view weapons and armor, check out the gilded coaches ridden in by kings, and look at coronation outfits, some dating from the 16th century. *Skattkammaren*, the **Royal Treasury ★★**, contains one of the best-known collections of crown jewels in Europe, including a dozen crowns, scepters, and orbs, along with stunningly beautiful pieces of antique jewelry. The most outstanding exhibit here is King Erik XIV's coronation regalia from 1561. Gustav III's collection of sculpture from the Roman Empire can be viewed in the **Antikmuseum (Museum of Antiquities).**

Kungliga Husgerådskammaren. ⓒ**08/402-61-30.** www.kungahuset.se. Combination ticket to all parts of palace except the Royal Armory 140SEK adults, 70SEK students and children 18 and under. Entrance to the Royal Armory 50SEK, free for students and children 18 and under. May close without warning for state visits and royal receptions. Mid-Sept to mid-May noon–3pm; early May and Sept 10am–4pm; June–Aug 10am–5pm.T-bana: Gamla Stan. Bus: 2, 43, 55, 71, or 76.

Moderna Museet (Museum of Modern Art) ★★ On the tiny island of Skeppsholmen, this museum focuses on contemporary works by Swedish and international artists, including kinetic sculptures. In addition to changing exhibitions that have been known to kick up controversy, there's a small but excellent collection of cubist art by Picasso, Braque, and Léger; Matisse's *Apollo* decoupage; the famous *Enigma of William Tell,* by Salvador Dalí; and works by Brancusi, Max Ernst, Giacometti, Arp, and more. Other works include the 12-foot-high (3.6m) *Geometric Mouse,* by Claes Oldenburg; *Fox Trot,* an early Warhol; and *Total Totality All,* a huge sculpture by Louise Nevelson.

Skeppsholmen. ⓒ**08/519-55-200.** www.modernamuseet.se. 80SEK adults, 60SEK students/seniors, free for children 18 and under. Tues 10am–8pm; Wed–Sun 10am–6pm. T-bana: Kungsträdgården. Bus: 65.

Nationalmuseum (National Museum of Art) ★★ Had Queen Christina retained her crown and continued building her collection, Stockholm would surely have had a Prado or a Louvre. This museum isn't the Prado—nor is it the Uffizi—but it does contain a vast Swedish collection of masterpieces and is one of the most outstanding art museums in Northern Europe, filled with the works of old masters such as Rembrandt and Rubens.

A WALK BACK IN time

Gamla Stan ★★★, or the Old Town of Stockholm, is spread over four islands and contains two of our top sights: the Royal Palace and Riddarholm Church. But with its narrow lanes and medieval buildings, Gamla Stan is a major attraction in its own right. The old shops are well worth the trip, and they are backed up by a number of attractive, mainly expensive restaurants.

Stortorget, the old marketplace, is the center of Gamla Stan. Dominated by a rococo palace, most of its buildings date from the 16th and 18th centuries (the red building was constructed during the reign of the famous queen Christina). The **Stock Exchange** is housed in an 18th-century building and contains a museum (© **08/534-81-818;** www.nobelmuseum.se) open to the public.

The **Storkyrkan Church ★★,** or **Great Church,** the oldest church in Stockholm, was founded in the 13th century but has been rebuilt many times since. It became Lutheran Protestant in 1527, 7 years after its darkest event, in which a Danish king invited 80 Swedish noblemen to dinner and had them beheaded in the courtyard, leaving their heads in a pile to warn dissidents. It is the scene of royal coronations, christenings, and weddings. The most celebrated sculpture is the immense *St. George and the Dragon ★★★,* dating from 1489. The royal pews have been in service for 3 centuries, and the ebony-and-silver altar, dating from 1652, is stunning. You can also see the *Last Judgment,* which is said to be one of the largest paintings on earth. This is still an operating church, so confine your sightseeing to times when no services are being conducted. It's open from 9am to 7pm Monday through Saturday, 9am to 5:30pm on Sunday; admission is free.

Located at the tip of a peninsula on Södra Blasieholmshamnen, a short walk from the Royal Opera House, the Renaissance-style building houses world-class masterpieces from the early Renaissance to the beginning of the 20th century.

The first floor is devoted to applied arts (silverware, handcrafts, porcelain, Empire furnishings, and the like), but first-time visitors may want to head directly to the second-floor collection of masterpieces, which includes a notable collection of rare 16th-century Russian icons and Lucas Cranach's most amusing painting, *Venus and Cupid.*

The most important room in the entire gallery has one wall devoted to the works of Rembrandt (*Portrait of an Old Man* and *Portrait of an Old Woman*), along with his impressions of a maid (one of the more famous works in Stockholm). Other rooms offer exceptional paintings by Flemish, English, and Venetian masters. Exhibited also are important modern works—Manet's *Parisienne;* Degas's dancers; Rodin's nude male *(Copper Age);* van Gogh's *Light Movements in Green;* and paintings by Renoir, notably *La Grenouillère.*

Södra Blasieholmshamnen. © **08/519-54-300.** www.nationalmuseum.se. 100SEK adults, 80SEK students and seniors, free for children 18 and under. Tues 11am–8pm (also on Thurs Sept 1–May 31); Wed–Sun 11am–5pm. T-bana: Kungsträdgården. Bus: 46, 62, 65, or 76.

Nordiska Museet (Nordic Museum) ★★ On the island of Djurgården, the outstanding Nordic Museum houses an impressive collection of more than a million implements, costumes, and furnishings depicting life in Sweden from the 1500s to the present day. Highlights of the rich and varied collection include dining tables laid with food and all the implements, one from each century, and period costumes ranging from matching garters and ties for men to the purple flowerpot hats of the strolling ladies of the 1890s. Anglers head for the basement, where there's an extensive exhibit of the tools of the Swedish fishing trade, plus relics once used by nomadic Lapps.

Djurgårdsvägen 6-16, Djurgården. © **08/519-546-00.** www.nordiskamuseet.se. 80SEK adults, free for children 18 and under. Sept–May Mon–Fri 10am–4pm, Sat–Sun 11am–5pm; June–Aug daily 10am–5pm. Bus: 44 or 47.

Prins Eugens Waldemarsudde ★★   The once-royal residence of the "painting prince," Prince Eugen (1865–1947), is today an art gallery, surrounded by a sculpture garden and overlooking the water. Donated by the prince to the city in his will, Waldemarsudde is on Djurgården. The prince was one of Sweden's major landscape painters, and his most high-profile works are the murals inside City Hall. In the garden are statues by such sculptors as Rodin, and the house itself is a treasure to behold. At one time, Prince Eugen possessed the largest art collection in Sweden, and some of it—works by Edvard Munch, for one—is on display.

Prins Eugens Väg 6. © **08/545-837-00.** www.waldemarsudde.se. Admission 95SEK adults, 75SEK seniors and students, free for children 18 and under. Tues–Sun 11am–5pm (Thurs until 8pm). Closed Mon. Bus: 47.

Riddarholm Church ★   The second-oldest church in Stockholm is on the tiny island of Riddarholmen, next to Gamla Stan. It was founded in the 13th century as a Franciscan monastery. Almost all the royal heads of state are entombed here, except for the elusive Christina, who is buried in Rome. Her father, Gustavus Adolphus II, who saw Swedish power reach its peak, is buried in a Dutch Renaissance chapel. There are three principal royal chapels, including one, the Bernadotte, that belongs to the present ruling family.

Riddarholmen. © **08/402-61-30.** www.royalcourt.se. Admission 30SEK adults, 15SEK students and children 7–18, free for children 6 and under. June–Aug daily 10am–5pm; May 15–31 and Sept 1–14 daily 10am–4pm; closed rest of year. T-bana: Gamla Stan.

Skansen ★★★   Stockholmers call this 75-acre (30-hectare) open-air museum, with more than 150 antique buildings from the 17th and 18th centuries, "Old Sweden in a Nutshell," because it represents all of Sweden's provinces, from Lapland in the north to Skåne in the south. Founded in 1891, Skansen is the world's oldest open-air museum and comes complete with a zoo featuring Scandinavian fauna. Exhibits range from a windmill to a manor house to an entire town quarter. Browsers can explore the old workshops where craftspeople such as silversmiths and glassblowers plied their trades. These handicrafts are demonstrated here, along with more humble occupations such as weaving and churning butter. In summer, international stars perform at the auditorium here, and special events such as folk dancing and concerts are staged.

Djurgårdsslätten 49-51. © **08/442-80-00.** www.skansen.se. Admission varies seasonally. 120SEK-150SEK adults, 50SEK children 6–15, free for children 5 and under. Special events attract higher charges. Historic buildings Jan–Apr daily 10am–4pm; May and Sept daily 10am–8pm; June–Aug daily 10am–10pm; Oct–Dec daily 10am–3pm (to 4pm Sat–Sun). Bus: 47 from central Stockholm. Ferry from Slussen.

Vasamuseet (Royal Warship Vasa) ★★★   On a bright, sunny Sunday, August 10, 1628, the Royal Flagship *Vasa*—ordered built by Gustavus Adolphus II—set sail on its maiden voyage and, much to the horror of onlookers, promptly keeled over and sank into the murky Stockholm harbor.

The *Vasa* was finally salvaged by Anders Franzén, an amateur marine archaeologist, in 1961. To everyone's amazement, it was fantastically well preserved. More than 4,000 coins, carpenter's tools, "Lübeck gray" sailor pants, fish bones, and other seagoing articles for the truncated trip were found aboard. All of the *Vasa* sculptures—97% of the 700 were found—are back on the ship, which looks stunning now that it is once again carrying grotesque faces, lion masks, fish-fashioned bodies, and other carvings, some with the original paint and gilt still gleaming.

The great cabin of the ship has been rebuilt with the original oak panels decorated with elegant woodcarvings and ingenious foldout beds. Visitors can walk right through the cabin. Also, a 16-foot-long (4.8m) interior exposed-view model has been built; 90 dolls representing soldiers and crew show life aboard.

Galärvarvsvägen 14, Djurgården. ☎ **08/519-54-800.** www.vasamuseet.se. Admission 110SEK adults (80SEK Sept–May), 80SEK students, free for children 18 and under. June–Aug daily 8:30am–6pm; Sept–May Wed 10am–8pm, Thurs–Tues 10am–5pm. Closed Jan 1 and Dec 23–25. Bus: 44, 47, or 69. Ferry from Slussen year-round, from Nybroplan in summer only.

Where to Dine

Bakfickan ★ 🍴 SWEDISH   In-the-know local foodies gravitate to Bakfickan, which is far more affordable than its more glamorous neighbor, Operakällaren, even though both restaurants use the same kitchen. Self-titled "the hip pocket," it's a help-yourself affair handing over authentic Swedish specialties such as reindeer, elk, and even delectable saffron-gold Arctic cloudberries. With only 28 eating stools set up around a counter, it fills up quickly in winter but has space outside during the warmer months.

Jakobs Torg 12. ☎ **08/676-58-09.** www.operakallaren.se. Reservations not accepted. Main courses 140SEK–280SEK. AE, DC, MC, V. Mon–Fri 11:30am–midnight, Sat 12:30pm–midnight. Sun 3–8pm. Closed Jan 1, 6–7; Dec 24–26, 31; and July 12–Aug 4. T-bana: Kungsträdgården.

Berns Asian ★ MODERN ASIAN   Located in the swank Bern Hotel, this classic restaurant might have opened in 1860 as a "pleasure palace," but it's changed with the times and now looks to Asia for its inspiration. Three monumental chandeliers light the main hall, while the plush furniture described by August Strindberg in the Red Room (*Röda Rummet*) is still here. Dishes are plucked from across the Continent and range from dim sum to tempura to raw meats and fish.

Näckströmsgatan 8. ☎ **08/566-32-222.** www.berns.se. Reservations recommended. Main courses 150SEK–425SEK. AE, DC, MC. Mon–Fri 7–10am; Sat–Sun 7:30–11am; Sun–Thurs 11:30am–1am; Fri–Sat 11:30am–3am. T-bana: Östermalmstorg.

Cattelin's 🍴   Since 1897, this old favorite has been feeding frugal Stockholm-ers—and feeding them well—from its location on a historic street about a half-mile (.8km) south of Central Station. Cattelin has survived not only wars but also changing tastes and still sticks to the tried and true, using fresh ingredients laced into grand-mother's favorite salmon, veal, chicken, and beef dishes—all served in a convivial but noisy setting.

Storkyrkobrinken 9. ☎ **08/20-18-18.** www.cattelin.com Reservations recommended. Main courses 128SEK–295SEK. AE, DC, MC, V. Mon–Fri 10am–9pm; Sat–Sun noon–10pm. T-bana: Gamla Stan.

Divino ★ TUSCAN   This elegant and pricey Italian restaurant is one of Stockholm's finest. The Tuscan menu, which includes dishes such as suckling pig with cauliflower and truffles, grilled tuna with lukewarm early spring salad, and scallops with avocado purée, is light-years away from your local trattoria. The wine cellar is particularly noteworthy. If the prices frighten you, check out the adjacent **Divino Deli & Bar** (same address) for something less elaborate, and for the best cappuccino in Stockholm.

Karlavägen 28. © **08/611-02-69.** www.divino.se. Reservations recommended. Main courses 265SEK-295SEK. Fixed-price menus from 380SEK. AE, DC, MC, V. Mon-Sat 6-11pm. Bus: 1, 42, 44, 55, or 56.

Eriks Bakfica ★ ◢ SWEDISH   Swedes looking for *husmanskost* (wholesome home cooking) have been coming here since 1979. We always check out the array of daily herring appetizers, but what really attracts us is the tantalizing "archipelago stew," a ragout of fresh fish (it varies daily) prepared with tomatoes and served with garlic mayonnaise. If you drop in for lunch, ask for Erik's cheeseburger with "secret sauce" (it's not on the menu, so you need to request it).

Fredrikshovsgatan 4. © **08/660-15-99.** www.eriks.se. Reservations recommended. Main courses 250SEK-300SEK. AE, DC, MC, V. Tues-Fri 11:30am-midnight; Sat and Sun 5-11pm. Bus: 47.

Grand Veranda ★ SWEDISH   Opposite the Royal Palace, the 1874 Grand Hotel, the finest in Sweden, is the setting for this first-class restaurant with panoramic views of the harbor. The chefs here are celebrated for their fabled smörgåsbord, offering up all the classic meats, fish, and cheeses, including herring and gravalax, plus some hot options. An a la carte menu is also served, with dishes ranging from sirloin of reindeer with artichoke terrine to seared filet of pike-perch with roasted beetroot.

In the Grand Hotel, Blasieholmshamnen 8. © **08/679-35-86.** www.grandhotel.se. Reservations required. Main courses 145SEK-335SEK, Swedish buffet 455SEK. AE, DC, MC, V. Daily 7am-11pm. T-bana: Kungsträdgården. Bus: 46, 55, 62, or 76.

Mälardrottningen ★ ⛴ INTERNATIONAL   A rare chance to dine aboard the famous motor yacht once owned by Woolworth heiress Barbara Hutton, who entertained her husbands, including Cary Grant, aboard the vessel. Converted into a hotel and restaurant, it is an atmospheric dining choice with an international menu that changes seasonally but always uses very fresh produce. Service is formal, and you can feast upon an array of top-notch dishes. Choose the less expensive option of breakfast to get a cheaper look at the boat.

Riddarholmen. © **08/545-187-80.** www.malardrottningen.se. Reservations recommended. Main courses 145SEK-325SEK. AE, DC, MC, V. Mon-Sat 6-11pm. T-bana: Gamla Stan.

Prinsens ★ SWEDISH   This enduring (it opened in 1897) and atmospheric restaurant has long been popular with artists and what used to be called "the bohemian fringe," and forcefully emphasizes good Swedish home cooking. Delights such as homemade lingonberry preserves go brilliantly with the game dishes of autumn. Seating is on two levels but spills out onto the sidewalk when the summer sun shines.

Mäster Samuelsgatan 4. © **08/611-13-31.** www.restaurangprinsen.com. Reservations recommended. Main courses 189SEK-379SEK. AE, DC, MC, V. Mon-Fri 11:30am-11:30pm; Sat 1-11:30pm; Sun 5-10pm. T-bana: Östermalmstorg.

Roxy ★ INTERNATIONAL   A restaurant-bar that's as cool as the surrounding Nytoget neighborhood and a hotspot on the gay scene (though it attracts a mixed and harmonious crowd). The menu is an interesting mix of Mediterranean and Scandinavian influences. Weekends at Roxy are lively, so call ahead to make reservations for the dining room. If you can't get a table, the food in the bar is excellent, and you'll get great music and a friendly staff thrown in for free.

Nytorget. ✆ **08/640-96-55.** www.roxysofo.se. Reservations recommended. Main courses 190SEK–240SEK. AE, MC, V. Sun–Thurs 1pm–midnight; Fri–Sat 1pm–1am. T-bana: Medborharplatsen.

Shopping

The quality of Swedish glass is known around the world, and functional Swedish design in furniture, often made of blond pine or birch, enjoys equal renown. Many visitors shop for handicrafts, especially woolen items. The favorite place for shopping is the network of cobblestone streets in **Gamla Stan,** near the Royal Palace, especially along **Västerlånggatan.** In central Stockholm, one of the main shopping drags is **Hamngatan.**

For pottery, try **Blås & Knåda,** Hornsgatan 26 (✆ **08/642-77-67;** www. blasknada.com), a cooperative of more than 40 Swedish ceramic artists and glassmakers selling high-quality products.

For one-stop shopping, visit one of Stockholm's major department stores, including its largest, **Åhléns City,** Klarabergsgatan 50 (✆ **08/402-80-00;** www.ahlens.com), which has a celebrated food department and first-class gift shop, along with a department selling Orrefors and Kosta Boda crystal. Its major competitor, in business since 1902, is **Nordiska Kompaniet (NK),** Hamngatan 18–20 (✆ **08/762-80-00;** www. nk.se), which also has a major department devoted to the sale of high-quality Swedish glass. In the basement you'll find thousands of various handicrafts. A final shopping stop that might interest you is **PUB Shopping Arcade,** Hötorget 13 (✆ **08/789-19-30;** www.pub.se), filled with boutiques and specialty departments selling a lot of middle-priced clothing and high-quality housewares. Greta Garbo worked here before she became a famous actress.

One of the great showcases of Swedish handcrafts is **DesignTorget,** in the Kulturhuset, Sergelgången 29 (✆ **08/219-150;** www.designtorget.se), which retails the work of nearly 200 Swedish craftspeople. This center is especially rich in pottery, furniture, textiles, clothing, pewter, and crystal.

Yet another artisan outlet is **Svensk Hemslojd,** Sveavägen 44 (✆ **08/23-21-15**), headquarters for the Society for Swedish Handcrafts, with a wide selection of elegant glassware, pottery, gifts, and wooden or metal handcrafts by some of Sweden's best-known artisans.

For home furnishings Swedish style, the best outlet is **Nordiska Galleriet,** Nybrogatan 11 (✆ **08/442-83-60;** www.nordiskagalleriet.se), with two floors of beautifully styled yet functional furniture. One of Sweden's most prominent stores for home furnishings, **Svenskt Tenn,** Strandvägen 5 (✆ **08/670-16-00;** www.svenskt tenn.se), has been a tradition since 1924. Look for one of Stockholm's best selections of furniture, printed textiles, lamps, glassware, china, and gifts.

Finally, and just for fun, head for **Östermalms Saluhall,** Östermalmstorg (**www. ostermalmshallen.se**). Sweden's most colorful indoor market is filled with vendors hawking cheese, meat, fresh vegetables, just-caught fish, and more. Plan to have lunch at one of the food stalls.

Nightlife

The greatest after-dark event is a performance at **Drottningholm Court Theater,** Drottningholms (✆ **08/759-0406;** www.dtm.se), founded by Gustavus III in 1766 (p. 730). On Lake Mälaren, outside Stockholm, but easily reached by public transportation, it stages operas and ballets with performances in regalia, wigs, and period costumes from the 1700s. The theater's original stage, machinery, and nearly three dozen sets are still in use. Seating 450 patrons, the theater charges 275SEK to 895SEK for its hard-to-get tickets. The season runs from May to September, with performances beginning at 4 and 7:30pm.

Another major cultural venue, **Kungliga Operan (Royal Opera House),** Gustav Adolfs Torg (© **08/791-44-00;** www.operan.se), was also founded by Gustavus III, who was later assassinated here at a masked ball. This is the home of the Royal Swedish Opera and Royal Swedish Ballet. Tickets cost 80SEK to 550SEK for most performances.

In summer, head for **Skansen,** Djurgården 49–51 (© **08/442-80-00;** www. skansen.se), which often stages folk dancing performances from June to August at 7pm. During the same period, outdoor dancing—everything from tango to ballroom—with live music takes place from Monday to Saturday, from 8pm to around midnight. In summer there are also concerts, singalongs, and guest performances by leading artists. See Skansen under "Top Attractions & Special Moments" (p. 733) for information on getting there and entrance fees (although evening events often attract higher prices).

MUSIC CLUBS One of the most frequented nightclubs in Stockholm is **Café Opéra,** Operahuset, Karl XII's torg (© **08/676-58-07;** www.cafeopera.se), which has an elegant dance floor open nightly from 10pm to 3am, charging a cover of 200SEK.

The leading jazz club in town is **Stampen,** Stora Nygatan 5 (© **08/20-57-93;** www.stampen.se), attracting lovers of Dixieland played by the hottest jazz bands around. There's a dance floor downstairs. It's open Monday to Saturday 5pm to 1am (weekends until 2am), with a cover of 140SEK on weekends. **Engelen,** Kornamnstorg 59 (© **08/20-10-92;** www.wallmans.com), is a combination pub and nightclub charging a cover of 70SEK to 100SEK after 8pm. Live performances—soul, funk, rock, whatever—fill the night. The pub is open Tuesday to Thursday 4pm to midnight, Friday and Saturday 4pm to 3am, Sunday 5pm to 3am; the nightclub's open daily from 10pm to 3am.

BARS Stockholm's most unusual bar is **Icebar,** Nordic Sea Hotel Vasaplan 4–7 (© **08/5056-3000;** www.nordichotels.se), the world's first permanent ice bar, with temperatures kept at 27°F (–5°C) year-round. Even the cocktail glasses here are made of pure, clear ice shipped down from the Torne River in Sweden's Arctic north. Admission is 140SEK to 200SEK, which includes warm clothes and a welcome drink. Guests enter in 45-minute shifts. Booking is recommended, although between 9:45pm and 1am on a Friday or Saturday night, you can simply stop by without calling ahead.

Perhaps Stockholm's favorite bar—certainly the most central—is **Sturehof,** Stureplan 2 (© **08/440-57-30;** www.sturehof.com), a tradition since 1897. Housed in a covered arcade, with a live music and performance venue upstairs in the Obar, it is open Monday to Friday 11am to 2am, Saturday noon to 2am, and Sunday 1pm to 2am. Supermodels and a bevy of TV actors flock to **Blue Moon Bar,** Kungsgatan 18 (© **08/20-14-11;** www.bluemoonbar.se), with its black leather upholstery and chic atmosphere. You get recorded dance music for the cover of 130SEK. It's open Monday to Saturday 7pm to 3am.

An Excursion to Uppsala

On the Fyrisån River, the ancient university city of Uppsala—easily reached by train—is 42 miles (68km) north of Stockholm and is the most popular day trip outside the capital. An important Viking settlement, Uppsala is also visited for its celebrated 15th-century cathedral and its 16th-century castle.

With its 40,000-plus students, Uppsala still reigns as one of the greatest centers of learning in Europe, as well as the ecclesiastical capital of Sweden. It enjoys a lovely setting in an urban environment of grand old churches and footbridges. One of its attractions is the former home of Swedish botanist Carl von Linné, with a predictably amazing garden. Film buffs already know Uppsala as the birthplace of Ingmar Bergman and the setting for his film classic *Fanny and Alexander*.

GETTING THERE During the day, trains leave approximately every 45 minutes from Stockholm's Central Station to Uppsala, making the trip in 40 minutes. It's possible to go to Uppsala early in the morning, see the major attractions, and be back in Stockholm for dinner. Those with a valid railpass ride for free; otherwise, a second-class one-way ticket costs about 70SEK.

Trains arrive in the heart of the city at the Uppsala Central Station, which is within easy walking distance of all the city's major attractions except for Gamla Uppsala (see below). The latter can be reached by bus no. 2 departing from the train terminal. The bus costs 30SEK per ride on the bus or 20SEK in the station.

VISITOR INFORMATION The **Uppsala Tourist Information Office** is at Fyris torg 8 (© **018/727-48-00;** www.uppland.nu), a 5-minute walk from the train station. It's open Monday to Friday 10am to 6pm, Saturday 10am to 3pm, and from July to mid-August Sunday noon to 4pm as well.

TOP ATTRACTIONS & SPECIAL MOMENTS

The crowning glory of Uppsala is **Domkyrkan ★★**, Domkyrkoplan 5(© **018/18-71-53;** www.uppsaladomkyrka.se), a Gothic cathedral—the largest in Scandinavia— whose twin spires dominate the skyline at 400 feet (120m). Once severely damaged in a fire in 1702, it has been restored in the old style. Finished in 1270, for 3 centuries the cathedral was the coronation church for Sweden's monarchy; a dozen Swedish royals were crowned under the Coronation Vault between 1441 and 1719. Much of the original Gothic work can still be seen in the doorways.

The cathedral's greatest treasure is the 1710 **Baroque pulpit ★★★**, which was carved by Burchardt Precht based on designs of Nicodemus Tessin the Younger. King Gustav Vasa is buried in the medieval Lady Chapel, and the Finsta Chapel is the setting for the display of the gilt and silver **Reliquary of St. Erik ★★★**, made in 1579 and dedicated to the patron saint of Sweden. A **museum ★★** in the north tower shelters a splendid collection of rare textiles, which date from the 12th century, as well as royal burial regalia from the Vasa tombs. Rare artifacts include a gold embroidered brocaded robe from the early 15th century that once belonged to Queen Margrethe.

Admission to the cathedral is free; admission to the museum costs 30SEK adults. Children up to 16 enter free. The cathedral is open daily 8am to 6pm. The museum is open May to September Monday to Saturday 10am to 5pm, Sunday 12:30 to 5pm. From October to April, hours are Tuesday to Saturday 10am to 4pm, Sunday 12:30 to 4pm.

The Swedish botanist Carl von Linné (1707–78)—also known as Carolus Linnaeus—lived and worked at the **Linnaeus Garden & Museum,** Svartbäcksgatan 27 (© **018/471-25-76;** www.linnaeus.uu.se), where he developed a classification system for the world's plants and flowers still used today. His house is now a museum adjacent to a botanical garden with some 1,600 different plants. When von Linné died, curators found detailed sketches and descriptions of his garden, which has been authentically restored. Entrance to the museum and gardens costs 60SEK, free for children 15 and under. The museum and shop are open daily 11am to 5pm. The gardens are open May to September daily 11am to 8pm.

At the end of Drottinggatan is the **Carolina Rediviva (University Library),** Drottninggatan (© **018/471-39-00;** www.ub.uu.se), which houses over 2 million volumes and more than 40,000 manuscripts, many from the medieval era and among the rarest in Europe. This is the largest library in Sweden, and the home of the celebrated **Silver Bible Codex Argenteus ★★**, written in silver and gold letters on 187 leaves of purple parchment sometime around A.D. 520. It is the only extant book in the old Gothic script in the world. Among other rare treasures is the **Carta Marina,** a fairly accurate map of Scandinavia from 1539. Another rare treasure is **Codex Uppsaliensis,** the oldest manuscript (around 1300) of Snorre Sturtasson's *Edda.* Admission is 20SEK adults, free for children under 12 from May 11 to September 13. It's open mid-June to mid-August Monday to Friday 9am to 6:30pm, Saturday 10am to 5pm, and Sunday 11am to 4pm.

If you have time, make your way to **Gamla Uppsala ★**, 3 miles (4.8km) north of the center of Uppsala, which was the capital of the Svea kingdom some 15 centuries ago. An archaeological site includes a trio of **Royal Mounts ★★★** dating from the 6th century and believed to contain the pyres of three Swedish kings. On the site of an early pagan temple stands a badly damaged 12th-century parish church that was never properly restored. Swedish kings were crowned here before that role fell to Uppsala Cathedral. **Gamla Uppsala Museum,** Disavägen (© **018/23-93-00;** www.raa.se), opened in 2000, helps to put the burial mounds and ancient stones in context, offering historical insights into this once-powerful pagan kingdom. Admission is 60SEK for adults, 50SEK seniors, 40SEK for children 7 to 18 and students, and free for kids aged 6 and under.

WHERE TO DINE

If you're in Uppsala for lunch, head for the **Domtrappkällaren ★★**, Sankt Eriksgränd 15 (© **018/13-09-55;** www.domtrappkallaren.se), in the center city, an atmospheric choice constructed on the remains of an ecclesiastical compound from the 12th century. The dining room is made up of a series of rooms, some with vaulted ceilings, as well as one narrow room where unruly students were imprisoned in medieval times. The chefs don't depend on the mellow old atmosphere alone, but turn out finely tuned Swedish cuisine made with fresh ingredients, including freshly caught salmon or else reindeer from the north, with game as an autumn specialty. Main courses cost 165SEK to 310SEK, and hours are Monday to Friday 11am to 11pm and Saturday 5 to 11pm.

An alternative choice is **Restaurant Odinsborg ★**, near the burial grounds in Gamla Uppsala (© **018/323-525;** www.odinsborg.com), housed in a farmhouse built in the late 1890s. As befits its setting near a Viking royal graveyard, the restaurant uses an early medieval theme in its decor. Order traditional preparations of Swedish favorites, including smoked eel, fried herring, or marinated salmon. Main courses cost 159SEK to 199SEK, with the summer smorgasbord (served May–Aug) going for 165SEK. It's open daily from 6pm until late, with a cafe providing sustenance during the day.

GOTHENBURG

Göteborg (in Swedish) is Sweden's major port and largest city, as well as the gateway to Northern Europe. Located at the mouth of the Göta River, it's especially convenient for the rail traveler, as it lies equidistant from three Scandinavian capitals. Stockholm can be reached in 3 hours, Oslo in 4 hours (these trains are not frequent), and Copenhagen in 3 to 4 hours.

Although filled with heavy industry, there is much in Gothenburg of interest to the visitor, including numerous museums and a huge summer amusement park. Gothenburg is also the best center for excursions to the fishing villages and holiday resorts strung along the western coast of Sweden.

Station Information

GETTING FROM THE AIRPORT TO THE TRAIN STATION

Many residents of Sweden's west coast consider Copenhagen's airport more convenient than Stockholm's for getting to Gothenburg. For information on getting to Copenhagen, see "Getting There" in chapter 6.

Planes arrive from other areas of Europe at **Landvetter Airport** (© 031/94-10-00; www.lfv.se), 16 miles (26km) east of Gothenburg. An airport bus *(Flygbuss)* departs every 20 minutes (during peak times) for the half-hour ride to the city's central bus terminal, just behind Gothenburg's main railway station. Buses run daily between 5am and 12:30am. A one-way trip costs 80SEK. For more information, see **www.flygbussarna.se**.

INSIDE THE STATION

Trains arrive from all over Scandinavia at **Central Station** (© 0771/75-75-75), on one side of Drottningtorget. The station has an office of the national railroad company, SJ, selling rail and bus tickets for connections to nearby areas. Office hours are 7am to 10pm daily. You will also find all the usual conveniences of a major rail hub station, including currency exchange, luggage storage, and newsstands.

Information Elsewhere in the City

The **Gothenburg Tourist Office** is at Kungsportsplatsen 2 (© 031/61-25-00; www.goteborg.com). Open June and mid-August to late August daily 9:30am to 6pm; July to mid-August daily 9:30am to 8pm; September to April Monday to Friday 9:30am to 5pm, Saturday 10am to 2pm. The staff here can make reservations in a hotel for a fee of 60SEK per person, or you can book the Gothenburg Package without a charge. The package includes a stay in a hotel, breakfast, and a Gothenburg Pass (see below). Booking hotels through the tourist office online is also free.

Warning: The area around the station attracts a lot of unsavory characters at night, many intent on baiting visitors into hookups with prostitutes or else mugging them. Take precautions or a cab if you need to get to the station at night.

Getting Around

Visitors usually find that the cheapest way to explore Gothenburg (besides on foot) is to buy a **Göteborgskortet (Gothenburg Pass).** Available at hotels, newspaper kiosks, and the city's tourist office (see above), it entitles you to unlimited travel on

ACCOMMODATIONS ■

Best Western Hotel Eggers **4**
Best Western Tidbloms Hotel **1**
Hotel Onyxen **17**
Hotel Opera **3**
Hotel Örgryte **5**
Hotel Royal **7**
Novotel Göteborg **10**
Quality Panorama Hotel **17**
Radisson SAS Scandinavia
  Hotel **6**

DINING ◆

A Hereford
  Beefstouw **12**
Brasserie Lipp **16**
Café Husaren **14**
Fiskekrogen **9**
Froken Olssons Café **8**
La Gondola **15**
Restaurang Räkan **19**
Restaurant 28+ **21**
Solrosen (Sunflower) **13**

ATTRACTIONS ●

Feskekörka (Fish Church) **11**
Guldhedens Vattentorn
  (Water Tower) **22**
Göteborgs Konstmuseum **23**
Göteborgs Maritima Centrum **2**
Liseberg Park **18**
Röhsska Konstslöjdmuseet **20**

local trams, buses, and ferries. The card also covers many sightseeing attractions (including Liseberg Amusement Park), discounts at some shops and restaurants, and other extras (such as two-for-one airport bus travel), which makes the card worthwhile. A ticket valid for 24 hours costs 245SEK for adults, 170SEK for children; a 48-hour ticket is 390SEK for adults and 270SEK for children.

A single tram ticket costs 25SEK; a 24-hour travel pass (the "red day card") is 65SEK, 3 days is 130SEK, and a single adult ticket can cover an additional three children under the age of 20. If you don't have an advance ticket (recommended, as it makes tram travel much cheaper; simply buy them from a Pressbyrån shop or kiosk near the tram stops), you can buy a ticket on board the tram. Make sure you have some change ready.

Taxis are not as plentiful as you might like. However, you can always find one by going to the Central Station. To call a **taxi,** dial Taxi **Göteborg** at ⓒ **031/65-00-00.** A taxi ride within the city limits costs 155SEK to 275SEK.

Bus and tram numbers and routes are currently in flux in Gothenburg. The bus and tram route numbers below were correct at the time of going to press but may have changed by the time you are reading this. Consequently, we recommend checking transport options with the tourist information office or staff at your chosen destination before you set off.

Where to Stay

Best Western Hotel Eggers ★ 📇   Built in 1859, this is the second-oldest hotel in Gothenburg, and it's still a favorite and going strong. Even better for rail travelers, it's right near Central Station. The hotel retains some of its old architectural allure—wood paneling, elaborate staircases, and stained-glass windows—though everything has been modernized. The individually decorated bedrooms vary in size but are attractive and comfortable, with large bathrooms.

Drottningtorget, S-401 25 Göteborg. ⓒ **800/528-1234** in the U.S. and Canada, or 031/333-44-40. www.hoteleggers.se. Fax 031/333-44-49. 67 units. Mid-June to mid-Aug and Fri-Sat year-round 995SEK-1,530SEK double; rest of year 1,780SEK-2,305SEK double. Rates include breakfast. AE, DC, MC, V. Tram: 1, 3, 4, 5, 6, 7, 8, or 9. Bus: 40. **Amenities:** Restaurant; bar; smoke-free rooms. *In room:* No A/C.

Best Western Tidbloms Hotel ★ 📇   There aren't enough affordable hotels in the city center, so if you're here in summer, you may want to take a tram to this hotel, located in a residential neighborhood 2 miles (3.2km) east of the rail station. The hotel dates from 1897 but has been completely modernized and enjoys the benefits of a tranquil and safe neighborhood. A conical tower, elaborate brickwork, and other 19th-century adornments are still in place. The midsize bedrooms with wooden floors are comfortably furnished, each equipped with a good-size bathroom. Guests like to meet each other in the little British-style library. The on-site **restaurant,** inspired by Scottish design and set in a cozy and inviting vault, is a local favorite.

Olskrosgatan 23, S-416 66 Göteborg. ⓒ **031/707-50-00.** Fax 031/707-50-99. www.tidbloms.com. 42 units. Sun-Thurs 1,450SEK double; Fri-Sat 1,100SEK double. Rates include breakfast. AE, DC, MC, V. Tram: 1, 3, or 6. **Amenities:** Restaurant; bar; rooms for those w/limited mobility; smoke-free rooms.

Hotel Onyxen ⬧   This family-owned and -run hotel is set inside a late-19th-century building that has been reconfigured into a more modern format. It's a good-value choice that's only a short tram ride from Central Station. The decor is more efficient than stylish. The midsize bedrooms rest under white, high ceilings and have shower-only bathrooms that are small but clean.

Sten Sturegatan 23, S-412 52 Göteborg. ✆ **031/81-08-45.** Fax 031/16-56-72. www.hotelonyxen.com. 34 units. Weekday double from 1,490SEK, weekend double from 1,090SEK. Extra bed 200SEK. Rates include breakfast. AE, DC, MC, V. Tram: 4, 5, 6, or 8. **Amenities:** Bar; smoke-free rooms. *In room:* No A/C.

Hotel Opera Created from two 19th-century buildings that were joined together, renovated, and modernized, this well-run hotel appeals equally to business and leisure travelers. It's ideal for rail travelers, as it's only a couple of minutes' walk from Central Station. The midsize bedrooms are individually decorated and comfortably furnished; each has a small bathroom.

Nils Ericsonsgatan 23, S-411 06 Göteborg. ✆ **031/80-50-80.** Fax 031/80-58-17. www.hotelopera.se. 75 units. 1,200SEK–1,900SEK double. Rates include breakfast. AE, DC, MC, V. Tram: 1, 4, 5, 6, 7, 8, or 9. **Amenities:** Restaurant, bar; smoke-free rooms. *In room:* No A/C.

Hotel Örgryte This family-owned and -run hotel is a local favorite dating from the 1960s but massively upgraded in the 1990s. It's in the residential district of Örgryte, 1 mile (1.6km) east of the historic district, but is easily reached by a short bus ride. The hotel has streamlined, rather functional midsize bedrooms, although some are large enough to have sitting areas. The bathrooms are a bit small. The place is decent, well maintained, and affordable.

Danska Vägen 68–70, S-416 59 Göteborg. ✆ **031/707-89-00.** www.hotelorgryte.se. Fax 031/707-89-99. www.hotelorgryte.se. 70 units. Sun–Thurs 1,560SEK double, mid-June to mid-Aug and Fri–Sat 990SEK double. Rates include breakfast. AE, DC, MC, V. Bus: 60 or 62. **Amenities:** Restaurant; bar, sauna; smoke-free rooms. *In room:* No A/C.

Hotel Royal Just ¼ mile (.4km) from the train station, this is the oldest hotel in Gothenburg, dating back to 1852. The owners, the Oddestad family, have completely renovated it and added all the modern comforts, though the entrance hall is still imbued with a rich aura of the 1800s, with a painted glass ceiling and a staircase with wrought-iron banisters. The guest rooms come in various shapes and sizes, each with a good-size shower-only bathroom.

Drottninggatan 67, S-411 07 Göteborg. ✆ **031/700-11-70.** Fax 031/700-11-79. www.hotel-royal.com. 82 units. 1,595SEK–1,795SEK double. Discounts may apply for weekends and summer. Rates include buffet breakfast. AE, DC, MC, V. Tram: 1, 3, 4, 5, or 6. Bus: 60. **Amenities:** Smoke-free rooms. *In room:* No A/C.

Novotel Göteborg ★ This stylish, converted brewery is now one of the best hotels in Gothenburg, run by the French outfit Accor. Even though it lies 2½ miles (4km) from the center, it is easily reached by a series of trams and buses. Its style and comfort make it worth the trek outside the suggested inner core of the city. The 148 bedrooms contain many built-in pieces, all tasteful and inviting, and each room has a small bathroom with tub and shower. The sauna is a popular facility here.

Klippan 1, S-414 51 Göteborg. ✆ **031/720-22-00.** Fax 031/720-22-90. www.novotel.se. 149 units. Mon–Thurs 1,660SEK–1,790SEK double; Fri–Sat 1,090SEK–1,190SEK double. Limited number of discounted rooms in summer. Rates include breakfast. AE, DC, MC, V. Tram: 3 or 9. Bus: 91 or 92. **Amenities:** Restaurant; bar; rooms for those w/limited mobility; smoke-free rooms. *In room:* No A/C.

Quality Panorama Hotel ★ 📠 Only a 10-minute walk from the city center, this 13-story hotel is one of the tallest buildings in Gothenburg. The best and most accessorized rooms are on floors 7 to 13. The larger ones were refurbished in 2005. The plant-filled lobby, lit by a skylight, is home to a mezzanine restaurant and a piano bar. Bedrooms are well furnished and bright, each featuring wooden floors and double-glazed windows. Bathrooms, though small, are neatly kept, with adequate shelf space.

Eklandagatan 51–53, S-400 22 Göteborg. ☎ **031/767-70-00.** Fax 031/767-70-70. www.panorama.se. 338 units (some with shower only). 1,200SEK–1,800SEK double. Rates include breakfast. AE, DC, MC, V. Closed Dec 21–Jan 7. Tram: 4 or 5. Bus: 40 or 51. **Amenities:** Restaurant; bar; smoke-free rooms. *In room:* No A/C.

Radisson SAS Scandinavia Hotel ★★★ If you can afford it, this hotel offers some of the best living in Gothenburg and is ideally located opposite the rail station. Surrounding a large atrium, it opened in 1986 but has kept abreast of the times ever since; many of the rooms received a touch-up in 2006–07. The bedrooms are spacious and luxuriously appointed, with well-maintained bathrooms. The hotel's health club has an indoor pool, and the whole building has free Wi-Fi.

Södra Hamngatan 59–65, S-401 24 Göteborg. ☎ **800/333-3333** in the U.S., or 031/758-50-00. Fax 031/758-50-01. www.gothenburg.radissonsas.com. 349 units. 1,390SEK–2,150SEK double; from 2,500SEK suite. Rates include breakfast. AE, DC, MC, V. Tram: 1, 3, 4, 5, or 7. Bus: 40. **Amenities:** Restaurant; bar; pool; rooms for those w/limited mobility; smoke-free rooms. *In room:* No A/C.

Top Attractions & Special Moments

If you're here in summer, be sure to enjoy a cup of coffee at one of the cafes along **Kungsportsavenyn ★**, the pulsating artery of Gothenburg, which stretches from Götaplatsen north for ½ mile (1km) to the canal and Kungsportsplatsen. To walk this tree-lined boulevard (known locally as "The Avenyn") is to experience the "living room" of Gothenburg. Winter visitors can explore some of Gothenburg's numerous museums, including **Göteborgs Konstmuseum,** the **Göteborg Maritime Center,** and the **East India House.**

Göteborgs Konstmuseum ★★★ This is the leading art museum of western Sweden. If your time is limited, take the elevator to the **Fürstenberg Gallery ★★★,** established by arts patron Pontus Fürstenberg (1827–1902) to display works by Scandinavian artists living as expats in Paris in the 1880s. All the big names in Swedish art, including Prince Eugen and Carl Larsson, are on parade here, and the collection is also rich in the National Romantic movement of the 1890s. The other highlight of the museum is the octagonal **Arosenium Room ★★★,** which is a delightful romp showcasing the whimsical paintings of artist Ivar Arosenius (1878–1909).

Colorful lyricism explodes in the rooms beyond, as they are devoted to the "Göteborg Colorists," including Karl Isakson (1878–1922) and Carl Kylberg (1878–1952). Old masters, including Rembrandt and Rubens, are also on exhibit, as are such contemporary achievers as Henry Moore and Francis Bacon. The gallery has an impressive collection of international art, notably French Impressionists, along with Bonnard, Cézanne, van Gogh, and Picasso, as well as sculpture by Carl Milles and Auguste Rodin.

Götaplatsen. ☎ **031/368-35-00.** www.konstmuseum.goteborg.se. Admission 40SEK adults, free for people 24 and under. Tues and Thurs 11am–6pm; Wed 11am–9pm; Fri–Sun 11am–5pm. Tram: 4 or 5. Bus: 40.

Göteborgs Maritima Centrum This maritime museum is appropriately located on the harbor. This is a true floating museum of nearly a dozen ships, of which the destroyer, *Småland,* is the most formidable. Other highlights of the fleet include the submarine *Nordkaparen,* along with tugboats, a lightship, steamships, and other watercraft. When not sailing to Stockholm, the famous Göta Canal boats are berthed here, including the 1874 *Juno,* the 1912 *Wilhelm Tell,* and the 1931 *Diana.*

SCENES FROM Gothenburg life

Early risers can visit the daily **Fish Auc-tion ★** at the harbor, the largest fishing port in Scandinavia. The entertaining sale begins at 7am sharp. You can also visit the **Feskekörka (Fish Church),** on Rosenlundsgatan, which is in the fish market. It's open Tuesday through Thursday from 9am to 5pm, Friday from 9am to 6pm, and Saturday from 10am to 2pm.

The traditional starting point for seeing Gothenburg is the cultural center, **Götaplatsen.** Its *Poseidon Fountain* is the work of Carl Milles, one of Sweden's most important sculptors. The big trio of buildings here is the Concert Hall, the municipally owned theater, and the Göteborgs Konstmuseum.

For a quick orientation to Gothenburg, visit the 400-foot-tall (120m) **Guldhedens Vattentorn (water tower),** Syster Estrids Gata (*(* **031/82-00-09**); take tram 13 or bus 60 from the center of the city, about a 10-minute ride. The elevator ride up the tower is free, and there's a cafeteria/snack bar at the top. The tower is open May to September daily noon to 10pm.

Packhuskajen 8. *(* **031/10-59-50.** www.goteborgsmaritimacentrum.com. Admission 80SEK adults, 40SEK children 5–15, free for children 4 and under. Family (2 adults, 2 kids) 210SEK. Apr, Sept–Oct Fri–Sun 10am–4pm; May–Aug daily 10am–6pm. Closed Nov–Apr. Tram: 5 to Lilla Bommen.

Liseberg Park ★★   This amusement park is Sweden's number-one tourist attraction, drawing more than three million visitors annually. Launched in 1923, it has been amusing, wining, and dining Gothenburgers ever since, with its "gardens of delight," including splashing fountains, pleasure pavilions, festive lighting, and beds of flowers. Open-air vaudeville shows and musical performances are presented on various stages, and there are dozens of rides, including a brand-new wooden roller coaster—Scandinavia's largest. The park is dominated by the 492-foot-high (148m) **Liseberg Tower ★**; the ride to the top is accompanied by sound and light, and it climaxes with a vast panoramic view of Gothenburg.

Korsvägen. *(* **031/40-01-00.** www.liseberg.se. Admission 70SEK–80SEK, free for children 6 and under. Ask about special passes. Opening hours are roughly June–Aug Mon–Fri 11am–11pm, Sat 11am–midnight, Sun 11am–10pm; Sept and May Thurs–Sun 11am–10pm; early Oct and late Apr Sat–Sun 11am–8pm. See website for more details. Tram: 4 or 5 from the city.

Röhsska Konstslöjdmuseet ★★   Two Gothenburgers, the Röhss brothers, launched this leading arts and crafts museum in 1916 with a bequest to the city. Pass through the entrance to this Romantic–style building—flanked by a pair of marine lions from the Ming dynasty—and you'll find temporary exhibitions of modern arts and crafts on the main floor. The highlights of the permanent collection of contemporary arts and crafts are on the second landing, where the exhibits are particularly rich with treasures of the 17th through the 19th centuries. Upstairs are exhibits devoted to silver, glassware, exquisite porcelain, furnishings, and antique textiles. On the top floor is an array of East Asian art.

Vasagatan 37–39. *(* **031/368-31-50.** www.designmuseum.se. Admission 40SEK adults, free for children 18 and under. Tues noon–8pm; Wed–Fri noon–5pm; Sat–Sun 11am–5pm. Tram: 3, 4, 5, 7, or 10. Bus: 42, 45, or 49.

Where to Dine

A Hereford Beefstouw ★ 🍴 STEAK Gothenburg's best steakhouse is part of a successful chain serving mostly Australian beef and specializing in a 17-ounce T-bone—finish it at your own risk. Backed up by an excellent salad bar, the menu offers a selection of sauces to go with your beef, including the classic Béarnaise, as well as a garlic butter or parsley sauce. A wide array of other cuts, including filet steaks, tenderloins, and veal sirloins, is also featured.

Linnégatan 5. ✆ **031/775-04-41.** www.a-h-b.dk. Reservations recommended. Main courses 225SEK-480SEK; salad bar as a main course 173SEK. AE, DC, MC, V. Mon-Fri 11:30am-2pm and 5-10pm; Sat 4-10pm; Sun 3-9pm. Closed frequently in July and early Aug; call ahead to check. Tram: 1, 3, 4, or 9.

Brasserie Lipp SWEDISH/FRENCH On Gothenburg's main promenade, this bustling eatery, established in 1987, is as close as the city gets to having a bistro evocative of the Left Bank in Paris. Although much of the menu is French inspired, such as the escargots in garlic butter and entrecôte of beef with a Dijon mustard sauce, other dishes are strictly homegrown, including fresh fish caught off the coastal waters of Gothenburg. The best *choucroute garnie* (sauerkraut with sausage and pork) in the city is served here.

Kungsportsavenyn 8. ✆ **031/10-58-30.** www.brasserielipp.com. Reservations required. Main courses 200SEK-300SEK. AE, DC, MC, V. Mon-Wed 11:30am-1am; Thurs-Fri 11:30am-3am; Sat noon-3am; Sun noon-midnight. Tram: 1, 4, 5, or 6. Bus: 40.

Café Husaren INTERNATIONAL This former pharmacy/milliner/bank is the best-known and most animated cafe in the Haga district of Gothenburg. The century-old decor includes a reverse-painted glass created in the mid-1890s. Place your order for well-stuffed sandwiches, freshly made salads, and pastries, which include the biggest and most succulent cinnamon roll in town. You carry your food to one of the indoor or, in summer, outdoor tables. The shrimp salad is very good here.

Haga Nygata 28. ✆ **031/13-63-78.** www.cafehusaren.se. Sandwiches 20SEK-45SEK; pastries 12SEK-32SEK. Mon-Thurs 9am-8pm; Fri 9am-7pm; Sat-Sun 9am-6pm. Tram: 3, 6, 9, or 11.

Fiskekrogen ★★ SEAFOOD Across the canal from the Stadtsmuseum, this restaurant is your best choice for seafood in the central city. Against a nautical backdrop, the restaurant offers a well-stocked fresh seafood bar, with plenty of lobster, clams, crayfish, mussels, and oysters. The chefs take a bold approach to harmonizing flavors and offer fragrant, light sauces as part of their finely tuned repertoire.

Lilla Torget 1. ✆ **031/10-10-05.** www.fiskekrogen.se. Reservations recommended. Main courses 275SEK-355SEK; set menus (ordered per table) 645SEK-845SEK. AE, DC, MC, V. Mon-Fri 11:30am-2pm and 5:30-11pm; Sat 1-11pm. Closed Sun and July 11-Aug 11. Tram: 2 or 5.

Froken Olssons Café SWEDISH This local favorite is conveniently located 2 blocks from Kungsportsavenyn, the major city artery. In summer, tables overflow onto a wide terrace, although there is ample space inside as well. Come here to feast on light cafe cuisine: well-stuffed baguettes and an array of homemade soups and fresh salads, plus desserts such as fruit cheesecakes and meringues. It can get a bit noisy and crowded at lunchtime.

Östra Larmgatan 14. ✆ **031/13-81-93.** www.forkenolsson.se. Coffee 24SEK; *dagens* (daily) menu 50SEK-69SEK; salad buffet 60SEK; sandwiches 30SEK-70SEK. MC, V. Mon-Fri 9am-10pm. Tram: 1, 4, 5, or 6. Bus: 40.

📷 A picnic IN THE PARK

Across the canal from the Central Station is an ideal spot for a picnic: **Trädgårdsföreningen** ★★ (🕿 031/ 365-58-58; www.tradgardsforeningen. se), with entrances on Slussgatan. This park boasts a large *rosarium* with some 10,000 rose bushes of 4,000 different species, the centerpiece being the Palm House, a large greenhouse where subtropical plants grow year-round. There's a Butterfly House where these stunning creatures live in a simulation of a natural habitat. Entrance to the park costs 20SEK, free for children under 17, and free for all mid-September through mid-April. The park is open daily from 7am to 8pm mid-April to mid-September and 7am to 6pm the rest of the year.

For the makings of an elegant picnic, go to **Saluhallen,** Kungstorget, which was built in 1888. This is the city's colorful indoor market. Shops sell meat, fruit, vegetables, and delicatessen products. You can buy all sorts of game, including moose and reindeer, and even lamb from Iceland. The produce (including exotic fruit) comes from all over the world. There are four restaurants and one coffee bar in the building. Much of the food is already cooked and can be packaged for you to take out. The hall is open Monday to Friday 9am to 6pm, Friday 8am to 6pm, and Saturday 9am to 2pm. Take tram 1, 3, 4, 5, 7, or 10 to Kungsportsplatsen.

La Gondola ITALIAN   Some of the best pizzas and classic Italian dishes in Gothenburg are dished up here. It's a little piece of Venice in Scandinavia, with its striped poles, outdoor seating area, and ample menu. All the old favorites turn up, including the house specialty, *saltimbocca* (veal and ham), along with such grilled specialties as tender and juicy steaks. Try the freshly made minestrone and save room for one of the delicious desserts.

Kungsportsavenyn 4. 🕿 **031/711-68-28.** www.lagondola.se. Reservations recommended. Main courses 105SEK–250SEK; *dagens* (daily) lunch 80SEK–170SEK. AE, DC, MC, V. Sun–Tues noon–10pm; Wed–Thurs noon–11pm; Fri–Sat noon–midnight. Tram: 1, 4, 5, or 6. Bus: 38 or 75.

Restaurang Räkan/Yellow Submarine ★ SEAFOOD   This is one of the city's finest seafood joints, as well as a wonderfully goofy treat. Its nautical decor taken to extremes, the restaurant offers not just the usual wooden plank tables and buoy lamps, but also a re-creation of a Swedish "lake." Your seafood platter arrives on a battery-powered boat, with you directing the controls. Kids, naturally, adore the place. If all this sounds too gimmicky, know that the fish is fresh, perfectly cooked, and lightly seasoned, especially the prawns, mussels, and Swedish lobster.

Lorensbergsgatan 16. 🕿 **031/16-98-39.** www.rakan.se. Reservations recommended. Main courses 225SEK–325SEK. AE, DC, MC, V. Mon–Sat 4–11pm; Sun 3–10pm. Tram: 1, 4, 5, or 6. Bus: 40.

Restaurant 28+ ★★★ INTERNATIONAL   Chic and stylish, this restaurant's three dining salons are romantically lit by candles and have soaring ceilings. It's hip, it's fashionable, the service is exceptional, and the food is good, if a little pricey. You're assured some of the most imaginative and fabulously fresh cuisine in town, so if you have a demanding palate that needs satisfying, this restaurant is worth the expense.

Götabergsgatan 28. 🕿 **031/20-21-61.** www.28plus.se. Reservations recommended. Fixed-price menus 795SEK–895SEK; main courses 295SEK–445SEK. AE, DC, MC, V. Mon–Sat 6–11pm. Closed for much of the summer. Bus: 40. Tram: 1, 4, 5, or 6.

Solrosen (Sunflower) 🌻 VEGETARIAN   This is the best vegetarian restaurant in Gothenburg. It's been going for decades, but there's still a good wholesome buzz about the place. Diners take advantage of the all-you-can-eat salad bar and the unlimited coffee. Beer and wine are also available. The Sunflower blooms in the Haga district, a low-rise neighborhood of 18th- and early-19th-century buildings. You serve yourself at the counter.

Kaponjärgatan 4. © **031/711-66-97.** Main courses 50SEK–130SEK. Daily platters 50SEK–75SEK. AE, DC, MC, V. Mon–Thurs 11:30am–10:30pm; Fri 11:30am–11:30pm; Sat 1–11:30pm; Sun 2–7:30pm. Tram: 1, 6, or 9.

Shopping

For one-stop shopping, visit **Nordstan,** one of the largest shopping malls in Scandinavia, with more than 150 shops, stores, restaurants, coffee shops, banks, a post office, and travel agencies. **Kungsgatan** and **Fredsgatan,** a hugely long pedestrian mall in Sweden, stretches for 2 miles (3.2km). Another major shopping artery is **Kungsportsavenyn,** called the "Avenyn" by Gothenburgers. From early spring to autumn, this is the most bustling avenue in Gothenburg, and it's flanked with shops, restaurants, and cafes. Also check out the recently revitalized working district of **Haga Nygatan,** now home to the rich and trendy, who've been followed by a load of funky/chic shops.

The biggest department store is **Bohusslöjd,** Teatergatan 19 (© **031/16-00-72;** www.bohusslojd.se), with one of the city's most carefully chosen selection of Swedish handcrafts, including hand-woven rugs and pine or birch bowls. Since 1866, **C. J. Josephssons Glas & Porslin,** Korsgatan 12 (© **031/17-56-15;** www.josephssons. se), has been a leading name in Swedish glassmaking. Many of its finest pieces are the work of some of the country's best-known designers.

Gothenburg's most popular store is **Nordiska Kompaniet (NK),** Östra Hamngatan 42 (© **031/710-10-00;** www.nk.se), carrying more than 200,000 items for sale. It's especially well stocked in Kosta Boda and Orrefors crystal, along with pewter items and many, many crafts.

A permanent exhibit center for some 30 potters and glassmakers, **Lerverk,** Södra Larmgatan 2 (© **031/13-13-49;** www.lerverk.se), offers beautifully crafted items of the highest quality.

Nightlife

Liseberg Park (see "Top Attractions & Special Moments," above) is the leading nighttime venue in summer, with all sorts of family-style entertainment. The cultural highlight is **Göteborgsoperan** (the Gothenburg Opera House), Packhuskajen (© **031/10-80-00;** www.opera.se), a relatively new opera house opened by the king in 1994 that features opera, operettas, musicals, and ballet. A short walk from Central Station, it opens onto views of the water and has five bars and a cafe on its premises. Prices depend on the event being staged.

The largest and most comprehensive nightclub in Gothenburg is **Trädgår'n,** Nya Allén (© **031/10-20-80;** www.tradgarn.se), where no one under 25 is admitted. Its two-story interior is filled with a dance club, a cabaret, and a restaurant. The cover charge for the dance club is 100SEK to 140SEK, with a dinner and access to the cabaret going for 530SEK. The dance club is open Friday and Saturday 11pm to 4am, the restaurant Monday to Friday 2pm to 10pm, and Saturday 5pm to 10pm, with the cabaret kickoff at 8pm.

In a former fire station, **Oakley's Country Club,** Tredje Långgatan 16 (✆ **031/ 42-60-80;** www.oakleys.nu), is a supper club offering a changing array of dancers and impersonators who work hard to keep the audience amused. Expect a changing array of musical acts, plenty of musical and show-biz razzmatazz, and imitations of Swedish pop stars you've probably not heard of. An automatic cover charge of 120SEK per person is added to the cost of your meal.

For a taste of the local rock scene, head to **Sticky Fingers,** Kaserntorget 7 (✆ **031/701-00-17;** www.stickfingers.nu), where you'll find four floors of music ranging from hip-hop to hard rock, and a band playing live nearly every night. Previous performers have included Motorhead and Queens of the Stone Age. Cover sticks at around 60SEK to 80SEK but is usually free between 9 and 10pm if you want to simply pop in for a look. It's open Wednesday 8pm to 2am (summer only), Thursday 8pm to 2am, and Friday and Saturday 8pm to 4am.

Finally, one of Gothenburg's newer nightspots is **Tranquilo,** Kungstorget 14 (✆ **031/13-45-55;** www.tranquilo.se), a fun, colorful Latino spot attracting a super-attractive crowd usually found nibbling on South American dishes or sipping *caipirinhas,* Brazil's national cocktail. Dining goes on until about 10:30pm, while the bar stays open until between 1 and 3am, depending on business.

SWITZERLAND

18

S witzerland occupies a position on the rooftop of the continent of Europe, with the drainage of its mammoth Alpine glaciers becoming the source of such powerful rivers as the Rhine and the Rhône. The appellation "the crossroads of Europe" is fitting, as all rail lines, road passes, and tunnels through the mountains lead here. From the time the Romans crossed the Alps, going through Helvetia (the old name for today's Switzerland) on their way north, the major route connecting Northern and Southern Europe has been through Switzerland. The old roads and paths have developed into modern highways and railroads.

The tourist industry as we know it started in Switzerland, and the tradition of welcoming visitors is firmly entrenched in Swiss life. The first modern tourists, the British, began to come here "on holiday" in the 19th century, and other Europeans and some North Americans followed suit, so that soon the small federal state became known as "a nation of hotel-keepers." Swiss hospitality, based on years of experience, has gained a worldwide reputation, and the entire country is known for its cleanliness and efficiency.

Switzerland has many great museums and a rich cultural life, but that's not why most people visit. They come mainly for the scenery, which is virtually unrivaled in the world, from Alpine peaks to mountain lakes, from the palm trees of Ticino to the "Ice Palace" of Jungfrau. And, especially important to the rail traveler, Switzerland is renowned for the breadth and number of its scenic train routes (see "Switzerland's Famous Scenic Rail Lines," at the end of this chapter, for the lowdown on eight of our favorites).

Highlights of Switzerland

Most European capitals completely dominate the attractions list of their countries, as in the case of London or Paris. Not so in Switzerland, which has four cities of equal tourist allure—Zurich, Geneva, Bern, and Lausanne—all of which we explore by rail in this section. Each city deserves at least 2 days of your time, and because Switzerland is so small, you can travel quickly by rail from one city to another in just a matter of a few hours.

Most airplanes from North America arrive in **Zurich,** which is the major rail transportation hub of Switzerland and an ideal place to embark upon your train tour of the Alps. At the foot of the large **Lake Zurich,** the city of Zurich is one of the most beautiful in Europe, spreading out along both banks of the Limmat River. Zurich can be visited for its remarkably preserved **Altstadt,** or Old Town, alone. You can spend a morning walking

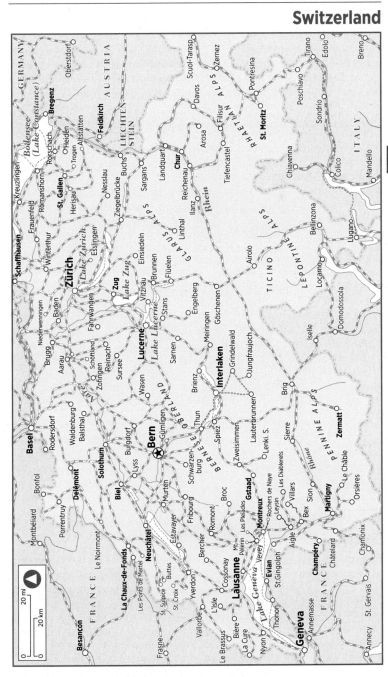

the Limmat's right bank and exploring its guild houses from the 16th and 17th centuries.

Switzerland's largest city, the former home of Thomas Mann, James Joyce, and Lenin, is filled with attractions, none more notable than the quays along the river. Its two chief churches are **Fraumünster** and **Grossmünster,** and its greatest museums are the **Landesmuseum (Swiss National Museum)** and **Kunsthaus Zurich,** a fine-arts museum that is one of the most important in Europe. Even on the shortest of visits, save time to walk the beautiful—and superexpensive—**Bahnhofstrasse,** the world's greatest shopping street, running from the main train station to the lake.

It's an hour's ride from Zurich to the capital city of **Bern,** which is even lovelier than Zurich because it embraces one of the greatest medieval districts in Europe. In Bern you get scenery, culture, and history, and the most idyllic gateway for exploring the **Bernese Oberland,** a summer and winter playground, with its Alpine skiing, clear blue lakes, and **Jungfraujoch,** at 11,333 feet (3,400m), where a train from **Interlaken** will take you to the highest railway station in Europe.

Walking the arcaded streets of the **Altstadt** is Bern's major drawing card. The special places include **Bärengraben (Bear Pits);** the **Cathedral of St. Vincent,** dating from 1421; and the **Kunstmuseum** or Fine Arts Museum, with an impressive collection of both Swiss and international works. For a final goodbye to the city, head for the belvedere atop **Mount Gurten,** at 2,815 feet (845m).

On your fifth day in Switzerland, head by rail to the lakeside town of **Lausanne,** usually a ride of about 1 hour. This is your best center for exploring **Lake Geneva,** one of the world's most beautiful bodies of water. You can spend 1 day discovering Lausanne itself, including Switzerland's most impressive Gothic building (**Lausanne Cathedral**), and the next day touring the lake by boat.

Devote your final 2 days in Switzerland to the serene city of **Geneva,** which is located near the French border and can be reached from Lausanne in about 45 to 50 minutes. Called the most international city in the world, Geneva is the center of the European United Nations, the birthplace of the International Red Cross, and is the capital of French-speaking Switzerland.

Although devoid of world-class attractions, the city and its beautiful lakeside setting is an attraction in and of itself. You come here to buy a watch, walk the lakeside quays, and spend a night in *Vieille Ville* (Old Town) clustered in narrow streets around **Cathédrale St-Pierre.** Geneva is also a good base for exploring the Alps and Lake Geneva.

ESSENTIALS

Getting There

Switzerland is situated at the center of Europe and, thus, is a focal point for international air traffic. The busy intercontinental airports of Zurich and Geneva can be reached in 7 to 8 hours from the East Coast of North America, in less than 3 hours from London, and in less than 2 hours from Paris.

Swiss International Air Lines Ltd. (© **877/359-7947** in the U.S., or 0848/700-700 in Switzerland; www.swiss.com), simply called **Swiss,** is the major carrier for Switzerland. Most flights from North America land in Geneva or Zurich.

Other airlines that offer service to Switzerland out of North America include **American Airlines** (© **800/433-7300;** www.aa.com), **Delta Airlines** (© **800/221-1212;** www.delta.com), and **Air Canada** (© **888/247-2262;** www.aircanada.com).

FESTIVALS & special events

On the third Monday in April, members of all the guilds dress in costumes and celebrate the arrival of spring at **Sechseläuten** ("Six O'Clock Chimes") in Zurich. The festival climaxes with the burning of Böögg, a straw figure symbolizing winter. There are also children's parades. The **Zurich Tourist Office** (✆ **044/215-40-00;** www.zuerich.com) shows the parade route on a map. (Böögg is burned at 6pm on Sechseläutenplatz, near Belevueplatz.)

At the **Fêtes de Genève,** in Geneva, highlights include flower parades, fireworks, and live music all over the city. Call ✆ **022/909-70-00** for more information, or surf the Web to **www.fetes degeneve.ch.** The festival runs from late July through early August.

Last, the famous "onion market" fair, **Zibelemärit,** takes place in Bernon the fourth Monday in November. Call ✆ **031/328-12-12** for more information.

If none of the major carriers above service your airport, you can also fly into London or Manchester, and from there connect to either Zurich or Geneva on **British Airways** (✆ **0844/493-0787** in Britain, or 800/AIRWAYS [247-9297] in the U.S.; www.britishairways.com), **easyJet** (✆ **0871/244-2366** in Britain, or 0870/6-000-000 in the U.S.; www.easyjet.com), or **Aer Lingus** (✆ **800/474-7424;** www.aer lingus.com).

Switzerland by Rail

PASSES

For information on the **Eurail Global Pass, Eurail Global Pass Flexi,** and other multicountry options, see chapter 2.

SWISS PASS/SWISS FLEXIPASS The most practical and convenient ticket for your trip to Switzerland is the **Swiss Pass,** which entitles you to unlimited travel on the entire network of the Swiss Federal Railways, as well as on lake steamers and most postal motor coaches linking Swiss cities and resorts. The pass also provides free entrance to more than 400 museums in Switzerland and provides a 50% discount on most Swiss mountain railways. Note that the **Swiss Flexipass** also offers the 50% mountain railway discount, and you don't have to use a day on your pass to take advantage of this discount. For prices and more information on the Swiss Pass, the Swiss Flexipass, and the free **Swiss Family Card** that allows children under 16 to travel free with a paying parent (and only a parent), see chapter 2. All of these passes should be purchased in North America before you leave on your trip and can be obtained through **Rail Europe** (✆ **888/438-7245** in the United States, ✆ 800/361-7245 in Canada; www.raileurope.com) or your travel agent.

SWISS REGIONAL RAILPASSES One of the country's most unusual transportation bargains is offered in the form of regional passes that divide Switzerland into about half a dozen districts. Passes, most of which are good for 5 days of unrestricted rail travel, are offered for the Lake Geneva region, the Graubunden (Grisons), the Ticino, central Switzerland, and the Bernese Oberland. If you plan to devote a block of days to exploring one of these specific regions, you might find one of these passes a great savings.

One of the most popular of these passes is the **Bernese Oberland Regional Pass** (Regional Pass für das Berner Oberland), which allows for 3 travel days out of 7 days, and 5 travel days out of 15 days. You can buy the pass at any railway station or tourist office in the Bernese Oberland. You can also purchase it by phone from **Reisezentrum BLS, Bern** (✆ 031/327-3271), or on the Web at **www.regiopass-berneroberland.ch**. The 3-day option sells for 230F in second class and 279F in first class. The 5-day option costs 277F in second class and 332F in first class. The pass provides free transport during the appropriate time frames on all but a handful of the cog railways, buses, cable cars, ferryboats, and SBB trains within the region.

SWISS CARD   This pass, valid for 1 month, entitles the holder to a free transfer from any Swiss airport or border point to any destination within Switzerland, and a second free transfer from any destination in Switzerland to any Swiss airport or border point. Each transfer must be completed within 1 day. Additionally, the Swiss Card gives the holder unlimited half-fare trips on the entire Swiss travel system, including trains, postal coaches, lake steamers, and most (but not all) excursions to mountain-tops. The pass costs $236 for first class or $169 for second class and is available from Rail Europe. Children under 16 ride free with a *parent* if you request the free **Swiss Family Card** (see above) when you purchase your Swiss Card.

SWISS TRANSFER TICKET   Like the Swiss Card, this offers one transfer from any Swiss airport or border point to any destination in Switzerland, and a second transfer from any destination in Switzerland to any Swiss airport or border point. The ticket costs $178 per adult in first class, $118 in second class. Children under 16 ride free with a *parent* if you request the free **Swiss Family Card** (see above) when you purchase your ticket.

FOREIGN TRAIN TERMS

The two most popular languages in Switzerland are German and French. English, however, is widely spoken and understood by Swiss nationals, who learn to speak it in grade school, so there's no need to learn any foreign train terms. Most Swiss time-tables in railway stations usually have a section written in English.

PRACTICAL TRAIN INFORMATION

The **Swiss Federal Railway** has one of the most extensive rail systems on the Continent, and its trains are noted for their comfort and cleanliness. Most of the electrically operated trains have first-class and second-class compartments. International trains link Swiss cities with other European centers. InterCityExpress trains arriving from Holland and Germany usually require a change at Basel's station, where a connection is normally available on the same platform. Mostly InterCity trains (also some ICE and TGVs) offer the fastest connections, and because trains leave the Basel station half-hourly on the major routes, there's never too long a wait.

One of the busiest rail links in Europe stretches from Paris to Geneva and Lausanne. Almost as busy are the rail routes between Paris and Zurich. Most of the trains assigned to these routes are part of Europe's network of high-speed trains. (The French refer to them as *trains à grande vitesse*, or TGV.) From Paris's Gare de Lyon, four trains a day depart Lausanne. Travel time for the 9 daily trains to Geneva is about 3 hours; travel time to Lausanne is about 4 hours. Trains from Paris to Zurich depart five times a day from Paris's Gare de l'Est (travel time to Zurich on the TGV is about 4½ hr.).

Ironically, miles traveled by train within Switzerland are proportionately more expensive than equivalent distances within France, so ongoing fares from Zurich or

Trains & Travel Times in Switzerland

From	To	Type of Train	# of Trains	Frequency	Travel Time
Zurich	Bern	InterCity, InterRegio	55	Daily	1 hr.
Zurich	Geneva	InterCity	23	Daily	2 hr., 45 min.
Zurich	Lausanne	InterCity	25	Daily	2 hr., 10 min.
Geneva	Lausanne	EuroCity, InterCity, InterRegio, RegioExpress	96	Daily	40 min.

Geneva to other points within Switzerland might come as an unpleasant surprise. Consequently, many travelers who anticipate lots of rail travel are well advised to consider the purchase of any of Rail Europe's passes. Note, however, that a number of Switzerland's best-known trains are privately owned and do not accept Eurail passes, though passholders will get a discount on fares. Swiss railpasses cover all scenic trains.

RESERVATIONS These are absolutely necessary on Switzerland's special scenic trains (see the last section in this chapter for details). On most Swiss trains, however, reservations aren't usually necessary, although you can make one for about $11 through Rail Europe if you want to ensure yourself a seat, especially during the busy holiday season. Having a railpass doesn't guarantee you a seat. Fares for EuroCity and InterCity trains within Switzerland are included in a railpass, but on EC trains into Italy, you'll be assessed a supplement (which depends on the train you take and your ultimate destination), which is included in the mandatory reservation.

Sleepers and couchettes are available on most international routes running through Switzerland, and accommodations on these trains can be reserved at least 90 days to 6 months in advance through Rail Europe. These sleeper services aren't available on domestic routes within Switzerland itself.

SERVICES & AMENITIES All major train stations in Switzerland have food and drink for sale. We recommend that you avail yourself of their offerings, taking along bottled water or a picnic lunch to enjoy as you watch Alpine scenery. Most trains have minibars, but they are expensive and not for the frugal rail traveler.

Many trains making longer runs also have self-service buffets, which are far more affordable than eating in one of the dining cars, where prices are lethal. If your train has one, a self-service buffet is the way to go if you didn't bring a picnic lunch.

[FastFACTS] SWITZERLAND

Area Code The country code for Switzerland is **41.** City area codes are as follows: **01 and 044** for Zurich, **031** for Bern, **021** for Lausanne, and **022** for Geneva.

Business Hours **Banks** are usually open Monday to Friday 8:30am to 4:30pm (closed on legal holidays). Foreign currency may be exchanged at major railroad stations and airports daily from 8am to 10pm. Most **business offices** are open Monday to Friday 8am to noon and 2 to 6pm. **Shops** are usually open Monday to Friday 8am to 12:15pm and

1:30 to 6:30pm, and on Saturday 1:30 to 4pm. In large cities, most shops don't close during the lunch hour, although many do so on Monday morning.

Climate The temperature range is about the same as in the northern United States, but without the extremes of hot and cold. Summer temperatures seldom rise above 80°F (27°C) in the cities, and humidity is low. Because of clear air and the lack of wind in the high Alpine regions, sunbathing is sometimes possible even in winter. In southern Switzerland, the temperature remains mild year-round, allowing subtropical vegetation to grow. June is the ideal month for a tour of Switzerland, followed by either September or October, when the mountain passes are still open. In summer, the country is usually overrun with tourist traffic.

Documents Required

Every traveler entering Switzerland must have a valid passport, although it's not necessary for North Americans to have a visa if they don't stay longer than 3 continuous months. For information on permanent residence in Switzerland and work permits, contact the nearest Swiss consulate.

Electricity
Switzerland's electricity is 220 volts, 50 cycles, AC. Some international hotels are specially wired to allow North Americans to plug in their appliances, but you'll usually need a transformer for your electric razor or hair dryer. You'll also need an adapter plug to channel the electricity from the Swiss system to the flat-pronged American system. Don't plug anything in without being certain your appliances and the electrical outlets are compatible.

Embassies & Consulates
Most embassies are located in the national capital, Bern; some nations maintain consulates in other cities, such as Geneva. The embassy of the **United States** is located at Sulgeneckstrasse 19, Bern (✆ **031/357-70-11;** http://bern.usembassy.gov), with consulates in Zurich at Dufourstrasse 101 (✆ **043/499-29-60**), and in Geneva at rue Versonnex 7 (✆ **022/840-51-60**). The **Canadian embassy** is at Kirchenfeldstrasse 88, Bern (✆ **031/357-32-00;** www.canadainternational.gc.ca/switzerland-suisse/index.aspx?lang=eng).

Health & Safety
Medical care and health facilities in Switzerland are among the best in the world. Note that Swiss authorities require immunization against contagious diseases if you have been in an infected area during the 14-day period immediately preceding your arrival in Switzerland.

Crimes of violence, such as muggings, are rare in Switzerland. It is generally safe to walk the streets of cities day and night. The most common crime reported by visitors is a picked pocket.

Holidays
The legal holidays in Switzerland are New Year's (Jan 1–2), Good Friday, Easter Monday, Ascension Day, Whit Monday, Bundesfeier (the Swiss Independence Day; Aug 1), and Christmas (Dec 25–26).

Legal Aid
This may be hard to come by in Switzerland. The government advises foreigners to consult their embassy or consulate (see "Embassies & Consulates," above) in case of a dire emergency, such as an arrest. Even if your embassy or consulate declines to offer financial or legal help, it will generally offer advice on how to obtain help locally.

Mail
Post offices in large cities are open Monday to Friday from 7:30am to noon and 2 to 6:30pm, and on Saturday 7:30 to 11am. If you have letters forwarded to a post office to be collected after you arrive, you'll need a passport for identification. The words *"Poste Restante"* must be clearly written on the envelope. Letters not collected within 30 days are returned to the sender. Letters are either first class, meaning air mail, or surface mail, rated second class.

Police & Emergencies
Dial ✆ **117** for the police (emergencies only) and ✆ **118** to report a fire.

Telephone
The telephone system is entirely automatic and connects the entire country. **Helpful numbers** to know are: **111** for directory assistance, **120** for tourist information and snow reports, **140** for help on the road, **162** for weather forecasts, and **163** for up-to-the-minute information on road conditions. Hotels add substantial

service charges for calls made from your room; it's considerably less expensive to make calls from a public phone booth.

To use a **coin-operated telephone,** lift the receiver and insert 40 centimes to get a dial tone. Be sure to have enough coins on hand, as you must insert more for each message unit over your initial deposit. If you insert more coins than necessary, the excess amounts will be returned.

To make a local call, dial directly after you hear the dial tone (no area code needed); for other places in Switzerland, dial the area code and then the number. To call a foreign country, dial the code of the country first, then the area code, and then the number.

Tipping   A 15% service charge is automatically included in most hotel and restaurant bills, although some people leave an additional tip for exceptional service. For taxis, a tip is usually included in the charges (a notice will be posted in the cab).

ZURICH ★★★

Zurich is not only the largest city in Switzerland and one of the most beautiful on the Continent, but it is also Switzerland's major rail hub and one of the country's two major airport terminals for air traffic from North America. Most rail passengers fly into Zurich to begin their rail tour of Switzerland.

Zurich is well connected to many of Europe's major cities, with four trains per day arriving from Munich (trip time: 4½ hr.), trains arriving every 2 hours from Milan (trip time: 3½ hr.), five TGV trains per day from Paris (trip time: 4½ hr.), four trains from Salzburg (trip time: 4 hr., 20 min.), and four trains from Vienna (trip time: 8 hr.). Zurich is also a hub for overnight trains to many international cities, including Amsterdam, Berlin, Prague, Barcelona, and Vienna. From Zurich, high-speed trains also race you anywhere you're going within Switzerland.

Called the "city by the lake," Zurich lies on both banks of the Limmat River and its tributary, the Sihl. Quays line the riverbanks and the lake, making for some of the grandest scenic promenades in Europe. Though the capital of a canton (district), Zurich has not been the capital of Switzerland since 1848 (that's Bern). It was, however, a great center of liberal thought, having attracted Linen, Carl Jung, James Joyce, and Thomas Mann. The Dadaist school was founded here in 1916.

Even though it's a German-speaking city, nearly all Zurichers speak English. Although there is much here of interest to the visitor, Zurich is essentially a city of commerce and industry, with briefcase-carrying, Armani-attired executives heading for the world's fourth-largest stock exchange or the world's largest gold exchange. Because of all this money changing hands, Zurich also offers some of the most upper-crust shops in Europe, along with a bevy of top-quality, posh restaurants. On the downside, the city caters to the wealthy, and prices are appropriately up there. No need to worry, though—we recommend dining and hotel options for all budgets in this section.

Station Information

GETTING FROM THE AIRPORT TO THE TRAIN STATION

Zurich International Airport (© 043/816-22-11; www.zurich-airport.com) is the biggest airport in Switzerland and the most popular gateway to the country; in fact, it's among the 10 busiest airports in Europe. It's located approximately 7 miles (11km) north of the city center.

The best and cheapest way to get to the center of the city is to hop a train at the airport; for 24F, you'll arrive in less than 10 minutes at the Zurich Hauptbahnhof, the

Zurich

RIGHT BANK

Klosbachstrasse
Eidmattstrasse
Hammerstrasse
Neptunstrasse
Minervastrasse
Forchstrasse
Merkurstrasse
Zeltweg
Kreuz-platz
Zollikerstrasse
Kreuzbühlstrasse
Mühlebachstrasse
Feldeggstrasse
Seefeldstrasse
Höschgasse
Florastrasse
Mainaustrasse
Dufourstrasse
Othmar-str.
Kreuzstrasse
Bellerivestrasse
Goethe-str.
Falkenstr.
Seehof-str.
Seefeldquai
Theaterstrasse
Opera House
Utoquai
Bellevue-platz
Quaibrücke
Bürkli-platz

Zürichsee/ Lake Zürich

Claridenstr.
Beethovenstr.
Stockerstr.
Gen.-Guisan-Quai
Dreikönigstrasse
Tödistr.
ARBORETUM
Mythenquai
Breitingerstr.
Alfred-Escher-Strasse
BELVOIR PARK
Lavaterstrasse
Tunnelstrasse
Tessinerplatz
Seestrasse
Bahnhof Enge
Grütlistrasse
RIETER PARK
Bürglistrasse
Scheideggstrasse
Brunaustrasse
Bederstrasse
Schulhausstrasse
ENGE
Gablerstrasse
Waffenplatzstrasse
Rieterstrasse
Hugelstrasse
Sihlpromenade
Lessingstrasse
Nationalstrasse 3

Basel ● **Zurich**
Bern ✪ **SWITZERLAND**
● Geneva

ACCOMMODATIONS ■
Hotel Bristol **1**
Hotel Kindli **7**
Hotel Rössli **15**
Hotel Walhalla **3**
Lady's First **17**

DINING ◆
Bierhalle Kropf **10**
Brasserie Lipp **6**
Kaufleuten **5**
Mére Catherine **13**
Restaurant Reithalle **4**
Zunfthaus Zur Zimmerleuten **12**

ATTRACTIONS ●
Fraumünster **11**
Grossmünster **14**
Landesmuseum (Swiss National Museum) **2**
Lindenhof **8**
Münsterhof **9**
Zurich Kunsthaus (Fine Arts Museum) **16**

ⓘ Information

0 ———— 1/4 mi
0 ———— 0.25 km

main railway station. The train runs every 15 to 20 minutes between 5am and 12:40am. The ride is covered by your railpass, though it's unwise to waste a day on your pass for such an inexpensive trip.

A trip to the central rail station by taxi will cost you between 50F and 60F.

INSIDE THE STATION

Zurich Hauptbahnhof (✆ 0900/300-300) is a major European rail hub and one of the cleanest and safest stations on the Continent. Trains arrive from and depart to a number of major European cities, including Munich, Milan, and Paris, from this station.

On the same level as the train tracks is the **Rail Travel Centre,** opposite track 13. You can get your railpass validated here, and the staff provides information for rail travel throughout Switzerland, sells tickets, and makes reservations. It's open Monday to Friday from 9am to 7pm, and Saturday from 10am to 5pm (closed Sun). Take a number from the machine as you enter and wait your turn. A list of departing trains is displayed on digital boards within the station.

On the left side of the main arrival hall is a **Money Exchange** kiosk, open daily from 6:30am to 9:30pm. The staff will convert your currency into Swiss francs. The Swiss prefer to use their own francs in transactions, shunning the euro and the dollar. You can store your luggage one level below (take the escalator). The cost is 5F per day, and the counter is open daily from 7am to 9pm. There are also public showers at the train station, costing 12F; they're open 6am to midnight.

The **Zurich Tourist Office,** Bahnhofplatz 15 (✆ 044/215-40-00; www.zuerich. com), is based inside the main railway station and offers tourist information, maps, and brochures. It's open November to April Monday to Saturday 8:30am to 7pm and Sunday 9am to 6pm; May to October Monday to Saturday 8am to 8:30pm, and Sunday 8:30am to 6:30pm.

Hotel reservations can be made here, or you can e-mail the staff in advance at **hotel@zuerich.com**. Vacancies in hotels are posted on an electronic hotel reservations board at the front of the station; otherwise, the tourist office will find rooms for you after 10:30am.

On the bottom level of the station are a number of shops and fast-food outlets.

The Bahnhof is also the hub for Zurich's public transportation system. You can catch trams or buses here to wherever you are going in the city.

Getting Around

The public transport system of Zurich is operated by VBZ Züri–Linie, or **Zurich Public Transport** (✆ 0848/988-988; www.stadt-zuerich.ch), and is the best and cheapest way to get around town. The modern and extensive network of trams and buses (there is no subway) runs daily from 5:30am to 12:30am. You should have to wait no longer than 6 minutes during rush hours. Most trams and buses connect at the Zurich Hauptbahnhof, in the heart of the city.

You can buy tickets from automatic vending machines located at every stop. You must have a ticket before you get on a vehicle; if you're caught without one, you'll pay a fine of 80F on the spot.

For a trip of up to four stops, the fare is 2.50F, and 4F for longer journeys. Visitors will get the most for their money by buying a *Tageskarte* (1-day ticket), which costs 8F and allows you to travel on all city buses and trams for 24 hours.

Taxis are very expensive in Zurich. The budget-conscious will want to use them only as a last resort. Your hotel will usually be glad to call a taxi for you, but if you're making the call yourself, call **Taxi 444** (© **044/444-44-44**). The basic charge before you even get into the vehicle is 6.50F, plus 3.80F for each kilometer you travel.

Biking is a good way to get around Zurich, especially in the outlying areas. Bikes can be borrowed at the baggage counter of the railway station through **AOZ** (© **043/288-34-45;** www.zuerirollt.ch). This service is free if you return the bike the same day; each additional day costs 10F.

Where to Stay

Note: Virtually no hotels in Zurich have air-conditioning, so unless specified below, assume none of the properties in this section have it.

Hotel Bristol ★ 🏃 Close to the Bahnhof, this affordable (a rarity in superexpensive Zurich!) hotel is a bit lean on facilities, but the helpful staff will quickly ease you into life in Zurich. The midsize bedrooms are well maintained and frequently renovated. This is also one of the few lower-priced hotels that is accessible to those with limited mobility.

Stampfensbachstrasse 34, CH-8035 Zurich. © **044/258-44-44.** Fax 044/258-44-00. www.hotel bristol.ch. 53 units. 250F double; 280F triple. Rates include continental breakfast. AE, DC, MC, V. Tram: 11 or 14. **Amenities:** Rooms for those w/limited mobility.

Hotel Kindli ★ This hotel is set inside a restored 16th-century building in the Altstadt's (Old Town) pedestrian zone. The structure might be antique, but the hotel was drastically overhauled and turned into one of the better choices for those seeking good comfort and a bit of atmosphere, enhanced by the use of Laura Ashley fabrics throughout. Bedrooms are midsize, each with a different color scheme and completely modern plumbing.

Pfalzgasse 1, CH-8001 Zurich. © **043/888-76-76.** Fax 043/888-76-77. www.kindli.ch. 20 units. 380F–460F double. Rates include continental breakfast. AE, DC, MC, V. Tram: 7, 11, or 13. **Amenities:** Restaurant.

Hotel Rössli ★ This antique building in the Oberdorf section of Zurich, about a mile (1.6km) from the train station, was massively overhauled and turned into a modern hotel that attracts a hip, young crowd. The midsize bedrooms are tastefully and comfortably furnished. A special feature here is a suite with a separate living room, kitchen, three bedrooms, and roof terrace offering lovely views. The bar is a popular gathering point for Zurich's artists and musicians.

Rössligasse 7, CH-8001 Zurich. © **044/256-70-50.** Fax 044/256-70-51. www.hotelroessli.ch. 18 units. 290F–320F double; 450F suite. Rates include buffet breakfast. AE, DC, MC, V. Tram: 4 or 15. **Amenities:** Bar.

Hotel Walhalla 🏃 Only a short walk from the Bahnhof, this hotel is a bargain by Zurich standards. It is spread across two five-floor buildings. One of these structures is relatively modern; the other is a bit more antiquated, although some prefer its higher ceilings and architectural details. The midsize bedrooms are comfortably furnished and well maintained, though beyond a bathroom, expect almost no in-room amenities but a TV.

Limmatstrasse 5, 8005 Zurich. © **044/446-54-00.** Fax 044/446-54-54. www.walhalla-hotel.ch. 48 units. 235F double. AE, DC, MC, V. Tram: 3 or 14. **Amenities:** Rooms for those w/limited mobility; smoke-free rooms.

Lady's First ★ 🛏 Pia Schmid, a well-known local architect, took an 1880s town house and successfully converted it into this charming boutique hotel, equipped with a first-class spa and a rooftop terrace with panoramic views of the cityscape. The midsize to spacious bedrooms are handsomely furnished with high ceilings and parquet floors. The summer rose garden is alluring, as is the blazing fireplace in the winter lounge. One other special feature: The hotel reserves its top two floors just for women.

Mainaustrasse 24, Kreis 8, CH-8008 Zurich. © **044/380-80-10.** Fax 044/380-80-20. www.ladysfirst.ch. 28 units. 275F–375F double. Rates include breakfast. AE, DC, MC, V. Tram: 2 or 4. **Amenities:** Breakfast room; rooms for those w/limited mobility.

Top Attractions & Special Moments

In the center of Zurich, the world-famous **Bahnhofstrasse** ★★★ is the world's most beautiful shopping street. Planted with linden trees, the street was built on the site of what used to be a "frogs' moat." The exclusive street is relatively free of traffic, except for trams, which Zurichers have labeled "holy cows."

Beginning at the Bahnhofplatz, the street extends for nearly 4,000 feet (1,219m) until it reaches the lake. The drab **Bahnhofplatz,** the hub of Zurich's transportation network, is the railway station square and is home to the Hauptbahnhof (the German word for central railway station), which was built here in 1871.

With your back to this railway terminus, head up Bahnhofstrasse, which is filled with banks and shops selling luxury merchandise, such as Swiss watches. Select a favorite cafe and people-watch when you get tired of shopping. Incidentally, if you do

A summer walk ALONG THE QUAYS OF ZURICH

To walk the **Quays of Zurich** ★★★ is an attraction rivaled in the city only by the Swiss National Museum. These promenades have been built along the Zurichsee (Lake Zurich) and the Limmat River. The most famous is **Limmat Quai,** in the virtual heart of Zurich, beginning at the Bahnhof Bridge and extending east to the Rathaus (town hall) and beyond. These quays have lovely gardens planted with beautiful trees such as the linden. The Swiss are known for their love of flowers, which is much in evidence as you join Zurichers for a stroll on the promenade, an especially invigorating experience when spring comes to the city.

Uto Quai is the major lakeside promenade, running from Badeanstalt Uto Quai, a swimming pool, to Bellevue Square and Quai Brucke. The graceful swans you see in the lake aren't just a scenic attraction. Zurichers have found that they're an efficient garbage disposal system, keeping the lake from being polluted as it laps up on their shores. If you stroll as far as **Mythen Quai,** you'll be following the lake along its western shore and out into the countryside where vistas open onto the Alps and, on the far horizon, the Oberland massifs.

shop, take along plenty of cash or else a gold-plated credit card. The merchandise here is exquisite, but it's also some of the most expensive in the world.

Fraumünster   On the left bank, this church, with its slender blue spire, overlooks the Münsterhof, the former pig market of Zurich. It was founded as an abbey by the Emperor Ludwig (Louis the German, grandson of Charlemagne) in 853 but dates mainly from the 13th and 14th centuries in its present incarnation. In the undercroft are the remains of the crypt of the old abbey church. The chief attractions here are five **stained-glass windows ★**—each with its own color theme—by Marc Chagall dating from 1970. Obviously, they are best seen in bright morning light. The church is also celebrated for its elaborate organ. The Gothic nave is from the 13th to the 15th centuries, and the basilica has three aisles. In the Romanesque and Gothic cloisters are 1920s paintings depicting old Zurich legends about the founding of the abbey.

Fraumünsterstrasse. ☏ **044/211-41-00.** www.fraumuenster.ch. Free admission. April–Oct Mon–Sat 10am–6pm, Sun noon–6pm; Nov–Mar Mon–Sat 10am–4pm, Sun noon–4pm. Tram: 4 to City Hall.

Grossmünster ★   The Romanesque and Gothic cathedral of Zurich was, according to legend, founded by Charlemagne, whose horse bowed down on the spot marking the graves of three early Christian martyrs. Rising on a terrace above the Limmatquai, the cathedral has twin three-story towers, a city landmark. On the right bank of the Limmat, the present structure dates principally from 1090 to 1180 and from 1225 to the dawn of the 14th century. The cathedral is dedicated to those Christian missionaries and the patron saints of Zurich: Felix, Regula, and Exuperantius.

The cathedral was once the parish church of Zwingli, one of the great leaders of the Reformation. He urged priests to take wives (he was married himself) and attacked the "worship of images" and the Roman doctrine of Mass. This led to his death at Kappel in a religious war in 1531. The public hangman quartered his body, and soldiers burned the pieces with dung. That spot at Kappel is today marked with an inscription: "They may kill the body but not the soul." If you visit the choir, you'll come upon stained-glass windows Giacometti completed in 1933. In the crypt is the original (but weather-beaten) statue of a 15th-century figure of Charlemagne. A copy of that same statue crowns the south tower.

Grossmünsterplatz. ☏ **044/252-59-49.** www.grossmuenster.ch. Cathedral free; towers 4F adults, 2F students, seniors, and children 16 and under. Cathedral Mar 1–Oct 31 daily 10am–6pm; Nov 1–Feb 28 daily 10am–5pm. Towers Mar 1–Oct 31 Mon–Sat 10am–5pm, Sun 12:30pm–5:30pm (weather permitting); Nov 1–Feb 28 Mon–Sat 10am–4:30pm, Sun 12:30pm–4:30pm (weather permitting). Tram: 4.

Landesmuseum (Swiss National Museum) ★★★   This museum, located in a big, sprawling gray stone Victorian building in back of the Zurich Hauptbahnhof, offers an epic survey of Swiss culture, art, and history. The collection of artifacts starts off in dim unrecorded time and carries you to the present day. It's like a storybook history of all the cantons that you turn page by page as you go from gallery to gallery.

Religious art sounds a dominant theme, and especially noteworthy are the 16th-century stained glass that was removed from Tänikon Convent and the frescoes from the church of Müstair. Some of the museum's Carolingian art dates from the 9th century. Altarpieces—carved, painted, and gilded—bring back the glory of the Swiss medieval artisan. Several rooms from Fraumünster Abbey are also on view.

The museum's prehistoric section is exceptional, dipping back to the 4th millennium. Switzerland's history as a Roman outpost is explored in several exhibits. And

DISCOVERIES ALONG medieval streets

Even if you have to skip a museum or two, head for the **Alstadt (Old Town)** ★★★, known for its romantic squares, narrow cobblestone streets, winding alleyways that aren't as sinister as they look, fountain-decorated corners, medieval houses, art galleries, boutiques, colorfully quaint restaurants, shops, a scattering of hotels, and antiques stores. The Old Town lies on both sides of the Limmat River, and you might begin your exploration at the **Münsterhof**, or former swine market. Excavations have turned up houses here that date back to the 1100s. Once it was the tarrying place of Charlemagne, and to walk its old streets is to follow in the footsteps of historic figures ranging from Mozart and Lenin to Einstein and Carl Jung.

Shaded by trees, the belvedere square of **Lindenhof** is one of the most scenic spots in Zurich, especially favored at twilight time by those who believe in "young love." It can be reached by climbing medieval alleyways from the Fraumünster. Once the site of a Celtic and Roman fort, Lindenhof is a good point to watch the crossing of the Limmat River. The lookout point is graced with a fountain, of course. There's also a good view of the medieval Old Quarter, which rises in layers on the right bank. Many excellent restaurants are located in this vicinity.

Directly south of Münsterbrücke is a Gothic church, rather austere, called the **Wesserkirche**, or "water church." When it was built in 1479, it was surrounded by water.

the displays of utensils and furnishings of Swiss life over the centuries are staggering: medieval silverware, 14th-century drinking bowls, tiled 18th-century stoves, 17th-century china, Roman clothing, painted furniture, costumes, even dollhouses. Naturally, arms and armor revive Switzerland's military legacy, from 800 to 1800, although some weapons date from the late Iron Age.

Museumstrasse 2. ⏱ **044/218-65-11.** www.musee-suisse.ch. Admission 10F adults, 8F students and seniors, free for children 15 and under; free admission on the last Sun of every month. Tues–Wed 10am–5pm; Thurs 10am–7pm; Fri–Sun 10am–5pm. Tram: 3, 4, 5, 11, 13, or 14.

Zurich Kunsthaus (Fine Arts Museum) ★ This museum is devoted to works mainly from the 19th and 20th centuries, although many of its paintings and sculpture dip back to antiquity. Dating from Victorian times, the collection has grown and grown, and is today one of the most important in Europe.

As you enter, note Rodin's *Gate of Hell.* Later on, you can explore one of our favorite sections, the **Giacometti wing** ★, showcasing the artistic development of the amazing Swiss-born artist (1901–66), whose works are characterized by surrealistically elongated forms and hallucinatory moods.

All the legendary names of modern art can be found in the galleries, including a collection of the works of Norwegian artist **Edvard Munch** ★★, the largest outside of Oslo. Old masters such as Rubens and Rembrandt are suitably honored, and one salon contains 17 Rouaults.

Heimplatz 1. ⏱ **044/253-84-84.** www.kunsthaus.ch. Admission 14F adults, 10F seniors, free for children 16 and under; combination ticket for special exhibitions 24F adults, 16F seniors. Tues 10am–6pm; Wed–Fri 10am–8pm; Sat–Sun 10am–6pm. Tram: 3 (marked "Klusplatz").

Where to Dine

Bierhalle Kropf ★ SWISS/BAVARIAN   *Der Kropf* is everyone's favorite beer hall, installed in one of the oldest burgher houses in Zurich, only a short walk from Paradeplatz. Locals flock here for the large portions and affordable prices. Against an old-fashioned Swiss backdrop of stag horns and stained glass, robust and well-prepared platters of mountain favorites, such as mammoth pork shanks, stewed meats, chopped veal, and the famous *rösti* (Swiss-style hash browns) are served.

In Gassen 16. ℭ **044/221-18-05.** www.zumkropf.ch. Reservations recommended. Main courses 20F–45F. AE, MC, V. Mon–Sat 11:30am–10pm. Closed Easter, Christmas, and Aug 1. Tram: 2, 8, 9, or 11.

Brasserie Lipp SWISS/FRENCH   This bustling bistro was inspired by the world-famous Art Nouveau Brasserie Lipp in Paris. The atmosphere of Paris is re-created here, as is the cuisine; you'll find such old-time classics as peppery steaks and sole meunière on the menu. It's a bustling place, with waiters scurrying about, often bringing in heaping platters of sauerkraut with pork products just as they do in the real thing on the Left Bank of Paris.

Uraniastrasse 9. ℭ **043/888-66-66.** www.brasserie-lipp.ch. Reservations recommended, especially Fri–Sat. Main courses 39F–65F. AE, DC, MC, V. Mon–Thurs 11am–midnight (to 12:30am Fri–Sat); Sun 11:45am–11pm. Tram: 6, 7, 11, or 13.

Kaufleuten INTERNATIONAL   Only a few steps from the Bahnhofstrasse, this enduring favorite roams the globe for its culinary inspiration, serving everything from a platter-size Wiener schnitzel fried a golden brown, to a fiery coconut and chicken curry from Thailand. It is strong in its freshwater fish dishes, especially salmon, sole, and sea bass, which are prepared almost close to perfection and never allowed to dry out. The restaurant is also a nightlife venue.

Pelikanstrasse 18. ℭ **044/225-33-33.** www.kaufleuten.ch. Reservations recommended. Main courses 25F–60F. AE, DC, MC, V. Sun–Fri 11:30am–2pm; daily 6:30pm–11pm (to 1am Fri–Sat). Tram: 6, 7, 11, or 13.

📷 sailing LAKE ZURICH

At some point during your stay in Switzerland's largest city, you'll want to take a lake steamer for a tour around Lake Zurich. Walk to Bahnhofstrasse's lower end and buy a ticket at the pier for any of the dozen or so boats that ply the lake waters from late May to late September. The boats are more or less the same, so it doesn't matter which one you take. Most of the steamers contain simple restaurant facilities, and all have two or three levels of decks and lots of windows, for wide-angle views of the Swiss mountains and shoreline. During peak season, boats depart at approximately 30-minute intervals. The most distant itinerary from Zurich is to **Rapperswil,** a historic town near the lake's southeastern end. A full-length, round-trip tour of the lake from Zurich to Rapperswil takes 2 hours each way, plus whatever time you opt to spend exploring towns en route. Many visitors opt for shorter boat rides encompassing only the northern third of the lake, where the total trip takes about 90 minutes.

A full-length tour of the lake costs 23F in second class and 38F in first class. The shorter boat ride on the northern third of the lake costs only 8F. For information, call ℭ **044/487-13-34.**

Mère Catherine PROVENÇAL/FRENCH   One of the Alstadt's favorite bistros is nestled in a quiet courtyard, its tranquil cafe tables evoking the Left Bank of Paris. The unpretentious French cooking features fresh fish along with an ever-changing roster of daily specials. Try to arrive early for an aperitif at the Bar Philosophe next door before going to your table to partake of delights that will make you salivate with pleasure.

Nägelihof 3. ℂ **044/250-59-40.** www.commercio.ch/mere-catherine. Reservations required. Main courses 30F–47F. MC, V. Kitchen daily 11:30am–2pm, 5:45–10:30pm; bar 11:30am–midnight. Tram: 4 or 15.

Restaurant Reithalle 🍴 INTERNATIONAL   In a former stable on a small island in the heart of Zurich, this local favorite is a friend of the frugal rail passenger. In fair weather, its cobblestone courtyard is mobbed with fun-loving drinkers and diners. Expect a robust and hearty cuisine prepared with fresh ingredients, based on recipes from around the world—even from as far away as Iran. The interior becomes a dance club every Saturday from 11pm to 3am (except during the summer months), and restaurant patrons enter free (otherwise, there's a cover of 15F).

In the Theaterhaus Gessnerallee, Gessnerallee 8. ℂ **044/212-07-66.** www.restaurant-reithalle.ch. Reservations not necessary. Lunch main courses 20F–25F; dinner main courses 20F–35F. AE, DC, MC, V. Mon–Fri 11:45am–2pm, 6–10:30pm; Sat 6–11:30pm; Sun 6–10:30pm. Tram: 3.

Zunfthaus Zur Zimmerleuten ★ SWISS   The foundations of this 1708 building date from 1336, when it was originally the carpenters' guildhall. An architectural showpiece, it's now one of the Zurich's most enduring restaurants. A flight of baroque stairs leads from the street level to the elegant dining room, which is decorated with rows of leaded-glass windows and an impressive collection of hunting trophies. Menu items include morel toasts; freshwater bouillabaisse; filet of pike-perch poached in Savoy cabbage; and a local specialty, *ratsherrentopf,* composed of three different filets with rösti and butter sauce. The reward for the kitchen's vigilance is a loyal clientele with discerning palates who enjoys the full-bodied dishes.

Limmatquai 40. ℂ **044/250-53-63.** www.zimmerleuten.ch. Reservations recommended. Main courses 35F–50F. AE, DC, MC, V. Daily 11:30am–2pm and 6–11:30pm. Tram: 4 or 15.

Shopping

Zurich has been called a shopper's Valhalla, if that's not too pagan a term for such a Protestant city. Within the heart of Zurich are 25 acres (10 hectares) of shopping, including the exclusive stores along the **Bahnhofstrasse,** previewed on p. 762. Along this gold-plated street, you can walk with oil-rich sheiks and their families in your search for furs, watches, jewelry, leather goods, silks, and embroidery. If your own oil well didn't come in, you can still shop for souvenirs.

Your shopping adventure might begin more modestly at the top of the street, the **Bahnhofplatz.** Underneath this vast transportation hub is a complex of shops known as **"Shop Ville."**

Bally Schuhfabriken AG, Bahnhofstrasse 66 (ℂ **044/224-39-39**), is the largest official outlet of the famous Swiss chain, occupying a prominent place in a big-windowed store on this shopping artery. For lovers of Bally shoes, this is the place to buy them, although the merchandise is not necessarily cheaper than at other Bally outlets. You'll find the most complete line of Bally shoes here in the world, along with accessories and clothing (most, but not all, of which are made in Switzerland).

If your heart is set on buying a timepiece in Zurich, try **Beyer,** Bahnhofstrasse 31 (ℂ **043/344-63-63;** www.beyer-ch.com/en), located midway between the train station and the lake. Besides carrying just about every famous brand of watch made in Switzerland, such as Rolex and Patek Philippe, they have a surprising museum in the basement, containing timepieces from as early as 1400 B.C. Another sure bet in Zurich is **Bucherer AG,** Bahnhofstrasse 50 (© **044/211-26-35;** www.bucherer.com). A longtime name in the Swiss watch industry, this store carries an impressive collection of jewelry as well.

Jelmoli Department Store, Seidengasse 1 (© **044/220-44-11;** www.jelmoli. ch), is a Zurich institution, selling everything a large department store should, from cookware to clothing. Founded 150 years ago by the Ticino-born entrepreneur Johann Peter Jelmoli, the store and the success of its many branches is a legend among the Zurich business community.

Musik Hug, Limmatquai 28–30 (© **044/269-41-41;** www.musikhug.ch), is the kind of shop that musicians will love, particularly if they need sheet music for anything from flugelhorn concertos to yodeling duets. It might be the largest repository of Alpine musical tradition anywhere, as well as a commercial music shop stocking woodwind recorders of all sizes and pitches, along with flugelhorns and French horns.

Schweizer Heimatwerk, Uraniastrasse 1 by the Rudolf Brun-Brücke (© **044/217-83-17;** www.heimatwerk.ch), is only one of a chain of similar stores throughout Zurich. Most of them have the same basic collection of, for example, hand-painted boxes in charmingly naïve patterns with or without music mechanisms, bookends, china, decorative stoneware plates, a wide range of textiles, and the obligatory cowbells in all sizes. This particular store has a large selection of glass, embroidery, and woodcarvings, among other items. The English-speaking staff is particularly helpful in suggesting "little gifts."

Nightlife

The Zurich Opera is the most outstanding local company, performing at **Opernhaus,** Falkenstrasse 1 (© **044/268-66-66;** www.opernhaus.ch), near Bellevueplatz in the center of the city. The opera house is also a repertory theater, hosting ballets, concerts, and recitals, although it shuts down in July and August. Tickets cost 20F to 300F, and the box office is open Monday to Saturday 11:30am to 6pm. The **Zurich Tonhalle Orchestra** performs at the Tonhalle Gesellschaft, Claridenstrasse 7 (© **044/206-34-34;** www.tonhalle-orchester.ch), a 1,500-seat theater that is also the venue for many internationally known soloists. Tickets range from 20F to 175F, and the box office is open daily 10am to 6pm.

More boisterous nightlife is found at the 160-seat **Bierhalle Wolf,** Limmatquai 132 (© **044/251-01-30;** www.bierhalle-wolf.ch), the best-known beer hall in the city, known for its "evergreen music" (folk) played by an oompah band. You can also dine here on the kitchen's robust fare. Cover starts at 7F, and hours are Monday to Wednesday 11am to 12pm, Thursday to Saturday 11am to 1am, and Sunday 11am to 11pm. The largest nightclub in Zurich, and one of the best, is **X-tra,** in the Limmathaus, Limmatstrasse 118 (© **044/448-15-00;** www.x-tra.ch). With a long bar and an outdoor terrace, it features some of the best rock groups in Europe. The cover ranges from 30F to 50F, depending on the performers.

House and garage music are featured at **Kaufleuten,** Pelikanstrasse 18 (© **044/225-33-22**), which has four different bar areas and an on-site restaurant. British or Irish pubs are all the rage in Zurich, including **James Joyce Pub,** Pelikanstrasse 8 (© **044/221-18-28;** www.jamesjoyce.ch), boasting the furnishings and paneling of an 18th-century pub in Dublin, and **Oliver Twist,** Rindermarkt 6

(© **044/252-47-10**; www.pickwick.ch), attracting a fun-loving young crowd that overflows into a summer courtyard.

BERN ★★★

Bern, set in the heart of Switzerland, has been the country's capital since 1848. A city of diplomats, it is one of the loveliest places to visit in the country, surrounded on three sides by the River Aare, a body of water to which it is linked symbolically as much as Paris is to the Seine.

Built between the 12th and 18th centuries, Bern is one of the few great medieval cities left in Europe that hasn't been destroyed, torn down, or bombed in wars. In 1983, the United Nations declared it a "World Landmark." It's a city of arcades, nearly 4 miles (6.4km) of them running along the streets of the old sector, and they're weatherproof and traffic free. Underneath these arcades are shops, everything from exclusive boutiques to department stores, from antiques dealers to jewelers. It's a city of fountains and oriel windows, and its old sandstone steps have been trodden for centuries.

The city is a stop on many international rail routes. Trains from France, Italy, Germany, and even Spain all pass through Bern, making it a great stopover point on a cross-continental train trip. The TGV high-speed train, for example, connects Paris with Bern in just 4½ hours. Bern is also situated on most major rail lines in Switzerland, particularly those connecting Geneva (90 min.) and Zurich (1 hr.). We place it second on a rail trip through Switzerland because most people fly into Zurich or Geneva first, though Bern has its own airport at Belpmoos.

Bern can also be your gateway to the Alpine region of central Switzerland, the Bernese Oberland. Trains leave every hour for Interlaken, the capital of the Bernese Oberland, where you can make all sorts of rail connections into the mountains, especially if you want to take the train trip to Jungfraujoch, which, for many rail passengers, is the most dramatic and scenic trip in all of Switzerland.

Station Information

GETTING FROM THE AIRPORT TO THE TRAIN STATION

The **Bern-Belp Airport** (© **031/960-21-11;** www.alpar.ch) is 6 miles (9.6km) south of the city in the town of Belpmoos. International flights arrive from London, Paris, and Nice, but transatlantic jets are not able to land here. Fortunately, it's a short hop to Bern from the international airports in Zurich and Geneva.

A taxi from the airport to the city center costs about 42F, so it's better to take the shuttle bus that runs between the airport and the Bahnhof (train station) in the city center. The shuttle trip costs 5.80F one-way.

INSIDE THE STATION

The **Bahnhof** rail station, on Bahnhofplatz, is right in the center of town near all the major hotels.

The **Rail Information Center** inside the station is open daily from 6am to 9pm. Here you can also make reservations and validate your railpasses. The location of the office is across the passageway from the tourist center. Many visitors who arrive in Bern choose to visit the Jungfrau, the famous mountain outside Interlaken, whose train station, at 13,638 feet (4,158m), is the highest in Europe. Your railpass will take you from Bern to Interlaken, but at the Interlaken station you must purchase a

Bern

ACCOMMODATIONS ■
Hotel Ambassador **2**
Hotel City am Bahnhof **4**
Hotel Continental **8**
Hotel Metropole **9**
Hotel National **3**

DINING ◆
Arlequin **15**
Frohsinn **12**
Gourmanderie
Café Moleson **6**
Kornhaus Keller/
Kornhauscafé **10**
Ratskeller **16**

ATTRACTIONS ●
BärenPark **17**
Bernisches Historisches
Museum **1**
Cathedral of St. Vincent **14**
Käfigturm **5**
Kunstmuseum **7**
Zähringen Fountain **13**
Zeitglocken **11**
Zentrum Paul Klee **17**

separate ticket on a private railroad for the final trip to Jungfrau. For more rail information and schedules, call ℂ **0900/300-300.**

On the ground level of the station, there are money exchange offices, including an ATM. The Swiss Railroad operates one of these offices, labeled Change SBB, which is open Monday through Friday from 7am to 7:30pm, Saturday from 7am to 7pm, and Sunday from 9am to 7pm. The station also offers baggage storage facilities downstairs, which are open from 6am to 1am; lockers cost between 5F and 8F.

The **Bern Tourist Office** is located inside the Bahnhof, on Bahnhofplatz (ℂ **031/328-12-12;** www.bernetourism.ch). It's open June to September daily 9am to 8:30pm; October to May Monday to Saturday 9am to 6:30pm, and Sunday 10am to 5pm. If you need help finding a hotel room, the tourist office can make a reservation for you in the price range you select. The office also sells hotel packages for 2, 3, or 4 nights in hotels rated anywhere from two to five stars, the latter almost paralyzingly priced.

If your luggage is light, you can walk to your hotel; otherwise, take one of the taxis waiting outside the station.

Getting Around

The public transportation system, **Stadtische Verkehrsbetriebe (SVB),** is a reliable 48-mile (77km) network of buses and trams. Before you board, purchase a ticket from one of the automatic machines (you'll find one at each stop), because conductors don't sell tickets. If you're caught traveling without one, you'll be fined 80F on the spot, in addition to the fare for the ride. A short-range ride (within six stations) costs 2F; a normal ticket, valid for 45 minutes one-way, goes for 3.80F.

To save time and money, purchase a **Bern Card** for 20F, which entitles you to unlimited travel on the SVB network for 24 hours. Forty-eight- and 72-hour cards are also available. One-day tickets are available at the **ticket offices** at the Railcity Tourist Center, the railway station, and some hotels and museums. The card also gives you discounts at museums and the zoo.

Bern: A CENTER FOR RAIL TRIPS

Bern is a center for several rail trips that are among the most spectacular in Europe. You'll probably need help from someone at the tourist office to organize one of these itineraries, but the staff at the Bern Tourist office is now capable of crafting and selling tickets for either one-way or circular itineraries that will take you through some of the most vertiginous landscapes in Europe. One of our favorites involves traveling from Bern through its Oberland region, with rail junctions in towns that include Interlaken, Lauterbrunnen, Wengen, and Kleine Scheidegg; then over the Jungfraujoch via Grindelwald and Interlaken; and back to Bern. Jungfraujoch, at 11,152 feet (3,346m), has the highest railway station in Europe and offers panoramic views over glaciers and the Alps, including the so-called Ice Palace. The cost for this particular itinerary, which is self-conducted, self-guided, and self-scheduled, assuming that participants begin and end their journeys in Bern, is $240 in second class and $288 in first class. For anyone holding a valid Swiss Pass, the price of this itinerary is reduced to $113.

You can catch a taxi at the public cab ranks or call a dispatcher; two cab companies you can try are **Nova Taxi** (✆ **031/331-33-13;** www.novataxi.ch) and **Bären Taxi** (✆ **031/371-11-11;** www.baerentaxi.ch). The first kilometer of any taxi ride in Bern costs from 6.80F to 12F, and every kilometer after that costs an additional 3.80F to 4.20F, depending on how fast the traffic is moving and the time of day. The "average" taxi ride within Bern will probably cost about 18F to 28F.

Where to Stay

Hotel Ambassador ★   This nine-floor hotel close to the Bundeshaus, the seat of the Swiss government, is one of the best and most affordable of the moderately priced hotels in Bern. True, its rooms are a bit small and the furnishings are only functional, but they are reasonably comfortable and very well maintained. Rooms like this you expect in Switzerland, but what comes as a surprise is the on-site teppan restaurant with Japanese specialties, including a garden evocative of Tokyo. Unusual for Bern, the hotel also has a private pool with sauna. It's a 5-minute tram ride from the train station (the tram stops right in front of the hotel).

Seftigenstrasse 99, CH-3007 Bern. ✆ **031/370-99-99.** Fax 031/371-41-17. www.fhotels.ch. 99 units. 220F–350F double. AE, DC, MC, V. Tram: 9. **Amenities:** Restaurant.

Hotel City am Bahnhof   This hotel takes its name from the train station, which is only 2 blocks away. If your luggage is light, you can walk straight here from the depot. The hotel is equally popular with business clients and visitors to Bern. The midsize bedrooms with acceptable—hardly exciting—furnishings are far from luxurious, but the maintenance level is high. Rooms come with a minibar and TV, but little else. Breakfast is the only meal served.

Bahnhofplatz 7, CH-3011, Bern. ✆ **031/311-53-77.** Fax 031/311-06-36. www.fhotels.ch. 58 units. 198F–235F double. AE, DC, MC, V. **Amenities:** Breakfast lounge.

Hotel Continental   This is one of the better, though still fairly impersonal, government-rated three-star hotels clustered around the Bern Bahnhof. It charges very fair prices—at least, by the standards of high-priced Bern—for its comfortably furnished bedrooms. The rooms, although small, are well maintained and outfitted in both contemporary and traditional pieces; flower boxes outside the bedroom windows are a nice touch. In fair weather, breakfast is taken under a canopied terrace.

Zeughausgasse 27, CH-3011 Bern. ✆ **031/329-21-21.** Fax 031/329-21-99. www.hotel-continental.ch. 43 units. 150F–245F double. Rates include buffet breakfast. AE, DC, MC, V. Tram: 3 or 9. **Amenities:** Lounge; smoke-free rooms.

Hotel Metropole   This hotel is situated between the Bern Bahnhof and the Altstadt, so it's convenient to most attractions and all transportation. The hotel's small bedrooms are comfortably furnished in both traditional and contemporary style, and have equally small bathrooms. Don't expect too many amenities—minimalism is the word here.

Zeughausgasse 26, CH-3011 Bern. ✆ **031/311-50-21.** Fax 031/312-11-53. www.hotelmetropole.ch. 58 units. 170F–196F double. Rates include buffet breakfast. AE, DC, MC, V. Tram: 9. **Amenities:** Smoke-free rooms.

Hotel National ⚑   Originally built in 1908 as a brewery, and later transformed into a textile factory, this simple but dignified hotel enjoys a consistently high occupancy, thanks to its good value and well-scrubbed interior. The reception area lies one floor above street level, and to reach it, you'll either take the stairs or a "historically significant" elevator that might remind you of a rather quaint birdcage. Accommodations are sober but reliable, utterly devoid of any contemporary fashion statements or accessories, and occupied by a value-conscious clientele. Of particular note are the bedrooms on the uppermost floor, where a recent renovation exposed some of the massive timber trusses that form the exterior's mansard roof.

Hirschengraben 24, CH-3011 Bern. © **031/381-19-88.** Fax 031/381-68-78. www.nationalbern.ch. 46 units, 32 with private bathroom. Double with shared bathroom 130F; double with private bathroom 150F–170F. AE, MC, V. Tram: 3, 5, or 9. **Amenities:** Restaurant. *In room:* No phone or TV in rooms w/no bathroom.

Top Attractions & Special Moments

Marktgasse is the principal artery of the Old Town, and it's lined with luxurious shops and boutiques, the number of florists revealing the Bernese love of flowers. In this traffic-free sector, you can stroll at your leisure, shopping and admiring the 17th- and 18th-century houses. Eventually, you'll come to **Junkerngasse,** the most prestigious street in Bern, lined with patrician houses.

Marktgasse rolls on until it becomes **Kramgasse,** the first street to the right of the city's clock tower. It has many antiques shops and art galleries. You'll also view many turrets and oriel windows, and you'll come upon the 1535 **Zähringen fountain,** showing a bear, the city's mascot, in armor. The **Käfigturm** (prison tower) on Marktgasse marked the boundary line of Bern in the 13th century. Restored in the 18th century, it stands at the top of the Marktgasse.

To the east stands the **Zeitglocken,** or Clock Tower, which was built in the 12th century and restored in the 16th century. Until 1250 it was the west gate of Bern. Four minutes before every hour, crowds gather for what has been called "the world's oldest and biggest horological puppet show." Mechanical bears (the little bear cubs are everybody's favorite), jesters, and emperors put on an animated show—it's one of the longest-running acts in show business, staged since 1530.

BärenPark ★ From the early 16th century through late 2009, Bern's beloved bears resided in the city's famous Bärengraben (bear pits) on the banks of the River Aare. After two bears had to be put down due to poor health, a new, more spacious home for the city's mascots was opened just down the street. The city bears can still access the large bear pit, but they now also roam freely in 6,000 square meters of open-air park on the river banks. Meanwhile, tourists have free reign of the smaller bear pit, through which they must pass to access the BärenPark shop.

Grosser Muristalden. © **031/357-15-25.** www.baerenpark-bern.ch. Free admission. Park accessible 24/7; shop daily 8:30am–4:30pm. Bus: 12.

Bernisches Historisches Museum (Bern Historical Museum) ★★ This neo-Gothic castle, built in the Swiss fortress style of the 16th century, contains historical relics, along with archaeological, ethnographic, and numismatic collections. The main attraction is a series of seven 15th-century tapestries. A tapestry called *The Thousand Flowers,* plus four others telling the story of Julius Caesar, once belonged to the dukes of Burgundy. A number of rural and urban rooms, filled with period furnishings and artifacts, are also open to the public.

Helvetiaplatz 5. © **031/350-77-11.** Admission 13F adults; 8F students, seniors, and children 6–16; free for children 5 and under; combination ticket for special exhibitions 18F–24F. Tues–Sun 10am–5pm. Tram: 3 or 5.

Cathedral of St. Vincent ★   The church was begun in 1421, although its tower wasn't completed until 1893. Its **belfry ★★**, dominating Bern, is 300 feet high (90m), and at the top a panoramic sweep of the Bernese Alps unfolds. You can climb a staircase, some 270 steps, to the platform tower. You'll also have a great vista over the Old Town and its bridges, and a view of the **Aare.**

The cathedral, or Münster, is one of the newer of the Gothic churches of Switzerland. Its most exceptional feature is the **tympanum ★★** over the main portal, with more than 200 figures. Some of them are painted, and the vanquished ones in this Last Judgment setting are singled out for particularly harsh treatment. The mammoth stained-glass windows in the chancel were created in the 15th century. The choir stalls (ca. 1523) brought the Renaissance to Bern. Inside the Matter Chapel is a curious stained-glass window, the *Dance of Death,* constructed in the closing year of World War I but based on a much older design.

Münsterplatz. ✆**031/312-04-62.** Cathedral free; viewing platform 4F adults, 2F children. Cathedral Easter to Oct Tues–Sat 10am–5pm, Sun 11:30am–5pm; off season Tues–Fri 10am–noon and 2–4pm, Sat 10am–noon and 2–5pm, Sun 11:30am–2pm. Viewing platform closes half an hour before cathedral. Bus: 12.

Kunstmuseum ★   The museum has both Swiss and foreign works, placing its emphasis on the 19th and 20th centuries. Some of its paintings, however, go back to the 14th century. There is a collection of Italian "primitives," such as Fra Angelico's *Virgin and Child.* Swiss primitives include one from the Master of the Carnation (Paul Löwensprung, d. 1499), who signed his work with either a red or a white carnation.

The romantic painter Hodler is represented by allegorical frescoes, depicting *Day* and, conversely, *Night.* Several Impressionists are represented, including Monet, Manet, Sisley, and Cézanne; you'll also find works by such artists as Delacroix and Bonnard.

Hodlerstrasse 12. ✆**031/328-09-44.** www.kunstmuseumbern.ch. Permanent collection 7F adults, 5F seniors; special exhibitions up to 15F extra. Tues 10am–9pm; Wed–Sun 10am–5pm. Bus: 20.

The Paul Klee Collection (Zentrum Paul Klee) ★★★   The painter was born in Switzerland in 1879. The local collection of his works includes 40 oils, 2,000 drawings, and many gouaches and watercolors. Klee had a style characterized by fantasy forms in line and light colors. Until around 2004, most of the artworks within this museum were contained within an overcrowded series of rooms within the also-recommended Kunstmuseum. That was before they were moved into a museum created expressly for them by Renzo Piano, one of the most celebrated architects of Italy. Today, in a location about 3 miles (4.8km) east of Bern's Alstadt, more than 4,000 works by the artist are proudly displayed as a kind of homage to Bern's "local son who made good."

Monument in Fruchtland 3. ✆**031/359-01-01.** www.paulkleezentrum.ch. Entrance 22F adults, 20F students and seniors, 10F children 6–16, free for persons 5 and under. Tues–Sun 10am–5pm. Tram: 5. Bus: 12.

Where to Dine

Arlequin SWISS/ITALIAN   Artists, writers, and frugal diners frequent this informal restaurant, which sets out tables on a pergola-shaded, open-air terrace in summer. From Wednesday to Friday, the chef sautés a platter-wide Wiener schnitzel—the best in town—a golden brown. At other times of the week, you can dig into a lot of

ON THE hoof THROUGH BERN

Bern is a walking city, and your own two feet are the only practical means of exploring Altstadt and its many attractions. You can see what there is to see here in about 2½ hours.

Don't overlook the possibility of walks in Greater Bern, including Bern's own mountain, **Gurten,** a popular day-trip destination reached in 25 minutes by tram 9 and a rack railway. Eurail passholders and Swiss Passholders get a 50% discount on the railway. Once here, you'll find many walking paths and can enjoy a panorama over the Alps. There's also a children's playground.

In and around Bern, you'll find 155 miles (250km) of **marked rambling paths.** One of the most scenic runs along the banks of the Aare through the English gardens, the Dählhölzli Zoological Gardens, Elfenau Park, and the Bremgarten woods.

For **jogging and running,** the best spots are the Aare River Run (Dalmaziquai), stretching 2¼ miles (3.6km), and the Aare River Run–Bear Pits, which is 3 miles (4.8km) long.

old-time Swiss favorites, such as goulash soup, and even some specialties from south of the border in Italy.

Gerechtigkeitsgasse 51. ℂ **031/311-39-46.** Reservations recommended. Main courses 15F–38F. AE, MC, V. Daily 11am–11:30pm. Tram: 9.

Frohsinn ★ 🏠 SWISS/CONTINENTAL   Small and intimate, this bistro sits in the shadow of the Bern Clock Tower. Its intimate atmosphere and good, moderately priced food has attracted a loyal following of journalists and national politicians. Sometimes the chefs dip across the borders into neighboring countries, especially France and Italy, for their recipes, which are prepared with first-rate ingredients purchased at the market that day.

Münstergasse 54. ℂ **031/311-37-68.** www.froh-sinn.ch. Reservations required. Main courses 21F–38F. AE, DC, MC, V. Mon–Sat 10am–2pm and 6–10pm. Tram: 54.

Gourmanderie Café Moleson ★ 🏠 INTERNATIONAL   This looks like your basic cafe, but the food at this joint is rather un-cafe-like. Market-fresh ingredients and skilled preparation combine to produce good-tasting dishes that attract everyone from politicians to artists. The friendly English-speaking staff will guide you through the specials of the day. Try such dishes as a sautéed filet of beef in a paprika cream sauce with fresh mushrooms, or else grilled organic chicken breast with a rich salad bowl of bacon, eggs, pineapple, cashew nuts, and a homemade dressing.

Aarbergerasse 24, 3011 Bern. ℂ **031/311-44-63.** www.moleson-bern.ch. Reservations not required. Main courses 28F–50F; fixed-price dinner 69F 3 courses, 79F 4 courses. AE, DC, MC, V. Mon–Fri 11:30am–2:30pm; Mon–Sat 6–11:30pm.

Kornhauskeller/Kornhauscafé SWISS/MEDITERRANEAN   With a pedigree dating from the 1700s, this is the most famous restaurant and beer cellar in Bern. Installed in a converted grain warehouse, this veteran favorite hardly serves the best food in Bern, although the acceptable, rib-sticking fare is dished out in heaping portions. The 450-plus-seat dining room is filled every night, and the restaurant keeps patrons in a convivial mood by presenting folk music from the Alps. Most diners come here for the good times under the soaring vaulted ceilings—you won't find a more jovial atmosphere elsewhere in Bern.

Kornhausplatz 18. ℂ **031/327-72-72.** www.kornhauskeller.ch. Reservations recommended in cellar-level restaurant, not necessary in cafe. Main courses in cellar 34F–55F; platters and snack items in cafe 10F–36F; glasses of wine and cocktails in cafe 7F–18F each. AE, DC, MC, V. Cafe Mon–Sat 8am–12:30am, Sun 9am–11:30pm. Cellar daily noon–2pm, 6–11pm (closes at 10pm Sun). Cellar-level bar 6pm–12:30am or 2am, depending on business.

Ratskeller ☺ SWISS   This historic establishment offers old masonry, modern paneling, and a battalion of busy waitresses serving ample portions of good, rib-sticking food. This dining room has long been the family favorite of generations of locals. Specialties include rack of lamb *a la diable* for two, an omelet soufflé aux fruits, veal kidneys Robert, and *côte de veau* (veal steak) in butter sauce. Your best bet is the tiny filet of perch (*egli* in German) with white sauce on a bed of spinach. Prized by gourmets, this tiny fish is native to the lakes around Bern.

Gerechtigkeitsgasse 81. ℂ **031/311-17-71.** www.platingastro.ch. Reservations recommended. Main courses 18F–49F. AE, DC, MC, V. Mon–Sat 8:30am–10pm; Sun 9am–9:30pm. Tram: 9.

Shopping

You'll find stores of all types along Bern's 4 miles (6.4km) of arcades. The main shopping streets are **Spitalgasse, Kramgasse, Postgasse, Marktgasse,** and **Gerechtigkeitsgasse.**

With a few exceptions, stores in the city center are open on Monday from 2 to 6:30pm; on Tuesday, Wednesday, and Friday from 8:15am to 6:30pm; on Thursday from 8:15am to 9pm; and on Saturday from 8:15am to 4pm. They're closed on Sundays.

You might begin your shopping excursion at **Globus,** Spitalgasse 17 (ℂ **031/313-40-40;** www.globus.ch), a major department store that has been compared to Bloomingdale's, with departments for everything. Many people from the Bernese Oberland come into Bern just to shop at Globus.

The best handicrafts, souvenirs, and gifts are found at **Heimatwerk,** Kramgasse 61 (ℂ **031/311-30-00**), located on a historic street near the Clock Tower. This outlet sells handicrafts from all over Switzerland, including textiles, woodcarvings, music boxes, and jewelry.

Nightlife

Bern Guide, distributed free by the tourist office, keeps a current list of cultural events.

The **Bern Symphony Orchestra** (www.bsorchester.ch), one of the finest orchestras in Switzerland, is conducted by the acclaimed Russian-born Andrey Boreyko, whose services are supplemented by frequent guest conductors from around the world. Concerts by the orchestra are usually performed at the concert facilities in the **Bern Casino,** Herrengasse 25 (ℂ **031/328-02-28;** www.kultur-casino.ch). Except for a summer vacation usually lasting from July until mid-August, the box office is open Monday through Friday from 12:30 to 3pm. Tickets range from 20F to 65F.

Major opera and ballet performances are usually staged in what is Bern's most beautiful theater, the century-old **Stadttheater,** Kornhausplatz 20 (ℂ **031/329-51-11;** www.stadttheaterbern.ch). Performances are often in German and, to a lesser degree, in French, but the language barrier usually won't get in the way of enjoying a performance. The Stadttheater closes for the summer at the beginning of July, reopening in mid-August.

Klötzlikeller, Gerechtigkeitsgasse 62 (© **031/311-74-56;** www.kloetzlikeller. ch), the oldest wine tavern in Bern, is near the Gerechtigkeitsbrunnen (Fountain of Justice), the first fountain you see on your walk from the Bärengraben (Bear Pits) to the Zytgloggeturm (Clock Tower). Watch for the lantern outside an angled cellar door. The well-known tavern dates from 1635 and is leased by the city to an independent operator. Some 20 different wines are sold by the glass; the menu is changed every 6 weeks. In summer, hours are Tuesday to Saturday 4 to 11:30pm, off season Monday to Saturday 4 to 11:30pm.

Marians Jazzroom, Engerstrasse 54 (© **031/309-61-11;** www.marians jazzroom.ch), has its own separate entrance from the Innere Enge Hotel. Unique in Bern, it serves up not only food and drink, but the finest traditional jazz performed live by top artists from around the world. Hours are Tuesday through Thursday 7pm to midnight, Friday 7:30pm to 1am, and Saturday 7pm to 2am. Showtimes are Tuesday through Saturday at 7:30pm and 10pm, and on some Sundays there is a Jazz Brunch from 10am to 1:30pm. Cover ranges from 15F to 50F, depending on the act. Closed from early June to early September.

Come Back Bar, Rathausgasse 43 (© **031/311-77-13;** www.comebackbar.ch), is a tavern that's cosmopolitan and tolerant, and likely to attract lots of genuinely cool artists and hipsters in Bern. It occupies the cellar vaults below the medieval buildings of the Rathausgasse. Inside, blinking lights frame a discreet dance floor and a long bar functions as a local hangout for many of the gay and gay-friendly residents of the Old Town. It's especially crowded on weekends, with a calmer, more low-key approach to things during weeknights. Open Sunday and Monday 6pm to 12:30am, Tuesday through Thursday 6pm to 2am, and Friday and Saturday 6pm to 3:30am.

LAUSANNE ★★★

Lausanne, the second-largest city on Lake Geneva and the fifth-largest city in Switzerland, rises in tiers from the lake. A haunt of international celebrities, Lausanne is 134 miles (216km) southwest of Zurich and is easily reached by rail. Either Lausanne or Geneva (see later) can be your base for exploring Lake Geneva, which the Swiss call Lac Léman.

Many rail passengers even use Lausanne as a base for a day trip to Geneva, as trains connect these two lakeside cities every 10 to 20 minutes (trip time: 35–50 min.). If you're in France and want to visit Switzerland next door, you can also take one of four trains per day (trip time btw. Paris and Lausanne is approx. 4 hr.).

This university city has been inhabited since the Stone Age and was the ancient Roman town of Lousanna. In 1803, it became the 19th canton to join the Confederation and is today the capital of the canton of Vaud.

Ouchy, once a sleepy fishing hamlet, is now the port and hotel resort area of Lausanne. The lakefront of Lausanne consists of shady quays and tropical plants spread across a lakefront district of about half a mile (.8km). The **Château d'Ouchy** stands on place de la Navigation; from here, place du Port adjoins immediately on the east. **Quai de Belgique** and **quai d'Ouchy** are lakefront promenades bursting with greenery and offering the best views of the lake.

Haute Ville, or the Upper Town, is the most ancient part of Lausanne and is best explored on foot (see box below). The Upper and Lower towns are connected by a small Metro, or subway.

Station Information

GETTING FROM THE AIRPORT TO THE TRAIN STATION

Lausanne doesn't have an airport, so most visitors fly to Geneva–Cointrin Airport in Geneva (p. 783) and then travel on to Lausanne. The train from Geneva leaves for Lausanne every 10 to 20 minutes (trip time: about 45 min.). Call © **0900/300-300** for **train** schedules.

In addition, between late May and late September, a lake steamer cruises several times a day in both directions between Geneva and Saint-Gingolph, Lausanne, Vevey, Montreux, and Nyon. Sailing time from Geneva is about 3½ hours. Round-trip transit from Geneva costs 68F in first class, 50F in second class, with 50% discounts for children between 6 and 16; it's free to passholders. For information, contact the **Compagnie Générale de Navigation (CGN),** 17 av. de Rhodanie (© **0848-811-848**).

Lausanne's railway station is a steep 20-minute uphill climb from the ferryboat terminal and recommended only for the enthusiastic and the very fit. More appealing is a 7-minute Metro ride, priced at 2.60F per person, between the stations of **Embarcadère** (immediately adjacent to the ferryboat terminal) and **Gare CFF.**

INSIDE THE STATION

Trains arrive at the **Lausanne Train Station,** place de la Gare (© **0900/300-300**), with arrivals from Basel every 2 hours (trip time: 2¼ hr.) or from Zurich via Biel every hour (trip time: 2¼ hr.).

The **Lausanne Tourist Office** (© **21/613-73-73;** www.lausanne-tourisme.ch) is located in the main hall of the train station and is open daily 9am to 7pm in high season (closes at 6pm off season). The multilingual staff here will make hotel reservations for a 3% commission. They'll also sell you passes to Lausanne's Metro (see "Getting Around," below).

There is also a **currency exchange kiosk** at the station (© **021/312-38-24**), which charges only a 4F commission or else no commission on traveler's checks. If your credit card allows it, the office also makes cash advances during its daily business hours: Monday to Friday 8am to 6:30pm, Saturday 9am to 6pm, and Sunday 10am to 1pm and 3 to 6pm.

Getting Around

To avoid the crawling pace of the city's trams, take the Metro, the city's subway system. The trip between the heart of the Haute Ville and Ouchy takes 6 minutes. Departures are every 6 minutes Monday to Friday from 6:15am to 11:45pm. During off-hours and on weekends and holidays, trains run every 10 minutes. A one-way ride from the town center to Ouchy costs 2.60F; a day ticket (valid from the time of purchase until midnight that day) sells for 7.60F. If you're staying at a hotel or hostel in Lausanne, you'll need to cover only the cost of your initial trip there, as you will receive a Lausanne Transport Card upon check-in. Offered through a special agreement between the city and its hotels, this card entitles you to unlimited travel on the Metro for the duration of your stay.

The **TL (Lausanne Public Transport Company)** has a well-designed network of trams and buses whose routes complement the city's subway line. The tram or bus fare is 2.60F, regardless of the distance, for a single trip completed within 60 minutes on lines 1 to 50 of the TL urban network on the Lausanne-Ouchy Metro.

You can purchase or stamp your tickets at the automatic machines installed at most stops, or just ask the driver. (A surcharge is collected if you get your ticket from the driver at a stop that has a machine.) A 1-day ticket for unlimited rides costs 7.60F for adults, 5.70F for children.

Lausanne has dozens of taxi stands, where you'll usually find a long line of people waiting for a cab. Alternatively, you can telephone **Taxi Services** (*© 0844/814-814*) for a cab. The meter starts at 6.20F; each kilometer traveled adds 3F during daylight hours in town, or 3.80F in town on weekends or at night between 8pm and 6am. For trips outside the town limits, each kilometer traveled costs 5F, regardless of the time of day. Most cab drivers accept credit cards, but ask before you get in the cab, as this is not always the case. For heavy luggage, 1F is charged per suitcase. You may also use the **Fast Baggage service,** which offers same-day luggage delivery between 45 destinations in Switzerland (cost starts at about 19F). Passengers can check in their luggage at the train station no later than 9am and collect it at the final destination from 6pm or later the same day (hours vary, so check before you use the service). For more information on the service and on luggage restrictions, contact **Rail Europe** (*© 888/438-7245* in the United States, *©* 800/361-7245 in Canada; www.raileurope.com).

You can rent bikes at the baggage-forwarding counter of the railroad station (*© 051-225-14-82*). It's open daily from 8am to 7pm. The cost is 33F per day. You can easily bike around the Lower Town—the part that borders the lake is relatively flat—but it isn't recommended in the Upper Town, where the streets are very steep.

Where to Stay

Beau-Rivage Palace ★★★ One of Switzerland's most legendary hotels, this *beaux-arts* luxury property sits directly beside Lac Léman, surrounded by 10 acres (4 hectares) of lush gardens. If you plan on splurging on a hotel room in Switzerland, here's the place to do it. Built in 1861 and enlarged in 1908, the hotel has been frequently renovated, but always with a sense of respect (reverence, even) for its original architecture. It's among the last bastions of formal Europe, attracting *la grande bourgeoisie.* In the tradition of the grand hotels of the early 20th century, rooms come in a wide range of styles. Even the least expensive units have Oriental carpets, a mixture of genuine antiques with convincing reproductions, and private balconies overlooking Lac Léman.

1719 place du Port, CH-1006 Lausanne-Ouchy. *©* **800/223-6800** in the U.S., or 021/613-33-33. Fax 021/613-33-34. www.brp.ch. 169 units. 480F–700F double; 1,185F–1,335F suite. AE, DC, MC, V. Parking 30F. Metro: Ouchy. **Amenities:** 3 restaurants; 2 bars.

Hotel Agora ★ For rail travelers, this hotel is the most convenient base in town, as it's only 900 feet (270m) from the Lausanne train depot. Opened in 1987, the six-story structure brings a futuristic look to old Lausanne—its architecture of sculpted marble has been compared by locals to the facade of a spaceship. The small to mid-size bedrooms are set behind soundproof windows and offer comfortable furnishings and modern plumbing.

9 av. du Rond-Point, CH-1006 Lausanne. *©* **021/555-59-55.** Fax 021/555-59-59. www.fhotels.ch. 82 units. 215F–260F double; 420F junior suite. AE, DC, MC, V. Bus: 1, 3, or 5. **Amenities:** Smoke-free rooms.

Hotel Aulac ✦ This hotel, on the Ouchy lakefront, is housed in a mellow old baroque-styled mansion with a three-story Renaissance-influenced porch. It dates from the turn of the 20th century, as evoked by its mansard roof with tiles and its towering Victorian clock tower. The bedrooms are among the least expensive along the waterfront, although hardly the best. They never rise to more than those found in a low-rent motel, but maintenance is high and the furnishings comfortable.

4 place de la Navigation, CH-1000 Lausanne-Ouchy. © **021/613-15-00.** Fax 021/613-15-15. www.aulac. ch. 84 units. 200F–260F double; 300F suite. Rates include continental breakfast. AE, DC, MC, V. Metro: Ouchy. **Amenities:** Restaurant.

Hotel Continental Across from the Lausanne train station, the Continental competes with the Agora (see above) for the most convenient hotel for passengers arriving by train. Because it's cheaper, the Agora is often fully booked, so the larger Continental is a viable alternative, as it, too, is a contemporary hotel. The accommodations here range from midsize to large, and are well maintained and comfortably furnished with modern pieces, soundproof windows, and tiled bathrooms.

2 place de la Gare, CH-1001 Lausanne. © **021/321-88-00.** Fax 021/321-88-01. www.hotelcontinental.ch. 116 units. 380F double; 550F junior suite. AE, DC, MC, V. Rates include buffet breakfast. **Amenities:** Restaurant; bar; rooms for those w/limited mobility; smoke-free rooms.

Hotel Elite ★ Though located in the center of Lausanne and a short uphill walk from the train station, this white-painted, five-story hotel has a tranquil atmosphere and a small garden with fruit trees. Originally built as a villa in the late 1890s, it was turned into a hotel in 1938 and has been successfully run by the same family ever since. The midsize bedrooms, some with air-conditioning and one with a kitchenette, are clean and neatly furnished. Bathrooms have either a shower, a bath, or both. The best units are those on the fourth floor, as they open onto views of the lake.

1 av. Sainte-Luce, CH-1003 Lausanne. © **021/320-23-61.** Fax 021/320-39-63. www.elite-lausanne.ch. 33 units. 205F–260F double; 375F–425F junior suite. Rates include buffet breakfast. AE, DC, MC, V. Bus: 1, 3, or 5. **Amenities:** Breakfast lounge; all smoke-free rooms.

Minotel AlaGare Taking its name from the nearby train station *(gare)*, this hotel offers affordable and convenient, if basic, accommodations for rail travelers. It's especially inviting in summer, when its window boxes burst into bloom with geraniums. The paneled public rooms lead to a series of small but clean and comfortable bedrooms, each with modern plumbing.

14 rue du Simplon, CH-1006 Lausanne. © **021/617-92-52.** Fax 021/617-92-55. www.alagare.com. 45 units. 165F–250F double. Rates include buffet breakfast. AE, DC, MC, V. Bus: 1, 3, or 5. **Amenities:** Restaurant; smoke-free rooms.

Top Attractions & Special Moments

Château de Beaulieu et Musée de l'Art Brut ★ If you find the bizarre art in this gallery "disturbing," know that it was painted by disturbed individuals. Located on the northwestern side of town, this château dates from 1756 and was once occupied by Madame de Staël. The museum displays what the artist Jean Dubuffet called *art brut* in the 1940s. This curious mélange of artwork was collected by the painter from prisoners, the mentally ill, and the criminally insane. It's a bizarre twilight zone of art, often dubbed "psychopathological," especially the art by schizophrenics. Dubuffet despised the pretentiousness of the avant-garde art scene around him and, as a form of protest, decided to begin this collection of the works of "nonartists," many of whom he found superior to the more established artists of his day.

11 av. des Bergières. © **021/315-25-70.** www.artbrut.ch. Admission 10F adults, 5F seniors and students, children 15 and under free. Free admission first Sat of each month. Tues–Sun 11am–6pm. Bus: 2 to Beaulieu.

Lausanne's Upper Town, or **Haute Ville ★★**, still evokes the Middle Ages—a night watchman even calls out the hours from 10pm to 2am from atop the cathedral's belfry. Walking through the old town of Lausanne is one of its major attractions and the best way to absorb the medieval atmosphere. It's easy to get lost—and that's part of the fun. If you don't want to be so carefree, you can also take an organized walking tour (see below). This area is north of the railroad station; you can reach it by strolling along rue du Petit-Chêne.

The focal point of the Upper Town, and the shopping and business heart of Lausanne, is **place Saint-François.** The Church of St. François, from the 13th century, is all that remains of an old Franciscan friary. Today the square is regrettably filled with office blocks and the main post office. While vehicles are permitted south of the church, the area to the north is a pedestrian-only zone; it has more than 1¼ miles (2km) of streets, including **rue de Bourg,** northeast of the church, the best street for shopping. Rue de Bourg leads to the large, bustling rue Caroline, which winds north to **Pont des Bessières,** one of the three bridges erected to connect the three hills on which Lausanne was built. From the bridge, you'll see the Haute Ville on your right, with the 13th-century

Cathedral of Lausanne, opening onto place de la Cathédrale. From the square, rue du Cité-de-Vant goes north to the 14th-century **Château Saint-Marie,** on place du Château—once the home of bishops and now housing the offices of the canton administration.

From here, avenue de l'Université leads to **place de la Riponne,** with the **Palais de Rumine** on its east side. From place de la Riponne, rue Pierre-Viret leads to the **Escaliers du Marché,** a covered stairway dating from the Middle Ages. You can also take rue Madeleine from the place de la Riponne, continuing south to place de la Palud. On the side of place de la Palud stands the 17th-century **Hôtel de Ville** (town hall).

South of place de la Palud is rue du Pont, which turns into rue Saint-François (after crossing rue Centrale). Nearby, at **place du Flon,** you can catch the subway to Ouchy. In recent years, place du Flon, with its cafes and bars, has become a favorite evening hangout.

Lausanne's civic authorities conduct a **guided walking tour** of their city, lasting 1 to 2 hours, Monday to Saturday May to September. Departure is from place de la Palud, adjacent to the city hall, at 10am and 2:30pm. The cost is 10F for adults, 5F for seniors. Students and children are free. For reservations, call ✆ **021/320-12-61.**

Lausanne Cathédrale ★★★   The focal point of the Upper Town is one of the finest medieval churches in Switzerland—in fact, one of the most beautiful Gothic structures in Europe, standing 500 feet (152m) above Lake Geneva. Construction began in 1175; in 1275, the church was consecrated by Pope Gregory X. The doors and facade of the cathedral are luxuriously ornamented with sculptures and bas-reliefs. The architect Eugène Viollet-le-Duc began a restoration of the cathedral in the 19th century—and it's still ongoing. The interior is relatively austere except for some 13th-century choir stalls; the rose window also dates from the 13th century. The cathedral has two towers; you can climb the 225 steps to the observation deck of one of the towers.

Place de la Cathédrale. ✆**021/316-71-61.** Free admission cathedral; tower 2F adults, 1F children 12 and under. Apr–Sept Mon–Sat 7am–7pm, Sun 8am–7pm; Oct–Mar Mon–Sat 7am–6pm, Sun 8am–6pm. Visits not permitted Sun morning during services. Bus: 7 or 16.

Where to Dine

À la Pomme de Pin ★★TRADITIONAL FRENCH/SWISS   Our favorite restaurant in Lausanne's old town lies within a 17th-century setting between the back side of the cathedral and the château. There are actually two restaurants here, including a brasserie with leather banquettes and a more expensive and formal restaurant, where prices are at least 25% higher and the cuisine is more elaborate and "gastronomic" than in its cheaper counterpart. Main courses in the brasserie are likely to include filet of fera (a whitefish from the nearby lake) prepared with white wine, parsley, and tomatoes. Main courses in the restaurant include rack of Emmenthaler Valley veal with a mousseline of potatoes and foie gras.

11 rue Cité Derrière. ✆**021/323-46-56.** Reservations recommended. In the brasserie, main courses 19F–32F; in the restaurant, main courses 28F–58F. AE, DC, MC, V. Mon, Tues, Thurs–Fri 8am–midnight; Wed 8am–3pm; Sat 6pm–midnight. Closed late July and Aug.

Buffet de la Gare CFFSWISS/FRENCH   Surprising as it may seem, one of the town's best inexpensive restaurants is inside the Lausanne railway station itself, and frugal city dwellers often come here for a good brasserie dinner. This is not a rail station fast-food joint, but an informal restaurant offering well-prepared dishes cooked to order and made from market-fresh ingredients. There is both a brasserie section for more casual dining (it's more fun) and a more formal restaurant area (more sedate), although the prices and the kitchens are the same.

In the train station, 11 place de la Gare. ✆**021/311-49-00.** www.buffetdelagare.ch. Reservations recommended in the restaurant only. Main courses 16F–40F. MC, V. Restaurant daily 7am–9pm; brasserie daily 5pm–midnight. Bus: 1, 3, or 5.

Le Jardin d'Asie ★PAN-ASIAN   This is the best Pan-Asian restaurant in the city, drawing heavily from the culinary influences of both Japan and China, but also including some zesty Malaysian specialties for greater variety. The atmosphere appropriately evokes a garden setting, and the widely spaced tables allow for private conversations. Servers stylishly present sushi, sashimi, and many specialties such as chicken in peanut sauce to a satisfied clientele. There are also uniformed teppanyaki chefs standing by, knives at the ready, to prepare your dinner in front of you.

7 av. du Théâtre. ✆**021/323-74-84.** www.jardindasie.ch. Reservations recommended. Main courses 15F–38F; fixed-price Chinese menu 42F–75F; fixed-price Japanese menu 45F–80F. AE, DC, MC, V. Mon–Sat noon–2pm and 7–10pm; Sun only 7–10pm. Bus: 7 or 16.

Pur CONTINENTAL   Catering to the young, the restless, and the emotionally available, this restaurant and bar is a popular meeting place among Lausanne's 20- and 30-somethings and counterculture crowd. At least some of its atmosphere of openness results from long communal tables, illuminated by night with candles artfully arranged in candelabras. There's an impressive list of cocktails and a winning selection of wines from around Europe, each sold by the glass, which taste especially good when accompanied by menu items that seem designed to be shared. Examples include a *panna cotta* of foie gras with port-flavored cream sauce, cabbage rolls with enoki mushrooms and satay (peanut) sauce, and roasted strips of duck with truffled potato slices and stewed eggplant. Be warned, however, that if you miss mealtime at this place by even as much as a minute or two, the staff will have already made a stampede to shut down the kitchens, and no amount of coaxing will prompt them to bring out any food.

17, Port-Franc (Place de l'Europe). © **021/311-99-33.** www.pur-flon.ch. Main courses 18F–44F. AE, DC, MC, V. Mon–Thurs 8am–midnight; Fri 8am–2am; Sat 9am–2am; Sun 9am–midnight. Bus: 7 or 16.

Shopping

Shoppers in Lausanne tend to be much more concerned with the commercialized glamour of Paris than with kitschy mountain souvenirs. That being the case, you'll find lots of emphasis on high-profile outfits such as luggage and leather maker **Louis Vuitton,** 30 rue de Bourg (© **021/312-76-60**), or haute jeweler **Cartier,** 6 rue de Bourg (© **021/320-55-44**). But if handmade souvenirs from the region appeal to you, head for **Heidi's Shop,** 22 rue du Petit-Chêne (© **021/311-16-89**).

The biggest jeweler in Lausanne, with a well-established international recommendation, is **Bucherer,** rue de Bourg 1 (© **021/312-36-12;** www.bucherer.ch). Competitors, especially for Swiss watches, include **Junod,** 8 place St-François (© **021/312-27-45;** www.junod-lausanne.ch), carrying Blancpain watches, among others.

Nightlife

A good way to spend an evening in Lausanne is by hanging out in any of the cafes and bars ringing the **Espace Flon,** a cluster of restaurants and shops at place Flon. Lots of hideaways, frequented by strollers of all ages, will be here to tempt you, but one of the most appealing is **Le Grand Café,** allée Ernest-Ansermet 3 (© **021/320-40-30**), inside the Casino of Lausanne. Here, in an American-inspired space that contains some of the glitz and razzle-dazzle of a celebrity haunt, you can meet a cross-section of virtually every night owl in town.

Attractive and popular discos include **Mad,** rue de Genève 23 (© **021/340-69-69**), where the fads and preoccupations of nocturnal Paris filter quickly in from the west via an under-30 crowd. **Ouchy White Horse Pub,** 66 av. d'Ouchy (© **021/616-75-75;** www.whitehorse.ch), draws the crowds at night who in summer enjoy the terrace with views of the water. There's beer on tap, and a range of tapas and burgers are sold. It's the most authentic pub atmosphere in town.

Lausanne is also a city of culture. With Geneva, it shares the Orchestre de la Suisse Romande and also occasionally hosts the legendary ballet company of Maurice Béjart. For information on what's happening during the time of your visit, contact the local tourist office (discussed earlier). Most performances of major cultural impact take place at the **Théâtre–Municipal Lausanne,** avenue du Theatre (© **021/310-16-00;** www.opera-lausanne.ch). **Beaulieu,** at 10 av. des Bergières (© **021/643-22-11;** www.theatredebeaulieu.ch), is also a venue for dance concerts, operas, and orchestral music presentations. For more information, call the Théâtre–Municipal Lausanne.

GENEVA ★★★

Switzerland's second-largest city, French-speaking Geneva is situated at the lower end of Lake Geneva, aka Lac Léman. Located on the Rhône at the extreme western tip of Switzerland, but right in the heart of Europe, Geneva is at the crossroads of the Continent. Often deemed the "most international of cities" because of all the international organizations (such as the Red Cross) that have their headquarters in the city, Geneva is linked to the outside world by a vast network of airlines and railways, and is an ultraconvenient stop on any rail passenger's itinerary.

In addition to enjoying good rail connections to all of Switzerland, Geneva receives five trains (all of them requiring at least one connection) per day from Vienna (trip time: 10–12 hr.) and four direct trains per day from Milan (trip time: 4 hr.). The city is also the terminal point for the Paris–Geneva train, seven of which arrive daily in the city after a journey of about 3½ hours. Geneva also rivals Lausanne (see earlier) as the best base for exploring Lake Geneva.

A lively, cosmopolitan atmosphere prevails in Geneva, a city of parks and promenades. In summer it becomes a virtual garden. It's also one of the healthiest cities in the world—the north wind blows away any pollution. The situation, in a word, is magnificent, not only lying on one of the biggest Alpine lakes, but within view of the pinnacle of Mont Blanc.

Geneva is virtually surrounded by French territory. It's connected to Switzerland only by the lake and a narrow corridor. For that and other reasons—the city was actually unwillingly annexed by France in 1798 before being set free during Napoléon's collapse in 1814—Geneva is definitely a Swiss city, but with a decided French accent.

Station Information
GETTING FROM THE AIRPORT TO THE TRAIN STATION
The **Geneva-Cointrin Airport** (✆ 022/717-71-11; www.gva.ch), although busy, is quite compact and easily negotiated. The national airline, **Swiss** (✆ 877/359-79-47; www.swiss.com), serves Geneva more frequently than any other airline. Other international airlines that partner with North American–based airlines and fly into Geneva include **Air France** (✆ 800/237-2747), with seven flights daily from Paris; and **British Airways** (✆ 800/217-9297), with seven daily flights from London.

You can easily get to the center of Geneva from the airport by rail. Trains leave from the airport terminal about every 10 to 30 minutes from 5:12am to 12:12am for the 6-minute trip to **Gare Cornavin,** the main train station. The one-way fare is 3F, but if you're arriving by plane, you can pick up a free ticket at the luggage station. Railpasses cover this line, though you may not want to waste a day on a pass for such a short and inexpensive trip.

A taxi into town will cost 45F and up, or you can take bus no. 5 or 10 for 3F.

Note: From late May to late September, there are frequent daily arrivals in Geneva by Swiss lake steamers from Montreux, Vevey, and Lausanne (you can use a railpass for the trip). If you're staying in the Left Bank (Old Town), get off at the Jardin Anglais stop in Geneva; Mont Blanc and Pâquis are the two Right Bank stops. For more information, call ✆ 0848/811-848. To get to the Jardin Anglais stop from the railway station, take bus no. 8, getting off (both stops are appropriate) at either the Quai du Mont-Blanc stop or the Metropole stop. If you prefer to go on foot, the walk from the railway station to the quays will take only 5 to 10 minutes.

INSIDE THE STATION
Geneva's **CFF (Chemins de Fer Fédéraux)** train station in the town center is **Gare Cornavin,** place Cornavin (✆ 0900/300-300 for ticket information), which is a major international and local hub.

Geneva

ACCOMMODATIONS ■
Best Western Strasbourg & Univers **9**
Hôtel Bernina **8**
Hôtel Edelweiss **26**
Hôtel International & Terminus **7**
Hôtel Lido **12**
Hôtel Moderne **11**

DINING ◆
Brasserie Lipp **13**
Café du Centre **20**
Chez Ma Cousine **10**
La Favola **19**
Le Sumo Yakitori **6**
Windows **27**

ATTRACTIONS ●
Brunswick Monument **25**
Cathédrale de Saint-Pierre **15**
Flower Clock **23**
Hôtel-de-Ville **17**
Ile Rousseau **21**
Jardin Anglais **22**
Jardin Botanique **3**
Jet d'Eau **28**
La Perle du Lac **4**
Maison Tavel **18**
Mouettes Genevoises Navigation **24**
Musée d'Art et d'Histoire (Museum of Art and History) **14**
Musée de l'Ariana **1**
Palais des Nations **2**
Parc Mon-Repos **5**
Temple de l'Auditoire **16**

Basel ● Zurich

Bern ✦

SWITZERLAND

Geneva ●

Lac Léman
(Lake Geneva)

1/4 mi

0.25 km

ⓘ Information

Quai Cologny

Rampe de Cologny

Route de Vandœuvres

Place de
Traînant

FRONTENEX

Plateau de Frontenex

Quai Gustave Ador

**PARC DES
EAUX-VIVES**

Route de Frontenex

Chemin Frank Thomas

**PARC
LA GRANGE**

Av. Rosemont

Avenue W. Favre

MONTCHOISY

Woodrow Wilson

Rue Plantamour

Jacquet

Rade de
Genève

26 ❽ 27

Rue des Eaux-Vives

Rue de Montchoisy

Rue de Vollandes

**Gare des
Eaux-Vives**

❽ 28

Quai Gustave Ador

rue du 31 Décembre

Route de Frontenex

Route de Chêne

Ch. de la Petite Boissière

Promenade Martin

25

Sq. du
Mont-
Blanc

Quai du Mont-Blanc

LES EAUX-VIVES

R. de la Marie

Av. de l'Amandolier

24

**Pont du-
Mont-Blanc**

**JARDIN
ANGLAIS**

R. F-Versonnex

Av. Pictet De Rochemont

Rue Agasse

21

**ILE
ROUSSEAU**

22 23

Place des
Eaux-Vives

**Pont des
Bergues**

Quai Général Guisan

**RIVE
GAUCHE**

Rue de la Terassière

Place du
Rhône

Rue du Rhône

20

R. De Rive

Cours de Rive

rd.-pt
de Rive

RUES BASSES

R. de la
Croix-d'Or

R. Lachenal

R. de la
Confédération

R. du
Marché

19

R. De Rive

13

15

Rue Hodler

Pl. Em.
Guyenot

Route de Malagnou

**VIELLE VILLE
(OLD TOWN)**

18

R. de la Fontaine

R. Jacques Dalcroze

14

Ch. Galland

Chemin Rieu

la Corraterie

17

16

Grand Rue

R. de l'Hôtel-
de-Ville

Place
du
Bourg-
de-
Four

Bd. Helvétique

Bd. des Tranchées

FLORISSANT

**Place
Neuve**

**Hôtel de
Ville**

R. de la Croix Rouge

Rue de l'Athénée

Route de Florissant

Dufour

Promenade
des Bastions

Cours des Bastions

Rue de l'Athénée

**PARC
A. BERTRAND**

Favon

Université

R. de Candolle

R. St. Léger

Place Ed.
Claparède

Avenue Bertrand

Avenue Peschier

**PLAINE DE
PLAINPALAIS**

Rd.-pt. de
Plainpalais

Bd. des Philosophes

Rue A. Lombard

Avenue de Champel

Avenue Louis Aubert

du Mail

R. Henri Dunant

R. de
Carouge

Boulevard du Pont d'Arve

R. Prévost-
Martin

Rue Bd. de la Cluse

CHAMPEL

Avenue de Miremont

LA CLUSE

The city's tourist office maintains a free direct phone line to most Geneva hotels at the station, with a digital board listing accommodations available. For comprehensive service and general information, however, you'll need to head for the main tourist office (see below).

Also on-site is a luggage storage kiosk, open Monday to Friday 7am to 7:30pm, Saturday and Sunday 8am to 12:30pm and 1:30 to 6:45pm, which charges 9F per day. You may also send your luggage on to your next destination using the **Fast Baggage service** (p. 778). The locker area charges from 4F to 7F and is open daily 4:30am to 12:45am. There are also several ATMs at the station.

Public transportation is readily available right outside the train station.

Information Elsewhere in the City

A 5-minute walk from the rail station, Geneva's tourist office, the **Office du Tourisme de Genève,** is located at 18 rue du Mont-Blanc (© **022/909-70-00;** www.genevetourisme.ch). The staff provides information about the city and can also arrange hotel reservations, both in Geneva and throughout Switzerland, and refer you to other establishments specializing in tour bookings. They can also give you details about audio-guided visits to the city's Old Town. The tourist office is open year-round Monday from 10am to 6pm, Tuesday through Saturday from 9am to 6pm, and Sunday from 10am to 4pm.

Getting Around

Walking is the cheapest and most practical form of transportation within Geneva, and it's also the most advantageous method for the rail traveler to view this beautiful city. That said, there will be times you'll need to get someplace a little more quickly than a leisurely stroll will allow, and the city has a couple of transportation methods to choose from.

BY PUBLIC TRANSPORTATION Most of Geneva's public tram and bus lines begin at the central place Cornavin in front of the main railroad station. From here, you can take bus F or 8 to the Palais des Nations. Local buses and trams operate daily from 5am to midnight, and you can purchase a ticket from a vending machine before you board; instructions are given in English. **Transport Publics Genevois** (© **0900/022-021;** www.unireso.com), next to the tourist office in Gare Cornavin, offers free maps of local bus routings. Trips that stay within zone 10, enveloping most of Geneva, cost 3F, with unlimited use of all zones costing 10F for 1 day. The latter is particularly useful, as most of the city's noteworthy attractions are in the suburbs.

BY TAXI The meter on whatever cab you take in Geneva will automatically begin calculating your fare at 7F, and then add between 3F and 3.80F for every kilometer you travel, depending on the time of day or night. No tipping is required. To summon a **taxi,** call © **022/331-41-33** or 022/320-20-20.

Where to Stay

Best Western Strasbourg & Univers ★ A 2-minute walk from Gare Cornavin, this is one of Geneva's best moderately priced hotels. The building itself dates from 1900 but has been renovated and modernized over the years. Bedrooms range from large (on the lower floors) to a bit cramped. Rooms are comfortably furnished with a lot of wood pieces and have decent tiled bathrooms. The hotel is run by a local family and doesn't have the feel of a chain hotel, despite its affiliation with Best Western.

10 rue J-J-Pradier, CH-1201 Genève. ℰ**800/780-7234** in the U.S. and Canada, or 022/906-58-00. Fax 022/906-58-14. www.bestwestern.com. 51 units. 250F–270F double; 500F suite. Rates include a buffet breakfast. AE, DC, MC, V. Bus: 1, 2, 3, 4, 8, 12, 13, or 44. **Amenities:** Breakfast lounge.

Hotel Bernina Rail passengers often check in here because of the convenience of its location across from Gare Cornavin and its reasonable prices (considered inexpensive in this costly town). Although guests get clean, comfortably furnished bedrooms under high ceilings, they don't enjoy a lot of style, as the place is rather sterile, especially the lobby, which evokes a dull airport waiting room. The soundproof windows, however, are welcome in this heavily congested part of Geneva.

22 place de Cornavin, CH-1211 Genève. ℰ**022/908-49-50.** Fax 022/908-49-51. www.bernina-geneve. ch. 80 units. 250F–350F double. Rates include breakfast. AE, DC, MC, V. Bus: 10.

Hotel Edelweiss This hotel enjoys a scenic location near quai du President-Wilson, one of the most scenic quays of Geneva, and is about a half-mile (.8km) from Gare Cornavin. Built in the 1960s, it was upgraded and renovated in the '90s and is a winning choice for its blend of rustic alpine decor, modern exterior, and completely up-to-date amenities. Most of the bedrooms are small and rather functionally furnished, but they are well kept and comfortable. The friendly staff greets guests in traditional costumes.

2 place de la Navigation, CH-1201 Genève. ℰ**022/544-51-51.** Fax 022/544-51-99. www.manotel.com. 42 units. 220F–420F double. AE, DC, MC, V. Bus: 1. **Amenities:** Restaurant; bar.

Hotel International & Terminus This hotel, originally built in 1900, is a winning choice for rail travelers, as it's just across the street from the main entrance to Gare Cornavin. Maintenance in the spacious accommodations is high (it completed major renovations in the summer of 2010), windows are double-glazed, and the furnishings are comfortable and modern—though the bathrooms are rather cramped. The hotel's **La Veranda** restaurant is frequently patronized by rail travelers tired of the train depot's fast-food outlets.

20 rue des Alpes, CH-1201 Genève. ℰ **022/906-97-77.** Fax 022/906-97-78. www.international-terminus.ch. 60 units. 160F–280F double. Rates include buffet breakfast. AE, DC, MC, V. Bus: 6, 10, or 33. **Amenities:** Restaurant.

Hotel Lido Only 2 blocks from Gare Cornavin, this hotel dates from 1963 and has never overcome the architectural dullness of that era. Nonetheless, the hotel is convenient for train travelers and charges reasonable rates for its basic bedrooms. Furnishings are functional—not stylish—but there is comfort and cleanliness here, along with full bathrooms. Expect very few amenities, however, especially in the rooms, although they are soundproof.

8 rue Chantepoulet, CH-1201, Genève. ℰ **022/731-55-30.** Fax 022/731-65-01. www.hotel-lido.ch. 31 units. 160F–190F double. Rates include continental breakfast. AE, DC, MC, V. Bus: 10. **Amenities:** Breakfast room.

Hotel Moderne One of many acceptable choices near Gare Cornavin, this seven-story hotel is within easy walk of the quays. The hotel's public areas are Nordic style and modern. Behind soundproof windows, the midsize bedrooms are sunny and furnished in a standard but comfortable manner. The small bathrooms are spotless and have either a shower or a tub. Breakfast is served in a glassed-in extension.

1 rue de Berne, CH-1211 Genève. ℰ **022/732-81-00.** Fax 022/738-26-58. www.hotelmoderne.ch. 55 units. 215F double. Rates include buffet breakfast. AE, DC, MC, V. Bus: 10. **Amenities:** 2 restaurants; smoke-free rooms.

Top Attractions & Special Moments

If you arrive in Geneva in summer, begin your tour of the city by heading east from the rail station along rue du Mont-Blanc until you arrive at quai du Mont Blanc, and begin a long promenade along the **Quays of Geneva ★★★**. The one sight you can't miss—even if you tried—is the **Jet d'Eau ★★**, the famous fountain that is the trademark of the city and is located on a concrete platform in the middle of the lake. Visible for miles around from April to September, it throws water 460 feet (138m) into the air above the lake. The *bise* (wind) blows the spume into a feathery, fluttery fan, often wetting those below who stand too close. The Genevese call the fountain the *jeddo*. It dates from 1891 but was much improved in 1951. The engineering behind the fountain used to be a secret, until Saudi Arabia managed to acquire it. It pumps 109 gallons of lake water at 125 mph (201kmph).

The quays, with their luxuriantly planted flower gardens, are dotted with ancient buildings. The aquatic population consists of seagulls, ducks, and swans. A fleet of small boats, called ***Mouettes genevoises*** (**© 022/732-29-44;** www.mouettes genevoises.ch), shuttles visitors from one quay to another every 10 minutes between 7:30am and 7:30pm. Rides are free with a public transit pass, Eurail Pass, or Swiss Pass; otherwise, rides that last 30 minutes or less cost 2F adults and 1.80F children, and rides lasting 30 to 60 minutes cost 3F adults and 2.20F children.

Like the water jet, the **Flower Clock** in the **Jardin Anglais (English Garden)** is another Geneva trademark. Its face is made of flowers, and it keeps perfect time (what else would you expect in this world-famed center of watchmaking?). The Jardin Anglais is at the foot of the Mont Blanc Bridge, which spans the river at the point where the Rhône leaves Lake Geneva. It was rebuilt in 1969. To get here from the Jet d'Eau, stroll south on quai Gustave-Ador and then bear right.

After leaving the garden, cross the Mont Blanc bridge and turn left onto the quai des Bergues, and stroll as far as the bridge, Pont des Bergues. If you cross this bridge, you'll come to **Ile Rousseau,** with a statue of Geneva's most famous son done by Pradier in 1834. This island, the former stamping ground of the philosopher, is home to any number of ducks, swans, and other aquatic fowl such as grebes. In the middle of the Rhône, it was once a bulwark of Geneva's river defenses.

You can continue crossing the bridge and can then turn right on the Bezanson Hugues quay until you reach rue de Moulins and the **Tour-de-l'Ile,** farther downstream. Built in 1219, a château that once stood here was used as a prison by the

 A Lakeside City of Parks & Gardens

If you head north along rue de Lausanne from Gare Cornavin, you'll arrive at some of the lushest parks in Geneva. **Parc Mon-Repos ★★** is off avenue de France, and La Perle du Lac is off rue de Lausanne. Directly to the right is the **Jardin Botanique (Botanical Garden),** which was established in 1902. It has an Alpine garden, a little zoo, greenhouses, and exhibitions, and can be visited for free from April to October daily from 8am to 7:30pm and November to March daily from 9:30am to 5pm.

If you leave the **Jardin Botanique** on the Left Bank, you can head west, along avenue de la Paix, to the Palais des Nations in the **Parc de l'Ariana**. It's located about a mile (1.6km) north of Gare Cornavin.

counts of Savoy. A wall plaque commemorates the visit of Caesar in 58 B.C. The tower is all that remains of the 13th-century castle. It was here that freedom fighter Philibert Berthelier was decapitated in 1519. Nowadays, the Geneva Tourist Office is located on the island. You can also explore the old markets, where there are often exhibitions of the works of contemporary Genevese artists.

If you walk east along the quai des Bergues, you'll return to the Pont du Mont-Blanc. To your left, when facing the lake, is the **Brunswick Monument,** the tomb of Charles II of Brunswick, who died in Geneva in 1873. The duke left his fortune to the city, provided it built a monument to him. Geneva accepted the cash and modeled the tomb after the Scalieri tombs in Verona, Italy.

VIEILLE VILLE ★★★

"Old Town" in Geneva is one of the most remarkable in Switzerland and has been called Europe's best-kept secret. It's situated on the city's Left Bank, where the cultural life of Geneva flourishes. Its ancient streets are home to art galleries, antiques shops, booksellers, and tiny bistros. Follow the Grand'Rue, about ¾ mile (1.2km) from Gare Cornavin, where Jean-Jacques Rousseau was born at 40 Grand'Rue, and wander back in time.

The old quarter is dominated by the **Cathedral of St. Pierre ★,** Cour St-Pierre (℡ **022/311-75-75;** www.saintpierre-geneve.ch), originally built between the 10th and 13th centuries and partially reconstructed in the 15th century. The church looks out over Geneva from its hilltop perch. It became Protestant in 1536. The interior is austere, just the way Calvin preferred it (his seat is on the north side). The church has seen much recent renovation, and it has a modern organ with 6,000 pipes. If you don't mind the 157 steps, you can climb to the north tower for a splendid vista of the city, its lake, the Alps, and the Jura mountains.

Recent excavations have disclosed that a Christian sanctuary was located here as early as A.D. 400. To enter the St. Pierre archaeological site, called **Site Archéologique de St-Pierre** (www.site-archeologique.ch), go through the entrance in Cour St-Pierre, at the right-hand corner of the cathedral steps. The underground passageway extends under the present cathedral and the High Gothic (early-15th-c.) **Chapelle des Macchabées,** which adjoins the southwestern corner of the church. The chapel was restored during World War II, after having been used as a storage room following the Reformation. Excavations of the chapel have revealed baptisteries, a crypt, the foundations of several cathedrals, the bishop's palace, 4th-century mosaics, sculptures, and geological strata.

The cathedral and the chapel are open June to September Monday to Saturday from 9:30am to 6:30pm and Sunday noon to 6:30pm, October to May Monday to Saturday 10am to 5:30pm and Sunday noon to 5:30pm. There is no admission charge to visit the cathedral, although donations are welcome; tower admission is 4F for adults, 2F for children ages 7 to 16, free for children 6 and under. Sunday service is held in the cathedral at 10am, and an hour of free organ music is presented on Saturdays at 6pm from June to September. The archaeological site is open Tuesday to Saturday from 10am to 5pm; the admission charge is 8F adults, 4F students and seniors. Take bus no. 3, 5, or 17, or tram 12.

Next door to the cathedral is a Gothic church where Calvin preached, known as the **Temple de l'Auditoire,** or Calvin Auditorium. It was restored in 1959 in time for Calvin's 450th anniversary.

After leaving the cathedral, strike out across the Cour St-Pierre, turning left onto the rue St-Pierre, where at no. 4 you'll encounter **Maison Tavel,** 6 rue du Puits-St-Pierre (✆ **022/418-37-00**), the oldest house in Geneva. First built in 1303, according to dim records, it was apparently rebuilt in 1334. It's decorated with amusing carved heads and a fine turret, and has a 12th-century cellar, which predates the original building. It's open Tuesday to Sunday 10am to 6pm; admission is free. Temporary exhibits cost 3F for adults and 2F 18 and under.

Hôtel de Ville (city hall), a short walk from the cathedral, dates from the 16th and 17th centuries. It has a cobbled ramp instead of a staircase. The **Salle d'Alabama** is the salon where arbitration between America and England in 1872 (over England's support of the Confederacy during the American Civil War) was peacefully resolved. Its Baudet Tower was constructed in 1455. Incidentally, the Red Cross originated here in 1864.

Across from the city hall is the **Arsenal,** an arcaded structure dating from 1634. In the courtyard of the building is a cannon cast in 1683.

OTHER ATTRACTIONS

Musée d'Art et Histoire (Museum of Art & History) ★★   If you can visit only one museum while in Geneva, make it this one, the city's most important. The collections offer a little bit of everything and include prehistoric relics, Egyptian relics, Greek vases, medieval stained glass, 12th-century armory, and many paintings of the Flemish and Italian schools. The Etruscan pottery is impressive, as is the medieval furniture. See the altarpiece by Konrad Witz from 1444, showing the "miraculous" draught of fishes. Swiss timepieces are duly honored, and many galleries contain works by such world-famous artists as Rodin, Renoir, Hodler, Vallotton, Le Corbusier, and Picasso.

2 rue Charles-Galland (btw. bd. Jacques-Dalcroze and bd. Helvétique). ✆**022/418-26-00.** www.ville-ge.ch/mah/?langue=eng. Free admission; temporary exhibitions 5F adults, 3F for children. Tues–Sun 10am–5pm. Bus: 1, 3, 5, 8, or 17.

Musée de l'Ariana ★★   This is one of the top three museums devoted to porcelain and pottery in Europe, and the headquarters for the international academy of ceramics. Located west of the Palais des Nations, the museum building is in the Italian Renaissance style and was built in 1877 for P. F. Revilliod, the 19th-century Genevese writer who began the collection. Here you'll see Sèvres at its best, along with the celebrated Delft faïence, Meissen porcelain, and many superb pieces from Japan and China.

10 av. de la Paix. ✆**022/418-54-50.** www.ville-ge.ch/mah/index.php?content=8. Free admission permanent collection; temporary exhibitions 5F adults, 3F students, free for children 17 and under. Wed-Mon 10am–5pm. Bus: 8 or F.

Palais des Nations ★★   The former home of the defunct League of Nations, about a mile (1.6km) north of Mont Blanc Bridge, is the present headquarters of the United Nations in Europe. The monumental compound was constructed between 1929 and 1936, and the complex of buildings is the second largest in Europe after Versailles. Tours, conducted in English, last about an hour and depart from the visitors' entrance at 14 av. de la Paix, opposite the Red Cross building. To join the tour, you'll need to show your passport. The highlight of the tour is the Assembly Hall, with a balcony made entirely of marble and lofty bays looking out over the Court of Honor. A Philatelic Museum displays collections of stamps relating to the League of Nations or the United Nations, and a League of Nations Museum documents the history of the precursor to the United Nations.

SAILING THE WATERS OF Lac Léman

More interesting than the monuments of Geneva itself is a sail across Lake Geneva (Lac Léman). You'll enjoy sweeping waterside views of the surrounding hills, and some of the most famous vineyards in Switzerland, many of which seem to roll down to the historic waters. Because of bad weather and low visibility in winter, cruises run only between April and late October and, in some cases, only between May and September.

Mouettes Genevoises Navigation, 8 quai du Mont-Blanc (© **022/732-47-47;** www.swissboat.com), specializes in small-scale boats carrying only 100 passengers at a time. An easy excursion that features the landscapes and bird life along the uppermost regions of the river Rhône draining into the lake is the company's **Tour du Rhône (Rhône River Tour).** The trip originates at a point adjacent to Geneva's Pont de l'Ile and travels downstream for about 9 miles (14km; 2 hr., 45 min.) to the Barrage de Verbois (Verbois Dam) and back.

Between May 1 and September 30, tours depart Wednesday through Sunday at 2:15pm, and also on Wednesday, Thursday, Saturday, and Sunday at 10am. In April and October, tours depart on Wednesday, Saturday, and Sunday at 2:15pm only. The tour costs 25F for adults and 18F for children 4 to 12; it's free for children under 4. The same company also offers 1¼-hour tours (four times a day) out onto the lake. These tours cost 15F for adults and 9F for children. No stops are made en route.

Parc de l'Ariana, 14 av. de la Paix. © **022/917-48-96.** www.unog.ch. Admission 10F adults, 8F students and seniors, 5F for children, free for 5 and under. July–Aug daily 10am–5pm; Sept–Mar Mon–Fri 10am-noon and 2–4pm; Apr–June daily 10am–noon and 2–4pm. Bus: 5, 8, 18, F, V, or Z.

Where to Dine

Brasserie Lipp FRENCH/SWISS   Named after the most famous brasserie on the Left Bank of Paris, this restaurant serves a similar type of cuisine, specializing in fresh oysters—the best in the city—and large platters of sauerkraut. When you see the waiters in long white aprons and black jackets, you'll think you've been miraculously transported over the border. That impression is reinforced when the actual food is served, including all our favorite classics, such as a Toulousian cassoulet and three kinds of pot-au-feu.

In Confédération-Centre, 8 rue de la Confédération. © **022/311-10-11.** www.brasserie-lipp.com. Reservations recommended. Main courses 37F–50F; *plats du jour* 19F–37F lunch only; fixed-price menus 65F–84F. AE, DC, MC, V. Daily noon–midnight. Bus: 2, 7, 12, or 16.

Café du Centre CONTINENTAL/SWISS   Established in 1871, this is still the busiest cafe in Geneva, with an outdoor terrace that's always packed in fair weather. The atmosphere inside evokes a time-blackened brasserie in Old Lyon. The menu (it comes in English) is the largest in town, with nearly 140 different items offered every day. Carnivores will be especially happy with the tender and well-flavored meat platters (the best and most tender cut is called *onglet*).

5 place du Molard. © **022/311-85-86.** www.cafeducentre.ch. Reservations recommended. Main courses 27F–78F; fixed-price *assiette du jour* 19F at lunch Mon–Fri only. AE, DC, MC, V. Mon 6am–midnight; Tues–Fri 6am–1am; Sat 9am–10pm; Sun 9am–midnight. Tram: 12.

Chez Ma Cousine 🍴 FRENCH/SWISS What you'll find here is an amiable but stringently unpretentious venue of spartan-looking wooden tables and chairs, and an open kitchen. Despite a very limited menu, the place does a roaring business. A free salad accompanies most main courses, and the only option for potatoes is "Provençal style." Platters include several variations of grilled chicken, the house specialty.

5 rue Lissignol. 🕾 **022/731-98-98.** www.chezmacousine.ch. Reservations unnecessary. Main courses 14F–18F. Mon–Fri 6:30am–2:30pm and 6:30–11:30pm. Bus: 1.

La Favola ★ TUSCAN/ITALIAN The habitués of the finest Italian restaurant in the city, just a few steps from the Cathedral of St. Pierre, complain only that it doesn't serve on weekends. This family-run restaurant is warm and inviting, its tables placed in two cramped—and always packed—rooms, through which waiters scurry back and forth while carrying heaping platters of food. The seasonal menu is small and deliberately limited, to ensure fresh ingredients. Look for such delightful dishes as carpaccio of beef; lobster salad; and a luscious version of tortellini stuffed with ricotta, meat juices, red wine, and herbs. Don't even think of coming here without making reservations well in advance.

15 rue Jean-Calvin. 🕾 **022/311-74-37.** www.lafavola.com. Reservations required. Main courses 20F–60F. AE, MC, V. Mon–Fri noon–2pm and 7–10pm. Closed 2 weeks in July–Aug and 1 week at Christmas. Tram: 12.

Le Sumo Yakitori ★ 🍴 JAPANESE This is a dining oddity that's well known to many cost-conscious residents of Geneva, and almost always overlooked by foreign tourists, most of whom might find the culinary format of this tiny place baffling. The fact that it doesn't serve sushi or sashimi, coupled with its claustrophobic dimensions (it seats only 22 diners at a time) and open galley-sized kitchen makes it unusual. You'll be happiest if you ask lots of questions of the English-speaking Japanese staff at this place before you order. Menu items include marinated and roasted quail, grilled shrimp, Bali-style jasmine rice, and all-vegetarian versions of grilled eggplant with garlic sauce.

15 rue Monthoux. 🕾 **022/731-19-50.** Reservations not accepted. Brochettes 2F–5F each, platters 10F–17F. Fixed-price menus 35F–50F. AE, MC, V. Wed–Sat 7–10:30pm. Bus: 1.

Windows ★ CONTINENTAL Flooded with sunlight from large panoramic windows, and permeated with an undeniably upscale but discreet sense of old-fashioned exclusivity, this charming restaurant attracts a clientele of politicians, film industry personnel, writers, and the merely rich. Menu items change with the seasons, but you might find orange-marinated chicken cutlets with a yogurt-flavored avocado sauce and bulgur wheat; or roasted *omble chevalier*, a whitefish from the nearby lake, served with a reduction of carrot juice and a passion fruit–flavored butter sauce.

In the Hotel Angleterre, 17 quai du Mont-Blanc. 🕾 **022/906-55-14.** www.dangleterrehotel.com/dining/restaurant. Reservations recommended. Main courses 51F–74F. AE, DC, MC, V. Daily noon–2pm and 7–10pm. Bus: 1.

Shopping

Geneva practically invented the wristwatch. In fact, watchmaking in the city dates from the 16th century. Be sure to avoid purchasing a Swiss watch in one of the souvenir stores; legitimate jewelers will display a symbol of the Geneva Association of Watchmakers and Jewelers. Here, more than in any other Swiss city perhaps, you should be able to find all the best brands, including Vacheron & Constantin,

Longines, Omega, and Blancpain, to name just a few. Most salespeople you'll encounter speak English and are very helpful.

A shopping spree might begin at **place du Molard,** once the harbor of Geneva before the water receded. Merchants from all over Europe used to bring their wares to trade fairs here in the days before merchants immigrated to richer markets in Lyon.

If you walk along rue du Rhône and are put off by the prices, go 1 block south to rue du Marché, which in various sections becomes rue de la Croix-d'Or and rue de Rive, and is sometimes referred to by locals as "la rue du Tram" because of the many trolleys that run along its length. Comparison shopping is the way to go in Geneva— many stores jack up prices for visitors.

Store hours vary. Most are open Monday to Friday from 8am to 6:30pm and Saturday from 8am to 5pm. For one-stop shopping, head for one of the big department stores, such as **Bon Genie,** 34 rue du Marché (✆ **022/818-11-11;** www.bongenie-grieder.ch/#/home), located on place du Molard. This department store sells mostly high-fashion women's clothing. Its storefront windows display art objects from local museums alongside designer clothes. There's also a limited selection of men's clothing, as well as furniture, cosmetics, and perfumes. **Globus-Grand Passage,** 48 rue du Rhône (✆ **022/319-50-50**), is one of the largest department stores in Geneva, with many boutique-style departments and a self-image that's firmly patterned after the Galeries Lafayette in Paris. Expect glamour and lots of upbeat cheerfulness.

Bucherer, 45 rue du Rhône (✆ **022/319-62-66;** www.bucherer.com), located opposite the Mont Blanc Bridge, is a chrome-and-crystal store selling deluxe watches and diamonds. The store offers such name brands as Rolex, Piaget, Ebel, Baume & Mercier, Omega, Tissot, Rado, and Swatch. The carpeted third floor is filled with relatively inexpensive watches. You'll also find a large selection of cuckoo clocks, music boxes, embroideries, and souvenirs, as well as porcelain pillboxes and other gift items.

Gübelin Jewelers, 1 place du Molard (✆ **022/310-86-55;** www.guebelin.ch), dates from 1854. This family-run establishment is known mainly for its brand-name watches, although it also sells beautiful precious stones and jewelry. You can also buy reasonably priced gifts, such as pen and pencil sets.

Nightlife

Geneva has more nightlife than any other city in French-speaking Switzerland. Most activity centers around **place du Bourg-de-Four,** which used to be a stagecoach stop during the 19th century and is located in the Old Town. Here you'll find a host of outdoor cafes in the summer.

Geneva has always attracted the culturally sophisticated, including Byron, Jean-Baptiste, Corot, Victor Hugo, Balzac, George Sand, and Franz Liszt. Ernst Ansermet founded Geneva's great **Orchestre de la Suisse Romande** (www.osr.ch), whose frequent concerts entertain music lovers at **Victoria Hall,** 14 rue du Générale-Dufour (✆ **022/418-62-45;** www.ville-ge.ch/culture/victoria_hall). For opera, there's the 1,500-seat **Grand Théâtre,** 5 place Neuve (✆ **022/418-30-00;** www.geneveopera.ch), which welcomes Béjart, the Bolshoi, and other ballet companies, in addition to having a company of its own. For a preview of events at the time of your visit, pick up a copy of the monthly *List of Events* issued by the tourist office.

Au Chat Noir, 13 rue Vautier (✆ **022/307-10-40**), is easy to reach by tram 12 from place Bel-Air. The club lies in the suburb of Carouge and is the best spot for funk, rock, salsa, jazz, and some good old New Orleans blues. Live music is presented from September through May Wednesday and Thursday at 9pm, and Friday and Saturday at 10pm. The cover ranges from 16F to 20F.

Scandale, 24 rue de Lausanne (© **022/731-83-73;** www.lescandale.ch), attracts the young, the restless, and the rebellious 20- and 30-somethings of Geneva to a wholesale rejection of the glittering sense of posh that prevails within more upscale neighborhoods beside the city's lakefront. There's an elongated bar where you're likely to meet hipsters from all over Europe and the Middle East, and a blend of house and electro-jazz music that keeps everybody hopping. Don't even ask about the gender preferences of the clientele here—everyone seems way beyond even attempting an easy and pat self-definition.

If you're barhopping, drop in at **Mr. Pickwick Pub,** 80 rue de Lausanne (© **022/731-67-97;** www.mrpickwick.ch), which also serves British food. Mostly patrons come here to drink and converse, listen to American or British music, or enjoy an Irish coffee. The best piano bar at night is **Le Francis,** 8 bd. Helvetique (© **022/346-32-52;** www.lefrancis.ch), which is an elegant place for a rendezvous, with live music Tuesday through Friday beginning at 10pm (restaurant and night club open seven nights a week).

SWITZERLAND'S FAMOUS SCENIC RAIL LINES ★★★

Switzerland offers not only Europe's most dramatic Alpine scenery but also eight of the greatest train rides in the world. If you take one or all of these train trips, be assured that they will be among the most memorable of your life. All of the trains below can be booked through **Rail Europe** (© **888/438-7245** in the United States, © 800/361-7245 in Canada; www.raileurope.com) or your travel agent.

GLACIER EXPRESS   One of the most evocative trains in the country, the **Glacier Express** (www.glacierexpress.ch) connects two fabled ski resorts—St. Moritz in the east and Zermatt in the west—while passing through the resorts of Chur, Andermatt, and Brig. On the 7½-hour trip, your train will pass through 91 tunnels and cross 291 bridges, peaking at 6,669 feet (2,001m) at the towering Oberalp Pass. There is no more memorable way to travel across the Alpine heartland of the country, past mountain lakes, vast forests, and cow-filled pastures. *Note:* Glacier Express trains do not run from late October through mid-December.

The Swiss Pass covers the full ride, while the Eurail Global Pass offers a discount. Prices start at $221 one-way in first class or $133 in second class. Seat reservations are required (book as soon as they become available—90 days prior!) and cost an additional 33F in the summer or 13F in the winter. If you begin your trip in Zermatt, you can reach the resort by rail from Geneva in just 4 hours; otherwise, tack on an additional 3½ hours for the trip from Zurich to St. Moritz.

BERNINA EXPRESS   Another dramatic ride is the **Bernina Express** (www.rhb. ch), a 2½-hour trip from St. Moritz through a lunar landscape of Ice Age glaciers and stone-studded fields and pastureland to the palms and foliage of Tirano in Italy. All cars on this train (run by the Rhäetische Bahn Authority) have panoramic windows so you won't miss the views. The ride may be short, but you won't soon forget the breathtaking scenery passing by your window as you go through wild gorges, across towering bridges, and into foreboding loop tunnels, moving past dozens upon dozens of snowcapped glaciers. At the rail junction in Tirano, a bus will take you on the 3-hour journey to Lugano (Apr to late Oct only), one of the finest lake resorts of Switzerland's Italian-speaking Ticino district. *Note:* Although we recommend you pick up the Bernina Express in St. Moritz, it actually starts off in Chur.

A one-way fare from St. Moritz to Lugano, including the bus fare, is 74F in first class or 55F in second class; the trip is covered by the Eurail Global Pass and the Swiss Pass. Seat reservations on both the train and bus are required and cost an additional $24 when made through Rail Europe. St. Moritz is a 3½-hour train ride from Zurich. For more information on the Bernina Express, head online to **www.rhb.ch**.

CENTOVALLI RAILWAY   The **Centovalli Railway** (www.centovalli.ch) offers one of the most dramatic train rides in Ticino, the Italian-speaking part of Switzerland in the south of the country bordering Italy. Running through the region's scenic "Hundred Valleys," the railway links Locarno (one of the country's most popular resorts) with the town of Domodossola in northern Italy, on the southern side of the Alps at the foot of the Simplon Pass.

The 2-hour trip features the lush, wonderful countryside of southern Switzerland, filled with mountain landscapes, flowering meadows, and magnificent forests.

No reservations are required. The trip is covered by the Eurail Global Pass and the Swiss Pass; otherwise, prices start at 66F in first class or 40F in second class. Locarno, the starting point of the trip, is about a 3-hour train ride from Zurich. For more information, check online at **www.centovalli.ch**.

GOLDEN PASS LINE   The **Golden Pass Line** (www.goldenpass.ch) is the natural and panoramic route linking Central Switzerland with Lake Geneva, and because it features some of the country's greatest lakes and evocative mountain scenery, the line is often called "Switzerland in a Nutshell." The train ride covers 149 miles (240km), from the shores of Lake Lucerne and over the Brünig Pass to the chic resort of Montreux on Lake Geneva. Three trains run along various legs of the route, and to cover the entire route, you'll need to change trains twice (track variances prevent a single train from running the entire length of the route). The **Zentralbahn** runs from Lucerne to Interlaken, the **BLS** from Interlaken to Zweisimmen, and the **GoldenPass Panoramic–MOB** from Zweisimmen to Montreux.

Reservations are recommended for each leg of the trip (they cost 5F per leg), though if you plan on traveling the whole route, you can get them for 17F for the whole stretch from Montreux to Interlaken Ost at any Swiss train station or online at **www.goldenpass.ch**. If you buy in advance from Rail Europe, it will cost you $18 per leg. The trip is covered by the Eurail Global Pass and the Swiss Pass; otherwise, the cost for a round-trip ticket for all three legs is 228F in first class or 138F in second class. To start your run in Lucerne, take a 50-minute train to the city out of Zurich. For more schedules and information on this railway line, see **www.goldenpass.ch** and **www.mob.ch**.

CHOCOLATE TRAIN   A real novelty is the so-called **"Chocolate Train,"** which offers luxurious first-class travel in vintage Belle Epoque 1915 Pullman cars or modern panoramic cars from May through October (and only on Mon, Wed, and Thurs in Apr, May, Sept, and Oct). You depart from Montreux on Lake Geneva for the medieval city of Gruyères, where you are given time to tour the city's castle and famous cheese factory. Then it's back on the train and off to the Cailler-Nestlé chocolate factory in Broc, where you're given a tour and a tasting of some of the factory's delicious chocolate before reboarding your train and returning to Montreux. Along the way,

Switzerland's Famous Scenic Rail Lines

your train will pass stunning views of Lake Geneva vineyards and other beautiful landscapes. Complimentary croissants and coffee are served on the train.

A first-class Swiss Pass or Eurail Global Pass covers the train ride and all entrance fees; passholders can obtain the mandatory seat reservations for $40 on the train's website at **www.goldenpass.ch/goldenpass_chocolate_train** or at **www.rail europe.com**. Those without passes can buy a ticket online or at any Swiss train station for 89F in first class, 59F in second class. The round-trip train ride, including stopovers, takes more than 8 hours to complete, and there's only one train per day. Montreux, the starting point of the trip, is a 1-hour train ride from Geneva. For more information on the train, see **www.goldenpass.ch/goldenpass_chocolate_train**.

WILLIAM TELL EXPRESS   The **William Tell Express** links the German-speaking part of the Switzerland with the Italian-speaking Ticino region. Your trip begins in Lucerne when you board a historic paddle-steamer for a 3-hour cruise of Lake Lucerne and a first-rate meal. At the little town of Fluelen, you'll abandon ship and board a panoramic train that runs through towering cliffs and steep ravines of the Reuss Valley, including passage through the Gotthard Tunnel—a historic railway tunnel that is Europe's most important north-south gateway. After passing a number of old-fashioned Swiss villages, the train plunges south into the valleys that open onto the lakeside resort of Locarno (passengers bound for Lugano change at Bellinzona to a regional train).

The journey takes just over 5 hours. The trip is free for holders of the Swiss Pass; holders of a Eurail Pass will receive 50% off of the boat fare, though reservations are required and cost $40 (which includes your meal on the boat and a souvenir). A regular one-way passage (most rail travelers don't do the round-trip) for the journey from Lucerne to Lugano costs $130 in first class or $82 in second class. To get to the starting point in Lucerne, take a 50-minute train out of Zurich. You can do the trip in reverse direction as well.

MOUNT PILATUS COG RAILWAY   One of the most stunning mountain rail journeys in Switzerland is the **Mt. Pilatus Cog Railway** (www.raileurope.com), located about 9 miles (14km) south of Lucerne, a city only a 50-minute train ride from Zurich. The regular round-trip fare on the cog railways is 62F. The Swiss Pass and the Eurail Global Pass offer a 25% discount on the regular fare.

Between May and mid-November, weather permitting, the cog railway operates between Alpnachstad, at the edge of the lake, and the very top of Mount Pilatus. From the quays of Lucerne, take a lake steamer for a scenic 90-minute boat ride to Alpnachstad. If you have a railpass, you will get a 50% discount on the steamer fare.

At Alpnachstad, transfer to the electric cog railway, which runs at a 48% gradient—the steepest cogwheel railway in the world. Departures are every 45 minutes daily from 8:15am to dusk May to November only (trip time: 45 min.). At Pilatus-Kulm, you can get out and enjoy the view. There are two mountain hotels and a belvedere offering views of Lake Lucerne and many of the mountains around it. For the descent from Mount Pilatus, some visitors prefer to take a pair of cable cars that terminate at Kriens, a suburb of Lucerne. Here you can take bus no. 1 (covered by the Swiss Pass), which will carry you into the heart of Lucerne. If you opt to go down by the cable cars, the round-trip fare on the cog railway and cable cars is 64F. Eurail passholders get a 30% reduction on the cable cars.

A similar excursion to Pilatus is possible in the winter, but because the cog railway is buried in snow, you must alter your plans. You'll have to ascend and descend by cable car, which many visitors find exhilarating. From the train station at Lucerne, take bus no. 1 to the outlying suburb of Kriens. At Kriens, transfer to a cable car that glides over meadows and forests to the village of Fräkmüntegg, 4,600 feet (1,380m) above sea level. The trip takes half an hour. At Fräkmüntegg, switch to another cable car, this one much more steeply inclined than the first. A stunning feat of advanced engineering, it swings above gorges and cliffs to the very peak of Mount Pilatus (Pilatus-Kulm). Unlike the cog railways, these cable cars operate year-round. The round-trip ride by cable car from Kriens to Fräkmüntegg costs 36F.

JUNGFRAUJOCH   A train trip from Interlaken to **Jungfraujoch,** at an elevation of 11,333 feet (3,400m), is the most dramatic rail journey in Switzerland. For more than a century, it's been the highest railway station in Europe. It's also one of the most expensive: A ticket costs $177 in first class or $166 in second class. Holders of Swiss and Eurail passes are granted a 25% discount; Swiss Card holders get a 50% discount. Note that families with Swiss Pass or Card can fill out a Family Card form, available at the railway station, which allows children 16 and under to ride free. For more information, see **www.raileurope.com.**

Take a train from either **Zurich** (2 hr.) or **Geneva** (3 hr.) to get to Interlaken's East Station (you'll need to transfer in Bern in both directions), and then allow 2 hours and 20 minutes for the journey from Interlaken to the Jungfraujoch. To check times, contact the sales office of **Jungfrau Railways** (© **033/828-72-33;** www.jungfrau bahn.ch).

The trip is comfortable, safe, and packed with adventure. First you'll take the **Wengernalp railway (WAB),** a rack railway that opened in 1893. It will take you to Lauterbrunnen, at 2,612 feet (784m), where you'll change to a train heading for the Kleine Scheidegg station, at 6,762 feet (2,029m)—welcome to avalanche country. The view includes the Mönch, the Eiger Wall, and the Jungfrau, which was named for the white-clad Augustinian nuns of medieval Interlaken (Jungfrau means "virgin").

At Kleine Scheidegg, you'll change to the highest rack railway in Europe, the **Jung-fraubahn.** You have 6 miles (9.6km) to go; 4 miles (6.4km) of them will be spent in a tunnel carved into the mountain. You'll stop briefly twice, at **Eigerwand** and **Eis-meer,** where you can view the sea of ice from windows in the rock (the Eigerwand is at 9,400 ft./2,820m, and Eismeer is at 10,368 ft./3,110m). When the train emerges from the tunnel, the daylight is momentarily blinding, so bring a pair of sunglasses to help your eyes adjust. Notorious among mountain climbers, the Eigernordwand (or "north wall") is incredibly steep.

Once at the Jungfraujoch terminus, you may feel a little giddy until you get used to the air. There's much to do in this eerie world up in the sky, but take it slow—your body's metabolism will be affected and you may tire quickly.

Behind the post office is an elevator that will take you to a corridor leading to the famed **Eispalast (Ice Palace).** Here you'll be walking inside "eternal ice" in caverns hewn out of the slowest-moving section of the glacier. Cut 65 feet (20m) below the glacier's surface, these caverns were begun in 1934 by a Swiss guide and subsequently enlarged and embellished with additional sculptures by others. Everything in here is made of ice, including full-size replicas of vintage automobiles and local chaplains.

After returning to the train station, you can take the Sphinx Tunnel to another eleva-tor. This one takes you up 356 feet (107m) to an observation deck called the **Sphinx Terraces,** overlooking the saddle between the Mönch and Jungfrau peaks. You can also see the **Aletsch Glacier,** a 14-mile (23km) river of ice—the longest in Europe. The snow melts into Lake Geneva and eventually flows into the Mediterranean.

Have a meal in one of the five **restaurants** at the top of the peak. As a final adventure, you can take a **sleigh ride,** pulled by stout huskies.

On your way back down the mountain, you'll return to Kleine Scheidegg station, but you can vary your route by going through **Grindelwald,** which offers panoramic views of the treacherous north wall.

Note: A new ice railway that ascends up to 13,000 feet (3,960m) will open in 2012 as part of the celebrations for the centenary of the Jungfraujoch. Also opening will be an additional restaurant, a hiking trail along the Eiger that will lead to a museum focusing on climbing, and a new historical exhibit. For up-to-date information on all the additions, check out **www.jungfrau.ch**.

EASTERN EUROPE, GREECE & THE BALKANS

T
hough this book covers the primary rail destinations of Europe, there are a number of other European countries, primarily in Eastern Europe, where change is always in the air and today's rail traveler can see history in the making.

From the Baltic to the Black Sea, the nations of Eastern Europe stretch across one of the most diverse regions on earth. Freed from the Soviet umbrella, the last in a line of 2 millennia of conquerors, these nations have changed their politics and identities—or have been created from scratch—since the epochal year of 1989. You'll be treated to some remarkable attractions, as every country or region is completely different.

The nations of Eastern Europe are a land of great culture, folklore, and attractions, both man-made and natural. Expect stunning landscapes, a fascinating but turbulent history, and some of the friendliest people in Europe, as you travel from the snowcapped Tatra Mountains of Poland to the wide beaches of the Bulgarian Black Sea coast. Not only that, but you'll encounter prices a lot cheaper than in the West. On the downside, trains in these countries can be unpredictable, slow, less safe, and a whole lot less comfortable than rail service in Western Europe.

BULGARIA

Occupying the eastern half of the Balkan Peninsula, Bulgaria is a land of great beauty, from its Black Sea coast to its villages still somewhat living in the Middle Ages, from its rugged and mountainous interior to its fertile Danube plains, from its fishing villages to its Roman ruins and lush valleys. At the crossroads of Europe, it's naturally had a violent history. Its recent past has been blighted by its record as the closest ally of the former Soviet Union, but today it turns toward Western Europe, embracing capitalism and democracy and welcoming visitors to come see what Bulgaria is all about.

Not as touristy as its neighbors Greece and Turkey (with the notable exception of the Black Sea coast), Bulgaria today is a bulwark of Balkan culture, a country existing for 13 centuries with impressive mosques, rustic villages, flamboyantly decorated churches, and an enduring folklore, the latter a holdover from the days when the country fancied itself a "guardian" of Balkan Christian tradition.

Its climate is continental, meaning long, hot, and dry summers, when everybody who can afford it races toward the cooling Black Sea coast, followed by bitterly cold winters, which are a less than ideal time to travel. The only travelers who brave Bulgaria's winters are skiers attracted to Bulgaria's major ski resorts, which generally offer plenty of snow from mid-December to mid-April and feature improving but not yet world-class facilities like those found in Austria and Switzerland. Visitors not at the beach in summer can be found hiking along 22,991 miles (37,016km) of marked trails, many cutting through virgin national parks and pristine nature reserves.

Bulgaria by Rail

PASSES

Rail Europe offers the **European East Pass,** which covers Bulgaria; see chapter 2 for more on this pass. See below for details on the **Balkan Flexipass,** which covers not only Bulgaria but other countries as well.

PRACTICAL TRAIN INFORMATION

The country's main rail operator, **Bulgarian State Railways** (**BDZ;** http://bdz. creato.biz), oversees a network of some 2,658 miles (4,279km) of track, fanning out to all parts of the country. Buses are generally quicker and more common, but riding the rails is more comfortable and offers far more panoramic views.

Train travel is cheap by Western standards, and nearly all cities, towns, and resorts are accessible by rail (though traveling up or down the seacoast is possible only by bus, boat, or car). Facilities and standards, however, lag behind the West, except for **InterCity Express** trains running between Sofia, Varna, and Burgas. There are three types of trains: express, called *ekspresen;* fast moving, known as *bârz;* and, to be avoided, in our view, the snail-like *pâtnicheski,* or slow-moving vehicles, that stop at every cow pasture. Slow trains are made even slower because of the often mountainous terrain.

InterCity trains are about the only vehicles that are stocked with a buffet car, so you may need to bring along your own food and water on some runs. ***Note:*** Reservations are mandatory on all express trains. A reservation is called *zapazeno myasto* in Bulgarian.

It's not always easy to find a national rail timetable on the ground, and even if you do, don't count on its accuracy. Timetables are written sloppily—unusually in Cyrillic—on a paper hastily pasted to the window of the ticket office. If you're close to a computer, BDZ has a good online route planner on its website (**http://bdz.creato. biz**).

Trains that run long distances at night offer a couchette and/or a sleeper, which are most affordable and far cheaper than a hotel (though, admittedly, far less comfortable than their Western counterparts). Reservations for these accommodations must be made at least 2 days in advance, and possibly earlier in heavily booked July and August.

A daily train runs between Istanbul, Turkey, and Bucharest, Romania, crossing year-round through a slice of Bulgaria. The **Balkan Express** also travels between Sofia and Belgrade. The **Rila International Travel Agency** (see below) maintains an online timetable of international routes on its website, at **www.bdz-rila.com**.

Eastern European Rail Routes

The main train station for rail information—and for the purchase of tickets—is **Tsentralna Gara (Central Station)**, in Sofia, at Maria Luiza 112 (✆ **02/931-11-11**), which is your point of arrival for most international trains. Tickets are also sold and information dispensed at **Rila International Travel Agency,** General Gurko 5 (✆ **02/987-07-77;** www.bdz-rila.com), in Sofia. The same service is provided in the center of Sofia at the **Natzionalen Dvoretz na Kulturata (National Palace of Culture),** 1 Bulgaria Sq. (✆ **02/865-71-86;** www.ndk.bg).

Highlights of Bulgaria

Culturally and historically rich, **Sofia ★**, the capital of Bulgaria, is ripe for discovery. If you overlook its occasionally dreary Soviet-era architecture, you'll find Roman churches, Ottoman and Byzantine mosques, superb ballet and opera, varied restaurants, and even an exciting nightlife with enough bars and dance clubs to satisfy a New Yorker. Is a new "Prague" waiting to be discovered by hipsters?

Sitting on a 1,788-foot (536m) plateau, at the foot of Mount Vitosha, Sofia is the highest capital in Europe with a population of around 1.2 million. For centuries the center of trans-European routes, Sofia sits midway between the Black Sea and the Adriatic. The hub of Bulgaria's rail network, Sofia deserves at least 2 days of your time.

The major attraction is **Hram-pametnik Alexander Nevski (Alexander Nevski Memorial Cathedral)** ★★, Ploshtad Alexander Nevski (© **02/987-76-97**), a neo-Byzantine structure with glittering interlocking domes, constructed at the dawn of the 20th century. Try to visit the crypt, which is filled with a stunning collection of icons.

The other noteworthy house of worship is **Tsentralna Sofiiska Sinagoga (Central Sofia Synagogue)** ★, 16 Ul. Ekzarh Yosif at Bul. Washington (© **02/983-12-73**), in a beautifully restored 1909 synagogue celebrated for its Moorish turrets and gilt domes. It's dedicated to the Russians who fell liberating Bulgaria from the Ottoman Empire.

Among the city's 10 or so other top attractions, the most notable is **Natzionalen Archeologicheski Musei (National Archaeological Museum)** ★, Ploshtad Alexander Batenberg (© **02/988-24-06**), housed in a former Great Mosque and filled with artifacts of the country's cultural history—notably the gold treasure of **Vulchi Trun** ★★, a masterpiece of Thracian workmanship on 13 vessels of gold.

In summer, most visitors make a dash for the country's Black Sea resorts (the sea is actually a brilliant blue with sandy beaches), centered on the ancient city of **Varna** ★, 282 miles (454km) east of Sofia and 7 hours away by train. Cosmopolitan and cultivated, it is the third-largest city of Bulgaria and is known for its parks, gardens, wide tree-lined boulevards, and a beachfront boardwalk.

Another great Bulgarian city is **Plovdiv** ★, 104 miles (167km) southeast of Sophia on the main route from the capital city to the Turkish border. Skip the tacky environs and head at once to the heart of the old city, with some of Bulgaria's most romantic National Revival architecture from the 18th and 19th centuries. Spend a day here wandering its cobblestone streets free of cars. Some of its museums are rich in Thracian artifacts from as far back as 4000 B.C. Plovdiv is 2½ hours by train from Sofia.

If time remains, try to visit one of the most stunning cities in the Balkans—**Veliko Târnovo ★★**, 144 miles (232km) northeast of Sofia. This was the capital of the Second Bulgarian Kingdom from the 12th to the 14th centuries, when it was hailed as "a second Constantinople." Known as the City of the Czars, it's a virtual museum city with panoramic vistas at every turn. The ruined fortress of **Tsarevets** was once a royal palace and cathedral, and in summer the most spectacular sound-and-light show in Bulgaria takes place here. Take the train from Sofia toward Varna and change at the town of Gorna-Orjahovitza. Trip time from Sofia is roughly 5½ hours.

For More Information

Tourism information is found at the **Bulgarian Tourism Authority,** 1 Sveta Nedelia Sq. Sofia (𝒞 **02/933-58-45;** www.bulgariatravel.org), open Monday to Friday 9am to 5:30pm. Another source of information is the **Bulgarian Tourist Chamber,** 8 Sveta Sofia (𝒞 **02/987-40-59;** www.btch.org), in Sofia.

CROATIA

For decades, Croatia's gorgeous Adriatic seacoast drew tens of thousands of holiday-makers each year from around Eastern Europe. The stark beauty of the Venice-inspired coastal resorts, the clean sand and rock beaches, and the crystal clear water made the then-Yugoslav republic a kind of open secret among those in the know. Just as Croatia declared its independence in 1992 and was about to go international, however, the Yugoslav wars of the 1990s practically destroyed the tourism industry altogether.

Now with more than a decade of peace, the coastal resorts have made a big come-back and are more popular than ever. Altogether, there are around 1,110 miles (1,787km) of pristine coastline and an astounding 1,000 islands, of which around 60 are inhabited year-round. The medieval stone city of Dubrovnik (which was partially damaged in the war) has been completely renovated and spiffed up. This is the main attraction along the coast, which also includes a string of holiday islands and the city of Split. Beachgoers descend en masse from mid-May to late September, when the country's beaches are ideal for swimming.

Wherever you go, fresh seafood will be found on the menu. Of course, as a Balkan nation, Croatia naturally offers such old favorites as spit-roasted lamb and other grilled meats.

 Your Pass to Exotic Countries

A trail of ancient cities, mosques, and natural wonders can be made most affordable through a **Balkan Flexipass,** granting you unlimited travel through Bulgaria, Greece (but there are currently no international connections to and from Greece), Macedonia, Romania, Turkey, and Serbia/Montenegro. You can travel for 5, 10, or 15 days within a 1-month period, with prices starting at $256. Travel is in first class only, and there are special fares for passengers under 26 or more than 60 years of age. The Balkan Flexipass is available through **Rail Europe** (𝒞 **888/438-7245** in the United States, 𝒞 **800/361-7245** in Canada; www.raileurope.com) and most travel agents.

In addition to the long coastline, the country's capital and transportation hub, Zagreb, merits a visit for a sprinkling of historical sites and its exciting, cosmopolitan feel. Zagreb is the country's road and rail hub and is usually the starting point for most tours.

Croatia by Rail

PASSES

For information on the Eurail Select Pass, see chapter 2. The **Eurail Austria–Croatia–Slovenia Pass** offers 4 to 10 days of unlimited first-class travel in Austria, Slovenia, and Croatia within a 2-month period. Passes start at $269 for adults; children ages 4 to 11 get a discounted rate, and kids under 4 travel free. Longer passes are also available.

Another option is the **Eurail Croatia–Slovenia Hungary Pass,** which offers anywhere from 5 to 10 days of unlimited first-class travel in Hungary, Slovenia, and Croatia within a 2-month period. Prices start at $249, and children 4 to 11 get a discounted rate.

Both passes should be purchased through either Rail Europe or a travel agent before leaving North America.

PRACTICAL TRAIN INFORMATION

Croatian Railways, Mihanovićeva 12, 10000 Zagreb (✆ **01/3782-532**), is the main state rail operator. The company oversees a mostly dilapidated system of track and rolling stock, though recent years have brought some improvements. Most notably, these include faster travel times from the capital, Zagreb, to the coastal resorts along the Adriatic. Travel time between Zagreb and Split, for example, has been cut down to around 6 hours now, when the journey previously took something like 9 hours.

Rail Europe represents the Croatian railway system through its sales and information network. For more information, contact Rail Europe (✆ **888/438-7245** in the United States, ✆ 800/361-7245 in Canada; www.raileurope.com).

Although Croatia's train network is slow (buses are the preferred option for most locals), international connections are fine and much more comfortable than buses. Tickets are cheaper here than in most other parts of Europe, so if you're planning on traveling only within Croatia, you won't get much value for your railpass.

There are three types of trains: fast-moving ones, called *ubrazni*; locals, known as *putnicki*; and first-class-only trains, called *poslovni*. The first-class trains of Croatia are capacity controlled, with a rudimentary system of seat reservations that limit the number of passengers so that no one will be without a seat, although that luxury doesn't apply to the *ubrazni* and the *putnicki* trains mentioned above. The word for arrivals is *dolazak,* and departures are *odlazak* or *polazak*. A transfer is known as *presjedanje.*

It might be difficult to lay your hands on a hard (printed) copy of a Croatian timetable, even within Croatia, and even that may not always be accurate. Croatian Railways posts a helpful electronic version on their website at **www.hznet.hr** (you may have to poke around the site a bit to find the English version).

The main train station for rail information—and for the purchase of tickets—is the recently renovated **Zagreb Glavni kolodvor** in Zagreb, at Trg kralja Tomislava 12, which is also your point of arrival for most international trains. There are eight other major train stations around the country: **Željeznički kolodvor Knin,** Trg Ante

Starčevića 2; **Željeznički kolodvor Metković,** Andrije Hebranga bb; **Željeznički kolodvor Ploče,** Trg Tomislava 19; **Željeznički kolodvor Šibenik,** Fra Jerolima Milete 24; **Željeznički kolodvor Split,** Zlodrina polijano 20; **Željeznički kolodvor Zadar,** Ante Starčevića 3; **Željeznički kolodvor Pula,** Kolodvorska 5; and **Željeznički kolodvor Rijeka,** Trg Kralja Tomislava 1. For train information once you are in Croatia, call ✆ **060/333-444.**

Highlights of Croatia

The capital of Croatia, the history-rich city of **Zagreb,** lies on the fringe of the Pannonian plain on the Sava River. For most of its centuries of existence, it consisted of two separate towns—one on the high ground and secular, the other religious. These two towns, Kaptol and Gradec, were finally joined in 1850. The population today hovers around 780,000, almost 52,000 of whom are enrolled at the University of Zagreb.

A major attraction is **Hrvatski Povijesni Muzej (Croatian History Museum),** 9 Matoševa (✆ **01/4851-900;** www.hismus.hr). Located in the 18th-century Baroque palace, Vojković-Oršić-Rauch, and the old site of the National Museum, this place now houses more than 140,000 artifacts dating from the Middle Ages. The collection includes fine art, firearms, flags and uniforms, everyday objects, religious artifacts, and a plethora of other relics.

The city's other noteworthy museum is **The Archaeological Museum,** 19 Nikola Subic Zrinski Sq. (✆ **01/487-3101;** www.amz.hr). Permanent exhibits here include extensive collections from the prehistoric era and ancient Egypt. There is also a **Numismatic collection** that draws many visitors. The museum itself is beautiful and worth the price of admission.

Among the city's 10 or so other top attractions, the most notable is **Hrvatsko Narodno Kazalište u Zagrebu (Croatian National Theater in Zagreb),** Trg Marsala Tita 15 (✆ **01/488-8418;** www.hnk.hr), which was opened in 1895 by Emperor Franz Joseph I. Today it is the cultural epicenter of Zagreb and the site of ballet, musicals, comedies, dramas, contemporary dance, and opera performances. Ticket prices are reasonable.

In summer, most visitors make a dash for **Dubrovnik ★★★,** 243 miles (391km) southeast of Zagreb in southern Dalmatia. People refer to this beautiful part of the Adriatic coast as "The New Riviera . . . but cheaper." On a visit here in 1929, George Bernard Shaw explained: "If you want to see heaven on earth, come to Dubrovnik." With its white pebble beaches, craggy shoreline, and pristine sea, today's visitors are finally seeing what Shaw meant. There is no connection to the rail network in Dubrovnik, so your best bet is to take a train to Split and the bus or ferry to Dubrovnik (bus trip time: 1 hr., 20 min.).

Another great city of Croatia is **Split ★,** 156 miles (251km) south of Zagreb, and reached by a scenic train ride (trip time: 5½ hr.) that is a virtual preview of Croatia in its entirety. Set against a backdrop of crystal-clear waters, dense forests, and barren

19

EASTERN EUROPE, GREECE & THE BALKANS

Croatia

mountains, Split, founded in the 3rd century A.D., is the second-most-populous city in Croatia. Thanks to its vibrant cafe life and beach scene, it is still more of a cultural center than a resort.

The city's attractions can easily fill 2 busy days of your vacation. Chief among these is **Diocletian's Palace (Obala Hrvatskog Norodnog Preporoda) ★★**. These ruins are all that remain of the palace that Roman Emperor Diocletian built at the end of the 3rd century on the Bay of Aspalathos. He spent the last 2 years of his life here, following his abdication in A.D. 305. Much altered over the centuries, the remains combine the quality of a luxurious villa with those of a military camp.

Other attractions include the **Cathedral of St. Dominius Peristil,** whose main site is a 3rd-century octagonal mausoleum built as a shrine to Emperor Diocletian. Its 200-foot (60m) bell tower, designed in the Romanesque-Gothic style, dates from the 12th century. At the cathedral, you can ask to visit **Jupiter's Temple,** Kraj Sv. Ivana at Grad, an ancient Roman temple that was converted into a baptistery during medieval times. The city's main museum, **Gradski Muzej,** Papaličeva 1 at Grad, houses a stunning collection of medieval weaponry.

One local tradition is the *Splitski Sir,* which is a nightly trip through the city checking to see who is at which of the cafes and what is going on there. The best cafe for people-watching is the outdoor terrace of the **Luxor Café,** Peristil, at Grad. While enjoying your drink, you'll take in a view of monuments in the distance that go back 2,000 years.

For More Information

Tourism information is found at the **Hrvatska Turisticka Zajendica** (Croatian National Tourist Board), Iblerov trg 10/IV, 10000 Zagreb (© **01/469-9333;** www.croatia.hr), open Monday to Friday 9am to 5:30pm. There is a U.S. office at 350 Fifth Ave., Ste. 4003, New York, NY 10118 (© **212/279-8672**).

GREECE

Though better known for its islands, Greece does have attractions on its rail-served mainland. With the 2004 Olympics as the impetus, much of the rail network and stations around Greece received upgrades. Unfortunately, the country's recent and well-publicized economic woes have taken their toll on its rail networks; all international rail service to and from Greece was canceled on January 1, 2011, and internal rail travel has taken a hit as well. So though it is possible to travel by rail in Greece and domestic rail travel offers spectacular sightseeing, it's not a perfect method of getting around.

Greece by Rail

PASSES

If your rail journey is limited to the Greek mainland, buying point-to-point tickets or an in-country pass instead of an international pass might be cheaper, as train travel in Greece is inexpensive. For information on the **Eurail Global Pass, Eurail Global Pass Flexi, Eurail Select Pass, Eurail Greece–Italy Pass,** and **Eurail Saver,** see chapter 2; for information on the Balkan Flexipass, see p. 803. The Eurail Greece Pass provides 3 to 10 days of nonconsecutive, first-class travel on Greece's national rail network. Prices start at $130 for adults. Check online for ferry, hotel, and tour discounts.

All of the above passes should be purchased before departing for your trip; you can buy them from **Rail Europe** (ⓒ 888/438-7245 in the United States, ⓒ 800/361-7245 in Canada; www.raileurope.com) or your travel agent.

Domestic **discount railpasses** can also be purchased through OSE once you are in Greece. If you buy six journeys on InterCity trains, you get one bonus trip. There are also family discount cards; cards for people over 60; and for multiple journeys used within 10, 20, or 30 days anywhere in Greece, but only in second class on regional trains. The **Multiple Journey Card** (*Karta Polaplon Taxidion* or *Karta Sindromis*) for one person for 10 days costs 48€; a card for two people costs 80€. A 20-day card for one person costs 72€, and a 30-day card costs 96€. There are no discount cards for those under 26, but you get a discount if you show ID.

PRACTICAL TRAIN INFORMATION

The **Hellenic Railway Organization** (**OSE; www.ose.gr**) has a bilingual website for schedule information (but not always up-to-date on routes currently in service), augmented by a help line with English-speaking operators to assist travelers. You can also call ⓒ **1440** for ship, airline, train. and long-distance bus timetables information; ⓒ **185** for urban bus timetables; or ⓒ **210/821-0872** for Attica bus schedules. Route information, prices, and so on can be obtained in English by dialing ⓒ**1110** from any phone in Greece. But not all is perfect in Greece for rail travelers, and visitors should take that into account. You can speak to operators only when you're inside the country. Furthermore, there is no system to reserve seats or sleepers directly with OSE online or if you are outside the country (even through Rail Europe), although you can try and reserve through a hotel or OSE-affiliated travel agency. Tickets must be paid within 48 hours of departure; otherwise, your reservation will be canceled. It's not exactly tourist-friendly for a European Union country that relies on tourism for some 15% of its GDP. (For example, I could book a sleeper long-distance to Victoria Falls in Zimbabwe 8 years ago.)

In Athens, tickets can be purchased at all stations or the two Hellenic Railways Organization ticket offices: Karolou 1, open Monday to Friday 8am to 3pm; and Sina 6 (international travel ⓒ **210/362-7947;** domestic travel ⓒ **1110,** or **210/362-1039** if calling from abroad), open Monday to Saturday 8am to 3:30pm. All signs on the rail network are in both Greek and English, but, with the exception of the Athens metro system and airports, announcements—usually inaudible anyway—are only in Greek. Schedules are posted at stations, while railway staff will certainly understand "ticket," "information," "how much," and the usual (polite) sign language for "how many." ***Note:*** What you might want to ask, however, is if there is a toilet on the train (*E*-hi toe *tre*-no tooa-*le*-ta?). As with the long-distance buses, often there are not, especially on the newer trains.

Before the rail system was upgraded, first-class travel in Greece was worth the extra cost, but second-class seating is now equally comfortable, at least on routes with new cars. You can call ⓒ **1110** for information on which lines have new "wagons," as train cars are called here in English. Overhead rails for duffle bags and small suitcases are available; larger baggage should be checked. There are three sleeper services on the Athens–Thessaloniki route, prices ranging from 54€ in a single compartment to 20€ in a six-bed.

Highlights of Greece

If you're flying into Greece, your first stop will likely be **Athens ★★★,** the capital and a major airport hub. It is home to about half of the country's 11 million people, the nation's total more than doubling in summer with tourists. Athens is the center of the country's north-south railway axis. It's main rail station, **Larissa Station** (*Stathmos Larissis*), shares its name with the metro station in front of it, and is the hub for northern Greece rail lines as well as the Peloponnese in the south. A luggage storage office, restaurant, and platform cantina are pretty much all the facilities this relatively small station has to offer, as well as a train information desk.

The city's underground **metro** lines, some with antiquities on display at the stations, have made it easy to explore the city's ancient glory on modern public transport. A quick ride will take you near the **Acropolis ★★★** hill, Dionysiou Areopagitou St. (*©* **210/321-0219**) and the renowned monuments upon it, including its crown jewel, the 2,500-year-old **Parthenon ★★★.** In the shadow of the ancient hill, the touristy **Plaka** and **Monastiraki** districts provide ample opportunities to shop, eat, and relax amid scattered antiquities. A pedestrian walkway loops around the Acropolis past **Thissio,** with arguably one of the best views in the world, and links many of the sites, including classical Athens's cemetery, **Kerameikos,** Ermou 148 (*©* **210/346-3553**) and the trendy/sophisticated **Gazi** district across the street (Pireos). If you're a museum lover, then you can't miss The **New Acropolis Museum ★★★**, 15 Dionisiou Aeropagitou (*©* **210/900-0901;** www.theacropolismuseum.gr), featuring a stunning collection of artifacts (and what Greece keeps hoping will house the Elgin Marbles if they can get the British to return them); or **The National Archaeological Museum ★★★**, Patission 44, Museo (*©* **210/821-7717**), which houses one of the world's greatest collection of antiquities. In the summer, enjoy a concert or theatrical performance at the **Herodion Atticus Theater** (*©* **210-324-2121** or 210/323-2771)**,** built around A.D. 160 and located below the Acropolis.

When you've had enough of the city buzz and chaos, travel southwest to enjoy a bird's-eye view of the impressive **Corinth Canal** as you head toward **Corinth ★** to visit the ancient sites; the ancient theater at **Epidaurus ★★★** (*©* **27530/22-006,** 27530/22-666, or 27530/23-009) can be experienced with a theatrical performance by night or as an archaeological site by day, perhaps together with **Mycenae ★** as an excursion from Athens.

The port town of **Patras** will likely be the starting point of your trip if you come to Greece via ferry from Italy (p. 506). You can head west or south to the **beaches** along the Peloponnesian coast, taking a detour at Pyrgos to **Ancient Olympia ★★,** birthplace of the Olympic Games. The archaeological site—where the Olympic flame is lit and the ancient Olympics were held—and the superb archaeological museum, with its unique Olympics-related contents, are some of Greece's prime attractions. If you need to head to Athens, you'll need to take bus service (not covered by a railpass).

If you take the main line north from Athens, you'll reach Greece's second-largest city, **Thessaloniki ★★,** which is also accessible by plane and ferry, and serves as a rail base for east-west trips in northern Greece, as well as points north and east out of the country.

Southwest of Thessaloniki, **Mount Olympus,** where Zeus and the other mythological gods dwelled, can prove a challenge to hikers and a rewarding escape for nature lovers, with **beaches** located less than 4 miles away from the mountain town of **Litohoro** "base camp" and other interesting sites nearby, such as **Ancient Dion, Pella,** and **Vergina.** Or travel east from Thessaloniki through the breathtaking **Nestos river valley,** which looks even better when hiked.

For More Information

On the Web, search the **Greek National Tourism Organization** site at **www. greektourism.com**.

In Athens a desk of the **Greek National Tourism Organization** (**GNTO,** also known by its Greek initials, EOT) at the arrivals terminal of **Athens International Airport** (✆ **210/353-0445** or 210/353-0048), is open from 9am to 7pm on week-days, 10am to 4pm on weekends in high season. There is a GNTO outlet at Amalias 26 (✆ **210/331-0392** or 210/331-0529; www.gnto.gr). It's open Monday through Friday from 9am to 7pm and weekends 10am to 4pm. Its staff can provide maps, transportation schedules, and glossy booklets on Athens, as well as more general information on other parts of Greece, although that information may not always be up-to-date.

For information in the U.S., contact the **Greek National Tourism Organiza-tion,** Olympic Tower, 645 Fifth Ave., Ste. 903, New York, NY 10022 (✆ **212/421-5777;** fax 212/826-6940; info@greektourism.com). In Canada, the GNTO is at 1500 Don Mills Rd., Toronto, ON M3B 3K4 (✆ **416/968-2220;** fax 416/968-6533; grnto.tor@on.aibn.com).

MACEDONIA

A troubled but beautiful land, this former Yugoslav republic is now charting an uncer-tain future as one of Europe's newest countries. Lying to the west of Bulgaria, Mace-donia is a relatively poor country that has been beset by racial and ethnic tensions—and often violence—as it's inhabited by pockets of Turks, Serbs, Bulgars, and Albanians. The political situation remains somewhat unstable, and while the threat of violence is small, both the U.S. and Great Britain advise their citizens to travel here only with caution and at their own risk.

Macedonia lies on the main rail line between Western Europe and Greece (though currently the line to and from Greece has been severed), so many passengers stop here briefly before continuing farther south and east. Even though it's been fought over by other nations for centuries—it was once part of the Ottoman Turkish Empire—most of the country's monuments, including ancient monasteries, mosques, old churches, historic buildings, and archaeological "gardens," remain relatively intact. Even so, Macedonia is only for the most adventurous of travelers.

Macedonia by Rail

PASSES

Macedonia has no railpasses of its own—nor would you need one for the limited amount of travel you're likely to do in the country. Rail Europe offers a **Balkan Flexi-pass** (p. 803) that covers travel in Macedonia, among several other countries.

PRACTICAL TRAIN INFORMATION

International trains tend to run more or less on time in Macedonia, but domestic trains proceed at a snail's pace (for travel within Macedonia, buses are often much quicker). Trains are operated by **Makedonski Aheleznici** (Macedonian Railways). The principal line, and the route the average visitor will travel, is the north/south rail link between Belgrade and Skopje (pop. 600,000), the capital of Macedonia.

Thessaloniki (p. 808), incidentally, is the capital of a Greek province that also calls itself "Macedonia" (as opposed to the country of Macedonia). Both sides claim the right to the name, leading to confusion and rivalry (indeed, in the U.N., the country of Macedonia is often referred to as FYROM, for "former Yugoslav republic of Macedonia)."

International train travel is limited. The only connection runs through Belgrade and northward to Vienna and Hungary. Reservations are required on all international lines passing through Macedonia. For night travel, you must also reserve a couchette or sleeper on any international trains traveling through Macedonia. International lines serve food and drink, but if you're traveling on domestic services in Macedonia, bring your own supplies for the trip.

The best source of rail assistance is the **Skopje Railway Station** (© 02/234-255) in the capital. Most of the staff at Feroturist Travel Agency, inside the train station, will provide rail data and sell international and domestic tickets. They also book couchettes and sleepers—say, on the train to Belgrade.

Highlights of Macedonia

Skopje, the capital of Macedonia, is on the banks of the Vardar River in the historic core of the Balkans. Disasters have historically beset the city, none worse than the earthquake of 1963, which destroyed much of Skopje. But there is still much in the rebuilt city to admire, with its minarets, mosques, and Turkish-style domes in the old town.

All the major sights unfold as you make your way out of the train depot, walking northwesterly toward the old city, with its 15th-century **Turkish Baths** and other attractions. The ancient **Oriental Bazaar** is worth an hour of your time, as you shop for regional handicrafts or watch them being made at this atmospheric souk.

Near the Turkish Bridge is Skopje's best museum, the **Municipal Art Gallery.** The **Museum of Macedonia,** filled with regional artifacts, is also worth a visit. The **Church of Sveti Spas** is visited mainly for its impressive collection of icons, many from the 1700s, and there is also a local mosque, **Mustafa Pasha,** where you can scale the minaret for the most panoramic view of Skopje. Across the street from this mosque lies **Fort Kale,** now in ruins but dating from the 10th century.

Outside the capital, the most scenic rail route is a 2-hour trip to the town of **Bitola ★**, which is relatively undiscovered and well worth a night or two. You'll definitely feel you're in Turkey here, and there are many relics to explore, including the Roman ruins of **Heraclea,** along with an early **Christian palace.** Other highlights—all on Marshal Tito Square (named for Yugoslavia's former dictator)—are the **Mosa Pijade Art Gallery,** installed in an old mosque, and the 16th-century **Bezistan Bazaar.** Wander at your leisure through the district of bazaars known as **Stara Charshiya,** making your way to the city market.

The greatest attraction of Macedonia is not on a rail line but can be reached by frequent buses from Bitola. The old town of **Ohrid ★★** is a charmer filled with red-roofed houses, sidewalk cafes, and rustic fish restaurants surrounding the world's second-deepest lake after Lake Baikal in Russia. Ohrid is acclaimed as one of the true beauty spots in all of Europe, and UNESCO has declared it a World Heritage Site. Trip time from Bitola to Ohrid is 90 minutes (via bus).

Although you'll want to spend most of your precious time on the lake, you can stroll the streets of Ohrid for hours, taking in such notable churches as **Sveti Kilment** and **Sveti Sofija** before heading west to the **Amphitheater** constructed by the Romans. After a visit, walk over to the walls of the old **citadel** for a panoramic view of the district before continuing south to the ruins of an ancient basilica whose mosaics can still be seen.

For More Information

Getting information on rail travel in Macedonia before you get here is almost impossible; it's difficult enough even when you're in the country.

The **Macedonian National Tourism Board** operates an excellent website at **www.exploringmacedonia.com**, with information on travel tips, accommodations, and cultural events.

Because it's so hard to obtain information before you go, visitors often contact their **Macedonian embassy.** In North America, the Embassy of the Republic of Macedonia is at 2129 Wyoming Ave. NW, Washington, DC 20008 (© **202/667-0501**).

POLAND

A member of NATO since 1999 and the European Union since 2004, Poland is shaking off its tragic past at the hands of the Nazis and the Soviet Union, and forging greater ties with Western Europe and a close bond with America. Although it has a troubled image abroad because of its disastrous history, it offers an abundance of natural and cultural attractions. These range from the bustling, post-socialist charm of Warsaw, its capital, to the beautifully restored old city of Gdańsk, from the Renaissance arcades of 1,000-year-old Kraków to the grim Nazi concentration camps of Auschwitz and Birkenau.

Poland by Rail

PASSES

Unlike most other Eastern European countries, rail travel is not incredibly cheap in Poland, though it's still a lot less expensive than in Western Europe. It's estimated that, on some long runs, the cost of a regular rail ticket is practically that of a discounted airplane ticket. Therefore, railpasses are the way to go here if you plan to do extensive rail travel in Poland.

Rail Europe offers a **European East Pass** that covers travel in Poland (see chapter 2), and the **Poland Pass,** which allows unlimited travel on the entire network of the Polish rail system. The Poland Pass varies in duration from 5 to 15 days of travel in a 1-month period; a first-class pass (recommended) starts at $166. Passengers under 26 years old can purchase a Poland Youth Pass for about 30% less.

PRACTICAL TRAIN INFORMATION

Berlin and Warsaw, both virtually destroyed in World War II, today enjoy one of the most famous rail connections in Europe, the fastest train running from Berlin in the west to Warsaw in the east in just 5½ hours. Four trains arrive daily from Berlin. The scenery is pleasant without being spectacular, and the rail lines go along the Piast Trail, linking such historic towns as Rzepin and Poznan.

Berlin is the western rail gateway to Warsaw, but there are many other options, notably three daily trains linking Warsaw to Prague in 10 to 12 hours, depending on connections. Two daily trains also run between Vienna and Warsaw (via Katowice) that take 7 to 9 hours, depending on the train. Most North American rail passengers take the train from Berlin.

Staying Safe

Regrettably, safety is an issue when traveling the rails in Poland. International trains to Poland are mostly safe, but theft of valuables, including luggage, has been reported in the past. For night train travel, our advice would be to get a sleeping car and lock the door.

Polish trains are faster and more efficient than they've ever been, though still lagging behind rail service in, say, Germany. Opt whenever possible for InterCity, EuroCity, or *Ekspresowe* trains, which offer restaurant cars, more comfort (some even have air-conditioning), and fewer delays. Avoid the snail-like *Osobowe* or *Pospieszne* categories, though if you get stuck, make sure to stock up on food and drink before getting on the train. Reservations are vital on all express trains. We definitely recommend that you go first class when traveling in Poland. The extra comfort and the security of actually having a reserved seat are worth the money. If you're taking a night train, opt for a sleeping car instead of a couchette.

Reservations can be made through Rail Europe or at ticket offices within each of the country's major railway stations. You can also buy rail tickets and make reservations at any branch of the **Orbis Polish Travel Bureau,** which are found in all major cities and towns. This agency is especially recommended for North Americans, as it places great importance on hiring people who speak English. It's sometimes—but not always—possible to pay for a ticket with a credit card. With the purchase of a ticket, reservations are free. When you obtain a ticket, look at it carefully. If there's an R positioned inside a box, it means that reservations are mandatory; an R that's not encased within a box means that seat reservations are required in only part of the train.

In Warsaw, the main dispenser of information for rail travel in Poland is **Warszawa Centralna,** or Central Station at Jerozolimskie 54, Śródmieście (✆ 022/19-757; for information on InterCity travel ✆ 0801/022-007). International trains arrive at the Central Station. Domestic departures are most often at the adjoining station, Warszawa śródmieście, Jerozolimskie, śródmieście (✆ 022/628-47-41). Online, go to the excellent online Polish rail timetable at **http://rozklad-pkp.pl**.

Highlights of Poland

Your rail adventure begins in **Warsaw ★**, where you can wander for a day around the Old Town that was destroyed by the Nazis but reconstructed in the 1950s. The city is the political center of the country and its geographical heart since 1611. Try to ignore the drabness of the surrounding Soviet-style architectural horror, and concentrate on the nuggets, which include **Rynek Starego Miasta (Old Town Square) ★★**, the hub of Old Town life where arts and crafts are sold in summer and spontaneous musical performances take place. The best way to see Old Town is to take a horse-drawn carriage from here, which passes by such attractions as **Zamek** Królewski **(Royal Palace)** ★, Pl. Samkowy 4, Stare Miasto, the royal castle dating from the 14th century.

After a look at Warsaw, most visitors head 170 miles (274km) south to **Kraków** ★★★, home to 100,000 students and almost as many pubs. Hourly trains make the 3-hour journey each day from Warsaw. Kraków is more intriguing than Warsaw, since its Stare Miasto (Old Town), with its towers, facades, and ancient churches, was spared from Hitler's devastation. The streets of its Old Town are likened to a living museum. On a grim note, you can journey to **Auschwitz–Birkenau** ★★, 38 miles (61km) west, to visit this infamous death camp for Jews, Polish political prisoners, Russian POWs, gypsies, and others deemed undesirable by the Nazis. Several buses a day leave from Kraków for Auschwitz; buses will drop you off close to the entrance to the museum at the death camp. Several tourist groups also run day trips from Kraków.

If time remains, try to see the city of **Gdańsk** ★★, 219 miles (353km) north of Warsaw. More than a dozen trains make the 4- to 5-hour trip every day. On the Baltic Coast at the mouth of the Vistula River, this was once the free city of Danzig. The birthplace of Solidarity, it is the center of the Polish Riviera and the gateway to "castle country," such as the fortress of the Teutonic Knights of Malbork (easily accessible by train from Gdańsk). In the area to the far east of Gdańsk (toward Belarus) are 1,000 lakes.

For More Information

On the Web, search the **Poland National Tourist Board** site at **www.poland. travel**.

In Warsaw, information is available at **The Center for Tourist Information,** Zamkowy 1/13, Stare Miasto (✆ **022/635-18-81**); and at the **Warsaw Tourist Information Office,** Krakówskie Przedmieście 15/17, Śródmieście (✆ **022-474-1142;** www.warsawtour.pl).

In Kraków, the city maintains a helpful network of tourist offices around town, including a main office in the Town Hall Tower on the Main Square (✆ **012/433-73-10;** www.krakow.pl), and at Józefa 7 (✆ **012/422-04-71**).

For information in North America, contact the **Polish National Tourist Office,** 5 Marine View Plaza, Hoboken, NJ, 07030 (✆ **201/420-9910;** www.poland.travel).

ROMANIA

The most beautiful country in Eastern Europe—a nation the size of Oregon—has a lot going for it: medieval villages, cosmopolitan cities (its capital, Bucharest, was once known as "The Paris of the East"), Count Dracula's Transylvania, a history-rich landscape, snowy peaks, and a Black Sea coastline. There are 2,000 old monasteries alone, including the fabled painted monasteries of Bucovina. From its mysterious Carpathian Mountains to its UNESCO World Heritage Site monuments, Romania calls out for your attention and time.

There are problems here, mainly those caused by the country's painful transition from the Communist dictatorship of the brutal Nicolae Ceaușescu to a market economy and liberal democracy. Sure, there's natural and man-made beauty, but tourist facilities lag far behind and there is much that is derelict, not working, and definitely not operating on a time clock. But entry into the European Union in 2007 has definitely spurred public and private investment, and every year brings new improvements to the tourism infrastructure.

The weather is a big determining factor when timing your visit. Because summers are blistery hot and winters are bitterly cold, spring and fall are ideal.

Note: Americans and Canadians can stay in Romania without visas for 90 days.

Romania by Rail

PASSES

Rail Europe offers a **Balkan Flexipass** (p. 803) that covers travel in Romania. They also offer a **Romania Pass** that covers 5 or 10 days of first-class travel in Romania over a 2-month period. Prices start at $195 per adult; children 4 to 11 pay a discounted price, and children under 4 travel for free. The passes should be purchased in North America.

The **Eurail Global Pass** is now good for Romania. Also available is the **Hungary–Romania Pass.**

PRACTICAL TRAIN INFORMATION

Train fares in Romania are reasonable, and rail travel is a good way to move from city to city (though buses are helpful for reaching small towns and villages within regions). The country's 7,021-mile (11,304km) rail network is operated by the **Romanian State Railway,** generally known as CFR. Western travelers find Romania's timetables confusing, or "bizarre," as one irate traveler described them to us. Some trains are in poor condition, often derelict, and passengers are frequently left sweltering in the heat or freezing in the cold. Trains also tend to get crowded, so try to reserve seats in advance and travel first class when practical. To compensate, some rail routes are especially scenic, especially those making their way across the Transylvanian landscape.

Opt for the InterCity or *rapide* services, which stop at only the major towns and usually have a dining car (bring some food and drink with you anyway, just to be on the safe side). Advance bookings for these fast trains are vital. Avoid the slow and often derelict *tren de personae* trains. Most long-distance overnight trains have couchettes or sleeping cars, which require reservations. Tickets are sold at rail depots only an hour, sometimes 2 hours, before departure times—expect long lines. CFR operates a network of in-town ticket offices in major cities where you can buy tickets in advance and get general train information, though English language sometimes is lacking.

 Staying Safe

Traveling by train in Romania is relatively safe, but crimes do occur, mostly nonviolent ones such as petty theft, pickpocketing, and confidence scams. Organized groups of thieves and pickpockets sometimes operate in the train stations, on trains, and on the Bucharest subway. A number of thefts and assaults occur on overnight trains, including thefts from passengers in closed compartments. One popular scam involves an individual posing as a plainclothes policeman approaching a potential victim, flashing a badge, and asking for his/her passport and wallet, which the thief then grabs and flees with.

Bucharest's main station, the **Gara de Nord,** offers numerous international train connections, and facilities on these trains are usually quite good. One of the most popular routings from the west is the Budapest–Bucharest train journey, which takes around 12 hours. Some of the international trains that run through the Hungarian capital and the Romanian capital include the *Pannonia Express* (out of Prague), the *Dacia Express* (out of Vienna; it offers nice views of the Transylvanian countryside), and the *Ister* (a EuroNight train with modern sleeping compartments). There is also train service between Belgrade and Bucharest (trip time: 12–13 hr.), and a slow train between Sofia and Bucharest, which covers a distance of 319 miles (514km) in 12 hours.

You can seek more information on CFR, the Romanian Railways, at **www.cfr.ro**. In Bucharest, you can check with Agentia de Voiaj CFR at Str. Domnita Anastasia 10–14 (© **021/313-2643**). You can also get train information and reservation by phone on © **021/9521** or 021/9522). As there will no doubt be a language problem, ask an English-speaking member of your hotel staff to make the call for you. A helpful rail timetable in English is offered online at **www.mersultrenurilorcfr.ro**.

Highlights of Romania

You will likely arrive in the country's bustling, grimy, but still fascinating capital city of **Bucharest ★**. Ceauşescu tried to have bulldozers destroy much of the French flavor of the old city with his grotesque Communist state–inspired architecture, but restoration is underway to recapture some of the former essence of Bucharest.

Allow at least a day to see the monuments and to partake of some of the city's lively new restaurants and burgeoning nightlife. You can't see it all in a day, but you should definitely see the attractions we list below if your time is limited. **Biserica Stavropoleos ★**, Strada Stavropoleos, is uniquely Romanian, the best example of what is known locally as Brancovenese architecture, a curvy style created in both stone and wood and blending late Renaissance with Byzantine motifs. The remarkable church, with its fresco-adorned walls and impressive dome, was constructed between 1724 and 1730.

For the best introduction to the varied architecture of Romania, head for Muzeul Naţional al Satului ★, a village museum at şos Kiseleff 28–30, filled with workshops of craftspeople, old churches, and the most typical of regional housing, each furnished authentically. Another folkloric museum is Muzeul Ţăranului Român ★, a Romanian regional museum with nearly 100,000 artifacts on display at şos Kiseleff 3. The 19th-century **Palatul Cotroceni ★**, Blvd. Geniului 1, was the home of the royal family from 1893 until 1947, when they were chased out by the Communists. Rebuilt after a 1977 earthquake, it is lavishly furnished and houses many personal items left by the fleeing royals.

Finally, you might want to go by the **Palatul Parlamentului ★★**, or the Parliament Palace (sometimes also called by its former name, the House of the People), Calea 13 Septembrie, a mammoth contemporary structure that can be blamed on Ceauşescu's megalomania. It is the second-largest building in the world, a true Stalinist monstrosity that has several of its 3,000 rooms open to the public. Note that tours must be booked in advance (© **021/311-3611**). Yes, that's 24-karat gold on the ceiling.

The true charm of Romania lies not in Bucharest but in its countryside, especially a trip to Transylvania, with its mountainous settings and Saxon-built towns, villages and churches. Another popular destination is the **Danube Delta (Delta Dunării) ★★**, a UNESCO World Heritage Site and Europe's largest wetland reserve. The delta embraces an area of 3,604 square miles (5,800 sq. km) and shelters some 300 species of birds and 160 species of fish. One of the best centers for exploring the delta is **Tulcea,** lying 163 miles (263km) northeast of Bucharest, reached best by bus or by a slow daily express train (trip time: 5 hr.).

The western province of Romania, **Transylvania ★★★**, the land of the fictional Count Dracula (inspirer Vlad the Impaler, however, was all too real), continues to spark the imagination of the world. It is a land of forest-covered mountains, historic villages, fortified churches, and an unspoiled landscape. The best way to see this province is to take one of 15 daily trains out of Bucharest and make the 3- to 4-hour trip to **Braşov ★★**, a medieval city that's an ideal Transylvanian gateway. From Braşov, your itinerary can continue west to **Sighişoara** and **Sibiu** and north to **Cluj** before pressing on to **Deva, Hunedoara, Arad,** and **Timişoara ★**. The center of Romania's once-numerous German population, **Sibiu ★★**, is another good base city and a good place to get information about traveling in Transylvania (see below). Sibiu is serviced by seven trains per day from Bucharest; the trip takes around 6 hours.

Romania's northeastern province of **Moldavia** is visited mainly for its fabled monasteries. The nearest major city for exploring the monasteries is **Suceava**, which can be reached by rail from **Cluj** or **Iaşi,** but plan on a long trip.

For More Information

The **Official Romanian Tourist Board** website is **www.romaniatourism.com**. Amazingly, Bucharest has no tourist office, although there is a booth in the Gara de Nord train station. Many hotels keep helpful brochures to distribute to their clients. Private travel agents fill the gap.

A good source for information about Transylvania is the **Tourist Information Office** in Sibiu, S. Brukenthal 2 (✆ **0269/208-913;** www.primsb.ro).

For information before you leave home, contact the **Romanian National Tourist Office,** 355 Lexington Ave., 19th Floor, New York, NY 10017 (✆ **212/545-8484;** www.romaniatourism.com).

SERBIA & MONTENEGRO

Serbia and Montenegro are actually two countries now, having separated in the past decade as the last act of the splitting apart of the former Yugoslavia.

Serbia is a turbulent Balkan country with a lively capital city, Belgrade, and some picturesque mountain scenery. Montenegro is a pint-sized state bordering the Adriatic Sea, with one of Europe's most beautiful and as yet undiscovered seacoasts. Though both are still suffering the aftershocks of civil war and economic transformation, the tourist industry is slowly coming back. Travel is generally safe, with the exception of the former Serbian province of Kosovo, where travel is still not advised.

There is much to see in both countries, and for the traveler with a sense of adventure, it's worth the effort. Because of the varied terrain, the climate is very different depending on the region. In the north, with its fertile plains, a continental climate prevails, meaning hot and very humid summers, with bitterly cold winters. To the southeast, moving toward Montenegro and its mountains, an Adriatic climate prevails along the coast, with hot, dry summers lasting until October and cold winters with lots of snowfall inland.

The short Montenegrin coast stretches for just 93 miles (150km). The splendid **Tara Canyon** in Montenegro is the largest in Europe, and the **Bay of Kotor** is the only real fjord in the south of Europe.

North American citizens don't need a visa. Belgrade is the major rail terminus from other international destinations.

Serbia & Montenegro by Rail

PASSES

Rail Europe offers a **Balkan Flexipass** (p. 803) and the **Eurail Select Pass** (see chapter 2), which cover rail travel through Serbia and Montenegro. There is no single railpass for either country, nor is one really needed, as most travelers pass through here en route to somewhere else—often Bulgaria.

PRACTICAL TRAIN INFORMATION

International trains run through Serbia (not Montenegro) and go on to some of the former Yugoslav republics and surrounding countries. The main rail link coming down from Hungary arrives in Belgrade and goes on to Macedonia or Bulgaria. Even international lines tend to be slow moving and overcrowded. Domestic trains are often a physical disaster, in poor condition, even more overcrowded than international trains, and subject to endless delays. Reservations made at the departure station are absolutely essential on all international trains.

Two trains link Belgrade with Budapest (7 hr.), and daily trains run to Vienna (11 hr.). The Balkan Express goes from Belgrade to Sofia in Bulgaria in 9 hours; the trip from Belgrade to Istanbul takes 23 hours.

International trains from Belgrade include stops at Novi Sad and Subotica for places in the north and west, and they also stop at Nis for passengers heading east. Montenegro is easily accessed from Belgrade, with regular service to the Montenegrin capital Podgorica and the coastal town of Bar, the country's major port. A total of four fast (and we use the term loosely) passenger trains make the run daily between Belgrade and Bar via Podgorica. From Belgrade to Bar, figure on a minimum trip time of 8 hours.

Although international lines are generally safe (the usual precautions are advised), domestic train travel through the country should be undertaken with care, as assaults and robberies of visitors have been reported.

For information about rail travel in Serbia and Montenegro, go to the main Belgrade rail station on Savski Trg (© **011/3614-811;** www.serbianrailways.com).

Highlights of Serbia & Montenegro

From its low mountains off the Adriatic Coast to the highlands of Serbia, there is much to see and explore here, including a wide variety of architectural styles ranging from Romanesque to Gothic, from Renaissance to baroque. Throughout the land are great monuments or else their ruins, including fortresses, ancient churches, Byzantine-style basilicas, and Roman amphitheaters. If you're pressed for time, spend a day exploring Belgrade and the rest of your time taking in Montenegro, which has a far greater scenic allure.

With a population of two million, **Belgrade ★**, on the southern tier of the Carpathian Basin where the River Sava links up with the Danube, is your gateway to the country. The city has been "the capital of the Serbs" since 1403, when the Turks drove the Serbs northward. The train station lies on the south side of Belgrade. From the station, tram 1, 2, or 13 heads for the **Kalemegdan Citadel ★**, a major attraction on the north side of town. A Roman camp in the 1st century A.D., today this is a complex of Orthodox churches, Turkish baths, Muslin tombs, and a big military museum presenting a warlike view of the country.

The art and culture of Serbia are showcased at the **National Museum,** Trg Republike 1A, which displays everything from ancient artifacts to Picasso. Serbian folkloric costumes are best seen at the **Ethnographical Museum,** Studentski Trg 13. A section of great charm is **Skadarlija ★**, originally settled by gypsies but later turned into a retreat for Bohemians. Much of its 19th-century artistic flavor remains intact.

In contrast to Serbia, **Montenegro ★★★** is sometimes called "the jewel of Europe." Train arrivals are in **Bar,** a port city of only minor interest. From here, buses fan out to the area's major scenic wonders. From June to September, all of Montenegro is a popular holiday spot, centering on the beautiful **Lake Skadar ★★★**, the largest lake in the Balkans and a major bird sanctuary. **Kotor ★** is a major resort town situated at the head of southern Europe's deepest fjord. It's a walled medieval city that is a UNESCO World Heritage Site. The other town of interest is **Budva ★★**, built by the Venetians in the Middle Ages. Today it is Montenegro's leading beach resort. Its old walled town, destroyed by two earthquakes in 1979, has been reconstructed.

For More Information

The **National Tourist Organization of Serbia** operates a helpful website, **www. serbia.travel**. The official website for the **National Tourism Organization of Montenegro** is www.visit-montenegro.com.

The **Belgrade City Office** operates an information service at Masarikova 5, Belgrade (✆ **011/3061-699;** www.beograd.rs).

SLOVAKIA

Slovakia broke away from Czechoslovakia on January 1, 1993, and has been trying to hard to forge an independent identity ever since. While Slovakia lacks a world-class city like Prague and doesn't have the three-star attractions its neighbor does, it does offer some beautiful natural resources, including a short but authentic range of Alpine peaks in the eastern part of the country.

In addition to its charming capital city of Bratislava, Slovakia is home to the High Tatra Mountains, which are spread out over an area of 300 square miles (777 sq. km). With its waterfalls, caves, and canyons, this is one of the great national parks of Europe, the mountains peaking at 8,694 feet (2,608m). Combined with all this majestic glory are quaint villages and castles on the Danube, charming towns of the Little Carpathians, and beautiful 18th-century churches in the east of the country.

Slovakia by Rail

PASSES

Rail Europe offers a **European East Pass** (see chapter 2) that covers travel in Slovakia. No other pass is accepted.

PRACTICAL TRAIN INFORMATION

Zeleznice Slovenskej Republiky (Slovak State Railways; ✆ **02/18-188; www. zsr.sk**) is the country's central rail administrator. The railway network is less dense than in the Czech Republic, but trains are a good way of traveling between major

Staying Safe

Statistics cite Slovakia as having "medium crime," mostly picked pockets and purse and cellular phone snatchings. Armed robbery and the drugging and robbing of unsuspecting victims at nightspots or bars are extremely rare. Most thefts occur at crowded tourist sites or on trains or buses. Occasional thefts are reported from couchettes on international train journeys, so keep a careful eye on your belongings or get a sleeper car with a lockable door.

cities, as well as accessing the High Tatras (through the city of Poprad). You'll also find some of Central Europe's most scenic rail lines in Slovakia, including a stunning ride on an electric train into the High Tatras.

Although it's not the transportation hub for central Europe that Prague is, Bratislava is well connected. The best routing into Slovakia is the 5-hour trip from Prague to Bratislava's **Hlavná Stanica** (✆ **02/2029-7538**); there are several trains per day. From Vienna's Suedbahnhof, hourly trains make the 1-hour run to Bratislava. If you're in Hungary, seven trains per day make the 3-hour trip from Budapest to Bratislava.

Reservations are essential, especially on express trains, which are labeled **R** or **Míst.** Reservations can be booked ahead of time on Slovak trains through Rail Europe. It's also essential to reserve sleepers—called *lahatkovy vozen*—and couchettes on long trips. These should both be booked as far in advance as possible (again, Rail Europe can book these as well). In all cases, you should book the direct lines, which are called *rýchlik*, as these trains stop only at cities or larger towns. Unless you've got endless time, avoid the local trains, called *osobný vlak,* though travel on these snail-paced trains is 50% cheaper. On express trains, and if you're willing to pay 50% more for your tickets, you can go first class—if you can afford it, we advise it, as second-class travel is often overcrowded and uncomfortable. Only express trains have dining cars, so bring food and drink along with you on other trains. In general, the network is reliable, with trains running on time.

Highlights of Slovakia

On the banks of the Danube, **Bratislava ★** is the rail hub of Slovakia and also its capital. Its Old Town, or **Starý Mesto,** is looking better than ever now that it's brightening up its dreary Communist-era gray concrete high-rise projects. On the city's outskirts are castles and vineyards. The Old Town, with its cobblestone streets, invites hours of exploration relieved by fashionable cafes, bars, and restaurants.

A highlight is **Bratislava Castle ★**, or Brastislavsky Hrad, Zámocka U1, Starý Mesto, a four-towered landmark overlooking Old Town from a hill just outside the city. Its 18th-century glory was reconstructed by the Communists on foundations laid in the 9th century. Under the Hungarian kings and later the Habsburgs, the edifice was further expanded as a fortress against the Turkish menace from the east. You're free to climb up to the Castle garden, but entry may be restricted, as the building is undergoing a thorough long-term renovation.

Another gem awaiting you is **Primaciálny Palác ★**, or Primates' Palace, Primaciále Nam, 1 Starý Mesto, a pale pink baroque palace celebrated for its **Hall of Mirrors ★★**, where the peace treaty of Pressburg was signed in 1805 by Napoleon and Franz I, the Austrian emperor. You can also enjoy the lush antiques and intricately woven tapestries from the 1600s. The massive Gothic church of **Dom Svätého Martina ★**, or St. Martin's Cathedral, Rudnayovo Nám, Starý Mesto, was consecrated in 1452. Once Hungary's coronation cathedral (Slovakia was part of the Austro-Hungarian Empire until 1918), it witnessed the crowning of 17 royals here between the 16th and 19th centuries.

After Bratislava, the country's main attraction is the **Tatras Mountains ★★★**, but reaching them by train will take at least 5 hours. Once you finally get here, the district is compact, about 20 miles (32km) from end to end, containing 35 mountain lakes with clear but very cold waters. Your gateway to the Tatras is the city of **Poprad,** located 204 miles (328km) east of Bratislava. The town is a bit of a Soviet-era architectural horror, but there's beauty at its doorstep. An electric railroad here takes you to the more fascinating attractions and tourist facilities that lie 19 miles (31km) to the north.

For More Information

On the Web, consult **www.slovakia.travel**. In the Tatras Mountains, tourist information is available at all resort towns, including **Satur,** Námestie Sv. Egídia 3006/116, Poprad (© **052/7721-740**). In Bratislava itself, **Satur** is one of Slovakia's largest travel agencies, with offices at Jesenského 5, Starý Mesto (© **02/5441-0131**).

The Slovak national tourist board does not maintain an office in North America. For information, send e-mail to info@slovakia.travel or see **www.slovakia.travel**.

SLOVENIA

Of all the breakaway republics of old Yugoslavia (it declared its independence from Yugoslavia in 1991 and met only meager resistance from Belgrade), Slovenia is the most prosperous and safest to visit.

Without a doubt, Slovenia is one of the most beautiful countries in all of Europe. From its Adriatic shores to its Alpine peaks, Slovenia is loaded with natural treasures. Many European vacationers here spend all their time with a beach towel on the country's small strip of emerald blue coast. But there is so much more to see inland, ranging from mountains and lakes to old vineyards and undulating farmland. The standard of living here is much like that of Western Europe. The culture reflects the long occupation of Habsburg control (before the Habsburgs, Slovenia was part of the Roman Empire for nearly 5 c.).

Slovenia is bordered by Austria, Hungary, Croatia, and Italy. Seemingly ignoring the neighbors to which it was once united, the country has turned its eyes to the West and joined the European Union and NATO in 2004. About 90% of the population is made up of a single ethnic group, the Slovenes, so the country is not as sharply divided by ethnic minorities as some of its neighbors.

Spring and autumn are the best times to explore this small Slavic nation. July and August are the obvious months to visit if you're planning on spending time at its beaches.

Slovenia by Rail

PASSES

For information on the **Eurail Select Pass,** see chapter 2.

The **Eurail Austria–Croatia–Slovenia Pass** offers 4 days of unlimited first-class travel in Austria, Slovenia, and Croatia within a 2-month period. Passes start at

$269 for adults, children ages 4 to 11 pay a special rate, and kids under 4 travel free. Up to 6 extra days may be purchased for $40 each day. Another option is the **Eurail Hungary–Croatia–Slovenia Pass,** which offers anywhere from 5 to 10 days of unlimited first-class travel in Hungary, Slovenia, and Croatia within a 2-month period. The cost starts at $249 for an adult; children ages 4 to 11 pay a special rate, and kids under 4 travel free.

Both passes should be purchased through either Rail Europe or a travel agent before leaving North America.

PRACTICAL TRAIN INFORMATION

Rail travel isn't the most time-efficient mode of transportation in Slovenia (most locals leave the trains to the tourists, preferring to take buses instead), but it will get you from point A to point B without too many stops. Tickets here are inexpensive, so if you plan to travel only in Slovenia, purchasing a railpass makes no financial sense. Do not fall into the trap of buying tickets on the train unless you absolutely have to. Supplements for such purchases can run you more than the actual ticket.

Slovenian Railways (✆ 01/29-13-332; www.slo-zeleznice.si) operates several types of trains. The modern high-speed tilting trains, known as **InterCity Slovenian trains (ICS),** offer greater comfort than the other rail types. Additional services on these trains include wheelchair transport, telephones, a restaurant, and a free parking place at the rail station. Seat reservations are mandatory. **EuroCity (EC)** trains are high-quality international trains with a superfluity of services. **InterCity trains (IC)** connect longer distances within Slovenia. There are also lower-quality international trains (designated MV on timetables). Local and regional trains are the slowest of the Slovenian rail network and cover the shortest distances. **Note:** Figuring out timetables, if there are any at the station, is a challenge. Departures are usually listed on a yellow chalkboard titled ODHAD or ODHODI VLAKOV. Arrivals are listed on a white chalkboard titled PRIHOD or PRIHODI VLAKO. Be forewarned that there is a small chance that the times listed will be wrong. Helpful Slovene words include *peron* (platform), *sedez* (seat), and *smer* (direction). If you're having trouble, many people speak English in Slovenia, so try asking for help. Getting off a train at the right spot has also proved tricky for travelers in Slovenia, because no announcements are made over a speaker system to announce a coming stop and smaller stations usually have only one sign. Ticket checkers will be happy to help you find the right stop, or you could go by the estimated travel time, though we don't recommend that.

Tickets are for sale at various tourist agencies. In Ljubljana, call the railway station directly at ✆ **01/29-13-332** for information daily 6am to 10pm. If you're traveling

---

 Staying Safe

Political demonstrations have been known to occur in city centers in Slovenia, most often in Ljubljana around *Kongresni Trg* (Congress Sq.). These demonstrations are, for the most part, peaceful in nature, but in the past there have been anti-American incidents. Once demonstrators threw paint balloons and eggs at the American Embassy. The U.S. Department of State urges Americans to stay away from such rallies. Information on the security and political climate of the country can be obtained by calling the U.S. Department of State at ✆ **888/407-4747** from 8am to 8pm Monday to Friday, except federal holidays.

from the west into Slovenia, the best crossing is at the town of Jesenice on the Austrian border. This is the railway entry that's closest to Ljubljana. If you have a railpass that is valid in Austria but not in Slovenia, you'll have to pay a nominal amount, depending on your ticket, for the short transit.

Highlights of Slovenia

According to an ancient legend, the capital, **Ljubljana ★**, was founded by the Greek prince Jason and his Argonauts. The story goes that while the motley crew was trying to escape King Aites, the man from whom they had stolen the Golden Fleece, they sailed on the Sava into Ljubljana. Culture and a rich history are two components that have made this city a favorite among both locals and visitors.

Set in a basin between the Karst and Alpine regions, this city is one of the least populous capitals in Europe, with only 278,000 inhabitants. Despite the small size, however, Ljubljana has everything that most other European capitals have—just on a smaller scale.

A major attraction is the **National Museum,** 20 Prešernova 1000 (✆ **01/241-4400;** www.narmuz-lj.si). This national landmark was established in 1821 and has been the Slovene center for artifacts and other historical items ever since. In front of the building is a monument honoring nobleman and scholar Janez Vajkard Valvasor. A member of the Royal Society of London, Valvasor's true fame came when he penned *Slava vojvodine Kranjske (The Glory of the Duchy),* which described Slovenia in great detail, essentially putting it on the map.

Another noteworthy museum is the **Virtualni Muzej,** Ljubljanski grad 1000 (✆ **01/232-9994;** www.ljubljanafestival.si/sl/ljubljanski_grad/virtualni_muzej). This innovative museum presents the visitor with a ticket into the past through virtual reconstructions of the Emona Forum (in A.D. 388), Ljubljana (in 1580), the Town Square (in 1780), Congress Square (in 1886), Marija Square (in 1913), Vegova Street/Napoleon Square (in 1941), and Revolution Square (in 1984). Using virtual technology, visitors can also examine Slovenian artifacts more closely than they would be able to anywhere else because of security restraints.

> **Changing Currency**
>
> Note that Slovenia is one of the few Central and Eastern European countries to use the E.U.'s common currency, the euro.

Among the city's other top attractions is the **Grand Casino Ljubljana,** 154 Dunajska cesta (✆ **05/907-8600;** www.casino-lj.si/en), with plenty of slot machines and live gaming tables, and built in accordance with international gaming standards.

The capital of the Štajerska region, **Maribor,** 64 miles (103km) northeast of Ljubljana, is the second-most-important city in Slovenia. Tourist areas have popped up at the feet of the vineyard-covered hills that blanket the city. There are 31 miles (50km) of wine roads lined with shops and restaurants selling homemade treats, allowing visitors a close look at the most dominant product of the region. The area is perfect for cyclists and horseback riders.

Bled ★★★, 34 miles (55km) northwest of Ljubljana, is the best mountain resort in the country. Surrounded by the Julian Alps, it opens onto Lake Bled, which has a small island in its center that's part of Bled itself. The most popular excursion in Bled involves going over to the island to visit the **Church of the Assumption.** Boats can be rented to take you over, or you can take a round-trip on a gondola. Some visitors swim over.

European aristocrats made Bled a fashionable destination in the 1800s, although its thermal springs have been known for their healing powers since the 1600s. Many recreational facilities have opened here in the time since Slovenia achieved its independence, with the lake and its island turned into a virtual playground, offering windsurfing, rowing, and sailing. Horse-drawn carriages carry you for a ride along the lakefront promenade, as swans glide by on the water. Bled is surrounded by the mountains of **Triglav National Park.** Within its borders, you'll find waterfalls, roaring rapids, and nature trails cut through the forests. **Bled Castle,** built in 1004, houses a museum with artifacts unearthed in the region.

For More Information

Tourist information is found at the **Slovenian Tourist Information Centre,** 10 Krekov trg, SI-1000 Ljubljana (© **01/306-45-75** or 01/306-45-76; www.slovenia. info), open Monday to Friday 9am to 5:30pm. There is an office of the Consulate General in the United States at 600 Third Ave., 21st Floor, New York, NY 10016 (© **212/370-3006;** www.slovenia.info).

For information on Bled, head online to **www.bled.si**.

USEFUL TERMS & PHRASES

GLOSSARY OF FRENCH-LANGUAGE TERMS

BASICS

English	French	Pronunciation
Yes/No	Oui/Non	**wee/nohn**
Okay	D'accord	**dah-*core***
Please	S'il vous plaît	**seel voo *play***
Thank you	Merci	**mair-*see***
You're welcome	De rien	**duh ree-*ehn***
Hello (during daylight hours)	Bonjour	**bohn-*jhoor***
Good evening	Bonsoir	**bohn-*swahr***
Goodbye	Au revoir	**o ruh-*vwahr***
What's your name?	Comment vous appellez-vous?	**ko-mahn voo za-pell-ay-*voo*?**
My name is . . .	Je m'appelle . . .	**jhuh ma-*pell* . . .**
Happy to meet you	Enchanté(e)	**ohn-shahn-*tay***
Miss	Mademoiselle	**mad-mwa-*zel***
Mr.	Monsieur	**muh-*syuh***
Mrs.	Madame	**ma-*dam***
How are you?	Comment allez-vous?	**kuh-mahn tahl-ay-*voo*?**
Fine, thank you, and you?	Très bien, merci, et vous?	**tray bee-ehn, mare-ci, ay *voo*?**
Very well, thank you	Très bien, merci	**tray bee-ehn, mair-*see***
So-so	Comme ci, comme ça	**kum-*see*, kum-*sah***
I'm sorry/excuse me	Pardon	**pahr-*dohn***
I'm so very sorry	Désolé(e)	**day-zoh-*lay***
That's all right	Il n'y a pas de quoi	**eel nee ah pah duh kwah**

20

GETTING AROUND/STREET SMARTS

English	French	Pronunciation
Do you speak English?	Parlez-vous anglais?	**par-lay-voo ahn-*glay*?**
I don't speak French	Je ne parle pas français	**jhuh ne parl pah frahn-*say***
I don't understand	Je ne comprends pas	**jhuh ne kohm-*prahn* pas**
Could you speak more loudly/more slowly?	Pouvez-vous parler un peu plus fort/plus lentement?	**poo-vay-voo par-lay un puh ploo for/ploo lan-te-*ment*?**
Could you repeat that?	Répetez, s'il vous plaît?	**ray-pay-*tay,* seel voo *play***
What is it?	Qu'est-ce que c'est?	**kess kuh *say*?**
What time is it?	Qu'elle heure est-il?	**kel uhr eh-*teel*?**
What?	Quoi?	**kwah?**
How? or What did you say?	Comment?	**ko-*mahn*?**
When?	Quand?	**kahn?**
Where is . . . ?	Où est . . . ?	**ooh eh . . . ?**
Who?	Qui?	**kee?**
Why?	Pourquoi?	**poor-*kwah*?**
Here/there	ici/là	**ee-*see*/lah**
Left/right	à gauche/à droite	**a goash/a drwaht**
Straight ahead	tout droit	**too drwah**
I'm American/Canadian/British	Je suis américain(e)/canadien(e)/anglais(e)	**jhe sweez a-may-ree-*kehn*/can-ah-dee-*en*/ahn-glay (*glaise*)**
Fill the tank (of a car), please	Le plein, s'il vous plaît	**luh plan, seel voo *play***
I'm going to . . .	Je vais à . . .	**jhe vay ah . . .**
I want to get off at . . .	Je voudrais descendre à . . .	**jhe voo-*dray* day-son-drah ah**
I'm sick	Je suis malade	**jhuh swee mal-*ahd***
airport	l'aéroport	**lair-o-*por***
bank	la banque	**lah bahnk**
bridge	pont	**pohn**
bus station	la gare routière	**lah gar roo-tee-*air***
bus stop	l'arrêt de bus	**lah-*ray* duh boohss**
by means of a bicycle	en vélo/par bicyclette	**ahn *vay*-low/par bee-see-*clet***
by means of a car	en voiture	**ahn vwa-*toor***
cashier	la caisse	**lah *kess***
cathedral	cathédral	**ka-tay-*dral***
church	église	**ay-*gleez***
dead end	une impasse	**ewn am-*pass***
driver's license	permis de conduire	**per-mee duh con-*dweer***
elevator	l'ascenseur	**lah-sahn-*seuhr***
stairs	l'escalier	**les-kal-*yay***

English	French	Pronunciation
entrance (to a building or a city)	une porte	**ewn port**
exit (from a building or a freeway)	une sortie	**ewn sor-*tee***
fortified castle or palace	château	**sha-*tow***
garden	jardin	**jhar-dehn**
gasoline	du pétrol/de l'essence	**duh pay-*trol*/de lay-*sahns***
ground floor	rez-de-chausée	**ray-de-show-*say***
highway to . . .	la route pour	**la root por**
hospital	l'hôpital	**low-pee-*tahl***
insurance	les assurances	**lez ah-sur-*ahns***
luggage storage	consigne	**kohn-*seen*-yuh**
museum	le musée	**luh mew-*zay***
no entry	sens interdit	**sehns ahn-ter-*dee***
no smoking	défense de fumer	**day-*fahns* de fu-may**
on foot	à pied	**ah pee-*ay***
1-day pass	ticket journalier	**tee-kay jhoor-nall-ee-*ay***
one-way ticket	aller simple	**ah-*lay* sam-pluh**
police	la police	**lah po-*lees***
rented car	voiture de location	**vwa-*toor* de low-ka-see-on**
round-trip ticket	aller-retour	**ah-*lay*-re-*toor***
second floor	premier étage	**prem-ee-*ehr* ay-*taj***
slow down	ralentir	**rah-lahn-*teer***
store	le magasin	**luh ma-ga-*zehn***
street	rue	**roo**
subway	le Métro	**le *may*-tro**
telephone	le téléphone	**luh tay-lay-*phone***
ticket	un billet	**uh *bee*-yay**
ticket office	vente de billets	**vahnt duh bee-*yay***
toilets	les toilettes/les WC	**lay twa-*lets*/lay vay-*say***
tower	tour	**toor**

NECESSITIES

English	French	Pronunciation
I'd like . . .	Je voudrais . . .	**jhe voo-*dray* . . .**
a room	une chambre	**ewn *shahm*-bruh**
the key	la clé (la clef)	**la *clay***
I'd like to buy . . .	Je voudrais acheter . . .	**jhe voo-dray ahsh-*tay* . . .**
aspirin	des aspirines/des aspros	**deyz ahs-peer-*eens*/deyz ahs-*prohs***
cigarettes	des cigarettes	**day see-ga-*ret***
condoms	des préservatifs	**day pray-ser-va-*teefs***

English	French	Pronunciation
dictionary	un dictionnaire	**uh deek-see-oh-*nare***
dress	une robe	**ewn robe**
envelopes	des envelopes	**days ahn-veh-*lope***
gift (for someone)	un cadeau	**uh kah-*doe***
handbag	un sac	**uh sahk**
hat	un chapeau	**uh shah-*poh***
magazine	une revue	**ewn reh-*vu***
map of the city	un plan de ville	**unh plahn de *veel***
matches	des allumettes	**dayz a-loo-*met***
necktie	une cravate	**eun cra-*vaht***
newspaper	un journal	**uh jhoor-*nahl***
phone card	une carte téléphonique	**ewncart tay-lay-fone-*eek***
postcard	une carte postale	**ewn carte pos-*tahl***
road map	une carte routière	**ewn cart roo-tee-*air***
shirt	une chemise	**ewn che-*meez***
shoes	des chaussures	**day show-*suhr***
skirt	une jupe	**ewn jhoop**
soap	du savon	**dew sah-*vohn***
socks	des chaussettes	**day show-*set***
stamp	un timbre	**uh *tam*-bruh**
trousers	un pantalon	**uh pan-tah-*lohn***
writing paper	du papier à lettres	**dew pap-pee-*ay a let*-ruh**
How much does it cost?	C'est combien? / Ça coûte combien?	**say comb-bee-*ehn*?/sah coot comb-bee-*ehn*?**
That's expensive	C'est cher/chère	**say share**
That's inexpensive	C'est raisonnable/C'est bon marché	**say ray-son-*ahb*-bluh/say bohn mar-*shay***
Do you take credit cards?	Est-ce que vous acceptez les cartes de credit?	**es-kuh voo zaksep-*tay* lay kart duh creh-*dee*?**

NUMBERS & ORDINALS

English	French	Pronunciation
zero	zéro	**zare-*oh***
one	un	**uh**
two	deux	**duh**
three	trois	**twah**
four	quatre	***kaht*-ruh**
five	cinq	**sank**
six	six	**seess**
seven	sept	**set**
eight	huit	**wheat**
nine	neuf	**nuf**

English	French	Pronunciation
ten	dix	**deess**
eleven	onze	**ohnz**
twelve	douze	**dooz**
thirteen	treize	**trehz**
fourteen	quatorze	**kah-*torz***
fifteen	quinze	**kanz**
sixteen	seize	**sez**
seventeen	dix-sept	**deez-*set***
eighteen	dix-huit	**deez-*wheat***
nineteen	dix-neuf	**deez-*nuf***
twenty	vingt	**vehn**
twenty-one	vingt-et-un	**vehnt-ay-*uh***
twenty-two	vingt-deux	**vehnt-*duh***
thirty	trente	**trahnt**
forty	quarante	**ka-*rahnt***
fifty	cinquante	**sang-*kahnt***
sixty	soixante	**swa-*sahnt***
sixty-one	soixante-et-un	**swa-*sahnt*-et-*uh***
seventy	soixante-dix	**swa-sahnt-*deess***
seventy-one	soixante-et-onze	**swa-sahnt-et-*ohnze***
eighty	quatre-vingts	**kaht-ruh-*vehn***
eighty-one	quatre-vingt-un	**kaht-ruh-vehn-*uh***
ninety	quatre-vingt-dix	**kaht-ruh-venh-*deess***
ninety-one	quatre-vingt-onze	**kaht-ruh-venh-*ohnze***
one hundred	cent	**sahn**
one thousand	mille	**meel**
one hundred thousand	cent mille	**sahn meel**
first	premier	***preh*-mee-ay**
second	deuxième	***duhz*-zee-em**
third	troisième	***twa*-zee-em**
tenth	dixième	***dees*-ee-em**
twentieth	vingtième	***vehnt*-ee-em**
thirtieth	trentième	***trahnt*-ee-em**
one-hundredth	centième	***sant*-ee-em**

THE CALENDAR

English	French	Pronunciation
Sunday	dimanche	**dee-*mahnsh***
Monday	lundi	***luhn*-dee**
Tuesday	mardi	***mahr*-dee**
Wednesday	mercredi	***mair*-kruh-dee**

English	French	Pronunciation
Thursday	jeudi	*jheu*-dee
Friday	vendredi	*vawn*-druh-dee
Saturday	samedi	*sahm*-dee
yesterday	hier	ee-*air*
today	aujourd'hui	o-jhord-*dwee*
this morning/this afternoon	ce matin/cet après-midi	suh ma-*tan*/set ah-preh-mee-*dee*
tonight	ce soir	suh *swahr*
tomorrow	demain	de-*man*

GLOSSARY OF ITALIAN-LANGUAGE TERMS

USEFUL ENGLISH-ITALIAN PHRASES

English	Italian	Pronunciation
Thank you	Grazie	*graht*-tzee-yey
You're welcome	Prego	*prey*-go
Please	Per favore	*pehr* fah-*vohr*-eh
Yes	Si	see
No	No	noh
Good morning or Good day	Buongiorno	bwohn-*djor*-noh
Good evening	Buona sera	*bwohn*-ah *say*-rah
Good night	Buona notte	*bwohn*-ah *noht*-tay
It's a pleasure to meet you.	Piacere di conoscerla.	pyah-*cheh*-reh dee *koh*-nohshehr-lah
My name is ____.	Mi chiamo ____.	mee *kyah*-moh
And yours?	E lei?	eh lay
Do you speak English?	Parla inglese?	*pahr*-lah een-*gleh*-seh
How are you?	Come sta?	*koh*-may *stah*
Very well	Molto bene	*mohl*-toh *behn*-ney
Goodbye	Arrivederci	ahr-ree-vah-*dehr*-chee
Excuse me (to get attention)	Scusi	*skoo*-zee
Excuse me (to get past someone)	Permesso	pehr-*mehs*-soh

GETTING AROUND

English	Italian	Pronunciation
Where is . . . ?	Dovè . . . ?	doh-*vey*
the station	la stazione	lah stat-tzee-*oh*-neh

English	Italian	Pronunciation
a hotel	un albergo	oon ahl-*behr*-goh
a restaurant	un ristorante	oon reest-ohr-*ahnt*-eh
the bathroom	il bagno	eel *bahn*-nyoh
I am looking for . . .	Cerco . . .	*chehr*-koh
a porter	un facchino	oon fahk-*kee*-noh
the check-in counter	il check-in	eel check-in
the ticket counter	la biglietteria	lah beel-lyeht-teh-*ree*-ah
arrivals	l'area arrivi	*lah*-reh-ah ahr-*ree*-vee
departures	l'area partenze	*lah*-reh-ah pahr-*tehn*-tseh
gate number	l'uscita numero	loo-*shee*-tah *noo*-meh-roh
the waiting area	l'area d'attesa	*lah*-reh-ah daht-*teh*-zah
the men's restroom	la toilette uomini	lah twa-*leht woh*-mee-nee
the women's restroom	la toilette donne	lah twa-*leht dohn*-neh
the police station	la stazione di polizia	lah stah-*tsyoh*-neh dee poh-lee-*tsee*-ah
a security guard	una guardia di sicurezza	*ooh*-nah *gwahr*-dyah dee see-koo-*ret*-sah
the smoking area	l'area fumatori	*lah*-reh-ah foo-mah-*toh*-ree
the information booth	l'ufficio informazioni	loof-*fee*-choh een-*fohr*-mah-*tsyoh*-nee
a public telephone	un telefono pubblico	oon teh-*leh*-foh-noh *poob*-blee-koh
an ATM/cashpoint	un bancomat	oon *bahn*-koh-maht
baggage claim	il ritiro bagagli	eel ree-*tee*-roh bah-*gahl*-lyee
a luggage cart	un carrello portabagagli	oon kahr-*rehl*-loh *pohr*-tah-bah-*gahl*-lyee
a currency exchange	un cambiavalute	oon *kahm*-byah-vah-*loo*-teh
a cafe	un caffè	oon kahf-*feh*
a restaurant	un ristorante	oon ree-stoh-*rahn*-teh
a bar	un bar	oon bar
a bookstore	una libreria	*oo*-nah lee-breh-*ree*-ah
a duty-free shop	un duty-free	oon duty-free
To the left	A sinistra	ah see-*nees*-tra
To the right	A destra	ah *dehy*-stra
Straight ahead	Avanti (*or* sempre diritto)	ahv-*vahn*-tee (*sehm*-pray dee-*reet*-toh)

DINING

English	Italian	Pronunciation
Breakfast	Prima colazione	*pree*-mah coh-laht-tzee-*ohn*-ay
Lunch	Pranzo	*prahn*-zoh

English	Italian	Pronunciation
Dinner	Cena	*chay*-nah
How much is it?	Quanto costa?	*kwan*-toh *coh*-sta
The check, please	Il conto, per favore	eel kon-toh *pehr* fah-*vohr*-eh

A MATTER OF TIME

English	Italian	Pronunciation
When?	Quando?	*kwan*-doh
Yesterday	Ieri	ee-*yehr*-ree
Today	Oggi	*oh*-jee
Tomorrow	Domani	doh-*mah*-nee
What time is it?	Che ore sono?	kay *or*-ay *soh*-noh
It's one o'clock.	È l'una.	*eh loo*-nah
It's two o'clock.	Sono le due.	*soh*-noh leh *doo*-eh
It's two-thirty.	Sono le due e mezzo.	*soh*-noh leh *doo*-eh eh *mehd*-dzoh
It's noon.	È mezzogiorno.	*eh* mehd-dzoh-*johr*-noh
It's midnight.	È mezzanotte.	*eh* mehd-dzah-*noht*-teh
It's early.	È presto.	*eh prehs*-toh
It's late.	È tardi.	*eh tahr*-dee
in the morning	al mattino	ahl maht-*tee*-noh
in the afternoon	al pomeriggio	ahl poh-meh-*reed*-joh
at night	di notte	dee *noht*-the

DAYS OF THE WEEK

English	Italian	Pronunciation
Monday	Lunedì	loo-nay-*dee*
Tuesday	Martedì	mart-ay-*dee*
Wednesday	Mercoledì	mehr-cohl-ay-*dee*
Thursday	Giovedì	joh-vay-*dee*
Friday	Venerdì	ven-nehr-*dee*
Saturday	Sabato	*sah*-bah-toh
Sunday	Domenica	doh-*mehn*-nee-kah

MONTHS & SEASONS

English	Italian	Pronunciation
January	gennaio	jehn-*nah*-yoh
February	febbraio	fehb-*brah*-yoh
March	marzo	*mahr*-tso
April	aprile	ah-*pree*-leh
May	maggio	*mahd*-joh
June	giugno	*jewn*-nyo
July	luglio	*lool*-lyo

English	Italian	Pronunciation
August	agosto	ah-*gohs*-toh
September	settembre	seht-*tehm*-breh
October	ottobre	oht-*toh*-breh
November	novembre	noh-*vehm*-breh
December	dicembre	dee-*chehm*-breh
spring	la primavera	lah pree-mah-*veh*-rah
summer	l'estate	lehs-*tah*-teh
autumn	l'autunno	low-*toon*-noh
winter	l'inverno	leen-*vehr*-noh

NUMBERS

English	Italian	Pronunciation
one	uno	*oo*-noh
two	due	*doo*-ay
three	tre	tray
four	quattro	*kwah*-troh
five	cinque	*cheen*-kway
six	sei	say
seven	sette	*set*-tay
eight	otto	*oh*-toh
nine	nove	*noh*-vay
ten	dieci	dee-*ay*-chee
eleven	undici	*oon*-dee-chee
twenty	venti	*vehn*-tee
twenty-one	ventuno	vehn-*toon*-oh
twenty-two	venti due	*vehn*-tee *doo*-ay
thirty	trenta	*trayn*-tah
forty	quaranta	kwah-*rahn*-tah
fifty	cinquanta	cheen-*kwan*-tah
sixty	sessanta	sehs-*sahn*-tah
seventy	settanta	seht-*tahn*-tah
eighty	ottanta	oht-*tahn*-tah
ninety	novanta	noh-*vahnt*-tah
one hundred	cento	*chen*-toh
one thousand	mille	*mee*-lay
five thousand	cinque milla	*cheen*-kway *mee*-lah
ten thousand	dieci milla	dee-ay-chee mee-lah

Index

A

Abades (Seville), 690
Abbaye de Notre Dame de
  Lérins (Ile St-Honorat), 307
Abbey Theatre (Dublin), 454
A Brasileira (Lisbon), 647
Accommodations
  tips on, 75–78
  types of, 44–46
Acropolis (Athens), 808
Adega Machado (Lisbon), 646
Adolfo Domínguez (Barcelona),
  714
Aéroport Roissy-Charles de
  Gaulle (Paris), 253
AghaRTA Jazz Centrum
  (Prague), 187
Åhléns City (Stockholm), 736
Ainola Ainolantie (Helsinki), 238
Air travel, 63, 70–72
Aix-en-Provence, 301–304
Ajuntament (Barcelona), 708
Akavriet (Bergen Aquarium),
  617–618
Aker Brygge (Oslo), 610
Akershus Festning og Slott
  (Akershus Castle and Fortress;
  Oslo), 607–608
Akhnaton (Amsterdam), 585
A la Mort Subite (Brussels), 144
Albaicín (Granada), 698
Albert Cuyp Markt (Amsterdam),
  584
Albertina Museum (Vienna), 99
Alcazaba (Granada), 697
Alcázar de los Reyes Cristianos
  (Córdoba), 693
Alcázar (Toledo), 685
Alexander Nevski Memorial
  Cathedral (Sofia), 802
The Alfama (Lisbon), 639
The Algarve, 652–656
Alhambra (Granada), 697–698
Alien (Rome), 509
A l'Imaige de Nostre-Dame
  (Brussels), 144
Alpenzoo (Alpine Zoo;
  Innsbruck), 122–123
Alstadt (Old Town; Zurich), 764
Altar of the Holy Blood
  (Rothenburg), 385
Alte Pinakothek (Munich),
  359–360
Altes Museum (Berlin), 339–340
Altes Presshaus (Grinzing), 107
Altmarkt Galerie Dresden, 380
Altstadt (Old City)
  Innsbruck, 120
  Vienna, 91
Amalienborg Museum and
  Palace (Copenhagen), 210–211
Amalienburg (Munich), 362
Amboise, 289–291

Ambrosiana Library & Picture
  Gallery (Milan), 557
American Express, 73
Amphithéâtre (Arles), 300
Amsterdam, 569–587
  accommodations, 574–576
  canal-boat tours, 581
  excursion to Haarlem,
    586–587
  getting around, 573–574
  nightlife, 584–586
  restaurants, 581–583
  shopping, 583–584
  sights and attractions,
    576–581
  special Amsterdam
    experiences, 580
  train station information, 572
  visitor information, 573
Amsterdam Diamond Center,
  584
Amsterdamse Bos, 581
Amsterdams Historisch Museum
  (Amsterdam Historical
  Museum), 576
Ana Salazar (Lisbon), 647
Ancient Olympia, 808
Ancona, 506
Andersen's Childhood Home
  (Odense), 221
Anna Lowe (Paris), 277
Anne Frankhuis (Amsterdam),
  576–577
Anta (Edinburgh), 431
Antico Caffè Greco (Rome), 508
Antigo Mercado de Escravos
  (Lagos), 654
Antiguedades Artur Ramón
  (Barcelona), 714
Antiquarium (Munich), 363
Antiquarium (Pompeii), 516
Antiques Market (Brussels), 143
Antwerp, 147–149
Antwerp Royal Museum of Fine
  Arts, 148
Appartamenti Reali (Florence),
  526
Arc de Triomphe (Paris), 266
The Archaeological Museum
  (Zagreb), 805
Archaeological Park (Syracuse),
  515
Arche Scaligere (Verona), 550
Architecture Museum (Munich),
  362
Arch of Constantine (Rome),
  499
Arch of Titus (Rome), 501
Arciliuto (Rome), 509
ARCO (Madrid's International
  Contemporary Art Fair), 660
Arena di Verona, 551
Århus, 200, 222–224
Århus Domkirke, 223
Århus Festival Week, 200
Arles, 299–301
Artesia Night Train, 44
Artesian (London), 419

Arthur's Seat (Edinburgh), 427
Art Picasso (Barcelona), 714
A Severa (Lisbon), 646
Astronomical Clock (orloj;
  Prague), 182
Atelier de Cézanne (Aix-en-
  Provence), 302
Ateneum Art Museum (Helsinki),
  237–238
Athens, 807–808
ATMs (automated teller
  machines), 73
Atomium (Brussels), 139
A Trane (Berlin), 349
Au Bon Vieux Temps (Brussels),
  144
Au Chat Noir (Geneva), 793–794
Augsburg, 386–388
Augustinerbräu (Munich), 368
Augustiner Bräustübl (Salzburg),
  118–119
Augustiner Keller (Vienna), 106
Au Lapin Agile (Paris), 278
Au Printemps (Paris), 277
Au Sauvignon (Paris), 279
Auschwitz-Birkenau, 813
Austria, 79–125
  area codes, 85
  business hours, 85
  climate, 85
  documents required, 85–86
  electricity, 86
  embassies and consulates, 86
  ferries, 65
  festivals and special events,
    82
  highlights of, 79–80
  mail, 86
  police and emergencies, 86
  by rail, 81–84
  telephone, 86–87
  tipping, 87
  traveling to, 81–85
Austria-Croatia-Slovenia Pass,
  55, 804, 820
Austria-Czech Republic Pass,
  55, 166
Austria-Germany Pass, 55
Austria-Hungary Pass, 56
Austrian Railpass, 53, 55
Austria-Switzerland Pass, 56, 83
Avignon, 295–299
Axis & the Lobby Bar (London),
  419
Azay-le-Rideau, 288

B

Baccarat (Paris), 276
Baerum Verk (Oslo), 612
Bahnhofplatz (Zurich), 762–763
Bahnhofstrasse (Zurich),
  762, 766
Baiser Salé (Paris), 279
Baker's (Helsinki), 244
Balkan Flexipass, 56, 60, 77,
  800, 803
Bally Schuhfabriken AG (Zurich),
  766

Baltic Herring Market (Helsinki), 228

Bangsbo Museum (Frederikshavn), 224

Baptismal Font (Liège), 158

Baptistery (Battistero)
Florence (Battistero San Giovanni), 523
Milan, 557-558
Pisa, 532
Siena, 534

Barbican Hall (London), 418

Barcelona, 700-717
accommodations, 704-707
getting around, 704
nightlife, 714-716
restaurants, 711-713
shopping, 713-714
sights and attractions, 707-710
train station information, 701
visitor information, 701

Barcelona Pipa Club, 716

BärenPark (Bern), 772

Bargello Museum (Museo Nazionale del Bargello; Florence), 523

Bari, 506

Bar (Montenegro), 818

Bar of the Café Alcántara (Lisbon), 650

Baroque Theater (Český Krumlov Château), 194

Bar Pilar del Toro (Granada), 700

Barrio Latino (Paris), 280

Bar Rumba (London), 419

Basilica di San Giovanni in Laterano (Rome), 496

Basilica di San Lorenzo (Florence), 523

Basilica di San Marco (Venice), 544-545

Basilica di San Pietro (St. Peter's Basilica; Rome), 497

Basilica di Santa Maria Novella (Florence), 524

Basilica di Sant'Antonio (Padua), 549

Basilica of Our Lady (Maastricht), 593

Basilica of St. Servatius (Maastricht), 593

Basilica of the Holy Blood (Bruges), 152

Basilica San Zeno Maggiore (Verona), 550-551

Basiliek van het Heilig Bloed (Bruges), 152

Basilique du Sacré-Coeur (Paris), 266, 267

Bateaux-Mouche (Paris), 272

Batofar (Paris), 279

Battistero. See Baptistery

Battlefield Panorama (Waterloo), 145

Bavarian State Opera (Munich), 368

Bayerisches Nationalmuseum (Munich), 360

Beaulieu (Lausanne), 782

Befani e Tai (Florence), 530

Belém, 640-642

Belfort en Hallen (Belfry and Market Halls; Bruges), 150, 152

Belfort en Lakenhalle (Ghent), 146

Belfry and Cloth Hall (Ghent), 146

Belgian Center for Comic-Strip Art (Brussels), 140-141

Belgium, 126-163
area codes, 130
business hours, 130
climate, 130
documents required, 130
electricity, 130-131
embassies, 131
festivals and special events, 128
health and safety, 131
highlights of, 126-127
holidays, 131
mail, 131
police and emergencies, 131
taxes, 131
telephone, 131
tipping, 131
traveling to, 127-130

Belgrade, 817

Benelux, suggested itinerary, 4-6

Benelux-France Pass, 56

Benelux Pass, 56, 59, 60, 128, 566

Bergen, 597, 614-623

Bergen Aquarium (Akvariet), 617-618

Bergen Folklore, 622

Bergen International Festival (Bergen Festspill), 596

Bergen Kunstmuseum (Bergen Art Museum), 618

The Berggruen Collection: Picasso and His Era (Berlin), 338-339

Bergisel (Innsbruck), 124

Berle Bryggen (Bergen), 622

Berlin, 327-351
accommodations, 336-338
getting around, 333-336
layout, 332-333
nightlife, 348-349
restaurants, 344-347
shopping, 347
sights and attractions, 338-344
train station information, 330, 332
visitor information, 332

Berliner Trödelmarkt und Kunstmarkt (Art and Junk Market; Berlin), 347-348

Berlin-Mitte, 339-341

Berlin Wall, 342

Berlin Wall Documentation Center, 342

Berlin WelcomeCard, 333

Berlin Zoo (Zoologischer Garten), 344

Bermuda Bräu (Vienna), 107

Bern, 768-776

Bern Casino, 775

Bernina Express, 794-795

Bernisches Historisches Museum (Bern Historical Museum), 772

Bern Symphony Orchestra, 775

Beyer (Zurich), 766-767

Biblioteca Medicea Laurenziana (Florence), 523-524

Biblioteca-Pinacoteca Ambrosiana (Milan), 557

Bierhalle Wolf (Zurich), 767

Big Ben (London), 407

Big Mama (Rome), 509

Biking
Copenhagen, 208
Vienna, 92-93

Bill Baber (Edinburgh), 431

Bimhuis (Amsterdam), 585

Binnenhof (The Hague), 588

Biserica Stavropoleos (Bucharest), 815

Bitola, 810

Black Friar (London), 419

Black Tower (České Budějovice), 196

Black Virgin (Montserrat), 717

Blås & Knåda (Stockholm), 736

Bled, 822

Bled Castle, 823

Blois, 291-292

Bloody Tower (London), 412

Blue Moon Bar (Stockholm), 737

Blues Café (Lisbon), 647-648

Blue Vans (Paris), 256

Boarding your train, 62

Boboli Gardens (Florence), 527

Bob's Special Tours (Salzburg), 113

Bohemia (Czech Republic), 188-197

Bohusslöjd (Gothenburg), 748

Bond Street (London), 416

Bon Genie (Geneva), 793

Bonnefanten Museum (Maastricht), 594

The Book of Kells (Dublin), 447-448

Boom Chicago (Amsterdam), 585

Borghese Gardens (Rome), 501

Bourbon Street (Amsterdam), 585

Boutique de Tintin (Brussels), 143

Boutique Lalique (Paris), 276

BOZAR (Brussels), 144

Brandenburg Gate (Berlin), 339

Brașov, 816

Bratislava, 819

Bratislava Castle, 819

Brazen Head (Dublin), 454

Brera Picture Gallery (Milan), 557

Bridge of Sighs (Venice), 542

British Airways London Eye, 405
British Museum (London), 405–406
BritRail passes, 52, 53, 56, 59, 60, 392–394, 397
BritRail Pass + Ireland, 56
Bröhan Museum (Berlin), 338
Brouwerij De Halve Maan (Bruges), 154
Brown cafes (Amsterdam), 585–586
Bruges, 149–156
Bruges Museum-Liberty of Bruges, 152
Bruggemuseum-Brugse Vrije (Bruges), 152
Brunate (Como), 561
Brunswick Monument (Geneva), 789
Brussels, 132–149
    accommodations, 136–138
    attractions and special moments, 138–141
    excursion to Antwerp, 147–149
    excursion to Ghent, 145–147
    getting around, 133, 136
    information, 133
    nightlife, 143–145
    restaurants, 141–143
    shopping, 143
    station information, 132
    train stations, 132–133
Brussels Park, 140
Bryggen Brukskunst (Bergen), 622
Bryggens Museum (Bergen), 618
Bucharest, 815
Bucherer
    Geneva, 793
    Lausanne, 782
    Zurich, 767
Buckingham Palace (London), 406–407
Budapest, 460–477
    accommodations, 466–469
    coffeehouses, 475
    Danube Bend excursions, 477–481
    getting around, 464–466
    nightlife, 476–477
    restaurants, 472–475
    shopping, 475–476
    sights and attractions, 469–472
    train station information, 460–464
    visitor information, 464
Budapest Autumn Festival, 456
Budapesti Történeti Múzeum (Budapest History Museum), 469
Budapest Spring Festival, 456
Budapest Summer Music Festival, 456
Budějovický Budvar (České Budějovice), 197
Budva (Montenegro), 818
Bulgaria, 799–803

Bulgaria Pass, 53
Bundestheaterkassen (Vienna), 106
Burberry (London), 417
Burg (Bruges), 152
Burgmuseum (Salzburg), 111
Burgundian Treasure (Vienna), 98
Bus travel, 63–64
Butte du Lion (Waterloo), 145

C
Cabaret du Casino Ruhl (Nice), 313
Cabo de São Vicente, 654
Ca' d'Oro (Venice), 541
Café Bazar (Salzburg), 117
Café Beaubourg (Paris), 275
Café Central (Madrid), 684
Café Chris (Amsterdam), 586
Café Cova (Milan), 560
Café de Chinitas (Madrid), 683
Café de Flore (Paris), 275
Café de la Musique (Paris), 275
Café de la Opera (Barcelona), 715
Cafè de Paris (Rome), 508
Cafe Hoppe (Amsterdam), 586
Café Opéra (Stockholm), 737
Café Rivoire (Florence), 531
Café Rosati (Rome), 508
Café Tomaselli (Salzburg), 117
Café Zurich (Barcelona), 715
Caffè Florian (Venice), 547
Caffè Sant'Eustachio (Rome), 508
Caffè Torino (Turin), 562
Campanile
    di Giotto (Florence), 525
    di San Marco (Venice), 541
    Pisa (Leaning Tower of Pisa), 532
Campidoglio (Rome), 497–498
Campo del Príncipe (Granada), 700
Camposanto (Pisa), 532
Cannes, 304–308
Canova Café (Rome), 508
Capela d'Ossos (Faro), 655
Capilla de Villaviciosa (Córdoba), 693
Capilla Real (Granada), 698
Capitoline Museum (Rome), 497–498
Cappella degli Scrovegni (Padua), 549
Cappella Palatina (Palatine Chapel; Palermo), 515
Cappelle Medicee (Florence), 526
Ca' Rezzonico (Venice), 541–542
Carlsbad (Karlovy Vary), 189–192
Carnevale masks (Venice), 546
Carnevale (Venice), 484
Carnival (Nice), 248
Carolina Rediviva (University Library; Uppsala), 739
Carpet of Flowers (Brussels), 128

Car rentals, 58–59, 68–70
Carte Mobilis (Paris), 259
Cartier (Lausanne), 782
Car travel, 65–70
Casa dei Cervi (Herculaneum), 516
Casa dei Vettii (Pompeii), 515
Casa-Museu Gaudí (Barcelona), 710
Casa Patas (Madrid), 683
Casa Ramón (Seville), 690
Casa y Museo de El Greco (Toledo), 686
Casemates (Luxembourg City), 162
Casino Gran Madrid, 684
Castel Nuovo (Naples), 512
Castelo de São Jorge (Lisbon), 638
Castel Sant'Angelo (Rome), 498–499
Castelvecchio (Old Castle; Verona), 551
Castles and palaces, suggested itinerary, 2–4
Catedral
    Barcelona, 707
    Granada, 698
    Mezquita-Catedral de Córdoba, 692–693
    Seville, 688–689
    Toledo, 685
Cathedral. See also Duomo and entries starting with Catedral, Cathédrale, Cattedrale, Sé, and Dom
    of Lausanne, 780
    of Our Lady (Antwerp), 148
    of St. Clemens (Århus Domkirke), 223
    of St. Dominius Peristil (Split), 806
    of St. Nicholas (Prague), 182
    of St. Pierre (Geneva), 789
    of St. Vincent (Bern), 773
Cathédrale de Notre-Dame, Luxembourg City, 163
Cathédrale des Sts-Michel-et-Gudule (Brussels), 139–140
Cathédrale Notre-Dame des Doms (Avignon), 298
Cathédrale Orthodoxe Russe St-Nicolas à Nice, 311
Cathédrale Ste-Croix (Orléans), 282–283
Cathédrale St-Gatien (Tours), 286
Cathédrale St-Sauveur (Aix-en-Provence), 302
Catherine (Paris), 277
Celetná Crystal (Prague), 186
Cellphones, 78
Centovalli Railway, 795
Central Helsinki Railway Station, 233
Central Market Hall (Központi Vásárcsarnok; Budapest), 476
Central Sofia Synagogue, 802

Centre Belge de la Bande-Dessinée (Brussels), 140–141
Centre Comercial Barcelona Glòries, 714
Centre Pompidou (Paris), 267
Centro de Anticuarios Lagasca (Madrid), 682
České Budějovice, 196–197
Český Krumlov, 192–195
Český Krumlov Château, 194, 195
Chambord, 292–293
Champs-Elysées (Paris), 258, 264
Changing of the Guard (London), 407
Chapelle des Macchabées (Geneva), 789
Chapelle du Rosaire (Vence), 315
Chapelle St-Jean (Avignon), 297
Chapelle St-Nicolas (Avignon), 296
Chapel of St. Hubert (Amboise), 290
Chapel Royal of St. Peter ad Vincula (London), 411
Charles Bridge (Prague), 180
Charles de Gaulle Airport (Paris), 253
Charlottenburg Palace and Museums (Berlin), 338–339
Château d'Azay-le-Rideau, 288–289
Château de Beaulieu et Musée de l'Art Brut (Lausanne), 779
Château de Chambord, 292–293
Château de Chaumont, 294
Château de Chenonceau, 294–295
Château de Jallanges (Vouvray), 289
Château de Versailles, 280–281
Château du Clos-Lucé, 290–291
Château Royal d'Amboise, 290
Château Royal de Blois, 291–292
Château Saint-Marie (Lausanne), 780
Chenonceaux, 293–295
Chiesa degli Eremitani (Padua), 549
Children, families with, 60–61
Children's fares, 51
Chinese Pavilion (Stockholm), 730
Chinon, 293
Chocolate Train, 795–796
Chrám sv. Víta (Prague), 179
Christ Church Cathedral (Dublin), 448
Christiania, 211
Christian Müller Organ (Haarlem), 587
Christiansborg Palace (Copenhagen), 211–212
Churchill Arms (London), 419
Church of Our Lady, Bruges, 153
Church of St. Bartholomew (Liège), 158
Church of St. Mary Magdalene (Karlovy Vary), 191

Church of St-Séverin (Paris), 265
Church of the Assumption (Bled), 822–823
Cip's (Venice), 548
Citadella (Budapest), 472
Cité de la Musique (Paris), 278
Cittie of Yorke (London), 418–419
CityNightLine, 44
City Park (Városliget; Budapest), 472
C. J. Josephssons Glas & Porslin (Gothenburg), 748
Clamores (Madrid), 684
Cloud Castle (Fellegvár; Visegrád), 480–481
Club der Visionaere (Berlin), 349
Coimbra, 648–649
Colete Encarnado (near Lisbon), 625
Collezione Peggy Guggenheim (Venice), 542
Collins Barracks (Dublin), 448
Colonne de Juillet (Paris), 265
Colosseo (Colosseum; Rome), 499
Columbus Pub (Budapest), 477
Come Back Bar (Bern), 776
Como, Lake, 560–561
Concertgebouw (Amsterdam), 584
Conciergerie (Paris), 268
Connolly Station (Dublin), 442
Copenhagen, 198, 204–222
  accommodations, 208–210
  getting around, 205, 208
  nightlife, 217–218
  restaurants, 215–217
  shopping, 217
  sights and attractions, 210–215
  train station information, 204
  visitor information, 205
Copenhagen Card, 205
Copenhagen Jazz Festival, 200
Copenhagen JazzHouse, 218
Córdoba, 692–694
Corinth, 808
Corral de la Morería (Madrid), 683
Couchettes, 44
Couple discounts, 60–61
Cours Mirabeau (Aix-en-Provence), 302
Court of Lions (Granada), 697
Court of the Myrtles (Granada), 697
Covent Garden Market (London), 416
Cow's Lane Fashion and Design Market (Dublin), 453
Crazy Horse Saloon (Paris), 278
Credit cards, 74
Cristal Discovery (Liège), 159
Cristallino (Prague), 186
Croatia, 803–840
Croatian History Museum (Zagreb), 805

Croatian National Theater in Zagreb, 805
Croatia Pass, 53, 60
Croatia-Slovenia-Hungary Pass, 56
Crystal Worlds (Wattens), 123
Currency, 72
Czech Flexipass, 53
Czech Philharmonic (Prague), 186
Czech Railways (České Dráhy), 167
The Czech Republic, 164–197
  area codes, 169
  business hours, 169
  climate, 169
  currency, 169
  documents required, 170
  electricity, 170
  embassies, 170
  festivals and special events, 166
  health and safety, 170
  highlights of, 164–165
  holidays, 170
  mail, 170
  police and emergencies, 170
  by rail, 166–169
  telephone, 170–171
  tipping, 171
  traveling to, 165–166
Czech Republic-Germany Pass, 56

D

Dachau, 370
Dahab (Prague), 185
Damasquinados Suarez (Toledo), 686
Dandoy (Brussels), 143
Danish Maritime Museum (Helsingor), 219
Danube Bend excursions, 477–481
Danube Delta, 815–816
Danube Island Festival, 82
Danube River cruises (Vienna), 101
DART (Dublin Area Rapid Transit), 444
De Bijenkorf (Amsterdam), 584
De Karpershoek (Amsterdam), 586
Delft, 591–592
Déli Station (Budapest), 464
Den Fynske Landsby (Odense), 220–221
Den Gamle By (Århus), 223
Den Lille Havfrue (Copenhagen), 215
Denmark, 198–225
  area code, 202
  business hours, 202
  climate, 202
  currency, 202–203
  documents required, 203
  electricity, 203
  embassies, 203

health and safety, 203
highlights of, 198–200
legal aid, 203
mail, 203
police and emergencies, 203
telephone, 203
tipping, 203
train travel, 201–202
traveling to, 200–201
Denmark-Germany Pass, 56, 201
Denmark Pass, 53, 60, 201
Den Norske Husfliden (Oslo), 612–613
Den Norske Opera (Oslo), 613
DesignTorget (Stockholm), 736
Det Blå Pakhus (Copenhagen), 217
Det Hanseatiske Museum (Bergen), 618
Det Lille Apotek (Copenhagen), 218
Deutsche Oper Berlin, 348
Deutsches Apotheken-Museum (Heidelberg), 372
Deutsches Historisches Museum (Berlin), 340
Deutsches Museum von Meisterwerken der Naturwissenschaft und Technik (Munich), 360–361
Deux Magots (Paris), 275
De Vos Almshouse (Bruges), 154
Diamond Quarter (Antwerp), 148–149
Diana Lookout Tower (Karlovy Vary), 191
Die Bahn (DB), 35
Die Sammlung Berggruen: Picasso und Seine Zeit (Berlin), 338
Diocletian's Palace (Split), 806
Di Rienzo (Rome), 508
Dirty Dick's (Barcelona), 715
Disabilities, travelers with, 62
Dohány Synagogue (Budapest), 471
Dom, Salzburg, 112
Domkyrkan (Uppsala), 738
Domplatz (Salzburg), 112
Dom St. Kilian (Würzburg), 383
Dom St. Maria (Augsburg), 387
Dom Svätého Martina (Bratislava), 820
Donatello bronzes (Padua), 549
Donauinselfest, 82
Dorotheum (Vienna), 105
Dresden, 375–382
Driving tips, 65
Drottningholm Palace and Theater (Stockholm), 720, 730, 736–737
Dublin, 438–454
accommodations, 445–447
crime, 443
getting around, 443–445
nightlife, 453–454
restaurants, 451–453
shopping, 453

sights and attractions, 447–450
train station information, 439, 442–443
visitor information, 442–443
Dublin Castle, 448
Dublinia (Dublin), 448–449
Dublin International Airport, 439
Dublin Writers Museum, 449
Dubrovnik, 805
Ducal Palace (Venice), 542
Duomo (Cattedrale)
Como, 561
Florence (Cattedrale di Santa Maria del Fiore), 526
Milan, 557–558
Pisa, 532
Siena, 534
Turin (Cattedrale di San Giovanni), 563
Duomo Museum (Museo dell'Opera del Duomo; Florence), 524

E
Eastern Europe, suggested itinerary, 9
East Side Gallery (Berlin), 342
EasyJet, 63
Edinburgh, 419–432
accommodations, 423–425
getting around, 422–423
nightlife, 431–432
restaurants, 428–431
shopping, 431
sights and attractions, 425–428
traveling to, 422
visitor information and room reservations, 422
Edinburgh Castle, 425–426
Edinburgh Festival Theatre, 432
Edinburgh International Festival, 390, 431, 432
Eduskunta (Finnish Parliament; Helsinki), 238
Edvard Munch Museum (Oslo), 607
Eglise St-Barthélemy (Liège), 158
Egon Schiele Centrum (Český Krumlov), 194
Egyptian Museum (Berlin), 340
Egyptian Museum (Turin), 562
Eiffel Tower (Paris), 268
Eispalast (Ice Palace; Jungfraujoch), 797
El Agua Casa de Vinos (Granada), 700
El Arco de los Cuchilleros Artesania de Hoy (Madrid), 682
El Arenal (Seville), 691
Elbe River cruises, 379
El Born (Barcelona), 715
El Corte Inglés
Barcelona, 713–714
Seville, 690

El Corte Inglés (Madrid), 682
Elipsos Trenhotel, 43–44
El Patio Sevillano (Seville), 691
El Perro (Dresden), 381
El Postigo (Seville), 690
El Rastro (Madrid), 682
El Rinconcillo (Seville), 690
El Tablao de Carmen (Barcelona), 716
Engelen (Stockholm), 737
Englischer Garten (Munich), 363–364
English National Ballet (London), 418
English National Opera (London), 418
Enjoy Rome, 491
Epidaurus, 808
Erlebniszug, 84
Escalera del Agua (Granada), 698
Escaliers du Marché (Lausanne), 780
Escolanía (Montserrat), 717
Espace Dalí (Paris), 266
Espace Flon (Lausanne), 782
Espai Barroc (Barcelona), 715–716
Estação Cais do Sodré (Lisbon), 635
Estação Entrecampos (Lisbon), 635
Estação Oriente (Lisbon), 634–635
Estação Rossio (Lisbon), 634
Estação Santa Apolónia (Lisbon), 634
Estates' Theater (Prague), 187
Esterházykeller (Vienna), 107
Estoril Festival, 625
Esztergom, 479–480
Esztergom Cathedral, 479–480
Eurail Czech Republic Pass, 166
Eurail Drive Pass 'n Drive, 59
Eurail Global Pass, 58, 77, 83, 166, 201, 229, 249, 323, 392, 627, 661, 720
Eurail Global Pass Flexi, 58, 77, 83, 661, 720
Eurail Select Pass 'n Drive, 59
EuroCity (EC) trains, 38
Eurolines, 64
Europa Center (Berlin), 347
European East Pass, 57, 59, 60, 166, 456, 800, 811, 818

F
Fábrica Viuva Lamego (Lisbon), 647
Fabric (London), 419
Fado (Portugal), 646
Families with children, passes for, 60
Family discounts, 60–61
Fare discounts, 50–51
Farnese Armory (Naples), 512
Farnese Gardens (Rome), 501
Faro, 655

Fasching (Carnival; Munich), 322
Fat Mo's Music Club (Budapest), 477
Fauchon (Paris), 277
Feira da Ladra (Lisbon), 645
Fellegvár (Cloud Castle; Visegrád), 480–481
Feria de Sevilla, 660
Fernsehturm (Berlin), 349
Ferries, 64–65
Feskekörka (Fish Church; Gothenburg), 745
Festas dos Santos Populares (Lisbon), 625
Festival d'Automne (Paris), 248
Festival d'Avignon, 248
Festival Fringe (Edinburgh), 390, 432
Festival International des Jardins (Chaumont-sur-Loire), 294
Festival of the Five-Petaled Rose (Česky Krumlov), 166
Festspielhaus (Salzburg), 118
Festung Hohensalzburg (Salzburg), 111
Festung Marienberg (Würzburg), 384
Fêtes de Genève (Geneva), 753
Fiesta de San Isidro (Madrid), 660
Finland, 226–244
    area code, 231
    business hours, 231
    climate, 231
    currency, 231
    documents required, 231
    electricity, 231
    embassies and consulates, 231
    festivals and special events, 228
    health and safety, 231
    highlights of, 228
    holidays, 231–232
    mail, 232
    police and emergencies, 232
    rail travel, 229–230
    telephone, 232
    tipping, 232
    traveling to, 228–229
Finland Pass, 54, 229
Finland-Sweden Pass, 57
Finnish National Opera (Helsinki), 244
First and second class, 39–40
Fish Auction (Gothenburg), 745
Fiskerkylyngen (Frederikshavn), 224
Fisketorget (Fish Market; Bergen), 621
Flåm, 620
Flamenco
    Barcelona, 716
    Madrid, 683
    Seville, 690
Flandria Line (Antwerp), 148
Flea Market (Brussels), 143

Florence, 517–535
    accommodations, 521–522
    getting around, 520–521
    nightlife, 530–531
    restaurants, 527–530
    shopping, 530
    sights and attractions, 522–527
    train station information, 517, 520
    visitor information, 520
Flower Clock (Geneva), 788
Flower Market (Amsterdam), 584
Folies-Bergère (Paris), 278
Folkart Craftman's House (Budapest), 475
Fontana dei Draghi (Tivoli), 510
Fontana dei Quattro Fiumi (Rome), 500
Fontana dell'Organo Idraulico (Tivoli), 510
Fontana del Moro (Rome), 500
Fontana di Nettuno (Rome), 500
Fontana di Trevi (Trevi Fountain; Rome), 499
Fontana di Vetro (Tivoli), 510
Fonte Gaia (Siena), 533
Fonte Luminosa (Lisbon), 642
Fonts-Baptismaux (Liège), 158
Fori Imperiali (Imperial Forums; Rome), 499–500
Foro Romano (Roman Forum), 500–501
Fortaleza de Sagres, 654
Forum of Augustus (Rome), 500
Forum of Julius Caesar (Rome), 500
Forum of Nerva (Rome), 500
Forum of Trajan (Rome), 500
Forum (Pompeii), 516
Forum Shopping Center (Helsinki), 244
Fotballpuben (Bergen), 622–623
Foundation Maeght (St-Paul-de-Vence), 314
Fountain of Glass (Tivoli), 510
Fountain of Neptune
    Florence, 523
    Rome, 500
Fountain of Sampson (České Budějovice), 196
Fountain of the Dragons (Tivoli), 510
Fountain of the Four Rivers (Rome), 500
Fountain of the Hydraulic Organ (Tivoli), 510
Fountain of the Moor (Rome), 500
Fouquet's (Paris), 275
Frágil (Lisbon), 650
Frammuseet (Oslo), 609
France, 245–319
    area code, 251
    business hours, 251
    climate, 251
    documents required, 251

electricity, 251
    embassies and consulates, 251–252
    festivals and special events, 248
    health and safety, 252
    highlights of, 245–246
    holidays, 252
    mail, 252
    police and emergencies, 252
    rail travel, 248–251
    telephone, 252
    tipping, 252
    traveling to, 247–248
France Rail 'n Drive, 59
France Railpass, 54
France-Spain Pass, 57
Frans Hals Museum (Haarlem), 587
Frauenkirche (Dresden), 379
Fraumünster (Zurich), 763
Frederikshavn, 224–225
Free City of Christiania, 211
French Riviera, 295–319
French Riviera Pass, 310
Friedrich IV, palace of (Heidelberg), 372
Frilandsmuseet (Copenhagen), 212
Fuggerei (Augsburg), 387
Fundaçao de Serralves (Porto), 649
Fundació Joan Miró (Barcelona), 708
Funen Village/Den Fynske Landsby (Odense), 220–221
Fürstenbaumuseum (Würzburg), 384
Fürstenzug (Procession of Princes; Dresden), 379

G
Galeria d'Arte Rinascimento (Amsterdam), 584
Galeries Royales St-Hubert (Brussels), 143
Galleria Borghese (Rome), 501–502
Galleria d'Arte Moderna (Florence), 527
Galleria degli Uffizi (Florence), 524–525
Galleria dell'Accademia
    Florence, 525
    Venice, 542–543
Galleria Palatina (Florence), 526
Galleriet (Bergen), 622
Gamla Stan (Old Town; Stockholm), 730
Gamla Uppsala, 739
Gamla Uppsala Museum, 739
Gamle Bergen, 619
Garden on the Ramparts (Prague), 182
Gardens of Versailles (Versailles), 281
Gare d'Austerlitz (Paris), 257

Gare de l'Est (Paris), 257
Gare de Lyon (Paris), 257
Gare du Nord (Paris), 256–257
Gasteig (Munich), 368
Gate Theatre (Dublin), 454
Gatwick Airport (near London), 392
Gatwick Express (London), 397
Gdańsk, 813
Gellért Hegy (Gellért Hill; Budapest), 471
Gemäldegalerie Alte Meister (Dresden), 378
Gemäldegalerie (Picture Gallery; Berlin), 342–343
Gemeentemuseum Den Haag (The Hague), 588
Generalife (Granada), 697–698
Geneva, 782–794
    accommodations, 786–787
    getting around, 786
    nightlife, 793–794
    restaurants, 791–792
    shopping, 792–793
    sights and attractions, 788–791
    train station information, 783, 786
    visitor information, 786
Geoffrey (Tailor) Highland Crafts (Edinburgh), 431
Georg Bräu (Berlin), 349
Georg Jensen (Copenhagen), 217
German Historical Museum (Berlin), 340
German Pharmaceutical Museum (Heidelberg), 372
German Rail 'n Drive, 59
German Railpass, 54
Germany, 320–388
    area codes, 326
    business hours, 326
    climate, 326
    documents required, 326
    electricity, 326
    embassies and consulates, 326
    ferries, 65
    festivals and special events, 322
    health and safety, 326–327
    highlights of, 320–322
    holidays, 327
    mail, 327
    police and emergencies, 327
    rail travel, 323
    telephone, 327
    tipping, 327
    traveling to, 322–326
Germany-Poland Pass, 57
Germany-Switzerland Pass, 57
Ghent, 145–147
Giant's Hall (Innsbruck), 122
Giardini di Boboli (Florence), 527
Gilli's (Florence), 531
Giotto frescoes (Padua), 549

Giotto's Bell Tower (Florence), 525
Glacier Express, 794
Global Refund, 75
Globus (Bern), 775
Globus-Grand Passage (Geneva), 793
Godshuis de Vos (Bruges), 154
Goldenes Dachl (Golden Roof; Innsbruck), 120
Golden Lane (Prague), 179
Golden Pass Line, 795
Götaplatsen (Gothenburg), 745
Göteborgs Konstmuseum (Gothenburg), 744
Göteborgs Maritima Centrum (Gothenburg), 744–745
Göteborgsoperan (Gothenburg), 748
Gothenburg, 740–749
Gotische Zaal (Gothic Room; Bruges), 152
Grachtenfestival Canals Festival (Amsterdam), 565
Granada, 694–700
Grand Café (Prague), 185
Grand Canal (Venice), 543
Grand Casino Ljubljana, 822
Grande Ecourie (Versailles), 281
Grandhotel Pupp (Karlovy Vary), 191
Grand-Place (Brussels), 138
Grands Appartements (Versailles), 281
Grand Théâtre (Geneva), 793
Grand Trianon (Versailles), 281
Gran Teatre del Liceu (Barcelona), 715
Gravensteen (Ghent), 146
Great Britain, 389–432
    area codes, 394
    business hours, 394
    climate, 394–395
    currency, 395
    documents required, 395
    electricity, 395
    embassies and consulates, 395
    festivals and special events, 390
    health and safety, 395
    holidays, 395
    legal aid, 395
    mail, 395–396
    police and emergencies, 396
    rail travel, 392–394
    telephone, 396
    tipping, 396
    traveling to, 392–394
Great Church (Stockholm), 732
Greece, 806–809
    ferries, 65
Greece-Italy Pass, 57, 806
Greece Pass, 54, 77
Green Vault (Dresden), 376, 378
Grieghallen (Bergen), 622
Grinzing, *heuriger* of, 107

Groc (Barcelona), 714
Groeninge Museum (Bruges), 152
Grossmünster (Zurich), 763
Grote Kerk (Haarlem), 587
Grote Markt (Haarlem), 586
Group discounts, 60–61
Grünes Gewölbe (Dresden), 376, 378
Gruuthuse Museum (Bruges), 153
Gübelin Jewelers (Geneva), 793
Guldhedens Vattentorn (water tower; Gothenburg), 745
Gun Park (Heidelberg), 372
Gurten, 774

H

Haarlem, 586–587
Hadrian's Villa (Tivoli), 509–510
The Hague, 587–592
The Hague Municipal Museum, 588
Half-Moon Brewery (Bruges), 154
Hall of Mirrors Building (Heidelberg), 372
Hall of Mirrors (Versailles), 281
Hall of Shells (Potsdam), 351
Hallwylska Museet (Hallwyl Museum; Stockholm), 730
Hamlet's Castle (Helsingor), 218–220
Hamleys (London), 417
Handpets (Szentendre), 478
Harlem Jazz Club (Barcelona), 715
Harrods (London), 417
Harry's Bar
    Rome, 508
    Venice, 548
Harry's New York Bar (Paris), 280
Hash Marihuana & Hemp Museum (Amsterdam), 577
Haus der Musik (Vienna), 99–100
Haute Ville (Lausanne), 776, 780
Havel's Market (Prague), 186
H.C. Andersen's Barndomshjem (Odense), 221
H.C. Andersen's Hus (Odense), 221
Health and safety, Austria, holidays, 86
Heathrow Airport (near London), 392
Heathrow Express (London), 397
Heaven (London), 419
Heidelberg, 371
Heidelberg Castle, 372
Heidi's Shop (Lausanne), 782
Heimatwerk (Bern), 775
Heimen Husflid (Oslo), 613
Hekticket (Berlin), 348
Hellabrunn Zoo (Munich Zoo), 364
Hellbrunn Palace (Salzburg), 114
Helsingor (Hamlet's Castle), 218–220

Helsinki, 232–244
accommodations, 236–237
getting around, 236
nightlife, 244
restaurants, 241–243
shopping, 243–244
sights and attractions, 237–241
station information, 233
visitor information, 233, 236
Helsinki Card, 236
Helsinki City Museum, 238–239
Helsinki Festival, 228
Helsinki-Vantaa Airport, 233
Henie Onstad Kunstsenter (Oslo), 608
Henry Wood Promenade Concerts (The Proms; London), 390
Herculaneum, 516–517
Herend Shops (Budapest), 476
Herr Nilsen (Oslo), 613
Heuriger, Grinzing, 107
Heuston Station (Dublin), 442
High season, 33
High-speed trains, 37
first and second class, 40
Historical Museum (Museo Storico; Rome), 497
Historiska Museet (Museum of National Antiquities; Stockholm), 730–731
Hjertholm (Bergen), 622
Hofburg Kaiserappartements (Vienna), 97–98
Hofburg Palace Complex (Vienna), 97–99
Hofburg Silberkammer (Vienna), 97–98
Hofgarten Cafe (Innsbruck), 125
Hofkirche (Innsbruck), 122
Hohensalzburg Fortress (Salzburg), 111, 118
Hohenschwangau Castle, 369–370
Holland. See The Netherlands
Holland Casino Scheveningen, 590
Holmenkollen Ski Festival (near Oslo), 596
Holocaust Memorial (Berlin), 339
Holyrood Park (Edinburgh), 427
Holy Shroud (Turin), 563
Holy Week
Italy, 484
Seville, 686
Hospital de Santa Caridad (Seville), 689
Hôtel des Invalides (Paris), 268–269
Hôtel de Ville
Brussels, 140
Geneva, 790
Hôtel-de-Ville, Arles, 299
Hôtel Groslot (Orléans), 283–284
Hotel Råže (Český Krumlov), 193

Hotel Thermal (Karlovy Vary), 190–191
House of Livia (Rome), 501
House of the Mysteries (Pompeii), 515
House of the Vestal Virgins (Rome), 501
House of the Vettii (Pompeii), 515
Houses of Parliament (London), 407–408
Hrampametnik Alexander Nevski (Alexander Nevski Memorial Cathedral; Sofia), 802
Hrvatski Povijesni Muzej (Croatian History Museum; Zagreb), 805
Hrvatsko Narodno Kazaliste u Zagrebu (Zagreb), 805
Hugh Lane Municipal Gallery of Modern Art (Dublin), 449
Hundertwasser Haus (Vienna), 100
Hungarian National Museum (Nemzeti Múzeum; Budapest), 469
Hungarian State Opera House (Magyar Allami Operaház; Budapest), 470, 476, 477
Hungary, 455–481
business hours, 459
climate, 459
currency, 459
documents required, 459
electricity, 459
embassies and consulates, 459
festivals and special events, 456
health and safety, 459–460
highlights of, 455
holidays, 460
police and emergencies, 460
rail travel, 456–459
telephone, 460
tipping, 460
traveling to, 455–459
Hungary Pass, 54, 56, 456
Hungary-Romania Pass, 57
Hungerburg (Innsbruck), 123

I

Iarnrod Eireann, 436
Ibsen, Henrik, apartment of (Oslo), 609
Icebar (Stockholm), 737
Ice Palace (Eispalast; Jungfraujoch), 797
Iconos (Seville), 690
Iglesia de Santo Tomé (Toledo), 685
Igreja de Nossa Senhora do Monte do Carmo do Faro, 655
Igreja de Santa Clara (Porto), 649
Igreja de Santo António (Lagos), 654–655

Il Duomo. See Duomo
Ile de la Cité (Paris), 264
Ile Rousseau (Geneva), 788
Ile Ste-Marguerite, 306–307
Iles de Lérins, 306–307
Ile St-Honorat, 307
Ile St-Louis (Paris), 264
Illum (Copenhagen), 217
Il Piccolo Mondo (Venice), 548
Imperial Apartments (Vienna), 97–98
Imperial Court Palace (Innsbruck), 121–122
Imperial Forums (Fori Imperiali; Rome), 499–500
Imperial Silver Collection (Vienna), 97–98
Infante Dom Henrique Archaeological Museum (Lagos), 655
Ingreja de Santa Maria (Lisbon), 640
Innsbruck, 80, 119–125
InterCity (IC) trains, 39
International Film Festival (Cannes), 306
International Palace Tournament (Visegrád), 456
Ireland, 433–454
area codes, 437
business hours, 437
currency, 437
electricity, 437
embassies and consulates, 437
festivals and special events, 433
health and safety, 437–438
mail, 438
police, 438
rail travel, 435–437
telephone, 438
tipping, 438
traveling to, 433–437
Ireland Pass, 54, 59, 393, 435
Itaca (Barcelona), 714
Italy, 482–563
area code, 487
climate, 487–488
documents required, 488
electricity, 488
embassies and consulates, 488
festivals and special events, 484
health and safety, 488
highlights of, 482–484
holidays, 488–489
legal aid, 489
mail, 489
police and emergencies, 489
rail travel, 485–487
telephone, 489
tipping, 489
traveling to, 484–487
Italy Pass, 54, 57, 485
Italy Rail 'n Drive, 59
Italy-Spain Pass, 57

Itineraries
1-week, 1–13
  castles and palaces, 2–4
  Eastern Europe, 9–11
  Scandinavia, 11–13
  scenic route, 6–9
  small cities of the
    Benelux, 4–6
2-week, 13–28
  art and architecture,
    16–19
  for food lovers, 19–22
  grand tour, 26–28
  great cities, 23–26
  for history and culture
    buffs, 13–16

J

Jahn-Markl (Salzburg), 117
Jamboree (Barcelona), 715
James Joyce Pub (Zurich), 767
James Pringle Woolen Mill
  (Edinburgh), 431
J. & L. Lobmeyr (Vienna), 105
Jardin Anglais (English Garden;
  Geneva), 788
Jardin Botanique (Botanical
  Garden; Geneva), 788
Jardin Exotique (Monaco), 318
Jazzclub Unterfahrt (Munich),
  368
Jazz-Fest Berlin, 322
Jazzland (Vienna), 108
Jelmoli Department Store
  (Zurich), 767
Jet d'Eau (Geneva), 788
Jewish Museum Berlin, 341
The Jewish Museum (Prague),
  180
Joalharia do Carmo (Lisbon),
  645
Joe's Wirthaus zum Löwen
  (Berlin), 349
Jorritt Heinen (Amsterdam), 584
Jubilee Market (London), 416
Judería (Córdoba), 693
Jüdisches Museum Berlin, 341
Jungfraujoch, 797
Junod (Lausanne), 782
Jupiter's Temple (Split), 806
Jutland, 222–225

K

Käfigturm (Bern), 772
Kaiserappartements (Innsbruck),
  122
Kaiserliche Hofburg (Innsbruck),
  121–122
Kaiser-Wilhelm Gedächtniskirche
  (Kaiser Wilhelm Memorial
  Church; Berlin), 343
Kalemegdan Citadel (Belgrade),
  817–818
Kalke Village (Vienna), 100
Kantcentrum (Bruges), 153
Kapital (Madrid), 683
Karlovy Vary, 164–165

Karlovy Vary (Carlsbad), 189–192
Karlstejn Castle, 164, 188
Käthe-Kollwitz Museum (Berlin),
  343
Kaufhaus des Westens (KaDeWe;
  Berlin), 347
Kaufleuten (Zurich), 767
Kavárna Slavia (Prague), 185
Keleti Station (Budapest), 461
Kensington Palace (London),
  408
Kiasma (Museum of
  Contemporary Art; Helsinki),
  239
Kilmainham Gaol Historical
  Museum (Dublin), 449
King Matthias Museum
  (Visegrád), 480
King's Road (London), 417
King's Theatre (Edinburgh), 432
King St. Stephen's Day
  (Hungary), 456
Klötzlikeller (Bern), 776
Kloverhuset (Bergen), 622
Kobenhavn Hovedbanegård
  (Copenhagen), 204
Komische Oper (Comic Opera;
  Berlin), 348
Kongeliege Stalde & Kareter
  (Copenhagen), 211
Koninginnedag (Queen's Day;
  the Netherlands), 565
Koninklijke Porceleyne Fles
  (Delft), 592
Koninklijk Kabinet van
  Schilderijen (The Hague), 588
Koninklijke Museum voor Schone
  Kunsten Antwerpen
  (Antwerp), 148
Koninklijk Paleis (Royal Palace;
  Amsterdam), 577
Kon-Tiki Museum (Oslo),
  609–610
Kontoret Pub (Bergen), 623
Konzerthaus Berlin, 348
Kotor, 818
Központi Vásárcsarnok (Central
  Market Hall; Budapest), 476
Krah Krah (Vienna), 107
Kraków, 813
Kriminalmuseum (Rothenburg),
  386
Kronborg Slot, 219
Ku'damm (Kurfürstendamm;
  Berlin), 347
Kungliga Operan (Stockholm),
  737
Kungliga Slottet (Royal Palace)
  and Museums (Stockholm),
  731
Kungsportsavenyn
  (Gothenburg), 744
KunstHausWien (Vienna), 100
Kunsthistorisches Museum
  (Vienna), 100
Kunsthof (Dresden), 381
Kunstmuseum (Bern), 773
Kupferstich-Kabinett (Dresden),
  378

Kurpfälzisches Museum
  (Heidelberg), 373
Kustaanmiekka, 241
KZ-Gedenkstätte Dachau
  (Dachau), 370

L

La Alicantina (Seville), 690
La Balajo (Paris), 279
Lace Center (Bruges), 153
Lac Léman (Lake Geneva), 791
La Coupole (Paris), 275
La Fondation Angladon-
  Dubrujeaud (Avignon), 298
La Fontaine (Copenhagen), 218
La Giralda (Seville), 688
Lagos, 654
La Gran Taberna (Granada), 700
Lake Como, 560–561
Lake Geneva (Lac Léman), 791
Lake Zurich, 765
Lambert van Meerten (Delft),
  592
Landesmuseum (Swiss National
  Museum; Zurich), 763–764
La Paloma (Barcelona), 716
La Rambla (Barcelona), 710
L'Archiduc (Brussels), 144
Largo das Portas do Sol
  (Lisbon), 639
La Rinascente (Florence), 530
La Sagrada Família (Barcelona),
  708
La Scala (Milan), 560
The Last Supper of Leonardo da
  Vinci (Milan), 558
Laterna Magika (Prague), 187
La Tuile à Loup (Paris), 276–277
Lausanne, 776–782
Lausanne Cathédrale, 780–781
La Vinya del Senyor (Barcelona),
  714–715
Leaning Tower of Pisa
  (Campanile), 532
Le Château (Nice), 310
Le Falstaff (Brussels), 144
Le Francis (Geneva), 794
Le Grand Café (Lausanne), 782
Le Louvre des Antiquaires
  (Paris), 276
Le Marais (Paris), 264–265
Leopold Museum (Vienna),
  100–101
Le Petit Journal (Paris), 279
Lérins Islands, 306–307
Lerverk (Gothenburg), 748
Les Alyscamps (Arles), 300
Le Sancerre (Paris), 279–280
Les Arènes Romaines (Arles),
  300
Les Bains Douches (Paris), 279
Le Scimmie (Milan), 560
Les Égouts (Paris), 271
Les Grands Appartements du
  Palais (Monaco), 316
Le Sounds (Brussels), 144
Leute (Munich), 367

Liberation Monument (Budapest), 471
Liberty (London), 416–417
Lido de Paris (Paris), 278
Liège, 156–159
Limerick Bill's Irish Pub (Innsbruck), 125
Limmat Quai (Zurich), 762
Lindenhof (Zurich), 764
Linke Wienzeile market (Vienna), 105–106
Linnaeus Garden & Museum (Uppsala), 738–739
Lion Mound (Waterloo), 145
Lisbon, 632–652
    accommodations, 636–638
    excursion to Sintra, 650–652
    getting around, 635–636
    nightlife, 646, 647–650
    restaurants, 643–645
    shopping, 645, 647
    sights and attractions, 638–643
    train station information, 632, 634–635
    visitor information, 635
Liseberg Park (Gothenburg), 745
The Little Mermaid (Copenhagen), 215
Livrustkammaren (Stockholm), 731
Ljubljana, 822
Loewe (Madrid), 682
Loggia dei Cavalli (Venice), 544
Loggia dei Lanzi (Florence), 523
Loggia del Consiglio (Verona), 550
Logis du roi (Amboise), 290
Loire Valley, 281–295
London, 397–419
    accommodations, 403–405
    getting around, 401–402
    nightlife, 417–419
    restaurants, 413–416
    shopping, 416–417
    train station information, 397, 400–401
    visitor information, 401
London Symphony Orchestra, 418
The Long Hall (Dublin), 454
Loos American Bar (Vienna), 107
Lorry (Oslo), 613–614
Los Tarantos (Barcelona), 716
Louis Vuitton (Lausanne), 782
Ludwig Museum (Budapest), 477
Lurblæserne (Copenhagen), 213
Luso (Lisbon), 646
Lutheran Cathedral (Tuomiokirkko; Helsinki), 239
Luxembourg City, 159–163
Luxury sleepers, 43–44
Luz de Gas (Barcelona), 716

M

Maastricht, 592–594
Macedonia, 809–811

Mad (Lausanne), 782
Madrid, 665–686
    accommodations, 672–674
    bullfighting, 675
    excursion to Toledo, 684–686
    getting around, 672
    nightlife, 682–684
    restaurants, 679–682
    shopping, 682
    sights and attractions, 674–679
    train station information, 670–671
    visitor information, 671
Madurodam (The Hague), 588
Magasin (Copenhagen), 217
Magestic Imperator, 82–83
Maggio Musicale (Florence), 530
Magyar Allami Operaház (Hungarian State Opera House; Budapest), 470, 476
Mainfränkisches Museum (Würzburg), 384
Maisel Synagogue (Prague), 180
Maison Antoine (Brussels), 143
Maison Jeanne-d'Arc (Orléans), 284
Maison Tavel (Geneva), 790
Maloe Melo (Amsterdam), 585
Manneken-Pis statue (Brussels), 139
Mannerheim Museum (Helsinki), 239
Manufacture Belge de Dentelles (Brussels), 143
Maps, road, 70
Marché aux Fleurs (Nice), 311
Marché aux Puces (Brussels), 139
Marciano Museum (Venice), 544
Maremagnum (Barcelona), 714
Margit Kovács Museum (Szentendre), 478
Mariakirke (St. Mary's Church; Bergen), 619
Marians Jazzroom (Bern), 776
Maribor, 822
Marienkirche (Würzburg), 384
The Market Bar (Dublin), 454
Marks & Spencer (London), 416
Marktgasse (Bern), 772
Markt (Market Square; Bruges), 150
Marktplatz, Würzburg, 383
Marktplatz (Heidelberg), 372–373
Marolles district (Brussels), 141
Marstallmuseum (Munich), 362
Martian (Seville), 690
Mátyás Templom (Matthias Church; Budapest), 471
Mauermuseum-Haus am Checkpoint Charlie (Berlin), 341–342
Mauritshuis (The Hague), 588
Max Emanuel Brauerei (Munich), 368
Max Krug (Munich), 367
Mayer am Pfarrplatz (Grinzing), 107

Medici Chapels (Florence), 526
Medici Laurentian Library (Florence), 523–524
Meidling station (Vienna), 90
Meissener Porzellan am Fürstenzug (Dresden), 379
Melkweg (Amsterdam), 585
Memling in Sint-Jan (Bruges), 153
Memorial de la Déportation (Paris), 264
Mercato Centrale (Mercato San Lorenzo; Florence), 530
Mercato della Paglia (Mercato Nuovo; Florence), 530
Mexuar (Granada), 697
Mezquita-Catedral de Córdoba, 692–693
Michelangelo
    Medici Chapels (Florence), 526
    Medici Laurentian Library (Florence), 523–524
    Sistine Chapel (Rome), 503
    St. Peter's dome (Rome), 497
Midsummer Eve (Sweden), 720
Milan, 552–563
Military Tattoo (Edinburgh), 390, 432
Mini-Europe (Brussels), 141
Mirador Torre de Collserola (Barcelona), 707
Miradouro de Santa Luzia (Lisbon), 639
Mobile phones, 78
Moderna Museet (Museum of Modern Art; Stockholm), 731
Moldavia, 816
Monaco, 315–319
Monasterio de las Descalzas Reales (Madrid), 674
Monasterio de San Juan de los Reyes (Toledo), 685
Monastery of Nossa Senhora da Assunção (Lagos), 655
Mönchsberg Lift (Salzburg), 114
Mondonovo (Venice), 546–547
Money matters, 72–75
Montenegro, 816–818
Montmartre (Paris), 265–266
Montserrat, 716–717
Morrison's Irish Pub (Cannes), 308
Moser (Prague), 185
Mosteiro dos Jerónimos (Lisbon), 640
Moulin Rouge (Paris), 278
Mount Olympus, 808
Mount Pilatus Cog Railway, 796–797
Mozart, Wolfgang Amadeus
    Birthplace (Salzburg), 113
    festival (Würzburg), 383
    Residence (Salzburg), 113–114
Mozarteum (Salzburg), 118
Mozart Geburtshaus (Salzburg), 113–114
Mozart-Wohnhaus (Salzburg), 113–114

Mr. Pickwick Pub (Geneva), 794
MUMOK (Museum of Modern Art
 Ludwig Trust Vienna), 101
Munch, Edvard, 607, 618, 764
Münchner Puppenstuben und
 Zinnfiguren-Kabinett
 (Munich), 367
Münchner Stadtmuseum
 (Munich), 361
Munich, 351–370
  accommodations, 357–359
  getting around, 355, 357
  layout, 355
  nightlife, 368
  restaurants, 364–367
  shopping, 367
  sights and attractions,
   359–364
  train station information, 354
  visitor information, 354
Munich Zoo (Hellabrunn Zoo),
 364
Municipal Baths (Herculaneum),
 516–517
Münsterhof (Zurich), 764
Musée d'Anthropologie
 Préhistorique (Monaco), 318
Musée d'Art Ancien (Brussels),
 138
Musée d'Art et Histoire
 (Geneva), 790
Musée d'Art Moderne (Brussels),
 138
Musée de la Castre (Cannes),
 306
Musée de la Mer (Ile Ste-
 Marguerite), 307
Musée de l'Ariana (Geneva), 790
Musée de l'Arles et de la
 Provence antiques, 300
Musée de l'Art Wallon (Liège),
 158
Musée de la Vie Wallonne
 (Liège), 158
Musée de la Ville de Bruxelles,
 138
Musée de l'Océanographie
 (Monaco), 318
Musée de Matisse (Cimiez), 312
Musée des Beaux-Arts
  Nice, 311
  Orléans, 284
  Tours, 286
Musée des Cires (Waterloo), 145
Musée des Tapisseries (Aix-en-
 Provence), 302
Musée d'Orsay (Paris), 269
Musée du Cristal Baccarat
 (Paris), 276
Musée du Louvre (Paris),
 269–270
Musée du Palais du Prince
 (Souvenirs Napoléoniens et
 Collection d'Archives;
 Monaco), 317–318
Musée du Petit Palais (Avignon),
 297–298

Musée National Auguste Rodin
 (Paris), 270
Musée National d'Art Moderne
 (Paris), 267
Musée National de Monaco, 318
Musée National d'Histoire et
 d'Art (Luxembourg City), 163
Musée National Message
 Biblique Marc-Chagall
 (Cimiez), 311–312
Musée Picasso (Paris), 270
Musée Réattu (Arles), 300
Musées Royaux des Beaux-Arts
 de Belgique (Brussels),
 138–139
Musée Wellington (Waterloo),
 145
Musei Vaticani (Vatican
 Museums; Rome), 502–503
Museo Archeologico Nazionale
 (Naples), 511–512
Museo Archeologico Regionale
 (Palermo), 515
Museo Arqueológico Nacional
 (Madrid), 674–675
Museo Arqueológico y
 Etnológico de Córdoba, 693
Museo Barbier-Mueller Art
 Precolombí (Barcelona), 709
Museo Bellas Artes en la
 Alhambra (Granada), 697
Museo Capitolino (Rome),
 497–498
Museo Civico Correr (Venice),
 543
Museo Civico di Padova (Padua),
 549
Museo da Fundacão Calouste
 Gulbenkian (Lisbon), 647
Museo de Bellas Artes de
 Córdoba, 693–694
Museo de Bellas Artes de Sevilla,
 689
Museo degli Argenti (Florence),
 527
Museo de la Alhambra
 (Granada), 697
Museo de la Real Academia de
 Bellas Artes de San Fernando
 (Madrid), 675–676
Museo della Santissima Sindone
 (Turin), 563
Museo dell'Opera del Duomo
 (Florence), 524
Museo del Prado (Madrid),
 676–677
Museo di San Marco (Florence),
 527
Museo e Gallerie Nazionale di
 Capodimonte (Naples), 512
Museo-Hospital de Santa Cruz
 (Toledo), 685
Museo Lázaro Galdiano (Madrid),
 677
Museo Nacional Centro de Arte
 Reina Sofía (Madrid), 677
Museo Nacional d'Art de
 Catalunya (Barcelona), 709

Museo Nazionale di San Martino
 (Naples), 512
Museo Nazionale di Villa Giulia
 (Rome), 503
Museo Storico (Historical
 Museum; Rome), 497
Museo Thyssen-Bornemisza
 (Madrid), 677–678
Museu Calouste Gulbenkian
 (Lisbon), 642–643
Museu d'Art Contemporani de
 Barcelona (Barcelona), 709
Museu de Marinha (Lisbon),
 640–641
Museu de Montserrat, 717
Museu de Santo Antóniano
 (Lisbon), 638–639
Museum der Moderne Salzburg
 Mönchsberg (Salzburg), 114
Museum Het Rembrandthuis
 (Amsterdam), 577
Museum of Art & History
 (Geneva), 790
Museum of Contemporary Art
 (Kiasma; Helsinki), 239
Museum of Fine Arts
  Budapest (Szépművészeti
   Múzeum), 470
  Vienna (Kunsthistorisches
   Museum), 100
  Zurich (Kunsthaus), 764
Museum of Foreign Art
 (Helsinki), 240–241
Museum of Modern Art
 (Stockholm), 731
Museum of National Antiquities
 (Stockholm), 730–731
Museum of Silver (Florence), 527
Museum of the City of Brussels,
 138
Museum of the Palatinate
 (Heidelberg), 373
Museum of Walloon Art (Liège),
 158
Museum of Walloon Life (Liège),
 158
Museu Municipal Dr. José
 Formosinho (Lagos), 655
Museu Nacional de Arte Antiga
 (Lisbon), 643
Museu Nacional dos Coches
 (Lisbon), 641
Museu Picasso (Barcelona),
 709–710
Musik Hug (Zurich), 767
Muziekgebouw aan 't IJ
 (Amsterdam), 585
Muziektheater (Amsterdam), 584
Myrdal, 620
Mythen Quai (Zurich), 762

N

Nachtgalerie (Munich), 369
N.A.L.L. Art Association (Vence),
 315
Naples, 510–517
Národní divadlo (Prague), 187
Naschmarkt (Vienna), 106

Nasjonalgalleriet (Oslo), 608
National Archaeological Museum
  Athens, 808
  Naples, 511–512
  Sofia, 802
National Ballet (Amsterdam),
  584
National Gallery
  London, 408–409
  Prague, 181
National Gallery of Ireland
  (Dublin), 449–450
National Gallery of Scotland
  (Edinburgh), 426
Nationalmuseet (Copenhagen),
  212
National Museum
  Belgrade, 818
  Copenhagen, 212
  Ljubljana, 822
National Museum & Gallery of
  the Capodimonte (Naples), 512
Nationalmuseum (National
  Museum of Art; Stockholm),
  731–732
National Museum of Art and
  History (Luxembourg City),
  163
National Museum of Finland
  (Helsinki), 239–240
National Museum of Ireland
  (Dublin), 450
National Museum of San Martino
  (Naples), 512
National Museum of Scotland
  (Edinburgh), 426
National Theater Ballet (Prague),
  187
Nationaltheater (Munich), 368
Nationaltheatret (Oslo), 613
Natural History Museum
  (London), 409
Natzionalen Archeologicheski
  Musei (Sofia), 802
Neckar Valley, 373
Necropolis Vaticana (Rome), 497
Nemzeti Múzeum (Hungarian
  National Museum; Budapest),
  469
The Netherlands, 564–594
  area codes, 568
  business hours, 568
  climate, 568
  documents required, 568
  electricity, 568
  embassies and consulates,
    568
  festivals and special events,
    565
  health and safety, 568–569
  highlights of, 564
  holidays, 569
  mail, 569
  police and emergencies, 569
  telephone, 569
  tipping, 569
  traveling to, 565–568
Netherlands Dance Theater
  (Amsterdam), 584

Netherlands Opera
  (Amsterdam), 584
Neue Pinakothek (Munich), 361
Neues Museum (Berlin), 340
Neues Palais (Potsdam), 351
Neuhaus (Brussels), 143
Neuschwanstein, 369–370
Neustadt (New City), Salzburg,
  111
New Acropolis Museum
  (Athens), 808
Nice, 308–319
Nieuwe Kerk (New Church;
  Delft), 591–592
Night trains, 40–43
Nikolaiviertel (Berlin), 341
Nobel Peace Prize Ceremony
  (Oslo), 596
Nordiska Galleriet (Stockholm),
  736
Nordiska Kompaniet (New
  Brunswick), Stockholm, 736
Nordiska Kompaniet (NK),
  Gothenburg, 748
Nordiska Museet (Nordic
  Museum; Stockholm), 732–733
Nordkette cable railway
  (Nordkettenbahn), 123
Norelene (Venice), 547
Norsk Folkemuseum (Oslo), 610
Norsk Sjofartsmuseum (Oslo),
  610
North Sea Jazz Festival
  (Rotterdam), 565
Norway, 595–623
  area code, 600
  business hours, 600
  climate, 600
  currency, 600
  documents required, 600
  electricity, 600
  embassies and consulates,
    600
  festivals and special events,
    596
  health and safety, 600
  holidays, 600–601
  legal aid, 601
  mail, 601
  police and emergencies, 601
  telephone, 601
  tipping, 601
  traveling to, 597–599
Norway Designs (Oslo), 613
Norway Pass, 54
Notre-Dame Cathedral
  Luxembourg City, 163
  Paris, 270–271
Notre-Dame des Doms
  (Avignon), 298
Nouveau Casino (Paris), 278
Ny Carlsberg Glyptotek
  (Copenhagen), 212–213
Nyhavn (Copenhagen), 213
Nyhavn 17 (Copenhagen), 218
Nymphenburg Palace (Munich),
  362
Nyugati Station (Budapest),
  461, 464

O

Oakley's Country Club
  (Gothenburg), 749
Obala Hrvatskog Norodnog
  Preporoda (Split), 806
ÖBB Vorteilscard, 83
Obidos, 648
Oceanario de Lisboa (Lisbon),
  642
Octave of Our Lady of
  Luxembourg (Luxembourg
  City), 163
Odense, 220
Odeon (Amsterdam), 585
Off season, 33
Ohrid, 811
Oktoberfest (Germany), 322
  Munich, 363
Old City. See also Altstadt
  Liège, 156
Old Jewish Cemetery (Prague),
  180
Old Man's Pub (Budapest), 477
Old-New Synagogue (Prague),
  180
Old Town Square (Prague),
  181–182
Oleana (Bergen), 622
Oliver St. John Gogarty (Dublin),
  454
Oliver Twist (Zurich), 767–768
Olympiastadion (Helsinki), 240
Ommegang (Brussels), 128
Ons' Lieve Heer op Solder
  (Amsterdam), 578
Onze-Lieve-Vrouwbasiliek
  (Maastricht), 593
Onze-Lieve-Vrouwekathedraal
  (Antwerp), 148
Onze-Lieve-Vrouwekerk
  (Bruges), 153
Open-Air Museum, Copenhagen,
  212
Opéra Bastille (Paris), 277–278
Opéra de Nice, 313
Opéra Garnier (Paris), 277
Opera House (Versailles), 281
Opernhaus (Zurich), 767
Orchestre de la Suisse Romande
  (Geneva), 793
Orlandostrasse (Munich), 367
Orléans, 282–285
Orly Airport (Paris), 256
Oslo, 601–614
  accommodations, 605–606
  getting around, 605
  nightlife, 613–614
  restaurants, 611–612
  shopping, 612–613
  sights and attractions,
    607–611
  train station information, 601,
    604
  visitor information, 604
Ostbahn (Vienna), 90
Östermalms Saluhall
  (Stockholm), 736
Österreichische Bundesbahn
  (ÖBB), 83

Ottheinrich Building (Heidelberg), 372
Ouchy White Horse Pub (Lausanne), 782
Oude Kerk (Old Church)
  Amsterdam, 578
  Delft, 591
Our Dynamic Earth (Edinburgh), 426–427
Ovetari Chapel (Padua), 549
Ö.W. (Österreichische Werkstatten; Vienna), 105
Oyster Card (London), 402

P

Pachá (Madrid), 683
Package tours, 71–72
Padua, 548–550
  excursions from, to Verona, 550–551
Palace of Arts (Budapest), 476–477
Palace of Friedrich IV (Heidelberg), 372
Palace of Holyroodhouse (Edinburgh), 427
Palace of the Conservatori (Rome), 498
Palace of the Grand Dukes (Luxembourg City), 162–163
Palace of the Normanni (Palace of the Normans; Palermo), 514
Palace of the Prince-Bishops (Liège), 158
Palacio Museo de Viana (Córdoba), 693
Palacio Nacional de Pena (Sintra), 651
Palacio Nacional de Sintra, 651
Palacio Real (Royal Palace; Madrid), 678
Palais des Nations (Geneva), 790–791
Palais des Papes (Avignon), 296–297
Palais des Prince-Evêques (Liège), 158
Palais Grand-Ducal (Luxembourg City), 162–163
Palais Royal (Royal Palace), Brussels, 140
Palatine Hill (Rome), 501
Palatul Cotroceni (Bucharest), 815
Palatul Parlamentului (Bucharest), 815
Palau de la Generalitat (Barcelona), 708
Palazzo dei Conservatori (Rome), 497–498
Palazzo del Governo (Verona), 550
Palazzo Ducale (Venice), 542
Palazzo Pitti (Florence), 526–527
Palazzo Pubblico (Siena), 533–534
Palermo, 514, 515

Palm Beach Casino (Cannes), 308
Panama (Amsterdam), 585
Panorama Bar (Lisbon), 647
Panorama de la Bataille (Waterloo), 145
Panorama Museum (Salzburg), 114–115
Panteón de Goya (Madrid), 678
Pantheon (Rome), 503
Pantomime Theater (Copenhagen), 217
Papeneiland (Amsterdam), 586
Papyrus Collection (Berlin), 340
Paradiso (Amsterdam), 585
Parc de Bruxelles (Brussels), 140
Parc Güell (Barcelona), 710
Paris, 253–281
  accommodations, 260–263
  arrondissements in brief, 258–259
  cafes, 275
  getting around, 259–260
  layout, 258
  nightlife, 277–280
  restaurants, 272–276
  shopping, 276–277
  sights and attractions, 263–272
  train station information, 253, 256–257
  visitor information, 257–258
Paris Shuttle, 256
Paris-Visite, 259
Parliament
  Budapest, 470
  London, 407–408
Parreirinha de Alfama (Lisbon), 646
Parthenon (Athens), 808
Passes, 51–61
  all-Europe
    consecutive-day passes, 57–58
    nonconsecutive passes, 58
  discounts, 59–61
  one-country
    consecutive-day, 52
    nonconsecutive passes, 52–55
  point-to-point tickets vs., 47–51
  rail-drive, 58–59
  regional, nonconsecutive passes, 55–57
Patio de los Naranjos (Seville), 688
Patras, 808
The Paul Klee Collection (Zentrum Paul Klee; Bern), 773
Pauly & Co. (Venice), 547
Penhaligon's (London), 416
Pergamon Museum (Berlin), 340
Petit Trianon (Versailles), 281
Philharmonie (Berlin), 348
Philosophenweg (Philosophers' Way; Heidelberg), 373

Phoenix Park (Dublin), 450
Piazza dei Signori (Verona), 550
Piazza del Campo (Siena), 533
Piazza della Signoria (Florence), 523
Piazza Navona (Rome), 500
Piazza San Carlo (Turin), 562
Piazza San Pietro (St. Peter's Sq.; Rome), 497
Piazzetta San Marco (Venice), 541
Picasso, Pablo
  Berggruen Collection: Picasso and His Era (Berlin), 338–339
  Musée Picasso (Paris), 270
  Museu Picasso (Barcelona), 709–710
Pinacoteca di Brera (Milan), 557
Pinacoteca Nazionale (Siena), 534
Pinacoteca (Rome), 502
Pinakothek der Moderne (Munich), 361–362
Pio Clementino Museum (Rome), 502
Piper (Rome), 509
Pisa, 531–533
Place de la Concorde (Paris), 263–264
Place de la République (Arles), 299
Place des Vosges (Paris), 265
Place du Forum (Arles), 299
Place Saint-Michel (Paris), 265
Place Vendôme (Paris), 264
Planning your trip, 29–78
  finding your rail route, 35–36
  visitor information, 29–32
  weather, 33–34
  when to go, 32–34
Plaza Mayor (Madrid), 678–679
Plaza Monumental de Toros de las Ventas (Madrid), 675
Plovdiv, 802
Poble Espanyol (Barcelona), 710
Poland, 811–813
Poland Pass, 54, 57, 811
Pompeii, 513–516
Pont des Bessières (Lausanne), 780
Ponte dei Sospiri (Venice), 542
Ponte Vecchio (Florence), 525
Poprad, 820
Porcelain Cabinet (Berlin), 339
Porto, 649
Portobello Road Market (London), 417
Portugal, 624–656
  area codes, 630
  business hours, 630
  climate, 630
  electricity, 630
  embassies and consulates, 630
  festivals and special events, 625
  health and safety, 630–631

Portugal *(cont.)*
highlights of, 624–626
holidays, 631
legal aid, 631
mail, 631
police and emergencies, 631
telephone, 631–632
tipping, 632
traveling to, 626–629
Portugal-Spain Pass, 57
Porzellansammlung (Porcelain Collection; Dresden), 378
Porzellansammlung (Porcelain Collection; Munich), 362
Potsdam, 350–351
Powder Tower (Prague), 179
Powerscourt Townhouse Centre (Dublin), 453
The Prado (Madrid), 676–677
Prague, 164, 171–188
accommodations, 177–179
cafes, 185
finding addresses in, 175
getting around, 175–176
nightlife, 186–188
restaurants, 182–185
shopping, 185–186
sights and attractions, 179–182
station information, 171, 174–175
visitor information, 175
Prague Castle (Pražský Hrad), 179–180
Prague Spring Festival, 186
Prague Spring International Music Festival, 166
Prague Symphony, 186
Prater (Vienna), 101–102
Primaciálny Palác (Bratislava), 819–820
Princely Beguinage of the Vineyard (Bruges), 153–154
Prinselijk Begijnhof ten Wijngaarde (Bruges), 153
Prins Eugens Waldemarsudde (Stockholm), 733
Procópio (Lisbon), 647
Promenade des Anglais (Nice), 310
Promenade des Rocher-des-Doms (Avignon), 298
The Proms (London), 390
Provence, 295–319
PUB Shopping Arcade (Stockholm), 736
Puppet shows, Brussels, 144

Q
Quadri (Venice), 548
Quai des Etats-Unis (Nice), 310
Quartier Latin (Paris), 265
Quasimodo (Berlin), 348–349
The Queen's Gallery (London), 409
Queen's Hall (Edinburgh), 432
Quinta das Lagrimas (Coimbra), 648

R
Rabensteig (Vienna), 107
Rådhuset (Town Hall), Århus, 223
Rådhus (Town Hall), Copenhagen, 213
Rafael Ortiz (Seville), 690
Rail Europe, 35, 47
Railjet, 82
Rail 'n drive passes, 59
Rail passes, 51–61
all-Europe
consecutive-day passes, 57–58
nonconsecutive passes, 58
discounts, 59–61
one-country
consecutive-day, 52
nonconsecutive passes, 52–55
point-to-point tickets *vs.*, 47–51
rail-drive, 58–59
regional, nonconsecutive passes, 55–57
Rainermuseum (Salzburg), 111
Raphael Rooms (Rome), 502
Rapperswil, 765
Rathaus (Town Hall), Rothenburg, 385
Rathen, 379
Razzmatazz (Barcelona), 716
Real Alcázar (Seville), 689
Red Light District (Amsterdam), 580
Reduta Jazz Club (Prague), 187
Regional Museum (Český Krumlov), 193
Reichsstadtmuseum (Rothenburg), 385–386
Reichstag (Parliament; Berlin), 341
Renaissancezaal (Renaissance Hall; Bruges), 152
Reservations, 46–47
Residenz
Salzburg, 112
Würzburg, 383
Residenzgalerie (Salzburg), 112
Residenz Museum (Munich), 363
Residenz Prunkräume (Salzburg), 112
Residenzschloss (Royal Palace; Dresden), 376
Restaurant cars, 42
Ribeira Nova market (Lisbon), 641
Rick's (Brussels), 144–145
Rick's Café (Bergen), 622
Riddarholm Church (Stockholm), 733
Ridderzaal (Hall of the Knights; The Hague), 588
Riesenrad (Vienna), 101–102
Rijksmuseum (Amsterdam), 578–579
Ringstrasse (Vienna), 91

Road maps, 70
The Rock (Copenhagen), 218
Rockefeller Music Hall (Oslo), 613
Rodin, Auguste, Musée National (Paris), 270
Röhsska Konstslöjdmuseet (Gothenburg), 745
Rolling Stone (Milan), 560
Roman Amphitheater (Syracuse), 515
Roman Forum (Foro Romano), 500–501
Romania, 813–816
Romania Pass, 54, 57, 59, 77, 814
Romantic Road (Romantische Strasse; Germany), 382–388
Rome, 490–510
accommodations, 494–496
getting around, 491, 494
nightlife, 507–508
restaurants, 504–507
shopping, 507
sights and attractions, 496–504
train station information, 490–491
visitor information, 491
Rome Opera Ballet, 508
Rome Opera House (Teatro dell'Opera), 508
Ronnie Scott's (London), 419
Room of a Hundred Columns (Barcelona), 710
Rosenborg Castle (Copenhagen), 213–214
Rosenkrantztårnet (Bergen), 619
Roskilde Festival, 200
Rosse Buurt (Amsterdam), 580
Rothenburg ob der Tauber, 385–386
Royal Apartments
Florence, 526
Stockholm, 731
Royal Armoury (Livrustkammaren; Stockholm), 731
Royal Ballet (London), 418
Royal Botanic Garden (Edinburgh), 427
Royal Cabinet of Paintings (The Hague), 588
Royal Ceremonial Dress Collection (London), 408
Royal Concertgebouw Orchestra (Amsterdam), 584
Royal Copenhagen Porcelain, 217
Royal Garden (Prague), 182
Royal Lyceum Theatre (Edinburgh), 432
Royal Mile (Edinburgh), 425
Royal Museum (Edinburgh), 426
Royal Museum of Fine Arts (Copenhagen), 214
Royal Museums of Fine Arts of Belgium (Brussels), 138–139
Royal National Theatre (London), 418

Royal Opera House
  London, 418
  Stockholm, 737
Royal Opera (London), 418
Royal Palace
  Amsterdam, 577
  Madrid, 678
  Prague, 179–180
  Stockholm, 731
  Warsaw, 813
Royal Route (Prague), 179
Royal Shakespeare Company (London), 418
Royal Stables & Coaches (Copenhagen), 211
Royal Treasury (Stockholm), 731
The Royal Yacht *Britannia* (Edinburgh), 427–428
Rubenshuis (Rubens House; Antwerp), 148
Rudolfinum (Prague), 186
Ruota della Fortuna (Verona), 550–551
Rust (Copenhagen), 218
Rüstkammer (Armory; Dresden), 378
Ryanair, 63
Rynek Starego Miasta (Old Town Square; Warsaw), 812

S

Sabauda Gallery (Turin), 562–563
Sagres, 654
St. Agnes Convent (Prague), 181
St. Bartholomew, Church of (Liège), 158
St. Bavo, Church of (Haarlem), 587
St. Bavo's Cathedral (Ghent), 146
St. Canute's Cathedral (Odense), 221
Ste-Chapelle (Paris), 271–272
Ste-Croix, Cathédrale (Orléans), 282–283
St. Dominius Peristil, Cathedral of (Split), 806
St-Gatien, Cathédrale (Tours), 286
St. George's Basilica (Kostel sv. Jirí), 179
St. George's Convent at Prague Castle, 181
St. Giles Cathedral (Edinburgh), 428
St. Jacob, Church of (Rothenburg), 385
St. Jakobskirche (Rothenburg), 385
St. John's Church (Maastricht), 593
St. Kilian, Dom (Würzburg), 383
St. Mark's Basilica (Venice), 544–545
St. Mark's Museum (Florence), 527
St. Mary Magdalene, Church of (Karlovy Vary), 191

St. Nicholas Church (České Budějovice), 196
St. Patrick's Cathedral (Dublin), 450
St. Patrick's Dublin Festival, 433
St-Paul-de-Vence, 313
St. Paul's Cathedral (London), 410
St. Peter's Basilica (Basilica di San Pietro; Rome), 497
St. Petersburg, 243
St. Peter's Church (Salzburg), 112–113
St. Peter's Square (Piazza San Pietro; Rome), 497
St. Peter's tomb (Rome), 497
St. Pierre, Cathedral of (Geneva), 789
St-Sauveur, Cathédrale (Aix-en-Provence), 302
St. Servatius Bridge (Maastricht), 593
St-Séverin, Church of (Paris), 265
St. Stephen's Cathedral (Stephansdom; Vienna), 102
St. Stephen's Church (Szent István Bazilika; Budapest), 471, 477
St. Vincent, Cathedral of (Bern), 773
St. Vitus Cathedral, Prague, 179
Sala Parés (Barcelona), 714
Salle d'Alabama (Geneva), 790
Salón de Embajadores (Granada), 697
Salon de Embajadores (Seville), 689
Saluhallen (Gothenburg), 747
Salzburg, 80, 108–119
  accommodations and restaurants, 115–116
  attractions and special moments, 111–115
  coffeehouses and pastry shops, 117
  getting around, 110
  nightlife, 117–119
  shopping, 116–117
  station information, 108, 110
  traveling to, 108
  visitor information, 110
Salzburg Card, 111
Salzburg Cathedral, 112
Salzburger Heimatwerk (Salzburg), 117
Salzburger Marionettentheater (Salzburg), 118
Salzburger (Salzburg), 118
Salzburger Schlosskonzerte (Salzburg), 118
Salzburg Festival, 82, 118
Salzburg Hauptbahnhof, 110
Sanatorium Baths III (Karlovy Vary), 190
San Giovanni in Laterano (Rome), 496
Santa Maria del Fiore, Cattedrale di (Florence), 526

Santa Maria delle Grazie (Milan), 558
Santa Maria Novella, Basilica di (Florence), 524
Santa Maria Novella rail station (Florence), 520
Sant'Ambroeus (Milan), 560
Sant Joan (Montserrat), 717
Santo Tomé, Iglesia de (Toledo), 685–686
Santuario della Scala Santa (Rome), 496
San Zeno Maggiore, Basilica (Verona), 550–551
Savoy Gallery (Turin), 562–563
Scalinata di Spagna (Spanish Steps; Rome), 503–504
Scandale (Geneva), 794
Scandinavia, suggested itinerary, 11–13
Scandinavia Pass, 57, 201, 229, 597, 720
Schaezlerpalais (Augsburg), 387
Schatzkammer (Treasury; Munich), 363
Schatzkammer (Vienna), 98
Scheveningen, 588, 590–591
Schiele, Egon, 100
  Egon Schiele Foundation and Egon Schiele Centrum (Český Krumlov), 194
Schilling (Barcelona), 715
Schloss Charlottenburg (Berlin), 339
Schloss Sanssouci (Potsdam), 350–351
Schönbrunn (Vienna), 96–97
Schumann's Bar am Hofgarten (Munich), 369
Schweizer Heimatwerk (Zurich), 767
Science Academy Building (Turin), 562
Science Museum (London), 409–410
Scottish Ballet (Edinburgh), 432
Scottish Chamber Orchestra (Edinburgh), 432
Scottish Opera (Edinburgh), 432
Scott Monument (Edinburgh), 425
Scuola di San Giorgio degli Schiavoni (Venice), 543
Scuola di San Rocco (Venice), 543–544
Seasons, 32–33
Sé (Cathedral)
  Faro, 655
  Lisbon, 639
Sechseläuten (Zurich), 753
Second class, 39–40
Select Italy, 524
Selfridges (London), 416
Semmering Pass Railway, 84
Semper Opera House (Dresden), 381
Senior passes, 59
Serbia, 816–818

Serbian Orthodox Blagovestenska Church (Szentendre), 478

Seurasaari Open-Air Museum (Helsinki), 240

Sé Velha (Coimbra), 648

Seven Stars (London), 419

Seville, 686–692

Seville Fair, 660

Sewers of Paris (Les Égouts; Paris), 271

Shakespeare's Globe Theatre (London), 418

Shoulder seasons, 33

Showers, 46

Sibelius, Jean, 238

Sicily, 514

Siena, 533–535

Silberne Kapelle (Silver Chapel; Innsbruck), 122

Silver Bible Codex Argenteus (Uppsala), 739

Sinagoga de Santa Maria la Blanca (Toledo), 686

Sinebrychoff Art Museum (Helsinki), 240–241

Sint-Baafskathedraal (Ghent), 146

Sint-Bavokerk (Haarlem), 587

Sint-Janskerk (Maastricht), 593

Sint-Pietersberg (Mount St. Peter; Maastricht), 594

Sintra, 650–652

Sint-Servaasbasiliek (Maastricht), 593

Sint-Servaasbrug (Maastricht), 593

Sisi Museum (Vienna), 97–98

Sistine Chapel (Rome), 503

Site Archéologique de St-Pierre (Geneva), 789

Skansen Folk Museum (Stockholm), 730

Skansen (Stockholm), 733, 737

Skattkammaren (Royal Treasury; Stockholm), 731

Skopje, 810

Sleeping accommodations, 35, 41, 43
luxury, 43–46

Slovakia, 818–820

Slovenia, 820–823

Slovenian Tourist Information Centre (Ljubljana), 820

Slovenia pass, 54, 55, 804, 820, 821

Smetana Hall (Prague), 186–187

Smoking coffee shops (Amsterdam), 586

Smuget (Oslo), 613

Society of International Railway Travelers, 72

Sofia, 801–802

Solar do Vinho do Porto (Lisbon), 647

Southbank Centre (London), 418

Space Electronic (Florence), 531

Spain, 657–717
area codes, 663
business hours, 663
climate, 663
documents required, 663
electricity, 664
embassies and consulates, 664
festivals and special events, 660
health and safety, 664
highlights of, 657–660
holidays, 664
legal aid, 664
mail, 664–665
police and emergencies, 665
telephones, 665
tipping, 665
traveling to, 660–663

Spain Pass, 54–55, 57, 77, 661

Spanische Reitschule (Spanish Riding School; Vienna), 98–99

Spanish Steps (Rome), 503–504

Split, 805–806

Staatsoper Unter den Linden (Berlin), 348

Stabian Thermae (baths; Pompeii), 516

Stadhuis (Town Hall), Bruges, 152

Stadttheater (Bern), 775

Stadtturm (Innsbruck), 120–121

Stampen (Stockholm), 737

State Apartments (London), 408

Staten-Generaal (States General; The Hague), 588

Statens Museum for Kunst (Copenhagen), 214

State Rooms (Salzburg), 111

Stazione Centrale (Naples), 510–511

Stazione Pisa Centrale (Pisa), 531

Stazione Termini (Rome), 490–491

Stedelijk Museum (Amsterdam), 579

Stedelijk Museum Het Prinsenhof (Delft), 592

Steen & Strom (Oslo), 613

Steffl Kaufhaus (Vienna), 105

Stephansdom (St. Stephen's Cathedral; Vienna), 102

Sternberk Palace (Prague), 181

Sticky Fingers (Gothenburg), 749

Stiftskirche St. Peter (Salzburg), 112–113

Stockholm, 723–739
accommodations, 728–729
getting around, 727–728
nightlife, 736–737
restaurants, 734–736
shopping, 736
sights and attractions, 729–734
train station information, 726
visitor information, 727

Stockholm Jazz Festival, 720

Stockmann (Helsinki), 244

Storkyrkan Church (Stockholm), 732

Stortorget (Stockholm), 732

The Story of Berlin, 343–344

Storyville (Helsinki), 244

Stranger's Galleries (London), 407–408

Striezelmarkt (Dresden), 380

Studentenkarzer (Student Prison; Heidelberg), 373

Sturehof (Stockholm), 737

Suburban Baths (Herculaneum), 517

Suburban trains, 39

Sunday Art Market (Amsterdam), 584

Suomenlinna Fortress, 241

Susisaari, 241

Svensk Hemslojd (Stockholm), 736

Svenskt Tenn (Stockholm), 736

Swarovski Kristallwelten (Wattens), 123

Swarovski Store Wien (Vienna), 105

Sweden, 718–749
area code, 722
business hours, 722
climate, 722
currency, 722
documents required, 722
electricity, 722–723
embassies and consulates, 723
health and safety, 723
highlights of, 719
holidays, 723
legal aid, 723
mail, 723
police and emergencies, 723
rail travel, 720–722
telephone, 723
tipping, 723
traveling to, 719–720

Sweden Pass, 55–57, 60, 720

Swiss Card, 58, 754

Swiss Flexipass, 55, 60, 753

Swiss Pass, 52, 60, 78, 753, 794

Switzerland, 750–798
area code, 755
business hours, 755
climate, 755–756
documents required, 756
electricity, 756
embassies and consulates, 756
festivals and special events, 753
health and safety, 756
highlights of, 750, 752
holidays, 756
legal aid, 756
mail, 756
police and emergencies, 756
rail travel, 753–755
scenic rail lines, 794–798
telephone, 756–757

tipping, 757
traveling to, 752–753
Syracuse, 515
Szabó Marzipan Museum (Szentendre), 478
Szántó Jewish Memorial House and Temple (Szentendre), 478
Széchenyi Baths (Budapest), 469–470
Szentendre, 477–479
Szent István Bazilika (St. Stephen's Church; Budapest), 471
Szépművészeti Múzeum (Museum of Fine Arts; Budapest), 470

T

Tablao Los Gallos (Seville), 690
Taormina, 515
Tartan Gift Shop (Edinburgh), 431
Tate Britain (London), 410–411
Tate Modern (London), 411
Tatras Mountains, 820
Teatro Comunale di Firenze (Florence), 530–531
Teatro de la Maestranza (Seville), 691
Teatro dell'Opera (Rome Opera House), 508
Teatro Goldoni (Venice), 547
Teatro Greco (Syracuse), 515
Teatro La Fenice (Venice), 547
Teatro Nacional São Carlos (Lisbon), 647
Teatro Real (Madrid), 682–683
Telecafe (Berlin), 349
Temple Bar Book Market (Dublin), 453
Temple Bar Food Market (Dublin), 453
Temple de l'Auditoire (Geneva), 789
Temple of the Dioscuri (Rome), 501
Temple of Venus and Roma (Rome), 499–500
Théâtre Antique (Arles), 299–300
Théâtre-Municipal Lausanne, 782
Théâtre Royal de la Monnaie (Brussels), 143–144
Théâtre Royal de Toone (Brussels), 144
Theresien-Bräu (Innsbruck), 125
Thessaloniki, 808
Thick Tower (Heidelberg), 372
Thomas Cook European Timetable, 35
Tibidabo Mountain (Barcelona), 707
Timetables, 35
Time zones, 33
Tiroler Abend (Innsbruck), 125
Tiroler Heimatwerk (Innsbruck), 125

Tiroler Landestheater (Innsbruck), 125
Tiroler Volkskunstmuseum (Innsbruck), 122
Tivoli, 509–510
Tivoli Gardens (Copenhagen), 214–215, 217
Tivolis Koncertsal (Copenhagen), 217
Toledo, 684–686
Torre de Belém (Lisbon), 641–642
Torre de la Vela (Granada), 697
Torre del Mangia (Siena), 533
Tour-de-l'Ile (Geneva), 788–789
Tour de Suquet (Cannes), 306
Tours (France), 285–288
Tower Bridge (London), 411
Tower Craft Design Centre (Dublin), 453
The Tower of London, 411–412
Town Hall. *See* **Hôtel de Ville; Stadhuis**
Trädgårdsföreningen (Gothenburg), 747
Trädgår'n (Gothenburg), 748
TRAFO (Budapest), 477
Train stations, 61–62
Trajan's Column (Rome), 500
Tranquilo (Gothenburg), 749
Transylvania, 816
Travel agents, 71–72
Traverse Theatre (Edinburgh), 432
Treasury
Esztergom (Kincstár), 479
Munich, 363
Vatican (Rome), 497
Vienna, 98
Treppenhaus (Würzburg), 383
Trevi Fountain (Fontana di Trevi; Rome), 499
Triglav National Park, 823
Trocadéro (Paris), 264
Troldhaugen (Bergen), 619
Trooping the Colour (London), 390
Tsarevets, 803
Tsentralna Sofiiska Sinagoga (Sofia), 802
't Smalle (Amsterdam), 586
Tulcea, 816
Tuomiokirkko (Lutheran Cathedral; Helsinki), 239
Turin, 561–563
Tyrolean Folk Art Museum (Innsbruck), 122

U

U Fleků (Prague), 187
United Kingdom, 389–432
area codes, 394
business hours, 394
climate, 394–395
currency, 395
documents required, 395
electricity, 395

embassies and consulates, 395
festivals and special events, 390
health and safety, 395
holidays, 395
legal aid, 395
mail, 395–396
police and emergencies, 396
rail travel, 392–394
telephone, 396
tipping, 396
traveling to, 392–394
Uppsala, 737–739
Usher Hall (Edinburgh), 432
Uto Quai (Zurich), 762
U zlatého jednorožce (Prague), 188

V

Vali Folklór (Budapest), 475
Val Saint Lambert (Liège), 158
Value-added tax (VAT), 74–75
Van Gogh Museum (Amsterdam), 579
Varna, 802
Városliget (City Park; Budapest), 472
Vasamuseet (Royal Warship Vasa; Stockholm), 733–734
Vasa Ship Museum (Stockholm), 729
Vatican Museums (Musei Vaticani; Rome), 502–503
Vega (Copenhagen), 218
Veletržní Palace (Prague), 181
Veliko Târnovo, 803
Vence, 314–315
Venice, 535–551
accommodations, 539–541
excursions from, to Padua, 548–550
getting around, 538–539
gondola rides, 543, 544
nightlife, 547
restaurants, 545–546
shopping, 546–547
sights and attractions, 541–545
train station information, 535, 538
visitor information, 538
Venini (Venice), 547
Verona, 550–551
Versailles, 280–281
Vesuvius, 516
Viaduc des Arts (Paris), 276
Victoria and Albert Museum (London), 412
Victoria Bar (Berlin), 349
Victoria Hall (Geneva), 793
Vieille Ville (Geneva), 789–790
Vieille Ville (Nice), 311
Vienna, 80, 87–108
accommodations, 93–96
getting around, 91–93
layout, 91

Vienna *(cont.)*
  nightlife, 106–108
  restaurants, 102–105
  shopping, 105–106sights and
    attractions, 96–102
  station information, 87, 90
  visitor information, 87, 90–91
Vienna Boys' Choir, 99
Vienna Card, 94
Vienna Festival, 82
Vienna International Airport,
  87, 90
Vigelandsparken and Museum
  (Oslo), 608
Vikingskiphuset (Viking Ship
  Museum; Oslo), 610–611
Viktualienmarkt (Munich), 367
Villa Adriana (Tivoli), 509–510
Villa dei Misteri (Pompeii), 515
Villa d'Este (Tivoli), 510
Vinçón (Barcelona), 714
Vinorant Alter Hof (Munich), 369
Vino Vino (Venice), 548
Virtualni Muzej (Ljubljana), 822
Visegrád, 480–481
Visitor information, 29–32
Vista Alegre (Lisbon), 647
Vondelpark (Amsterdam), 580
Vrídlo (Karlovy Vary), 191
Vrijthof (Maastricht), 593
Vyšehrad (Prague), 182

W

Warsaw, 812–813
W. A. Sarmento (Lisbon), 645
Waterloo, 145

Waterlooplein Flea Market
  (Amsterdam), 584
Wattens, 123
Waverley Station (Edinburgh),
  422
Waxworks Museum (Waterloo),
  145
Weather, 33–34
Weihnachtsland am Zwinger
  (Dresden), 380
Wellington Museum (Waterloo),
  145
Welt der Marionetten (Salzburg),
  112
Wengernalp railway (WAB), 797
Westbahnhof (Vienna), 90
Westerkerk (West Church;
  Amsterdam), 579–580
Westminster Abbey (London),
  412–413
Wheel of Fortune (Verona),
  550–551
Whispering Gallery (London),
  410
White Tower (London), 411
Wiener Festwochen, 82
Wiener Porzellanmanufaktur
  Augarten Gesellschaft
  (Salzburg), 117
Wiener Sängerknaben (Vienna),
  99
Wiener Staatsoper (Vienna), 106
Wiener Volksoper (Vienna), 106
William Tell Express, 796
Willi's Wine Bar (Paris), 280
Wimbledon Lawn Tennis
  Championships (London), 390
Wine Vat Building (Heidelberg),
  372

World Clock (Copenhagen), 213
Würzburg, 382–384

X

X-tra (Zurich), 767

Y

Youth passes, 59

Z

Zagreb, 805
Zähringen fountain (Bern), 772
Zamek Królewski (Royal Palace;
  Warsaw), 813
Zeitglocken (Bern), 772
Zeneakadémia (Budapest), 477
Zibelemärit (Bernon), 753
Zillemarkt (Berlin), 349
Zillertaler Trachtenwelt
  (Innsbruck), 125
Zollpackhof (Berlin), 349
Zoologischer Garten (Berlin
  Zoo), 344
Zsolnay (Budapest), 476
Zum Roten Ochsen (Heidelberg),
  375
Zum Sepp'l (Heidelberg), 375
Zurich, 757–768
Zurich, Lake, 765
Zurich Kunsthaus (Fine Arts
  Museum), 764
Zurich Tonhalle Orchestra, 767
Zurich-Vienna alpine run, 83
Zwiebelfisch (Berlin), 349
Zwinger (Dresden), 378
Zwölf Apostelkeller (Vienna),
  106